Drugs

Drugs

MIND, BODY, AND SOCIETY

SECOND EDITION

MARTHA S. ROSENTHAL

New York   Oxford

OXFORD UNIVERSITY PRESS

Oxford University Press is a department of the University of Oxford.
It furthers the University's objective of excellence in research, scholarship,
and education by publishing worldwide. Oxford is a registered trade mark of
Oxford University Press in the UK and certain other countries.

Published in the United States of America by Oxford University Press
198 Madison Avenue, New York, NY 10016, United States of America.

For titles covered by Section 112 of the US Higher Education
Opportunity Act, please visit www.oup.com/us/he for the latest
information about pricing and alternate formats.

CIP data is on file at the Library of Congress.
ISBN 9780197585283

Printed by Marquis, Canada

This book is dedicated to Christopher Michaels, BS, JD, MBA, PITA

Brief Table of Contents

Table of Contents

Section 1   Foundations

Section 3	Legal Psychoactive Drugs

Section 4   Commonly Used Prescription and Nonprescription Drugs

Chapter 13   Drugs for Treating Psychological Disorders   316

Section 5   Addiction, Prevention, and Treatment

Preface

Drugs are fascinating. We ascribe a nearly mythic status to these tiny bits of chemicals sprinkled around the earth that can change our behavior and our personality—and that can kill us or cure us. When our bodies, minds, or souls are ailing, we often seek relief by ingesting pills and potions and prescriptions, with a fervent belief in their necessity and efficacy. In some ways, we live in a drugstore society—we wander the aisles searching for the chemical combination to make us happy, or thin, or smart, or funny, or relaxed enough to deal with the task at hand.

Every day, we are bombarded with information about drugs, from highway billboards hawking alcohol, to films in which a protagonist fires up a joint, to direct-to-consumer ads that encourage us to ask our doctors if this or that drug is right for us. How can we evaluate this material?

Additionally, our perceptions and understanding of drugs are undergoing widespread changes. New information about the brain, changing laws regarding illegal drugs, and innovative pharmaceutical options are only a few of the ways the field continues to evolve. Because drugs have such a momentous impact on our physical and psychological health, on our relationships, and on society, open and honest communication about them is essential. It is my sincerest wish that *Drugs: Mind, Body, and Society* will help you learn the skills to evaluate the overabundance of data you encounter every day, so that you can make intelligent decisions that improve the quality of your life.

Throughout this endeavor, interested friends and colleagues have asked me which chapter was my favorite. I must admit that some chapters were more fun to write than others. Some made me grab my phone to share fun facts, while others made me stomp around the house waving my arms around in frustration. What I learned throughout the process, however, is that I am—as I ever was and ever shall be—both a teacher and a student. My greatest joy is helping to guide other students on their journeys to become lifelong learners. Thank you for embarking on this journey with me.

Approach

Drugs: Mind, Body, and Society is designed to help you understand the diverse foundations of drugs and drug use, and to provide you with skills to evaluate current research and data about drugs. My hope is that through reading this book you will

- expand your understanding of drugs and their effects on our minds, our bodies, and our society;
- learn to critically evaluate topics of concern today and in the future;
- gain greater knowledge of the world in which we live and the people with whom we share it; and
- recognize your own values and points of view and respect those of others.

As such, the framework of this book is built upon an emphasis on critical thinking skills; a multidisciplinary, integrated approach; a clear presentation of biological foundations; and a contemporary, accessible voice.

- **Emphasis on critical thinking skills.** "Critical thinking" is a buzz word bandied about quite a lot these days. But what is it really? Critical thinking involves maintaining a certain degree of skepticism about information, analyzing claims and arguments based on evidence, and recognizing and evaluating the value assumptions that may underlie a given position. Today, we are exposed to more drug information than ever before. But, as with any commodity, as the supply increases, the value decreases. It's essential that you learn to evaluate and assess the value of the information you encounter. Because critical thinking is not only a set of skills to be learned, but also a way of relating to the world, *Drugs: Mind, Body, and Society* gives you exercises designed to help you become an intelligent consumer of information by encouraging you to examine your own values, to seek out the sources of the data, and to ask pertinent questions so you can discern fact from opinion.
- **A multidisciplinary, integrated approach.** A comprehensive discussion about drugs and their effects on our mind, body, and society requires a multidisciplinary approach, which *Drugs: Mind, Body, and Society* provides. The study of drugs is a tapestry woven from the threads of physiology, neuroscience, pharmacology, psychology, society, culture, media, history, law, and religion. If one of those threads were lost, the fabric would no longer be whole. Our understanding of the effects and influence of drugs is made much richer by integrating these diverse views.
- **Biological foundations.** My students often consider the biological components of drug action to be the most difficult (and most boring) part of the course; however, this is the foundation upon which all the other factors interact. Knowledge of the biological foundations is crucial for a full understanding of drug action. However, I do have sympathy for students bemoaning the necessity of understanding the neuroscience and pharmacokinetics behind it all, as well as for the faculty who have to listen to all the bemoaning. As such, I tried to be very selective with the pharmacological and physiological information that I included and limited it to the facts that are necessary for readers to understand the ways that drugs affect our bodies and minds. *Drugs: Mind, Body, and Society* breaks down biological topics in a clear, organized, and easy-to-understand way for students of all levels.
- **Contemporary, accessible voice.** In this book, I hope to tell you not only what you need to know, but also what you want to know. I wrote *Drugs: Mind, Body, and Society* as if I were speaking to you individually. I have tried to be nonjudgmental and welcoming, as well as informal, conversational, and humorous, although I recognize that not all of you will appreciate my humor. As I was typing away at my computer, I cracked myself up a number of times, but some stories or phrases were deemed a bit too much and are now safely ensconced in my desktop trashcan (thank goodness for wise editors). It is my sincere hope that you enjoy reading this book as much as I enjoyed writing it.

Organization of the Book

Drugs: Mind, Body, and Society is divided into six sections:

- The first section covers the topic that lies at the heart of this book—"thinking critically about drugs." This section discusses how drug research is done, and how to critically evaluate the information about drugs and other topics that touch our lives every day.

- Section 1 provides an overview of the main themes of the text: the significant effect that drugs have on our lives and the influence of society on our drug use and attitudes about drugs (Chapter 1); drug laws and policies (Chapter 2); and the biological foundations needed to understand the effects of drugs on the body (Chapters 3 and 4).
- Section 2 reviews the physiological, pharmacological, historical, legal, political, societal, and cultural aspects of legally restricted psychoactive drugs, such as stimulants (Chapter 5), hallucinogens (Chapter 6), opioids (Chapter 7), sedatives (Chapter 8), and cannabis (Chapter 9).
- Section 3 covers the same for legal psychoactive drugs, such as tobacco (Chapter 10), caffeine (Chapter 11), and alcohol (Chapter 12).
- Section 4 discusses commonly used prescription and nonprescription drugs, including drugs to treat psychological disorders (Chapter 13); drugs to enhance physical and academic performance, such as anabolic steroids, and drugs to treat attention-deficit/hyperactivity disorder (ADHD) (Chapter 14); over-the-counter drugs (Chapter 15); and drugs that affect the reproductive system (Chapter 16).
- Section 5 examines addiction (Chapter 17), as well as the prevention and treatment of problematic drug use and abuse (Chapter 18).

The use of, attitudes about, and laws governing many drugs are undergoing a profound transformation, and the latest edition of *Drugs: Mind, Body, and Society* reflects those changes. A short three years ago, when the first edition was published, cannabis was legal in a fraction of the states in which it is now legal, ketamine had not been approved for use to treat depression, and COVID-19 didn't exist. The new edition of the book has been revised to include the most up-to-date information available and includes hundreds of new references. Some significant additions include

- the increased use and acceptance of psychedelic drugs as a therapeutic treatment option;
- recent lawsuits against opioid-manufacturing pharmaceutical companies;
- the evolving laws and expanded understanding of cannabis;
- an analysis of the risks and benefits of electronic nicotine delivery systems;
- the use of hormone replacement therapy for transmen and transwomen;
- drugs that have been developed to treat hypoactive sexual desire disorder in women; and
- the impact of COVID-19 on drug use, substance use disorders, and mental health disorders.

Features of the Book

Each chapter of *Drugs: Mind, Body, and Society* includes a host of features and pedagogical tools to help you learn and remember the fascinating content you encounter.

At the Start of Each Chapter:
- *Learning Objectives*—The key principles and ideas that you should know and understand after reading the content provide a framework for approaching the material.

- *Summary Box*—Each drug-specific chapter includes a summary box with pharmacological facts about each drug.
- *True/False Questions*—Three provocative true/false questions (and answers) challenge commonly held misconceptions about the material.

Within Each Chapter:

- *Critical Evaluations*—Critical thinking is an active process. These in-depth evaluations ask controversial questions about drugs and then provide research and questions that encourage you to consider the information from several different perspectives. Some examples of questions asked and debated include the following:
  - Should pharmaceutical companies be allowed to produce direct-to-consumer ads? (Chapter 1)
  - Does long-term cannabis use cause cognitive deficits? (Chapter 9)
  - Does alcohol increase aggression? (Chapter 12)
  - Is addiction a disease? (Chapter 17)
- *Straight Dope*—Boxes include profiles of real people and cases; self-knowledge tests; historical, biographical, and anecdotal topics of interest; and points of clinical or cultural relevance to each chapter.
- *"Ask yourself" Questions*—Pull-quote questions included throughout each chapter encourage you to think critically about how the content affects your life.
- *Quick Hits*—Shorter notes and fun facts include drug trivia from various disciplines.
- *Acute Effects Figures*—Infographics in each of the main drug chapters help you to visually identify the common acute effects of specific drugs.
- *Running Glossary*—Definitions of each of the key terms appear on the page where they are bolded in the text.

At the End of Each Chapter:

- *Chapter Summary*—The bulleted takeaways of each major section help you to remember the most important points of each chapter and study for exams.
- *Quiz Yourself!*—Multiple choice, true/false, and short-answer questions enable you to test your understanding of the material.
- *Additional Resources*—Websites, videos, movies, and books are included to help jump-start your own research into each chapter topic.

Ancillaries

For Students
Oxford Learning Link

Oxford Learning Link is your central hub for a wealth of engaging digital learning tools and resources to help you get the most of your Oxford University Press course material. The Oxford Learning Link includes the following for each chapter:

- Enhanced e-book
- Video Vignettes

- Interactive Figures, Tables, and Activities
- Matching Exercises
- Animations
- Videos
- Flashcards
- Further Readings

Enhanced e-book

Oxford's Enhanced e-books combine high quality text content with a rich assortment of integrated multimedia and self-assessment activities in order to deliver a more engaging and interactive learning experience.

The Enhanced e-book version of *Drugs: Mind, Body, and Society* is available via RedShelf, VitalSource, and other leading higher education e-book vendors and includes self-assessment questions, embedded animations and videos, interactive activities, figures, and tables, and flashcards.

For Instructors

An extensive and thoughtful supplements program offers instructors everything they need to prepare their course and lectures and to assess student progress, including lecture slides, an instructor's manual, figure slides, and a test bank in Word, Respondus, and Common Cartridge formats.

The Oxford Digital Difference

The Oxford Digital Difference is the flexibility to teach your course the way that you want to. At Oxford University Press, content comes first. We create high quality, engaging, and affordable digital material in a variety of formats and deliver it to you in the way that best suits the needs of you, your students, and your institution.

Oxford Learning Link

Oxford Learning Link is your central hub for a wealth of engaging digital learning tools and resources to help you get the most of your Oxford University Press course material.

Available online exclusively to adopters, the Oxford Learning Link includes all of the instructor resources that accompany *Drugs: Mind, Body, and Society* 2e.

Instructor's Manual

The Instructor's Manual, written by the author and based on her experience teaching the course, includes the following for each chapter:

- Chapter outline
- Chapter summary including an outline of each section, take-home messages, questions to pose to your class, and tidbits and trivia
- Discussion questions
- Challenges you may face and hints on how to deal with them
- Homework ideas
- Critical thinking exercises
- Classroom activities
- Classroom games

- Suggested video clips
- Tips for teaching this course

The Instructor's Manual has been updated for the second edition, and includes even more games, activities, homework ideas, as well as suggestions to optimize online instruction.

PowerPoints

Complete lecture outlines for each chapter are available and ready for use in class. These include coverage of all important facts and concepts presented in each chapter.

Test Bank

A complete test bank provides instructors with a wide range of test items for each chapter, including multiple choice, fill-in-the-blank, true/false, matching, short-answer, and essay questions. The test bank has been significantly expanded for the second edition and includes almost 2,000 questions. In addition, questions have been added that cover the connections and intersections of multiple chapters, so students can consider similarities and differences between classes of drugs. Each question is tagged to a learning objective from the book. The test bank is available in multiple formats including Word, Respondus, and Common Cartridge (for import into learning management systems).

Oxford Learning Link Direct

Oxford Learning Link Direct brings all of the high-quality digital teaching and learning tools for *Drugs: Mind, Body, and Society* right to your local learning management system. Instructors and their LMS administrators simply download the Oxford Learning Link Direct cartridge from Oxford Learning Link, and, with the turn of a digital key, incorporate engaging content from Oxford directly into their LMS for assigning and grading. This cartridge includes all digital resources for this title, as well as matching quizzes and multiple choice quizzes that can only be accessed through the cartridge.

Oxford Learning Cloud

Ideal for instructors who do not use a LMS or prefer an easy-to-use alternative to their school's designated LMS, Oxford Learning Cloud delivers engaging learning tools within an easy-to-use, mobile-friendly, cloud-based courseware platform. Learning Cloud offers pre-built courses that instructors can use "off the shelf" or customize to fit their needs. A built-in gradebook allows instructors to see quickly and easily how the class and individual students are performing. This Learning Cloud includes all digital resources for this title, as well as matching quizzes and multiple choice quizzes that can only be accessed through the Learning Cloud.

Acknowledgments

I am so grateful to everyone at Oxford University Press for their hard work, patience, and dedication. First and foremost, Jess Fiorillo, executive editor extraordinaire. You've been my rock! You're also way cool, smart, and fun, which is a bonus. I'd also like to thank Ryan Amato, editorial assistant;

Karissa Venne, digital resource development editor; Allison Bland, digital resource development assistant; Malinda Labriola, editorial assistant; Joan Lewis-Milne, marketing manager; Melissa Yanuzzi, senior production editor, amazing project manager Brad Rau and copyeditor Jennifer McIntyre, and everyone else at Oxford who made this a reality. I'm also grateful for the wonderful people who helped get the first edition launched—Lisa Sussman, Jane Potter, Larissa Albright, Micheline Frederick, Joyce Helena Brusin, and Wesley Morrison.

Thank you to the following reviewers:

Peter Adler, University of Denver
Claire Advokat, Louisiana State University
David S. Anderson, George Mason University
Carolyn Baird, Robert Morris University
Scot B. Boeringer, University of South Florida
Scott E. Bowen, Wayne State University
Nancy K. Brown, University of South Carolina
Chris Jones-Cage, College of the Desert
Jeffrey L. Calton, California State University, Sacramento
Suzanne Clerkin, SUNY Purchase
Jennifer L. Cobuzzi, University of Pennsylvania
Carolyn Cohen, Northern Essex Community College
Chris Correia, Auburn University
Marc Dingman, Pennsylvania State University
Margaret S. Dobbs, Northeastern State University
Kevin Doyle, University of Virginia
Ceymone Dyce, University of Florida
Mitch Earleywine, University at Albany
Amanda ElBassiouny, Spring Hill College
Julie A Fink, Old Dominion University
Perry Fuchs, University of Texas, Arlington
Marc D. Gellman, University of Miami
Gilbert W. Gipson, Virginia State University
Joshua M. Gulley, University of Illinois, Urbana-Champaign
Sue Hart, Lees-McRae College
Lara Heflin, New Mexico Highlands University
Kelly Helm, Valparaiso University
Emily Hensleigh, University of Nevada Las Vegas
Shawn Hrncir, Arizona State University
Kim L. Huhman, Georgia State University
Jessica G. Irons, James Madison University
Denise Jackson, Northeastern University
Shepherd Jenks, Central New Mexico Community College
Chandrika Johnson, Fayetteville State University
Robert Keel, University of Missouri-St. Louis
Mark Kilwein, Clarion University of Pennsylvania
Kirsten Lupinski, Albany State University
Michael Madson, University of Southern Mississippi
Darlene Mosley, Pensacola State College
Geoffrey L. McIntyre, University of Toledo
Peter J. McLaughlin, Edinboro University of Pennsylvania

Bill Meil, Indiana University of Pennsylvania

Dr. Bennie Prince, University of Arkansas at Little Rock

Matthew Quinlan, California State University,
  San Bernardino

Pamela Richards, Central College

John A. Sanford, Laramie County Community College

Jacqueline Schwab, Pennsylvania State University
  Mont Alto

Wendy Seegers, University of Wisconsin Colleges

Donald J. Stehouwer, University of Florida

Anne Strouth, North Central State College

Dr. Purcell Taylor, Jr., University of Cincinnati

Paige Telan, Florida International University

Jennifer Thomson, Messiah College

Karin Walton, University of North Dakota

Toni Watt, Texas State University

Judeth Forlenza Wesley, Rutgers University

Joseph D. Wolfe, University of Alabama at Birmingham

Rebecca Vidourek, University of Cincinnati

Nickolas Zaller, Rhode Island College

Tracy Zeeger, University of Maryland, College Park.

I'd also like to thank the following people:

- **Students:** Ultimately, it's all for you. You were my inspiration through-out this long process. You gave me the drive to go on when I wanted to run away from my computer and become a beet farmer. Your questions and comments were intelligent, poignant, thought-provoking, and inspirational.
- **Instructors:** I am so thankful for all the wise suggestions and feed-back you gave me. I am grateful that you took time out of your busy days to share your knowledge and experience. You have made this book so much stronger than it would otherwise have been.
- **To my friends and family:** I am grateful for your gifts of love, laugh-ter, and support over these many years. Maria Roca—more than twenty years later, you are still there for me. Chris Michaels—I'm grateful for your steadfast support, love, and kindness. You are right. (That's all I need to say, isn't it?) And to my family: Melissa Rosenthal Somosky, Bruce Press, Matthew Rosenthal, Amy Rosenthal, Ron and Judy Rosenthal, and nieces, nephews, aunts, uncles, cousins, and sib-lings in-law too numerous to name. Also, a shout out to Leila, Baxter, Chloe, Mickey, (and forever Buddy), who helped by walking across the computer keyboard or by insisting I take breaks to give belly rubs. I love you all so very much. You all know me better than anyone, yet you still invite me to family gatherings. Having you as my family is the best gift a person could ever receive.

About the Author

Martha S. Rosenthal spends her time studying drugs, sex, brains, and bodies, and therefore believes she has the best job in the whole wide world. Dr. Rosenthal is a professor at Florida Gulf Coast University, where she teaches courses in drugs and society, cannabis and its impact, human physiology, neuroscience, and human sexuality, as well as courses that focus on critical thinking and the development of values. She received her bachelor's degree in biology from the University of Virginia, her master's degree in neuropharmacology from Brown University, and her PhD in neuroscience from UCLA.

Dr. Rosenthal believes that no topic can be understood in a vacuum and that all disciplines influence one another, so she has spent a lifetime in multidisciplinary study. Dr. Rosenthal is the coauthor of *Discoveries in Human Systems* and the author of *Human Sexuality from Cells to Society*. In addition to textbooks, she has written and presented on the use of games in the classroom, and developed FGCU's cannabis research, education, and workforce initiative.

Dr. Rosenthal has been honored to receive the teacher of the year award at both the University of Florida and at Florida Gulf Coast University; to have her sexuality textbook chosen as "the most promising new text of 2013"; and to have been selected to present a TEDx talk about sex and gender. Dr. Rosenthal's mother would like it mentioned that she played violin at Carnegie Hall when she was nine years old. When not writing, Dr. Rosenthal enjoys reading, watching movies, playing the harp, spoiling her dogs and cats, and spending time with family and friends.

Thinking Critically about Drugs

1.
True or false? The most accurate experiments are those involving participants who hear about the project and volunteer to take part in the study.

2.
True or false? Internet sources are always unreliable.

3.
True or false? The alcohol industry spends almost $1 billion per year on all media advertising.

Answers: 1. F, 2. F, 3. F (it spends almost $2 billion per year)

....

Learning Objectives

- Define the terms *population, sample, representative sample, sampling bias, volunteer bias, independent variable, dependent variable, control, double-blind, internal validity, external validity, confounding factor, generalizability,* and *informed consent.*

- Contrast and compare various sampling methods.

- Assess the pros and cons of various research methods.

- Identify the control, dependent variables, and independent variables in a controlled experiment.

- Summarize the pros and cons of animal research.

- Distinguish between brain imaging techniques that give information about structure and those that show brain activity.

- Define the terms *ad hominem, ad populum, appeal to emotion, tautology, red herring, searching for perfect solutions, inappropriate appeals to authority, appeal to ignorance, false dilemma, hasty generalization,* and *slippery slope.*

- Apply the skills of critical thinking to recognize the strengths and weaknesses in an argument.

- Consider the significance of the prevalence and effect of drug and alcohol portrayals in the media.

- Define the term *direct-to-consumer advertising.*

We are born with an innate curiosity about the world and our place in it. In order to function in and adapt to our surroundings, we make observations, create a hypothesis, test our ideas, and draw conclusions. This is the scientific method in its simplest form. In order to learn about the mysteries of the brain and the actions of various drugs, scientists need to understand aspects of biology, biochemistry, psychology, neuroanatomy, neurophysiology, neuropharmacology, endocrinology, and computer science. They need to develop research techniques and critical thinking skills, which are refined through many years of work. In designing research, scientists must carefully consider who and what they are studying, the methods by which they will test their hypotheses, and how to ensure the validity of their findings.

It is not only scientists who need these skills. Every day in our society, we are inundated with messages about drugs, and some of these messages are more accurate than others. Think about some of the controversial issues related to drugs that come across your newsfeed. Should marijuana be legalized? Is vaping safe? Are antidepressant drugs effective? Does the Pill affect sex drive? The answers to these questions affect not only your own health and well-being but also society's. How can we pry out the most accurate answer from the overwhelming amount of information to which we are exposed? In this section, we will consider ways for you to do just that. We will encourage you to be an intelligent consumer of information about drugs, and to critically evaluate the information you obtain from scientists, friends, the internet, and the media.

Pharmacological Research

In this section, we will consider how pharmacological research is done, and how the selected population, the methods used, and even the wording of the query can all affect the results. To "do good science," you must ask specific questions using precise language; carefully consider your study population; choose an appropriate method of investigation; use valid and precise measurements; ensure that your study is safe, ethical, and unbiased; maintain objectivity; and consider the quality of and vetting of information.

Ask Specific Research Questions

High-quality research requires asking specific questions and using precise language. Consider the question, "Are drugs harmful?" A term or phrase is ambiguous if its meaning is left uncertain or open to interpretation. As stated, the word *drug* might refer to heroin, antibiotics, alcohol, or aspirin. And how about "harmful"? Does harm in this case refer to physical, emotional, societal, or financial harm? Harm to whom, and by whose standards? Given the inherent emotional, political, and legal ramifications of drugs, it is particularly important to clearly define one's terms and to ask precise questions. A better and more specific research question in this instance might be, "Does two ounces of alcohol a day cause liver damage in college students?"

Carefully Consider Your Study Population

When doing research, you must first choose your **population**, or the group you want to investigate, such as college students in the United States, pregnant women, or adolescent boys. It is usually impossible to obtain information from all people in your chosen population, so scientists usually rely on data obtained from a **sample** or subset of individuals in the target population. Deciding on who the sample participants are is one of the most critical aspects of an experiment, given that using different sampling techniques may produce very different results (Table A). There are two general sampling approaches: probability sampling and nonprobability sampling.

Probability sampling uses some form of random selection. In a **simple random sample**, each member of your population has an equal likelihood of being selected. Perhaps every person is assigned a number, and then a random number generator selects the subjects. One type of probability sample is a **stratified random sample**, in which the population is divided up into similar subgroups—perhaps by race, age, gender, and religion—and then a simple random sample is chosen from each subgroup in the same proportions as they exist in the population. In that way, researchers can try to obtain a **representative sample**, in which the characteristics of the sample match the population being studied with regard to specific demographic characteristics.[1]

There may be times when obtaining a random sample is not practical or feasible. In nonprobability sampling, subjects are not chosen at random. In a

purposive nonprobability sample, a participant is selected because he or she reflects a specific purpose of the study. For example, if a tobacco company wanted to ascertain the effectiveness of a media campaign for smokeless tobacco, they might choose males from the southern and western United States, because this subset is their target audience.

In **self-selection samples**, participants volunteer to take part in a study. Perhaps the sample consists of those who respond to an ad, or students who choose to partake in a professor's experiment. Given that people who are willing to volunteer for drug studies (or for any experimental studies, for that matter) do not necessarily represent the attitudes, behaviors, and beliefs of the general population, **volunteer bias** may occur. To illustrate the concept of volunteer bias, consider whether you yourself would take part in any of the following drug studies:

- Fill out an anonymous survey about your personal drug attitudes and experiences.
- Undergo a 30-minute, face-to-face interview, during which the researcher will ask you questions about your drug attitudes and experiences.
- Consume a specified amount of alcohol prior to performing coordination tests in the laboratory.
- Smoke a specified amount of marijuana prior to performing a memory test in the laboratory.
- Test an unapproved medication as part of a clinical trial on the efficacy of the drug.

Population: The group of individuals being studied.

Sample: A subset of individuals in the population.

Simple random sample: A sample in which each member of the population has an equal probability of participating.

Stratified random sample: A sample in which the population is divided into subgroups of certain characteristics and a random sample from each group is taken in a number proportional to what is seen in the larger population.

Representative sample: A sample that has similar characteristics (such as age, gender, ethnicity, education) to those of the population from which it was drawn.

Purposive nonprobability sample: A sample in which participants are selected because they reflect a specific purpose of the study.

Self-selection sample: A sample in which participants volunteer to take part in the study.

Volunteer bias: The tendency for those who volunteer for research to be different in some way from those who refuse to participate.

TABLE A.   A Comparison of Various Sampling Methods[2,3]

Type of Sample	Description	Advantages	Disadvantages
Simple random sample	Each member of the population has an equal chance of being selected.	For very large samples, this gives the best chance of an unbiased/representative sample.	For large populations, this is time-consuming. It is hard to truly get a random sample, because participants with computers or landline phones may be more likely to be selected.
Stratified random sample	The population is divided into subcategories such as age, gender, and race, and members are selected in the proportion that they occur in the population.	Representative sample. Can be generalized to the general population.	Time-consuming. Subcategories have to be identified and their proportions calculated.
Purposive samples	Investigator purposely chooses participants based on certain characteristics.	Economical and less time-consuming. Can focus on subjects with relevant characteristics.	Selection bias can threaten external and internal validity.
Self-selection/volunteer	People self-select to participate—those who respond to an ad or show up for a study.	Convenient, quick, and economical.	Nonrepresentative. Volunteer bias can threaten external validity and internal validity, because differences in participants may underlie results.
Convenience sample	Sample those who are available at the time.	Convenient, quick, and economical.	Nonrepresentative. Volunteer bias and selection bias can threaten external validity and internal validity.

Many researchers use **convenience samples**—a sample that is easily accessible although not necessarily representative of the population. These samples are not ideal, although they are probably used more often than any other kind of sample.[4] Be particularly cautious when generalizing results using nonprobability samples. These samples can lead to **sampling bias**, which is when some members of the population—such as middle-class North American college students of European descent—are overrepresented, while others—elderly people, certain minority groups, and people with disabilities—are excluded or under-represented. Consider your own classroom population: How closely does your classroom conform to a representative sample of the population of the United States?

The size of the sample is also important. Larger samples usually give more reliable results, because they generally vary less from the mean (average) of the population than small samples do.[5] Using a large sample, however, does not necessarily mean that the group of subjects you are studying is representative of the larger population.

Convenience sample: A sample that is not necessarily representative of the population, but that is easily accessible to the researcher.

Sampling bias: The tendency for some members of the population to be over-represented and others to be excluded from a sample.

Research methods: A systematic approach to gathering information and evaluating the findings.

Choose an Appropriate Method of Investigation

How would *you* learn about drugs? If you were given the assignment to find out about drug use in this country, how would you conduct your research? Would you ask your friends? Listen to a story about "my cousin's friend's sister who got so wasted last night"? Slip some LSD into your friend's drink and watch how her behavior changes? (Please don't.) Different questions call for different means of study. Scientists need to assess which method best serves their purpose, weigh the advantages and disadvantages, and evaluate the practicality and ethical concerns of each of these methods. The most common **research methods** employed by those who investigate drugs are surveys, observational studies, and controlled experiments.

Surveys

Surveys are a way to study the attitudes, opinions, and behaviors of individuals. Survey participants are presented with a number of questions. In written surveys, participants choose from a list of responses, while interview questions are often open-ended. It is important to note that surveys are usually **cross-sectional** in nature; that is, they obtain data from respondents at one point in time and, therefore, cannot be used to examine trends in drug taking or other types of behavior over a longer period of time. There are longitudinal studies as well, which will be discussed later in this section.

The Office of Applied Studies, within the Substance Abuse and Mental Health Services Administration (SAMHSA), annually conducts the *National Survey on Drug Use and Health* (NSDUH). A random sample of all U.S. households is selected, and a professional interviewer visits each of the chosen households. Residents answer a few general questions and then may be asked to participate in the survey. This survey polls approximately 70,000 individuals age 12 years and older, in households from all 50 states and the District of Columbia, about the use of tobacco, alcohol, and illicit drugs, including nonmedical use of prescription drugs. Data are gathered by both surveys and interviews. NSDUH strives to provide accurate data about drug use, track trends in drug use, assess the consequences of use, and identify high-risk groups.

For well over a quarter of a century, the *Monitoring the Future* survey has measured tobacco, alcohol, and drug use among eighth-, tenth-, and twelfth-grade students in the United States. Survey participants report their drug use behaviors across three different periods of time: within the past month, within the past year, and within the participant's lifetime. The survey is funded by the National Institute of Drug Abuse (NIDA), a branch of the National Institutes of Health (NIH), and conducted by the University of Michigan.

Surveys—both written and oral—are a fairly easy and inexpensive way to obtain information from large groups of people. Scientists hoping to learn about drug use, attitudes, or behaviors from either questionnaires or interviews should, however, be aware of the weaknesses of this method of investigation. Imagine you asked, "How many alcoholic drinks did you consume last month?" Although you might think that people would be honest in an anonymous survey, the fact is that people don't always tell the truth when asked about drug use for fear of consequences, or because of worry that confidentiality might not be protected. It may not always be intentional; people may forget or misunderstand the question, or they may give the answer that they think the researcher wants to hear (this is referred

FIGURE A. How much wine is in a glass? The amount of wine in "a glass of wine" depends on the size of the glass.

to as social desirability bias). Also, ambiguity further muddies the waters. How much is a "drink?" Different bartenders may pour different amounts, and the amount of alcohol in a glass of wine depends on the size of the glass (Figure A).

QUICK HIT

The wording of a survey can significantly affect the result. A survey asking, "Have you ever tried [a drug]?" gives a much larger percentage of affirmative responses than one that asks, "Have you ever used [a drug]?" perhaps because many respondents will acknowledge trying it, but do not consider themselves to be drug users.[6]

....

Cross-sectional: Surveys that obtain data from respondents at one point in time; cannot be used to examine trends over a longer period of time.

Observational Methods

In observational methods, investigators observe participants in a particular situation and record and interpret the outcome.[7] Researchers may observe participants in a laboratory, or in a more natural environment. For example, a scientist may go to a bar and observe how flirtations between bar patrons change as they become more inebriated.

The data from observational studies may be more reliable and less susceptible to misinterpretation than survey data, but observational studies are more expensive and time-consuming than surveys. Also, if participants know they are being observed, they may alter their behavior; this is known as an **observer effect**. Finally, observations can be subject to the witnesses' interpretation. One scientist may view a couple's interaction as an attempt to hook up, while another might see it as a casual conversation.

Longitudinal studies are one form of observational study. A longitudinal study involves repeated observations of the same variables over long periods of time. For example, one longitudinal study done in New Zealand has followed over 1,000 participants for more than 40 years, and observed the correlation of various factors with measures of physical and mental health. These studies can be difficult and costly because participants must be tracked and observed for long periods of time.

Controlled Experiments

Cause-and-effect relationships can be only identified using the experimental method, and even then, it is almost impossible to definitively prove one thing *causes* another. An **experiment** (conducting an investigation) begins with a **hypothesis**, which is a prediction about the world based on observations. Each experiment has at least two variables. A **variable** is anything that can vary or change, such as an attitude or a behavior. The **independent variable** is a factor that is controlled and manipulated by the researcher, while the **dependent variable** is observed and measured. What happens to the dependent variable *depends* on what the independent variable is. Although it is problematic in research to say that one variable causes another, for our purposes you might say that the independent variable is the presumed cause, while the dependent variable is the presumed effect; when you change the independent variable (the presumed cause), you observe the effect on the dependent variable.[8]

Controlled experiments require a **control group,** which is a group of participants used in the experiment as a standard of comparison in order to determine the actual effects of the independent variable. For example, imagine you have developed a new weight-loss drug. Participants take the pill once a day for six months, while maintaining a low carbohydrate diet and initiating an exercise regimen. After six months, you find that your participants have lost an average of 20 pounds. Does this mean that you've discovered a miracle drug and are going to be rich beyond your wildest dreams? Probably not. You neglected to use a control group, a group of participants who are treated identically to the experimental group in every way, except that they are not exposed to the independent variable (the drug). The use of a control group allows you to determine the actual effects of your independent variable. This control group should use a **placebo** pill—one that looks identical but contains no pharmaceutically active compounds. If you had used a control group in the weight-loss drug experiment, you may have found that many of your participants lost weight due to the effects of the low-carb diet and exercise plan rather than solely because of the pill.

Let's use another example to illustrate the terms we have learned. Suppose you want to learn about the effect alcohol has on perceptions of attractiveness in the opposite sex. Your hypothesis may read: *All else being equal, alcohol consumption causes heterosexual subjects to rate photos of members of the opposite sex as more attractive.* Suppose 150 female volunteer participants come to the laboratory. Half of them consume a drink of vodka and club soda, and the other half drink club soda only. Participants do not know which they are

---

Observer effect: The effect that the presence of the observer has on a participant's behavior.

Longitudinal study: The same group of participants is observed, measured, or tested over time.

Experiment: A controlled test or investigation, designed to examine the validity of a hypothesis. Also, the act of conducting an investigation.

Hypothesis: A proposed explanation for facts or observations.

Variable: Anything that can vary or change, such as an attitude or a behavior.

Independent variable: The variable that is manipulated in an experiment.

Dependent variable: The variable that is observed and measured and that may change as a result of manipulations to the independent variable.

Control group: The group of participants who are not exposed to the independent variable.

Placebo: A substance or procedure that has no therapeutic effect and may be used as a control in experimental research designs or to reinforce a patient's expectation of recovery.

TABLE B.   Balanced Placebo Design

		Beverage participants actually received	
		Alcohol	**Placebo**
Beverage subjects told they received	Alcohol	Group 1	Group 3
	Placebo	Group 2	Group 4

drinking, as the soda masks the taste of the vodka. Twenty minutes later, they are asked to rate the attractiveness of men in a series of photographs.

In this study, the independent variable (the causal agent) is the alcohol. It is this variable that is manipulated: The test participants will drink alcohol, and those in the control group will only drink club soda. The dependent variable is the effect: How attractive did the women rate the photos of men? If you properly account for variables that may change along with the independent variable (known as confounding factors and discussed in more detail in the next section), and other potentially important differences between the experimental and control groups, and you find that the group of women who consumed alcohol rated the males as more attractive than the control group did, you can say that your results are consistent with the hypothesis.

Participants also have preconceived notions and are susceptible to suggestion. The use of **blinded studies**—a research design in which the investigator or participant (or both) are unaware whether the participant is in the experimental group or in the control group—is one way to reduce bias. In a **single-blinded study**, participants do not know if they are receiving the treatment or intervention, but the researchers do. If neither the participant nor the investigator is aware of who is in the control group and who is in the experimental group, it is called a **double-blinded study**.

As an example, imagine your company has designed a drug to reduce social anxiety. You administer the drug to a number of participants. If you knew which participants received the drug, you might rate their social interactions as more successful. Likewise, if participants believed they had received the drug, they might feel more confident and less apprehensive with other people; this is referred to as an **expectancy effect**.

In a double-blinded study such as this, participants would be given either the experimental drug to reduce anxiety or a placebo identical in size, shape, color, etcetera, to ensure that neither the researchers nor the participants knew which pill contained the experimental drug. Double-blinded studies are used to reduce the influence of the placebo effect and of observer bias (discussed previously).

In order to separate the effects of the drug itself, and the effects due to *expectations* of drug use, it may be best to use a balanced placebo design. The balanced placebo design can simultaneously evaluate the effects of the drug as well as expectancy effects. In a balanced placebo design, shown in Table B, four distinct conditions are created:

- Group 1: Participants receive the active drug (alcohol) and are told they received the active drug (alcohol).
- Group 2: Participants receive the active drug (alcohol) and are told they received the placebo.
- Group 3: Participants receive the placebo and are told they received the active drug (alcohol).
- Group 4: Participants receive the placebo and are told they received the placebo.

Although they can be time consuming and expensive, experiments are the best method for identifying potential causal inferences. They also give us the opportunity to control for unwanted variables. One must remember, however, that not all findings can be generalized to the "real world." The artificiality of the surroundings—for example, the fact that the experiment is conducted in a laboratory rather than in a real bar—may influence your results. Also, results are subject to volunteer bias. Participants who volunteer for a drug study may not be representative of people in the general population.

Blinded study: A research design in which the investigator or participant (or both) are unaware whether the participant is in the experimental group or the control group.

Single-blinded study: An experimental procedure in which the participants do not know whether they have received the treatment being tested.

Double-blinded study: An experimental procedure in which neither the investigator nor the participants know who is in the experimental group and who is in the control group.

Expectancy effect: An effect that may occur when a research participant's expectation of a certain result affects the outcome of the experiment.

Use Valid and Precise Measurements

Imagine you want to learn the effects of a new antidepressant. You give your drug to depressed patients and ask them, "Do you feel better?" How would you measure such a subjective phenomenon? By their self-assessment (known as "self-report" in research terminology) of their mood? By how well they perform on a mood questionnaire? By reports from their family and friends? Each of these standards will give you a different perspective; you need to choose which will best answer your question.

Your means of measurement needs to be accurate and consistent over repeated tests of the same participant. You will also need to make sure that your project is designed to measure only the questions in which you are interested. For instance, in studying the effects of the antidepressant, you need to control for other factors that might influence the results, such as the participant's hormone levels, drug use, and family dynamics. By using accurate and consistent measurements throughout the study and controlling for other factors that might influence the study's results, you will help ensure the **validity** of your experiment. Validity refers to how well the study was run, how closely it actually measures the variables it intends to study, and how generalizable it is.

Internal validity is the degree to which a research design enables one to be confident of a causal relationship between the independent variable and the changes in behavior. If other explanations are possible—for example, if someone's improvement in mood is due to the passage of time, or to seeing a particular doctor, or to other lifestyle changes—then the experiment may not be internally valid. Just because two factors occur together does not mean that one causes the other. It is important not to confuse **correlation**, a relationship between two variables, with **causation**—when one variable causes another.

In an experiment, we try to tightly control as many variables as possible. Factors other than the dependent and independent variable may change throughout an experiment and may influence the outcome. An extraneous variable is a factor that is not the focus of the experiment but can influence the results.[9] A **confounding factor** is an extraneous variable that changes along with the independent variable, such that it is hard to determine what caused the result.

As an example, let's consider the fact that murder rates and ice cream sales are positively correlated. There are three possible explanations for this phenomenon[10]:

1. Buying ice cream causes murder. Perhaps after eating ice cream, brain freeze causes one to lash out in a murderous rage.
2. Murder causes people to buy ice cream. Maybe killing induces a chemical change that can only be sated by the ingestion of sweet cream and sugar.
3. Perhaps there is a third variable—a confounding variable—that causes both the increase in murder and ice cream sales. When it is hot outside, people eat more ice cream. They are also more likely to be outside, interacting with each other, and getting into potentially dangerous situations.

As another example, early studies of postmenopausal women suggested that hormone replacement therapy (HRT) might reduce the risk of coronary heart disease (Chapter 16). Later randomized and controlled studies found that HRT does not decrease heart disease; instead, women who use HRT tend to be in a higher socioeconomic class and, therefore, receive better medical care, exercise more, and follow a healthier diet, and it is these factors that reduce the risk of heart disease.[11]

External validity is a measure of how well the findings of the experiment apply to other settings—are these findings applicable in the real world? The higher the external validity, the more **generalizable** the findings are.

To what degree can we generalize from one population to the next? Do the results found in college students apply to an elderly population? Can animal studies give us information about our own bodies and behaviors? Because our behaviors are a complex amalgam of biological, psychological, and environmental forces, the generalizability of findings depends on many factors. External validity exists on a continuum, and some experiments are more externally valid than others.[12]

Validity: An indication of how reliable the research is.

Internal validity: The degree to which an experiment avoids confounding factors.

Correlation: A complementary, parallel, or reciprocal relationship between two variables.

Causation: When one variable causes the other.

Confounding factor: A variable that is not the focus of the experiment, but which changes along with the independent variable, making it difficult to determine causal factors underlying the result.

External validity: The degree to which the findings can be applied in other settings.

Generalizable: The degree to which the results of the study represent the results that would be obtained from the entire population.

Externally valid experiments can be replicated, meaning that other scientists can recreate the original findings. Scientists need to describe their research methods clearly so that other researchers can replicate their results.

Conduct a Safe, Ethical, and Unbiased Study

All researchers are required to protect the rights and safety of their participants. In 1979, the Belmont Report summarized the ethical standards for doing research with human participants, including the need to show respect for participants, to maximize participants' safety, and to administer procedures fairly. Today, wherever scientific research is conducted in the United States, an independent Institutional Review Board (IRB) reviews research projects. These committees are guided by the principles of the Belmont Report. They evaluate and monitor research proposals to determine the potential value of the research against any possible risk to the participants, and ensure that the studies are scientifically sound, ethical, and safe.[13]

Research participants must give their **informed consent**, a process by which a participant confirms his or her willingness to participate after being told what to expect in study-related procedures, any likely risks or benefits, how the information will be used, how anonymity or **confidentiality** will be assured, and to whom they might address questions. Participants must not be compelled in any way to participate in the study; for example, college students should not be required to take part in any specific experiment in order to receive course credit. Participants also have the right to withdraw from a study at any time.

Maintain Objectivity

Science may be objective, but all scientists are not (Figure B). Every person involved in a scientific study, both as participant and investigator, comes into the

LOOK, HALF THE WORK IS DONE! ALL YOU NEED TO DO IS FILL IN THE TOP PART SO WE CAN LEGALLY SAY THE BOTTOM PART

CHOCOLATE CO-OP INC.

RESEARCH AND DEVELOPMENT

DATA:

CONCLUSION: EATING CHOCOLATE WILL MAKE YOU LOOK YOUNGER AND THINNER

© Wiley Ink, inc./Distributed by Universal Uclick via Cartoonstock

CartoonStock.com

FIGURE B. Science should be objective. Except when the results support eating more chocolate.

study with his or her own experiences and values that may affect the design or interpretation of the work. To illustrate, if a scientist truly believes that marijuana is harmful, when interviewing people who have smoked marijuana, he or she may unconsciously look for evidence to support that point of view and interpret a participant's answers based on this preconception. **Confirmation bias** is the tendency to search for, favor, and remember information that confirms one's beliefs. Sometimes, researchers have a conflict of interest—for

Informed consent: The process by which a study participant is informed of any risks, benefits, or other ramifications when participating in a study.

Confidentiality: How a patient's relevant information from the study will be kept private.

Confirmation bias: The tendency to interpret evidence as confirmation of one's preexisting beliefs

example, if they are funded by the pharmaceutical company that produces the drug they are evaluating. A review of research articles about the effectiveness of Tamiflu found that 88 percent of articles written by scientists who had financial ties to the pharmaceutical company that sells Tamiflu found the product to be effective, compared to only 17 percent among those without a financial conflict of interest.[14] Objectivity is an important ideal of scientific research. To make their studies as objective as possible, researchers can carefully examine research that presents opposing viewpoints; consider using a variety of methods of data collection; report any personal, financial, or other conflicts of interest; and have their research undergo the peer review process.

Consider the Quality of and Vetting of Information

When evaluating studies of drugs—or any studies—you need to consider the project design. Did the study use the best method to achieve its goals? Was the sample appropriate and the methodology clear? Were the statistics used appropriately? Has the study been replicated? Were the data published in a respected, peer-reviewed journal such as *The Journal of Neuroscience* or *The Lancet*, or were the data published in *Scooter's Way Cool Journal of Science Stuff*? High-quality research goes through the **peer review process**, by which a scholar's work is subjected to the scrutiny of others who are experts in the field. Independent reviewers assess the value of the work and check for inconsistencies.

Techniques in Neuropharmacological Research

Now that we have discussed ways that scientists conduct research, let's consider some of the scientific techniques they use to study the effects of drugs on the brain. You will encounter many of these brain imaging techniques in later chapters.

Animal Research

Before drugs are tested on humans, most neuropharmacological research initially is performed on animals. Animal behavior can give us insight into many

Peer review process: The means by which experts in the field check the quality of a research study

conditions that affect humans. Administering drugs to animals can provide animal models of psychiatric disorders, show us the effects of drugs on behavior, and allow us to test new medications. We also can observe animals as they self-administer drugs. In these types of experiments, drugs are automatically injected into an animal's body when it presses a bar. The animal learns that pressing the bar means they get the drug. This technique can show researchers which drug an animal prefers or measure the degree to which the drug causes physical dependence.

Stereotaxic surgery is one way to investigate brain activity in a living animal. The animal's head is stabilized and specific skull markers are used so procedures can be performed with precision. Scientists may place an electrode in a specific area of the animal's brain, stimulate the area, measure the neural activity, and record the animal's behavior. The brain can also be chemically stimulated. Small amounts of psychoactive substances can be injected directly into the brain to help identify the areas that mediate these chemicals' effects. Conversely, researchers may lesion (destroy) a particular area, either physically or chemically, to observe the effect. Scientists must be careful in their interpretation of the results from such experiments—one can't always imply function from behavior, just as one can't always imply cause from effect. As an example, imagine that you taught a frog to jump when it heard a sound. You then lesioned the frog's auditory nerve. When you next played the sound, the frog did not jump, so you (incorrectly) concluded that the auditory nerve controls the frog's motor activity.

Neuropharmacologists sometimes measure the neurotransmitters released in a specific area of the brain while an animal is engaged in a certain behavior. Radioligand binding allows researchers to quantify and locate the neurotransmitters and receptors in the central nervous system (CNS). Researchers dissect out the specific regions of the animal's brain that they are interested in, grind up the tissue, and add a radioactively labeled drug or chemical. They then measure the amount of radioactively labeled substance that is bound to the tissue.

Using animals permits scientists to study phenomena that could not ethically or legally be observed in humans, as well as to test drugs and procedures that save the lives of animals. Examples of drugs and procedures first tested on animals include:

- Untried drugs and procedures
- Insulin and antibiotics

- Open-heart surgeries and coronary bypass surgeries
- Vaccines for smallpox, polio, measles, and rabies

Another advantage of using animals is that it enables scientists to set up a rigorously controlled research design, in which the animal's diet, environment, age, and genetic history are all known and controlled. A disadvantage of animal research is its generalizability. Although there are many similarities between some animal and human systems, a rat is not human, and a drug tested on one animal may have a different effect on other animals or humans. There are also ethical concerns. Laboratory animals have no autonomy and do not choose to participate in research studies. They are also often bred for research and sacrificed once the study is complete.

Animal rights groups protest the use of animals in research (Figure C). Radical groups such as the Animal Liberation Front and Negotiation Is Over have broken into research laboratories and released the animals. Members of these groups have physically threatened researchers, placed bombs on the doorsteps of scientists' homes, and firebombed their cars. The head of one radical group wrote, "If you spill blood, your blood should be spilled as well. . . . If I have my way, you'll be praying to us for mercy."

Ask yourself: Do you believe that humans have the right to do research on animals? On some animals but not others? If so, what differentiates these animals? If you are against animal research, do you eat meat, wear leather, or take medications that were previously tested on animals? Which of these (if any) is acceptable and why?

Brain Imaging Techniques

Researchers use several techniques to give us insights into how the human brain works and reacts to various substances, treatments, and interventions. With today's tools, we can see which brain regions are activated with specific behaviors. A number of techniques give us structural information about the brain, including CT scans and MRIs. Other technologies such as EEGs, PET scans, and fMRIs, provide us with information about the activity of the brain.

Computerized Tomography (CT)

Also called CAT scans or CT scans, computerized axial tomography uses a series of X-ray beams that rotate around the head and are passed through the skull, creating a cross-sectional image of the brain. CT scans provide a three-dimensional image and a sharper picture than X-rays, which makes them helpful in evaluating many structural problems of the brain, such as tumors or trauma (Figure D).

Magnetic Resonance Imaging (MRI)

MRI uses strong magnetic fields, instead of X-rays, to distinguish different body tissues based on their water

FIGURE C. Using animals in research. People feel passionately about both sides of the issue of animal research.

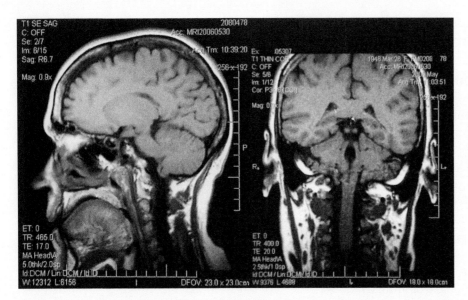

FIGURE D. **Brain imaging techniques.** CT scans give sharp, 3-dimensional images of the brain.

content. MRIs produce higher-contrast images of soft tissues than CT scans, and they are especially good for detecting tumors, infections, and degenerative diseases. However, MRIs are expensive to use. They cannot be used in patients with metallic devices, such as pacemakers, insulin pumps, or cochlear implants, because the strong magnetic field can suck metal objects through and from the body. MRIs are loud, and may be difficult for claustrophobic patients, who need to lie still in a tight, enclosed space.

Structural information about the brain is helpful for making medical diagnoses, but not as helpful in pharmaceutical research. Techniques that give us insight into the brain's activity are more useful in discovering the effects that drugs might have on human behavior.

Electroencephalograms (EEGs)

EEGs let us record the electrical activity of the brain (Figure E). Action potentials (the process by which nerve signals are transmitted; see Chapter 3) produce voltage changes in neurons, and electrodes record this activity. Microelectrodes can record the electrical activity of individual neurons, and macroelectrodes record electrical activity of large portions of neural tissue. EEGs are used to assess states of consciousness, seizure disorders, sleep states, degenerative diseases, and brain activity.

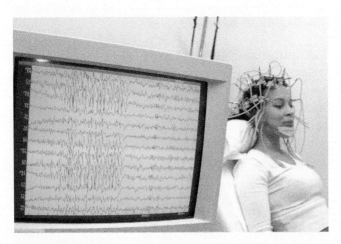

FIGURE E. **EEG.** Electroencephalograms record the electrical activity of the brain.

Positron Emission Tomography (PET)

PET scans are one method of measuring the brain's metabolic activity. In a PET scan, a patient is injected with a radioactive substance called 2-deoxyglucose (2-DG), which resembles glucose and is taken up into cells, especially in the brain. When 2-DG decays, it emits subatomic particles called positrons, which are detected by a scanner. The scanner identifies which areas of the brain have taken up the most 2-DG; these are the most metabolically active areas. A computer then produces a colored picture of that section of the brain (Figure F). PET scans provide

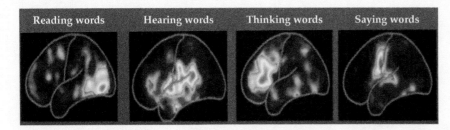

FIGURE F. **PET scans show brain activity.** The PET scan on the left shows that the primary visual cortex of the occipital lobe is particularly active (seen in red and yellow) when people read words. The second scan shows areas of the temporal lobe that fire when people hear words. Scan number 3 shows where brain activity is highest when people think about words, and scan 4 shows areas of the brain involved in saying words.

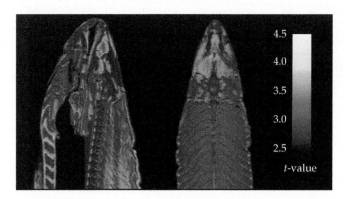

FIGURE G. Brain imaging techniques are not perfect. An fMRI of a dead salmon "perceiving" human emotions.

functional, not just anatomical, information about the brain. They can show where radioactively labeled drugs bind in the brain, and can determine which parts of the brain are active during certain behaviors or processes. However, PET scans are expensive, fairly slow, and not as readily available as CT scans or MRIs.

Functional MRI (fMRI)

The fMRI is a modification of the traditional MRI that provides both an anatomical and functional view of the brain. fMRI measures brain activity by detecting levels of oxygen in the brain's blood vessels. fMRI is faster than PET scans, has a higher resolution, is noninvasive, and does not use a radioactive tracer. Its accuracy, however, has been called into question.[15]

In one study, published in the *Journal of Serendipitous and Unexpected Results*, researchers placed a dead salmon into the apparatus and showed it a series of photographs of people in social situations.[16] Tongue firmly in cheek, the researchers asked the deceased fish to determine what emotion the person in the photo was feeling. Imagine the researchers' surprise when areas of the salmon's brain showed increased activity (Figure G)! So, using your critical thinking skills, which is more likely: that a dead salmon can perceive a human's emotional state; or that the analysis tool is not perfect, and scientists must be careful in interpreting the data?

Critical Thinking

Although scientists use many specialized techniques to conduct research and then explain that research, they are not the only ones who present an argument to prove a position. Every day, we are bombarded with opinions, beliefs, and viewpoints. How do we know if those positions have value? To illustrate, a recent Google search

of "drugs" produced 2,090,000,000 sites, including the U.S. Food and Drug Administration (FDA) web page, a site on how to buy pharmaceutical drugs illegally from Mexico, an ad for the latest sexual enhancement tablet, and advice on how to make a bong out of an apple. People today are exposed to more drug information than ever before, but as with any commodity, as the supply increases, value decreases. In order to become an intelligent consumer of information, you must learn to think critically.

Dr. Richard Paul, a noted authority in the area of critical thinking, once said, "Critical thinking is thinking about your thinking while you're thinking in order to make your thinking better." Critical thinkers don't just accept what they are told; they question and analyze. They are aware of their own and others' biases and assumptions. They try to judge ideas and actions in their historical and cultural context, and explore the implications and consequences of ideas. Critical thinkers evaluate arguments and statements based on evidence, and recognize the difference between "strong" evidence and "weak" evidence. Critical thinking entails both a set of skills, as well as a mindset. This section lays out some of the skills you need in order to evaluate the barrage of drug information to which you are constantly exposed.[17,18,19] To illustrate how critical thinking can be done, let's consider an example. How much do you know about dihydrogen monoxide (DHMO)?

DHMO has been used:

- As an industrial solvent and coolant
- In nuclear power plants
- In producing and distributing pesticides
- In the rallies and marches of the KKK and the death camps run by the Nazis

Some of the dangers associated with DHMO are:

- Acid rain
- Severe burns from exposure to its gaseous form
- Presence in biopsies of precancerous tumors
- Death (caused by inhaling even small quantities)

Despite these dangerous side effects, DHMO is used as an additive in many food products, including soups, sodas, baby formula, and even supposedly "all-natural" fruit juices; in cough medicines; in personal hygiene products; and in certain brands of coffee. Studies show that even after careful washing, food that has been exposed to DHMO remains tainted.[20]

Tom Way, at the dihydrogen monoxide research division, writes, "Research conducted by award-winning U.S. scientist Nathan Zohner concluded that roughly

86 percent of the population supports a ban on dihydrogen monoxide. Although his results are preliminary, Zohner believes people need to pay closer attention to the information presented to them regarding dihydrogen monoxide. He adds that if more people knew the truth about DHMO, then studies like the one he conducted would not be necessary."[21]

Are you angry? Ready to march on Washington to ban DHMO? Hold on there. Dihydrogen monoxide—H_2O—is water. All the facts previously listed are true—water *is* a component of acid rain, and inhalation can cause death—but it is important to consider the context in which these facts are presented. By presenting the facts out of context, the authors can fool some unsuspecting and uninformed individuals into thinking that water should be banned. Learning to think critically will help you to gather and analyze the necessary information to make an informed and intelligent opinion. It also will allow you to laugh at the people who are caught by the hoax, which is always fun.

The internet is a convenient source of information for many people. Most internet sites, however, do not undergo peer review. For example, Wikipedia can be amended by almost anyone who chooses to do so and is more likely to have inaccuracies and flaws than Encyclopedia Britannica or other recognized reference guides.[22] Evaluation of the Wikipedia articles for the 20 most frequently prescribed drugs were found to be inaccurate and incomplete, especially regarding information on contraindications, precautions, and adverse drug events.[23] As you encounter information, be sure to check out the sources and verify the data.

Ask yourself: How readily do you trust information you find on the internet? What criteria have you used in the past to determine whether the information on a website is trustworthy?

Primary source: The original publication of a scientist's data, results, and theories

Jim Kapoun has developed some criteria to help you determine whether a website is a good source of information.[24] First, evaluate the accuracy and authority of the web documents.

- What is the purpose of the document and why was it produced?
- Who wrote the page? Is he or she a qualified expert? Does she provide contact information?
- Is the domain .edu or .gov (more reliable), or is it .com?

Next, consider how objective the documents are.

- Why was the site written, and for whom?
- How detailed is the information presented?
- Does the author express personal opinions?
- Is the page a mask for advertising?

You also should check to see how old the site is, when it was produced and last updated, whether the links are up to date and active, and whether you need to pay to access the site.

QUICK HIT

About 1.5 million people click on Erowid.org (www.erowid.org) each month for information about drugs. (Its name was assembled from Proto-Indo-European roots that together mean "Earth wisdom" or "knowledge of existence.") Erowid contains more than 63,000 pages of information about psychoactive substances, both legal and illegal. The information comes from a variety of resources, including experts, published literature, and the general public. The information is fact checked by dozens of volunteers.

Erowid is a well-respected site and has been cited in scientific journals, by numerous authors, and in the media. Some people, however, fear that the site minimizes adverse effects of drugs.

Many people obtain important health information from the media. When research is presented in the popular media, however, the press may distort or simplify its meaning. Whenever possible, seek the **primary sources** of the information. Other print sources that provide accurate information about drugs include

---

STRAIGHT DOPE   Nathan Zohner

So who is this award-winning scientist Nathan Zohner? In 1997, Zohner, then a 14-year-old middle school student in Idaho, presented 50 of his classmates with some of the information regarding DHMO and then surveyed them regarding their opinions. Forty-three voted to ban the substance. Zohner presented his findings at his school's science fair and won first prize. The term *Zohnerism* now means "the use of a scientific fact to guide an uninformed public to a false conclusion."

the *Physician's Desk Reference,* which includes chemical information, action of drugs, indications and contraindications, side effects, and warnings about the drugs; package inserts from pharmaceuticals; and the United States Pharmacopoeia, which sets the standards of identity, strength, purity, packaging, storage, and labeling for drugs.

Recognize Underlying Value Assumptions

Everyone has views about the way the world should be. A value assumption is a position so taken for granted by an author that he or she does not feel the need to state it as part of an argument.[25],[26] So how can one discover an author's value assumption if it is not stated in his or her argument? Let's give an example.

- "We should not legalize recreational drugs. These drugs cause too much street crime."

The author's conclusion is that recreational drugs should not be legalized. The reason is that illegal drugs cause street crime. But the unspoken value assumption is that *public safety is more important than personal freedom of choice.*[27] You may or may not agree with the conclusion, but if you can identify the author's value assumption, you can better evaluate the argument. Using the same example, if you *do not* feel that public safety is more important than personal choice, then the author's rationale is not valid for you, regardless of your feelings about recreational drugs.

- "The government should prohibit the manufacture and sale of cigarettes. More and more evidence has demonstrated that smoking has harmful effects on the health of both the smoker and those exposed to smoking."

The author's conclusion is that cigarettes should be prohibited, because they are physically harmful. The unspoken value assumption is that *the government, rather than an individual, should regulate its citizens' health.* Some common value assumptions we will see in this book include the conflicting ideas of individual responsibility versus collective responsibility, public safety versus freedom of choice, success versus happiness, and security versus excitement.

Evaluate the Strength of the Argument

Fallacies of reasoning are arguments based on unreliable, irrelevant, or insufficient evidence. These fallacies undermine the strength of an argument. As critical thinkers, you can learn to recognize these errors.

Fallacies of Relevance

When an argument fails to address the facts and, instead, focuses on irrelevant and unrelated matters, this is known as a **fallacy of relevance**. Examples of these include *ad hominem* and *ad populum* arguments, appeals to emotion, tautologies, red herrings, and searching for perfect solutions.[28],[29]

In an *ad hominem* argument, the author attacks the background or the motives of a person.

- "Senator Latham gave a speech about the failure of the war on drugs, but he smoked pot in college, so he's clearly biased" [attacking the senator and not discussing the facts about the issue, which is the war on drugs].

An *ad populum* argument gives the popular opinion. Just because "most people agree" doesn't mean that they're right. This is the "if your friends jumped off the Brooklyn Bridge, would you?" argument.

- "Most Americans drink alcohol. Therefore, drinking is harmless." [Just because most people do something doesn't mean it's harmless.]

An *appeal to emotion* hopes to persuade by presenting the issue in an emotionally charged way.

- "This adorable puppy is named Fluffy. Fluffy is trapped in a cage at a pharmaceutical company, where he receives daily injections of a potentially dangerous drug. Please stop the monsters who torture puppies and vote to ban animal testing." [This argument presents no data about any potential benefits of animal testing, nor does it discuss any actual harms done to the animal; instead, it goes right to the emotional gut punch of a sad puppy.]

When a conclusion is supported only by itself, the argument is known as *circular reasoning*, or a *tautology*.

- "Only criminals use illegal drugs." [If one does something illegal, one is by definition a criminal. If drugs were legal, all of a sudden, the users wouldn't be criminals.]

A *red herring* diverts the reader's attention to another issue rather than the facts at hand.

- "People may claim that SSRIs help people with depression, but what they don't realize is that most of the bottles the drugs come in are made

Fallacy of relevance: An argument that is irrelevant to the matter at hand.

of nonrecyclable material and are hurting our environment" [the red herring—whether or not the bottles are recyclable—has nothing to do with the issue, which is the effectiveness of the SSRIs].

When a person assumes that a resolution to a problem does not deserve support unless it solves the problem completely, that person is said to be *searching for a perfect solution*.

- "Drug testing has not eliminated drug use in America; therefore, it should be abolished."

Fallacies of Insufficient Evidence

When an argument addresses the facts but does not provide sufficient evidence to support the conclusion, this is referred to as a **fallacy of insufficient evidence**. Examples include inappropriate appeals to authority, appeals to ignorance, false dilemmas, hasty generalizations, and slippery slope arguments.[30],[31]

Some sources of information are more reliable than others. For instance, if you were hoping to obtain information about the neuropharmacological effects of MDMA (also known as ecstasy), the National Institute for Drug Abuse would be a more trustworthy source than, say, Lindsey Lohan. Arguments that are based on the statements of "experts" who are not qualified to make reliable claims are *inappropriate appeals to authority*.

- "Justin Bieber says it's safe to drive if you've had fewer than six drinks, so I'm good to go."

An *appeal to ignorance* assumes that if we haven't proven that something is true, then it must be false (or vice versa). The absence of evidence is not the same as evidence of absence.

- "This study did not find evidence that our new antidepressant Dammitol causes cancer; therefore, it is safe."

If the argument is designed such that there are only two possible outcomes: *either* this *or* that will happen, then the author has created a *false dilemma* or *either/or fallacy*.

- "Either we send drug users to jail or our children will be shooting up heroin at recess."

Hasty generalizations are some of the most common fallacies in reasoning that people make. We often give more credence to personal experiences than to data and evidence. When people make generalizations, they may be guilty of **egocentrism**, the practice of regarding one's own opinions as most important. Some examples of hasty generalizations include:

- "Prozac didn't work for me. So Prozac is a useless drug."
- "People who smoke marijuana have no ambition and don't make anything of themselves."
- "All smokers will get cancer."

A *slippery slope* argument is one in which it is claimed that one small step leads to an ever-intensifying chain of events, culminating in a catastrophic result:

- "If a woman uses cocaine while she is pregnant, she can be held accountable for endangering her unborn child. What's next? Will we punish women for drinking caffeine, or not getting enough exercise? Will pregnant women go to jail if they don't get enough calcium?"

Critically Evaluate Graphs and Data

Sometimes, graphs and statistics can be manipulated to present results that can be easily misinterpreted. As critical thinkers, be on the lookout for suspect data.

Does the Graph Accurately Represent the Data?

Consider a fictitious press release from Mendax Pharmaceuticals raving about their new weight-loss drug Adipnope. Mendax publishes the graph shown in Figure H. This drug looks great! But wait a second. . . check out the Y-axis. There is only a tenth of a pound difference between those who took the drug and those who did not. If the Y-axis were changed, as shown in Figure I, the graph might better represent the true effectiveness of Adipnope.

Fallacy of insufficient evidence: An argument that does not provide sufficient evidence to support the conclusion

Egocentrism: The practice of regarding one's own experiences or opinions as most important.

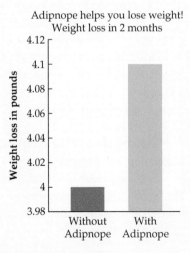

FIGURE H. Evaluating graphs. Be sure to check the scale of the axes.

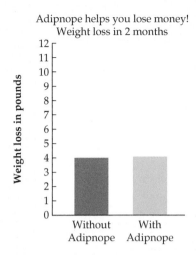

Adipnope helps you lose money!
Weight loss in 2 months

FIGURE I. Evaluating graphs. Changing the scale of the axes can make a 2.5% increase look like a 500% increase.

Are the Statistics Used Appropriately?

"Anticapitis works 50 percent better in easing your headache pain!" Better than what? Better than other drugs? Better than using nothing? Better than a kick in the head? A contextual framework is necessary in order to interpret statistics. Be on the lookout for the following contextual clues:

- *Historical context.* How have the data varied over time, and what time period is being investigated? Is the latest figure an indication of a trend, or is it an anomaly?
- *Population context.* How does the value compare to the overall population in question?[32] Imagine that a new drug—"Mellow Yellow"—becomes popular. One million New Yorkers have taken the drug, compared with only 200,000 Vermonters. Before you decide that New Yorkers must be crazed drug fiends, keep in mind that the population of New York State is 20 million, while Vermont has only 600,000 residents. This means that 5 percent of New Yorkers used Mellow Yellow, but a whopping 33 percent of Vermonters did.
- *Absolute value context.* What does the percentage mean in the real world? In 1995, the British Committee on Safety of Medicines issued a warning that some brands of hormonal contraceptive pills raised the

risk of dangerous blood clots by 100 percent. Many women stopped taking the pill due to fears of life-threatening thrombosis. In reality, the relative risk *was* increased by 100 percent—from 1 in 7,000 women to 2 in 7,000 women, but the absolute, "real world" risk of blood clot was still very low. The pill scare led to an increase in unplanned pregnancies and abortions the following year in the United Kingdom.[33]

Drugs in the Media

We are exposed to about 10 hours of media a day—thousands of ads, hundreds of web pages, and hours of television and movies. Movies, television, and music portray the full range of human activity—love, sex, violence, jealousy, crime, family, work, and, yes, drugs. Drug references are rife in the media, and the images they present influence our beliefs, values, and behavior. Therefore, it is important to critically evaluate the messages communicated in movies, television, music, and advertisements.

Movies

In the 2009 movie *The Hangover*, four friends take a trip to Las Vegas for a bachelor party (Figure J). After

Ask yourself: Which of the various media—movies, television, music, or advertisements—would have the most powerful influence on our attitudes about drugs? Why do you feel that way?

FIGURE J. The movie *The Hangover* minimizes the deleterious effects of alcohol.

they imbibe an enormous amount of alcohol, chaos ensues. In reality, if someone lost a tooth, found a tiger in the bathroom, and angered Mike Tyson, it would be very upsetting, but the movie illustrates how society idolizes and admires alcohol use and downplays the problematic effects connected to its consumption. Alcohol portrayals are common in film, even in G-rated films intended for children, and positive references about alcohol outnumber negative ones by more than 10 to 1.[34]

Movies also both glamorize and demonize illegal drugs. There are stoner films (*Cheech and Chong, Harold and Kumar, Pineapple Express*); stories about dealing, crime, and the war against drugs (*Traffic, Blow, Midnight Express, Scarface*); cautionary tales about addiction (*Reefer Madness, When a Man Loves a Woman, Requiem for a Dream*); and rehab stories (*28 Days, Clean and Sober*). Films about addiction are often melodramas with a hero and an adversary, in which addiction serves as the adversary. The hero may find redemption and defeat addiction, or lose the battle, ending up in jail or dead. Often, these films present a complicated situation as morally clear with no middle ground.[35]

Television

Drug and alcohol use are also commonly depicted on television, although the way these are portrayed on network TV differs from their portrayal on pay channels (such as HBO) or online programming (like Amazon, Hulu, or Netflix). Network television has tighter governmental controls over its content, needs to satisfy its advertisers, and seeks to have the broadest appeal to viewers, making it therefore more likely to avoid extremes in portrayals that might offend viewers.[36] Alcohol consumption is more commonly shown on television than tobacco or drug use.

When researchers analyzed the content of the top 18 prime-time TV shows in the 2004–2005 season, alcohol was present in every program investigated.[37] Until fairly recently, drinking alcohol typically was shown as a positive, routine, problem-free activity, and alcohol was most likely to be consumed by the characters who were attractive and high status.[38] Today, however, prime-time television is more likely to present mixed messages when it comes to alcohol, with direct references

Ask yourself: In what ways do you think drug and alcohol depiction in movies is accurate? In what ways is it inaccurate?

Ask yourself: What messages about alcohol and other drugs have you seen in network television shows as opposed to shows on pay channels? What underlying agendas might explain any dissimilar depictions?

being associated with negative consequences and more positive messages being presented subtly or in the background of the action.[39]

Illegal drug use also is frequently depicted. Drug portrayal on pay or cable channels is often grittier than on network television. Shows such as *Breaking Bad* and *Weeds* subvert the racial and cultural stereotypes of drugs and drug users from society's entrenched notions of these stereotypes.[40]

Music

Drug and alcohol references are ubiquitous in popular music. How prevalent are these references today? In one study, researchers looked at 279 of the best-selling songs in five genres: rap, country, R&B/hip-hop, rock, and pop.[41] Of the 279 songs, 33.3 percent portrayed substance use, with an average of 35.2 substance references per song-hour. Given that the average adolescent listens to over two hours of music a day, he or she is exposed to approximately 84 daily references to explicit substance use in his or her music. Alcohol was referenced the most, followed by marijuana, illicit drugs, and last of all, tobacco. Over two-thirds of the songs that contained references to substance use portrayed positive consequences more than negative consequences. Alcohol, for example, is typically associated with sex and partying, and is portrayed as positive, fun, and free of consequences.[42] Only 4 percent of songs gave explicit messages against substance use, and none contained messages of substance refusal. The prevalence of drug references varied greatly by genre. Some 9 percent of pop songs and 14 percent of rock songs contained drug references. One in every five R&B songs contained references to drugs, as did 36 percent of country songs. In the case of rap music, 77 percent of songs contained drug references.

Hundreds of studies have documented a relationship between media exposure and the attitudes and

Ask yourself: Does the widespread portrayal of drugs and alcohol in the media necessarily influence behavior?

behavior of young people.[43] Studies have shown that media exposure to tobacco;[44] alcohol;[45,46,47,48] and illegal drugs[49] is linked to increased use. Researchers theorized that the link between exposure and consumption may be due to three factors:

- People are wired to imitate other people's behaviors.
- Viewers observe beautiful, glamorous actors and musicians using alcohol and other drugs and learn to idealize their use.
- Media references also might teach people to associate drugs and alcohol with certain behaviors or events, such as drinking champagne on New Year's Eve.

QUICK HIT

People have always sung about alcohol and drugs. The first drinking song dates from the eleventh century. Over 80 years ago, Cab Calloway sang about the "reefer man," and the Memphis Jug Band crooned about those "cocaine habit blues." The 1950s gave us "one bourbon, one scotch, and one beer," and popular songs of the 1970s included the lyrics "sister morphine" and "legalize it." In this century, Afroman sang "because I got high" and Amy Winehouse sang about "rehab."

Advertising

Ads are everywhere. We encounter them on television, in movie theaters, on the internet, and in magazines, billboards, and even bathroom stalls. The average American is exposed to hundreds if not thousands of ads a day. And many of those ads encourage us to use drugs and alcohol.

Alcohol Advertising

Media expenditures for alcoholic beverages have increased by 400 percent since 1971.[50,51] The alcohol industry spends well over $2 billion per year on all media advertising; if one were to include sponsorship, point-of-sale materials, product placement, and brand-logoed items, total expenditures would equal about $6 billion or more. The alcohol industry also uses social networking platforms such as Facebook, Twitter, and YouTube, as well as text messages, cellphone apps, and downloadable ringtones to market their products.[52] Evidence suggests that exposure to alcohol ads predicts when nondrinkers will start drinking, as well as increased drinking by existing drinkers.[53]

Alcohol ads link drinking to socially desirable attributes, as well as to desirable outcomes such as success,

fun, sex, and adventure. The alcohol industry targets different products to specific audiences. Beer and whiskey ads are typically aimed at men, and they play up many stereotypical male characteristics. Lighter alcohols such as liqueurs or "umbrella drinks" largely target the female population, and often highlight romance, relationships, and pictures of women being the center of male attention.

Some alcoholic products, and the ads that market them, are designed to appeal to children. Each year, children see about 300 alcohol ads on television, and many more in magazines and on billboards.[54] Youth are especially drawn to alcohol ads that include musical elements, animal and human characters, celebrities, and humor.[55]

Some alcohol companies place "responsibility" ads to deliver messages about underage drinking or drinking safely. But for every single "don't drink" campaign ad they see each year, teenagers will see 50 to 96 times more ads that promote drinking.[56] In 2006, Congress unanimously passed a law that would allow for a governmental agency to review and track young people's exposure to advertisements and other media messages that may promote alcohol use, and to report their findings. To date, Congress has not appropriated any funds for this program, and no reports have been made.

Direct-to-Consumer Pharmaceutical Ads

Direct-to-consumer (DTC) advertising flooded the American airwaves in 1997, when the FDA eased the regulations controlling pharmaceutical ads. In these ads, the pharmaceutical companies directly market their product to consumers rather than to physicians. Banned in almost all other industrialized nations, DTC ads are allowed only in the United States and in New Zealand. DTC ads often describe a disease and then tell the viewer about the specific drug that can treat it.

Ask yourself: Why might the fact that alcohol is a legally available product, whose taxes support our economy, make it difficult to restrict its advertising? Should alcohol be restricted given that (as we will see in later chapters) it creates more personal, social, economic, and legal problems than all other drugs combined? If so, in what ways? If not, why not?

Direct-to-consumer advertising: A form of marketing promotion used by pharmaceutical companies aimed at patients rather than healthcare professionals.

These ads are required to provide a summary of a drug's actions, indications, and potential adverse effects, although the ads can refer consumers to web pages or phone numbers to obtain the information.

In 1997, there were about 79,000 ads for pharmaceuticals; by 2016, that had soared to over 4.6 million ads. Drug companies spend over $6 billion each year on DTC ads, and every dollar spent on advertising prescription drugs is estimated to increase the drug company's retail sales by $4.20 (incidentally, drug companies spend more on DTC ads each year than the total budget allocated to the FDA, the agency that oversees the pharmaceutical industry).[57],[58] By the time a 30-second commercial airs, the company has conducted months of studies on how best to market the drug, and has spent many billions of dollars on free samples and marketing the drug to physicians.[59]

Companies do not shell out tens of billions of dollars annually on campaigns that are not effective. Up to 30 percent of adults in the United States have asked their doctors about an advertised drug, and 44 percent of those reported receiving the requested drug.[60] A 10 percent increase in DTC ads translates to a 1 percent increase in sales for that class of drugs.[61] In fact, patients' requests for drugs are a powerful driver of prescribing decisions. Many times, physicians will prescribe a requested medicine, even though they may be ambivalent about the choice of treatment. Physicians may feel pressured by patient requests to prescribe drugs they would not ordinarily prescribe.[62] The pros and cons of DTC ads will be discussed in Chapter 1. Not all advertisements encourage drug use, however, and some are designed to decrease the use of illicit drugs and tobacco. These ads are discussed in Chapter 18.

Critical thinking skills are useful not only in evaluating the material in the rest of this textbook, but in evaluating the information and arguments you're presented with for the rest of your life. In subsequent chapters, you will be presented with real examples of research as well as arguments for and against controversial issues related to drugs. Critically evaluate these positions using the ideas and skills presented in this section.

Chapter Summary

- **Pharmacological Research**
  - » Scientific studies must be carefully designed to be as clearly defined, properly controlled, and unbiased as possible.
  - » High-quality research requires precise and unambiguous language.
  - » The proper sample, or subset of the population being investigated, must be selected. Probability sampling uses some form of random selection, and in non-probability sampling, participants are not chosen at random.
  - » The most common research methods in drug studies are surveys, observational studies, and controlled experiments. In a survey, information is gathered through questionnaires or interviews. In observational studies, investigators observe participants in particular situations and record and interpret the outcomes.
  - » Controlled experiments are the only way to identify cause-and-effect relationships. A controlled experiment includes an independent variable, a dependent variable, and a control group.
  - » Measurements should be valid and precise. Validity is the measure of how reliable an experiment is. Internal validity is the degree to which an experiment avoids confounding factors, and external validity is a measure of how well the findings can be applied in other settings. When interpreting results, it is important not to confuse correlation and causation.
  - » Institutional review boards and rules about proper research protocols are in place to ensure that studies are safe, ethical, and unbiased.
- **Techniques in Neuropharmacological Research**
  - » Many techniques are used to investigate the effects that drugs have on the brain and body.
  - » Animal research provides important information about the ways drugs work. Animal testing enables scientists to set up rigorously controlled research designs, and can allow us to test the effects of drugs on a living body before they are tested on humans. Their generalizability to humans can be questioned, however, as can the ethics of using animals against their will.
  - » Some techniques, including CT scans and MRIs, give us information about the structure of the brain, while EEGs, PET scans, and fMRIs let investigators see brain activity.
- **Critical Thinking**
  - » Critical thinking entails both a set of skills as well as a mindset.
  - » Value assumptions are the unspoken positions that may underlie an author's opinion.
  - » Fallacies of relevance are arguments that are irrelevant to the matter at hand. They include *ad hominem* and *ad populum* arguments, appeals to emotion,

tautologies, red herrings, and searching for perfect solutions.

» Fallacies of insufficient evidence are arguments that do not provide sufficient or appropriate evidence to support themselves. Examples are inappropriate appeals to authority, appeals to ignorance, false dilemmas, hasty generalizations, and slippery slope arguments.

» Consider whether the graphs and statistics accurately represent the data.

• **Drugs in the Media**

» Drug references are common in the media. Many studies suggest that media exposure to tobacco, alcohol, and illegal drugs is linked to use.

» Pharmaceutical companies market many drugs to consumers with direct-to-consumer ads.

Key Terms

Blinded study (p.xxxv)
Causation (p.xxxvi)
Confidentiality (p.xxxvii)
Confirmation bias (p.xxxvii)
Confounding factor (p.xxxvi)
Control group (p.xxxiv)
Convenience sample (p.xxxii)
Correlation (p.xxxvi)
Cross-sectional (p.xxxiii)
Dependent variable (p.xxxiv)
Direct-to-consumer advertising (p.xlvii)
Double-blinded study (p.xxxv)
Egocentrism (p.xliv)
Expectancy effect (p.xxxv)

Experiment (p.xxxiv)
External validity (p.xxxvi)
Fallacy of insufficient evidence (p.xliv)
Fallacy of relevance (p.xliii)
Generalizable (p.xxxvi)
Hypothesis (p.xxxiv)
Independent variable (p.xxxiv)
Informed consent (p.xxxvii)
Internal validity (p.xxxvi)
Longitudinal study (p.xxxiv)
Observer effect (p.xxxiv)
Peer review process (p.xxxviii)
Placebo (p.xxxiv)
Population (p.xxxi)
Primary source (p.xlii)

Purposive nonprobability sample (p.xxxi)
Representative sample (p.xxxi)
Research methods (p.xxxii)
Sample (p.xxxi)
Sampling bias (p.xxxii)
Self-selection sample (p.xxxi)
Simple random sample (p.xxxi)
Single-blinded study (p.xxxv)
Stratified random sample (p.xxxi)
Validity (p.xxxvi)
Variable (p.xxxiv)
Volunteer bias (p.xxxi)

Quiz Yourself! (Answers to the Quiz Yourself! questions may be found at the back of the book.)

1. Dr. Washington wants to understand about prescription drug use in American women. She will study a sample of this population. Which best describes a representative sample of this population?

    A.   All female students in her class

    B.   All female readers of *Time* magazine

    C.   A group of women that represents the race, age, and religion distribution of American women

    D.   All American women

2. True or false? Thirty students from Dr. Michael's advanced calculus class take a survey about drug use. Because the topic of drug use is important to study, this survey has good external validity.

3. Dr. Brown wants to see the relationship between drinking alcohol and a man's attitudes toward violence against women. One hundred and fifty male volunteer participants come to his laboratory. Half of them consume a drink of vodka and club soda (the taste of the vodka is masked by the club soda), and the other half drinks club soda only. They are then told to complete a questionnaire regarding their attitudes about women, sex, and violence.

    A.   What in this experiment is the independent variable?

    B.   What in this experiment is the dependent variable?

    C.   What in this experiment is the control?

4. True or false? An MRI gives information about brain structure, and PET scans give information about brain activity.

5. Match the statement to the type of fallacy.

1. Your honor, I know it's my third time caught driving drunk, but I shouldn't be punished because I'm going through a divorce, I have a cold, and they killed off my favorite character on *Game of Thrones*.

2. Dr. Stewart claims that nicotine is dangerous. But he's obnoxious and has a bad combover, so who cares what he says.

3. Nothing has proven that Ritalin stunts growth; therefore, it doesn't.

4. It is a proven scientific fact that cold medicine corrupts adolescent boys. Researchers gave cold medicine to teenaged boys and later found that they all had sexual thoughts at times. Therefore, cold medicine causes sexual thoughts.

A. *Ad hominem* argument

B. Inappropriate appeals to authority

C. False dilemma/either-or

D. Appeals to ignorance

E. Appeal to emotion

F. *Ad populum* argument

G. Red herring

H. Confusing correlation and causation

I. Slippery slope

J. Hasty generalization

5. If we legalize marijuana, then what's next? Legalizing cocaine? Heroin? The very fabric of our nation will be destroyed.

6. My hairdresser says antidepressants cause autism, so I'm going to stop taking my Prozac prescription immediately.

7. I know three people from Colorado who have taken cocaine. Clearly, people from Colorado are all druggies.

8. Most Americans have driven drunk at some time in their lives; therefore, driving drunk isn't as bad as everyone says.

9. If we don't give Gardasil to all preteen girls, then they will all get cervical cancer.

10. Sure, this new drug has been clinically proven to reduce symptoms of Parkinson's disease, but the bottle it comes in is not recyclable, so it's a bad drug.

6. Which is true about drug and alcohol portrayals in the media?

A. G-rated films are not allowed to portray alcohol use.

B. Drug and alcohol references in popular music were most common in the 1980s; today, fewer than 5 percent of songs reference drugs or alcohol.

C. Only about 40 percent of prime-time television programs portray alcohol use.

D. All of these are true.

E. All of these are false.

Additional Resources

Books

Almossawi, A. (2013). *An illustrated book of bad arguments*. New York: The Experiment Publishing.

Browne, M.N., & Keeley, S. (2014). *Asking the right questions: A guide to critical thinking* (11th ed.). Saddle River

Learn more with this chapter's digital tools at www.oup.com/he/rosenthal2e.

Drugs: Mind, Body, and Society

True or false?

1.
True or false? Withdrawal from chronic heavy alcohol use is more dangerous than withdrawal from long-term heroin use.

2.
True or false? Eating a poppy seed bagel may cause you to test positive for opioids on a drug test.

3.
True or false? The United States consumes 65 percent of the world's supply of illicit drugs.

Answers: 1.T, 2.T, 3.T

....

Learning Objectives

- Identify demographic factors that raise one's risk of drug use.
- Name some of the factors that explain fluctuations in drug use over time.
- Specify some reasons why people use drugs.
- List some problems associated with both short-term and long-term drug use.
- Define the terms *psychoactive*, *drug*, *illegal*, *illicit*, and *recreational*.
- Differentiate among endogenous substances, natural drugs, and synthetic drugs.
- Explain the difference between a drug's generic name and its trade name.
- Distinguish among schedule I and schedules II, III, IV, and V.
- Describe the process by which a new drug is approved by the FDA.
- Evaluate the advantages and disadvantages of direct-to-consumer advertising.

Psychoactive: A substance that affects the mind. Psychoactive substances often produce feelings of euphoria or altered perception.

How many drugs do you take a day? You might have responded to that question with an indignant "I don't do drugs" or a drawn out, red-eyed "Duuuuude." But the reality is that few Americans ingest *no* drugs. Although the word *drug* may bring to mind heroin syringes and crack pipes, the elegant woman sipping her red wine over dinner is openly doing drugs, and the barista at Starbucks is a drug dealer. Have you ever taken an aspirin? Are you on the Pill? You take drugs.

Drugs are fascinating. We ascribe a nearly mythic status to these tiny bits of chemicals sprinkled around the earth that can change our behavior and our personality, and which can kill us or cure us. When our bodies, minds, or souls are ailing, we often seek relief by ingesting pills and potions and prescriptions, with an almost religious belief in their necessity and efficacy (as a former professor of mine was wont to say, "A headache is not a sign that your body is low on aspirin"). In some ways, we live in a drugstore society—we wander the aisles searching for the chemical combination to make us happy or thin or smart or funny or relaxed enough to deal with the task at hand.

Drug use is universal. People in every human society in every age of history have used one or more **psychoactive** drugs to alter their thoughts, moods, emotions, and behavior. If you include prescription drugs and caffeine, 95 percent of the adult U.S. population is currently using some type of psychoactive drug.[1] And although drug use is ubiquitous in human societies, the specific drugs used, the amounts, and the context of their use can vary greatly; a drug that is celebrated in one culture may invoke the death penalty in another.[2]

Our attitudes about drugs—whether they are harmful or helpful, socially acceptable or reprehensible—depend upon so many factors: the drug's effect; the time and place of taking it; the reason for taking the drug; even the age, sex/gender, and profession of the user. One of the goals of this book is to help you develop the critical thinking skills to best evaluate the messages you receive about drugs.[3]

Over the course of the next 18 chapters, we will consider physiological, pharmacological, historical, legal, political, societal, and cultural aspects of drugs. As we proceed, we will question, analyze, and explore the information regarding these fascinating molecules that have such a powerful effect on our minds and bodies, and on society itself.

What Is a Drug?

Kathy loves her white powder, which powerfully affects her body and mood, and she will go out of her way to get some, even though it hurts her health. What is the white powder? Sugar.

It can be difficult to define exactly what a **drug** is. Some define a drug as a substance that produces significant changes in the body, mind, or both (Figure 1.1). But this definition easily can include food and water. And it is true—foods certainly cause significant changes to the body. Under different conditions, a glass of orange juice can cause either life-threatening or lifesaving changes to someone suffering from diabetes.

The World Health Organization defines a drug as "any chemical entity or mixture of entities, other than those required for the maintenance of normal health (like food), the administration of which alters biological function and possibly structure."[4]

Does the purpose for which a substance is taken determine whether it is a drug? Human bodies naturally produce human growth hormone, but it is considered a drug if taken to increase one's muscle mass above what normally occurs. Is there a difference between a drug and a medicine, or between a medicine and a poison? If a drug helps, it is considered a medicine. If it hurts, it is a poison. But the difference between medicine and poison is not that simple. Under certain conditions or dosages, all medicines can be harmful, and many potentially harmful substances can be useful. For example, chemotherapeutic drugs kill fast-dividing cells. Even though many chemotherapeutic drugs cause a plethora of side effects, because their benefits outweigh their harms they are considered medicines. On the other hand, psilocybin mushrooms typically only make the user feel lethargic and dreamy, but they are illegal and considered toxic.

QUICK HIT

"In wise hands, poison is a medicine. In foolish hands, medicine is a poison." — Casanova, 1725–1798

Ask yourself: Do you consider foods to be drugs? Under which circumstances? If you do, should there be limitations on the availability of these foods? Why or why not?

It is also difficult to differentiate between *drug use* and *drug abuse*. As physician and author Andrew Weil says, "Any drug can be used successfully, no matter how bad its reputation, and any drug can be abused, no matter how accepted it is."[5] Drug abuse often depends on the relationship a person has with that drug. A good relationship includes an honest awareness of what the drug does to one's body; freedom from adverse effects on one's physical, emotional, and social well-being; and an ability to stop using the drug if need be.

How Prevalent Is Drug Use?

People of all ages, genders, races, and nationalities use drugs. Drug use is not evenly distributed across countries; a nation's laws, traditions, and religious proscriptions can influence the drug use of its citizens. Other demographic factors such as age, sex/gender, and race also influence the type and amount of drug used.

Global Drug Use

According to the United Nations Office on Drugs and Crime's *World Drug Report*, a comprehensive survey of the world's illicit drug markets, in 2020, 5.5 percent of the world's adult population (275 million people) reported having used an illicit drug at least once, and the most widely used illicit drug was cannabis (marijuana), followed by opioids, and then amphetamines and prescription stimulants.[6] An **illicit** drug is one whose use has been legally prohibited, such as cocaine, heroin, or marijuana, or the misuse of a prescription medication or household substance, such as prescription pain medications or glue. Drug use is not evenly distributed across countries, and prevalence of drug use is not simply related to drug policy. It is not the case that countries with more liberal policies have higher levels of drug use than countries with harsher illegal drug policies.[7] The United States sees some of the highest rates of illicit drug use in the world, despite having harsher policies than other comparable countries (Figure 1.2).[8]

Alcohol use is more prevalent in the Americas, Europe, Japan, and New Zealand than it is in the Middle East, Africa, and China. Alcohol and tobacco use are especially high in Eastern Europe (Figure 1.3).

Drug: Any chemical entity or mixture, other than those required for the maintenance of normal health (such as food), that alters biological function or structure when administered.

Illicit: Forbidden by laws, rules, or customs. Illicit drugs are not necessarily illegal; they are illicit when taken outside of their regulated or medically prescribed use.

FIGURE 1.1. Under the influence. Bryan Lewis Saunders is an artist who took a different drug every day and drew a self-portrait under the influence of the drug. Some of the drawings are shown here: (a) alcohol, (b) Ambien, (c) cocaine, (d) bath salts, (e) LSD, (f) marijuana, (g) heroin, (h) nitrous oxide, (i) PCP.

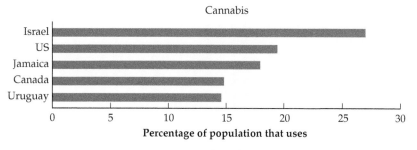

Cannabis

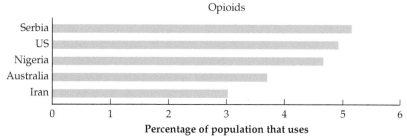

Opioids

Prescription stimulants

FIGURE 1.2. The top five drug-using countries, by annual drug use. The United States has among the highest rates of illicit drug use in the world.

Source: United Nations Office on Drugs and Crime. (2020). World drug report, 2020. United Nations publication, sales no. E.20.XI.6. https://wdr.unodc.org/wdr2020/en/index.html

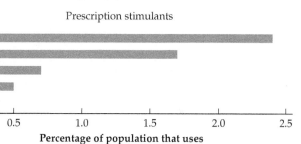

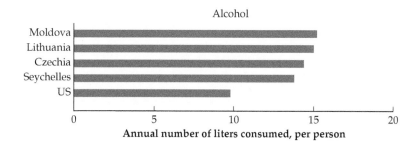

Alcohol

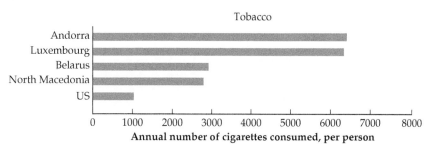

Tobacco

FIGURE 1.3. The top four alcohol- and tobacco-using countries. The United States, although not in the top five, is included for comparison.

Source: World Health Organization. (2018). Global status report on alcohol and health, 2018. World Health Organization. https://apps.who.int/iris/handle.10665/312318

Demographics of Drug Use in the United States

The United States has 4.4 percent of the world's population but consumes 65 percent of the world's supply of illicit drugs. In 2019, over 60 percent of those age 12 and older in the United States reported using a substance (tobacco, alcohol, kratom, or an illicit drug) in the previous month.[9] The United States also accounts for one-quarter of drug-related deaths worldwide.[10] Each year, about 600,000 people die due to alcohol, tobacco, prescription medication, or illegal drug use—and well over 90 percent of these deaths are due to tobacco and prescription drugs.[11]

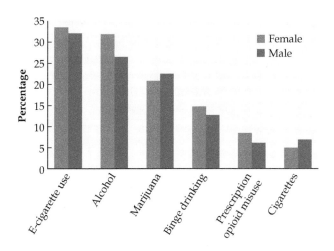

FIGURE 1.5. Current use of selected drugs in high school students. Although high school boys are more likely overall to have used illegal drugs such as cocaine, methamphetamine, and heroin, high school girls have a higher prevalence of current use of many drugs, including alcohol and e-cigarettes.

Sources: Jones, C.M., Clayton, H.B., Deputy, N.P., Roehler, D.R., & Ko, J.Y., et al. (2020). Prescription opioid misuse and use of alcohol and other substances among high school students—Youth Risk Behavior Survey, United States, 2019. MMWR, 69(1): 38–46.

Creamer, M.R., Jones, S.E., Gentzke, A.S., Jamal, A., & King, B.A. (2020). Tobacco product use among high school students—Youth Risk Behavior Survey, United States, 2019. MMWR, 69(1): 56–63.

The Substance Abuse and Mental Health Administration (SAMHSA) is a branch of the U.S. Department of Health and Human Services. Every year, they publish a national survey on drug use and health-related practices. The 2019 survey included data from 67,500 persons age 12 years and older. The survey questions participants about alcohol, tobacco, and illicit drug use, which includes illegal drugs as well as the nonmedical use of prescription drugs. Demographic factors such as age, sex/gender, race, and education all influence drug use.

Age

Those age 21–25 years had the highest rate of current illicit drug use according to the SAMHSA survey. This was followed by those age 26–29, and then by 18- to 20-year-olds (Figure 1.4).[17] From 2018 to 2019, illicit drug use increased among almost all age groups, and there is reason to believe that rates will increase even more in 2020, in part due to the physical and emotional stressors of COVID-19.[18]

Drug Use in Teens. The Youth Risk Behavior Surveillance Survey[19] (YRBSS) was developed in 1990 to monitor activities that affect the health of youth and adults in the United States. From 1991 through 2019, the YRBSS collected data from more than 4.9 million high school students in more than 2,100 separate surveys. The *Monitoring the Future* survey has studied the behaviors, attitudes, and values of American students since 1975.[20] Each year, about 50,000 students in the 8th, 10th, and 12th grades in 400 secondary schools nationwide are questioned about their drug use. Alcohol is the drug most widely used by today's teens. Marijuana is the most widely used illicit drug, and this has been true throughout *Monitoring the Future*'s history. Figure 1.5 shows the prevalence of current drug use among high school students.

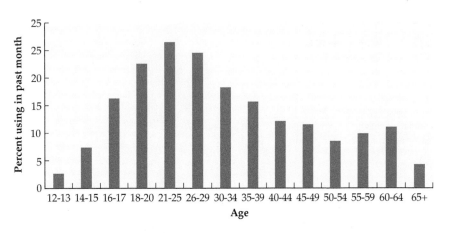

FIGURE 1.4. Illicit drug use in the United States over the past month, by age. Illicit drug use is highest in those age 18–29.

Source: SAMHSA. (2020). Results from the 2019 National Survey on Drug Use and Health: Detailed Tables. Rockville, MD: Center for Behavioral Health Statistics and Quality.

Ask yourself: Why do you think men are more likely than women to use most illicit drugs?

Initiation of Use. In 2019, an estimated 6.5 million persons age 12 years and older—about 18,000 people a day—used alcohol or cigarettes for the first time.[21] This number is significantly lower than in in previous years.

- About 4.9 million people used alcohol for the first time. Of those, 78 percent were younger than 21, and almost half were younger than 18.
- Almost 1.6 million people smoked a cigarette for the first time, three-quarters of whom were under the legal age.

Millions of people also used an illicit drug for the first time. Among those first-time users, marijuana was the most common drug with 3.5 million new users, followed by pain relievers with 1.6 million new users. As adult use of cannabis is legal in many states, its status as an "illicit" drug is ambiguous. For now, however, surveys still categorize marijuana as an illicit drug, regardless of its legal status.

Gender
In the United States, men are more likely to use illicit drugs than are women. Of those age 12 years and older, 15.5 percent of men and 10.7 percent of women report that they have used an illicit drug in the past 30 days.[22]

Race
Drug use varies among members of different racial groups. Among adults, Asians have the lowest rates of illicit drug use; their rates are more than four times lower than those who identify as belonging to two or more races (Figure 1.6).[23]

Education
Among those age 18 and older, college graduates showed the lowest rates of current illicit drug use, followed by those without a high school diploma, and then high school graduates. Drug use was highest among those who attended but did not finish college.[24] Perhaps their drug use interfered with their education, or perhaps people who are the type to not finish school, due to personality or social factors, are more likely to use drugs.

Most Commonly Used Drugs
The most commonly used drugs in America are alcohol, tobacco, marijuana, and nonmedical use of prescription drugs. Use of these four drugs far outweighs the use of other illicit drugs, and most illicit drug use is due to

marijuana and prescription drugs. In the United States, more people drink alcohol each month—some 140 million people—than use all illicit drugs combined. Current illicit drug use is summarized in Figure 1.7.

Prescription Drugs
Nearly half of all Americans took at least one prescription drug in the past 30 days, which is actually a slight improvement from 10 years prior.[25] This varies by age—89 percent of adults age 65 and older take at least one prescription medication, compared to 75 percent of those age 50–64, 51 percent of those age 30–49, and 38 percent of 18- to 29-year-olds.[26] The types of drugs also vary by age group (Figure 1.8). ADHD drugs and medication to treat asthma are most common among children and adolescents; antidepressants are the most common prescription drug for adults under age 60; and older Americans are most commonly prescribed drugs to treat high cholesterol, cardiovascular disease, and diabetes.[27] Each year, approximately 128,000 individuals die from properly prescribed and administered

Ask yourself: Although many presidential administrations have cited a "drug-free America" as their goal, prescription drug use is rampant and much more accepted than recreational drug use. Why do you think people are more accepting of pharmaceutical drug use than recreational drug use?

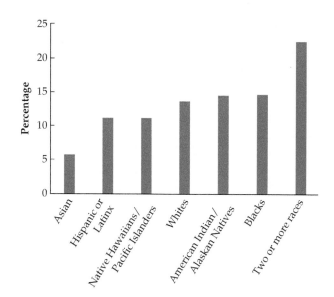

FIGURE 1.6. Current illicit drug use in those age 12 and older, by race. Asians typically report the lowest rates of illicit drug use.

Source: SAMHSA. (2020). Results from the 2019 National Survey on Drug Use and Health: Detailed Tables. Rockville, MD: Center for Behavioral Health Statistics and Quality.

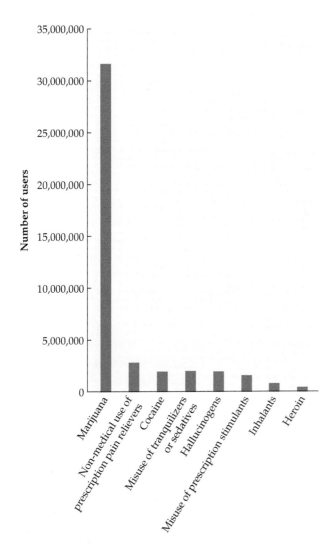

FIGURE 1.7. Past month illicit drug use in those age 12 and older, by drug. Marijuana is the most popular illicit drug used by Americans age 12 and older. Alcohol and tobacco, however, are much more widely used. In recent years, the use of cannabis, hallucinogens, heroin, and inhalants has increased, and the misuse of prescription pain medications has fallen.

Source: SAMHSA. (2020). Results from the 2019 National Survey on Drug Use and Health: Detailed Tables. Rockville, MD: Center for Behavioral Health Statistics and Quality.

drugs, and there are as many as 2.7 million hospitalizations due to serious side effects.[28] This does not include deaths from prescribing errors, overdose, or legal drugs that were not medically prescribed, but instead obtained for recreational purposes.

Nonmedical use of pharmaceutical drugs is a significant problem in the United States. In 2018, there were over 67,000 deaths due to a drug overdose, and almost one in five of those deaths were caused by overdoses of prescription opioids.[29] In a 2015 survey, approximately 12 million Americans reported nonmedical use of a prescription drug in the past month,

but the actual incidence may be much higher.[30] This growth in the nonmedical use of prescription drugs may be due to the fact that there are more prescriptions being written today than in the past. In addition, because they are so widely used for legitimate purposes, and because they are advertised directly to the consumer, prescription drugs may be perceived as less dangerous than street drugs.[31]

Variations in Drug Use over Time

Drug use fluctuates over time. As the use of one substance diminishes, another rises, due to a combination of social, political, and economic factors. Stimulant use increases in times of industry, depressants during times of stress, and hallucinogens during times of exploration.[32] Although the popularity of individual drugs may change, the proportion of those who use any drug is more stable.[33] Some of the factors underlying the fluctuations in drug use as well as in the popularity of individual drugs include the following:

- *Penalties for use.* U.S. drug policy has largely been to impose harsh penalties for drug use in the hopes that such penalties will decrease use. As we'll see in Chapter 2, this policy has been largely unsuccessful.
- *Presentation of drugs in the media.* Individual drugs may be presented in a positive, negative, or neutral light, which impacts our desire to use or avoid the drug. Alcohol, America's most popular drug, is depicted as sexy, cool, and fun. Until the later part of the twentieth century, tobacco was presented as glamorous and sophisticated; as its portrayal has become more negative, use has decreased. Cocaine use was high in the late 1970s and early 1980s, when it was presented as the drug of the rich, famous, and beautiful, but it declined after 1986, when the appearance of crack—a smokable form of cocaine—led to a barrage of negative messages from the media.
- *Perceived risk and accessibility.* Drug use may be influenced by how accessible a drug is, based on its price, risk, or local laws. Over time, cannabis use has risen as its perceived risk and disapproval have fallen and its availability has increased.
- *Patriotic sensibilities.* Marijuana use temporarily declined after September 11, 2001, when terrorists attacked the United States. Drug use is, in part, a rebellion against authority, and Americans were not feeling particularly rebellious against the government at this time. Decreases in drug use also occurred during World War I and World War II.[34]

DRUG-FREE AMERICA

©Signe Wilkinson.

AGE 0-4	4-12	12-18	18-24	24-38	38-65	65 —
AMOXICILLIN	RITALIN	APPETITE SUPPRESSANTS	NO-DOZ	PROZAC	ZANTAC	EVERYTHING ELSE

FIGURE 1.8. Prescription drug use is extremely common in the United States. Many organizations have a zero-tolerance policy for recreational drugs, but pharmaceutical drug use is much more accepted.

- *Social activities and lifestyle.* Some drugs typically are used as part of a social activity, while others more often are used alone. Teenagers today have less free time than ever before. Over the past 25 years, "structured time"—such as participating in sports teams and music lessons—has doubled, and "unstructured time" has declined by 50 percent among all socioeconomic groups. Adults also work more hours, and they often work two jobs. Social interactions increasingly occur online rather than in person. Such constraints on free time and social time can influence which drug is used. The increased popularity of prescription pills may be due, in part, to these changes. Pills are quick and easy to take; all one needs is a glass of water. There is no social ritual involved. Amphetamines or Adderall can keep people awake for a long night of interactive gaming or web surfing, and Xanax can ease stress and help people get to sleep.

Why Do People Use Drugs?

Drugs have both powerful rewards and devastating consequences. Why do people use drugs, even when faced with the possibility of incredible loss? There are probably as many reasons for drug use as there are people who use drugs. Some of the most common reasons follow.

To Feel Pleasure and to Avoid Feeling Pain

Sometimes drugs simply make a person feel good. And Americans need some pleasure—we work hard. On average, Americans work 135 hours more each year than the average Briton, 240 more than the typical worker in France, and 370 hours—9 weeks—more than the average German.[35] Whether sipping a beer at a ballgame or taking a hit of Molly at a rave, users may feel like the drug will enhance their recreational pursuit.

Sometimes drugs are used to relieve depression, anxiety, lethargy, loneliness, insomnia, or boredom—to numb the body and escape both physical and emotional pain. As Edgar Allan Poe said, "I have absolutely no pleasure in the stimulants in which I sometimes so madly indulge. It has not been in the pursuit of pleasure that I have periled life and reputation and reason. It has been the desperate attempt to escape from torturing memories, from a sense of insupportable loneliness and a dread of some strange impending doom."[36]

It is important to remember that the drug itself does not contain sensations or emotions. The sensation and perception are all in one's brain; drugs are just a delivery system for a sensation. Nonpharmacological pursuits—meditation, music, movement— can often deliver the same sensation without the negative side effects.

To Change the State of Consciousness

Have you ever watched five-year-old children spin and spin until they get so dizzy that they fall down, laughing hysterically as they watch the world reel around them? A desire to alter our perceptions may be innate. Sensory pleasure becomes dulled with repetition; some people use drugs to make familiar experiences seem new and interesting again. Some seek out drugs to stimulate creativity. Many artists, writers, and musicians have taken drugs hoping for inspiration; many of these artists also died because of the drugs.

Alcohol and Religion

Alcohol has had a more widespread effect on society than any other drug, as it also plays a fundamental role in many of our religious ceremonies. For instance, wine plays an important role in Judaism. The weekly Sabbath service both commences and concludes with a prayer delivered over a cup of wine. Circumcisions, weddings, funerals, and the Passover celebration all incorporate wine. On Purim, which recognizes the Jews' deliverance from a plot to destroy them, the faithful are instructed to drink so much wine that they can't tell the difference between "cursed is Haman" (the deadly enemy) and "blessed is Mordechai" (the devoted friend).

For the first 1,800 years of the Christian Church, alcohol was a part of everyday life as well as a religious sacrament. Most looked upon wine as a gift from God, although overindulgence was considered a sin. The ceremony of the Eucharist, wherein wine represented the blood of Christ, was at the heart of early Christianity. The gospels say that Jesus's first miracle was turning water into wine at the wedding feast at Cana. Today, however, some Christian denominations, such as Methodists,

Pentecostals, Southern Baptists, and Mormons, believe that adherents should abstain from alcohol.

Islam was born in a region of drinkers, but over time, attitudes about alcohol changed. Alcohol was first mentioned in the Qur'an as a blessing, alongside water, milk, and honey. In its next appearance in the Qur'an, alcohol was decreed as sinful but having some useful qualities. Finally, strong drink was described as an abomination of Satan. But faithful Muslims are reminded to not despair, because there will be wine in heaven.

Hinduism generally shies away from absolute regulations and strives to deal with individual cases. To Hindus, moderate wine consumption can have health benefits for some, but not all. Refraining from intoxicants enables the faithful to release from the material world and its cycles of rebirth. Buddhists typically avoid consuming alcohol, which can disrupt mindfulness and impede one's progress toward enlightenment.

Source:

Gately, I. (2008). Drink: A cultural history of alcohol. *New York: Gotham Books.*

To Enhance Spiritual, Religious, or Mystical Experiences

For millennia, people have used drugs to transcend their sense of separateness and to feel more at one with God, nature, and the universe. Drugs like peyote, marijuana, psilocybin, and alcohol have played a role in religious ceremonies, and some people have believed that the substances themselves had spiritual powers and mystical properties.[37] Drugs also are used to commemorate liminal experiences (periods of transition between one stage and another) such as birth, death, a bar/bat mitzvah, or a wedding ceremony. We often use drugs as part of the ritual to celebrate these events—new fathers pass out cigars at the birth of their children, we drink to celebrate the beginning of a marriage and to honor the end of a life, and some Native Americans may take hallucinogenic mushrooms as part of a manhood ritual.

To Facilitate and Enhance Social Interactions

Sharing drugs is often an excuse for intimacy—people may meet for coffee, take a cigarette break, or go to happy

Ask yourself: Of the people you know who have used drugs, what are the major reasons that they use? If you use drugs, why do *you* use them?

hour together. Sharing illegal drugs may strengthen the connection even more as users bond over their shared defiance of authority. Pharmacologically, drugs can enhance social interactions as they can lower inhibitions and relieve feelings of awkwardness or anxiety.

Peer pressure also plays a role in drug use.[38] People often feel a strong need to fit in and be accepted. They may begin to use a drug in order to go along with the crowd. On the other hand, some people use drugs to demonstrate their individuality and to rebel against the norm.

To Alter and Improve the Body

Some may take drugs to improve physical performance—cocaine and amphetamines can enhance endurance, and anabolic steroids can increase strength. Weight-loss drugs, anabolic steroids, and GHB can (temporarily) reduce body fat and increase muscle mass. And of course, many drugs of abuse, including opium, morphine, heroin, cocaine, and alcohol, were once widely prescribed by physicians to alleviate various ailments.

For all these rewards associated with drugs, one cannot forget the obvious and sometimes devastating problems that can occur with drug use. These problems can occur with acute (short-term) or chronic (long-term) use, and they can hurt both the individual and society.

How Does Drug Use Affect Individuals and Society?

When individuals abuse a drug for many years, they can experience a variety of problems. But even a single experience with a drug can lead to devastating consequences.

Individual Problems with Acute Use

When drugs are obtained illegally, it is often impossible to know how much to take, or what else is in the substance. Users need to rely on the honesty of their dealer, who may not have the user's best interests at heart. Impurities in the drug can lead to allergic reactions, infection, and other problems. Even if the drug itself is pure, some routes of administration can be problematic—intravenous injections can lead to infections, and smoking freebase cocaine can cause burns. Additionally, the user may underestimate how much he or she is taking and overdose. Overdoses (ODs) can occur even with a known quantity; for example, if a heroin addict takes the same dose of heroin, by the same route of administration every day, but one day takes the same amount in a new environment, he or she can die of an overdose.

Legally obtained drugs can be misused as well. A person who crushes his or her prescribed Ritalin and snorts it for a faster high, someone who takes prescription pain medication long after pain has subsided, or someone who guzzles 10 shots of whiskey at once are all at risk of developing dependence or suffering an overdose.

Individual Problems with Chronic Use

Years of drug use can lead to chronic health problems. Long-term heavy drinkers may damage their livers, and years of smoking can significantly raise one's risk of many forms of cancer. Some drugs can increase one's risk of psychiatric problems such as paranoia, depression, and even psychosis. Long-term drug use, abuse, or addiction can wreak havoc with personal relationships, occupation, and financial status. Finally, because most drugs of abuse are illegal, use will increase a user's chances of running afoul of the law. At best, this will cost time, money, and embarrassment, but at worst, a user may lose not only her or his job, but possessions and freedom as well.

Societal Problems Associated with Drug Use

In the United States, abuse of tobacco, alcohol, and illicit drugs is estimated to cost over $740 billion dollars annually, when considering healthcare expenses, lost productivity, and legal costs.[39] This number is hard to conceptualize, but if you were to spend $1 million a day, it would take over 2,027 years to equal the annual expense of addiction. And these cold equations can't adequately express the pain felt due to a drug-related loss of a family member or friend. Drug use can cause direct and indirect injury to others, as seen in drug-related violence, car accidents, or fetal harm. The increased crime and incarceration rates can destroy communities and tax the criminal justice system to its breaking point. Illicit drug manufacturing and use can cause environmental damage through toxic waste or infected needles.

How Are Drugs Classified?

Drugs can be classified in many ways, including by their legality, by whether or not they are licit, by their purpose, and by their origin. **Illegal** drugs are drugs that are restricted at any level of government or authority by laws. Illicit drugs, by contrast, may be forbidden by laws, rules, or customs, but they are not necessarily illegal. For example, nonmedical use of prescription drugs or underage drinking may be considered illicit use, even though the drugs themselves are not illegal when used properly. **Recreational drugs** are psychoactive substances taken for nonmedical purposes. They may be legal or illegal. Tobacco and alcohol are examples of legal recreational drugs, while cocaine and heroin are examples of illegal recreational drugs. Finally, drugs may be classified by their chemical structure, therapeutic use, mechanism of action (the way they work in the body), origin (whether they are natural or synthetic), and what schedule they are (how they are classified by the federal government). In the sections that follow, we will explore in more detail just a few of these ways of classifying drugs: by origin, naming, and scheduling.

It bears mentioning that these classifications are not always clear-cut. Cannabis, for example, occupies an ambiguous status in our society (Chapter 9). In some states it is legal, but the federal government still classifies it as illegal. Most surveys of drug use classify marijuana as an illicit drug, but if an adult is using cannabis in accordance with the laws of their state, should it be considered illicit? Finally, cannabis can have an

Illegal: Restricted at some level of government or authority—national, state, county, or in the individual institution, school, or work site.

Recreational drugs: Drugs that are taken for nonmedical purposes.

(a)   (b)

FIGURE 1.9. Many drugs are derived from animal sources. Isolation of compounds from the venom of the (a) Brazilian pit viper *Bothrops jararaca* and saliva from the (b) Gila monster *Heloderma suspectum* were critical in the development of some life-saving drugs.

intoxicating effect, but many adults use it for medicinal purposes. Does that mean cannabis is recreational if taken for pleasure, but not recreational if taken for pain? After all, one's body doesn't necessarily know (or care) *why* a person takes a drug.

Drug Types

Drugs may be categorized in many different ways. One useful way to categorize drugs is by their origin—whether they are made within the body, derived from a particular plant or substance, or synthesized in a laboratory.

Endogenous Drugs

Our bodies make powerful chemicals that affect our thoughts, moods, and behaviors. In the 1950s, researchers began to realize that many psychoactive drugs fit into receptor sites on nerve cells (Chapter 3). Morphine, an opioid used to alleviate pain, is one example—it binds directly into receptors in parts of the brain that control pain and mood. These receptors exist because our bodies produce substances that fit into them.

An **endogenous** substance is one that is produced within an organism. In 1975, an endogenous form of morphine—*endorphin*—was discovered. Endorphins are neurotransmitters produced in the brain in response to pain, fear, or stress. They bind to receptors to promote analgesia, produce feelings of euphoria, and enhance immune response, along with other effects. Another endogenous substance is *anandamide*—our body's natural form of cannabis. Anandamide

Endogenous: Produced or originating from within an organism.

binds to receptors in the brain and body that affect mood, appetite, memory, reproduction, and immune function.

Natural Drugs

About 50 percent of all medicines on the market are derived from what are called natural products—molecules produced by living organisms for a variety of functions, from feeding to mating to defense.[40] Many new drugs are derived from lower organisms such as bacteria or fungi. Antibiotics such as penicillin and streptomycin came from bacteria and mold, and rapamycin, an immunosuppressant for organ transplants, derives from a bacterium found in the soil on the island of Rapa Nui.[41]

Some substances originate from animals. The blood pressure drug captopril was first derived from the venom of the Brazilian pit viper, and Gila Monster (a venomous lizard) saliva contains a substance used to treat patients who suffer from diabetes (Figure 1.9).

Most psychoactive drugs originally come from plants. It seems odd that plants would produce substances that have such a powerful effect on the human mind, but evolution may play a role. If a plant evolved to produce a substance that made an animal eating it fall ill or feel peculiar, the animal might avoid that plant. The plant would then be less likely to be eaten and more likely to reproduce and survive. Many of the recreational drugs we'll discuss—tobacco, marijuana, cocaine, and opium, just to name a few—are derived from plants.

Oftentimes, after the active substance in the plant has been identified, it is purified and synthesized in a lab. Morphine is a purified form of opium, cocaine comes from the coca leaf, and mescaline (a hallucinogen) is purified from the peyote cactus. Natural drugs tend to be more complex than refined and synthesized forms of the drugs. Peyote has at least 55 pharmacologically active substances, and cannabis has about 500 identified substances, all of which contribute to the overall effect. However, the synthetically manufactured versions of these drugs—mescaline and THC (the main psychoactive ingredient in cannabis)—are chemically very simple.[42] In many cases, the natural form of the drug is less potent and less toxic.

QUICK HIT

Of the half a million or so known species of plants, about 4,000 have psychoactive properties.[43] Additionally, many household plants, including buttercup, mistletoe, daffodils, rhododendron, oleander, tulip, iris, and morning glory, are poisonous.

Synthetic Drugs

To create a synthetic drug, a chemist often takes a purified form of a natural drug and changes its chemical structure to vary its properties. For instance, heroin is made by adding two acetyl groups onto a morphine molecule. This makes the drug more fat-soluble and able to enter the brain more easily.

Pharmaceutical companies are not allowed to patent a natural drug for exclusive manufacture and sale. Therefore, these companies would rather develop, patent, and sell a synthetic drug to which they have exclusive rights. Because of this, there is less effort to evaluate the benefits of natural drugs, given that they cannot be patented. As a result, natural drugs that have been declared illegal tend to remain illegal, because there is often no financially powerful lobby pushing for legalization. New synthetic drugs are aggressively marketed due to their high profit potential.[44]

Drug Naming

Over the course of our journey through this textbook, you will encounter many drugs. In order to be on a "first-name basis" with these drugs, let us take a moment to discuss how pharmaceutical drugs get their names.

When a drug is first discovered, it is given a chemical name, which describes the molecular structure of the drug. After a patent application has been filed for a drug, it is given a **generic name**—its official name—and a **brand or trade name** that is used by the company that has filed the patent for the drug. Patents expire 20 years from the date that the inventor first applies for approval. Because it can take many years until the

application is approved, the actual patent on a marketed drug often lasts for much less than 20 years. When the drug is approved, the company sells the drug under its brand name, but when the patent expires, other companies can apply to the FDA (the Food and Drug Administration) to sell the drug under its generic name, or they can market the drug under their own brand name.

Generic names are not capitalized. The names often provide clues to the nature of the drug. For example, most barbiturates end in -al, like phenobarbital or secobarbital; some local anesthetics end in -caine, such as lidocaine and prilocaine (brand name Novocaine); and many cholesterol-lowering drugs end in -vastatin. Generic drugs are often less expensive than drugs that remain under patent, but they are usually the same chemical formula as the brand names.

Trade names are capitalized. They often are chosen to give the buyer a sense of the drug's characteristics: Lopressor lowers blood pressure, Glucotrol controls blood glucose, and drugs to aid sleep often contain the letter "Z," perhaps to bring to mind a happily snoring individual. Latin and Greek roots often are used to enforce certain associations; Paxil, an antianxiety drug, contains the Latin word for peace—pax. Viagra sounds like both "vigorous" and "virile." In addition, medications marketed to men are more likely to contain a "hard" sound like "T," "G," or "K," and drugs marketed to women more often contain the "soft" letters "S," "M," "L," and "R." Examples of chemical names, generic names, and trade names of some drugs are shown in Table 1.1, and a more comprehensive listing is provided in the Appendix of this book.

Drug Scheduling

In 1970, President Nixon signed the Controlled Substances Act (CSA) into law. The CSA created five **drug schedules** that classified drugs based on their potential for abuse, medical benefits (if any), and likelihood of

Ask yourself: If you could design any drug in the world, what would it do? If you could eliminate any one drug from the world forever, which would it be and why? What do your choices suggest about what you value?

Generic name: The nonproprietary drug name that is in general public use. It is not subject to trademark rights.

Brand or trade name: A proprietary trademarked name that a company gives a drug.

Drug schedules: The five categories into which drugs are classified based upon the drug's accepted medical use and its potential for abuse and addiction.

TABLE 1.1. Drug Naming

Chemical Name and Formula	Generic Name	Trade Name	Street Name	Function
7-chloro-1,3-dihydro-l-methyl-5-phenyl-2H-l,4-benzodiazepin-2-one $C_{16}H_{13}ClN_2O$	diazepam	Valium	V's, Benzos	Antianxiety
d-amphetamine saccharate and d, l-amphetamine aspartate monohydrate $C_9H_{13}N$	dextroamphetamine	Adderall	Addys, Beans, Bennies, Speed	Treat attention- deficit/hyperactivity disorder
4,5α-epoxy-14-hydroxy-3-methoxy-17-methylmorphinan-6-one hydrochloride $C_{18}H_{21}NO_4$	oxycodone HCl	OxyContin	Oxys, O's, Cotton	Analgesic

producing physical or psychological dependence. A schedule I drug is considered the most dangerous, and schedule V is thought to be the least dangerous. A schedule I drug is one believed to have a high potential for abuse, no currently accepted medical uses in the United States, and a demonstrated lack of safety, even under medical supervision. Schedule II drugs also have a high potential for abuse, and their use may lead to severe physical or psychological harm, but these drugs do have a currently accepted medical use. Schedules III, IV, and V drugs have decreasing abuse potential and risk. Descriptions of the schedules, as well as some examples of each, are listed in Table 1.2.

The decision as to whether a drug should be scheduled, and if so, what schedule it should be, is made by agents working in the FDA in conjunction with the secretary of the Department of Health and Human Services and the Drug Enforcement Agency (DEA). The FDA provides the secretary of the Department of Health and Human Services with a scientific and medical evaluation of a drug to decide in which schedule it belongs, and the DEA determines the schedule and enforces the penalties.[45] Interested parties can petition the DEA to add, delete, or change the schedule of a drug.

TABLE 1.2. Drug Schedule

	Abuse Potential	Effects	Medical Use	Examples
Schedule I	Highest	Lack of accepted safety for use even under medical supervision.	No currently accepted medical use in the United States.	Heroin, LSD, DMT, marijuana, peyote, psilocybin, methaqualone, MDMA
Schedule II	High	Abuse may lead to severe physical and/or psychological dependence.	Some accepted medical use; may be severe restrictions on use.	Cocaine, PCP, methamphetamine, Ritalin, Adderall, opium, morphine, codeine, oxycodone, fentanyl, pentobarbital, amobarbital
Schedule III	Medium	Less potential for abuse than drugs in higher schedules. Abuse may lead to moderate or low physical dependence or high psychological dependence.	Has a currently accepted medical use in the United States.	Codeine with aspirin or acetaminophen, anabolic steroids, ketamine
Schedule IV	Low	Less potential for abuse than drugs in higher schedules. Abuse may lead to limited physical or psychological dependence.	Has a currently accepted medical use in the United States.	Xanax, Valium, Rohypnol, Ambien, Librium
Schedule V	Lowest	Less potential for abuse than drugs in higher schedules. Abuse may lead to limited physical or psychological dependence.	Has a currently accepted medical use in the United States.	Lomotil, cough syrups containing low quantities of codeine, Lyrica

As we learn more about the specific drugs listed in Table 1.2, you may notice that the characteristics of some drugs don't always align with their schedule. Some drugs listed in schedule I (such as psilocybin and marijuana) have little to no potential to cause physical harm, appear to have medical benefits, and have never caused a known overdose, while other, more dangerous drugs, such as alcohol and tobacco, are excluded from the CSA. This exclusion is due, in part, to the fact that when the CSA was established alcohol and tobacco already had specific tax provisions, but also because of the strong political influence of the tobacco and liquor lobbies. If they were not excluded, alcohol and tobacco might certainly be classified as schedule I or II. Caffeine is also exempt; if scheduled, it might be classified as schedule IV or V.

How Are New Drugs Developed?

Every year, dozens of new drugs appear on the U.S. market. They usually come from three sources[46]:

- The rediscovery of traditional uses of various naturally occurring products
- The accidental observation of an unexpected drug effect
- The synthesis of known or novel compounds

FDA Drug Development and Approval

The FDA is an agency of the Department of Health and Human Services. It is responsible for regulating the safety of food, prescription and over-the-counter pharmaceuticals, tobacco products, dietary supplements, vaccines, and medical devices. Pharmaceuticals go through a rigorous process in order to be approved for the U.S. market.

When a compound is believed to have clinical value, it is first tested on animals. The compound then undergoes limited experimental studies on healthy human volunteers and on clinical patients. If all goes well, these clinical trials are expanded. If the drug's benefits outweigh its risks, the drug may be approved for licensing and marketing. Finally, there are after-market evaluations of the drug's clinical use, where its long-term and short-term effects are more fully evaluated. Let's look at these steps in more detail (Figure 1.10).[47]

QUICK HIT

For each drug that makes it to market approval, 5,000 to 10,000 have been screened, 250 enter clinical testing, and 5 enter clinical trials.[48,49] The average cost to develop a new drug, including the cost of failures, is $2.6 billion, and this cost doubles every 9 years.[50] The U.S. pharmaceutical industry reported that in 2018, it spent $80 billion on research and development of new drugs.[51]

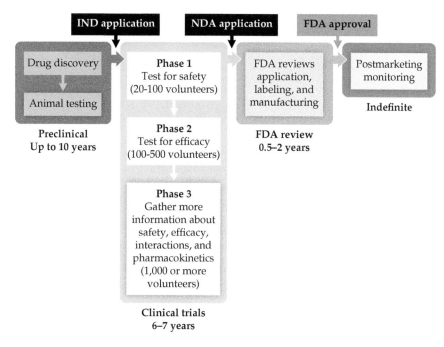

FIGURE 1.10. **The FDA drug approval process.** The process of developing a new drug involves many steps and typically takes 10–20 years.

Preclinical Stage

The first stage of drug development lasts for 2–10 years and includes the initial synthesis and development of the drug and preclinical trials. The drug is tested on at least two animal species to determine whether it is safe enough to test on humans. If at this point the compound is deemed to have therapeutic potential, the drug developer applies to the FDA for the new product to be considered an IND—an Investigational New Drug.

Clinical Stage

If the IND is approved, the drug can begin the three phases of clinical testing. Clinical testing can last six to seven years and costs an average of $40 million.

1. *Phase 1 clinical trials* establish the drug's safety. Human reactions to the drug are tested in about 20–100 healthy volunteers. Scientists evaluate the drug's toxicity, side effects, and pharmacokinetic characteristics. These tests typically take around two years. About 70 percent of INDs get through this stage.
2. *Phase 2 clinical trials* emphasize effectiveness. The drug is tested on 100–500 patients with the target disease, to see how effective it is in treating the disorder. If these tests indicate that the experimental drug is effective and not toxic, it enters the final stage of clinical testing. About 33 percent of INDs make it through phase 2 testing.
3. *Phase 3 clinical trials* are typically double-blinded, placebo-controlled studies on 1,000 or more patients in order to determine the drug's effectiveness, appropriate dosage, potential adverse reactions, and labeling requirements. This stage can last three years or more. About 27 percent of INDs will then go on for FDA review.

FDA Review

If—many years and tests and dollars later—the drug appears to be safe and effective, the manufacturer can submit a *New Drug Application* (NDA) to the FDA. Once the application is presented, the FDA performs either a standard review, which takes about 10 months, or an accelerated review, which will be completed in about 6 months. Drugs may be put on the fast track to facilitate the development and review of medications that treat serious conditions and fill an unmet medical need.[52] The FDA reviews the drug's labeling, as well as the facilities in which it will be manufactured. FDA review typically takes up to two years. If the new drug is approved, the developer can market the drug in the United States. If the application is not approved, the manufacturer must spend more time and money to correct the problems and may then file a new application for approval. As few as 20 percent of new drugs tested reach final approval; the vast majority of new drugs are eliminated after time-consuming and expensive testing.[53]

Ask yourself: Do you think the process by which a drug gains approval in the United States is too rigorous or too lax? What are the ramifications of making it more difficult for a drug to be approved? What are the ramifications of making it easier?

Sometimes the process fails, as when pharmaceutical companies fabricate data, don't turn over all their scientific records to the FDA during the NDA process, or deceptively market the drug. These fraudulent practices were behind the Vioxx tragedy in the early 2000s (Figure 1.11).

Postmarketing Analysis

Once a drug is approved by the FDA, the drug enters the marketplace. During postmarketing analysis, the drug's effectiveness, side effects, adverse effects, and drug interactions are monitored. If concerns arise, the drug may be pulled from the market, as occurred with the drugs Vioxx, Zelnorm, and Darvocet. At this point, pharmaceutical companies distribute and advertise their drugs, and this is the most prominent type of health communication the public encounters.[54] It is important for thoughtful consumers to critically evaluate the information presented in these advertisements.

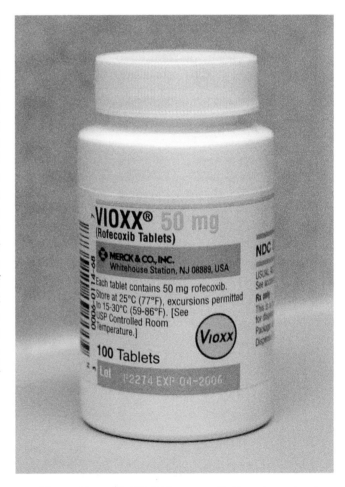

FIGURE 1.11. Vioxx. The NSAID Vioxx was pulled from the marketplace in 2004 due to serious adverse reactions.

The Rise and Fall of Vioxx

The nonsteroidal anti-inflammatory (NSAID) drug Vioxx was released by Merck in 1999. The ad campaign, which cost $160 million, claimed falsely that Vioxx controlled pain better than existing, less expensive anti-inflammatories. By the following year, Vioxx was the number one direct-to-consumer advertised drug. Although it was new, relatively untested, expensive, and intended for a small population of specialized patients (those whose stomachs were sensitive to other NSAIDs), it became the default prescription for adult arthritis pain.

By 2003, Vioxx had sales revenues of $2.5 billion. Twenty million Americans and 80 million people worldwide were prescribed Vioxx at some time, before it was found to nearly double the risk of heart attack or stroke. Before it was taken off the market in 2004, between 88,000 and 140,000 serious cardiovascular events and up to 60,000 deaths worldwide were attributed to Vioxx.

This was not a surprise to those who reviewed the drug. Preliminary studies (not published in reports included in medical journals) showed that Vioxx caused a four- to fivefold increase in the risk of heart attack. Additionally, one of the researchers of the drug admitted that he fabricated the data for 21 studies in order to exaggerate Vioxx's pain-relieving effects.

In 2008, Merck was found liable for using deceptive marketing tactics to promote Vioxx. The company agreed to pay $950 million and pled guilty to a criminal misdemeanor charge of illegal promotion of the drug and deception about its safety. As of 2014, the company has paid nearly $6 billion in litigation settlements. During the time the drug was on the market, Merck recorded more than $11 billion in sales of Vioxx.

Sources: Critser, G. (August 4, 2008). The Vioxx scandal. The New York Times. Accessed on November 30, 2012 from http://roomfordebate.blogs. nytimes.com/2009/08/04/should-prescription-drug-ads-be-reined-in/

Lurie, P. (2008). DTC advertising harms patients and should be tightly regulated. In R. Goldberg (Ed.), Taking sides: Clashing views in drugs and society (10th ed.) (pp. 283–301). Dubuque, IA: McGraw-Hill/Dushkin.

The Cost of Drugs

The autoinjector syringe EpiPen contains about $1 worth of epinephrine, but its value is immeasurable to those patients who may die without it. When the pharmaceutical company Mylan purchased the rights to EpiPen in 2007, they raised its list price from about $50 each to about $600 for a two-pack, meaning that some people lost access to the lifesaving drug. In an even more egregious move, when Martin Shkreli became CEO of Turing Pharmaceuticals, he raised the price of Daraprim, a drug used to treat HIV-positive patients, from about $13.50 per pill, to $750 per pill, making the cost about $75,000 per month.

According to the Organisation for Economic Co-operation and Development (OECD), an organization of 35 countries in North and South America, Europe, Asia, and the Pacific, the United States spends more on pharmaceuticals on a per capita basis than all other countries—an average of $1,026 per year per person—compared with an average of $515 per person for other countries, and this rate has risen rapidly over the past four decades.[55,56] For example, a 30-day supply of the multiple sclerosis-treating drug Tecfidera costs $5,089 in the U.S., compared to $1,855 in the U.K. and $663 in Switzerland.[57] The U.S. Department of Health and Human Services (HHS) reports that the 10 most commonly advertised drugs in the U.S. have list prices ranging from $488 to $16,983 per month.[58] Almost one in four Americans say it is difficult for them to afford their medications, especially those age 50–64, those with a lower annual income, those who take more medications, and those who are in fair or poor health. Almost 30 percent of Americans reported not taking a medication as prescribed at some point in the past year because of the cost.[59]

In 2019, the HHS ruled that pharmaceutical companies would have to list their prices in TV ads if the price was greater than $35 per month (the approximate average insurance company copayment for a preferred-brand drug). Days before this was scheduled to take effect, the rule was struck down by a judge, who ruled that the HHS does not have the authority to institute such a policy.

Direct-to-Consumer Pharmaceutical Advertising

Pan in on a handsome, distinguished-looking man. He speaks sincerely to us. "Just because I'm a doctor doesn't mean I don't worry about my cholesterol." The voiceover informs us that this is Dr. Robert Jarvik, inventor of the artificial heart. Dr. Jarvik goes on to tell us that for some people, diet and exercise are not enough, so he recommends that people use Lipitor to lower their cholesterol. As he rows confidently across a serene lake, we are left with the impression that Lipitor will keep us healthy and safe—Dr. Jarvik says so! Pfizer spent almost $260 million on this very effective ad campaign. Alert critical thinkers will note that this is an inappropriate appeal to authority (see "Thinking Critically about Drugs" at the start of this book). Although Dr. Jarvik is a pioneer in development of the artificial heart, he is not a cardiologist; he is not even

Direct-to-consumer (DTC) advertising: A form of marketing promotion used by pharmaceutical companies aimed at patients rather than healthcare professionals.

licensed to practice medicine. It turns out Dr. Jarvik is also not a rower, so the company used a body double in the rowing scenes.[60]

In **direct-to-consumer (DTC) advertising,** pharmaceutical companies market their products directly to patients rather than to healthcare professionals. In recent years, the U.S. pharmaceutical industry spent about $6 billion per year advertising prescription drugs to consumers.[61]

Critical Evaluation

Should pharmaceutical companies be allowed to produce direct-to-consumer ads?

Only two nations—the United States and New Zealand—allow DTC advertising. DTC advertising is a highly contentious issue and has both benefits and disadvantages. Use your critical thinking skills to consider the issues at hand.

Type of information for consumers. The FDA requires that DTC ads be accurate, reflect the balance of harms and benefits, and make claims only supported by evidence. However, a recent analysis of DTC ads showed that over the past decade, these ads have presented substantially less factual information about the conditions being addressed, less evidence, and fewer alternative treatments, and are instead increasingly likely to focus on lifestyle and to show happy people engaged in physical activities such as yoga and hiking.[62] How much control over the material and the way it's presented should be enforced in these ads?

Availability of information for consumers. DTC pharmaceutical advertising allows consumers to recognize symptoms, learn about diseases, and seek medical attention for conditions that might otherwise go unidentified or untreated. Do the benefits of increased awareness outweigh the risks of people seeking a potentially unnecessary or inappropriate drug? Is an investor-owned company likely to provide objective, unbiased information about the product it sells? Do those watching DTC ads focus on the possible risks of the drug to the same extent as on the potential benefits? How accurate are the ads?

DTC ads often oversell the benefits and undersell the risks of the drug. Is this a case of "buyer beware," or should drug companies be held to a higher standard than companies that sell cars, makeup, or fast food? Why or why not?

The only way for a consumer in the United States to obtain a prescription drug is through his or her physician. It makes sense for pharmaceutical

companies to advertise to physicians, but does it make sense for pharmaceutical companies to advertise to consumers?[63] Is the average consumer—without a background in medicine or research—knowledgeable enough to understand the drug company's literature? The complete list of adverse effects is listed on the company's web page, but how many consumers will search out that information? If they don't, is that the fault of the consumer or the drug company?

The responsibility of pharmaceutical companies. Drug companies are a business, not a nonprofit organization. They spend hundreds of millions of dollars on research and have only a limited time to recoup their expenses. Do they have the right to advertise their product as they see fit to maximize profits? Do they have a responsibility to promote nonpharmaceutical treatments or generic drugs that are cheaper, have been around longer, and have longer safety records?

Most of the DTC ads are not for life-threatening and treatable diseases such as hypertension. There also aren't many ads for drugs such as antibiotics, where there is often no need for refills, or for cancer drugs, which are chosen by physicians, not patients. Instead, many ads focus on "lifestyle" problems such as thin eyelashes, insomnia, toenail fungus, and erectile dysfunction,[64] conditions which are not usually detected or addressed by physicians. These ads can also medicalize and stigmatize normal attributes or aging processes. Should the ubiquity of an ad be related to its health impact on users?

Views of physicians. Most physicians have negative views about DTC ads, and in 2015, the American Medical Association (AMA) voted to ban DTC prescription drug commercials. Physicians cited concerns that these ads don't provide enough information about adverse effects, change patient expectations of their doctors, and encourage consumers to demand new and expensive treatments despite the effectiveness of less expensive older drugs. To what degree should physicians' concerns be taken into account when considering DTC ads?[65]

Freedom of speech. Is advertising a matter of free speech? Can you advertise any product? Why or why not? Should DTC pharmaceutical ads have to be approved by the FDA before they are broadcast?

Communication with physicians. DTC ads encourage patients to discuss their health concerns with their doctors. However, they also may lengthen office visits and require time for the physician to correct misperceptions.[66] How do we weigh the advantages and disadvantages of patients having a little bit of knowledge? Do you think that if a patient goes to his or her doctor and requests a drug by name, the physician would be more likely to prescribe that drug rather than a cheaper generic equivalent or a more time-tested alternative? Do you think DTC ads could encourage patients to bypass their doctors and instead seek out drugs from online pharmacies or other unauthorized sources? What would be the result of this? If a patient receives an inappropriate or unnecessary prescription, who is at fault—the consumer requesting the drug, the physician who prescribes it, or the pharmaceutical company for advertising it to consumers? Who ultimately decides the best treatment for the patient—the physician or the patient? Is it the physician's role to dictate what treatment is appropriate or, instead, to explain to the patient the various options and let the patient decide? Why?

Many people support a ban on DTC ads, but such a campaign would face strong resistance from the pharmaceutical companies and years of legislative and legal challenges. Richard Friedman, director of the psychopharmacology clinic at Cornell, suggests another alternative—that drug companies provide information about how the drug's cost and effectiveness compare with similar medications.[67] He believes that DTC ads and drug labels should show information about (Figure 1.12) the following:

- the monthly cost of a drug;
- the "number needed to treat": the number of people that need to be treated in a clinical trial for one person to benefit from a drug. The lower the number, the more effective the drug;
- how many total clinical trials were conducted for the drug, and how many of those trials had a positive or negative outcome compared to placebo; and
- how these figures compare with those of older drugs.

Antipsychotics For bipolar depression

DRUG NAME, DOSE RANGE (MILLIGRAMS)	MONTHLY COST, LOWEST TO HIGHEST	NUMBER OF PEOPLE NEEDING TREATMENT IN CLINICAL TRIALS … … FOR **ONE PERSON** TO BENEFIT FROM DRUG	TOTAL CLINICAL TRIALS: POSITIVE	TOTAL CLINICAL TRIALS: NEGATIVE
GENERIC Prozac/Zyprexa 20 Prozac (antidepressant) + 5 Zyprexa	$21.79	4	?	?
GENERIC Seroquel 300 – 600	$50.89 – 101.78	6	?	?
Symbyax 25 Prozac (antidepressant) + 6 Zyprexa	$402.30	4	?	?
Latuda 20 – 80	$921.90	5	?	?

Costs set by manufacturers; pharmacy costs may vary.

Benefit = positive antidepressant response

FIGURE 1.12. Ways to compare and contrast drug efficacy and cost. Richard Friedman suggests that DTC ads and drug labels could contain information about a drug's efficacy and cost. Some missing data that he believes should be easily available include statistics on how many people have serious side effects, as well as the results of both positive and negative clinical trials of the drug.

Source: Friedman, R.A. (2016). What drug ads don't say. New York Times. http://www.nytimes.com/2016/04/24/opinion/sunday/what-drug-ads-dont-say.html?_r=0]

Chapter Summary

- **Introduction**
  - » Drugs are ubiquitous and have a powerful effect on many aspects of our lives.
  - » All drugs have the potential to have both positive and negative ramifications.
- **What Is a Drug?**
  - » The World Health Organization defines a drug as "any chemical entity or mixture of entities, other than those required for the maintenance of normal health (e.g., food), the administration of which alters biological function and possibly structure."
  - » It can be difficult to differentiate between drug use and abuse. Drug abuse often depends on the relationship a person has with the drug.
- **How Prevalent Is Drug Use?**
  - » Drug use is not evenly distributed across countries. Prevalence of drug use is related to a country's policies, history, religion, and other factors.
  - » The United States has some of the highest rates of illicit drug use.
  - » In the United States, drug use is highest among persons 21–25 years of age, followed by those age 26–29.
  - » Among today's teens, alcohol is the most widely used drug and marijuana is the most widely used illicit drug.
  - » Men are more likely to use illicit drugs than are women.
  - » Asians have the lowest rates of illicit drug use, while those of mixed race and American Indian/Alaskan Natives have the highest.
  - » The most commonly used drugs in America are alcohol, tobacco, marijuana, and nonmedical use of prescription drugs.
  - » Nonmedical use of pharmaceutical drugs is a significant problem in the United States.
  - » Drug use fluctuates over time. Some of the factors underlying the fluctuations in drug use include penalties for use, how drugs are presented in the media, their perceived risk and accessibility, social activities and lifestyle, and even feelings of patriotism.
- **Why Do People Use Drugs?**
  - » People use drugs for many different reasons, including to feel pleasure, to avoid feeling pain, to change their state of consciousness, to enhance spiritual experiences, to facilitate social interactions, and to improve the body.

- **How Does Drug Use Affect Individuals and Society?**
  - » Problems can occur with drug use, affecting both individuals and the larger society. These problems may occur with a single occurrence of drug use or may be due to chronic use.
- **How Are Drugs Classified?**
  - » Drugs can be classified by their legality, by whether or not they are licit, by their origin, or by many other factors.
  - » Endogenous substances, such as endorphin and anandamide, are produced and secreted within the body.
  - » Naturally occurring drugs come from bacteria, fungi, plants, or animals, and synthetic drugs are created in a lab.
  - » When a drug is first discovered, it is given a chemical name that describes the molecular structure of the drug.
  - » A drug's generic name is its official, nonproprietary designation. The company that produces it chooses a proprietary trade name.
  - » The Controlled Substances Act classifies drugs into five categories, based on their potential for abuse, medical benefits (if any), and likelihood of producing physical or psychological dependence.
  - » The decision as to whether a drug should be scheduled, and, if so, what schedule it should be, is made by agents in the FDA and DEA.
- **How Are New Drugs Developed?**
  - » The process of drug development is prolonged and expensive. Preclinical testing, involving the basic discovery and research as well as animal studies, can take up to 10 years. If a drug is approved by the FDA as an Investigational New Drug, it then enters clinical trials, which involve three phases and take up to six or seven years.
  - » If, after clinical trials, the drug appears to be safe and effective, the manufacturer can submit a New Drug Application to the FDA. If approved, the FDA will take up to two years to review the drug. If the new drug is approved by the FDA, the developer can begin to market the drug in the United States, although it is subject to postmarketing monitoring.
  - » Pharmaceutical companies produce direct-to-consumer advertisements. There are both advantages and disadvantages to these ads.

Key Terms

Brand or trade name (p.13)

Direct-to-consumer (DTC) advertising (p.18)

Drug (p.3)

Drug schedules (p.13)

Endogenous (p.12)

Generic name (p.13)

Illegal (p.11)

Illicit (p.3)

Psychoactive (p.2)

Recreational drugs (p.11)

Quiz Yourself!

1. True or false? Compared to the rest of the world, the United States consumes far less than its share of illicit drugs.

2. True or false? Both globally and in the United States, lifetime use of alcohol and most other drugs is higher for men than for women.

3. Which of the following age groups has the highest rate of current illicit drug use in the United States?

   A. 16- to 17-year-olds

   B. 18- to 20-year-olds

   C. 21- to 25-year-olds

   D. 35- to 39-year-olds

4. Rate the following drugs in order of prevalence of use in the United States: Alcohol, cocaine, marijuana, nonmedical use of prescription drugs, tobacco.

5. Name three reasons people use drugs.

6. True or false? Naturally occurring drugs are usually more potent and more toxic than synthetically manufactured versions of the drug.

7. Match the substance to its origin.

   _____ Tobacco   A. Endogenous

   _____ Captopril   B. Naturally occurring

   _____ Endorphins   C. Synthetic

   _____ Heroin

   _____ Opium

8. Matching: For the following drug, identify the type of name:

   _____ Adderall   A. Chemical name or

   _____ $C_9H_{13}N$ formula

   _____ Addys   B. Generic name

   _____ dextroamphetamine   C. Trade name

   sulfate   D. Street name

9. Which of the following drugs is NOT a schedule I drug?

   A. Marijuana

   B. Heroin

   C. Cocaine

   D. LSD

10. Put the following steps for new drug development in order: clinical trials, postmarketing analysis, NDA application, animal testing, FDA approval, IND application, FDA review

Additional Resources

Websites

Erowid. www.erowid.org. Erowid is an organization that provides information about psychoactive substances, both legal and illegal.

Bryan Lewis Saunders. http://bryanlewissaunders.org/drugs/ Saunders is an artist who drew self-portraits while under the influence of various drugs.

ProCon.org. Should Prescription Drugs be Advertised Directly to Consumers? https://prescriptiondrugs.procon.org/

Videos

Spiders on Drugs. https://www.youtube.com/watch?v=sHzds FiBbFc

Books

Gahlinger, P. (2004). *Illegal drugs: A complete guide to their history, chemistry, use, and abuse*. New York: Plume.

Learn more with this chapter's digital tools at www.oup.com/he/rosenthal2e.

2 Drug Laws and Policies

True or false?

1.
True or false? The government can confiscate anything (not just drugs) in your possession at the time of a drug arrest.

2.
True or false? Blacks use drugs at about the same rates as whites but are incarcerated at six times the rate of whites.

3.
True or false? When the minimum legal drinking age in the United States goes up, drunk driving deaths go down.

There never has been, and there never will be, a drug-free society. For hundreds of years, governments have tried various approaches to reduce the personal and societal harm that may come from using drugs. Some policies prohibit the use of certain drugs, and invoke severe penalties for their production, distribution, or use. Other policies acknowledge that they can't eradicate all drug use, and instead try to reduce harm by emphasizing safer use practices such as ride-share programs, needle exchanges, and drug replacement and maintenance therapy. Alternatively, drugs may be legalized and regulated through government agencies.

In this chapter, we will investigate the laws and policies used to reduce the use of illicit drugs. These policies may make you examine some of your deeply held values. As you read through this chapter, ask yourself some of the following questions:

- What is the purpose of drug laws? To stop all drug use, or only "problematic" use?
- What determines "problematic" use? Should we be more concerned with drug use that causes personal harm, or use that causes harm to the larger society?
- How should we treat someone who abuses a drug? As a criminal who breaks the law or as a person with a medical condition—addiction—that needs treatment?
- What is the role of government? To prevent its citizens from using drugs? To help them to recover from the effects of drugs? To educate them about the pros and cons of drug use so they can make an informed decision? Is it the government's job to prevent people from engaging in self-destructive behaviors? All self-destructive behaviors? Or self-destructive behaviors that are illegal?
- Are drug laws an effective deterrent?

Learning Objectives

- Describe some of the most important drug policies and laws enacted throughout U.S. history.
- Compare and contrast the rates of drug use and drug arrests for different races.
- Identify some of the federal agencies involved in creation, oversight, and enforcement of drug laws.
- Define *misdemeanor, felony, possession,* and *trafficking.*
- Summarize the principles and practices that underlie harm reduction policies.
- List some collateral sanctions that may be incurred with a drug conviction.
- Sort the most commonly used drugs based on their level of harm.
- Assess the pros and cons of legalizing drugs.
- Evaluate the advantages and disadvantages of lowering the minimum legal drinking age.
- Consider the issues involved in enforcing potential penalties against pregnant women who use drugs.

History of Drug Policy

The U.S. government has been imposing policies and laws on drug use since the nation was first founded. In the best of all worlds, these laws are driven by the desire to ensure the optimal physical and mental health of the nation's citizens. It cannot be denied, however, that economic, racial, and political motivations play a role as well. In this section, we examine some of the most influential federal drug acts and laws passed in the United States. Some of these laws will be discussed in later chapters dealing with specific drugs:

- **1906 Pure Food and Drug Act.** Forced the patent medicine industry to label the amount of alcohol, opium, cocaine, and other habit-forming drugs contained in the compound. This act was the first law to allow the government some oversight of the drug marketplace (Chapter 7).
- **1914 Harrison Narcotics Act.** Decreed that physicians and pharmacists had to be licensed to prescribe narcotics, that they must register with the U.S. Treasury Department and keep records of the narcotic drugs they dispensed, and that they could prescribe only in the course of their medical practice (Chapter 7).
- **1920–1933 Prohibition.** The 18th Amendment to the Constitution prohibited the manufacture, sale, or transportation of alcoholic beverages in the United States (Chapter 12). During the 13 years that it was the law of the land, Prohibition successfully reduced the consumption of alcohol, but encouraged the growth of organized crime and a general disregard for the law. The government also lost billions of dollars in potential tax revenues.
- **1937 Marijuana Tax Act.** Banned recreational use of marijuana but allowed for medicinal or industrial use, provided the user paid for a license (Chapter 9). The U.S. government, however, made it effectively impossible to acquire the necessary tax stamp. The Act was ruled unconstitutional in 1969, in the case of *Leary v. United States*.
- **1938 Food, Drug, and Cosmetics Act.** Required drug companies to prove their products were both safe and effective, to label the product with adequate directions for safe use, and to determine if the drug should be sold over the counter or by prescription (Chapter 15). This law gave the U.S. Food and Drug Administration (FDA) more authority and responsibility.

1950s: Increasing Penalties for Drug Crimes

Organized crime flourished during Prohibition and, after its repeal, became more involved with the illegal distribution of drugs, resulting in an expanding drug problem. In an attempt to reduce drug use, Congress es-

calated the penalties for narcotics violations. In 1951, Congress passed the Boggs Act, which established the first mandatory minimum prison sentences for drug crimes, with harsher penalties for repeat offenders. The 1956 Narcotics Control Act made drug-related penalties more severe. The Act

- increased mandatory minimum sentences;
- forbade judges from suspending sentences or imposing probation in cases where they felt a prison sentence was inappropriate; and
- denied the right to parole consideration for those imprisoned for drug offenses (although murderers, child molesters, and serial rapists were still granted parole).

1970 Controlled Substances Act

By 1970, the legislative patchwork of over 200 drug laws was hard to keep track of and did not effectively address the country's drug problems. In an attempt to remedy this, President Nixon signed the **Controlled Substances Act** (CSA) into law in 1970. The CSA repealed, replaced, and consolidated all previous federal drug laws. It was the first law to control drugs directly, rather than through taxes.

The CSA created five classifications of drugs—called schedules—based on the drug's potential for abuse, its medical benefits (if any), and its likelihood for producing dependence (Chapter 1). This classification made it easier to administer—the government could enact criminal penalties by referring to a schedule rather than listing all related substances within the text of a law. In addition, the CSA made it possible to add or remove a drug from a schedule rather than changing the entire drug law.

In 1971, President Richard Nixon identified drug abuse as "public enemy number one." He was the first to use the term **war on drugs** to refer to the U.S. government's campaign to reduce the importation, production, distribution, and consumption of illegal drugs. This campaign included harsh penalties for sellers and users, as well as military interventions to reduce the illegal drug trade. Nixon's drug policies actually began as a public health crusade and focused on prevention and treatment. In later years, especially under President Ronald Reagan, the focus changed to one of **interdiction** (interception of illegal drugs being

Controlled Substances Act (CSA): The federal policy under which the manufacture, importation, distribution, possession, and use of certain substances is regulated.

War on drugs: The U.S. government's campaign to reduce the importation, manufacture, sale, and use of illegal drugs.

Interdiction: The action of intercepting and preventing access to a prohibited substance.

smuggled into the country), law enforcement, and punishment, and subsequent administrations would enact many laws to further this goal.

1984–1988 Drug Abuse Control Acts

Throughout the 1980s, the rhetoric against drugs increased. Congressman Thomas Arnett declared, "Drugs are a threat worse than nuclear warfare or any chemical warfare waged on any battlefield."[1] Upon taking office, President Reagan appropriated an additional $1.7 billion to fund the war on drugs. New legislation was enacted that was directed at drug users, not just at manufacturers or distributors. Penalties for possession and distribution increased dramatically, and the prison population soared (Figure 2.1).

The Anti-Drug Abuse Act of 1986 strengthened federal anti-drug policies in a number of ways. The Act

- encouraged other countries to eradicate their illicit drug crops and halt international drug traffic;
- provided for substances that are structurally or functionally similar to existing schedule I and II drugs (analogues) to be treated as though they were already in those schedules, meaning drugs could be declared illegal without the need to demonstrate their abuse;
- reinstated mandatory minimum sentences for all drug offenses, without the possibility of suspended sentences, probation, or parole for prisoners; and
- strengthened the forfeiture laws. The government can confiscate anything in one's possession—a car, boat, house, currency, or other belongings—at the time of

a drug arrest. This seizure does not require conviction of a crime, or even an official criminal charge to be filed; it is often very difficult to get one's assets back, and people have no recourse if their assets are damaged.[2] The seized assets are used, in part, to fund the police, which means the police can seize property or funds to finance their own operations.

The penalties enacted in 1986 were not considered punitive enough to stem the drug problem, so the Drug Abuse Act of 1988

- established the Office of National Drug Control Policy (ONDCP), in order to coordinate the efforts of the federal agencies involved in drug regulation and drug law enforcement;
- lowered the blood alcohol content (BAC) standard for DUI from 0.10 to 0.08 percent;
- permitted the death penalty for anyone who kills another while committing or planning a felony-level drug crime;
- increased the penalties for possession; and
- permitted the withholding of federal benefits for drug crime offenses, which means that someone convicted for any drug-related crime could lose any and all grants, loans, and professional licenses provided by the United States.

Ask yourself: Do you think that mandatory minimum sentences for drug crimes are more beneficial or more harmful for our society? Why?

The 1990s and Beyond

When George H.W. Bush became president in 1989, he announced a major escalation of the war on drugs with renewed focus on marijuana offenders. The prison population continued to rise and showed no signs of slowing when President Bill Clinton assumed office in 1993. The number of jail sentences nationwide for marijuana offenders during Clinton's two terms was 800 percent higher than during the 12 years under Presidents Reagan and George H.W. Bush.[3] President Clinton also signed legislation that prevented students with drug charges from receiving federal aid and student loans for colleges and universities.

These drug laws were not applied evenly and consistently, however. Minorities and people of lower socioeconomic status bore the brunt of the penalties. Blacks use drugs at a lower rate than whites (Figure 2.2) but are arrested for drug charges at more than twice times the rate of whites, and are incarcerated for drug crimes at more than six times the rate of whites.[4,5,6,7]

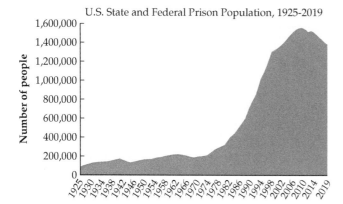

U.S. State and Federal Prison Population, 1925-2019

FIGURE 2.1. The U.S. prison population, by year. In the 1980s, less than one-quarter of U.S. prisoners were incarcerated for drug offenses. Today, the number of people in state prisons for drug offenses is 10 times greater than in 1980, and almost half of those in federal prison are serving time for drug offenses, mostly possession.

Source: The Sentencing Project. (2021). Trends in U.S. Corrections. https://www.sentencingproject.org/publications/trends-in-u-s-corrections/

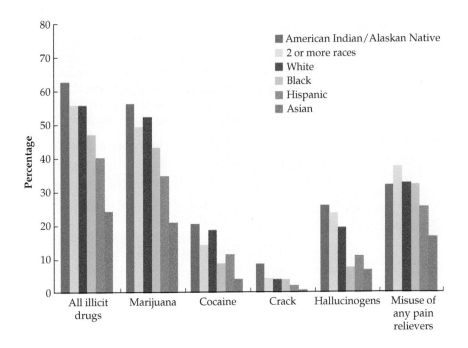

FIGURE 2.2. **Percent of U.S. population who has ever used a drug, by race.** Those whose heritage includes two or more races and American Indians/Alaska natives have the highest rate of drug use. Whites have a higher rate of drug use than Blacks, Hispanics, or Asians for every drug listed except crack.

Source: SAMHSA. (2020). Results from the 2019 national survey on drug use and health: Detailed tables. Rockville, MD: Center for Behavioral Health Statistics and Quality.

Current Drug Laws

Why are some drugs illegal, while others are not? The government establishes drug laws to reduce the harmful effects of drugs—to the user, to others, and to society. Drug laws also have been used for political and economic reasons.

Federal Agencies that Create and Enforce Drug Control Laws

Our nation's drug policies are complex and far reaching, and they require the interaction and cooperation of many federal agencies. Table 2.1 summarizes some of the agencies involved in the creation, oversight, and enforcement of some of our drug laws.

QUICK HIT
The director of the ONDCP is known as the "drug czar."

Federal Drug Laws

The CSA of 1970 established the federal drug laws regulating many illicit drugs. For the most part, the U.S. government tries to deter drug use with a prohibitionist policy that includes strategies to reduce both the supply of and demand for drugs, and by exacting high penalties for drug law violations.[8]

Types of Drug Crimes

Drug crimes may be charged as a misdemeanor or as a felony. Most states define a **misdemeanor** as a minor

Misdemeanor: A lesser crime punishable by no more than one year in prison.

crime that might result in a fine, public service, or a prison sentence of less than a year, while a **felony** is considered a more serious crime, punishable by at least a year in prison.

Drug **possession** is when a person knowingly or intentionally has any controlled substance without a valid prescription. Possession also may mean that the drugs are within a person's control. A person may be considered to be in possession of drugs if the drugs are found in their house or car. Possession of small quantities may be deemed "simple possession," while possession of large amounts may result in a charge of "possession with intent to distribute," which carries stiffer penalties upon conviction. The police also may presume an "intent to distribute" if the possessor has drug paraphernalia, packaging material, large amounts of money, or communications from customers. Drug possession laws also criminalize the possession of chemicals or certain accessories used in the manufacture of some drugs, as well as drug paraphernalia such as bongs, syringes, or crack pipes.

Drug **trafficking** refers to the unauthorized manufacture, import, export, distribution, or dispensation of a controlled substance, or possession of a controlled substance with intent to distribute. Simply handing a package of drugs to someone can be considered distribution, even if money is not exchanged.

Possession: The crime of having illegal or nonprescribed controlled substances under one's control.

Felony: A serious crime, typically punishable by at least a year in prison

Trafficking: The unauthorized manufacture, distribution, or sale of any controlled substance.

TABLE 2.1.   Federal Agencies Involved in Drug Control Laws

Executive Office of the President	The Office of National Drug Control Policy (ONDCP)	• Establishes policies and actions to eradicate illicit drug use, manufacturing, and trafficking, and to reduce crime, violence, and health consequences associated with illicit drugs. • Evaluates, coordinates, and oversees anti-drug efforts in the United States and internationally, including the National Youth Anti-Drug Media Campaign.
The Department of Justice (DOJ)	FBI	• Investigates multinational organized crime networks.
	Bureau of Alcohol, Tobacco, and Firearms (ATF)	• Prevents illegal trafficking of alcohol and tobacco products.
	Immigration and Customs Enforcement (ICE) and the U.S. Coast Guard	• Involved in interdicting drugs and deporting foreign drug traffickers.
	Justice Tax Division	• Prosecutes crimes involving money laundering or other tax evasion cases related to drugs.
	Federal Bureau of Prisons	• Maintains prisons and manages the treatment, education, and rehabilitation programs for prisoners.
	Drug Enforcement Agency (DEA)	• The lead agency for domestic enforcement of the Controlled Substances Act. The agency also works in conjunction with the FBI, ICE, and foreign law enforcement agencies to combat drug smuggling and conduct international drug investigations.
The Department of Transportation	Federal Aviation Administration (FAA)	• Works with other agencies to restrict the transport of drugs.
	National Highway Traffic Safety Administration (NHTSA)	• Regulates and enforces drunk driving laws.
The Department of Health and Human Services	Food and Drug Administration (FDA)	• Helps regulate and supervise the safety of prescription and over-the-counter pharmaceutical drugs, tobacco products, vaccines, dietary supplements, medical devices, food, and other products. • Works with the DEA to determine which drugs are added to or removed from the schedules of drugs.

A person who associates with those who possess or sell drugs can be convicted of **conspiracy**. A person can be charged with drug conspiracy without ever having bought, sold, or possessed any type of illegal drug. Lending a drug-dealing friend your car, cashing their check, or allowing a dealer to use your telephone can be considered conspiracy. To prove conspiracy, the government must prove that there was an agreement between the parties and that each alleged conspirator knew of the unlawful agreement and joined in it.

Penalties for Drug Offenses

The penalties for drug crimes depend on several factors. These include the specific drug, the quantities involved, whether it is a first offense, and if the crime is possession or trafficking.

Possession. The penalties for possession of some drugs, such as marijuana, vary greatly from state to state, although the federal law states that a person who is convicted of a possession charge is subject to the following:

- First offense: A maximum of one year in prison and a fine of not less than $1,000.

Conspiracy: An agreement between two or more people to violate the federal drug laws.

- Second offense: Between 15 days and 2 years in prison, and a fine of $2,500 to $10,000.
- Third offense: Between 90 days and 3 years in prison, and a fine of no less than $5,000.

For a first offense of simple possession, the court has the option to put the individual on probation for up to a year. If there is no violation of the conditions of the probation, the charge may be dismissed and the conviction erased. Judges sometimes require the accused to successfully complete a drug treatment program, and to undergo periodic drug testing to guarantee that they are not using drugs. Conviction of any drug charges, even possession, may make one ineligible to receive federal student loans or other federal benefits.

Drug Trafficking. The penalties for drug trafficking depend on the specific drug, what schedule it is, its quantity, and whether it's a first, second, or third offense. Other factors also affect the sentencing. Distribution of drugs to a person under age 21 by those age 18 or older, distribution within 1,000 feet of a school or college, and/or if death or bodily injury results from the use of the substances will instigate greater than normal penalties. Drug trafficking penalties are included in Table 2.2.

TABLE 2.2.   Federal Penalties for Drug Trafficking (U.S. Codes 841, 960, 962) as of 2015

Drug (Schedule)	Quantity	Penalties*	Quantity	Penalties	Quantity	Penalties
Cocaine (II)	Less than 500 grams	First offense: Up to 20 years in prison Fine: $1/$5 million ***Second offense:*** Up to 30 years; if death or serious injury, 20 years to life Fine: $2/$10 million	500 to 4,999 g mixture	First offense: 5–40 years; if death or serious injury, 20 years to life Fine: $5/$25 million ***Second offense:*** 10 years to life; if death or serious injury, life imprisonment Fine: $8/$50 million	5 kg or more mixture	First offense: 10 years to life; if death or serious injury, 20 years to life Fine: $10/$50 million ***Second offense***: 20 years to life; if death or serious injury, life imprisonment Fine: of $20/$75 million
Crack (II)	Less than 28 grams		28 to 279 g mixture		280 g or more mixture	
Heroin (I)	Less than 100 grams		100 to 999 g mixture		1 kg or more mixture	
Fentanyl (II)	Less than 40 grams		40 to 399 g mixture		400 g or more mixture	
Fentanyl analogue (I)	Less than 10 grams		10 to 99 g mixture		100 g or more mixture	
LSD (I)	Less than 1 gram		1 to 9 g mixture		10 g or more mixture	
Methamphetamine (II)	Less than 5 grams pure or less than 50 grams mixture		5 to 49 g pure or 50 to 499 g mixture		50 g or more pure or 500 g or more mixture	
PCP (II)	Less than 10 grams or less than 100 grams mixture		10 to 99 g pure or 100 to 999 g mixture		100 g or more pure or 1 kg or more mixture	

Drug	Quantity	Penalties
Any other schedule I and II drugs	Any amount	First offense: Up to 20 years; if death or serious injury, 20 years to life Fine: $1/5 million Second offense: Up to 30 years; if death or serious injury, life imprisonment Fine: $2/10 million
Schedule III drugs	Any amount	First offense: Up to 10 years; if death or serious injury, not more than 15 years Fine: $500,000/$2.5 million Second offense: Up to 20 years; if death or serious injury, not more than 30 years Fine: $1.5/5 million
Schedule IV drugs	Any amount	First offense: Up to 5 years. Fine: $250,000/$1 million Second offense: Up to 10 years. Fine: $500,000/$2 million
Schedule V drugs	Any amount	First offense: Up to 1 year. Fine: $100,000/$250,000 Second offense: Up to 4 years. Fine: $200,000/$500,000

Drug	Quantity	First offense	Second offense
Marijuana (schedule I)	1,000 kg or more mixture, or 1,000 or more plants	10 years to life; if death or serious injury, 20 years to life Fine: $10/$50 million	20 years to life; if death or serious injury, mandatory life Fine: $20/$75 million
	100–999 kg mixture, or 100–999 plants	5–40 years; if death or serious injury, 20 years to life Fine: $5/$25 million	10 years to life; if death or serious injury mandatory life Fine: $20/$75 million
	50–99 kg marijuana mixture, 50–99 plants, more than 10 kg hashish, or more than 1 kg hashish oil	Up to 20 years; if death or serious injury, 20 years to life Fine: $1/$5 million	Up to 30 years; if death or serious injury, mandatory life Fine: $2/$10 million
Marijuana/hashish/ hashish oil (schedule I)	1–49 plants, or less than 50 kg mixture marijuana	Up to 5 years Fine: $250,000/$1 million	Up to 10 years Fine: $500,000/$2 million
	1 kg or less hash oil		
	10 kg or less of hashish		

Penalties

- A reference to a fine of $5/$25 million means a fine of no more than $5 million for an individual and no more than $25 million for a defendant other than an individual, such as a business or corporation.
- A reference to 5–40 years means a term of not less than 5 years and not more than 40 years. Note that for trafficking offenses, there is a mandatory prison sentence even for a first offense.
- Other factors that affect sentencing:
  - Distribution to a person under age 21 years by those age 18 or older is punishable by a greater than normal penalty.
    - First offense: up to twice the normal penalties otherwise authorized
    - Second offense: up to three times the penalties otherwise authorized
    - Third conviction: mandatory life in prison
  - Distribution within 1,000 feet of school or college:
    - First offense: up to twice the normal penalties otherwise authorized, and at least one year in prison
    - Second offense: up to three times the penalties otherwise authorized and at least three years in prison
    - Any offense involving methamphetamine: Other sentence imposed plus imprisonment for no more than 20 years

Source: https://www.dea.gov/sites/default/files/drug_of_abuse.pdf

State and Local Drug Laws

The CSA set the federal drug laws. Technically, states can determine their own laws, but if a state law conflicts with federal law, the federal law overrides the state law. States are allowed some flexibility in how they decide to enforce (or not enforce) the CSA. Since 2009, many states have taken some action to ease their drug laws. Some have reclassified drug possession from a felony to a misdemeanor, while others have rolled back mandatory minimum sentences. On the other hand, some states have toughened their drug laws.[9] Many states have passed laws legalizing or decriminalizing marijuana, but since these laws directly contradict the CSA, there is ambiguity in how different presidential administrations choose to enforce the law.

Sometimes, drug laws vary greatly from state to state, for scheduled as well as nonscheduled drugs. There may be differences regarding the minimum age at which it is acceptable to drink in one's home; the days, hours, and locations when alcohol can be sold; whether it is acceptable to drink in public; or whether adults are allowed to consume alcoholic beverages at all—there are more than 500 municipalities in the United States that are dry, meaning that it is illegal to buy or sell alcohol (Figure 2.3). (In some jurisdictions, it is even illegal to possess alcohol.)

Violations of drug laws can lead to either federal or state charges, but most drug-related offenses are prosecuted at the state level. State prisons house more than six times as many prisoners as federal prisons.[10]

International Drug Laws and Policies

When the World Health Organization surveyed over 85,000 subjects in 17 countries about their drug use, they found that drug use was not solely related to drug laws; countries with harsher drug policies did not have lower levels of drug use.[11,12] British officials came to a similar result when they investigated the drug use and policies in 11 countries around the world (Figure 2.4).[13]

FIGURE 2.3. "Wet" and "dry" counties in the U.S. Some counties in the United States are dry; nearly all are located in the south. On this map, blue represents a "wet" county where alcohol is not banned; yellow counties are partially dry and have some alcohol controls; and red counties have strict controls on alcohol.

Source: Data from NABCA. (2014). Wet and dry counties: Control and license states. http://www.nabca.org/assets/Docs/Research/December%202014%20WetDry%20Counties.pdf

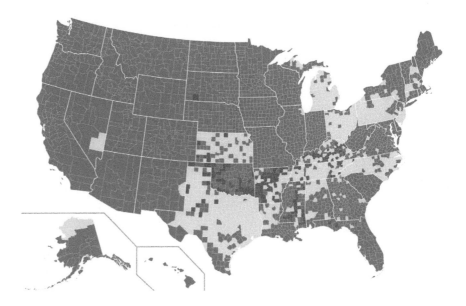

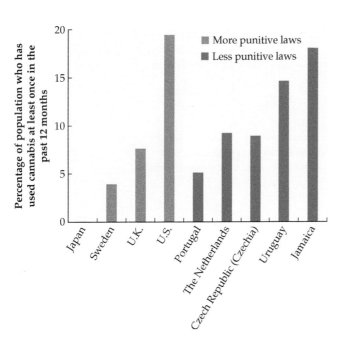

FIGURE 2.4. Annual cannabis use, by country. There is no clear relationship between the severity of a country's laws and its level of drug use.

Sources: World Drug Report. (2020). Annual prevalence of drug use. Accessed on November 5, 2020, from https://wdr.unodc.org/wdr2020/

International Comparators. (2014). https://www.gov.uk/government/publications/drugs-international-comparators UNODC. (2012). World drug report, 2011. Vienna, Austria. https://www.unodc.org/documents/data-and-analysis/WDR2011/World_Drug_Report_2011_ebook.pdf

The British study found a wide range of approaches to drug possession, from zero tolerance (Japan and Sweden) to decriminalization (Portugal and the Czech Republic) and legalization (Uruguay).

- Japan has a zero-tolerance policy for drug possession, and substances are more strictly controlled in Japan than in many other countries. Some products that are available over the counter (OTC) in other countries (such as cold and flu remedies) are banned. Possession of even small amounts of drugs is punishable by a lengthy imprisonment. Illegal drug use is very low, but alcohol and tobacco use are widespread.
- Sweden has a drug-free society policy. Drug offenses are categorized as minor, ordinary, or serious. Even minor cases are still punishable by up to six months in prison. Ordinary offenses can result in sentences of three years, and serious offenses can mean up to 10 years in prison. Cannabis use is low, but it is not significantly lower than in some countries with more lenient approaches.
- In the Czech Republic, possession of drugs is illegal, but possession of small amounts is treated as an administrative penalty, punishable with a fine.
- Portugal removed criminal sanctions for possession and use of small amounts of any drug in 2001, but possession is still considered illegal. Those found in possession of small amounts of any drug (less than a 10-day supply) are referred to a dissuasion commission panel that evaluates the personal circumstances of individuals and refers them to appropriate services, which may include treatment.
- In Uruguay, drug use or possession for personal consumption is not criminalized. In 2014, Uruguay became the first country in the world to legalize and regulate the production, supply, and recreational use of cannabis, which is sold in pharmacies.

Many factors can influence drug use in a country—the time frame, economics, religion, and culture. When Portugal first decriminalized drugs, there was an upswing in drug use—but that level declined over time, and drug use is now lower than it was prior to decriminalization (as are the number of drug-related deaths and HIV infection rates among drug users).[14] The laws codifying penalties for possession in the Czech Republic were only introduced in 2010, but the lifetime rates of cannabis use have declined since 2010.[15]

Drug use is typically very low in Japan, but it is hard to know whether that is due to Japan's harsh drug laws, or because drug use has long been considered taboo in Japan and conformity is important in the Japanese culture. It is clear that factors other than legislation and enforcement influence a country's drug use.[16]

Ask yourself: The United States has harsh drug laws, and some of the highest rates of drug use. Why do you think this is so? What factors influence the relatively high prevalence of illicit drug use in the United States?

Harm Reduction Policies

Many countries believe that the "war on drugs" cannot be won. Instead of spending enormous resources trying to reduce the supply of drugs or punishing the drug user, they have dedicated resources to reducing the harm that can come from drug use. For example, there are four major objectives in The Netherlands' drug policy: (1) to diminish the use of recreational drugs and to help recreational drug users get the help they need; (2) to reduce harm to users; (3) to decrease drug-related disruptions of public order and safety; and (4) to reduce the manufacturing and sale of recreational drugs. In the United States, some states and communities have implemented harm reduction policies as well. Some of the principles that underlie harm reduction policies include

- accepting, for better or worse, that drug use is a reality;
- considering drug use to be a complex, multifaceted phenomenon;
- recognizing that sex/gender, race, socioeconomic status, and other social factors affect people's capacity to deal effectively with drug-related harm;

- acknowledging that not all drugs or ways of using drugs are comparable; and
- regarding the quality of life of both the individual and the community as the criteria for policies.

Most harm reduction policies seek to reduce the health risks associated with drug use, reduce the overcrowding of prisons, and focus on treatment rather than punishment.

Reduce Health Risks Associated with Drug Use

Harm reduction programs acknowledge that drug use, both legal and illegal, occurs, but they try to reduce the associated negative consequences. For example, providing nicotine patches helps those who wish to quit tobacco, and establishing safe-ride programs can cut down on DUI offenses. Needle exchange programs for intravenous (IV) drug users can lower rates of HIV and hepatitis B transmission. Methadone maintenance programs, or providing naloxone to opioid addicts, may reduce the number of fatalities due to overdose. Some countries have established drug consumption rooms—facilities into which drug users can bring illicitly purchased drugs for supervised consumption—which may reduce public drug use, provide a safer injecting environment, decrease the incidence of drug-related infection, and increase users' access to social, health, and drug treatment services.

Reduce Prison Overcrowding

Laws that focus on incarceration not only crowd our prisons, but they may drive drug users away from health and social support services. Eliminating mandatory minimum sentences can give judges more leeway to consider the best course of action for each individual, taking into consideration the defendant's personal history and circumstances. Appropriate actions may include incarceration, fines, drug rehabilitation programs, counseling, vocational training, or other therapeutic approaches. Since decriminalizing drugs in 2001, Portugal has seen a significant decline in the burden on criminal justice system resources.[17] The number of people convicted for drug trafficking has remained fairly stable, but the number imprisoned for possession has declined dramatically.

Focus on Treatment Rather than Punishment

Some states have initiated acts that allow nonviolent drug offenders to enter drug treatment and educational programs rather than go to prison. Treatment has reduced drug abuse recidivism (reoffending), and those who have been through treatment programs commit fewer crimes.[18,19] Compared to incarceration, treatment also has been found to be a more cost-effective way to deal with drug offenders. Maryland's state sentencing commission found that while the annual cost to incarcerate an offender was $20,000, the annual cost of treatment was only $4,000; furthermore, jurisdictions that increased the number of drug offenders sent to treatment rather than jail saw a significant drop in violent crime.[20,21] California and Arizona also have programs that allow for nonviolent drug offenders to enter substance abuse treatment programs rather than prison, and these states have seen lower recidivism rates, and significant savings to taxpayers.

Ask yourself: Do you think a convicted drug user who is forced to enter rehab would be more or less likely to be successful in quitting drugs than a drug user who checks him- or herself into rehab voluntarily? Why?

Ramifications of Drug Laws

Drug laws have far-reaching ramifications. These extend beyond affected individuals and families to society at large.

Individual Ramifications

Any drug conviction will permanently affect your life whether or not you are sentenced to serve time in prison. Having a drug conviction on one's record erects barriers to future employment; a felony conviction can lower a person's subsequent annual income by as much as 30 percent.[22] In many states, a person may be not hired, or may be fired from a position, regardless of qualifications or actual work performance, for any drug conviction—be it misdemeanor or felony.

If a person is convicted of a drug crime, the punishment doesn't stop with the penalty directly imposed by the judge. The individual also may experience a range of collateral sanctions that are automatically triggered by the conviction.[23] In most cases, conviction on a felony drug charge—even one for marijuana— triggers the same concomitant penalties that one might experience after a conviction for murder, rape, or kidnapping. In many cases, the collateral penalties for a drug conviction actually exceed those for a violent crime.[24]

Societal Ramifications

The United States represents 4.4 percent of the world's population . . . and almost 25 percent of the world's prisoners. Although the rate of incarceration in the United States has declined over the last few years, our nation has more prisoners than any other industrialized country (Figure 2.5). Over 14 percent of the state prison population and 47 percent of the federal prison population are incarcerated for drug charges (Figure 2.6).[25]

QUICK HIT

Among white males age 18 years and older, 1 in every 251 is incarcerated, as is 1 in every 100 Hispanic males, and 1 in every 43 Black males. Black people, who represent 13.4 percent of the U.S. population and 14.6 percent of regular illicit drug users, account for over 60 percent of those in prison for drug crimes.[26,27] Among U.S. residents born in 2001, the lifetime likelihood of imprisonment is 1 in 17 for white men, 1 in 6 for Latino men, and 1 in 3 for Black men.[28]

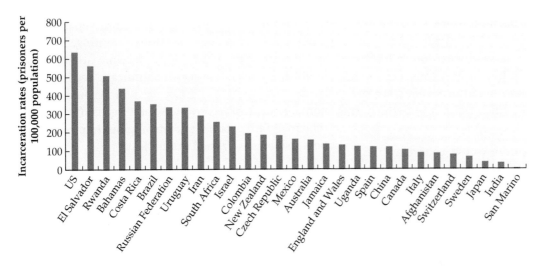

FIGURE 2.5. Incarceration rates (prisoners per 100,000 population) of various countries. The United States has the highest per capita incarceration rate in the world.

World Prison Brief: International Center for Prison Studies. (2020). https://www.prisonstudies.org/world-prison-brief-data

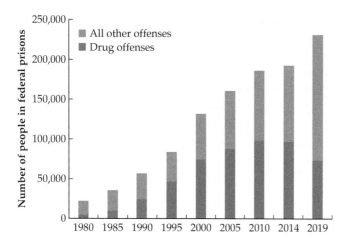

FIGURE 2.6. **The proportion of federal prisoners incarcerated for drug offenses.** The number of people in federal prison for drug offenses has increased greatly since 1980, from 21.5% in 1980 to almost 60% in 1995. It has since fallen and is now about 46%.

The Sentencing Project. (2021). Trends in U.S. Corrections. https://www. sentencingproject.org/publications/trends-in-u-s-corrections/

In 2019, there were over 1.5 million drug arrests made in the United States—one arrest every 20 seconds—over 86 percent of them for possession.[29] Marijuana offenses accounted for over one-third of all drug arrests.[30] The United States incarcerates more people for drug offenses than the European Union incarcerates for all crimes combined (and their population is 100 million more than the United States).

Drug incarceration represents an enormous cost to society, not only due to millions of damaged lives, but also due to the financial burden on law enforcement and prisons. The national average annual cost to incarcerate one inmate in a state prison is $33,286, the average cost for federal prisoners is $36,299; this is a cost of almost $10 billion each year just to house the drug prisoners.[31,32] If one adds in the drug-related spending on police and court personnel used to try drug offenders, the annual cost is about $40 billion. Drug laws also occupy the time of police officers. The minimum average amount of time spent by one police officer to make and process a marijuana possession arrest is 2.5 hours.[33]

International Ramifications

Drug policies also have international ramifications. Since the 1980s, the U.S. government has deployed combat forces to foreign countries to destroy their drug supplies, and it has enacted mandatory sanctions against countries that refused to cooperate fully with antinarcotics efforts.[34] The United States also regularly sponsors spraying of large amounts of toxic herbicide over the jungles of Central and South America in order to eradicate drug production.[35] The pesticides also eradicate

---

STRAIGHT DOPE **Collateral Sanctions for Drug Convictions**

If convicted of a drug offense, additional penalties can include the following:

- *Loss or suspension of professional licenses.* Attorneys, physicians, pharmacists, psychologists, social workers, architects, paramedics, midwives, certified public accountants (CPAs), contractors, electricians, plumbers, hair stylists, taxi drivers, or funeral directors, among others, may all lose their licenses if convicted of drug offenses. In 20 states, it is possible to lose your professional license based on a misdemeanor drug conviction, such as possession of marijuana.

- *Suspension of driver's license.* In some states, a drug conviction will lead to suspension of your driver's license for at least six months.

- *Loss of educational aid.* Any drug conviction, even misdemeanor possession, can result in the loss of federal aid, student loans, and some scholarships. Each year, approximately 20,000 to 40,000 college students are denied federal financial aid or had that funding delayed as a result of a drug conviction. Drug offenses are the only crimes that result in exclusion from financial aid.

- *Loss of welfare benefits.* In 1996, President Bill Clinton signed legislation that allowed states to deny public housing and food stamps to those convicted of felony drug offenses. This ban, which particularly impacts women, children, and minorities, is imposed for no other offenses but drug crimes.

- *Ineligibility to vote.* In 48 states, drug-related felonies will result in being barred from voting for at least some time. In nine states, this bar on voting may last for life.

- *Bars on adoption.* In some states, a misdemeanor marijuana conviction can prevent one from adopting a child.

Sources: American Civil Liberties Union (ACLU). (2015). Injustice 101: Higher education denies financial aid to students with drug convictions. Retrieved on August 3, 2015 from https://www.aclu.org/injustice-101-higher-education-act-denies-financial-aid-students-drug-convictions

Boire, R.G. (2007). Life sentences: The collateral sanctions associated with marijuana offenses. http://www.mpp.org/assets/pdfs/library/The-Collateral-Sanctions-Associated-with-Marijuana-Offenses.pdf

ProCon.org. (2019). State felon voting laws. Accessed on October 14, 2019 from https://felonvoting.procon.org/view.resource.php?resourceID=000286

food crops, destroy fragile ecosystems, and expose the local farmers to unhealthy levels of toxic chemicals.

In 1988, Congress passed a resolution proclaiming its goal of "a drug-free America by 1995." Despite the full efforts of the government and law enforcement officials and a huge monetary outlay, America is not even close to being drug free. Many organizations believe that such a goal is not only unattainable, but that it is doing much more harm than good. In 1998, over 350 people from 44 countries, including 11 Nobel Prize winners, 7 heads of state, and the past Secretary General of the United Nations, wrote an open letter to the Secretary General of the United Nations. The letter stated the authors' belief that "the global war on drugs is now causing more harm than drug abuse itself." No legislators from the United States—the country that controls the global drug war—signed the letter.

In 2011, the Global Commission on Drug Policy released a report saying "the global war on drugs has failed, with devastating consequences for individuals and societies around the world." The report went on to state that even though enormous amounts of money, time, and resources have been spent fighting the manufacturers, sellers, and users of illegal drugs, their supply or consumption has not been reduced significantly. In addition, once one drug source is eliminated, another source emerges almost instantly to fill the void. The authors found that repressive efforts directed at consumers impeded public health measures and increased some harmful consequences of drug use.[36] Not only has the war on drugs been a failure, but it has been an expensive failure. In 2015, state and federal expenses to incarcerate people charged with drug-related offenses equaled about $10 billion a year—over $27 million per day. Why are there such forceful efforts to eliminate drugs? Is it because drugs can be harmful to our bodies, or is it because of their detrimental effects on society?

Critical Evaluation

What is the relationship between drugs and crime?

The relationship between drugs and crime is complex. It's important to consider many factors when trying to understand their interactions.

Defining terms. It is easy to make a statement like "drugs cause crime." But which drugs? Alcohol, which is legal, is actually associated with more crime than all other drugs combined; the U.S. Department of Justice estimates that most criminal offenders were under the influence of alcohol alone when they committed their crimes. On the other hand, hallucinogens and marijuana are actually associated with a *decrease* in violent crime. And what types of crimes are being considered? Given that controlled substances are illegal in the United States, the crime-drug relationship may be an artifact of the laws themselves. What if we suddenly declared it illegal to be over age 30? All of a sudden, we would have millions of criminals! And they're all over age 30! Oh no—age causes crime!

Correlation is not causation. There is a positive correlation between drugs and crime—as the use of certain drugs increases in a community, so does the occurrence of certain types of crimes. But do the drugs cause the crime? Or, does hanging out with a criminal element put one in an environment that encourages drug use? Or, perhaps both crime and drug use are due to a third factor, such as genetic traits, psychological conditions, poverty, unemployment, lack of opportunities, or poor family dynamics.

Underlying factors. If drugs do indeed lead to criminal activity, what factors underlie this association? Is it the psychopharmacological properties of the drugs that lead to crime? Alcohol, methamphetamine, cocaine, and PCP may increase aggression, paranoia, and violence. Or, maybe drugs lead to crime because drug users rob to support their habit; when drug prices are high, the incidence of drug-related property crimes rise. Or, maybe it is the drug laws. If a drug is illegal, it is more lucrative. As penalties escalate, drug dealers' risks increase, which forces them to charge more for their product to compensate for the increased risk. Finally, maybe the fact that drugs are illegal makes them more attractive than they would otherwise be. As the old expression says, "forbidden fruit tastes the sweetest."

Ask yourself: Have you ever passed a wall with a sign that said "Wet Paint: Do Not Touch" and then suddenly had a strong urge to reach out and touch the wall, just because the sign forbade it? How effective do you think our current drug laws are?

Legalization

The decision as to whether a drug should be scheduled under the CSA is made by the Secretary of the Department of Health and Human Services (HHS) in consultation with the FDA and other agencies that may provide scientific information about the drug. Two decisions must be made: Should the drug be scheduled? And, if so, what schedule should the drug be? If it is determined that the drug should be scheduled, the Drug Enforcement Agency (DEA) administrator decides the drug's schedule based on its pharmacological actions, potential for abuse, the current scientific knowledge about its effects, and what danger it may pose to public health, among other factors. The DEA administrator then sends his or her recommendation to the Secretary of HHS, who evaluates the decision and forwards the recommendation to the Attorney General, who sends the decision back to the DEA for implementation.

The proposal is then published in the *Federal Register*. All interested parties are invited to file comments with the DEA or request a hearing regarding the scheduling. At the hearing, the DEA discusses the issues with the interested group and tries to reach a compromise. If a compromise can't be reached, a hearing is held before an administrative law judge, who considers the evidence on factual issues and hears arguments on legal questions about the drug. The judge then submits a recommendation to the DEA administrator, who evaluates the document, prepares another report, and publishes the final order in the *Federal Register*. All citizens

then have 30 days to issue an appeal to the U.S. Court of Appeals. If no appeals are considered, the final order becomes law.[37,38]

Factors Considered When Evaluating a Drug's Legal Status

Several recent studies have evaluated the harm caused by a variety of drugs. Lachenmeier and Rehm[39] considered the ratio between the dose that causes adverse effects and the dose that people typically use—a measurement similar to the therapeutic index. In their study, alcohol presented the highest risk of death, followed by nicotine, cocaine, and heroin. Marijuana was the safest recreational drug in the study. One also could consider what percentage of users die from specific drugs. Figure 2.7 shows the rates of drug use compared to the percentage of users who die annually; in this measurement, although there are only about 15,000 heroin-related

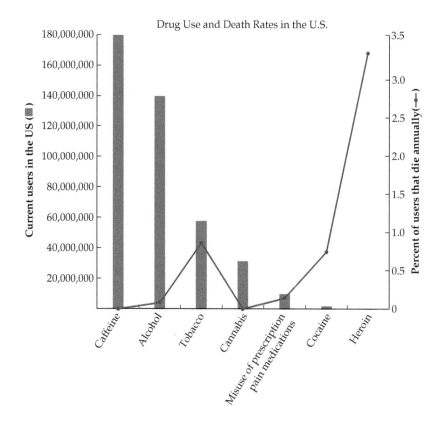

FIGURE 2.7. Drug use and death rates in the United States. The bars and left axis show the number of current users for each drug, and the line and right axis represent the percentage of users who die each year due to the drug.

Centers for Disease Control and Prevention. (2020). Drug overdose deaths in the United States, 1999–2018. NCHS Data Brief, no 356. Hyattsville, MD: National Center for Health Statistics.

SAMHSA. (2020). Results from the 2019 national survey on drug use and health. Rockville, MD: Center for Behavioral Health Statistics and Quality.

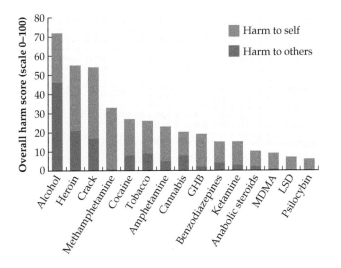

FIGURE 2.8. Levels of harm of different drugs. Researchers considered physical, psychological, and social harm to the user and to society.

Source: Data from: Nutt, D.J., King, L.A., Phillips, L.D. (2010). Drug harms in the UK: A multicriteria decision analysis. Lancet, 376(9752): 1558–65.

deaths each year, as a percentage of current users, heroin fatality rates are highest, followed by tobacco, cocaine, and prescription pain medications.

Members of the Independent Scientific Committee on Drugs rated 20 different drugs on 16 criteria related to the harms that the drug produced in the user and to others.[40] Overall, alcohol was the most harmful drug, followed by heroin and crack cocaine. Mushrooms and LSD were found to be least harmful (Figure 2.8). Alcohol, heroin, crack cocaine, and tobacco were the most harmful to others, and crack, heroin, methamphetamine, and alcohol were the most harmful to the user.

This study only considered harm, not benefits. All drugs have some benefits to the user, at least initially; otherwise, they would not be used. Some drugs, such as alcohol and tobacco, also have economic benefits to society.

Ask yourself: What factors should be considered to determine which drugs should be illegal? Medical and scientific data? The drug's potential to produce dependence? Its potential risks and benefits? Its effects on society? How should we weigh each of these factors in our consideration?

Public Opinion on Drug Laws

Americans' attitudes about drugs and drug laws are changing. Current surveys show that that a majority of adults believe that the government should focus more on treating people who use illegal drugs rather than on prosecution, and that nonviolent drug offenders should

not receive mandatory prison sentences.[41] This is quite a change from 1990, when 73 percent of Americans favored a mandatory death penalty for major drug traffickers and 57 percent said police should be allowed to search houses of "known drug dealers" without a warrant.

Americans also are much more accepting of marijuana than they were in the past. Survey respondents viewed alcohol as significantly more harmful to health and to society than marijuana.[42] There is also growing support for legalization of marijuana (Chapter 9). As of 2021, over one-third of Americans live in a state with legal adult use of cannabis.

To illustrate just how much attitudes about drugs are changing, in November 2020, Oregon passed Measure 110, a ballot initiative that decriminalized the personal use of all drugs. Underlying this proposal was the belief that low-level drug offenses should be treated as a public health issue rather than as a problem for the criminal justice system. Under Measure 110, possession of all drugs, including heroin, cocaine, and methamphetamine, carries a maximum fine of $100 and a requirement to complete a health assessment within 45 days. The measure also establishes drug treatment and recovery programs funded in part by the state's tax revenue from legal sales of cannabis and from state prison savings.

QUICK HIT

By law, the director of the ONDCP must oppose any attempt to legalize the use of illicit drugs, and must ensure that no federal funds shall be used for any study relating to the legalization of any schedule I drug.

Issues Related to Legalizing Drugs

Regarding the legalization of drugs, there are strong arguments in favor of legalization, as well as against it. Some of these arguments are summarized in Table 2.3.

As we've seen with the rapidly changing laws regarding marijuana, our laws and attitudes about drugs are in flux. It is unlikely that the United States will legalize all drugs in the near future, but some drugs may be rescheduled and available by prescription. We also may see a change in the mandatory minimum sentences, giving the judicial system more discretion when it comes to punishments for drug crimes.

Ask yourself: Should we legalize drugs? If so, which ones? By what criteria? Would you be more tempted to use a previously illegal drug if it became legal?

TABLE 2.3.   Issues Related to the Legalization of Drugs

Issue	Pro-legalization	Anti-legalization	Other Issues to Consider
Economic	• Legalizing drugs could add billions of dollars to the U.S. economy, from tax revenue and law enforcement savings.	• Legalizing drugs would be costly due to lost productivity and increased funding to treat addiction.	• How should we assess the risks and benefits of increased economic rewards versus potentially higher addiction rates?
Health	• The government could regulate and monitor drug quality and provide safe implements for their use.	• Drugs cause physical harm to the user.	• Many things are harmful that are not illegal. How much harm does a drug have to cause to the user before it is made illegal?
Crime	• Legalizing drugs will decrease crime, given that the war on drugs supports criminal activity and organized crime networks. • Our prisons are severely overcrowded, mostly with drug offenders.	• There is a positive correlation between drugs and crime. • Some drugs have pharmacological actions that increase violent behavior.	• The relationship between drugs and crime is complex and multifaceted. How can we best weigh the pharmacological, psychological, social, and economic factors involved?
Social Ramifications	• Minorities are particularly affected and punished by our drug laws. • Some of the harm from drugs comes from the penalties if arrested for using them (legal and otherwise) rather than from the drugs.	• Racially biased laws are a product of our society, not the drugs or laws themselves. Solutions other than legalization can be used to address this inequality. • Legal alcohol and tobacco cause more medical, social, and personal problems than all illegal drugs combined.	• Simply because a law isn't perfect, does that mean we should eliminate the laws and legalize drugs? • How might we weigh the harm due to the direct effects of drugs versus the harm due to their illegality? • Is the harm caused by alcohol and tobacco due to the fact that they are inherently worse drugs, or due to the fact that they are legal and, therefore, easily available?
Role of Government	• Drug laws take away personal freedoms. Current drug laws do not stem from a constitutional amendment, and because states and individuals retain all rights not delegated to the federal government, drug enforcement practices can be considered unconstitutional.	• One role of the government is to protect its citizens. We can't purchase uranium or drive 150 mph. We accept that some laws exist to keep us safe.	• How should we balance our personal freedoms against public safety? Which is more important to you—individual rights, or the safety of the nation's citizens?
Effects on Prevalence of Use	• Criminalization doesn't stop drug use. People still use drugs, so drug laws don't work. • If drugs are no longer "forbidden fruit," people might not be as tempted to use them. Additionally, if there is less social stigma about drugs, more people may seek treatment. • States and countries with harsher drug laws do not have fewer persons using drugs.	• Keeping drugs illegal deters their use. If the legal, economic, and physical cost of illicit drugs decreased, more people might use them, leading to more addiction and death. • Legalizing drugs might implicitly condone their use. If drugs are perceived as OK, use may increase. Marijuana use increases in high school students after perception of its risk falls.	• Do we have to "search for perfect solutions"? Does a law have to eliminate all drug use to be effective? • Can we compare drug use in different states and countries, considering the significant effects that cultural mores have on drug use?

Social Policies Related to Drug Use

Drug laws and policies have far-reaching social ramifications. How should we balance these laws with the rights of individuals? Some social policy issues discussed in this section include the minimum legal drinking age, driving while intoxicated, and drug use during pregnancy.

Minimum Legal Drinking Age

After Prohibition ended, most states set the minimum legal drinking age (MLDA) at 21 years. In 1971, the voting age was lowered to 18 years, and many states decreased the minimum age for other privileges of adulthood, including marriage, legal age of consent, and purchase of alcoholic beverages.[43] By the end of 1975, 38 states had lowered their MLDA, usually to 18. In these states, the number of alcohol-related motor

Critical Evaluation

Should the U.S. minimum legal drinking age be lowered?

The MLDA has changed throughout the years and continues to be a topic of debate. Use your critical thinking skills to analyze some of the factors involved.

18-year-olds are legal adults. Those who are 18 years of age can vote, go to war, and get married, but they can't legally drink. Does this mean we should lower the drinking age, or should we raise the age at which those other privileges and responsibilities of adulthood occur? Are all 18-year-olds ready for these responsibilities? Are all those under 18 not yet ready? Should all responsibilities of adulthood be considered equal?

MLDA laws are correlated with a decrease in motor vehicle accidents. Since the early 1980s, alcohol-related traffic deaths have been cut in half. The greatest proportional declines occur among persons age 16–20. The U.S. Department of Transportation estimates that MLDA laws prevent 1,000 traffic deaths each year. How do we balance the loss of personal freedoms associated with a higher MLDA with the value of the lives saved? Which is more important—the personal freedom to drink as an adult, or the lives saved by enacting this law?

On the other hand, the United States has the highest MLDA in the Western world, yet it still has significant drinking-related problems. In Europe, drinking ages are much lower, and they don't have high rates of traffic fatalities. Does the United States' high MLDA *cause* drinking problems? Or are the lower traffic fatalities in Europe due to other factors, such as higher legal driving ages? For example, public transportation is more available in many European countries, so is it appropriate to compare those rates with the United States? Would drinking problems in the young be even worse if the MLDA were lowered?

A lower minimum drinking age would decrease the time between when a person learns to drive, and when he or she is allowed to legally drink. Although younger drivers are less likely to drive after drinking alcohol than adults are, when younger people do drive under the influence, their crash risk is substantially higher than an adult's.[48] Is this, in part, due to their inexperience with drinking, driving, and combining the two? How are the appropriate ages for these activities best determined? Whose right or responsibility is it to determine them?

Underage drinkers are more likely to binge drink than those over age 21. Perhaps younger drinkers are more irresponsible. If they had legal access to alcohol, would there be an epidemic of binge drinking? Or is it because they have less opportunity to drink legally that when they do drink, they make it "count" more?

A higher MLDA is associated with decreased alcohol consumption. Between 1976 and 1981, high school seniors drank more in states that had an MLDA of 18 than in states with an MLDA of 21. Is this directly due to the lower MLDA or to other factors?

A high MLDA is not a deterrent. High school and college students still drink. About half of high school seniors report being drunk at least once in their lives, and almost 19 percent of Americans age 12–20 report current alcohol use.[49,50] But just because a high MLDA doesn't entirely eliminate underage drinking, does that mean we should throw out the law?

Drinking violations are costly. With fines, legal fees, and possible imprisonment, drinking violations are costly. How do we compare the costs of prosecuting underage drinkers with the social and medical costs that would occur by lowering the MLDA?

vehicle fatalities among people age 18–21 years increased. Because of this, between 1976 and 1979, eight states raised their MLDA again, after which they saw a reduction in crash rates.[44]

Because the 21st Amendment to the U.S. Constitution gave the states the right to regulate alcohol, the federal government could not enact a national MLDA of 21 years. Instead, in 1984, Congress passed the Uniform Drinking Age Act. This act reduced federal highway funding to states without an MLDA of 21 by October 1, 1987. All states complied, which essentially and effectively raised the national minimum legal drinking age to 21.[45] Today, only 12 countries throughout the world, including Micronesia, Samoa, Palau, Sri Lanka, and the United States—have set the MLDA at age 21. Nineteen countries, including Bolivia, Jamaica, Morocco, and Cambodia have no MLDA. In most countries, the legal drinking age is between 16 and 19.

Raising the MLDA to age 21 has reduced drunk driving in underage drivers. When roadside breathalyzer surveys of weekend nighttime drivers under age 21 were conducted in 1973, 11 percent of underage drivers had a blood alcohol content (BAC) of 0.05 or higher. By 1986, that number had fallen to 5 percent and continues to drop.[46,47]

Ask yourself: Do you think a culture in which children were exposed to alcohol at an early age would be more or less likely to have a high rate of alcohol abuse? How can we as a nation teach moderation in drinking? How can we reduce drunk driving?

Drunk Driving

In 2019, almost 8 percent of those over age 16—or over 20 million people—drove under the influence of alcohol in the previous year, according to the national survey on drug use and health.[51] This accounts for about 112 million annual incidents of drunk driving.[52] Men were almost twice as likely as women to drive under the influence, accounting for the majority of alcohol-impaired drivers who were involved in a fatal crash.[53] The highest incidence of drunk driving was among those age 21–34 (Figure 2.9). During the 30 days before responding to the survey, 5.4 percent of high school students who had driven a car in the past month indicated that they had driven under the influence of alcohol, and 16.7 percent of students had ridden in a motor vehicle driven by someone who had been drinking alcohol.[54]

A drunk driver is 13 times more likely to cause an accident than a sober one. When intoxicated, drivers

- Process information more slowly
- Are less likely to use peripheral vision
- Show worse coordination
- Demonstrate slower reaction times
- Have poorer judgment
- Are less able to attend to multiple sources of information
- Underestimate hazards and take longer to detect and respond to them

Every day, 29 people in the United States die in a motor vehicle crash involving an alcohol-impaired driver. That's one death every 50 minutes.[55] Most alcohol-related traffic fatalities occur between 12 a.m. and 6 a.m. on weekend nights, when as many as one in every seven drivers are intoxicated.

In 2017, over 1 million drivers were arrested for driving under the influence of alcohol or narcotics, which is only 1 percent of the 111 million self-reported episodes of alcohol-impaired driving among U.S. adults each year.[56] Many of those who are arrested or convicted of driving under the influence of alcohol are repeat offenders; in fact, an average drunk driver has driven drunk 80 times before his first arrest.[57]

A person with a BAC of 0.08 is considered legally intoxicated in the United States (although in 2016, the National Transportation Safety Board recommended

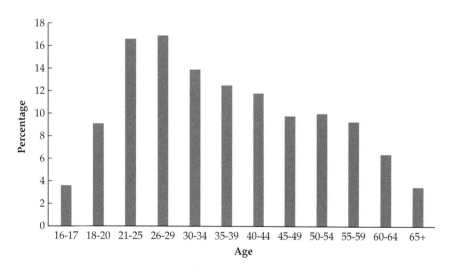

FIGURE 2.9. **Percentage of those who drove under the influence at least once in the past year, by age.** Those age 21–34 are most likely to drive under the influence of alcohol.

Source: SAMHSA. (2016). 2015 Survey on drug use and health: Detailed tables. Rockville, MD: Center for Behavioral Health Statistics and Quality.

lowering the legal limit to 0.05 or less). Anyone who drives on public roads or highways has, by that action, tacitly consented to a field sobriety test or breathalyzer to determine intoxication. This is called **implied consent.** A driver who refuses these tests may face suspension of his or her driver's license.

Ask yourself: Should the BAC be the main criteria for determining if someone is driving under the influence, or should a person's degree of impairment matter more? What should be the penalty for drunk driving? Have you ever driven drunk or been a passenger in a car where the driver was impaired? If so, why did you do it?

Implied consent: Any person who operates a motor vehicle on a public road has, by that action, consented to a chemical test to determine his or her blood alcohol concentration

The greater a person's BAC, the higher the risk of fatal injury in a single-vehicle crash. Each 0.02 percentage increase in the BAC of a driver with any alcohol in their system nearly doubles the risk of being in a fatal crash.[58] The relationship between a person's BAC and their likelihood of a motor vehicle accident is complex, and it interacts with both age and driving experience. The likelihood of a fatal crash is about eight times higher for a driver with a BAC over 0.1 percent than for a sober driver. Table 2.4 shows the approximate BAC and its relation to driving.

Drug Use during Pregnancy

Drugs can be harmful to the adult body, so imagine what they can do to a 1-pound fetus not yet able to metabolize the substances. Drugs taken during pregnancy can affect the fetus in many ways. They can alter the fetus's development, or affect the placenta such that the blood vessels constrict and reduce the supply of oxygen

TABLE 2.4.   BAC Table: Approximate Blood Alcohol Percentage (by Volume)

Drinks		90	100	120	140	160	180	200	220	240	Condition
					Body Weight in Pounds						
0	Male	.00	.00	.00	.00	.00	.00	.00	.00	.00	Only safe driving limit
	Female	.00	.00	.00	.00	.00	.00	.00	.00		
1	Male		.04	.03	.03	.02	.02	.02	.02	.02	Driving skills significantly affected
	Female	.05	.05	.04	.03	.03	.03	.02	.02	.02	
2	Male		.08	.06	.05	.05	.04	.04	.03	.03	
	Female	.10	.09	.08	.07	.06	.05	.05	.04	.04	
3	Male		.11	.09	.08	.07	.06	.06	.05	.05	Legally intoxicated Criminal penalties
	Female	.15	.14	.11	.10	.09	.08	.07	.06	.06	
4	Male		.15	.12	.11	.09	.08	.08	.07	.06	
	Female	.20	.18	.15	.13	.11	.10	.09	.08	.08	
5	Male		.19	.16	.13	.12	.11	.09	.09	.08	
	Female	.25	.23	.19	.16	.14	.13	.11	.10	.09	
6	Male		.23	.19	.16	.14	.13	.11	.10	.09	
	Female	.30	.27	.23	.19	.17	.15	.14	.12	.11	Death possible
7	Male		.26	.22	.19	.16	.15	.13	.12	.11	
	Female	.35	.32	.27	.23	.20	.18	.16	.14	.13	
8	Male		.30	.25	.21	.19	.17	.15	.14	.13	
	Female	.40	.36	.30	.26	.23	.20	.18	.17	.15	
9	Male		.34	.28	.24	.21	.19	.17	.15	.14	
	Female	.45	.41	.34	.29	.26	.23	.20	.19	.17	
10	Male		.38	.31	.27	.23	.21	.19	.17	.16	
	Female	.51	.45	.38	.32	.28	.25	.23	.21	.19	

Subtract 0.01% for each 40 minutes of drinking

1 drink = 1.25 ounces 80 proof liquor, 12 ounces beer, or 5 ounces wine

to the developing fetus. How a drug affects a fetus depends on the specific drug, its dose, and at which stage of pregnancy the drug is taken. Drugs taken early in the pregnancy are more likely to raise the risk of miscarriage and of physical malformations in a child, while drugs taken during the last trimester are more likely to lead to premature birth, low birth weight, and neurological damage.

Many drugs are potentially harmful to a fetus. Cocaine damages the placenta, restricts blood flow to the fetus, and increases the risk of miscarriage, premature labor, and stillbirth (Chapter 5). A baby born to a mother who used heroin throughout her pregnancy may go through withdrawal when he or she is born (Chapter 7). Alcohol increases the risk of fetal alcohol syndrome, characterized by multiple deformities, learning problems, and poor coordination (Chapter 12). Tobacco constricts blood vessels and decreases the supply of oxygen to the fetus (Chapter 10), resulting in pregnancy complications, miscarriages, stillbirths, low birth weight, and increased incidence of Sudden Infant Death Syndrome (Figure 2.10).

Medications also can be harmful. Aspirin can harm a fetus's heart; the antibiotic tetracycline can cause permanent brown stains on a child's teeth; phenytoin, an anticonvulsant, can increase the risk of cleft lip, cardiac defects, and mental deficiencies; and the acne treatment Accutane can cause brain, heart, and facial deformities in the fetus if a woman takes it while pregnant.

Pregnant women are much less likely to use illicit drugs than are nonpregnant women. Over 16 percent of all nonpregnant women in the United States are current illicit drug users, but only 5.8 percent of pregnant women are current drug users.[59] This is highly depen-

dent on a woman's age (Figure 2.11). Pregnant women age 15–17 years are actually *more* likely to use illicit drugs than are nonpregnant women of the same age.[60,61]

About 9.6 percent of pregnant women use tobacco, compared with 19.4 percent of nonpregnant women of the same age. As with illegal drugs, younger women who are pregnant are more likely to smoke than are their nonpregnant counterparts.[62] About 9.5 percent of pregnant women age 15–44 report current alcohol use.[63] Women who are most likely to drink during pregnancy tend to be younger, single, less educated, and unemployed.

In some states, women are prosecuted for drug use during pregnancy under statutes that deal with child abuse, chemical endangerment, delivery of a controlled substance to a minor, felony assault, and murder. These charges are legally problematic for many reasons. No statute or law clearly indicates when or if an embryo or fetus would be considered a minor.[64] Also, what is the timeline to determine if the baby has been harmed? One week? One year? Eighteen years? The American College of Obstetricians and Gynecologists and the American Medical Association have issued statements objecting to these laws, because they believe they will deter pregnant women from seeking prenatal care or help with their drug dependence.

Women who are found guilty of these charges may face criminal prosecution, be forced into treatment, or lose their parental rights. In some states, it's possible

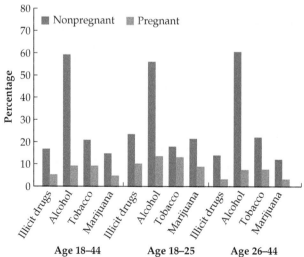

FIGURE 2.11. Percentage of women age 18–44 who use illicit drugs, alcohol, tobacco, or marijuana. Pregnant women are less likely to use drugs than nonpregnant women, but this depends on the woman's age as well as the drug.

Source: SAMHSA. (2020). Results from the 2019 national survey on drug use and health. Rockville, MD: Center for Behavioral Health Statistics and Quality.

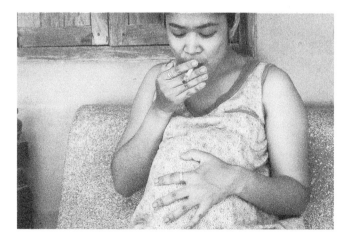

FIGURE 2.10. Smoking while pregnant. Smoking has been linked to 115,000 miscarriages and 5,600 infant deaths a year.

for a child to be taken from a mother if she has had just one positive drug test, regardless of whether the newborn shows any symptoms of drug exposure or whether the mother had a doctor's prescription for the drug, and in the absence of any other evidence to suggest that she has a substance use disorder, or that she would be an unfit parent.[65]

As you will see in chapters throughout this book, race affects how drug laws are enforced. Researchers examined the records of 8,487 women who gave birth.[66] Of those, 3 percent were tested for illicit drug use. Black women and their newborns were 1.5 times more likely to be tested for illicit drugs than non-Black women. There was no difference between Black and non-Black women in the likelihood of having a positive test for drug use. In Florida, reports to child protective services were made 10 times more against Black women who tested positive for illicit drugs compared with white or Hispanic mothers who tested positive. Socioeconomic factors also play a role. Pregnant women who are poor, unmarried, or unemployed, or who have less than a high school education are more likely to be drug tested, and if found to be positive for drug use, are more likely to be punished than treated.

Obviously, drug use during pregnancy is a highly contentious issue. Here are just some of the questions to consider[67]:

- Should women be prohibited from taking drugs while pregnant? All drugs?
- Should pregnant women be punished for using drugs, even if there is no certainty that harm will come to the unborn baby from the mother's drug use?
- Whose rights come first—the baby's or the mother's? Why? Do you feel that a woman gives up her own freedoms when she is pregnant?
- Should the government play a role in regulating healthy behaviors for pregnant women? If so, should the government regulate healthy behaviors for *all* people?
- Drug use by males could potentially affect their sperm and the health of future children. Should men be penalized for using drugs if they happen to get a woman pregnant? Why or why not?

Chapter Summary

- **History of Drug Policy**
  - » The 1906 Pure Food and Drug Act was the first law to give the government some oversight of the drug marketplace. It required that a drug's ingredients be labeled.
  - » The Harrison Narcotics Act of 1914 decreed that physicians and pharmacists must be licensed to prescribe narcotics. They had to register with the U.S. Treasury Department and keep records of the narcotic drugs they dispensed, and they could only prescribe in the course of their medical practice.
  - » The Marijuana Tax Act of 1937 essentially banned the use of marijuana. The impetus for this law was largely political.
  - » The FDA gained more authority and responsibility with the passage of the Food, Drug, and Cosmetics Act of 1938, which increased the accountability of drug companies regarding the safety of drugs.
  - » Throughout the 1950s, Congress escalated the penalties for narcotics violations in an attempt to not only reduce drug use, but to diminish the influence of organized crime.
  - » The CSA of 1970 repealed, replaced, and consolidated all previous federal drug laws. It created five schedules of drugs.
  - » The Drug Abuse Control Acts of the 1980s strengthened federal anti-drug policies.
  - » Drug laws are not applied evenly and consistently. Minorities are significantly more likely to be arrested for a drug charge.
- **Current Drug Laws**
  - » Our nation's drug policies are complex and require the interaction and cooperation of many federal agencies, including the ONDCP, DEA, and FDA.
  - » Federally, drug crimes may be charged as a misdemeanor or a felony. Common drug crimes include possession and trafficking.
  - » The federal penalties for drug crimes depend on several factors. These include the specific drug, the quantities involved, whether it is a first offense, and whether the crime is possession or trafficking.
  - » States are allowed some flexibility in how they decide to enforce or not enforce federal drug laws. Sometimes there is great variation in the drug laws from state to state, for scheduled as well as nonscheduled drugs.
  - » Countries with harsher drug policies do not have lower levels of drug use. Many factors, including economics, religion, and culture, influence the drug use in a country.

- **Harm Reduction Policies**
  - » Instead of spending enormous resources trying to reduce the supply of drugs or punishing the drug user, many countries focus on harm reduction policies.
  - » These policies may try to reduce the health risks associated with drug use, reduce prison overcrowding, and focus on treatment rather than on punishment.
- **Ramifications of Drug Laws**
  - » Drug laws have consequences for individuals, families, and societies.
  - » Conviction for drug crimes results in the penalty imposed by the judge, as well as a range of collateral sanctions that are automatically triggered by the conviction. These penalties include loss of professional licenses and driver's licenses, loss of educational aid and welfare benefits, and bans on voting.
  - » The United States has a higher percentage of its population in prison than any other country. Most prisoners in the United States are in for drug crimes.
- **Legalization**
  - » Members of the DHHS, FDA, and DEA work together to make the decision as to whether a drug should be scheduled under the CSA.
  - » These laws are based on physical as well as economic, political, and social factors.
  - » Americans' attitudes regarding drugs have changed; a majority now believe the government should focus on treatment rather than punishment, that cannabis should be legalized, and that alcohol is more harmful than marijuana.
- **Social Policies Related to Drug Use**
  - » The United States is one of the few countries in the world to set the minimum legal drinking age at 21 years. There are both positive and negative results of this law.
  - » A BAC of 0.08 is considered legally intoxicated in the United States. The greater one's BAC, the higher the risk of a motor vehicle accident.
  - » Both legal and illegal drugs that are taken during pregnancy can affect the fetus in numerous ways, many of which are potentially harmful.
  - » Pregnant women are much less likely to use illicit drugs than are nonpregnant women, yet some do use drugs. In some states, pregnant women who use drugs may be charged with child abuse, delivery of a controlled substance to a minor, or even murder. Compared to white women, Black women and their newborns are more likely to be tested for illicit drugs, and more likely to be reported to child protective services.

Key Terms

Conspiracy (p. 27)
Controlled Substances Act (CSA) (p. 24)
Felony (p. 26)

Implied consent (p. 40)
Interdiction (p. 24)
Misdemeanor (p. 26)

Possession (p. 26)
Trafficking (p. 26)
War on drugs (p. 24)

Quiz Yourself!

1. What is the name of the law that established the scheduling of drugs, and what year was it implemented?

2. True or false? There were one-fifth as many jail sentences for marijuana offenders under Bill Clinton's presidency than during the 12 years of Ronald Reagan and George H.W. Bush's presidencies.

3. True or false? All drug policies and laws in the United States are created and enforced by just two departments—the DEA and the FBI.

4. True or false? A person may be charged with drug conspiracy if he lends his car to a friend who uses the car to transport drugs.

5. At what BAC is a person considered legally intoxicated in the United States?

6. Which of the following is true?

   A. The more severe a country's drug laws, the lower the drug use.

   B. Portugal allows for the death penalty for possession of small amounts of any drug.

   C. Sweden has some of the most lenient drug laws in the world.

   D. In Uruguay, drug use or possession for personal consumption is not criminalized.

7. Which of the following penalties does NOT occur with conviction for a drug-related crime?

   A. Loss of federal student loans

   B. Forbidden from having a credit card

C. Suspension of driver's license

D. Ineligibility to vote

E. Bans on adopting a child

8. True or false? About 5 percent of people have driven drunk at least once.

9. Which of the following drugs has the highest death rate as a percentage of use (the highest percent of users who die of the drug)?

A. Alcohol

B. Caffeine

C. Cocaine

D. Heroin

E. Marijuana

F. Tobacco

10. True or false? Most Americans believe that marijuana is more harmful to health than alcohol is.

11. Match the drug to the problem it can cause during pregnancy:

1. Alcohol	A. Harms the fetus's heart
2. Heroin	B. Causes fetal alcohol syndrome
3. Aspirin	C. Decreases oxygen supply to the fetus
4. Tetracycline	D. Causes the baby to go through opioid withdrawal
5. Tobacco	E. Permanently stains the child's teeth

Additional Resources

Websites

Drug Policy Alliance. http://www.drugpolicy.org/Organization promoting drug policies that are grounded in science, compassion, health, and human rights.

Videos

Drug policy reformist Ethan Nadelmann's TED Talk about ending the war on drugs. https://www.ted.com/talks/ethan_nadelmann_why_we_need_to_end_the_war_on_drugs

Books

Robinson, M.B. (2013). *Lies, damned lies, and drug war statistics (2nd ed.). A critical analysis of claims made by the Office of National Drug Control Policy*. Albany: SUNY Press.

Learn more with this chapter's digital tools at www.oup.com/he/rosenthal2e.

The Nervous System

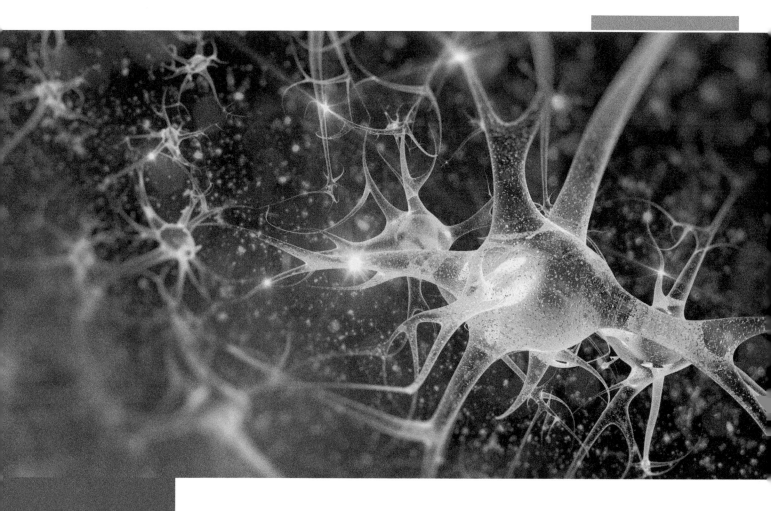

True or false?

1.
True or false? There are up to 86 billion neurons in the brain.

2.
True or false? The area of the brain that is most involved in rational decision-making and planning is not fully developed until well into a person's twenties.

3.
True or false? We use only 10 percent of our brains.

Answers: 1. T, 2. T, 3. F

Learning Objectives

- Define the terms *neuron*, *soma*, *neurotransmitter*, *axon*, *dendrites*, *myelin*, *axon terminal*, *synapse*, *receptors*, and *vesicles*.

- Label a neuron and describe the function of the various areas.

- Define the terms *action potential* and *reuptake*.

- Trace the process of neuronal transmission at a chemical synapse.

- Understand the ways the nervous systems are organized, their functions, and their relationships to each other.

- Define the terms *central nervous system*, *peripheral nervous system*, *somatic nervous system*, *autonomic nervous system*, *sympathetic nervous system*, and *parasympathetic nervous system*.

- Identify the function of the cortex, basal ganglia, hippocampus, thalamus, hypothalamus, midbrain, pons, cerebellum, medulla oblongata, and spinal cord.

- Reassess some of the common myths about the brain.

- Compare the capillaries of the central nervous system with the capillaries that feed other organs of the body.

- Identify the primary functions of the major neurotransmitters discussed, as well as some drugs that affect them.

Neuron: A nerve cell that receives and sends signals within the body.

Sensory neuron: A nerve cell that carries information into the brain and spinal cord.

Motor neuron: A nerve cell that sends instructions from the brain and spinal cord out to nerves, muscles, and glands.

Take a minute to think about the cool gadgets in your life. You may have a smart phone, an Xbox, a tablet. Oh, yeah—and you also have what might be the most complex living structure in the world, nestled there in your skull. Your brain grows, repairs, and reconfigures itself to adapt to changes. It coordinates the vital functions of your body; senses and reacts to the world; stores, organizes, and retrieves past experiences; makes decisions; sings songs; falls in love; and plans for the future. And this marvelous device was included as standard equipment when you were born! Given that almost all of the drugs discussed in this book affect the brain and influence the way your body and mind function, in this chapter, we will investigate the form and function of this amazing organ.

The Structure and Function of Neurons

The various parts of our body need to communicate in order to provide information about what the body is experiencing, and to produce an appropriate response. **Neurons** are cells that process and transmit information to aid communication throughout the body. They receive and integrate vast amounts of information from both the outside world and the internal environment, and they change constantly to adapt to the body's demands, sensations, and environmental influences. **Sensory neurons** carry information into the brain and spinal cord, and **motor neurons** transmit signals from the brain and spinal cord out to our muscles, nerves, and glands in order to produce a response.

QUICK HIT

If you were to line up all the nerve fibers in your brain in a straight line, they would stretch for approximately 100,000 miles.

When most other cells (such as liver cells or skin cells) die, they are replenished, but most neurons are not—the neurons you have now are the same ones you had as a baby. It was once thought that adults had all the neurons they would ever have, and if you lost a few million after a particularly busy Saturday night, well, there goes all your knowledge of, say, the Stamp Act. But in the 1990s, scientists discovered that the human brain *does* create new neurons in certain areas of the brain, although most do not live long or integrate into the working brain. The production of new neurons, or **neurogenesis**, predominantly occurs in several bursts: during a person's first three years of life, during puberty, and then in young adulthood. Learning and physical exercise promote neurogenesis, while various types of stress can suppress the production of new neurons.[1, 2]

The brain is not only made up of neurons. **Neuroglia**, which account for up to 90 percent of brain tissue, provide neurons with nutrients and oxygen, clean up debris, protect and insulate neurons, and aid in the transmission of information.

There is a saying (originally from architecture, but co-opted by biologists) that "form follows function." This means that a cell's function determines its structure. If you look at a neuron, it resembles a long wire, and indeed, just like a telephone wire, the neuron is designed to carry information from one location to the next (Figure 3.1).

Neurons generate electrical signals (called *action potentials*), which travel down the long, wire-like axon. Chemical messengers called **neurotransmitters** are then released from the end of an axon and bind to receptors on the tree-like branches of the dendrites of the subsequent neuron. Most neurons are a few millimeters long—although some may be as short as a few hundred micrometers, and others stretch for as much as a meter or more.

QUICK HIT

At some stages of prenatal brain development, a fetus creates about 250,000 neurons per minute.

....

The **soma**, or cell body, contains the neuron's machinery that keeps it functioning. The soma includes the **nucleus**, which contains genes that code for proteins such as neurotransmitters and enzymes, as well as other organelles that keep the cell operational.

Ask yourself: The axon of neurons resembles a wire because its function is communication. Given that form follows function, how would you imagine a muscle cell would look? Or a skin cell?

The **axon** is the long, wire-like component of the neuron. Neurons have only one axon, but the axon can split into numerous branches called collaterals; in this way, they can influence many more cells. The axons of most neurons are covered by a white, fatty substance called **myelin**, which insulates the axon and speeds electrical transmission. About every millimeter or so, there are gaps along the axon that are not covered by myelin. These gaps, about a micrometer long, are called **nodes of Ranvier** (ron-vee-AY), and are the site of electrical signal generation. The electrical impulse hops down the axon from node to node.

Neurogenesis: The production of new neurons.

Neuroglia: Nerve cells that support neurons and aid in neurotransmission.

Neurotransmitter: A chemical substance released from a neuron that binds to a receptor and affects another cell.

Soma: The cell body of a neuron.

Nucleus: The part of a cell that contains genes that code for proteins.

Axon: The long, wire-like part of a neuron along which electrical impulses are conducted away from the cell body.

Myelin: A white, fatty material that encloses and insulates some axons and speeds neurotransmission.

Node of Ranvier: A gap in the myelin sheath of an axon, where action potentials are propagated.

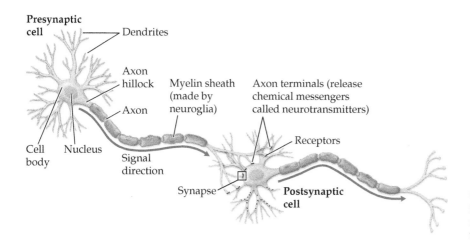

FIGURE 3.1. **The structure of a neuron.** This diagram illustrates one neuron interacting with one other neuron, but in reality, one neuron may receive signals from thousands of other neurons.

Electrical signals travel down the axon until they reach the **axon terminal**. The axon terminal contains little sacs called **vesicles**, each of which is filled with several thousand molecules of neurotransmitters. Vesicles allow for the release of a predetermined amount of neurotransmitter, and they also protect the neurotransmitter from degradation by enzymes within the nerve terminal. When the electrical signal reaches the axon terminal, neurotransmitter is released. The neurotransmitter enters the **synapse**, or space between neurons, and then binds to receptors on the next neuron's dendrites.

Dendrites are branched outgrowths from the soma. Most of a neuron's **receptors**—proteins with specific size, shape, chemical, and electrical properties—are located on the dendrites. The dendrites receive many signals—some excitatory, some inhibitory—all of which are added together. The resultant signal is sent toward the soma and axon, which will fire another signal or not, as directed.

QUICK HIT

The dendrites of a single neuron have been shown to connect with the axons of as many as 50,000 other neurons.

Neuronal Transmission

Neuronal transmission is electrochemical. Information travels down an axon in the form of a change in the electrical charges around a neuron's plasma membrane. Once the electrical signal reaches the axon terminal, the signal causes a neurotransmitter to be released. The neurotransmitter binds to receptor sites on the next

Axon terminal: The end of the axon, which contains vesicles of neurotransmitter.

Vesicle: A small sac in the axon terminal that contains neurotransmitter molecules.

Synapse: The gap between two nerve cells.

Dendrites: The branched outgrowths from the soma; they are the main receptive surface of the neuron.

Receptor: A protein molecule located on or in a cell, which responds specifically to a particular neurotransmitter, hormone, or drug.

Action potential: The short-term change in electrical potential between the inside and outside of a neuron that leads to transmission of nerve signals.

Depolarization: When the charge across the neuron is reversed; in a neuron, depolarization refers to the inside of a neuron becoming more positively charged compared with the outside.

neuron, which causes electrical changes in that neuron, and so the information travels from cell to cell.

Action Potentials

Information travels down an axon as a change in voltage known as an **action potential**. The movement of ions (charged particles) into and out of the cell causes this voltage change. The plasma membrane that surrounds the neuron contains protein channels that allow certain ions to cross into and out of the neuron. At rest, the inside of the neuron is more negatively charged than the outside, but when a neuron is stimulated, special voltage-gated channels open in the nodes of Ranvier, and positively charged sodium ions rush into the neuron such that, for a brief period of time, the inside of the nerve cell experiences **depolarization** (become positively charged) compared with the outside. These voltage-gated sodium channels then close, and other changes occur, bringing the voltage back to what it was at rest. The change in voltage (the action potential) is how information travels down an axon (Figure 3.2).

QUICK HIT

One millimeter of a neuron contains several hundred million sodium channels, each of which admits 100 million ions per second. So, in a space about the size of the period at the end of this sentence, hundreds of quadrillions of ions cross per second. Now realize that you have 100,000 miles of nerve fibers in your brain alone, and you'll better appreciate the sentiment "I might look like I'm doing nothing, but at the cellular level, I'm really quite busy."

Actions at a Chemical Synapse

The neuron that releases neurotransmitter is called the presynaptic neuron, and the neuron that the neurotransmitter affects is called the postsynaptic neuron. A single neuron can receive a signal from many thousands of other neurons, and can itself contact as many as a thousand other cells. This means there are at least 100 trillion synaptic connections in your brain, which is at least one thousand times the number of stars in our galaxy.

Neurotransmission involves several steps (Figure 3.3). At the start of neurotransmission, the neurotransmitter is produced and packaged into vesicles (1), which are stored in the axon terminal. When an action potential travels down the axon and reaches the axon terminal, it opens voltage-gated calcium channels (2). Calcium enters the axon terminal from the extracellular fluid and causes vesicles containing

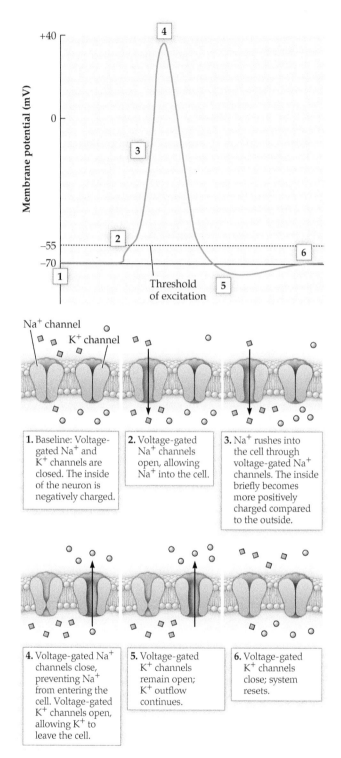

1. Baseline: Voltage-gated Na+ and K+ channels are closed. The inside of the neuron is negatively charged.

2. Voltage-gated Na+ channels open, allowing Na+ into the cell.

3. Na+ rushes into the cell through voltage-gated Na+ channels. The inside briefly becomes more positively charged compared to the outside.

4. Voltage-gated Na+ channels close, preventing Na+ from entering the cell. Voltage-gated K+ channels open, allowing K+ to leave the cell.

5. Voltage-gated K+ channels remain open; K+ outflow continues.

6. Voltage-gated K+ channels close; system resets.

FIGURE 3.2. Protein channels open and close to control the movement of ions across a neuron's plasma membrane. This voltage change can lead to an action potential.

neurotransmitter to fuse with the presynaptic membrane (3). The neurotransmitter is then released into the synapse (4). (Neurotransmitters will be discussed more fully later in the chapter, but some common

neurotransmitters are dopamine, norepinephrine, serotonin, acetylcholine, gamma-aminobutyric acid [GABA], and glutamate.)

Next, the neurotransmitter binds to receptors that are located on the dendrites of the postsynaptic neuron (5). When a neurotransmitter binds, it can cause ion channels on the postsynaptic neuron to open or close, allowing ions to flow into or out of the cell (6). Depending on the neurotransmitter, the target organ, and other factors, the effect on the postsynaptic cell may be either excitatory or inhibitory. For example, if a neurotransmitter binds and causes a sodium channel to open, positively charged sodium may flow into the postsynaptic cell, making it more likely for that cell to fire an action potential (excitatory). But if a neurotransmitter binds and opens a chloride channel, negatively charged chloride may flow in. The postsynaptic cell is now slightly more negatively charged, and less likely to fire an action potential (inhibitory).

As will be discussed at greater length in Chapter 4, neurotransmitters or drugs can bind to receptors that are themselves an ion channel. These receptors are called **ionotropic receptors**, and when a substance binds, the receptors quickly open and an ion such as sodium or chloride rushes into the cell. Conversely, substances can bind to receptors that are separate from ion channels. If a substance binds to these **metabotropic receptors**, it may open a separate ion channel or cause another change in the cell, but it happens comparatively slowly.

Receptors are not only found on the dendrites. **Presynaptic autoreceptors** are found on the membrane of the axon terminal. These autoreceptors help to self-regulate the amount of neurotransmitter released from the axon. When a neurotransmitter is released, it can bind to these autoreceptors, which detect their presence in the synapse and send a signal to halt synthesis and/or release of the neurotransmitter.

Ionotropic receptor: A type of receptor that is also an ion channel; when a substance binds, the receptor quickly opens, and an ion such as sodium or chloride rushes into the cell.

Metabotropic receptor: A type of receptor that is separate from an ion channel; if a substance binds to the receptor, a series of events may open a separate ion channel or cause another change in the cell, but it happens relatively slowly.

Presynaptic autoreceptor: A type of receptor located on the presynaptic membrane, which detects the presence of neurotransmitter in the synapse and sends a signal to inhibit synthesis or release of that neurotransmitter.

1. Neurotransmitter is synthesized and stored in vesicles.

2. Action potential reaches the presynaptic axon terminal, opening voltage-gated Ca^{2+} channels.

3. Influx of Ca^{2+} causes vesicles to travel to presynaptic membrane.

4. Vesicles release neurotransmitter into the synapse.

5. Neurotransmitter binds to receptor on postsynaptic membrane.

6. Ion channels in the postsynaptic neuron open or close, leading to an excitatory or inhibitory change in voltage in the postsynaptic cell.

7. The signal is terminated, usually by reuptake (a) or by enzymatic degradation (b).

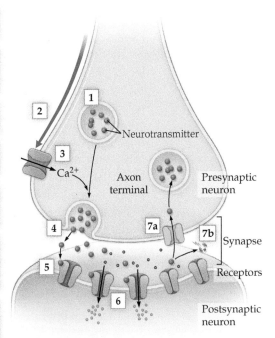

FIGURE 3.3. The process of neurotransmission.

Ask yourself: Neurotransmission is a complex occurrence, involving an intricate cycle of events. Does learning about its complexity make you more or less interested in the action of drugs in the brain?

Drugs that bind to autoreceptors, therefore, decrease synthesis and release, and ultimately inhibit the neurotransmitter's actions. Drugs that block presynaptic autoreceptors interrupt this feedback loop, and increase the neurotransmitter's synthesis and release.

Neurotransmission stops when the neurotransmitter is removed from the receptor. There are three main mechanisms by which neurotransmission stops: reuptake, enzymatic degradation, and diffusion.

Reuptake: The process by which a presynaptic neuron reabsorbs a neurotransmitter that it has released.

Central nervous system (CNS): The brain and spinal cord.

Peripheral nervous system (PNS): All the nerves going to and from the brain and spinal cord.

Somatic nervous system: Part of the PNS, the somatic nervous system consists of nerves that carry sensory information into the CNS, as well as nerves that carry motor signals from the CNS to skeletal muscle cells.

Most termination occurs when the neurotransmitter undergoes **reuptake** into the presynaptic neuron (7a). Transporter proteins in the presynaptic membrane (or neuroglia cells) carry the neurotransmitter back into the presynaptic axon terminal, where the chemical is destroyed or repackaged into vesicles. During enzymatic degradation (7b), enzymes associated with the postsynaptic membrane or in the synapse break down some neurotransmitters. Finally, with diffusion, a process by which molecules move from areas of greater concentration to areas of lesser concentration, the neurotransmitter drifts to areas lacking receptors, where it is broken down and is removed by the general circulation of fluids in the brain.

Many of the actions that drugs have on the nervous system are due to changes produced at the synapse. The numerous ways that drugs can influence neurotransmission are summarized in Table 3.1.

The Peripheral and Central Nervous Systems

The nervous systems are the control centers of the body. These systems gather information and coordinate a response. The brain and spinal cord together form the **central nervous system (CNS)**. The **peripheral nervous system (PNS)** is made up of all the nerves going to and from the brain and spinal cord (Figure 3.4).

The Peripheral Nervous System

The PNS is further divided into the somatic nervous system and the autonomic nervous system. The **somatic nervous system** consists of neurons that carry sensory information (from the eyes, ears, nose, mouth, and sense of touch) into the CNS, as well as nerve fibers that carry motor signals from the CNS to skeletal muscle cells. The site at which motor neurons from the somatic

TABLE 3.1. Ways that Drugs Can Affect Neurotransmission

Excitatory Effect on Receptor Activation	Examples of Drug's Effects on Neurotransmitters
Increases synthesis of neurotransmitters	L-DOPA (dopamine)
	Tryptophan (serotonin)
Increases release of neurotransmitters	Black widow spider venom (acetylcholine)
	MDMA (serotonin)
	Amphetamines (dopamine and norepinephrine)
Binds to receptor	Nicotine (acetylcholine)
	Morphine (opioids)
	THC (cannabinoids)
Block presynaptic autoreceptors	Yohimbine (dopamine, norepinephrine, serotonin)
Blocks reuptake of neurotransmitters	Prozac and Zoloft (serotonin)
	Cocaine (dopamine, norepinephrine, serotonin)
Block enzymes that break down neurotransmitters	MAO-I (dopamine, norepinephrine, serotonin)
	Nerve gases (acetylcholine)
Inhibitory Effect on Receptor Activation	**Examples of Drug's Effects on Neurotransmitters**
Decreases synthesis of neurotransmitters	PCPA (serotonin)
Decrease storage of neurotransmitters in vesicles	Reserpine (dopamine, norepinephrine, serotonin)
Decreases release of neurotransmitters	Botulinum toxin (acetylcholine)
Blocks the receptor	Curare (acetylcholine)
	Antipsychotics (dopamine)
Stimulates presynaptic autoreceptors	Clonidine (norepinephrine)

nervous system **innervate** skeletal muscles is called the **neuromuscular junction (NMJ)**. Drugs such as curare and high doses of nicotine work at the NMJ.

The **autonomic nervous system (ANS)** is a series of neurons that innervate (and either excite or inhibit) heart muscle, glands, and smooth muscle (smooth muscle can be found in the walls and sphincters of the gut, the uterus, the urinary bladder, the hair follicles of the skin, the pupils, and in blood vessels). The ANS regulates visceral functions such as heart rate, blood pressure, digestion, defecation, and urination. This system functions in-

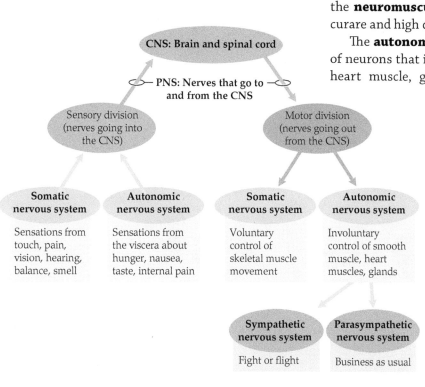

FIGURE 3.4. **The organization of the central and peripheral nervous systems.**

Innervate: To supply a part of the body with nerves, or to stimulate an area by a nerve.

Neuromuscular junction (NMJ): The site at which motor neurons from the somatic nervous system influence skeletal muscles.

Autonomic nervous system (ANS): Part of the PNS, the ANS consists of nerves that go to and from smooth muscle, heart muscle, and glands.

dependently, involuntarily, and continuously without conscious effort. Many drugs, including atropine and amphetamine, affect the ANS.

The ANS is further divided into the sympathetic and parasympathetic nervous systems (Figure 3.5). The **sympathetic nervous system** is sometimes called the "fight or flight" system. It helps to mobilize our bodies in case of emergency. You can remember the letter "E" for the

functions of the sympathetic system: emergency, energy expending, exercise, excitement, and embarrassment. There is extensive communication among sympathetic fibers, which means that the initial signal can have a widespread effect. This is advantageous because it allows the whole body to mobilize in times of emergency. Imagine that you are walking to class, and all of a sudden, a tiger rushes at you (don't you just *hate* when that happens?). It would be inefficient to have to send a separate signal to increase heart rate, dilate your pupils and lung bronchi, and decrease blood flow to the kidneys and gastrointestinal

Sympathetic nervous system: Part of the PNS, the sympathetic nervous system regulates "fight or flight" impulses.

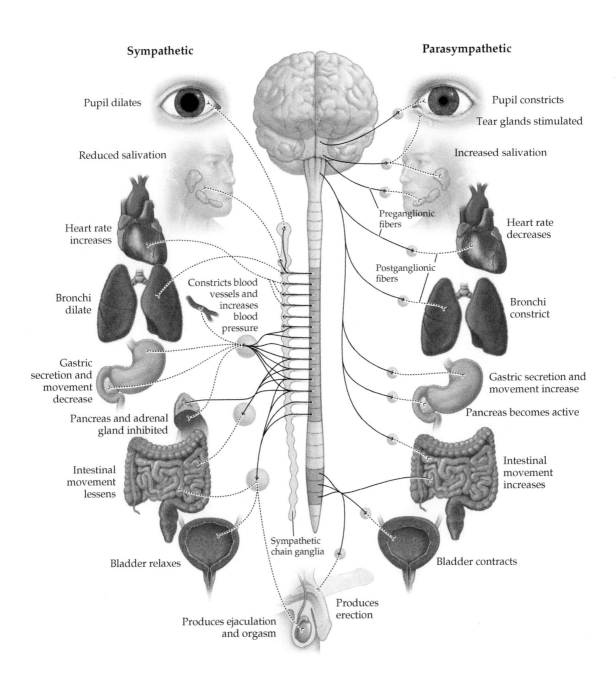

FIGURE 3.5. Overview of sympathetic and parasympathetic nervous systems.

(GI) tract—instead, the fight-or-flight system is wired together, so your body responds quickly to escape from the emergency. (Although orgasm and ejaculation are also sympathetic nervous system responses, they function independently from the rest, and luckily, will not be firing as you try to run away from the tiger.)

The **parasympathetic system** is for ordinary, restful situations. The functions of this system can be remembered by the letter "D": digestion, defecation, diuresis, dozing, and downtime. Fibers in the parasympathetic system are highly targeted and discrete. This allows the organs innervated by the parasympathetic system to work independently. To illustrate how advantageous this is, let's imagine that your significant other comes over for dinner one night. You've had a nice evening, and now the two of you are relaxing on the couch. If your parasympathetic system were mobilized as one, similar to the way the sympathetic nervous system is, your heart rate and blood pressure would fall so you'd collapse in your chair, all the while defecating, urinating, and drooling. With an erection. Not a pretty picture.

The Central Nervous System

The CNS is composed of the brain and spinal cord. The spinal cord is the major conduit of information

Ask yourself: Later in the book, we will describe some drugs as "sympathomimetic," meaning that their actions mimic the sympathetic nervous system. Given what you've just learned about this system, at this stage in your learning, which drugs would you guess are sympathomimetic?

from the skin, joints, muscles, and viscera (internal organs) to and from the brain. The brain is functionally and anatomically divided into the forebrain, the midbrain, and the hindbrain. The forebrain contains the **cerebrum** (which includes the cerebral cortex, hippocampus, and basal ganglia), thalamus, and hypothalamus. The midbrain includes the tectum and tegmentum. The pons, cerebellum, and medulla make up the hindbrain. Table 3.2 and Figure 3.6 highlight the main areas of the CNS and the drugs that affect them.

Parasympathetic nervous system: Part of the PNS, the parasympathetic nervous system regulates restful, "business as usual" impulses.

Cerebrum: Part of the forebrain containing the cerebral cortex, basal ganglia, and hippocampus.

TABLE 3.2.   Areas of the Central Nervous System and Some Drugs that Affect Them

Division	Area	Function	Drugs that Affect
Forebrain	Cerebral cortex	Outermost portion of brain Frontal, parietal, temporal, occipital, and insular lobes Sensory information, reasoning, thought	Marijuana, LSD, alcohol, and other psychoactive drugs
	Basal ganglia	Fine tuning of movements Emotions	Anti-Parkinson's drugs
	Hippocampus	Memory	Marijuana Antidepressant drugs
	Thalamus	Relay station for incoming sensory information	LSD
	Hypothalamus	Hormonal control Control of autonomic nervous system Control of sex drive, hunger, body temperature, pleasure, fear	Antidepressant drugs Weight loss drugs Hormonal contraceptives Ecstasy, cocaine, marijuana, and other psychoactive drugs
	Pituitary gland	Produces and secretes hormones	Hormonal contraceptives
	Pineal gland	Biological clock	Melatonin
Midbrain	Tectum and tegmentum	Visual and auditory reflexes Reward and motivation	Almost all psychoactive drugs affect the "addiction pathways" of the midbrain
Hindbrain	Cerebellum	Balance, posture, coordination	Alcohol, marijuana
	Pons	Sleep, smooths the breathing pattern	Opioids
	Medulla oblongata	Basic vegetative processes: breathing, heartbeat, swallowing, coughing	Opioids, alcohol
Spinal cord	Spinal cord	Sensory and motor pathways to and from body	Opioids

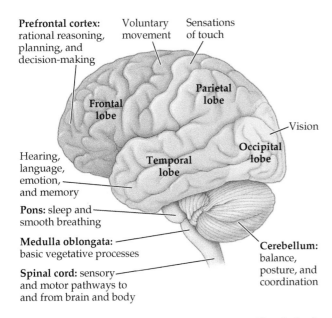

Prefrontal cortex: rational reasoning, planning, and decision-making

Voluntary movement

Sensations of touch

Frontal lobe

Parietal lobe

Vision

Occipital lobe

Temporal lobe

Hearing, language, emotion, and memory

Pons: sleep and smooth breathing

Medulla oblongata: basic vegetative processes

Spinal cord: sensory and motor pathways to and from brain and body

Cerebellum: balance, posture, and coordination

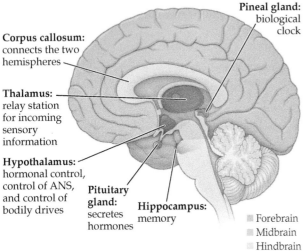

Pineal gland: biological clock

Corpus callosum: connects the two hemispheres

Thalamus: relay station for incoming sensory information

Hypothalamus: hormonal control, control of ANS, and control of bodily drives

Pituitary gland: secretes hormones

Hippocampus: memory

■ Forebrain
■ Midbrain
■ Hindbrain

FIGURE 3.6. The forebrain. The forebrain consists of the cerebral cortex, basal ganglia, thalamus, hypothalamus, hippocampus, and other areas. The midbrain contains the tectum and tegmentum. The hindbrain includes the pons, medulla, and cerebellum.

Forebrain

The forebrain is the largest part of the brain, and it includes the cerebrum, thalamus, hypothalamus, and limbic system. The first thing you notice about a brain is that it's wrinkly. The **cerebral cortex**, the outermost portion of the brain, is highly folded, which increases its surface area. In fact, two-thirds of the surface of the cortex is hidden in grooves. Every person has a different folding pattern in his or her brain—the folds of the brain are more individual than a person's fingerprints. Cortical folding is not

Cerebral cortex: The outermost portion of the brain hemispheres; cortex translates to "bark."

random. As the network of nerve fibers develops, they physically pull the cortex into a specific shape.

QUICK HIT

The folding of the brain affects its wiring, which can indicate different disorders. The brain begins to fold around the sixth fetal month, and premature babies don't have as much folding (or as large a brain) as full-term infants. People with autism show increased folding, and a larger surface area of the brain. Those with schizophrenia have overall less folding, as well as atypical folding patterns. The way the brain is folded in a patient suffering from schizophrenia may indicate how well they respond to different antipsychotic drugs.[3]

The brain and spinal cord are made up of neurons and neuroglia. The dendrites and cell bodies of the neurons are called "gray matter" and the axons (covered with white myelin) are called "white matter." As mentioned previously, sensory neurons carry information into the CNS, and motor neurons send instructions out from the CNS to the muscles, glands, and other neurons. As an example, imagine you are relaxing on the couch when a piece of fringe from a pillow touches your leg. Sensory neurons carry information about tickle or itch to your brain, and signals traveling down motor neurons to your arms allow you to brush the fringe away. Simple, right? Sorry to lull you into a false sense of security, but when we're dealing with the brain—which has up to 86 billion interconnected neurons—things are rarely simple.

To illustrate, let's imagine that you are relaxing on the couch when, instead of pillow fringe, a spider lands on your leg. Sensory neurons carry signals to a vast network of cells in your brain and spinal cord. Some signals go to areas that process touch and vision, and others to areas that control emotions and memory. Although the stimulus was simple—a spider on your leg—the factors that influence your response are incredibly complex. Depending on your memories, your emotional state, whether you are alone or not, and whether or not you ever read the book *Charlotte's Web*, your response may be to gently flick the spider away, to squish it with a maniacal gleam in your eyes, or to flail your arms and legs wildly while shrieking like a little girl. As biologist Lyall Watson once said, "If the brain were so simple that we could understand it, we would be so simple that we couldn't."

The cerebrum is the largest part of the brain and is divided into two hemispheres that are each concerned with sensory and motor functions for the opposite side of the body. The hemispheres are mostly symmetrical but not entirely equal in function. About 70–90 percent of the population is left-brain dominant (and usually right-handed). The left hemisphere is involved with analysis of a sequence of stimuli, so that you can recognize and control a consecutive series of events and behavior. Language is largely a sequential event, and the left hemisphere is specialized for speech. Reading, writing, vocabulary, and understanding language, as well as some math skills, are all primarily located in the left hemisphere. The right hemisphere is for synthesis—putting isolated elements together as a whole. Spatial perceptions, map reading, geometry, art, and music appreciation are localized to the right brain, as are emotions, intuitions, understanding emotional tone in speech, and recognition of faces.

QUICK HIT

People who stutter can often *sing* what they want to say without difficulty, because language is mostly located in the left hemisphere, but music is located in the right hemisphere.

The two hemispheres are connected by the **corpus callosum**. Neuroscientist Roger Sperry performed a series of experiments on patients who had their corpora callosa cut to treat their severe epilepsy. (He won the Nobel Prize in 1981 for his work.) Sperry found that each hemisphere is a conscious, individual system in its own right.

The cerebral cortex is traditionally divided into four anatomical and functional lobes: frontal, parietal, temporal, and occipital, although a fifth lobe, the insula, is now being recognized as an important area (Figure 3.7). The **frontal lobe** is responsible for planning, programming, speech, and initiating voluntary movements. In humans, the **prefrontal cortex** is larger and more advanced than in other animals. It is the prefrontal cortex that is responsible for reasoning, judgments, and decision making.

The prefrontal cortex can be disconnected from the rest of the brain in a procedure called a prefrontal lobotomy. Thousands of prefrontal lobotomies were performed on patients from the 1930s through the 1960s. During this outpatient procedure, an ice pick was thrust through the patient's upper eye socket, and then twirled like a swizzle stick. This procedure did show some degree of success in some patients with depression, anxiety, obsessive-compulsive disorder (OCD), and schizophrenia. Other patients, however, were left irreparably damaged. Bus driver Howard Dully was lobotomized at the age of 12 after his stepmother complained that he was difficult. His doctor's notes about the patient, used to justify his lobotomy, state, "He objects to going to bed but then sleeps well ... He does a good deal of daydreaming and when asked about it says 'I don't know.' ... He turns the room's lights on when there is broad daylight outside."[4]

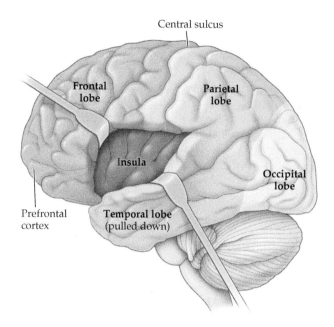

FIGURE 3.7. **The lobes of the brain.**

Ask yourself: In the middle of the twentieth century, frontal lobotomies were considered cutting edge medicine. We now consider the procedure to be unscientific and inhumane. Are there any medical procedures done today that you think future generations will repudiate?

QUICK HIT

The prefrontal cortex is not fully developed until approximately age 26, which, in part, explains why teenagers do not always make good decisions and may not be able to see the consequences of their actions.

The **parietal lobe** contains the primary somatosensory area of the cortex, where sensations such as pain, temperature, and touch are processed. Sensory information from the left side of the body is mapped out onto the right parietal lobe, and vice versa. Abstract

Parietal lobe: The part of the cerebrum that contains the primary somatosensory area of the cortex, where sensations such as pain, temperature, and touch are processed.

Corpus callosum (plural: corpora callosa): A band of nerve fibers that connect the left and right hemispheres of the brain.

Frontal lobe: The part of the cerebrum responsible for planning, programming, speech, and initiating voluntary movements.

Prefrontal cortex: The part of the cerebrum responsible for reasoning, judgments, and decision making.

Phineas Gage was the foreman of a railway crew in 1848. Friendly, capable, and efficient, Gage was at work one day when an explosion caused a 13-pound iron rod to shoot through his skull, blasting through his left eye and out the top of his head (Figure 3.8). Although the facts of the case are disputed, there is general agreement that the severing of his frontal lobe caused profound changes in Phineas Gage's personality. No longer mild-mannered and responsible, Gage became impulsive, unreliable, and ill-tempered, unable to make appropriate emotional responses or wise decisions, or plan for the future. This is cited as perhaps the first case to suggest that damage to specific parts of the brain might affect one's personality.

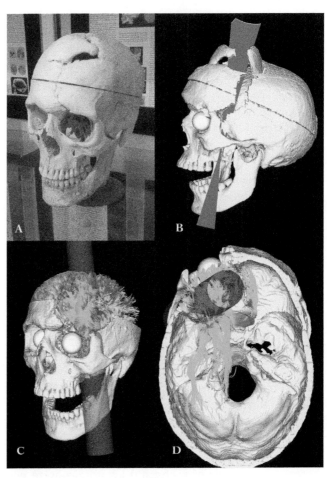

FIGURE 3.8. Phineas Gage's personality changed when an iron bar separated his prefrontal cortex from the rest of his brain.

concepts such as mathematics also might be housed in the parietal lobe. The **temporal lobe** processes hearing, memory, and the integration of sensory functions. The **occipital lobe** is where visual images are sent.

For a long time, the fifth lobe—the **insula**—was ignored, perhaps because it is tucked deep inside the brain, and is, therefore, hard to test with electrodes. Newer brain imaging techniques, however, allow us to observe it. Located beneath the frontal and temporal lobes, the insula is involved with mind–body integration. The insula receives and responds to internal sensations (such as pain or a full stomach) and translates

Temporal lobe: The part of the cerebrum that processes hearing, memory, and integration of sensory functions.

Occipital lobe: The part of the cerebrum where visual images are sent.

Insula: The fifth lobe of the cerebrum that receives and responds to internal sensations and translates these into a conscious, subjective experience.

these into a conscious, subjective experience, which affects what you do about those feelings. For example, imagine you have the sensation of hunger. What do you do? Do you get a sandwich? Or do you feel guilty and get on the treadmill? Another person touches you. Do you feel lust? Disgust? What actions do you undertake because of your subjective feelings? The insula helps to process social emotions such as disgust, pride, guilt, lust, and humiliation. It also plays a role in intuition, empathy, and our capacity to respond emotionally to music.

QUICK HIT

Scientists who analyzed Albert Einstein's brain found that the part of his parietal lobe responsible for mathematical thought and visuospatial cognition had unusual patterns of ridges and grooves.[5]

QUICK HIT

Those with damage to the insula can give up cigarettes easily, immediately, and without relapse.[6] Scientists are unsure what role the insula plays in addiction, but it may convince the body that smoking is a bodily need.

As we move deeper into the forebrain, we encounter the basal ganglia, limbic system, thalamus, hypothalamus, pituitary gland, and pineal gland. The **basal ganglia** are a group of connected nuclei that influence muscle movement, emotions, and mood. These nuclei are especially important in starting, stopping, regulating, and monitoring movements ordered and executed by the cortex. Impairment leads to disturbances in posture and muscle tone, and slowness and stiffness, as well as involuntary movements. Parkinson's disease and Huntington's disease are movement disorders of the basal ganglia. The basal ganglia also are involved in what are called overlearned sensory motor pathways, such as typing, driving, or playing a musical instrument. When one first learns these behaviors, one's cortex is largely in control, but after they become well-learned motions, the cortex essentially flips on autopilot and turns over these motor behaviors to the basal ganglia.

The **nucleus accumbens** (a-COME-benz) is an area in the basal ganglia that plays a vital role in reward, pleasure, motivation, and addiction. Drugs that increase activity in the nucleus accumbens may have a strong addictive potential.

The **limbic system** includes the hypothalamus, hippocampus, amygdala, and other areas. It is involved in

the control of emotions and memory. The hippocampus plays a vital role in memory. The amygdala is involved with rage and fear. The **hypothalamus**, an almond-sized structure in the middle of the brain, is said to control the four F's: fighting, fleeing, feeding, and, uh, mating. The hypothalamus integrates and controls the ANS, and helps regulate blood pressure, heart rate, respiratory rate, body temperature, pupil diameter, and water balance. The hypothalamus also produces hormones and coordinates the response between our emotional state and our physical response to the emotion. Finally, the hypothalamus is involved with such biological drives as hunger, sleep, pleasure, and addiction. The medial forebrain bundle is a dopamine-rich (dopamine is a neurotransmitter) bundle of fibers that runs through the hypothalamus and carries signals related to pleasure and reward. Many drugs influence the limbic system, including cocaine, amphetamines, ecstasy, nicotine, antidepressant drugs, marijuana, and opioids.

Finally, the forebrain also contains the thalamus, pineal gland, and pituitary gland. The **thalamus** is said to be the relay station of the brain. When sensory signals (except for olfaction [smell]) enter the brain, they are first sent to the thalamus, which sorts them and sends them to the appropriate area of the cortex. The **pineal gland** is one of our biological clocks. It produces a substance called melatonin, which may be involved in sleep and depression. The **pituitary gland** is sometimes called the master gland because it releases

Basal ganglia: A group of connected nuclei that influence muscle movement, emotions, and mood.

Nucleus accumbens: An area in the basal ganglia that plays an important role in reward, pleasure, and addiction.

Limbic system: Involved in the control of emotions and memory, this entity includes the hypothalamus, hippocampus, and amygdala, among other areas.

Hypothalamus: Part of the limbic system; it integrates and controls the autonomic nervous system, and helps regulate blood pressure, heart rate, respiratory rate, body temperature, and pupil diameter, as well as emotions, food intake, water balance, and sleep; it is also involved with such drives as pleasure and addiction.

Thalamus: Part of the forebrain that serves as the relay station of the brain; it sorts many sensory signals and sends them to the appropriate areas of the cortex.

Pineal gland: One of our biological clocks that produces a substance called melatonin, which is involved in sleep and depression.

Pituitary gland: Sometimes called the master gland, it releases many important hormones.

so many important hormones, such as growth hormone, thyroid-stimulating hormone, and oxytocin.

Midbrain

The midbrain is composed of the tectum and the tegmentum. The **tectum** contains nuclei that control eye movements, pupillary response to light, and reactions to moving stimuli, as well as auditory reflexes. The **tegmentum** is a neural network involved in many reflexive and homeostatic pathways. It includes the **periaqueductal gray**, **substantia nigra**, **ventral tegmental area (VTA),** and **reticular formation**.

- The periaqueductal gray is important in the modulation of pain. Opioids work here to diminish pain.
- The substantia nigra is a cluster of cell bodies that affect the basal ganglia and are important in movement. Some drugs that treat Parkinson's disease are targeted to this area.
- The VTA is composed of dopaminergic cells (cells that release the neurotransmitter dopamine) involved in addiction, reward, and rational

Tectum: Part of the midbrain that contains nuclei that control eye movements, pupillary response to light, and reactions to moving stimuli, as well as auditory reflexes.

Tegmentum: A neural network in the midbrain that is involved in many reflexive and homeostatic pathways.

Periaqueductal gray: An area of the midbrain involved in pain control.

Substantia nigra: Part of the midbrain that plays an important role in movement.

Ventral tegmental area (VTA): An area of the midbrain involved in addiction, reward, and rational processing.

Reticular formation: A network of nuclei involved in mediating levels of arousal and attention.

Pons: Part of the brainstem that contains respiratory nuclei that help smooth out breathing patterns; it is also important in sleep and arousal.

Brainstem: Part of the brain that includes the medulla oblongata, pons, and midbrain and controls basic vegetative processes and other automatic activities of the body.

Medulla oblongata: Part of the brainstem that controls basic vegetative processes such as heart rate, blood vessel diameter, respiratory rate, coughing, swallowing, and sneezing.

Cerebellum: Part of the hindbrain that helps control balance, posture, and coordination.

Spinal cord: A longitudinal system of neurons and supporting tissue that carries signals between the brain and the peripheral nervous system.

processing. Neurons in the VTA connect with many areas of the brain, including the nucleus accumbens, the prefrontal cortex, and the hippocampus. The VTA–nucleus accumbens pathway plays an important role in addiction; nearly all rewarding behaviors, including food, sex, and addictive drugs, influence this pathway.

- A collection of nuclei called the reticular formation is important for arousal, attention, sleep, muscle tone, and other homeostatic pathways. Some of the drugs thought to influence these pathways include LSD and drugs to treat attention-deficit/hyperactivity disorder (ADHD).

Hindbrain

The hindbrain contains the pons, medulla, and cerebellum. The **pons** is part of the **brainstem**, and contains respiratory nuclei that help to smooth out breathing patterns. The pons is also important in sleep, arousal, and attention. The **medulla oblongata** controls basic vegetative processes such as heart rate, blood vessel diameter, respiratory rate, coughing, swallowing, and sneezing. When a person dies of an overdose of alcohol, heroin, or other drugs, it is often due to depression of respiratory cells in the medulla.

When you see someone pulled over by the side of the road, eyes shut, standing on one leg, with a police officer looking on suspiciously, he or she is most likely being tested for alcohol intoxication. Alcohol inhibits cells in the **cerebellum** that help control balance, posture, and coordination. The cerebellum takes in sensory information and figures out the best way to coordinate force, direction, extent of muscle contraction for smooth, appropriate, coordinated movements based on incoming information.

Spinal Cord

The **spinal cord** is a longitudinal system of neurons and supporting tissue that carries signals between the brain and the peripheral nervous system. About 18 inches long and three-quarters of an inch wide, the spinal cord is protected by the bony vertebral column.

Protection of the Central Nervous System

The brain, which controls our every action, thought, and desire, is a soft, easily damaged tissue. Many layers of supportive tissue are needed to protect this irreplaceable and vulnerable organ. The brain is protected by the bony skull, three layers of meninges, cerebrospinal fluid, and by the blood–brain barrier.

Three layers of connective tissue, called the meninges, cover the brain and spinal cord. These three layers

STRAIGHT DOPE

Top 10 Myths About the Brain

1. **We use only 10 percent of our brain.** Although our brains are less than 2 percent of our body weight, they use about 30 percent of our energy. It does not make sense that 90 percent of this magnificent organ would just sit idle. In fact, damage to small areas can have profound consequences. (Conversely, some people have lost huge amounts of brain tissue—an entire hemisphere, in some cases—with seemingly minor effects.) So where did this common misapprehension come from? Some cite American psychologist William James, who said, "The average person rarely achieves but a small portion of his or her potential."

2. **The brain is solid tissue.** In truth, the three pounds of mush in your skull has the consistency of cold oatmeal and could not even support its own weight if it were not suspended in a bath of cerebrospinal fluid.

3. **Your brain is gray.** Sure, parts are gray (hence the term *gray matter*), but other parts are white, or red, or black, or blue. The cell bodies and dendrites appear to be a beigeish gray, but the axons, which are covered in myelin, appear white. The substantia nigra of the midbrain contains a pigment called neuromelanin, which makes the area appear black. The locus coeruleus, located in the brainstem, looks dark blue. And finally, many parts of the brain appear red, due to the many blood vessels traversing our brains.

4. **Memories are accurate, detailed, precise, and unchanging.** Have you ever discussed a shared memory (a family gathering, a party with friends) with other people who experienced it with you? How clear is your memory? How closely do the details of your story match? You may think you precisely remember the events of that day, and of other important days, but memories actually change over time. Although many believe that human memory works like a video recorder—recording events and playing them back exactly—in fact, memories are reconstructed rather than replayed. Memory expert Elizabeth F. Loftus says that memory is "more akin to putting puzzle pieces together than retrieving a video recording."

5. **It's all downhill after 40.** Sure, for some things. Trust me, in 30 years your knees are going to make some interesting crackling sounds when you go up and down stairs. Children and young adults *are* better at some cognitive tasks: language acquisition, judging whether two objects are the same or different, memorizing lists of random words, and the ever-important counting backward by sevens. But take heart—older adults excel at other cognitive tasks: they have a bigger vocabulary, and they're better at judging character, settling conflicts, gauging the appropriate response in a social situation, and regulating their own emotions.

6. **We have five senses.** We all learned this one in elementary school—sight, sound, taste, touch, and smell. But what about proprioception, the sense of where our bodies are located in space and how we're moving? And what about the sense of time? If you had to, you'd probably have a pretty good idea of estimating when five minutes had passed. If not for your sense of time passing, there would be nothing to keep you from standing in the shower for hours on end.

7. **Brains are like computers.** No, brains are much more magnificent. Computers can't laugh at a joke, write a poem about how they feel, fall in love, or deal with a power failure. They (literally) cannot work outside the box to access new tools and processes when one does not work. Also, the more information a computer stores, the more slowly it runs. But the more data that goes into your brain, the quicker you can process information.

8. **The brain is hard wired.** Although certain areas of the brain are specialized for certain tasks, the brain is changeable. It responds to experience by learning, and reorganizes its neurochemistry and connections to deal with new situations. In blind people, parts of the brain that normally process sight can be devoted to hearing. The brain adapts and changes with ever-changing stimuli.

9. **Our senses give us a precise and accurate view of the world.** Humans are not passive recipients of information. We search for patterns, turn ambiguous scenes into ones that fit our expectations, and miss details that we do not expect. In one famous psychology experiment, when asked to count the number of times people playing basketball pass the ball, about half of all viewers fail to notice a man *wearing a gorilla suit* and pounding his chest as he walks among people playing basketball.

10. **Men are from Mars; women are from Venus.** People today embrace the myth that men and women are vastly different creatures. This applies to scientists who study brain differences between the sexes. It is true that there are neuronal differences in men and women, but the reality may be that we are born with some small differences that are exacerbated by our life experiences. Expectations play a huge role in cognitive performance. For example, when female participants in studies are told that women perform worse on a math test than men do, lo and behold, the female participants perform worse than men. But when they are told that women perform as well or better than men do, then perception becomes reality.

Sources: Arkowitz, H., & Lilienfeld, S.O. (2010). Why science tells us not to rely on eyewitness accounts. Scientific American.com. http://www.scientificamerican.com/article.cfm?id=do-the-eyes-have-it

Helmuth, L. (2011). Top ten myths about the brain. Smithsonian.com. http://www.smithsonianmag.com/science-nature/Top-Ten-Myths-About-the-Brain.html

(from outermost to innermost: the dura mater, arachnoid mater, and pia mater) support and protect the CNS. They also provide a space for circulation of cerebrospinal fluid, a clear acellular fluid that reduces brain weight and protects and nourishes the brain.

Blood does not pour into our organs from our capillaries like water from a hose. Instead, substances in the blood seep across capillary walls. The capillaries that feed many organ systems, such as the liver and kidneys, have pores in them to allow substances easy access to these organs. However, although the brain has a rich blood supply, the capillaries of the brain are highly selective about the hormones, chemicals, and substances that they will allow in. The walls of the **blood–brain barrier (BBB)**—a name for the specialized capillaries of the brain—are surrounded by cells that are not only tightly joined together, but also are covered by a layer of glial cells, which limit the access of blood-borne materials into the brain (Figure 3.9). Nutrients, oxygen, CO_2, and lipid-soluble drugs can pass through the BBB and access the brain, while wastes, proteins, toxins, and most drugs cannot.

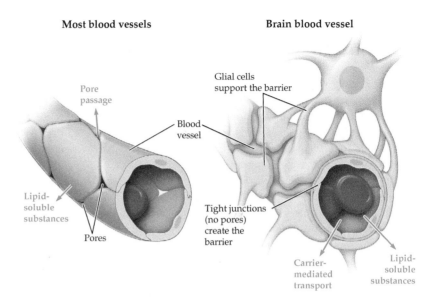

Most blood vessels

Brain blood vessel

Pore passage

Glial cells support the barrier

Blood vessel

Lipid-soluble substances

Pores

Tight junctions (no pores) create the barrier

Carrier-mediated transport

Lipid-soluble substances

FIGURE 3.9. The blood–brain barrier. Capillaries that feed the brain have tight junctions to prevent many blood-borne substances from entering the brain.

QUICK HIT

The BBB is absent or weak in some areas of the brain, such as the hypothalamus, posterior pituitary gland, and pineal gland. Blood-borne substances also have easy access to the medulla's *area postrema,* the vomiting center of the brain, which protects animals by eliminating toxic substances from the stomach before more harm can be done.

Neurotransmitters

As mentioned earlier in this chapter, neurotransmitters are chemicals that are released from the axon terminal of one neuron and bind to the receptors on another cell. When the neurotransmitter binds to its specific receptor, this causes a brief change in the electrical properties of the target cell.

Blood–brain barrier (BBB): The specialized capillaries that carry blood to the CNS, blocking the entry of certain substances.

GABA: Gamma-aminobutyric acid is the major inhibitory neurotransmitter of the brain.

Until fairly recently, scientists believed that a given neuron produced only a single type of neurotransmitter. We now know that most, if not all, neurons synthesize and release two, three, or more different transmitters. These co-transmitters often are physically segregated from one another within a synaptic terminal and are released at different times and due to different stimulation. Neurons often are named for the primary neurotransmitter they release. For example, cholinergic neurons produce and release acetylcholine, serotonergic neurons produce and release serotonin, and GABAergic neurons produce and release GABA.

The first neurotransmitter was discovered a century ago; today, well over 100 neurotransmitters have been identified. Some neurotransmitters are simple chemicals, and others are large and complex molecules. In general, the smaller, simpler neurotransmitters such as GABA and glutamate are responsible for most neural transmission in the brain, and larger neurotransmitters such as beta-endorphin and oxytocin work more slowly by regulating the strength and effectiveness of other systems. Table 3.3 summarizes the major neurotransmitters and their functions.

GABA

GABA (gamma-aminobutyric acid) is a small neurotransmitter that acts as the major inhibitory neurotransmitter of the brain. As many as 40 percent of the synapses in the CNS use GABA as their primary neurotransmitter.

TABLE 3.3. Major Neurotransmitters and Their Functions

Neurotransmitter	Actions	Location	Examples of Drugs that Directly Affect
GABA	Inhibitory Involved in sleep, general relaxation	Up to 40 percent of neurons in brain	Valium, Xanax, Rohypnol, barbiturates, alcohol
Glutamate	Excitatory Sensory signals, brain excitability, brain plasticity, learning and memory	Most common excitatory neurotransmitter in the brain—over half of all synapses in the brain release glutamate	Alcohol, PCP, ketamine
Norepinephrine	Actions similar to sympathetic nervous system, arousal, mood, sex, appetite	Locus coeruleus Almost every region of the brain receives input from adrenergic neurons	Cocaine, amphetamine
Dopamine	Involved in arousal, mood, sex, appetite, motor function, reward and addiction	Basal ganglia, ventral tegmental area of midbrain	Cocaine, amphetamine, anti-Parkinson's drugs, antipsychotics
Serotonin	Involved in sleep, appetite, mood, aggression, sex, hallucinations	Raphe nuclei of the brainstem Many locations all over brain and body	Antidepressants, MDMA, LSD
Acetylcholine	Involved in movement of skeletal muscles and ANS, sleep, and memory	NMJ, ANS Brain areas related to motor control, learning, memory, and addiction	Nicotine, atropine, curare, botulinum toxin
Opioids	Emotions, pain reduction, sleep, respiration, reward	Brainstem, limbic system, pituitary gland, and spinal cord	Morphine, heroin
Endocannabinoids	Movement, perception and cognition, sleep, appetite, emotions, memory, analgesia, reproduction	Many locations all over brain and body	Marijuana

Synthesis, Release, and Termination of GABA

GABA is synthesized from the amino acid glutamate (glutamate is both an amino acid and a neurotransmitter). After being released, GABA is transported from the synapse into nearby glial cells, where it is transformed to glutamate, carried into the axon terminal, and converted back into GABA. GABA also is transported directly back from the synapse into the presynaptic terminal by protein carriers.

QUICK HIT

Vitamin B_6 is a necessary ingredient in the synthesis of GABA. In the 1960s, vitamin B_6 was omitted from a batch of infant formula. The lack of this cofactor caused a significant depletion of GABA in the brains of the babies who drank it, and the subsequent loss of inhibition had tragic consequences as these infants experienced hyperexcitability and seizures that in some cases were fatal.

Location and Function of GABAergic Neurons

GABA is located in many areas, but is most highly concentrated in the basal ganglia, hypothalamus, hippocampus, and brainstem. GABA decreases the activity of neurons that it binds to, helps to regulate neuronal excitability in the CNS, affects memory, and decreases pain signals. GABA also is found outside of the CNS, in the GI system, reproductive system, kidney, lung, and liver.

There are two classes of GABA receptors. Metabotropic $GABA_B$ receptors are indirect and slow, while ionotropic $GABA_A$ receptors are direct and fast (Chapter 4). When GABA binds to the $GABA_A$ receptor, it opens a chloride channel. Chloride rushes into the cell, which makes it more negatively charged and less likely to fire an action potential, which leads to inhibition.

Drugs that Affect GABAergic Neurons

Many drugs bind to the $GABA_A$ receptor. Barbiturates such as phenobarbital and benzodiazepines such as Xanax bind to the receptor. When these drugs bind, they affect the chloride channel in a way that allows more chloride to enter the cell, leading to neuronal inhibition (Chapter 8).

Steroids such as progesterone bind to the receptor and have an overall sedative effect. Alcohol also has an effect on GABA, but its actions are quite complex (Chapter 12).

Glutamate

Glutamate is not only an amino acid; it is also the major excitatory neurotransmitter in the CNS. Over half of all brain synapses release glutamate.

Synthesis, Release, and Termination of Glutamate

Glutamate is synthesized from the amino acid glutamine, which is released by glial cells. The glial cells pump glutamine into the axon terminal, where it is converted into glutamate. After glutamate is released, transporters present in the presynaptic terminal and in nearby glial cells remove it from the synapse. Glial cells contain enzymes that convert glutamate back into glutamine, and the process begins again.

Location and Function of Glutamatergic Neurons

Glutamate is involved in sensory signals, brain excitability, brain plasticity (the ability of the brain to change its own structure and function following changes in the body or external environment), and higher cognitive functions such as learning and memory. Overactivation of glutamate receptors can cause neurological damage via excitotoxicity.

There are various types of glutamate receptors. Three of the best known are AMPA, kainate, and NMDA. Most fast excitatory responses to glutamate are mediated by stimulation of **AMPA** (α-amino-3-hydroxy-5-methyl-4-isoxazole propionic acid . . . do yourself a favor and just call it AMPA) **receptors**. When glutamate binds to an AMPA receptor, a sodium channel opens. Sodium enters the cell through this channel, which depolarizes the cell and excites it. Kainate (KAY-in-ate) receptors also control a Na^+ channel.

NMDA (N-Methyl-D-aspartate) **receptors** are more complex than other glutamate receptors. They require two neurotransmitters to stimulate the receptor—glutamate plus either glycine or serine must bind in order to open the ion channel. Once stimulated, both sodium and calcium enter through the ion channel. The story is even more complex, though. At rest, the ion channel is blocked by magnesium, so sodium and calcium

---

Glutamate: The major excitatory neurotransmitter in the central nervous system.

AMPA receptors: The most common type of glutamate receptor.

NMDA receptors: N-Methyl-D-aspartate is an important class of glutamate receptors that are involved in memory.

Catecholamine: Neurotransmitters, including dopamine, norepinephrine, and epinephrine, all of which have a similar structure and function.

---

cannot enter the channel, even if glutamate and glycine are present. Magnesium leaves the pore only when the membrane is depolarized, usually when AMPA channels are activated. Therefore, at a single synapse, NMDA receptors usually coexist with either AMPA or kainate receptors.[7] In some ways, NMDA is a biological coincidence detector. The channel only opens when two events occur close together in time—when glutamate and its co-transmitter bind to the receptor, and when the cell membrane is concurrently depolarized by a different excitatory receptor.

QUICK HIT

Domoic acid is a toxin that activates glutamate receptors. Made by several species of marine algae, it can be ingested and concentrated by certain fish and shellfish, and then passed on to humans who eat the tainted food. A person who ingests domoic acid may experience vomiting, cramps, diarrhea, headache, dizziness, muscle weakness, mental confusion, and sometimes even death. Alfred Hitchcock's movie *The Birds* reportedly was based on a 1961 incident in the coastal town of Capitola, California, where domoic acid–poisoned seabirds began crashing into, and seemingly attacking, people, buildings, and cars. It is thought that the birds were weak and disoriented due to ingestion of the toxin.[8]

Drugs that Affect Glutamatergic Neurons

Some of the drugs that bind to glutamate receptors include PCP, ketamine, ethanol, and dextromethorphan. When the dissociative anesthetics PCP and ketamine bind to the receptor, they block the channel and prevent glutamate's effects (Chapter 6). Ethanol (Chapter 12) also inhibits the effects at NMDA receptors, as do high doses of dextromethorphan (Chapter 15).

Catecholamines

Dopamine, norepinephrine, and epinephrine are **catecholamines**. These neurotransmitters are structurally similar to one another and also have some similarities in their functions.

Synthesis, Release, and Termination of Catecholamines

Catecholamines are synthesized from the amino acid tyrosine, which is found in many high-protein foods. Tyrosine is converted into a chemical called DOPA, from which dopamine is synthesized. Dopamine is then converted into norepinephrine, and norepinephrine into epinephrine. Dopamine, norepinephrine, and epinephrine are similar in structure to tyrosine, but each has a small, yet significant, chemical modification that alters its effects. After these neurotransmitters are released from the axon terminal, they are removed from the synapse by reuptake, and are returned into the presynaptic nerve terminal by transporter proteins. Some molecules are then repackaged into vesicles for re-release, while others are broken down and eliminated. The metabolic enzymes MAO and COMT break down these neurotransmitters and play a role in discontinuing their postsynaptic effects.

QUICK HIT

Norepinephrine and epinephrine-releasing neurons are sometimes referred to as "adrenergic." This is because in Europe, epinephrine is known as adrenaline, and norepinephrine is called noradrenaline. In the United States, we call them epinephrine and norepinephrine, because Adrenalin is a trademarked name for a product. The terms *adrenaline* and *epinephrine* both come from the same root. Epinephrine/adrenaline is released from a gland that rests on top of the kidney. The Greek word for kidney is *nephros,* and the Latin word is *ren* (from which we get the word *renal*.) Epi-nephron and ad-renal both translate to "on the kidneys."

Location and Function of Catecholaminergic Neurons

Almost every region of the brain receives input from adrenergic neurons, and so norepinephrine and epinephrine have widespread effects. These neurotransmitters are involved in regulating attention, arousal, sleep-wake cycles, learning and memory, emotions, mood, sex, appetite, and pain. Most norepinephrine in the brain is synthesized in an area of the pons called the locus coeruleus (LOH-cus suh-ROO-lee-us). Neurons here are primarily excited by new and unexpected stimuli and help us to focus our attention. Drugs that treat ADHD increase norepinephrine levels in the locus coeruleus to improve focus (Chapter 14). Norepinephrine and epinephrine also are released outside of the CNS. Stimulation of the sympathetic nervous system releases these neurotransmitters, and they produce the fight-or-flight response in many organs of the body.

Dopamine is involved in coordinating and integrating fine muscle movements, memory, cognitive processes, and emotions. There are three main dopaminergic pathways in the brain (Chapter 13). The nigrostriatal pathway of the basal ganglia helps control movement. This pathway is degenerated in the motor disorder Parkinson's disease. The mesolimbic path-

way, which runs from the dopaminergic cell bodies of the midbrain to the limbic system, is important in regulating mood, emotions, motivation, drive, reward, and addiction. Many pleasurable events—including food, sex, and drugs such as cocaine, heroin, and nicotine—result in release of dopamine in this pathway. Finally, the mesocortical pathway runs from the midbrain to the prefrontal cortex. It is important for problem solving, planning, short-term memory, and attention. The symptoms of schizophrenia may be related to excessive dopamine levels in the mesocortical pathway (Chapter 13).

Drugs that Affect Catecholamines

Some drugs that increase the effects of dopamine and norepinephrine include cocaine, amphetamine, drugs that treat ADHD, and some antidepressant drugs. Parkinson's disease is associated with a loss of dopaminergic cells in the basal ganglia, and anti-Parkinson's drugs increase dopamine production and its breakdown. On the other hand, dopamine levels may be elevated in those who suffer from schizophrenia; some antipsychotic drugs block dopamine receptors.

Serotonin

Also called 5-HT (5-hydroxy tryptamine), **serotonin** is an inhibitory neurotransmitter found throughout the brain and body. Serotonin got its name from "sero" (blood) and "tonin" (tone) due to its effects on vascular tone.

Synthesis, Release, and Termination of Serotonin

Serotonin is synthesized from tryptophan, an essential amino acid found in grains, meat, and dairy. Tryptophan is converted to 5-hydroxytryptamine, which is then converted into serotonin. After it is released into the synapse, serotonin is taken back into the presynaptic terminal by a transporter protein. Serotonin's actions also are terminated by enzymatic degradation.

QUICK HIT

Estrogen increases activity of an enzyme involved in the synthesis of serotonin and, therefore, helps to reduce anxiety and depression. During PMS (premenstrual syndrome) and after a woman gives birth, when estrogen is low, some women experience depression and anxiety.

Serotonin: A neurotransmitter found throughout the brain and body, involved in many functions, including mood, sleep, appetite, and visual perception.

Location and Function of Serotonergic Neurons

Serotonin is found all over the brain and body. Most of the body's serotonin is located in the gut, where it helps to regulate intestinal movement. Serotonin also is found in blood platelets. In the brain, most serotonin is located in the raphe (raa-FAY) nuclei of the brainstem. The raphe nuclei are part of the reticular activating system and project throughout most of the brain. They play an important role in sleep and wakefulness.

Serotonin modulates raw information and gives it emotional tone. For example, other neurotransmitters tell us when our stomachs are full; serotonin lets us know whether we feel satisfied. Other neurotransmitters let us see a glass of water and perceive the water level; serotonin helps us decide whether we think the glass is half full or half empty. One of the oldest signaling molecules, serotonin is even found in single-celled paramecia.[9] Serotonin plays a variety of roles in the body, including regulation of sleep and arousal, appetite, alcohol intake, migraine, mood, aggression, sexual activity, hallucinations, perception of social rank, learning, and memory, as well as nausea, body temperature, pain response, vasoconstriction, and GI functions. There are at least 14 serotonin receptor subtypes, which are found in different areas of the brain and are responsible for different functions.

Drugs that Affect Serotonergic Neurons

Many drugs affect serotonin. Both MDMA (also known as ecstasy or Molly) and LSD affect serotonin (Chapter 6). Prozac, Zoloft, and other selective serotonin reuptake inhibitors (SSRIs) elevate serotonin levels (Chapter 13).

Acetylcholine

Acetylcholine, the first neurotransmitter to be discovered, is also the most common neurotransmitter in the body (although GABA and glutamate are more common in the brain).

Synthesis, Release, and Termination of Acetylcholine

Acetyl coenzyme A (acetyl-CoA) and choline are converted into acetylcholine in the axon terminal, stored in vesicles, and released into the synapse. Unlike other small molecule neurotransmitters, there is no reuptake of acetylcholine. Instead, acetylcholine is broken down by the enzyme acetylcholinesterase (AChE), which is found in various locations and forms. AChE breaks ace-

Acetylcholine: The first neurotransmitter to be discovered and the most common neurotransmitter in the body.

tylcholine down into acetic acid and choline, and the choline is then taken up into the presynaptic axon terminals by a transporter.

Location and Function of Cholinergic Neurons

Acetylcholine is released into the neuromuscular junction from all motor neurons in the somatic nervous system and from all fibers in the parasympathetic nervous system. Acetylcholine also plays an important role in the sympathetic nervous system. In the CNS, acetylcholine is found in brain areas related to learning, memory, motor function, and sleep.

There are two acetylcholine receptor types: nicotinic and muscarinic. Nicotinic receptors are found in the neuromuscular junction, the ANS, and in the heart and blood vessels, as well as in the brain, where they enhance the release of other neurotransmitters from nerve terminals. Nicotinic receptors are ionotropic and fast, also serving as an ion channel; when acetylcholine binds, the channel opens quickly and sodium and calcium rush into the cell. The specific proteins that compose the nicotinic receptors are different in neurons and muscles. Muscle nicotinic receptors are not as sensitive to nicotine as are the nicotinic receptors in the brain and ANS. This allows smokers to obtain the psychological effects of nicotine (by stimulating brain receptors) without experiencing muscle contractions or spasms.

Muscarinic receptors are metabotropic, meaning the receptors are separate from the ion channel; these receptors produce slower and more prolonged actions. Muscarinic receptors are found in the heart, lungs, GI tract, bladder, sweat glands, and pupils. They also are found in parts of the brain related to motor control, synaptic plasticity, addiction, learning, and memory.

Many drugs work at cholinergic receptors. Nicotine, the active ingredient in tobacco, binds and activates nicotinic receptors (Chapter 10). Curare, a poison extracted from various South American plants, blocks these receptors and causes muscle paralysis (including the muscles that are necessary for breathing). Black widow spider venom causes a massive release of acetylcholine at the neuromuscular junction, leading to muscle pain, abdominal cramps, nausea, vomiting, salivation, sweat, tremors, and respiratory problems. Ounce for ounce, black widow spider venom is 15 times more toxic than prairie rattlesnake venom. But a single spider bite is rarely fatal to a healthy adult, because only a small amount of venom is injected.[10] Botulinum toxin is a neurotoxin produced by the bacterium *Clostridium botulinum*. This anaerobic bacterium can grow in oxygen-free environments, such as improperly

STRAIGHT
DOPE

The Discovery of Acetylcholine

Acting on an idea that came to him in a dream, an Austrian scientist named Otto Loewi rushed to his lab one night in 1926 and performed a single but conclusive test that showed that information can be transferred from one neuron to the next by means of a chemical signal. In this experiment, he used two frog hearts, one of which (heart #1) was still attached to its vagus nerve and one (heart #2) that was not. Heart #1 was placed in a saline-filled container, which was connected to a second chamber that housed heart #2 (Figure 3.10). The fluid from the first chamber was allowed to flow into the second chamber. As he expected, when Loewi electrically stimulated the vagus nerve of heart #1, its heart rate decreased. But Loewi observed that after a delay, heart #2 also slowed down, even though its vagus nerve had been removed. From this experiment, Loewi hypothesized that the vagus nerve regulates heart rate by releasing a chemical, which flowed from chamber 1 to chamber 2 and affected the rate of heart #2. Loewi called this substance "vagusstoff"; we know it today as acetylcholine. In 1936, Loewi received the Nobel Prize for his discovery. When Hitler moved into Austria in 1938, Loewi (who was Jewish) lost his job and was arrested by Nazis. He was released on the condition that he leave the country and turn over to the Nazis all his research, Nobel Prize winnings, and possessions.

Loewi moved to the United States, where he lived until his death in 1961.

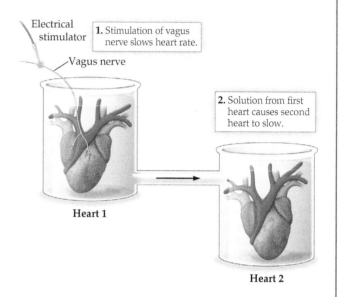

FIGURE 3.10. Otto Loewi's experiment was the first to demonstrate the existence of neurotransmitters.

canned foods. Botulinum blocks the release of acetylcholine from the neuromuscular junction. Symptoms of botulinum poisoning include muscle weakness and paralysis, blurred vision, difficulty in swallowing, and GI distress. Injection of botulinum toxin is an approved medical treatment for some disorders, including strabismus (crossed eyes), muscles spasms on one side of the face, migraines, and heavy sweating. Botox, the injection that temporarily prevents wrinkles, is actually an injection of botulinum toxin. It works by paralyzing the muscles of facial expression.

QUICK HIT

Botulinum toxin is one of the most poisonous substances on earth. One gram, about the weight of a dollar bill, is enough to fatally poison 3 million people.

Muscarine is a compound found in the mushroom *Amanita muscaria* (Chapter 6). It binds and activates muscarinic receptors. Muscarine can be used to treat glaucoma and postoperative urinary retention. Atropine, which blocks muscarinic receptors, speeds the heart, dilates pupils, inhibits salivary and mucous glands, and can produce dizziness, blurred vision, nausea, confusion, and hallucinations (Chapter 6).

QUICK HIT

Atropine comes from the deadly nightshade *Atropa belladonna*. Women used to put belladonna drops in their eyes to dilate their pupils. "Belladonna" translates to "beautiful woman"; when a person is attracted to you, his or her pupils dilate—and what is more beautiful than a person who is attracted to you?

Some drugs work on both nicotinic and muscarinic receptors. Organophosphates such as insecticides and nerve gases inhibit acetylcholinesterase, which prevents the breakdown of acetylcholine. As acetylcholine accumulates, muscles overstimulate. They can't relax, which leads to muscle weakness, cramps, and paralysis. The mnemonic SLUDGEM can help you to remember the effects of organophosphate poisoning: salivation, lacrimation, urination, defecation, GI motility, emesis, and miosis (pupil constriction).

Ask yourself: Our bodies produce endogenous forms of opioids. Heroin is an opioid and a schedule I drug. Is it fair for the government to regulate substances that also exist naturally in the human body? Why or why not?

Opioids

Drugs such as morphine, codeine, and heroin bind to **opioid** receptors. (Although the term *opiate* often is used as a synonym, *opioid* is the broader and more appropriate term). Opioids are large chemicals with a complex synthetic pathway. In general, the synthesis and release of larger neurotransmitters is slower and more complex than that of smaller neurotransmitters. As such, a description of their synthesis and termination is beyond the scope of this chapter.

There are four classes of endogenous opioids—β-endorphins, enkephalins, dynorphins, and endomorphins—and three principal classes of opioid receptors—mu (μ), delta (δ) and kappa (κ) (Chapter 7).

Endogenous opioids are found in many areas of the brain including

- the brainstem, where they reduce pain and slow breathing;

Opioid: Any natural, synthetic, or endogenous substance that binds to the opioid receptor.

Cannabinoid: A diverse group of physiologically active compounds found in cannabis and the human body that bind to cannabinoid receptors.

- the hypothalamus, where they affect hormonal regulation, sleep, body temperature, appetite, mood, and reward;
- the cortex, where they influence sensory processing;
- the eye, where they constrict the pupils;
- the spinal cord, where they reduce pain; and
- the intestinal tract, where they cause constipation.

Endocannabinoids

In the late 1980s, scientists discovered that THC, one of the psychoactive substances in marijuana, bound **cannabinoid** receptors in the brain. As we'll discuss at greater length in Chapter 4, receptors do not exist in our brain on the off chance that we might happen upon a plant and smoke it; if there are receptors in our brain for a substance, that means that our bodies produce a natural form of that chemical. Endocannabinoids are produced naturally by the body, and include substances such as anandamide and 2-AG (2-arachidonoylglycerol) (Chapter 9).

Cannabinoid receptors are all slow and metabotropic. They are categorized as CB-1 and CB-2. CB-2 receptors are located in the periphery and are thought to play a role in immune function. CB-1 receptors are widespread in the CNS—in fact, the brain has more CB-1 receptors than any other type of metabotropic receptor. CB-1 receptors are found in the basal ganglia and cerebellum, areas that regulate motor function and coordination; the cortex, where they affect perception and cognition. They are also found in the limbic system, which controls sleep, thermoregulation, appetite, emotions, and memory. CB-1 receptors also play a role in alleviating pain, and in helping the embryo implant in the uterus after fertilization.

Chapter Summary

- **The Structure and Function of Neurons**
  - » Neurons are cells that receive and send signals throughout the body.
  - » Sensory neurons carry information into the brain and spinal cord, and motor neurons transmit signals from the brain and spinal cord out to our muscles, nerves, and glands in order to elicit a response.
  - » Neuroglia are nerve cells that support neurons and aid in neurotransmission.
  - » The soma or cell body contains the neuron's machinery that keeps it functioning. The electrical signal travels down the wire-like axon. A chemical

neurotransmitter is released from the axon terminal into the synapse, which then binds to receptors located on the dendrites of the postsynaptic neuron.

- **Neuronal Transmission**
  - » Information travels down an axon as a change in voltage known as an action potential. For a brief time, the inside of the neuron becomes more positively charged than the outside.
  - » When this change in voltage reaches the axon terminal, it causes a neurotransmitter to be released into the synapse.

- » The neurotransmitter binds to receptors on the post-synaptic cell. Once bound, it typically causes effects by opening or closing an ion channel, thus changing the voltage in the postsynaptic cell.
- » Effects at the postsynaptic receptors are terminated by reuptake, enzymatic degradation, or diffusion.

- **The Peripheral and Central Nervous Systems**
  - » The brain and spinal cord together form the central nervous system (CNS). The peripheral nervous system (PNS) is made up of all the nerves going to and from the brain and spinal cord.
  - » The PNS is further divided into the somatic nervous system and the autonomic nervous system (ANS).
  - » The somatic nervous system consists of neurons that carry sensory information into the CNS and motor signals from the CNS to skeletal muscle cells.
  - » The ANS consists of neurons that carry information to or from heart muscle, smooth muscle, and glands.
  - » The ANS is further divided into the sympathetic nervous system (fight or flight) and the parasympathetic nervous system (business as usual).
  - » The forebrain contains the cerebrum (which includes the cerebral cortex, hippocampus, and basal ganglia), thalamus, and hypothalamus.
  - » The midbrain includes the tectum and tegmentum.
  - » The pons, cerebellum, and medulla make up the hindbrain.
  - » The brain is very soft tissue, so it is protected by the bony skull, three layers of connective tissue called meninges, cerebrospinal fluid, and the blood–brain barrier (BBB). The BBB describes the specialized capillaries of the CNS that prevent the entry of certain substances.

- **Neurotransmitters**
  - » In general, the smaller, simpler neurotransmitters such as GABA and glutamate are responsible for most neural transmission in the brain, and larger neurotransmitters such as beta-endorphin and oxytocin work more slowly by modulating the strength and efficacy of other systems.

- » GABA is the major inhibitory neurotransmitter of the brain. Some drugs that affect GABA include barbiturates, benzodiazepines, and alcohol.
- » Glutamate is the major excitatory neurotransmitter of the brain. It is involved in sensory signals, brain excitability, the ability of the brain to change its own structure and function following changes in the body or external environment, learning and memory. Some drugs that affect glutamate include PCP, ketamine, and alcohol.
- » Catecholamines include dopamine, norepinephrine, and epinephrine. They have widespread effects and are involved in regulating attention, arousal, sleep-wake cycles, learning and memory, emotions, mood, sex, appetite, and pain. Some drugs that affect catecholamines include cocaine, amphetamines, and drugs to treat ADHD, Parkinson's disease, and schizophrenia.
- » Serotonin is located in many areas in the brain and body. Serotonin modulates raw information and gives it emotional tone. Some of the functions it influences include regulation of sleep and arousal, appetite, mood, sexual activity, hallucinations, nausea, body temperature, pain response, vasoconstriction, and GI functions. Some drugs that affect the serotoninergic systems include LSD, MDMA, and SSRIs such as Prozac and Zoloft.
- » Acetylcholine is the most common neurotransmitter in the body. It is found in the neuromuscular junction, the ANS and in brain areas related to learning, memory, motor function, and sleep. Some drugs that affect acetylcholine include nicotine, atropine, and curare.
- » Opioids include morphine, codeine, and heroin. They affect pain, respiration, and mood.
- » Endocannabinoids bind to cannabinoid receptors in the brain and body. These receptors affect coordination, perception and cognition, pain, sleep, appetite, and memory; they also play a role in helping the embryo implant in the uterus after fertilization. THC, the psychoactive substance in marijuana, binds to cannabinoid receptors.

Key Terms

NMDA receptors (p.62)
Node of Ranvier (p.47)
Nucleus (p.47)
Nucleus accumbens (p.57)
Occipital lobe (p.56)
Opioids (p.66)
Parasympathetic nervous system (p.53)
Parietal lobe (p.55)
Periaqueductal gray (p.58)
Peripheral nervous system (PNS) (p.50)
Pineal gland (p.57)

Pituitary gland (p.57)
Pons (p.58)
Prefrontal cortex (p.55)
Presynaptic autoreceptor (p.49)
Receptor (p.48)
Reticular formation (p.58)
Reuptake (p.50)
Sensory neuron (p.46)
Serotonin (p.63)
Soma (p.47)
Somatic nervous system (p.50)

Spinal cord (p.58)
Substantia nigra (p.58)
Sympathetic nervous system (p.52)
Synapse (p.48)
Tectum (p.58)
Tegmentum (p.58)
Temporal lobe (p.56)
Thalamus (p.57)
Ventral tegmental area (VTA) (p.58)
Vesicle (p.48)

Quiz Yourself!

1. Label the following diagram:

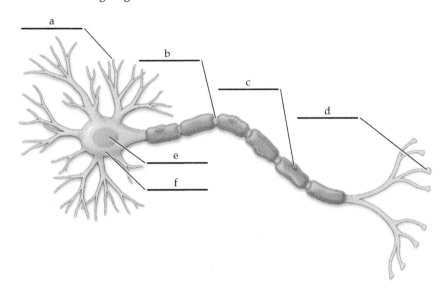

2. The space between two neurons is called a _____.

3. Which of the following is NOT a way that the effects at the postsynaptic receptor are terminated?

   A. Reuptake into the presynaptic cell

   B. Release of a chemical that destroys the postsynaptic receptors

   C. Enzymatic breakdown of the neurotransmitter

   D. Diffusion of neurotransmitter away from the receptor

4. The central nervous system is made up of the _____ and _____.

5. Which is true about the sympathetic nervous system?

   A. It is part of the central nervous system.

   B. It is part of the autonomic nervous system.

   C. It increases heart rate.

   D. Its actions may be increased by cocaine.

   E. A, C, and D are true.

   F. B, C, and D are true.

   G. All of the above are true.

6. **Matching**: Match the area of the brain with its function. There is only one correct answer per blank. Choices are only used once or not at all.

1. _____	Frontal lobe of the cortex	A.	Vision
2. _____	Hypothalamus	B.	Balance, posture, and coordination
3. _____	Basal ganglia	C.	Controls autonomic nervous system and hormone release, sex, emotions, temperature regulation, feeding behavior
4. _____	Cerebellum	D.	Smoothing, programming, initiating and terminating movements; degenerated in Parkinson's disease
5. _____	Medulla	E.	Sensation of touch
6. _____	Occipital lobe of cortex	F.	Reasoning, judgments, decision making
		G.	Keeps you alive: breathing, heartbeat, swallowing

7. True or false? The cerebellum includes the cerebral cortex, hippocampus, and basal ganglia.

8. Which of the following is most involved in pleasure, reward, and addiction?

   A. The nucleus accumbens

   B. The medulla oblongata

   C. The ventral tegmental area

   D. The cerebellum

   E. A and C

   F. B and D

9. True or false? The capillaries of the CNS are very leaky, so all substances in the blood can have access to the neurons in the brain.

10. Which of the following would most likely be the result of a drug that increases the neurotransmitter GABA?

    A. Increases heart rate

    B. Increases sleep

    C. Increases pain

    D. Increases the strength of muscle contraction

Additional Resources

Websites
Neuroscience for kids. http://faculty.washington.edu/chudler/neurok.html It's not just for kids! A wonderful reference to help you review and understand neurons, action potentials, drugs, and many of the concepts in this textbook.

Videos
Selective attention test. This is the video referenced in the straight DOPE feature "Top 10 Myths About the Brain." https://www.youtube.com/watch?v=vJG698U2Mvo

Two-minute neuroscience: The neuron. https://www.youtube.com/watch?v=6qS83wD29PY

Two-minute neuroscience: Neuronal transmission. https://www.youtube.com/watch?v=WhowH0kb7n0

Two-minute neuroscience: Divisions of the nervous system https://www.youtube.com/watch?v=q3OITaAZLNc

Two-minute neuroscience: The lobes of the brain https://www.youtube.com/watch?v=LQ4DlE1Xyd4

Books
The Human Brain Coloring Book. (1985). *Diamond, M.C., Scheibel, A.B., & Elson, L.M.* New York: Collins Reference. A way to learn the basics of the brain by coloring. The knowledge sneaks in while you're having fun.

Learn more with this chapter's digital tools at www.oup.com/he/rosenthal2e.

4 Pharmacology: How Drugs Work

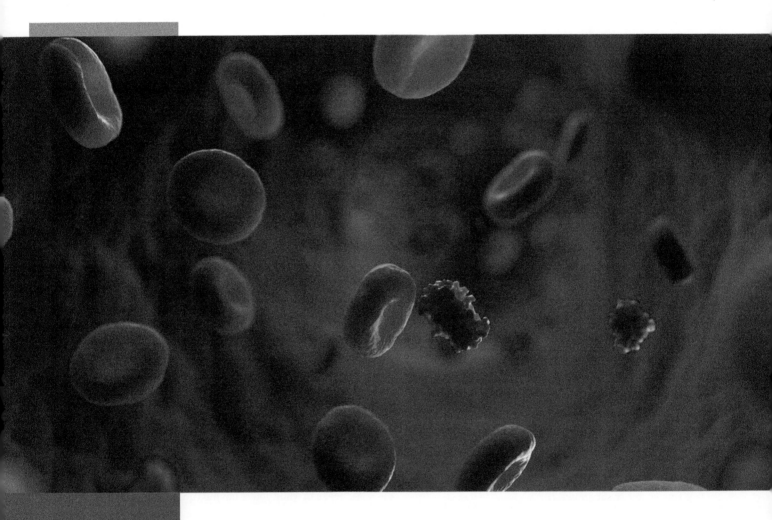

True or false?

1.
True or false? A drug that is smoked gets to the brain faster than one that is injected.

2.
True or false? A fake pill that a patient is told costs $100 will have more of an effect than a fake pill that the patient is told costs $5.

3.
True or false? Drug tolerance takes months to develop.

Answers: 1. T, 2. T, 3. F

J amie has a headache. She goes to her medicine cabinet and swallows two aspirin. About 30 minutes later, she notices that her headache is gone. But how did the aspirin exert its effects? How did it "know" to go to her head and not her toe? What did it do when it got there? And how did her body process these pills? In this chapter, we will investigate the mechanics of **pharmacology**—the scientific study of the actions of drugs and their effects on a living organism. Pharmacology encompasses both the way the body processes the administered drug (pharmacokinetics), and the effects the drug has on the body (pharmacodynamics).

Learning Objectives

- Define *pharmacokinetics, bioavailability, absorption, distribution, metabolism,* and *elimination.*
- Compare and contrast the various routes of administration.
- Explain the effect of drug depots.
- List some factors that influence the rate of metabolism.
- Describe the first-pass effect and its significance with regard to drug action.
- Define *pharmacodynamics, agonist, antagonist, ionotropic,* and *metabotropic.*
- Summarize the various ways a drug may act as an agonist or an antagonist.
- Define *placebo, potency, efficacy, therapeutic index, margin of safety,* and *tolerance.*
- Explain the ways that set and setting can influence a drug's actions.
- Analyze a dose-response curve.

Pharmacokinetics

What happens to a drug after we take it? **Pharmacokinetics** is the study of how drugs are handled by the body—how they are absorbed into the bloodstream, distributed throughout the body, transformed into different chemicals, and excreted.

Absorption
Absorption is the process by which drugs pass from the external world into the bloodstream. Many factors affect how well a drug is absorbed, including the dosage, its route of administration, whether the drug is **fat-soluble** (dissolves in fats or oils) or **water-soluble**, its pH, as well as characteristics of a tissue, including the amount of blood circulating to the tissue and its surface area. Regardless of how well a drug is absorbed, the primary concern is with its **bioavailability**—the extent to which a drug reaches its site of action. If a drug is easily absorbed across the wall of the stomach, but then is broken down into inactive products before it reaches general circulation, its bioavailability is low.[1]

Dosage
In the sixteenth century, Swiss physician Paracelsus (Chapter 7) coined the adage *Sola dosis facit venenum*, meaning "The dose makes the poison." The amount of a drug that is taken will influence the effect it has on the body. The difference between a night

Pharmacology: The scientific study of the actions of drugs and their effects on a living organism.

Pharmacokinetics: The branch of pharmacology concerned with the actions of a body on an administered drug.

Absorption: The process and mechanisms by which drugs pass from the outside world into the bloodstream.

Fat-soluble: Also called lipid-soluble, this refers to substances that dissolve in fats or oils.

Water-soluble: Substances that dissolve in water.

Bioavailability: The degree to which the original drug dose reaches its site of action.

out in which you sip one beer and an outing during which you chug 11 of them can be the difference between a pleasant evening and a morning in which you wake up with some really embarrassing pictures posted online or, much worse, in the hospital. But dosage determines more than the extent of a drug's actions; dosage can completely change the drug's effect on your body. For example, at small doses, atropine (a drug that blocks acetylcholine receptors) slows heart rate, but at large doses, it speeds the heart up. A small dose of morphine can decrease your pain, but a large dose will inhibit the respiratory centers of your brain.

So how does a pharmacologist compute the proper dose? This depends on the nature of the drug, the person's body weight, the person's prior experience with the drug, as well as other factors such as age and health. For example, in heavier persons, the drug is less concentrated than in smaller individuals. Dosage is typically expressed in milligrams (or micrograms) of drug

Route of administration (ROA): The method by which a drug is taken into the body.

per kilogram of body weight. A milligram is 1/1,000 of a gram, and a microgram is 1/1,000,000 of a gram. As an example, imagine two patients need pain relief and are both given intravenous (IV) morphine. One patient weighs 150 pounds and the other 200. The doctor prescribes a dose of 0.1 mg/kg. The smaller patient might obtain pain relief with 6.8 mg of morphine, but the heavier patient would need 9 mg to alleviate the pain.

Route of Administration

Humans have sniffed, snorted, smoked, swallowed, smeared, and shot drugs into their system (Figure 4.1). In all of these methods, the drug crosses the membranes of the body to enter the bloodstream (Figure 4.2). The **route of administration (ROA)** is one factor that determines how much of a drug reaches its site of action and how quickly the drug takes effect.

The best route of administration for a drug depends on many factors, including the characteristics of the drug, the goals of administration, and the particular circumstances involved. Even cultural considerations play a role. For example, a doctor on one particular

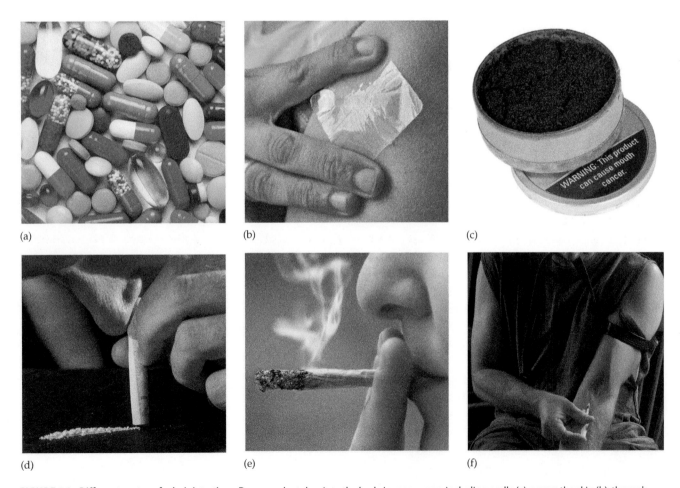

FIGURE 4.1. Different routes of administration. Drugs can be taken into the body in many ways, including orally (a); across the skin (b); through the mucus membrane of the mouth (c) or nose (d); smoked (e); or injected (f).

FIGURE 4.2. **Routes of administration.** Drugs enter the bloodstream in a variety of ways. The route of administration is one factor that influences how much of a drug reaches its site of action and how quickly the drug takes effect.

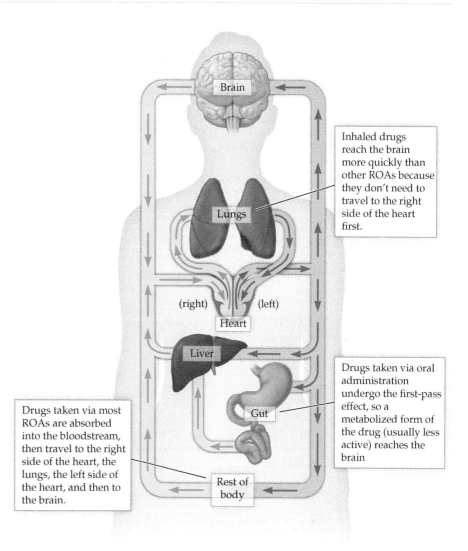

Inhaled drugs reach the brain more quickly than other ROAs because they don't need to travel to the right side of the heart first.

Drugs taken via oral administration undergo the first-pass effect, so a metabolized form of the drug (usually less active) reaches the brain

Drugs taken via most ROAs are absorbed into the bloodstream, then travel to the right side of the heart, the lungs, the left side of the heart, and then to the brain.

ocean liner bemoaned the problem of stocking the ship's pharmacy, saying that he needed to stock three times as many products as when working on land: "Tablets for the Brits, shots for the Yanks, and suppositories for the French."[2] Routes of administration also go in and out of fashion. Snuff is a form of ground-up tobacco leaves that is snorted into the nose (Chapter 10). In the eighteenth century, snuff was the tobacco product of the elite, enjoyed by such aficionados as Emperor Napoleon, Queen Charlotte of England, and Pope Benedict XIII. This ROA is much less popular today. Each route of administration has advantages and disadvantages (Table 4.1).

Oral Administration

Drugs administered orally can take many forms— liquids, pills, tablets, and capsules. After the drug is swallowed, it first goes to the stomach, where it dissolves in the gastric fluids. Not all drugs can be taken orally; the active ingredient must be resistant to destruction by stomach acids and enzymes. For example, stomach acids destroy insulin and local anesthetics.

From the stomach, the drug passes into the small intestine, where it is absorbed into the bloodstream and sent to the liver. In the liver, the drug is metabolized and converted into a new form. The altered drug is then carried through the circulatory system to the heart and on to the brain and other organs. A drug administered orally generally takes 20–30 minutes to reach the brain, and some of its effects might not be felt for an hour or longer.

QUICK HIT

Pills are a mixture of active and inactive ingredients. Because a typical drug dose is measured in milligrams, a pill that only contained the drug and nothing else would be tiny. Therefore, pill manufacturers add fillers and binders to hold it together, as well as disintegrators such as corn starch to ensure that the pill will break open when it comes in contact with digestive juices. Other substances are added for color— and these colors are carefully chosen. New antibiotics tend to be red or purple to suggest strength, while anxiety-relieving drugs tend to have soft shapes and calm, pastel colors.[3]

TABLE 4.1.   Routes of Administration

Route of Administration	Examples	Advantages	Disadvantages
Oral	alcohol, caffeine, LSD, PCP, cannabis, MDMA, amphetamines, barbiturates, benzodiazepines	Safe, easy, compact, economical, self-administered	Slow and highly variable absorption, subject to first-pass effect, some people have difficulty swallowing, not good in emergencies
Rectal	diazepam, acetaminophen, laxatives	Can be used if patient is vomiting or unconscious, quicker absorption than oral administration	Slightly variable absorption, uncomfortable for some
Vaginal	estrogen cream, Monistat, misoprostol, NuvaRing	Steady drug levels, can go directly to affected tissue, quicker than oral administration	Tissue irritation
Sublingual and buccal	nitroglycerin, chewing tobacco	Rapid absorption, higher bioavailability than oral administration	Can be inconvenient, small doses only, may taste unpleasant, can irritate the mouth
Intranasal	cocaine, heroin, powdered tobacco, nasal decongestants, calcitonin, and sumatriptan for migraines	Rapidly absorbed, both local and systemic effects	Irritation of the nasal mucosa
Eye drops, ear drops	drugs to treat ear and eye infections, glaucoma, dry eyes, and swimmer's ear	Goes directly to affected tissue	Administration can be difficult
Transdermal	cortisone cream, estrogen and progesterone, LSD, scopolamine, nicotine, fentanyl	Easy to administer, noninvasive, slow and continuous drug delivery	Not appropriate for all drugs, hard to control accuracy of dose, may irritate the skin
Inhalation/smoke/vape	cannabis, nicotine, cocaine, heroin, PCP	Very rapid onset of action	Irritation of lungs and nasal passages
Intravenous (IV)	heroin, amphetamines, PCP	Rapid, most accurate blood concentration	Expensive, painful, requires sterile equipment and trained personnel, can't be readily reversed
Intramuscular (IM)	vaccines (measles, diphtheria, HPV, tetanus, flu), antibiotics	Slow and even absorption, sustained release possible	Pain, local irritation at site of injection, requires sterile equipment and trained personnel
Subcutaneous (SubQ)	insulin, heroin	Slow and prolonged absorption, patient can administer	Variable absorption depending on blood flow, small doses only, can be painful

Much of the effect of an oral drug is lost before it reaches the brain. Due to a phenomenon called the **first-pass effect**, metabolism by the liver changes the form of the drug before it enters the systemic circulation. In most cases, the drug is inactivated, reducing its bioavailability. Examples of drugs that undergo a significant first-pass effect include morphine (Chapter 7), the benzodiazepine diazepam (Valium) (Chapter 8), and the antidepressant imipramine (Tofranil) (Chapter 13).

First-pass effect: The phenomenon by which orally administered drugs are metabolized by liver enzymes before they reach the general circulation, which usually reduces their bioavailability.

Oral administration is the most common method of drug administration. There are many advantages to this ROA: it is easy, convenient, and economical. It is also relatively safe compared with other ROAs—if a toxic dose has been taken, there may be time to induce vomiting or to pump the stomach before all of the drug has been absorbed. There are, however, several disadvantages. The user must be cooperative and conscious in order to swallow the drug. Absorption from the gastrointestinal (GI) tract is slow and highly variable; because of this, sometimes individuals may take more of a drug if they feel it isn't having the desired effect quickly enough, which can increase the risk of overdose. In addition, the environment of the stomach—both the acidic pH and the presence of some foods—makes it difficult to control drug absorption accurately. Oral administration is also subject to the first-pass effect, which can diminish the drug's concentration. Finally, oral administration is not ideal for drugs that treat nausea and vomiting.

Absorption across the Mucous Membranes or Skin

Drugs can be absorbed across the skin or across the mucous membranes of the rectum, vagina, mouth, eye, ear, or nose. **Transdermal administration** is the ROA by which drugs are delivered across the skin and then enter the bloodstream. Drugs can be applied to the surface of the skin as a cream, gel, lotion, spray, or patch, and may treat a localized skin condition such as eczema, or a systemic condition.[4] Drug-containing patches can be adhered to the skin and deliver their drugs slowly and continuously as long as the patch is worn. Some drugs that come in the form of a patch include nicotine for those who are trying to quit smoking, scopolamine to treat motion sickness, and contraceptive estrogen and progesterone (Chapter 16).[5] Patches are an easy and noninvasive way to slowly administer a drug over time. Not all drugs can be absorbed across the skin, however, and some patches can cause skin irritation.

Drugs also can be administered as a rectal suppository. To create this form, a drug is combined with a waxy substance that dissolves after being inserted into the rectum. The drug is readily absorbed because the blood supply is rich and the walls of the rectum are thin.[6] This may be an advantageous ROA if the patient is vomiting, unconscious, or unable to swallow pills, such as the case with infants. Rectal administration of drugs allows for a faster onset and shorter duration than oral administration. The first-pass effect is reduced by about one-half to two-thirds, which means that a greater concentration of unaltered drug will reach the circulatory system. Many people, however, may be squeamish to administer drugs in this way, and drugs administered this way can irritate the membranes that line the rectum. Some medications that may be administered rectally include diazepam (Valium), for seizures; acetaminophen (Tylenol), for fever (Chapter 15); and laxatives such as Dulcolax, for constipation (Chapter 15).

Some drugs are given as vaginal suppositories. These are generally creams, foams, gels, or tablets, which are absorbed into the bloodstream across the vaginal wall. Vaginal administration allows for lower, less frequent doses and steady drug levels, although tissue irritation

or allergic reactions can occur.[7] Some drugs administered vaginally include drugs to treat yeast infections, estrogen creams, drugs to induce labor, and hormonal contraceptive rings (Chapter 16).

Drugs can be absorbed across the mucous membrane of the mouth as well. In **sublingual administration**, drugs such as nitroglycerin (which dilates blood vessels and is used to treat chest pain) are placed under the tongue and are dissolved in saliva and absorbed directly into the small blood vessels that lie beneath the tongue. Sublingual drugs are absorbed more quickly than those that are swallowed, and this ROA avoids the first-pass effect. Not all drugs are efficiently absorbed sublingually, however, and there may be an unpleasant taste. Other drugs may be absorbed through the mucosal membranes lining the cheek (**buccal administration**). For instance, the nicotine in chewing tobacco is absorbed across the lining of the cheek and gums, although there is less absorption through the cheek lining than the sublingual area.[8]

Drugs can be administered into the eyes, ears, and nose. Eye drops are almost always used for their local effects on the eye, such as to treat dry eyes, conjunctivitis, or glaucoma. Ear drops similarly treat ear infections. Intranasal drugs are breathed in and absorbed through the mucous membrane that lines the nasal passages, where they quickly enter the bloodstream. Nasally administered drugs, such as cocaine powder (Chapter 5) and snorted heroin, typically take three to five minutes to reach the brain. Some of these drugs can irritate the delicate membranes that line the nose.

Inhalation

Inhalation is a means of introducing drugs through the respiratory system in the form of a vapor or gas. The heat of combustion breaks down the drug preparation—it destroys some components, frees others, and creates new ones. Absorption by inhalation is very rapid and effective. In fact, inhalation gets drugs to the brain in less than 10 seconds, even faster than IV injection. However, only certain drugs can be delivered this way. The drug must be fat-soluble and needs to form a vapor or gas when heated. Only a small amount of

Transdermal administration: The administration of drugs to the skin as creams or patches.

Sublingual administration: The administration of drugs under the tongue.

Buccal administration: The administration of drugs across the mucous membrane of the cheek.

the drug is typically absorbed in one administration, and it is therefore relatively short-acting. Also, small particles are inhaled, which can inflame and damage the lungs. Some drugs that are inhaled include nitrous oxide, chloroform, and airplane glue vapors (Chapter 8), as well as drugs that are burned or vaporized and inhaled such as tobacco, crack cocaine, and cannabis.

Parenteral Administration

Drugs are also administered by injection. Before a drug can be injected, it has to be in liquid form so that it can pass through the needle. But most drugs are originally in a crystalline or dry powder form (in fact, the word *drug* comes from the French word *drogue*, meaning "dry powder").[9] The powder must be dissolved in liquid (called the "vehicle") before it can be injected. Water, saline solution, or oil are typically used as vehicles, depending on the solubility and chemical characteristics of the drug. With all injections, sterile equipment must be used to reduce the risk of infection.

Although **intravenous (IV) injection** is the most direct way to get a drug into the bloodstream, it is not the fastest way to get drugs to the brain. When drugs are administered intravenously, the venous blood first returns to the right side of the heart, where it is pumped to the lungs, then flows to the left side of the heart, and then travels to the brain. Smoked drugs immediately enter the lungs, and then travel to the left side of the heart, then through the aorta to the brain. IV injection is rapid, so it is good for emergency use. IV also allows for the most accurate measurement of dosage and can be given to a patient who is unconscious. Finally, IV administration is acceptable for large volumes. However, IV injections may be expensive, inconvenient, and painful. Also, due to the immediate appearance of the drug in the bloodstream, there is a risk of accidental overdose, because there is little time to react to an unexpected drug reaction.

Drugs can also be administered by **intramuscular (IM) injection**. An IM injection allows slow and

Intravenous (IV) injection: The administration of drugs by injecting them into a vein.

Intramuscular (IM) injection: The administration of drugs by injecting them into a muscle.

Subcutaneous (SubQ) injection: The administration of drugs by injecting them directly underneath the skin.

Distribution: The transport of drugs to their site(s) of action in the body.

Drug depot: An area of the body in which a drug can be accumulated or stored.

Ask yourself: People may have different attitudes about drugs based on their route of administration. Would you have a different response to someone who snorted cocaine compared to someone who smoked it or injected it? Why? What factors underlie your response?

even absorption. The absorption rates depend on the amount of blood flow to the muscle into which the drug is injected. IM injections are usually made into the shoulder, thigh, or buttock muscles. These injections can be painful, and there can be irritation at the site of injection. The Gardasil vaccine (Chapter 16) is one example of a drug that can be administered IM.

Subcutaneous (SubQ) injections are administered under the skin and are the easiest type of injection, providing a relatively slow and constant rate of absorption. Absorption rates, however, depend on blood flow to the site of injection. Also, this method is not appropriate for large volumes or irritating substances. Insulin (used to treat diabetes) and some hormones can be administered subcutaneously.

Distribution

Once absorbed into the bloodstream, the circulating blood carries the drug throughout the body, distributing it to the fluids or tissues. Many factors will influence the **distribution** of a drug, including its ability to cross membranes and pass through tissues, its molecular size (smaller molecules are more easily distributed), and its solubility (fat-soluble drugs reach their sites of action more easily).

Drugs may be distributed to body fluid or tissues. Body fluids include blood, intracellular fluid, extracellular fluid, cerebrospinal fluid, and urine. Drugs also distribute to body tissues. Generally, parts of the body that receive the most blood—such as the liver, kidney, heart, lungs, and brain—will have the highest concentration of the drug, and may, therefore, be particularly vulnerable to its toxic effects. As an example, heroin and amphetamines accumulate in the kidney and are especially damaging to this organ, while alcohol (Chapter 12) has a strong effect on the liver. Tissues with less blood flow may take longer to receive the drug, but may act as a drug depot.

A **drug depot** is an area of the body that can accumulate and store a drug, but where no significant biological effect of the drug occurs. Some examples of drug depots include muscle and fat, as well as when drugs are bound to proteins that circulate in the plasma. When a drug is stored in a depot or bound to **plasma proteins**, the drug is temporarily unable to reach its target site, which slows its onset of action and reduces its effect. In addition, the stored drug does not reach the liver to be metabolized, which can prolong its action. Accumulating in drug depots or binding to plasma proteins is reversible. When the liver metabolizes molecules of the drug that are free in the blood (i.e., not bound to plasma proteins or stored in depots), the plasma concentration of the drug decreases. When that happens, drugs that were previously bound or stored are released into the bloodstream and travel to target organs where they can have their intended effect.

Many drugs bind to plasma proteins, muscle, and fat. Some examples of drugs that bind to plasma proteins are aspirin, barbiturates such as phenobarbital (Chapter 8), benzodiazepines such as Valium, the antidepressant Prozac, and the antiseizure drug phenytoin. Some drugs that are stored in body fat include benzodiazepines, PCP (also known as angel dust) (Chapter 6), and tetrahydrocannabinol (THC), the active ingredient in marijuana (Chapter 9). Digoxin, a heart medication, is a drug that accumulates in muscle tissue.

Because so many drugs are held inactive in depots, a high dose of one drug may displace another drug from its depot, resulting in higher than expected drug action. For example, phenytoin is highly protein-bound. But aspirin binds plasma proteins more easily, and thus can displace some phenytoin from the plasma proteins to the bloodstream, which can elevate plasma levels of phenytoin to potentially toxic concentrations.[10]

In order to enter the organs of the body, drugs need to pass through the walls of the capillaries in the circulatory system. As we learned in Chapter 3 (refer back to Figure 3.9), the capillaries that feed many organ systems allow blood-borne substances to access these organs easily. You don't want every substance in your blood to affect your brain, however, so the capillaries in the CNS (called the blood–brain barrier [BBB]) are very selective in what they allow to enter the brain. Their design reduces the diffusion of most water-soluble substances such as proteins, wastes, toxins, and most medications into the brain. However, fat-soluble substances, including THC, cocaine, caffeine, nicotine, LSD, and benzodiazepines, can easily cross the BBB.

The BBB does not cover every area of the brain. It is absent or weak around the hypothalamus and posterior pituitary gland, thus allowing water-soluble neurohormones entry into these glands. The BBB also is absent around a region of the medulla called the **area postrema**, the vomiting center of the brain. It is a marvel of evolution that the BBB is absent around this chemical trigger zone. When a toxic substance enters the bloodstream, it can easily access the area postrema to induce vomiting, thus eliminating the toxic substance from the stomach before more harm can be done.

Unfortunately, the placenta is not an effective barrier to drug distribution; almost all the drugs that enter a mother's blood supply will enter the fetus's circulation. Organ damage can occur in the fetus if drugs are ingested as early as two weeks after fertilization; this could happen before a woman even knows she's pregnant. The first two months of pregnancy are when the embryo is most sensitive to the damaging effects of drugs. If you are pregnant, it is best to discuss the use of any drug or medication with your healthcare provider.

QUICK HIT

Some of the drugs that are harmful to the developing embryo or fetus include alcohol, tobacco, thalidomide, aspirin, Accutane (an acne medication), tetracycline (an antibiotic), phenytoin, warfarin (an anticoagulant), and lithium (a mood stabilizer).

Metabolism and Biotransformation

How does the body deal with the wide array of pharmaceutically active agents that people take? The process by which the body accepts a drug, alters it chemically, and prepares it for excretion is called **biotransformation** or **metabolism**. Typically, when the body encounters a foreign substance, it will make the compound more water-soluble, which will lead to faster excretion through the urine. **Metabolites** are byproducts of the biotransformation process—structurally modified forms of the original chemical.

Metabolism can activate or deactivate the original chemical. Usually substances become less active, but some substances, such as diazepam, acetaminophen, fluoxetine (Prozac), chloral hydrate, psilocybin (psychedelic

Plasma proteins: Proteins found in the blood that serve many functions, including transport of some substances.

Area postrema (also known as the chemical trigger zone): The vomiting center of the brain.

Biotransformation or metabolism: The biochemical modification(s) made by an organism on a chemical compound in order to make it easier to be excreted by the body.

Metabolites: Chemical products of metabolism.

mushrooms) (Chapter 6), and THC, are made more active by liver enzymes.

The liver is the most important organ for metabolism. It contains hundreds of enzymes that synthesize, alter, and deactivate drugs. These enzymes can be regulated and modified by genes and by experience. The **cytochrome P450 (CYP450)** family of enzymes is the major enzyme group involved in drug metabolism, accounting for about 75 percent of the metabolism of all drugs.[11] CYP450 is a large and diverse group of enzymes that metabolize and deactivate many biochemical substances. This family of enzymes originated more than 3.5 billion years ago and has since diversified to process many chemicals, toxins, and drugs.[12] This diverse enzyme system is one of the most important defenses that evolved in our ancestors to protect against a wide array of potentially harmful xenobiotics (substances foreign to the human body) to which they were exposed.

For most drugs, the rate of elimination from the body is proportional to the amount of drug in the body. In other words, a constant percentage of the drug is lost per unit of time. So when drug levels are high, the drug is cleared from the body more rapidly. As drug levels drop, the clearance rate is reduced. This is called **first-order kinetics**. In **zero-order kinetics**, the drug is cleared from the body at a constant rate, regardless of the drug concentration (Figure 4.3). One way to visualize this is to imagine a busy bank on a Friday afternoon. In the National Bank of First-Order Kinetics, when the line of customers grows longer, more teller windows are opened. But in the Bank of Zero-Order Kinetics, no matter how long the line of customers grows, no more windows are opened.[13] Ethanol is a drug that undergoes zero-order kinetics. About 1 ounce of 100-proof alcohol is removed from the body per hour, regardless of the concentration of alcohol in the blood. Large doses of aspirin and the blood thinner warfarin also undergo zero-order kinetics.

A drug's **half-life** is the time it takes for the amount of drug in the body to be reduced by 50 percent. Drugs with a long half-life stay in the body for longer periods of time at close to their full strength (Table 4.2).

Cytochrome P450 (CYP450): A superfamily of enzymes that play a role in many activities, including metabolism of drugs and toxins.

First-order kinetics: The rate of the drug's metabolism is proportional to the concentration of the drug.

Zero-order kinetics: The rate of the drug's metabolism is constant over time and independent of the concentration of the drug.

Half-life: The time it takes for the amount of drug in the body to be reduced by 50 percent.

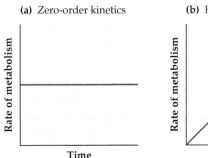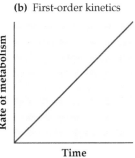

(a) Zero-order kinetics   **(b)** First-order kinetics

FIGURE 4.3. **Zero-order kinetics.** Alcohol undergoes zero-order kinetics (a) in which the rate of metabolism is independent of the concentration of alcohol. Most other drugs undergo first-order kinetics (b), in which the rate of metabolism is proportional to the concentration of the drug.

Our bodies are far from identical robot machines processing drugs in the same ways and producing the same results. Many factors—genetic, physiological, environmental, and dietary—influence the rate of metabolism and biotransformation.

Genetic and Racial Factors

Genetic variations among individuals can produce multiple forms of a given protein, including enzymes that metabolize drugs. Some individuals have a genetically fast or slow metabolism for specific drugs. For example, about 5–10 percent of whites have very low levels of the enzyme CYP-2D6 (a member of the CYP450 family), which metabolizes amphetamine and MDMA (ecstasy), and, therefore, may have a toxic or even fatal reaction to these drugs.[14]

Individuals of different races have varying levels of specific drug-metabolizing enzymes. Many individuals of Asian descent have less alcohol dehydrogenase and, therefore, metabolize alcohol more slowly. About 50 percent of those of Asian descent are also less able to metabolize acetaldehyde, a toxic byproduct of alcohol metabolism, and, therefore, experience flushing, a rapid heartbeat, decreased blood pressure, and nausea when they drink. Asians also metabolize some antipsychotics

TABLE 4.2.	The Half-Lives of Various Drugs
Aspirin	15 minutes
Cocaine	0.5–1.5 hours
Morphine	1.5–2 hours
Nicotine	2 hours
Naproxen	12 hours
THC	20–35 hours
Fluoxetine	2–4 days—but the active metabolite's half-life is 7–15 days

and mood-stabilizing drugs such as haloperidol, tricyclic antidepressants, and lithium more slowly than whites.[15,16] Black smokers of African descent metabolize nicotine slower than white smokers.[17,18] Black people are also less responsive to the hypotensive effects of propranolol, a cardiac drug, than are whites and Asians.

Physiological Factors

A person's size influences a drug's action. The concentration of a drug in the blood depends on how much blood and other body fluids are in the body. More fluids dilute the absorbed drug. Heavier people have more fluids, and so the drug is less concentrated. Also, heavier people may have more fat or muscle, which can act as drug depots.

Males and females metabolize drugs at different rates. Many drugs remain active in women longer than in men. For one, women are often smaller than men, and have a higher percentage of body fat and less body fluid. Alcohol is one example of a drug that affects women more than men. In addition to being more concentrated in a woman's body, women have less gastric alcohol dehydrogenase, one of the enzymes that break down alcohol.

Age also impacts how well our bodies metabolize drugs. Children and the elderly are less able to metabolize drugs and are, therefore, more sensitive to them than are adults. For the first year of life, the enzyme systems that break down some drugs may not be fully developed. In the elderly, by contrast, some liver enzyme systems may be impaired, which increases the duration of drug action. Older adults also may have decreased renal function and hepatic blood flow, compromising elimination and increasing the time the drug has to exert its effects. Additionally, we produce fewer plasma proteins as we age, so there can be higher levels of unbound drug, thus increasing the concentration of drug in the bloodstream, as well as the risk of toxicity.

Even the time of day we take a drug can influence its action. Our circadian rhythms affect our sleep, body temperature, and hormone secretion. Corticosteroids (such as cortisone or prednisone) are typically taken in the morning to mimic the body's own daily hormone cycle. The bronchodilator theophylline may be most effective against asthma at night, when airways are the narrowest.

Cross-Reaction Factors

Many drugs influence their biotransformation by cross-reacting to each other. Some drugs increase the activity of metabolic enzymes, thereby *decreasing* the effect of the drug action. This might mean that a previously effective dose won't reach therapeutic levels. Carbamaze-

pine, an antiseizure drug also used to treat bipolar disorder, will stimulate the production of one of the CYP450 enzymes, thus decreasing its own effectiveness, as well as the effectiveness of other drugs such as phenobarbital, phenytoin, and St. John's wort, necessitating higher doses of these drugs when taken together.[19]

Some drugs, including certain SSRI antidepressants, inhibit metabolic enzymes, thus *increasing* the effect (and toxicity) of other drugs, such as oral contraceptives, methadone, and some antipsychotics (Chapter 13).[20] Taking a drug that inhibits CYP450 enzymes also can *decrease* the effect of another drug if that second drug needs to be activated by CYP450. For example, much of codeine's analgesic effects occur because CYP450 converts codeine into morphine, a more potent analgesic. If someone took the antidepressant fluoxetine at the same time as codeine, fluoxetine would inhibit the CYP450 enzymes, codeine would not be fully converted into morphine, and the patient would experience less pain relief.

Still other drugs compete for the same metabolic enzymes. Because there are a limited number of enzyme molecules, if levels of one drug are high, this can reduce the metabolism of another drug that uses the same system. As an example, alcohol and Tylenol are both metabolized by the same CYP450 enzymes, so when these drugs are taken together, they are not broken down as efficiently and blood levels can reach toxic doses.[21]

Environmental and Dietary Factors

Drug metabolism also is influenced by environmental and dietary factors. Exposure to environmental pollutants and industrial chemicals such as polychlorinated biphenyls (PCBs) and benzenes influence drug metabolism,[22] as do dietary factors. For instance, vitamins are necessary for the synthesis of proteins and lipids, both of which are part of the drug-metabolizing enzyme system.[23] Many foods also can influence the metabolism of certain drugs. For example, a substance in grapefruit juice inhibits some CYP450 enzymes, thus raising the blood levels of drugs that are metabolized by these enzymes, sometimes to toxic levels. Other food–drug interactions will be discussed later in this chapter.

Elimination

Drugs leave the body through the kidneys, GI tract, lungs, and skin. Drugs are **eliminated** either unchanged or after being metabolized into pharmacologi-

Elimination: The process of substances leaving the body, usually through urine, breath, digestion, and sweat.

cally inert, water-soluble byproducts. Our excretory organs (except the lungs) more efficiently eliminate water-soluble substances, so fat-soluble drugs are not readily eliminated until they are metabolized to become more water-soluble.

QUICK HIT

The acidity of urine can influence the elimination of a drug. Amphetamine is excreted unchanged in urine. However, clinicians can add ammonium chloride (a salt highly soluble in water) to the urine to make it more acidic, which significantly increases the rate of amphetamine excretion. Emergency room physicians sometimes use this method to help eliminate amphetamines from a patient who has overdosed.

The kidney is the most important organ for elimination of drugs and their metabolites. Once the liver has metabolized most drugs into water-soluble substances, their metabolites leave the body in the urine. Drugs also can be eliminated in feces and bile. Only highly volatile or gaseous agents, such as general anesthetics and small amounts of alcohol, leave the body through the lungs. About 1 percent of the body's alcohol is eliminated in the breath; this is what is measured with a breathalyzer. Small amounts of drug also leave the body through sweat, saliva, and tears. Some drugs also can be detected in hair, while other drugs, including alcohol, nicotine, cocaine, tranquilizers, oral contraceptives, aspirin, tetracycline, and laxatives, are eliminated in breast milk and are passed from mother to baby during breastfeeding.

QUICK HIT

Some drugs and their metabolites can be eliminated into hair follicles. Traces of arsenic were found in Napoleon's hair 150 years after its administration, and traces of mercury were detected in Mozart's hair, which may explain his manic behavior during the preparation of his last major work. [24]

Pharmacodynamics: The branch of pharmacology concerned with the actions of an administered drug on an organism.

Drug action: The molecular changes produced by a drug when it binds to a receptor, and the physiological or psychological changes that occur as a result.

Ligand: From the Latin word *ligare*, meaning "that which binds," a ligand is any manmade or natural substance, such as a drug or neurotransmitter, which binds to a receptor.

Endogenous: Produced or originated from within an organism.

Pharmacodynamics

Thus far, we've talked about how drugs are metabolized, but we still have not touched on how drugs *work*. **Pharmacodynamics** is the study of what a drug does to the body and the mechanisms by which it exerts its effects. **Drug action** refers to the specific molecular changes produced by a drug when it binds to a receptor and the physiological, psychological, and behavioral changes that occur as a result. Drugs can have many actions—including stimulant, depressive, hypnotic, analgesic, antidepressant, antipsychotic, and hallucinogenic—and many drugs produce more than one effect. Drug action is determined by interactions among the drug's biochemical and pharmacological properties, the individual taking the drug, and the environment in which the drug is taken.

Receptors

Drugs exert their effects by binding to specialized proteins called receptors, which are located on the surface of or within a cell. A typical neuron may have millions of receptors on its surface with dozens of different types—50,000 of one type, 20,000 of another, 200,000 of a third, and so on.[25] A **ligand** is any molecule, manmade or natural, that binds to a receptor. When a ligand comes upon a receptor into which it fits, it temporarily binds, producing a physical change in the shape of the protein, which initiates a series of intracellular events that ultimately generate an effect. Some drugs closely resemble existing neurotransmitters and bind to receptors for those transmitters. For instance, the drug GHB fits almost perfectly into the GABA receptor. Other drugs do not resemble the neurotransmitter and instead produce their effects by increasing the release or by blocking reuptake of neurotransmitters.

Morphine binds to opioid receptors in our bodies. Humans did not develop opioid receptors on the off chance that some person might one day decide to suck the sap out of that pretty red poppy flower and smoke it. No, if a receptor exists, it means we have an **endogenous** neurotransmitter—our own body's form of the drug (one name for endogenous opioids is *endorphins*). A given drug may be more specific for a set of receptors than the endogenous neurotransmitter. For example, serotonin binds to all of the 14 (as yet discovered) serotonin receptors. But a specific drug such as LSD may attach only to one or two of those specific receptors.[26]

Drugs bind in receptor sites like a key that unlocks or locks a door. When a ligand binds to a receptor, it may initiate an action in a cell (unlock), but it may also diminish the cell's response (lock). If you have another key—a skeleton key—that is similar enough to the shape of the lock, it can open or close the door even though it is not an exact match. Drugs that are not identical, but which are similar in structure to the receptor, can similarly bind to the receptor. Sometimes many different drugs can fit into the same receptor and compete for the receptor site: which one binds depends on the drug concentration and on the **affinity** of the drug for the receptor. To continue with the metaphor, you could also make sure the door stays shut by putting a large boulder in front of it. These analogies describe the different ways drugs can influence activity at receptor sites.

How Ligands Bind: Agonists and Antagonists

An **agonist** is a drug that mimics the effects of a neurotransmitter. This effect can be excitatory or inhibitory. Agonists can work in a variety of ways. Direct agonists fit directly into the postsynaptic receptor (like a key in a lock). Indirect agonists increase the effect at the synapse without binding to the postsynaptic receptor; for example, they may increase release of a neurotransmitter into the synapse or block reuptake of the neurotransmitter. Examples of agonists include morphine, which is an opioid agonist that directly binds to opioid receptors, and nicotine, a cholinergic agonist that binds to acetylcholine receptors. **Full agonists** bind directly to the receptor and produce the maximal effect. Heroin is an example of a full agonist at opioid receptors. A **partial agonist** is a chemical, such as buprenorphine, that binds to and partially activates a receptor. Some partial agonists will be discussed in Chapters 7, 9, and 13.

An **antagonist** does not itself cause a response in the postsynaptic cell; instead, the antagonist prevents a neurotransmitter from having its effect, like glue in a lock. Direct antagonists do this by directly binding and blocking a postsynaptic receptor; indirect antagonists affect sites other than the postsynaptic receptor, perhaps by blocking synthesis or release. Atropine is an example of an antagonist at cholinergic receptors. It binds to cholinergic receptors and prevents ACh from binding, causing dry mouth, rapid heartbeat, and dilated pupils (Chapter 6) For a review of the ways that drugs can act as agonists and antagonists, refer back to Table 3.1.

Some receptors have a baseline level of activity even when there's no substance bound to it. These receptors aren't only "on or off," but instead are more like a dimmer switch. An **inverse agonist** not only blocks an agonist from binding, it also blocks this baseline activity. When an inverse agonist binds to a receptor, the effect is the opposite of what you typically see with an agonist. Naloxone is an opioid inverse agonist. Emergency

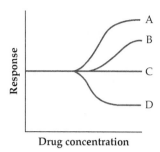

FIGURE 4.4. Dose-response curves for agonists and antagonists. Full agonists (A) bind fully to the main receptor site and produce the maximal response; partial agonists (B) activate this receptor site but bind incompletely, producing a lower response; antagonists (C) prevent an effect; and when an inverse agonist (D) binds to the receptor, it produces the opposite effects to that of an agonist.

room physicians may administer naloxone to patients who have overdosed on heroin—the administration of naloxone occupies the opioid receptors and reverses the depressive effects that heroin has on the respiratory system (Chapter 7). The relationship of agonists, antagonists, and inverse agonists is illustrated in Figure 4.4.

Some drugs act as **allosteric modulators**. These substances can change the receptor's response to a stimulus. They do this by binding to a site on the receptor which is separate from the site the endogenous agonist typically binds. Positive allosteric modulators fit into an alternate site and enhance the agonist's effect, perhaps by increasing the ability of the agonist to bind to its receptor. Benzodiazepines such as Xanax are positive allosteric modulators at $GABA_A$ receptors; they bind to an alternate site and increase the effect that GABA has on the main receptor site (Chapter 8). Negative allosteric modulators bind to an alternate site and decrease the effect of the agonist. CBD is a negative allosteric modulator at CB1 receptors; it interferes with THC's ability to activate these receptors, reducing some of THC's side effects (Chapter 9).

Affinity: How well a drug binds to its target.

Agonist: A chemical or drug that mimics the effects of a neurotransmitter.

Full agonist: A substance that binds to and activates a receptor, producing a maximal response.

Partial agonist: A chemical that binds to and activates a receptor, but not as completely as a full agonist.

Antagonist: A chemical or drug that blocks a receptor and inhibits the effects of a neurotransmitter.

Inverse agonists: Substances that bind to the main receptor site and produce the opposite effect that an agonist does.

Allosteric modulators: Substances that bind to alternate sites and influence the binding of agonists to the main receptor site.

Types of Receptors

Neurotransmitters cause postsynaptic effects by binding to receptors, which often work by opening or closing ion channels on the postsynaptic cell. There are two main classes of receptors: ionotropic receptors and metabotropic receptors (Figure 4.5).

Recall from Chapter 3 that, in ionotropic receptors, the receptor molecule itself is also an ion channel. The receptor spans the membrane and has subunits with a pore. When the neurotransmitter is not bound, the pore is usually closed. When the neurotransmitter binds, the receptor changes shape, which opens the pore. Ionotropic receptors cause fast postsynaptic responses, which usually last only a few milliseconds. Most glutamate and GABA receptors, as well as half of acetylcholine receptors, are ionotropic.

In metabotropic receptors, the receptor and the ion channel are two separate molecules. The ion channels will open or close via the activation of molecules called G proteins and second messengers. (Sometimes stimulating these receptors produces a different effect, not involving an ion channel.) Metabotropic receptors produce slower postsynaptic effects that last longer and are more diverse. Most receptors, including all catecholamine and neuropeptide receptors, most serotonin receptors, and half of acetylcholine receptors are metabotropic.

Drug Expectations and the Placebo Effect

Sir William Osler, the father of modern medicine, said, "The cure of tuberculosis depends more on what the patient has in his head than what he has in his chest." Indeed, one's expectations have a powerful effect on a drug's actions.

In a classic study that probably could not be replicated today due to ethical concerns, college students were given an injection of adrenaline, but were not told what they had received. Participants were then put in a waiting room with another student, who was actually working for the researcher (this student is called "the confederate"). Half of the time, the confederate acted happy, and half the time the confederate student acted angry. The physical effect of the adrenaline on the participants was the same—increased heart rate, blood pressure, and agitation—but the participants

Set: The effect of a person's expectations on drug effect.

Placebo: A substance or procedure that has no therapeutic effect and may be used as a control in experimental research designs or to reinforce a patient's expectation of recovery.

Placebo effect: When a placebo treatment produces a perceived or actual improvement in a medical condition.

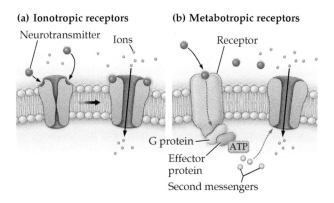

FIGURE 4.5. Ionotropic and metabotropic receptors. (a) In ionotropic receptors (e.g., GABA), the receptor itself is also an ion channel. When a drug such as Valium binds to the receptor, it opens the chloride channel and chloride rushes into the cell. (b) In metabotropic receptors (e.g., most serotonin receptors), the receptor is separate from the ion channel. When a drug such as psilocybin binds to the 5-HT$_{2A}$ receptor, it initiates a series of events that may open up an ion channel (or activate an enzyme, or produce other changes) that are located separately from the receptor.

who were in a room with an angry confederate attributed their physical sensations to anger, and those who were in a room with a happy confederate attributed the very same physical sensations to happiness and excitement.[27] So the physical response was the same, but the brain interpreted the response and assigned it an emotion based on the stimulus.

What people believe about a drug powerfully influences the drug's effect. Expectations can sometimes have an even stronger effect than the pharmacological actions of the drug; remember, the drug does not cause sensation, your brain does. The **set** relates to a person's unique biological and psychological qualities, as well as their expectations about what a drug will do. Expectations come from people's previous experiences with the drug—either through their own use or by hearing about a drug by "word of mouth"?, advertising, television, or other media.

A **placebo** is a pharmacologically inert substance that can sometimes elicit a significant therapeutic response. Stop and think for a moment about how intriguing this concept actually is. A patient comes to a doctor with an ailment. The doctor gives the patient a fake drug—a tablet with no active ingredients in it—*and the patient gets better.* The ramifications of the **placebo effect** are fascinating—our bodies must have some innate knowledge of healing that they can turn on, simply by believing that the healing process has begun.

Placebos also are used as controls in research studies to determine the effectiveness of a medicinal drug. The placebo effect is not limited to drugs. A surgical placebo test was performed on patients with osteoarthritis in the knee. Half received real arthroscopic surgery, and the other half just had holes drilled in their knees and, unknowingly, did not receive any actual surgical repair. The placebo group and the surgical repair group showed no difference in reports of pain or function.[28]

A number of mechanisms—biological, psychological, and environmental—underlie the placebo effect. Biologically, placebo analgesia involves endogenous opioids as well as other factors. Release of a person's endogenous opioids probably underlies part of the analgesic effect of a placebo, because this effect is blocked by the opioid inverse agonist naloxone. However, there may be different brain areas and mechanisms involved in opioid analgesia and placebo analgesia.[29] For example, the digestive hormone cholecystokinin (CCK) may be involved. CCK has an anti-opioid action; CCK antagonists can increase the analgesic effects of the placebo.[30]

Genetic differences may exist in those who respond to placebos compared to those who do not.[31] Neuroanatomical differences also may affect a person's response to placebo analgesia. Pain alleviation seems to be related to the density of gray matter in several brain regions, including the ventral striatum, insula, and prefrontal cortex.[32]

A patient's experiences and expectations also influence his or her susceptibility to the placebo effect. Many patients have had an experience of taking a pill and finding relief from their symptoms. It may be that they associate relief with the experience of taking medicine, and the placebo effect is, in part, due to a conditioned reflex response. Also, receiving a prescription from a physician, getting instructions from a pharmacist, or receiving other familiar cues may set up the patient's expectation that the drug will be effective. Even personality can have an influence; individuals who are thrill seekers are more responsive to placebo effect.[33]

QUICK HIT

Placebos work better if they are bigger, brightly colored, bitter rather than sweet, and more expensive rather than economical.[34] Capsules are more effective than tablets, and injections are more effective than pills.[35] Red, yellow, and orange pills lead to an expectation that the drug will stimulate; blue and green pills lead the patient to expect a calming effect; and white is preferred for analgesics.[36,37]

Medical care generally takes place in a particular context. The clinician's personality, as well as the treatment setting, may influence the patient's response.[38] A patient's pain is as equally diminished by a hidden injection of morphine as by a saline injection in full view of the patient.[39] The doctor's attitude toward a drug also has a powerful effect. Patients respond more to treatments when their physician says, "It does work" rather than "It may work."[40] Interestingly, placebos may even work when patients are explicitly told that they are taking a placebo. When physicians informed patients with irritable bowel syndrome (IBS) that they would be treated with a pill containing no active ingredients, but that the body often responds to the action of taking a pill and that the placebo effect was powerful and effective, patients reported less pain on placebo, even when they knew they were taking a placebo.[41] It is important to note that in this study, the doctors were described as warm, caring, and responsive—this might have had a significant effect on the effectiveness of the sham treatment.

Placebos are probably more effective for conditions that are strongly affected by the mind–body connection, such as IBS or depression, and conditions that are measured on a subjective continuum, such as pain and mood, than for objective binary measurements like cholesterol levels or tumor growth.[42] In a survey of physicians in the United States, about half of the internists and rheumatologists said they prescribed placebo treatments regularly. Most (62 percent) believed the practice was ethical.[43] Prescribing placebos is discouraged by the American Medical Association, however, because the practice does not allow for the informed consent of patients.

Setting

Imagine you've just downed four glasses of wine. How do you feel? Wait a minute—won't your response depend on the environment in which you drank the wine? What might your physical and psychological response to alcohol be if you drink with a group of friends? Now imagine that you've had most of a bottle of wine all alone in your room. Do you think you would have the same feelings that you do when you're drinking with friends? The **setting**—the physical, social,

Ask yourself: Should doctors be allowed to prescribe placebos? Why or why not? How do you balance the ethical principles of respect for patient autonomy and informed consent with a placebo's potential beneficial effects?

Setting: The physical, social, and cultural environment in which a drug is used.

and environmental context in which a drug is taken—can greatly influence a person's drug experience.

Effects and Side Effects of Acute Drug Use

There is no such thing as a "magic bullet"—a drug that goes directly to the desired target in the body, produces only the effect for which it was taken, and has no side effects. Every drug has main effects (the effect for which the drug is taken), as well as side effects.

Side effects are pharmacological actions that occur in addition to the main action. The main effect and side effect can reverse depending on the reason the drug is taken. For example, if a person takes opioids to control pain, then constipation is an undesirable side effect. But if a person were to take an opioid to treat diarrhea, then the constipating effects of the drug are the much-appreciated main effect. Additionally, side effects are not necessarily bad or dangerous. Topamax is a medication used to treat epilepsy and migraine headache. One side effect of this drug is weight loss; many people are pleased with this unexpected result.

The average pharmaceutical drug has 69 potential side effects. The most commonly prescribed drugs average around 100 side effects each, and some contain as many as 525 listed reactions. Side effects send more than 700,000 people in the United States to hospitals every year.[44]

QUICK HIT

Viagra was originally developed to treat high blood pressure and heart disease. It produced the side effect of penile erections. This effect was discovered during drug testing when the male subjects did not want to return their drug samples after the study was completed. Viagra is now marketed to treat erectile dysfunction, and its hypotensive effects are considered a side effect.

Drug Effectiveness

The **dose-response curve** measures the magnitude of a drug's effect as a function of the amount administered. As seen in Figure 4.6, the X-axis is the dose of the drug, and the Y-axis represents the magnitude of the

Side effects: Pharmacological actions that occur in addition to the main drug action.

Dose-response curve: A measure of a drug's effectiveness as a function of the dose administered.

Potency: The minimum dose of a drug that yields its desired effect.

Efficacy: The maximum effect that can be produced by a drug; the peak of the dose-response curve.

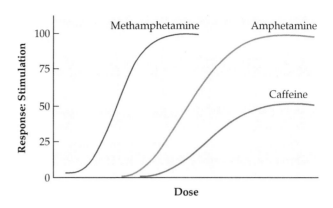

FIGURE 4.6. The dose-response curve. According to this curve, methamphetamine is the most potent, followed by amphetamine, and then caffeine. Methamphetamine and amphetamine have the same efficacy because they both can produce the same maximum effect, albeit at different doses. Finally, since the slope is steeper for methamphetamine and amphetamine than it is for caffeine, there is less of a difference between the smallest effective dose and the maximal or toxic dose for amphetamine than for caffeine.

drug's effect. Usually, as the dose increases, the effect increases until it reaches a plateau, or maximum effect.

The minimum dose of a drug that produces the desired effect is called the **potency** of a drug. The smaller the amount needed to obtain the particular effect, the more potent the drug is. The location along the X-axis reflects the potency of a drug. Amphetamine and methamphetamine are both powerful stimulants with a similar chemical structure. Methamphetamine's additional methyl group makes it more lipid-soluble, giving it a greater behavioral effect than amphetamine at the same dosage and making it a more potent drug. But potency is not necessarily important clinically, as long as the required dose can be conveniently given. If 50 mg of one drug produces the same effect as 25 mg of another drug, but both drugs can be administered in one tablet, it is not really important that one drug is more potent than the other. In this case, a drug's efficacy may be more clinically significant.

A drug's **efficacy** represents the maximum effect that can be produced by a drug. Even at high doses, caffeine cannot exert the same intensity of CNS stimulation as amphetamines, and aspirin cannot give the same pain relief as morphine. A drug may not be able to achieve its maximal efficacy if there are too many undesired side effects.

The slope, or steepness, of the dose-response curve reflects the range of doses that are useful for achieving a clinical effect. If the slope is steep, there is only a small difference between the dose that has a minimal effect and a dose that has a maximal, or potentially toxic, effect.

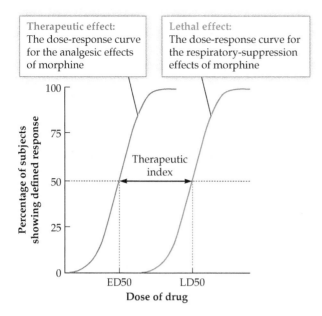

Therapeutic effect:
The dose-response curve for the analgesic effects of morphine

Lethal effect:
The dose-response curve for the respiratory-suppression effects of morphine

FIGURE 4.7. The therapeutic index. The therapeutic index is a measure of how safe a drug is, and it is expressed by the ratio LD50/ED50. The lower the therapeutic index, the more potentially dangerous the drug may be.

At high enough doses, almost all drugs are toxic. The **therapeutic index** is a measure of the safety of a drug. It can be expressed as the LD50 divided by ED50, as shown in Figure 4.7. The LD50 is the dose that is lethal

to 50 percent of the test animal population, while the ED50 is the effective dose—the amount required to produce the desired effect in half the population.

In Figure 4.7, the curve on the left represents the dose of morphine necessary to alleviate pain in a population of mice, while the curve on right is the dose that would cause a lethal suppression of respiration in a similar population. The distance between the curves is the therapeutic index. The narrower the distance, the greater the overlap between the effective and toxic doses, the lower the therapeutic index, and the more dangerous the drug may be.

The therapeutic index often is used as a clinical measure in animal studies, but it is not safe enough for human use, so instead we measure the **margin of safety**, which is the LD1/ED99, or the amount of drug that is lethal (or toxic) to 1 percent of the population divided by the amount of drug that causes the desired

Therapeutic index: A measure of a drug's safety given as the ratio of the average lethal dose of a drug divided by the therapeutic dose; LD50/ED50.

Margin of safety: An index of a drug's effectiveness and safety; LD1/ED99.

STRAIGHT DOPE

Therapeutic Index of Some Drugs

- Lithium: 1.5–2
- Digoxin: 2–3
- Heroin: 6
- Alcohol: 5–10
- GHB: 8
- Phenobarbital: 10
- Methamphetamine: 10
- Cocaine: 15
- MDMA: 16
- Codeine: 20
- Methadone: 20
- Nicotine: 21
- Mescaline: 24
- Rohypnol: 30
- Ketamine: 38
- Morphine: 70
- Prozac: 100
- Valium: 100 or more
- Nitrous oxide: 150

- Aspirin: 199
- Fentanyl: 400
- Caffeine: 1,000—about 100 cups of coffee
- Psilocybin: 1,000 or more
- LSD: 1000–4800
- Remifentanil (opioid analgesic) = 33,000
- Marijuana = Some estimate it as high as 40,000 (no human fatalities ever recorded)

The estimates of the average effective dose are for a normal healthy 70-kg adult who has not developed tolerance to the drug. These estimates do not take environmental stressors or individual differences into account.

Sources: Gable, R.S. (2004). Comparison of acute lethal toxicity of commonly abused psychoactive substances. Addiction, 99: 686–96.

Advokat, C.D., Comaty, J.E., & Julien, R.M. (2014). Julien's primer of drug action (13th ed.). New York: Worth Publishers.

Stanley, T.H. (2000). Anesthesia for the 21st century. Baylor University Medical Center Proceedings, 13(1): 7–10.

Gable, R.S. (2004). Comparison of acute lethal toxicity of commonly abused psychoactive substances. Addiction, 99: 686–96.

effect in 99 percent of the test population. Because people have different enzymes and receptor levels, in a given population, the drug dose that produces a therapeutic effect in most people will usually overlap with the dose that produces a toxic effect in some people.[45] The wider the margin, or higher the therapeutic index, the pharmacologically safer the drug is.

Drug Interactions

Nearly three-fourths of Americans take at least one prescription drug.[46] Add that to the fact that most Americans drink alcohol and many also consume additional illicit drugs, and the degree for potential drug interactions is staggering.

Pharmacokinetic drug interactions occur when one drug alters the absorption, distribution, metabolism, or excretion of another. Morphine and other opioids slow the activity in the GI tract and may increase the absorption of some drugs. As one example, iron binds to Synthroid (used to treat hypothyroidism) in the GI tract and reduces its absorption, lowering Synthroid's effectiveness. An example of one drug affecting the distribution

Additive effects: The combined effect of drugs is equal to the sum of each drug's effect alone.

Synergistic: The combined effect of drugs is greater than the sum of each drug's effect alone.

Antagonism: The combined effect of drugs is less than the sum of each drug's effect alone.

of another drug is when aspirin displaces the anticoagulant warfarin from its binding to plasma proteins. This raises the amount of free warfarin in the bloodstream to dangerous levels. As previously discussed, many drugs affect the metabolism of other drugs. Finally, an example of drugs interfering with excretion occurs when carbonic anhydrase inhibitors (a class of drugs that treat glaucoma, epilepsy, and other conditions) make the urine more alkaline and consequently decrease the elimination of drugs like pseudoephedrine or amphetamines, which raises their toxicity.

Pharmacodynamic drug interactions occur when one drug alters the pharmacological effect of another, usually at the receptor site. At the receptor level, drug interactions can be additive, synergistic, or antagonistic. **Additive effects** occur when drugs taken together produce an acute effect that is equal to the sum of each drug administered separately. For example, if a person takes one aspirin and one Advil at same time to treat a headache, the effect on their pain may be the same as if they took two aspirin tablets. When two drugs are **synergistic**, the effects of taking them together are greater than the effects of taking either drug alone. Taking alcohol and Xanax together has a potentially dangerous synergistic effect on respiration and sedation. In **antagonism**, one drug (such as naloxone) cancels or blocks the effects of another drug (such as heroin). Figure 4.8 illustrates these relationships.

STRAIGHT DOPE   Food–Drug Interactions

Food can influence the way our bodies process drugs. This interaction can be beneficial or harmful. Here are just a few food–drug interactions:

- *Grapefruit juice* inhibits some CYP450 enzymes, thus raising the blood levels of drugs that are metabolized by these enzymes, sometimes to toxic levels. (This effect occurs because grapefruit contains compounds that block some of the CYP450 enzymes. Other fruit juices do not have this effect.) Occasionally, physicians will instruct their patients to take certain drugs with grapefruit juice to enhance the drug's effect. Grapefruit juice enhances the absorption of vinblastine (a chemotherapeutic agent), digoxin (used to treat congestive heart failure), losartan (a blood pressure medication), Lipitor (a cholesterol-lowering drug), and cyclosporine (an immunosuppressant drug used by organ

transplant recipients). Grapefruit juice also inhibits the metabolism of Xanax, Valium, Zoloft, Prilosec, Synthroid, Viagra, and oxycodone.

- *Milk* blocks the absorption of iron and the antibiotic tetracycline from the stomach.

- MAO inhibitors should not be taken with foods that are high in the amino acid tyramine, such as wine, cheese, yogurt, and chocolate, because it can lead to a hypertensive crisis.

- When certain antibiotics like Cefotan are taken with alcohol, the unlucky imbiber will suffer flushing, headache, sweating, a rapid heartbeat, and nausea. People taking drugs like Zantac or Tagamet also should avoid alcohol, because these antacids block the enzyme that breaks down alcohol, increasing its effects on the body.

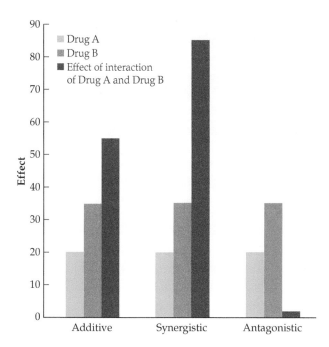

FIGURE 4.8. Different ways that drugs may interact. Ingesting one drug may increase, decrease, or otherwise change the effects of another drug.

Effects of Chronic Drug Use

Chronic drug use can have widely varied effects, depending on the drug, the physical and psychological conditions of the individual, as well as environmental factors. In some cases, individuals can take a drug every day with no significant effects on their lives. In other cases, chronic drug use can destroy a person's health, relationships, career, and bank account.

Chronic drug use can lead to both psychological and physical dependence on the drug. Physical dependence occurs when chronic drug use produces tolerance and withdrawal. Psychological dependence—craving—may be even stronger than physical dependence. Drug dependence and addiction are discussed in greater length in Chapter 17.

Tolerance

In the movie *The Princess Bride*, the hero Westley challenges the villain Vizzini to a duel of wits (Figure 4.9). Westley takes two glasses of wine and pours iocane powder, a powerful (and fictitious) poison into one of them. He invites Vizzini to use his intellect to deduce which glass the poison is in, after which they will both drink. One will survive, and the other will succumb to the poison. After Vizzini chooses and drinks, Westley informs him he chose incorrectly. Vizzini triumphantly

FIGURE 4.9. Inconceivable! *The Princess Bride* movie demonstrates the tolerance phenomenon.

crows, "You only think I guessed wrong! I switched glasses when your back was turned! Ha ha ha ha ha ha ha!" . . . and falls over dead. When questioned by Princess Buttercup, Westley explains, "They were both poisoned. I spent the last few years building up an immunity to iocane powder." You should realize that by watching this movie, you are not simply avoiding your homework; instead, you are learning a valuable lesson about the nature of drug **tolerance**, a phenomenon whereby chronic use of a drug can decrease the drug's effects.

Tolerance depends on the dose and frequency of drug use, as well as on individual factors and the environment in which it occurs. Tolerance is reversible; if a person abstains from drug use, his or her sensitivity to the drug returns. This can lead to tragic outcomes. If a person who is addicted to a drug enters rehab and goes off of the drug for a time, his or her sensitivity will return. If he or she relapses and takes the same dose of the drug as before rehab, his or her tolerance may be gone, and he or she may die of a drug overdose.

Tolerance can develop rapidly, or not at all. Tolerance to LSD occurs very quickly; users will become tolerant to its hallucinogenic effects within a day or two. Individuals can develop a tolerance to opioids and barbiturates within weeks, and may require escalating doses fairly rapidly. Those on antipsychotics never become tolerant to their effects. There are several different types of tolerance, including acute, metabolic, cellular, and behavioral tolerance.

Tolerance: A phenomenon whereby chronic use of a drug can decrease the drug's effects.

Acute tolerance. Tolerance can occur within a single exposure to a drug. For example, **acute tolerance** can occur over a night of drinking, such that a person may feel more intoxicated at a certain blood alcohol level at the beginning of the night than at the same blood alcohol level toward the end of the night.

Metabolic tolerance. Repeated use of a drug can cause the body to speed up the metabolism of the drug in order to eliminate it faster, thus reducing the amount of the drug available at the target tissue. One example of **metabolic tolerance** is the way that the body deals with alcohol. The presence of alcohol in the liver induces the synthesis of metabolizing enzymes, which breaks down alcohol faster. Alcohol is eliminated from the body at a constant rate, but in long-term, heavy drinkers, that constant rate may be faster than in someone who rarely drinks. This means that chronic drinkers must ingest larger quantities of alcohol in order to maintain the same level of drug in the body. Metabolic tolerance also occurs with chronic use of barbiturates, morphine, and nicotine.

Acute tolerance: Tolerance that occurs within a single exposure to a drug.

Metabolic tolerance: Tolerance that occurs when the body speeds up the metabolism of a drug by increasing the production of certain liver enzymes.

Cellular tolerance: Tolerance that occurs when cells adapt to the presence of a drug by changing receptor density.

Homeostasis: The tendency of the body to try to maintain equilibrium, even when faced with external changes.

Downregulation: The process by which a cell decreases the number of receptors in response to an increased amount of neurotransmitter in the synapse.

Upregulation: The process by which a cell increases the number of receptors in response to less neurotransmitter in the synapse.

Cellular tolerance. With chronic use, neurons and other cells adapt to the continued presence of a drug, either by reducing the number of receptors available, or by reducing their sensitivity to the drug. This alters the amount of drug that is able to exert its effects on the brain and body, and it can occur very rapidly—within the course of a single dose of a drug—or over time.

Acute **cellular tolerance** can occur after a single use of cocaine, amphetamines, ephedrine, and MDMA. Psychedelics such as LSD and psilocybin also demonstrate very rapid acute cellular tolerance. In many cases, people are unable to feel the effects of these hallucinogens two days in a row. Acute cellular tolerance might involve the rapid release of neurotransmitters and subsequent emptying of vesicles, which need time to be refreshed.

When tolerance occurs after regular or chronic administration of a drug, the mechanism of protracted cellular tolerance involves the change in the number of receptors available to bind neurotransmitters or hormones. This occurs because the body wants to maintain **homeostasis**. If someone were to take morphine regularly, the opioid receptors would be continually bathed in more opioids than normal, producing sedation and euphoria. To compensate for this, the body would decrease the number of opioid receptors to try to get the body back to its normal condition. This phenomenon is called **downregulation** (Figure 4.10). In downregulation, receptors are chronically exposed to more neurotransmitter, which stimulates the postsynaptic cell more than usual. In response, the number of receptors decreases. This will produce tolerance—although there is more neurotransmitter or drug available, there are fewer receptors for the drug to bind to, so the overall effect is diminished. Conversely, when less neurotransmitter is available to the receptors over a relatively long period of time, the postsynaptic cell responds by increasing the number of receptors to try to maintain the normal levels of the drug—a process called **upregulation**.

Behavioral tolerance. Every day, Chris and Alex both smoke marijuana. Each day at 4:20, Chris lights up a joint and smokes it before leaving the dorm and then wanders down to the cafeteria. Alex also smokes a joint every day, but at different times, with different people, and in different locations. Based on cellular tolerance, Chris and Alex took in the same amount of drug and should have similar tolerance. But in the real world, Chris is more tolerant to marijuana's effects. When a

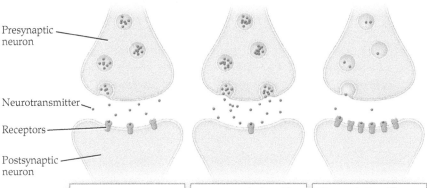

Presynaptic neuron

Neurotransmitter

Receptors

Postsynaptic neuron

Normal: An axon terminal releases a normal amount of neurotransmitter onto a normal amount of receptors on a post-synaptic surface.

Downregulation: The postsynaptic neuron is exposed to more neurotransmitter over a relatively long period of time, which stimulates the post-synaptic cell more than usual. In response, the number of postsynaptic receptors decreases.

Upregulation: The postsynaptic neuron is exposed to less neurotransmitter over a relatively long period of time. The postsynaptic cell responds by increasing the number of postsynaptic receptors to try to maintain homeostasis.

FIGURE 4.10. Cellular tolerance, down-regulation, and upregulation. Exposure to more or less neurotransmitter than usual can change the number of available receptors for that neurotransmitter, a process which can lead to cellular tolerance.

person takes a drug under similar conditions, his or her body compensates with a reflex-like response, a sort of homeostatic counter-reaction, even before the person ingests the drug.

Learning is involved in this form of **behavioral tolerance**.[47] The cues associated with drug use become associated with the effects of the drug. So just seeing a razor blade and mirror may cause someone's body to prepare for the influx of cocaine. Cocaine elevates a user's heart rate and blood pressure; when a chronic user sees the drug paraphernalia, his or her body elicits a conditioned homeostatic response—lowered heart rate and blood pressure—in order to prepare for the physiological change it has learned is coming.

There is also an element of learning to "handle yourself" while high. In a classic study, alcohol was given to rats while they walked on a treadmill. Initially, they stumbled about, but eventually they learned to walk while intoxicated. But was this due to learning or to metabolic or cellular tolerance? To find out, another group of rats was given the same number of alcohol treatments and the same number of practice sessions on the treadmill, but they received their alcohol after they walked on the treadmill. This second group of rats performed worse on the belt after they drank, compared to the rats that had become used to walking while intoxicated.[48] This study demonstrated that behavioral tolerance was at work. Because both sets of rats received

Ask yourself: A regular heavy drinker can become tolerant to ethanol's motor effects. So although his or her blood alcohol level may mean that he or she is legally drunk, he or she may be less impaired than someone who is not a regular drinker. Should DUI laws reflect behavioral impairment or be based solely on the blood alcohol level? What might be some of the consequences of your position?

the same amount of alcohol, they should have experienced the same metabolic or cellular tolerance. But because one group of rats learned to walk drunk, they grew more tolerant to the physical effects of alcohol.

Other Forms of Tolerance. If a person develops tolerance to one drug, he or she also may develop tolerance to closely related drugs, even if he or she has never taken them. This phenomenon is called **cross tolerance**. It is usually seen between members of the same

Behavioral tolerance: Tolerance that occurs when people learn to "handle themselves" while on a drug by developing resistance to the drug's effects.

Cross tolerance: Resistance to the effects of a drug as a result of tolerance previously developed to a pharmacologically similar compound.

class of drugs, and it usually means that the drugs have a common mechanism of action. As an example, someone who drinks heavily may have cross tolerance to CNS depressants and/or anesthetics, which might make it difficult to find a therapeutically effective dose during surgery. Repeated use of a drug also can cause an *increased* sensitivity to it, in a phenomenon called **reverse tolerance** (also called sensitization or kindling). Long-term cocaine users, for example, become more sensitive to the drug's motor effects.

In **select tolerance**, the body develops tolerance to different aspects of the drug at different rates. Chronic users of heroin will become rapidly tolerant to the nausea and vomiting that afflict first-time users. However, they will never develop tolerance to the constipation and pupil constriction the opioid causes. Tolerance may develop fairly rapidly to the calming and

Reverse tolerance: Also called sensitization or kindling, this is when repeated use of a drug causes increased sensitivity to its effects.

Select tolerance: When the body develops tolerance to different aspects of the drug at different rates.

Withdrawal: The physical symptoms that occur upon abrupt discontinuation of a chronically used drug.

relaxing effects of barbiturates, so a user may take a higher dose of the drug to try to recapture that sensation. Unfortunately, he or she does not develop tolerance to the depressant effects that barbiturates have on the respiratory system, which can lead to a fatal overdose.

Withdrawal

After chronic use of a drug, withdrawal can occur. **Withdrawal** is the group of symptoms that occurs upon the abrupt discontinuation or decrease in the dose of a drug. Withdrawal symptoms are typically opposite those of the direct effects of the drug. So if Ambien causes sleepiness, withdrawal will produce insomnia. Opioids have a constipating effect; those withdrawing from heroin and OxyContin may experience explosive bouts of diarrhea. Withdrawal can be a powerful factor driving drug dependence (Chapter 17), because people may keep taking a drug to avoid the physical effects of withdrawal. Just because a person goes through withdrawal, however, does not mean he or she is addicted to the drug, just that his or her body and brain have been altered by its presence. Patients on antidepressants are warned to not go "cold turkey" off their medication, because a rebound depression can occur.

Chapter Summary

- **Pharmacokinetics**
  - » Pharmacokinetics is the study of how drugs are handled by the body—how they are absorbed into the bloodstream, distributed throughout the body, transformed into different chemicals, and excreted.
  - » Absorption is the process by which drugs pass from the external world into the bloodstream. Factors that affect absorption include dosage, route of administration, solubility, and pH.
  - » The dose of a drug will influence the effect it has on the body. Dosage depends on the nature of the drug, as well as the person's body weight and any prior experience with the drug.
  - » Routes of administration include oral, rectal, vaginal, sublingual, intranasal, transdermal, and inhalation, as well as IV injection. The best route of administration for a drug depends on many factors, including the characteristics of the drug, the goals of administration, and the particular circumstances involved.
  - » Once absorbed into the bloodstream, the drug is distributed throughout the body. Generally, parts of the body that receive the most blood will have the highest concentration of the drug.

  - » A drug depot is an area of the body that can accumulate and store a drug, but where no significant biological effect of the drug occurs. Some drug depots include muscle or fat, and when drugs are bound to plasma proteins.
  - » The blood–brain barrier is a system of capillaries that prohibits most water-soluble substances from entering the brain.
  - » Metabolism is the process by which the body accepts a drug, alters it chemically, and prepares it for excretion. The liver is the most important organ for metabolism. Many drugs are metabolized by cytochrome P450 enzymes.
  - » Many factors influence the rate of metabolism, including genetics, size, age, sex, other foods or drugs, and environment.
  - » The kidney is the most important organ for elimination.
- **Pharmacodynamics**
  - » Pharmacodynamics is the study of the mechanisms by which a drug exerts its effects.
  - » Drugs exert their effects by binding to receptors, which are located on the surface of or within a cell.

» An agonist is a drug that mimics the effects—either excitatory or inhibitory—of a neurotransmitter. An antagonist does not itself cause a response; instead, it prevents a neurotransmitter from having its effect.

» A person's expectations can have a powerful effect on a drug's actions.

» A placebo is a pharmacologically inert substance that can sometimes elicit a significant therapeutic response.

» The setting in which a drug is taken can greatly influence a person's drug experience.

» Side effects are pharmacological actions that occur in addition to the main action.

» The dose-response curve measures the magnitude of a drug's effect as a function of the dose. The lower the dose necessary to produce the desired effect, the more potent the drug is. The efficacy is the maximum effect that can be produced by a drug.

» The therapeutic index and margin of safety are measures of the safety of a drug. The lower they are, the more dangerous the drug.

» Many drugs interact with each other. Pharmacokinetic drug interactions occur when one drug alters the absorption, distribution, metabolism, or excretion of another. Pharmacodynamic drug interactions occur when one drug alters the pharmacological effect of another, usually at the receptor site.

» Tolerance occurs when more drug is needed to produce the same response. There are various types of tolerance, including acute, metabolic, cellular, and behavioral.

» Withdrawal refers to the physical symptoms that occur upon abrupt discontinuation of a chronically used drug.

Key Terms

Absorption (p. 71)
Acute tolerance (p. 88)
Additive effects (p. 86)
Affinity (p. 81)
Agonist (p. 81)
Allosteric modulator (p. 81)
Antagonism (p. 86)
Antagonist (p. 81)
Area postrema (p. 77)
Behavioral tolerance (p. 89)
Bioavailability (p. 71)
Biotransformation or metabolism (p. 77)
Buccal administration (p. 75)
Cellular tolerance (p. 88)
Cross tolerance (p. 89)
Cytochrome P450 (CYP450) (p. 78)
Distribution (p. 76)
Dose-response curve (p. 84)
Downregulation (p. 88)
Drug action (p. 80)

Drug depot (p. 76)
Efficacy (p. 84)
Elimination (p. 79)
Endogenous (p. 80)
Fat-soluble (p. 71)
First-order kinetics (p. 78)
First-pass effect (p. 74)
Full agonist (p. 81)
Half-life (p. 78)
Homeostasis (p. 88)
Intramuscular (IM) injection (p. 76)
Intravenous (IV) injection (p. 76)
Inverse agonist (p. 81)
Ligand (p. 80)
Margin of safety (p. 85)
Metabolic tolerance (p. 88)
Metabolites (p. 77)
Partial agonist (p. 81)
Pharmacodynamics (p. 80)
Pharmacokinetics (p. 71)
Pharmacology (p. 71)

Placebo (p. 82)
Placebo effect (p. 82)
Plasma proteins (p. 77)
Potency (p. 84)
Reverse tolerance (p. 90)
Route of administration (ROA) (p. 72)
Select tolerance (p. 90)
Set (p. 82)
Setting (p. 83)
Side effects (p. 84)
Subcutaneous (SubQ) injection (p. 76)
Sublingual administration (p. 75)
Synergistic (p. 86)
Therapeutic index (p. 85)
Tolerance (p. 87)
Transdermal administration (p. 75)
Upregulation (p. 88)
Water-soluble (p. 71)
Withdrawal (p. 90)
Zero-order kinetics (p. 78)

Quiz Yourself!

1. Give two advantages and two disadvantages of the following routes of administration: oral, intravenous (IV), transdermal.

2. What is the name of the enzyme family of the liver that metabolizes many drugs?

3. Which of the following best relates to pharmacodynamics?

A. The route by which a drug is administered

B. The effect that food has on the absorption of the drug

C. The ability of a drug to bind to a receptor and exert an effect

D. Whether the drug undergoes the first-pass effect

4. Matching:

  1. Increases synthesis   A. Agonist

  2. Increases release   B. Antagonist

  3. Blocks reuptake

  4. Blocks postsynaptic receptors

5. True or false? The environment in which a drug is taken has very little influence on the drug's effect.

6. True or false? All side effects are harmful.

7. On the following dose-response curve for analgesia, which curve represents aspirin, which fentanyl, and which morphine?

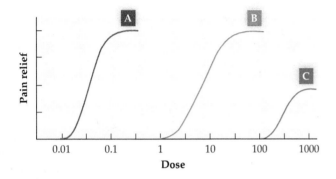

8. If the therapeutic index of a drug is 50, and the effective dose is two tablets, how many tablets would be lethal in 50 percent of the population?

9. What is the name for the phenomenon when a cell decreases the number of its receptors in response to an increased amount of neurotransmitter?

10. True or false? Withdrawal symptoms are typically opposite to those of the direct effects of the drug.

Additional Resources

Websites

ABCs of Pharmacology https://www.nigms.nih.gov/education/Booklets/medicines-by-design/Documents/Booklet-Medicines-by-Design.pdf#page=8

Videos

Two-minute neuroscience: Receptors and ligands. https://www.youtube.com/watch?v=NXOXZ-kaSVI

Books

Goodman and Gilman's Pharmacological Basis of Therapeutics is the "bible" of pharmacology. A free online version of the latest edition is available from http://freepages.school-alumni.rootsweb.ancestry.com/~dpok/Goodman%20&%20Gilman's%20The%20Pharmacological%20Basis%20of%20Therapeutics,%2012th%20Edition.pdf

Learn more with this chapter's digital tools at www.oup.com/he/rosenthal2e.

Stimulants: Cocaine and Amphetamines

CHAPTER

5

True or false?

1.
True or false? Coca-Cola once contained cocaine.

2.
True or false? Significantly more Blacks than whites use illegal stimulants.

3.
True or false? Prenatal cocaine use is worse for the unborn child than any other drug.

Answers: 1. T, 2. F, 3. F

- Recognize the factors that historically have increased or decreased the popularity of cocaine and amphetamines.
- Identify the various forms of cocaine.
- Compare the onset of action for cocaine and amphetamines when administered orally, intranasally, by smoking, and intravenously.
- Explain the mechanism of action of cocaine and amphetamines.
- Describe the physiological and psychological effects of cocaine and amphetamines.
- List the potential adverse effects from the use of cocaine and amphetamines.
- Specify the approved medical uses for cocaine and amphetamines.
- Evaluate the effects of prenatal cocaine use on a child's future behavior.
- Assess the treatment options for cocaine and amphetamine dependence.
- Describe the effects of khat and bath salts.

Stimulants are a popular class of drug that activate the sympathetic nervous system and make people feel more alert, energetic, and euphoric. Stimulants include such drugs as cocaine, amphetamines, methylphenidate (Ritalin) (Chapter 14), ephedrine, and khat. These drugs have both therapeutic and recreational uses.

Cocaine

Cocaine is a strong stimulant used mostly as a recreational drug. Public perception of the drug has fluctuated over the years; at various times it has been considered a miracle cure, a harmless euphoriant, and one of the most dangerous drugs known to humankind.

History of Cocaine

For thousands of years, South American natives would chew the leaves of the coca plant to increase their alertness and endurance at the high altitudes of the Andes Mountains. Chewing coca was an important component of religious and ceremonial occasions.[1] When Spanish missionaries arrived during the sixteenth century, they tried to ban the use of coca; they felt it was idolatrous and interfered with their ability to convert the natives to Catholicism. But the Spaniards found that without the coca, the Incans could not work as long or as hard in the mines and in the fields, so coca cultivation and chewing were restored.

In 1855, the German scientist Friedrich Gaedcke isolated the active ingredient in coca. He named it *erythroxyline*, from the genus name for coca, but we now know it as cocaine.[2] Five years later, Albert Niemann, a graduate student in Germany, improved the process for isolating and purifying cocaine. In 1884, purified cocaine became commercially available in the United States. Pharmaceutical company Parke-Davis marketed coca cigarettes, powders, and injectable mixtures that came with a hypodermic needle. They claimed that their cocaine products would "[take the place of] food, make the coward brave, the silent eloquent and render the sufferer insensitive to pain."[3]

Doctors considered cocaine to be a medical miracle. Its first medical use was as a local anesthetic. When you consider that eye surgeries were once performed without anesthesia, by strapping down patients and slicing their eyes, you can better appreciate why cocaine was considered to be such a great discovery. In 1884, William Stewart Halsted, one of the founders of Johns Hopkins Hospital, performed the first nerve block (which desensitized the nerve) using cocaine as an anesthetic. (Halsted was also the first cocaine-impaired physician on record. He was able to kick his cocaine addiction with the use of opiates . . . but subsequently

Cocaine and Amphetamines

Type of drug: Stimulant

Chemical structure:
- Cocaine: $C_{17}H_{21}NO_4$
- Amphetamine: $C_9H_{13}N$

Routes of administration:
Ingested, injected, snorted, smoked (cocaine also applied topically)

Duration of effect:
- Cocaine: 1–3 hours (powder), 5–30 minutes (crack)

- Amphetamine: 2–12 hours, depending on type

Neurotransmitters directly affected: Dopamine, norepinephrine, serotonin

Tolerance: Moderate, with some reverse tolerance

Physical dependence: moderate

Psychological dependence: Intense

Withdrawal symptoms:
Depression, anxiety, drug craving

Schedule: II

Slang:
- Cocaine (powder): coke, blow, candy, nose candy, flake, snow
- Crack cocaine: rock, hubba
- Amphetamine: speed, bennies, uppers
- Methamphetamine: meth, crystal, crystal meth, crank, ice (smokable form)

STRAIGHT DOPE | Cocaine in Popular Beverages

Cocaine intrigued French chemist Angelo Mariani. In 1863, he steeped coca leaves in wine and began selling Vin Mariani, which he promised would restore health, strength, energy, and vitality (Figure 5.1). Vin Mariani contained about 6.5 mg of cocaine per ounce of alcohol and was used by such luminaries as Thomas Edison, Czar Nicholas of Russia, Jules Verne, and Pope Leo XIII. In addition to Mariani, other enterprising men developed their own cocaine-laced wines.

One of those men was Dr. John Pemberton, an Atlanta pharmacist. During the second half of the nineteenth century, the temperance movement in the United States had intensified, and in 1886, Atlanta became first major U.S. city to prohibit the sale of alcohol. Pemberton took advantage of the alcohol ban by creating a syrup containing extracts of coca leaves and flavoring from the kola nut. In 1903, the formula was changed to use de-cocainized coca leaves, which eliminated the cocaine but kept the coca flavoring. Today, 1.9 billion servings of Coca-Cola are sold every day.

How does the Coca-Cola Company obtain the coca needed for their formula? Each year, a firm in New Jersey, sanctioned by the government and monitored by the DEA, receives 175,000 kilograms of coca leaves from Peru. Workers, who have gone through extensive background checks, remove the cocaine from the coca leaves, netting about 1,750 kilograms of cocaine (equivalent to 20 million hits of crack, worth $200 million on the illicit market). The extracted cocaine is then used to make legitimate medicines such as local anesthetics, and the de-cocainized leaves go to Coca-Cola.

Sources: Spillane, J.F. (2000). Cocaine: From medical marvel to modern menace in the United States, 1884–1920. Baltimore: Johns Hopkins University Press.

Coca-Cola at a glance: Infographic. http://www.coca-colacompany.com/our-company/infographic-coca-cola-at-a-glance/(2016)

Miller, M.W. (1994, October 17). Quality stuff: Firm is peddling cocaine, and deals are legit. Wall Street Journal, pp. A1, A14.

FIGURE 5.1. Cocaine-containing beverages. An advertisement for Vin Mariani, a cocaine-laced wine popular in the 19th century.

became addicted to morphine.) In addition to being used as an anesthetic, cocaine also was used to treat morphine addiction (rife at the time), exhaustion, depression, tuberculosis, and allergies.

QUICK HIT

In 1886, the Hay Fever Association declared cocaine to be its official remedy.

One of the reasons for cocaine's enormous popularity was Sigmund Freud. In 1884, Dr. Freud read about the benefits of cocaine in a medical journal. Freud did not know at the time that the journal was owned and controlled by the pharmaceutical company Parke-Davis and was essentially an advertising brochure. In any case, Freud tried cocaine and was an immediate advocate. His first major publication was called "Über Coca," in which he promoted the use of cocaine as a local anesthetic and as a treatment for depression, fatigue, indigestion, asthma, syphilis, autism, wasting disease, morphine addiction, and alcoholism.[4] Freud also gave cocaine to a friend to help him kick his opiate addiction, but after the friend died of cocaine poisoning, Freud's enthusiasm for the drug diminished.

Nevertheless, for many years to come, cocaine's popularity continued to soar. By 1909, the United States was importing more than 10 tons of cocaine each year. And as long as wealthy white people were using it, cocaine was perceived to be a beneficial substance. Soon, however, cocaine became popular with southern African American laborers, who had to work long shifts of uninterrupted, monotonous, arduous toil. Although opiates could offer relief from the pain, they made it difficult to maintain the energy necessary to work. Cocaine—compact, easily transported, and easily administered—allowed laborers to work long, pain-free hours and keep their energy and spirits high. Additionally, with local alcohol prohibition laws in the south, cocaine was more accessible to them than alcohol.[5]

Cocaine use soon began to spread throughout urban districts and into less reputable neighborhoods. It was blamed for the bolder attitude of a new generation of young urban Blacks.[6] In 1903, the *American Journal of Pharmacy* reported that "the negroes, the lower and immoral classes are naturally most readily influenced."[7] The perception was that most cocaine users were gamblers, prostitutes, and criminals. When ap-

Crack: A potent, smokable form of cocaine.

pearing before Congress on federal antinarcotic laws in 1914, Dr. Christopher Koch of the Pennsylvania State Pharmacy Board testified, "Most of the attacks upon the white women of the south are the direct result of a cocaine-crazed Negro brain."[8] Cocaine, the "miracle medicine," was now believed by some to transform otherwise law-abiding Black men into violent animals. Following passage in 1914 of the Harrison Narcotics Act regulating and taxing the production, importation, and distribution of opiates and cocaine, cocaine's popularity diminished for the next few decades.

By the 1970s, however, the dangers of cocaine seemed to have been forgotten by society. In 1974, a prominent drug expert (who would later become President Carter's chief drug advisor) wrote "Cocaine . . . is probably the most benign of illicit drugs currently in widespread use. At least as strong a case could be made for legalizing it as for legalizing marijuana."[9] That year, 5 million Americans had tried cocaine in one form or another. By 1982, that number had risen to more than 10 million.[10] Cocaine was associated with wealth, fame, glamour, and beauty. The conventional wisdom about cocaine said that it was safe and nonaddictive.

In 1984, however, a new form of cocaine—**crack**—appeared. The media focused on the use of crack by Black urbanites, much as it had focused on "cocaine-crazed Negroes" in the early twentieth century. Crack cocaine use was reported to be a frightening epidemic, causing addiction, violence, and crime. In the 1970s, cocaine was the glamorous drug of the rich and famous (and white), but when poor minorities consumed it, it was considered the scourge of the nation.

In 1986, Congress passed the Anti-Drug Abuse Act. The Act established mandatory minimum sentences for specific quantities of cocaine. Distribution of just 5 grams of crack cocaine carried the same sentence (a minimum of five years in federal prison) as distribution of *500* grams of powder cocaine. This law was expanded in 1988 to impose a five-year minimum prison sentence for simple possession of 5 grams of crack. Compare this to a sentence of no more than one year in prison for possession of *any* amount of powder cocaine or any other drug.[11]

There was no scientific or penological justification for this 100:1 ratio, which seemed to encourage unfair discrepancies based largely on race. Before the passage of the Anti-Drug Abuse Act, the average federal drug sentence for a Black offender was 11 percent higher than for a white offender. After 1986, the average federal drug sentence was 49 percent higher for Blacks than for whites.[12] According to the American Civil Liberties Union (ACLU), compared with whites, minorities were more likely to be prosecuted for drug offenses; when prosecuted, minorities were more likely to be convicted; and, if convicted, minorities were more likely to be sent to prison.[13]

In 2010, President Obama signed the Fair Sentencing Act into law, which reduced disparities in minimum sentences for crack and powder cocaine and eliminated the mandatory five-year sentence for simple possession of crack. As a result, the ratio went from 100:1 down to 18:1; in other words, 500 grams of powder and 28 grams of crack both carry a five-year minimum sentence.

Prevalence of Cocaine Use

Approximately 0.4 percent of the global adult population—about 19 million people age 15–64—used cocaine in 2018.[14] The United States is one of the world's largest consumers of cocaine, after the United Kingdom.[15]

QUICK HIT

Every day in the United States, over 1,800 people try cocaine for the first time. The average age of initiation is 21½ years.[16]

According to the 2019 National Survey on Drug Use and Health, in 2019, 41.4 million Americans age 12 years and older (over 15 percent of the population) had used cocaine at least once in their lives, and over 9 million had ever smoked crack.[17] About 0.7 percent of the U.S. population, or 2 million people, have used cocaine within the past month.[18] Although use has significantly declined since the 1980s, the United States remains one of the largest national cocaine markets in the world. One factor underlying the increase in cocaine use may be the fact that since 2012, the average retail price per gram of cocaine has decreased by over 28 percent from $213 per gram to $153 per gram, and its average purity has increased by 39 percent, from 46 percent pure to 64 percent pure.[19]

In terms of demographics, men are more likely than women to use cocaine.[20] African Americans are significantly less likely than whites to use powder cocaine or methamphetamine, and are equally likely to use crack cocaine.[21] Use of cocaine by U.S. high school students has decreased since the 1980s, when it was the most popular of illegal stimulants; nevertheless, in 2020, 4.1 percent of twelfth graders in the United States had ever used cocaine.[22,23]

Source and Forms of Cocaine

Cocaine comes from a plant native to South America. It can be taken in many forms, which have varying effects on the body.

Sources of Cocaine

Erythroxylum coca is a shrub native to the hot and humid eastern slopes of the Andes Mountains, from Colombia into Peru and Bolivia (Figure 5.2). About 1 percent of the weight of the leaf is cocaine, but the higher the altitude, the higher the percentage of cocaine the coca

(a)

(b)

FIGURE 5.2. Source of cocaine. (a) The coca plant grows in the Andes Mountains of South America. (b) The map shows 19 areas known for coca cultivation. (Colombia = red; Peru = green; Bolivia = blue).

Source: Map created with ArcGIS advanced software (Environmental Systems Research Institute). http://www.nature.com/articles/srep23520

(a)   (b)   (c)

FIGURE 5.3. Forms of cocaine. Cocaine comes in many forms, including coca leaves (a), powder cocaine (b), and crack (c).

plant is likely to contain. The coca leaf also contains other substances that modify the stimulating effect of the cocaine, as well as B vitamins and compounds that allow the body to stabilize blood sugar. Coca leaves contain more iron and calcium than any of the food crops grown in the Andes and may have helped the native Indians survive.[24]

Colombia leads the world in cocaine production, producing up to three-fourths of the world's annual yield.[25] Every two to three months, native farmers harvest the coca leaves, which are dried for a day or two and then crushed into small pieces. There are three main steps in the process of isolating the cocaine from the coca leaves:

- First, the crude coca paste is extracted from the leaf.
- Second, the coca paste is purified to a coke base.
- Third, the coke base is converted into cocaine HCl.[26]

Each of these steps typically occurs in a separate laboratory. Coca paste and coke base are often created in thousands of small operations across Colombia, Peru, and Bolivia, while cocaine HCl is usually produced in large, sophisticated, centralized laboratories.

Cocaine HCl is shipped from South America to the Caribbean, Miami, or other eastern ports, or is transported via land routes through Central America and Mexico. Most cocaine enters the United States across the Mexican border. People who carry cocaine across the border are called **drug mules**. They strap packages of cocaine to their waist or legs, or swallow condoms full of cocaine, to be excreted and retrieved once they cross the border.

In the early part of the twenty-first century, coca cultivation in Colombia was in a significant decline. But in 2016, the Colombian government and

Drug mule: A person who transports illegal drugs by swallowing them or concealing them in a body cavity.

the country's main insurgency group signed a peace accord. As part of this negotiation, the Colombian government changed its approach to drug policy and ended aerial spraying to eradicate coca crops. Since then, coca plant cultivation and cocaine production are at record high levels, and, consequently, the cost of cocaine in the United States has fallen.[27] Although more cocaine is produced and use has risen in the past few years, cocaine use hasn't increased as sharply as production has, since cocaine seizures are also at a record high.[28]

Forms of Cocaine

Cocaine can be taken in many forms. The leaves of the coca plant can be chewed, cocaine powder can be snorted or injected, and freebase or crack can be smoked (Figure 5.3).

Coca Leaves. A typical coca leaf contains only a small amount of cocaine, just enough to give a coffee-like lift. Users will chew the leaves, along with an alkaline substance such as ash or lime (a mineral derived from limestone), in order to enhance absorption. Most men in the Andes take cocaine this way, and there is very little abuse with this method of administration.

Powder Cocaine. Powder cocaine is water soluble and can be administered orally, intranasally, by intravenous (IV) injection, or dissolved in solution to be applied topically. It cannot be smoked, because it breaks down at high temperatures. Powder cocaine contains a much higher percentage of cocaine than do coca leaves. Users snort cocaine from a tiny spoon, or from lines that are laid out on a hard, flat surface such as a mirror. Lines are typically one-eighth of an inch wide and one to two inches long, and inhaled through a straw or a rolled-up piece of paper. Users might snort 25–100 mg at a time.

Powder cocaine is typically cut or diluted with other white powders such as cornstarch, talcum powder, lactose, mannitol, chalk, Epsom salts, laundry detergent, meat tenderizer, or laxatives. Local anesthetics, caffeine, or amphetamines also may be cut into the cocaine. In 2011, the Drug Enforcement Agency (DEA) reported that over 80 percent of cocaine shipments seized entering the United States were cut with levamisole, a drug used to treat parasitic worm infections in humans and animals.[29] Levamisole enhances the psychoactive effects of cocaine and also prevents the bone marrow from producing white blood cells.

Freebase. When cocaine HCl is separated from the acid—when you *free* the *base*—its lipid solubility increases, and it more easily crosses the blood–brain barrier. The alkaline form also vaporizes at a lower temperature than powder cocaine, so it can be smoked. To produce freebase, cocaine HCl is heated in water with a base. An organic solvent such as ether is added, and the liquid separates into layers, with cocaine dissolved in ether in the top layer. The top layer can be drawn off with an eyedropper and placed in a dish to evaporate, leaving almost pure cocaine crystals. The result is a base that is smokable, lipid soluble, and highly flammable.

QUICK HIT

Comedian Richard Pryor learned how flammable freebase was when he set himself on fire smoking it in 1980; he had burns over more than half of his body.

Crack. Freebase is potent and intense, but dangerously flammable. Therefore, enterprising drug users developed a technique to create a safer form of freed cocaine base. Rather than extracting pure cocaine, powder cocaine is dissolved in baking soda and water, and the mixture is boiled and cooled. The solids settle and are then removed, dried, and broken into small yellowish-white chunks that are smoked in a glass pipe. The chunks make a cracking sound when heated, giving the drug its name. Crack is safer than freebase in terms of flammability, and gives a quick and more intense high than powder.

Pharmacokinetics of Cocaine

The effects of cocaine depend on how much of the drug enters the brain. The dose, route of administration, distribution throughout the body, metabolism, and elimination all influence cocaine's effect.

Cocaine doses commonly range between 50 and 150 mg, but this depends on the purity of the drug administered. The amount of cocaine that is absorbed into the bloodstream also depends on the route of administration.

Routes of Administration

The way cocaine is administered has a powerful effect on how easily it enters the bloodstream and makes its way to the brain (Table 5.1).

Topical. Cocaine may be dissolved into solution or made into a paste for medical use as a local anesthetic. Its peak anesthetic effects occur within two to five minutes, and its effects last for up to an hour. The cocaine is then absorbed into the bloodstream and can cause systemic effects.

Oral. Cocaine is not particularly well absorbed into the bloodstream when taken orally, because it constricts the blood vessels of the mouth (vasoconstriction) and is broken down in the acidic stomach. When mixed with an alkaline substance, absorption in the mouth is relatively equal to that of the intranasal route (about 20–30 percent), but the cocaine-containing juice from the leaves that is swallowed and absorbed in the stomach undergoes the first-pass effect in the liver, which metabolizes 70–80 percent of the cocaine before it reaches the brain.

TABLE 5.1.   The Influence of the Route of Administration on the Pharmacokinetics of Cocaine

Route of Administration	Onset of Action	Peak Effect	Duration of Action	Strength of Effect
Oral/chewed leaf	10–30 minutes	60 minutes	1–2 hours	Minor
Snorted/powder	3–5 minutes	15–30 minutes	1–2 hours	Moderate
Injection	15–30 seconds	3–5 minutes	10–30 minutes	Very potent
Smoked	7–8 seconds	1–5 minutes	5–30 minutes	Very potent

Sources: Hanson, G.R., Venturelli, P.J., & Fleckenstein, A.E. (2012). Drugs and Society (11th ed.). Burlington, MA: Jones and Bartlett Learning.
Hecht, A. (2011). Understanding drugs: Cocaine and crack. New York: Chelsea House.
Burnett, L.B. (2012). Cocaine toxicity in emergency medicine. http://emedicine.medscape.com/article/813959-overview

Snorting (Insufflation). Cocaine's potent vasoconstricting effects limit its absorption when snorted. Cocaine crystals are absorbed across the mucous membranes of the nose and throat, pass into the bloodstream, and reach the brain within several minutes.

Smoking. Powder cocaine cannot be effectively smoked. Cocaine HCl does not vaporize until it reaches 197 degrees, at which point the drug decomposes. Crack cocaine, however, can be smoked because it vaporizes at around 98 degrees, below the boiling point of water. Users often smoke crack out of a glass tube or pipe (Figure 5.4). Crack is rapidly absorbed into the bloodstream of the lungs, from where it travels to the left side of the heart and directly on to the brain (and other organs) within seconds; by this route of administration the drug reaches the brain even faster than injection.

Injection. Injection leads to the highest blood levels in the shortest amount of time, although it actually takes longer for injected cocaine to reach the brain than smoked cocaine. The reason injected cocaine takes longer to reach the brain is that it must first travel in the bloodstream to the right side of the heart before being pumped to the lungs, sent to the left side of the heart, and then finally passed on to the brain and other organs of the body.

FIGURE 5.4: Crack pipes. The glass pipes in which "love roses" are sold at gas stations and convenience marts are often used as crack pipes.

Distribution, Metabolism, and Elimination

Once it enters the bloodstream, cocaine is widely distributed through body tissues, and it is metabolized by the cytochrome P450 system of the liver (a family of enzymes that metabolize many drugs). Liver and blood enzymes degrade about half of the dose of cocaine in about an hour, although the activity of metabolic enzymes differs from person to person. Excreted in the urine, sweat, saliva, and breast milk, cocaine metabolites are detectable in urine for two to three days after administration, and for up to two weeks in chronic users.

Mechanism of Action of Cocaine

In addition to blocking sodium channels, which interferes with the transmission of action potentials in pain pathways, cocaine exerts its effects in the body by blocking the reuptake of dopamine, norepinephrine, and serotonin. Remember, when a neurotransmitter is released from the presynaptic neuron, it crosses the synapse and binds to a receptor on the postsynaptic cell (Chapter 3). Its effect on the cell then needs to be terminated. One of the major mechanisms of termination is a process called reuptake, whereby a transporter molecule picks up the neurotransmitter from the synapse and carries it back into the presynaptic neuron to be recycled. Therefore, if reuptake is inhibited, the neurotransmitter stays bound to the receptor longer, which increases its postsynaptic effects (Figure 5.5).

Many of cocaine's effects are due to elevated dopamine levels. Cocaine increases dopamine levels in the basal ganglia, prefrontal cortex, ventral tegmental area (VTA), and nucleus accumbens (Chapter 3):

- The basal ganglia help to control motion, and elevated dopamine levels in the basal ganglia may lead to repetitive and compulsive movements.
- Dopamine in the prefrontal cortex influences planning, problem-solving social behavior, and decision-making.
- The dopaminergic pathway that runs from the VTA to the nucleus accumbens is involved with reward and motivation, and it is thought to be key to dopamine's role in addiction.

Serotonin also plays a role in the rewarding and addictive aspects of cocaine. When rats that genetically lack a dopamine transporter but retain serotonin receptors receive cocaine, they still self-administer the drug.[30] Serotonin also is involved in regulating mood, sleep, appetite, and body temperature, all of which are affected by cocaine.

In addition, cocaine raises synaptic levels of norepinephrine, which is the primary neurotransmitter of the sympathetic nervous system. Norepinephrine prepares the body and mind for emergencies—it makes the heart beat faster, dilates the bronchi, brings glucose and oxygen to the muscles, and helps with attention and arousal. Cocaine also increases the effects of the excitatory neurotransmitter glutamate on reward synapses in the VTA. By making dopaminergic neurons more responsive to glutamate, cocaine causes a hypersensitivity that may enhance addiction.[31]

Acute Effects of Cocaine

Cocaine has powerful physiological, psychological, and behavioral effects. Some of these effects are shown in Figure 5.6.

Physiological Effects of Cocaine at Low and Moderate Doses

Cocaine is **sympathomimetic**—it mimics the effects of the sympathetic nervous system and:

- Increases heart rate, respiratory rate, and blood pressure
- Promotes blood clot formation
- Dilates bronchi and the pupils
- Constricts blood vessels
- Increases body temperature and sweating
- Mobilizes the breakdown of fat
- Causes dry mouth and headache
- Decreases appetite
- Delays the onset of sleep

Individuals taking cocaine move and fidget more than usual, and they may itch and pick at their

Sympathomimetic: A substance whose actions mimic those of the sympathetic nervous system.

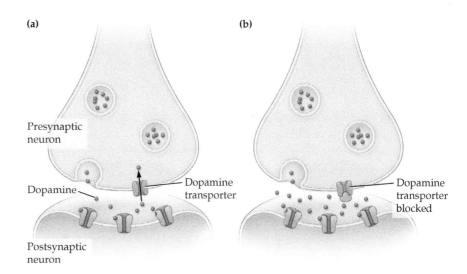

FIGURE 5.5. **The mechanism of action of cocaine.** In normal transmission (a), dopamine is released from the presynaptic neuron, crosses the synapse, and binds to the postsynaptic receptor, exerting its effects. These effects are terminated, in part, because dopamine undergoes reuptake—it is removed from the synapse and taken back into the presynaptic neuron via a transporter protein. When cocaine is present (b), dopamine remains in the synapse longer because the transporter protein is blocked.

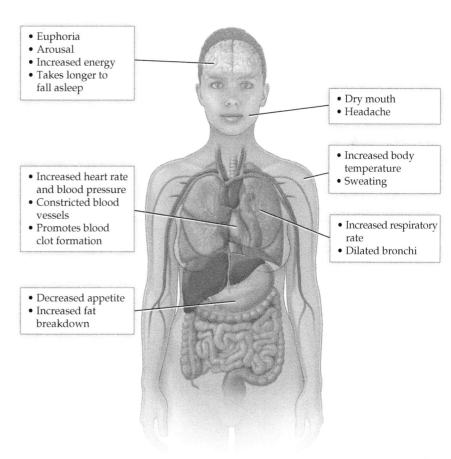

FIGURE 5.6. **Acute effects of cocaine.**

skin. Some people report heightened sexual interest, but expectation strongly affects a person's response to a drug.[32] This means that if someone expects to become sexually aroused while on cocaine, arousal may be more likely.

Behavioral and Psychological Effects of Cocaine at Low and Moderate Doses

Cocaine produces euphoria, elation, arousal, and heightened energy and endurance. Individuals taking cocaine sometimes become very talkative and sociable. They may experience inflated self-esteem and self-absorption, and become overconfident in their abilities. Cocaine can enhance physical strength and increase a person's performance on tasks that require physical endurance. Users of cocaine may become engrossed in repetitive and compulsive physical behaviors, such as sorting and resorting items, or cleaning a small area over and over.

Cocaine users can focus more intently and feel mentally sharp. However, those who think that cocaine will help their academic performance are bound to be disappointed. Cocaine and other stimulants have a negative effect on cognitive performance and can lead to impairments in memory, attention, abstract thinking, spatial processing, and the ability to manipulate information.[33]

Medical and Therapeutic Uses of Cocaine

Cocaine is a schedule II drug (Chapter 1). It is approved for use as a local anesthetic. Other local anesthetic drugs such as lidocaine and Novocain do not stimulate the central nervous system and are preferred for most medical uses. But, since cocaine is well absorbed in mucous membranes, it is still used in oral and eye surgeries. Cocaine's vasoconstrictor properties also make it effective for oral and facial surgery, as it diminishes bleeding in these highly vascular areas. Every year, cocaine is used for tens of thousands of operations in the United States.

Myocardial infarction: Also called a heart attack, a myocardial infarction is when the arteries supplying blood to the heart become blocked, and the heart muscle is starved of oxygen. During a heart attack, the heart continues to pump blood throughout the body.

Cardiac arrest: The normal electrical rhythm of the heart fails, preventing the heart from pumping blood to the body, which can lead to sudden death.

Formication: The delusion that insects are crawling on or under one's skin; usually associated with high doses of cocaine or amphetamines.

Adverse Effects of Cocaine

Cocaine causes an intense, short-term high. It also, however, produces some powerful adverse effects. Physically, cocaine can cause overstimulation of the central nervous system and the cardiovascular system, as well as damage to other organs. Cocaine lowers the threshold for seizure, and cocaine users are 14 times more likely to experience a stroke than nonusers.[34] Cocaine also can suppress the flow of blood to cardiac tissue, which can lead to dangerous cardiovascular situations. Cocaine increases a person's risk of arrhythmias (irregular heart rhythms), **myocardial infarction**, and **cardiac arrest**. Approximately one-quarter of heart attacks in people age 19–45 years can be attributed to frequent use of cocaine.[35] Because there is significant individual variation in the uptake and metabolism of cocaine, a lethal dose is hard to estimate, but most cocaine-related deaths due to heart-related malfunctions occur in patients who use low or modest levels of cocaine.[36] In addition, cocaine also can lead to perforation of the nasal septum, stomach, and intestinal wall; pulmonary edema; and renal failure.

Cocaine can lead to irritability, hostility, anxiety, fear, and restlessness. Cocaine users may also suffer from more serious psychological effects, including depression, aggression, and paranoia. They may be confused and disoriented and experience delusions or hallucinations. Some users undergo delusional parasitosis, also called **formication**, a delusion that insects are crawling in and under one's skin.

Different routes of administration can lead to distinctive side effects.[37] When the cocaine reaches the gastrointestinal (GI) tract after oral administration, vasoconstriction can reduce the blood supply to the large intestines, leading to tissue damage. Bacteria can then infect the dead and dying tissue and cause the intestines to decompose. Those who snort cocaine may experience nosebleeds, runny nose, and/or perforation of the nasal septum, the wall that runs down the middle of the nose, separating the two halves. Injection of cocaine can lead to allergic reactions at the site of injection, as well as increased risk of HIV or hepatitis from shared needles. Not surprisingly, smoking crack is hard on the lungs. The smoke irritates the lung tissue and causes inflammation that is not responsive to antibiotics. This inflammation can give rise to chest pains, difficulty breathing, bleeding from the lungs, scarring, and permanent damage. Sharing a crack pipe can also transmit diseases such as tuberculosis. And, because a user's lips are in close contact with the burning bowl, smoking cocaine can cause cracked and blistered lips.[38]

Overdose. Cocaine use can be fatal. Cocaine's therapeutic index is about 15, which means that a dose 15 times larger than the typical recreational dose will be fatal in 50 percent of users.[39] Cocaine greatly increases blood pressure and heart rate, which can cause stroke, cardiac arrest, or even rupture the aorta.[40] Cocaine overdose deaths have risen sharply in the United States in recent years (Figure 5.7). In 2019, over 22 percent of all drug overdose deaths involved cocaine. The increase is mostly due to the presence of opioids,

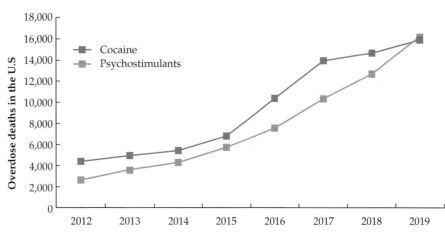

FIGURE 5.7. Annual overdose deaths for cocaine and psychostimulants in the United States.

Source: Centers for Disease Control and Prevention. (2020). Drug overdose deaths in the United States, 1999–2018. NCHS Data Brief, no 356. Hyattsville, MD: National Center for Health Statistics.

specifically fentanyl, either through poly-drug use or because fentanyl was mixed into the cocaine without the user's knowledge.[41,42,43] And unlike opioids, there is no way to reverse the effects of a cocaine overdose.

Drug Interactions. Cocaine often is taken with alcohol and other drugs, which can heighten the danger and lead to an increased risk of death. Between 30 and 60 percent of those who use cocaine combine it with alcohol.[44]

- When taken with cocaine, alcohol forms a new compound in the body called cocaethylene (CE). CE has pharmacological properties similar to cocaine, but it causes greater euphoria, enhances stimulation of the cardiovascular system, and is more toxic. Cocaine and alcohol taken together increase a person's risk of immediate death 18–25 times over that of cocaine alone, usually due to cardiovascular complications, hepatotoxicity, convulsions, and behaviors leading to injury.[45]
- Snorting or injecting heroin immediately after using cocaine (a combination called a *speedball*) may enhance the effects of both drugs. Those addicted to crack sometimes use heroin to reduce the effects of withdrawal.
- Nicotine, like cocaine, produces hypertension and tachycardia (an abnormally rapid heart rate). The combination of these drugs is particularly hard on the cardiovascular system. Nicotine also seems to increase the euphoric effects of cocaine.[46]
- The antiepileptic phenytoin, which also treats some cardiac arrhythmias, enhances cocaine's effects.

- When taken with cocaine, monoamine oxidase (MAO) inhibitors and tricyclic antidepressants can produce a large increase in norepinephrine, which can lead to a hypertensive crisis.
- When combined with cocaine, capsaicin (found in pepper spray) can lead to potentially fatal consequences, perhaps due to intense activation of the sympathetic nervous system.[47]

Chronic Effects of Cocaine

Long-term use of cocaine has negative effects on the brain and body. Its effects depend on the amount and form of the drug, and the length of time the drug has been used.

Tolerance

Chronic use of cocaine leads to both tolerance and reverse tolerance (also known as sensitization). Chronic users of cocaine develop reduced responsiveness to cocaine's euphoric effects and to some of its stimulant effects. This acute tolerance can develop after a single use. Prior administration of cocaine, however, *increases* a person's susceptibility to effects such as hyperthermia, convulsions, and stereotyped movements.

Withdrawal

Abrupt discontinuation of many drugs of abuse, such as alcohol and opioids, produces withdrawal symptoms. It is unclear, however, whether this occurs with cocaine. An old, yet commonly cited reference reported that cocaine withdrawal was associated with three distinct phases—crash, withdrawal, and extinction—and symptoms could last for many weeks.[48] Other studies, however, have found that withdrawal is fairly short-lived.[49]

Most often, cocaine withdrawal is associated with short-term depressed mood, appetite changes, sleep disturbances, lethargy, and irritability.[50] Users may experience **craving**—a powerful desire for the drug—particularly when they encounter cues, such as people, places, or paraphernalia, that they associate with cocaine. These triggers even can lead to physiological responses similar to effects of cocaine—arousal, palpitations, chest tightness, ringing in ears, or the taste of cocaine in the back of the throat. Although it is by no means pleasant, cocaine withdrawal is not as intense or dangerous as withdrawal from other barbiturates, opioids, or alcohol.

Adverse Effects from Chronic Use of Cocaine

Long-term cocaine use may speed up the aging of the brain, with some abusers in their thirties exhibiting changes in the brain normally seen in individuals who are over 60.[51] Individuals who are addicted to cocaine are also likely to have higher rates of brain shrinkage than those who do not use. These losses are seen in the prefrontal and temporal cortices, areas important for decision-making and memory (Chapter 3).[52]

Sexual dysfunction, associated with decreased sexual performance and a loss of desire, is also common in heavy users. In addition, chronic cocaine use may increase a person's risk of developing an autoimmune disease such as lupus or scleroderma, perhaps due to the contaminant levamisole.[53,54,55] Chronic use of cocaine also can lead to scarring and death of heart tissue, and cause tears in the aorta, the main vessel leaving the heart.[56] Rates of premature death are up to eight times higher in chronic users than in the general population.

Effects of Cocaine when Taken during Pregnancy

Pregnant women who use cocaine have higher rates of miscarriage and stillbirths. Cocaine readily crosses the placenta and affects the developing fetus. A potent vasoconstrictor, cocaine constricts blood flow to the placenta, decreasing the amount of oxygen and nutrients that are delivered to the fetus. The drug also may cause the placenta to separate prematurely from the uterine wall, which shuts off the fetus's blood supply and can lead to premature labor. Cocaine reduces the mother's appetite, and poor maternal nutrition can slow fetal growth.

Babies born of women who used cocaine during pregnancy may have a low birth weight and a smaller head than babies of non-drug-using mothers. As they grow, however, the brains and body sizes of these babies generally catch up to those of their peers. Cocaine babies are more irritable, jittery, and overly sensitive to sensory stimuli at birth, but this too usually improves as they develop. These babies may have motor problems and shorter attention spans, as well as a higher risk of seizures and sudden infant death syndrome.

Cocaine Dependence and Addiction

Cocaine's addictive potential is a bit paradoxical. Until as recently as the 1970s, cocaine was not considered to be addictive. For many years, addiction was defined by physical withdrawal symptoms, and cocaine users do not experience dramatic withdrawal. Most people who try cocaine do not become addicted to or abuse the drug.[62] Some do not enjoy the experience—they feel too anxious or dislike the loss of control. For others, the drug is too expensive or difficult to find. The social and legal consequences of cocaine use deter others.

Although cocaine is not extremely physically addictive, its potential for psychological dependence is high, and about 10–15 percent of those who use cocaine intranasally eventually become cocaine abusers (addiction rates are higher when cocaine is smoked or injected). There are over 1 million actively dependent cocaine users in the United States, many of whom have experienced substantial social and economic impairment due to its use (Chapter 17).[63]

Cocaine has powerful reinforcing effects. One way to test the addictive potential of a drug is to train an animal so that when it presses a bar, it can self-administer the drug. Once the animal becomes dependent on the substance, the scientist increases the number of times the animal needs to press the bar to receive the drug. The researcher will continue to raise the number. With most drugs, at some point the animal seems to decide it's not worth the effort and stops pressing the bar. Not with cocaine. One chimp pressed the bar 12,800 times in his fruitless quest for more cocaine.[64] Additionally, when allowed to self-administer drugs, most animals will not overdose on alcohol, nicotine, or heroin, but they will self-administer cocaine until they die. One population of rats was taught to bar press to self-administer a drug. Half received heroin; the other half received cocaine. The rats that received heroin became dependent and incorporated their heroin use into their normal lifestyle of eating, sleeping, and grooming. For most of them, their body weight remained normal and

Craving: A powerful desire to use a drug.

Critical Evaluation

What are the long-term effects of prenatal cocaine use on children's future behavior?

Conventional wisdom holds that cocaine use by pregnant mothers will cause lifelong deficits in children born to these mothers. However, studies that control for many factors seem to contradict this wisdom. A study of over 4,000 cocaine-exposed children age 4–13 years showed no statistically significant difference in IQ scores or language development compared to kids whose mothers never used the drug.[57] A meta-analysis of studies on cocaine children found that after controlling for confounders such as the use of other drugs and prenatal care, there was no consistent negative association between exposure to cocaine in the womb and later physical growth, developmental test scores, language, or child behavior.[58,59] As you critically evaluate the effects of prenatal cocaine exposure, consider these issues.

Confounding factors. How can you determine if any deficits in the child are due to cocaine, or due to other factors? For instance, a pregnant woman who smokes crack is probably not taking her prenatal vitamins or eating only the freshest organic food. How might you control for the effects of poverty, access to health care, and parenting skills? Women who use cocaine also drink more alcohol and smoke more cigarettes than women who do not use cocaine. And crack babies' most common problems—low birth weight and subtle developmental delays in childhood—are the same as those experienced by children of women who smoke cigarettes. A number of studies suggest that many of the perinatal adverse effects commonly attributed to cocaine are actually caused by the use of other drugs taken during pregnancy.[60] Finally, what problems, if they exist, might result from labeling these children as handicapped, thus creating a self-fulfilling prophecy?

Severity of the problem. Cocaine's effects on the fetus are comparable to those of tobacco and are less severe than those of alcohol.[61] In addition, many more women smoke tobacco and drink alcohol during pregnancy than use cocaine. How do we best address the issue of any prenatal drug use?

Accuracy of studies on drug use and childhood behaviors. When evaluating the development of children whose mothers used cocaine, it is possible that more dysfunctional caregivers may be less responsible in bringing their children to be assessed, which could underplay the effects of cocaine. On the other hand, caregivers of children with obvious impairments may be more willing to stay in the program for assessments, which would overestimate the risk of poor outcomes. How can we best take these factors into account? How truthful are caregivers likely to be when reporting drug use? Should we trust self-reports, as we did in the past, or should we rely on the more invasive, yet more accurate hair drug tests?

Ask yourself: Pregnant women who use illegal drugs, but not alcohol or tobacco, commonly lose custody of their children. The organization CRACK (Children Requiring a Caring Kommunity) raises money to give mothers with a history of illegal drug use financial incentives to undergo sterilization. There is not a similar drive to sterilize women who smoke or drink while pregnant, and teachers do not dread having a "tobacco kid" in their class. Why do you think these discrepancies exist?

they were generally healthy. The rats that were given access to cocaine, however, did nothing but press the bar to receive cocaine. They did not eat, groom, or mate; they did nothing but self-administer cocaine until they died.[65] Cocaine is similarly reinforcing in humans and psychologically addictive, especially with frequent use.

Treatment of Cocaine Addiction

Some who seek relief from cocaine addiction enter an inpatient facility for intense treatment with medical supervision and psychological counseling. Others enter outpatient programs, remaining at home but traveling frequently to the facility for treatment. Outpatient programs are less expensive than inpatient rehabilitation facilities, but the user remains in his or her everyday environment, which may expose him or her to drug cues. Addicts also can seek out self-help programs such as Cocaine Anonymous or Narcotics Anonymous. Treatment for addiction is described in more detail in Chapter 18.

The Food and Drug Administration (FDA) has not approved any medications for cocaine addiction, but some substances have been shown to help alleviate cocaine cravings. Disulfiram (Antabuse) may reduce cravings, and may be particularly effective in addicts with a particular genotype.[66] The heart medication propranolol also eases withdrawal symptoms, and modafinil, a drug used to treat narcolepsy, may alleviate cravings.

Ibogaine is a naturally occurring psychoactive substance found in the roots of a shrub in western Africa (Chapter 6). Indigenous peoples use low doses of ibogaine to alleviate fatigue, hunger, and thirst, and in higher doses as part of religious rituals. Anecdotal reports claim that a single dose of the drug decreases cravings and assists with abstinence from addictive substances, including cocaine and opioids.[67] Tests in animals support this finding,[68,69] and human tests have similarly shown that a single injection of ibogaine significantly decreased craving for cocaine and heroin during inpatient detoxification and reduced symptoms of depression. Potential adverse effects, however, may limit ibogaine's clinical usefulness.[70,71,72]

Scientists also are investigating the use of a vaccine to prevent cocaine addiction (Chapter 18). In this vaccine, antibodies bind to cocaine, making it too large to cross the blood–brain barrier and thus preventing its euphoric effects. Administration of the cocaine vaccine reduced cocaine use in 38 percent of patients in one trial.[73] Patients who attained high levels of IgG anticocaine antibodies refrained from cocaine use more than patients who did not make sufficient antibodies. Some subjects, however, began using massive amounts of cocaine in efforts to overcome the effects of the vaccine.[74] In addition, some subjects were unable to make sufficient antibodies after receiving the vaccine to produce an effect.

Gene therapy may be potential treatment for addiction. Butyrylcholinesterase (BChE) is an enzyme that breaks down cocaine into harmless byproducts. Normally, though, the enzyme does not work quickly and does not linger long enough in the bloodstream to help those addicted to the drug. Scientists edited the DNA of skin stem cells of mice so that they would synthesize a modified form of the enzyme that is 4,400 times more potent than the naturally occurring enzyme. They then implanted these genetically modified stem cells back into the mice, who subsequently sought cocaine less than the untreated animals, and were able to withstand normally fatal doses of the drug.[75]

Amphetamines

Globally, amphetamines are more popular than cocaine, in part because their effects are more potent and sustained, they can be administered by several routes, and they can be easily and inexpensively synthesized.[76] As many as 27 million people around the world use amphetamine, methamphetamine, and other amphetamine-type stimulants.[77]

QUICK HIT

"Amphetamine" has a double meaning in Chinese—besides the name for the drug, *an fei ta ming* also means "Is this not his fate?"

History of Amphetamines

For more than 5,000 years, *ma huang* (Figure 5.8) has been used to treat asthma and other breathing problems. *Ma huang* is the Chinese name for the leafless *Ephedra sinica* shrub, which grows throughout the desert regions of Asia and North America. Ephedrine, the active ingredient of *ma huang*, was isolated in 1885 (the other active ingredient is pseudoephedrine).[78] Ephedrine is less fat-soluble than amphetamine and cocaine, so it has fewer psychostimulating effects, although it does increase heart rate and blood pressure. Ephedrine has been used for many years as

FIGURE 5.8. *Ma huang.* The Chinese herb *ma huang* is the source of the stimulant ephedrine.

an appetite suppressant, and in the nineteenth century, it became a popular and effective treatment for asthma.

In 1887, Romanian chemist Lazar Edeleano, seeking a more efficient asthma treatment than ephedrine, synthesized amphetamine. He called the substance "phenylisopropylamine" but later switched the name to "alpha-methylphenethylamine," which was shortened to "amphetamine."[79] Despite Edeleano's work, amphetamine received little attention and languished on the shelf until 1927, when UCLA researcher Gordon Alles investigated its therapeutic potential.

Alles resynthesized amphetamine, injected himself, and, feeling rather delightful, declared the drug a success. He began injecting asthma sufferers with amphetamine to test its effects. Although it proved disappointing in treating asthma, amphetamine was marketed in the 1930s to treat congestion, narcolepsy, and depression.[80] The drug also became popular in the 1930s with college students cramming for exams, dieters, long-distance drivers, and factory workers, who found that amphetamine decreased their appetite and their need for sleep. During World War II, 200 million tablets were supplied to U.S. troops to keep them alert. Amphetamine was considered a miracle drug; by the 1940s, there were 39 clinical conditions for which amphetamine could be used, including asthma, obesity, narcolepsy, alcoholism, bed-wetting, depression, schizophrenia, radiation sickness, morphine and cocaine addiction, head injuries, seasickness, and persistent hiccups.

Ask yourself: Novelist Chuck Palahniuk said, "Amphetamines are the most American drug. You get so much done. You look terrific, and your middle name is Accomplishment." Do you think amphetamine's enduring popularity is because it seemingly supports so many American values?

Henry Ford considered giving amphetamines to his employees to keep his workers focused and working longer hours. Hollywood producers used it as a chemical tool to reduce budgets and keep stars animated for long hours. Judy Garland, who played Dorothy in *The Wizard of Oz*, was regularly given amphetamines to keep her energy high and her weight low, and to help her get through 12-hour all-singing, all-dancing shoots. Producers then provided her with barbiturates to help her sleep (Figure 5.9).[81]

FIGURE 5.9. Judy Garland. Garland, who played Dorothy in *The Wizard of Oz*, was regularly given amphetamines to keep her energy high. Producers then provided her with barbiturates to counteract the amphetamines and help her sleep. Garland ultimately died from a barbiturate overdose in 1969.

STRAIGHT DOPE

Famous People Who Have Used Amphetamines

For many years in the mid-twentieth century, amphetamines were socially accepted, and many famous authors, actors, musicians, and politicians partook of the drug. In Ian Fleming's book *Moonraker*, James Bond popped a pill and said, "Benzedrine. It's what I shall need if I'm going to keep my wits about me tonight." David O. Selznick took amphetamines while filming *Gone with the Wind*, and choreographer-director Bob Fosse's amphetamine use was portrayed in his autobiographical movie *All That Jazz*. President John F. Kennedy used speed, as did Winston Churchill. Adolf Hitler injected himself with methamphetamine up to eight times a day.

Sources: Farren, M. (2010). Speed Speed Speedfreak: A fast history of amphetamine. Port Townsend, WA: Feral House.

Eventually, the medical community became aware of the dangers of amphetamine use. The phrase "speed kills" became popular, and amphetamines began to fall out of favor . . . until the 1990s, when methamphetamine, a more potent form of the drug, soared in popularity. In 1984, fewer than 4 million Americans had tried meth; by 1999, that number swelled to more than 9 million. Today, that number is over 16 million.[83]

Prevalence of Amphetamine Use

In the United States, more than 18 million people age 12 years and up have used stimulants in the past year.[84] Some 4.9 million people report having misused prescription stimulants, such as Adderall, Vyvanse, or Ritalin, in the past year.[85] The United States consumes 85 percent of the world's medically prescribed amphetamines, with 80 percent being prescribed to those under the age of 18. Stimulant drugs used to treat attention-deficit/hyperactivity disorder (ADHD) are discussed in Chapter 14. Although methamphetamine is legally available by prescription, most methamphetamine used in the United States is produced and distributed illicitly. About 2 million people each year report illicit methamphetamine use.[86] Use is most common on the West Coast and in the Midwest, and Black people are least likely to use methamphetamine (Figure 5.10).[87,88]

Source and Forms of Amphetamines

Amphetamines come in a variety of chemical forms. Amphetamine (Benzedrine) is a mixture of both right- and left-handed amphetamine molecules. The left-handed derivative (levo-amphetamine) raises blood pressure, opens nasal passages, and causes headaches, but does not have significant mood-elevating effects. The right-handed isomer—dextro-amphetamine (Dexedrine)—has stronger effects in the brain, elevates mood, and enhances energy. Replacing a hydrogen atom on dextro-amphetamine with a methyl group

(thus producing methamphetamine) increases its lipid solubility and potency and leads to even stronger effects in the brain.

The components to produce methamphetamine are readily available. Most labs use pseudoephedrine or ephedrine, available in over-the-counter (OTC) cold and sinus medicines, as the key chemical precursors. In 1996, Congress passed the Comprehensive Methamphetamine Control Act, placing pseudoephedrine under the same regulations that apply to ephedrine. Controls were tightened further with the Combat Methamphetamine Epidemic Act (CMEA) of 2006. These laws regulate the sale of any products that contain pseudoephedrine and ephedrine. These drugs are kept behind the pharmacy counter, purchases are recorded, and sales often are limited to three packages per customer.

Regulations that target small-scale producers—such as those that limit access to cold and sinus medicine—have not led to a decrease in methamphetamine production, although they are still beneficial given that the chemicals used to make methamphetamine are corrosive, highly flammable, and toxic (Figure 5.11).[89] Instead, amphetamine production has shifted from homegrown labs to drug trafficking organizations in Mexico.[90] It is now estimated that as much as 90 percent of methamphetamine consumed in the United States is produced in large Mexican labs.[91] Laws that target large-scale producers have been shown to reduce methamphetamine-related arrests and hospital admissions more so than regulations that target small-scale, independent producers.[92] In part due to the shift away from homegrown production, the purity of amphetamine has increased, from 39 percent pure in 2008 to

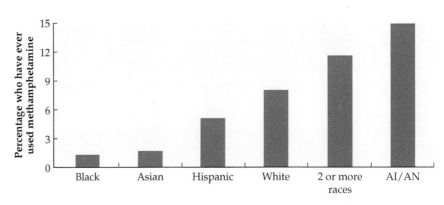

FIGURE 5.10. Use of methamphetamine, by race and ethnicity. African Americans are least likely to report using methamphetamine; American Indians/Alaskan natives report the highest use.

Source: (SAMHSA). (2019). Key substance use and mental health indicators in the United States: Results from the 2018 national survey on drug use and health. *Rockville, MD: Center for Behavioral Health Statistics and Quality.*

FIGURE 5.11. *Breaking Bad.* *Breaking Bad* tells the story of a high school chemistry teacher who begins producing and selling methamphetamine.

98 percent pure in 2019. The price has also decreased and is now about $56 per gram.[93,94]

Pharmacokinetics of Amphetamines

Amphetamines' dose and effect depends on its form. Dextro-amphetamine is three to four times more potent than levo-amphetamine, and methamphetamine is more potent than dextro-amphetamine. Therapeutic doses typically range from 2.5 to 40 mg per day for ADHD, and from 5 to 60 mg per day for narcolepsy. Common abused doses are 100–1,000 mg/day, but binge users may take as much as 5,000 mg/day.

Amphetamine and methamphetamine can be ingested, injected, snorted, and smoked. Just as with cocaine, smoking has the fastest onset of action, followed by injection, then snorting, and finally, oral administration. The time it takes for effects to first occur is slightly slower compared with cocaine, but the peak effects are greater and the duration of action is longer with amphetamines than with cocaine. Methamphetamine is more lipid-soluble than amphetamine, and it is, therefore, better able to penetrate the blood–brain

barrier. **Ice** is the freebase concentrated, smokable form of methamphetamine; ice is to methamphetamine as crack is to cocaine. Unlike crack, ice has a very long half-life (about 12 hours), resulting in an intense, persistent high.

Amphetamine is well absorbed from the nasal cavity, lungs, and GI tract. It is absorbed fastest when smoked or injected, but unlike cocaine, amphetamine also is effective when swallowed. Once absorbed, amphetamine is distributed to the brain, kidneys, and spleen. Methamphetamine is metabolized to amphetamine via the cytochrome P450 enzyme system in the liver. The liver metabolizes amphetamine more slowly than it does cocaine, which increases amphetamine's duration of action, as well as its toxicity.

Amphetamine's effects can last for about 12 hours, and methamphetamine's for about 8. These drugs are excreted by the kidney, as well as in the sweat and saliva. Amphetamine is alkaline, so when urine is more acidic, the drug is leached out of the blood into the urine and excreted more rapidly. Consumption of large amounts of vitamin C, vinegar, or acidic fruit juices can speed up the elimination of amphetamines.

Mechanism of Action of Amphetamines

Amphetamine and methamphetamine increase postsynaptic levels of dopamine, norepinephrine, and serotonin to a larger degree than does cocaine. They do this via a number of mechanisms: increasing release; blocking reuptake; and, at high concentrations, by inhibiting MAO, the enzyme that breaks down monoamine neurotransmitters such as dopamine, norepinephrine, and serotonin.[95]

Amphetamine increases monoamine levels by binding to transporter proteins. Amphetamine not only binds to the transporter protein, thus blocking reuptake and increasing neurotransmitter levels in the synapse, but because it is similar in structure to dopamine, amphetamine is able to hitch a ride on the transporter pump into the presynaptic terminal. Once there, it causes dopamine to be released from inside the vesicles into the cytoplasm of the nerve terminal (Figure 5.12). The dopamine is then released into the synapse by a reversal of the dopamine transporter protein.[96,97] Amphetamines also increase release of serotonin and norepinephrine.[98]

High levels of norepinephrine are probably responsible for amphetamine's sympathomimetic effects, while serotonin may be particularly to blame for the

Ice: A potent, smokable form of methamphetamine.

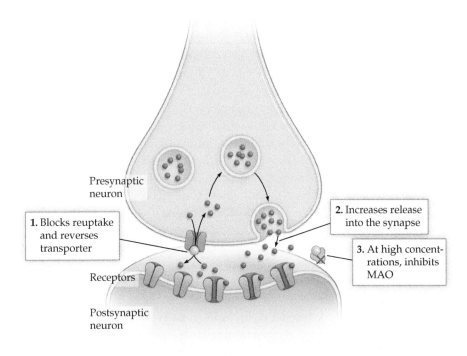

Presynaptic neuron

1. Blocks reuptake and reverses transporter

2. Increases release into the synapse

3. At high concentrations, inhibits MAO

Receptors

Postsynaptic neuron

FIGURE 5.12. The mechanism of action of amphetamine. Amphetamine increases the levels of monoamine in the synapse in 3 ways. (1) It blocks reuptake, (2) it increases release, and (3) at high doses it inhibits MAO.

Stimulant-related deaths are on the rise (Figure 5.7). In 2019, psychostimulants (including amphetamine, methamphetamine, ADHD drugs, MDMA, and caffeine) accounted for almost 23 percent of all drug overdose deaths.[99] From 2009 to 2019, the rate of deaths involving psychostimulants (the number of people who have died per 100,000 population) increased nearly ten-fold. Amphetamine-related toxicity is usually due to an increased risk of cardiac arrest or cerebrovascular hemorrhage.

Chronic Effects of Amphetamines

Long-term use of amphetamines can have negative effects on the user. These effects may be physical, psychological, and social.

delusions and perceptual disturbances produced. Elevated dopamine leads to amphetamine's locomotor effects, psychotic side effects, and its potent reinforcing characteristics.

Acute and Adverse Effects of Amphetamines

The physiological and psychological effects of amphetamine closely resemble those of cocaine, although there is a slower onset of effects and a longer duration. Amphetamine and methamphetamine are classified as schedule II drugs, which means they have medically approved therapeutic uses, including for ADHD, narcolepsy, and short-term weight reduction. Amphetamines reduce appetite, food intake, and body weight, but tolerance quickly develops and these effects are lost.

Combining amphetamines with over-the-counter decongestants can lead to a dangerous elevation in blood pressure. Phenobarbital, phenytoin, and MAOI antidepressants slow the metabolism of amphetamines and enhance their stimulant effects.

The side effects and withdrawal seen with amphetamines are similar to those of cocaine. Upon withdrawal, users may experience craving, depression, lethargy, muscle pain, and abnormal sleep patterns.

Tolerance

With high doses of amphetamines, rapid tolerance can occur. Because amphetamines work, in part, by displacing dopamine, norepinephrine, and serotonin from their presynaptic storage sites, a dose of amphetamine can deplete neurotransmitter levels enough such that another dose might produce a reduced effect. This tolerance can last for days or longer.

Adverse Effects from Chronic Use of Amphetamines

Chronic users of amphetamines may experience:

- Weight loss
- Skin sores that do not heal
- Poor oral hygiene, including tooth deterioration
- Liver disease
- Hypertensive disorders
- Cerebral hemorrhage
- Cardiac arrhythmias
- Myocardial infarction
- Kidney damage
- Seizures

It's not always possible to tell which of these symptoms are due to the drug and which are due to poor nutrition and other unhealthy habits associated with the lifestyle. Chronic amphetamine users face the risk of psychiatric disorders, long-term neurological damage, addiction, and sudden death.

Repeated use of amphetamines over days or weeks can lead to a psychotic state of hallucinations, hostility, panic, and paranoia that resembles schizophrenia.[100] Amphetamine psychosis can persist for weeks or even months after the drug has been withdrawn. These psychological deficits can be much more severe than the psychosis associated with cocaine use, due to amphetamines' higher potency and longer half-life.

Sustained administration of high doses of amphetamines (and especially of methamphetamine) can produce persistent, and possibly irreversible, damage to dopaminergic and serotonergic nerve endings, an effect that does not seem to occur with cocaine use. Amphetamine enters the presynaptic terminal and ejects dopamine from its vesicle into the cytosol, which may begin to kill the cell. The duration of damage is not yet known. In some cases, dopamine depletion persists even in users who have abstained from amphetamine use for years,[101,102] but other studies report some degree of recovery[103] (Figure 5.13). This dopamine loss is espe-

cially significant in brain areas responsible for movement, memory, and decision-making. Hyperthermia, another effect of amphetamine use, enhances this neurotoxicity.[104]

Amphetamine Dependence and Addiction
Although small doses of orally administered, medically prescribed amphetamines usually do not result in addiction, large doses that are smoked or injected for the purpose of getting high may. Not all users become addicted, and many users of methamphetamine stop abusing the drug without formal substance abuse treatment.[105] National surveys suggest, however, that over 1.5 million Americans are addicted to methamphetamine or prescription stimulants.[106] When addiction does develop, it can be hard to treat, given that the drug significantly impairs a person's decision-making ability. Many of those who enter treatment are forced into it by the court system. Successful treatment typically requires more than a year of intense intervention consisting of drug abstinence, antidepressant medications, and psycho-behavioral interventions to modify thinking patterns, improve cognitive skills, change expectations, and learn how to cope with life's stressors. For more information on treatment of addiction, see Chapter 18.

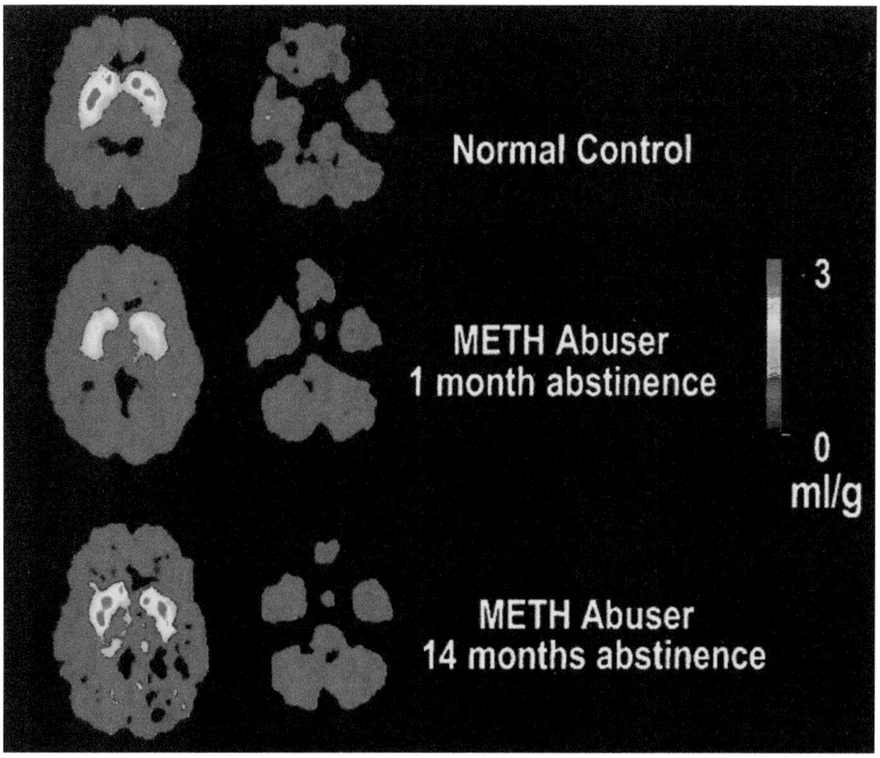

Other Stimulants
Khat and MDPV (bath salts) are other stimulants that sometimes are used recreationally.

Cathinone/Khat
Catha edulis is a leafy shrub native to East Africa and the southern part of the Arabian Peninsula. The use of khat (pronounced "cot") was documented by Arab scribes as far back as the thirteenth century.[107] Khat is one of the most popular stimulants worldwide; up to 10 million people use it daily. It is especially popular in Yemen, where 70–80 percent of Yemenis between the ages of 16 and 50 chew khat at least occasionally.

FIGURE 5.13. **Effects on the brain after stopping methamphetamine.** One study showed that abstinence produced some recovery in the brains of methamphetamine addicts, although this physical recovery was not associated with functional recovery

Source: Volkow, N.D., Chang, L., Wang, G-J., Fowler, J.S., Franceschi, D., & Sedler, M., et al. (2001). Loss of dopamine transporters in methamphetamine abusers recovers with protracted abstinence. Journal of Neuroscience, 21(23): 9414–18.

Its popularity in North Africa may be due to the fact that it is more acceptable to Muslim users than alcohol.

The fresh leaves of the shrub contain the active ingredient *cathinone*, which is structurally similar to amphetamine. As the leaves mature or dry, cathinone is converted to cathine, which is about one-tenth as potent. Because the leaves are pharmacologically active only when they are fresh, the use of khat remained a local phenomenon until recently, when air transport allowed exportation.[108] Methcathinone ("cat") is a synthetic variant that is more potent than cathinone. Methcathinone was patented by Parke-Davis in 1957 but was never marketed because of its many side effects.[109] Methcathinone is similar to methamphetamine and is more potent and addictive than cathinone. Cathinone and methcathinone are both schedule I drugs.

A typical khat user chews the leaves for a few minutes, then tucks the softened mass into a ball in his or her cheek and slowly swallows the juice. Khat also can be snorted, injected, or smoked, and its effects are much more intense with these routes of administration. Methcathinone powder can be snorted, dissolved in water and then drunk, or injected. A user can also smoke methcathinone for a particularly intense and rapid high. Cathinones work similarly to amphetamines, by raising the levels of dopamine, norepinephrine, and serotonin in the synapse, blocking reuptake, and increasing release of these neurotransmitters.

When taken orally and in moderation, khat is a mild stimulant, much like coffee. When it is snorted, smoked, or injected, khat's effects are more similar to those of amphetamines. Exhilaration, euphoria, elevated energy, hyperactivity, talkativeness, thirst, and appetite suppression are all effects associated with khat. Elevated heart rate, elevated blood pressure, and constipation also may occur. Larger doses of khat may lead to manic behavior, delusions, paranoia, and/or hallucinations, while withdrawal may cause mild depression, irritability, or lethargy.

QUICK HIT

Chronic use of cathinone or methcathinone causes a distinctive, very disagreeable body odor as metabolic breakdown products are exuded from the skin.

Bath Salts

Synthetic derivatives of cathinone, such as mephedrone, methylone, and MDPV (3,4-methylenedioxypyrovalerone), are psychoactive substances similar to khat. Also known as bath salts, plant food, magic, MTV, MCAT, meow meow, ivory wave, or vanilla sky, these powders are usually sold in gas stations and head shops and are labeled "not for human consumption" to circumvent drug abuse legislation (Figure 5.14).[110]

Bath salts can be swallowed, snorted, smoked, injected, or inserted rectally. The rush reaches its peak at one and a half hours, and the effects last three to four hours. The average dose is 5–20 mg, but there is a high risk of overdose because packets often contain 500 mg and suggest users use 50 mg.[111]

The desired effects reported by users include euphoria, increased energy, wakefulness, enhanced motivation, empathy, mental stimulation, sociability, and increased libido.[112] Unfortunately, bath salts also produce several undesirable effects and have been described as combining the worst characteristics of LSD, PCP, MDMA, cocaine, and methamphetamine.[113] The more common effects include rapid heart rate, high blood pressure, insomnia, nausea, GI distress, teeth grinding, hyperthermia, headache, dizziness, and ringing in the ears. People may feel agitated, confused, paranoid, and panicked, and experience delusions, violent behavior, and suicidal thoughts. Kidney failure, liver failure, seizures, heart attacks, and death have occurred due to the use of bath salts, which are now classified as schedule I compounds.

FIGURE 5.14. Bath salts. Synthetic derivatives of cathinone, sometimes called "bath salts," are sold under a variety of names.

Chapter Summary

- **Cocaine**
  - » Cocaine was very popular in the early part of the twentieth century but fell out of favor with the passage of the Harrison Narcotics Act, before regaining popularity in the 1970s and early 1980s.
  - » The United States is one of the world's largest consumers of cocaine. About 2 million Americans have used cocaine within the last month.
  - » Cocaine comes from a shrub native to the Andes Mountains.
  - » Cocaine can be ingested in many forms, including coca leaves, powder cocaine, freebase, and crack.
  - » The amount of cocaine that is absorbed into the bloodstream depends on the route of administration. Cocaine enters the brain fastest when it is smoked, followed by injection, snorting, and oral administration.
  - » Cocaine works by blocking reuptake of dopamine, norepinephrine, and serotonin. Cocaine exerts most of its effects in the basal ganglia, prefrontal cortex, ventral tegmental area, and nucleus accumbens.
  - » Cocaine is a schedule II drug, and it is approved for medical use as a local anesthetic.
  - » Cocaine mimics the effects of the sympathetic nervous system. It also produces euphoria, elation, arousal, and heightened energy and endurance.
  - » After chronic use, cocaine users may undergo a fairly short-lived withdrawal period. They may experience side effects such as irritability, hostility, anxiety, fear, and restlessness, or more serious effects such as heart attack or seizures.
  - » When taken during pregnancy, cocaine constricts blood flow to the placenta, thus decreasing the amount of oxygen and nutrients that are delivered to the fetus.

  Its long-term effect on children of mothers who used cocaine during pregnancy is unclear.
  - » Cocaine does not produce strong physical dependence, but it does produce powerful psychological dependence.
- **Amphetamines**
  - » Amphetamines come in a variety of forms. Left-handed and right-handed derivatives have different effects. Methamphetamine is more lipid-soluble, enters the brain faster, and is more addictive.
  - » As with cocaine, amphetamine's route of administration determines its onset of action.
  - » Amphetamines increase postsynaptic levels of monoamines by a variety of methods. They block reuptake of dopamine, norepinephrine, and serotonin; increases their release; and at high doses, blocks MAO, the enzyme that degrades monoamines.
  - » The physiological and psychological effects of amphetamines closely resemble those of cocaine, although there is a slower onset of effects and a longer duration.
  - » Amphetamines are schedule II drugs and are approved to treat ADHD and narcolepsy, and to aid in short-term weight reduction.
  - » Chronic use of amphetamines can cause significant physical and psychological damage.
- **Other Stimulants**
  - » Cathinone (khat) is one of the most popular stimulants worldwide. It is structurally and functionally similar to amphetamine.
  - » Bath salts are synthetic derivatives of cathinone, such as mephedrone, methylone, and MDPV. They can produce devastating physical and psychological effects.

Key Terms

Cardiac arrest (p. 102)
Crack (p. 96)
Craving (p. 104)

Drug mule (p. 98)
Formication (p. 102)
Ice (p. 109)

Myocardial infarction (p. 102)
Sympathomimetic (p. 101)

Quiz Yourself!

1. True or false? Crack is made by treating powder cocaine with baking soda.

2. True or false? Possession of 5 grams of crack cocaine carries a much harsher sentence than possession of 5 grams of powder cocaine.

3. Rate the following forms of cocaine in order, from fastest onset of action to slowest: injected, smoked, snorted, oral.

4. What is the mechanism by which cocaine increases dopamine in the synapse?

5. True or false? Drinking alcohol can help a person come down off cocaine.

6. True or false? Cocaine is no longer approved for medical use.

7. Which gets into the brain faster—amphetamine or methamphetamine?

8. Which of the following is NOT a mechanism by which amphetamine exerts its effects?

   A. Blocks reuptake of dopamine

   B. Blocks reuptake of norepinephrine

   C. Increases release of dopamine

   D. Blocks postsynaptic dopamine receptors

9. Name two conditions for which amphetamines are approved for medical use.

10. True or false? Bath salts, a synthetic form of cathinone, are schedule V and relatively safe.

Additional Resources

Websites
The faces of meth http://www.facesofmeth.us/main.htm

Self-help sites:
Cocaine Anonymous http://www.ca.org
Narcotics Anonymous http://www.na.org

Videos
Two-Minute Neuroscience: Effects of Cocaine https://www.youtube.com/watch?v=dBuIliNAixg

Movies
Blow. (2001). 124 minutes. The story of George Jung, the man who established the American cocaine market in the 1970s. Starring Johnny Depp.

Cocaine Cowboys. (2006). 118 minutes. A documentary about the rise of cocaine in Miami in the 1970s and 1980s.
Crack: Cocaine, Corruption, and Conspiracy. (2021). 89 minutes. A documentary about the crack epidemic in the 1980s, its origins, and its results.

Books
Streatfeild, D. (2003). *Cocaine: An unauthorized biography*. New York: Picador.

Learn more with this chapter's digital tools at www.oup.com/he/rosenthal2e.

Hallucinogens

True or false?

1.
True or false? LSD and psilocybin are highly addictive and have a dangerously low therapeutic index.

2.
True or false? Nutmeg contains a hallucinogenic substance.

3.
True or false? MDMA may be an effective treatment for post-traumatic stress disorder.

Learning Objectives

- Define the term *hallucinogen*.
- Categorize hallucinogens as psychedelics, deliriants, or dissociatives.
- Describe the roles that Albert Hofmann and Timothy Leary played in promoting the popularity of LSD.
- Assess the pros and cons of classifying hallucinogens as schedule I drugs.
- Distinguish among the mechanisms of action of psychedelic hallucinogens, MDMA, deliriants, and dissociatives.
- Summarize the acute physiological and behavioral effects of hallucinogenic drugs.
- List some of the potentially fatal effects of MDMA.
- Identify some of the potential therapeutic uses of hallucinogens.
- Explain why there is a relatively low risk of addiction to hallucinogenic drugs.
- Evaluate the effects of chronic MDMA use on cognition in humans.

Hallucinogen: From the Latin *alucinare*, meaning "to wander in mind, to idle, or prate," a hallucinogen is a drug that distorts one's perceptions of reality

Hallucination: An experience involving the perception of something that may not actually be present.

Illusion: A perceptual alteration, in which an actual object is seen in a distorted form.

Hallucinogens are powerful psychoactive substances that can affect thoughts, mood, perceptions, and other mental processes.[1] For thousands of years, people have used hallucinogenic substances for healing, divination, to expand their creative expression, to aid their search for a connection to the universe, or to enhance their personal development, but their therapeutic uses are only now being rediscovered. Scientists, shamans, and scholars have scaled the heights of inventiveness when trying to name this category of drugs. Although the term *hallucinogen* is not perfect, it is the term most commonly used in the scientific literature, and has thus won its role as the title of this chapter. We will define **hallucinogens** as those drugs that distort one's perceptions of reality at relatively low doses.

As a class, hallucinogens are paradoxical drugs whose mechanisms of action are not entirely understood. They show incredible diversity in chemistry, mechanism of action, and use. Even the same drug, taken by the same person, at the same dose can have unpredictable effects depending on the setting and on the person's mindset. Finally, although these drugs are generally physiologically safe and nonaddictive, hallucinogens are typically classified as schedule I.

A **hallucination** is a sense perception for which there is no external stimulus—the perception occurs in the absence of environmental stimulation, as might occur in a dream or psychotic state. Although they may produce true hallucinations when taken in high doses, most hallucinogens produce **illusions** rather than hallucinations; they alter and distort perceptions, thoughts, and feelings, or give a sense of increased insight or awareness. To further muddy the situation, some drugs that are not classified as hallucinogenic (such as amphetamines and cocaine) *can* produce hallucinations at a high enough dose.

This chapter is organized differently than the others in this section. In other chapters, each drug or category of drug is covered independently, while in this chapter, all of the various types of hallucinogenic drugs are discussed together under the various headings ("Mechanism of Action," "Pharmacokinetics," etc.). The chapter was organized this way to avoid redundancies and to better highlight the commonalities and differences among the various hallucinogenic drugs.

Hallucinogens

Type of drug: Hallucinogen; some have stimulant properties as well

Chemical formula:
- Psilocybin: $C_{12}H_{17}N_2O_4P$
- LSD: $C_{20}H_{25}N_3O$
- Mescaline: $C_{11}H_{17}NO_3$
- MDMA: $C_{11}H_{15}NO_2$
- PCP: $C_{17}H_{25}N$
- Ketamine: $C1_3H_{16}ClNO$

Routes of administration:
- Psilocybin: Ingested
- LSD: Ingested, injected, absorbed across skin
- DMT: Smoked, injected
- Peyote and mescaline: Ingested
- MDMA: Ingested, snorted, injected
- PCP and ketamine: Ingested, smoked, snorted, injected

Duration of effect:
- Psilocybin: 3–6 hours
- LSD: 6–12 hours
- DMT: 1 hour
- Peyote and mescaline: 4–12 hours
- MDMA: 3–6 hours
- PCP and ketamine: 8 hours

Neurotransmitters directly affected:
- Psilocybin, LSD, mescaline, peyote: Serotonin
- MDMA: Serotonin, dopamine
- Anticholinergics: Acetylcholine
- PCP and ketamine: Glutamate

Tolerance: Develops rapidly

Physical dependence: None

Psychological dependence: Moderate

Withdrawal symptoms: Minimal
- MDMA: Depression, fatigue

Schedule:
- Schedule I: Psilocybin, LSD, DMT, ibogaine, peyote, mescaline, MDMA
- Schedule II: PCP
- Schedule III: Ketamine
- Unscheduled: *Atropa belladonna*, datura, henbane, mandrake, salvia, *Amanita muscaria*

Slang:
- Psilocybin: Shrooms, magic mushrooms
- LSD: Acid, Alice, blotter, windowpane, trip
- DMT: Businessman's high, businessman's special
- Peyote: Buttons
- Mescaline: Mesc, moon, cactus
- MDMA: Ecstasy, E, X, XTC, rave, love drug, Molly
- Ayahuasca: Yage
- PCP: Angel dust, cyclones, gorilla biscuits, zombie dust
- Ketamine: Special K, vitamin K, jet, purple, L.A. coke
- Salvia: Sally-D, magic mint

History of Hallucinogens

Hallucinogens have a long and varied history. Some hallucinogenic plants have been used for thousands of years, while some synthetic psychedelics were created within the last few decades. In Indian tribes of North and South America, shamans—specially trained individuals who act as liaisons between the human and spirit worlds—largely control the use of hallucinogens.[2] They use psychedelic drugs to facilitate healing, communicate with spirits, locate missing objects or people, and guide rites of passage.

History of LSD and Psilocybin

In December 1691, in Salem, Massachusetts, eight young girls suddenly developed "unknown distempers" of disoriented speech, odd postures and gestures, and convulsive fits.[3] Accusations of witchcraft began, followed by trials. By September of 1692, more than 150 people were convicted of being witches, and 20 were executed.

Linnda Caporael and Mary Matossian are two scholars who support the theory that ergotism may explain the events that took place in Salem.[4,5] **Ergot** is a group of fungi that grow on grains such as rye and barley and produce **alkaloids** (Figure 6.1). Ergot contains

Ergot: A family of fungi that grows on rye and barley and produces alkaloids when consumed, which may result in hallucinatory effects.

Alkaloid: A nitrogen-containing compound of fungal or plant origin that produces physiological effects in humans.

FIGURE 6.1. Ergot fungus. The dark ergot fungus replaces the grain on rye or barley.

lysergic acid, a chemical precursor of LSD, and produces hallucinatory convulsive effects. Many of the conditions exhibited by the "possessed" girls were symptoms of ergotism—burning and tingling of the skin, sensory disturbances, and hallucinations. Additionally, the spring and summer of 1691 were warm and rainy, conditions that favor the growth of the ergot fungus, and 72 percent of the households in Salem with an afflicted member were located close to a riverbank or swamp.

Others find fault with this theory.[6,7] Most of the typical symptoms of ergotism, such as a voracious appetite, vomiting, diarrhea, bruised skin color, and limbs that will not straighten, were not exhibited at Salem. Also, many of the individuals living in the same household as the afflicted girls, and who presumably would have eaten the same bread, showed no symptoms.

Although we may never know what led to these behaviors, ergotism is not just a bygone phenomenon. In 1951, in the small French village of Pont-Saint-Esprit, hundreds of townspeople went completely berserk, running through the streets and jumping from windows. Some died, and those who survived suffered strange aftereffects for weeks. These phenomena were thought to be due to the villagers' ingestion of ergot-contaminated rye flour.[8]

Albert Hofmann

Albert Hofmann worked as a chemist for Sandoz, a large pharmaceutical company in Switzerland. In 1938, he was studying an ergot derivative—lysergic acid—as a way to treat problems associated with childbirth. LSD-25 was the 25th compound synthesized, and he tested it on animals, but saw no commercially interesting properties, so LSD remained on the shelf until

Ask yourself: Many drugs have been brought to light after scientists purposely ingested a newly discovered chemical. Do you think the potential benefits of such an action justify the risks? Why or why not?

April 16, 1943, when Hofmann accidentally spilled a tiny amount on his hand. Hofmann described that as he lay "in a dazed condition with eyes closed there surged up from me a succession of fantastic, rapidly changing imagery of a striking reality and depth, alternating with a vivid, kaleidoscopic play of colors."[9] Curious as to how such a small amount of a substance could have produced such intense symptoms, three days later Hofmann intentionally swallowed 250 micrograms (what we today know to be three to eight times the normal effective dose). After some initial anxiety, he began to enjoy the intense visual images and personal insights he experienced.[10] Believing that the substance could be a powerful psychiatric tool, Hofmann wrote of his discovery. In 1947, Sandoz first marketed LSD under the trade name Delysid.

The CIA and LSD

During World War II, the Office of Strategic Services (the precursor to the CIA) began a top-secret research program to develop a truth serum. They thought LSD might be useful "for eliciting true and accurate statements from subjects under its influence during interrogation," while also producing amnesia, so the enemy would not remember sharing its military secrets.[11] LSD did not work as planned, but the odorless, colorless, tasteless, and powerful drug was too compelling to abandon.

In 1953, the CIA began the MKUltra program, which was concerned with "the research and development of chemical, biological, and radiological materials capable of employment in clandestine operations to control human behavior."[12] CIA agents began to test how individuals would respond to LSD if they took it under "normal" conditions without being warned in advance.[13] The technical services staff of the CIA began slipping acid into the drinks of unsuspecting fellow agents. In November 1953, army scientist Dr. Frank Olsen experienced panic, paranoia, and delusions for two weeks after his experience. Before Olsen could be moved to a psychiatric hospital, he committed suicide by jumping out of a tenth-story window.[14]

The next step of MKUltra was to give LSD to unsuspecting civilian targets in real-life situations. In "Operation Midnight Climax," prostitutes were hired to slip LSD into the drinks of customers so that the CIA could then watch and record their behaviors. Victims were hesitant to report their experiences, because they would have had to admit to visiting a prostitute when the incidents occurred.[15] The CIA's experiments with LSD eventually ended when the drug was deemed too unpredictable.

Psychiatric Use of LSD and Psilocybin in the 1950s and 1960s

Until the 1950s, most psychiatric medications were tranquilizers that dampened one's awareness of problems and conflicts. Hallucinogens, by contrast, enhanced awareness. Sandoz began marketing LSD and psilocybin as a way to help psychiatric patients resolve their problems and access repressed memories.[16] Patients on these hallucinogens were found to be less defensive and to respond more effectively. By 1965, an estimated 40,000 patients had received LSD and psilocybin in a psychotherapeutic context, and over 1,000 articles—most highly favorable—were published on the subject. Yet, by the end of the 1960s, for political reasons, hallucinogens were considered to be among the most dangerous drugs in existence.[17] Today, the idea of using hallucinogenic drugs to treat psychological disorders is making a comeback, and many states have decriminalized the use of psilocybin and other psychoactive plants and fungi.

Timothy Leary and the 1960s Counterculture

One of the reasons for the change in society's awareness of and attitudes about LSD stemmed from the actions of Dr. Timothy Leary (Figure 6.2). In 1960, Leary, a 39-year-old lecturer in clinical psychology at Harvard, went to Mexico and tried psilocybin mushrooms. These mushrooms—called *teonanacatl*, or "flesh of the gods" by Central and South American Indians—were an important part of social and religious rituals for these tribes for many thousands of years. About his experience with the psilocybin mushrooms, Leary said, "It was above all and without question the deepest religious experience of my life . . . I learned more in the six or seven hours of this experience than in all my years as a psychologist . . . I came back a changed man . . . You are never the same after you've had the veil drawn."[18]

Timothy Leary returned to Harvard and, with fellow psychology professor Richard Alpert, began testing psilocybin on graduate students. At first, they did these experiments in a laboratory setting, with a physician present. They soon became less scientific in their approach, and began to take the drug along with their students, at home, without a physician present; eventually they switched to using LSD. Due to growing concerns about their research, Leary and Alpert were fired from Harvard University in 1963.[19]

Timothy Leary's departure from Harvard did not lessen his commitment to the drugs, as he encouraged young people to "turn on, tune in, and drop out," a phrase that became the philosophy of the youth movement of the 1960s.[20] Throughout the decade, LSD became associated with cultural and political rebellion. And although protesters could not be arrested for gathering and speaking, they *could* be arrested for drug use. Just as marijuana was vilified in the 1930s, LSD was demonized in the press as "a monster in our midst" and "the greatest threat facing the country today . . . more dangerous than the Vietnam War."[21] As a result of this

FIGURE 6.2. Timothy Leary. Due to his vocal endorsement of the use of hallucinogenic drugs, Timothy Leary (center) often encountered opposition from law enforcement agencies.

media campaign, Sandoz Pharmaceuticals recalled all the LSD and psilocybin they had distributed to scientists for research, bringing to a halt nearly all government-sponsored research in the United States (except for the CIA's clandestine research). Illegal labs stepped in to supply the demand, and the market was soon flooded with cheap and widely available LSD.

LSD use declined throughout the 1970s and 1980s, before picking up again in the 1990s, only to make a sharp decline at the start of the century. Today, MAPS—the Multidisciplinary Association for Psychedelic Studies— and the Johns Hopkins Center for Psychedelic and Consciousness Research promote research that shows potential clinical applications for hallucinogenic drugs.

History of Peyote/Mescaline

Aztecs of pre-Columbian Mexico considered the peyote cactus magical and divine. They used it to treat illnesses, communicate with spirits, and as a centerpiece of religious ceremonies. In the late nineteenth century, German pharmacologist Arthur Heffter isolated the major psychoactive substance in peyote and named it "mescaline" after the Mescalero Apache Indians who provided the peyote. In 1919, Ernst Spath was the first to synthesize mescaline (MESS-ka-lin) in the laboratory. Mescaline entered mainstream American culture when author and philosopher Aldous Huxley published his experiences with it in 1954.

History of MDMA

In 1912, Anton Köllisch, a chemist working at the German pharmaceutical company Merck, sought to create a new medication to stop bleeding. The drug company Bayer already had a patent on the antihemorrhagic substance hydrastinine, so Köllisch tweaked the chemical structure of hydrastinine and developed methyl-hydrastinine. MDMA (3,4-methylenedioxy-methamphetamine; today known as ecstasy or Molly) was an intermediate step in the synthesis of methyl-hydrastinine.[22] It was not until the 1950s, however, when the U.S. Army funded secret testing of MDMA and other drugs for their potential as brainwashing weapons, that MDMA was tested on humans.[23]

In the 1960s, Alexander Shulgin, a biochemist at Dow, synthesized MDMA and tested it as a psychotherapeutic agent. Shulgin published the first scientific articles on the effects of MDMA on humans in the 1970s and recommended the drug to psychiatrist Leo Zeff.[24] Dr. Zeff extolled its benefits, and it soon became popular with California psychotherapists who used it as an aid during talk therapy—to increase empathy and trust during the therapeutic process.[25]

During the 1980s, the recreational use of MDMA began in earnest, as people could order the drug by calling a toll-free number or purchasing it at nightclubs. In 1984, the Drug Enforcement Agency (DEA) announced its intention to declare MDMA a schedule I drug. Although there were no double-blind, placebo-controlled studies examining its clinical efficacy, at hearings in 1985, many psychiatrists, therapists, and scientists spoke of MDMA's therapeutic benefits. In 1986, Judge Francis Young handed down his opinion—he thought MDMA had an accepted medical use and should be classified as schedule III, which would allow clinical work, research, and further testing to proceed. Despite Young's recommendation, in 1988, the DEA permanently classified MDMA as schedule I.[26]

In 2001, the U.S. Congress passed the Ecstasy Anti-Proliferation Act, which increased the penalties for the manufacture, importation, exportation, and trafficking of MDMA by nearly 3,000 percent. The new Act made one gram of MDMA (about four pills) equivalent to one gram of heroin for sentencing purposes.[27]

History of PCP and Ketamine

PCP and ketamine were first marketed in the early 1960s as surgical anesthetics, and ketamine, in particular, was used on the battlefield in Vietnam.[28] Compared with other anesthetics, PCP and ketamine had a higher, and therefore safer, therapeutic index. Initial tests were promising because the drugs did not produce respiratory depression or cardiac irregularities. Upon awakening, however, so many patients experienced negative effects, such as hallucinations, delirium, paranoia, agitation, and changes in body perception, that PCP was withdrawn from use for humans in 1965. PCP began to emerge as a recreational drug in the United States in 1967, while ketamine gained popularity as a club drug during the 1980s. Today, ketamine is still used as a short-acting general anesthetic in both human and veterinary medicine, and a form of ketamine is approved for treatment-resistant depression (Chapter 13).[29]

Prevalence of Hallucinogen Use

Drugs go in and out of fashion, and hallucinogens are no exception. LSD and psilocybin's popularity peaked in the late 1960s and early 1970s and then began to taper off due to a number of factors, including cultural changes and diminished availability.[30] Since 2013, LSD use is on the rise again; reported use of LSD in the past year has more than doubled, especially in those with college degrees.[31,32]

In 2019, over 1.2 million persons age 12 years and older used hallucinogens—including LSD, MDMA, and PCP—for the first time; or over 3,300 initiates per day. About 44 million people—16 percent of the U.S. population—have ever used a hallucinogen.[34]

MDMA (ecstasy, Molly) became increasingly popular in the 1990s and 2000s, particularly at raves—large-scale, all-night dance parties with electronic music and light shows, which were often held in empty warehouses or airplane hangars. MDMA use declined in the early part of the twenty-first century, but is now on the rise again.[35] Today, over 20 million individuals in the United States and millions more worldwide have used MDMA.[36]

Ask yourself: Some drugs, such as LSD and ecstasy, go in and out of vogue. What factors do you think affect how popular a drug is?

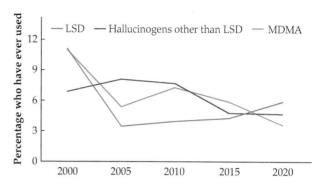

FIGURE 6.3. Hallucinogenic use in high school seniors. The popularity of hallucinogenic drugs changes over time, but in general, their popularity among high school students has fallen in the past 20 years.

Source: Meich, R.A., Johnston, L.D., O'Malley, P.M., Bachman, J.G., & Schulenberg, J.E., et al. (2021). Monitoring the Future: National survey results on drug use 1975–2020. Ann Arbor: Institute for Social Research, The University of Michigan.

Illicit use of PCP peaked in the United States in 1979, when lifetime use was around 14 percent among those age 18–25. Its popularity has fallen significantly, but still, some 5.5 million U.S. residents age 12 years and older have used PCP at least once in their lifetime.[37] Figure 6.3 illustrates the trends in the use of some hallucinogenic drugs by high school seniors over the last 20 years.

Source and Forms of Hallucinogens

The natural world contains hundreds of different species of psychedelic plants and fungi, about 150 of which are used for hallucinogenic purposes. Still more

Psychedelics: Drugs that produce a vivid perceptual experience. These include hallucinogens such as LSD and psilocybin that are structurally similar to serotonin, as well as substances such as peyote, mescaline, and MDMA that structurally resemble dopamine.

Deliriants: Drugs that produce extreme mental confusion and a loss of touch with reality. These include deadly nightshade, mandrake, and henbane.

Dissociatives: Drugs that produce analgesia, amnesia, catalepsy, and a sense of detachment. These include PCP and ketamine.

Catalepsy: A medical condition characterized by a trance-like stare, rigidity, and diminished responsiveness.

hallucinogenic substances are synthesized in laboratories. Hallucinogens may be classified as **psychedelics**, which produce a vivid sensory experience and altered perceptions; **deliriants**, which result in mental confusion and the inability to differentiate reality from fantasy; and **dissociatives**, which cause analgesia, amnesia, **catalepsy**, and a sense of detachment from the environment. Table 6.1 identifies the sources of some hallucinogenic substances, and Table 6.2 summarizes characteristics of many of the drugs discussed in this chapter.

Psychedelic drugs are classified based on their structural resemblance to neurotransmitters. *Indole-amines* are structurally similar to serotonin, while *phenylethylamines* are structurally similar to dopamine and norepinephrine.

Indoleaminic Psychedelic Hallucinogens

Some of the best known hallucinogens are substances, both natural and synthetic, which are structurally similar to serotonin. These include LSD, psilocybin, morning glory seeds, DMT, ayahuasca, ibogaine, and bufotenine.

LSD

Lysergic acid diethylamide-25, also known as LSD or acid, is a synthetic derivative of lysergic acid, a component of the fungus ergot. LSD is a complex molecule that is difficult to synthesize. Due to its potency, however, a small quantity can easily supply the hallucinogenic demands of thousands of people. Odorless and colorless, with a slightly bitter taste, LSD often is packaged by placing drops of the solution onto blotter paper or sugar cubes. LSD also can be incorporated into a thin gelatin square called a windowpane, or in microdots, which are tiny LSD-containing tablets (Figure 6.4).

Psilocybin

(SIL-oh-SIGH-bin; 4-phosphoryloxy-N,N-dimethyl-tryptamine) is a hallucinogen found in three genera

TABLE 6.1. Sources of Hallucinogenic Substances

		Psychedelics	Deliriants	Dissociatives
Naturally Occurring	Plants	• Morning glory (family Convolvulaceae) contains lysergic acid amide • Peyote cacti (*Lophophora williamsii*) contain mescaline • *Psychotria viridis* vines contain DMT • *Anadenanthera peregrine* trees and *Virola* trees contain DMT and bufotenine • *Banisteriopsis caapi* vine contains harmine and harmaline • *Myristica frangrans* tree contains nutmeg • Ibogaine is found in the roots of the *Tabernanthe iboga* tree	• Deadly nightshade (*Atropa belladonna*) • Jimson weed (*Datura stramonium*) • Henbane (*Hyoscyamus niger*) • Mandrake (*Mandragora officinarum*)	• *Salvia divinorum*
	Fungi	• *Psilocybe, Panaeolus,* and *Conocybe* genus of mushrooms		• *Amanita muscaria* mushrooms
	Animals	• The skin of the Colorado River toad contains bufotenine		
Synthetic Sources		• LSD • MDMA		• PCP • Ketamine

TABLE 6.2. Summary of Hallucinogenic Drugs

Categories		Drug Name	Source	Primary Mechanism of Action	Acute Effects	Legal Status
Psychedelics	Indoleamines	LSD	Synthetic	Serotonergic agonist	Sympathomimetic, alterations in perception and sensation, visual illusions, altered time perception, changes in perception of self, cognitive alterations, enhanced emotionality	Schedule I
		Psilocybin	Fungus			Schedule I
		Morning glory seeds	Plant			Seeds are legal in most states, but active ingredient LSA is schedule III
		DMT	Plant			Schedule I
		Ibogaine	Plant			Schedule I
		Bufotenine	Animal		Heart palpitations, drooling, raised blood pressure, muscle cramps, headache, blurred vision	Schedule I
	Phenylethylamines	Peyote	Plant		Similar to other psychedelics, but fewer mood changes, more headaches, nausea, and vomiting	Schedule I
		Mescaline	Plant			Schedule I
		Nutmeg and mace	Plant		Disorientation, confusion, perceptual distortions	Uncontrolled
		MDMA	Synthetic	Serotonergic agonist, also increases dopamine and oxytocin	Sympathomimetic, increased empathy, self-acceptance, emotional warmth. Fluid retention and hyperthermia	Schedule I
Deliriants		*Atropa belladonna*	Plant	Antagonist at muscarinic acetylcholine receptors	Increased body temperature, dilated pupils, dry skin and mouth, increased heart rate and blood pressure, agitation, confusion, delirium, hallucinations	Uncontrolled
		Datura	Plant			
		Henbane	Plant			
		Mandrake	Plant			
Dissociatives		*Salvia divinorum*	Plant	Agonist to kappa opioid receptors	Altered perceptions, vivid visual imagery, sensory and time distortions, dizziness, nausea, disconnection	Not scheduled, but some states have laws against its use
		Amanita muscaria	Fungus	GABA agonist, agonist at NMDA glutamate receptors	Changes in visual perception, hallucinations, muscle spasms, increased sweat, salivation, constricted pupils, lowered body temperature, drowsiness	Unscheduled
		PCP	Synthetic	NMDA antagonist, increases dopamine release	Varied effects—can be stimulant, depressant, analgesic, anesthetic, convulsant, hallucinogenic. Often gives a sense of detachment from the self, the world, and reality.	Schedule II
		Ketamine	Synthetic			Schedule III

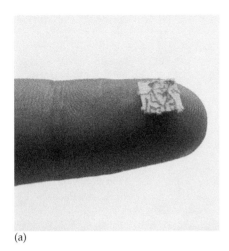
(a)

(b)

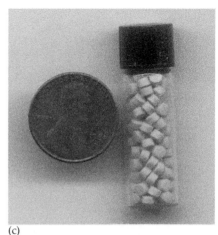
(c)

FIGURE 6.4. Forms of LSD. LSD can be taken dissolved on blotter paper (a), sugar cubes (b), or microdots (c).

of mushrooms—*Psilocybe, Panaeolus,* and *Conocybe,* with a total of about 200 different species of psilocybin-containing mushrooms among them (Figure 6.5). These mushrooms grow in the warm, damp climates of Southeast Asia, Central America, South America, and the Gulf Coast and Pacific Northwest of the United States. Even trained professionals can have difficulty distinguishing the mushrooms from one another, and there is no way to tell that a mushroom is poisonous by its taste or initial physical effects. Therefore, amateur mushroom hunters run the risk of mistaking poisonous mushrooms, which can cause death or permanent liver damage within hours of ingestion, for ones that contain psilocybin.[38]

Psychoactive compounds in the hallucinogenic mushrooms are found in both the cap and stems. The fungus's potency varies between species, between specimens of one species, and between different parts of the fungus. Younger, smaller mushrooms tend to have higher concentrations of drug compared with larger, more mature mushrooms. Because 90 percent of the mushroom is water, drying will increase the concentration tenfold.[39] Also, the drug is more stable in dried mushrooms than in fresh. Psilocybin is not as potent as LSD.

Morning Glory Seeds

The seeds of the morning glory flower contain lysergic acid amide (LSA, also called ergine). The Aztecs used these seeds for healing and as a part of their religious rites. LSA is much less potent than LSD, and it would take several hundred seeds to produce any noticeable psychedelic effect. When swallowed whole, the seeds have no effect, because the hard, indigestible seed coat must be cracked in order to access the psychoactive

FIGURE 6.5. Psilocybin-containing mushrooms. *Psilocybe Mexicana* is one species of hallucinogenic mushroom.

substance. Morning glory seeds are available to the public, but to prevent recreational use, suppliers have coated them with a toxin that cannot be removed by washing; this coating can lead to nausea, vomiting, and severe abdominal pain.

DMT

Dimethyltryptamine—DMT—is a short-acting psychedelic found in the bark, leaves, and seeds of several varieties of trees native to Central America, South America, and the Caribbean (small amounts of DMT also occur naturally in mammalian blood, brain tissue, and cerebrospinal fluid). DMT is ineffective when taken orally, because the enzyme monoamine oxidase (MAO) breaks down DMT in the stomach before it can enter the bloodstream. When smoked, snorted, or injected, DMT's effects begin within seconds, producing colorful and visually intense hallucinations that typically last less than one hour.

Ayahuasca

The Incans called ayahuasca "the vine of the soul" or "the vine of the spirits." Ayahuasca is an herbal tea made from two plants that grow in the jungles of South America, one of which contains DMT. Ayahuasca produces powerful visions, emotional reactions, and profound personal, spiritual, and mystical insights.[40] Quechuan Indians would drink ayahuasca during initiation rites, before a hunting expedition, or before making any major tribal decisions. Ingestion of ayahuasca often causes vomiting or diarrhea, which led South American shamans to believe this represented the elimination of negative energy and emotions built up over years. In fact, ingestion of these substances might have helped users purge their body of worms and parasites.[41]

Ibogaine

Ibogaine is a serotonergic hallucinogen that comes from a rainforest shrub that grows in Central Africa. The roots of the plant are psychoactive.[42] Ibogaine may help treat addiction to cocaine, alcohol, and heroin by blocking receptors in the addiction pathway of the brain. Unfortunately, not enough is known about the risks of using the drug. There is some evidence that ibogaine may damage the cerebellum, cause severe motor tremors, and increase the risk of heart attack and seizures, so the FDA has not approved the drug for treatment of addiction.

Bufotenine

The skin of some toads, such as the Colorado River toad and the cane toad, contains the hallucinogenic substance 5-hydroxy dimethyltryptamine (Figure 6.6).[43] Licking these toads can produce some slight hallucinogenic effects, but because the active ingredients do not easily cross the blood–brain barrier, they mainly cause intense drooling, heart palpitations, elevated blood pressure, oxygen depletion, cramped muscles, blurred vision, a splitting headache, and toad breath, so this practice has not really caught on as the next big drug. In fact, any

---

STRAIGHT DOPE

Hallucinogens in Biblical Times

1. "And Aaron cast down his rod before Pharaoh and his servants, and it became a serpent."—Exodus 7:10

2. "And the angel of the lord appeared unto him in a flame of fire out of the midst of a bush. And he looked, and behold, the bush burned with fire, and the bush was not consumed."—Exodus 3:2

Based on the imagery from the Bible story of Moses' experience on Mount Sinai, as well as geographical, religious, and cultural explanations, Hebrew University Professor Benny Shanon proposes that Moses may have been hallucinating when he received the Ten Commandments on Mount Sinai. Religious ceremonies of the Israelites often included the use of psychoactive materials, and two of the plants that grow in the Sinai Peninsula and southern Israel contain the same psychoactive substances found in ayahuasca. In addition, much of the imagery from the story of Moses' experience on Mount Sinai seems to match the descriptions of what some users of ayahuasca have reportedly experienced:

- Encountering the divine and feelings of profound spirituality.

- Seeing lights and hallucinations of serpents.

- Experiencing an altered sense of time: Shanon suggests that Moses may have looked at a burning bush and believed he was looking at it for a long time—long enough for it to be consumed—when in reality, the period of time may have been much shorter.

Of course, we might never know if Moses and the Israelites were hallucinating, but it certainly gives a new perspective to Proverbs 23:33: "Your eyes will see strange sights, and your mind will imagine confusing things."

Source: Shanon, B. (2008). Biblical entheogens: A speculative hypothesis. Time and Mind: The Journal of Archaeology Consciousness and Culture, 1(1): 51–74.

FIGURE 6.6. **Toad skin.** The skin of the Colorado River toad contains bufotenin. As appealing as this may appear, please do not lick one.

FIGURE 6.7. **The peyote cactus.** This small, round, gray-green cactus has fuzzy tufts instead of spines.

hallucinogenic effects that may occur are probably due to decreased oxygen flow to the optic nerve.

Phenylethylamine Psychedelic Hallucinogens

While indoleaminic psychedelics have a structure similar to serotonin, phenylethylamines are structurally similar to dopamine and norepinephrine. Peyote and mescaline are naturally occurring, and MDMA is synthetic. The synthetic drugs are more potent and more toxic than the naturally occurring ones, and they typically act as stimulants at low doses but have psychedelic effects at higher doses.

Peyote and Mescaline

Used for religious rituals for more than 10,000 years, peyote (pay-OH-tee) is the top of a small, spineless, flowering cactus native to Mexico, northern South America, and the southwestern United States (Figure 6.7). The cactus has a long, carrot-like root; users cut the cactus at the soil level, leaving the root intact. The cactus is then sliced and dried into hard, bitter-tasting peyote buttons, which are chewed raw or cooked and eaten. There are more than 30 psychoactive alkaloids in peyote, the major one being mescaline.

Structurally related to amphetamines, mescaline—3,4,5-trimethoxyphenethylamine—was isolated from peyote in 1896. Mescaline produces vivid visual hallucinations similar to those experienced by LSD users, but also more negative side effects, such as nausea and vomiting. Although some licensed members of the Native American Church are allowed to legally harvest peyote, peyote and mescaline are both schedule I drugs.

Nutmeg and Mace

Nutmeg is the seed of a tropical tree, native to the spice islands of Indonesia. The outer covering of the seed is ground into a spice called mace. *Myristicin* and *elemicin* are the pharmacologically active ingredients in nutmeg and mace, which are structurally similar to mescaline. These substances are converted in the body to an amphetamine-like psychedelic.

Several teaspoons of nutmeg can lead to a very mild hallucinogenic state that includes disorientation, confusion, feelings of unreality, perceptual distortions, and euphoria. At high enough doses to cause hallucinations, these substances also lead to facial flushing, dizziness, apprehension, and intense nausea and vomiting; the sense of unreality can persist for days.

MDMA (Ecstasy, Molly)

MDMA (3,4-methylenedioxymethamphetamine), also known as ecstasy or Molly, is structurally similar to both amphetamines and mescaline and, as such, has some amphetamine-like characteristics as well as some hallucinogenic properties. MDMA is characterized as an *empathogen*, a type of drug that produces feelings of empathy. Ecstasy is a schedule I drug not currently approved for any medical treatments, but many therapists believe it greatly aids the therapeutic process and can even cure post-traumatic stress disorder (PTSD) (Chapter 13).[44,45]

The primary precursor for MDMA is oil from the sassafras tree, which grows in the jungles of Southeast Asia. The roots of the sassafras tree are broken up into small pieces, boiled in a large pot, and the highly toxic sassafras oil is distilled out. The oil is then chemically treated to synthesize MDMA.

Ecstasy is typically taken orally, as a tablet, while Molly is a white powder or crystalline substance that is sometimes snorted and sometimes enclosed in a capsule. When pure, ecstasy and Molly are the same—both are MDMA. The amount of actual MDMA in the tablet or capsule can vary. A good quality pill will contain 75–100 mg of MDMA. The average retail price of an MDMA tablet in the United States is $15–$35.[46,47]

Anticholinergic Deliriants

Deliriant hallucinogens produce extreme confusion in users and an inability to differentiate reality from fantasy. Users may awaken from a dream-like trance of which they retain little or no memory. Anticholinergic deliriants are found in plants that are part of the Solanaceae (nightshade) family, such as belladonna, jimsonweed, henbane, and mandrake. (Potatoes, tomatoes, eggplants, and peppers are also part of the nightshade family.) Three pharmacologically active alkaloids are responsible for the effects of these plants—daturine (l-hyoscyamine), atropine (dl-hyoscyamine), and scopolamine (l-hyoscine). These alkaloids block muscarinic cholinergic receptors in the body, dilate pupils, greatly increase heart rate, and dry secretions. High doses—near toxic doses—are needed to produce hallucinations and delirium.

Atropa belladonna

Native to Central and Southern Europe, Northern Africa, and the Middle East, deadly nightshade is one of the most toxic plants found in the eastern hemisphere (Figure 6.8). The root contains the highest concentration of atropine, scopolamine, and daturine, but the leaves and soft, blue-black berries are also toxic.

QUICK HIT

Anticholinergic deliriants are known to cause dreams and hallucinations in which one is flying. *Atropa belladonna*, datura, and other deliriants are well absorbed through mucous membranes, such as in the vagina, and hundreds of years ago, these drugs were important tools in a healing woman's arsenal. Many historians believe that wise women (sometimes known as witches) would make an ointment of deadly nightshade, which they would spread on a stick and straddle. This may be the origin of the image of witches flying through the night on broomsticks.[48]

Datura

Also called locoweed, stinkweed, angel's trumpet, and jimsonweed, *Datura stramonium* is a tall, leafy, flowering

FIGURE 6.8. Nightshade. During the Roman Empire and in the Middle Ages, the deadly nightshade plant was frequently used as a poison. Ingestion of as few as 12 berries or less can be fatal. Belladonna dilates the pupils, speeds heart rate, and gives the sensation of flying.

plant containing anticholinergic alkaloids (Figure 6.9). Datura has been used for centuries in many cultures as a poison and hallucinogen.[49] Most parts of the plant contain poisonous substances, but the seeds are particularly toxic—as little as half a teaspoon can be fatal.

Mandrake

In herbology classes at the fictional Hogwarts School of Witchcraft and Wizardry, Harry Potter and his classmates work with mandrakes, which are described as plants with roots that look human-like. Harry learns that mandrakes can be used to make powerful potions and that a mature mandrake's cry can be fatal to any person who hears it. Author J.K. Rowling was referencing the actual mandrake, *Mandragora officinarum*, a potato-like plant with a long, forked root that is native to southern Europe, North Africa, western Asia, and the Himalayas. According to legend, when the plant was pulled from the ground, it would shriek, with dire results for anyone within hearing distance. Low doses can relieve anxiety and induce sleep, but high doses cause hallucinations, amnesia, and muscular paralysis.

Dissociative Hallucinogens

Dissociative hallucinogens are anesthetics that produce a sense of detachment from the surrounding environment—both the body and the outside world. These drugs, including *Amanita muscaria*, salvia, PCP, and ketamine, also produce analgesia, amnesia, and catalepsy.

FIGURE 6.9. ***Datura stramonium.*** Datura is also called Jimsonweed, a contraction of "Jamestown weed." British troops who were sent to the Jamestown colony of Virginia in 1676 to suppress a rebellion ate the leaves of the datura plant and suffered adverse effects for days.

Amanita muscaria Mushrooms

The *Amanita muscaria* mushroom is one of the world's oldest intoxicants (Figure 6.10). Native to many regions of the Northern Hemisphere, *Amanita* mushrooms now also grow throughout most areas of the world. *Amanita* mushrooms were widely used by shamans and many indigenous peoples of Siberia. The mushroom's active ingredient is excreted unchanged in urine. Because mushrooms could be scarce and expensive, this led to the practice of recycling—the Siberian shaman would ingest the mushrooms and the others would drink his urine to experience the hallucinogenic properties.[50] *Amanita muscaria* mushrooms act as sedative/hypnotics, depressants, deliriants, and dissociatives. Death may occur with ingestion of approximately 15 caps.

Salvia

Salvia divinorum, or Mexican sage, is a member of the mint family native to Mexico. Reaching about three feet tall, salvia has large leaves, a hollow square stem, and light blue flowers. Salvia's Latin name means "savior of the seers," and Mazatec Indians in Mexico used it for centuries for healing and spiritual practices.

Ask yourself: Azaleas are poisonous, as are larkspur, foxglove, hyacinth, oleander, and many other flowers/ plants. Yet, all of these are legal and grow with abundance in suburban yards across the country. How do you think governments determine which plants should be banned? How should they decide?

(a)

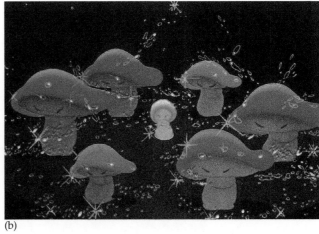
(b)

FIGURE 6.10. ***Amanita muscaria.*** (a) The *Amanita muscaria* mushroom has a bright red cap speckled with white dots. (b) The dancing mushrooms in the surreal Disney cartoon *Fantasia* were reportedly based on *Amanita.*

People typically chew the leaves of the salvia plant and swallow them. The active ingredient in salvia is salvinorin-A, which is the only known hallucinogen that is not an alkaloid.[51] Salvia (both the drug and the plant) is illegal in some states, and there are currently efforts to classify *Salvia divinorum* as a schedule I drug.

PCP and Ketamine

Phencyclidine (fen-SIGH-klih-deen; 1-[1-phenylcyclohexyl] piperidine hydrochloride), otherwise known as angel dust or PCP, is a hard drug to classify. It has anesthetic, analgesic, stimulant, depressant, convulsant, and hallucinogenic effects, depending on the dose and route of administration.[52] PCP comes as a pill and as a white, crystalline powder that dissolves easily in water or alcohol.

Ketamine shows the same anesthetic qualities as PCP but is less psychoactive and shorter acting. Like PCP, ketamine produces delusions, hallucinations, and feelings of being disconnected from one's self and from the environment. PCP is currently a schedule II drug, while ketamine is schedule III.

Cultural and Religious Influence of Hallucinogens

The psychedelic era of the 1960s was a time of broken rules—in terms of music and fashion as well as traditional beliefs and values. The influence of psychedelic drugs can be seen in the artwork, fashion, literature, movies, and music of the 1960s (Figure 6.11).

Literature

In 1953, when Aldous Huxley, author of the novel *Brave New World*, took 400 mg of mescaline, it not only changed his life, but also influenced the direction of literature for years to come. Huxley wrote *The Doors of Perception* the year after his first mescaline trip. The title was taken from a line from William Blake's poem— "if the doors of perception were cleansed everything would appear to man as it is, infinite." Huxley's book was one of the first of a wave of psychedelic-inspired literature. Allen Ginsburg wrote his poem "Howl" after a night on peyote. Some of his other poems include "Lysergic Acid," "Mescaline," and "Laughing Gas." Tom Wolfe published *The Electric Kool-Aid Acid Test* in 1968 as a firsthand account of the experiences of Ken Kesey and his band of Merry Pranksters as they traveled the United States in a brightly colored bus. The book describes the parties in which participants drank LSD-laced Kool-Aid in order to trip together. In *Fear and Loathing in Las Vegas*, Hunter S. Thompson describes his trip to Las Vegas, during which he and a companion ingest a truly staggering amount of hallucinogens and other recreational drugs.

Music

The music of the 1960s was strongly influenced by hallucinogenic drugs. The rock band The Doors took their name from Aldous Huxley's book. Some of the popular songs of the time thought to reference psychedelic trips include "White Rabbit" by Jefferson Airplane, "A Girl Named Sandoz" by The Animals, "Too Much to Dream Last Night" by The Electric Prunes, "Purple Haze" by Jimi Hendrix, "Eight Miles High" by The Byrds, "Journey to

(a)   (b)   (c)

FIGURE 6.11. The influence of psychedelics. Psychedelics influenced the (a) artwork, (b) clothing, and (c) music of the 1960s.

the Center of My Mind" by The Amboy Dukes, and, not surprisingly, "LSD" by The Pretty Things. John Lennon has claimed that the song title "Lucy in the Sky with Diamonds" did not come from the abbreviation LSD but from a drawing that his son's young classmate did; however, Lennon admitted that the song itself was inspired by the countless acid trips he had been on.

Religion

Hallucinogenic drugs have long been used to produce spiritual experiences. Timothy Leary led a double-blind study in which 20 divinity school students were divided into two groups—one of which took psilocybin, and one of which took a placebo—90 minutes before attending a religious service on Good Friday.[53] Participants who took psilocybin reported significantly more mystical experiences than did the control group. Twenty-five years after the experiments, all of the participants who took psilocybin reflected on their experience as having had elements of a "genuine mystical nature" and as being "one of the high points of their spiritual life."[54]

The Huichol tribe of Mexico believes peyote to be the physical manifestation of God, increasing the energy force that creates life. For the Huichol, peyote is more than a drug; it's a central feature of their lives and a part of all of their sacred religious and cultural practices.[55]

The Native American Church of North America, chartered in 1918, combines traditional tribal practices with Christian morality. Its membership includes as many as 250,000 Native Americans in the United States and Canada. The use of peyote is considered a sacrament, although recreational and social use is considered sacrilegious (Figure 6.12).

For many years, members of the Native American Church were able to use peyote legally in the United States for religious reasons, but in 1990, the U.S. Supreme Court ruled in *Employment Division v. Smith* that individual states could ban peyote, even when it was associated with religious use.[56] In 1993, Congress passed the Religious Freedom Restoration Act to ensure the protection of religious freedoms. Currently, the laws regulating peyote

Ask yourself: Should drugs be allowed to be used in religious ceremonies? Does it matter which drugs are used? Which religion is affected? (During Prohibition, Americans were allowed to drink sacramental wine, even though alcohol was illegal.) How do you balance the freedom of religion guaranteed in the First Amendment of the Constitution with existing drug laws?

use by members of the Native American Church vary from state to state.

Pharmacokinetics of Hallucinogens

As might be expected with such a diverse group of drugs, there is great variety among hallucinogens when it comes to pharmacokinetics. Hallucinogens vary in the required dosage, potency, routes of administration, and duration of action.

Dosage

It can be hard to definitively describe the amount of fungal or plant matter that has a physiological effect, given that the drug content depends on the species, age of the fungus or plant, and which part is consumed.

FIGURE 6.12. Peyote ceremony. Peyote is considered a sacrament in the Native American Church.

TABLE 6.3. Effective Doses of Hallucinogenic Drugs

Substance	Dose	Miscellaneous
Psilocybin	5–20 mg	This dose can be found in 10–50 grams of fresh mushrooms (about 2–4 mushrooms) or 1–5 grams of dried mushrooms.
LSD	75–125 mcg	Higher doses tend to intensify rather than lengthen the experience.
Mescaline	200–500 mg	This dose can be found in about 5–15 peyote buttons.
MDMA	5–300 mg	Usual doses range from about 80 to about 160 mg.
PCP	1–10 mg	70 mg may induce seizures.
Atropine	0.5–10 mg	The lethal dose in adults is unknown, but the fatal dose in children may be as low as 10 mg.
Salvinorin-A	100–500 mcg	Salvia is one of the most potent of any naturally occurring hallucinogen.

Typical doses of some hallucinogens can be found in Table 6.3.

QUICK HIT

LSD is the most psychoactive substance known; it takes only 25 micrograms to produce effects. To put that into perspective, a postage stamp weighs 60,000 micrograms, or 2,400 times as much. Of the 25 micrograms, only about 0.01 percent, or 1/10,000, of the LSD actually reaches the brain, where it remains for only about 15 minutes before it is metabolized. LSD is about 100 times stronger than psilocybin, and 3,000 times more potent than mescaline.

QUICK HIT

Microdosing is the practice of taking very small doses of hallucinogens like psilocybin or LSD for therapeutic purposes. The dose is too small to produce a hallucination, but may be large enough to have an effect on one's mood. Typical microdoses of LSD are 10–20 micrograms of LSD, or 0.2–0.5 grams of dried psilocybin mushrooms.

Routes of Administration

- Psilocybin mushrooms are typically eaten raw, boiled into tea, or cooked with other foods, while peyote buttons may be eaten fresh or dried, and steeped into tea. Both psilocybin mushrooms and peyote cactus have a revolting bitter taste, and some users become nauseated.
- LSD is a clear or white, water-soluble crystal that can be crushed into powder and dissolved in liquid. The liquid is then put on blotter paper, into capsules, or on sugar cubes, where it is easily absorbed across the mucous membranes of the body. LSD can also be inhaled or injected.
- MDMA is usually taken orally as a tablet or capsule, but it also can be snorted or injected.

- Anticholinergic drugs such as belladonna and datura often are ingested, but they can also enter the bloodstream when applied to mucosal surfaces of the body, such as the nose, eye, anus, and vagina.
- PCP and ketamine can be ingested, snorted, smoked, or injected. Smoking is the most popular route of administration for PCP, while ketamine is primarily snorted or taken as a pill.

Absorption, Distribution, Metabolism, and Elimination

When taken orally, hallucinogenic drugs typically take effect in 20–60 minutes; onset of action is faster when drugs are snorted, smoked, or given intravenously. A drug's duration of action depends on many factors, including the dosage, purity, and drug taken (Figure 6.13). Hallucinogens are metabolized by the liver and mostly excreted in the urine.

Mechanism of Action of Hallucinogens

More than 60 years ago, Aldous Huxley believed that hallucinogens inhibited the brain's ability to selectively filter out sensory input, emotions, memories, and thoughts. He was not too far off. Although the mechanisms of action vary, hallucinogenic drugs likely affect the normal screening of sensory information to our brain, which influences the amount of sensory information we process and the way we construct our reality.

Microdosing: Taking a sub-hallucinogenic dose of LSD or psilocybin, often for therapeutic purposes.

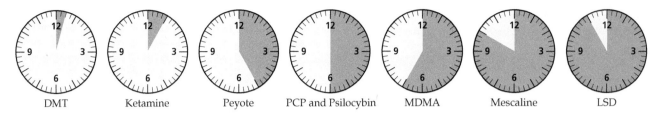

FIGURE 6.13. Duration of action of some hallucinogenic drugs. DMT's effects last for only about 30 minutes, but an LSD trip can last for up to 11 hours.

Psychedelic Hallucinogens

The classic psychedelic hallucinogens—psilocybin, LSD, and mescaline—largely work by affecting serotonergic receptors (especially 5-HT$_{2A}$ receptors) in the thalamus, locus coeruleus, and cortex (Figure 6.14).

- The thalamus is the brain's "relay station," sending incoming sensory information to the appropriate sites in the brain to be processed.
- The locus coeruleus is an area of the pons that receives and integrates input from all major sensory systems and sends information to the cortex. Under the influence of classic psychedelic drugs, the locus coeruleus is more sensitive to sensory input.
- Under the influence of LSD, the visual cortex communicates more than it normally does with other areas of the brain, which is one reason underlying the vivid visual hallucinations associated with psychedelic drugs.[57]
- Hallucinogens alter the connections between different areas of the brain.[58, 59] They strengthen some connections, and decrease activity in others. Imagine you live in a city where you primarily talk only to those in your neighborhood.

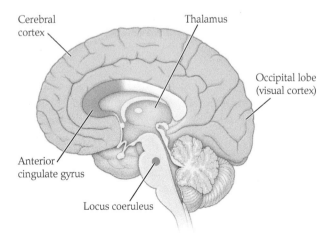

FIGURE 6.14. Areas of the brain affected by classical hallucinogenic drugs.

Then one day, you stop talking with them and instead communicate with other people across town. This might lead to new perspectives, and novel ways of looking at yourself and at the world around you. Hallucinogens can have a similar effect on the brain.[60] When hallucinogens lead to more communication among disparate areas of the brain, this increased global connectivity can cause users to feel a greater sense of connection with people and of being "at one with the all."[61]

Psilocybin also works in areas of the brain that affect emotions and social judgments. In one study of 30 participants, all of whom had previous experience with hallucinogenic drugs, half received an intravenous (IV) injection of psilocybin, while half received a placebo.[62] Scientists found that participants who were given psilocybin had decreased blood flow relative to the control group in the cingulate gyrus and medial prefrontal cortex.

- Negative personal and social assessments are made in the cingulate gyrus, which means that people on psilocybin may judge others less harshly.
- The anterior cingulate gyrus and medial prefrontal cortex normally inhibit the limbic system, but hallucinogenic drugs reduce their activity; this may lead to greater activity in the limbic system, and perhaps stronger emotional responses.[63]
- Some areas of the brain show enhanced activity in those with clinical depression. Hallucinogens lower activity in these overactive areas, and may have an effect on mood.

MDMA

MDMA's mechanism of action is similar to amphetamines (Chapter 5): MDMA increases release of serotonin into the synapse, blocks serotonin's reuptake, and inhibits the degradative enzyme MAO (Figure 6.15). The combination of these actions floods the synapse with serotonin (5-HT). Serotonin's widely varying actions occur in part because it binds to many different types of receptors. MDMA's effects on body temperature, as well as its minor hallucinogenic effects, are due to MDMA's slight affinity for 5-HT$_2$ receptors. Binding to 5-HT$_{1B}$ receptors may produce feelings of calmness.

Unlike psilocybin and LSD, MDMA seems to markedly deplete the amount of serotonin in the presynaptic cell and to inactivate the enzyme necessary to synthesize new serotonin. As a result, cells cannot replenish their serotonin levels for 24 hours. With a single dose of MDMA, brain serotonin levels recover within a day, but higher doses can cause sustained depletion of serotonin that may last for up to 12 months in the rat.[64] MDMA also appears to produce long-term effects on serotonin in the human brain.

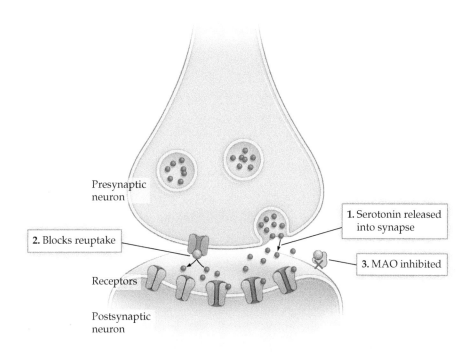

FIGURE 6.15. MDMA's mechanism of action. MDMA (1) increases release of serotonin into the synapse, (2) blocks its reuptake, and (3) inhibits MAO. As a result, postsynaptic serotonin levels are greatly increased.

To a lesser extent, MDMA also causes the release of dopamine[65] and may increase levels of oxytocin (a hormone involved in sex, love, and trust), prolactin (a hormone that plays a role in reproductive health), and cortisol (the "stress" hormone).[66] The surge in oxytocin may be, in part, responsible for MDMA's empathic effects.[67] MDMA may lead to positive social interactions because it improves users' ability to recognize positive emotions in others, while decreasing their ability to recognize negative emotions.[68] In addition, MDMA activates the ventral striatum, an area involved in reward expectation, and decreases activity in the amygdala, which processes fear and rage.[69]

Deliriants and Dissociatives

Anticholinergics such as atropine and scopolamine prevent acetylcholine from binding to muscarinic receptors, which are found in the heart, lungs, digestive tract, and glands, as well as in the brain. It was once thought that the active ingredient in *Amanita muscaria* mushrooms was muscarine, and that they therefore exerted their actions by affecting acetylcholine, but the levels of muscarine are actually insignificant. *Amanita's*

main psychoactive substances are two structurally related compounds—muscimol and ibotenic acid. Muscimol is a GABA$_A$ agonist responsible for most of the mushroom's effects, such as confusion, disorientation, and sensory disturbances. Ibotenic acid, some of which is converted into muscimol after ingestion, binds to NMDA glutamate receptors, which are involved in learning, memory, and allowing the brain to change in response to external stimuli.

Salvinorin-A, found in the dissociative hallucinogen salvia, binds to kappa opioid receptors that regulate perception.[70] The dissociative anesthetics PCP and ketamine bind to and block glutamatergic NMDA receptors, especially in the cortex and hippocampus, which leads to a sense of disconnection from one's body and surroundings. This inhibition of the NMDA receptor can trigger production of brain-derived neurotrophic factor (BDNF), which stimulates the growth of new brain cells in the hippocampus.[71] Dissociative anesthetic drugs also increase the synthesis and release of dopamine, leading to agitation, stimulation, and increased motor activity. This dopaminergic effect explains why PCP and ketamine have an addictive potential, while the classic hallucinogens do not.

Synesthesia: When stimulation of one sense leads to sensations in a different sense.

Acute Effects of Hallucinogens

An old adage says, "We do not see things as they are; we see them as *we* are." This is particularly true for hallucinogenic drugs. More than virtually every other class of psychoactive drug, the effects of hallucinogens are often unpredictable and are heavily dependent on the *set*—the intentions, expectations, mental, and physical capacities of the user—and the *setting*—the user's physical and interpersonal environment.[72]

Physiological and Psychological Effects of Psychedelic Hallucinogens

LSD is considered the prototypical psychedelic hallucinogen, and so we will focus on its effects first (Figure 6.16).[73] Some have categorized the experiences of a trip into distinct stages, but be aware that these hallucinatory experiences are extremely variable, and depend on the dose taken, the environment, as well as the user's previous experience, personality, and state of mind.

The first stage develops gradually over 20 minutes. During this stage, there are some physiological changes, which are usually mild and brief. Psychedelic hallucinogens are sympathomimetic, and therefore elevate heart rate, blood pressure, blood sugar, respiratory rate, and body temperature, and cause sweating, dilated pupils, loss of appetite, and sleeplessness. Users sometimes feel dizzy and nauseated. These drugs can cause muscular tremors and make muscles feel weak, twitchy, or numb. LSD and psilocybin also can cause uterine contractions, making LSD dangerous for pregnant women.

The second stage begins 30 minutes to 2 hours after

ingestion. The physiological effects diminish as altered sensations begin. Common objects or experiences may take on a significant, strange, exaggerated, or mystical appearance, and the users' perception of space and time is altered, making minutes seem like hours. Sensory perceptions are exaggerated and heightened. Colors can seem more intense, and textures look especially clear. Spirals, tunnels, and checkerboard patterns are common illusions, as are flashes of light, visual trails, and a sense of movement in stable objects. These images can be seen with eyes open or closed. Sounds, smells, and tastes are also intensified, and users may experience an overlap of the senses called **synesthesia.** Someone experiencing synesthesia may taste music or hear colors. Synesthesia may occur because the thalamus does not route sensory information to its proper destination.

Three to five hours after the start of the trip, the third stage begins. Visual illusions, as well as distortions of space and time continue, and users also may experience abnormalities in the perception of self—they may

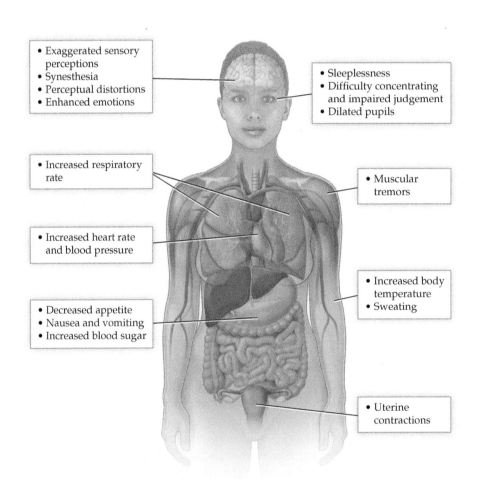

- Exaggerated sensory perceptions
- Synesthesia
- Perceptual distortions
- Enhanced emotions

- Sleeplessness
- Difficulty concentrating and impaired judgement
- Dilated pupils

- Increased respiratory rate

- Muscular tremors

- Increased heart rate and blood pressure

- Increased body temperature
- Sweating

- Decreased appetite
- Nausea and vomiting
- Increased blood sugar

- Uterine contractions

FIGURE 6.16. Acute effects of LSD.

feel that their mind is disconnected from their body, or that their body appears oddly distorted. They may lose their sense of self, or feel they have a deeper sense of themselves.

Cognitive alterations also occur. A person on a psychedelic trip may have difficulty focusing, maintaining attention, and concentrating. They may be preoccupied with trivial thoughts, experiences, or objects. Judgment may be impaired, and they may believe that they can speak to God, telepathically understand others' thoughts, or communicate with animals. Individuals on a psychedelic trip may feel they are undergoing a profound mystical or religious experience.

People on a psychedelic trip may experience great swings of emotion from exaltation to panic. Albert Hofmann, the first person to synthesize and ingest LSD, recalled[74]:

My surroundings had now transformed themselves in more terrifying ways. Everything in the room spun around, and the familiar objects and pieces of furniture assumed grotesque, threatening forms . . . I was seized by the dreadful fear of going insane. I was taken to another place, another time . . . Kaleidoscopic, fantastic images surged in on me, alternating, variegated, opening and then closing themselves in circles and spirals . . . It was particularly remarkable how every acoustic perception, such as the sound of a door handle or a passing automobile, became transformed into optical perceptions. Every sound generated a vividly changing image, with its own consistent form and color.

The enhanced emotionality may sometimes lead someone to psychological insights. However, highly adverse reactions including frightening hallucinations, confusion, disorientation, agitation, depression, and/or terror can occur as well when someone experiences a **bad trip**. A bad trip may be terrifying and can leave long-lasting psychological scars.[75] Users can be overcome by disturbing images that they cannot control, or they may experience intense anxiety, panic, and paranoia. Users may fear that they are losing their mind or their identity, or that reality no longer exists.

Typically, LSD users cannot consciously control whether they have a good or bad trip. However, bad trips are more likely when the drug is taken in an uncomfortable setting—especially if the user is taking the drug for the first time or consuming a high dose. Bad trips can be alleviated with benzodiazepines such as Xanax.

There is no evidence that a bad trip will lead to long-term psychiatric problems, but if taken while someone is depressed or anxious, LSD can exacerbate a preexisting psychiatric illness or affective disorder. The incidence of LSD-related psychosis is about 0.08 percent.[76] When mental breakdowns do occur, they typically involve people who were unaware that they were taking LSD, showed unstable personality characteristics prior to taking LSD, or were experiencing LSD under hostile or threatening circumstances.[77]

Some LSD users also have **flashbacks**, visual disturbances such as trails or flashes of color that occur long after the drug has left the body. Flashbacks are typically brief and mild, and appear and disappear spontaneously, although they may be brought on by stress, fatigue, anxiety, emergence into a dark environment, or marijuana use.[78] Flashbacks are more common in heavy hallucinogen users: 30–60 percent of those who have taken 20 or more trips have experienced a flashback.[79] Flashbacks tend to diminish in frequency and intensity with time, and do not usually occur more than a year after the original drug experience. Psilocybin users do not typically experience flashbacks.

There is no evidence that LSD causes damage to any human body organ.[80] LSD's therapeutic index is quite high (many reports estimate it as well over 1,000). There are, in fact, no documented toxic fatalities from LSD use, but some of the behavioral consequences associated with these drugs may be fatal. People have jumped off buildings believing they could fly, violently attacked others, or even committed suicide after a bad trip. In addition, because hallucinogens may only be obtained illegally, dealers can dissolve many toxic substances onto blotter paper, or provide pills of unknown composition.

Compared with LSD, psilocybin produces effects that are warmer, more relaxing, less isolating, and not as emotionally intense. A psilocybin trip is more strongly visual and more euphoric, and is associated with fewer panic reactions and less chance of paranoia. The risk of overdose is low with psilocybin; a 130-pound person would need to take 40–50 pounds of fresh psilocybin mushrooms to produce a lethal effect.[81]

Bad trip: A disturbing and frightening psychological experience associated with the use of a psychedelic drug.

Flashback: A phenomenon in which an individual re-experiences perceptual elements of a psychedelic episode long after the effects of LSD have worn off.

Ask yourself: How do you measure the danger of a drug? LSD isn't physically toxic, but strong negative psychological effects may result. How do these effects figure in to your assessment of what schedule the drug should be classified as or how safe the drug is?

The onset of a mescaline trip is more gradual. Users experience fewer changes in mood and the sense of self; they also experience more side effects, such as headaches, nausea, and vomiting, than with LSD or psilocybin use. Mescaline is also more toxic; its therapeutic index is approximately 7–30.[82] Mescaline deaths are due to convulsions and respiratory arrest.

Physiological and Psychological Effects of MDMA

MDMA's effects reflect its unique structure—a combination of amphetamine-like stimulation and the altered perception associated with hallucinogens. Like the classic hallucinogens, MDMA has sympathomimetic effects—it increases heart rate and blood pressure, dilates the pupils and bronchioles, and increases sweating. After taking MDMA, many experience muscle tension and tremor, headache, jaw tension, and teeth grinding. Although ecstasy is called the "love drug" because users may experience a sense of empathy and closeness to other people as well as increased energy and arousal, in actuality the drug reduces a person's ability to achieve orgasm. Ecstasy also suppresses the appetite, elevates the body temperature, and can decrease one's sensitivity to pain.

Users may experience a sense of inner peace, self-acceptance, emotional warmth, compassion, and forgiveness toward others. They also may feel more sociable and talkative and be able to discuss normally anxiety-provoking topics with ease. In addition, MDMA can lead to feelings of euphoria, self-confidence, and decreased fear. However, aggression, defensiveness, jealousy, anxiety, and insecurity are also common. The psychoactive effects of MDMA appear stronger in women.[83] Women experience more perceptual changes, thought disturbances, toxic reactions, and greater fear

Hyponatremia: Low sodium concentration in the blood.

Serotonin syndrome: A potentially life-threatening reaction that can occur when medications cause large amounts of serotonin to accumulate in the body.

of loss of body control.[84,85,86] Most side effects are fairly minor and short-lived, and mostly are related to the drug's amphetamine-like properties.

Most toxic reactions to MDMA occur with high doses or multiple doses. Psychologically, a person who has taken a high dose may experience panic, anxiety, paranoia, disorientation, confusion, hallucinations and delusions, and cognitive and memory impairment. Physiological reactions to an MDMA overdose include muscle twitching, over-reactive reflexes, rapid breathing and/or shortness of breath, heart palpitations, cardiac arrhythmias, hemorrhage, stroke, loss of consciousness, organ failure, coma, and death. The therapeutic index of MDMA is about 14–16.[87] Often, the toxic reactions are due not solely to the MDMA, but to the circumstances in which the drug was taken.

MDMA intoxication can cause hyperthermia; body temperatures of over 104 degrees are not uncommon, and some have been reported as high as 110 degrees. Significantly elevated body temperature is the most dangerous side effect of MDMA, and most MDMA-related deaths result from persistent hyperthermia and the resulting organ failure.[88] The high potassium levels that occur due to kidney failure can lead to fatal heart rhythms and death.[89] MDMA's effect on hyperthermia is strongly affected by ambient temperature, so MDMA use is much more dangerous at a crowded dance party than under laboratory conditions.

MDMA increases secretion of antidiuretic hormone, which causes the user to retain fluid and have overall lower plasma levels of sodium, a condition known as **hyponatremia**. When a user is dancing at a crowded party, he or she may drink large amounts of water, exacerbating this effect. Hyponatremia can lead to headache, nausea and vomiting, muscle cramps, weakness, fatigue, confusion, seizures, and cerebral edema. Often, those with MDMA-induced hyponatremia will lose their ability to speak, even before they lose consciousness. Estrogen exaggerates MDMA's effect on antidiuretic hormone, so women are more likely to be affected by hyponatremia.[90] Hyponatremia can occur with just a single dose of ecstasy. Nearly 20 percent of those who report this complication die. Others experience permanent brain damage.[91]

MDMA use can lead to cardiac complications such as hypertension, tachycardia, cardiac arrhythmias, and increased blood coagulation. In those who already have heart disorders, this effect can be fatal.

Finally, because MDMA triggers an excessive release of serotonin, **serotonin syndrome** sometimes results. Serotonin syndrome is characterized by cognitive symptoms, such as headache, agitation, confusion, and hallucinations; autonomic indications, including elevated blood pressure and heart rate, diarrhea, shivering, sweating, and hyperthermia; and somatic signs, such as muscle rigidity and twitching, heightened reflexes, and tremor. In severe cases, heart rate, blood pressure, and body temperature may elevate enough to cause seizures, muscle breakdown, renal failure, and death. Serotonin syndrome is fatal 10–15 percent of the time.[92] The condition is more severe in patients who have taken other drugs such as antidepressants that increase synaptic serotonin.

Physiological and Psychological Effects of Deliriant Hallucinogens

"Hot as a hare, blind as a bat, dry as a bone, red as a beet, and mad as a hatter." This phrase, memorized by medical students the world over, summarizes the physiological effects of deliriants, including deadly nightshade, datura, mandrake, and henbane. These anticholinergic drugs produce hyperthermia, dilated pupils and blurred vision, dry skin and mouth, flushed skin, and delirium, as well as elevated heartbeat and blood pressure, agitation, confusion, urinary retention, and constipation.

Unlike other psychedelics that mostly produce illusions, such as alterations in color, shape, and movement, deliriants produce visions that more closely match the traditional definition of a true hallucination—experiencing phenomena that are not actually there. The hallucinations tend to be very unpleasant. Coupled with the high risk of unintentional overdose, the anticholinergic deliriant drugs are not a popular choice among recreational drug users.

Anticholinergic deliriants have a low therapeutic index. A dose capable of producing hallucinations is close to the lethal level for these drugs, and death can occur due to respiratory failure. Deliriant overdose can be treated with drugs that elevate the levels of acetylcholine in the synapse.

Physiological and Psychological Effects of Dissociative Anesthetics

When Alice was wandering in Wonderland, she came upon a mushroom. Eating from one side of the mushroom made her shrink, while the other side caused her neck to stretch and grow. Many believe that *Amanita muscaria* mushrooms were Lewis Carroll's inspiration, as they can cause the user to perceive that

his or her body parts appear larger or smaller than they are.[93] These mushrooms can produce euphoria, a sense of lightness and dizziness, as well as vividly colored hallucinations. Physiologically, they cause muscular twitches and spasms, numb feet, sweat, salivation, constricted pupils, lowered blood pressure, and drowsiness. Effects appear 30–90 minutes after ingestion and peak within 3 hours. The user typically recovers within 12–24 hours, but some effects—such as headache, retrograde amnesia, and sleepiness—can last for days. The effects of the *Amanita* mushroom are variable and depend upon the person's size, the amount ingested, what part of the fungus is consumed, and the season in which the mushroom is picked, among other factors.

Salvia's effects range from a subtle alteration of consciousness to a full-blown psychedelic trip. Users may experience vivid visual imagery, sensory disturbances, and time distortions; they may feel as though they are disconnected from their body and traveling through space and time. Users also can experience dizziness, nausea, incoordination, slurred speech, chills, and decreased heart rate. Very high doses can cause lesions in the brain and exacerbate psychiatric illnesses.[94] Salvia's effects can last from 15 minutes to 2 hours, depending on the dose and route of administration.

PCP is one of the most complex psychoactive drugs with a wide array of effects—stimulant, depressant, analgesic, anesthetic, convulsant, and hallucinogen—all of which depend upon the dose, environment, and characteristics of the user. A low dose—less than 5 mg—produces drunken behavior, drowsiness, slurred speech, numbness of the extremities, and poor coordination. At doses of 10 mg or more, the effects become more difficult to predict. The user may experience muscle rigidity, agitation, radical mood swings, combative behavior, and a feeling of strength and invulnerability. Heart rate, blood pressure, and sweating may increase, along with pupil dilation and nausea and vomiting. Individuals on PCP may experience alterations in the sense of time and distance, as well as visual and auditory hallucinations. These hallucinations differ from those experienced by users of LSD. There are fewer reports of intense visual experiences, and more reports of body perception changes, paranoia, and disorganized thinking. As their eyes twitch rapidly from side to side or stare blankly ahead, some PCP users feel completely detached from their body and from external reality.

There is no evidence that PCP increases strength, but it does cause a dose-dependent loss of pain sensitivity. Picture someone running around intoxicated, uninhibited, paranoid, and insensitive to pain; it is not surprising then that PCP-intoxicated people frequently find themselves in trouble with the law.[95] The effects of PCP typically last for four to six hours, but delirium, confusion, paranoia, and impaired memory can linger for days or even weeks. Users often have no memory of the events after they recover from the experience.

PCP's therapeutic index is about 10–15. High doses of PCP—20 mg or more—can cause convulsions, respiratory failure, coma, and death. However, most PCP deaths result from the aftermath of drug-induced delusions, such as a leap from a tall building, accidents, or suicide.

Ketamine's effects are similar to those of PCP, with fewer hallucinations and a shorter duration of action.[96] Like PCP, ketamine gives the user a feeling of being separated from one's body and cut off from reality, a phenomenon called "going down a K hole." About 2 mg/kg can cause anesthesia; those taking ketamine for depression receive a dose of about 0.5 mg/kg.

Drug Interactions

A number of drugs interact with hallucinogens. Some of these effects are summarized in Table 6.4.

Medical and Therapeutic Uses of Hallucinogens

Psilocybin, LSD, and mescaline are classified as schedule I, and so they involve very burdensome procedures for research approval.[99] Finding funding for hallucinogen research is also difficult—both the pharmaceutical companies and the U.S. government are reluctant to fund the research. Many researchers turn to private donors, who often do not have the resources to allow for large-scale human trials.[100] Hallucinogen research may have turned a corner, however. In 2019, philanthropists gave $17 million to fund the Johns Hopkins Center for Psychedelic and Consciousness Research. Although it is an onerous process for American scientists and doctors to study hallucinogens, these drugs have many therapeutic uses.

A cluster headache is one of the most painful conditions a human can experience; it is described as worse than amputating a limb without anesthesia. The pain may be related to dilation of the blood vessels in the brain. Cluster headaches, which predominately affect men, come in cycles—an excruciating pain on one side of the head that may occur at the same time each day for weeks, followed by a pain-free period lasting weeks, months, or years. Sub-hallucinogenic microdoses of LSD and psilocybin can reduce the pain from cluster headaches and also interrupt the cluster headache cycle. In some cases, a single dose may be enough to induce remission.[101,102] Psilocybin and LSD's effectiveness in treating cluster headaches may be due to the fact that serotonin can cause vasoconstriction.[103]

Psilocybin and LSD also have been used to improve the psychological adjustment in dying patients.[104] In studies of patients with cancer, patients who received psilocybin showed significantly less depression and anxiety, and these effects lasted for months after

TABLE 6.4.   Some Hallucinogenic Drug Interactions

Drug	Effect	Mechanism
MAO inhibitors	Prolong and enhance the effects of psilocybin. Can cause serotonin syndrome when taken with MDMA	Increased levels of serotonin
Selective serotonin reuptake inhibitor (SSRI) antidepressants	Decrease effects of LSD, psilocybin, MDMA	SSRIs, which have extremely long durations of action, bind to the serotonin transporter and prevent the psychedelic drug from binding[97,98]
Antipsychotics, MDMA, LSD, anticholinergics	When any of these are taken in combination, potentially lethal hyperthermia may result	Affect temperature regulation areas of the brain
Alcohol	Potentially fatal when combined with PCP or ketamine	Cause respiratory depression

Sources: Malberg, J.E., & Bonson, K.R. (2001). How MDMA works in the brain. In J Holland (Ed.), Ecstasy: The complete guide. Rochester, VT: Park Street Press.

Farre, M., Abanades, S., Roset, P.N., Peiro, A.M., Torrens, M., et al. (2007). Pharmacological interaction between 3,4-methylenedioxymethamphetamine (ecstasy) and paroxetine: Pharmacological effects and pharmacokinetics. Journal of Pharmacology and Experimental Therapeutics, 323(3): 954–62.

treatment. There were no clinically significant adverse effects in patients who received the psychedelic.[105,106] A single dose of LSD also improved the psychological adjustment of dying patients by reducing anxiety, improving their responsiveness with family members, and making their everyday lives more enjoyable.[107,108] Cancer patients who no longer responded to conventional pain treatments also experienced relief with LSD. Their pain disappeared for 12 hours and was reduced for two to three weeks, with no adverse medical reactions.[109]

When psychedelics first made it into the public eye in the middle of the twentieth century, they were embraced by some psychotherapists for helping reduce patient defensiveness, facilitating recollection of repressed memories, helping patients gain insight into their condition, and breaking down emotional barriers. Current clinical trials both within and outside the United States offer promising findings with respect to the use of psilocybin, ketamine, and other psychedelic drugs for the treatment of depression, anxiety, and obsessive-compulsive disorder.[110,111,112,113,114,115, 116] In 2018, the FDA designated an experimental psilocybin-based compound as a "breakthrough treatment" for depression in order to fast-track the drug development and review process. Breakthrough treatment status is given to a drug if preliminary clinical evidence suggests that it might be significantly better than available treatments. In 2019, the FDA approved a form of ketamine for the treatment of depression. It can be administered only in a medical office where the patient can be closely monitored. Recent clinical trials demonstrate that medically monitored MDMA, given along with psychotherapy, significantly reduces PTSD symptoms in patients, and these benefits persist in many patients for years.[117,118, 119,120] The use of psychedelic drugs to treat mood disorders is discussed further in Chapter 13.

Hallucinogens also have been used to treat alcohol, cocaine, opioid, and tobacco addiction (Chapters 5, 7, 10, 12, and 18).[121,122, 123,124] Studies have found that a majority of cigarette smokers had abstained from smoking for over a year after a psilocybin-facilitated treatment.[125, 126] A single dose of ibogaine may promote long-term drug abstinence from alcohol, cocaine, and opioid addiction.[127,128,129] LSD and ketamine may help reduce alcohol dependence as well. After receiving a single dose of LSD, 59 percent of participants reported lower levels of alcohol misuse, compared with 38 percent of those who received a placebo.[130] Six months after leaving treatment, those who took LSD were 15 percent

Ask yourself: Unlike other psychiatric drugs, LSD isn't guaranteed to relieve a specific symptom, and its effects largely depend on the context in which it is taken. Should therapeutic uses of LSD be investigated, or is it too risky? Why?

more likely to be sober. Ketamine may help significantly reduce alcohol consumption in heavy users by interrupting positive memories about drinking.[131]

The context of psychedelic use is important, however. Having someone who is dependent upon alcohol take LSD at home is not a cure for alcohol dependence; the psychedelic drug needs to be administered in a rehabilitation facility under psychiatric guidance. In addition, this research is preliminary. Many of these studies have a very small sample size, some do not include a control group, and double-blind studies are rare, given that the effects of psychedelic drugs are obvious to the participants.[132]

Anticholinergics also have medical therapeutic uses. For example, atropine can be used for the management of peptic ulcer and gastroesophageal reflux disease. Ophthalmologists use anticholinergics to dilate their patient's pupils so they can examine the retina, and anesthesiologists employ them during surgery to inhibit excessive salivation and airway secretions. Scopolamine is an ingredient in anti–motion sickness medications, and daturine can help alleviate some symptoms of Parkinson's disease. Because it does not suppress cardiac output or respiratory function nearly as much as other anesthetics, ketamine is still used as an emergency surgical anesthetic, or during short surgical procedures involving the head or neck.

Chronic Effects of Hallucinogens

For the most part, hallucinogenic drugs have a low potential for abuse. Chronic administration of classic psychedelics such as LSD is not associated with significant organ damage, although there is some organ damage associated with MDMA and dissociative hallucinogens.[133,134]

Tolerance
Tolerance to the behavioral effects of hallucinogens develops—and dissipates—very quickly; when

schizophrenics were treated with LSD on a daily basis, tolerance was evident by the second day and complete by the third day. After four to six days of abstinence from LSD, the user could once again experience the full effect of the drug.[135] Tolerance develops more slowly to mescaline. The psychedelic hallucinogens show cross tolerance, meaning that users of one of these drugs also become tolerant to the effects of the other psychedelic drugs. Chronic users quickly develop tolerance to MDMA's enhancement of empathy, but some of the unpleasant amphetamine-like effects become *more* pronounced with subsequent use.[136]

Adverse Effects of Chronic Use

Chronic use of LSD and psilocybin do not appear to cause damage to any organ systems, although long-term use is associated with an increased risk of flashbacks. Hallucinogen users are also disproportionately represented among psychiatric inpatients, although it might be that those with an underlying psychiatric condition are more likely to use hallucinogens.

Chronic use of MDMA occasionally has been associated with erosion of the tooth enamel due to grinding, liver damage, and depression.[137] However, the relationship between MDMA use and depression is confusing and contradictory. While some studies show that heavy users do have higher rates of depression,[138,139] others do not.[140,141] If chronic MDMA use is indeed correlated

Neurotoxic: Something that damages nervous tissue.

with higher rates of depression, it does not necessarily mean that MDMA *causes* later depression; it might be that those with depression are more likely to use MDMA. Additionally, most MDMA users also take other illicit drugs, and depression could be correlated with the use of these other drugs.[142]

Many studies show that MDMA is **neurotoxic** in animals, which means it has a poisonous effect on the nerves and nerve cells.[143,144,145,146] Administration of high doses of MDMA produces a loss of serotonin and serotonergic nerves, which may be temporary with low doses, but permanent when high doses are administered. Figure 6.17 shows the effect of MDMA on the amount of serotonin in monkey brains. A high dose of MDMA resulted in depletion of serotonin two weeks after administration of the drug; seven years later there was some recovery, but not to the initial level before administration of the MDMA.

MDMA also appears to produce neurotoxicity in humans. Habitual ecstasy users have low levels of serotonin, as evidenced by lower levels of serotonergic metabolites in their cerebrospinal fluid, fewer serotonin transporters, and less serotonin bound to serotonin transporters.[147,148]

Many studies suggest that the use of MDMA, even moderate use, can cause cognitive and memory deficits in humans. One study examined 149 people who had used MDMA only five or fewer times. These participants took a series of tests of learning and memory. One year later, the participants were retested. Some had not used

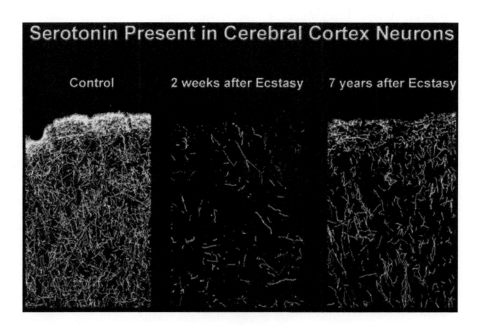

FIGURE 6.17. The effect of MDMA on the brain. Heavy MDMA use is associated with significant damage to serotonin neurons in the brain.

Source: Image courtesy of Dr. GA Ricaurte, Johns Hopkins University School of Medicine.

MDMA in the past year, and others had (members of this group had taken an average of 33.6 tablets in the past year). Researchers found that even light use of MDMA might cause subtle memory deficits up to a year later.[149]

A recent study compared the cognitive skills of 52 MDMA users against 59 matched nonusers.[150] The researchers considered many of the shortcomings in past experiments and eliminated many confounding factors. They controlled for exposure to other drugs, and participants were drug-tested to assure that they were truthful about drug use or abstinence. Groups were compared based on such factors as age, gender, race, ethnicity, childhood history of conduct disorder, and attention-deficit/hyperactivity disorder (ADHD). In addition, all participants were part of the rave culture, so all were exposed to similar noise, sleep, and temperature conditions. This well-controlled study found no short- or long-term differences in cognitive skills in MDMA users compared to controls. They did find that MDMA users had poorer strategic self-regulation and possible increased impulsivity, but this could reflect a characteristic of MDMA users rather than a result of the drug.[151]

Unlike the use of other hallucinogens, long-term PCP and ketamine use is associated with memory loss,

Critical Evaluation

Is MDMA neurotoxic in humans, and does it cause cognitive damage?

Chronic MDMA use depletes brain levels of serotonin, which may have subtle but important long-term effects on cognition and mood.[152] But simply because MDMA causes serotonergic losses, does this cause actual cognitive impairment? The role of neuronal degeneration in the brain and cognitive deficits in humans is highly controversial.

Dose needed to produce neurotoxicity. Laboratory animals typically receive higher doses of MDMA than humans take with recreational use. MDMA is also administered subcutaneously to lab animals, a route that is two to three times more neurotoxic than the oral route typically used by humans. If MDMA does produce cognitive deficits in humans, at what dose do these deficits occur?

Heavy MDMA users who reported minimal exposure to other drugs showed significant neuropsychological deficits compared with nonusers, while moderate users did not.[153] But what is "moderate" use? "Heavy" use? Who makes the determination and based on what?

Significance in the real world. Simply because there is a difference on a test in a laboratory situation does not necessarily mean that in "real life" it would cause cognitive problems in an MDMA user. How can we measure the real-world significance if a deficit does exist?

Duration of deficit. Many studies followed regular MDMA users and tested them after they had not taken the drug for three to five months; these studies found that MDMA users scored more poorly on a number of cognitive tests.[154,155] But what if the damage was only short-term? If there is a deficit, how long does it last? When researchers used PET scans to look at serotonin transporter binding in former MDMA users who had not used the drug for at least a year, users of multiple recreational drugs who had never taken MDMA, and 19 controls who reported no illicit drug use, they found no significant differences in depression, anxiety, or IQ among these groups.[156]

Quality of research. In 2002, a paper published in the prestigious journal *Science* reported that a recreational dose of MDMA destroyed dopamine neurons and could potentially cause Parkinson's disease.[157] Unfortunately, the scientists only *thought* they were administering MDMA to the animals; a bottle was mislabeled, and they were actually giving the animals methamphetamine, which *has* been found to destroy dopaminergic cells. Although the paper was retracted, the impression that ecstasy is neurotoxic to dopaminergic cells remained. How can we evaluate the quality of research? What are some negative repercussions from bad research?

In addition, many studies are based on self-reports of drug use. How can we tell if subjects are telling the truth about their drug use? How accurate is their memory about how many times they actually took the drug?

The effect of other drugs. MDMA is illegal and is only obtainable from illicit sources. When a user swallows a hit of ecstasy or Molly, he or she does not actually know how much MDMA, if any, was in the tablet. Participants in these studies have likely been exposed to varied amounts of MDMA. In addition, most ecstasy users also use other drugs. How can a researcher be sure that the cognitive effects being measured are due to MDMA rather than the concurrent use of marijuana, alcohol, or other drugs?

The role of the environment. MDMA is often taken at raves or dance clubs, so use is often associated with dancing all night in a loud and hot environment. How can we know if the cognitive effects are due to the drug, or if they are due to a lack of sleep, a barrage of noise, or constant exposure to high temperatures?

Correlation versus causation. Many studies have found diminished serotonin in MDMA users. But low serotonin concentrations have been linked to impulsivity and sensation seeking, which might predispose someone to seek out MDMA. Perhaps those with memory problems, depression, or low serotonin are more likely to use MDMA. Is the low serotonin an effect of MDMA use, or the cause of it?

---

persistent speech problems, delusional thinking, and, in ketamine users, urinary tract dysfunction that can be irreversible and result in renal failure.[158] Long-term dissociative hallucinogen users may also experience flashbacks of their dissociative trip and/or chronic and severe anxiety and depression.

Hallucinogen Dependence and Addiction

Psilocybin, LSD, and mescaline are not considered addictive, because they do not produce drug-seeking behavior, and users do not go through withdrawal after use.[159] Some possible reasons for this lack of compulsive use include the long duration and significant emotional expense that a trip often entails; the rapid development of tolerance, such that repeated ingestion is useless; and the inconsistent, uncontrollable, and context-dependent effects.

MDMA has a slight potential for dependence. Some people will use ecstasy regularly, but usually in a certain context, such as at a party. They may experience a small withdrawal effect; a few days after use, they may feel drowsy, fatigued, anxious, and depressed. They may find it difficult to concentrate and be less motivated to finish tasks. The backlash one experiences from withdrawal after ecstasy use has been coined "Terrible Tuesday."

Some moderate degree of dependence is seen with PCP and ketamine. Given the chance, animals will self-administer PCP. There also may be some physical dependence in humans, but most dependence in humans is psychological.[160] Dependence to ketamine is more likely if the user has easier access to the drug, such as those who work in a surgical setting, laboratory, veterinary clinic, or club.

Chapter Summary

- **History of Hallucinogens**
  - » Psilocybin mushrooms were an important part of social and religious rituals of Central and South American Indians for thousands of years. Aztecs considered the peyote cactus to be sacred.
  - » LSD was first synthesized and ingested by Albert Hofmann. Psychologists investigated LSD in the 1950s and 1960s as a therapeutic tool, and the CIA performed clandestine experiments with LSD, giving it to unsuspecting victims. Timothy Leary, once a professor at Harvard, championed the use of LSD and psilocybin.
  - » MDMA was developed in 1912 and tested as a psychotherapeutic agent in the 1960s. It found a degree of popularity in the 1970s and 1980s as an aid to the therapeutic process but was declared a schedule I drug in 1988.

- » PCP and ketamine were first marketed as anesthetics that did not depress respiration or cause cardiac irregularities, but they produced hallucinations, paranoia, and other frightening psychological effects and were consequently withdrawn from therapeutic use.
- **Prevalence of Hallucinogen Use**
  - » LSD and psilocybin's popularity peaked in the late 1960s and early 1970s and then began to taper off. MDMA was most popular in the early 2000s, then fell in popularity, and is rising once again.
- **Source and Forms of Hallucinogens**
  - » Some hallucinogens are synthesized; others occur naturally in some plants, fungi, and animals.
  - » Psychedelic hallucinogens alter perceptions while still allowing the person to communicate with the present

world. They are divided into indoleamines, such as LSD and psilocybin, which are structurally similar to serotonin; and phenylethylamines, such as mescaline and MDMA, which are structurally similar to dopamine and norepinephrine.

» Deliriants such as belladonna and datura produce mental confusion and the inability to differentiate reality from fantasy.

» Dissociatives such as PCP and ketamine produce analgesia, amnesia, catalepsy, and a sense of detachment from the environment.

- **Cultural and Religious Influence of Hallucinogens**
  » The influence of psychedelic drugs can be seen in the artwork, fashion, literature, movies, and music of the 1960s.
  » Hallucinogens have been used in religious ceremonies for thousands of years. Many users report that they enhance spiritual or mystical experiences. The Native American Church of North America considers the use of peyote to be a sacrament.

- **Pharmacokinetics of Hallucinogens**
  » Doses of hallucinogens vary greatly. LSD is the most psychoactive substance known; it takes only 25 micrograms to produce effects.
  » Psilocybin and peyote are usually eaten or steeped into tea.
  » LSD is typically dissolved in liquid, which is put on blotter paper or sugar cubes.
  » MDMA is usually taken as a tablet.
  » PCP and ketamine can be ingested, snorted, smoked, or injected.

- **Mechanism of Action of Hallucinogens**
  » Psychedelic hallucinogens largely work by affecting serotonin. They affect brain areas related to sensory processing, personal and social assessments, emotions and mood, and higher executive processing.
  » MDMA increases levels of serotonin, dopamine, and oxytocin.
  » Deliriants such belladonna and datura prevent acetylcholine from binding to its receptors; *Amanita muscaria* mushrooms bind to GABA and glutamate receptors; and PCP and ketamine bind to and block glutamatergic NMDA receptors.

- **Acute Effects of Hallucinogens**
  » There are three stages to an LSD trip: (1) the sympathetic nervous system is activated; (2) alterations in perceptions and sensations occur; and (3) the user's self-perceptions may change, leading to distortions of space and time and emotional swings.

» During a bad trip, users can be overcome by disturbing or terrifying images, or negative emotions that they cannot control. Some LSD users have flashbacks.

» Psilocybin and LSD have a very high therapeutic index, and there is no evidence that these drugs damage any body organ.

» MDMA is associated with sympathomimetic effects, as well as a sense of empathy and closeness to others. Toxic reactions to MDMA, including hyperthermia, low plasma levels of sodium, cardiac complications, and serotonin syndrome, usually occur when high doses or multiple doses are taken.

» Deliriant hallucinogens lead the user to feel "hot as a hare, blind as a bat, dry as a bone, red as a beet, and mad as a hatter."

» PCP's effects vary. Depending on the dose, environment, and characteristics of the user, it may act as a stimulant, depressant, analgesic, hallucinogen, and anesthetic. High doses can cause convulsions, respiratory failure, coma, and death. Ketamine's effects are similar to those of PCP.

- **Medical and Therapeutic Uses of Hallucinogens**
  » Psilocybin, LSD, mescaline, and MDMA are all classified as schedule I drugs, yet they may have therapeutic uses. Some of the uses for which they are being investigated include relief of cluster headache, depression, PTSD, and drug and alcohol addiction, and to ease the psychological trauma in end-of-life patients.
  » Anticholinergics such as atropine can be used to treat peptic ulcers and gastric reflux, to dilate pupils, and to inhibit salivation during surgery.

- **Chronic Effects of Hallucinogens**
  » Tolerance to the behavioral effects of hallucinogens develops and dissipates very quickly.
  » Psilocybin, LSD, and mescaline are not considered addictive, but MDMA, PCP, and ketamine may have a slight potential for dependence.
  » Chronic use of MDMA has been associated with depression and cognitive deficits. Many factors must be considered to accurately assess MDMA's role in long-term cognitive damage.
  » Long-term PCP and ketamine use are associated with memory loss, persistent speech problems, and delusional thinking.

Key Terms

Alkaloid (p. 117)
Bad trip (p. 135)
Catalepsy (p. 122)
Deliriants (p. 122)
Dissociatives (p. 122)
Ergot (p. 117)

Flashback (p. 135)
Hallucination (p. 116)
Hallucinogen (p. 116)
Hyponatremia (p. 136)
Illusion (p. 116)
Microdosing (p. 131)

Neurotoxic (p. 140)
Psychedelics (p. 122)
Serotonin syndrome (p. 136)
Synesthesia (p. 134)

Quiz Yourself!

1. List five naturally occurring plants or fungi that are hallucinogenic.

2. True or false? Mescaline is to peyote as morphine is to the opium poppy.

3. True or false? MDMA is chemically related to amphetamine.

4. Which of the following has the highest therapeutic index?

    A. Belladonna

    B. MDMA

    C. LSD

    D. PCP

5. True or false? LSD was first synthesized by the CIA.

6. True or false? It takes a relatively high dose of LSD to produce an effect.

7. Match the drug to the *primary* neurotransmitter it affects:

    1. _____ LSD   A. Acetylcholine

    2. _____ MDMA   B. GABA

    3. _____ *Amanita muscaria*   C. Glutamate

    4. _____ Psilocybin   D. Serotonin

    5. _____ Belladonna

    6. _____ PCP

8. Which of the following is NOT a mechanism by which MDMA exerts its effects?

    A. Increases release of serotonin into the synapse

    B. Increases actions of the enzyme MAO

    C. Blocks reuptake of serotonin

    D. Increases release of dopamine

9. What is the word that describes the phenomenon that occurs when stimulation of one sense leads to sensations of a different sense, such as tasting music or hearing colors?

10. Which of the following is one of the potential severe side effects of MDMA?

    A. A significant increase in body temperature

    B. Dehydration

    C. Slowed heart rate

    D. None of the above—there are no severe side effects associated with MDMA

Additional Resources

Websites

Multidisciplinary Association for Psychedelic Studies (MAPS). www.maps.org

Johns Hopkins Center for Psychedelic and Consciousness Research. https://hopkinspsychedelic.org/

Videos

Hallucinogens: How psychedelics, dissociatives, and deliriants differ. https://www.youtube.com/watch?v=FByE-ppYIkI

Bicycle Day: The discovery of LSD. https://www.youtube.com/watch?v=L32mAiLXnLs

Movies

Go. (1999). 102 minutes. A movie about a girl, a rave, and some ecstasy. Starring Katie Holmes, Sarah Polley, Scott Wolf, Jay Mohr, and Timothy Olyphant.

Books

Lee, M.A., & Shlain, B. (1994). *Acid dreams: The complete social history of LSD: The CIA, the sixties, and beyond.* New York: Grove Press.

Learn more with this chapter's digital tools at www.oup.com/he/rosenthal2e.

Opioids

True or false?

1.
True or false? In the eighteenth century, Britain went to war with China in order to force them to buy opium.

2.
True or false? Heroin was once marketed as a safe, nonaddictive cough suppressant.

3.
True or false? Americans consume about 80 percent of the global opioid supply.

Answers: 1. T, 2. T, 3. T

Learning Objectives

- Identify the major components of opium.
- Trace the history of opioid use.
- List the five main factors that caused opiate addiction to greatly increase during the nineteenth century.
- Clarify the ways that race and socioeconomic status influenced the development of drug laws in the United States.
- Describe how heroin is chemically different from morphine.
- Compare and contrast the natural, semi-synthetic, and synthetic forms of opioids.
- Explain the way opioids interact with the opioid receptor and the effects this produces in the body.
- Outline the acute physiological and behavioral effects of opioids.
- Describe some physiological and social effects of long-term opioid use.
- Explain the significance of the Rat Park experiment.
- Evaluate the pros and cons of needle exchange programs.

Opiate: A drug derived from opium.

Opioid: Any natural, synthetic, or endogenous substance that binds to the opioid receptor.

Narcotic: From the Greek word *narke*, meaning "numbness" or "stupor" (which gives rise to the word "stupid"), a narcotic is a drug that relieves pain, induces sleep, and reduces sensibility.

The highest highs. The lowest lows. A God-given gift of relief. A scourge of Satan. Opioids have been considered all these and more. **Opiates** are drugs, including opium, morphine, and codeine, which occur naturally in the opium poppy. **Opioids** is a comprehensive term that refers to any natural, synthetic (manufactured), or endogenous (produced by the body) substance that binds to the opioid receptor. Opioids are also sometimes referred to as narcotics. Although often used inappropriately to refer to any illicit psychoactive drug that causes some degree of dependence, such as cocaine, amphetamine, or marijuana, a **narcotic** is a drug that dulls the senses, relieves pain, and induces sleep.

History of Opioids

Opium is one of the oldest drugs in the world, having been cultivated for at least 6,000 years. Throughout the centuries, opium and its derivatives have both alleviated pain and caused great suffering.

Early Opioid Use

Archeological evidence suggests that Neanderthals may have used the opium poppy 30,000 years ago. The first known written reference to the plant is in an ancient Sumerian text from around 4000 BCE that refers to the opium poppy as *hal gil*, or "joy plant." Opium use spread throughout the Middle East, North Africa, and Greece. Alexander the Great gave his army opium to help them march longer and sleep more restfully, and the Greek physician Hippocrates wrote of opium's sleep-inducing properties.

Although the Muslim religion frowned on the use of alcohol and other intoxicants, opium was enthusiastically used and traded. Between the eleventh and fifteenth centuries, opium spread from the Middle East throughout India, Asia, and Western Europe.

In 1524, the Swiss physician Paracelsus created laudanum (from the Latin meaning "to praise"), a medicinal drink that combined opium, wine, musk, crushed pearls, and spices. Physician Thomas Sydenham introduced his own formulation in 1680, which greatly increased in popularity over the next two centuries. Sydenham is quoted as having said, "Among the remedies which it has pleased the Almighty God to give to man to relieve his sufferings, none is so universal and efficacious as opium."[1]

Opioids

Type of drug: Narcotic

Chemical formula:
- Morphine: $C_{17}H_{19}NO_3$
- Heroin: $C_{21}H_{23}NO_5$

Routes of administration:
Ingested, smoked, snorted, injected

Duration of effect: 2–6 hours

Neurotransmitters directly affected: Endogenous opioids

Tolerance: Intense

Physical dependence: Intense

Psychological dependence: Moderate

Withdrawal symptoms:
Vomiting, sweating, cramps, diarrhea, depression, irritability, gooseflesh

Schedule (depends on specific formulation):
- I: Heroin, fentanyl
- II: Morphine, opium, codeine, hydrocodone, hydromorphone, methadone
- III: Buprenorphine

Slang:
- Opium: Aunti, poppy
- Morphine: M, morpho, Miss Emma
- Codeine: Schoolboy
- Heroin: Big daddy, China white, garbage, H, horse, junk, skag, smack
- Hydrocodone: Vikes, hydro
- Oxycodone: OC, oxy, OxyContin, roxies, hillbilly heroin
- Fentanyl: Chinagirl, apache, murder 8
- Methadone: Dollies
- Tramadol: Chill pills, ultra

Smoking Opium

Although it was popular to ingest opium via drinks such as laudanum, the growing popularity of smoking tobacco also led people to smoke opium, which provided a more rapid, intense, and addictive means of experiencing the drug. Opium smoking was a communal experience, and opium dens became social meeting places (Figure 7.1).

In the early eighteenth century, sailors and traders introduced China to the practice of smoking opium, and widespread opium addiction followed.[3] In 1750, Britain assumed control of opium growing districts in India, and for the next several decades, England held a monopoly on the sale of opium. England's desire to

QUICK HIT

Opium dens had benches or upholstered couches on which smokers would relax on their sides while holding the long pipe. Because they would recline for hours as the drug took effect, many addicts developed sore hips. Smoking opium came to be called "on the hip" or just "hip." Eventually, "hip" became associated with being avant-garde. In the 1960s, people who wanted to be hip became known as "hippies." "Yen" is another word that derived from the opium den. To have a yen for something means to desire it. Yen, or *yen-yen*, comes from the Chinese word for "craving for opium."[2]

FIGURE 7.1. Opium den. Opium smoking was typically a social rather than a private event. Many opium dens had couches or beds on which users could recline as the drug took effect.

maintain their lucrative opium trade to China would eventually lead to not one, but two wars.

Opium Wars

By the 1830s, the opium habit was associated with so much crime and corruption that the Chinese government banned its use and importation. Meanwhile, England's drug of choice was tea, which it imported from China. However, because the Chinese considered Westerners to be barbarians, English products were not in high demand. Trade, therefore, occurred mainly in one direction, leading to a steady drain of British assets.[4] To maintain the trade balance, Britain smuggled the forbidden, yet still highly desired, opium into China for lucrative profits.

In 1839, the emperor of China sent Commissioner Lin Tse-Hsu to the port of Canton, where he seized and destroyed over 20,000 chests of opium.[5] In retaliation, and in what would become the start of the first opium war (Britain called it "The War for Free Trade"), England sent warships to the China coast and massacred between 20,000 and 25,000 Chinese soldiers, losing only 69 British sailors in the process. The city of Shanghai fell to Britain in 1842, whereupon China signed the Treaty of Nanking, which forced the Chinese to reopen five ports to traders, cede Hong Kong to Britain for 155 years, and pay England millions of dollars for the cost of the war and loss of income.

When the opium trade resumed, with it came piracy, smuggling, and addiction, which by 1856 were at an all-time high. The Chinese were again desperate to end trade, but England wanted to legalize opium in China and open all of China to British merchants. The second opium war began in 1856, and this time French and American forces joined British soldiers to once again defeat China. Among other conditions, the terms of the Convention of Peking, which ended the war, legalized the opium trade. By 1900, half of the adult male population of China was addicted to opium.[6]

Opioids in the Nineteenth Century

Opiate addiction in the Western world also skyrocketed during the nineteenth century. This was due to a number of factors, including:

- *Isolation of morphine.* In 1803, at the age of 20, pharmacist's assistant Friedrich Sertürner isolated and identified the active ingredient in opium. He named it morphine, after Morpheus, the Greek god of dreams, who often is depicted clutching a handful of opium poppies. Because morphine is more potent than opium, it is also more addictive.
- *Invention of the hypodermic syringe.* In 1853, Dr. Alexander Wood invented the hypodermic syringe. Because it enters the bloodstream directly, intravenous morphine produces stronger and more rapid feelings of relief and euphoria than when it is ingested.
- *Influx of Chinese immigrants.* When gold was discovered in California in 1848, some 300,000 people flocked to the state to seek their fortunes. To aid this migration, a railroad line was built from Iowa to San Francisco, and Chinese immigrants performed most of the manual labor. Many of these laborers came from Canton, where opium trafficking was particularly intense. After their grueling days of work, they often would gather together to smoke opium, for social interactions and relaxation. After the railroads were completed, many of these workers eventually settled in San Francisco and other West Coast cities where opium dens became popular.
- *War.* Battlefield surgeons often had to amputate injured limbs quickly due to the excruciating pain, but with morphine, the physicians could sedate the patients and have more time to better perform surgeries. It is not surprising that morphine was called "God's Own Medicine." Due to its widespread use, however, by the end of the Civil War, an estimated 400,000 veterans were addicted.[7]
- *Patent medicines.* The three leading causes of death in the nineteenth century were pneumonia, tuberculosis, and diarrhea, and opium was a drug that alleviated symptoms of them all! Opium and morphine were found in many medicines, wines, and enemas, easily and legally available, socially acceptable, and inexpensive. Opium also was used (often ineffectively) as a treatment for cholera, malaria, smallpox, syphilis, headache, toothache, earache, painful menstrual periods, mental illness, fatigue, measles, bedwetting, morning sickness, hemorrhoids, masturbation, photophobia (sensitivity to light), nymphomania (compulsive sexual behavior), and hiccups.[8,9]

QUICK HIT

Throughout much of the nineteenth century, opioid use was common among the British writing elite. Charles Dickens, who authored *Great Expectations* and *Oliver Twist*, used opioids, as did poets Percy Bysshe Shelley, John Keats, and Elizabeth Barrett Browning.

Social Factors Influencing Opiate Laws

In nineteenth-century Britain, opium was sold over the counter. Less expensive than alcohol, opium was consumed mainly by men, women, and children of the lower classes. On the other hand, the more powerful and potent morphine was controlled by the medical profession and was used mainly by the upper classes. During the mid-nineteenth century, a temperance movement against opiates arose. The movement was aimed at the poor; the reasoning being that wealthy people could control themselves, but the lower classes could not. In 1868, the British Parliament passed the Pharmacy Act, which restricted the sale of opiates to pharmacists and doctors. This meant that the wealthy could go to a doctor to obtain their morphine, but it was more difficult for the poorer people to obtain their less addictive and less potent opium. In reality, administration of morphine by a physician was more likely to lead to addiction than consumption of opium in a patent medicine.[10]

A similar phenomenon occurred in the United States, where morphine was enthusiastically consumed and regarded as a valuable and legitimate tool in a doctor's pharmacopeia, while smoking opium was thought to be an appalling vice, with no therapeutic purpose, practiced by degenerates. The first drug law in the United States—the 1875 San Francisco Ordinance—was specifically aimed at outlawing Chinese opium dens.

Synthesis of Heroin

Heroin was first synthesized in 1874 by British chemist Charles Adler Wright. After initial tests, Wright shelved the drug, and heroin went unnoticed for 23 years, until chemist Felix Hoffman, working at the Bayer Company, resynthesized it.

Felix Hoffman played a key role in creating two of Bayer's most famous drugs. Hoffman added two acetyl groups to morphine and created diacetylmorphine, eventually to be named heroin. Later that year, Hoffman added an acetyl group to salicylic acid, thus creating aspirin. Hoffman's supervisor, Heinrich Dreser, thought aspirin was a worthless product (Chapter 15), but he had confidence in heroin's commercial potential and marketed the drug as a remedy for tuberculosis, laryngitis, and cough (Figure 7.2).

Opioids in the Twentieth Century

By the beginning of the twentieth century, opium and its derivatives were found in more than 50,000 medicines, and up to 1 percent of Americans were addicted. The U.S. government began to introduce measures to crack down on drug use. As they did in England, U.S. drug laws reflected a racial and class bias.

Early Federal Government Actions

In 1901, Henry Cabot Lodge introduced a resolution, adopted by the Senate, which forbade the sale of opium and alcohol to "aboriginal tribes and uncivilized races . . ." and was later extended to include "uncivilized elements . . . such as Indians, Alaskans, the inhabitants of Hawaii, railroad workers, and immigrants at ports of entry."[11]

Ask yourself: Do you think class and socioeconomic status still play a role today in our views of opioid use? What are some examples to support your position?

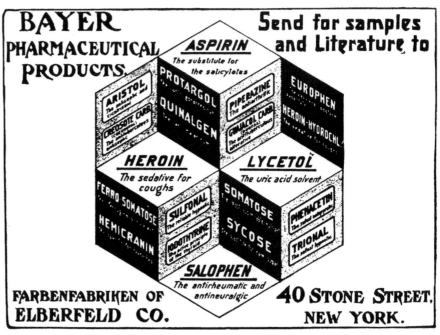

FIGURE 7.2. **Bayer Company's ad for aspirin and heroin.** Heroin was marketed as a safe and non-addictive cough suppressant.

In 1905, the U.S. Congress banned the use of opium, and the following year Congress passed the Pure Food and Drug Act, which required pharmaceutical manufacturers to label the contents of their patent medicines. President Teddy Roosevelt appointed Hamilton Wright to be the U.S. opium commissioner. Wright believed that if the United States could organize and lead a series of international conferences about opium trafficking, China would reward the United States with favorable trade concessions. In 1912, a drug control treaty was signed at The Hague International Opium Convention, and Wright convinced the participants to pledge to pass laws regulating opium, morphine, and cocaine.[12]

The Harrison Narcotics Act and Its Ramifications

To address drug use in the states, Hamilton Wright worked with Congressman Francis Harrison to introduce the **Harrison Narcotics Act**. This act decreed that physicians and pharmacists had to be licensed to prescribe opium, morphine, and cocaine; that they must register with the U.S. Treasury Department and pay a nominal tax; that they should keep records of the narcotic drugs they dispensed; and that they could only prescribe in the course of their medical practice. This act was signed into law in 1914.

The Harrison Narcotics Act left the status of the addict uncertain. Addiction itself was not illegal, and physicians could prescribe narcotics to their patients. But could a physician prescribe narcotics simply to maintain an addict's habit? Later Supreme Court decisions declared that addiction was *not* a disease and made it illegal for physicians to prescribe opioids to help users maintain their addiction. As a result of the Harrison Narcotics Act, doctors were fined, jailed, and ruined, and the characteristics of the typical opioid addict changed—from a middle-class white woman who obtained the drug from her doctor, to a young, lower-class criminal male.[13] By 1924, the U.S. Treasury Department's narcotics division had banned all legal narcotic sales, including heroin, which was faster-acting than morphine, more potent, and less expensive. Heroin became the perfect black-market drug because it was compact and odorless, and because it could be cut and diluted, which increased profits.

Harrison Narcotics Act: Signed into law in 1914, this act regulated and taxed the production, distribution, and prescription of opium, morphine, and cocaine.

QUICK HIT

During the early 1920s, a number of New York City heroin addicts supported themselves by picking through industrial dumps for scraps of copper, lead, and other metals, which they collected in a wagon and sold to a dealer. The term *junkie* came from these junkmen.[14]

Heroin use remained at a relatively low level until the end of World War II, when it began to increase, especially in inner-city ghettos. In the 1950s, in an effort to stop the spread of communism in Asia, America made alliances with tribal commanders of "the golden triangle," which included Myanmar (previously known as Burma), Thailand, and Laos. As part of those alliances, the United States supplied tribal commanders with guns and ammunition, as well as air transport for opium. The flow of illegal heroin into the United States exploded.[15] Throughout the 1960s and 1970s, the use of heroin and all drugs accelerated, due in part to the counterculture and to our military presence in Vietnam.

The 1960s until Today

Heroin use was rife in Vietnam. About one-third of army-enlisted men fighting in Vietnam from 1970–1971 had tried heroin, and 20 percent of soldiers felt they were dependent on or addicted to the drug.[16] The heroin available in Vietnam in the 1960s was about 95 percent pure, compared with the heroin in the United States, which was 2–10 percent pure. Because the heroin in Vietnam was so pure, most users were able to mix heroin with marijuana or tobacco and smoke it, rather than injecting the drug.[17] In addition, heroin in Vietnam was inexpensive: a soldier could purchase 250 mg of pure heroin for $10; in the United States, the same amount of highly diluted heroin would cost 50 times as much. Finally, many of the soldiers were underage, and military rules prevented underage soldiers from buying alcohol, so heroin was actually more accessible for these soldiers than alcohol.[18]

Because of the epidemic use of heroin among America's fighting men, President Richard Nixon established Operation Golden Flow in 1971. Any military personnel due to leave Vietnam were required to undergo a drug test and submit a clean urine sample before being allowed to return home. If he tested positive, the soldier was sent to a detox program for about a week. Almost 11 percent of enlisted men's urine tested positive at departure.[19]

In the 1990s, Afghanistan increased its poppy cultivation and became the major source of opium around the world. In 2000, the Taliban banned poppy cultivation, which cut Afghanistan's production by 94 percent. But in 2001, American and British troops removed the Taliban, and poppy cultivation and heroin production increased once again. Today, Afghanistan is the world's largest supplier of heroin, producing more than 90 percent of the world's opium, although the majority of heroin consumed in the United States comes from Mexico.[20]

QUICK HIT

- The price of a gram of heroin around the world[21, 22]:
- New Zealand: $567
- United States: $307
- Japan: $267
- Finland: $168
- Ireland: $155
- China: $80
- Spain: $64
- Germany: $48
- The Netherlands: $45
- Portugal: $30
- Greece: $24
- Afghanistan: $5

Currently, opioid use is still very prevalent, although use has fallen in recent years.

Prevalence of Opioid Use

Each year, the world consumes about 7,400,000 pounds of opium, which is the weight of Seattle's space needle. Almost 83 million Americans age 12 and older—30 percent of the population—report using prescription pain relievers in the past year, and almost 10 million people report misusing these drugs.[23] The total economic burden of the opioid crisis in the United

States from 2015 to 2018 was at least $631 billion, including costs related to health care, the criminal justice system, child and family assistance programs, education programs, and lost productivity.[24]

Prescription Opioids

Gram per gram, individuals in the United States consume more narcotic medication than any other nation worldwide; Americans consume about 80 percent of the global opioid supply.[25,26] Hundreds of millions of opioid pain prescriptions are dispensed to patients each year in the United States; in fact, clinicians in the United States are more likely to prescribe opioids, and to prescribe higher doses of opioids, than doctors in other countries, even though recent studies suggest that opioids are often less effective than non-opioid analgesics.[27,28] In recent years, physicians have been prescribing less opioid analgesics to their patients (Figure 7.3). The downside of this is the possibility of under-treating patients in pain, as well as the possibility that opioid-addicted patients will seek out heroin or other black-market opioids.

Opioid medications, which can be beneficial when prescribed and taken legitimately for pain relief, are often abused. The nonmedical use of prescription painkillers has soared in the past few decades. Figure 7.4 shows where users of nonmedically indicated pain relievers generally obtain their drugs.[29]

Over half a million American youth between the age of 12 and 17 reported misuse of opioids in the past year.[30] People who are most likely to abuse prescription

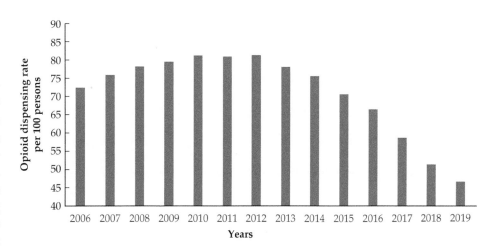

FIGURE 7.3. **Opioid prescription rate in the United States: Prescribing rate per 100 patients.** Physicians in the United States are prescribing fewer opioid analgesic prescriptions to their patients. At its peak in 2012, there were over 255 million opioid pain prescriptions dispensed.

Sources: CDC (2021). U.S. opioid prescribing rate maps. Accessed on June 27, 2021 from https://www.cdc.gov/drugoverdose/maps/rxrate-maps.html

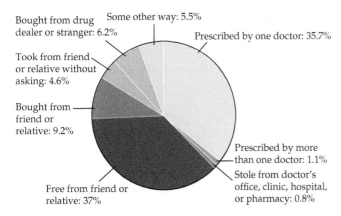

FIGURE 7.4. Drug sources for nonmedical use. Most people who use nonmedically indicated pain relievers obtain them for free from a friend or relative.

Source: Substance Abuse and Mental Health Services Administration (SAMHSA). (2020). Results from the 2019 National Survey on Drug Use and Health: Detailed tables. Rockville, MD: Center for Behavioral Health Statistics and Quality.

pain medications tend to live in rural areas, are often unemployed, and are often less educated.[31,32,33,34]

Heroin

Worldwide, between 15 and 21 million people age 15–64 use heroin. According to the National Survey on Drug Use and Health, almost 5.7 million Americans report having tried heroin at least once in their lives; about two in every thousand Americans over the age of 11—431,000 people—have used heroin in the past month; and every day, 136 people try heroin for the first time.[35] Many researchers believe this survey vastly understates heroin use; an analysis by researchers at the RAND corporation estimated that there were about 1 million daily heroin users in the United States.[36]

Heroin use greatly increased over the last decade, but has declined a bit over the past few years (Figure 7.5). One reason for the surge in use is the increased use of prescription pain medications; in fact, 80 percent of new heroin users started out misusing prescription pain medications.[37] Some people who abuse prescription opioids may find that heroin is easier to obtain, more potent, and less expensive.[38]

Ask yourself: The media often report on the epidemic of nonmedical opioid use among middle- and upper-class families. Yet, these drugs are most often abused by those of lower socioeconomic status in rural areas. What do you think accounts for this discrepancy in media reporting versus what the data show?

In the mid-1990s, a gram of highly adulterated heroin (heroin that has many impurities or is cut with a large amount of other substances) cost about $1,000. Today, a gram that is about 32 percent pure can be purchased for around $300.

The demographic composition of heroin users also has changed. In the past, heroin use was largely seen in inner-city minority populations, but use has spread to the suburbs and rural towns, where it is primarily used by young, white men and women in their late twenties.[39]

Source and Forms of Opioids

Opioids come from many sources. Some opioids occur naturally in the poppy plant, while others require some chemical modification. Some opioids are entirely synthetic, while still others are endogenous, occurring naturally in the body (Table 7.1).

The primary source for naturally occurring opioids is the poppy flower, *Papaver somniferum* ("The poppy that brings sleep"). Native to southern Europe and western Asia, the poppy flower is now cultivated all over the world. The plant, which grows to a height of about 3–4 feet, produces red, white, or purple flowers. Nearly 100 different kinds of poppies exist, but only *Papaver somniferum* produces a sufficient quantity of opium.

Even though it happened to Dorothy in Oz, a person can't just walk through a poppy field and get high. Harvesting the opium from the poppy is a difficult and labor-intensive process. Opium can only be collected during a few days of the plant's life cycle. After the poppies bloom, the flower petals wither and fall, leaving the one- to three-inch, ripe and swollen green seedpod (Figure 7.6). When cut, the walls of the seedpod ooze a milky fluid. The next day, this fluid oxidizes and hardens into a reddish-brown sticky substance. This gummy substance—opium—is scraped off of each poppy plant and dried into small tar-like, bitter balls. Each year, the United States legally imports hundreds of tons of opium powder for medical use. This powder is then refined to produce opioid medications.

Natural Opiates

Over 40 pharmacologically active alkaloids have been identified in opium. The three most common of these are morphine, codeine, and thebaine.

Raw opium has a morphine content that ranges from 3–10 percent, depending on where it is cultivated and

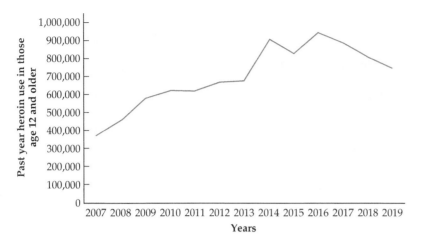

FIGURE 7.5. **Heroin use from 2007–2019.** The use of heroin has greatly increased in recent years.

Source: SAMHSA. (2020). Results from the 2019 National Survey on Drug Use and Health: Detailed tables. Rockville, MD: Center for Behavioral Health Statistics and Quality.

FIGURE 7.6. **Opium poppy.** After the poppies bloom, the flower petals wither and fall, leaving the 1- to 3-inch ripe and swollen green seedpod. When cut, the walls of the seedpod ooze a milky fluid.

how it is processed.[40] Morphine, which is about 10 times more potent than opium, is extracted by dissolving opium in hot water and then adding lime and ammonium chloride to cause the morphine to separate out of the solution. Morphine is a soluble white powder that can be taken orally, or mixed with water and injected.

When compared with morphine, codeine is one-twelfth as effective as an analgesic. Therefore, codeine sometimes is given in combination with nonsteroidal anti-inflammatory drugs (NSAIDs) to increase the analgesic effects. Codeine produces less sedation and respiratory depression, is better absorbed orally, and is a more effective cough suppressant than morphine.

Thebaine has no psychoactive properties and is not a drug of abuse. Thebaine is, however, widely employed in the manufacture of many semisynthetic opioids.

Semisynthetic Opioids

Semisynthetic opioids are created by chemically modifying natural opiates. Semisynthetic opioids include diacetylmorphine (heroin), hydromorphone (Dilaudid), oxymorphone (Opana), oxycodone (Percodan, Percocet, OxyContin), hydrocodone (Vicodin), and buprenorphine (Subutex, Butrans).

The conversion of morphine to heroin is a fairly simple and inexpensive procedure. Two acetyl groups are added to morphine, making it more potent and more lipid-soluble than the original morphine, so that it enters the brain faster.

Before it is sold, heroin is often combined with various contaminants, such as talc, baking powder, or lactose to increase its bulk and mannitol to counteract heroin's constipating effects. Heroin is naturally bitter; if the drug has been cut with sweet lactose, sometimes dealers add quinine to restore the bitter taste. But quinine can be a deadly adulterant, and can cause vascular damage, depressed respiration, and potentially lethal disturbances in the heartbeat. Quinine poisoning is characterized by froth oozing from the nose and mouth.

Heroin is colored from white to brown to black, depending on the source and on the quality of the preparation technique. Pure heroin is white, and colors may be due to the presence of adulterants or imperfections

TABLE 7.1. Comparison of Major Opioids

Category	Generic Name	Brand Name	Slang	Potency (Compared to Morphine)	Duration of Action (hours)	Schedule*	Miscellaneous
Natural	morphine	MS-Contin	Morpho, Miss Emma	1	4–5	II, III	First pure drug ever extracted from a plant
Natural	codeine	Codeine sulfate	Schoolboy	0.1	4–6	II, III, V	Most commonly used narcotic in the world
Semi-synthetics	heroin		H, snow, horse, skag, junk	2–5	3–4	I	Enters the brain 100 times faster than morphine
Semi-synthetics	hydrocodone	Vicodin, Lortab	Vikes, hydro, fluff, scratch	1–1.5	5–7	II, III	The third most prescribed drug in the United States in 2016
Semi-synthetics	hydromorphone	Dilaudid	Dillies, hospital heroin	6–10	4–5	II	Elvis Presley was addicted to Dilaudid in his later years
Semi-synthetics	oxycodone	Percodan, Percocet, Oxy-Contin	Oxy, OC, roxies, percs, hillbilly heroin	1–2	4–5	II	Percodan and Percocet include NSAIDs; Oxy-Contin is the delayed-release form of the drug
Semi-synthetics	buprenorphine	Subutex, Butrans	Bupe, subs	40	24–60	III	Higher doses are used to treat opioid addiction
Synthetic	methadone	Dolophine	Dollies	1	12–36	II	Used as a maintenance drug for opioid addiction
Synthetic	meperidine	Demerol	Doctors	0.1	2–4	II	Has cardiotoxic qualities. Michael Jackson received an injection the night before he died of cardiac arrest
Synthetic	fentanyl	Sublimaze, Actiq	China white, China girl, apache, murder 8	100	1–3	II	In 2002, a fentanyl-based gas was used as a bioterrorism agent against Chechen rebels
Synthetic	carfentanil	WildNil (veterinary use only)	Elephant tranquilizer, drop dead	10,000		II	The most potent opioid used commercially. Intended as a large animal anesthetic. It has been found in the heroin supply in the U.S.
Synthetic	tramadol	Ultram	Chill pills, ultra	0.1	2–6	IV	Tramadol affects not only opioid receptors, but serotonin, norepinephrine, and other neurotransmitters as well; may be used in patients who do not respond well to other opioid pain relievers

*Sometimes the scheduling depends on the purpose and formulation of the drug (see Chapter 2).

in the processing techniques. When heroin first enters the United States, it is typically 95 percent pure, but the purity of heroin sold on the streets ranges from 3–70 percent.

Oxycodone is about as strong as morphine and commonly blended with an NSAID to enhance its analgesic properties. Oxycodone's delayed-release form is Oxy-Contin. When Purdue Pharma presented OxyContin to the FDA, they claimed the drug gave longer pain relief, was less addictive, and less subject to abuse than other opioids. Although there was no data to back up these claims, OxyContin was approved by the FDA in 1995. Used to treat chronic and severe pain, OxyContin was formulated to be delivered over a longer period of time than Percocet or Percodan. But when crushed and snorted, all 12 hours of opioid are delivered at once,

---

STRAIGHT DOPE · Lawsuits against Opioid Manufacturers

The opioid crisis has cost tens of billions of dollars and caused over half a million overdose deaths since the year 2000. As such, cities, counties, states, and individuals across the nation have filed more than 3,000 lawsuits against opioid manufacturers—over $2 trillion worth—to help recoup the cost of opioid abuse. Many drug manufacturers and distributors, including Insys Therapeutics, Johnson & Johnson, and Purdue Pharma, have been sued.

Insys Therapeutics sold a fentanyl-based painkiller, up to 100 times as strong as morphine. Company executives bribed doctors to write prescriptions for a much wider pool of patients than the drug was approved for. In addition, sales reps for Insys would call insurance companies, pretend to be doctors' assistants, and make up false diagnoses so the drug would be approved. A former sales representative testified that her boss, the regional sales director, was a former exotic dancer who gave a lap dance to a physician to encourage him to prescribe the drug. In 2019, top executives at Insys were found guilty of racketeering charges. Their CEO was sentenced to 66 months in prison, and Insys settled for $225 million in order to avoid further criminal and civil investigations.

Johnson & Johnson, the makers of the Duragesic fentanyl patch and other opioids, were found guilty of promoting misleading and dangerous marketing campaigns that contributed to opioid addiction and deaths. In 2019, they were ordered to pay $572 million in damages, after a judge ruled they had fueled opioid addiction in Oklahoma. In June 2021, Johnson & Johnson agreed to pay New York State over $230 million for treatment and prevention, and agreed to permanently stay out of the opioid business in the United States.

Purdue Pharma knew their product OxyContin was dangerous and had a high abuse potential, but they concealed the information and aggressively marketed OxyContin, especially in states with less restrictive prescription regulations. When marketing to physicians, Purdue paid for physicians' trips to luxury locales, all while telling them that OxyContin was a safer, less addictive alternative to other opioids. In 2007, Purdue pled guilty to a felony charges of misrepresenting its risk of abuse and paid $634 million in fines. After this settlement, Purdue continued their aggressive marketing techniques, and in 2019, Purdue agreed to pay an additional $270 million. In 2020, Purdue pled guilty to felony charges of defrauding federal health agencies and violating anti-kickback laws, and agreed to an $8.3 billion settlement. Purdue Pharma will be dissolved as part of the settlement, and assets will be used to create a public benefit company, which will continue to produce and sell opioids, but will also make overdose rescue drugs available at a steep discount to communities dealing with the opioid crisis.

Other lawsuits have been filed as well. Drug manufacturer Teva Pharmaceuticals and three of the nation's biggest drug distributors agreed to a settlement of $48 billion to provide addiction treatment and paramedic services.

Sources:

Emanuel, G. & Thomas, K. (2019). *Top executives of Insys, an opioid company, are found guilty of racketeering.* The New York Times. *Accessed on October 20, 2020, from https://www.nytimes.com/2019/05/02/health/insys-trial-verdict-kapoor.html*

Frakt, A. (2020). *Damage from OxyContin continues to be revealed.* New York Times *https://www.nytimes.com/2020/04/13/upshot/opioids-oxycontin-purdue-pharma.html*

Isidore, C. (2020). *OxyContin maker to plead guilty to federal criminal charges, pay $8 billion, and will close the company. Accessed on October 21, 2020, from https://www.cnn.com/2020/10/21/business/purdue-pharma-guilty-plea/index.html*

Jones, J.S. (2019). *For big pharma, a history of profiting from manufactured addiction.* Undark. *Accessed on December 3, 2019, from https://undark.org/2019/03/05/big-pharma-history-profit-manufactured-addiction/*

Meier, B. (2018). *Origins of an epidemic: Purdue Pharma knew its opioids were widely abused.* New York Times. *Accessed on December 3, 2019, from https://www.nytimes.com/2018/05/29/health/purdue-opioids-oxycontin.html*

Muldoon, M. (2020). *Notable opioid settlements. Accessed on October 20, 2020, from https://www.addictioncenter.com/opiates/opioid-epidemic/notable-opioid-settlements/*

making OxyContin as potent and addictive as heroin. OxyContin has since been reformulated.

Hydrocodone (Vicodin) is often formulated in combination with acetaminophen and is about 1.5 times as potent as morphine. In 2016, hydrocodone (with acetaminophen) was the third most prescribed drug in the United States with 97 million prescriptions written.[41]

Low doses of buprenorphine (Subutex, Butrans) relieve mild to moderate pain, but higher doses are used to treat opioid addiction. Buprenorphine relieves opioid cravings but does not tend to cause dependence itself and can be given alone or combined with naloxone.

Etorphine is an extremely potent opioid discovered in 1960 in an Edinburgh lab when some scientists accidentally stirred their morning tea with a glass rod used in an experiment. The unsuspecting scientists were knocked into a coma. Once they recovered, they analyzed the compound and found it up to 3,000 times as strong as morphine. Etorphine is not used medically for humans; instead, it is the key ingredient in dart guns used to stun elephants and rhinos.

Synthetic Opioids

Synthetic opioids are entirely man-made and are not all chemically related to the natural opiates. Some synthetic opioids include meperidine (Demerol), methadone (Dolophine), propoxyphene (Darvon, Darvocet), fentanyl (Sublimaze), and carfentanil (WildNil).

Meperidine (Demerol) is about as strong as codeine. Shorter-acting and less potent than morphine, meperi-dine is used for relief of moderate to severe pain, particularly in obstetrics and after surgery.

German scientists invented methadone (Dolophine) as a substitute for morphine during World War II when natural opium could not be obtained from the Far East. Methadone is chemically different than morphine, is better absorbed orally and longer lasting, and provides pain relief with little to no euphoria. Tolerance, dependence, and withdrawal do develop to methadone, but at a slower rate than with morphine.

When addicts are given methadone instead of heroin or other fast-acting opioids, methadone not only blocks the effects of heroin, but its gradual and mild onset of action staves off withdrawal without the intense highs and lows of heroin. Today, methadone is used for relief of chronic pain, but it is most commonly used as a maintenance drug for opioid addicts.

Fentanyl (Sublimaze, Actiq) is highly lipid-soluble, and so it has a rapid onset and short duration of action. Fentanyl can be administered intravenously for general anesthesia, and in the form of patches and lollipops to treat chronic pain. Easy and cheap to produce and similar in form and color to heroin, fentanyl is sometimes added to batches of heroin, illicitly created versions of drugs such as oxycodone or Xanax, or other drugs such as cocaine.[42] Because it is up to 50 times more potent than heroin, however, fatal overdose is possible, and fentanyl-related deaths are on the rise (Figures 7.7, 7.11). When taken intravenously, fentanyl can paralyze the muscles of the chest wall, which prevents breathing, and can kill within minutes.[43]

Carfentanil is the most potent opioid used commercially. It is intended as an anesthetic for elephants, rhinos, and other large animals. Carfentanil is 100 times as potent as fentanyl and 10,000 as potent as morphine. Reports of fatal overdoses involving carfentanil have increased substantially in recent years.

FIGURE 7.7.   Prince. In 2016, pop superstar Prince died from an accidental overdose of fentanyl. Investigators believe that the fentanyl may have been added to the illicitly created counterfeit oxycodone tablets he took to control his chronic pain.

Ask yourself: Should the potential abuse of a drug and other social factors be considered when a drug is undergoing Food and Drug Administration (FDA) approval, or should the FDA confine its decision to the physiological and pharmacological effects of the drug? Why?

Pharmacokinetics of Opioids

As with all drugs, an opioid's effects depend on how it is handled by the body. The drug's route of administration, lipid solubility, and interactions with other substances will all influence the opioids actions in the body.

Routes of Administration

The route of administration has important implications for a drug's duration of action, as well as the user's risk of dependence, susceptibility to infection, and route-specific health complications.[44] Opioids can be eaten; absorbed rectally, sublingually (under the tongue), or transdermally (across the skin); snorted; smoked; or injected. The speed of the drug's onset of action depends on its route of administration (Table 7.2).

Absorption, Distribution, Metabolism, and Elimination

Orally administered opioids are much less effective than those given by injection. Morphine is alkaline, so it is not rapidly absorbed from the gastrointestinal (GI) tract. In addition, oral opioids undergo a significant first-pass effect, in which the liver metabolizes the drug and greatly reduces the concentration of active drug that reaches the brain. Codeine and methadone are better absorbed orally than morphine.

High-purity heroin produces its effects when it is snorted or smoked. Because heroin is more fat-soluble than morphine, it can be absorbed across the mucosal lining of the nose to allow for the snorting or inhalation of the drug. When smoked, heroin is vaporized, and the user inhales the resulting fumes.

QUICK HIT

Smoking heroin and inhaling its vapor is sometimes called "chasing the dragon," because the spiraling smoke is thought to resemble a dragon's tail. Chasing the dragon also refers to the idea that opioid users may never quite repeat the thrill of their first high. The availability of high-purity heroin and the desire to avoid using needles has increased the incidence of vaporizing heroin.

Intravenous (IV) injection is the method by which heroin enters the bloodstream fastest. Most heroin users begin by snorting or "popping" the drug—injecting the needle under the skin rather than into a vein. Intravenous heroin users add several drops of water to the heroin powder in an improvised container such as a bottle cap or spoon. They dissolve the powder by shaking it lightly while holding the container over a small flame. They then draw the fluid into the syringe through a small wad of cotton to filter out large contaminants.

Sometimes users will crush up OxyContin or other pills, dissolve them in saline, and inject the suspension, which is very dangerous. Some components of the pills are insoluble in saline. Injecting these insoluble particles into blood vessels can irritate the vessels, leading to vascular inflammation and permanent damage. Particles can also lodge in a small vessel and block blood supply, which can cause a stroke.

After absorption into the bloodstream, opioids accumulate in the liver, lungs, spleen, muscles, and GI tract. Because most opioids are not very lipid-soluble, they do not easily cross the blood–brain barrier. In fact, less than 0.1 percent of an opioid typically reaches its active site in the central nervous system. Drugs like heroin and fentanyl are more fat-soluble, so they reach the brain faster. Once heroin reaches the brain, it is converted back into morphine—heroin is essentially just a more effective delivery system for morphine. Opioids are metabolized in the liver, and some metabolites are more potent analgesics than morphine. Once metabolized, most opioids are eliminated in the urine and feces.

TABLE 7.2. Onset of Opioid Effects Based on Route of Administration

Smoking	7–10 seconds
Intravenous injection	10–20 seconds
Intramuscular injection	5–8 minutes
Snort or sublingual	5–15 minutes
Oral ingestion	30–45 minutes
Transdermal patch	Up to 16 hours

Ask yourself: Consider the fact that heroin is converted into morphine once it reaches the brain; what factors underlie the differences between how society views the use of morphine and how it views the use of heroin?

Mechanism of Action of Opioids

Once opioids are absorbed into the bloodstream, they travel through the body and bind to opioid receptors. These receptors exist because the human body itself produces opioids.

Opioid Receptors

In the 1960s, chemists slightly altered the morphine molecule and produced a substance called naloxone, which reversed the effects of morphine. Scientists assumed that naloxone and morphine must act at a common brain receptor site. In the early 1970s, scientists Sol Snyder and Candace Pert found brain receptors that respond selectively to opioid drugs. These opioid receptors are distributed throughout the body and mediate a number of processes, including analgesia, euphoria, respiratory depression, digestion, and reward.

Opioid receptors are located both presynaptically (on the neuron that releases the neurotransmitter) and postsynaptically (on the neuron that the neurotransmitter directly influences) (Figure 7.8). When opioids bind to presynaptic opioid receptors, they act as neuromodulators and affect the release of neurotransmitters such as dopamine, norepinephrine, GABA, histamine, acetylcholine, and possibly others. When opioids bind to postsynaptic receptors, they themselves act as neurotransmitters and directly alter membrane potential. The body's response to an opioid depends on which receptor it binds to, its affinity for the receptor, whether the opioid is endogenous or medically used, and whether the opioid is an agonist (initiating a physiologic response) or antagonist (blocking a physiologic response).[45]

There are four principal classes of opioid receptors: mu, delta, kappa, and nociceptin (NOP). These receptors are summarized in Table 7.3.

Endogenous Opioids

Once opioid receptors were discovered, researchers asked why the neurons in our brains had binding sites

Endorphin: A morphine-like substance originating from within the body that blocks pain transmission. Endorphins got their name by combining "endogenous," meaning "from within the body," and "morphine."

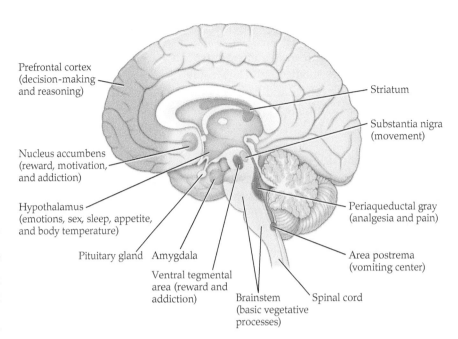

FIGURE 7.8. The location of some opioid receptors in the brain.

for substances that come from the poppy. If our brains have receptors for specific compounds, it must mean that our bodies produce a similar chemical that binds to those receptors. So scientists went looking for an endogenous substance in the brain that could serve as a natural activator of these receptors.

In 1974, two different laboratories identified a naturally occurring peptide that mimicked opioid action, bound to opioid receptors, and was found in high concentrations in brain areas similar to those in which opioid receptors are found. Other endogenous opioids were also found. Overall, there are 18 different molecules endogenous to the brain that can act like morphine. As a group, these endogenous opioids are called **endorphins**, and they may be involved in pain transmission and perception, modulating emotional response, euphoria, eating behaviors, memory, stress, seizures, and the use of alcoholic beverages.[46] Endogenous opioids have a higher affinity for receptors than exogenous opioids because they are an exact fit for the receptor.

Acute Effects of Opioids

Opioids affect almost every part of the body. An opioid's effects depend on many factors, including the dose and potency, the route of administration, the environment in which the drug is taken, the user's degree of toler-

TABLE 7.3. Opioid Receptors in the Brain

Receptor	Location	Corresponding Effects of Opioids	Relevant Opioid Substances that Bind
Mu	• Ventral tegmentum and nucleus accumbens • Periaqueductal gray • Hypothalamus • Locus coeruleus • Medial frontal cortex • Brainstem • Spinal cord • Pupils • GI tract	• Reward and addiction • Analgesia • Euphoria • Alleviation of anxiety; easing of withdrawal • Clouds decision making • Inhibition of respiration, lowering of blood pressure, nausea • Analgesia and itch • Constriction • Constipation	Endorphins Enkephalins Most clinically used opioids are relatively selective for mu receptors
Delta	• Neocortex • Striatum and substantia nigra • Olfactory bulb • Nucleus accumbens	• Sensory perception, spatial reasoning, conscious thought • Abnormal movement • Antidepressant • Addiction	Enkephalins
Kappa	• Pituitary gland • Hypothalamus • Periaqueductal gray • Spinal cord • Also, many of the areas above	• Hormone release, pair bond maintenance, increased urine production • Sedation, dysphoria, depression, disorientation, depersonalization • Modest analgesia	Endorphins Dynorphins PCP and ketamine
NOP	• Limbic system • Spinal cord	• Anxiety, depression, appetite • Pain modulation	Nociceptin Buprenorphine

ance, the user's expectations, and whether or not the user is in pain.

Physiological Effects at Low and Moderate Doses

Opioids cause muscles to relax and limbs to feel heavy. Body temperature generally falls, and skin may flush. Opioids also release histamine, which can cause itching over the entire body. In addition to these acute effects, opioids may affect pain, mood, breathing, digestion, urination, sleep, and reproduction (Figure 7.9).

Central Nervous System

Opioids bind to many areas of the brain and spinal cord, including regions that control pain, mood, cognition, reward, and addiction. They bind to nuclei in the midbrain that cause the pupils to constrict. When first administered, opioids also stimulate

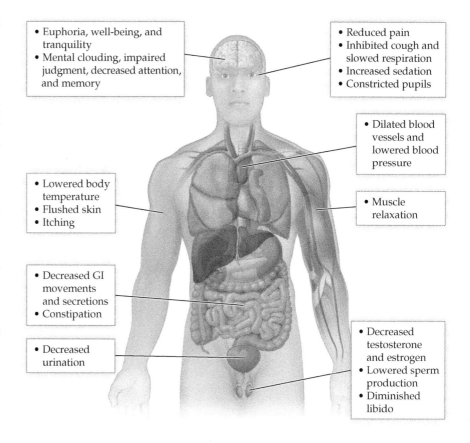

FIGURE 7.9. Acute effects of opioids.

Sol Snyder and Candace Pert

Sol Snyder (Figure 7.10) wandered into research as a means to avoid being drafted to fight in Vietnam. He did graduate work with Nobel Prize–winning scientist Julius Axelrod and, at 31 years of age, became the youngest full professor at Johns Hopkins University. Snyder studied receptors in the brain, and he developed a technique—ligand binding—to aid in his work. In 1973, Snyder, along with graduate student Candace Pert (Figure 7.10), discovered the opioid receptor. For this work, Snyder was awarded one of the most respected science prizes in the world—the Lasker Award—in 1978. Snyder later identified the existence of endogenous opioids in the brain. Today, Snyder is considered one of the most influential living American scientists.

Although Candace Pert discovered the receptor with Snyder—in fact, she was first author on the paper—she was not awarded the Lasker prize, which was instead given to two other males who worked with Snyder. Until her death in 2013, Candace Pert studied psychoneuroimmunology, a science that investigates the link between the mind and the body. Rather than seeing the mind and the

FIGURE 7.10. Sol Snyder and Candace Pert. These doctors developed a technique known as ligand binding and discovered the opioid receptor.

body as separate, she recognized the powerful interactions that occur between the two. Pert also appeared in the 2004 film *What the #$8! Do We Know?*

the area postrema, which is the vomiting center of the brain. Some people find this effect so distressing that they never take heroin or other opioids again. Others find the euphoria so powerful that they ignore the vomiting. Tolerance rapidly develops to this effect, and then opioids suppress vomiting.

Cardiovascular and Respiratory

Opioids suppress the coughing reflex and slow respiration by making cells in the respiratory center of the brainstem less responsive to carbon dioxide. Fortunately, the analgesic effects of opioids usually occur at doses below that which significantly suppresses respiration. Opioids also dilate the blood vessels, decrease blood pressure, and cause flushing of the skin.

QUICK HIT

In the movie *Pulp Fiction*, one character's heroin overdose was treated by an injection of adrenaline into the heart. In reality, this would be ineffective and dangerous, because opioids have little direct effect on the heart.

Neonatal abstinence syndrome: A group of conditions that occur when a baby withdraws from opioid drugs he or she was exposed to as a fetus.

Gastrointestinal and Renal

Opioids decrease the movement of food through the stomach and intestines, and they inhibit secretions from the pancreas and gall bladder, which slows the digestion and passage of food through the system and leads to constipation. Opioids also make urination difficult; they constrict the ureter and the sphincter muscles of the bladder and stimulate the release of antidiuretic hormone.

Sleep

Sedation and drowsiness occur with opioid use. Opioids themselves do not actually increase sleep. If pain is keeping someone awake, the alleviation of pain may allow him or her to sleep. When people take narcotics to sleep, they often have lighter and less restful sleep, sometimes with frequent, vivid dreams.

Reproduction and Effects on the Newborn

Opioids inhibit the release of the hormone GnRH, which lowers levels of the reproductive hormones LH, FSH, testosterone, and estrogen. These hormonal changes can decrease libido, and lead to impotence, amenorrhea (absence of menstruation), and decreased sperm production.

Since 1999, the incidence of babies born with **neonatal abstinence syndrome (NAS)**, a pattern of postnatal drug withdrawal primarily caused by maternal opioid use, has increased more than five-fold.[47, 48, 49, 50, 51] Some newborns who are exposed to opioids in utero will experience withdrawal symptoms that include irritability, vomiting, diarrhea, seizures, and respiratory distress. NAS infants are also more likely to have a low birth weight than other babies.

There's no clear consensus on how to best care for babies going through opioid withdrawal. Many spend weeks in the neonatal intensive care unit (NICU) and are treated with opioids to wean them off the drug. Recently, some hospitals have found better success by letting these infants stay in their parents' arms in quiet, dark environments, rather than in the bright, noisy NICU.[52] When withdrawing babies are in a calm, quiet environment where they are held by a loving individual, the average length of hospital stay and the percentage of babies given opioids plummet.[53]

Long-term effects of prenatal opioid use on a child are hard to accurately assess. Some studies suggest that these children may have poorer academic performance in high school compared to age-matched controls, but it is difficult to differentiate the effects that are due to the opioid exposure versus the effects of poverty, poor childhood nutrition, prenatal exposure to alcohol or other drugs, or other medical risk factors that may accompany opioid use in pregnant women.[54, 55]

Behavioral and Psychological Effects at Low and Moderate Doses

The effects of opioids are not solely physical. Opioids also affect mood and cognitive function, and the resulting euphoria may lead to compulsive use and addiction.

Mood

Opioids cause a sense of euphoria. Many of these narcotics indirectly increase dopamine release in neurons that project from the ventral tegmental area to the nucleus accumbens, also known as the "reward pathway" of the brain, which makes these drugs potentially addictive. Opioids also make the user feel a sense of contentment, well-being, tranquility, and relaxation, as they bind to receptors inhibiting the locus coeruleus, an area of the midbrain that plays a role in panic and anxiety.

Cognitive Function

Opioids lead to mental clouding, impaired judgment, diminished attention and memory, and overall confusion. People on opioids may have slurred speech, dimin-

ished social function, and a sense of disconnectedness. Smoking heroin also has been linked to leukoencephalopathy, an incurable neurological disease that leads to paralysis and death.

Drug Interactions

Most opioid deaths are not due to the ingestion of morphine or heroin alone, but are instead due to the combination of opioids with alcohol, benzodiazepines, or other drugs that amplify their lethal effects.[56] Opioids are particularly dangerous when taken with other respiratory suppressants such as alcohol or Xanax.

Overdose

Each year, thousands of people die from opioid overdose. Opioid-related overdose deaths are one of the leading causes of preventable death in the United States, killing about 170 Americans every day.[57] In 2016, among those age 15–24, more than one in every 8 deaths was attributable to opioids. Among those age 24–35, one in five deaths was attributable to opioids.[58]

As seen in Figure 7.11, there are three waves in opioid overdose deaths in the United States. The first wave began in the 1990s, with increased prescribing of opioids throughout the early part of the new century. The second wave began in 2010; as prescription opioids became more difficult to obtain, there was a rapid increase in opioid overdose deaths involving heroin. In 2013, the third wave began as significantly more overdose deaths involved synthetic opioids, especially fentanyl.

From 1999 to 2018, some 230,000 people died in the U.S. due to prescription opioid overdose. Overdose death of prescription opioids was almost five times higher in 2018 than in 1999.[59] Some groups are particularly vulnerable to prescription opioid overdose. Those most at risk include people who take high doses or otherwise misuse prescription painkillers, people who obtain multiple controlled substance prescriptions from multiple providers ("doctor shopping"), those currently using benzodiazepines, low-income people and those living in rural areas, and those with mental illness and/or a history of substance abuse.[60, 61]

Heroin overdose deaths have risen eight-fold since 2000 (Figure 7.11).[62] Several factors underlie this increased death rate (Figure 7.12):[63]

- Increased number of users, many of whom began with prescription opioids
- Inconsistencies in the purity of illegally obtained heroin, which can lead to accidental overdose

Opioid Overdose Deaths, by type and year

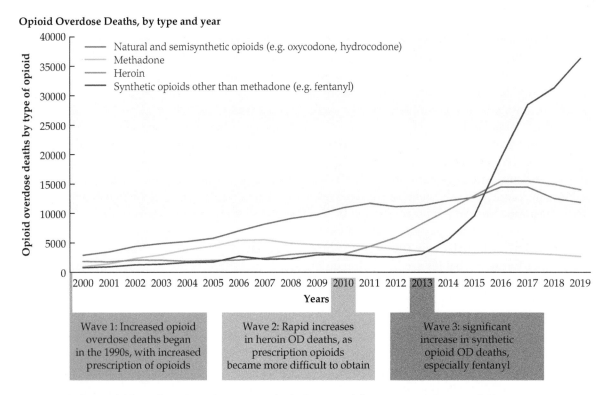

FIGURE 7.11. Deaths from opioid overdose. Since the year 2000, deaths from opioids have increased almost ten-fold.

Sources: Centers for Disease Control and Prevention. (2020). Drug overdose deaths in the United States, 1999–2018. NCHS Data Brief, no 356. Hyattsville, MD: National Center for Health Statistics.

Mattson, C.L., Tanz, L.J., Quinn, K., Kariisa, M., & Patel, P., et al. (2021). Trends and geographic patterns in drug and synthetic opioid overdose deaths—United States, 2013-2019. MMWR, 70(6): 202-07.

- Potentially dangerous impurities found in heroin
- The concurrent use of alcohol or other sedatives
- Heroin use that occurs after a chronic user has gone weeks or months without heroin, and then injects the same amount he or she used before, not realizing tolerance has worn off.

The **opioid triad** of coma, depressed respiration, and pinpoint pupils is the classic sign of opioid poisoning. Very high doses of opioids also can lower one's seizure threshold and cause convulsions. Death from overdose usually occurs when respiration ceases, but depressed respiration generally occurs slowly and is preventable with administration of an opioid antagonist such as naloxone. Naloxone is a short-acting opioid receptor blocker that crosses the blood–brain barrier and

enters the brain faster than heroin or morphine. Once there, it has a higher affinity for the receptor. Therefore, when naloxone is administered, it binds to the receptor in place of those drugs. Naloxone is typically administered by injection or nasal spray, and immediately reverses the life-threatening respiratory suppression of breathing. Studies have found that deaths resulting from narcotic overdose can be prevented by distributing naloxone to heroin users or their families and instructing them about resuscitation techniques.[64,65, 66] In most states, Narcan, an FDA-approved nasal form of naloxone, is available in CVS and Walgreens pharmacies without a prescription.

There is an enormous variation in the therapeutic index of different opioids. Heroin's therapeutic index is about 6. Codeine and methadone have a therapeutic index of 20, while morphine's is 70. The therapeutic index of fentanyl is 400, and that of the opioid analgesic Remifentanil is 33,000.[67]

Opioid triad: The symptoms of coma, depressed respiration, and pinpoint pupils, which are indicative of opioid poisoning.

Acute pain is essential in helping us to avoid physical (and emotional) damage. But chronic or long-term pain has no ostensible purpose; chronic pain is a disease in and of itself. Over 20 percent of adults in the U.S.—some 50 million people—suffer from chronic pain; in about 40 percent of these people, the pain frequently limits their life or work activities.[68] The financial cost to treat pain ranges from $560 billion to $635 billion per year.[69]

FIGURE 7.12. Heroin overdose deaths. Heroin overdose has been responsible for the deaths of many celebrities, including actors Chris Farley, John Belushi, and Philip Seymour Hoffman (pictured).

Medical and Therapeutic Uses of Opioids

Opioids, once called "God's own medicine," are used to treat a number of conditions. They are potent analgesics, cough suppressants, and can alleviate diarrhea.

Pain

When a person is exposed to a stimulus that is causing, or could potentially cause, tissue damage, he or she experiences pain. The sense of pain is different than our other senses. Several types of stimuli—touch, pressure, temperature, light, sound, or even smell—that stimulate **nociceptors** can produce pain. Pain is also highly subjective and dependent on many other factors, including expectations, emotions, environmental stimuli, and stress.

Opioids are an effective analgesic, more so with dull, chronic pain than with sharp, intermittent pain. They bind and activate inhibitory neurons in the spinal cord that impede the transmission of pain up to the brain. They also bind to receptors in the periaqueductal gray (PAG), an area of the midbrain that helps alleviate pain. Women have fewer opioid receptors in the PAG, which is one of the reasons the same stimulus elicits more pain in women than in men.

Although millions of Americans are in pain every day of their lives, some physicians are hesitant to treat their patients' pain due to the fear that patients could become addicted or that they are solely drug-seeking, even though the vast majority of those taking prescription pain medications use them responsibly and do not become addicted.[70] Many chronic pain patients feel dismissed, mistrusted, and judged. Oncologist Dan Brookoff says, "Pain does not have a moral value. Drugs do not have a moral value. Life is good . . . to be cherished, promoted and supported. We, as physicians, should not be moralizing about pain or its treatments."[71]

Nociceptor: A sensory receptor for painful stimuli.

Scientists are working to develop new drugs that effectively alleviate pain but produce fewer side effects and a lower risk of addiction than classic opioids. For example, researchers discovered that the type of opioid receptors targeted by most narcotics sends two messages—one to alleviate pain, and another that controls the development of tolerance and many of the side effects. Blocking a protein that controls the second message stream could give pain relief without many of the negative effects of opioids.[72] In animal studies, one potentially beneficial opioid activates NOP receptors to alleviate pain without the dangerous side effects or risk of addiction.[73]

QUICK HIT

Despite the need for effective analgesics, drug companies are finding it more difficult to shepherd new painkillers through clinical trials. This is not because these new drugs are necessarily less effective, but because the response of participants to placebos has increased over the years, which diminishes the difference in perceived effectiveness between the experimental group and the control group. Pain researcher Jeff Mogil believes that as clinical trials get longer and more expensive, they may be enhancing participants' expectations of their effects, thus boosting the placebo effect. Interestingly enough, this enhanced placebo response is seen only in American participants. America not only has long, large clinical trials, but it is also one of only two countries in the world that permits direct-to-consumer advertising, which may increase people's expectations of a drug's potential benefits.[74]

Ask yourself: How does a physician balance his or her desire to alleviate pain with the reluctance to potentially encourage addiction? Right now, heroin is more readily available to someone seeking it on the street than it is to a terminally ill cancer patient in constant pain. Heroin is currently a schedule I drug, but many doctors feel that heroin should be reclassified as schedule II so it can be prescribed for end-of-life pain relief, because it is more effective than morphine and there is no risk of addiction when a patient has only weeks to live. Heroin is currently legal for medical use in the United Kingdom, Switzerland, Germany, the Netherlands, and Denmark. What do you think? Should heroin be reclassified as a schedule II drug? Why or why not?

Cough Suppressant

Opioids suppress the cough reflex and are especially helpful for dry and nonproductive cough. Dextromethorphan, found in such drugs as Robitussin, NyQuil, and TheraFlu, is an opioid derivative that suppresses cough, and at medically recommended doses it has almost no psychoactive effects. At high doses, dextromethorphan can have dissociative properties. Due to its potential for recreational use and abuse, some retailers in the United States have moved dextromethorphan-containing products behind the pharmacist's counter (Chapter 15).

Diarrhea Treatment

Opioids cause constipation, but physicians are understandably hesitant to use most opioids to treat diarrhea. Loperamide (Imodium) binds to opioid receptors in the intestine, but although it crosses the blood–brain barrier, loperamide is immediately pumped back out again, preventing any euphoric effects and posing little threat of potential abuse.

Chronic Effects of Opioids

With long-term use, the chronic opioid user will experience tolerance. In addition, the risk of physical and psychological dependence on opioids increases with prolonged use.

Tolerance

With repeated opioid use, tolerance develops. And although the process begins with the first dose, tolerance develops at different rates for different effects and does not usually become clinically significant until after two to three weeks of frequent use. For opioid's analgesic effects, euphoria, respiratory suppression, sedation, nausea, and vomiting, tolerance develops rapidly. On the other hand, tolerance to the itching and urinary retention that accompanies opioid use occurs less rapidly. Tolerance occurs most rapidly when high doses are taken at short intervals, and tolerance can be so powerful that users may ingest 10, 100, or even 1,000 times the recommended dose.[75]

Three different types of tolerance to opioids may develop: metabolic, cellular, and behavioral. With chronic use, the liver becomes able to metabolize opioids faster. On a cellular level, downregulation (loss) of opioid receptors occurs with habitual opioid administration, meaning a user will have to use ever-increas-

STRAIGHT DOPE

Kratom

Kratom comes from the leaves from the *Mitragyna speciosa* tree, a member of the coffee plant family native to Southeast Asia. In recent years, kratom has gained popularity in the U.S., where it is usually marketed as a dietary or herbal supplement. It is estimated that 1.3 percent of adults in the U.S.—some 3.4 million people—have used kratom at some point. Some take it recreationally, and others believe it helps them manage chronic pain or help with opioid withdrawal symptoms. The chopped leaves may be brewed into a tea or taken as an extract or pill. Effects begin about 15 minutes after consumption, and last for 1–5 hours.

Kratom's two main active ingredients—mitragynine and 7-hydroxymitragynine—are partial agonists at opioid receptors in the brain. In fact, 7-hydroxymitragynine is 13 times as potent as morphine. Kratom also affects norepinephrine and serotonin. At low to moderate doses, kratom is a mild stimulant, increasing alertness and boosting physical energy. At moderate to high doses, kratom has opioid-like effects, causing analgesia, pleasure, and sedation. Very high doses can lead to stupor and seizure. Common side effects include loss of appetite, sweating, high blood pressure and increased heart rate, dry mouth, hair loss, constipation, increased urination, nausea and vomiting, and erectile dysfunction. More serious adverse effects include seizures, respiratory depression, hallucinations, liver toxicity, and psychosis. Between 2016 and 2017,

there were 152 deaths in the U.S. involving kratom overdose. Most, but not all, of these deaths involved other substances as well.

Kratom is considered to be addictive. Users may build tolerance and go through withdrawal when they stop taking the drug. Symptoms of withdrawal are similar to opioid withdrawal.

Kratom is not yet a controlled substance, but the FDA has issued a public health advisory regarding its use, and the DEA stated that there is no evidence that kratom is safe or effective for treating any medical condition. Kratom is not approved for human consumption, and as it is not regulated or overseen by the FDA, users should exercise great caution in its use.

Sources:

Olsen, E.O., O'Donnell, J., Mattson, C., Schier, J.G., & Wilson, N. (2019). Notes from the field: Unintentional drug overdose deaths with kratom detected—27 states, July 2016–December 2017. MMWR, 68(14): 326–7.

Prozialeck, W.C., Jivan, J.K., & Andurkar, S.V. (2012). Pharmacology of kratom: An emerging botanical agent with stimulant, analgesic, and opioid-like effects. Journal of the American Osteopathic Association, 112(12): 792–99.

Schimmel, J., Amioka, E., Rockhill, K., Haynes, C.M., & Black, J.C., et al. (2020). Prevalence and description of kratom (Mitragyna speciosa) use in the United States: A cross-sectional study. Addiction, doi: 10.1111/add.15082

Veltri, C. & Grundmann, O. (2019). Current perspectives on the impact of Kratom use. Substance Abuse and Rehabilitation, 10: 23–31.

ing doses to achieve the same effect. Most interesting is behavioral tolerance. Long-time opioid users show increased tolerance to the drug if they take it in locations other than where they have previously repeatedly taken the drug.

In a classic experiment,[76,77] Shepard Siegel injected rats with heroin every other day in a particular environment. After 15 such injections, the rats were given a much larger dose of heroin. Half of the rats received this large injection in the environment previously associated with heroin use, and the other half received the injection in a different location. Most of the rats who received their injection in the new environment died of an overdose, while most of the rats that were injected in the familiar environment lived. These rats learned to associate the environment with heroin injection. Conditioned reflexes occurred that counteracted some of the physiological effects of the drug. Glutamatergic NMDA receptors, which are involved in associative learning and memory, seem to be involved in behavioral tolerance of opioids. Giving an NMDA agonist along with morphine is associated with the develop-

ment of tolerance, while co-administration of NMDA antagonists with opioids reduces the development of tolerance.[78]

Cross tolerance to other opioids also can occur. When heroin addicts are given methadone, for example, they do not experience the emotional peaks, because they are already tolerant to the opioid's euphoria and side effects. Likewise, when those who are dependent on opioids undergo a painful medical procedure, administering enough medication to alleviate their pain can be difficult.

Adverse Effects of Chronic Use

Unlike alcohol, amphetamines, and barbiturates, which are harmful to the body with long-term use, heavy use of (safely administered) opioids, including heroin, even after a lifetime of addiction, does not damage or destroy the organs of the body.[79] With the exception of being chronically impotent and constipated, a user may be able to function quite well and live a long life.[80]

This is not to say that chronic opioid use has no ill effects. Long-term opioid use may lead to difficulties

A Bad Batch of Heroin Leads to Paralysis

In 1976, Barry Kidston, a graduate student in chemistry, tried to whip up a batch of MPPP—a synthetic opioid with morphine-like effects—in his garage. Instead of MPPP, he unknowingly produced the neurotoxin MPTP. Within three days of injecting himself with the drug, Kidston began to display severe Parkinsonian symptoms, a disease that normally affects the elderly. Two years later, Kidston died of a cocaine overdose (possibly intentional), and an autopsy showed a loss of dopamine neu-rons in the substantia nigra. In 1982, another batch of MPPP was manufactured illegally in California. Six young men showed up in the ER with bent, twisted, and largely paralyzed bodies. These cases were also ultimately linked to the use of MPPP batches tainted with MPTP.

Source: Jackson-Lewis, V., Lester, D., Kozina, E., Przedborski, S., & Smeyne, R.J. (2010). From man to mouse: The MPTP model of Parkinson disease. In M.S. LeDoux, Ed., Movement disorders (2nd ed.). London: Elsevier.

in problem solving and decision making. Opioids' analgesic properties may conceal early symptoms of illnesses such as pneumonia. Opioids may interfere with the body's ability to repair damaged DNA and may even stimulate the growth and spread of cancer cells. Finally, and ironically, long-term use of opioid painkillers may make a person more sensitive to pain over time.[81]

Rather than the direct effects of the drug, it may be the lifestyle of the opioid abuser that is most dangerous. Opioid addicts may not be taking exemplary care of themselves. They may be malnourished and less able to access health care. When heroin users share needles, they potentially expose themselves to septicemia and abscesses, as well as blood-borne diseases such as HIV and hepatitis. About 25 percent of new HIV transmissions in the United States are due to sharing a needle.

Also, because heroin is illegal in the United States, a user is never sure about the potency or purity of the drug. Black-market heroin may be laced with synthetic opioids such as fentanyl, which has led to a dramatic increase in overdose deaths.[82] Heroin also can contain adulterants and toxins.

Heroin addiction often means a hard life associated with crime. One study followed 581 heroin addicts over 33 years.[83] The heroin addicts had a death rate 50–100 times the rate of the general population for the same age. The most common cause of death was accidental poisoning or overdose. Of those who survived, 20.7 percent were still using heroin, another 9.5 percent refused to be tested, and 14 percent were in prison. The addicts also had high rates of other drug use, mental health problems, and involvement in the criminal justice system.

Opioid Use Disorder and Addiction

Opioids are highly addictive. Not only do they produce feelings of euphoria, they also boost dopamine's ef-fects in the reward and addiction pathway of the brain (Figure 7.13).

Because prescription pain pills may be habit-forming, physicians are often hesitant to prescribe enough pain reliever to adequately alleviate their patients' suffering. However, the fact is that most people who take prescription opioids for pain do *not* become addicted. And if addiction does occur, it typically takes 5–18 months to develop. In a meta-analysis of over 88,000 patients, fewer than 5 percent of patients who were prescribed narcotics for chronic pain became addicted.[84] An earlier study of 11,882 hospitalized patients who received opioids found only four cases of subsequent new addictions—an incidence of 0.03 percent.[85] Even with heroin, considered one of the most addictive drugs in the world, only about 23 percent of users become addicted.[86] Factors that influence addiction include which opioid is used, the size of the dose, the route and frequency of administration, and characteristics of the individual. The following factors may make opioid use disorder more likely:

- Frequent use
- Higher dosage
- A family history of substance abuse problems
- A history of alcohol and other drug use beginning in adolescence and the young adult years
- A dependence on nicotine, alcohol, or sleeping pills
- A past history of depression or other mental illness
- Opioid use as a means of dealing with life's difficulties—to alleviate feelings of anxiety, depression, or boredom[87]

Environmental and psychosocial factors are also very important in the development of opioid use disorder. As discussed earlier in this chapter, about one in every five American soldiers fighting in Vietnam became addicted to heroin. These soldiers were required to detox before returning to the United States, but government officials were justifiably concerned, given that clinical studies found that 90 percent of heroin addicts relapse, most within the first 6 months. However, only 3 percent of the returning soldiers had resumed regular heroin use two years after returning from the war, which is about the same percentage of individuals who were found to be using narcotics when inducted into the service.[88] One reason for these low relapse numbers is that heroin use is, in part, related to the user's environment; although the soldiers used heroin in the war-torn jungles of Southeast Asia, they did not use heroin when they returned to their civilian lives because they were in a different environment. Why, then, are opioids considered to be so addictive?

One reason opioids are thought to be so addictive has to do with studies performed on rats. When caged laboratory rats are given opioids, they quickly become addicted. Professor Bruce Alexander thought that perhaps the problem was environmental rather than chemical. Rats are highly social and curious animals. Yet, in laboratory studies, they are usually isolated in small, bare, metal cages. Alexander and his colleagues, therefore, created "Rat Park," a 200-square-foot area with cedar shavings to nest in; tin cans, balls, and running wheels to play on; and a group of male and female rats to interact with (Figure 7.14).[89] Some of the experimental rats lived alone in small, bare, metal cages, while the others resided in the Rat Park colony. All rats were given two sources of water, one pure and the other laced with bitter morphine. Rats could drink all they wanted, at any time, and devices recorded how

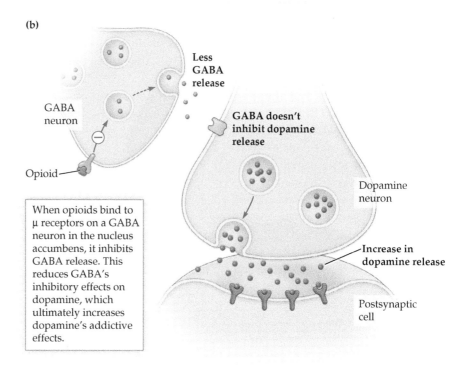

(a)

GABA receptor

GABA neuron

μ opioid receptor

GABA normally acts on the cell bodies of dopaminergic neurons to inhibit dopamine release in the nucleus accumbens / VTA , to reduce reward and addiction

Dopamine neuron

Dopamine release inhibited

Dopamine receptors   Postsynaptic cell

(b)

Less GABA release

GABA neuron

Opioid

When opioids bind to μ receptors on a GABA neuron in the nucleus accumbens, it inhibits GABA release. This reduces GABA's inhibitory effects on dopamine, which ultimately increases dopamine's addictive effects.

GABA doesn't inhibit dopamine release

Dopamine neuron

Increase in dopamine release

Postsynaptic cell

FIGURE 7.13. Opioids boost dopamine's reinforcing effects. (a) GABA normally acts on the cell bodies of dopaminergic neurons to inhibit dopamine release in the nucleus accumbens/VTA, to reduce reward and addiction. (b) When opioids bind to GABA neurons in the nucleus accumbens, less GABA is released. This reduces GABA's inhibitory effects on dopamine, which ultimately increases dopamine's reinforcing effects.

FIGURE 7.14. Rat Park. (Left) Professor Bruce Alexander and his colleagues created "Rat Park," a large area with cedar shavings to nest in; tin cans, balls, and running wheels to play on; and a group of male and female rats to interact with. (Right) Rats confined to a bare metal cage were significantly more likely to use morphine than rats that lived in Rat Park.

much of each supply of water was consumed. The cage-isolated rats tried both types of water, and showed a strong preference for the morphine-laced supply. After a few tastes, the colony rats would rarely or never drink from the bitter morphine water; rats do not like the taste of bitter, although the caged rats drank it anyway. To get the colony rats to drink morphine-laced water, the researchers dosed the morphine solution with sugar, which rats relish. When sugar was added to the morphine water, caged males drank 19 times more morphine than colony males. Rat Park rats resisted drinking the morphine-laced water, no matter how sweet it was. When Alexander and his colleagues added the opioid antagonist naloxone to the sweet water, thus blocking morphine's effects, the rats that lived in the colony happily drank the water. Colony rats avoided the opioid that interfered with their ability to play, mate, and eat, but they would consume the sweetened water as long as they did not get "high."

Opioid addiction also is considered to be so relentless because the effects of withdrawal are so horrible. The Rat Park researchers investigated the force of withdrawal on their rats. The scientists took two sets of rats and kept one set in their isolated cages, while the others lived in Rat Park. Both sets of rats were given only morphine-laced water to drink (with some days off) for enough time to produce tolerance and physical withdrawal. Colony rats and caged rats were then supplied with both plain and morphine water. The caged group continued to drink morphine water. But the Rat Park rats, even when they already were addicted, did not choose the morphine solution regularly and de-

creased their use of it, even though they were going through withdrawal.

The Rat Park experiments showed that rats naturally avoid opioid drugs. Extreme experimental pressure (sugar, forced habituation, or isolation) is required before laboratory rats want to consume opioids at all. This is hardly consistent with the "seductively addictive and dangerous" reputation of heroin, but then again, rats are not humans.

Of course, preventing addiction is not as simple as making sure everyone has enough toys to play with. Addiction is a multifactorial problem, involving biological, psychological, societal, and environmental factors (Chapter 17). Although Rat Park has been criticized on methodological grounds,[90] its finding is still compelling.

When addiction to opioids occurs, it can be devastating. Scientists are investigating ways to provide pain relief without the potential for addiction. Rats given (+)-naloxone (a synthetic mirror isomer of naloxone that blocks opioid receptors) before receiving morphine experienced pain relief but did not exhibit behavior linked to addiction and had much less dopamine release in their brains compared with rats that received only morphine.[91]

Ask yourself: What are the larger ramifications of the Rat Park experiments? What do the experiments tell us about the social or economic foundations of addiction?

Treatment for Opioid Use Disorders and Addiction

Many factors underlie the development of addiction; therefore, a multifaceted approach involving a combination of therapies is often best, as discussed in Chapter 18. Some treatments for opioid dependence include medications, psychotherapy or self-help programs, and social programs.

Medications to treat opioid use disorder are typically antagonists (such as naltrexone) that block opioid receptors and interfere with opioids' rewarding effects, long-acting agonists (such as methadone) that activate opioid receptors, and partial agonists (such as buprenorphine) that bind to opioid receptors but produce a diminished response.[92] Self-help therapies such as Narcotics Anonymous can help users change their behaviors. Needle exchange programs have shown some success in harm reduction in some communities. Other treatments, such as vaccines to make users immune to opioid effects, are also being tested (Chapter 18).

Withdrawal

To stop using drugs, opioid addicts must first undergo detoxification by going through withdrawal. Withdrawal from opioids is miserable, but unlike withdrawal from alcohol or sedative hypnotics, it is not life-threatening. Withdrawal symptoms can appear after only a week or two of chronic use, but the longer the drug has been used, and the higher the dose taken, the more severe the withdrawal symptoms. Withdrawal begins 6–12 hours after the last dose, peaks in 48–72 hours, and is usually over within 5–10 days. Withdrawal symptoms are typically opposite those of the direct effects of the drug (Table 7.4).

Withdrawal from opioids generally follows these stages:

- About six hours after the last dose of heroin (or 24 hours after methadone—the length of time until withdrawal depends on the pharmacology of the drug), the user will experience craving and anxiety.
- A few hours later, yawning, sweating, watery eyes, and a runny nose will occur.
- Twelve hours to two days after the last dose, a user's pupils will dilate, and he or she will have alternating bouts of shivering and sweating, along with a fever. Abdominal cramps, nausea, vomiting, and diarrhea are likely. The user may have goose bumps—this is the origin of the expression "going cold turkey."
- Two to four days into withdrawal, a user will still be undergoing many of the previously mentioned symptoms, along with weakness and depression. He or she may experience insomnia, restlessness, and an elevated blood pressure, heart rate, and breathing rate. The user's bones may ache, and he or she may have muscle spasms that cause restless legs and spontaneous kicking (the origin of the phrase "kicking the habit."). Erections and spontaneous ejaculations and orgasms also may occur.
- Within five days, symptoms of withdrawal start to subside.

TABLE 7.4.   Acute Effects and Rebound Withdrawal Effects of Opioids

Acute Action	Withdrawal Symptoms
Analgesia	Pain and irritability
Euphoria, relaxation, and calm	Dysphoria, depression, restlessness, anxiety
Stupor and sleep	Insomnia
Respiratory depression	Hyperventilation, yawning, panting, sneezing
Decreased blood pressure	Increased blood pressure
Pupil constriction	Pupil dilation
Constipation	Diarrhea
Lowered body temperature	Elevated body temperature
Secretions dry	Watery eyes, runny nose
Reduced sex drive	Spontaneous ejaculations and orgasms
Peripheral vasodilation, flushed and warm skin	Chilliness and goosebumps ("going cold turkey")
Muscular relaxation	Restlessness, twitching, involuntary kicking ("kicking the habit")

Treatments to Aid Withdrawal

Naltrexone (ReVia, Vivitrol) blocks opioid receptors for about three days and helps patients overcome opioid addiction by blocking the drug's euphoric effects (Table 7.5). If a user were to take heroin or another opioid while on naltrexone, she or he would not only *not* experience any of the opioid's reinforcing effects, but would also be put immediately into withdrawal, thus discouraging the use of opioids. Naltrexone can cause nausea and liver toxicity when taken daily. Also, naltrexone has poor patient compliance; patients must be highly motivated to quit.

Clonidine is an alpha$_2$-adrenergic agonist. Typically marketed for the treatment of hypertension, clonidine also suppresses many of the signs and symptoms of opioid withdrawal. Symptoms of opioid withdrawal are modulated by excessive discharge of norepinephrine neurons in the locus coeruleus (LC), which is involved in physiological responses of panic and anxiety.[93] Clonidine inhibits norepinephrine receptors in the LC that are involved in the expression of opioid withdrawal. Because opioids also inhibit norepinephrine-sensitive neurons, the LC remains relatively calm while a person is taking opioids. When the opioid is withdrawn, however, these norepinephrine-sensitive neurons become hyperactive and lead to fear, anxiety, chills, watery eyes, yawning, nausea, stomach cramps, diarrhea, and sweating. Clonidine suppresses noradrenergic hyperactivity and helps relieve these symptoms.

Ultra-Rapid Opioid Detoxification

The more time it takes opioid drugs to be removed from opioid receptors, the longer it takes for withdrawal symptoms to subside. So, when someone addicted to opioids simply stops using the drug, opioid receptors may remain bound with drug for days, prolonging the time course of withdrawal. When another drug such as naloxone competes for the receptor, heroin is removed,

Ultra-rapid opioid detoxification (UROD): A detoxification procedure in which a person who is addicted to opioids quickly goes through opioid withdrawal while under anesthesia.

and withdrawal happens more quickly. In **ultra-rapid opioid detoxification (UROD)**, a person who is addicted to opioids is put under general anesthesia or heavy sedation, and then given clonidine, as well as enough naloxone to completely block the opioid receptors. When he or she awakens a few hours later, withdrawal and detoxification are complete.[94] General anesthesia or heavy sedation are used because the more rapid the withdrawal, the more severe the symptoms.[95, 96]

All patients who undergo UROD will successfully detox. Although 30–91 percent of patients drop out of traditional inpatient detoxification programs before completing withdrawal, there are no reports of patients dropping out of treatment while they are under anesthesia.[97]

There are, however, a number of risks associated with the UROD procedure. Anesthesia is always hazardous, and its dangers are magnified by the possibility of the patient vomiting due to withdrawal. Another risk involves the user's loss of tolerance to opioids. Once a chronic user has detoxed, if he or she resumes opioid use, there is a strong potential for death by overdose. One must also consider the high cost of the procedure relative to other methods of detoxification. Finally, many of these programs offer little follow-up for underlying psychological issues, which may put the opioid abuser at risk of returning to heroin use. Reports are inconsistent regarding UROD's efficacy compared to conventional methods of detoxification, and the CDC recommends against using UROD, stating that it has substantial risks and little to no evidence to support its use.[98, 99, 100, 101]

Substitution Opioids

In 1964, scientists at Rockefeller University pioneered opioid maintenance treatment for heroin addiction. In substitution therapy, the goal is not abstinence from opioids, but rather for addicts to be able to function as normally as possible in society: increase their employment, eliminate criminal behavior, and reduce harm by providing a safer route of administration. As with tobacco, much of the danger from the drug comes from

TABLE 7.5	The Differences between Naloxone, Naltrexone, and Buprenorphine
Naloxone	A short-acting opioid antagonist used to reverse opioid overdose in emergency situations. Naloxone has a higher affinity for the opioid receptor than morphine or heroin, so when administered it replaces the drug bound to the receptor.
Naltrexone	A longer-acting opioid antagonist used to treat alcohol and opioid addiction.
Buprenorphine	A partial agonist. When bound to an opioid receptor, it will not cause an opioid response, but because it is occupying the receptor, other opioids are prevented from binding.

the way it is administered. Although it would be ideal for cigarette users to quit entirely, until they do, a nicotine patch can provide the drug they are addicted to in a safer manner. Opioid substitution therapy does the same thing. Although opioid substitution therapy replaces a heroin habit with another opioid dependency, the addict has a chance at a much-improved lifestyle; many studies have shown that substitution opioids lower the risk of relapse or overdose.[102,103,104]

Methadone

Methadone is an orally administered, long-acting opioid. Those on methadone therapy typically report to a clinic once a day to obtain their methadone pill. Because methadone is relatively long-acting, it offers users a more constant blood level, does not produce the euphoric highs of heroin, and allows the user to avoid the cravings and withdrawal associated with heroin.

If a methadone user stops taking methadone, he or she will still go through withdrawal, but symptoms take longer to appear. Six hours after the last dose of heroin, a user will feel cravings and anxiety; with methadone, the cravings and anxiety will take about 24 hours to appear. Other withdrawal symptoms such as fever, chills, and cramps can take two to three days to develop.

Methadone is medically safe even with long-term use, and it does not interfere with one's daily activities. One study followed 610 heroin users for one year after admission to a methadone maintenance program.[105] By the end of the year, just over half of the participants were still on methadone, while just under half had dropped out of the program and were no longer taking methadone. Those on methadone reported significantly fewer days of IV drug use, crime, and needle sharing, as well as more days of productive activity.

Finally, methadone substitution therapy is cost-effective. Two years of methadone therapy, including the drug and the substance abuse services used to maintain someone on methadone, costs approximately $14,000 (which is similar to the cost of other drug maintenance programs). However, when one considers societal costs such as criminal activity and loss of work productivity, two-year costs associated with *untreated* opioid dependence are estimated to be over $200,000.[106] One study found that every dollar spent on methadone therapy generated $38 in related economic benefits.[107]

Ask yourself: Do you think opioid substitution therapy serves the needs of the individual or of society? Both? Neither? Why?

Buprenorphine (Subutex)

The partial agonist buprenorphine (Subutex) is a long-lasting, semisynthetic narcotic that may be more effective and safer than methadone. As discussed in Chapter 4, partial agonists bind to a receptor, but produce a lesser effect than a full agonist. When buprenorphine is bound to an opioid receptor, withdrawal is prevented, as is the euphoria of a high. However, because the drug is occupying the receptor, other opioids cannot bind. When given in conjunction with counseling, those on buprenorphine have significantly lower illicit opioid use and stay in treatment longer.[108] Buprenorphine is less addictive than other opioids, and it does not suppress respiration, but does have some risks.

Buprenorphine increases the risk of seizures. It is not well absorbed when taken as a pill, so it is often given sublingually in a water-soluble form, which presents the potential for abuse if injected. In 2016, the FDA approved a matchstick-like insert of buprenorphine that is designed to be inserted under the skin and to release the drug slowly for up to six months.[109]

Buprenorphine Plus Naloxone (Suboxone)

Suboxone, which is a combination of buprenorphine and naloxone, was approved in 2002 as the first office-based treatment for opioid addiction. Rather than visiting a methadone clinic, narcotic addicts can be treated by certified physicians at their medical offices. The addition of naloxone to the formulation discourages users from abusing buprenorphine, because it will block any pleasurable sensations. In order to administer Suboxone, practitioners must meet certain qualifications, which limits the places patients can go for treatment.

Heroin

Another option in treating heroin addiction is . . . heroin. Some assert that it is the lifestyle of the addict, as well as the fact that drugs are illegal and expensive, rather than the drug itself that is dangerous. For years, doctors in Switzerland, the Netherlands, and other countries have been allowed to provide some addicts with a prescription form of heroin as an alternative to buying drugs on the street. These heroin addicts have a significantly lower mortality rate, less illicit drug use and illegal activity, and a higher rate of retention in addiction treatment programs.[110,111]

A study in Canada found that prescription heroin administration was more cost-effective than methadone administration, mainly due to fewer relapses and to the reduction in criminal activity.[112] As addicts report to a clinic for their fix, this can also act to reduce

Critical Evaluation

Should needle exchange programs be funded by the federal government?

In 1988, the U.S. Congress banned federal funding for needle exchange programs (NEPs). This ban was overturned in 2009, but reinstated in 2011. Congress has approved a measure that allows locally raised tax dollars to be spent on NEPs. In 2011, there were at least 220 NEPs operating in the United States. Over 90 percent of them are legally authorized to operate, but many still report some form of police interference, including client harassment and confiscation of the client's syringes.

Medical considerations. Providing clean syringes for intravenous drug users reduces the transmission of blood-borne viruses such as HIV and hepatitis.[113] Currently in the United States, about 10 percent of new HIV infections are due to IV drug use, and the Centers for Disease Control and Prevention (CDC) estimates that at least 30 percent of those could be prevented by NEPs. NEPs also provide disinfecting agents and other supplies, and they teach users how to treat injection site infections and wounds safely. NEPs reduce the risk of death following overdose. Some sites provide clean and safe areas for addicts to inject, and the staff are trained in CPR (cardiopulmonary resuscitation) and other emergency procedures. Are these health benefits enough of a justification to provide clean needles to addicts?

Legal considerations. Heroin is illegal. Does handing out clean needles to addicts legitimize their addiction and give the appearance of condoning IV drug use? But illegal or not, it is a reality—some people inject heroin. Do they no longer deserve medical intervention? Should heroin addicts be seen as criminals to be incarcerated or victims to be treated with compassion?

Cultural considerations. Scientists compared the HIV infection rates among IV drug users in 81 cities around the world. In cities without NEPs, HIV rates increased an average of 5.9 percent per year. In cities with NEPs, HIV rates decreased by 5.8 percent per year.[114] There are 11 percent fewer HIV-positive individuals in cities that have established NEPs compared with cities without NEPs. Are we confusing correlation and causation?

What other cultural considerations may affect HIV rates in countries that have NEPs?

Economic considerations. There are costs associated with providing clean syringes to IV drug users, as well as costs if clean syringes are not provided. There are more than 36 million syringes distributed annually in the United States. Each needle costs about $0.97 at an exchange clinic.[115] It costs approximately $169,000 for one site to operate for a year, and about $37.5 million for all the NEPs operating in the United States.

The HIV drug Truvada costs about $64 for a 1-day supply.[116] The annual cost of HIV care per person in the United States is between $15,000 and $40,000, and lifetime healthcare costs are between $303,000 and $619,000.[117,118] The CDC estimates that every case of HIV that is prevented through needle exchange saves an estimated $178,000. How should we assess the cost of NEPs? How do we weigh the cost of the materials against the potential personal and medical benefits?

Social considerations. The American Medical Association, the American Bar Association, the U.S. Conference of Mayors, and others support NEPs, although federal funding of these programs is prohibited. How much should the endorsement of these professional associations matter?

Proponents assert that NEPs will reduce drug-related crime, lessen the amount of drug paraphernalia on the street, and provide an arena where addicts can obtain health and social services. They say that NEPs will promote positive social networks and improve the status of IV drug users in society. But when it's time to put your money where your mouth is, would you want one in your neighborhood? Why or why not? Is it someone else's responsibility to help needy people in society? Whose responsibility should it be?

Philosophical considerations. Should society provide syringes for diabetics who inject insulin? Is that different than providing clean needles for IV drug users? How much responsibility should society take to help drug addicts? How would you analyze the risk/benefit relationship of NEPs? For the individual? For society? Which is more important?

the perceived glamour of drugs, given that "sickness is generally less attractive than sin."

Programs to Help Quit Opioids

Recovering addicts can also temporarily stay in a therapeutic community, a drug-free residential setting with treatment stages that change depending on the member's level of personal and social responsibility. Therapeutic community members interact with one another and with counselors to relearn or reestablish healthy habits and social skills. Users who successfully complete treatment in a therapeutic community have lower levels of alcohol and illegal drug use, depression, unlawful behavior, and unemployment than they had before treatment.

Narcotics Anonymous is a 12-step program formed in 1953. Its principles, including the steps to recovery, group meetings, and sponsor-sponsee relationships, are similar to those of Alcoholics Anonymous (Chapter 18). Narcotics Anonymous helps people who feel helpless against all drugs, including alcohol.

Needle Exchange Programs

There are around 13 million intravenous drug users (IDUs) around the world. About 13 percent of IDUs are HIV positive, and about 67 percent test positive for hepatitis C.[119]

A **needle exchange program (NEP)** is a service wherein IDUs can obtain clean, new syringes and a safe place to dispose of used needles. Many syringe exchange programs also provide other services, such as tests to screen for HIV, hepatitis C, and other sexually transmitted infections (STIs); referrals to substance abuse treatment programs; prevention supplies such as condoms, alcohol pads, and other materials; and education about STI prevention and safer injection and vein care.

Needle exchange program (NEP): An intervention program that provides clean needles to IV drug users in return for used syringes, which are destroyed.

Chapter Summary

- **Introduction**
  - » Opiates are drugs that occur naturally from the opium poppy.
  - » Opioids are natural, semisynthetic, synthetic, or endogenous substances that bind to the opioid receptor.
- **History of Opioids**
  - » Opium is one of the oldest drugs in the world.
  - » In the nineteenth century, Britain went to war against China to force them to purchase opium. China lost and had to make significant concessions to the West.
  - » Opiate addiction skyrocketed during the nineteenth century due to the isolation of morphine, the development of the hypodermic syringe, the importation of Chinese laborers, war, and the popularity of patent medicines.
  - » Racial and socioeconomic factors played a key role in the development of laws against opioid use.
- **Prevalence of Opioid Use**
  - » Almost 83 million Americans age 12 and older report using prescription pain relievers in the past year, and almost 10 million people in the United States report misusing these drugs.
  - » The nonmedical use of prescription painkillers has greatly increased in the past few decades.
  - » About 431,000 people report current use of heroin, although some researchers believe that is an underestimation. Heroin use among adolescents and young

adults may be increasing due to the availability of cheaper, purer heroin.
- **Source and Forms of Opioids**
  - » Opium comes from the poppy and contains morphine, codeine, thebaine, and other substances.
  - » Heroin is synthesized from morphine by adding two acetyl groups. This makes the substance more lipid-soluble.
- **Pharmacokinetics of Opioids**
  - » The routes of administration, lipid solubility, and interactions with other substances affect opioid actions in the body.
  - » Opioids can be ingested; absorbed rectally, sublingually, or transdermally; snorted; smoked; or injected.
- **Mechanism of Action of Opioids**
  - » Opioids bind to opioid receptors throughout the body. These receptors are classified as mu, delta, kappa, and NOP.
  - » Endogenous opioids include enkephalins, endorphins, and dynorphins.
- **Acute Effects of Opioids**
  - » Opioids diminish pain, suppress respiration, decrease gastrointestinal activity, increase sleep, cause euphoria, impair cognitive function, and exert many other effects throughout the body.

» Thousands of people in the United States die each year of an overdose of opioids. Among those age 24–35, 20 percent of deaths were attributable to opioids.

- **Medical and Therapeutic Uses of Opioids**
  » Opioids are used to treat a number of conditions. They are effective analgesics, cough suppressants, and can alleviate diarrhea.
- **Chronic Effects of Opioids**
  » Unlike with some other drugs, the organs are not damaged or destroyed even with long-term, heavy use of narcotics. Rather than the direct effects of the drug, it may be the lifestyle of the addict that is most dangerous.
  » Metabolic, cellular, and behavioral tolerance, as well as cross tolerance, develops in chronic opioid users.

» Opioids are addictive. Addiction is due to physical, environmental, and psychosocial factors.

- **Treatment for Opioid Use Disorders and Addiction**
  » Withdrawal symptoms are typically opposite those of the direct effects of the drug.
  » Treatments to aid withdrawal include naltrexone, clonidine, and ultra-rapid opioid detoxification.
  » Sometimes substitution opioids such as methadone or buprenorphine are given to help stop heroin use. Users also can stay in therapeutic communities or attend Narcotics Anonymous meetings to try to end their addictive behaviors.
  » Needle exchange programs provide clean needles to IV drug users in return for used syringes, which are destroyed.

Key Terms

Endorphin (p. 158)
Harrison Narcotics Act (p. 150)
Narcotic (p. 146)
Needle exchange program (NEP) (p. 173)

Neonatal abstinence syndrome (NAS) (p. 160)
Nociceptor (p. 163)
Opiate (p. 146)
Opioid triad (p. 162)

Opioid (p. 146)
Ultra-rapid opioid detoxification (UROD) (p. 170)

Quiz Yourself!

1. True or false? Deaths from heroin and prescription opioids have doubled since the year 2000.

2. Which of the following does NOT naturally occur in the poppy plant?
   A. Morphine
   B. Heroin
   C. Codeine
   D. Thebaine

3. Arrange the following opioids in order of increasing potency, from least potent to most potent: codeine, carfentanil, heroin, morphine, OxyContin

4. List the five main factors that caused opiate addiction to soar during the nineteenth century.

5. True or false? Heroin is converted to morphine in the brain.

6. Which of the following is a physiological effect of opioids?
   A. Pupil dilation
   B. Diarrhea

C. Itching
D. Increased urination
E. All of the above

7. True or false? Long-term, heavy use of opioids is damaging to almost every organ system in the body.

8. True or false? Opioid users experience metabolic and cellular tolerance, but no behavioral tolerance.

9. What did the Rat Park experiments show?

10. Which of the following is not an effect of opioid withdrawal?
    A. Pain and irritability
    B. Insomnia
    C. Spontaneous ejaculations and orgasms
    D. Constipation
    E. Goosebumps

11. Extra credit bonus! What are the names of the scientists who discovered opioid receptors in the brain?

Additional Resources

Websites

Information about Rat Park. http://www.stuartmcmillen.com/ blog/bustle-cagerow-making-rat-park/

The story of many in an Ohioan High School who were hit hard by the opioid epidemic. https://www.nytimes.com/interactive/ 2019/12/02/us/opioid-crisis-high-school-teenagers.html

Movies

The Basketball Diaries. (1995). 102 minutes. Leonardo DiCaprio stars in this story of an athlete's fall into drug addiction.

Trainspotting. (1996). 94 minutes. A black comedy/drama about a group of Scottish friends and their passage through life as heroin addicts.

Permanent Midnight. (1998). 88 minutes. Ben Stiller stars in this story based on Jerry Stahl's real-life story of addiction.

Requiem for a Dream. (2000). 102 minutes. A brilliant and shattering portrait of addiction, starring Jared Leto, Ellen Burstyn, Jennifer Connolly, and Damon Wayans. Directed by Darren Aranofsky.

The Pharmacist. (2020). 4 episodes. After his son's tragic death, a Louisiana pharmacist goes to extremes to expose the rampant corruption behind the opioid addiction crisis. Netflix Series.

Videos

The All-American Drug: Heroin in Suburbia and the Heartland. 2006. 18 minutes. Item # 40018. Films for the Humanities and Sciences.

Opium: A Blessing and a Curse. 2010. 78 minutes. Item # 43751. Films for the Humanities and Sciences.

Books

Quinones, S. (2016). *Dreamland: The true tale of America's opiate epidemic*. New York: Bloomsbury Press.

Learn more with this chapter's digital tools at www.oup.com/he/rosenthal2e.

Sedatives, Hypnotics, and Inhalants

True or false?

1.
True or false? Benzodiazepines (such as Xanax) are more dangerous than barbiturates (such as secobarbital).

2.
True or false? Insomnia (difficulty sleeping) and sleep disturbances play a role in the development of depression, attention-deficit/ hyperactivity disorder, diabetes, and obesity.

3.
True or false? Inhalants are less toxic than all other recreational drugs.

Throughout recorded history, humans have sought chemical agents to alleviate the harsh realities of the world. They have guzzled gin, consumed kava, and popped pills, all to ease the stress of their daily lives. Central nervous system (CNS) depressants are a diverse group of drugs that slow physical and mental activities, relieve anxiety, diminish awareness, and increase sleep. Sedatives and hypnotics are two types of CNS depressant drugs. Inhalants are volatile solvents, anesthetics, or nitrites that are sniffed or inhaled, and give a feeling of dizziness, disorientation, and impairment of judgment and coordination. Many inhalants produce a depressant effect similar to sedative/hypnotics.

Learning Objectives

- Define the terms *sedative* and *hypnotic*.
- Identify some of the uses of sedative/hypnotic drugs.
- Compare and contrast the long-acting and short-acting sedative/hypnotics.
- Describe the GABA$_A$ receptor.
- Distinguish between the mechanism of action of barbiturates and benzodiazepines at the GABA$_A$ receptor.
- Outline the acute physiological and behavioral effects of sedative/hypnotic drugs.
- Assess the medical risks and benefits of sedative/hypnotic drugs.
- Summarize the actions and effects of low doses and high doses of GHB.
- List some of the sources of inhalants.
- Categorize inhalants as volatile substances, anesthetics, or nitrites.
- Evaluate the causes of cognitive impairments associated with inhalant use.

Sedatives and Hypnotics

Sedatives are drugs that relieve anxiety, cause relaxation, and produce mild depression of the CNS, and **hypnotics** induce drowsiness and sleep (*hypnos* is the Greek word for "sleep"). Two popular classes of sedative/hypnotics are barbiturates and benzodiazepines. **Barbiturates** (bar-BIT-chur-ates) are used mainly for anesthesia and treatment of seizure disorders, while **benzodiazepines (BZDs)** are used mainly as muscle relaxants and to reduce anxiety. Other sedative and tranquilizer drugs include muscle relaxants and "Z drugs."

History of Sedatives and Hypnotics

Stress and sleeplessness are not new phenomena. Pacific Islanders have long used an extract of the kava plant to reduce anxiety and help them sleep (Chapter 15).[1] Valerian root has been used for thousands of years as a remedy for insomnia. And of course, for centuries, people would use alcohol (Chapter 12) and opium (Chapter 7) for their sedative properties.

Chloral hydrate was the first synthetic drug that could truly be classified as a hypnotic. Synthesized in 1832, chloral hydrate quickly induces a long, deep sleep. Today, the drug is classified as schedule IV and is sometimes given to infants as a sedative prior to surgical or EEG procedures, or to help people withdraw from opioid or alcohol addiction.[2]

QUICK HIT

During the mid-nineteenth century in California, many sailors arriving in San Francisco would desert their ships and their harsh conditions to seek their fortunes panning for gold, making it difficult for ships to find enough crewmen to set sail. Runners would, therefore, offer liquor or other inducements to get sailors to come to a certain saloon. Once there, the sailors would be drugged with liquor spiked with laudanum or chloral hydrate. Relieved of their clothes and belongings, they were rowed unconscious to a waiting ship. When the sailors regained consciousness, they were already far out to sea.[3]

Sedative: A drug taken to promote relaxation and calm.

Hypnotic: A sleep-inducing drug.

Barbiturates: A group of sedative/hypnotic drugs used mainly for anesthesia and treatment of seizure disorders.

Benzodiazepines (BZDs): A group of sedative/hypnotic drugs used mainly as antianxiety agents, sleep inducers, and muscle relaxants.

Sedatives and Hypnotics

Type of drug: Depressant

Chemical formula:
- Pentobarbital: $C_{11}H_{18}N_2O_3$
- Alprazolam: $C_{17}H_{13}ClN_4$
- Quaalude: $C_{16}H_{14}N_2O$
- GHB: $C_4H_8O_3$

Routes of administration:
- Barbiturates, BZD: Ingested, injected, snorted, suppository
- GHB: Ingested, injected
- Quaalude: Ingested

Duration of effect:
- Barbiturates, BZD: Variable
- GHB: 2–6 hours
- Quaalude: 4–8 hours

Neurotransmitters directly affected:
- Barbiturates, BZD, Quaaludes: GABA

- GHB: At low doses: excitatory GHB; at high doses: GABA

Tolerance:
- Barbiturates, BZD, Quaaludes: Moderate-high
- GHB: Moderate

Physical dependence:
- Barbiturates, BZD, Quaaludes: High
- GHB: moderate

Psychological dependence:
- Moderate

Withdrawal symptoms:
- Restlessness, anxiety, agitation, confusion, tremor, insomnia, vomiting, seizures, delirium, disorientation, delusions, paranoia

Schedule:
- Barbiturates: Schedule II, III, IV
- BZD: Schedule IV
- Quaaludes: Schedule I
- GHB: Schedule I (Xyrem, schedule III)

Slang:
- Barbiturates (downers, goofballs): Pentobarbital (yellow jackets); secobarbital (reds, red devils); amobarbital (bluebirds, blue dolls, blue devils)
- Benzodiazepines (benzos): Valium (V, tranqs); Xanax (bars, footballs, zannies); Rohypnol (roofies, rape, Mexican Valium)
- GHB: Grievous bodily harm, Georgia home boy, liquid X, liquid E, easy lay, and G
- Methaqualone: Quaalude, ludes, love drug, sopes

In 1864, Adolf von Baeyer, a German scientist, synthesized barbituric acid by combining malonic acid from apples with urea, a waste product found in urine. Although barbituric acid itself isn't pharmacologically active, slight modifications of the molecule produce the family of chemicals known as barbiturates.

QUICK HIT

There are a number of stories as to why Adolf von Baeyer named his product barbituric acid. Some say that after inventing it, he and his colleagues retired to a tavern, where army officers were celebrating the feast of St. Barbara, their patron saint. One officer is said to have combined the words "Barbara" with "urea," thus christening the compound. Others claimed that Barbara was the woman who donated the urine used in von Baeyer's discovery.[4]

Patented in 1903 by the Nobel Prize-winning German chemist Emil Fischer, diethylbarbituric acid (called Veronal) was one of the first barbiturates to be marketed as a sleeping aid. After the United States entered into World War I against the Germans in 1917, Congress passed the Trading with the Enemy Act, which gave America free rein to manufacture patent-protected German products, modifying their generic name, and taking the profits.[5] The American Medical Association (AMA) approved the name "barbital" for this drug. (To this day, the generic names of most barbiturates end in "barbital.") Since the early part of the twentieth century, more than 2,500 barbiturates have been synthesized. At the height of their popularity in the mid-twentieth century, enough barbiturates were produced in the United States to provide 10 million adults with a sleeping pill every night of the year.[6] In the 1950s, about 50 barbiturates were marketed for human use. Today, only about a dozen are still available.

Although barbiturates were once popular sedatives, they are quite dangerous. As a result, scientists began the search for a safer substance. In 1955, Leo Sternbach discovered chlordiazepoxide (Librium), a benzodiazepine (BZD). (He later went on to invent Valium, Dalmane, Rohypnol, and Klonopin.) Since their discovery, over 3,000 different forms of BZDs have been synthesized. Librium became the top-selling prescription drug in the United States until the 1970s, when it was supplanted by the more potent Valium. In 1973 alone, there were 100 million prescriptions written for BZDs. These drugs were predominantly marketed to women, to help them deal with the stress of daily life (Figure 8.1).

At first, benzodiazepines were viewed as extremely safe and free from the problems of tolerance, dependence, and withdrawal. But you, the observant reader, have probably noticed that this is a common pattern—a drug that was once thought to be safe and nonaddictive is later shown to have significant dangers. BZDs are relatively safe when used for short periods (and are much safer than barbiturates), but long-term use can cause tolerance, dependence, and withdrawal problems. Although the use of BZDs to treat insomnia is waning, and newer drugs such as Ambien are gaining in popularity, the search for a CNS depressant that alleviates stress and anxiety without dependence or harmful side effects is not yet over.

Prevalence of Sedative and Hypnotic Use

The use of sedative/hypnotics has increased considerably in the past 20 years.[7,8] In 2019, over 44 million Americans—16 percent of the population of those age 12 and older—reported using tranquilizers or sedatives in the past year, and 5.9 million reported misusing them, including taking them without having a prescription of their own, or using in greater amounts, more often, or longer than instructed by their physician.[9] Sedative/hypnotic use increases with age, and although women use them more than men, men are more likely to abuse sedatives and tranquilizers.[10,11,12]

Source and Forms of Sedatives and Hypnotics

Barbiturates and benzodiazepines are synthetically manufactured. Approximately 300 tons of barbiturates are legally produced every year in the United States. There are thousands of different types of barbiturates, yet only a few are typically available for medical use. BZDs are much more commonly prescribed; there are more than 15 different types of BZDs currently available in the United States (Figure 8.2).

FIGURE 8.1. Mother's little helper. The Rolling Stone's song "Mother's Little Helper" was about the surge in popularity of sedative/hypnotics, which were marketed to women as a way to deal with everyday stress.

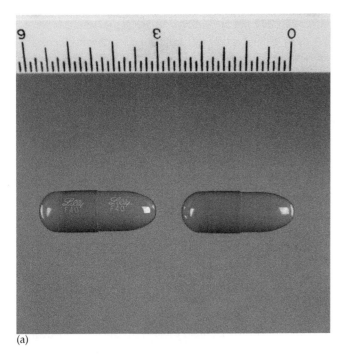
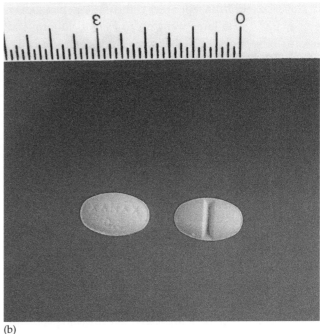

(a)   (b)

FIGURE 8.2. Benzodiazepines and barbiturates. (a) Barbiturates come in bright colors like the bright red of Seconal. (b) Benzodiazepines often come in soothing pastel colors, like the peach color of Xanax.

Barbiturates

Barbiturates are categorized as long-acting, intermediate-acting, short-acting, or ultra-short-acting, based on their duration of action (Table 8.1). Shorter-acting drugs are more lipid-soluble and take effect rapidly, because they quickly enter the bloodstream and easily cross the blood–brain barrier. They are then cleared from the system faster than longer-acting compounds. These short-acting barbiturates are more likely to be abused.

Epilepsy: A neurological disorder characterized by a predisposition to experience seizures.

Anxiolytic: A drug used to reduce anxiety.

The duration of action of barbiturates determines their best clinical use. Longer-acting drugs are best used as anticonvulsants in the treatment of **epilepsy** or to prevent or reduce anxiety (drugs that reduce anxiety are called **anxiolytics**). Intermediate- and shorter-acting drugs are used to treat insomnia, for emergency management of seizures, and as a preanesthetic sedative. Ultra-short-acting barbiturates can be used to rapidly anesthetize a patient in emergency situations, and to bring them out of anesthesia quickly as well. Not only do they reduce awareness, but ultra-short-acting barbiturates also leave the patient with no memory of the experience.

TABLE 8.1. Common Barbiturates

Category	Duration of Action	Examples	Uses
Long-acting	>6 hours	phenobarbital (Luminal)	Anticonvulsant Anxiolytic
Intermediate-acting	4–6 hours	amobarbital (Amytal)	Insomnia Emergency management of seizures Preanesthetic sedative
Short-acting	2–4 hours	pentobarbital (Nembutal) secobarbital (Seconal)	Insomnia Emergency management of seizures Preanesthetic sedative
Ultra-short-acting	<30 minutes	thiopental (Pentothal)	Rapid surgical anesthesia

TABLE 8.2. Common Benzodiazepines

Category	Duration of Action	Examples	Uses
Long-acting	Long (half-life up to 200 hours)	chlordiazepoxide (Librium) diazepam (Valium) flurazepam (Dalmane)	Preanesthetic sedative Antianxiety Anticonvulsant Chronic alcohol withdrawal Muscle relaxation Status epilepticus (IV)
Intermediate- and short-acting	Short/Intermediate (half-life typically 5–24 hours)	alprazolam (Xanax) clonazepam (Klonopin) lorazepam (Ativan) temazepam (Restoril)	Antianxiety Antidepressant Anticonvulsant Insomnia Chronic alcohol withdrawal Muscle relaxant Preanesthetic sedation Status epilepticus (IV)
Ultra-short-acting	Very short (half-life 1–3 hours)	midazolam (Versed) triazolam (Halcion)	Insomnia Preanesthetic sedation Anticonvulsant Muscle relaxant Antianxiety

Benzodiazepines

Benzodiazepines are divided into four categories, based on their duration of action and time it takes them to be eliminated. Long-acting BZDs have a median half-life of over 24 hours due to their pharmacologically active metabolites. In the elderly, and in those with impaired liver function, the effects of long-acting BZDs can be felt for days or even weeks. Intermediate-acting BZDs last for less than 24 hours, and short-acting BZDs have a half-life of less than 12 hours. The half-life of ultra-short-acting BZDs is between one and five hours. Table 8.2 summarizes some of the popular BZDs.

QUICK HIT

A new designer benzodiazepine has hit the black market. Clonazolam, a chemical combination of clonazepam (Klonopin) and alprazolam (Xanax) is 100 to 1000 times as potent as standard BZDs. Doses as low as 0.5 mg can lead to an overdose.[13]

Pharmacokinetics of Sedatives and Hypnotics

The lipid solubility of a sedative significantly influences its absorption, distribution, speed of onset, metabolism, and elimination from the body. Physicians will prescribe sedatives with different pharmacological properties based on the patient's specific needs and characteristics.

Routes of Administration

Sedatives can be administered rectally or by injection, but they are most commonly administered orally. Some anesthetic medications or drugs given to treat emergency seizures or status epilepticus (epileptic seizures following one another in which the sufferer remains unconscious) are administered intravenously.

Absorption and Distribution

Sedative/hypnotics are readily absorbed into the bloodstream after oral administration. Barbiturates are absorbed in the stomach, while benzodiazepines are absorbed in the small intestine; this means that BZDs are absorbed into the bloodstream more slowly than are barbiturates. Drugs that elevate gastric pH, such as antacids or proton pump inhibitors (Chapter 15), may further reduce the absorption of BZDs. When absorption occurs more slowly, this decreases the drug's onset of action (how quickly the drug takes effect).

Once in the blood, a sedative's distribution is determined by its lipid solubility. Barbiturates are more fat-soluble than BZDs; as a result, barbiturates are better able to cross the blood–brain barrier, leading to a faster onset of action. Shorter-acting barbiturates are especially lipid-soluble. Their effects may begin rapidly, but diminish just as fast—not because the drug is metabolized, but rather because its level in the brain quickly falls as the barbiturate is redistributed and stored in the fatty tissues of the body. From these body fat deposits, the barbiturate is released slowly into the blood. The amount of body fat a person has can influence her or his response to barbiturates and BZDs. Although the initial effects of a short-acting barbiturate may recede quickly, the drug may be released from body fat deposits and then circulate at low levels in the blood for a significant period of time.

Sedative/hypnotics can cross the placenta and also enter breast milk, where they exert their depressant effects on the fetus or infant (discussed more fully later in this chapter). Longer-acting sedatives/hypnotics are less lipid-soluble and enter the brain more slowly. These sedative/hypnotics are less likely to be absorbed by body fat. As a result, their effects depend entirely on the metabolism of the drug rather than on redistribution.

Metabolism and Elimination

Barbiturates and benzodiazepines are metabolized in the liver. When these drugs enter the bloodstream, some of them bind to plasma proteins. Only unbound molecules of the drug are free to bind to receptor sites and exert an action. As the unbound molecules of barbiturates are metabolized and excreted, the drug that was previously stored in fat or that was bound to plasma proteins becomes free and available for metabolism. The balance between the free and bound forms of the drug is responsible for the varying durations of action for different barbiturates.

Benzodiazepines undergo two major pathways of metabolism: oxidation and conjugation. Those BZDs that are conjugated are metabolized to pharmacologically inactive, water-soluble products that are excreted in urine. But BZDs that are oxidized, such as diazepam (Valium), chlordiazepoxide (Librium), and flurazepam (Dalmane), produce active metabolites, prolonging their duration of action until they are further detoxified by metabolism and then excreted. The active metabolites are chemically modified more slowly than the parent compound, so the duration of action of many BZDs bears little relationship to their stated half-life. As an example, Librium's half-life in plasma is 5–30 hours, but the half-life of one of its major active metabolites can be more than eight days.

Metabolism is decreased in infants, pregnant women, those with liver disease, and the elderly. The elderly, in particular, are susceptible to the sedating effects of this class of drugs, with the potential for dangerous BZD accumulation. For a long-acting drug like Valium, the elimination half-life can be as long as 10 days, so elderly patients may not be drug free for months after discontinuing the drug. Longer-term use of BZDs in the elderly can produce confusion and delirium that may be confused with Alzheimer's disease.

Mechanism of Action of Sedatives and Hypnotics

Sedative/hypnotics are typically GABA agonists; they exert their effects by binding to GABA receptors. Barbiturates and BZDs both work on the receptor, but by slightly different mechanisms.

GABA Receptor

GABA receptors respond to gamma-aminobutyric acid (GABA), the primary inhibitory neurotransmitter in the CNS. As we learned in Chapter 4, $GABA_A$ receptors are ionotropic, meaning that the receptor itself is an ion channel. The membrane-spanning receptor contains five subunits arranged around a chloride-conducting pore (Figure 8.3). When GABA binds to the receptor, the shape of the receptor changes and the chloride channel opens. Negatively charged chloride ions then enter the cell (making the cell more negatively charged inside) and inhibit new action potentials from firing.

The $GABA_A$ receptor consists of different combinations of alpha (α), beta (β), and gamma (γ) subunits.[14] There are six different types of alpha subunits (1–6), three types of beta subunits (1–3), three gamma subunits (1–3), and others. These subunits can combine in various ways. There are about 30 different forms of $GABA_A$ receptors, each made up of different combinations of subunit subtypes, which have unique distributions in the brain, and distinct physiological and pharmacological properties.[15] So $GABA_A$ receptors that contain the $alpha_1$ subunit have a different pharmacology than those with $alpha_2$ or $alpha_3$ subunits.

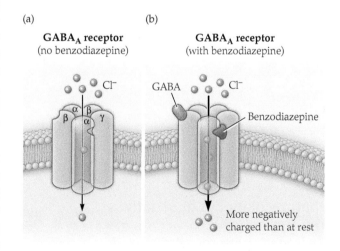

FIGURE 8.3. **The GABA$_A$ receptor.** (a) The receptor has 5 subunits arranged around a chloride-conducting pore. GABA binds between alpha and beta subunits. (b) BZDs bind between alpha and gamma subunits in those receptors that contain these subunits.

The GABA$_A$ receptor complex has two binding sites for GABA, as well as distinct sites where BZDs, barbiturates, ethanol, and other substances bind.

Benzodiazepines' Interaction with the GABA$_A$ Receptor

Some GABA$_A$ receptors have a binding site for benzodiazepines.[16] When a BZD binds to a GABA receptor, the shape of the receptor changes, increasing the frequency of chloride channel openings, and enhancing GABA's inhibitory effects. BZDs that bind to alpha$_1$ subunits are effective hypnotics, while BZDs with a higher affinity for alpha$_2$ or alpha$_3$ subunits are better suited to treat anxiety.[17] Because Valium, Xanax, and other BZDs bind to a specific receptor, this means there is most likely an endogenous BZD-like substance in the body; one naturally occurring substance may play an important role in suppressing seizures.[18]

GABA receptors that contain BZD binding sites are located in the brain, primarily in the limbic system, reticular activating system, and cortex (Chapter 3). The GABA receptors that control respiration and other vegetative processes do not have many BZD sites, so BZDs do not suppress respiration as much as barbiturates do. There are also GABA receptors with BZD binding sites in the peripheral nervous system, which modulate the immune system and are involved in the body's response to injury.

In addition to their actions on GABA, BZDs also slightly block the reuptake of the inhibitory neurotransmitter adenosine, which acts to increase adenosine's activity at the synapse and is responsible for some of the anticonvulsant, anxiolytic, and muscle relaxant effects of BZDs.

Barbiturates' Interaction with the GABA$_A$ Receptor

Unlike benzodiazepines, barbiturates do not seem to act at a specific single site on the GABA$_A$ receptor; instead, they bind to multiple cavities on the surface of the receptor. Barbiturates have a more general effect that enhances the inhibitory activity of GABA. When low concentrations of barbiturates bind to the GABA receptor, they enhance the affinity of the receptor for GABA, which increases the duration of time that the chloride channel is open, leading to inhibition of neural activity. High concentrations of barbiturates can directly increase the duration of channel opening, even in the absence of GABA. This may in part explain why barbiturates are more dangerous than BZDs. BZDs can only open the chloride channel if GABA is present, providing a ceiling effect that is missing with barbiturates.

Because barbiturates have a more general effect on GABA receptors, they have more widespread sedating effects than do the BZDs. Along with widespread CNS depression, barbiturates can suppress cognitive function, muscle activity, and respiration.

Acute Effects of Sedatives and Hypnotics

Sedative/hypnotics produce physiological and psychological effects ranging from mild relaxation, to sleep, to death. An individual's response may depend not only on sex, age, and health but also on his or her mood, expectation, and the environmental setting.

Physiological and Psychological Effects at Low and Moderate Doses

Barbiturates and BZDs are CNS depressants (Figure 8.4). The effects of sedatives are dose-dependent. Lower doses can lead to relaxation, decreased anxiety, and drowsiness. As the dose increases, the user may experience euphoria and disinhibition, as well as sedation, dizziness, staggering, and sleep. Still higher doses can lead to unconsciousness, respiratory depression, coma, and death.

Sedatives and hypnotics help people to fall asleep faster, and they increase a person's total sleep time. But these drugs decrease the time spent in REM sleep (dream sleep), as well as the time spent in deep sleep. Therefore, although most hypnotics increase total sleep time, the sleep they produce is not as restful and restorative as normal slumber. Withdrawal from these drugs can produce both insomnia and longer and more frequent REM periods with vivid and excessive dreams.

Barbiturates and BZDs have no significant effect on the cardiovascular system, except for minor decreases in blood pressure. Barbiturates tend to slightly lower the heart rate slightly, while BZDs may elevate it somewhat. Although barbiturates depress the respiratory drive and lower one's breathing rate, BZDs have minimal effects on the respiratory system and are, therefore, safer than barbiturates. When taken with alcohol or other CNS depressants, however, the drugs act synergistically, and a potentially fatal suppression of respiration can occur.

Sedatives are muscle relaxants. These drugs can impair coordination and response time, which is why users should not operate motor vehicles while on these drugs. Moderate doses of barbiturates and higher doses of BZDs can cause incoordination, staggered gait, and slurred speech.

Sedatives and hypnotics produce mood changes that are similar to alcohol. They reduce anxiety and give a sense of relaxation and mellowness. People on sedatives

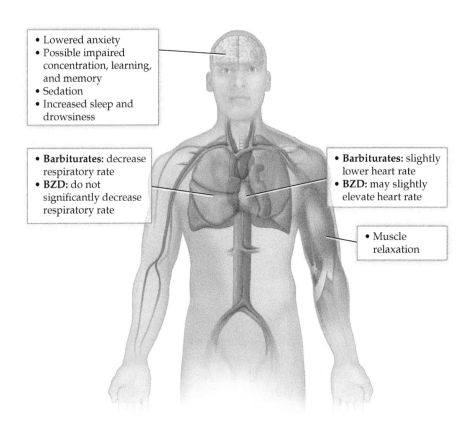

FIGURE 8.4. Acute effects of sedative/hypnotic drugs.

- Lowered anxiety
- Possible impaired concentration, learning, and memory
- Sedation
- Increased sleep and drowsiness

- **Barbiturates:** decrease respiratory rate
- **BZD:** do not significantly decrease respiratory rate

- **Barbiturates:** slightly lower heart rate
- **BZD:** may slightly elevate heart rate

- Muscle relaxation

may have difficulty thinking clearly and making rational judgments. Their learning and memory may be impaired. Disinhibition—the release of bizarre, uninhibited behaviors, or of hostility or rage—may occur, and users sometimes become emotionally unstable.

Sedatives can also be addictive. They bind to GABA receptors that modulate the firing of neurons in the addiction pathways of the brain. Abuse and dependence are more likely to occur with faster-acting agents than with those that have long-lasting effects.

Barbiturates have a narrow therapeutic index; a high potential for tolerance, dependence, and abuse; and are lethal in overdose. Barbiturates also interact in a dangerous way with other drugs. Although BZDs are much safer, they also have significant side effects and other risks. Barbiturates and BZDs are particularly dangerous in those with liver disease or compromised kidney function, and in the elderly.

Side Effects

Side effects are similar in barbiturates and BZDs, but they are more severe in barbiturates. Common side effects of barbiturates and BZDs include

- Drowsiness
- Lethargy

- Dizziness
- Confusion
- Reduced libido
- Diminished concentration
- Incoordination and impairment of driving skills

Barbiturates may also lead to

- Gastrointestinal distress
- Joint pain
- Skin rash
- Impotence and menstrual irregularities
- Staggered gait
- Impaired thinking
- Anterograde amnesia

At higher doses, side effects of barbiturates are life-threatening, and include

- Suppressed respiration
- Lowered heart rate and blood pressure
- Shock
- Coma
- Death

With BZDs, however, respiration is not severely depressed even at high doses. Even attempted suicides are rarely successful unless the BZD is taken with opioids, alcohol, or other CNS depressants.[19]

Halcion and Adverse Psychotic Reactions

In 1988, a 57-year-old woman taking the BZD Halcion shot her 83-year-old mother eight times. She claimed that the Halcion she was prescribed made her psychotic and was responsible for the murder. Charges against the woman were ultimately dismissed, but she sued Upjohn, the manufacturer of Halcion, for $21 million. The lawsuit was settled out of court for an undisclosed amount. At the time, Halcion was widely prescribed. Complaints from others began to accumulate, however, reporting that Halcion led to amnesia, confusion, paranoia, hostility, and adverse psychiatric reactions. The drug was banned in five countries, but the Food and Drug Administration concluded that its benefits outweighed its risks, and Halcion is still available today in the United States, although its popularity is nowhere near what it once was.

Source: Cobb, K. (1994). Former Utahn kills herself 6 years after killing mom. Deseret News. http://www.deseretnews.com/article/366520/FORMER-UTAHN-KILLS-HERSELF-6-YEARS-AFTER-KILLING-MOM.html?pg=all

One study found that sedative/hypnotic drugs were associated with an elevated risk of death and cancer.[20] The researchers followed 10,529 patients who received hypnotic prescriptions and 23,676 matched controls for an average of 2.5 years. The researchers controlled for many factors, including age, sex, smoking, body mass index, ethnicity, marital status, and alcohol use. They discovered that patients prescribed any hypnotic were more likely to die, when compared to those prescribed no hypnotics.

However, the researchers did not control for depression or anxiety and the effects that these debilitating disorders have on one's health. The researchers also did not address the fact that many of these patients taking sleeping aids suffered from insomnia. Poor sleep has significant health ramifications and would certainly contribute to an increased health risk. Finally, sedatives affect judgment, coordination, and driving skills, another factor that can negatively impact one's health. Although long-term use of sedatives may be detrimental to one's health, it is possible that the underlying psychiatric ailments or insomnia have a more powerful negative effect than do the drugs.

A similar study followed almost 35,000 people who filled prescriptions for BZDs and "Z drug" sleep aids (such as Ambien), and compared them with over 69,000 control subjects over the course of seven years. After adjusting for confounding factors such as sex, age, sleep disorders, anxiety disorders, medical morbidity, and other drugs, the researchers found that people who took sedative/hypnotic drugs had more than double the risk of death compared to age and sex-matched controls.[21]

Sometimes users of sedative/hypnotic drugs experience paradoxical adverse effects, such as aggression, violence, and impulsivity. Sedatives/hypnotics may lead to loss of inhibition and control.

Benzodiazepines and barbiturates may interfere with cognitive function. A meta-analysis found that long-term users of BZDs were consistently more impaired than controls.[22] But it's important to evaluate this finding critically. Were the cognitive impairments due to the drug, or due to the underlying condition for which users were taking the drug? Anxiety, depression, and insomnia can all lead to confusion, muddled thinking, and poorer test performance. Participants with an anxiety disorder might be particularly prone to test anxiety, and perform more poorly as a result. Additionally, some of the cognitive tests were administered while subjects were actively undergoing withdrawal or being treated for emotional disorders. Once again, it is difficult to tease out the effects of the drug from the effects of the underlying condition.

That being said, BZDs do have at least a short-term effect on the formation and consolidation of memories. They can cause anterograde amnesia and interfere with the storage of new memories. One BZD in particular—flunitrazepam, also known as Rohypnol, or roofies—is particularly effective at impairing memory formation and has been used as a date rape drug.

Rohypnol (Figure 8.5) is a colorless, odorless, tasteless drug that is 5–10 times stronger than Valium. When slipped into an unsuspecting victim's drink, Rohypnol can lead to blackouts, unconsciousness, and complete memory loss. The unsuspecting victim is not only powerless to resist the sexual assault, but he or she has a poor recollection of the event and cannot testify against the assailants. Rohypnol is not approved for use in the United States, but it is available in Europe. Hoffman-La Roche, the manufacturer of Rohypnol, changed its formulation so that it dissolves more slowly and turns blue in solution. In 1996, the Drug-Induced Rape Prevention and Punishment Act established penalties up to 20 years in prison for giving a date rape

FIGURE 8.5. Rohypnol has been used as a date rape drug.

drug with the intent to commit a crime of violence, including rape. Another potential date rape drug, GHB, is discussed later in this chapter.

Effects on the Fetus

About 3 percent of pregnant women use benzodiazepines.[23,24] Some pregnant women take BZDs out of medical necessity; for example, for some women with epilepsy, anticonvulsant drugs are essential to their daily living. Taking antiepileptic drugs during pregnancy is thought to increase the risk of congenital malformations.[25] However, advising a pregnant woman to discontinue medication exchanges one risk for another—it swaps the risk to the fetus of medication exposure for the risk of untreated maternal illness. Untreated maternal illness, whether epilepsy or psychological illness, can result in reduced prenatal care, inadequate nutrition, increased alcohol use, reduced mother–infant bonding, and disruptions within the family environment.[26] There is currently insufficient

data to determine whether the benefits of BZD use to the mother might outweigh the risks to the fetus; much depends on which drug is taken, when, and for how long.[27]

Some studies have found an increased risk of miscarriage in women who take BZD during early pregnancy.[28] On the other hand, a number of recent studies have found that, except for a potential increased risk of cleft palate (a congenital malformation of the face and mouth), prenatal exposure to BZDs did not significantly raise the risk of major malformations.[29,30,31] There is some chance, however, that prenatal BZD exposure may sensitize GABA receptors in the infants and lead to an increased susceptibility to anxiety when they are adults.[32]

If a pregnant woman takes BZDs during her third trimester, the baby may go through withdrawal. Withdrawal starts several days or even weeks after delivery and can last for up to three to six months. Babies undergoing BZD withdrawal may experience irritability with constant crying, poor sleep patterns, trouble feeding, diarrhea, vomiting, tremors, bradycardia (slow heart rhythm), cyanosis (blue skin due to lack of oxygen), and slow growth.[33] If a mother uses BZDs shortly before delivery, the infant may experience floppy infant syndrome, with symptoms that include withdrawal, hypothermia, lethargy, and difficulty breathing or sleeping.

It is difficult to accurately assess the long-term risks for the baby of a BZD user during pregnancy. Many of the women who take BZDs during pregnancy are also taking other drugs. In addition, some women who take BZDs during pregnancy suffer from epilepsy or a psychiatric illness, which in itself may provide an intrinsic risk to the fetus.

Drug Interactions

Barbiturates and benzodiazepines have a synergistic effect with other depressants, in which the combined result is greater than the sum of the effects of each drug alone. That means that when users take these sedatives with other CNS depressants such as alcohol, opioids, or general anesthetics, there is a chance they may stop breathing. The concurrent use of BZD and opioids increases one's risk of dying of an opioid overdose five-fold.[34]

Both barbiturates and BZDs are metabolized by the cytochrome P450 (CYP450) enzymes of the liver and, therefore, may interact with other substances that use the same enzyme system. Sedatives may interact with drugs such as oral contraceptives, some antibiotics, antidepressants, anticonvulsants, fungal agents, vitamins

 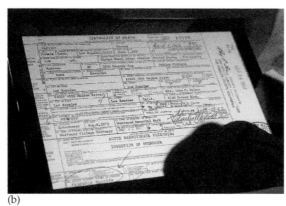

(a)   (b)

FIGURE 8.6. Marilyn Monroe. (a) Many famous people, including Marilyn Monroe, have died from using sedative/hypnotic drugs. (b) Marilyn Monroe's death certificate lists "acute barbiturate poisoning" as the cause of death.

K and D, steroids, and the blood thinner warfarin. Chronic barbiturate use increases the activity of the CYP450 liver enzyme system, enhancing the metabolism of barbiturates and other substances that use the same enzyme system, which leads to the development of tolerance.

Overdose

One of the reasons barbiturates are so dangerous is that their lethal dose is not significantly higher than their effective dose. The exact lethal dosage depends on one's tolerance, age, size, and other drugs that have

been taken. Symptoms of a barbiturate overdose include sluggishness, incoordination, confusion, slurred and slowed speech, sleepiness, staggering, and shallow breathing, leading to coma and death (Figure 8.6). If you suspect someone has overdosed on barbiturates, do not give them anything, and call 911.

BZDs are safer compounds, but by no means are they risk-free. The number of deaths attributable to benzodiazepine overdose increased ten-fold from 1999 to 2017, although it has decreased in recent years (Figure 8.7).[35,36] In 2019, BZDs were involved in almost 14 percent of all fatal drug overdoses in the United States.[37] Over the last few years, the BZD overdose mortality rose at a faster rate than the overall increase in usage. This may be related to the increase in opioid prescriptions over the same period; opioids are involved in about three-quarters of the overdose deaths involving BZDs.[38,39] When overdose occurs, it's usually related to respiratory depression, which typically occurs only in special circumstances, such as when the drug is given as a rapid IV injection, with severe liver dysfunction or concurrent lung disease, or when taken

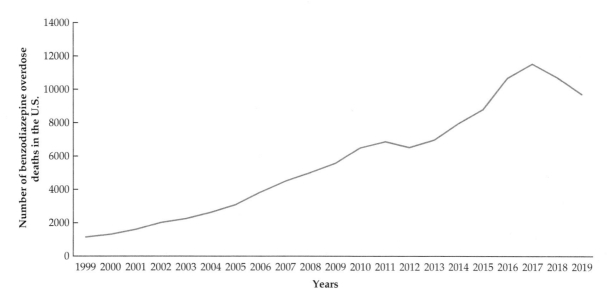

FIGURE 8.7. Number of overdose deaths attributable to benzodiazepines. The number of deaths attributable to benzodiazepine overdose has risen almost ten-fold in the past two decades.

Source: NIDA. (2021). Overdose death rates. Accessed on June 27, 2021, from https://www.drugabuse.gov/related-topics/trends-statistics/ overdose-death-rates

in combination with alcohol, opioids, or other CNS depressant drugs. Symptoms of BZD overdose are similar to barbiturate overdose, and include drowsiness, slowed and slurred speech, rapid involuntary eye movements, incoordination, respiratory depression, and coma. Flumazenil, a competitive antagonist to the GABA$_A$ receptor, can be administered to treat a BZD overdose.

Medical and Therapeutic Uses of Sedatives and Hypnotics

Benzodiazepines and barbiturates have been used to treat many conditions, including

- Insomnia
- Anxiety disorders
- Seizure disorders
- Withdrawal from chronic alcohol use
- As general anesthetics and preanesthetic medications.

BZDs have for the most part replaced barbiturates as the drug of choice for these conditions, because BZDs have more specific effects than barbiturates, fewer side effects, a much wider margin of safety, less potential for abuse or tolerance, less effect on REM sleep, and minimal effects on the respiratory center of the brainstem.

The therapeutic uses of a given BZD depend on the BZD's half-life. Longer-acting BZDs may be used to control anxiety disorders, and their relaxing effects can last as long as two to three days. Intermediate- and short-acting forms are better suited to treat insomnia. A drug used for insomnia would ideally work quickly when taken at bedtime, facilitate sustained sleep throughout the night, and be out of the person's system by morning. A short-acting BZD like midazolam (Versed) may be used before some surgical procedures to reduce anxiety and cause forgetfulness.

Sleep

Sleep is an important, insistent biological drive that is necessary for both physical and mental health. Sleep is so important that even though people can choose to stop eating or drinking until they die, individuals cannot voluntarily sleep-deprive themselves to death. Sleep is so insistent that sometimes people will fall asleep even in situations (such as driving a car) in which they know that falling asleep will be potentially fatal.

But what is sleep? Sleep is divided into five stages—Non-REM (NREM) stages 1, 2, 3, and 4; and REM

Orexin: A neurotransmitter that promotes appetite and wakefulness.

Insomnia: Difficulty falling asleep or staying asleep.

sleep—which are characterized by specific brain wave patterns and other physiological properties. One advances through these stages in cycles throughout the night, and there is more deep sleep early in the night and more REM sleep toward morning. As one progresses from NREM stage 1 to NREM stage 4, sleep becomes progressively deeper and more restorative. REM sleep is a unique stage, characterized by fairly active brain waves, a loss of skeletal muscle tone, a loss in the body's ability to regulate body temperature, erections of the clitoris and penis, rapid eye movements (from whence the stage gets its name), and dreams. REM dreams are long, more visual, and often bizarre—for example, you may be skateboarding with Elvis, but he suddenly turns into your first-grade teacher and you decide to go out for fondue. NREM dreams are shorter, less emotional, and more related to events in one's life—for example, in a NREM dream, you might recite lists of neurotransmitters and the drugs they affect.

Sleep changes across the lifespan. As people age, they generally go to sleep earlier and wake earlier, but they have decreased total sleep time. Adolescents and young adults undergo a natural change in their sleep cycle; their biological clocks shift so they stay up later and awaken later. The cycle tends to revert back in a person's late twenties. Over 25 percent of high school and college students are sleep deprived. In 2014, the American Academy of Pediatrics issued a statement recommending later start times for middle and high school students to better align the school schedules with the biological sleep rhythms of adolescents.[40]

Different neurotransmitters and drugs affect our sleep/wake cycle. Glutamate, norepinephrine, acetylcholine, and **orexin** all increase wakefulness, as do the drugs (such as amphetamines and cocaine) that stimulate them. Non-REM sleep is increased by GABA, the main inhibitory neurotransmitter of the CNS. Adenosine also promotes sleep, as do a number of other substances, including insulin, and (possibly) serotonin.

Insomnia is an inability to fall asleep or to stay asleep as long as desired and is particularly common in the elderly. Insomnia can occur over the short term, and may be due to pain or illness, changes in one's sleep environment, drugs, or stress. Chronic insomnia—an inability to consistently sleep well for a month or longer—may be the primary disorder or it may be related to another disorder such as depression. At least 20 percent of the U.S. population experiences insomnia at some point in time, and 10 percent have chronic insomnia.[41]

Insomnia can have widespread consequences. Sleeplessness can increase the risk of memory and learning problems, inflammation, diabetes, weight gain, and mood disorders. Both depression and ADHD are associated with insufficient sleep. In the past, scientists assumed that these disorders led to sleeping problems, but it now appears that there is a bidirectional relationship and these disorders may also occur *because* of insufficient sleep.[42] In one study, about half of the adults with sleep apnea (a chronic condition that disrupts sleep by interrupting breathing) also scored low on attention tests. When their apnea was treated and their sleep improved, 60 percent showed significant improvement in attention scores.[43] Another study followed male medical students for 34 years. The men who had insomnia as students were twice as likely to develop depression.[44] Recent studies bear this relationship out—insomnia increases one's risk of developing depression.[45,46,47]

In our drugstore society, people often seek pharmacological help for insomnia. There are both prescription and over-the-counter (OTC) pharmacological remedies for insomnia (Table 8.3).

Benzodiazepines may be prescribed to help treat insomnia. Although BZDs help individuals to fall asleep faster, increase total sleep time, and decrease the number of times people awaken during the night, they decrease the amount of time spent in deep sleep, so the sleep is unlikely to be as satisfying or restorative.[48]

Since the late 1980s, prescription non-BZD sleeping aids, such as zolpidem (Ambien and Intermezzo), eszopiclone (Lunesta), and zaleplon (Sonata), have become more popular. Structurally, these **Z drugs** are not BZDs, but they bind to the same place on the GABA receptor, and their effects are primarily hypnotic rather than anxiolytic. Z drugs produce a sleep rhythm that more closely matches one's natural sleep cycle. The shorter-acting Z drugs are best for initiating sleep, while the longer-acting or controlled-release forms can help maintain sleep. Users may experience a hangover effect the next day, including sleepiness, and impaired motor and cognitive function, and often experience insomnia again when stopping the drug. From 2005–2010, the number of zolpidem-related emergency room visits increased by 220 percent, and the use of Ambien accounted for 20 percent of ER visits among those age 65 and older, more than any other single medication.[49,50] Additionally, because the Z drugs are cross tolerant (tolerance to one drug results in tolerance to another similar drug) with ethanol, overdose can occur if the Z drugs are combined with alcohol or other CNS depressants.

QUICK HIT

Most of the non-benzodiazepines that promote sleep have the letter "z" in their name (zolpidem, eszopiclone, zaleplon). In cartoons, it is not uncommon to see a series of Zs (zzzzzzzzzz) used to indicate that a person is sleeping or snoring. Perhaps scientists bestowed these names on the "Z drugs" hoping to evoke the image of slumber.

Users of non-BZD hypnotics should be particularly careful when operating motor vehicles. A group of scientists examined the use of hypnotic drugs in Norway and determined that the use of these drugs

Z drugs: Nonbenzodiazepine hypnotic drugs such as Ambien, Lunesta, and Sonata, often used to treat insomnia.

TABLE 8.3. Summary of Sleep Aid Medications

Class	Examples	Mechanism of Action	Selected Side Effects	Schedule
Benzodiazepines	diazepam (Valium) alprazolam (Xanax) lorazepam (Ativan)	Bind to GABA receptors and increase GABA's effects	Sleepiness in the morning, confusion, incoordination, tolerance, withdrawal, dependency	IV
Z drugs	zolpidem (Ambien) eszopiclone (Lunesta) zaleplon (Sonata)	Bind to GABA receptors and increase GABA's effects	Tolerance, sleep driving, sleep eating	IV
Orexin antagonists	suvorexant (Belsomra)	Blocks orexin receptors	Sleepiness in the morning, muscle weakness, trouble driving, intense and vivid dreams and nightmares	IV
Melatonin agonists	ramelteon (Rozerem) OTC melatonin	Binds to melatonin receptors	Can influence the biological clock	Unscheduled
Antihistamines	doxylamine (Unisom) diphenhydramine (Benadryl)	Blocks histamine receptors in the CNS	Sleepiness in the morning Tolerance may develop	Unscheduled

STRAIGHT DOPE   Ways to Relieve Insomnia without Medication

Rather than running to the medicine cabinet when you can't sleep, consider trying nonpharmacological methods to combat insomnia.

- Establish and maintain a regular bedtime and wake time.
- Avoid looking at your computer, tablet, or smart phone screen for at least an hour before bedtime.
- Don't use your bed for anything but sleep and sex—no homework, no TV.
- Prepare a relaxing sleep environment—make sure your bedroom is dark, quiet, and set at a comfortable temperature.
- Once you're in bed with the lights off, try to relax and clear your mind of the worries and stresses of your day. Try some meditative practices, relaxation therapy, or cognitive behavioral therapy.

- Avoid lying awake in bed for long periods. If you can't sleep within 30 minutes, get out of bed and do something relaxing. Or put your pillow at the foot of bed and try to sleep at the other end.
- Avoid caffeine within eight hours of bedtime.
- Don't nap during the day.
- Exercise regularly, but not late at night. In fact, regular, moderate exercise meets the criteria of the perfect sleep aid: exercise encourages a normal night of sleep; there is no sedation or rebound anxiety the next day; exercise won't negatively interact with other medications; and you can use exercise long-term, without dependence or rebound insomnia upon discontinuation.

was correlated with traffic accidents.[51,52] This is particularly true in women. Women are five times more likely to get into a motor vehicle accident the morning following Ambien use.[53,54] Due to this increased risk, in 2013, the U.S. Food and Drug Administration (FDA) required the manufacturers of some of these drugs to lower the recommended dose.

Ambien and other non-BZD hypnotics have also been tied to the unusual phenomenon of sleepwalking, sleep eating, sleep sex, and sleep driving. Some users have awoken to find the refrigerator emptied and the stove on from a late-night baking and eating spree. Others have abashedly realized that they had ordered thousands of dollars of items from the internet while asleep. Still others have reported going to sleep, only to wake up arrested on the side of the road in their pajamas.[55] In 2006, a class action lawsuit was filed against Sanofi-Aventis, the makers of Ambien, by those who said that the company had failed to adequately warn consumers about the risk of these behaviors. Due to this suit, in 2007, the

Ask yourself: Is a bad reaction to a drug a reasonable defense for a crime? Should someone who gets into a car accident while sleep driving due to Ambien use be charged with a crime? If someone turns over and hits a bed partner in his sleep, is he guilty of assault? How do these two situations compare?

FDA began to require that the labels for all prescription sleep aids clearly warn users of potential side effects.

Rozerem (Ramelteon) is a different category of prescription hypnotic. This drug works at melatonin receptors to help regulate the sleep-wake cycle. It has not been shown to produce dependence or abuse, and it is approved for long-term use. Rozerem has been associated with decreases in testosterone levels and increases in prolactin (hormone that stimulates breast development and milk production in women) levels, and patients may experience difficulties associated with these hormonal changes.

Orexin is a substance that regulates wakefulness and appetite. Suvorexant (Belsomra), approved by the FDA in 2014 to treat insomnia, works by blocking orexin receptors.[56] Side effects of suvorexant include sleepiness the next morning, difficulty driving, and vivid dreams or nightmares.

Over-the-counter drugs to treat insomnia include melatonin (a hormone produced by the brain's pineal gland), antihistamines, and herbal remedies (Chapter 15). For those who suffer from insomnia, however, nonpharmacological methods are often superior to pharmacological approaches. Drugs address the symptoms of insomnia, not the underlying problems that cause the sleeplessness. Not only that, but the drugs themselves may cause additional problems and side effects, and they are not always effective.

Antianxiety Drugs and Treatment

Anxiety is important for survival, warning us of danger and activating the sympathetic nervous system to help us deal with emergencies. Unfortunately, many of the dangers and stresses of today's world are not helped by the surging adrenaline, pounding heart, and increased blood flow that follows anxiety. In fact, anxiety may make stresses that are often best dealt with by restraint and control (don't punch your boss), clear thinking (take your exam), and fortitude (finish your oral presentation) worse. Sometimes, anxiety even becomes overwhelming and debilitating.

Anxiety disorders are the most common category of mental illness in the United States. An estimated 40 million adult Americans between the ages of 18 and 54 suffer from anxiety disorders. In any given year, 18 percent of Americans experience the symptoms of anxiety disorders such as generalized anxiety disorder (GAD), panic disorder, social anxiety disorder, or phobias. These anxiety disorders will be discussed at greater length in Chapter 13.

Benzodiazepines such as alprazolam and diazepam are effective as anxiolytics for short-term treatment. For longer-term treatment of GAD, phobias, and panic disorder, behavioral treatments such as cognitive behavioral therapy, exposure therapy, anxiety management, and relaxation exercises may be more effective (Chapter 13).

Anticonvulsants

Barbiturates and benzodiazepines are used to treat seizure disorders. These anticonvulsants are administered intravenously for the emergency treatment of convulsions due to tetanus, eclampsia, poisoning by convulsant drugs such as strychnine, or status epilepticus. Longer-acting sedatives such as phenobarbital or diazepam may be taken to alleviate or prevent seizures in epileptic patients.

Anesthesia

General anesthesia is a controlled state of unconsciousness that disrupts the communication between different parts of the brain, which stops the processing of higher-level information without shutting down the brain entirely.[57] Doctors have been putting patients to sleep for 150 years, but we still do not completely understand what happens in the brain during general anesthesia. We do know the patient loses awareness, the ability to move, the perception of pain, as well as memories, and anesthesiologists may vary the type and dose of the drugs used to effect these changes.

The ultra-short-acting barbiturate thiopental (Pentothal) is used as a general anesthetic and a preoperative

Ask yourself: Author Anthony Beal said, "I wonder when someone will grow the testicles to say to Americans everywhere, 'Enough with the self-medicating.' Seriously. What ever happened to dealing with life? Life is pain. Life is inconvenience. Life is a tall, cool glass of f**k you. Step away from the Prozac and Xanax and drink up, bitches. Refills are on the house." To what degree do you think using antianxiety drugs is a crutch or an escape, and to what degree do you feel it's a necessary medical aid? How glad are you that Beal did not pursue a career as a grief therapist?

anesthetic for minor surgery. BZDs are used as a presurgical medication to relieve anxiety, and to limit a patient's recollection of any details of the procedure.

Chronic Effects of Sedatives and Hypnotics

Long-term use of sedatives, especially of barbiturates, can be problematic, and is associated with daytime fatigue, accidents, and overall mortality.[58] Use is especially problematic in the elderly, and is associated with increased risk of falls, traffic accidents, and cognitive decline.[59] Except when they are used as anticonvulsants, barbiturates are typically recommended for only short-term use.

Tolerance to Sedatives and Hypnotics

Tolerance to barbiturates develops at different rates. Those who take daily or near-daily barbiturates over a period of weeks or months will need ever-increasing doses to achieve the desired sedative or hypnotic effects. Tolerance does not develop for the anticonvulsant effects, even after years of use. Tolerance also fails to develop for respiratory depression, so the margin of safety decreases dangerously as the user becomes tolerant to the drugs' sedative effects. Tolerance to barbiturates is both cellular and metabolic. Cellular tolerance occurs when the neurons in the brain adapt to the presence of the drug, and receptors downregulate (decrease in number). Metabolic tolerance occurs because barbiturates increase the activity of the liver's CYP450 enzymes that metabolize barbiturates; the more drug used, the faster it is metabolized.

Tolerance to BZDs is not as fast or complete. As with barbiturates, tolerance first develops to the sedative and hypnotic effects, although tolerance to the anxiolytic effects develops slowly and to a limited extent. When the sedative effects wear off, the disinhibitory effects become more prominent. This may be why some people show aggression and impulsivity—at first, there's drowsiness and slowing, but as that wears off, individuals express behaviors that had been suppressed by fear or anxiety.[60] Unlike barbiturates, BZDs do not increase the activity of the liver enzymes that normally metabolize the drug, so they show no metabolic tolerance. Both barbiturates and BZDs show cross tolerance with each other, as well as with other CNS depressants.

Sedative and Hypnotic Dependence and Addiction

When large quantities of barbiturates are taken for several weeks, physical dependence begins to develop. Benzodiazepines are not as strongly addictive. Most people who use BZDs as medically directed—even long term—do not become dependent. The risk of BZD dependence is higher in patients who are anxious or have sleep disorders, those who take large doses, individuals who abuse other drugs, and in users who obtain the drug illegally simply to get high.[61] Nevertheless, sedatives are second only to opioids as the most frequently abused group of prescription medications. In 2019, over 680,000 Americans age 12 years and older were thought to have a substance use disorder for tranquilizers or sedatives, and about 17 percent of those received treatment at a specialty facility.[62]

Psychological dependence occurs most powerfully when a drug reaches the brain quickly. Sedatives with a fast onset of action and a short half-life are typically more likely to be abused than slower-acting compounds. Those dependent on sedative/hypnotic drugs should see a medical professional and should not attempt to stop taking the drugs abruptly, because withdrawal can be life threatening.

QUICK HIT

Corey Haim, an actor and teen idol popular in the 1980s, said this about his Valium use: "But one led to two, two led to four, four led to eight, until at the end it was about 85 a day—the doctors could not believe I was taking that much." Haim is thought to have died of complications related to drug overdose.

Sedative and Hypnotic Withdrawal and Treatment

Withdrawal from sedatives occurs when a person has a physical dependence to these drugs, which can happen with long-term use, typically defined as daily use for at least three months. Not all long-term users will experience withdrawal symptoms upon discontinuation, and when they do, the onset of symptoms may be delayed for days or even weeks. Compounds with a fast onset of action and more rapid elimination may produce more intense withdrawal reactions than drugs that have a longer half-life.

A person withdrawing from sedatives may experience some of the same conditions the anxiolytics were originally treating:

- Insomnia
- Anxiety
- Irritability
- Tremor

He or she may also suffer from

- Nausea and vomiting
- Loss of appetite
- Headache
- Sweating
- Muscle pain
- Fever
- Confusion
- Memory problems
- Difficulty concentrating

Withdrawal from high doses, especially of barbiturates, is more severe, and can lead to

- Nightmares
- Hallucinations
- Tremors
- Seizures
- Death

Those who are dependent on sedative/hypnotic drugs should seek treatment for their addiction. Withdrawal should be medically supervised to monitor for potentially fatal symptoms. Professionals will generally taper down drug use, which involves decreasing the dose or transferring the user to a sedative with a longer half-life. Those seeking treatment can go through inpatient or outpatient therapy to address the psychological issues underlying dependence. Cognitive behavioral therapy teaches patients to monitor their thoughts, behaviors, and expectations to help adapt to a life without sedatives (Chapter 18).

Other Sedative/Hypnotic Drugs

Barbiturates, benzodiazepines, and Z drugs are some of the best-known and most widely used sedative/hypnotic drugs, but there are many others. In this section, we will discuss GHB, methaqualone, and propofol.

FIGURE 8.8. GHB. GHB is found in the human brain and body and is also made synthetically.

GHB

Gamma-hydroxybutyric acid (GHB) is both a naturally occurring substance and a synthetic drug (Figure 8.8). GHB occurs naturally in beef, wine, and some fruits, and in the body from the breakdown of GABA; in fact, GHB is considered a neurotransmitter in its own right. GHB has both therapeutic and recreational uses.

History of GHB and Prevalence of Its Use

Gamma-hydroxybutyric acid was first synthesized in 1960, when Dr. Henri Laborit, a French researcher, investigated the drug's properties as an anticonvulsant that could cross the blood–brain barrier more easily than GABA. Later, GHB was used in a limited capacity as an anesthetic. Although GHB does induce unconsciousness, it doesn't prevent pain, which makes it less than ideal for surgical use. In the United States, GHB gained popularity in the 1980s as a nutritional supplement for bodybuilders. Although GHB increases

the secretion of growth hormone, the drug has not been scientifically shown to increase weight loss or muscle growth, and in 1990, the FDA banned over-the-counter sales of GHB. The drug was classified as schedule I over concerns about overdoses and its use as a date rape drug. However, under the trade name Xyrem, GHB is a schedule III drug approved to treat narcolepsy. Illicit use of GHB declined dramatically following its categorization as a schedule I drug.[63,64]

Pharmacokinetics and Mechanism of Action of GHB

When given as a drug, GHB has effects similar to other CNS depressant drugs. It is an odorless, colorless, salty-tasting liquid that is rapidly absorbed into the bloodstream and easily crosses the blood–brain barrier. Effects are usually felt within 15 minutes and peak within 40 minutes.

Although a simple chemical compound, the mechanism of action of GHB is complex (Figure 8.9). GHB binds to excitatory GHB receptors as well as to inhibitory $GABA_B$ receptors. $GABA_B$ receptors are metabotropic, meaning that when GABA or a drug binds to the receptor, it starts a cascade of events leading to the opening of a separate ion channel located down the membrane. It's a slower and more complex process than the mechanism by which sedatives/hypnotics interact with the $GABA_A$ receptors. At low doses, GHB binds almost exclusively to GHB receptors, which are found in the cortex, substantia nigra, basal ganglia, hippocampus, and hypothalamus. Binding to these receptors stimulates the release of excitatory glutamate. As the dose of GHB increases, more GHB binds to and activates $GABA_B$ receptors, producing sedation and sleepiness. GHB has a relatively low affinity for GABA receptors; a high dose is required for GHB to have an effect at these inhibitory receptors.

GHB also affects other neurotransmitters:

- GHB has a biphasic effect on dopamine—low doses of GHB inhibit the release of dopamine, while high levels of GHB increase it.
- GHB increases levels of acetylcholine and serotonin.
- GHB also mediates opioid effects in the brain. The opioid antagonist naloxone blocks some of GHB's effects.

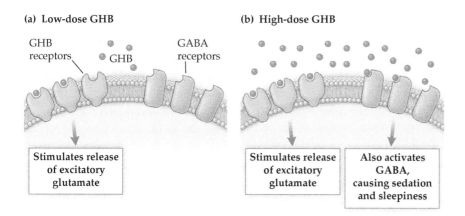

(a) Low-dose GHB

GHB receptors / GHB / GABA receptors

Stimulates release of excitatory glutamate

(b) High-dose GHB

Stimulates release of excitatory glutamate

Also activates GABA, causing sedation and sleepiness

FIGURE 8.9. Mechanism of action of GHB. (a) Low doses of GHB have a stimulatory effect, but at higher doses (b), GHB binds to GABA receptors and can cause sedation.

Ask yourself: If a drug is also a naturally occurring neurotransmitter, is it appropriate for the government to make it illegal? Why or why not?

These varied effects help to explain GHB's paradoxical mix of sedative and stimulatory properties.

Acute Effects of GHB

GHB can give the sensation of inebriation. A mild dose (1 gram or less) will cause relaxation, mild euphoria, a loss of inhibition, increased sociability, and short-term forgetfulness. The user may feel heightened sexual interest, although, like alcohol, GHB is actually associated with decreased sexual performance. A higher dose (2–3 grams) can cause lethargy, drowsiness, and sleep. Loss of muscle control, slurred speech, vomiting, dizziness, and visual disturbances, and amnesia also may occur.[65] Doses of 4–5 grams or more (about 1 teaspoonful) can lead to very deep sleep, depressed respiration, hypothermia, coma, and possibly death.

Coma, when it occurs, is generally of a short duration. Even deeply comatose GHB patients typically awaken, spontaneously and abruptly, within four to six hours after ingestion. This unusual effect might occur because as GHB levels decrease in the body, the concentration of GHB falls below the threshold level necessary to stimulate the GABA receptors, and instead mainly activates the excitatory GHB receptors. High doses of GHB not only cause rapid unconsciousness and coma, but also can produce convulsions, vomiting (and aspiration of vomit while unconscious), slow heart rate, reduced blood pressure, and depressed respiration, especially if taken with alcohol or another CNS depressant. These effects are potentially life-threatening.

....

QUICK HIT

Aqua Dots was a children's arts and crafts bead toy. In 2007, it was found that the popular toy's beads contained a chemical coating that metabolized into GHB.[66]

....

Because GHB produces rapid unconsciousness and suppresses memory, it has been used as a date rape drug. As with Rohypnol, GHB may be slipped into the drink of an unsuspecting person who may then black out and be vulnerable to sexual attack (Figure 8.10). Take caution in public settings by avoiding opened drinks from strangers or leaving drinks unattended.

(a)

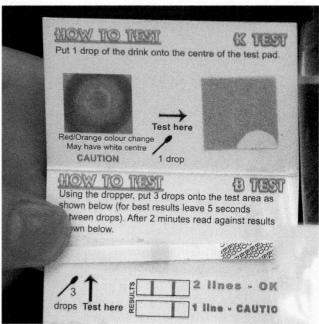

(b)

FIGURE 8.10. Date rape drug detection. (a) (b) There are a number of products on the market that claim to detect the presence of date rape drugs in a drink. But there are dozens of different date rape drugs, and none of the coasters, glasses, nail polishes, or other testing kits can detect them all. In addition, some of these products are not as effective with acidic beverages, results can take up to 30 minutes for some drugs, and the test kit's color change may be masked by the color of the beverage.

Medical and Therapeutic Uses of GHB

In Europe, GHB is approved for use as an anesthetic, sleeping aid, and as a treatment for opioid addiction and alcohol withdrawal, because it has been found to help relieve withdrawal symptoms and to reduce cravings. But estimates of GHB's beneficial and harmful effects when being used as a treatment for opioid addiction or alcohol withdrawal have not yet been established.[67,68]

In the United States, GHB's only approved use is for the treatment of narcolepsy. Narcolepsy is a condition characterized by excessive daytime sleepiness, especially during boring events. Cataplexy—a sudden loss of muscle tone during wakefulness—is another symptom of narcolepsy, one that can be triggered by exciting or emotional events. Scientists now think that narcolepsy is an autoimmune destruction of orexin cells.[69] Under the trade name Xyrem, GHB reduces the frequency of cataplexy and alleviates excessive daytime sleepiness.

FIGURE 8.11. Michael Jackson. In 2009, pop star Michael Jackson died of an overdose of benzodiazepines and propofol.

Quaaludes

Methaqualone (Quaaludes [KWAY-lewds]) was first introduced in the 1950s in India as an antimalarial drug. Although ineffective against malaria, methaqualone had hypnotic properties that interested drug manufacturers. Quaaludes were first marketed in America in 1965 and became quite popular in the late 1970s and early 1980s, in part because they were (falsely) rumored to be an aphrodisiac. Quaaludes were also incorrectly thought to be safe and nonaddictive.

Quaaludes are a CNS depressant that works as a positive allosteric modulator at $GABA_A$ receptors to produce sedation and sleepiness.[70] Some reported positive effects include relaxation, calm, a sense of well-being, a loss of inhibition, and increased self-confidence. Fairly common unwanted side effects include stomach pain, nausea and vomiting, sweating, dry mouth, rapid heartbeat, dampened sexual response, dizziness, anxiety, restlessness, depersonalization, and paranoia. Quaaludes can also be used as date rape drugs.

QUICK HIT

Actor and comedian Bill Cosby was accused of dozens of instances of sexual assault spanning over three decades. In 2018, Cosby was found guilty and sentenced to prison for these crimes. Court documents from 2005 show that Cosby admitted he gave Quaaludes to women he wanted to have sex with.[71]

An overdose can cause convulsions, renal failure, coma, and death. Methaqualone overdose resembles barbiturate poisoning, but with increased motor difficulties and a lower incidence of respiratory depression. Methaqualone was categorized as schedule I in 1984.

Propofol

Propofol (Diprivan) is a fast-acting anesthetic that was first synthesized in 1986. Administered intravenously, this white liquid often is used for induction (the beginning process) of anesthesia; for anesthesia during short procedures, such as endoscopy or colonoscopy; and to sedate individuals who are being put on mechanical ventilation (Figure 8.11). Propofol has a fast onset of action as well as a quick recovery time. Not only does propofol reduce awareness, it also leaves the patient with no memory of the experience; for this reason, propofol is sometimes called "milk of amnesia." Propofol acts as a positive allosteric modulator at $GABA_A$ receptors, and also increases actions of the endocannabinoid system.[72] Recreational use of propofol has risen in recent years, especially among anesthesiologists who have access to the drug.[73,74]

Inhalants

As mentioned at the start of this chapter, sedatives and hypnotics are not the only drugs to produce depressant effects. **Inhalants** are a class of drugs that may be found in kitchen and bathroom products, as well as in

Inhalants: Volatile substances, anesthetics, or nitrites that produce inhalable vapors that can have mind-altering effects.

products found in hardware stores and garages. Inhalants include a wide array of intoxicants and come in the form of volatile solvents, such as glues, paints, polishes, and fuels; anesthetics, such as chloroform, ether, halothane, and nitrous oxide; and nitrites. They are easily vaporized liquids or are gases at room temperature. High doses of inhalants can lead to effects similar to sedative/hypnotics, which is why they are included in this chapter.

History of Inhalants

The Temple of Apollo in Delphi was among the most sacred sites of ancient Greece, because it held the oracle. The oracle was a woman who went into a trance in order to allow the gods to speak through her. It has since been shown that there were hidden faults under the Delphic temple, and the oracle was probably inhaling ethylene gas, which, in lower doses, evokes a trance-like state leading to euphoria and mystical experiences.[75]

Since ancient times, people have inhaled the fumes of oils, incense, and gas to alter their consciousness. Ether and nitrous oxide were two anesthetics commonly inhaled as intoxicants. In the mid-twentieth century, recreational use of solvents became popular.

Ether

Spanish alchemist Raymundus Lullius is credited with the discovery of ether in 1275. In 1540, German physician Valerius Cordus developed a method of synthesizing diethyl ether, and called it "sweet oil of vitriol." Around the same time, Paracelsus (the Swiss physician who created laudanum) discovered ether's analgesic properties. Centuries later, William Morton, a Boston dentist, painlessly removed a patient's tooth under ether's anesthetic effects. Word of this achievement spread, and in 1846, a Boston surgeon demonstrated ether's use as an anesthetic at Massachusetts General Hospital. Before an amazed audience, a patient's tumor was removed with no pain, and with the patient's heart and respiratory functions remaining safely intact throughout the procedure.[76] Today, ether is rarely used in surgical procedures because it triggers nausea and vomiting and is highly flammable.

Nitrous Oxide

The English scientist Joseph Priestly first discovered nitrous oxide in 1772. In 1845, dentist Horace Wells investigated the effectiveness of the drug as a surgical anesthetic by having one of his own teeth extracted while breathing nitrous oxide. Excited by the drug's potential as an anesthetic, Wells gave a demonstration at Massachusetts General Hospital. Unfortunately, this demonstration did not go as well as the demonstration for ether. Wells did not fully understand the effective dosages of the drug, and his patient woke up and screamed in pain during the operation.[77] Nitrous oxide is not a strong enough anesthetic for use in major surgery, but today dentists sometimes may use the drug to relieve anxiety and pain during dental procedures.

Glue Sniffing

The first known print reference to glue sniffing appeared in newspapers in 1959. The article warned readers about the dangers of sniffing glue . . . but also informed adolescents that glue was a potential intoxicant. Ten months after the article appeared, there was a surge in the number of cases of glue sniffing. The first peer-reviewed journal article on recreational glue sniffing appeared in *JAMA* (the *Journal of the American Medical Association*) in 1962. Glue sales rose as media coverage of the glue sniffing "epidemic" increased. In 1971, The *New York Times* began an anti-inhalant campaign, warning of the dangers of inhalants, complete with a description of how to get high on aerosols and which products were most popular.[78]

Prevalence of Inhalant Use

Inhalants are often a young person's first introduction to a drug-induced alteration of consciousness. The average age of first-time use in 2019 was 18.4 years, younger than for all other drugs of abuse except alcohol.[79] About half of users were under age 18 when they first used inhalants. Inhalants are also one of the most commonly used drugs in middle school and high school, surpassed only by alcohol, vaping, and marijuana.[80] Perhaps this popularity is due to the fact that inhalants are readily available, inexpensive, legal to buy and possess, and easy to conceal. Also, their potential dangers are not as widely known as those for other drugs. Unfortunately, inhalants are also among the most toxic drugs.

Over 25 million Americans—9.1 percent of the population age 12 and older—have ever used inhalants.[81] Inhalant use disproportionately afflicts the poor, mentally ill, and young.[82] Unlike nearly all other classes of drugs, inhalant use is most common among younger adolescents and declines as they get older.[83] In 2019, 4.7 percent of eighth-graders, 2.8 percent of tenth-graders, and 1.9 percent of twelfth-graders reported inhalant use in the past year.[84] Females high school students were more likely to use inhalants than males.[85]

TABLE 8.4. Dangerous Compounds Found in Inhaled Substances

Substance	Sources	Adverse Effects
Acetone	Gasoline, glues, nail polish removers, paint removers, paint thinners, rubber cement, spray paints	Irritates and damages eyes and mucous membranes of respiratory tract; flammable
Benzene	Glues, nail polish removers, paint removers, paint thinners, rubber cement, spray paints	Bone marrow injury—increased risk of aplastic anemia and impaired immunological function; carcinogenic, increased risk of leukemia; menstrual irregularities, infertility, and birth defects
Butane	Air freshener, fabric spray, hair spray, lighter fluid, spray paint	Cardiac arrhythmias and sudden sniffing death syndrome; temporary memory loss; laryngospasm; flammable
Difluoroethane	Canned air, computer duster	Cardiac arrhythmias, sudden sniffing death syndrome, and coronary heart disease
Freon	Fluorinated hydrocarbons used in a number of products including refrigerators and air conditioners	Freeze injuries to skin and upper airway; respiratory obstruction, injury, and collapse; liver damage; cardiac arrhythmia and sudden sniffing death syndrome
Gasoline	Mixture of volatile chemicals, including toluene, benzene, triorthocresyl phosphate (TCP)	TCP can cause degeneration of motor nerve cells, spastic muscle disorders, and liver problems; problems associated with toluene and benzene; highly flammable
Hexane	Gasoline, glues, rubber cement	Peripheral nerve damage, muscular weakness and atrophy
Propane	Air freshener, barbecue gas tanks, hair spray, portable stoves, spray paint	Flammable
Toluene	Correction fluid, gasoline, glues, nail polish, nail polish removers, paint removers, paint thinners, rubber cement, spray paints	Reduction in short-term memory, myelin damage, loss of hearing and color vision, and cerebellar dysfunctions that can result in incoordination; liver and kidney damage; anemia; cardiac arrhythmias and sudden sniffing death syndrome
Trichloroethylene and trichloroethane	Antifreeze, correction fluid, degreasers, dry-cleaning fluid, glues, rubber cement, sealants	Kidney cancer; cirrhosis of the liver; reproductive complications and miscarriage; cardiac arrhythmias and sudden sniffing death syndrome
Nitrous oxide	Whippets—gas propulsion system in whipped cream	Brain anoxia and neurotoxicity
Butyl nitrite	"Poppers," "rush," "locker room"	Suppression of immunologic function; cardiac arrhythmias and sudden sniffing death syndrome

Source and Forms of Inhalants

More than 1,400 household products can be used as inhalants to get high (Table 8.4). They have little in common in their chemical structure, pharmacology, or mechanism of action; what joins them is that they are all taken by inhalation. Inhalants often are categorized as volatile substances, anesthetics, and nitrites.

Volatile Substances

Volatile substances are chemicals that are liquid at room temperature and give off fumes that are inhaled. They were never intended for internal consumption, and they are among the most toxic substances used as recreational drugs. The fumes of these substances may cause mild euphoria, dizziness, loss of inhibition, impaired judgment, nausea, incoordination, disorientation, distorted perceptions, and hallucinations. Some examples of volatile inhalants include

- Adhesives: glues and cements
- Aerosols: hair spray, spray paint, air freshener, household cleaning sprays, fabric protector sprays, computer cleaners
- Cleaning agents: dry-cleaning fluid, degreasers, spot removers
- Fuels: butane, propane, kerosene, gasoline
- Solvents: nail polish remover, paint remover, paint thinner, correction fluid, felt-tip marker fluid

Anesthetic Inhalants: Ether and Nitrous Oxide

Anesthesia has three main functions: pain relief, muscle relaxation, and loss of consciousness. Anesthetics that have been used recreationally include ether and nitrous oxide.

Huffing: Using inhalants in order to get high. Also, the act of soaking a rag or handkerchief with the chemical and then deeply inhaling from the cloth.

Ether ($C_4H_{10}O$) is a colorless, volatile, highly flammable liquid that was once used as a general anesthetic, but today is mostly used as a solvent and in the manufacture of a number of illicit drugs. Ether has a strong, distinctively sweet smell, and it can irritate the airway. High doses can trigger salivation, coughing, and vomiting, and chronic use can lead to dependence.

Nitrous oxide (N_2O) is a colorless gas with a sweet taste and odor. Sometimes called "laughing gas" due to its euphoric effects, nitrous oxide is the only anesthetic gas widely available enough to be a significant abuse concern. Nitrous oxide is available to dentists

FIGURE 8.12. Huffing. A girl is shown here sniffing glue. Inhalant use is portrayed in movies such as *Citizen Ruth, Blue Velvet, Little Shop of Horrors, Airplane,* and *Boys Don't Cry,* as well as in the television show *It's Always Sunny in Philadelphia,* and the book *Cider House Rules.* In the song *The Bitch is Back,* Elton John sings, "I get high in the evening sniffing pots of glue."

and other health professionals. Nitrous oxide is also available in *whippets,* small cartridges that are used to charge whipped cream dispensers.

Nitrites

The nitrites are yellow, volatile, flammable liquids with a fruity odor. Amyl nitrite and butyl nitrite also are known as "poppers," "amys," "rush," and "locker room," and they have both medicinal and recreational purposes. Amyl nitrite is a vasodilator that is sometimes used to treat angina (chest pain) in people with congestive heart failure or coronary artery disease, although its use has been mostly replaced by nitroglycerin and other organic nitrates. Amyl nitrite can be used to revive a person who has fainted and is also an antidote for cyanide poisoning. Amyl nitrite was used recreationally in the 1970s and 1980s, especially at dance clubs and gay bars, when approximately 250 million recreational doses were consumed yearly in the United States.[86] Part of amyl nitrite's popularity was due to reports of enhanced sexual pleasure and prolonged orgasm.

QUICK HIT

Amyl nitrite originally came in mesh-enclosed glass ampules. When crushed before use, these made a popping sound, hence their slang name "poppers."

Pharmacokinetics and Mechanism of Action of Inhalants

Users of inhalants will often sniff fumes out of a bag, from a rag saturated with the substance, or directly out of the original container in which the inhalants came. The process of sniffing fumes is known as **huffing** (Figure 8.12). The fumes of these substances often cause feelings similar to alcohol and anesthetics. When they are inhaled, these lipid-soluble substances are easily absorbed into the bloodstream and rapidly enter the brain. After entering the brain, drug levels peak within a few minutes and usually last for 15–30 minutes; they then are absorbed by the body fat.

Far less is known about the mechanism of action of inhalants than for other drugs.[87] Inhalants are a diverse group of substances with diverse mechanisms. Nitrous oxide may affect opioid systems, although this finding has been disputed. Due to some similarities in their acute effects, many volatile solvents are thought to have cellular actions in common with drugs such as barbiturates, benzodiazepines, and alcohol, but it may be that some inhalants have a more complex mechanism of action. To give one example, toluene may enhance GABAergic inhibition but also inhibit NMDA glutamate receptors and reinforce effects on dopamine.[88] Some inhalants probably do not exert their effects by binding to a specific receptor. Amyl nitrite's effects may be due to its ability to dilate blood vessels and relax smooth muscle. More research is needed to elucidate the mechanism of action of this class of drugs.

Acute Effects of Inhalants

The acute effects of many inhalants are similar to alcohol intoxication and the effects of high doses of some sedative/hypnotics.

- They may begin with euphoria, disinhibition, dizziness, and lightheadedness, followed by drowsiness, disorientation, and headache.
- As with alcohol, progressively heavier doses can cause slurred speech, poor coordination, lethargy, nausea and vomiting, double vision, ringing in the ears, delusions, and hallucinations.
- Very high doses can lead to unconsciousness, respiratory suppression, coma, and death.

Dangers from inhalants include hazards from the high doses taken, the ways in which the drugs are administered, the risks associated with the behavioral effects that follow their use, and the toxic effects of the substances themselves.[89] Use of these compounds typically involves exposure to concentrations 50–100 times greater than the maximum allowable concentration in industry exposure.[90] Hypoxia and asphyxiation can occur when a user inhales less oxygen than his or her body needs. When gases are stored under pressure, they cool abruptly when released, which can lead to frostbite upon contact. Additionally, many inhalants are highly flammable. About one in every four deaths associated with inhalant use is due to accidental burns.[91]

Using inhalants produces incoordination and diminished judgment. Unfortunately, this is paired with increased recklessness and feelings of omnipotence, which may lead to accidents and injuries. Finally, huffers risk the toxic effects of the inhaled substances, including vomiting (and the risk of choking on vomitus while unconscious), kidney damage, liver damage, anemia, seizures, cardiovascular problems, respiratory suppression, and death.

When it occurs, death is usually due to cardiac arrhythmia, hypoxia, accidents, or suicide. About 20 percent of people who die from inhalants are first-time users.[92] Inhalants make the heart more sensitive to the effects of adrenaline. If, after using inhalants, a person experiences sudden stress or vigorous activity, he or she may suffer a fatal cardiac arrhythmia, a condition called **sudden sniffing death syndrome**.

....

QUICK HIT

In order to help prevent recreational use, the Testor Corporation, a leading manufacturer of airplane glues and model cements, added oil of mustard to its formula. Oil of mustard gives horseradish its pungent smell and can irritate the eyes, nose, and throat, which deters some recreational users from sniffing the glue.

....

Acute Effects of Nitrous Oxide

Nitrous oxide produces mild euphoria, giddiness, and drowsiness, and also reduces pain and inhibitions. Some may experience a brief loss of consciousness and a sensation of flying. N_2O is fairly safe in clinical settings, but when used recreationally, there are four main dangers. First, although nitrous oxide itself is a nontoxic gas, when a person inhales N_2O without the addition of oxygen, severe hypoxia (low oxygen) may occur, which can be fatal. Second, administering nitrous oxide can cause physical damage to tissues due to the pressure of the expanding gas. Third, nitrous oxide may be neurotoxic, especially if it is used in combination with other NMDA antagonists such as alcohol, dextromethorphan, or PCP. Finally, long-term use can cause vitamin B_{12} deficiency, which can damage the bone marrow and nervous system, and impair memory and mental functioning.

Acute Effects of Amyl Nitrite

Amyl nitrite's vasodilatory effects cause a sudden fall in blood pressure, along with a rise in heart rate, warmth, and flushing of the skin. Users may feel mildly euphoric or dizzy and often see a bright yellow spot with purple radiations.[93] The anal sphincter dilates, and there is increased blood flow to the genitals. After inhaling amyl nitrite, users often feel nauseated, have short-term vision problems, and may experience a pounding headache. When inhaled, amyl nitrite has very low toxicity; when swallowed or injected, however, amyl nitrite can interfere with the ability of the blood to bind and transport oxygen.

Chronic Effects of Inhalants

The long-term effects of inhalant abuse are not well documented, because inhalant abuse usually occurs only sporadically, and typically does not last more than

Sudden sniffing death syndrome: Sudden death due to cardiac arrhythmias after using inhalants.

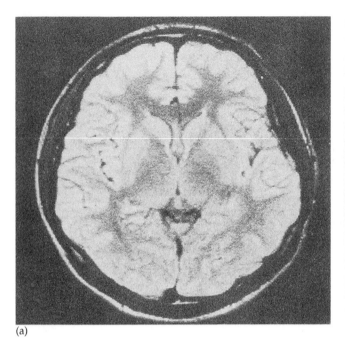
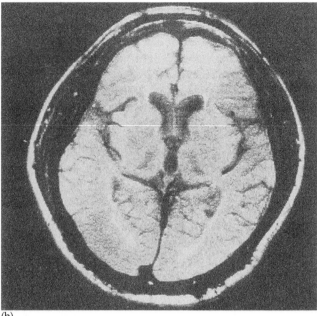

(a)   (b)

FIGURE 8.13. The brain of an inhalant abuser. Compared with the brain of an individual with no history of inhalant abuse (a) the brain of a chronic toluene abuser (b) is smaller and fills less of the space inside the skull.

Source: Rosenberg, N. (2012). NIDA Research Report (NIH 05-3818). https://teens.drugabuse.gov/sites/default/files/inhalantsrrs.pdf

a year or two. Tolerance may occur to the euphoric effects of some inhalants, and long-term use may lead to withdrawal symptoms, including nausea, tremors, irritability, anxiety, and sleep disturbances.

Repeated use can cause rashes around the nose and mouth, nosebleeds, weight loss, depression, hostility, and paranoia, and may damage the liver, kidneys, lungs, bone marrow, and brain. Additionally, many of these substances are carcinogenic.

Chronic inhalant abuse has been linked to widespread brain damage and cognitive abnormalities that range from mild impairment to severe dementia.[94,95] When scientists compared brain abnormalities and cognitive impairment among long-term inhalers of volatile solvents and cocaine abusers, they found inhalant abusers were more likely than cocaine users to have brain abnormalities, to have more extensive brain damage, and to have more memory, cognitive, and behavioral impairments. Brain areas that were especially affected include the basal ganglia, cerebellum, thalamus, and pons; inhalant users also had extensive loss of myelin in the brain (Figure 8.13).[96,97]

Critical Evaluation

Are the cognitive impairments seen in huffers due to inhalant use or to other factors?

Chronic inhalant abusers show signs of brain damage and cognitive abnormalities, even more so than chronic cocaine abusers. But are these differences due to the inhalants themselves, their pattern of use, or to differences in those who use inhalants?

Differing demographics between users and control group. One study that found cognitive impairments between users and nonusers did not control for racial demographics or for baseline mental health status. Also, most of the inhalant users, but only 28 percent of the control group, had previous psychiatric treatment.[98] Could the psychiatric conditions have influenced the cognitive differences?

Pattern of drug use. Inhalants are more often used by incarcerated or institutionalized people and those of a lower socioeconomic status.

Also, inhalant use typically starts at a younger age than that of other drugs. Are brain abnormalities due to the toxic effects of inhalants, or due to the use of a drug during adolescence, a time when the brain is developing and reorganizing?

More than half of solvent abusers described their use as continuous, which was defined as "staying intoxicated most of the day, every day," but only 26 percent of the control group said they used their drug of choice continuously.[99] Might the cognitive damage be due to *continuous use* of inhalants, and would continuous use of other drugs cause similar damage?

The use of other drugs. Only 16 percent of the huffers said that inhalants were the only drugs they abused, and 65 percent reported that they used another drug several times weekly or more.[100] How might you determine if the harmful effects are due to inhalants or to another drug?

Correlation versus causation. In a comparison of chronic solvent abusers and chronic cocaine abusers, both groups had similarly low intellectual function, but inhalant abusers performed significantly worse than cocaine abusers on tests involving memory, attention, planning, problem solving, and behavior control.[101] Could it be that those who are less able to plan and focus are more drawn to inhalants, and those differences were there before the drug use?

Chapter Summary

- **Sedatives and Hypnotics**
  - » Sedative/hypnotic drugs slow physical and mental activities, relieve anxiety, and increase sleep. Two of the best-known types are barbiturates and benzodiazepines (BZDs).
  - » Adolf von Baeyer synthesized barbituric acid, the compound from which barbiturates are developed. The first pharmacologically active barbiturate was marketed in 1903.
  - » The use of sedative/hypnotics has increased considerably in the past 20 years. In 2019, over 44 million Americans reported using tranquilizers or sedatives in the past year.
    - » BZDs have been one of the top-selling prescription drugs in the United States since their introduction in the mid-twentieth century.
    - » Female users outnumber male users.
  - » Barbiturates and BZDs are categorized based on their duration of action.
    - » More lipid-soluble barbiturates are shorter acting and more likely to be abused.
    - » Longer-acting barbiturates are used as anticonvulsants and (less commonly) as anxiolytics.
    - » Shorter-acting barbiturates are used as preanesthetic sedatives or to treat insomnia.
  - » Sedative/hypnotic drugs can be administered orally, rectally, or by injection. Their lipid solubility determines their absorption and distribution. Barbiturates and BZDs are highly bound to plasma proteins and are metabolized in the liver.
  - » Sedatives/hypnotics exert their effects by binding to GABA receptors.
    - » $GABA_A$ receptors have five subunits around a chloride-conducting pore.
    - » When GABA binds to the receptor, the pore opens, chloride enters the cell, and the cell is inhibited.
    - » BZDs bind to a site on the $GABA_A$ receptor, which increases the frequency of chloride channel openings.
    - » Barbiturates have a more general effect on GABA receptors. When barbiturates bind, they enhance the affinity of the receptor for GABA, which increases the duration of time that the chloride channel is open, leading to neuronal inhibition.
  - » Sedatives/hypnotics reduce muscle tone, impair coordination, and increase sedation and sleep. Although total sleep time is increased, REM sleep and restorative deep sleep are reduced.
  - » Sedatives/hypnotics reduce anxiety, learning, and memory, and can cause bizarre, uninhibited behaviors. These drugs may also be addictive.
  - » Barbiturates and BZDs have been used to treat insomnia, anxiety disorder, seizure disorder, alcohol withdrawal, and as anesthetics.
  - » Z drugs such as Ambien raise the risk of motor vehicle accidents, as well as the incidence of sleepwalking, sleep eating, sleep sex, and sleep driving.
  - » Common side effects of sedatives/hypnotics include drowsiness, lethargy, dizziness, confusion, reduced libido, diminished concentration, incoordination, and impairment of driving skills.
  - » Fetuses exposed to sedative/hypnotic drugs may have an increased risk of cleft palate, BZD syndrome, floppy infant syndrome, or drug withdrawal.
  - » Tolerance develops to barbiturates by both cellular and metabolic mechanisms. Tolerance to BZDs is not as fast or complete.

» Chronic use of barbiturates and BZD can lead to physical dependence. The number of deaths attributable to BZD overdose has risen significantly in the past two decades.

» Withdrawal from sedative/hypnotics should be done carefully under medical supervision. Withdrawal may lead to insomnia, anxiety, tremor, headache, confusion, and difficulty concentrating.

- **Other Sedative/Hypnotic Drugs**
  » GHB is both a neurotransmitter and an illegal drug. Low doses of GHB bind to GHB receptors and produce an excitatory effect, while high doses activate GABA receptors and produce sedation and sleepiness.

  » The sensation of GHB is similar to inebriation. High doses can lead to suppressed respiration, convulsions, coma, and death.

  » In the United States, GHB is a schedule I drug, except where it is approved for the treatment of narcolepsy, in which case it is schedule III.

  » Quaaludes are a CNS depressant that work at GABA receptors. They were very popular in the 1970s and 1980s, but are now classified as schedule I.

  » Propofol is a fast-acting anesthetic that affects both the GABA and endocannabinoid systems. It reduces awareness and leaves the patient with no memory of the experience.

- **Inhalants**
  » Ether and nitrous oxide are two anesthetics that were commonly inhaled as intoxicants.

  » Ether and nitrous oxide were first used as anesthetics during dental and surgical procedures.

  » Over 25 million Americans age 12 years and older have used inhalants. Inhalant use is most common among younger adolescents and declines as they age.

  » More than 1,400 household products can be inhaled to get high. They have little in common in their chemical structure, pharmacology, or mechanism of action but often are categorized as volatile substances, anesthetics, and nitrites.

  » Inhalants have effects similar to alcohol intoxication. They are dangerous not only due to their toxic effects, but due to their routes of administration and the incoordination and recklessness that often follow their use.

  » Long-term effects of inhalant abuse are not well documented, but use can cause nosebleeds, rashes, weight loss, depression, hostility, and paranoia. Inhalants can also increase the risk of cancer and damage the liver, kidneys, lungs, bone marrow, and brain.

  » Chronic inhalant abuse has been linked to cognitive impairments, but it is difficult to ascertain to what degree these effects are due to the inhalants themselves, their pattern of use, or to differences in the users.

Key Terms

Anxiolytic (p.180)
Barbiturates (p.177)
Benzodiazepines (p.177)
Epilepsy (p.180)

Insomnia (p.188)
Huffing (p.198)
Hypnotic (p.177)
Inhalant (p.195)

Orexin (p.188)
Sedative (p.177)
Sudden Sniffing Death Syndrome (p.199)
Z drugs (p.189)

Quiz Yourself!

1. True or false? There are more female BZD users than male users.

2. All else being equal, which of the following is most likely to lead to addiction or abuse?

   A. A short-acting barbiturate

   B. A long-acting barbiturate

   C. A benzodiazepine

3. Which of the following is NOT a BZD?

   A. Valium

   B. Xanax

   C. Seconal

   D. Ativan

4. When benzodiazepines bind to the GABA$_A$ receptor, they increase the _____ of chloride channel openings, but when barbiturates bind, they increase the _____ that the chloride channel is open.

5. Which of the following is true of sedative/hypnotic drugs?

   A. They improve concentration.

   B. They increase REM sleep and deep, restorative sleep.

   C. They have been proven to quadruple the fetus' risk of cleft palate.

   D. Benzodiazepines have a higher therapeutic index than barbiturates.

6. True or false? Barbiturates and BZDs are not recommended for use in the elderly because they are metabolized too fast and are therefore less effective.

7. True or false? At low doses, GHB has an excitatory effect, but at higher doses, it has a depressant effect.

8. True or false? Inhalants are some of the safest drugs used by adolescents.

9. In what three forms are inhalants often categorized? Give one example of each.

10. Which of the following is/are schedule I drugs? Phenobarbital, diazepam, Rohypnol, chloral hydrate, Quaaludes, amyl nitrite

Additional Resources

Websites

National Institute on Drug Abuse: Inhalants http://www.drugabuse.gov/drugs-abuse/inhalants

Videos

Inhalants. (2010). 18 minutes. Films for the Humanities and Sciences. BVL39502.

Sedatives. (1999). 32 minutes. Films for the Humanities and Sciences. BVL9286.

Structure and mechanism of action of the GABA receptor https://www.youtube.com/watch?v=hB-BxvUJTTM

Learn more with this chapter's digital tools at www.oup.com/he/rosenthal2e.

True or false?

1.
True or false? The U.S. Government filed for a patent on the use of cannabinoids as neuroprotective substances useful in the treatment of a variety of diseases.

2.
True or false? The human body makes an endogenous substance similar to THC.

3.
True or false? It is impossible to become dependent on cannabis.

Cannabis is a paradoxical and polarizing drug. Although some believe passionately in its safety and therapeutic properties, others feel just as strongly that it is harmful to the body, mind, and society. Cannabis is simultaneously legal and illegal in many of the United States. And although cannabis is America's most widely used illegal drug with no known fatal overdoses; it is classified among the most dangerous.

Some praise cannabis as a cure for a variety of human ailments, while others condemn it as a deadly and dangerous scourge. One of the largest cash crops in America, marijuana's prohibition also costs the United States many billions of dollars each year. Cannabis not only affects many parts of the brain and body, but its religious, legal, social, economic, and ethical ramifications are vast.

Learning Objectives

- Trace the various attitudes about cannabis throughout history.
- Describe the relationship between cannabis use and the perception of risk in high school students.
- Consider the social effects that result from marijuana's status as a schedule I drug.
- List some examples of phytocannabinoids, endocannabinoids, and synthetic cannabinoids.
- Distinguish between the effects that result from oral administration of cannabis compared to smoking cannabis.
- Define the endocannabinoid system.
- List the major locations of cannabinoid receptors in the brain and body.
- Summarize the acute physiological and behavioral effects of cannabis.
- Evaluate the effect of long-term cannabis use on cognitive deficits.
- Identify some of the potential therapeutic uses of cannabis.
- Compare cannabis's addictive potential to that of other psychoactive drugs.

History of Cannabis

Cannabis, also known as **marijuana**, has been cultivated since the Stone Age and may be the earliest non-food-bearing plant grown by humans.[1] Archeologists have found pots made of **hemp** fibers dating back more than 10,000 years. The first known reference to cannabis's medicinal use was in 2737 BCE, in the *Pen Ts'ao Ching*, the pharmacopeia of traditional Chinese medicine. Emperor Shen Nung, who introduced the world to tea drinking, recommended *ma* (marijuana) for more than 100 ailments. By 1000 BCE, cannabis use spread to India, where cannabis consumption has a long, rich tradition as an important medical and religious herb.

From India, cannabis use spread to the Middle East. The psychoactive substance in cannabis has been identified in the internal organs of Egyptian mummies from 950 BCE. In the ancient Persian religious text *Xend-Avesta*, cannabis is mentioned as *the most important of 10,000 medicinal plants*.[2,3]

Cannabis likely was introduced to the western hemisphere in the sixteenth century through the slave trade. The Portuguese were among the first Europeans to enslave Africans and

Cannabis: A tall plant with serrated leaves. Also refers to any of the preparations or chemicals derived from the plant. Both marijuana and hemp are cannabis but have different amounts of psychoactive chemicals.

Marijuana: A slang term for cannabis that contains enough psychoactive compounds to have an intoxicating effect. Also refers to the leaves and flowers of the female cannabis plant that are dried and shredded.

Hemp: A cannabis plant with low THC content primarily grown for industrial or food use. Hemp is non-intoxicating.

Cannabis

Type of drug: Part stimulant, sedative, analgesic, and hallucinogen

Chemical formula of THC:
$C_{21}H_{30}O_2$

Routes of administration: Ingested, smoked, inhaled with vaporizer

Duration of effect: 2–8 hours

Neurotransmitters directly affected: Anandamide, 2-AG, and others

Tolerance: Some

Physical dependence: Low

Psychological dependence: Some

Withdrawal symptoms: Irritability, restlessness, decreased appetite, weight loss, abnormal sleep

Schedule: Schedule I

Slang: Marijuana, pot, weed, grass, bhang, bud, blunt, bowl, cheeba, ganja, herb, joint, reefer, 420, tea, dope, Mary Jane, spliff, chronic, doobie, muggles

transport them to Brazil in the early 1500s.[4] Cannabis then spread through northern South America and into Mexico.

Seventeenth- to Nineteenth-Century America

English settlers planted cannabis in Jamestown in 1611. In 1619, King James I issued a royal decree that actually required every property owner in the Virginia colony to grow 100 hemp plants to be exported to Britain.[5] Both George Washington and Thomas Jefferson grew cannabis at their homes.[6]

QUICK HIT

Some of the rough drafts of the Declaration of Independence were written on hemp paper, and the first flag of the United States was made of hemp cloth.

Irish physician William O'Shaughnessy studied the medicinal uses of cannabis. He played an important role in promoting its therapeutic benefits to the Western world. Throughout the nineteenth century, cannabis was legal and widely available, and used as an analgesic, appetite stimulant, and muscle relaxant. Anyone could walk into a pharmacy and purchase a wide range of cannabis preparations, or place their cannabis order from the Sears Roebuck catalogue.[7]

Twentieth Century and Beyond

During the Mexican Revolution (1910–1920), Pancho Villa's guerilla army smoked marijuana during long marches and to celebrate successful campaigns. After the revolution, Mexican immigrants flooded into the United States, and smoking marijuana become common in Texas and California.[8] With the passage of Prohibition, marijuana use increased and became popular among jazz musicians. In Harlem, hundreds of "tea pads" opened, where people could gather to smoke marijuana.

QUICK HIT

A partially smoked marijuana joint is sometimes called a "roach." The Mexican folk song "La cucaracha" ("the cockroach") was written about Mexican soldiers who were unable to function unless they were high on marijuana. The chorus of the song translates to:

"The cockroach, the cockroach / is unable to walk / because he doesn't have any, / because he doesn't have any marijuana to smoke."

As the Depression deepened and the economy worsened, cannabis was a handy scapegoat for the fear and prejudice against African American musicians and against Mexican immigrants thought to be taking rare jobs away from "real" Americans. Just as the first opium laws in San Francisco were directed at a shunned minority (Chapter 7), and laws against cocaine began with the perception that African Americans were using cocaine (Chapter 5), early marijuana laws stemmed from fear and hostility toward foreigners rather than from the properties of the drug itself.[9]

In 1930, the Federal Bureau of Narcotics (FBN) was established, and Harry Anslinger appointed its first director. By 1934, however, the FBN was in financial trouble due to the Great Depression. Harry Anslinger set out to convince Congress and the American people that a terrible new drug menace was threatening the country—one that required a well-funded FBN.[10] Although cannabis had been used medicinally by many people, Anslinger referred to the drug as "marijuana," which sounded foreign and frightening. Anslinger vilified marijuana with a vengeance. He testified before Congress that marijuana was linked to criminal activity, insanity, and intellectual and moral decay. Anslinger called marijuana "the most violence-causing drug in the history of mankind." According to Anslinger, not only was marijuana deadly, addictive, and capable of turning innocent people into deranged violent psychopaths, but it also caused "white women to seek sexual relations with Negroes."[11] Harry Anslinger had an ally in publisher William Randolph Hearst, who launched a smear campaign in his newspapers against Mexican migrants and their "murder weed." Movies, books, and ads depicted the horrors that would supposedly come from smoking marijuana (Figure 9.1).

Congress passed the Marijuana Tax Act in 1937. This law acknowledged the medicinal use of marijuana and permitted a prescription following a tax payment of $100 per ounce (comparable to about $1,650 today).[12] The marijuana user simply had to show the government the marijuana, and he or she would receive a stamp. But the government did not actually make any tax stamps. So, when a hapless smoker brought weed in order to receive a stamp, he or she was guilty of the crime of possessing marijuana without a stamp. Punishments for illegal possession were a $2,000 fine, five years in prison, or both, but penalties got harsher over the years.[13]

(a)

(b)

FIGURE 9.1. Anti-marijuana messages in the media. Movies such as (a) *Reefer Madness* and books such as (b) *Marihuana* suggested that a single exposure to marijuana caused its unfortunate users to go insane and embark on murder sprees.

In the early 1940s, a committee of physicians, psychologists, sociologists, and scientists conducted a thorough and extensive study on the pharmacological, clinical, and sociological effects of cannabis. The La Guardia Report, published in 1944, found that cannabis was not addictive and that it produced no permanent negative effects to the user or to society. In contrast to what Harry Anslinger had argued, the report did not find that marijuana led to physical, mental, or moral decay, insanity, sexual deviance, violence, or criminal misconduct. The committee recommended that cannabis's medical uses be investigated. Anslinger rejected the findings; he called the authors "dangerous" and "strange" and instructed the FBN to investigate the commission members' own drug use.[14,15]

By the end of the 1940s, the Cold War was in full swing. Drug addiction was considered a threat to national security and a way to aid and abet communism. In 1948, Anslinger reversed his position on marijuana's violent influences and instead testified before Congress that marijuana was a threat because it would cause American boys to become so peaceful they would not want to fight, making the nation vulnerable to a Communist takeover.[16] Throughout the 1950s, drug laws proliferated with increased penalties for all drug offenses. The government put mandatory minimum penalties for drug offenses in place, and repeat drug offenders (unlike rapists, murderers, and child molesters) were denied parole.

In 1962, Harry Anslinger retired, and President Kennedy authorized a committee to study America's drug problem. In 1963, the White House Conference on Narcotics and Drug Abuse concluded that the hazards of smoking marijuana were exaggerated. Throughout the 1960s, attitudes about marijuana became more lenient, as more people tried it and found that the drug did not lead to insanity, homicide, or moral deterioration.

Although the Supreme Court struck down the Marijuana Tax Act in 1969, marijuana was not yet fully accepted. President Nixon felt that marijuana's popularity was due to "loudmouthed radical protestors" and "the Jews."[17] In 1970, the Controlled Substances Act was established, and marijuana was designated as a schedule I drug. Two years later, Nixon convened the Shafer Commission to study marijuana. He handpicked most of the members, many of whom believed in a strict criminal justice system and the war on drugs. Nixon clearly stated his desired outcome: "I want a goddamn strong statement on marijuana. Can I get that out of this sonofabitching, uh, domestic council? I mean one on marijuana that just tears the ass out of them."[18] The commission conducted the most comprehensive review of cannabis that had ever been produced by the federal government. They oversaw 50 research projects, and obtained data from scientists, doctors, law enforcement officials, and concerned citizens. They published their final report—all 1,184 pages of it—in March of 1972. Much to Nixon's dismay, the Shafer Commission found no evidence that marijuana causes physical or psychological harm, harsh withdrawal, birth defects, brain damage, a compulsion to use hard drugs, or death resulting solely from marijuana intoxication. They found the potential harm of getting arrested was much greater than any harm that might come from using the plant. The Shafer Commission recommended that state and federal laws be changed to remove criminal penalties for possession of marijuana for personal use. Nixon rejected the policy recommendations before he even finished reading the report.[19]

Despite the lack of presidential support, the tide began to turn, and in 1973, Oregon became the first state to decriminalize pot, making possession of under an ounce a civil offense akin to speeding. California followed in 1975. By 1978, 11 states had decriminalized small amounts of the drug. President Carter addressed Congress and said, "Penalties against drug use should not be more damaging to the individual than the use of the drug itself."[20]

In 1980, however, Ronald Reagan was elected president. Reagan described marijuana as "probably the most dangerous drug in the United States" and called for a "full scale anti-drug mobilization." His wife, Nancy, who led the "just say no" campaign, agreed. Nancy Reagan said, "There is no moral middle ground. If you're a casual user [of marijuana], you're an accomplice to murder."[21,22]

In 1982, the National Academy of Sciences published a report based on six years of research, which found "no convincing evidence" that cannabis damaged the brain or nervous system. It concluded that marijuana should be decriminalized. Reagan rejected these findings. Throughout the 1980s, the rhetoric against drugs increased, along with the penalties against them. In 1989, George H.W. Bush became president and promptly announced a major escalation of the war on drugs. His "drug czar," William Bennett, called for a "massive wave of arrests" and rapid expansion of the nation's prison system and urged prosecutors to go after weekend pot smokers.[23]

In the early 1990s, President Clinton further escalated the war on drugs. In 1994, he signed the Violent Crime Control and Law Enforcement Act, which encouraged more punitive laws and incentivized states to build more prisons. The number of jail sentences nationwide for marijuana offenders during Clinton's two terms was 800 percent higher than during the 12 years under Reagan and Bush senior.[24] Clinton also signed legislation that cut off federal aid to student marijuana offenders and other drug violators.

Yet, in the 1990s, the tide began to turn again, and cannabis use increased substantially. In 1996, California approved Proposition 215 and became the first state to legalize the medical use of marijuana. The Compassionate Use Act removed criminal penalties for the use, possession, and cultivation of medical marijuana and provided physicians with immunity from prosecution. As of this writing, medical marijuana is legal in 36 U.S. states as well as in Austria, Belgium, Canada, the Czech Republic, Finland, Israel, Netherlands, Spain, and the United Kingdom. As of this writing, over one-third of Americans live in a state in which cannabis use is legal for adults (Figure 9.2).

Ask yourself: Attitudes about cannabis are undergoing a significant change in the United States. What cultural and social factors do you think underlie this change?

Prevalence of Cannabis Use

Marijuana is the fourth most commonly used recreational drug in the world, surpassed only by tobacco, caffeine, and alcohol. Even though it is illegal in almost every country on earth, approximately 4 percent of the world's adult population, or 192 million people, use cannabis each year.[25] Cannabis use varies greatly among countries. Less than 2 percent of the population in Asia, 5.4 percent of Europe's population, almost 11 percent of the population in Australia, and 14.6 percent of those in North America report annual marijuana use.[26]

In the United States, cannabis is the most commonly used illicit drug. Americans consume about 10,000 tons of cannabis each year, and about half of all Americans have used cannabis at some time in their lives.[27, 28] In recent years, more people in the United States report both current (defined as use within the past month) and daily use of cannabis (Figure 9.3).[29,30]

Cannabis use differs by gender, race, and age. Men are more likely than women to use cannabis.[31] Those who are two or more races report the highest rates of marijuana use, followed by Blacks, whites, American Indians and Alaskan natives, and

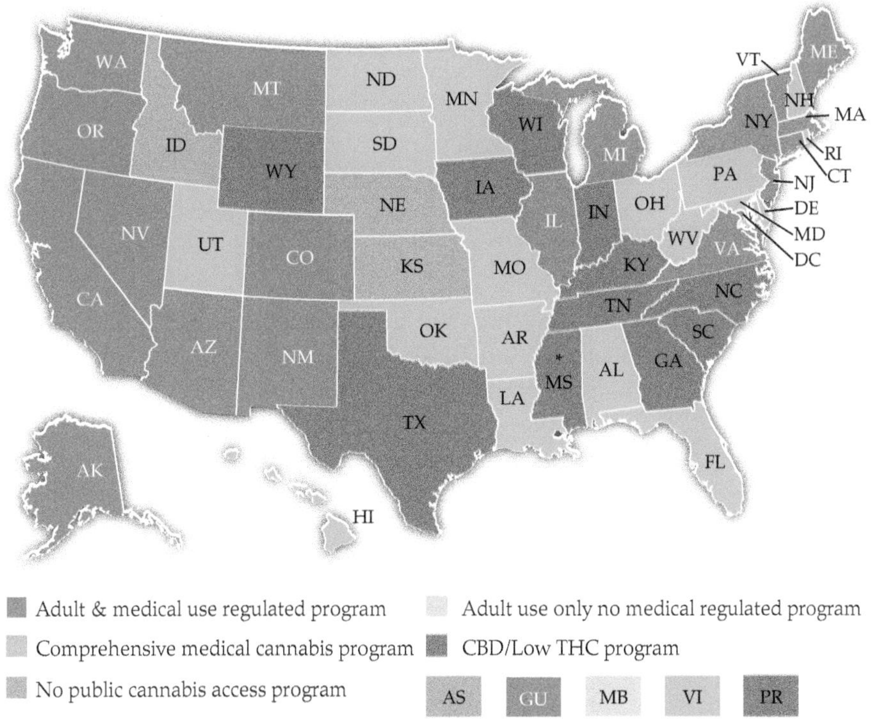

FIGURE 9.2. Cannabis laws by state as of July 2021. Laws vary greatly from state to state. Some states have legalized both recreational and medical use of marijuana; others allow medical marijuana to varying degrees, and some states don't permit any cannabis use.

Source: National Conference of State Legislatures. (2021). State medical marijuana laws. https://www.ncsl.org/research/health/state-medical-marijuana-laws.aspx

Legend:
- Adult & medical use regulated program
- Comprehensive medical cannabis program
- No public cannabis access program
- Adult use only no medical regulated program
- CBD/Low THC program
- AS GU MB VI PR

Ask yourself: There is an inverse relationship between the perceived risk and current use of cannabis among high school students. Do you think that a lower perception of risk increases cannabis's use? Or is it the case that as its use increases, people perceive the drug to be not as harmful?

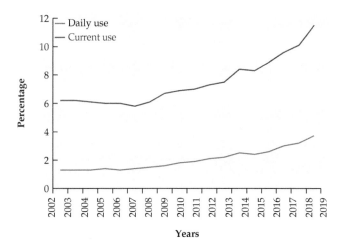

FIGURE 9.3. Current and daily use of cannabis. Over 31 million Americans age 12 and older report cannabis use within the past month, and over 10 million use cannabis every day or almost every day.

Source: SAMHSA. (2020). Results from the 2019 national survey on drug use and health. Rockville, MD: Center for Behavioral Health Statistics and Quality.

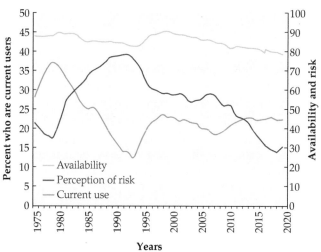

FIGURE 9.4. Marijuana use, perception of risk, and availability among high school seniors, 1975–2019. The percentage of high school seniors who have used marijuana in the last 30 days is charted on the left Y-axis, and the percentage of high school seniors who consider regular use of marijuana to be very risky and those who say marijuana is fairly easy or very easy to obtain is charted on the right Y-axis. Regular use among high school students began to rise in the 1960s and peaked in 1979. After declining fairly steadily for 13 years, use bottomed out in 1992, after which it began to rise again, with some fluctuations.

Sources: Johnston, L.D., Meich, R.A., O'Malley, P.M. Bachman, J.G., & Schulenberg, J.E., et al. (2020). Monitoring the Future: National survey results on drug use 1975–2019. Ann Arbor: Institute for Social Research, The University of Michigan.

Johnston, L.D., O'Malley, P.M., & Bachman, J.G. (1996). National survey results on drug use from the Monitoring the Future study, 1975–1995. Ann Arbor: Institute for Social Research, The University of Michigan).

Hispanics; Asians report the lowest rates of use.[32] Although cannabis use by Blacks is only 14 percent higher than use by whites, a Black person is 3.6 times more likely to be arrested for marijuana possession than a white person.[33,34] These disparities are especially strong in states in which cannabis has not been legalized; for example, in Montana, Black persons are almost 10 times more likely to be arrested for possession of marijuana than white persons.[35]

The average age among first-time users of marijuana is around 16.[36] Marijuana is widely available among high school students; consistently between 80 and 90 percent of high school seniors say marijuana is "fairly easy" or "very easy" to obtain, although these rates have fallen slightly in the past few years.[37] Figure 9.4 shows current marijuana use, the perception of its risks, and availability among high school seniors from 1975–2019.[38,39] Note the inverse relationship between perceived risk and current use.

QUICK HIT

The price of a gram of marijuana around the world, in U.S. dollars[40]:

- Tokyo: $32.66
- Dublin: $21.63
- Oslo: $19.14
- Washington, DC: $18.08
- New York City: $10.76
- Amsterdam: $7.89
- Toronto: $7.82
- Seattle: $7.58
- New Delhi: $4.38
- Quito: $1.34

Legal and Cultural Issues Related to Cannabis

Cannabis has had an enormous influence on today's society. References to marijuana are rife in popular culture, and both its cultivation and its prevention have a significant economic effect. In addition, thousands of people campaign vigorously for marijuana's legalization, while others fight just as hard to keep it illegal.

Legal Issues

Cannabis occupies an inconsistent and ambiguous legal status. Although medical marijuana is permitted in a majority of the United States, and recreational marijuana is permitted in some, according to federal law, marijuana is illegal and has no accepted medical uses.[41] This means that a person could have a recommendation from his or her physician for medical marijuana and use it according to the laws of their state, and still be arrested by federal agents for this use.

Cannabis Laws

Although cannabis is legal in many states, according to federal law, it is still illegal. Here are some laws that highlight cannabis's contradictory and confusing status in the U.S.

- Even when individuals or businesses are in compliance with state cannabis laws, they are still violating federal cannabis laws (Gonzales v. Raich, 2005).

- If you have a doctor's recommendation for medical marijuana and have acquired it according to the laws of your state, you can still get fired for testing positive for marijuana from your employer's mandated drug test (Coats v. Dish network, 2015).

- Although cannabis is a multi-billion-dollar industry, because marijuana is still a schedule I drug, many cannabis businesses have little to no access to federal banks, credit cards, or checking accounts, and are forced to be all-cash operations.

- Many of the normally accepted business tax deductions are disallowed for cannabis businesses (Internal revenue code 280§ E, Alterman v. Commissioner of Internal Revenue, 2018).

Since the war on drugs began in 1970, more than 39 million arrests for nonviolent drug offenses have been made. In 2019 alone, 545,601 people in America were arrested for marijuana—about 1 arrest every minute.[42] Of those arrests, almost 87 percent were for marijuana possession.[43] There has been an increase in cannabis arrests in the past few years, despite the fact that cannabis is legal in 15 states. Although the actual arrest rates of marijuana users are low compared to the number of users, and most of those convicted of simple possession receive a small fine and no jail time, drug penalties are not administered equally across the population. Whites and people of color use illegal drugs at about the same rate, but Blacks and Hispanics are arrested, prosecuted, and jailed at a much higher rate than whites.[44] Blacks are two to four times more likely to be arrested for marijuana possession than are whites.[45]

During the Reagan years, the incarceration of minorities began to skyrocket. By 1990, there were more young Black men 20–29 years of age in the prison system than Black men of the same age enrolled in college.[46] Today, the United States has a higher percentage of its population in prison than any other country—five times the world's average (Chapter 2).

So how is marijuana's legal status determined? What factors are, or should be, considered? Lawmakers may consider not only physical ramifications of use, but social consequences and the effectiveness of the laws as well. They also may look to other countries for perspective.

The Netherlands has embraced a policy of harm reduction. Although marijuana is not technically legal in the Netherlands, it is widely tolerated. There is no evidence that de-penalizing cannabis has increased its use among Dutch citizens.[47] In fact, many studies suggest use is lower in the Netherlands than in the United States.

Following the Netherland's success, most countries in Western Europe removed or ignored criminal penalties for cannabis. Italy and Spain decriminalized possession, and their rates of marijuana use are comparable to those in neighboring countries. But we must consider the fact that each country has its own social and cultural realities, and we can't necessarily generalize their results to the United States. Many officials will be keeping a close eye on the U.S. states in which marijuana use is legal to see how legalization affects life in those states.

Marijuana laws in America are inconsistent. In some states, possession is a misdemeanor, punishable by up to a year in prison. Other states have instituted **decriminalization**, which means that although the underlying law remains, the criminal or monetary penalties are reduced or removed. And in still other states, **legalization** of marijuana means that criminal penalties have been removed, and the drug can be fully regulated and taxed. Laws also depend on the amount of cannabis, location, and age. For example, many states provide harsher penalties if an individual is within a certain distance of a school or park.

Ask yourself: In what ways might the drug war be seen as a way to further disenfranchise minorities?

Decriminalization: To remove or reduce the criminal and/or monetary penalties associated with an action, although the underlying law remains.

Legalization: Removal of criminal penalties. Legalization allows for full taxation and regulation. Alcohol and tobacco are two examples of legal drugs.

A national poll in 2020 found that 68 percent of Americans support the legalization of marijuana (Figure 9.5).[48] Those who are more likely to approve of legalization include (Figure 9.6)[49]:

- Men more than women
- Blacks and whites more than Hispanics
- Democrats more than Republicans
- Younger adults more than older adults
- Those who have ever tried marijuana compared to those who had never used it

Over 70 percent of Americans also think that the costs of enforcing marijuana laws are not worth the effort, and 60 percent believe that in states where cannabis use is legal, federal laws prohibiting its use should not be enforced.[50] The pros and cons of legalizing marijuana and other drugs were discussed in Chapter 2.

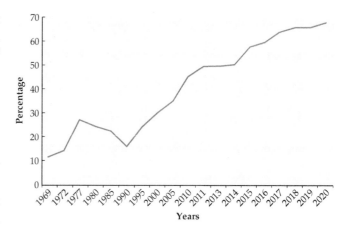

FIGURE 9.5. Percentage of Americans who believe marijuana should be legalized, by year.

Source: Gallup poll. (2020). Support for legal marijuana inches up to new high of 68%. Accessed on November 9, 2020, from https://news.gallup.com/poll/323582/support-legal-marijuana-inches-new-high.aspx

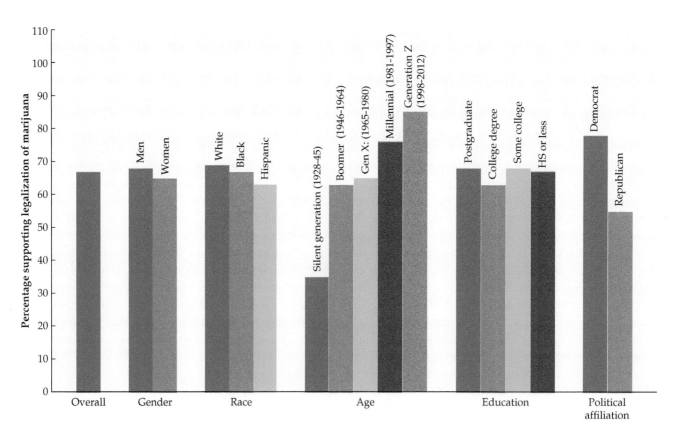

FIGURE 9.6. Americans' attitudes about marijuana legalization, by demographic.

Sources: Pew Research Center. (2019). Two-thirds of Americans support marijuana legalization. https://www.pewresearch.org/fact-tank/2019/11/14/americans-support-marijuana-legalization/

Quinnipiac. (2019). https://poll.qu.edu/images/polling/us/us03062019_uenh42.pdf

Ask yourself: What is your position on legalizing marijuana? Should it remain illegal, be legalized for medical use, be decriminalized, or be legalized entirely? What do you think the ramifications of legalization would be? Would you be more tempted to use the drug if it were legally available? Why or why not?

It's not just happy stoners who believe that cannabis should be legalized. Established in 2002, LEAP—Law Enforcement Action Partnership—is a group of former prosecutors, police officers, judges, prison wardens, Drug Enforcement Agency (DEA) agents, and civilians who believe that the war on drugs is a colossal failure that fosters crime, police corruption, social discord, and racial injustice, as well as wastes billions of tax dollars, clogs courtrooms and prisons, and impedes medical advances.

Some economists also favor the legalization of cannabis, although the estimates of its financial benefits vary widely. Approximations of economic gains due to a reduction in criminal justice costs, an increase in cannabis tax revenues, and sales of cannabis as a cash crop range from $5–$50 billion. However, there would be financial costs as well as savings, such as costs associated with regulating marijuana policies and increased healthcare costs for marijuana dependence.[51,52,53,54]

Cultural Issues

Even though cannabis was illegal for most of the twentieth century, it has had a huge cultural impact, making its mark in literature, art, music, television, and the movies. Alexandre Dumas and Victor Hugo used hashish, and the drug is mentioned in both *The Count of Monte Cristo* and *Les Miserables*. Oscar Wilde wrote about cannabis, as did Lewis Carroll, with his tale of a hookah-smoking caterpillar. Musical references to marijuana are not new. In 1933, Bessie Smith sang "gimmee a reefer," and Cab Calloway sang of the "Reefer Man." Ella Fitzgerald crooned, "When I get low, I get high." Peter Tosh urged the world to "legalize it"; Bob Dylan said, "Everybody must get stoned"; and C+C Music Factory encouraged its listeners to "Take a toke." Cypress Hill, Latino rappers from California, who wrote "Hits from the Bong," "Something for the Blunted," and "Stoned Is

the Way of the Walk," earned a lifetime ban from *Saturday Night Live*, after smoking pot on the stage during the live television broadcast.

The 1936 movie *Reefer Madness* warned of the perils of the killer weed. The movie portrays high school students who are lured by pushers to try marijuana. It doesn't end well. After taking one hit, these students mow people down with their cars, attempt rape, commit suicide, or bash their mothers to death with frying pans while laughing maniacally. Forty years later, Cheech and Chong smoked continuously in *Up in Smoke* and wandered around haplessly looking for weed and narrowly avoiding trouble. Marijuana also is featured prominently in the television show *Weeds* (Figure 9.7) and the films *Fast Times at Ridgemont High*; *Dazed and Confused*; *Half Baked*; *Dude, Where's My Car?*; *Harold and Kumar Go to White Castle*; and *The Pineapple Express*.

QUICK HIT

The number 420 (four-twenty) has come to be associated with the consumption of cannabis (Figure 9.8). A number of false rumors are associated with this term: that it refers to Bob Marley's birthday, or the date that Jim Morrison died, or that 420 is the number of chemical compounds in marijuana or the penal code section for marijuana use in California. Actually, the earliest use of the term began among a group of California teenagers in the early 1970s; 4:20 was the time they would meet up to smoke every day. In North America, April 20 is an unofficial holiday where people gather in celebration to consume cannabis.

FIGURE 9.7. *Weeds.* The television show *Weeds* is about a mother who begins selling marijuana to support her children after her husband dies suddenly. Over the course of the show, she and her family become increasingly involved in the drug trade.

FIGURE 9.8. **Four-twenty.** Thieves have stolen the mile marker 420 sign in Colorado and Idaho so often that both states have replaced it with one reading 419.9 in an attempt to stop the thievery.

Source and Forms of Cannabis

Marijuana comes from the *cannabis* plant, a hardy, adaptable plant that is native to Central Asia, but which now grows everywhere in the world except for Antarctica and the Arctic Circle. Nearly every part of the plant is useful—the stem and stalk provide fiber for cloth and rope; the seeds are a source of essential fatty acids and proteins; and the leaves and flowers have medicinal and psychoactive properties.[55]

Types of Cannabis Plant

There are different varieties of the cannabis plant. ***Cannabis sativa*** (CAN-a-bis suh-TEE-vuh) is a tall, slender plant with thin, light green leaves capable of reaching heights of 15–20 feet that grows in tropical or semitropical regions (Figure 9.9). The shorter (grows to a height of about 3–4 feet) and bushier ***Cannabis indica*** (CAN-a-bis IN-dik-uh) fares better than *sativa* in cooler climates and is cultivated in Afghanistan, Pakistan, and India. *Indica* has wider, darker, deeply serrated leaves and a compact and dense flower cluster. In order to fine-tune the effect, growers often produce unique hybrids by cross-pollinating *sativa* and *indica* plants; most strains available today are hybrids.

Cannabis sativa: A tall, slender plant with light green serrated leaves that grows in warm climates.

Cannabis indica: A shorter, bushier cannabis plant that grows in cooler climates.

FIGURE 9.9. *Cannabis sativa.* The plant is tall and slender with thin, light-green leaves that can reach a height of 15–20 feet.

Cannabis has a three- to four-month outdoor growing cycle. A hot, dry climate produces a plant with weaker fiber and more psychoactive resin, while cooler, humid conditions make less resin and more durable fiber. When cultivated indoors, the grower can control the conditions, including heat, light, temperature, and humidity, and also more easily avoid discovery and eradication of the crop.

Cannabis plants are either male or female. The female plants produce flower clusters (also called *buds*, or *flower*) with a sticky, psychoactive resin that protects the flowers from excessive heat and ultraviolet radiation, and catches the pollen produced by the male plants. Seeds are produced when pollen fertilizes the female flowers. After fertilization, the flower no longer needs the protective (and psychoactive) resin. But if it is not pollinated, the female plant continues to produce THC within the resin of the flowers. Because THC production decreases once pollination occurs, growers usually separate the male plants from the female ones.

Most of the world's cannabis is grown in the U.S. and Mexico. Sixty percent of the cannabis sold in the U.S. is produced in three counties in California, collectively known as the Emerald Triangle.[56]

Phytocannabinoids

Cannabinoids are substances that interact with the body's cannabinoid receptors. Some cannabinoids come from the cannabis plant (phytocannabinoids), and others are produced naturally by the body (endocannabinoids). Cannabis's green, serrated leaves and flowers of tiny, sticky hairs contain around 500 chemicals, over 140 of which are unique to the cannabis plant and collectively called **phytocannabinoids**. Phytocannabinoids include Delta-9-tetrahydrocannabinol (**THC**), Cannabidiol (**CBD**), CBG, CBN, THCV, and many others. These phytocannabinoids bind to the body's cannabinoid receptors. THC is the most intoxicating of the phytocannabinoids and is most abundant in the flowering heads and surrounding leaves of the female cannabis plant; the lower leaves, stalks, and roots contain little THC. CBD is not intoxicating, but it has antioxidant, anticonvulsant, anti-inflammatory, antianxiety, antipsychotic, and neuroprotective properties.

The amount of THC varies with the type of cannabis plant, growing conditions, timing of harvest, storage, and age of the plant.[57] As the plant matures, different chemicals predominate. In the young plant, cannabidiolic acid (CBDA) predominates. As the plant ages, this CBDA is converted to CBD, which is then converted to THC as the plant begins to flower. Not all the CBD is converted to THC, and the final amount determines the potency of the marijuana. The CBD:THC ratio varies in different genetic strains of cannabis, but generally, the more THC a strain has, the less CBD it has, and vice versa.[58] If plants are harvested at their peak floral stage, they produce a high ratio of THC to CBD and give a more stimulating and mental high, but if the plant matures past the peak, THC is converted into other cannabinoids and produces a heavier, more sedating experience. Growers can cultivate different strains to adjust for the degree of psychoactivity or therapeutic effects their users are seeking.

The cannabis plant contains substances other than phytocannabinoids, including **terpenes** and **flavonoids**. Terpenes are naturally occurring aromatic oils that give odor, color, and flavor to many plants. Some may produce sedation, while others elevate mood and alertness. Each plant has a distinctive terpene profile, and the unique combination of phytocannabinoids and terpenes in each plant produce a unique response. Flavonoids are components of the plant that also have physiological effects in humans.

THC and CBD interact with terpenes, flavonoids, and other phytocannabinoids to modify the effects, a phenomenon known as the entourage, or **ensemble effect**. Cannabinoids also interact with each other; CBD is known to diminish some of THC's more negative effects.[59,60]

QUICK HIT

CBD's legal status is ambiguous. Cannabidiol extracted from a hemp plant that has 0.3 percent THC or lower is legal to sell as a cosmetic ingredient, but is not federally approved for use as a dietary supplement or food additive. There is one CBD product that is approved for use as a drug; Epidiolex is used to treat some forms of seizure disorder, and is no longer a controlled substance. However, cannabidiol extracted from a cannabis plant that is greater than 0.3 percent THC remains a schedule I drug.

Types of Cannabis Products

Marijuana today has a significantly higher THC content than the marijuana that was available in the 1960s and 1970s, when levels averaged about 3 percent THC.[61] This means that users can smoke less to obtain the same effect, but the higher THC also increases the risk of adverse reactions such as panic attacks. Today, the average U.S. dispensary cannabis flower contains about 12–18 percent THC, although

Cannabinoid: A diverse group of physiologically active compounds found in cannabis and the human body that bind to cannabinoid receptors.

Phytocannabinoids: Naturally occurring plant compounds, such as THC and CBD, which bind to the body's cannabinoid receptors.

THC: Delta-9-tetrahydrocannabinol, the primary psychoactive substance in cannabis.

CBD: Cannabidiol is a biologically active, yet intoxicating compound in cannabis.

Terpenes: Aromatic oils that occur in plants and have physiological effects in humans.

Flavonoids: Components of plants that give color to plants and have antioxidant and anti-inflammatory effects.

Ensemble effect: Also called the "entourage effect," the compounds in cannabis interact synergistically to magnify the therapeutic effects of the plant's individual components, such that the whole is greater than the sum of its parts.

some strains are available with as much as 30 percent THC. Users can also purchase vape cartridges containing different cannabinoids, or cannabis concentrates such as **dab** or **shatter**.

The cannabis plant is also a source of hemp. Although anatomically the same species, hemp contains high amounts of CBD and only trace amounts of THC and is, therefore, not psychoactive. Hemp is a high-yield, low-maintenance crop that can flourish in a wide range of soil types, altitudes, and weather conditions, and is adaptable under stress. The plant is selectively bred to increase its fiber content and is a good source of fiber, fuel, and food.

Hemp is also ecologically friendly. According to a U.S. Department of Agriculture (USDA) study, an acre of fiber hemp grown during a four- to six-month season produced the same amount of paper as four to five acres of 20-year-old trees.[62] Hemp does not require pesticides and harsh fertilizers, and the plant enriches and replenishes the soil as it grows. Industrial hemp cultivation was prohibited in the United States until the passage of the 2018 Farm Bill.

Synthetic Cannabinoids

Dronabinol (Marinol) is a synthetic, FDA-approved THC pill intended to raise appetite and diminish nausea and vomiting in cancer and AIDS patients. One advantage to taking a pill is that oral administration avoids the potential respiratory damage that can occur with smoking marijuana. There are a number of disadvantages, however, to ingesting pure THC. First, when cannabis is ingested rather than smoked, it has the potential to actually *increase* nausea. Second, a person taking oral THC to treat nausea may vomit up the pill before it has had a chance to work. Third, the dose, onset, and duration of action are harder to control in an orally administered pill than with smoking because of delayed absorption of the pill and the first-pass effect. Finally, while cannabis is made up of hundreds of natural compounds and scores of cannabinoids, each with a unique medicinal impact, which interact synergistically, dronabinol contains only THC.[63]

Spice, also called K2, is a commercially available psychoactive product, containing one or more synthetic cannabinoids, which is sprayed onto dried, shredded plant material and then smoked or eaten.[64]

Dab: A highly concentrated THC which is vaporized on a heated metal plate.

Shatter: An extract of the cannabis plant in concentrate form.

These synthetic blends first appeared in the marketplace in the early 2000s, typically sold at gas stations, head shops, and on the internet, and they have since become the second most frequently used illicit substance (after cannabis) among adolescents and young adults.[65] Spice's popularity may be due to its easy access and affordability, a promise of a stronger high than with cannabis, the perception that it's legal, and the difficulty in detecting the drug in standard urine drug tests.[66]

Despite its appeal among young people, however, Spice can be dangerous. Spice and many other synthetic cannabinoids bind more fully to brain cannabinoid receptors than does THC and may produce more intense effects. It does not typically contain CBD, which in marijuana reduces many of THC's negative effects. As such, Spice produces more anxiety, agitation, panic, paranoia, and psychosis than marijuana. In 2015, Spice was responsible for more than 6,000 incidents reported to poison control centers in the United States, and the likelihood of seeking emergency medical treatment after using synthetic cannabinoid products is 30 times greater than with natural cannabis.[67,68]

As each new synthetic cannabinoid is classified as schedule I, manufacturers generate and substitute yet newer synthetic substances. Not only is there significant variability in the type and amount of cannabinoids in each batch of Spice, but the product may also contain preservatives, additives, or other potentially dangerous drugs.

Pharmacology of Cannabis

Pharmacokinetics of Cannabis

The route by which cannabis is administered can profoundly impact its effects. Additionally, cannabis has unique properties that make its absorption, distribution, and effect on receptors different from that of many other common recreational drugs.

Routes of Administration and Dosage

Cannabis is most commonly inhaled or ingested. The psychoactive parts of the cannabis plant are not water-soluble and, therefore, cannot be injected. Smoking and vaping are highly efficient routes of administration. THC is rapidly absorbed in the blood supply of the lungs and travels quickly and directly to the heart and then to the brain. Effects are felt within a few minutes, peak after 15–60 minutes, and gradually diminish over two to five hours.

Smokers typically use **joints** (hand-rolled marijuana cigarettes), pipes, **bongs** (water pipes that trap and cool the smoke until it is inhaled), or **vaporizers** (Figure 9.10). Some vaporizers heat plant material, while others heat an oil that contains an isolate of THC, CBD, or other phytocannabinoids. A vaporizer that uses plant material heats the cannabis flower to a temperature hot enough to vaporize cannabinoids and terpenes, but not hot enough to burn the remaining plant material. Vaporizing cannabis flower can produce different effects than smoking because different cannabinoids are vaporized at different temperatures. Vaporizers are more efficient than smoking, since more THC is destroyed by combustion. Other advantages of vaporizers over smoking are that they produce much less tar and they allow cannabis users to consume in public without being detected. In 2019, there was an outbreak of lung injury associated with vaping products, possibly due to vitamin E acetate or other substances used as a diluent in illicit vape cartridges (Chapter 10).[69] Users should be careful to use only laboratory-tested and approved products.

Some users also ingest cannabis. Cannabis must be heated to chemically activate THC, so nibbling on a leaf or tossing a handful into a salad would not get you high, but may have other physiological effects. Additionally, because cannabinoids are highly lipid-soluble, they do not dissolve well in digestive fluid. Adding oils to the plant material before consumption enhances absorption from the gastrointestinal tract.

Cannabis is commonly baked into foods such as brownies or cookies. When ingested, the first-pass effect (Chapter 4) causes the liver to metabolize most of the absorbed THC into 11-hydroxy-THC, which is four times more potent than THC. Orally administered cannabis has a delayed onset of action, but its effects last longer than smoking. Effects start within an hour or two, peak within five hours, and may last for up to 12 hours. Compared with smoking, the effects of ingested marijuana are less predictable and controllable.[70] Due to its long onset of action, inconsistent absorption, and potency of 11-hydroxy-THC, ingesting marijuana carries a higher risk of accidental overconsumption.

A typical joint contains about one-third of a gram of marijuana, and a single hit from a bong or vaporizer delivers about one-twentieth of a gram.[71,72] When marijuana is baked into foods, it is often unevenly distributed, so the dose is less consistent. Cannabis has a wide range of effective doses; due to the complexity of the body's response to cannabinoids, a similar dose may have a very different effect in different people. Additionally, cannabis has a biphasic dose response curve (Figure 9.11). A low dose may have little to no benefit. As they find their optimal dose, the user will experience the most benefit. But increasing the dose will reduce any positive effects. For this reason, when recommending cannabis, health care workers often advise their patients to "start low and go slow."

Absorption, Distribution, Metabolism, and Elimination

Cannabinoids are readily absorbed from the lungs and gastrointestinal (GI) tract. They enter the circulation, accumulate in fatty tissue, and then are gradually eliminated from the body. Absorption depends on the route of administration. About 20 percent of smoked THC is absorbed in the lungs, and significantly less is absorbed through the GI tract.

THC travels through the blood and is distributed to all areas of the body. Plasma levels decrease rapidly

Joint: A hand-rolled marijuana cigarette.

Bong: A filtration device generally used for smoking marijuana.

Vaporizer: An electronic device used to vaporize substances such as THC or nicotine, which are then inhaled.

(a)   (b)   (c)   (d)

FIGURE 9.10. Methods for ingesting cannabis. Joints (a), pipes (b), bongs (c), and vaporizers (d) are commonly used to smoke cannabis. Enterprising and desperate smokers have also found ways to use aluminum foil, apples, or soda cans to smoke cannabis.

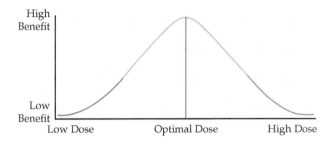

FIGURE 9.11. Cannabis has a biphasic dose-response curve.

Receptor	THC	CBD
CB1	Partial agonist	Negative allosteric modulator
CB2	Partial agonist	Negative allosteric modulator
GPR55	Agonist	Antagonist
5-HT$_{1A}$	Indirectly activates	Full agonist
5-HT$_{2A}$	Does not bind	Possibly weak antagonist
5-HT$_{3A}$	Negative allosteric modulator	Negative allosteric modulator
GABA	May indirectly activate	Positive allosteric modulator
Dopamine	Increases synthesis	Partial agonist
TRPV1	No effect	Full agonist
Glycine	Positive allosteric modulator	Positive allosteric modulator

TABLE 9.1. The Effects of Cannabinoids on Selected Receptors

as THC leaves the blood and is deposited in fatty tissues and the brain. The maximum subjective effects are usually reported while THC plasma levels are falling, because THC levels in the brain continue to increase as the drug leaves the blood and enters the brain and other tissues. THC is gone from the brain within a few hours, but it accumulates in the lungs, liver, kidney, spleen, adipose, and testes. Because cannabinoids are so lipid-soluble, they can remain in the body fat for days.

Metabolism begins in the lungs, if inhaled, and in the stomach, if ingested, but most occurs in the liver, where marijuana is metabolized by the cytochrome P450 system, as well as by other enzymes. THC and its metabolites have long half-lives; some metabolites may remain in the body for many days or even weeks after use. This has real-world ramifications; urinalysis drug tests typically measure levels of THC metabolites, which can be detectable even when the user no longer feels high or shows any behavioral effects. A person who smokes marijuana for the first time may test positive for a drug test for one to three days, and a frequent user can test positive for more than four weeks after use.

Pharmacodynamics of Cannabis

Cannabinoids interact with multiple receptors in a variety of ways. Cannabinoids not only bind to cannabinoid receptors, but to many other receptors in the body as well, including GABA, glutamate, serotonin, and others; in fact, CBD is thought to bind to and affect at least 60 different receptor systems throughout the body! Substances can act as full agonists, partial

Endocannabinoid System: A widespread physiological system involved in maintaining homeostasis in the body.

Homeostasis: The state of maintaining steady and stable physiological conditions despite fluctuations in the external environment.

agonists, antagonists, inverse agonists, and positive and negative allosteric modulators at these receptors (Chapter 4). Table 9.1 gives a brief summary of how THC and CBD interact with some receptors in the body.

Mechanism of Action of Cannabis

Cannabis affects the body in part because it interacts with the **endocannabinoid system (ECS)**—a system of neurotransmitters, enzymes, and receptors found in all animals. The ECS is one of the most important physiological systems that establishes and maintains human health and **homeostasis**. When there is a trigger such as illness, injury, or inflammation, the ECS tries to restore balance. Some of the processes regulated by ECS include inflammatory reactions, immune function, resilience to stress, protection of neurons, gastrointestinal activity, regulation of metabolism, cardiovascular activity, maintaining bone mass, pain perception, neurotransmitter modulation, regulation of hormones, control of fertility, and inhibition of tumor growth. The ECS is composed of cannabinoid receptors, endocannabinoids, and enzymes that synthesize and break down cannabinoids.

In the late 1980s, scientists discovered cannabinoid receptors CB1 and CB2 in the rat brain, and once discovered, these receptors proved to be widespread and ubiquitous.[73,74] CB1 receptors, which are present in all animals except for insects, predominate in the central nervous system, as well as in the eye, pancreas, liver, skin, uterus, and testes. CB2 receptors are found mostly in the spleen, tonsils, and cells of the immune system. Cannabinoids bind to CB1 and CB2 receptors (as well as other receptors) to exert their effects.

QUICK HIT

The ECS actually predates the cannabis plant. It is thought to have evolved in primitive animals as long as 600 million years ago. The cannabis plant, however, is thought to have evolved between 6 million and 34 million years ago.

As you'll remember from Chapter 7, endogenous receptors do not just exist on the off chance that we will happen upon a plant, dry it, and smoke it; there must be a naturally occurring agent to bind to these receptors. In 1992, Raphael Mechoulam and his colleagues discovered an endogenous cannabinoid (**endocannabinoid**) that mimics THC and binds to cannabinoid receptors (although it binds much more to CB1 receptors than to CB2 receptors). They called the substance "anandamide," from the Sanskrit word for "bliss." Anandamide, or arachidonoyl ethanolamide (AEA), is shorter-acting and 4–10 times less potent than THC.[75] Three years later, the group discovered 2-AG (2-arachidonoylglycerol), a second, more abundant endocannabinoid, which binds to both CB1 and CB2 receptors.

Endocannabinoids are not typical neurotransmitters. Most neurotransmitters are stored in the axon terminal in little sacs called vesicles. But endocannabinoids are too fat-soluble to be stored in vesicles—they would float right through the vesicle membrane; so, instead of being stored, they are rapidly synthesized as needed from components of the cell membrane,

and released in areas that require that particular compound when certain biochemical processes occur.[76] Additionally, endocannabinoids undergo *retrograde signaling*, in which they are synthesized and released from the postsynaptic neuron, travel backward across the synapse, and bind to CB1 receptors on presynaptic nerve terminals, where they help regulate the release of other neurotransmitters (Figure 9.12).[77]

Acute Effects of Cannabis

Marijuana's effects are more variable than many other drugs. Marijuana can be stimulatory or sedating. Some users become grumpy, some gleeful, some groggy, and some giggly. Its effect depends on many factors including the dose; the particular strain's potency and the ratio of THC to CBD; the user's previous experience, expectations, and mood; and the environment in which cannabis is used.

Endocannabinoids: Endogenous substances such as anandamide and 2-AG that bind to the body's cannabinoid receptors.

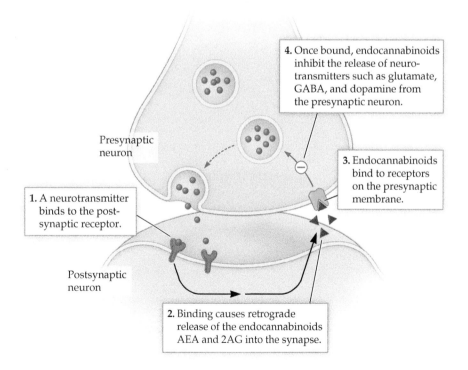

1. A neurotransmitter binds to the postsynaptic receptor.

2. Binding causes retrograde release of the endocannabinoids AEA and 2AG into the synapse.

3. Endocannabinoids bind to receptors on the presynaptic membrane.

4. Once bound, endocannabinoids inhibit the release of neurotransmitters such as glutamate, GABA, and dopamine from the presynaptic neuron.

Presynaptic neuron

Postsynaptic neuron

FIGURE 9.12. Retrograde signaling with endocannabinoids. Endocannabinoids help regulate the release of other neurotransmitters by retrograde signaling.

Physiological Effects at Low and Moderate Doses

Cannabinoid receptors are widespread in the brain and body. As a result, marijuana has many varied effects (Figure 9.13).[78,79]

Brain

Cannabinoid receptors are found in high concentrations in the hippocampus, which is important in the formation of new memories; the cerebellum and basal ganglia, which help control and regulate movement and coordination; the hypothalamus, where they modulate reward, emotions, hunger, sex, and sleep; the amygdala, where they may help alleviate anxiety and dampen painful memories; the periaqueductal gray, where they play a role in analgesia; and the cortex, where they affect perception and cognition. They are fairly rare in the brainstem, and don't seem to exist in brainstem areas that control respiration.

Cardiovascular

Cannabis produces a dose-related increase in heart rate, which means the higher the dose, the higher the heart rate. About 10–15 minutes after smoking, the effects on heart rate reach their peak. Marijuana can increase heart rate by 20–30 beats per minute or more.[80] Heart rate typically returns to baseline after about 90 minutes. When cannabis is ingested, the heart rate does not reach its peak for one to two hours and can stay elevated for at least four hours after drug administration. Acute administration of cannabis seems to raise blood pressure, but this effect is variable, and tolerance to the cardiovascular effects develops rapidly. Blood vessels that feed the skin dilate, leading to flushing, feelings of warmth, and lowered body temperature, and blood vessels of the salivary glands constrict, leading to dry mouth. Marijuana also dilates the blood vessels of the eye, making the eyes look reddened and bloodshot.

Hunger, Digestion, and Metabolism

Cannabis increases appetite, particularly for sweet food (often referred to as the "munchies"), and thirst, by working on appetite control centers in the hypothalamus, which contain many CB1 receptors. THC seems to cause these hypothalamic neurons to switch over from making a hormone that suppresses appetite to one that stimulates appetite.[81] CB1 receptors also are involved in insulin modulation in the pancreas and energy metabolism in the liver. When these receptors are blocked, less weight is gained even when the same food is consumed.[82] Marijuana is also gastroprotective, reducing abnormally high gastric secretions and GI inflammation.

Immune System

Cannabinoids are immunomodulators, which means they increase some immune

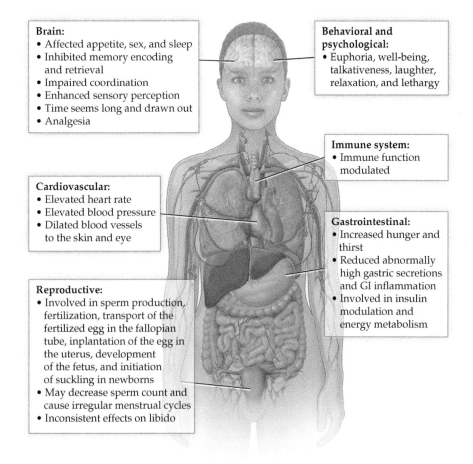

Brain:
- Affected appetite, sex, and sleep
- Inhibited memory encoding and retrieval
- Impaired coordination
- Enhanced sensory perception
- Time seems long and drawn out
- Analgesia

Cardiovascular:
- Elevated heart rate
- Elevated blood pressure
- Dilated blood vessels to the skin and eye

Reproductive:
- Involved in sperm production, fertilization, transport of the fertilized egg in the fallopian tube, inplantation of the egg in the uterus, development of the fetus, and initiation of suckling in newborns
- May decrease sperm count and cause irregular menstrual cycles
- Inconsistent effects on libido

Behavioral and psychological:
- Euphoria, well-being, talkativeness, laughter, relaxation, and lethargy

Immune system:
- Immune function modulated

Gastrointestinal:
- Increased hunger and thirst
- Reduced abnormally high gastric secretions and GI inflammation
- Involved in insulin modulation and energy metabolism

FIGURE 9.13. Acute effects of marijuana.

responses and decrease others. They modulate immune reactions in the brain as well as in the periphery, influence T cells, and play a role in inflammation. The dose and timing of delivery of cannabinoids, as well as the type of immune cell, lead to varied responses.[83]

Reproductive System

Endocannabinoids are important throughout the reproductive process. They play a role in sex drive, sperm production, fertilization, transport of the fertilized egg in the fallopian tube, implantation of the egg in the uterus, development of the fetus, and initiation of suckling in newborns.[84,85,86]

The effect of cannabis on libido and sexual activity is inconsistent and strongly dependent on the environment, expectations, and other factors. Some users report that marijuana enriches sexual pleasure, either due to its enhancement of sensory stimuli or more direct effects.[87] A study of over 50,000 men and women found that higher marijuana use was associated with more frequent sex.[88] This may be due to biological factors—cannabinoid receptors are found in the hypothalamus, a site important in regulating hormone release, emotional response, and sex drive. Cannabinoids also heighten sensory experiences and modulate the release of dopamine and serotonin, both of which are involved in the regulation of genital reflexes and sexual motivation.[89] On the other hand, it may be that those who are more likely to use drugs are also more likely to have frequent sex.

Other evidence suggests that cannabinoids may diminish sexual function. Cannabinoids suppress production of hormones that help regulate the reproductive system, which can lead to diminished sperm count in men and irregular menstrual cycles in women. Cannabinoid antagonists can increase erections, although there is no strong epidemiological connection between the frequency of cannabis use and erectile difficulties.[90]

Behavioral and Psychological Effects at Low and Moderate Doses

Although the experience of marijuana use is subjective and varies widely, most people find it to be pleasurable. Cannabis can produce a sense of emotional wellbeing, euphoria, talkativeness, laughter, relaxation, dreaminess, and lethargy. Everything might seem funny, and music, food, and sex can be more absorbing, as sensory perception is magnified. This enhanced sensory perception causes time to seem long and drawn out. Often, however, when people try to write

down or otherwise share their experience, it does not translate well. Learning, memory, and concentration are impaired. Users may feel an enhanced physical and emotional closeness to others, but anxiety and paranoia also can occur. Cannabis that is high in THC and low in CBD also disrupts short-term memory encoding and retrieval, affecting neuronal activity in the hippocampus, an area necessary for memory formation and consolidation.[91]

Potential Adverse Effects

According to the DEA's Administrative Law Judge, Francis Young, "marijuana, in its natural form, is one of the safest therapeutically active substances known to man."[92] Its therapeutic index is at least 1,000; in fact, some estimate it to be as high as 40,000, which would mean that one would have to consume nearly 1,500 pounds of marijuana in 15 minutes to produce a lethal response.[93,94] Nevertheless, every drug comes with risks, and cannabis is no exception. In addition to impairing judgment and coordination, marijuana may make some people feel anxious or paranoid. The increased heart rate can be dangerous for those with heart conditions. Also, marijuana may be covered in pesticides, and if the marijuana is illegally cultivated, no regulatory body oversees these pesticides. Sure, most of the fruits and vegetables we eat also are covered in pesticides, but while it's possible to wash off a tomato before taking a bite, weed can't be washed. And when ingesting a pesticide-laden tomato, the liver breaks down some of the toxins by first-pass metabolism, but no such mechanism occurs when cannabis is smoked.[95] Other potential physical, psychological, and cognitive adverse effects are also possible as a result of cannabis use.

Effects on the Respiratory System

Marijuana smoke contains as much or more tar, carbon monoxide, hydrocarbons, acetaldehyde, acetone, benzene, toluene, benzopyrene, and hydrogen cyanide as tobacco smoke.[96] Additionally, unlike cigarettes, joints do not have a filter, and the user holds the smoke in his or her lungs longer. Smoking marijuana on a regular basis is associated with an increased risk of chronic cough and bronchitis.[97] However, although it is well established that tobacco use leads to serious lung diseases and lower pulmonary function, smoking marijuana does *not* seem to be associated with an increased risk of developing lung cancer or chronic obstructive pulmonary disease.[98,99] In fact, a longitudinal survey of adults from 1985–2006 found no evidence of adverse pulmonary function for either light smokers (those who smoked cannabis two to three times a month) or heavy smokers (those who smoked an average of one joint per day for seven years, or one joint per week for 49 years).[100] One reason for this might be that the marijuana leaf burns at a lower temperature than the tobacco leaf, so less toxic substance enters the lungs, or it might be that cannabinoids have protective qualities. Marijuana also can be eaten or vaporized, which can eliminate or reduce the potentially harmful effects of combustion on the lungs.

Effects on Immunity

THC's role in immunity is inconclusive. There is some evidence that regular exposure to THC and CBD may have an anti-inflammatory effect.[101] But there has been no comprehensive evaluation of the effects of marijuana on overall immune function. The available evidence suggests that cannabis use is not associated with a higher incidence of any major infectious diseases or an increase in overall death rates.[102,103]

Reproductive Effects

The endocannabinoid system is important in many aspects of fertilization and reproduction. Laboratory studies have found that higher levels of endocannabinoids are associated with a reduced ability of a fertilized egg to attach to the uterus, impaired embryonic development, and increased incidence of miscarriage.[104] This might be because the ECS is involved with maintaining homeostasis and is triggered when there is inflammation, injury, or stress. Perhaps a disruption of the body's normal cannabinoid response is read as sign of injury or danger and therefore inhibits fertility. High THC suppresses the release of luteinizing hormone, which can suppress ovulation in women. In males, high THC lowers testosterone, reduces sperm count, and increases abnormal sperm. THC also may impede the way that sperm swim. While one might imagine that after smoking marijuana, a man's sperm would meander lazily around the uterus, searching for a bag of Doritos and the television remote; instead, THC makes sperm swim too fast.

Sperm have two types of movement—a forward swimming motion that gets them to the egg and a fast, sideways motion produced by a whipping of the flagella that helps the sperm thrust to push into the egg. The fast, sideways motion on the way toward the egg will impede the sperm's progress. In one study, men who used cannabis approximately 14 times a week for five years had lower rates of fertility than nonsmokers and more sideways movements in their sperm.[105] However, cannabis use seems to reduce sperm count only with extremely heavy use, and the effects do not seem to be permanent. Epidemiological studies of light or moderate users have not demonstrated a direct link between marijuana and infertility.[106]

Marijuana is the most commonly used illicit drug during pregnancy, and its use is increasing. From 2009 to 2016, rates of cannabis use in pregnancy increased from 4.2 percent to just over 7 percent.[107] Some of this may be due to pregnant women using cannabis to treat their morning sickness. Pregnant women with severe nausea and vomiting are almost 4 times more likely to use cannabis during pregnancy than pregnant women without morning sickness.[108] Prenatal exposure to cannabinoids does not produce malformations in the fetus or baby, but it is linked to lower birth weight.[109] However, studies on the effects of prenatal cannabis exposure on infants are contradictory. Some studies suggest that moderate levels of marijuana use in pregnant women are associated with higher levels of irritability and hyperactivity in infants; others find that marijuana use during pregnancy has no effect on neonatal behavior; and some even find that cannabis *improves* outcomes for babies.[110,111] In analyzing these results, it is important to consider the many confounding factors in play, including cultural, social, and economic influences; the varying strains and amounts of cannabis consumed; the use of other drugs; prenatal care; and the effects of marijuana use to increase appetite and decrease nausea, which can change the diet of the pregnant woman and consequently of the fetus. It is best to avoid the use of all unnecessary drugs during pregnancy.

Psychosis

Very large doses of cannabis can sometimes result in psychotic-like symptoms, such as auditory hallucinations, delusions of control or persecution, and grandiose identity, which resemble the "positive" symptoms of schizophrenia (Chapter 13). Additionally, people with schizophrenia use more cannabis than the general population, and schizophrenics who use marijuana are more difficult to treat effectively.[112,113]

Some studies have suggested that cannabis users are at a higher risk of schizophrenia.[114,115] One Swedish study of over 45,000 participants found that the relative risk of schizophrenia was 2.4 times higher in moderate cannabis users, and 6 times higher in heavy users.[116,117] In a susceptible minority who have a genetic predisposition for psychosis, repeated cannabis exposure may increase the risk of developing schizophrenia, or may lower the age at which symptoms first appear, especially if these individuals smoke strains that have a high THC-to-CBD ratio. In those with an established psychotic disorder, cannabinoids can make symptoms worse and even trigger relapse.[118]

But as you know, correlation is not causation. Although it's possible that marijuana use may increase one's risk of psychosis, it also may be that those who are predisposed to schizophrenia are more likely to smoke marijuana; indeed, in a large sample, the onset of schizoid symptoms generally preceded the onset of cannabis use.[119] Additionally, many people diagnosed with schizophrenia have never used cannabis, and the vast majority of marijuana users do not develop psychosis.[120,121,122] If cannabis directly caused schizophrenia, then the significant rise in marijuana use between 1990 and 2010 should have produced a 12–20 percent increase in schizophrenia cases, but the number of new schizophrenia cases over this time period has remained stable or declined.[123]

Cognitive Effects

Although there is moderate evidence supporting impairments in learning and memory soon after using marijuana,[124] there is no strong consensus regarding the effects of long-term use on cognitive performance.[125,126] The most frequently mentioned deficits are poorer perceptual motor coordination, slowed cognitive processing, impaired concentration, and memory dysfunction.

While some studies support the idea that long-term cannabis use impairs learning and memory,[127] other studies do not find a connection between chronic marijuana use and cognitive deficits, or find that effects are so small as to have no real-world ramifications, that the effects are age-related, or that any cognitive declines are short-term and disappear.[128,129,130,131,132] Some studies have found that cognitive performance may cause acute impairment in occasional users, but not in heavy users, who may become tolerant to the adverse cognitive effects of marijuana.[133,134] One problem with studying the effects of cannabis on intelligence is that it is hard to determine if the effects are short term or long term, if any

cognitive deficits were present before drug use began, and how to control for confounding factors such as socioeconomic status. One longitudinal study followed over 1,000 people in Dunedin, New Zealand, from birth until age 38.[135] This study reported that marijuana use decreased IQ, but the author later recanted this finding and determined that any fall in IQ was probably due to confounding factors rather than cannabis use.[136]

If cannabis does have a long-term effect on learning and memory, this effect might be because THC has been found to suppress the activity of hippocampal cells, an area important in the formation of new memories. Cannabinoids also inhibit a process known as "long-term potentiation," the cellular mechanism by which memories are stored.[137] Researchers also have found reduced blood flow to the temporal lobe, where the hippocampus is housed, and to the frontal lobe, where higher-level cognitive processes occur.[138]

Drug Interactions

Cannabis is metabolized in part by cytochrome P450 enzymes, and therefore may interact with many other drugs. Cannabis can enhance the sleep-inducing effects of barbiturates, benzodiazepines, alcohol, and other sedatives, and also may increase the hypertension and tachycardia that occur with cocaine and amphetamines. Those taking blood thinners should be cautious, as cannabinoids, and especially CBD, may increase its effects. Drinking alcohol when using marijuana increases the concentration of THC in the blood, which in part explains the increased impairment seen when marijuana and alcohol are combined.[139] When administered at the same time as morphine, codeine, or nonsteroidal anti-inflammatory drugs (NSAIDs), marijuana can increase the analgesic effect of these drugs. Administering THC at the same time as NSAIDs may also alleviate the memory and learning problems triggered by THC.[140]

Critical Evaluation

Does long-term cannabis use cause cognitive deficits?

As revealed in this section, there are a lot of contradictory data available regarding cannabis use and cognitive functioning. Given that some data suggests that cannabis use has no meaningful effect on cognition and other data suggests it may impair cognition, how should we best evaluate the long-term effects of cannabis use on cognition?

Defining terms. How much marijuana use constitutes "heavy use" or "casual use"? One study claiming that casual use of marijuana caused cognitive damage characterized those who smoked 11 joints per week or more as "casual users" rather than "regular users" or "heavy users." How would you determine the criteria for casual, regular, or heavy use?

Honesty of participants. Are the participants telling the truth? Marijuana is still illegal in most parts of the world. If you were to ask participants how much they smoked, some consumers might over- or under-estimate their use.

Type of cannabis. What exactly did the participants smoke? Different strains of cannabis, with different THC-to-CBD ratios may have different effects on cognition. For that matter, perhaps it is the process of smoking that has an effect.

Time since last use. How long since the subjects last consumed cannabis? Some of the studies that looked at heavy smokers compared to light smokers gave the memory tests after one to two days of abstinence, when heavy users still had marijuana in their system. Any cognitive differences might be due to the acute effects of cannabis on memory, rather than on long-term damage.

Underlying differences in heavy and light users. How do those who are classified as heavier users differ from lighter users? It may be that cannabis itself lowers IQ. On the other hand, it may be that people with attention, memory, and learning deficits are particularly attracted to cannabis. One study looked at brain volume and found that people who had smaller orbitofrontal cortexes when they were 12 years old were more likely to use marijuana later in life.[141] Or, perhaps other factors such as family dynamics or the use of other drugs underlie both the cannabis use and the poorer performance on tests. Other factors to consider include gender, education, socioeconomic status, diet, exercise, and other drug use.

Measuring cognitive effects. How were cognitive effects measured? With an IQ test? Many IQ tests are considered to be racially or economically biased. Also, some people experience test anxiety, which can hurt their score. If a regular user of cannabis is withdrawing from the drug, he or she may be even more anxious, and that anxiety may be detrimental to their performance on the test.

Age at start. At what age did the participants begin using cannabis? Although there are contradictory findings, the majority of the evidence suggests that cannabis use during adolescence is more detrimental than use in adulthood. Adolescence is a time of critical brain development, when neuronal systems mature and rearrange. THC disrupts the learning ability in adolescent animals far more potently than it does in adult animals.[142] THC also produces fewer unpleasant side effects in adolescents, which may encourage cannabis use in teens more than in adults. Although the exact effects of marijuana on learning and memory are unclear, any drug use in a developing brain has the potential to cause long-term changes.

Collateral Damage

Some of the adverse consequences of cannabis use come not from the drug itself, but from collateral effects of use. As written in the *Journal of the American Medical Association,* "At present, the greatest danger in medical use of marijuana is its illegality, which imposes much anxiety and expense on suffering people, forces them to bargain with illicit drug dealers, and exposes them to the threat of criminal prosecution."[143]

Cannabis also slows reaction time, and decreases attention, hand-eye coordination, and concentration, which may raise one's risk of a traffic accident. The data on the effects of cannabis on traffic accidents are inconsistent, with some reports suggesting cannabis users have a significantly higher risk of accidents than their nonsmoking peers[144,145], some reporting that there is only a slightly increased risk[146,147], and still other studies reporting that cannabis users actually drive more slowly, cautiously, and consistently than non-users, were more aware of their intoxication, increased the distance between their cars and the car in front of them, and were less likely to attempt to pass other cars.[148,149,150] Either way, stoned drivers fare much better than drunk drivers, who increase their speed and passing, decrease their following distance, and take more risks. However, stoned drivers are still less able to react to unexpected occurrences than those who are not impaired.

In an anti-drug public service announcement called "Pete's Couch," a teenager talks directly to the camera, as he sits next to his very droopy-looking friends. He says, "I smoked weed and nobody died. . . . Nothing happened. We sat on Pete's couch for 11 hours." The implication is that pot smokers do nothing except sit in sodden

Ask yourself: Is marijuana a gateway drug? Why or why not?

lumps on the couch until they're 86. **Amotivational syndrome** describes the decreased productivity, lack of interest, and inability to implement long-term plans in adolescent marijuana users. Evidence for amotivational syndrome is mostly from people's observations and personal stories. There are very few controlled studies investigating amotivational syndrome, and these studies have not shown strong evidence to support the phenomenon, primarily because it is hard to prove that marijuana causes apathy. One study found that poor performance in school preceded marijuana use,[151] while others suggest that the link between cannabis use in adolescence and decreased educational attainment is mostly dependent on the social context.[152]

Some also believe that marijuana is a **gateway drug**—that using marijuana leads to the use of other addictive drugs. And indeed, the younger teens are when they begin to use alcohol, cigarettes, and marijuana, and the more often they use these drugs, the more likely they are to use other drugs and to possibly develop a substance use disorder.[153] And while it is true that some people who use cannabis will use harder drugs later in life, no widely accepted study has satisfactorily shown that the use of cannabis *causes* the later use of harder drugs.

In 1999, and again in 2017, the Institute of Medicine issued a report stating that there is no conclusive evidence that effects of marijuana are causally linked to subsequent abuse of other illicit drugs.[154] In fact, the use of alcohol and cigarettes are better than cannabis at predicting later illicit hard drug use. Many of these studies look at marijuana use and later hard drug use, but most drug users begin with alcohol and nicotine before progressing to marijuana.[155]

There are other factors that may play a role. Because cannabis is readily available, adolescents may start with marijuana before they move onto harder drugs. Also, because marijuana is still illegal in most states, people who smoke marijuana are more likely to be in situations where they become acquainted with those

who use and sell other drugs. And, of course, it's important not to confuse correlation with causation. It is possible that marijuana causes neurological and psychological changes that incline someone to escalate to harder drugs, but it is more likely that those who are predisposed to drug use are more likely to use marijuana when they are young. Finally, a third factor, such as age, sex, socioeconomic status, employment, or psychological stress, may influence use.

Medical and Therapeutic Uses of Cannabis

There are a number of reasons why the federal government has been slow to recognize the medical uses of marijuana. There are concerns about its psychoactivity and its potential for abuse and dependence. For some conditions, there are not enough clinical, controlled, human studies showing its efficacy, and strains of marijuana are inconsistent with regard to their chemical composition. Because cannabis is not legally recognized as a medicine by the federal government, even in states where medical marijuana has been legalized, physicians may not prescribe it and pharmacists may not dispense it. Instead, healthcare professionals can recommend marijuana to their patients, who will then obtain it through co-ops, dispensaries, or by growing it themselves. "Recommendations" often do not specify the strain, route of administration, quantity, or frequency of use.[156]

Although both the National Academy of Sciences' Institute of Medicine and the American Medical Association have called for more research on medical marijuana, the U.S. government makes it extremely hard to do, and marijuana is one of the most tightly controlled substances under federal law. In order to perform cannabis research, scientists need to obtain approval from the FDA. Scientists then must apply to the National Institute of Drug Abuse, which holds a monopoly on all legally available research marijuana, but only very rarely dispenses it for medical research. All cannabis samples in federal research studies have to be purchased from the sole facility in the United States that cultivates research cannabis. This has limited generalizability, not only because the federally supplied cannabis has a much lower potency than cannabis available from retail dispensaries or found

Amotivational syndrome: A condition of apathy, loss of motivation, and unwillingness to work associated with prolonged heavy use of marijuana.
Gateway drug: A drug whose use is thought to lead to the use of a harder drug.

on the street, but because its quality is so poor that the FDA said this cannabis would not be approved for use in stage 3 clinical trials. Finally, researchers have to obtain a special license from the DEA. These licenses are expensive and take a long time to acquire.[157] It is considerably easier to obtain marijuana on the street than it is for scientists to study the drug in the lab. In 2016, the DEA denied a petition to remove marijuana from schedule I, but agreed to allow more universities to grow cannabis for approved scientific studies. Many facilities applied to be certified growers—and paid a $34,000 application fee—but as of 2021, none of these applications have been processed.

Cannabis has many therapeutic benefits, some well-documented and others less so. Substantial evidence exists that cannabis is effective for treating chronic pain, reducing nausea and vomiting, stimulating hunger, and alleviating the stiffness and muscle spasms experienced by patients with multiple sclerosis.[158] In addition, scientists are investigating marijuana's effectiveness against epilepsy, glaucoma, cancer, stroke, Parkinson's disease, Huntington's disease, amyotrophic lateral sclerosis (ALS), Alzheimer's disease, diabetes, inflammatory bowel disease, and depression. Although there is much that is still uncertain about cannabis's effects, what is clear is that far more research is needed.

Analgesia

There is considerable evidence that cannabis can effectively treat chronic pain in adults.[159,160]

Cannabinoids alleviate pain via multiple mechanisms.[161,162] They reduce sensitivity to both short-term (acute) and long-term (chronic) painful stimuli, and their potency and efficacy are comparable to opioids.[163,164] Substances in cannabis alleviate pain by acting as anti-inflammatories, reducing the release of pain-causing substances in the body, increasing the synthesis and release of endogenous opioids, stimulating CB1 receptors that block the transmission of pain signals to the brain, blocking receptors involved in pain perception, and by other mechanisms as well.[165] The body also releases its own stores of endocannabinoids when in pain; some scientists think that the runner's high is actually due to endocannabinoid release rather than endorphin release.[166,167] In addition, THC can act synergistically with other pain relievers. Cannabinoid and opioid receptors appear to interact and form complexes which play a role in analgesia.[168] The analgesic effects of morphine, codeine, and NSAIDs

such as acetaminophen are greatly magnified when given with the addition of a small dose of THC. In fact, acetaminophen (Tylenol) is converted by the liver into a substance that activates cannabinoid receptors. The reason why Tylenol does not lead people to experience a high is unknown.[169]

Nausea, Vomiting, and Appetite

Cannabis alleviates nausea and vomiting. Marijuana prompts a normal desire to eat, which can be of therapeutic benefit to chemotherapy patients and others who are suffering from wasting syndrome—a loss of body mass, muscle atrophy, fatigue, and weakness often associated with cancer, AIDS, or other conditions.

Epilepsy

Cannabis may be effective in reducing seizures.[170] This anticonvulsant effect is particularly evident in marijuana with a high CBD-to-THC ratio.[171,172,173] In a double-blind, placebo-controlled clinical trial, children with Dravet syndrome, a rare, severe form of epilepsy, were randomly assigned to receive either CBD or placebo in addition to standard antiepileptic treatment. In those children receiving CBD, the average number of seizures per month decreased from 12.4 to 5.9, as compared with a decrease from 14.9 to 14.1 in the placebo group.[174] Epidiolex is an FDA-approved prescription CBD used to treat some forms of seizure disorder.

Cancer

Cannabis may help manage many of the symptoms of cancer and side effects of chemotherapy due to its ability to stimulate the appetite, inhibit nausea and vomiting, provide pain relief, elevate mood, and give relief from insomnia.[175,176,177]

Although marijuana smoke contains carcinogenic hydrocarbons, there have been no convincing epidemiological associations between marijuana smoking and an increased incidence of most types of cancers[178] In fact, marijuana smokers may have a relatively *lower* risk of getting cancer. In one study, researchers analyzed data comparing nonsmokers, those who smoked only marijuana, those who smoked only tobacco, and those who smoked both marijuana and tobacco.[179] They found that not only did marijuana smokers have a significantly lowered risk of cancer compared with tobacco smokers, and that those who smoked marijuana and tobacco had a lower risk of developing cancer than those who smoked only tobacco, but marijuana smok-

Charlotte's Web

Charlotte Figi (Figure 9.14) had her first seizure when she was three months old. Diagnosed with a rare form of epilepsy, by the time she was five years old, she had more than 300 seizures each week. Charlotte could not walk, could say only a few words, could barely eat, and had gone into cardiac arrest more than once. Her parents had tried every available medical option, with no success. Charlotte's father heard of a similar case in which medical marijuana helped a boy's seizures, and the family decided to give it a try. Charlotte's parents gave her a few drops of an extract made from a cannabis strain that was high in CBD and low in THC. Her seizures stopped immediately. The strain, which was once named "hippie's disappointment" due to its lack of psychoactivity, is now known as "Charlotte's Web" and is well known among parents whose children suffer from epilepsy and other seizure disorders. For 7 years, CBD allowed Charlotte to engage in normal childhood activities. Tragically, Charlotte died in 2020 at the age of 13 after being hospitalized with respiratory complications most likely related to COVID-19. In her short life, she represented a beacon of hope to many struggling families.

FIGURE 9.14. Charlotte Figi and her dad. Charlotte's life-threatening seizures were controlled with medical marijuana.

ers also had a lower risk of developing cancer than nonsmokers.

In addition, cannabinoids might also directly inhibit cancer growth. Cannabinoids may reduce the risk of various types of cancers, including lung,[180] breast,[181] skin,[182] brain,[183,184] and squamous cell cancers of the head and neck.[185] There is evidence that cannabinoids may cause some tumor cells to die, decrease the proliferation and growth of cancer cells, inhibit metastasis, and prevent cancer cells from binding to normal tissues.[186,187,188]

Now, before lighting up a joint in the name of cancer prevention, we need to consider some serious limitations of the data.[189] Most of the scientific research investigating whether cannabinoids are an effective treatment for cancer has been done using animal models or cancer cells grown in a lab. We must be careful when extrapolating these results to live patients. Epidemiological studies have limitations as well, including under-reporting of marijuana use (especially in places where marijuana is illegal), small sample sizes, and inconsistent definitions of what constitutes moderate or heavy marijuana use. The length of the study is also important—did the study follow the participants for a long enough time for cancer to develop? It is also unclear which types of cannabi-

noids might be the most effective, which doses, and against which types of cancer. At this point, there is not enough evidence to support (or refute) the conclusion that marijuana is an effective treatment for cancer.[190] It is also important to consider other damage that marijuana may cause. Cannabinoids modulate the immune system. Immunotherapy is the standard of care for many types of tumors, and cannabis may interfere with this treatment. Also, although cannabinoids may prevent tumor metastasis by impeding blood vessel growth and development, impaired blood vessel growth can negatively affect wound healing, as well as heart and kidney function.

Brain Injury and Neurodegenerative Disorders

Traumatic brain injury is a leading cause of death in adolescents and young adults, especially in young men. Injury to the brain triggers the release of substances such as chemically reactive molecules that contain oxygen, cytokines, and glutamate, which induce neuronal cell death. Endocannabinoids, whose levels increase after brain injury, inhibit the release of these harmful substances.[191] Cannabinoids, especially CBD, are neuroprotective, and may prevent the damage that occurs due to traumatic brain injury, stroke, and epilepsy, as well as neurodegenerative disorders such as multiple sclerosis, Parkinson's disease, Huntington's disease, and ALS. Scientists are unsure of the mechanism by which marijuana may help these conditions, but it may be through its antioxidant capacity, or by its ability to inhibit the neuronal cell death that can occur due to over-release of glutamine.[192,193]

QUICK HIT

Although the U.S. government does not recognize any therapeutic benefits of marijuana, in 2003, the U.S. Department of Health and Human Services secured a patent titled "cannabinoids as antioxidants and neuroprotectants." This patent—number 6630507—states that "cannabinoids [are] useful in the treatment and prophylaxis of a wide variety of oxidation associated diseases, such as . . . stroke and trauma, or in the treatment of neurodegenerative diseases, such as Alzheimer's disease, Parkinson's disease and HIV dementia."

Multiple sclerosis patients who use cannabis report fewer muscle spasms and less pain.[194,195,196] Given that CB1 receptors are abundant in the basal ganglia and cerebellum, marijuana also may help treat movement disorders such as Parkinson's disease and Huntington's disease.

Alzheimer's disease is a progressive neurodegenerative disorder, and one of the most serious health problems in the industrialized world. The onset of Alzheimer's has been linked to the brain's failure to produce enough of its own neuroprotective endocannabinoids—CB1 receptors are diminished in Alzheimer's brains. Giving synthetic cannabinoids to rats reduced cognitive impairment and diminished the characteristic neuronal markers of the disease. THC also may boost acetylcholine levels, which might help lessen the symptoms of the disease.[197,198] At this point there is no clinical evidence that cannabinoids effectively treat Alzheimer's disease in humans, but there is preliminary evidence in animals that it may help to reduce the cognitive decline that occurs with aging.[199,200]

Diabetes

In a study of over 4,600 participants, current users of cannabis had better glucose control than did former users or those who had never used marijuana.[201] Current users also had lower fasting insulin levels and higher levels of "good" cholesterol. In a representa-

Ask yourself: Nondrinking alcoholics who switch to marijuana generally have lower rates of relapse and much more manageable lives than alcoholics do, but they are substituting one addiction for another. Which is more important—living a completely drug-free life or managing an addiction in a tolerable way? Why?

tive sample of almost 11,000 adults, after controlling for sociodemographic factors, participants who used marijuana had a lower prevalence of diabetes.[202] The phytocannabinoid THCV may be especially helpful in regulating insulin levels.

Other Potential Therapeutic Benefits

Cannabinoids may have other potential therapeutic effects. Some scientists believe that some diseases, including IBD, migraines, fibromyalgia, and depression are a clinical deficiency of the endocannabinoid system and may be helped with cannabis.[203,204,205,206,207,208] In addition, cannabis use enables some people to minimize or eliminate their use of more harmful substances such as alcohol or crack cocaine,[209] alcohol,[210] prescription painkillers,[211,212,213,214,215] benzodiazepines,[216,217,218,219] and antidepressants.[220,221,222]

Chronic Effects of Cannabis

A recent longitudinal study followed over 400 men from adolescence to age 36 and found that long-time chronic smokers of marijuana did not significantly differ in terms of physical health (such as respiratory or cardiovascular) or mental health (such as psychosis, depression, or anxiety) from nonsmokers.[223] Chronic use of any drug, however, may have some physiological, psychological, and interpersonal effects.

Tolerance

Regular use of marijuana will cause metabolic, cellular, and behavioral tolerance. With chronic exposure to THC, there is increased activity in the enzymes that metabolize THC, and a decrease in the number of CB1 receptors.[224,225] Tolerance is uneven, however. Different receptors downregulate at different rates, and tolerance develops to some of cannabis's effects and not others. Tolerance also depends on experience and the environment, and frequent users may show behavioral tolerance as they learn to deal with marijuana's effects. Chronic users are less responsive to marijuana's hypothermic, cardiovascular, analgesic, locomotor, and immune effects, but not to its memory effects.[226] Frequent smokers report less of a feeling of being high than inexperienced smokers do.

Dependence

Contrary to popular belief, users can become addicted to marijuana; up to 9 percent of users show signs of dependence.[227] Those who first tried marijuana before age 25 have higher rates of dependence.[228,229] In 2019, 1.8 percent of the adult population of the United States were currently considered to be dependent on marijuana, and 4.3 percent of Americans have been dependent on marijuana at some point in their lives.[230,231] Of the 4.4 million persons in the United States who reported problems with a cannabis use disorder, about 5 percent received treatment at a specialty facility.[232] Admissions for cannabis dependence were less likely than other drugs to be self-referred; instead, most people entering rehab for cannabis were arrested for possession and referred to treatment by the courts in lieu of prison.[233,234]

Although even heavy cannabis users do not typically become dependent, when it does occur, some aspects of marijuana dependence are similar to those of other drugs: use continues despite social, psychological, and physical impairments; users perceive themselves as unable to stop; and they have made a number of serious attempts at quitting without long-term success (Chapter 17).[235] Cannabinoids increase the release of dopamine in the addiction pathways of the brain, although to a much lesser degree than cocaine, opioids, alcohol, and nicotine. Cannabis dependence is also likely to be less severe than that of other drugs, and those with marijuana dependence typically have fewer dependence criteria according to the DSM-5.[236] Finally, cannabis produces dependence less readily than other drugs (Figure 9.15).[237]

Withdrawal

Not all heavy chronic users go through withdrawal upon cessation of marijuana, but if withdrawal symptoms occur, they are usually not as severe, perhaps because THC is easily stored in fat tissue and then is slowly released over time.[238] Unlike withdrawal from alcohol, opioids, or benzodiazepines, there are no major medical or psychiatric consequences from cannabis withdrawal.[239] Instead, when withdrawal occurs,

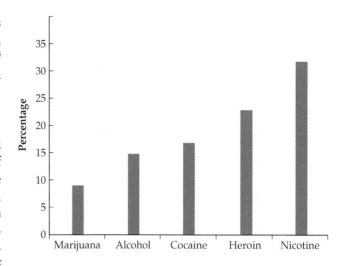

FIGURE 9.15. The percentage of those who tried a drug once and eventually fit a diagnosis of dependence. Marijuana is significantly less addictive than other drugs of abuse, such as alcohol, cocaine, heroin, and nicotine.

Sources: Anthony, J.V., Warner, L.A., & Kessler, R.C. (1994). Comparative epidemiology of dependence on tobacco, alcohol, controlled substances, and inhalants: Basic findings from the National Comorbidity Survey. Experimental and Clinical Psychopharmacology, 2:244–68.

Nutt, D.J., King, L.A., Phillips, L.D. (2010). Drug harms in the UK: A multicriteria decision analysis. Lancet, 376(9752): 1558–65.

it may be associated with a craving for cannabis; irritability, anger, and aggression; nausea; restlessness; depression; sleep difficulties and strange dreams; and decreased appetite and weight loss. Most symptoms begin 24–48 hours after abstinence, peak within four to six days, and last one to three weeks, although significant individual differences occur.

Treatment for Cannabis Dependence

Treatment for cannabis dependence typically involves psychological approaches. Users are encouraged to strengthen their motivation to quit, focus on skills relevant to quitting, and avoid situations that interfere with abstinence. Similar to what is seen with people seeking treatment for addiction to other substances, success rates are limited (Chapter 18). Only about 50 percent of people who enroll in a treatment program are successfully abstinent two weeks after leaving treatment, and among those, about half will resume marijuana use within the year.[240]

Ask yourself: What is the best way to help someone who is dependent on marijuana?

Chapter Summary

- **History of Cannabis**
  - » Cannabis has been cultivated for many thousands of years. Its use has a long tradition in many cultures as an important medical and religious substance.
  - » Harry Anslinger, the first director of the Federal Bureau of Narcotics, led the charge to convince the public that marijuana was a frightening and dangerous drug. William Randolph Hearst helped his campaign by printing terrifying (and spurious) tales of the drug. The Marijuana Tax Act was passed in 1937.
  - » Throughout the 1960s and 1970s, attitudes about marijuana eased, and the DEA strongly considered decriminalizing the drug. In the 1980s and 1990s, attitudes shifted and penalties increased. Since the mid-1990s, marijuana use has increased, and many states have decriminalized the drug, approved the use of medical marijuana, or legalized it entirely.

- **Prevalence of Cannabis Use**
  - » Cannabis is the most commonly used illicit drug in the United States. Use has increased in recent years.
  - » There is an inverse relationship between marijuana use and perception of its risk among high school students.

- **Legal and Cultural Issues Related to Cannabis**
  - » Although medical marijuana is legal in most states, and recreational marijuana is legal in many, federal law states that marijuana is illegal; in fact, it is a schedule I drug.
  - » Hundreds of thousands of people are arrested each year in America for cannabis possession. Blacks are arrested and incarcerated at rates significantly higher than are whites.
  - » A recent poll showed that most Americans support the legalization of marijuana.
  - » Cannabis has made its mark in American culture, and references can be found in literature, art, music, television, and movies.

- **Source and Forms of Cannabis**
  - » There are different varieties of the cannabis plant; two of the most common are *Cannabis sativa* and *Cannabis indica*.
  - » The cannabis plant contains phytocannabinoids such as THC and CBD; the percentage of the specific phytocannabinoids varies among different varieties of the plant. THC is an intoxicant, and CBD is antioxidant, anticonvulsant, anti-inflammatory, antianxiety, antipsychotic, and neuroprotective. Cannabis also contains terpenes and flavonoids.
  - » Marijuana today has been bred to contain higher THC content than in the past.
  - » Hemp contains only trace amounts of THC and is not psychoactive. It is a hardy, adaptable plant that is a source of fiber, fuel, and food.

- » Synthetic cannabinoids include dronabinol, a THC pill used to raise appetite and alleviate nausea and vomiting in cancer patients; and Spice, a term for a wide variety of synthetic cannabis products.

- **Pharmacology of Cannabis**
  - » Cannabis is most commonly smoked, vaporized, or eaten. It is highly fat-soluble and easily crosses the blood brain barrier. Compared to smoking, ingesting cannabis gives a slower onset of effect, less predictability of action, and less user control.
  - » Cannabis has a wide range of effective doses and exhibits a biphasic dose response curve. Some marijuana metabolites may remain in the body for days or even weeks after use.
  - » Cannabinoids interact with multiple receptors in a variety of ways.

- **Mechanism of Action of Cannabis**
  - » Cannabis affects the endocannabinoid system, a system of neurotransmitters, enzymes, and receptors found in all animals. The ECS is one of the most important physiological systems in the body and helps maintain homeostasis.
  - » The ECS is composed of cannabinoid receptors, endocannabinoids, and enzymes.
  - » Cannabinoid receptors are found in the basal ganglia, cerebellum, hippocampus, cortex, amygdala, eye, pancreas, testes, uterus, and immune system.
  - » Endocannabinoids include anandamide and 2-AG. These fat-soluble neurotransmitters are rapidly synthesized as needed, released from the postsynaptic neuron, and bind to receptors on the presynaptic neuron, to modulate the release of other substances.

- **Acute Effects of Cannabis**
  - » Cannabis's effects depend on many factors, including the dose; the particular strain's potency and the ratio of THC to CBD; the user's previous experience, expectations, and mood; and the environment in which it is used. Because the ECS is so widespread, cannabinoids affect almost every organ system in the body.
  - » Cannabis increases one's sense of well-being, enhances sensory perception, and impairs memory and concentration. It also reduces reactivity to pain, increases heart rate, boosts appetite, modulates the immune system, and plays a role in sperm production, fertilization, and development of the fetus.
  - » Cannabis has a very high therapeutic index, but nevertheless it has some potentially negative physical, psychological, and cognitive effects. Marijuana may impair fertilization and raise the risk of schizophrenia in a susceptible minority.
  - » Some of the adverse consequences of marijuana use come not from the drug itself, but from criminal penalties or harm due to one's diminished reaction time and coordination.

- **Medical and Therapeutic Uses of Cannabis**
  » Cannabis is known to alleviate pain, reduce nausea and vomiting, stimulate appetite, and help with the spasticity associated with multiple sclerosis.
  » Scientists are investigating marijuana's efficacy against seizure disorders, cancer, stroke, Alzheimer's disease, diabetes, inflammatory bowel disease, depression, and other disorders.

- **Chronic Effects of Cannabis**
  » Regular use of cannabis will cause tolerance.
  » Not all heavy chronic users go through withdrawal upon cessation of the drug, but if withdrawal symptoms occur, they are usually not severe.
  » Cannabis is less addictive than other drugs of abuse, but the drug can prove addictive in some individuals.
  » Most treatment for cannabis dependence typically involves psychological approaches.

Key Terms

Amotivational syndrome (p.225)
Bong (p.217)
Cannabidiol (CBD) (p.215)
Cannabinoids (p.215)
Cannabis (p.205)
Cannabis indica (p.214)
Cannabis sativa (p.214)
Dab (p.216)

Decriminalization (p.211)
Endocannabinoid system (p.218)
Endocannabinoids (p.219)
Ensemble effect (p.215)
Flavonoids (p.215)
Gateway drug (p.225)
Hemp (p.205)
Joint (p.217)

Legalization (p.211)
Marijuana (p.205)
Phytocannabinoids (p.215)
Shatter (p.216)
Terpenes (p.215)
THC (p.215)
Vaporizer (p.217)

Quiz Yourself!

1. Which of the following pairs has a higher percentage of THC?
   A. Male plants or female plants
   B. Hemp or marijuana
2. True or false? Cannabis use has been illegal in the United States since 1914.
3. True or false? In some American colonies, it was required that all households cultivate hemp.
4. Which of the following is true about cannabis?
   A. Cannabis is very water-soluble and is most effectively absorbed when eaten.
   B. Cannabis must be heated to chemically activate THC.
   C. After ingestion, cannabis remains in fatty tissues for as long as 12 hours.
   D. A vaporizer burns cannabis at a hotter temperature than smoking.
5. Give an example of a phytocannabinoid and an example of an endocannabinoid.
6. "Most cocaine users smoked marijuana when they were young; therefore, marijuana is a gateway drug that causes cocaine use." What fallacy of reasoning has been employed here?

7. True or false? Those who drive while high on marijuana tend to drive faster, decrease their following distance, and take more risks.
8. Which of the following is FALSE about the acute effects of cannabis?
   A. Raises heart rate
   B. Decreases motor activity and coordination
   C. Dilates blood vessels of the eye
   D. Increases sperm count
9. True or false? A majority of studies have proven that marijuana smokers have twice the rate of lung cancer than tobacco smokers.
10. A study compared two groups of participants: one that reported smoking "moderate" amounts of marijuana and another that smoked at least a pack of cigarettes a day for 10 years. The cigarette smokers had higher rates of lung cancer. The press published the headline, "Marijuana Cures Cancer!" Use your critical thinking skills to evaluate that statement.

Additional Resources

Websites

The National Organization for the Reform of Marijuana Laws. www.norml.org

Project CBD. https://www.projectcbd.org/

Leafly. www.leafly.com

Law Enforcement Action Partnership (LEAP). www.lawenforcementactionpartnership.org

Videos

Retired police captain Peter Christ discussing the War on Drugs https://www.youtube.com/watch?v=W8yYJ_oV6xk

Dr. Rachel Knox's TEDx Talk about the Endocannabinoid System https://www.youtube.com/watch?v=oJbOQ9P2NYQ&feature=youtu.be

Books

Caulkins, J.P., Kilmer, B., & Kleiman, M.A.R. (2016). *Marijuana legalization: What everyone needs to know* (2nd ed.). New York: Oxford University Press.

Lee, M.A. (2012). *Smoke signals: A social history of marijuana—Medical, recreational, and scientific.* New York: Scribner.

National Academies of Sciences, Engineering, and Medicine. (2017). *The health effects of cannabis and cannabinoids: The current state of evidence and recommendations for research.* Washington, DC: National Academies Press.

Games

CannaBoss. https://www.thegamecrafter.com/games/cannaboss-to-go:-just-a-dab-ll-do-ya

Learn more with this chapter's digital tools at www.oup.com/he/rosenthal2e.

Tobacco and Nicotine

True or false?

1.
True or false? More people smoke today than at any other time in human history.

2.
True or false? Studies prove that vaping (e-cigarettes) is the most effective way to quit smoking.

3.
True or false? Nicotine is one of the most addictive substances ever discovered.

Answers: 1. T, 2. F, 3. T

Learning Objectives

- Trace the history of tobacco use.

- Compare tobacco and nicotine use by gender, race, education, age, and socio-economic status, and among inhabitants of different countries.

- Identify factors that increase a person's chance of smoking.

- List some of the harmful substances in cigarettes and e-cigarettes.

- Describe the various forms of tobacco.

- Explain the way that nicotine interacts with the acetylcholine receptor and the effects this produces in the body.

- Outline the acute physiological and psychological effects of nicotine.

- List the adverse effects from chronic use of tobacco.

- Evaluate tobacco's legal status.

- Summarize some strategies for quitting tobacco and nicotine.

In May of 1933, the *Journal of the American Medical Association* published an article describing the story of a florist who spilled a nicotine-based insecticide onto a bench on which he was sitting. Fifteen minutes later, he began to experience nausea, vomiting, sweating, and difficulty breathing. His body temperature and blood pressure dropped. He was taken to the hospital, where he remained for four days. Upon discharge, the florist put on the clothes he had been wearing when he entered the hospital. The seat of his pants was still damp. An hour later, the florist suffered a second attack of nicotine poisoning.[1,2]

What a toxic substance! Yet more than 1 billion people around the world pay good money to voluntarily inhale about 6.5 trillion cigarettes each year—almost 18 billion cigarettes every day.[3] In fact, more people smoke today than at any other time in human history.[4] Tobacco is one of the most widely used drugs in the world, consumed by approximately 20 percent of the global adult population.

History of Tobacco

Native Americans cultivated tobacco for thousands of years. On October 11, 1492, Christopher Columbus landed in the Bahamas. Local tribal members met him and offered gifts including dried tobacco leaves. Columbus didn't understand the value of the leaves and tossed them overboard. Two weeks later, after reaching Cuba, explorers from the ship observed the natives inhaling smoke from a pipe and joined in. Columbus brought tobacco, as well as the concept of smoking as a drug-delivery system, to Europe.[5]

Early Tobacco Use in Europe

Tobacco use spread throughout Europe in the sixteenth century. In 1560, Jean Nicot, the French ambassador to Portugal, sent tobacco seeds to the Queen of France. The French began to call it the Nicotian herb, and when a French chemist isolated the active ingredient in 1809, he commemorated his countryman and named it nicotine.[6] In 1565, Sir Francis Drake and Sir Walter Raleigh introduced tobacco to England. Over the next few decades, tobacco's popularity spread, and European doctors recommended smoking the plant as a cure for toothaches, worms, halitosis, lockjaw, plague, and cancer.

Not everyone in England was immediately taken with tobacco, however. In 1604, King James I (the same King James who had the Bible translated) wrote *A Counterblaste to Tobacco*, calling it "[a] custom loathsome to the eye, hateful to the nose,

Nicotine

Type of drug: Stimulant

Chemical formula of nicotine:
- $C_{10}H_{14}N_2$

Routes of administration:
- Smoked, absorbed across skin and mucosal membranes of mouth and nose

• Duration of effect:
- Short. Half-life of two hours

• Neurotransmitters directly affected:
- Acetylcholine

Tolerance:
- Moderate/high

Physiological dependence:
- Moderate/high

Psychological dependence:
- Moderate/high

Withdrawal symptoms:
- Variable—craving, irritability, headache, increased appetite, abnormal sleep

Schedule:
- Legal

Slang:
- No slang for nicotine. Slang for tobacco or nicotine delivery products: smoke, butt, cigs, coffin nails, stogies, dip, chew, vape

harmful to the brain, dangerous to the lungs, and in the black stinking fume thereof, nearest resembling the horrible Stygian smoke of the pit that is bottomless." The king enacted heavy taxes on tobacco imports (a 4,000% tax increase), hoping to curtail the use of tobacco. And indeed, at first, only the wealthy could afford the drug. In 1598, a pound of tobacco cost over four British pounds (worth about $1,083 in today's currency).[7] But tobacco's popularity rose. By 1614, there were more than 7,000 tobacco shops in London alone.[8] Tobacco became one of England's richest sources of income, both from the heavy taxes received and from the wealth coming from the tobacco crops of England's American colonies.

Tobacco in Colonial America

Once King James recognized the financial benefits to be gained by growing tobacco, the mission of the English colony of Virginia became to grow as much tobacco as possible.[9] England reaped enormous profits from the American colony's production of tobacco, and the king passed acts that imposed heavy taxes on tobacco, prohibited the colonists from selling their tobacco to any nation other than England, and required that all goods imported from the American colonies be carried on British ships.[10,11] Colonists became dependent on England for revenue for their crops, and were forced to sell tobacco at prices favorable to British traders. Colonists'

bitterness at these restrictions and taxes on tobacco were among the factors that would eventually lead to America's declaration of independence from Britain. The resulting revolution was partially financed by the use of tobacco as collateral for loans.

Tobacco was also instrumental in the introduction of slavery to North America. Tobacco planting and harvesting is very labor-intensive. In 1619, Dutch traders kidnapped African men, women, and children and delivered them to the new world as slaves to toil in Virginia's tobacco fields. Slavery quickly became essential to Virginia's economy.[12]

Mechanization

Tobacco remained popular throughout the eighteenth and nineteenth centuries, and the growth of the U.S. cigarette industry was largely due to the efforts of two men: James Buchanan ("Buck") Duke and Richard Joshua ("R.J.") Reynolds. In the 1880s, Buck Duke took over his father's small cigarette company and acquired the license for the first cigarette-making machine. Invented by James Bonsack, the rolling machine could produce 200 cigarettes per minute—as many as 40 laborers could produce by hand, and at a much lower cost. (Today's machines can produce up to 20,000 cigarettes per minute.) Buck Duke was able to offer his cigarettes at a significant savings, and by 1890, he controlled 40 percent of the American cigarette market.

R.J. Reynolds was the son of a tobacco farmer. In 1891, he created the modern cigarette—a mix of American and Turkish tobacco leaves, flavoring, and saccharine to sweeten it and increase its shelf life. Additionally, at a time when most men rolled their own, R.J. Reynolds developed and marketed prepackaged cigarettes.

Tobacco in the Twentieth Century

Throughout the first half of the twentieth century, cigarette smoking was a national habit. Cigarettes and cigars were part of the ration for soldiers fighting during World War I. American General John Pershing, the supreme commander of U.S. troops, sent a cable to the U.S. War Department saying, "You ask what we need to win this war, I answer tobacco, as much as bullets. Tobacco is as indispensable as the daily ration. We must have thousands of tons of it without delay."[13] Soldiers smoked for physical, social, and spiritual reasons. Tobacco helped to suppress their hunger, ease their pain, and calm their nerves. It gave the soldiers the comfort of performing a normal sequence of actions that reminded them of home.

In the late 1920s, tobacco companies began marketing directly to women and linked smoking with women's right to vote (Figure 10.1). Advertising campaigns of the day called cigarettes "torches of freedom." Cigarettes were encouraged and ubiquitous throughout the 1930s and 1940s. But by 1950, some frightening data began to emerge.

Troubled Times for the Tobacco Industry

In the early 1950s, scientific studies were published showing the statistical link between smoking and lung cancer, and by 1954, 40 percent of the public believed that smoking caused lung cancer.[14] To combat the public perception that cigarette smoking was dangerous and to avoid a potential decrease in sales, a group of tobacco company executives formed the Tobacco Industry Research Committee. Although internal industry documents have shown that they were aware of cigarettes' cancer-causing properties, tobacco company executives embarked on a public relations campaign to encourage smokers to continue to smoke. They attacked scientific findings that suggested a link between cancer and smoking, financially supported research

FIGURE 10.1. Torches of freedom. In the late 1920s, tobacco companies began marketing directly to women.

that showed no link between cancer and smoking, and produced new brands with filters and lower tar. One popular new "safer" cigarette was Kent, which featured a micronite filter—made from asbestos.[15]

In 1964, at a time when 46 percent of all Americans smoked, the Surgeon General of the United States released a report, based on thousands of articles and years of research, that stated that smoking cigarettes caused serious illness and that cigarette packages should bear a warning of the potential for cancer. Tobacco industry supporters killed the bill on the grounds of aesthetics—because "cigarette packets were masterpieces of design and should not be defaced by crude statements of fact."[16] In 1966, the significantly watered-down warning "cigarette smoking may be hazardous to your health" was printed on cigarette packs. This weaker warning gave tobacco companies protection, in that if a customer fell ill with cancer the fault was his own, given that he had been warned.[17]

Assaults against the tobacco companies continued to mount. In 1971, all cigarette ads were banned from radio and TV. In 1975, Minnesota became the first state to pass a law restricting smoking in most public spaces (Today, most states have laws in effect dictating certain areas to be smoke free). In 1978, President Jimmy Carter's Secretary of Health, Education, and Welfare announced the start of a major antismoking campaign, which would include increased taxes, bans on smoking during airline flights, and education about tobacco's health hazards.

In 1998, Mississippi was the first state to instigate legislation against the four largest cigarette-producing companies, seeking compensation for tobacco-related healthcare costs. Florida, Minnesota, and Texas followed suit, settling their lawsuits for a combined total of $40 billion. The remaining 46 states and the District of Columbia joined together in a class action suit against Big Tobacco. This settlement required congressional action, as it was a binding contract on behalf of the states and government agencies against the tobacco industry. In 1998, the **Master Settlement Agreement (MSA)** was signed, and became the largest civil settlement in U.S. history. The MSA settled lawsuits against the tobacco companies and exempted them from private tort liability. In exchange, the tobacco companies agreed to make payments to compensate for some medical costs and to change some of their industrial practices.

The MSA was intended to reimburse states for expenses related to treatment of smoking-related illnesses. The MSA also contained provisions to reduce smoking prevalence, especially among youth.[18] The key elements of the pact included

- *Monetary payouts.* The industry agreed to pay $206 billion to the states over 25 years, $1.5 billion over 10 years to support antismoking measures, and $250 million to fund research into reducing youth smoking.
- *Industry changes.* Big Tobacco was ordered to make industry records and research accessible, disband tobacco trade organizations, and set the minimum pack size at 20 cigarettes.
- *Limitations on advertising, marketing, and promotion of cigarettes.* The MSA banned outdoor, billboard, and public transit advertising of cigarettes; prohibited the prominent placement of tobacco products in stores; and forbade the sale of merchandise bearing tobacco brand names. Big Tobacco agreed to refrain from marketing tobacco to those under the age of 18 and to work to restrict youth access to cigarettes.

Since the late 1990s, tobacco companies have experienced increasing restrictions, and tobacco use has fallen significantly (Figure 10.2).[19] Tobacco farmers no longer receive federal subsidies for growing tobacco, and CVS drugstores no longer sell tobacco products. In 2009, President Barack Obama signed the Family Smoking Prevention and Tobacco Control Act into law, thus granting the U.S. Food and Drug Administration (FDA) authority to regulate the tobacco industry. This law gives the FDA the authority to set and enforce standards for tobacco products, ingredients, and design; regulate tobacco marketing; require the presence and size of warning labels on tobacco packages and ads; prohibit flavored cigarettes (except menthol); and requires FDA premarket approval for certain new products. As of 2016, the FDA also regulates the sale and manufacture of electronic nicotine delivery systems (**ENDS**) such as e-cigarettes and vapes. The tobacco companies filed suit against the United States and the FDA for infringement of their rights. But, in 2012, the U.S. Supreme Court upheld the law.

Although it is waning, tobacco companies still exert enormous political power. They spend untold millions each year to influence public policy and regulation. In the United States, in 2019, tobacco interests spent over $28 million and employed 280 lobbyists in an attempt to directly influence political decisions.[20]

Master Settlement Agreement (MSA): A legal agreement between the four largest tobacco companies and 46 of the United States.

ENDS: Electronic nicotine delivery systems, such as e-cigarettes and vaporizers.

Ask yourself: If smokers become sick, who is responsible? The tobacco companies who lied about their product or the smoker, who, by now, should have knowledge of tobacco's risks? Are alcohol companies responsible for liabilities from use of their product? Is the situation different with tobacco, and if so, how? What factors influence your decision?

Prevalence of Tobacco Use

Although smoking is declining in most Western nations, it is on the rise in the developing world. Smoking is especially popular in Asia—40 percent of all cigarettes worldwide are smoked in China.[21] This increase might be due to increased social acceptability, continued economic development, population increases, lax regulation, and aggressive marketing.

QUICK HIT

The tiny island nation of Kiribati has the dubious distinction of having the highest percentage of its population who smoke tobacco.[22] But when you take the size of the population into consideration, the top five cigarette-consuming countries are China, Indonesia, the United States, the Russian Federation, and Japan. More cigarettes are consumed in China than in the next top 29 cigarette-consuming countries combined.[23,24]

In the United States, 58.1 million people age 12 years and older—21.1 percent of the population—have used tobacco in the past month.[25] Cigarettes are the most popular form of tobacco, with almost 46 million users, followed by cigars (11.7 million users), smokeless tobacco (8.5 million users), and pipes (1.9 million users).[26] About 4 percent of adults use electronic nicotine delivery systems (ENDS) every day or some days, meaning there

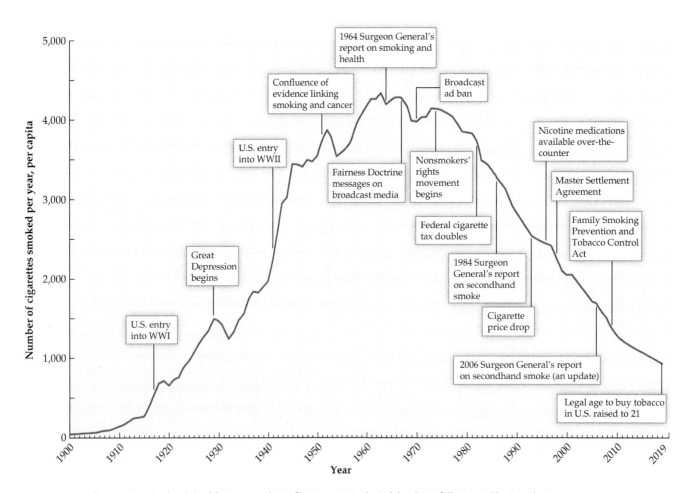

FIGURE 10.2. Cigarette use in the United States over time. Cigarette use in the U.S. has been falling steadily since the 1960s.

Sources: U.S. Department of Health and Human Services. (2014). The Health Consequences of Smoking—50 Years of Progress: A Report of the Surgeon General. Atlanta, GA: Centers for Disease Control and Prevention.

Federal Trade Commission Cigarette Report. (2019). Accessed on May 1, 2020, from https://www.ftc.gov/system/files/documents/reports/federal-trade-commission-cigarette-report-2017-federal-trade-commission-smokeless-tobacco-report/ftc_cigarette_report_2017.pdf

Ask yourself: Why do you think the form of tobacco use is so dependent on gender in our society?

are over 10 million e-cigarette users in the United States.[27] E-cigarette, or "vape", use is increasing in young adults—approximately 9 percent of those age 18–24 report use of e-cigarettes.[28,29] Next, we examine tobacco use by gender, race, education, employment and socio-economic status, mental health, and age.

Gender

Men are more likely to use tobacco than women are. According to the CDC, 24.8 percent of males and 14.2 percent of females age 18 years and older reported current use of a tobacco product of some kind.[30] Men are more likely to smoke cigarettes and use e-cigarettes, almost five times more likely to use pipes, about 7 times more likely to smoke cigars, and 20 times more likely to use smokeless tobacco (Figure 10.3).

Race

American Indians and Alaskan Natives have the highest rate of tobacco use, and Americans of Asian descent have the lowest (Figure 10.4).

Education

The more educated a person is, the less likely he or she is to smoke (Figure 10.5). About one in every four students who are currently in college use tobacco, but this rate is significantly lower than people of the same age who are not in college. Students at public universities report smoking more than those at private colleges.

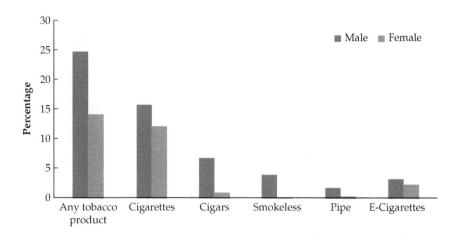

FIGURE 10.3. Percentage of adults reporting current use of any form of tobacco/nicotine use, by gender.

Source: Wang, T.W., Asman, K., Gentzke, A.S., Cullen, K.A., & Holder-Hayes, E., et al. (2018). Tobacco product use among adults—United States, 2017. MMWR, 67: 1225–32.

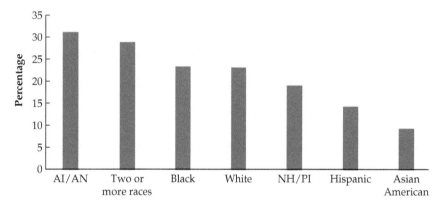

FIGURE 10.4. Percentage reporting current use of any tobacco product, by race. American Indians are more than three times more likely to use tobacco products than are Asian Americans.

Source: SAMHSA. (2020). Results from the 2019 National Survey on Drug Use and Health. Rockville, MD: Center for Behavioral Health Statistics and Quality.

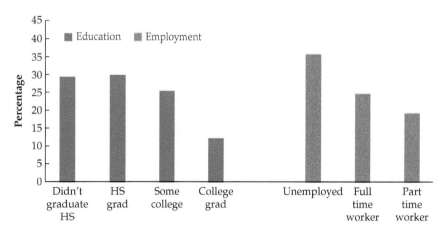

FIGURE 10.5. Demographics of tobacco users. Those with less education and those who are unemployed are more likely to smoke.

Source: SAMHSA. (2020). Results from the 2019 National Survey on Drug Use and Health. Rockville, MD: Center for Behavioral Health Statistics and Quality.

Employment and Socioeconomic Status

Smoking rates are highest for those who are poor and unemployed (Figure 10.5). Depending on where he or she lives, a pack-a-day smoker would spend somewhere between $2,000 and $5,000 per year on cigarettes.

Concurrent Use of Other Drugs

Compared with nonsmokers, current smokers are more likely to drink alcohol and use illicit drugs (Figure 10.6). This difference is even more pronounced in youth; among those age 12–17 who smoke cigarettes, current illicit drug use is nine times higher than among those who do not smoke.[31]

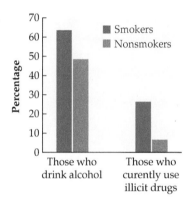

FIGURE 10.6. Association of cigarettes with alcohol and illicit drugs. Current smokers are more likely than nonsmokers to drink alcohol and use illicit drugs.

Source: SAMHSA. (2016). 2015 Survey on drug use and health: Detailed tables. Rockville, MD: Center for Behavioral Health Statistics and Quality.

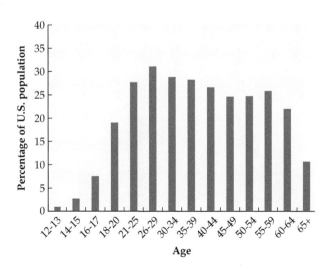

FIGURE 10.7. Tobacco use by age. The highest rates of current tobacco use are among those age 21–39.

Source: SAMHSA. (2020). Results from the 2019 National Survey on Drug Use and Health. Rockville, MD: Center for Behavioral Health Statistics and Quality.

Mental Health

Individuals who suffer from mental illness and affective disorders (Chapter 13) are significantly more likely to smoke cigarettes. Those with major depressive disorder are almost twice as likely to smoke every day compared to those without depression. One out of every five people with serious mental illness smokes daily compared to one out of ten people without.[32]

Age

Very few people say, "In honor of my 40th birthday, I think I'll start smoking!" Most addicted smokers picked up the habit when they were teenagers. Every day, 4,369 people begin smoking, and over 94 percent of them are age 25 or younger (Figure 10.7).[33]

In 2019, cigarette use among teens reached its lowest levels recorded in over 40 years.[34] In 1976, 39 percent of high school seniors had smoked cigarettes in the past 30 days; by 2019, this number had fallen to 5.7 percent (Figure 10.8). This fall may be related to a number of factors[35]:

- Higher disapproval of smoking
- Greater awareness of smoking's dangers
- Adverse publicity suffered by the tobacco industry
- The reduction in cigarette advertising

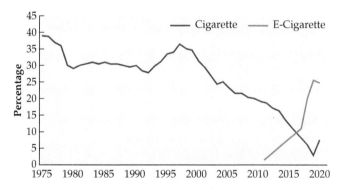

FIGURE 10.8. Cigarette use in high school seniors over time. Cigarette use in high school seniors over time. The percentage of high school seniors who smoked cigarettes in the past 30 days has fallen precipitously since 1997. In recent years, the fall in cigarette use has been offset by an increase in the use of e-cigarettes. The annual increases in current use of e-cigarettes are the largest ever recorded for any substances in the 45 years that Monitoring the Future has tracked adolescent drug use.

Sources: Meich, R.A., Johnston, L.D., O'Malley, P.M., Bachman, J.G., & Schulenberg, J.E., et al. (2021). Monitoring the Future: National survey results on drug use 1975–2020. Ann Arbor: Institute for Social Research, The University of Michigan.

Cullen, K.A., Gentzke, A.S., Sawdey, M.D., Chang, J.T., & Anic, G.M. et al. (2019). E-Cigarette use among youth in the United States, 2019. JAMA 322(21): 2095–2103.

- Smoking bans in public areas and schools
- Cigarettes' decreased availability due to increased prices and more rigorous controls over underage purchases
- An increase in the popularity of e-cigarettes—in 2019, 25.5 percent of high school seniors had used an e-cigarette to vape nicotine in the last 30 days.[36]

The earlier in life a person tries cigarettes, the swifter and stronger the addiction to nicotine generally is.[37] There are psychological, social, and biological reasons underlying this phenomenon.

Teens may smoke in order to feel mature or independent, because they're bored or curious, or because they lack the skills to resist pressures to smoke. They may smoke to gain social acceptance or to rebel. Exposure to tobacco advertisements or images of smoking or vaping in movies also encourages teen use of tobacco or nicotine.

Some adolescents are particularly at risk. Some factors that raise a teen's chance of smoking include the following:[38,39,40]

- Having parents, siblings, or friends who smoke
- Being from a single parent or low-income household
- Growing up with a household member who is mentally ill, abuses substances, or has been in jail
- Having suffered physical, emotional, or sexual abuse
- Having poor grades and/or low self-esteem
- Suffering from depression
- Being exposed to cigarette ads and images of smoking in movies

Biology plays a role as well. An adolescent's brain is different than an adult's brain. The frontal lobe—responsible for making rational, sensible decisions—is not yet fully developed. Teen brains are also more sensitive to the rewarding effects of nicotine than are those of older individuals.[41] Edward Levin and colleagues studied the self-administration of nicotine in rats. When rats were first given nicotine during adolescence, they self-administered significantly greater amounts of nicotine compared with rats who were first exposed to nicotine during adulthood.[42] This increased nicotine intake persisted into adulthood. In fact, many scientists consider nicotine to be a gateway drug. Cigarette use tends to precede initiation of other drugs, and it appears that nicotine may activate a gene that underlies the learning process involved in addiction. It may also enhance reinforcement in the brain, making it especially hard to quit.[43,44]

Ask yourself: What do you think is the most significant reason someone starts smoking? Given your answer, what would you recommend to decrease smoking's prevalence?

Economic, Legal, and Social Issues Related to Tobacco and Nicotine

Tobacco has a powerful influence on the U.S. economy. Each year, tobacco companies spend billions of dollars to promote their brands and products. In addition, tobacco-related medical expenses and lost workplace productivity costs the United States billions of dollars a year.

Economics

The global cigarette industry is one of the most profitable in the world; in 2018, cigarette retail was valued at over $713 billion, and over 80 percent of this market is controlled by just 5 transnational companies.[45] In 1959, the average price of a pack of cigarettes in California was 25 cents. Today, it's $8.76 and the national average price is $7.26 (Figure 10.9).[46,47] But when one considers the cost to the state's economy due to healthcare expenditures and workplace productivity loss, the cost

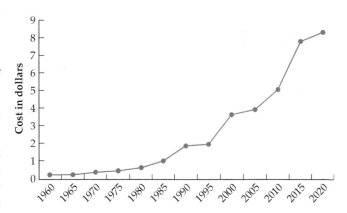

FIGURE 10.9. Average price of a pack of cigarettes in California, by year. Cigarette prices have risen dramatically in recent years. Costs are highest in New York, where a pack can cost as much as $14 or more.

Sources: Hirsig, R.J. (2009). Cigarette taxes, prices, and sales. Sacramento, CA: State Board of Equalization. http://www.boe.ca.gov/news/cigarette_price_effects_d2.pdf

Holmes, J. (2015). What a pack of cigarette costs, in every state. https://theawl.com/what-a-pack-of-cigarettes-costs-in-every-state-173b6cb1fb9#.68nhupjk3

World Population Review. (2020). Cigarette prices by state, 2020. Accessed on May 1, 2020, from https://worldpopulationreview.com/states/cigarette-prices-by-state/

is significantly higher.[48] In addition, when individuals spend money on tobacco, this often reduces resources available for food, health care, and education.

Electronic cigarettes also impact the economy. E-cigarettes generated $20 million in sales in 2008, $500 million in 2012, $2.5 billion in 2014, and $7 billion in 2019.[49]

Legal Considerations

Tobacco is legal for adult use in the United States. In 2019, legislation was enacted to raise the federal minimum age for purchasing any tobacco product, including cigarettes, cigars, and e-cigarettes, to 21.

Drug Testing

Some companies won't hire smokers, and many have potential employees take a nicotine test. This test can detect whether a person has cotinine, a nicotine metabolite, in their system. Companies do this to avoid paying higher health insurance premiums and present a health-positive public image.

Regulation of Tobacco and E-Cigarettes

Since 2009, the FDA has regulated the manufacture, import, packaging, labeling, advertising, promotion, sale, and distribution of cigarettes. Right now, there are about 8–15 mg of nicotine per cigarette, and the average smoker absorbs about 10 percent of that. In 2017, the commissioner of the FDA announced a comprehensive plan to substantially explore lowering the nicotine level in cigarettes to about 0.3–0.5 mg.[50] Studies suggest that lowering the nicotine levels in cigarettes to minimally addictive levels would mean that millions of people would quit and avoid becoming hooked, which

Critical Evaluation

Should tobacco be legal?

Many criteria are used to determine a drug's legal status. Its positive and negative physical effects, its potential for addiction, and its social and economic consequences may all be taken into account. Should tobacco's legal status be reconsidered?

Legal considerations. A schedule I drug is one that has a high potential for abuse, has no currently accepted medical use in the United States, and is not safe to use even under medical supervision. Unlike many of the drugs currently listed as schedule I, tobacco meets all of these criteria, and yet it is not only not a schedule I drug, it is unscheduled, legal, and freely available. Why is tobacco not classified as schedule I? Should it be? Why or why not?

Medical considerations. There are many factors to contemplate when analyzing a drug's safety and use. What are its risks? Its benefits? Do you think the benefits of tobacco outweigh its risks? How does one determine the "appropriate" risk-to-benefit ratio that makes a drug freely available?

Philosophical considerations. Everyone has views about the way the world should be, and these feelings color interpretations about many issues. What are the value assumptions underlying your beliefs about tobacco's legal status? How do you rate the relative value of personal freedoms, social responsibility, and the role of the government in protecting public safety? How do

your underlying feelings about these values affect your view of tobacco?

Historical considerations. Profits from tobacco sales helped to finance the War of Independence and thus helped pay for American independence. But tobacco was also one of the reasons African men, women, and children were first kidnapped and brought as slaves to America, which led to one of the darkest stains on our nation's history. Should these facts matter when considering a drug's legal status? Are these both red herrings, or are they relevant to tobacco's current legal status?

Economic considerations. The CDC estimates that tobacco smoking costs Americans over $300 billion a year, including direct medical care and lost productivity.[53] But on the other hand, heavy smokers might not live long enough to collect their Social Security benefits. How does one put a price on the medical, social, and psychological costs of smoking?

Social considerations. In general, Americans value the personal liberties and freedoms they are granted by being American citizens. And yet, Americans also depend on their government to keep them safe. Finding the right balance is often challenging. Does a person have the right to engage in self-destructive behavior? Or does society have a moral obligation to help individuals overcome their dangerous habits? Are smokers ultimately being helped or simply stigmatized by the establishment of nonsmoking areas?

would lead to a substantial reduction in tobacco-related death.[51]

Since 2016, the FDA is also responsible for regulating electronic nicotine delivery systems. However, as of 2020, the FDA has not evaluated most vaping devices or flavored liquids for safety. In 2017, then-President Trump appointed Scott Gottlieb as commissioner of the FDA. Gottlieb, who had previously served on the board of a chain of vaping lounges, gave the ENDS companies a 4-year reprieve before they would have to prove that their products were safe and effective.[52] This decision was overturned by a federal judge, and e-cigarette companies were required to submit evidence and apply for product approval in 2020, although many firms did not submit their pre-market applications.

You can further consider tobacco's legal status in the Critical Evaluation feature.

Advertising

Since 1971, when cigarette ads were banned in the U.S. broadcast media, the tobacco industry has exponentially increased the size of its marketing budget.[54] In 2017, tobacco companies spent $9.4 billion on ads and promotions.[55] This amounts to over $25 million *per day* on advertising. This budget includes promotional items such as lighters and T-shirts, as well as ads. Savvy marketers have also turned to social media to promote their product, and some companies pay influencers to post images using tobacco products or vapes, and to use hashtags for their product. In 2019, Facebook and Instagram banned influencers from getting paid to promote tobacco or vaping products.

Unlike traditional cigarettes, e-cigarettes and other ENDS can be advertised on TV and radio, and their marketing is unregulated. These products are highly marketed to youth and young adults. Studies suggest that when young people view promotional material for ENDS at retail stores or on television, they have a higher likelihood of initiating ENDS use later on.[56]

Despite spending billions of dollars on marketing, the tobacco companies claim that ads are not designed to make people start smoking, only to get people to switch brands. These claims notwithstanding, research indicates that exposure to advertising and promotional items does encourage smoking, and the ads are designed to attract specific markets (Figure 10.10).[57,58,59,60] Chris Reiter, R.J. Reynolds' campaign program manager, was famously quoted in 2003 as saying, "If you can market a product that kills people, you can sell anything."

FIGURE 10.10. **Cigarette ads are designed to appeal to specific markets.** In 1968, Virginia Slims cigarettes were introduced and marketed to women. In the 6 years that followed, the number of young women age 12–18 who smoked more than doubled. Lung cancer and COPD death rates in women increased almost four-fold in the decades following the introduction of Virginia Slims.

Tobacco companies target teens and young adults as "replacement smokers" for the more than 480,000 smokers who die each year from smoking-related diseases. They know that most smokers start in their teens. Excerpts from confidential company documents that were revealed to the public include "Today's teenager is tomorrow's regular customer" (Philip Morris); "The base of our business is the high school student" (Lorillard Tobacco); and the R.J. Reynolds statements "If our company is to survive and prosper, over the long term we must get our share of the youth market" and "Younger adult smokers are the only source of replacement smokers."[61] Many of the company's ads and promotions are aimed at youth—through magazines with young subscribers, sponsorship of sporting events favored by the young, and product placement in entertainment.[62]

Joe Camel first appeared in U.S. advertising in 1988 (Figure 10.11). At that time, 0.5 percent of smokers under age 18 smoked Camels. By 1991, almost 33 percent of teen smokers smoked Camels.[63] Joe Camel ads, which many believed were targeted at children and adolescents, were ubiquitous and effective. More than 91 percent of six-year-olds were able to correctly identify a picture of Old Joe and connect him with cigarettes; only Mickey Mouse was more widely recognized.[64]

In 1998, Philip Morris announced that it was prepared to spend $100 million a year in a U.S. campaign to reduce teen smoking, which sounds delightfully altruistic. In reality, however, exposure to Philip Morris's antismoking ads made teens less likely to hold negative attitudes about cigarettes and actually increased the youths' future likelihood of smoking.[65]

Ask yourself: If you were going to design an ad to prevent today's youth from smoking, what would it look like? On the other hand, if you were trying to encourage today's youth to smoke, what would that ad look like?

The Truth Campaign, on the other hand, was created by and for young people, and was designed to show the impact of tobacco in emotional ways. These ads *were* highly successful (Chapter 18). The percentage of youth age 12–17 years who were aware of anti-tobacco campaigns doubled in the first 10 months of The Truth Campaign. The percentage of young people using tobacco fell dramatically, from 36 percent in 1997 to 22 percent in 2003.[66] The Truth Campaign cost $324 million to develop, deliver, evaluate, and litigate but recouped its costs and averted about $1.9 billion in medical costs for society.[67]

Movies

Although cigarette smoking is rare on television, it is commonly depicted in films; in 2018, 46 percent of the top-grossing Hollywood films and 31 percent of films rated for young people portrayed smoking.[68] The total number of individual occurrences of tobacco use within movies has increased since 2010.[69] Although smoking has declined significantly in real life since the 1960s, in films today, adults are commonly shown smoking, and film heroes smoke significantly more often than their age, race, and gender matches in real life (Figure 10.12).[70]

FIGURE 10.11. Joe Camel was designed to attract young smokers. Joe Camel increased Camel Cigarette's market share among teen smokers by 6600%.

FIGURE 10.12. Films often portray the heroes smoking. Tobacco companies pay to have their products prominently displayed in movies. Here, Scarlett Johansson is shown smoking in the movie *The Black Dahlia*.

The depiction of smoking could be dismissed as "it's just a movie," except for the fact that the more teens are exposed to smoking in the movies, the more they are likely to experiment with smoking themselves.[71,72,73] In fact, tobacco use in films is the largest single factor influencing teen smoking—more than parents, peers, or cigarette ads.[74] Adolescents who watch movies in which characters smoke are almost three times more likely to start smoking as those who do not watch such movies[75,76] The Centers for Disease Control and Prevention (CDC) estimate that watching on-screen smoking in movies may encourage more than 6 million children to begin smoking—one-half of whom would ultimately die due to the habit.[77]

Why does seeing smoking in movies increase actual smoking? When adolescents see celebrities smoking, this makes the behavior more attractive. Adolescents may associate smoking with appealing qualities such as toughness, sexiness, and rebelliousness.[78] Also, when smokers watch movies in which actors smoke cigarettes, this may trigger cravings. Simply watching someone else smoke activates the part of the brain that plans hand movements, such as those required for lighting up.[79]

Sources and Forms of Tobacco and Nicotine

People ingest tobacco in many ways. They may smoke it in the form of cigarettes, cigars, or pipes, or they may use smokeless forms to snort it into their nostrils, chew it, or absorb it across their gums. No matter the source, however, all tobacco contains nicotine.

Nicotine is a poisonous and highly addictive alkaloid stimulant. A key ingredient in insecticides, nicotine is one of the most toxic of all drugs, about as toxic as cyanide. In fact, drop for drop, nicotine is deadlier than arsenic. About 40–60 mg is fatal to an adult. A typical cigar contains 120 mg of nicotine, but tobacco users do not absorb all of the nicotine into their bloodstream, as that would be almost instantly fatal. Nicotine occurs naturally from only one source—the leaves of the tobacco plant.

Growing, Harvesting, and Processing Tobacco

Tobacco plants are native to North America and other parts of the Western Hemisphere, but they are now grown primarily in Turkey, India, and Russia. There are two major forms: the taller, large-leafed *Nicotiana tabacum*, which is the principal source of modern-day tobacco (Figure 10.13); and the smaller *Nicotiana rustica*. The nicotine content of the leaves ranges from 0.3–7.0 percent, depending on the variety of plant, position of the leaf on the stalk (the higher the leaf, the more nicotine it contains), and the growing conditions. Nicotine's toxicity helps to protect the tobacco plant from being eaten by animals.

QUICK HIT

Tobacco is grown in at least 124 countries and occupies millions of acres of land that could otherwise be used to grow food crops. Many of the top tobacco-producing countries have undernourishment rates between 10 and 27 percent.[80]

After being harvested, the tobacco is dried, or cured. Tobacco can be air-cured, fire-cured, or flue-cured, each of which produces tobacco with different pH and nicotine levels. After the tobacco leaf is dried and shredded, manufacturers remoisten it with glycerin and pack it into huge silos, where the tobacco is stored for up to two years. Eighty-five percent of the tobacco grown in the United States is used for making cigarettes.

Smoking Tobacco

Cigarettes are the most common way, and the most toxic way, to use tobacco. Nearly one-fourth of the tobacco in a cigarette comes from tobacco scraps that

FIGURE 10.13. The tobacco plant. *Nicotiana tabacum* is the principal source of modern-day tobacco.

have been made into reconstituted sheets. These sheets are a pulp of mashed tobacco stems and other parts of the leaf that would otherwise be discarded. In order to control its flavor, color, moisture, and addictiveness, manufacturers spray this sheet with as many as 600 chemical additives, at least 250 of which are known to be harmful.[81,82]

Some of these harmful substances include hydrogen cyanide (used in lethal execution by gas), chlorofluorocarbons (refrigerants), acetylene (found in welding torches), phenol (a toilet bowl disinfectant), toluene (an industrial solvent), lead, cadmium (found in car batteries), ammonia (used to clean toilets), and formaldehyde (an embalming agent). Among these 250 harmful chemicals, more than 70 are known carcinogens, including arsenic, benzene (found in napalm), benzopyrene, the insecticide DDT, ethylene oxide, vinyl chloride, nitrosamines, polycyclic aromatic hydrocarbons, polonium-210 (found in nuclear waste), and uranium-235 (found in nuclear weapons).

Tobacco smoke contains over 4,000 chemicals, some gaseous and some particulate. The gaseous phase of tobacco smoke includes ammonia, hydrogen cyanide, acetone, acetaldehyde, carbon dioxide, and carbon monoxide (CO). Many people have CO detectors in their homes, which set off a piercing shriek when they detect the fatal substance. Many of these same people smoke cigarettes, thus inhaling CO directly into their lungs with each puff.

The small particles suspended in smoke include tar and nicotine. **Tar**, the brown, sticky, particulate matter generated by burning tobacco, clogs up the cilia in the airway, so contaminants and carcinogenic substances that would normally be cleared from the lungs are allowed to settle on the tissue. Tar contains dozens of carcinogens and is the substance that is mainly responsible for the diseases associated with long-term tobacco use.

Manufacturers adjust the nicotine content of cigarettes. Tobacco companies extract nicotine from the tobacco leaf and add it back to tobacco in controlled amounts, which results in an even distribution of nicotine in each cigarette. The process also ensures there is enough tobacco for smokers to become addicted.[83] Evidence strongly suggests that tobacco companies manipulated and controlled the amount of nicotine in cigarettes to make them more addictive. The nicotine content of domestic cigarettes in the United States has increased over the years, with an average increase of 1.78 percent per year.[84]

Tar: The particulate matter generated by burning tobacco.

Menthol is a substance found in mint that gives a cooling sensation. Menthol was first added to cigarettes in the 1920s, and the tobacco industry once marketed menthol cigarettes as being healthier than nonmentholated cigarettes. Menthol cigarettes are aggressively marketed to and purchased mostly by African American smokers—86 percent of African American smokers use mentholated cigarettes, compared to less than 30 percent of Caucasian smokers.[85] Scientists recently found a gene associated with a preference for menthol cigarettes. This gene—found only in people of African descent—is 5–8 times more frequent in smokers who use menthol cigarettes than in other smokers.[86] Not only are menthol cigarettes not healthier, but they may be more addictive than regular cigarettes. In 2021, the FDA announced a plan to ban the sales, manufacture, and import of menthol cigarettes. The ban could save 633,000 lives by the year 2050.

Cigars and pipes were most popular in the nineteenth century and into the early decades of the twentieth century. Pipes have a hollow stem and bowl. Tobacco is placed in the bowl of the pipe and lit; smoke travels up the stem and is pulled into the smoker's mouth. A cigar is a tightly rolled cylinder of dried tobacco leaves, which are held together by a binder leaf. Expensive cigars are rolled by hand, but most are mass marketed and machine rolled. Cigars come in different sizes. Small and slender cigars are called cigarillos; panatelas are longer and slim, and coronas are large and thick.

The Family Smoking Prevention and Tobacco Control Act of 2009 banned flavored cigarettes but was silent on flavored cigars, which are not only significantly less expensive than a pack of cigarettes, but are also available in chocolate, grape, strawberry, and pineapple flavors, making them popular among young smokers.

Electronic Nicotine Delivery Systems

Electronic cigarettes and vapes deliver the nicotine as an aerosol, so no tobacco is consumed. E-cigarettes typically contain three ingredients—nicotine, flavoring, and a humectant—a synthetic liquid such as propylene glycol in which the nicotine is heated. Almost all e-cigarettes contain nicotine, although many young e-cigarette users believe the device mostly contains flavoring.[87] In fact, e-cigarettes in the United States contain nearly 3 times the legal limit of nicotine allowed in ENDS in the European Union.[88] Until recently, users could choose from among more than 60 flavors of nicotine liquid. These flavors were particularly appealing to youth, but in 2020, the FDA began to enforce bans on some types of flavored e-cigarettes, allowing only tobacco and menthol flavors. (Although the FDA announced plans to ban menthol cigarettes, they have not yet committed to banning menthol-flavored vape products.) Although many of the humectants have been approved by the FDA for oral consumption, they are not approved for inhalation into the delicate tissues of the lungs, and the long-term effects on the lung are unknown.

The use of e-cigarettes, also called **vaping**, has greatly increased over the past few years, particularly among the young; more young people use e-cigarettes than any other nicotine-containing product.

ENDS come in many different forms. The first-generation resembled cigarettes, but people found there was still a stigma with using what looked like traditional cigarettes, so later generations were made to resemble pens or flash drives. Juul is the most popular brand of e-cigarette, controlling almost three-quarters of the market.[89] Juul has a sleek, high-tech design, rechargeable batteries, and significantly more nicotine than other e-cigarettes on the market. Juul uses protonated nicotine from tobacco rather than the more acidic form used in other e-cigarettes, so it is easier to inhale and is absorbed into the bloodstream almost 3 times faster than other e-cigarettes, increasing the risk of addiction. In 2021, Juul agreed to pay North Carolina $40 million to settle the first of several lawsuits which claimed that the company's marketing techniques led to widespread nicotine addiction among the young.[90] In 2020, the FDA banned flavored pods, but a loophole in the federal regulations allowed flavored vapes to be sold in disposable e-cigarettes. Since then, sales of disposable vaping products such as Puff Bars, which are available in kid-appealing flavors, have far surpassed Juul and other cartridge-based devices.[91]

The FDA has not yet evaluated e-cigarettes for safety or effectiveness. Vaping does indeed reduce the smoker's exposure to tar, but the long-term effects of regularly inhaling propylene glycol are unknown. Many of the compounds found in the vapor are potentially toxic, and the more the e-cigarette is used, the more harmful chemicals it emits.[92] "Dripping," a practice of pouring the e-liquid directly on the heating element of a vaping device and inhaling the thick vapor clouds, is increasingly popular among teens. Unfortunately, this practice exposes users to higher levels of toxic chemicals such as aldehydes.[93] Some researchers have found that e-cigarettes are linked to increased arterial stiffness, blood pressure, and heart rate, and may cause mutations in lung tissue.[94,95] Studies also have found that quality control processes governing ENDS might be substandard or nonexistent, and carcinogenic substances have been detected in the cartridges of some brands. The FDA issued warning letters to several distributors of e-cigarettes for violating the Federal Food, Drug, and Cosmetic Act. These violations included "unsubstantiated claims and poor manufacturing practices."[96] E-cigarettes are also dangerous due to the batteries, which can explode, and because exposure to the highly concentrated liquid nicotine in the canister can be lethal. In 2019, an outbreak of vaping-related lung illness led to many deaths.

Smokeless Tobacco

Over 8.5 million Americans, or 3.1 percent of the population, report current use of smokeless tobacco.[97] Some people use smokeless tobacco because it allows them to get their nicotine fix in situations where smoking is inconvenient or prohibited. There is also a (false) perception that smokeless tobacco is safe. In actuality, smokeless tobacco users are exposed to dozens of carcinogenic agents and suffer other health risks as well.

Smokeless tobacco comes in two main categories—chewing tobacco and snuff. **Chewing tobacco** is sweetened, loose tobacco leaves. The user can chew the leaves or hold a pinch between the cheek and gum. Because the tobacco is not ground, it must be manually crushed to release the flavor and nicotine. Smokeless tobacco stimulates the salivary glands, so the user needs to spit occasionally.

Snuff is finely ground tobacco that is mixed with salts, oils, flavorings, and other additives. Snuff can be moist or dry, and it is packaged in cans or sachets. Moist snuff, also called dipping tobacco or dip, is ground-up tobacco that is placed between the lower lip and gum. Snus, which comes in a pouch, is a steam-cured, moist, powdered tobacco product that is not fermented and does not stimulate the salivary glands, so it doesn't require spitting. Unlike dip, snus is usually placed between the upper lip and gum. Dry snuff is snorted into the nose. The user takes a pinch of tobacco dust between the thumb and forefinger and inhales sharply.

Vaping: The process of inhaling and exhaling the vapor produced by an electronic cigarette or similar device. The electronic cigarette itself is sometimes called a vape.

Chewing tobacco: A form of smokeless tobacco that is sold in packets of sweetened, loose tobacco leaves that are sometimes fashioned into long strands or twists.

Snuff: A form of finely ground and powdered smokeless tobacco that is snorted into the nose or inserted between the gum and lip.

In 2019, people started showing up in emergency rooms, dizzy, vomiting, and gasping for breath. One thing that these patients, most of whom were otherwise healthy, had in common was vaping.

E-cigarette or vaping product use-associated lung injury, also known as EVALI, was first recognized by the CDC in August of 2019. Most patients were young men who had used vaping products, some containing nicotine and some THC. Most of the THC-containing vape products used were counterfeit or illicitly obtained from friends, dealers, and online, but most patients who used nicotine-containing products acquired them from commercial sources.

As of February 2020, EVALI was associated with over 2800 hospitalizations and 68 deaths. At that point, the CDC stopped updating on EVALI deaths, in part due to the emergency of the COVID-19 pandemic. Vaping and tobacco may increase one's risk of infection with COVID-19; compared with non-users, those who reported the use of e-cigarettes or tobacco had a five- to seven-fold increased risk of a COVID-19 diagnosis. Additionally, nicotine might upregulate the ACE2 receptor, the point of entry for the CoV-2 virus.

Sources:

CDC. (2020). Outbreak of lung injury associated with the use of e-cigarette, or vaping, products. Accessed on April 29, 2020, from https://www.cdc.gov/tobacco/basic_information/e-cigarettes/severe-lung-disease.html.

Lancet Editorial Board. (2020). The EVALI outbreak and vaping in the COVID-19 era. The Lancet Respiratory Medicine, 8(9): p. 831.

Reagan-Steiner, S., Gary, J., Matkovic, E., Ritter, J.M., & Shieh, W-J., et al. (2020). Pathological findings in suspected cases of e-cigarette, or vaping, product use-associated lung injury (EVALI): A case series. The Lancet Respiratory Medicine, doi: 10.1016/S2213-2600(20)30321-0.

Ask yourself: Smokeless tobacco is more than twice as popular in the southern United States as it is in the Northeast. What is your perception of someone who uses smokeless tobacco, and how much does this correspond with regional differences?

Pharmacokinetics of Tobacco and Nicotine

How does the body process nicotine? And by what mechanisms does nicotine exert its effects? This section examines the dosage, absorption, distribution, metabolism, elimination, and drug interactions of nicotine.

Dosage, Absorption, and Distribution

A cigarette, pipe, cigar, dip, or (usually) vape is a drug-delivery system for nicotine. Unlike cocaine from the coca leaf or morphine from the opium poppy, nicotine from tobacco is almost never administered in its pure form. Nicotine is highly toxic and must be precisely controlled.

The average cigarette contains 8–15 mg of nicotine, and a smoker typically inhales 1.0–1.5 mg per cigarette.[98] Nicotine is rapidly absorbed into the bloodstream through the skin; the mucous lining of the nose, mouth, and gastrointestinal tract; and the lungs. The absorption of nicotine depends on a number of factors, including

- Route of administration
- Composition of tobacco and how densely it's packed into the cigarette or cigar
- Length of the cigarette and the presence and characteristics of a filter
- Number of cigarettes smoked throughout the day
- Volume of smoke inhaled
- pH of the tobacco

Because of the way it is cured, the tobacco used in cigarettes produces an acidic smoke, which allows for less absorption in the mouth and more absorption in the lungs. This is in contrast to cigar and pipe smoke, which is more alkaline, allowing for more absorption of smoke in the mouth (additionally, many cigar smokers take the smoke into their mouths, but do not inhale it into their lungs). In the 1970s, tobacco companies began adding ammonia to cigarettes to increase the absorption of nicotine. Ammonia makes the naturally acidic tobacco more alkaline, enabling the drug to pass more easily into the bloodstream.

Smoking is the most common route of administration, as well as the quickest and most efficient way to get nicotine to the brain. Smoking, whether through a cigarette, pipe, or cigar, delivers nicotine to the brain within 10–15 seconds, faster than with intravenous administration.

Nicotine is also absorbed in the oral cavity. After placing smokeless tobacco or nicotine gum in the mouth, the nicotine quickly enters the user's bloodstream through the blood vessels of the cheek and gum. Absorption is actually more complete with smokeless tobacco than with smoking, but it is delivered over a longer period of time. Typically, about 3–5 mg of nicotine enters the bloodstream when chew or dip is in the mouth continuously for 30 minutes.

Nicotine can also be absorbed across the mucous membranes of the nasal cavities, as snuff; absorbed across the skin, as transdermal patches; insufflated, as nicotine inhalers; and aerosolized, in e-cigarettes. Once absorbed, nicotine is concentrated in the brain, as well as in the liver, kidneys, salivary glands, and stomach.

Metabolism and Elimination

Nicotine is primarily metabolized in the liver, as well as in the kidneys and lungs. Nicotine has a half-life of about two hours, so blood levels begin to decline fairly rapidly and smokers quickly feel the urge for another cigarette. About 80 percent of nicotine is transformed by one of the cytochrome P450 system enzymes into two active metabolites, cotinine and nicotine-1-N-oxide.

Some factors that inhibit nicotine's metabolism, causing nicotine to stay in the system longer, include the following:

- *Food and drugs.* Menthol, grapefruit juice, some selective serotonin reuptake inhibitors (SSRIs), and smoking itself all inhibit nicotine metabolism.
- *Genetic differences.* People with low levels of the enzymes that break down nicotine are less likely to become smokers, and if they do smoke, they tend to smoke fewer cigarettes.
- *Age.* Newborns and the elderly metabolize nicotine more slowly than adults age 18–64.

Some factors enhance nicotine's metabolism, clearing nicotine from the system faster, including

- *Gender.* Women metabolize nicotine faster than men, and women who are either pregnant or who are currently taking oral contraceptives metabolize nicotine faster than nonpregnant women or women who are not on the Pill.
- *Race.* Despite smoking fewer cigarettes per day, Black men have higher levels of the nicotine metabolite cotinine than whites, as well as a higher incidence of and mortality from lung cancer than white men.

After nicotine is deactivated by liver enzymes, these products of deactivation are mostly eliminated by the kidneys, as well as by sweat, saliva, and breast milk. The pH of urine determines how much is excreted by the kidneys. The more acidic the urine, the more nicotine metabolites are eliminated.

Drug Interactions

Nicotine interacts with a number of drugs. For example, it speeds up the metabolism of the anxiolytic diazepam (Valium), the analgesic propoxyphene (Darvon), and the antidepressant imipramine (Tofranil), which means that these drugs are not as effective in smokers. Nicotine also changes the activity of certain enzymes, which increases cocaine addictiveness. Nicotine increases alcohol use, and people who are dependent on tobacco are 4–10 times more likely than nonsmokers to be addicted to alcohol. It may be that smokers just have a greater tendency toward addiction, or it may be that nicotine reinforces consumption of alcohol and other drugs. Recent studies support the latter hypothesis. Rats addicted to nicotine escalate their alcohol and cocaine use more quickly than rats that have not been exposed to nicotine.[99,100]

Mechanism of Action of Nicotine

Nicotine is a fairly simple molecule, yet it works in a complex way, affecting many neurotransmitters in both the central and peripheral nervous systems, including acetylcholine, dopamine, GABA, and glutamate. Nicotine binds to nicotinic cholinergic receptors, depolarizing and exciting them. Because it has such a high affinity for these receptors, nicotine stays bound, and the cell can't fire again until the nicotine is removed. This *prevents* transmission of information. So, nicotine, especially at high doses, has a biphasic effect that begins with stimulation, but then blocks nicotinic cholinergic activity.

Nicotine binds to cholinergic receptors in the autonomic nervous system, where it affects heart rate, blood pressure, and gastrointestinal activity; in the neuromuscular junction, where it causes skeletal muscle contraction; and in the central nervous system (CNS), where it affects focus and mood.

In the CNS, nicotine-sensitive acetylcholine receptors are located in the cortex and hippocampus, as well as in the midbrain. The reinforcing and addictive effects of nicotine are mediated through activation of the dopamine system of the midbrain, specifically in the ventral tegmentum and nucleus accumbens, the addiction centers of the brain. Cholinergic receptors in the nucleus accum-

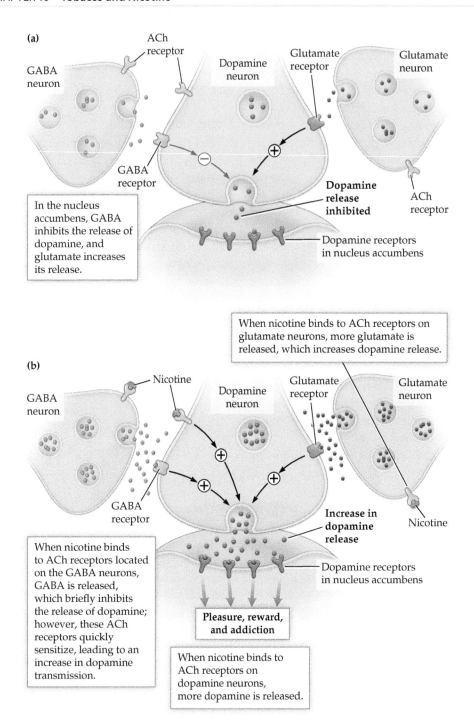

FIGURE 10.14. Nicotine affects the release of several neurotransmitters. (a) The release of dopamine in the nucleus accumbens is influenced by both glutamate and GABA. Glutamate increases the release of dopamine, and GABA inhibits its release. (b) There are nicotinic cholinergic receptors located on the nerve terminals of presynaptic dopamine, glutamate, and GABA neurons in the nucleus accumbens. When acetylcholine binds to receptors on the dopamine neurons, it increases the release of dopamine. Acetylcholine binding to glutamate receptors increases release of glutamate, thus boosting glutamate's excitatory effects on dopamine release. When acetylcholine binds to receptors on GABA neurons, it stimulates GABA's release, briefly inhibiting the release of dopamine; however, these acetylcholine receptors quickly sensitize, leading to a reduction in the inhibitory control of GABA on dopamine transmission.

bens are located on presynaptic nerve terminals of dopamine, glutamate, and GABA neurons, so nicotine affects the release of these neurotransmitters (Figure 10.14).[101] In addition, nicotine's effects on glutamate contributes to

the improvement in memory that some report. Nicotine also increases levels of beta-endorphins (analgesia), histamine (released by cells in response to injury or allergic reactions), and a number of hormones.

Acute Effects of Tobacco and Nicotine

Tobacco has complex and unpredictable effects. A person's ultimate response to nicotine depends on the sum of nicotine's excitatory and inhibitory effects, the route of administration and amount used, as well as a person's expectations and prior experience with the drug.[102]

Physiological Effects at Low and Moderate Doses

At low and moderate doses nicotine has several physiological effects (Figure 10.15). The central nervous, cardiovascular, respiratory, gastrointestinal, and endocrine systems, and muscles and skin, are all affected.

Central Nervous System

Nicotine produces alertness and arousal. It activates brain areas related to pleasure and reinforcement, which can lead to dependence. Tobacco use also can cause lightheadedness, dizziness, headache, sleep disturbances, and abnormal dreams.

Cardiovascular

Tobacco raises a user's heart rate and blood pressure, which increases the oxygen needs of the heart. As a result, the heart has to perform extra work with no extra oxygen, increasing a person's risk of heart attack and stroke, especially in women who are on oral contraceptives. The CO in cigarettes decreases the ability of blood to deliver oxygen to the tissues, exacerbating the situation. Finally, nicotine constricts the blood vessels of the hands and feet, limiting blood supply, and also increases the risk of blood clots, which further increases one's risk of heart attack and stroke.

Respiratory

When exposed to smoke, the bronchi of the lungs constrict in an effort to prevent the damaging smoke and particles from entering the lungs. Because this also limits the amount of air that enters the lungs, smoking decreases lung capacity.

Gastrointestinal

Nicotine stimulates the brain's vomiting center, and nausea and vomiting are common reactions the first few times a person uses tobacco, although users quickly become tolerant to these effects. Smokers may get dry mouth, as nicotine first stimulates salivary secretions and then inhibits them. Smoking or chewing tobacco may also reduce the function of the taste buds.

Nicotine increases the secretion of hydrochloric acid in the stomach and decreases gastrointestinal tone and muscle contraction in the intestine, which can lead to diarrhea. Nicotine suppresses the appetite, especially for sweet foods. Cigarette smokers weigh an average of 8–10 pounds less than gender- and age-matched nonsmokers, but this also may be due to smoking-related illnesses adversely affecting one's weight.

Endocrine

Nicotine affects many hormones in the body, increasing release of

- Epinephrine and norepinephrine (hormones of the sympathetic nervous system);
- Vasopressin (also known as antidiuretic hormone), which causes fluid retention and raises blood pressure;

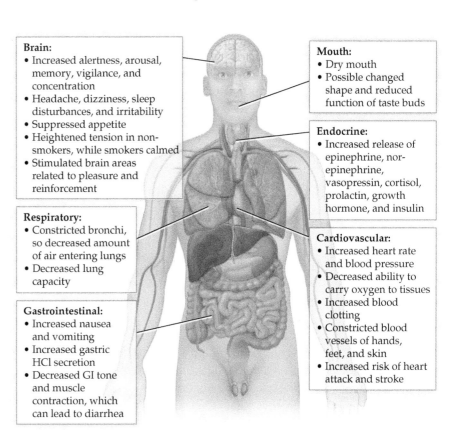

Brain:
- Increased alertness, arousal, memory, vigilance, and concentration
- Headache, dizziness, sleep disturbances, and irritability
- Suppressed appetite
- Heightened tension in nonsmokers, while smokers calmed
- Stimulated brain areas related to pleasure and reinforcement

Respiratory:
- Constricted bronchi, so decreased amount of air entering lungs
- Decreased lung capacity

Gastrointestinal:
- Increased nausea and vomiting
- Increased gastric HCl secretion
- Decreased GI tone and muscle contraction, which can lead to diarrhea

Mouth:
- Dry mouth
- Possible changed shape and reduced function of taste buds

Endocrine:
- Increased release of epinephrine, norepinephrine, vasopressin, cortisol, prolactin, growth hormone, and insulin

Cardiovascular:
- Increased heart rate and blood pressure
- Decreased ability to carry oxygen to tissues
- Increased blood clotting
- Constricted blood vessels of hands, feet, and skin
- Increased risk of heart attack and stroke

FIGURE 10.15. Acute effects of smoking tobacco.

- Cortisol (stress);
- Prolactin (stimulates milk production after childbirth);
- Growth hormone (stimulates growth and increases blood glucose levels); and
- Insulin (this hyperinsulinemia, as well as the increased blood sugar from growth hormone, can lead to insulin resistance and raise a tobacco-user's risk for type 2 diabetes).

Skeletomuscular and Skin

Low to moderate nicotine reduces muscle tone, while high doses can lead to tremors and joint pain. Nicotine constricts blood vessels to the skin and decreases skin temperature, so smokers do not blush as easily as nonsmokers.

Overdose

As mentioned previously, nicotine is toxic. Its therapeutic index is 21, which means that 50 percent of individuals who smoked an entire pack of cigarettes at once would die shortly thereafter. Nicotine is even more dangerous when combined with cocaine or other drugs that increase heart rate or reduce the oxygen-carrying capacity of the blood.

Overdose is rare but possible. Those suffering from nicotine poisoning will first feel dizzy, weak, and nauseated. Excessive salivation, sweating, and vomiting will follow, along with diarrhea, headache, mental confusion, and breathing difficulties. The poisoned victim's blood pressure will fall and his or her pulse will weaken. If untreated, he or she will undergo tremors, convulsions, and death from respiratory failure.

Behavioral and Psychological Effects at Low and Moderate Doses

Nicotine also has behavioral and psychological effects at low and moderate doses. Nicotine can affect both mood and cognitive function.

Mood

Nicotine heightens tension and irritability in nonsmokers, but calms and relaxes smokers. This may be because smokers find the ritual calming, or because nicotine eventually relaxes skeletal muscle, but it is probably due to the alleviation of withdrawal symptoms.

Smoking is associated with depression; heavy smokers are four times more likely to have a history of major depression. There is evidence that some depressed smokers may be unknowingly self-medicating—substances other than nicotine that are present in tobacco

Ask yourself: If smokers are more likely to have depression, does this mean that smoking causes depression? Or are those with depression more likely to smoke? How is it possible to determine the answer?

smoke inhibit MAO, an enzyme that breaks down dopamine and serotonin, so it may act as an antidepressant and improve some symptoms of depression.[103,104]

Cognitive Function

Nicotine may enhance memory, vigilance, sensorimotor performance, cognitive functioning, and rapid information processing for a brief time after its administration. When abstinent smokers were given nicotine, they performed better at cognitive tasks, especially those that required them to pay attention.[105] Of course, this might be due to relief from withdrawal symptoms, but there is some evidence that nicotine also enhances attention and cognitive function in nonsmokers.

Adults and adolescents with attention-deficit/hyperactivity disorder (ADHD) smoke much more frequently than those without. Just as people with depression may be self-medicating by smoking, those with ADHD may be unconsciously trying to improve their focus; nicotine administered by transdermal patch produces improved concentration and performance.[106] But if you're not a smoker, don't believe that smoking will help you study for exams! The nausea, dizziness, oxygen deficit, and CO are more detrimental to your cognitive abilities than nicotine's brief and unproven benefits can justify.

Chronic Effects of Tobacco and Nicotine

Chronic tobacco use has widespread effects on the entire body. Tolerance and dependence occur quickly, as do withdrawal symptoms when the user is deprived of the drug. Long-term use can lead to severe adverse effects including cancer, cardiovascular disease, and death.

Tolerance

The first time someone smokes, he or she will most likely experience dizziness, sweating, heart palpitations, and nausea. Fun! It does seem baffling as to why anyone would want to do that again, but obviously tobacco has a powerful appeal. Tolerance to some effects develops within hours, as compared to days or weeks for heroin and months for alcohol. So, a new smoker can go from a green, dizzy, nauseated, sweaty mess to a one-pack-a-day smoker within weeks. But smokers show little or no tolerance to nicotine's effects on increasing heart rate, tremor, and vasoconstriction to the skin and extremities.

Tobacco users undergo metabolic, cellular, and behavioral tolerance. In metabolic tolerance, the body speeds up its metabolism of a drug in order to eliminate the drug faster. Nicotine metabolism is indeed enhanced in smokers; nonsmokers excrete larger amounts of unchanged nicotine in their urine than do smokers. And smokers experience more of an effect from their first cigarette of the day compared to those smoked later in the day. Metabolic tolerance occurs because some substance in tobacco increases the activity of the liver enzymes that deactivate the drug. Tobacco also causes cellular tolerance; with continued tobacco use, nicotinic receptors, including ones that influence reinforcement and reward, are desensitized. Finally, tobacco leads to a small degree of behavioral tolerance, as learned cues associated with the drug—such as stepping outside to the smoking area—can cause the body to reverse some of nicotine's effects.

Withdrawal

Abstinent smokers experience withdrawal symptoms fairly rapidly. These symptoms include craving; mood changes, such as irritability, anxiety, restlessness, depression, and difficulty concentrating; physiological effects like headaches, drowsiness, insomnia, increased appetite and weight gain, and gastrointestinal disturbances; and cognitive symptoms, such as impaired concentration, judgment, and psychomotor performance.

Symptoms may begin within a few hours or days after the last cigarette, and may continue for weeks or even months. Physical symptoms are usually gone within two weeks, but psychological and social habits are powerful enticements, and many abstinent smokers resume the habit, even long after their physical withdrawal symptoms have passed.

Adverse Effects from Chronic Use

Tobacco addiction is the single greatest cause of premature death in the world. Around the world, a person dies every seven seconds due to smoking-related disease. The annual global death toll is over 7 million and climbing; this is mostly concentrated in low- and middle-income countries.[107,108]

One could argue that there are many other threats to global health. But, as researchers concluded in a report by the World Health Organization, unlike tobacco, "infectious diseases do not employ multinational public relations firms, there are no front groups to promote the spread of cholera, [and] mosquitoes have no lobbyists."[109]

QUICK HIT

There is no such thing as a safe use of tobacco. Tobacco is the only product advertised that is lethal when used as intended.

In the United States, tobacco remains the number one cause of preventable disease, disability, and death, killing 480,000 Americans each year—more than alcohol, illegal drugs, fires, motor vehicle injuries, homicide, suicide, and AIDS *combined*.[110,111] At least one out of every five Americans today will die due to tobacco (Figure 10.16),[112] and only about 40 percent of smokers will live past the age of 65 (Figure 10.17).[113] According to the CDC, adult male smokers lose 13.2 years of life, and female smokers lose 14.5 years of life.

QUICK HIT

Texas death row inmate Larry White asked for a last cigarette before his execution. His request was denied due to prison policy, on the grounds that it would have been bad for his health.[114]

Tobacco use has many adverse effects. Some, such as wrinkles and sexual dysfunction are unpleasant but not life-threatening. Other adverse effects may significantly diminish a smoker's quality of life. Smoking is causally associated with type 2 diabetes, cataracts and macular degeneration, hearing loss, liver and colorectal cancers, Crohn's disease, tuberculosis, rheumatoid arthritis, osteoporosis, inflammation, and impaired immune function.[115] Other life-threatening conditions that may result from chronic tobacco use include cardiovascular disease, cancer, and chronic obstructive pulmonary disease (COPD).

QUICK HIT

Over half of all lifetime smokers will ultimately die of a disease caused by smoking. For every 1,000 tons of tobacco produced, about 1,000 people will eventually die.[116]

(a)   (b)   (c)

FIGURE 10.16. Tobacco-related deaths. Many notable celebrities have died of smoking-related cancer, heart attacks, or other tobacco-related causes, including (a) comedian and actress Lucille Ball, (b) noted psychologist Sigmund Freud, and (c) animator, producer, and entrepreneur Walt Disney.

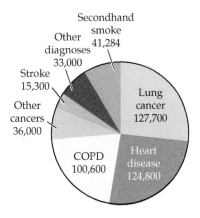

FIGURE 10.17. Incidence of smoking-related deaths. Smoking causes almost half a million deaths each year in the United States.

Source: CDC. (2018). Tobacco-related mortality. Accessed on May 4, 2020, from https://www.cdc.gov/tobacco/data_statistics/fact_sheets/health_ effects/tobacco_related_mortality/index.htm

Skin

Smokers have thinner, prematurely aged, and more wrinkled skin. This is because smokers' skin is starved of oxygen due to nicotine's constriction of the tiny blood vessels that nourish the underlying skin cells. Tobacco smoke also impairs the production of collagen.[117]

Cardiovascular disease: Also called heart disease, this is a broad term that includes a range of diseases that affect the heart, including coronary heart disease and ischemic stroke.

Reproductive Effects

Tobacco use can raise the risk of impotence, reduced sperm production, sluggish sperm motility, menstrual disorders, early menopause, ectopic pregnancy, miscarriage, and diminished libido in both men and women.

Cardiovascular Disease

Cardiovascular disease is the single biggest killer in the United States. Cardiovascular disease is a broad term that covers a range of conditions that affect the heart, including blood vessel diseases, heart infections and defects, and abnormal heart rhythms. Coronary heart disease (CHD) is one common type of cardiovascular disease in which the heart is damaged due to restriction of blood flow through narrowed or blocked coronary arteries. Without adequate blood flow, the heart becomes starved of oxygen, which increases its workload. This can lead to a myocardial infarction (heart attack). Smoking is implicated in 30 percent of all deaths from CHD. One's risk of CHD doubles if one smokes and quadruples if one smokes heavily. Ischemic stroke is another type of cardiovascular disease that involves an interruption or reduction of blood flow to the brain.

Chronic Obstructive Pulmonary Disease (COPD)

Smoking causes ash and sticky tars to be deposited on the delicate membranes of the lungs. This damages the airways, alveoli, and elastic fibers of the lung, and destroys the cilia that sweep out harmful particles. **Chronic obstructive pulmonary disease (COPD)** is a group of lung diseases characterized by chronic airflow obstruction, including chronic bronchitis, in which excess mucus builds up in the air passages, and emphysema, when the lung's air sacs lose their elasticity. These serious and irreversible diseases appear almost exclusively in smokers.

People with COPD experience shortness of breath, lung congestion, and increased susceptibility to illness, because the lungs are more vulnerable to inhaled pollutants and infections. Sixteen million adults in the United States have been diagnosed with COPD: millions more have it and are undiagnosed. Chronic lower respiratory diseases are the fourth leading cause of death in the United States after heart disease, cancer, and accidents.[118]

Gastrointestinal Effects

Chewing tobacco can lead to tooth decay, gum disease, excess saliva and drooling, and precancerous sores and patches in the mouth. Both smoking and chewing tobacco can stain teeth and cause bad breath. Nicotine's increased secretion of HCl elevates the incidence and severity of heartburn and ulcers.

Cancer

Cigarette smoking causes almost 50 percent of all cancer deaths in the United States.[119] This is not a new realization; as early as 1785, a physician reported that pipe smokers were particularly afflicted by lip cancer. The first American study confirming the statistical link between smoking and lung cancer was published in the *Journal of the American Medical Association* in 1950. Epidemiologist Morton Levin showed that the risk of lung cancer was 10 times higher for heavy long-term smokers than for nonsmokers. In the same issue, Ernst Wynder and Evarts Graham found that 96.5 percent of lung cancer patients interviewed were heavy smokers.[120]

Tobacco contains many carcinogenic substances that affect the activity of genes known to increase the risk of developing cancer.[121] For example, benzo(a)pyrene, one of the most potent carcinogens known, is metabolized to a substance that damages a cancer suppressor gene. Most of the cancer-causing substances are found in tar, but nicotine is also carcinogenic on its own. Nicotine has been found to promote the growth of colon cancer and to help tumors metastasize and grow.[122,123]

Cigarettes are responsible for about 80 percent of cancers of the lung, bronchi, larynx, and trachea, and 50 percent of cancers of the mouth, esophagus, and bladder.

Ask yourself: Should nonsmoking taxpayers have to pay for the medical costs of smokers? If so, what role does personal responsibility play? If not, should people who eat badly and don't exercise be similarly penalized?

They also increase one's risk of stomach, pancreatic, kidney, cervical, and testicular cancer.[124] About 20 percent of regular smokers will get lung cancer. Within two years, 75 percent of those diagnosed with lung cancer will die. The carcinogenic effects of tobacco are not limited to cigarettes. Using smokeless tobacco quadruples one's risk of mouth, throat, and esophageal cancer.

Prenatal and Postnatal Effects

About 8.7 percent of pregnant women smoke, compared with 17.2 percent of nonpregnant women age 15–44.[125] Smoking rates in pregnant women are usually much lower than rates in women who are not pregnant, except in those under age 25—in this age group, smoking rates were similar in pregnant and nonpregnant women (Figure 10.18).[126] Smoking is harmful to the fetus, infant, and children of smokers.

When a pregnant woman smokes, nicotine, carbon monoxide, cyanide, and other deadly substances pass from the mother's blood to the fetus. Nicotine constricts

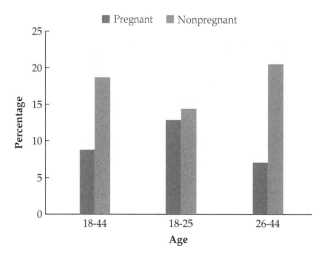

FIGURE 10.18. Cigarette use in pregnant and nonpregnant women. Pregnant women age 25 and under are more likely to smoke than are pregnant women over the age of 25.

Source: SAMHSA. (2020). Results from the 2019 National Survey on Drug Use and Health. Rockville, MD: Center for Behavioral Health Statistics and Quality.

Chronic obstructive pulmonary disease (COPD): A group of lung diseases that obstruct airflow and make breathing difficult. COPD includes emphysema and chronic bronchitis.

the blood vessels of the umbilical cord, which decreases the amount of oxygen available to the fetus. This can result in irreversible, long-term intellectual and physical deficiencies. Nicotine also may affect the developing reward system in the fetus's brain, which might predispose him or her to addictive behaviors later in life. This is what happened with rats in the research lab.

Researchers injected small doses of nicotine into pregnant rats. When the young rats who had been exposed to prenatal nicotine reached adolescence, they self-administered more nicotine, drank more alcohol, and ate more fatty foods than their unexposed peers.[127] Prenatal nicotine exposure produces changes in the brain that increase appetite, food intake, addiction, and other goal-directed behaviors. The use of nicotine patches or e-cigarettes during pregnancy could have a similar effect, given that this is due to nicotine itself, not to cigarettes.

Pregnant women who smoke have a higher risk of miscarriage, stillbirth, premature birth, and low infant birth weight. In 1969, when the U.S. Surgeon General's report confirmed the link between maternal smoking and low birth weight, the CEO of Philip Morris said that this was an advantage of smoking, because "some women would prefer having smaller babies."[128] Unfortunately, babies with a low birth weight may have an increased risk for many complications. Rates of cleft lip and cleft palate are higher in children born of women who smoked during pregnancy, as are rates of depression and ADHD. Sudden Infant Death Syndrome is more common in babies who live around smoke, but it is unclear whether this is due to their current or prenatal exposure to smoke. Pregnant women who do not smoke themselves but who are exposed to secondhand smoke are 20 percent more likely to give birth to a baby with a low birth weight.

Secondhand Smoke

When scientists were first developing methods to detect nicotine in the bloodstream, nicotine metabolites were found in the blood of nonsmokers. The researchers thought they were misinterpreting their analysis, but the nonsmokers who tested positive had been in the presence of smokers shortly before their tests.[129] **Secondhand smoke (SHS)**, also called passive smoke or environmental tobacco smoke (ETS), is a combination of mainstream smoke exhaled from the smoker, plus sidestream smoke that rises off the lit end of the cigarette, cigar, or pipe.

Secondhand smoke (SHS): Also called passive smoke or environmental tobacco smoke, secondhand smoke is a combination of mainstream smoke and sidestream smoke.

In 1993, the Environmental Protection Agency (EPA) declared environmental tobacco smoke to be a class A carcinogen. Sidestream smoke actually contains a higher concentration of tar, nicotine, CO, and carcinogens than the smoke that the smoker takes into his or her lungs. The burning end of the cigarette is so hot that more nicotine and CO are emitted compared to what is exhaled from the smoker. Also, sidestream smoke doesn't pass through a filter, so those exposed to SHS are exposed to more toxic substances than the smoker is. You may be exposed to toxicity even if no one smokes directly around you. Thirdhand smoke—smoke that lingers on a smoker's clothes and hair—also contains carcinogenic compounds and toxins.[130] Thirdhand smoke may be particularly harmful to infants.

Although exposure to SHS is half what it was in 2000, 25 percent of nonsmokers in the United States—58 million people—were exposed to SHS in 2017.[131] African American male workers, construction workers, blue-collar workers, and those living below the poverty line experience especially high levels of exposure.[132] The CDC estimates that SHS causes 34,000 heart disease deaths and 7,300 lung cancer deaths each year among adult nonsmokers in the United States.[133]

The first epidemiological studies linking SHS with heart disease were published in 1988 and 1991. Later studies have supported these early reports.[134,135] Lung cancer rates are higher for those who live with a smoker and for those who work in an environment with a lot of smoke, such as bars and restaurants. Nonsmokers married to smokers have three times the rate of heart attacks as those with nonsmoking spouses.

Exposure to SHS also leads to short-term adverse effects, such as eye and nose irritation, respiratory tract infections, asthma, chest discomfort, and cough, as well as heightened oxygen needs in heart tissue and increased platelet aggregation, both of which can lead to heart attack. Children of smokers may be at particular risk.[136] They are more likely to get respiratory tract infections such as colds, bronchitis, and pneumonia. They are also likely to have more frequent asthma attacks, ear infections, and school absences. Children of fathers who smoke are also more likely to develop childhood cancers than children of nonsmoking dads. These effects are probably due to direct exposure to carcinogenic substances in smoke, as well as prenatal factors, because smoking may damage the DNA in sperm in ways that could lead to cancer.

Secondhand smoke is even a danger to pets. Dogs who live with smokers are more likely to get lung cancer or nasal cancer; birds have higher rates of lung cancer, pneumonia, eye disorders, and cardiac problems; and higher oral cancer rates are found in cats that live with smokers. In addition, pets can eat tobacco products and suffer from nicotine poisoning.

In the past, not all scientists agreed that SHS was dangerous. However, when scientists reviewed numerous articles about SHS, they found that "the only factor associated with concluding that passive smoking is not harmful was whether an author was affiliated with the tobacco industry."[137] Compared with independent researchers, tobacco industry–affiliated scientists were 88 times more likely to conclude that SHS was not harmful. When scientists demonstrated that SHS increased atherosclerosis and heart disease, the tobacco companies withdrew their funding. Big Tobacco instead began to fund research whose objective was to show that SHS did not increase risk of disease.[138] Today, however, the link between SHS and health risks is accepted by the World Health Organization, the National Institutes of Health, the U.S. Surgeon General, the National Cancer Institute, the Environmental Protection Agency, the American Medical Association, the American Cancer Society, the American Heart Association, the American Lung Association, the American Academy of Pediatrics, and others.

Increased understanding about the dangers of SHS has led to prohibitions on public smoking. As of 2020, 36 states, along with the District of Columbia and many American territories, have laws in effect that require nonhospitality workplaces, and/or restaurants, and/or bars to be smoke free. Since smoke-free legislation has passed, many municipalities have seen a reduction in the number of hospital admissions for heart disease.[139, 140]

Tobacco and Nicotine Dependence and Addiction

Nicotine is one of the most addictive substances ever discovered.[141] Nicotine is the primary reinforcing substance in tobacco, and the Philip Morris Company had evidence that nicotine was addictive in the early 1980s. However, instead of publishing the results, they fired the researchers and increased nicotine levels in cigarettes.[142]

Addiction may start within a few days of starting to smoke and after just a few cigarettes, often before the onset of daily smoking.[143,144] Tobacco researchers suggest that the length of time before a person has his or her first cigarette of the day after waking up is a pretty reliable indicator of addiction. If a smoker needs to smoke within 30 minutes of getting out of bed, she or he is likely to be addicted.[145]

Tobacco is both biologically and psychologically addictive. Nicotine stimulates dopamine's release from the nucleus accumbens, the addiction center of the brain. Nicotine is quickly and frequently reinforcing. Each inhalation is a mini-bolus injection of nicotine into the smoker's system. If one takes 10 inhalations from each cigarette, someone who smokes a pack a day will receive almost 75,000 reinforcing hits each year. Even the most hardcore heroin user would not be exposed to that many hits of heroin per year. Nicotine also is quickly metabolized and cleared, which means the high does not last long. Withdrawal onset occurs rapidly, and tobacco users often seek out the drug to ease their withdrawal symptoms.

Biological forces are not the only ones driving addiction. Long after physical withdrawal symptoms have passed, people still smoke. Drug-related cues induce cravings, which may perpetuate drug use or trigger relapse in those who are trying to quit. Craving is impacted by drug availability and self-control, and smokers experience more craving when cigarettes are immediately available.[146] Smoking becomes a conditioned habit that often is associated with rewarding behavior—after a meal, while drinking, out with friends, after sex. Smokers associate the settings and circumstances with smoking, which leads to learned rewards. Additionally, there are many rituals associated with smoking, which strengthens the habit.

Social factors also conspire to enhance tobacco's biologically and psychologically addictive properties. Unlike other drugs, tobacco is legal and readily available. It is rare to see coworkers shooting up together in sanctioned "heroin zones," but smokers often gather together to share their drug. Tobacco is portable, easy to store, and needs no equipment other than a lighter or a match. Distinct from other addictive substances, tobacco is not mind-altering and produces no marked impairment in performance.

Quitting Tobacco and Nicotine

"Stopping smoking is easy; I've done it many times myself"—attributed to Mark Twain
"For thy sake, tobacco, I would do anything but die."—Charles Lamb, *A Farewell to Tobacco* (1805)

Ask yourself: Given what you now know about nicotine's addictive properties, what role if any do you think the rituals of smoking play in increasing the likelihood of cigarette addiction?

Most people who smoke want to quit. They are aware of the health risks or want to save money. Perhaps their school or work has become a nonsmoking environment, or maybe the nagging from loved ones has finally gotten through. Unfortunately, it's hard to quit tobacco.

According to the U.S. Department of Health and Human Services, 68 percent of smokers in the United States would like to quit; every year, more than half make a serious attempt to quit; but only a small portion of smokers who try to quit succeed.[147] Many people take multiple attempts until they successfully quit; many relapse due to nicotine withdrawal. Because the body's nicotine reserves drop by half every two hours, it can take up to three days for the blood to become nicotine free; three days is how long a person who quits typically lasts before resuming smoking.[148] Others succumb to stress, social pressure, or fears of gaining weight. Smokeless tobacco users actually have a lower success rate in quitting than smokers do, in part because smokeless tobacco users are exposed to higher levels of nicotine than are smokers. But take heart! Although it may take more than one attempt, more than 60 percent of adults who were ever cigarette smokers have quit smoking.[149]

Benefits of Quitting

If you are a smoker, the younger you are when you quit, the better the benefits. People who stop smoking at age 30 reduce their risk of dying from smoking-related diseases by more than 90 percent compared with someone who continues to smoke. If you quit smoking at age 50, you reduce your risk by 50 percent. Within eight hours of quitting, the CO levels in your blood drop to normal. Within a week, your heart, blood pressure, circulation, and breathing show improvement. Within nine months, your respiratory cilia regain their normal function. Your excess risk of coronary heart disease (CHD) is cut in half a year after you've stopped smoking, and 5–10 years later, your risk of stroke is reduced to that of a nonsmoker. Within 15 years, your risk of CHD is similar to that of nonsmokers, and your risk of lung cancer is half of what it is in those who continue to smoke.[150]

Methods of Quitting

If a smoker is ready to quit, physiological, behavioral, and psychosocial therapies can increase the likelihood of success.[151] Nicotine cessation products are a $16 billion global market.[152]

Nicotine Replacement Therapies

Nicotine withdrawal is one of an addict's major roadblocks to quitting tobacco, so nicotine replacement therapies provide safer routes of administration of nicotine, without the tar and CO. Nicotine replacement allows the user to make behavioral changes before experiencing nicotine withdrawal. Nicotine is available in patches, gum, nasal sprays, inhalers, and lozenges, as well as in e-cigarettes.

Nicotine gum has been on the market since 1984 and has been available over the counter since 1996. Nicotine gum slowly releases a small amount of nicotine into the bloodstream to help ease withdrawal symptoms. It is easy to use—the consumer can regulate the dose by controlling how much he or she chews, with the ultimate goal to gradually decrease the amount chewed each day to wean himself or herself off nicotine. Nicotine gum can cause a bad taste in the mouth, throat irritation, nausea if swallowed, jaw discomfort, and a racing heartbeat. Nicotine patches, available since 1996, release a continuous small dose of nicotine across the skin. It may lead to mild skin irritation. Nicotine inhalers and nasal sprays deliver nicotine into the bloodstream more rapidly than gum or patches, but these may cause nasal and sinus irritation. These are available by prescription.

Electronic nicotine delivery systems can deliver nicotine to ease tobacco withdrawal, but their effectiveness in helping users quit is undetermined. Some recent studies suggest they are equally or more effective than nicotine patches in helping smokers to quit.[153,154,155] Others report that e-cigarette users are less likely to quit compared to those who have never used e-cigarettes.[156,157,158,159] There are also fears that adult smokers will stay hooked longer now that they have exciting new gadgets to use, and because they can obtain a nicotine fix without the need to leave the building.[160]

Pharmacological Treatments that Do Not Replace Nicotine

Bupropion (Zyban or Wellbutrin) is an antidepressant that has been found to help people quit smoking. Side effects include dry mouth, insomnia, and skin rash. Bupropion also can increase risk of seizures, so it

Ask yourself: E-cigarettes may help attract young people to tobacco. Teens who previously used e-cigarettes are 4 times more likely to move on to conventional cigarettes than those who don't use ENDS, and the higher the nicotine concentration of the ENDS, the greater the frequency and intensity of later use.[161,162,163] In light of this, should people be allowed to smoke e-cigarettes in places where smoking is banned? Why or why not?

is contraindicated in those with epilepsy. Varenicline (Chantix) is a partial agonist at nicotinic receptors in the brain, so it both reduces cravings for and decreases the pleasurable effects of tobacco products. Varenicline may be more effective than bupropion in aiding smokers to quit.[164] Side effects include nausea, vomiting, constipation, flatulence, insomnia, and sometimes depression.[165] Hallucinogens may be effective as well. Two to three moderate to high doses of psilocybin, in conjunction with cognitive behavioral therapy, resulted in substantially higher 6-month smoking abstinence rates than other medications or CBT alone. Sixty percent of the former smokers were still abstinent 16 months later.[166]

Behavioral and Psychosocial Treatments

In *Quitters Inc.*, one of Stephen King's short stories, smokers sign up for a 100 percent guaranteed plan that will make them stop smoking forever. Once they sign the contract, they learn that they will be observed constantly, and if they ever smoke, their loved ones will be tortured. With increasing infractions, the punishments intensify. If the smoker commits a tenth infraction, he becomes part of "the unregenerate 2 percent," who are executed by the company. But, as the quitting counselor explains it, "even the unregenerate 2 percent never smoke again. We guarantee it."

Although this would be an effective means to encourage smokers to quit, it is a bit extreme. Approved behavioral and psychosocial techniques such as counseling, stress management, and behavior modification teach smokers to identify situations that are high risk for them and show them ways to break the habit. Combining pharmacological with behavioral/psychological treatments increases the odds that a smoker will successfully quit.[167] For example, when combined with nicotine patches, hypnosis is more effective in helping smokers quit than nicotine patches alone.[168] In addition, teaching young people to understand, analyze, and

Ask yourself: Should the government subsidize all those who want to quit tobacco by providing free therapy? What would be the pros and cons of such a program?

FIGURE 10.19. Pictorial cigarette pack warnings. Graphic images on cigarette packs have been shown to decrease smoking.

evaluate advertising and other media messages enables them to actively process media messages rather than passively remain media targets, and is associated with reduced smoking and reduced susceptibility to future smoking.[169]

A change in the design of cigarette packs also could help people quit smoking. In nearly 80 countries around the world, cigarette labels now include shocking and graphic pictures of the risks of smoking—rotted teeth, laryngeal tumors, and dangerously small newborn babies (Figure 10.19). Studies have found that adding pictorial warnings to cigarette packs increased users' attempts to quit and increased the success of those efforts.[170] The American tobacco industry has thus far blocked all attempts to include these images on cigarette packs sold in the United States.

Handy Hints to Help Someone Quit

Quitting tobacco is not easy! In fact, it is one of the more difficult drugs to quit.[171] If you or someone you know uses tobacco and wants to quit, here are some helpful ideas:[172]

- Prepare.
  » Make a list of all the reasons you want to quit, and keep it somewhere you can easily see your reasons.
  » Think about the times you smoke—what are your triggers? Places? People? Activities? Emotions? If you keep a record of this, you can prepare in advance for these situations and try to avoid triggers.

» Clean out your environment before your quit day. Throw out all cigarettes, lighters, matches, and ashtrays. Don't keep "just one last cigarette."

» Be prepared for the physical and psychological effects of withdrawal. Plan some activities (such as exercise) to distract yourself.

- Deal with cravings.
  » Remind yourself that cravings will pass.
  » Find a low-calorie oral substitute, such as gum, carrots, sunflower seeds, or celery.

- Seek support.
  » Find someone to encourage you and keep you focused on your goals. Share your plan with him or her, so he or she can hold you accountable.

- Learn new behaviors and routines.
  » Avoid situations that you normally associate with smoking. Develop new routines and habits.
  » Those who work in environments that implement smoke-free policies are almost twice as likely to quit smoking as those who work in settings that permit smoking everywhere. Adolescents who work in smoke-free environments are less likely to become smokers.

- Consider using pharmacological or psychological aids.
- Understand that relapses can happen.
  » It might take more than one attempt for you or someone you know to quit. Many people need two or three attempts before quitting successfully.
  » Keep at it—remember, the sooner you quit, the sooner you reap the benefits!

Chapter Summary

- **Introduction**
  » Tobacco is one of the most widely used drugs in the world, consumed by approximately 20 percent of the global population, most of whom live in developing nations.
- **History of Tobacco**
  » Tobacco has been cultivated in the Americas for thousands of years. Christopher Columbus brought tobacco back to the Old World, and its use spread.
  » In the seventeenth century, the English colony of Virginia cultivated this valuable crop, and African men, women, and children were kidnapped and delivered to Virginia as slaves to work the tobacco fields.
  » The development of the cigarette-rolling machine significantly boosted the production of cigarettes while lowering their cost, and their popularity soared.
  » In the early 1950s, scientific studies showed the link between smoking and cancer, and a 1964 U.S. Surgeon General report stated that cigarette use was related to a number of serious illnesses.
  » Lawsuits against the tobacco industry culminated in the Master Settlement Agreement, the largest civil settlement in U.S. history.
- **Prevalence of Tobacco Use**
  » In the United States, 21.1 percent of the population uses tobacco.
  » Tobacco use is more common in men, American Indians, those with a high school education or less, unemployed people, those who live below the poverty line, and people with mental illness.
  » Most smokers began using tobacco when they were teenagers or young adults.
- **Economic, Legal, and Social Issues Related to Tobacco and Nicotine**
  » The global cigarette industry is one of the most profitable in the world, valued at over $713 billion.

  » Cigarette smoking is estimated to be responsible for $300 billion in annual health-related costs in the United States.
  » In 2019, the minimum age for purchasing any tobacco or ENDS product was raised to 21. The FDA is considering lowering nicotine levels in cigarettes to reduce their addictive potential. As of 2020, most ENDS devices have not been evaluated by the FDA for safety.
  » The tobacco companies spend millions each day on advertising, with many ads aimed at youth or "replacement smokers."
  » Cigarette smoking is depicted in many films. Greater exposure to smoking in films is associated with greater smoking in adolescents.
- **Sources and Forms of Tobacco and Nicotine**
  » Tobacco smoke contains over 4,000 substances, including nicotine, tar, and CO.
  » Nicotine, found naturally only in the tobacco plant, is one of the most toxic of all drugs. Additionally, manufacturers add many harmful additives to tobacco.
  » Tar is the sticky brown particulate matter generated by burning tobacco.
  » Tobacco is most commonly ingested as cigarettes, but some people also use cigars, pipes, and smokeless tobacco.
  » Electronic nicotine delivery systems (ENDS) such as e-cigarettes and vapes have become popular. E-cigarettes typically contain nicotine, flavoring, and a humectant.
- **Pharmacokinetics of Tobacco and Nicotine**
  » A smoker typically inhales about 1 mg of nicotine per cigarette. Nicotine is rapidly absorbed into the bloodstream and easily crosses the blood–brain barrier.
  » Nicotine is metabolized more slowly in men, newborns, and the elderly.

- **Mechanism of Action of Nicotine**
  - » Nicotine binds to nicotinic cholinergic receptors and excites them. It then stays bound, which prevents neural transmission.
- **Acute Effects of Tobacco and Nicotine**
  - » Nicotine is a sympathomimetic that has widespread effects on the body.
  - » Overdose is rare but possible. Smoking 21 cigarettes at one time would be fatal in 50 percent of the population.
- **Chronic Effects of Tobacco and Nicotine**
  - » Tolerance to tobacco's diverse effects develops at different rates. Abstinent smokers experience withdrawal symptoms fairly rapidly.
  - » Chronic tobacco use is associated with life-threatening conditions, including cardiovascular disease, cancer, and chronic obstructive pulmonary disease (COPD).
  - » Smoking also is causally associated with type 2 diabetes, liver and colorectal cancers, Crohn's disease, tuberculosis, rheumatoid arthritis, and impaired immune function.

- » Smoking is harmful to the fetuses, infants, and children of smokers.
- » Exposure to SHS also is associated with a higher incidence of heart disease and lung cancer.
- **Tobacco and Nicotine Dependence and Addiction**
  - » Nicotine is considered one of the most addictive substances ever discovered.
  - » Tobacco is both biologically and psychologically addictive.
- **Quitting Tobacco and Nicotine**
  - » Most people who smoke want to quit. Smokers who try to quit unaided have a high failure rate, but pharmaceutical aids and cessation programs increase the odds of success.
  - » Smoking cessation aids include nicotine replacement therapies; pharmacological treatments that don't replace nicotine, such as bupropion; and behavioral and psychosocial treatments.

Key Terms

Cardiovascular disease (p.254)
Chewing tobacco (p.247)
Chronic obstructive pulmonary disease (COPD) (p.255)

Electronic Nicotine Delivery System (ENDS) (p.237)
Master Settlement Agreement (p.237)

Secondhand smoke (SHS) (p.256)
Snuff (p.247)
Tar (p.246)
Vaping (p.247)

Quiz Yourself!

1. True or false? More cigarettes are consumed in China than in any other country on earth.

2. True or false? In the United States, 13 percent of the population uses tobacco.

3. Which of the following is TRUE about tobacco?

   A. Nicotine itself is not harmful.

   B. Tar, the sticky brown matter generated by burning tobacco, contains dozens of carcinogens.

   C. Carbon monoxide harms cells by causing too much oxygen to be delivered to them.

   D. Cigarettes today have less tar than in the past, so the health risks from smoking are lower than they used to be.

   E. Smokeless tobacco is significantly safer than cigarette use.

4. Which of the following is NOT part of the Master Settlement Agreement?

   A. The tobacco industry agreed to pay $206 billion to the states over 25 years to reimburse them for smoking-related illnesses.

   B. The tobacco industry was required to reveal secret industry records and research.

   C. The minimum pack size was set at 20 cigarettes.

   D. All tobacco advertisements were banned.

5. Give at least three examples of the effects of tobacco on the cardiovascular system.

6. The therapeutic index of nicotine is about _____.

7. True or false? Cigarette smoking causes 20 percent of all cancer deaths in the United States.

8. In an analysis of research about tobacco, what was the only factor associated with the conclusion that SHS is not harmful?

9. List three different aids to help someone quit smoking.

10. True or false? The FDA has evaluated e-cigarettes and found them to be safe and effective.

Additional Resources

Websites

American Cancer Society. www.cancer.org
Tobaccofree. www.tobaccofree.org
The Tobacco Atlas. https://tobaccoatlas.org/

Videos

Smoking Kid. One of the most effective antismoking videos of all time. https://www.youtube.com/watch?v=gugjMmXQrDo

Movies

Thank You for Smoking. (2005). 92 minutes. Satirical comedy follows the machinations of Big Tobacco's chief spokesman, Nick Naylor, who spins on behalf of cigarettes.

Books

Gately, I. (2001). *Tobacco: A cultural history of how an exotic plant seduced civilization.* New York: Grove Press.

The Health Consequences of Smoking—50 Years of Progress: A Report of the Surgeon General. http://www.surgeongeneral.gov/library/reports/50-years-of-progress/fulls-report.pdf

Learn more with this chapter's digital tools at www.oup.com/he/rosenthal2e.

Caffeine

True or false?

1.
True or false? Most adults get their caffeine from carbonated soft drinks.

2.
True or false? Coca Cola, Pepsi, and Dr Pepper were all invented by pharmacists.

3.
True or false? Caffeine may protect against liver disease, diabetes, and cancer.

Learning Objectives

- Trace the history of the use of coffee, tea, chocolate, and soft drinks.
- Compare the caffeine consumption in people of different ages and in inhabitants of different countries.
- Identify the natural source of caffeine, as well as the forms from which caffeine is most commonly ingested.
- Understand the ways the body processes caffeine after it is ingested and some of the factors that affect its metabolism.
- Explain the way that caffeine interacts with the adenosine receptor and the effects this produces in the body.
- List the acute physiological and psychological effects of caffeine, at both moderate and high doses.
- Outline some therapeutic benefits of caffeine, coffee, tea, and chocolate.
- Evaluate the effect that caffeine has on a person's mortality.
- Describe the effects of caffeine withdrawal.
- Summarize some strategies for quitting caffeine.

Legend states that Kaldi, an Ethiopian goat herder who lived in the sixth or seventh century, noticed that his goats became unusually frisky after grazing on the fruit of certain wild bushes. He tried the berries himself, felt exhilarated, and brought them to an Islamic holy man, who disapproved of their use and tossed the beans into the fire, creating an enticing aroma. The story suggests that the monk raked the aromatic beans from the embers, ground them up, and dissolved them in hot water, thus creating the first cup of coffee.[1]

Caffeine is the world's most commonly used psychoactive drug, although if you mention this to someone as he sips his coffee, he may be very offended by the suggestion that he uses drugs. Caffeine is so ubiquitous that one must specifically *ask* for a soft drink or coffee that does not contain the drug, and it is so accepted that it has been added to juices, gum, mints, water, wine, and waffles. Caffeine's physical, economic, and social effects are far-reaching.

People use caffeine for many different reasons. It is a reinforcing substance that makes people feel good and is part of a pleasurable daily ritual. Caffeine also gives people the ability to regulate their bodies so they can meet physical and mental demands, without any loss of consciousness or rational thought.

History of Caffeine

Caffeine has a long, rich history. Over a cup of coffee or tea, people have debated poetry and politics, fomented dissent, and instigated revolution. We'll now consider the story of the most popular caffeine-containing substances.

Coffee

"A very wholesom and physical drink, having many excellent vertues, closes the orifice of the stomack, fortifies the heat within, helpeth digestion, quickneth the spirits, maketh the heart lightsome, is good against eye-sores, kings evil and many others."—English advertisement for coffee, 1657[2]

"Coffee leads men to trifle away their time, scald their chops, and spend their money, all for a little base, black, thick, nasty, bitter, stinking, nauseous puddle water."—The Women's Petition Against Coffee, 1674

Caffeine

Type of drug: Stimulant

Chemical name:
1,3,7-trimethylxanthine

Chemical formula: $C_8H_{10}N_4O_2$

Routes of administration: Oral

Duration of effect: Half-life
approximately five hours

Neurotransmitters directly affected: Adenosine

Tolerance: Some

Physiological dependence:
Some

Psychological dependence:
Some

Withdrawal Symptoms:
Anxiety, lethargy, headache,
fatigue

Schedule: Legal

Slang: No slang for caffeine, tea,
or chocolate. Coffee: joe, java,
cuppa, mud, wakey juice

Sometime between the twelfth and fifteenth centuries, Arabian people began to cultivate the *Coffea* tree. They would crush the beans, ferment the juice, and make a wine called "qahwa" (from the Arabic word for stimulating or invigorating; this is probably the root of our word "coffee"). Coffee spread throughout Egypt, North Africa, and Turkey, and from there to Europe.

Coffee began to gain in popularity among the avant-garde in Europe in the sixteenth century. Conservative Catholic clerics opposed the beverage, however, saying its use constituted a breach of religious law. Because coffee was used by Muslims, Christian priests associated the black brew with the devil and encouraged Pope Clement VIII to ban its use. Before rendering his decree, however, the pope insisted on trying some and was so delighted by its flavor and effect that he baptized the drink as suitable for Christian use.[3]

Coffee houses began sprouting up in England and France in the seventeenth century. They were popular sites for intellectual discourse—places for people to relax, speak their mind, and share the news of the day. King Charles II attempted to outlaw coffee houses in England, because he considered them to be dangerous places where the politically disaffected met to conspire against him. But due to the furious backlash to this proclamation, he reversed his ruling 11 days later.

Because tea became a symbol of English oppression, coffee became more popular in the United States after the Revolutionary War and has remained popular for centuries. Today, coffee is an $18-billion-a-year industry in the United States. Results from a national survey suggest that well over half of Americans drink coffee every day.[4]

Tea

"We advise tea for the whole nation and for every nation. We advise men and women to drink tea daily; hour by hour if possible; beginning with ten cups a day, and increasing the dose to the utmost quantity that the stomach can contain and the kidneys eliminate."—Dr. Cornelius Buntekuh, Dutch physician (who was in the pay of the Dutch East India Company), 1680[5]

The Chinese Emperor Shen Nung often is credited with the discovery of tea. The legend goes that one day, almost 5,000 years ago, the emperor was waiting for his drinking water to boil. The fire was made from branches of a *Camellia sinensis* tree, and a gust of wind carried some leaves into the pot, where they steeped. Shen Nung tasted the brew and liked it, and tea was born.

In 1606, Dutch traders shipped tea to Europe. Catherine of Braganza, the wife of King Charles II, took to the habit and helped spread its popularity. The tea trade became a major part of the British economy, accounting for about 10 percent of British tax income.[6] The British and Dutch battled for control of the tea trade, and the Dutch introduced tea to North America in New Amsterdam around 1650. But the British Parliament passed an act that required colonists to import their tea only from Great Britain. Britain's East India Company imported tea to England, and British firms bought the tea and exported it to the colonies. Tea imported into England was highly taxed. According to the constitution, British subjects couldn't be taxed without the consent of their elected representatives . . . but American colonists did not have any elected representatives in Parliament. The Boston Tea Party was, in part, a protest over the extent of the British Parliament's authority over the colonies.

Six decades later, tea played a role in yet another war. British citizens desired Chinese tea, yet the Chinese did not want Western goods, leading to a trade imbalance. England tried to force China to buy opium to balance the inequity, leading to the Opium Wars (Chapter 7).

Chocolate

"Chocolate is a divine, celestial drink, the sweat of the stars, the vital seed, divine nectar, the drink of the gods, panacea and universal medicine."— Geronimo Piperni, quoted by Antonio Lavedán, Spanish army surgeon, 1796

The Olmecs (1500–400 BC), who lived in the fertile coastal Mexican lowlands centuries before the Mayans arrived, harvested wild *kakawa* pods that they made into a chocolate drink.[7] (The word "cacao" is thought to come from kakawa; "cocoa" is a corrupted form of the word *cacao*.) In later centuries, the Mayan Indians of the Yucatan peninsula, the Aztecs of central Mexico, and the Incas of Peru cultivated the cacao tree, which they believed to be a gift of the gods. The Aztecs and Mayans made a warm, bitter drink from the cacao beans. The original chocolate drink was a very thick, unsweetened concoction that had to be eaten with a spoon.

Spanish explorers brought cacao pods back to Spain. At first, the Roman Catholic Church banned chocolate because of its reputation as a sexual stimulant; the ban did not last. King Charles V is credited with adding vanilla and sugar to the previously bitter concoction, and nutritious, delicious, filling, and stimulating chocolate became a popular drink. The chocolate drink was expensive, so its use was mainly limited to the wealthy and noble. They found that its flavor was strong enough to hide a variety of poisons, so chocolate also became the medium of choice throughout Europe for dispatching one's enemies.[8]

In 1828, the Dutch developed a process that removed much of the fat from the kernels to make a chocolate powder that was the forerunner of the cocoa we know today. Cocoa fat (cocoa butter, as it is now called) was later mixed with sugar. The first chocolate bars were produced in 1847, and milk chocolate appeared on the scene in 1876.

QUICK HIT

Did you know if you send chocolate to the author of this book, you will have good luck for the rest of your days? It's true! Try it and see!

Soft Drinks and Energy Drinks

"The bar is dead, the fountain lives, and soda is king!"—John Somerset, 1920

The first soft drink—water with lemon juice and honey—was marketed in the 1600s. In the eighteenth century, Joseph Priestly discovered a method to infuse water with carbon dioxide to make carbonated water. Others added flavors such as juice, wine, and spices to the carbonated water. During the nineteenth century, pharmacists began selling mineral waters infused with herbs—Coca Cola, Pepsi, Dr Pepper, ginger ale, and Hires root

FIGURE 11.1. Pharmacy soda fountains became popular gathering spots in the early 20th century. Their popularity increased when prohibition began and bars were closed.

FIGURE 11.2. Red Bull is the most popular energy drink in the word. In 2014, the company that produces Red Bull agreed to pay out $13 million following a class action lawsuit that accused Red Bull of making false advertising claims regarding its effects.

beer were all invented by pharmacists. Soda fountains at pharmacies became popular gathering spots (Figure 11.1). Bottled soft drink sales began to rise in the early twentieth century. Inventions such as aluminum cans, diet soda, safe pull-tabs, and others have facilitated the meteoric rise in the popularity of soft drinks.

Since the 1990s, energy drinks have soared in popularity, but the idea behind them is not new. At the beginning of the twentieth century, Coca Cola was marketed as an energy-boosting beverage; the cocaine the soda contained certainly had an energizing effect. In 1960, a Japanese pharmaceutical company created the first drink specifically targeted to increase energy. Containing mostly taurine and B vitamins, it was sold in small, brown glass medicine bottles. Jolt Cola, introduced in the United States in 1985, boasted that it contained "all the sugar and twice the caffeine." Red Bull, invented in 1987 and introduced to the United States in 1997, is the most popular energy drink in the world, initiating the meteoric surge in popularity of energy drinks (Figure 11.2). In 2001, the U.S. market for energy drinks was $8 million; by 2018, energy drinks accounted for almost $11 billion in sales in the U.S.

Because the United States limits the amount of caffeine per serving, energy drink manufacturers have gotten around this by increasing the caffeine content, while also enlarging the size of the bottles. As a result, these drinks can be sold containing multiple servings per container. Due to the deaths associated with energy drink use, some jurisdictions have tried to restrict the sale of energy drinks to individuals over 18 years of age.

Prevalence of Caffeine Use

Caffeine consumption from all sources is about 70–76 mg per person per day worldwide,[9] although this varies greatly by country and form of caffeine consumed (Figure 11.3). For example, Canadians and Brits drink about the same amount of caffeine each day, but Brits get 48 percent of their caffeine from tea, while that number is only 8.5 percent for Canadians.[10] After combining per capita information for coffee, tea, chocolate, and soft drinks,[11,12,13,14] some of the countries of northern Europe (Finland, Norway, and Iceland, in particular) have the highest caffeine consumption in the world.

Worldwide, 120,000 tons of caffeine are consumed annually, which adds up to 1.3 trillion cups of coffee and tea per year. This amount of caffeine is enough to spike 260 cups of coffee or tea for every man, woman, and child on Earth each year.[15]

Current estimates put U.S. caffeine consumption around 165 mg per day.[16] The exact amount is hard to measure, because caffeine is found in many sources and

Ask yourself: Although the U.S. Food and Drug Administration (FDA) monitors over-the-counter products that contain caffeine, such as NoDoz or Excedrin, it does not regulate energy drinks that have higher total caffeine content. This lack of oversight is also surprising given that the health consequences of energy drinks are unknown and that most drinkers are children, adolescents, and young adults. Do you think caffeine should be regulated as a food or as a drug? Why?

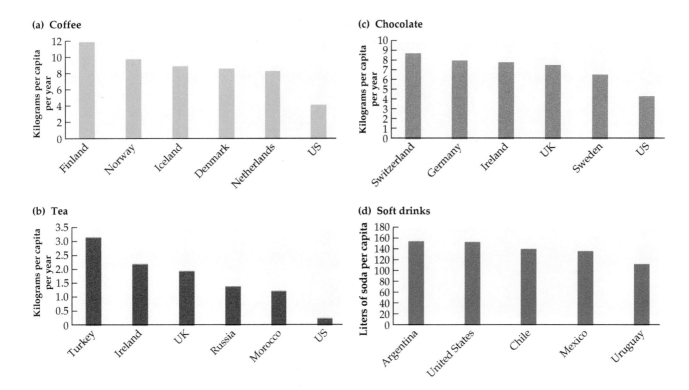

FIGURE 11.3. The top five consuming countries of (a) coffee, (b) tea, (c) chocolate, and (d) soft drinks. The United States is included for comparison.

Sources: World Atlas. (2018). The top coffee-consuming countries. Accessed on May 17, 2020, from https://www.worldatlas.com/articles/top-10-coffee-con-suming-nations.html

Ferdman, R.A. (2014). Where the world's biggest tea drinkers are. http://qz.com/168690/where-the-worlds-biggest-tea-drinkers-are/#int/words=dinner_supper&smoothing=3

Nag, O. (2018). Which countries eat the most chocolate? Accessed on May 18, 2020, from https://www.worldatlas.com/articles/which-countries-eat-the-most-chocolate.html

World Atlas. (2016). Countries with the highest levels of soft drink consumption. http://qz.com/168690/where-the-worlds-biggest-tea-drinkers-are/#int/words=dinner_supper&smoothing=3

because the way that caffeine-containing beverages are prepared can alter the caffeine content. Approximately 85 percent of the entire U.S. population, and over 90 percent of adults age 18 and older, consume caffeine.[17,18] Fewer than 5 percent of Americans are true abstainers from caffeine, and about 5 percent are occasional users.[19]

The most common sources of caffeine in the United States are coffee and soft drinks.[20,21] Since the year 2000, soft drink consumption as decreased from 53 gallons per person to just under 39 gallons per person in 2018.[22] Coffee consumption has remained fairly steady over that time, at around 10 pounds of coffee beans per person.[23] Most American adults are coffee drinkers, while soft drinks account for the most caffeine consumed by U.S. children and teenagers (Figure 11.4). Surveys suggest that almost three-quarters of

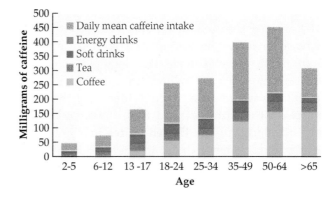

FIGURE 11.4. Caffeine consumption by age in the United States. Caffeine consumption is highest in those aged 50–64.

Source: Mitchell, D.C., Knight, C.A., Hockenberrry, J., Teplansky, R., & Hartman, T.J., (2014). Beverage caffeine intakes in the U.S. Food and Chemical Toxicology, 63: 136–42.

children and adolescents have caffeine every day, including about 58 percent of two- to five-year-olds.[24,25]

Energy drinks are most commonly consumed by those aged 13–24. Frequent consumers of energy drinks (consuming one on six or more days per month) are more likely to show excessive risk-taking and engage in risky behaviors such as smoking cigarettes, abusing prescription drugs and alcohol, being in physical fights, not wearing seatbelts, and engaging in unprotected sex.[28,29] Perhaps the high doses of caffeine cause these behaviors, or perhaps those who are risky and impulsive are more likely to drink highly caffeinated beverages. Or maybe a third factor, such as a lack of parental supervision, underlies both effects.

Source and Forms of Caffeine

Coffee, tea, and cola are the three most popular drinks in the world. Although they may differ in taste and smell, their common denominator is caffeine.[30] Caffeine is a methylated xanthine (ZAN-theen) found naturally in the seeds, leaves, and fruit of over 60 species of plants. Responsible for stimulating the central nervous system, skeletal muscle, and respiratory system, caffeine is also a natural pesticide, killing harmful bacteria and fungi and causing sterility in certain insects that feed on plants.

Caffeine enhances bees' memory so they can remember the flowers that have caffeine longer than they remember the ones without.[31] However, too much caffeine is toxic, so bees have receptors within their mouths that enable them to sense caffeine. As a result, bees avoid only the plants with high caffeine concentrations.[32]

Theophylline is a related xanthine found in cacao and tea. Meaning "leaf of the gods," it is more effective than caffeine as a cardiac stimulant, bronchodilator, and diuretic. Theobromine ("food of the gods") is found

Ask yourself: Do you think there should be an age limit for caffeine consumption? If so, what age? How would caffeine purchases and use be regulated?

in cacao, cola, and tea. Although weaker than caffeine and theophylline, theobromine can be used as a vasodilator, diuretic, and cardiac stimulant.

Coffee

Coffee comes from the beans of several species of *Coffea* plants—a shrubby tree native to Ethiopia, which is now cultivated in many tropical countries throughout the world. Most coffee comes from *Coffea arabica*, but some coffee comes from *Coffea robusta*, which produces beans with more caffeine but also a more bitter taste (Figure 11.5). The beans are roasted to enhance their flavor and then ground into powder. To decaffeinate the beverage, coffee is brewed and mixed with a solvent that absorbs the caffeine. The solvent,

FIGURE 11.5. Coffee beans. Most coffee comes from the plant *Coffea Arabica;* the coffee bean is the bright red berry.

FIGURE 11.6. **Tea leaves.** Tea comes from the leaf and bud of the *Camellia sinensis* tree.

along with the caffeine, is removed, and the remaining coffee is dried and prepared in the same manner as ordinary coffee.

Tea

Tea comes from the leaf and bud of the *Camellia sinensis* tree, which is native to China, India, Burma, Thailand, Laos, and Vietnam (Figure 11.6). There are three distinct methods of processing tea leaves, each resulting in a recognizably different product. The main difference depends on how long the leaves are allowed to oxidize (ferment) after picking.

In the case of black tea, the leaves are dried and then crushed, before oxidizing. Steaming the fresh leaves immediately after picking prevents oxidation; this produces green tea. Oolong tea is prepared like black tea, but the leaves are allowed to ferment for only a

Ask yourself: What assumptions do you make about a person depending on whether they prefer coffee or tea?

short time, giving oolong a flavor between the brighter green teas and the fuller-bodied black teas. Although the same tea plant can produce the three types of tea, certain regions typically specialize: green from Japan; black from India; and green, black, and oolong from China. The highest-quality teas use only the bud and first two leaves of each twig, while inferior-quality teas are made from the third and fourth leaves. The farther the leaf is from the bud, the less caffeine it contains.[33]

QUICK HIT

Iced tea was sold for the first time at the Louisiana Purchase Exposition in 1904. Iced tea now accounts for 85 percent of all tea consumed in the United States.[34]

Chocolate

Cocoa, which is the basis of chocolate, comes from the bean of the *Theobroma cacao* tree, which is native to South America, although most cocoa today comes from West Africa rather than South America (Figure 11.7). Cacao beans contain only a small amount of caffeine, but eight times as much theobromine. Cacao also contains phenylethylamine, a natural alkaloid that, in high enough quantities, is related to the feeling of infatuation, as well as a compound similar to THC (the psychoactive ingredient in cannabis). However, one would need to eat 25 pounds of chocolate in order to stimulate these receptors as much as a typical dose of marijuana.

Cacao is the raw or minimally processed form of the bean. After the cacao beans are harvested, they are fermented, before being dried, cleaned, and roasted. Pure cocoa is bitter, but when pressed into a powder and mixed with sugar and cocoa butter (the fat extracted from the cocoa bean), the cocoa becomes the chocolate with which we are more familiar. Milk chocolate

---

STRAIGHT DOPE   Coffee vs. Tea

Coffee and tea share much in common, from their composition, to the way they are served, to their pervasive availability. Yet, their cultural paths diverge. Coffee is stereotypically associated with masculinity, artistic endeavors, nonconformity, rebelliousness, and bohemianism. Coffee also is often linked to gossip, politics, intense conversation, excessive work, and coming down from a night of overindulgence. Tea, on the other hand, is associated with femininity, conventionalism, quietude,

spirituality, harmony, and tranquility. Tea is the drink of the elite, the elderly, and the meditative. Finally, while coffee has been banned many times by kings, sultans, police, and religious leaders, tea rarely makes an appearance on anyone's list of illegal substances.

Source: Weinberg, B.A., & Bealer, B.K. (2002). The world of caffeine: The science and culture of the world's most popular drug. New York: Routledge.

FIGURE 11.8. **Cola nuts.** The cola nut is the seed from the *Cola acuminate* and *Cola nitida* trees.

FIGURE 11.9. **There are more than 50 varieties of energy drinks on the market.** Energy drinks contain large amounts of caffeine.

FIGURE 11.7. **Cocoa beans.** Cocoa comes from the bean of the *Theobroma cacao* tree.

results when dried milk is added to the mixture; when cocoa butter is mixed with sugar and milk, but no cocoa solids, white chocolate results.

Soft Drinks and Energy Drinks

Soft drinks, also called soda, pop, and cola, are flavored drinks that typically contain water (usually carbonated), a flavoring agent, and a sweetener (sugar, corn syrup, fruit juices, or sugar substitutes). They also may contain caffeine, colorings, and preservatives.

The cola nut is the seed from the *Cola acuminate* and *Cola nitida* trees, which grow in West Africa, India, China, and South America (Figure 11.8). Cola nuts contain caffeine and are used as a flavoring ingredient in beverages, although most modern bottled cola drinks actually contain very little cola nut. Most soft drinks contain 30–60 mg of caffeine per 12-ounce serving. In the United States, the FDA limits soft drinks to 71 mg of caffeine per 12-ounce drink.

The FDA, however, does not regulate all energy drinks. Energy drinks are canned or bottled beverages, such as Red Bull, Full Throttle, Adrenaline Rush, Rockstar, Tab Energy, and Monster, which contain large amounts of caffeine (Figure 11.9). They also may contain sugar, B vitamins, taurine, and herbal stimulants such as ginseng or guarana; some of these substances can synergistically intensify the effects of the caffeine.

To confound the issue, some energy products, such as Red Bull, are sold as beverages, while others, such as 5-hour Energy and Monster Energy, are sold as dietary supplements.[35] Dietary supplements are regulated less strictly than beverages. Manufacturers of dietary supplements do not need to obtain FDA approval before selling their product, although they are required to report all serious adverse events associated with the use of the product to the FDA. On the other

Ask yourself: Do you think energy drinks should be classified as beverages or as dietary supplements? Why?

> **STRAIGHT DOPE**
>
> ## Caffeine Content of Common Foods, Drinks, and Medicines
>
> - Coffees
>   - Drip coffee (8 oz.): 65–330 mg
>   - Brewed coffee (8 oz.): 65–330 mg
>   - Instant coffee (8 oz.): 57–75 mg
>   - Espresso (1 oz.): 47–63 mg
>   - Decaffeinated coffee (8 oz.): 2–12 mg
> - Teas
>   - Black teas (8 oz.): 40–74 mg
>   - Oolong teas (8 oz.): 12–55 mg
>   - Green teas (8 oz.): 8–36 mg
>   - Arizona Iced Tea (20 oz.): 38 mg
> - Soft Drinks (12 oz. can)
>   - 7UP: 0 mg
>   - Coca Cola: 34 mg
>   - Pepsi Cola: 38 mg
>   - Diet Coke: 45 mg
>   - Mountain Dew: 54 mg
>   - Jolt Cola: 70 mg
> - Energy Drinks
>   - 5-hour Energy drink: 208 mg/1.9 oz.
>   - Red Bull: 83 mg/8.4 oz.
>   - Monster: 160 mg/16 oz.
>   - No Fear: 182 mg/16 oz.
>   - Full Throttle: 200 mg/16 oz.
>   - Wired X505: 505 mg/24 oz.
>   - 5150 Energy drink: 15,200 mg/32 oz.
> - Chocolate
>   - Hershey's chocolate bar: 9 mg/1.6 oz.
>   - Hershey's dark chocolate bar: 20 mg/1.5 oz.
>   - Starbucks hot chocolate: 25 mg/16 oz.
> - Over-the-Counter and Prescription Medications
>   - Anacin: 32 mg/tablet
>   - Excedrin Migraine: 65 mg/tablet
>   - Midol: 60 mg/tablet
>   - Vivarin: 200 mg/tablet
>   - Dexatrim: 200 mg/tablet
>   - NoDoz: 200 mg/tablet

hand, manufacturers of substances that are classified as beverages are not required to report resultant deaths or injuries to the FDA, but they are required to list the product's ingredients on the can.

Other Caffeine Sources

Guarana is a paste made from the seeds of a plant that grows in regions surrounding the Amazon River in South America. The paste is molded into bars and dried in the sun. It is usually sweetened with sugar. Guarana seeds contain twice the caffeine of coffee beans. The Maté tree of Argentina, southern Brazil, and Paraguay also contains caffeine.

How Much Caffeine Is in the Substances We Ingest?

How much caffeine is in a cup of coffee? That is not an easy question to answer, because it depends on so many variables. Which types of beans were used? Robusta beans have about twice the caffeine as Arabica. How were they roasted? The roasting process reduces the caffeine content of beans, so dark roast has slightly less caffeine than lighter roasts. How was the coffee brewed? Coffee prepared with a French press that steeps the grounds for a while before the plunger is depressed will have more caffeine than drip coffee. Finally, what is "a cup" of coffee? A delicate teacup or a big mug? A small cup of weak coffee might have as little as 50 mg caffeine, while a mug of infused coffee made with with *robusta* beans that have steeped for a long time might have as much as 350 mg. The average cup of coffee contains about 100–250 mg of caffeine per cup.[36]

When measured by dry weight, tea contains more caffeine than coffee. However, because tea is generally brewed weaker, a typical serving of tea contains less caffeine. The longer the tea leaves have been fermented, the greater their caffeine content. Unfermented green tea contains the least caffeine. Oolong is partially fermented, and has 50 percent more caffeine than green tea. Black tea is fully fermented and has three times as much caffeine as green tea. In addition, the longer a tea is brewed, the higher its caffeine content.

Pharmacokinetics of Caffeine

Once we consume our coffee, taste our tea, sip our soda, or chow on chocolate, how does the caffeine exert its effects in our bodies? In this section, we will consider the pharmacokinetics of caffeine, including the routes of administration, absorption, and distribution, as well as the metabolism and elimination of caffeine from the body.

Route of Administration, Absorption, and Distribution

Caffeine is almost always absorbed orally from the gastrointestinal tract. Caffeine in soft drinks is absorbed more slowly than caffeine from coffee and tea. Because caffeine is both water-soluble and fat-soluble, it is rapidly distributed throughout the body, including into the brain, placenta, and breast milk. Caffeine levels peak in the blood about an hour after consumption.

Metabolism, Elimination, and Drug Interactions

The cytochrome P450 (CYP450) enzyme system of the liver metabolizes caffeine to paraxanthine, theophylline, and theobromine, each of which has its own effects on the body. Paraxanthine increases the breakdown of fat, theophylline is a bronchodilator and cardiac stimulant, and theobromine is a vasodilator and diuretic. These metabolites are processed further and then eliminated. Water-soluble caffeine is quickly and easily eliminated within 12 hours. Most is excreted in the urine, and the rest in feces, saliva, semen, and breast milk.

Several factors affect the metabolism of caffeine. Metabolism is slower in men, infants, the elderly, pregnant women, Asians, Africans, and those with liver disease.[37] This means that caffeine stays in their system longer and has more of an effect.

Some drugs slow the metabolism of caffeine. Alcohol reduces the rate of caffeine metabolism, which means that drinkers feel the effects of caffeine more than nondrinkers. However, giving someone who is intoxicated large amounts of caffeine to sober them up can do them more harm than good. The drinker may feel that he or she is less impaired than he or she actually is and be more likely to try to drive or engage in other risky behaviors. Oral contraceptives decrease the rate of caffeine metabolism by one-half to two-thirds.[38] Many selective serotonin reuptake inhibitors (SSRIs) also inhibit the liver's CYP450 system. So those taking SSRIs may be particularly sensitive to caffeine. Finally, theobromine, found in chocolate, inhibits the metabolism of itself, of theophylline, and of caffeine, so if a person regularly consumes chocolate, then coffee or tea may have a stronger effect.

Ask yourself: Caffeine is the most commonly consumed drug in the world, and it may interact with many drugs, including antidepressants, thyroid medication, oral contraceptives, and some antibiotics. Has your physician or pharmacist ever discussed your caffeine use with you?

By contrast, smoking cigarettes doubles the rate at which caffeine is eliminated because substances in tobacco induce the CYP450 enzyme system. Therefore, smokers can drink more caffeine and feel it less than nonsmokers. When smokers stop smoking and no longer metabolize caffeine as quickly, they may be more sensitive to their caffeine intake, which can increase the anxiety that already exists due to quitting cigarettes.

Mechanism of Action of Caffeine

There are two main mechanisms of action of caffeine. Caffeine inhibits phosphodiesterase, an enzyme that inactivates cyclic AMP (cAMP). Cyclic AMP is a molecule that relays signals important in many biological processes. Caffeine's increase of cAMP affects sugar and lipid metabolism and stimulates the release of epinephrine (adrenaline). But these effects occur only at very high concentrations of caffeine.[39] The most likely mechanism of action is through caffeine's blockage of adenosine receptors.

Adenosine is an inhibitory neurotransmitter, with receptors in the brain, heart, kidney, smooth muscle, and adipose. In the central nervous system, adenosine causes sedation and sleep and acts as an anticonvulsant. In the peripheral nervous system, adenosine lowers blood pressure and heart rate, dilates cerebral blood vessels, constricts the vessels that serve the heart, and decreases urination and gastric secretion. Because caffeine blocks these receptors, the drug reverses these effects.

Adenosine also normally stimulates the neurotransmitter GABA, which helps to calm and relax us, and decreases the discharge rate of dopamine, norepinephrine, serotonin, acetylcholine, cortisol, and glutamate neurons. So by blocking adenosine, caffeine increases the activity of these neurotransmitters, hormones, and other stimulating substances. At high doses, caffeine increases endorphins, and at very high doses (over 500 mg), caffeine directly inhibits GABA, which leads to insomnia, anxiety, and a rapid heartbeat.

Acute Effects of Caffeine

Summarizing the effects of caffeine can be difficult. For one, caffeine is usually ingested in a beverage, rather than in its pure form. But coffee and tea contain so many pharmacologically active substances that there is no easy way to isolate the effects of caffeine from those of the other substances these beverages contain.[40] Also, the effects depend on the frequency with which a person takes caffeine.

In the United States, most adults consume caffeine in the form of coffee. Coffee contains more than caffeine; the bean also contains **polyphenols**, **diterpenes**, and **trigonelline**, all of which have effects on the body (Figure 11.10).[41]

Polyphenols: A class of compounds found in fruits, vegetables, cocoa, teas, and other plants, which are thought to have antioxidant, anti-inflammatory, and anticarcinogenic properties. There are many different subclasses of polyphenols, including flavanols.

Diterpenes: Chemical compounds with anti-inflammatory and antimicrobial properties.

Trigonelline: A substance found in many plants, including potatoes, hemp, and coffee, which may have hypoglycemic, antiviral, antibacterial, anticarcinogenic, and neuroprotective properties.

Flavanol: A type of polyphenol found in tea and chocolate, which is thought to have antioxidant, anti-inflammatory, and anticarcinogenic properties.

The cacao bean and the tea leaf also contain beneficial substances. Both chocolate and tea contain polyphenols, including the antioxidant **flavanol**, which provides many beneficial effects.

Physiological Effects at Low and Moderate Doses

Acute administration of caffeine in someone who has no tolerance can cause a temporary increase in blood pressure, respiratory rate, urine output, gastric secretions, adrenaline, and cortisol release (Figure 11.11). But with *regular* caffeine consumption, tolerance develops and these effects diminish.

Central Nervous System

Caffeine stimulates the central nervous system, enhances alertness and arousal, and diminishes fatigue. Caffeine is most potent for central nervous system stimulation, followed by theophylline, then theobromine.

Caffeine can decrease a person's total sleep time and make it take longer to fall asleep. A person who has taken caffeine may awaken more frequently and be more easily awakened by sudden noises. High doses can change the pattern of sleep and lead to less time spent in the deeper and more restful sleep stages.

Caffeine also has some analgesic effects.[42] This might be due to its ability to elevate mood, or because it increases release of beta-endorphins.

Cardiovascular and Respiratory

Caffeine has a biphasic effect on the heart. Doses below 200 mg may cause no effect or may slow heart rate, while doses above 500 mg speed up the heart. If a person is not tolerant to caffeine's effects, the heart rate can increase as much as 10–20 beats per minute, and high doses also increase blood pressure. Caffeine acts directly on the heart tissue, as well as on brain centers that regulate the cardiovascular system.

Caffeine dilates coronary arteries, which allows more oxygen to enter the heart. However, it also constricts cerebral blood vessels, which decreases blood flow to the brain by about 30 percent. This may help to reduce pressure in the brain; hence, caffeine can be used to treat migraines.

Caffeine
- Reduces liver fibrosis (scarring)
- May counter Parkinson's, Alzheimer's, and depression

Diterpenes (Cafestol and Kahweol)
- Fights certain carcinogens
- Antioxidant
- Anti-inflammatory
- Prevents the development of new blood vessels that cancer cells need in order to grow and spread

Polyphenols (Chlorogenic acids, caffeic acid)
- Reduces liver fibrosis (scarring)
- Boosts DNA repair
- May reduce formation of blood clots
- Boosts metabolic efficiency
- Lowers blood pressure
- Demethylating potential helps prevent cancer
- Antioxidant

Trigonelline
- Antioxidant
- Lowers blood sugar

FIGURE 11.10. The coffee bean. The coffee bean contains many physiologically active substances, many of which have beneficial effects.

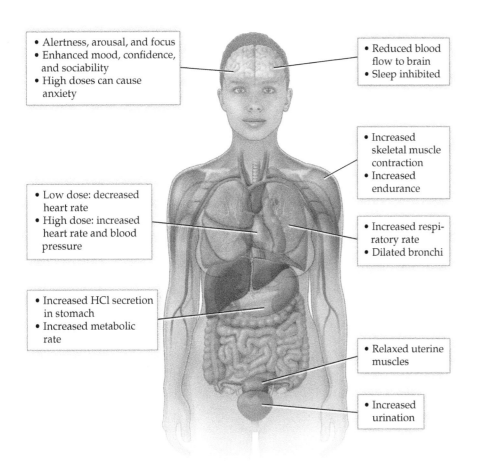

- Alertness, arousal, and focus
- Enhanced mood, confidence, and sociability
- High doses can cause anxiety

- Reduced blood flow to brain
- Sleep inhibited

- Increased skeletal muscle contraction
- Increased endurance

- Low dose: decreased heart rate
- High dose: increased heart rate and blood pressure

- Increased respiratory rate
- Dilated bronchi

- Increased HCl secretion in stomach
- Increased metabolic rate

- Relaxed uterine muscles

- Increased urination

FIGURE 11.11. Acute effects of caffeine.

Caffeine increases respiratory rate and dilates bronchi to the lungs. Theophylline has the greatest effect on the respiratory system compared to the other methylxanthines.

Gastrointestinal and Renal

The acids, oils, and caffeine in coffee can irritate the stomach lining and promote HCl secretion, leading to gastritis. Caffeine also increases basal metabolism. More than five cups of coffee per day can increase LDL ("bad") cholesterol as much as 15 percent, but when a paper filter is used, coffee does not elevate cholesterol as much.[43] This effect is probably due to an ingredient in coffee itself, and not due to the effect of caffeine.

Adenosine decreases urination, so when caffeine blocks these receptors, it acts as a diuretic. Caffeine also may slow the release of antidiuretic hormone from the pituitary gland.

Muscular

Caffeine boosts physical performance, by increasing the contraction of skeletal muscle, enhancing physical endurance, and delaying fatigue. Caffeine does this by releasing fats into the blood for use as energy.[44,45] This allows muscles to burn released fat for fuel and save the body's limited store of carbohydrates until later in the workout. Caffeine relaxes the smooth muscle of the uterus, bronchi, and coronary arteries.

Behavioral and Psychological Effects at Low and Moderate Doses

Caffeine's effect depends on dose. Although caffeine can increase alertness, improve concentration, and enhance mood, it also can lead to nervousness and agitation at higher doses.

Mood

Caffeine can elevate mood and cause people to feel energized, efficient, confident, and alert. They may feel a sense of well-being or increased sociability. But higher doses, or low doses in those who are sensitive, can lead to anxiety and stress. Caffeine can induce panic attacks in those who are vulnerable[46]; those who suffer from anxiety disorders tend to use less caffeine and may be hypersensitive to caffeine's anxiety-producing effects.[47,48] Caffeine increases the amount of adrenaline that is active in the body under stressful conditions, which can intensify stress and exacerbate panic attacks.

Cognitive Function

Caffeine seems to improve performance of simple, familiar, routine tasks, but it doesn't improve the accomplishment of complex, novel, and unpracticed tasks.[49] Solving many simple arithmetic problems or driving a car for long distances seem to be improved, and these effects are more apparent when people have been working at

Ask yourself: Why might the energy level and personality of a person play a role in whether caffeine boosts or diminishes performance?

their tasks for a while; caffeine doesn't improve performance when people are allowed to take breaks from their assignment. The personality of the user also may play a role. When presented with challenging mental tasks such as proofreading or solving math problems, impulsive and extroverted people get a boost in performance from caffeine, but introverts perform more poorly.[50] In short, caffeine's cognitive benefits seem to be a function of the energy level and personality of the subject as well as the cognitive nature and demands of the task.

Overdose

Over an extended period of time, and if taken in large doses, caffeine can lead to **caffeinism**, which results in an array of unpleasant symptoms in addition to caffeine dependency. Ingestion of over 300 mg of caffeine (about three cups of coffee) can cause difficulty sleeping, anxiety, and muscle twitches. More than 500 mg can lead to panic, chills, and nausea, while heavy consumption—10 cups of coffee or more per day—can produce agitation, tremors, and rapid breathing. Doses of over 1,000 mg per day can lead to severe anxiety, ringing in the ears, photophobia (extreme sensitivity to light), rambling thoughts and speech, confusion, elevated and irregular heartbeat, flushed face, fever, excessive urination, insomnia, vomiting, and diarrhea. Doses of 5–10 grams can result in seizures, respiratory failure, and death. Fatalities due to caffeine overdose are more frequent in infants, psychiatric patients, and athletes.[51] Caffeine's therapeutic index (TI) is about 1,000, or about 100 cups of coffee per day. (Remember, the TI is a ratio of the lethal dose over the effective dose of a drug.) Caffeine overdose is usually treated by alleviating the immediate symptoms, but with very high blood levels of caffeine, kidney dialysis may need to be implemented. Because of their high caffeine content, and because they often are consumed by adolescents and young adults, consumers should be especially wary of energy drinks.

Medical and Therapeutic Uses of Caffeine

Caffeine, other methylxanthines, and the foods that contain them seem to have many therapeutic benefits. Caffeine, coffee, tea, and chocolate have been shown to boost metabolism, reduce the risk of type 2 diabetes

Caffeinism: A toxic condition due to excessive caffeine consumption.

and liver disease, improve cognitive abilities, lower the risk of neurological disorders, protect against cancer, and improve mortality rates (Table 11.1).[52,53,54]

Although coffee, tea, and chocolate have been linked to medical benefits, it is important to clarify that any beneficial effects are thought to be due to the coffee or chocolate itself, not any added cream or sugar. As an example, black coffee has five calories, no fat, and no sugar. Many of coffee's purported health benefits would be lost with the consumption of a beverage such as Cold Stone Creamery's large Lotta Caramel Latte, which has 1,790 calories, 90 grams of fat, and 223 grams of carbohydrates.

Type 2 Diabetes

In both men and women, coffee, tea, and chocolate consumption are associated with a statistically significant reduction in risk of type 2 diabetes. Caffeine's role is controversial. Some report that caffeine itself helps reduce diabetes, and others say the protective effects of coffee and tea are independent of caffeine, and it is the other substances in coffee, tea, and chocolate that play a role in preventing diabetes.[55,56,57] Those who drink three to four cups of coffee per day have about a 25 percent lowered risk of developing type 2 diabetes.[58,59] This may be due to trigonelline, which lowers blood sugar, and to magnesium, which helps to increase insulin sensitivity.[60] Flavanols, present in tea and chocolate, improve insulin sensitivity. Those who consume at least three cups of tea per day,[61,62] or who eat dark chocolate on a weekly basis,[63] have a lower risk of developing type 2 diabetes. In addition, caffeine seems to have a dose-dependent protective effect on mortality among women who have diabetes.[64]

Liver

Alcohol, obesity, and the hepatitis virus can damage the liver. When the liver senses tissue damage, adenosine promotes the formation of tough collagen patches over the damaged areas. Over time, collagen scars (known as fibrosis) result, disrupting blood flow through the liver and ultimately leading to cirrhosis and liver failure.[65] Caffeine blocks adenosine and tamps down on collagen overproduction. Coffee consumption is associated with less severe liver fibrosis,[66] lower rates of liver cirrhosis,[67] less fatty liver,[68] and lower rates of liver cancer.[69] Green tea may also protect against various liver diseases.[70] Dark chocolate, which is particularly high in antioxidants, can improve circulation in the liver in patients with cirrhosis.[71]

TABLE 11.1. Some Potential Health Benefits of Caffeine, Coffee, Tea, and Chocolate

| Disease | Potential Mechanism by Which They Are Beneficial | | | |
	Caffeine Itself	Coffee	Tea	Chocolate
Metabolism	• Increases metabolic rate • Stimulates fat burning • Decreases appetite	• Polyphenols boost metabolic efficiency	• Polyphenols boost metabolic efficiency	• Polyphenols boost metabolic efficiency
Type 2 Diabetes	• May lower risk	• Trigonelline lowers blood sugar • Magnesium helps increase insulin sensitivity	• Flavanols and other polyphenols improve insulin sensitivity	• Flavanols and other polyphenols improve insulin sensitivity
Liver Disease	• Blocks adenosine receptors, which decreases fibrosis and slows liver damage	• Polyphenols block adenosine receptors, which decreases fibrosis and slows liver damage	• Tea polyphenols antioxidants prevent liver cell injury and death	• Cocoa flavanols improve liver circulation
Cognition	• May help performance of simple, routine tasks by boosting energy • May reduce risk of Alzheimer's disease by boosting acetylcholine levels in the brain and acting as an antioxidant	• Polyphenols improve cognitive function and cerebral blood flow • May lower risk of dementia and Alzheimer's disease	• Polyphenols improve cognitive function and cerebral blood flow • May lower risk of dementia and Alzheimer's disease	• Polyphenols improve cognitive function and cerebral blood flow
Parkinson's Disease	• Elevates dopamine levels in the brain			
Cardiovascular	• Slows cardiovascular damage • Constricts blood vessels in the brain to help treat migraines	• Polyphenols, magnesium, and potassium counteract the increase in blood pressure caused by caffeine • Polyphenols reduce blood clots	• Polyphenols and flavanols lower blood pressure	• Polyphenols and flavanols lower blood pressure
Respiratory	• Theophylline is a bronchodilator that can treat asthma and help stimulate breathing in premature infants			
Cancer		• Polyphenols boost DNA repair genes, act as antioxidants, and prevent the addition of cancer-triggering methyl groups to DNA • Diterpenes and trigonelline have antioxidant, anti-inflammatory, and anti-angiogenesis properties	• Tea flavanols have anti-inflammatory, antioxidant, and antitumor effects	

Cognitive Function

Caffeine may improve performance on some cognitive tasks, but any effects seem to be primarily due to enhanced energy and alertness. Some studies suggest that men and women who drink coffee or tea perform better on tests of mental acuity, and have a lower risk of cognitive decline, dementia, and Alzheimer's disease compared to those who don't imbibe.[72,73,74,75,76,77] This might be because of adenosine's effects on cholinergic neurons in the brain, because coffee and tea contain antioxidants, because polyphenols are neuroprotective, or because these beverages reduce the risk of diabetes, a disease that raises one's risk of dementia.[78,79] However, the effects of coffee and tea on mental acuity and cognitive decline are inconsistent.[80,81]

Many studies have demonstrated chocolate's ability to not only prevent cognitive impairment and decline in the elderly but also to improve memory, mental processing speed, abstract reasoning, and other measures of cognitive performance, with both short- and long-term use.[82,83,84] These effects may be due to the increased cerebral blood flow caused by cocoa flavanols.[85]

Parkinson's Disease

Coffee and tea consumption are associated with a lower incidence and slower progression of Parkinson's disease. Their beneficial effects are probably due to caffeine.[86,87] Parkinson's disease is a motor disorder associated with a loss of dopamine neurons in the brain. Adenosine normally inhibits dopamine production, and because caffeine blocks adenosine, it consequently boosts available dopamine.[88,89]

Cardiovascular Disease

Long-term coffee consumption may slightly lower one's susceptibility to heart disease.[90] Caffeine itself raises blood pressure, but the polyphenols and magnesium in coffee counteract that effect. Polyphenols found in both coffee and tea may also reduce the chance of dangerous blood clots and stroke.[91,92] However, one's risk of heart attack or stroke may be transiently elevated immediately after coffee intake, especially among infrequent drinkers.[93] Those who eat chocolate at least once a week have lower incidence of hypertension compared to those who never or rarely eat chocolate.[94]

Cancer

Coffee consumption is associated with a reduced risk of uterine, breast, mouth, throat, kidney, liver, and colorectal cancers.[95,96,97,98,99] Coffee's polyphenols may enhance the activity of genes that help repair genetic mutations that can lead to cancer, and also may prevent the addition of cancer-causing methyl groups to DNA. Diterpenes inhibit certain carcinogens, as well as act as anti-inflammatories and antioxidants. Diterpenes also suppress angiogenesis (the blood vessel growth that tumors need). Trigonelline also has antioxidant effects. The flavanol and other polyphenols found in tea have anti-inflammatory, antioxidant, and antitumor effects that may reduce the risk of various types of cancer, including ovarian and breast cancers.[100]

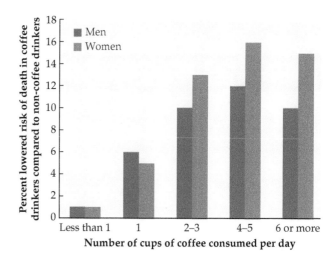

FIGURE 11.12. The effects of coffee on mortality. Studies have shown that drinking several cups of coffee every day may help people live longer. The risk of heart disease, diabetes, respiratory ailment, stroke, infections, and overall mortality goes down with the consumption of at least two cups a day.

Source: Freedman, N.D., Park, Y., Abnet, C.C., Hollenbeck, A.R., & Sinha, R. (2012). Association of coffee drinking with total and cause-specific mortality. NEJM, 366:1891–1904.

Mortality

As if all these benefits were not enough, drinking several cups of coffee every day may help you live longer. Although a study of over 400,000 people showed that coffee drinkers had a *higher* risk of death (perhaps because coffee drinkers were also more likely to smoke cigarettes), when researchers controlled for tobacco use and other confounding variables, they found that coffee consumption *lowered* mortality. Those who drank at least two cups of coffee per day were 10–16 percent less likely to have died than non-coffee drinkers (Figure 11.12).[101,102] Recent meta-analyses of studies involving over a million people support this finding.[103,104] Other studies also find reduced mortality associated with caffeine, regardless of the presence or absence of coffee.[105]

So, does this mean that non-coffee drinkers need to start forcing themselves to ingest the bitter brew? Should Red Bull replace orange juice at the breakfast table? Hold on. One survey found that those who consume a lot of coffee have a *greater* chance of dying early compared with people who don't imbibe as much.[106] In this study, researchers followed over 43,000 subjects for 17 years. They found that men under 55 years of age who drank at least 28 cups of coffee per week had a 21 percent higher risk of dying compared with their non-coffee-consuming peers. Clearly, we need to consider carefully the data regarding coffee's effect on mortality.

Critical Evaluation

Does caffeine increase or decrease a person's mortality?

Some studies suggest that caffeine helps us to live longer, while others propose that it lowers our life expectancy. There are many issues that must be considered in evaluating caffeine's effects on lifespan.

Empirical studies vs. longitudinal surveys. The gold standard for medical studies is the empirical double-blind, randomized, controlled trial, in which participants are randomly assigned to one testing condition, and neither they nor the researchers are aware of which group they are in. In an ideal empirical study, a scientist would gather thousands of participants, divided into groups that were identical with regard to age, sex, education, health, exercise, medical history, and social interactions. One group would drink only a specified amount of coffee at a certain time of day, one would drink tea, one would consume only soft drinks, and the last group would ingest no caffeine at all. All participants would be tightly controlled as to their diet, activity, drug use, and stress levels. To better manage the experiment, the participants would remain in the laboratory for 30 years, while scientists monitored their caffeine intake and subsequent health status.

Clearly, this is not only impossible, but laughable. Much of the research that investigates the long-term effects of caffeine on health consists of longitudinal studies in which participants are questioned about their habits and history and monitored over subsequent decades for the development of various diseases. Longitudinal surveys are not ideal, but they are one of the better tools at our disposal.

Limitations of surveys. Longitudinal studies are largely based on self-reports. For example, a participant may be given a survey that asks (among other things) about his or her coffee and tea consumption. But what is a "cup" of coffee or tea? There is great variation in the size of the cup and the amount of caffeine per cup. And, how accurate are participants' assessments of how much coffee they drink over the course of a lifetime likely to be?

It bears mentioning that many of these participants are elderly, and some are being evaluated for Alzheimer's disease. Will their assessment of their coffee or tea consumption be entirely accurate?

Many of the studies only measured coffee consumption at baseline and didn't assess changes in the subsequent years. Coffee use tends to be stable in adulthood, but how likely is it that at least some of the participants changed their caffeine intake over the following decades?

Participants. Human research participants are not genetically bred laboratory animals that are kept under identical conditions. Caffeine is metabolized differently depending on a person's age, size, and sex, as well as on other drugs that are ingested. Should the effects on one group be generalized to another?

Participants who consume caffeine are different in some way than those who do not drink caffeine. Do the non-caffeine imbibers have health problems that preclude them from using caffeine? Are those who drink coffee more susceptible to addictive substances and, therefore, more likely also to be addicted to other drugs?

The older subjects presumably did not consume as much caffeine in childhood as people do today. What might be the effects of caffeine consumption across the lifespan?

Correlation and causation. In these studies, most of the caffeine-consuming participants drank coffee rather than tea. Yet, the popular press sometimes reported about the effects of caffeine rather than the effects of coffee. In some studies, those who drank decaffeinated coffee received about the same benefits as those who drank caffeinated coffee. Are these effects due, then, to the caffeine or to the coffee itself?

Every research paper brings forth more questions than it answers. . . but this is a joy, not a burden. Think of all the mysteries out there still to be discovered. Let's consider these mysteries over a cup of coffee.

Some studies considered tea consumption, but found that tea did not provide the same benefits as coffee. Is this because the beneficial substances are found in coffee instead of tea? Or is it because a typical cup of tea contains less caffeine than a cup of coffee? Or is it because tea drinking is not as common, making the statistical power lower?

Perhaps the effects, whether beneficial or harmful, are related to other factors. Do people who are more stressed or more sleep-deprived drink more coffee? Or is the daily coffee or tea a person drinks part of a calming ritual that alleviates stress?

Many people who drink coffee or tea take it with milk and sugar. How do those substances influence health? Does coffee make them ingest more calories over the course of a day? Fewer calories?

Maybe those who drink coffee are more social and take time out to gather with others in coffee shops. A person who frequents a coffee shop many times a day will end up paying thousands of dollars a year to maintain a coffee habit. Does this have a significant influence on the person's overall health?

Chronic Effects of Caffeine

Just as the acute effects of caffeine can range from benign and beneficial with low and moderate doses to deadly with overdose, the chronic effects of caffeine are wide ranging. Tolerance and dependence may develop quickly, and withdrawal symptoms may vary in terms of duration and severity. In addition, adverse effects may develop with chronic use, and caffeine use also may impact an unborn fetus.

Tolerance and Dependence

A certain degree of tolerance and dependence on caffeine develops quickly, even in those who don't partake to excess, although the exact picture of caffeine tolerance is unclear. Tolerance seems to develop to the cardiovascular, respiratory, and sleep effects, but not to effects on mood. Physical dependence can occur quickly, but most use is noncompulsive and does not impair the user's daily activities.

Ask yourself: Most people in the world are dependent on caffeine, yet many don't even consider it a drug. If most people in a society use a drug, does that mean it is normal to use the drug and abnormal to abstain? How does a society's acceptance of a particular substance influence our laws and attitudes about that drug?

Withdrawal

When someone regularly consumes the adenosine antagonist caffeine, there is an increase in the number of adenosine receptors, such that there are about 10–20 percent more receptors than were there previously (a process called "upregulation"). When the person then suddenly stops using caffeine, there are a greater number of inhibitory adenosine receptors, but there is no caffeine to block them.

Withdrawal from caffeine usually begins 12–24 hours after cessation of use and can last for up to nine days.[107] There is considerable variability with regards to the symptoms, duration, and severity of caffeine withdrawal. Symptoms typically include headache, fatigue, sleepiness, decreased energy and alertness, impaired concentration, anxiety, irritability, and a craving for the drug.

Adverse Effects from Chronic Use

Caffeine has been implicated in causing or aggravating premenstrual syndrome and increasing the growth of benign breast cysts. There are, however, a number of flaws with these studies. Given the variations in source of caffeine, preparation methods, amount of caffeine consumed, as well as a lack of control for other health factors and lifestyle habits, it is difficult to adequately assess the effect of caffeine on PMS and breast disease.[108,109]

Effects on the Fetus

Most women drink caffeine during pregnancy.[110] More than 75 percent of infants tested exhibit detectable levels of caffeine in their blood at birth.[111] We are unsure of the effects of caffeine on the fetus. Some reports say it is associated with lower birth weight and miscarriage,[112,113,114,115,116] while other studies suggest that pregnancy is not adversely affected by consumption of less than 300 mg per day of caffeine.[117,118,119,120] One of the reasons it is so difficult to accurately assess caffeine's effect on a fetus is that it is hard to accurately determine a pregnant woman's caffeine consumption. In addition, smoking and caffeine are strongly correlated, and some symptoms of pregnancy may further confound the situation. For example, nausea is significantly less common in pregnancies that are lost to miscarriage. Women who are nauseated are less likely to drink caffeine.[121] Therefore, it's possible that it was not the caffeine that led to the miscarriage but rather because the fetus was less viable to begin with.

Although there is no definitive proof that caffeine can harm the fetus, it is best to err on the side of safety. Even if a pregnant woman ingests a small amount of caffeine, the fetus's body is so much smaller that serum concentrations will reach higher levels. Also, a fetus's liver is unable to metabolize caffeine, so the drug lingers in the fetus's system 15 times as long as it does in adults.[122] Remember also that caffeine metabolism slows significantly during gestation, so caffeine ingested during pregnancy stays in the mother's system two to three times longer than usual, elevating the unborn child's exposure to caffeine.

Quitting Caffeine

Melissa, 51, learns that she has atrial fibrillation, a common type of heart arrhythmia that is worsened by caffeine. Mark, 42, has just been laid off and needs to ease up on his $12-a-day Starbucks habit. Brandon, 24, has been having trouble sleeping. Thirty-year-old Amanda has recently discovered she is pregnant and wants to be as healthy as she can for her unborn baby. All these people have decided to quit caffeine. What advice can we give them?

- Write out your reasons for quitting, and keep them somewhere visible. This reminder may help you say "no" when the craving hits you.
- Start slowly. Unless otherwise instructed by your doctor, you can slowly cut down on your daily caffeine intake. Substitute some of your caffeinated drinks with decaffeinated coffee, herbal tea, or caffeine-free soft drinks. Write out a schedule you will follow to eliminate caffeine from your diet.
- Drink lots of water. Water will help you detoxify and stay hydrated. As you eliminate caffeine-containing drinks from your daily regimen, be sure to replace them with water.
- Be aware of hidden sources of caffeine—caffeine can be found in chocolate, energy water, and some headache medicines. Even decaffeinated coffee has small amounts of caffeine.
- Don't be surprised when you experience withdrawal symptoms such as sleepiness, headache, anxiety, irritability, and constipation. If possible, allow some time for rest and recuperation.
- Give yourself treats. Figure out how much money you spent on coffee or soft drinks and reward yourself with a noncaffeinated incentive.
- Give yourself some energy in nonpharmaceutical ways. Listen to upbeat music, take a walk, sit up straight, and breathe deeply.

Chapter Summary

- **Introduction**
  - » Caffeine is the world's most popular psychoactive substance.
  - » Worldwide, about 120,000 tons of caffeine are consumed annually.
- **History of Caffeine**
  - » Coffee began to be cultivated in Arabia between the twelfth and fifteenth centuries.
  - » Coffeehouses increased in popularity in Europe in the seventeenth century.
  - » Tea was discovered almost 5,000 years ago in China.
  - » In the early seventeenth century, the Dutch shipped tea to Europe; the tea trade became a major part of the British economy.
  - » The Mayans, Incas, and Aztecs cultivated the cacao tree and made a warm, bitter drink from its beans.
  - » Spanish explorers brought cacao pods back to Spain; after vanilla and sugar were added, the delightful brew became a popular drink.
  - » Soft drinks first became popular in the nineteenth century; pharmacists invented many of the brands that are still popular today.
  - » Over the last two decades, energy drinks have soared in popularity.
- **Prevalence of Caffeine Use**
  - » Approximately 85 percent of the entire U.S. population, and over 90 percent of adults age 18 and older, consume caffeine.
  - » Most American adults are coffee drinkers, while soft drinks account for most of the caffeine consumed by U.S. children and teenagers.
- **Source and Forms of Caffeine**
  - » Caffeine, theophylline, and theobromine are three chemically related xanthines that occur naturally in more than 60 species of plants.
  - » Coffee comes from the beans of several species of *Coffea* trees; the beans are roasted to enhance their flavor and then ground.
  - » Tea comes from the leaf and bud of the *Camellia sinensis* tree; black, green, and oolong tea differ in how long the leaves are allowed to oxidize after picking.
  - » Chocolate comes from the bean of the *Theobroma cacao* tree; cocoa beans contain a small amount of caffeine, but eight times as much theobromine.
  - » Many soft drinks contain cola nuts, which are the seeds from *Cola* trees. Soft drinks are classified as beverages and overseen by the FDA, but energy drinks are

classified as dietary supplements and, therefore, not regulated by the FDA.

» Not only do coffee, tea, chocolate, and soft drinks all contain different amounts of caffeine, but how much they contain depends on many variables.

- **Pharmacokinetics of Caffeine**
  » Caffeine is almost always absorbed orally from the gastrointestinal tract; its metabolism is influenced by a person's age, sex, and race, as well as by other drugs taken.
- **Mechanism of Action of Caffeine**
  » Caffeine's main mechanism of action is to block adenosine receptors, which causes overall stimulation.
- **Acute Effects of Caffeine**
  » Physiologically, low to moderate doses of caffeine increase heart rate, dilate bronchi, constrict cerebral blood vessels, and increase skeletal muscular contraction.
  » Caffeine also can enhance alertness, diminish fatigue, elevate mood, and improve concentration.
  » The effects of caffeine depend on whether a person has become tolerant to its actions.
  » Large amounts of caffeine can lead to caffeinism; about 100 cups of coffee in one day could be fatal.

- **Medical and Therapeutic Uses of Caffeine**
  » Caffeine and other xanthines can be used as a respiratory stimulant for premature infants, to treat asthma, and to help treat migraine headaches.
  » Caffeine may help to reduce the risk of type 2 diabetes, liver disease, Parkinson's disease, Alzheimer's disease, stroke, and cancer.
  » Some studies suggest that drinking several cups of coffee every day reduces a person's risk of mortality, while other studies have found the opposite. Many factors influence the results of these studies.
- **Chronic Effects of Caffeine**
  » A certain degree of tolerance and dependence on caffeine develops quickly, even in those who don't partake to excess.
  » Withdrawal from caffeine typically includes headache, fatigue, decreased energy, and irritability.
  » Most women drink caffeine during pregnancy; research on the effects of caffeine on the fetus is inconclusive.
- **Quitting Caffeine**
  » If you want to quit caffeine, it may help to slowly cut down on your daily intake, drink lots of water, and prepare for withdrawal symptoms.

Key Terms

Caffeinism (p.276)
Diterpenes (p.274)

Flavanol (p.274)
Polyphenols (p.274)

Trigonelline (p.274)

Quiz Yourself!

1. True or false? Those age 18–24 typically consume the most caffeine.
2. True or false? To produce green tea, leaves are oxidized longer than they are to produce black tea.
3. True or false? Caffeine raises a person's risk of type 2 diabetes.
4. What ingredient in chocolate is toxic to dogs?
5. Why is it so difficult to generalize how much caffeine is in a cup of coffee?
6. What are some factors that must be considered when evaluating caffeine's effects on mortality?
7. In each of the following pairs, who will experience slower metabolism of caffeine?
   A. A man or a woman?
   B. A nonpregnant woman or a pregnant woman?
   C. An Asian man or a Caucasian man?
   D. A woman on SSRI antidepressants or a woman not taking SSRIs?
   E. A man who smokes one pack of cigarettes a day or a nonsmoking man?
8. True or false? Caffeine binds to and stimulates adenosine receptors.
9. Which of the following is FALSE about caffeine's effects on the body?
   A. Caffeine may increase basal metabolism.
   B. Caffeine dilates cerebral blood vessels.
   C. Caffeine acts as a diuretic.
   D. Caffeine is a bronchodilator.
10. About _____ cups of coffee in a day would be fatal.

Additional Resources

Websites

The Effects of Caffeine: From the Neuroscience for Kids webpage. http://faculty.washington.edu/chudler/caff.html

Videos

Caffeinated. (2015). 80 minutes. A documentary on the story of coffee through the perspectives of people who have dedicated their lives to it.

Caffeine! Short video covering some details about caffeine. https://www.youtube.com/watch?v=Xl1XBJLfIDU&t=166s

The science of caffeine: the world's most popular drug https://www.technologynetworks.com/applied-sciences/videos/the-science-of-caffeine-the-worlds-most-popular-drug-311120

Books

Allen, S.L. (1999). *The devil's cup: A history of the world according to coffee.* New York: Soho Press.

Weinberg, B.A. & Bealer, B.K. (2002). *The world of caffeine: The science and culture of the world's most popular drug.* New York: Routledge.

Learn more with this chapter's digital tools at www.oup.com/he/rosenthal2e.

12 Alcohol

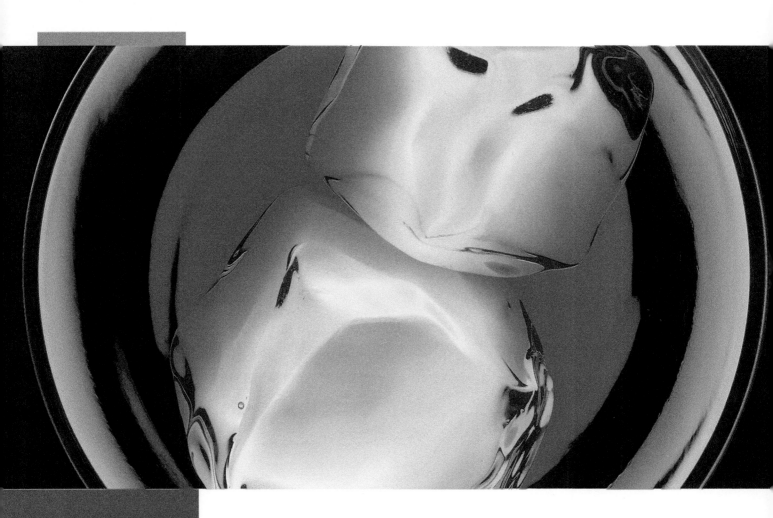

True or false?

1.
True or false? Humans are the only species that drinks alcohol.

2.
True or false? All else being equal, the same amount of alcohol will make a female more intoxicated than a male.

3.
True or false? Withdrawal from alcohol can be fatal.

"Alcohol is the cause of, and solution to, all of life's problems."
—Homer Simpson

A lcohol is one of the most widely consumed and popular psychoactive drugs in the world, used by millions of people every day. An ingrained part of American culture, we use it to celebrate our successes, grieve our losses, and commemorate rites of passage from birth to marriage to death. We drown our sorrows to mourn the end of one relationship and meet for a drink to initiate the beginning of another.

Alcohol is so deeply rooted in our society that we don't always remember that it is, in fact, a drug. Even the federal government differentiates between alcohol and drugs; the National Institute on Drug Abuse (NIDA) and the National Institute on Alcohol Abuse and Alcoholism (NIAAA) are separate organizations. Perhaps alcohol is given special status because it is openly and widely distributed, advertised, and sold. (Similarly, many people don't consider tobacco and caffeine to be drugs.) Maybe alcohol's long history of use, and the fact that parents and other role models imbibe, contributes to alcohol's special position in the pharmacological pantheon. Yet, alcohol *is* a drug—when used irresponsibly, it is one of the most dangerous and devastating drugs in the world. In the United States alone, alcohol abuse costs approximately $249 billion and causes over 95,000 deaths each year.[1,2,3]

Alcohol addiction is a complex, multifaceted condition with biological, psychological, social, and environmental foundations. Alcohol use disorders affect young and old, rich and poor, black and white, men and women. Almost 15 million Americans age 12 and older currently have a diagnosis of alcohol use disorder, but most are not treated. Alcohol addiction is discussed at greater length in Chapter 17, and prevention of problematic drinking and treatment of alcohol dependence and alcohol use disorders is covered in Chapter 18.

Learning Objectives

- Trace the history of alcohol use in the United States.
- Assess the positive and negative outcomes of Prohibition in America.
- Compare alcohol use in the United States by gender, age, race, and other demographic factors.
- Compare and contrast fermented beverages and distilled beverages.
- Describe the metabolic pathway of ethanol.
- Identify factors that affect the metabolism of alcohol.
- Summarize the way ethanol interacts with different neurotransmitter systems.
- Outline the acute physiological and behavioral effects of alcohol.
- Evaluate the medical benefits of alcohol and the effects of alcohol on aggression.
- List some effects of both acute and chronic heavy drinking.

History of Alcohol

Humans have consumed alcohol for millennia. Fermentation of fruits and grains produces ethanol, which acts as a powerful inebriant and also helps to preserve food.[4] In addition to humans, golden hamsters, elephants, wild pigs, baboons, birds, and bees often seek out alcohol-containing fermented fruits, consuming them until they become drunk.

Alcohol

Type of drug: Depressant	**Tolerance:** Moderate	**Schedule:** Legal
Chemical formula: CH_3CH_2OH	**Physical dependence:** Intense	**Slang:** Booze, hooch, liquor, brewski (for beer), adult beverage
Routes of administration: Oral	**Psychological dependence:** Moderate	
Duration of effect: Moderate		
Neurotransmitters affected: GABA, glutamate, dopamine, endogenous opioids	**Withdrawal symptoms:** Cramps, delirium, vomiting, sweating, hallucinations, seizures, delirium tremens (DTs)	

Early Alcohol Use

Humans most likely discovered alcohol during the late Stone Age, when a jar of fruit or honey fermented, and a lucky caveman enjoyed the effects. The development of agriculture around 8000 BCE enabled alcohol production to flourish. Lacking enough clean water for all inhabitants, alcohol sustained life.[5] Beer and wine helped distract people from the fatigue and boredom of life, alleviated pain, and were sources of pathogen-free liquid, which provided necessary vitamins, nutrients, and calories. It may be that people who drank fermented beverages lived longer and reproduced more, so the tendency to drink and the enzymes to metabolize alcohol were passed on. Wine and beer were an important part of the culture of Ancient Egypt and Israel, as well as Ancient Greece and the Roman Empire.[6]

The Middle Ages to the Early Modern Era

In the eighth century, Arab alchemists developed a safe process of alcohol **distillation**, which increases the ethanol content of a beverage. Arabs were traders, and they spread the skill and practice of alcohol distillation across the globe. Some suggest that early efforts at distillation were performed because it was easier to ship smaller amounts of liquid with higher alcohol content overseas. At the end of the voyage, the distilled beverage was meant to be diluted back to a lower alcohol concentration. But when the more potent beverage arrived, everyone liked it just fine as it was.[7]

By 1100 CE, distilled liquors had spread throughout Europe. Physicians investigated distilled alcohol as a treatment for many ailments. Alcohol was part of

Distillation: A process that concentrates the alcohol in a beverage.

meals and medicines, given to children and invalids, and played a role in religious ceremonies. Men, women, and children had ale, the only safe or easily available drink, for breakfast, with lunch, and before bed—about a gallon per person per day was the standard ration.[8] Water was often laden with pathogens, milk was used to make cheese or butter, and cider and wine were too rare or too expensive.[9] The widespread drinking of spirits surged after the Black Death of 1347–1351. Alcohol was completely ineffective as a cure for the plague, but it made the imbiber feel better. As a result, Europe emerged from the Middle Ages as a heavy-drinking culture. By the mid-eighteenth century, every man, woman, and child in London drank an average of more than a pint of gin per week.[10]

Puritans and Colonial America

In 1620, the Mayflower was scheduled to land in Virginia, but the seas were rough and the Pilgrims were running out of beer, so they decided to disembark in Massachusetts at Plymouth Rock. As the voyagers wrote, "We could not now take time for further search or consideration, our victuals being much spent, especially our Beere, and it being now the 19th of December."[11]

QUICK HIT

The name Manhattan is reputed to have alcohol-related origins. When Henry Hudson explored the region in 1609, he met some Indians and offered them a drink. One of the warriors took the drink and swallowed it in one gulp. After initially collapsing, he stood up, declaring the drink to be wonderful. His fellows joined in, drank, became intoxicated, and soon after, the place was named *Manahachtanienk*, "the island where we drank liquor."[12]

During the Colonial period, men, women, and children drank alcohol on a daily basis. The tavern in the middle of town was the center of social life, a place where one could find friends, food, drink, business, and local politics. The Continental Army supplied soldiers with a daily ration of rum, and employers provided workers with liquor. When Harvard College was being built, one of the first buildings constructed was a brewery, to assure that students would have an ample supply of beer.[13]

Alcohol also played an important role in the economic development of the nation. Farmers distilled excess grain, making it easier to ship and trade.[14] Rum became New England's largest and most profitable business. In the infamous "triangle trade," Yankees shipped rum to the west coast of Africa, where they traded it for slaves. The enslaved men, women, and children were sent to the West Indies and used as barter for sugar and molasses, which was then taken back to New England and converted into rum. Between 1680 and 1713, ships carried about 1.3 million gallons of spirits to Africa, which they exchanged for about 60,000 humans (Figure 12.1).[15]

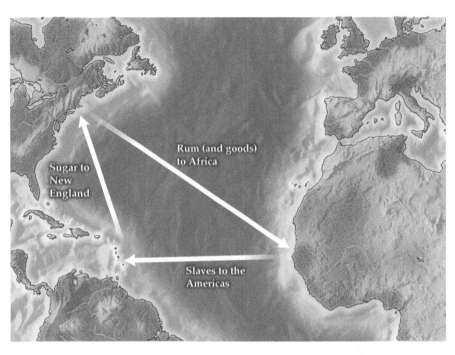

FIGURE 12.1. The Triangle Trade. In Colonial America, rum was traded for African slaves.

Temperance Movements in the United States (Nineteenth Century)

The early nineteenth century was a time of the heaviest drinking in the country's history, and alcohol was seen as a major cause of crime, violence, and immorality. Per capita consumption was about five drinks each day for each adult (about three to four times what it is today).[16] As the nineteenth century progressed, a number of **temperance movements** appeared. Early temperance groups focused on moderation; their goal was to temper (curtail or moderate) the use of distilled spirits, not to eliminate them. Beer and wine were still largely considered acceptable and healthy beverages.

In the 1830s and 1840s, the temperance movement experienced a significant groundswell. The American Temperance Society, 1.5 million members strong, helped reduce the per capita alcohol consumption in the United States. Millions of Americans took either the "short pledge" (abstinence from spirits) or the "long pledge" (total abstinence). In this hard-drinking time, those who abstained from alcohol did so bravely, taking risks with their health, given that most public water supplies were contaminated. Abstainers were even forced to pay higher premiums for life insurance.[17]

The Civil War took attention away from the temperance movement. States needed revenue from alcohol sales to help finance the war, and many of the prohibition laws passed in the 1850s were repealed by 1865. In the 1870s, however, temperance movements mobilized, and women often led the charge.

First organized in 1873, the Women's Christian Temperance Union (WCTU) became one of the most successful lobbying organizations in American history (Figure 12.2). The WCTU saw alcohol as both a cause and consequence of larger social problems. Members would march into saloons and stores that sold liquor and prevail upon customers to not buy alcohol. They visited elementary schools and warned students that if they started drinking, they would grow up to become a danger to themselves and others before dying young.[18]

As America entered the early twentieth century, anti-alcohol attitudes increased. It is said that Henry Ford immediately fired any worker who drank alcohol, even when the worker drank only while off-duty.[19] Several reasons—economic, religious, and nationalistic—underlie this shift in attitudes.

Temperance movement: A social program urging restrictions or prohibitions on the use of alcoholic beverages.

FIGURE 12.2. Carrie Nation. An ardent member of the temperance movement, Carrie Nation started a local branch of the WCTU in Kansas, but eventually turned to violence. She adopted the hatchet as her signature weapon, wrecking nearly 50 bars and causing hundreds of thousands of dollars in damage. Carrie was arrested 25 times and had her nose broken, head smashed, and wrist broken, among other injuries. She died in 1911, nine years before the implementation of National Prohibition.

- *Economic.* Between 1870 and 1915, the tax on liquor provided one-half to two-thirds of the internal revenue for the U.S. federal budget. But with the passage of the 16th Amendment in 1913 establishing the federal income tax, America's need for alcohol revenues decreased. Additionally, it was considered almost un-American to waste money on alcohol and other nonproductive ends.
- *Religious.* The religious revival sweeping the nation at the time gave people a sense of righteousness against evil alcohol.

Bootlegger: Someone who illegally distills or sells liquor.

Rumrunner: Someone who illegally smuggles liquor across a border.

Speakeasy: Illegal and clandestine nightclub and drinking spot.

- *Nationalistic.* In 1917, America went to war against Germany. Beer, with its German associations, fell out of favor. It was thought that liquor weakened the nation's strength and depleted grains that could be used for bread for our brave soldiers.

By 1912, a total of 12 states had amended their constitutions or introduced legislation to outlaw alcohol, and by 1919, some 34 states had passed prohibition laws. The following year, prohibition became the law of the land.

Prohibition

In 1917, the Senate adopted a resolution authored by Andrew Volstead, the Chairman of the House Judiciary Committee, to add a Constitutional amendment prohibiting the sale of alcohol in the United States. By January 16, 1919, forty-six of the forty-eight states ratified the amendment (Connecticut and Rhode Island rejected the amendment), and the 18th Amendment went into effect on January 16, 1920. Upon passage of Prohibition, members of the Yale Club, a private club in Manhattan whose members were alumni or faculty of Yale University, pragmatically laid down a stock of wine sufficient to last for 14 years.[20]

The 18th Amendment specified that the "manufacture, sale, or transportation of intoxicating liquors within, the importation thereof into, or the exportation thereof from the United States and all territory subject to the jurisdiction thereof for beverage purposes is hereby prohibited." This was the first addition to the U.S. Constitution to restrict rights rather than expand them. The Volstead Act set down the methods of enforcement of the 18th Amendment. Violators could be punished with substantial fines, prison terms, and confiscation of property. Medical patients and church members entitled to receive Communion were exempt, as were home brewing, cider making, and the distillation of alcohol for industrial purposes.[21]

The 18th Amendment did *not* forbid the use of alcohol; the crime was in supplying the alcohol. But criminals quickly stepped in to fulfill the demand, and illegal liquor flooded the nation. The Volstead Act required that chemicals be added to industrial alcohol to make it unpleasant and even dangerous to drink. **Bootleggers**, however, soon learned how to remove these chemicals (although they were not always successful) that could cause blindness, paralysis, and death.

Rumrunners illegally smuggled liquor across borders, and **speakeasies**—illegal and clandestine nightclubs and drinking spots—began to sprout up in cities.

In 1929, the New York police commissioner estimated there were 32,000 drinking spots in New York City—double the number of saloons and illegal joints the city had contained before Prohibition.[22]

QUICK HIT

William S. McCoy was considered to be the prince of rum-runners. He never watered down his liquor and never dealt with gangsters. His name gave birth to the term "the real McCoy" for an article of genuine quality.[23]

Alcohol was illegal, but Americans continued to purchase it. At the height of Prohibition, Americans spent about $5 billion a year on alcohol,[24] which would be about $69 billion in today's dollars. As such, Prohibition encouraged a general disregard for the law. Even President Harding drank whisky and beer in the White House bedroom.

The illegal trade of alcohol encouraged the growth of organized crime. Because alcohol was now illegal, citizens had to turn to criminals to get their liquor. The mobster Al Capone coordinated a vast bootlegging enterprise and oversaw the importation of alcohol from Canada, hundreds of illegal distilleries and breweries in the United States, and bodyguards to protect these investments. Capone said he broke the law to fill the nation's demand for liquor:

> I make my money by supplying a public demand. If I break the law, my customers, who number hundreds of the best people in Chicago, are as guilty as I am. The only difference between us is that I sell and they buy. Everybody calls me a racketeer. I call myself a businessman. When I sell liquor, it's bootlegging. When my patrons serve it on a silver tray on Lake Shore Drive, it's hospitality.[25]

The United States underwent enormous changes during the Prohibition era, many of which led to the demise of the 18th Amendment. Americans embraced consumerism, and the item that American consumers most wanted to buy was an automobile.[26] Not only did automobiles facilitate illegal alcohol distribution, but automobiles and airplanes also connected far-flung regions of the country, spreading sophisticated city values to small towns. During the 1920s, Americans enjoyed their independence. Women had recently won the right to vote, skirts were shorter, jazz was in, and sexual freedom was the word of the day. As such, people grew increasingly distasteful of the oppressive means by which the government enforced Prohibition,

as federal agents searched homes, tapped phones, and killed innocents.

It was the Great Depression, however, that tolled the death knell for Prohibition. During the 1920s, the federal government lost billions in potential tax revenues. By 1932, industrial production had fallen by more than half, and a quarter of the workforce was unemployed. If liquor were to be made legal and taxed again, the country could fill the gaping hole in its revenue sources.

In 1932, Franklin Delano Roosevelt included the repeal of the 18th Amendment as a plank of his platform for election, and he won by a landslide. By December 1933, some 35 states had passed a referendum to reinstitute drinking, and Utah became the 36th and final state to cast its ballot to officially end Prohibition. On December 5, 1933, the 21st Amendment to the Constitution was ratified, repealing the 18th Amendment and returning control over alcohol policies to the states. Prohibition lasted 13 years, 10 months, and 18 days, fifty-odd days less than the 14-year supply of wine laid down by the Yale Club in 1920.[27]

Prohibition saw the lowest alcohol consumption in U.S. history. There were fewer hospital admissions and deaths due to alcohol, fewer drunk-driving accidents, and fewer arrests for alcohol-related offenses. But Prohibition also led to the rise of organized crime, bribery, blackmail, corruption, and a reduced respect for the law.

Alcohol from World War II to Today

In a few short years, drinking went from being a criminal activity to being practically a civic duty. During World War II, brewers made sure to link alcohol to patriotism and what "our boys" were fighting for back home: steaks in the backyard and a cold beer.[28] One Seagram's ad implied that drinking whiskey was as patriotic an act as buying war bonds.

Throughout U.S. history, attitudes toward alcohol have alternated between tolerance and disapproval and back again in cycles roughly 70 years long.[29] Figure 12.3 shows per person alcohol consumption in the United States from 1780 through 2018.[30,31,32]

Ask yourself: What are cultural attitudes toward alcohol today? In what ways might it depend on a person's age, gender, profession, or other factors?

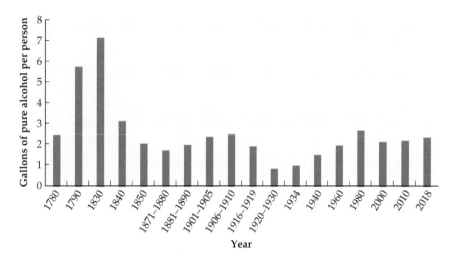

FIGURE 12.3.   Alcohol use in the United States over time. The early 19th century showed the highest alcohol use in our nation's history.

Sources: Goode, E. (2007). Drugs in American Society, 7th edition. *New York: McGraw Hill.*

Slater, M.E., & Alpert, H.R. (2020). Apparent per capita alcohol consumption: National, state, and regional trends: 1977–2018. Arlington, VA: NIAAA Surveillance Report.

Prevalence of Alcohol Use

"Salud." "L'Chaim." "Na zdrovie." These are just a few of the ways to say "cheers" in other languages. Alcohol is consumed in almost all countries on earth, although there is significant variation in the amount imbibed and attitudes about its use.

Global Alcohol Use

About 2.3 billion people around the globe are current drinkers, but the amount of alcohol consumed by each country varies greatly, from hard-drinking Eastern and Western Europe, to abstentious Islamic countries of the Middle East and Northern Africa (Figure 12.4).[33] Drinking behaviors, attitudes, and customs vary as well. Commonly held stereotypes suggest that Russians like to pound shots of vodka, Irish men bond over beers, and French and Italians sip wine decorously with their meals. In the Mediterranean, alcohol is associated with peaceful and harmonious interactions, while alcohol is often associated with violence in the United States, the United Kingdom, and Australia.[34] These differences often come from cultural beliefs and expectancies about alcohol rather than from the amount of alcohol consumed or inherent genetic differences.

Although there are cultural differences regarding who may drink, how much, of what, and in what context, cross-cultural research has revealed some

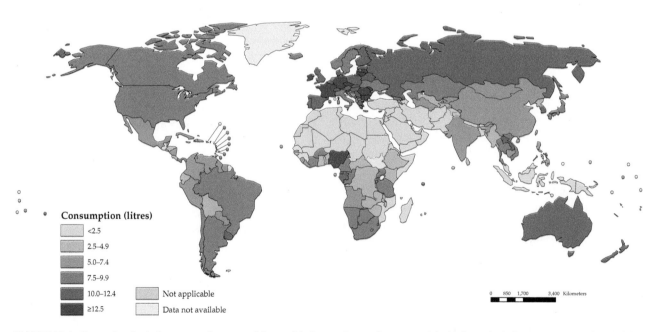

FIGURE 12.4.   Per capita alcohol consumption around the world. Eastern Europe has some of the highest alcohol consumption in the world; Northern African and Middle Eastern countries have some of the lowest.

Source: WHO. (2018). Global status report on alcohol and health, 2018. https://apps.who.int/iris/bitstream/handle/10665/274603/9789241565639-eng.pdf

near-universal constants in the social norms of alcohol consumption.[35] Most societies designate specific environments for communal drinking; these separate social worlds have their own customs and values. In addition, most societies have rules of conduct concerning

- Social control of intoxicated behavior
- Restrictions on female and underage alcohol consumption
- Proscription of solitary drinking

These 10 people represent the population of the United States.

These 10 bottles represent the total alcohol consumed in the United States

30% of the population does not drink at all

50% of the population drinks 20% of the alcohol

10% of the population drinks 20% of the alcohol

10% of the population drinks 60% of the alcohol

FIGURE 12.5. Distribution of alcohol consumption in the U.S. About 20% of the population consumes 80% of all alcohol sold in the United States.

Alcohol Consumption in the United States

Alcohol is America's most popular drug. With the exception of caffeine, more Americans use alcohol than any other legal or illegal drug. Each year, Americans consume an average of about one and a half standard drinks each day.[36] Obviously, not every man, woman, and child in America has a drink every day, which means that some people consume more than their share.

About 65–70 percent of the U.S. population consumes alcohol, and there are more than 10 million Americans who are alcohol dependent. But alcohol is not evenly consumed across the population. About one-third of the population does not drink at all, 50 percent of Americans (representing 70 percent of those who do drink) consume 20 percent of the alcohol sold, and the other 20 percent of Americans consume 80 percent of all alcohol sold in the United States (Figure 12.5).

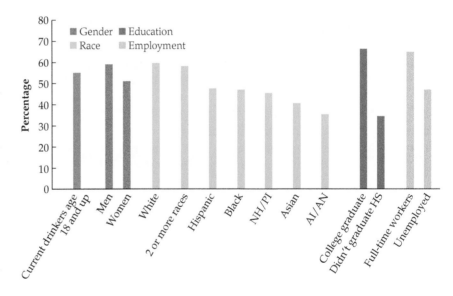

FIGURE 12.6. Demographics of current alcohol use in the United States in adults age 18 and older. Drinking rates are higher in men, whites, and college graduates.

Source: SAMHSA. (2020). Results from the 2019 national survey on drug use and health. Rockville, MD: Center for Behavioral Health Statistics and Quality.

Ask yourself: Many first dates typically involve meeting for a drink. What does it say about our culture that dating partners often choose to consume a drug together at their first meeting?

Current Alcohol Use

Almost 51 percent of the U.S. population age 12 years and older—or about 140 million people—are current drinkers.[37] Current use refers to having consumed at least one drink in the past month. Whites are more likely to drink than those of other races, younger adults more than older adults, and college-educated people are more likely to drink than those without a high school diploma (Figure 12.6).[38] Drinking rates are highest among those age 21–29 (Figure 12.7).

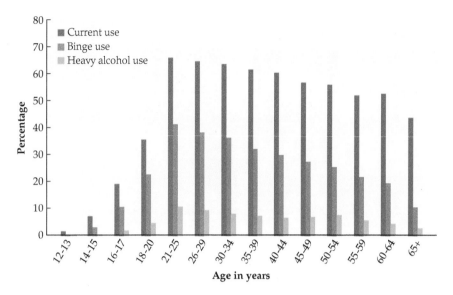

FIGURE 12.7. Alcohol use by age. Those age 21–29 have the highest rate of current, binge, and heavy alcohol use.

Source: SAMHSA. (2020). Results from the 2019 national survey on drug use and health. *Rockville, MD: Center for Behavioral Health Statistics and Quality.*

Binge Drinking

Excessive use of alcohol costs the United States $249 billion a year and accounts for about 10 percent of deaths among working-age adults in the United States, most often due to liver disease, motor vehicle accidents, or alcohol-related homicide or suicide.[39] Excessive use includes **binge drinking**, heavy weekly consumption, and any drinking by pregnant women or by those under 21 years of age.[40] Binge drinking is the most common form of excessive alcohol use and is responsible for over half the deaths and three-quarters of the economic costs of excessive drinking. Almost 25 percent of Americans age 12 and older—some 66 million people—report binge drinking in the past month, and binge drinking has increased almost 8 percent since 2000.[41,42]

Most studies in the United States define binge drinking as consuming five or more drinks on the same occasion on at least one day in the past month for a male and four or more drinks for a female.[43] If you were to ask the typical person on the street to describe binge drinking, however, they might be more likely to describe it as a bout of unrestrained alcohol consumption that lasted for at least a couple of days, during which time the intoxicated drinker ignored responsibilities,

Binge drinking: The consumption of five or more drinks on the same occasion on at least one day in the past month for a male, and four or more drinks for a female.

spent money, and engaged in risky and harmful behaviors.

Some problems with the standard American definition of binge drinking are that it does not account for differences in a person's weight or drinking history or whether the person consumed the alcohol with food or over a short or long period of time.[44] By the current definition, if you are a woman and you have two glasses of wine with dinner and then sip two more drinks over the course of five hours, this is considered binge drinking.[45] These inconsistencies make it difficult to assess the prevalence, significance, and consequence of binge drinking. This definition of binge drinking also may lead some young people to think binge drinking is more prevalent than it is, which can make them feel more social pressure to drink heavily. Additionally, any definition using a fixed cutoff implies that any alcohol consumption below that level is safe; for some people, any drinking is unsafe.[46] As we can see, the prevalence of binge drinking depends upon the definition we use to describe it, the people surveyed, as well as the way the questions are asked, and even the method used to contact survey participants.

Underage Drinking

Alcohol is the most widely used drug by today's teenagers. Underage drinking rates have declined significantly over the past 15–20 years, but still, over 61 percent of students have tried alcohol by the end of high school.[47] Adolescents have a greater vulnerability to alcohol than do adults. Not only are they physically smaller, but the brains of underage drinkers are especially vulnerable to alcohol's negative effects on cognition and memory. In addition, underage drinkers lack experience and have not yet built up a tolerance to alcohol.[48] A number of adverse effects result from underage drinking, especially binge drinking, including violence and illegal behavior; risk-taking behavior, such as unplanned and unprotected sex; psychological and physical impairment; poor academic performance; and injuries and death due to drunk driving.[49] Early drinking may also predispose someone to develop an alcohol dependency later in life.

Drinking by College Students

Each year, college students consume 430 million gallons of alcohol; this is enough to fill an Olympic-size swimming pool in every college and university in the United States.[50] College students drink an average of 5.42 drinks per week,[51] and they consume an estimated 4 billion cans of beer annually. If all these cans were lined up end to end, there would be enough to circle the globe more than 10 times.

For many people, alcohol is an integral part of college culture. Drinking may be considered the easiest way to fit in, form friendships, hook up, and blow off steam. Alcohol flows freely at many fraternity parties, and, indeed, there are many parties at college in which the entire point of the gathering is to get drunk.

Over 80 percent of college students report that they drink alcohol at least occasionally, and almost 53 percent drank in the past month.[52,53] Drinking rates are higher among 18- to 22-year-olds who are currently enrolled in college compared with those who are not in college (Table 12.1). Sixty percent of underage college students drink alcohol. Compared to students who are 21 or older, underage students drink alcohol less frequently, but when they do drink, they are more likely to binge drink or drink heavily, and more likely to say that the reason they drank was in order to get drunk.[54,55]

Those 4 billion cans of beer are not evenly distributed among all college students. Those who tend to consume more alcohol include[56,57,58,59,60]

- First-year students
- Whites
- Athletes
- Members of fraternities and sororities
- Lesbian, gay, bisexual, and transgender (LGBTQ) students
- Those who live on campus, especially in Greek (fraternity/sorority) housing

TABLE 12.1.   Drinking Rates in Those Age 18–22

	Those Currently in College (Full-Time)	Those Not in College
Current drinkers	52.5%	44.0%
Binge drinkers	33.0%	27.7%
Heavy drinkers	8.2%	6.4%

Source: SAMHSA. (2020). Results from the 2019 national survey on drug use and health. *Rockville, MD: Center for Behavioral Health Statistics and Quality.*

Source and Forms of Alcohol

Alcohol is produced when sugars—such as from fruits, honey, or molasses—are dissolved in water, left to stand in a warm place, and exposed to air. Yeast, a one-celled organism found in the environment wherever plants grow, floats through air and lands on the fruit. The yeast consumes the sugar and converts it into ethanol and carbon dioxide (CO_2). The CO_2 bubbles out of solution, and the alcohol remains. This naturally occurring process, known as **fermentation,** continues until the sugar is gone, usually when the substance reaches 10–15 percent alcohol. Grains such as corn, rice, or barley contain starch rather than sugar, so before fermentation begins, enzymes must convert the starch into sugar. An enzyme present in saliva can do this. In fact, some of the earliest beer was made by chewing corn into a pulp, spitting it into a clay pot, mixing it with water, and letting it ferment.[61]

QUICK HIT

The world's oldest written recipe is for beer. Written in the Sumerian language, the recipe was found on tablets that date to the third millennium BCE.

The chemical designation of "alcohol" may refer to several substances. Methyl alcohol (CH_3OH, also called methanol or wood alcohol), which is sometimes used in antifreeze, is toxic if consumed. Isopropyl alcohol (($CH_3)_2CHOH$), also called rubbing alcohol, is also unsafe to ingest. The alcohol we drink is ethyl alcohol, or ethanol. Ethanol (CH_3CH_2OH, also called grain alcohol) can also be dangerous to consume, but many of us do so anyway.

Fermented Beverages

Wine and beer are considered fermented beverages. Naturally fermented beverages do not exceed 15 percent alcohol, because the yeast will die at higher alcohol levels. Wines average about 12 percent alcohol, and beers are typically 4–8 percent alcohol.

To make wine, the grapes are harvested at the proper time, crushed, and pressed. Yeast is added for fermentation, and then the solids are removed from the product. Finally, the wine is aged and bottled. Different types of wines are produced from different grapes and

Fermentation: Production of alcohol from sugars through the action of yeast.

production procedures. Some of the most popular are white, red, blush, sparkling, dessert, and fortified.

Beer, the world's most widely consumed alcoholic beverage, is made from fermented grains, most commonly barley. The barley grain is soaked in water until it begins to flower, or germinate. Germination produces an enzyme that allows the starches in the grain to be converted into fermentable sugars, a process called malting. The partially sprouted grain is then dried into a substance called mash. Mash is mixed with hot water, and hops—the female flower of the hop plant—are added for flavor (Figure 12.8). After the substance is cooled, yeast is added to ferment the mixture, which is then filtered and processed into various types of beer, such as lager, ale, malt liquor, light beer, and nonalcoholic beer.

Distilled Beverages

All hard liquors are distilled. In order to distill a fermented beverage and increase its potency, the

Proof: The proportion of alcohol in a beverage, by volume.

FIGURE 12.8. Hops. The female flower of the hop plant is used to make beer.

Ask yourself: What does the alcoholic beverage that someone chooses to drink say about them? Are beer drinkers different than wine drinkers? Are scotch drinkers different than rum drinkers? How much of this difference is a factor of the drinks themselves, and how much is a factor of the media images of these beverages?

fermented mixture is heated until it boils. Because alcohol has a lower boiling point than water, the vapor has a higher alcohol content than what is left in the container. The condensed vapor is collected in a series of cooling tubes called a still. This condensate (the liquid formed by condensation) is hard liquor or distilled spirits. The process is repeated until the desired potency is achieved. Beverages also can be distilled by freezing a fermented product and removing the ice, thus concentrating the alcohol. This process is called freeze distillation or jacking. Table 12.2 provides information on several types of distilled beverages.

Alcohol Content of Standard Drinks

Wine, beer, and distilled spirits contain different amounts of alcohol. Drinking 12 ounces of beer would produce a very different effect than drinking 12 ounces of grain alcohol. Table 12.3 shows the "standard" size drink for different types of alcohol.

Alcoholic **proof** is the measure of how much ethanol an alcoholic beverage contains. The "proof" typically equals twice the percentage of alcohol; a beverage that is 40 percent alcohol is 80-proof. The strongest proof that any alcoholic beverage can be is 190. Above 95 percent alcohol, the beverage draws moisture from the air and self-dilutes.

TABLE 12.2.   Different Types of Distilled Beverages

Type of Liquor		How It's Made	Percent Alcohol in Standard Drink	Fun Facts
Brandy		Distilled from wine or fruit	40–45%	First distilled beverage, first produced as early as 100 BCE.
Rum		Distilled from molasses	40–75%	First invented in Barbados in the 1650s, it also was called "kill-devil."
Tequila, Mescal		Distilled from the Agave plant	Tequila: 8–40% Mescal: 40–50%	The mescal worm is an insect larva found in some types of tequila produced in Mexico. Contrary to urban legend, it does not cause hallucinations when eaten.
Vodka		Distilled from potato or other carbohydrate sources	35–50%	The word "vodka" means "little water" in Russian.
Gin		Distilled from any fermentable carbohydrate, such as wheat, corn, rye, barley, or potato; flavored by a second distillation with juniper berries	35–50%	First distilled in the 1600s.
Whiskey				Whiskey" is a Gaelic term translated as "water of life" or *usequebaugh*. Whisky was first distilled in Ireland and Scotland in the 1400s.
	Scotch	Distilled from fermented corn and malted barley	40–50%	For a whiskey to be labeled Scotch, it must be produced in Scotland.
	Bourbon	Distilled from fermented corn, plus rye and malted barley	40–50%	In 1964, the U.S. Congress declared bourbon to be the official alcohol of the United States.
	Rye	Distilled from rye plus malted barley	40–50%	Rye refers to either American rye whiskey or Canadian whiskey, which may or may not include any rye in its production process.

TABLE 12.3.   Standard Drink Volumes

Drink	Approximate Percentage of Alcohol	Standard Serving Size
Regular beer	5%	12 fluid ounces
Malt liquor	7%	8–9 fluid ounces
Wine	12%	5 fluid ounces
Fortified wine (sherry or port)	17%	3–4 fluid ounces
Cordial, liqueur, aperitif	24%	2–3 fluid ounces
Brandy	40%	1.5 fluid ounces
80-proof spirits	40%	1.5 fluid ounces

QUICK HIT

The term *proof* comes from an old British navy custom, wherein the sailors would test their ration of rum to ensure that it hadn't been watered down. To do so, they would douse gunpowder with their rum—if the alcohol content was 50 percent or greater, the gunpowder would burn. If the rum contained too much water, it wouldn't ignite. Burning was "proof" that their rum ration was at least 50 percent alcohol.

Pharmacokinetics of Alcohol

All alcohol consumption is not considered equal. The effects on a person depend on many factors, including the dose; how well the alcohol is absorbed into the blood stream; a person's age, sex, race, and tolerance; other drugs that are taken concurrently; and even the environment in which the alcohol is consumed.

Dosage

The amount of alcohol consumed greatly influences one's physical and mental state. Two drinks in an hour may make you feel happy and outgoing; eight may cause you to stagger and cry; twenty may kill you. Table 12.4 describes the physical and mental effects that typically occur based on one's **blood alcohol content (BAC)**. BAC is expressed as a percentage of alcohol in the blood. A BAC of 0.10 percent means that one-tenth of 1 percent of a person's blood is ethanol. The physical and mental effects described in the table are based on BAC rather than on the amount ingested, because the

Blood alcohol content (BAC):   The percentage of alcohol in the blood.

TABLE 12.4.   Acute Effects of Alcohol Associated with Increasing Blood Alcohol Content (BAC), in Drinkers Without Tolerance

BAC (mg/100 ml)	Physical and Mental Effects
0.01–0.02	• Sense of warmth and well-being • Relaxed • Talkative • Slight loss in fine motor coordination
0.03–0.04	• Relaxation • Mild euphoria • Talkative, boastful • Flushed skin • Mild impairment in motor skills, coordination, and reflexes
0.05–0.07	• Lowered inhibitions • Exaggerated changes in emotion • Feelings of remoteness • Impaired judgment • Impaired coordination • Rapid pulse
0.08–0.09	• Legally intoxicated • Slower reaction time • Impaired muscle coordination • Numbness in face and extremities • Increasingly impaired judgment
0.1	• Drowsiness • Impaired breathing • Emotional swings • Further deterioration in motor coordination and reaction time • Staggering • Slurred speech • Reduced visual and auditory acuity • Temporary erectile dysfunction • Risk of accident increases eightfold
0.15	• Less responsible behavior • Significant impairment in balance, movement, and reaction time • Major impairments in judgment • Distortions of perception
0.2	• Difficulty staying awake • Excessive and changeable emotions, easily angered, shouting, weeping • Stupor, blackout • Inability to recall events later • Greatly reduced motor and sensory capabilities • Slurred speech • Double vision • Difficulty standing or walking without assistance • Risk of accident increases 31-fold
0.3	• Confusion, stupor • Not likely to remember events the next day • Possible loss of consciousness • Difficulty comprehending events
0.4 and above	• Skin is sweaty and clammy • Unconscious • Depressed respiratory functions • Depressed circulatory functions • Half will fatally overdose without medical intervention

absorption, distribution, and elimination of alcohol are modified by many factors, and these pharmacokinetic effects influence the BAC. It is also important to note that the behavioral effects depend on a person's tolerance to alcohol. A chronic heavy drinker may be able to function with a BAC that would put others into a coma.

Absorption

Ethanol is a simple molecule, yet it produces such diverse effects. It is water-soluble enough to readily mix with water, and lipid-soluble enough to quickly cross the blood brain barrier.[62] After oral ingestion, alcohol enters the stomach and small intestine, where it is easily absorbed into the bloodstream. If vaporized, alcohol can also be absorbed in the lungs. Many things affect ethanol's absorption into the bloodstream, including the type of alcohol, the rate of consumption, and the presence of food in the stomach. Distilled liquors are absorbed the fastest, followed by sparkling wine, and then by wine. Beer is absorbed more slowly.

If a person's stomach is full, the alcohol mixes with the stomach contents, which are released a little bit at a time into the small intestine, where most absorption occurs. If there is no food in the stomach, contents pass directly into the small intestine for rapid absorption into the bloodstream. The type of food also can influence the rate of alcohol absorption. Fats are emptied from the stomach more slowly than are carbohydrates or proteins, so high-fat foods slow ethanol's absorption more so than high-carb or high-protein foods.

To illustrate this phenomenon, imagine you are the owner of a bar and grill. You want your patrons drinking, but you do not want them to be obnoxiously drunk. Therefore, you decide to serve food that helps you reach this goal. Salty foods make them thirsty, and fatty foods slow the absorption of alcohol. Consider the typical food served in drinking establishments: fried cheese, nachos, French fries, and other plates full of salty fat. Eating these dishes allows someone to keep drinking the alcohol (at an enormous price markup), often without getting drunk and disorderly.

Stress, anxiety, fear, and anger all can influence the rate of absorption, as can illness. If a person is dehydrated, it can result in a higher BAC. Estrogen and progesterone may also influence alcohol absorption. Some studies show that women absorb alcohol faster when they are premenstrual and their estrogen and progesterone levels are low.[63,64]

Distribution

Once absorbed, alcohol is freely distributed throughout all the body fluids and tissues, including the placenta, if a woman is pregnant. Alcohol easily crosses the blood brain barrier and distributes to the cerebral cortex, limbic system, cerebellum, hypothalamus, pituitary gland, and lastly, the medulla. Alcohol in the blood circulates through the lungs and vaporizes in air, so it is possible to estimate the alcohol level in the blood by measuring the alcohol vapor in exhaled air.

After drinking, larger people have a lower BAC compared with smaller people. Larger lean people will have an even lower BAC, because alcohol absorbs better in muscle than it does in fat, so less alcohol remains in the bloodstream. Given two people of equal body weight, the person with a higher percentage of body fat will have a higher BAC than the person with more muscle. Women tend to have more body fat and less body fluid than men, so if you were to give the same amount of alcohol to a woman and a man who weigh the same, the woman will usually have a higher BAC.

Metabolism

After being absorbed into the bloodstream, ethanol travels to the liver, where it undergoes oxidation. The rate of metabolism varies in each person, based on sex, size, age, race, tolerance, and many other factors. Unlike most other drugs, in which the rate of metabolism increases with a higher plasma concentration of the drug, the rate of alcohol metabolism remains constant over time (a phenomenon known as zero-order kinetics, described in Chapter 4). Typically, the liver can metabolize about one-third of an ounce of pure ethanol per hour (about an ounce of hard liquor); any unmetabolized alcohol circulates throughout the blood and BAC rises.

Enzymes Involved in Metabolism

Several enzymes are involved in the metabolism of ethanol, but two play a prominent role: alcohol dehydrogenase and aldehyde dehydrogenase (Figure 12.9). **Alcohol dehydrogenase (ADH)** breaks ethanol down into acetaldehyde, which is toxic and causes reddening of the skin, rapid heart rate, and nausea. But acetaldehyde also stimulates the reward areas of the brain, which is why a person may continue to drink despite negative consequences.

Alcohol dehydrogenase (ADH): An enzyme that metabolizes ethanol into acetaldehyde.

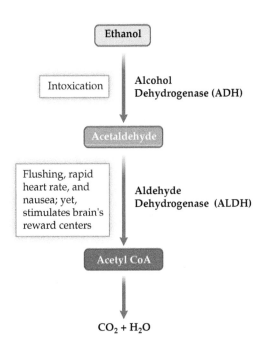

FIGURE 12.9. The metabolism of ethanol. Levels of alcohol dehydrogenase are lower in women, and both men and women produce less of this enzyme in the morning. Some people of Asian descent have an inactive from of the enzyme aldehyde dehydrogenase (ALDH).

Gastric (stomach) ADH metabolizes about 15–20 percent of alcohol, while hepatic (liver) ADH breaks down the rest. Genetic differences in these enzymes may play a role in why some groups of people have higher or lower rates of alcohol use disorders.[65,66] In addition, women have 50–60 percent less gastric ADH than men; as a result, BAC increases by about 7 percent in women when compared with men of the same size drinking the same amount of alcohol.

QUICK HIT

Humans, chimpanzees, gorillas, and bonobos have a gene mutation that improves ADH's ability to metabolize alcohol 40-fold over that of other animals, giving primates a much higher tolerance for alcohol than seen in other species. Some animals, such as elephants and dogs, have a nonfunctioning gene for ADH, such that a very small amount of alcohol may get them very drunk.[67]

Circadian rhythms also influence ethanol metabolism. Both men and women produce less ADH in the morning, so drinking before noon will have more of an effect on someone than it will later in the day.

Aldehyde dehydrogenase (ALDH): The enzyme that breaks down acetaldehyde.

The enzyme cytochrome P450 2E1 (CYP2E1) also breaks down alcohol into acetaldehyde. CYP2E1 normally accounts for only a small percentage of alcohol metabolism, but after chronic ethanol consumption, the activity of this enzyme can be increased 10- to 20-fold, which is one reason that chronic drinkers get less drunk on the same amount of alcohol than do infrequent imbibers.[68] The degree to which CYP2E1 is enhanced by chronic alcohol consumption varies among people, and may be genetically determined. Additionally, many other drugs are also broken down by the cytochrome P450 enzyme system, so when someone takes these drugs along with alcohol, competition for enzymes occurs, which can affect the amount of alcohol or drug in one's system.

Aldehyde dehydrogenase (ALDH) converts acetaldehyde to acetyl CoA, which is broken down into CO_2 and water. There are different genetic variants of ALDH.[69] The low activity form allows acetaldehyde to accumulate, leading to reddening of the skin, nausea, vomiting, dizziness, headache, sweating, confusion, and tachycardia. Disulfiram (Antabuse) is a drug that competes with acetaldehyde for ALDH, causing acetaldehyde levels to increase. This drug is sometimes given to those with alcohol use disorders to physiologically encourage them to avoid alcohol (Chapter 18).

Racial Differences in Metabolic Enzymes

Different racial groups may express different variants of ADH and ALDH. For example, some individuals of African descent carry a form of the gene for ADH that is associated with more rapid breakdown of alcohol, leading to a short-term accumulation of acetaldehyde. People carrying this gene are unlikely to respond well to alcohol and are less likely to suffer from alcohol use disorders.[70] As another example, about 10 percent of Asians have genes that code only for the inactive form of ALDH, causing aldehyde to accumulate. They do not tolerate alcohol well and are less likely to become dependent on alcohol.[71] About 40–50 percent of the Asian population has genes that code for both the active and inactive form, resulting in an unpleasant response to alcohol but not as bad as those with only the inactive form.

Elimination

The liver metabolizes 95 percent of the alcohol that reaches the general circulation, which is then eliminated in urine. The remaining 5 percent is eliminated unchanged in the breath, where it can be detected by a Breathalyzer. The proportion of exhaled ethanol stays constant enough to give an accurate estimate of how much alcohol is in the blood.

Drug Interactions

Alcohol–medication interactions may be a factor in at least 25 percent of all emergency-room admissions. Alcohol increases the effects of some drugs and diminishes the effects of others. In some cases, these interactions depend upon whether alcohol is used occasionally or chronically.

Alcohol influences the effects of several other medications, especially those that are metabolized by cytochrome P450 enzymes. These include analgesics, anesthetics, anticonvulsants, anticoagulants, antidepressants, antipsychotics, and sedatives. In addition, certain medications may impact the effects of alcohol on the body. Drugs shown to enhance the effect of alcohol include aspirin, antibiotics, nitroglycerin, sulfonylurea, oral contraceptives, and ulcer medications.

Mechanism of Action of Alcohol

Although it is a very simple molecule, ethanol has complex and widespread effects. Ethanol alters the composition of the plasma membrane that surrounds cells, disrupts normal electrical transmission, and affects many different neurotransmitter systems, including GABA, glutamate, dopamine, opioids, serotonin, and endogenous cannabinoids.

GABA

Ethanol increases GABA's inhibitory actions by binding to a portion of the GABA receptor and by increasing GABA's release. When GABA is bound to its receptor, alcohol binds to a subunit on the receptor and allows more negatively charged chloride ions to enter the cell, resulting in neuronal inhibition. With acute alcohol use, this leads to sedation, reduced anxiety, and incoordination. Chronic use can produce downregulation—a reduction in the number of GABA receptors, which can lead to the development of tolerance. However, in one brain region—the ventral tegmental area of the midbrain (VTA), which is important for reward and addiction—ethanol *decreases* GABA transmission. Dopaminergic cell bodies in the VTA are normally inhibited by GABA, so when ethanol decreases GABA transmission, this increases dopamine release, thereby enhancing the rewarding effects of alcohol (Figure 12.10).[72] *Chronic*

ethanol administration, on the other hand, has the opposite effect on the activity of GABA neurons in the VTA, leading to a reduction in dopaminergic activity, which may be related to some of the unpleasant psychological effects of withdrawal.[73]

Glutamate

Alcohol decreases glutamate's excitatory actions. An indirect antagonist to the NMDA glutamate receptor, alcohol also reduces glutamate release in the hippocampus. Given that glutamate is involved with both learning and memory, ethanol's antagonism may be responsible for the memory loss associated with intoxication. With long-term, chronic alcohol use, the cell responds to the reduced amounts of available glutamate by increasing the number of NMDA receptors. There is also a rebound increase in glutamate release. Upon withdrawal, this hyperexcitability can lead to seizures and brain damage.

Dopamine

Alcohol causes dopaminergic cells in the VTA to release dopamine to the prefrontal cortex, amygdala, and nucleus accumbens, which plays a significant role in reinforcement, addiction, and reward. This dopamine increase only occurs while a person's BAC is rising, not when it is falling; pleasure and reinforcement circuits are stimulated early when drinking, rather than later. Withdrawal from alcohol can reduce dopamine concentration, which may result in depression.

Opioids

If the dopaminergic cell bodies in the VTA are destroyed, animals will still self-administer ethanol. This suggests that dopamine is not the only neurotransmitter involved with ethanol's addictive properties. Endogenous opioids also play a role in alcohol addiction. Ethanol increases beta-endorphin release from the pituitary and hypothalamus, and may increase endorphin levels in the nucleus accumbens and VTA as well, which potentially increases the rewarding effects of alcohol.[74] A person's baseline levels of endorphins may be one factor that influences his or her susceptibility to alcohol use disorders. Both humans and rats with a genetic predisposition for alcohol dependence have low baseline levels of endorphins, and release significantly more endorphins from the hypothalamus when given alcohol compared to those with no genetic predisposition.[75] Chronic administration of alcohol may decrease endorphin levels and lead to the dysphoria seen during withdrawal.

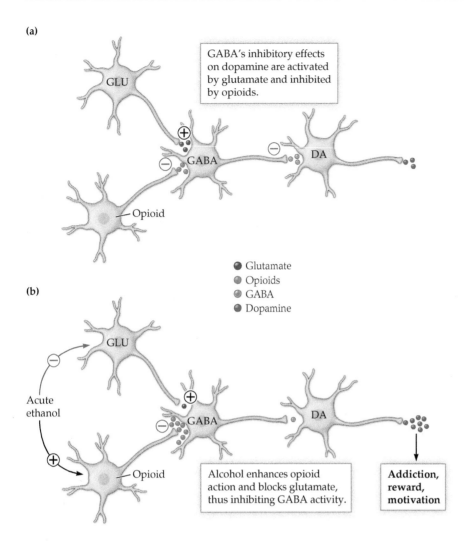

Serotonin

Serotonin also may play a role in alcohol's reinforcing effects. Those with low serotonin activity are likely to drink more alcohol.[77] In addition, SSRI antidepressants boost serotonin levels and reduce alcohol consumption and cravings, possibly by modulating dopaminergic activity in the midbrain.[78]

Endocannabinoids

Endogenous cannabinoids—naturally occurring compounds that mimic some of the psychoactive ingredients of marijuana—appear to enhance the ethanol-induced activation of the VTA, possibly through interactions with the opioid systems. Alcohol consumption and alcohol-induced dopamine release in the reward areas of the brain were reduced in mice lacking CB1 receptors, and cannabinoid antagonists reduced drinking behaviors in addicted rats.[79]

FIGURE 12.10. The mechanism of action of ethanol's reinforcing properties. (a) In the VTA and nucleus accumbens (nA), GABA normally inhibits the activity of dopamine neurons. GABA's effects on dopamine are activated by glutamate and inhibited by opioids. (b) Alcohol enhances opioid action and blocks glutamate, which both result in reduced GABAergic activity. Less inhibitory GABA means that dopamine activity in the VTA/nA is enhanced, potentially leading to addiction.

Acute Effects of Alcohol

In this section, we consider the physiological, behavioral, and psychological effects of alcohol and some of the dangers from heavy drinking, including hangover and overdose.

Ethanol's reinforcing properties are due to an interaction of dopamine, GABA, opioids, and glutamate. These actions are summarized as follows (Figure 12.10)[76]:

1. Release of dopamine in the VTA leads to reward.
2. GABA normally inhibits dopamine release in the VTA.
3. In the VTA, GABA's effects are activated by glutamate and inhibited by opioids.
4. Ethanol increases the inhibitory actions of opioids and blocks the activating effects of glutamate, both of which lead to reduced activity in GABAergic neurons, thereby freeing dopaminergic cells from their inhibition and leading to increased dopamine release in the VTA, which produces rewarding sensations.

Physiological Effects

For such a simple molecule, ethanol has widespread and varied effects on the human body. Low consumption is probably not harmful, but heavy drinking can be dangerous or even lethal.

Brain

Low to moderate doses of alcohol will slow the electrical activity of neurons in the brain. Alcohol changes the sleep cycle, decreasing the time it takes to fall asleep and suppressing both deep sleep and REM sleep. Depending on the dose, ethanol may block the transfer from short-term memory to long-term memory and cause blackouts. A **blackout** is a failure to recall events that occurred while drinking, even with no loss of consciousness. During a blackout, an intoxicated person is interacting with the environment in seemingly meaningful ways, but will have little to no recall of the events the next day. Women are more susceptible to blackouts and recover from ethanol's cognitive impairment slower than men. Fifty percent of college students who drink report having had a blackout.[80] Risky activities such as fighting, sex, and drunk driving often occur during blackouts.

Alcohol impacts sensory perception. Drinkers may experience a reduced ability to see distant objects, a loss of peripheral vision, and blurred and double vision. Taste and smell are not as discriminating, and sensitivity to pain begins to diminish at a BAC of 0.08.

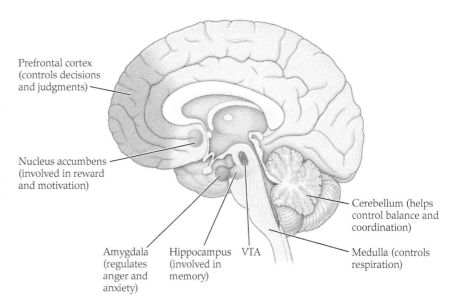

FIGURE 12.11. Brain areas affected by ethanol. Some of the areas of the brain affected by alcohol include the VTA/nucleus accumbens, the prefrontal cortex, the hippocampus, the amygdala, the cerebellum, the proprioception cells of the inner ear, and the respiratory centers of the medulla.

Even moderate alcohol consumption can shrink the brain and cause cognitive decline.[81,82] Those who drink more than 14 drinks per week lose approximately 1.6 percent of brain size compared to nondrinkers.[83] Parts of the brain that are particularly affected by alcohol include (Figure 12.11) the following:

- *The ventral tegmentum and nucleus accumbens* (motivation, reward, and dependence)
- *The prefrontal cortex* (alcohol impairs decisions and judgments)
- *The hippocampus* (impairs memory)
- *The amygdala* (affects anxiety and anger)

Higher doses interfere with the following:

- *The cerebellum* (balance and coordination)
- *The inner ear* (sense of one's location and movement). Alcohol changes the density of cells in the inner ear, giving the sensation of movement when there is none; "bed spins" is the popular name for this phenomenon.
- *The medulla.* Very high doses of alcohol suppress the respiratory centers of the brainstem.

Cardiovascular

Alcohol dilates the peripheral blood vessels of the skin, which increases heat loss and produces a flush as well as a feeling of warmth. By decreasing the ability of platelets to clump together, alcohol also reduces blood clotting. In addition, alcohol raises HDL levels—the "good" cholesterol that removes damaging "bad" cholesterol (LDL) from arterial walls.[84] Sometimes, a weekend of moderate to heavy drinking can lead to *holiday heart syndrome*—characterized by an irregular heartbeat, dizziness, and chest pain—that is more likely to occur during holidays or on Mondays after a weekend of binge drinking.

Gastrointestinal

Ethanol increases salivation and appetite and aids digestion. Ethanol stimulates the gastric secretion of HCl and pepsin, substances necessary for digestion. These substances, however, can erode the stomach lining at high doses (or at moderate doses in those with a peptic ulcer). High alcohol levels—typically BACs higher than 0.15 percent—can lead to nausea and vomiting.

Renal

Antidiuretic hormone (also called vasopressin) normally allows the kidneys to reabsorb and retain water. Alcohol inhibits the secretion of vasopressin, increasing urination. This leads to dehydration, one of the major causes of hangovers.

Blackout: An inability to recall events that occurred while drinking, even with no loss of consciousness.

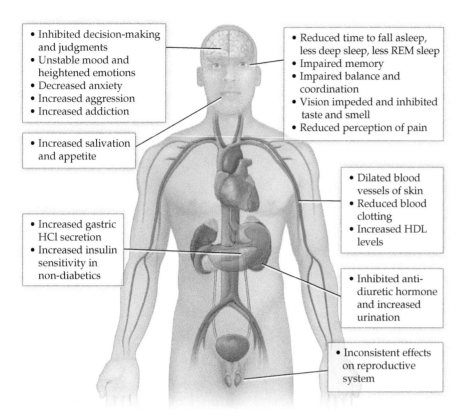

- Inhibited decision-making and judgments
- Unstable mood and heightened emotions
- Decreased anxiety
- Increased aggression
- Increased addiction

- Increased salivation and appetite

- Increased gastric HCl secretion
- Increased insulin sensitivity in non-diabetics

- Reduced time to fall asleep, less deep sleep, less REM sleep
- Impaired memory
- Impaired balance and coordination
- Vision impeded and inhibited taste and smell
- Reduced perception of pain

- Dilated blood vessels of skin
- Reduced blood clotting
- Increased HDL levels

- Inhibited anti-diuretic hormone and increased urination

- Inconsistent effects on reproductive system

FIGURE 12.12. Acute effects of alcohol.

Reproductive

Acute alcohol intoxication has inconsistent effects on erection, vaginal blood flow and lubrication, and the time it takes to achieve orgasm. Some reports show increased incidence of sexual dysfunction with higher BAC, while others do not.[85,86,87] Alcohol's short-term effects on sexual response are influenced by expectations, context, as well as past sexual experiences. Figure 12.12 summarizes some of the acute physiological effects of alcohol on the body.

Behavioral and Psychological Effects

Alcohol has a powerful influence on our mood and thought processes. These effects are mediated not only by the pharmacological effects of ethanol itself, but by the *set*—the person's expectation of what effect the drug will have—and by the *setting*—the physical environment in which the drug is consumed.

Cognitive Function

Self-perception and judgments are impaired by ethanol. Alcohol leads to disinhibition—a suppression of the part of the cortex that is responsible for social and behavioral restraints. This means that intoxicated people may do things they would not normally do—sing karaoke, text an old love interest, or have unsafe

sex—without fear of adverse consequences (Figure 12.13). In the words of author Erica Jong, "The superego is soluble in alcohol."[88]

Alcohol also may have long-term effects on risky behaviors. Those who drink during adolescence exhibit more risky behavior during adulthood. But does this mean that alcohol itself increases risky behavior, or are risk takers simply more likely to drink during adolescence? Although there is evidence that risk-taking individuals are more prone to alcohol use disorders, one study suggests that alcohol itself may actually cause neurobiological changes that encourage risky behavior. Researchers gave adolescent rats either alcohol or water for 20 days. When they grew up, both sets of rats were given a choice between rewards. Those exposed to alcohol when they were adolescents were more likely to take risks to get rewards, an effect that persisted months after alcohol access was discontinued. Therefore, adolescents exposed to alcohol may suffer from altered decision-making as adults.[89]

QUICK HIT

In England, pubs serve drinks in either pints or quarts. In old England, bartenders told their customers to mind their own pints and quarts, which is how the expression "mind your P's and Q's" originated.

Mood

When drinkers' BAC is rising, they may feel elated, expansive, jovial, relaxed, and self-confident. When their BAC is falling, they are more likely to feel angry and tired. At higher BACs, drinkers may be emotionally unstable and change abruptly from friendly to argumentative. Although low to moderate alcohol consumption can reduce stress, high doses ingested rapidly increase the release of the body's stress hormones.

Aggression

When people commit violent crimes, they are most often under the influence of alcohol. Alcohol significantly

FIGURE 12.13. **Alcohol impairs judgment.** Intoxicated people may do things they would not normally do, as indicated by this crosswalk sign.

increases the occurrence of aggression, in adult men and women, adolescents, members of a variety of ethnic groups, and in those with and without psychological disorders.[90] The co-occurrence of alcohol and violent crime is especially strong in men age 18–30; more than 50 percent of violent incidents perpetrated by males involved ethanol, compared with 27 percent of incidents with a female assailant.[91] Alcohol-related aggression is a phenomenon influenced by the interaction of many elements, including the pharmacological effects of alcohol, psychosocial factors, and situational and contextual influences.[92,93]

Pharmacological Effects of Alcohol on Aggression. Alcohol inhibits pathways in the frontal cortex and impairs higher-level cognitive processing, so an inebriated person exhibits lessened reasoning, self-monitoring, and problem-solving, along with heightened emotionality. Drinkers may act impulsively and be less able to consider the social, physical, or legal

consequences of their actions. Ethanol intoxication also affects brain regions responsible for preventing antisocial behaviors such as aggression. Normally, feelings of anxiety inhibit aggression, because we can recognize potential negative consequences of aggressive actions. But alcohol reduces anxiety—even the "healthy" anxiety that keeps us from acting in socially undesirable ways.

Psychosocial Factors that Influence Aggression. Temperament, mood, motivations, family and peer influences, and the presence of psychological disorders, can all influence a person's aggressive tendencies when intoxicated. Additionally, expectations about the relationship between alcohol and aggression can impact a person's behavior when drunk. Balanced placebo studies show that, in some cases, what individuals are *told* they are consuming is more important than what they actually consume.[94] Movies, TV shows, and stories from friends and relatives have encouraged the expectation that alcohol increases aggression, so drinkers may view drinking as an excuse to engage in aggressive or socially inappropriate behavior.

Situational and Contextual Influences that Affect Aggression. Social pressure affects the relationship between alcohol and aggression. If observers tolerate or encourage aggression, intoxicated participants are more likely to behave aggressively. If social pressure encourages peaceful behavior, however, alcohol does not seem to enhance aggression.[95] Environments in which drinking occurs, such as sporting matches, bars, and parties, are often more tolerant of aggressive behavior. One's culture also can influence the tendency to become aggressive when intoxicated. Some cultures define drinking occasions as a time out, holding people less responsible for their actions when drinking than when sober.[96,97]

The relationship between alcohol and aggression is a complicated one. Not only are scientists unsure what specific factors—be they pharmacological or environmental—underlie the relationship, but the causal nature of the relationship between alcohol and aggression is also uncertain.

Adverse Effects from Acute Heavy Drinking

Smashed. Wasted. Clobbered. Bombed. Plastered. Tanked. So many of the slang terms we use for being drunk suggest violence or damage. This may be more than coincidence. Alcohol affects every organ in the body and accounts for an estimated 95,000 deaths in the United States each year, which is more than all illicit

Critical Evaluation

Does alcohol increase aggression?

Although alcohol seems to be correlated with aggression, there are many factors underlying this relationship. Use your critical thinking skills to consider these dynamics.

Prevalence of the alcohol-aggression relationship. Estimates of what proportion of violent crimes are alcohol related vary widely, from 30–90 percent. For many reports, we have no reliable information about the amount of alcohol consumed, the BAC, the time frame of drinking, the presence of provocation, or other factors. Additionally, when perpetrators of violent offenses are questioned about their alcohol use, they may minimize the role of alcohol or inflate its role to blame their behavior on drinking.[98] What other metrics might help illuminate whether there is, in fact, a relationship between alcohol and aggression?

Generalizability of laboratory research. Participants in laboratory studies often know they are part of an experiment, and this may affect their behavior. How closely does giving someone alcohol in a lab and instructing them to shock a research partner correlate with aggressive behavior in "the real world"? Furthermore, most studies on alcohol and aggression are performed on college students. But how generalizable is this population? College students drink more than average, but most aggressive acts are not committed by college students.[99]

Research design. The expectations people have about alcohol and aggression may have a powerful influence on their behavior.[100] Perhaps research participants who are told they have been given alcohol act more aggressively due to their expectations, rather than because of the alcohol itself. Because of this, many scientists employ the "balanced placebo" design, which sorts participants into four groups: those who receive alcohol and believe they are drinking alcohol; those who receive alcohol and believe they are drinking club soda; those who receive club soda and believe they are drinking alcohol; and those who receive club soda and believe they are drinking club soda. But many participants may be familiar enough with the effects of alcohol to recognize whether they have received it, so how valuable are these designs?[101,102]

In most lab experiments, participants drink and then take part in aggression studies during the rising curve of BAC. However, where on the BAC curve does aggression occur? What about effects that occur during the descending curve? How would you design a laboratory study to measure alcohol's effect on aggression?

Correlation and causation. Although there may be a connection, alcohol is not necessary or sufficient for aggression to occur. Aggression occurs without alcohol, and people drink alcohol without resorting to aggression. What other factors influence this relationship?

If alcohol is correlated with aggressive behavior, this does not mean that alcohol *causes* aggression. Although drinking may lead to aggressive behavior, it also may be the case that aggression predisposes someone to drink. Or, other factors, such as impulsivity or hyperactivity, may be responsible for both drinking and aggression.

---

drugs combined, including opioids. The life expectancy of someone suffering from an alcohol use disorder is reduced by about 15 years. In this section, we will discuss some adverse effects that come from short-term heavy alcohol use.

Hangover

Although drinking may be fun in the moment, often the ramifications—such as headache, upset stomach, diarrhea, nausea, thirst, clumsiness, and fatigue—are not. A hangover occurs shortly after most of the alcohol has been metabolized.[103] Approximately 75 percent of persons who drink alcohol have experienced a hangover.[104,105]

We are not sure exactly why hangovers occur. Proposed mechanisms include a short-term withdrawal syndrome, a reaction to dehydration, toxicities related to elevated acetaldehyde levels, hormonal and nutritional disturbances, alcohol-induced gastric irritation, a rebound drop in blood sugar, sleep disruptions, personal susceptibilities relating to drinking behaviors, sex differences, and genetic differences.[106]

Chemicals that are produced during fermentation, which give color, flavor, and odor to alcohol (congeners),

STRAIGHT
DOPE

How to Use Alcohol Wisely

- The best way to avoid the adverse effects of alcohol is to not drink at all. Consider why you want to drink—do you want to be more comfortable around people? Do you want an "excuse" to talk to someone you like? Are there other ways you can achieve your goal rather than drinking?

- Don't spend time with people who drink to excess or encourage you to drink more than you want.

- If you do make the decision to drink, make rules about when and where it's OK. It's best to not drink every day.

- Learn to regulate the amount of alcohol in your bloodstream—food in your stomach slows absorption.

- If you plan to drink heavily, lessen the next day's hangover by remembering to drink plenty of water to offset fluid lost through urination.

- Be careful about falling into patterns of regular drinking to deal with ongoing emotional problems such as anxiety or depression. Alcohol may mask the symptoms temporarily, but it can't solve the problem. Emotional drinking may, in fact, increase your problems, because this kind of use is more likely to lead to dependence.

- If you begin to suspect you have a problem with drinking, or if people who know you think that you do, seek help from professionals. Whether you choose to go to rehab, rely on a self-help program such as Alcoholics Anonymous, or seek therapy, it is important that you have people you can lean on for support, encouragement, and guidance.

Source: Weil, A., & Rosen, W. (2004). From chocolate to morphine: Everything you need to know about mind-altering drugs. *Boston: Houghton Mifflin.*

may exacerbate hangovers. Bourbon, which has 37 times more congeners, may cause more frequent and severe hangovers than vodka.[107,108] Smoking cigarettes also may worsen a hangover. Controlling for the number of drinks, those people who smoke and drink on the same day are more likely to experience intense hangovers.[109]

The only treatment for a hangover is time. Staying hydrated and eating foods that are gentle on the stomach is also important. Taking acetaminophen is discouraged, as this interacts with ethanol and can cause significant damage to the liver. Remembering what a hangover feels like should make one reconsider how much, or whether, to imbibe next time.

QUICK HIT

People in every culture have experienced the misery of a hangover. The Germans call it *katzenjammer,* which translates to "the wailing of cats." Norwegians complain about *jeg har tommeermenn* ("the workmen in my head"), and Irish bemoan *ta dha cinn orm* ("There are two heads on me"). In France, drinkers experience "woody mouth" (*gueule de bois*) and Italians are "out of tune" (*stonato*). The isiZulu word for hangover is *isibhabhalazi,* which might be particularly difficult to say if you are experiencing one. Perhaps hangover is best expressed in Latin: *crapula.*

Overdose

Ethanol's therapeutic index is 5–10, which is similar to heroin's. Ethanol's average lethal dose corresponds to a BAC of 0.45 percent, which is five to six times the BAC that produces intoxication (0.08 percent). Or to put it another way, if the average person becomes intoxicated from four drinks in one hour, then 5–10 times that dose (i.e., 20–40 drinks in an hour) may be fatal in 50 percent of imbibers. Most people don't reach the lethal dose, because vomiting occurs (at around 0.15 percent BAC) or they pass out (0.35 percent BAC) before the lethal dose is met. But if someone drinks very rapidly, the liver can't metabolize the alcohol fast enough, and the BAC can reach lethal levels before he or she passes out. Death from alcohol overdose usually occurs from a suppression of the respiratory centers of the brainstem, or from inhaled vomit blocking one's airway.

Medical and Therapeutic Uses of Alcohol

Apart from recreation, alcohol has several therapeutic uses. Applied to the surface of the body, alcohol disinfects, kills bacteria, and cools the skin as it evaporates. Alcohol is a solvent, so a number of drugs, such as cough syrup, are dissolved in alcohol. Alcohol also can be injected close to sympathetic nerves to relieve chronic pain. Moderate alcohol consumption may also lower one's risk of a heart attack, perhaps by reducing the blood's clotting tendency, raising HDL levels, or by improving insulin sensitivity. The reduced risk also may be due to stress reduction or alcohol's vasodilating effects.

Ask yourself: Based on what you've read thus far, do you think moderate alcohol consumption is beneficial? Why or why not?

In the past, to ascertain the health benefits of drinking alcohol, most studies compared populations of people who drank with those who did not. Many of these studies reported that moderate drinkers lived longer than nondrinkers and had a reduced risk of death by stroke, cancer, diabetes, and other conditions. However, recent studies suggest that moderate alcohol consumption does not give the protective benefits once thought.[110] Instead, the association between cardiovascular health and moderate alcohol intake may have been confounded by other factors. One's mental health, socioeconomic status, and sources of emotional support may influence both alcohol consumption and overall health.[111] Moderate drinkers tend to be healthier, wealthier, more educated, and have access to better health care than those who drink heavily or those who abstain.[112] Moderation in drinking may reflect a healthy moderation in other aspects of life. Maybe moderate drinkers were thought to be healthier than nondrinkers not because alcohol itself provides a health benefit, but because those who are ill don't drink. People also tend to drink less when they get older and if they are sick, and these people are included in the abstainer category.[113] In this case, it's their age and ill health elevating their risk of heart disease, not the absence of alcohol.[114] A recent meta-analysis of thousands of articles investigating the relationship between alcohol consumption and health found that when studies controlled for these factors, the protective effects of alcohol disappear, and other recent large-scale studies suggest that the safest level of alcohol consumption is zero.[115,116]

Chronic Effects of Alcohol

Millions of people have an occasional drink. Unfortunately, even moderate alcohol consumption is linked to 60 acute and chronic diseases.[117] And when a person regularly consumes large amounts of alcohol, negative physical repercussions may occur, including tolerance, withdrawal, and organ damage.

Tolerance

When tolerance occurs, an individual needs to drink greater amounts of alcohol to attain the effect that was once achieved with less alcohol. Although some degree of tolerance occurs over the course of a single drinking experience, most tolerance occurs with chronic exposure to alcohol. Chronic drinkers develop tolerance to the sedative, anxiolytic, anticonvulsant, and hypothermic effects, as well as to the disruption of visual processing and motor coordination.

Acute tolerance occurs within a single exposure to alcohol. Because of this, many of alcohol's effects are more prominent when blood alcohol levels are rising than when they are falling. Acute tolerance has been observed in several behaviors, including motor coordination and reaction time, but not for more complex cognitive functions such as inhibitory control.[118] To illustrate the effects of acute tolerance, imagine that someone drinks enough to reach a BAC of 0.1 percent. As her BAC is rising, her impaired coordination and reaction time will negatively affect her driving ability as the alcohol curve approaches 0.08 percent. Her BAC peaks at 0.1 percent and begins to decline. When we again measure her driving skills at 0.08 percent, her motor coordination might not be as impaired as it was when her BAC was rising. It is very important to note, however, that her fatigue, impaired attention, and slowed cognitive functions—characteristics that do *not* show acute tolerance—still negatively affect driving. Acute tolerance also does not develop to alcohol's disinhibiting effects, so people whose BAC is declining are just as likely to make poor and impulsive decisions.

In metabolic tolerance, the body speeds up the metabolism of alcohol by increasing the production of certain liver enzymes. Although it normally plays only a minor role in alcohol metabolism, the CYP2E1 enzymes increase their activity after chronic ethanol consumption. This enzyme induction is limited and accounts for, at most, 25 percent of alcohol tolerance. Due to metabolic tolerance, a chronic drinker may need to drink more to achieve the desired mood changes, but the high BAC will still damage the body.

When neurons in the brain adapt to the continued presence of alcohol by changing the receptor density, cellular tolerance has occurred. People who develop this can have a BAC twice that of a nontolerant person and display a similar level of behavioral intoxication.

Over time, drinkers can develop resistance to alcohol's impairing effects. With behavioral tolerance, people learn to "handle themselves" while drunk. This also occurs in laboratory animals. In a classic study, one group of rats received alcohol while doing a motor coordination test on a treadmill, while the other received it in their cages. Both groups were then tested on the motor coordination test. Those rats that received alcohol while on the treadmill—and had therefore learned to walk while intoxicated—quickly developed tolerance, while those who received the alcohol in their cages did not.[119]

Finally, chronic alcohol use can increase the drinker's tolerance to barbiturates, benzodiazepines, anesthetics, or other sedatives, even if they had never used these other substances. Cross tolerance often occurs when drugs have a common mechanism of action; alcohol, barbiturates, benzodiazepines, and other sedatives all exert some of their effects by binding to the GABA receptor.

Withdrawal

Withdrawal symptoms typically appear within 12–72 hours after total cessation of drinking, but they can appear whenever the blood alcohol level drops below a certain point. Withdrawal reaches its peak intensity within the first few days, although symptoms can last for weeks.

Mild to moderate alcohol withdrawal is characterized by a craving for alcohol, anxiety, irritability, difficulty sleeping, vivid dreams, and decreased appetite. Tremors, sweating, headache, nausea and vomiting, and irregular and elevated heart rate may occur. These effects usually peak 24–36 hours after the cessation of drinking, and are generally over within 48 hours.

Less common, but more dangerous, **delirium tremens (DTs)** may occur in 5–10 percent of those withdrawing from chronic alcohol use. DTs are characterized by severe agitation; confusion; delusions; elevated heart rate, blood pressure, and body temperature; and seizures. Frightening visual, auditory, or tactile hallucinations can occur. DTs often are treated with benzodiazepines such as Valium until the symptoms

subside. Before modern pharmacotherapy, the mortality rate for those undergoing DTs was as high as 35 percent. Today, about 5–15 percent of individuals going through this severe form of alcohol withdrawal will die of it. In 2017, Nelsan Ellis, star of the show *True Blood*, died from alcohol withdrawal.

Adverse Effects of Chronic Heavy Drinking

Long-term heavy drinking is devastating to almost every organ system of the body. It is difficult, however, to ascertain definitively the long-term physical effects of drinking, given that every body is different and every body responds differently to alcohol's effects. Additionally, there is no consistent definition of what exactly "heavy drinking" entails. Obviously, there are great differences in the body's response to alcohol in someone who has five beers every Saturday night and someone who drinks a quart of whiskey every day. With that caveat in mind, here are some of the physiological effects of chronic heavy drinking.

Overall Mortality

In 2016, more than 3 million deaths around the world were due to alcohol (Figures 12.14, 12.15). This represents about 5 percent of global deaths, nearly 10 percent of deaths among those age 15-49, and over 13 percent of deaths among people in their 20s.[120,121] In the U.S., alcohol-related mortality increased significantly in the past two decades.[122,123] Although more men died of alcohol-related causes, the rate of death involving alcohol increased more for women since 1999.

Delirium tremens (DTs): A severe withdrawal symptom experienced by some chronic alcoholics, involving convulsions, disorientation, anxiety, and hallucinations.

(a)   (b)   (c)   (d)

FIGURE 12.14. Alcohol-related deaths. People who have died of alcohol-related causes include baseball player (a) Mickey Mantle, (b) artist Jackson Pollock, (c) singer Amy Winehouse, and (d) poet Dylan Thomas, whose last words were "I've had 18 straight whiskeys… I do believe that's a record."

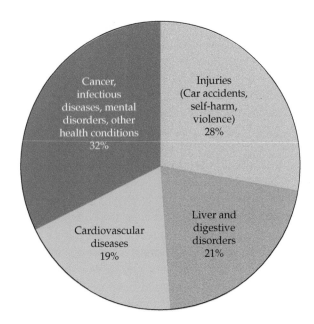

FIGURE 12.15. **Global deaths due to alcohol.** In 2016, more than 3 million people died due to alcohol.

Source: WHO. (2018). Global status report on alcohol and health. https:// www.who.int/substance_abuse/publications/global_alcohol_report/en/

An analysis of almost 600,000 drinkers around the globe found that compared to those who reported drinking 100 grams of pure alcohol or less per week (about 1 "standard" drink per day in U.S. measurements), a 40-year-old who drank 100–200 grams each week would cut their life expectancy by 6 months; a 200–350 gram/week drinker would lose 1–2 years of life, and someone who drank over 350 grams/week could expect to shorten their life expectancy by 4–5 years.[124]

Neurological

Over time, high doses of alcohol—perhaps five to six drinks a day for years—can cause neurological damage. Chronic heavy drinkers perform more poorly on tests of abstract thinking, problem-solving, memory, attention, concentration, learning, perception of emotions, and perceptual-motor speed. Those suffering from alcohol use disorders also have reduced brain weight compared with controls (Figure 12.16).[125,126] Most of the reduction is seen in the white matter, particularly in the prefrontal cortex, cerebellum, and hypothalamus. The brain damage that can occur after many years of heavy alcohol consumption is due to many factors, including the direct effects of alcohol, the toxic consequences of acetaldehyde exposure, and deficiencies in liver and digestive function. Chronic ethanol consumption also increases the brain's vulnerability to the potentially toxic effects of high glutamate.[127] Poor nutrition also may play a role. On average, ethanol accounts for a significant percentage of a chronic heavy drinker's caloric intake, displacing normal nutrients. Poor nutrition can, over time, cause widespread cognitive damage.

Alcohol interferes with the body's ability to absorb thiamine, a B vitamin that helps brain cells produce energy. **Wernicke's encephalopathy** (WURR-nik-keys en-sef-a-LOP-a-thee) is an acute reaction to severe thiamine deficiency. When levels get too low, neurons cannot generate enough

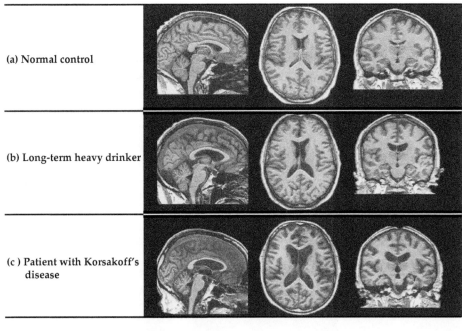

(a) Normal control

(b) Long-term heavy drinker

(c) Patient with Korsakoff's disease

FIGURE 12.16. **The effect of long-term heavy alcohol consumption on the brain.** As shown in the MRI scans of three brains, as alcohol consumption increases, brain tissue decreases.

Source: Zahr, N.M., Kaufman, K.L., & Harper, C.G. (2011). Clinical and pathological features of alcohol-related brain damage. Nature Reviews Neurology, 7(5): 284–94.

Wernicke's encephalopathy: A neurological disorder caused by a deficiency of thiamine, characterized by mental confusion, abnormal eye movements, and an unsteady gait.

energy to function properly. Wernicke's encephalopathy is due to damage in the thalamus and hypothalamus and is characterized by confusion, abnormal gait, loss of muscle coordination, abnormal voluntary eye movements, and vision problems. **Korsakoff's syndrome** (KOR-suh-coff) often follows Wernicke's encephalopathy, as thiamine deficiency leads to frontal lobe and hippocampal damage. This can cause hallucinations and vision problems, and make it difficult to remember recent events or to form new memories. Sufferers will confabulate—replace gaps in their memory with imaginary remembered experiences that they believe to be true. People with Wernicke-Korsakoff syndrome may seem drunk even when they are not. They may be confused, unsteady, and uncoordinated. Thiamine replacement can help reduce the coordination difficulties, vision problems, and confusion, but it will not restore memory loss or cognition.

Brain damage does not always require a lifetime of drinking to occur. The adolescent brain is particularly vulnerable to ethanol's toxic actions, because adolescence and young adulthood are important times of brain maturation. In an adolescent, there are strong connections formed between the striatum, which recognizes and seeks out rewarding experiences, and the prefrontal cortex, which regulates one's ability to consider consequences, overcome impulsiveness, and control behavior. As the prefrontal cortex develops, it regulates the reward-seeking effects of the striatum.[128]

Adolescents who drink heavily have abnormalities in brain structure, reduced volume, poorer white matter quality, and reduced cerebral blood flow, as well as deficits in memory, attention, information processing, and activation to cognitive tasks. These changes can occur in adolescents who have been consuming 20 drinks a month for as little as a year or two, especially if they consume more than four to five drinks on a single occasion.[129]

Cardiovascular

Alcohol consumption is associated with a higher risk of stroke, hypertensive disease, heart failure, and other cardiovascular diseases.[130] Heavy chronic alcohol use increases the risk of cardiomyopathy, a disease in which the heart muscle is abnormally enlarged and weakened, which reduces its ability to pump blood effectively. Alcoholic cardiomyopathy can lead to irregular heartbeat, high blood pressure, congestive heart failure, and stroke. Heavy drinkers also produce fewer red blood cells, which can lead to anemia; fewer platelets, which

can cause insufficient clotting; and a reduced number of white blood cells, which can lead to problems with the immune system. In addition, because alcohol dilates the blood vessels of the face, chronic heavy drinkers sometimes have broken blood vessels in the upper cheeks and nose ("gin blossom" is the slang term for these broken capillaries).

Immunity

Excess alcohol consumption may compromise the immune system and increase one's susceptibility to several infectious diseases, including pneumonia, meningitis, and tuberculosis, as well as increase the risk of contracting hepatitis C and HIV. Binge drinking may be particularly hard on the immune system. It damages the immune system by inhibiting the activity of the white blood cells that ingest and destroy invading microorganisms.[131] Even a single episode of binge drinking can cause bacteria to leak from the GI tract and enter the bloodstream. These bacterial toxins cause inflammation, tissue damage, and altered immune function.[132]

Gastrointestinal

When alcohol enters the stomach, the gastric secretion of pepsin and HCl increases. Therefore, moderate amounts of alcohol can aid digestion, but heavy or chronic drinking can increase one's risk of gastritis, pancreatitis, and ulcers. Ethanol reduces the amount of adipose that is oxidized, which can lead to a long-term increase in body fat, such as the dreaded "beer belly."

Heavy alcohol use is particularly damaging to the liver, whose job it is to metabolize the ethanol. Long-term alcohol abuse damages the liver and reduces its digestive and metabolic functions. In 2017, nearly one-third of alcohol-related deaths in the United States resulted from liver disease.[133] Almost 42,000 people died of chronic liver disease and cirrhosis in the United States in 2017.[134] Some alcohol-related liver disorders include fatty liver, alcoholic hepatitis, and alcoholic cirrhosis.

The liver normally metabolizes fatty acids, but if alcohol is present, the liver metabolizes alcohol first, causing fat to accumulate. If the stored fat droplets increase in size, they can rupture and kill liver cells.

Korsakoff's syndrome: A syndrome of severe mental impairment that features loss of coordination, disorientation, and a tendency to make up stories to cover memory loss of recent events.

Almost all heavy drinkers show evidence of **fatty liver**, but it is reversible with abstinence from drinking. If abstinence or moderation is maintained, fatty liver is not thought to lead to any chronic form of liver disease.

Up to one-third of heavy drinkers may eventually develop **alcoholic hepatitis**, which is characterized by the inflammation and death of liver cells. Mild cases can be reversed with abstinence, but severe cases are potentially lethal. Most alcoholic hepatitis patients already have, or eventually develop, alcoholic cirrhosis, the final stage of alcoholic liver disease.

Alcoholic cirrhosis develops gradually over time. Inflammation leads to irreversible scar tissue, which replaces healthy liver cells, and blocks the blood vessels that supply that liver with oxygen, leading to further cell death (Figure 12.17). With increased loss of liver function, nutrients are not processed, toxins and fluids accumulate, and immune function is compromised.

Cirrhosis occurs with long-term heavy drinking—at least 10 drinks a day for at least 10 years, and the liver damage is permanent. But even among heavy drinkers, only about 10–20 percent develop cirrhosis, leading researchers to believe some individuals may be genetically predisposed to the disease. After diagnosis, there is about a 50 percent mortality rate within five years.

Cancer

Alcohol, alone or with co-carcinogens, is thought to account for around 3–4 percent of cancer deaths in the United States each year.[135,136] The relationship between ethanol and cancer is complex, because the effects vary by quantity ingested and by the location and type of cancer. Alcohol consumption increases the risk of tongue, pharynx, larynx, esophageal, stomach, liver, lung, pancreas, colon, rectal, and breast cancer.[137,138,139,140]

Ask yourself: Should chronic heavy users of alcohol receive liver transplants? What about type 2 diabetics getting a new kidney? Is there a difference? What does your answer say about your value assumptions regarding alcoholism?

Fatty liver: A reversible condition in which large vacuoles of fat accumulate in the liver.

Alcoholic hepatitis: Inflammation of the liver due to excessive alcohol intake.

Alcoholic cirrhosis: A chronic liver condition characterized by replacement of liver cells with scar tissue, leading to loss of liver function.

FIGURE 12.17. Chronic alcohol use damages the liver. (Left) A healthy liver. Heavy drinking causes fat to accumulate in the liver (Middle). If heavy drinking continues for a long time, healthy liver cells are replaced with scar tissue, a condition called alcoholic cirrhosis (Right).

There are several proposed mechanisms by which ethanol may lead to cancer. The metabolism of ethanol produces acetaldehyde, which promotes tumor growth in the mouth, pharynx, stomach, and intestine.[141] Ethanol also may modify the actions of other cancer-causing agents. For example, ethanol serves as a solvent for tobacco metabolites. When alcohol and tobacco are used together, this increases one's risk of oral cancer 15 times above the risk for people who do not smoke or drink. Alcohol also may increase the risk of cancer by tissue irritation, nutritional deficiencies, induction of enzymes that activate other carcinogens, increased estrogen concentration, or by its immunosuppressive actions. One's risk of cancer increases with higher ethanol consumption, but there is no known safe threshold for alcohol and cancer risk.[142]

Reproductive

Sexual dysfunction in women and men is associated with alcohol use. In men, heavy chronic alcohol use is associated with decreased testosterone levels, lowered sperm count, reduced semen production, testicular atrophy, diminished erectile capabilities, ejaculatory incompetence, and impotence, as well as a loss of sexual desire. Long-term heavy drinkers entering outpatient counseling had over three times the prevalence of serious erectile dysfunction compared with nonalcoholic men.[143] Gynecomastia—the abnormal enlargement of a man's breasts—may occur, because liver damage causes estrogens to be reabsorbed into blood. Female heavy drinkers are more likely to experience painful intercourse and to have ovarian dysfunction, menstrual disorders, early onset of menopause, reduced libido, and infertility.[144]

Fetal Alcohol Syndrome

Fetal alcohol spectrum disorder (FASD) is an umbrella term used to describe the full range of neurological, cognitive, behavioral, and learning disabilities associated with prenatal alcohol exposure. Up to 5 percent of babies—perhaps 200,000 each year—are born with fetal alcohol spectrum disorder, ranging from minor cognitive and behavioral abnormalities to full-blown fetal alcohol syndrome.[145]

Fetal alcohol syndrome (FAS) is the most severe of the fetal alcohol spectrum disorders, and can result when a mother consumes an excessive amount of alcohol while pregnant. The disorder is characterized by reduced growth; cranial, facial, or neural abnormalities; and developmental disabilities. The prevalence of FAS is estimated to be up to 7.8 cases for every 1,000 live births. Rates are higher among Native American and African American mothers of low socioeconomic status.

Fetal alcohol syndrome is defined by four criteria: confirmed maternal exposure to alcohol; certain craniofacial anomalies in the child; pre- and postnatal growth retardation; and neurological abnormalities, which often are manifested as intellectual difficulties or behavioral problems (see Figure 12.18 and Table 12.5).[146] FAS is difficult to diagnose and has no biological markers that can confirm its diagnosis, so doctors may be more likely to look for and find the disorder in some groups rather than others.[147]

It is hard to obtain accurate self-reports from pregnant women about their drinking, but according to the latest national survey on drug use, 9.5 percent of pregnant women age 15–44 report current alcohol use, 4.8 percent report binge drinking, and 0.3 percent report heavy drinking.[148] Women who are most likely to drink during pregnancy tend to be younger, single, less educated, and unemployed.

Alcohol is a teratogen—a factor that causes malformation of an embryo or fetus. When a pregnant woman drinks, the ethanol easily crosses the placenta and enters the embryo or fetus's bloodstream. The fetus does not yet have well-developed liver enzymes to metabolize the alcohol, so it remains and wreaks havoc on the developing body and brain. There are several theories as to how ethanol and acetaldehyde cause prenatal damage. Ethanol constricts umbilical blood vessels, which diminishes blood flow to the fetus and reduces access to oxygen and nutrients. Ethanol also affects developing glutamate and GABA systems in the fetal brain and alters vitamin A metabolism and insulin regulation. Both ethanol and acetaldehyde can

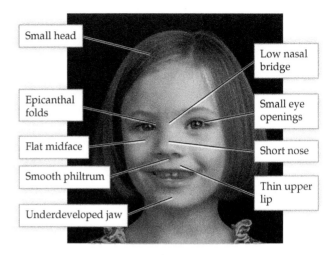

FIGURE 12.18. Fetal alcohol syndrome. A child with fetal alcohol syndrome (FAS) is likely to have several distinctive characteristics.

have toxic effects, and the brain is particularly sensitive to the neurotoxic effects of ethanol during its fetal period.[149,150]

The exact amount of alcohol a pregnant woman must consume to produce a child with FAS is unknown. Some of the factors that contribute to the variable consequences of maternal drinking include

- The amount of alcohol consumed.
- At what stage in the pregnancy the alcohol is consumed. Alcohol ingested during the first trimester probably causes the most severe damage, while alcohol use later in pregnancy affects the fetus's growth.
- The pattern of alcohol consumption. Binge drinking results in a high BAC that can be particularly destructive if it occurs during a critical period of brain development.[151]
- Differences in maternal metabolism.
- Genetic susceptibility.
- Variations in vulnerability of different brain regions.[152]

Because of these variables, the safest choice for women who are thinking about becoming pregnant or who are already pregnant is to abstain from alcohol. In 2016, the Centers for Disease Control and Prevention (CDC) released a controversial statement recommending that *all* sexually active women age 15–44 who are not on birth control abstain from alcohol.

Fetal alcohol syndrome (FAS): A collection of physical and behavioral abnormalities associated with prenatal alcohol exposure.

TABLE 12.5.	Diagnostic Criteria of Fetal Alcohol Syndrome
Maternal exposure to alcohol	Mother must exhibit a pattern of excessive alcohol use; either substantial, regular drinking, or heavy episodic drinking
Characteristic pattern of craniofacial abnormalities	Small head Small, wide-set eyes; drooping eyelids; skin folds across inner corners of eyes Short, upturned nose; flattened bridge; flat philtrum Thin, reddish upper lip Ears may be low-set and nonparallel
Prenatal or postnatal growth retardation	Low birth weight Retarded body growth rate Growth below 10th percentile
Neurological damage	Structural brain abnormalities • Reduced overall brain size • Damage to basal ganglia and cerebellum • Impaired development of the corpus callosum, a band of nerve fibers that connect the left and right halves of the brain. Approximately 7% of children with FAS may lack a corpus callosum, a rate 20 times higher than that found in the general population. • Inner ear abnormalities • Eye-related problems: increased risk of cataracts, color vision deficiencies, poor vision Cognitive and neurological abnormalities • Impaired fine motor skills • Slower reaction time • Poor coordination and low muscle tone • Language difficulties • Short-term memory problems • Deficiencies in problem-solving, organizing, planning • Visual-spatial learning difficulties » Intellectual disabilities Behavioral abnormalities • Hyperactivity • Short attention span • Poor impulse control • Problems with social integration
Other physical abnormalities	Kidney malfunctions Limb and joint irregularities Abnormal fingerprints or palm creases Undescended testicles Deformed cardiac blood vessels, heart murmurs, or holes in the heart

Sources: Armstrong, E.M. (2008). Conceiving risk, bearing responsibility: Fetal alcohol syndrome and the diagnosis of moral disorder. *Baltimore: Johns Hopkins University Press.*

NIAAA. (2000). Fetal alcohol exposure and the brain. *Alcohol Alert, 50. Washington, DC: National Institute on Alcohol Abuse and Alcoholism. http://pubs. niaaa.nih.gov/publications/aa50.htm*

Ask yourself: Should pregnant women be legally prohibited from drinking alcohol? Data do not demonstrate that the occasional drink causes FAS or other birth defects. And less than 10 percent of babies born to women who suffer from alcohol use disorders exhibit full-blown FAS. But the data also do not prove that a low level of alcohol use is safe. Should women be charged with child abuse if they drink while pregnant? Should they be charged with child endangerment if they breastfeed while drunk? Do the rights of the unborn or infant child outweigh the rights of the pregnant or nursing woman?

Chapter Summary

- **History of Alcohol**
  - » Alcohol is one of the most consumed and popular psychoactive drugs in the world.
  - » Alcoholic beverages have been around for many millennia. Alcohol production burgeoned with the spread of agriculture. Naturally fermented beverages helped sustain life by providing a source of pathogen-free liquid and nutrients.
  - » In the Colonial period, American men, women, and children drank alcohol daily, and alcohol played an important role in the social and economic development of the nation.
  - » Throughout the nineteenth century, temperance movements gained popularity in America.
  - » In 1920, the 18th Amendment to the Constitution, which banned the manufacture, sale, or transportation of intoxicating liquors, became the law of the land.
  - » Prohibition was repealed in 1933 with the passage of the 21st Amendment.
  - » Prohibition was associated with the lowest alcohol consumption in U.S. history, but it also led to the rise of organized crime.
- **Prevalence of Alcohol Use**
  - » Drinking prevalence, behaviors, attitudes, and customs vary enormously across different cultures.
  - » With the exception of caffeine, more Americans use alcohol than any other legal or illegal drug. About 65–70 percent of the U.S. population consumes alcohol.
  - » In the United States, males are more likely to drink than females, whites more than other races, younger adults more than older adults, and college-educated people more likely than those without a high school diploma.
  - » Binge drinking is consuming five or more drinks on the same occasion for a male and four or more for a female; it is most common in men, and in those age 18–34.
  - » The legal drinking age in the United States is 21, but most Americans first try alcohol when they are underage. Adolescents have a greater vulnerability to alcohol than do adults.
- **Source and Forms of Alcohol**
  - » Alcohol is produced when sugars are dissolved in water, left in a warm place, and exposed to air and yeast. The yeast consumes the sugar and converts it into ethanol and carbon dioxide in a naturally occurring process called fermentation.
  - » Naturally fermented beverages such as beer and wine can't contain more than 15 percent alcohol.
  - » Distillation is a process that concentrates the alcohol in a beverage.
  - » Wine, beer, and distilled spirits contain different amounts of alcohol.
- **Pharmacokinetics of Alcohol**
  - » The effects that alcohol has on a person depend on many factors, including the dose; how well it is absorbed into the bloodstream; a person's age, sex, race, and tolerance; other drugs that are taken concurrently; and even the environment in which it is consumed.
  - » Ethanol is broken down into acetaldehyde by an enzyme called alcohol dehydrogenase.
  - » Acetaldehyde is metabolized by aldehyde dehydrogenase.
  - » The levels of these enzymes differ from person to person, and will influence one's degree of intoxication, illness after drinking, and even likelihood of developing alcohol dependence.
  - » Alcohol can influence the metabolism of many other drugs and medications.
- **Mechanism of Action of Alcohol**
  - » Alcohol increases GABA's inhibitory actions.
  - » Alcohol acts as an antagonist at NMDA glutamate receptors.
  - » Alcohol increases the release of dopamine and endorphins in addiction pathways.
  - » Alcohol also affects serotonin as well as endogenous cannabinoids.
- **Acute Effects of Alcohol**
  - » Alcohol slows electrical activity in the brain.
  - » Ethanol dilates blood vessels of the skin, increases salivation and gastric secretion of HCl, and increases urination.
  - » Alcohol may enhance sexual arousal, but it diminishes sexual performance.
  - » Alcohol diminishes sensory perception and judgments.
  - » When BAC is rising, a person may feel happy, relaxed, and confident, but when it is falling, he or she is more likely to feel angry and tired.
  - » High BAC may lead to emotional instability.
  - » Alcohol is significantly correlated with the occurrence of aggression.
  - » Adverse effects of acute heavy drinking include hangover and overdose.
  - » Ethanol has a low therapeutic index.
- **Medical and Therapeutic Uses of Alcohol**
  - » Alcohol disinfects and cools the skin and may be correlated with a reduced risk of heart attack.
  - » In the past, it was thought that moderate alcohol intake was associated with health benefits, but recent studies do not support this finding, and even moderate alcohol use is associated with increased mortality.
- **Chronic Effects of Alcohol**
  - » Regular consumption of large amounts of alcohol may lead to tolerance, withdrawal, and organ damage.
  - » Chronic drinkers can experience acute, metabolic, cellular, as well as behavioral tolerance.
  - » Withdrawal from chronic alcohol use includes anxiety, difficulty sleeping, tremors, sweating, headache, nausea and vomiting, and irregular heartbeat. Potentially fatal delirium tremens also can occur.

» Long-term heavy drinking is devastating to almost every organ system of the body, especially the brain and the liver.

» Heavy alcohol use also may raise one's risk of cancer.

» Fetal alcohol syndrome can result from excessive alcohol consumption by a woman during pregnancy. It features slowed growth; cranial, facial, or neural abnormalities; and developmental disabilities.

Key Terms

Alcohol dehydrogenase (ADH) (p.297)
Alcoholic cirrhosis (p.310)
Alcoholic hepatitis (p.310)
Aldehyde dehydrogenase (ALDH) (p.298)
Binge drinking (p.292)
Blackout (p.301)

Blood alcohol content (BAC) (p.295)
Bootlegger (p.288)
Delirium tremens (DTs) (p.307)
Distillation (p.286)
Fatty liver (p.310)
Fermentation (p.293)
Fetal alcohol syndrome (FAS) (p.311)

Korsakoff's syndrome (p.309)
Proof (p.294)
Rumrunner (p.288)
Speakeasy (p.288)
Temperance movement (p.287)
Wernicke's encephalopathy (p.308)

Quiz Yourself!

1. Which amendment to the Constitution established Prohibition? Which amendment repealed Prohibition?

2. Which of the following is TRUE about distilled and fermented beverages?

   A. Beer and wine have a lower alcohol content than distilled beverages.

   B. Beer and wine are distilled beverages.

   C. If yeast is allowed to continue the fermentation process, it will eventually produce a liquid of 100 percent alcohol.

   D. Because of their ease of production, beer and wine historically have been seen as more dangerous than beverages such as gin and vodka.

   E. All of these statements are true.

3. True or false? A BAC of 0.08 means that 8 percent of a person's blood is ethanol.

4. Which of the following typically is associated with a higher BAC? Choose ALL that apply.

   A. Being a woman rather than a man

   B. Drinking while having a full stomach rather than an empty stomach

   C. A woman on oral contraceptives compared to a woman not on oral contraceptives

   D. Being dehydrated

   E. Weighing 150 pounds compared to weighing 250 pounds

   F. Having higher levels of alcohol dehydrogenase

5. True or false? People age 21–29 have the highest rates of alcohol use in the United States.

6. True or false? Drinking rates are lower among 18- to 22-year-olds who are currently enrolled in college compared with those who are not in college.

7. Name three neurotransmitters that are affected by ethanol.

8. Which of the following is NOT an effect of ethanol?

   A. Dilates blood vessels to the skin, which increases heat loss

   B. Increases secretion of hydrochloric acid in the stomach

   C. Increases levels of antidiuretic hormone

   D. At very high doses, suppresses respiratory centers in the brain stem

9. What is the therapeutic index of alcohol?

10. True or false? Current alcohol use among middle school and high school students has risen precipitously over the past 20 years.

Additional Resources

Websites
Alcohol: Medline Plus. http://www.nlm.nih.gov/medlineplus/alcohol.html

Videos
Alcohol and your brain. https://www.youtube.com/watch?v=zXjANz9r5F0

Fetal Alcohol Exposure: Changing the Future. (2006). 31 minutes. Item #BVL34864. Films for the Humanities and Sciences.

Getting Drunk: Body Hits, Series 1. (2003). 28 minutes. Item #BVL48655. Films for the Humanities and Sciences.

How many drinks to 0.08? https://www.youtube.com/watch?v=Umv8NXl1qCk&feature=youtu.be

Books
Black, R. (2010). *Alcohol in popular culture: An encyclopedia.* Westport, CT: Greenwood Publishing Group.

Gately, I. (2008). *Drink: A cultural history of alcohol.* New York: Gotham Books.

Rose, M.E., & Cherpitel, C.J. (2011) *Alcohol: Its history, pharmacology, and treatment.* Center City, MN: Hazelden.

Learn more with this chapter's digital tools at www.oup.com/he/rosenthal2e.

Drugs for Treating Psychological Disorders

True or false?

1.
True or false? It has been proven that major depressive disorder is due to a chemical imbalance.

2.
True or false? Schizophrenics have multiple personalities.

3.
True or false? About one-third of Americans will suffer from an anxiety disorder at some time in their lives.

Answers: 1. F, 2. F, 3. T

M ood fluctuations are normal and healthy. It is part of the human experience to sometimes feel sad, anxious, or even paranoid. Sadness allows us to recognize and honor loss; anxiety helps us to anticipate and avoid potential threats. But sometimes these emotions become overwhelming and unrealistic and interfere with our daily lives. Unfortunately, the defining line between normal emotions and mood disorders can be subjective, context dependent, and difficult to discern. In this chapter, we will discuss major depressive disorder, bipolar disorder, schizophrenia, anxiety disorders, and PTSD (a trauma- and stressor-related disorder), as well as the drugs used to treat them.

Learning Objectives

- List the symptoms of major depressive disorder, bipolar disorder, anxiety disorders, post-traumatic stress disorder (PTSD), and schizophrenia.

- Describe some of the biological, psychological, and social factors that underlie the development of major depressive disorder, bipolar disorder, schizophrenia, anxiety disorders, and PTSD.

- Provide some explanations for the increased rates of affective disorders in today's society.

- Analyze the evidence for and against the monoamine theory of depression.

- Compare the mechanism of action of MAOIs, TCAs, SSRIs, and atypical antidepressants.

- Evaluate the relationship between antidepressant drugs and suicide.

- List some nontraditional treatments for depression.

- Identify the most common pharmaceutical treatments for bipolar disorder.

- Differentiate between the positive and the negative symptoms of schizophrenia.

- Compare and contrast first- and second-generation antipsychotic drugs.

- Describe the major types of anxiety disorders.

Psychological Disorders in Today's Society

About half of all Americans will meet the criteria for a mental health disorder, including **affective disorders** (mood disorders), during their lifetime. In any 12-month period, about 20 percent of the U.S. adult population—over 47 million people—will suffer from a diagnosable mental illness. Although this is a huge number of people—enough to fill a standard baseball stadium 1,000 times—it is probably an underestimate. National surveys do not include the homeless or the institutionalized, so the mentally ill among those populations are not counted. Additionally, because mental illness is still stigmatized in our society, some survey participants may lie about their psychological status.

In our drugstore society, we mostly turn to drugs to treat these conditions. Currently, one in every six American adults report taking at least one psychiatric drug.[1] Each year, mood and psychiatric medications garner $25 billion in sales—more than the gross domestic product of the South American country of Paraguay.

Mental illness is more visible than ever before, but both the entertainment and news media present exceptionally dramatic and distorted images of mental illness that emphasize dangerousness, violence, and unpredictability (Figure 13.1).[2] Mentally ill characters are portrayed as significantly more violent than both non–mentally ill characters and mentally ill people in the real world. Media images often portray people with mental

Affective disorder: Mood disorder such as depression or anxiety, characterized by abnormalities in mood, behavior, sleep, and neurochemical equilibrium.

FIGURE 13.1. **Mental illness in the movies.** Mental illness has been portrayed in many films, including (a) *Silver Linings Playbook* (bipolar disorder), (b) *Ordinary People* (major depressive disorder), and (c) *Donnie Darko* (schizophrenia).

illness as having no occupation, no friends, no family, and being disenfranchised from society. Media images may also impair self-esteem, stop people from seeking help, lessen the likelihood that people will take their medication, and hurt overall recovery.[3]

Major Depressive Disorder

Also called "unipolar depression," **major depressive disorder (MDD)** is a debilitating condition character- ized by overwhelming sadness, feelings of worthless- ness, and a loss of interest in normally pleasurable activities (Figure 13.2). Depression is the most common mental disorder in adults and the major single cause of

Major depressive disorder (MDD): Also known as depression, or unipolar depression, MDD is an affective disorder characterized by overwhelming sadness, feelings of worthlessness, and a loss of interest in normally pleasurable activities.

medical disability in the world. Depression is respon- sible for up to 70 percent of psychiatric hospitalizations and about 40 percent of suicides.[4] The annual cost of de- pression in the U.S. is estimated to be over $210 billion, including medical, psychiatric, and pharmacological care, as well as decreased productivity, work absences, and mortality costs.[5]

Prevalence of Depression

More than 350 million people worldwide are affected by depression.[6] Prevalence of major depressive episodes tends to be higher in high-income countries such as the United States, France, and the Netherlands, and lower in low- to middle-income countries such as Mexico, India, and China.[7,8]

In the United States, lifetime prevalence of MDD is over 20 percent; 14.7 percent of men and 26.1 percent of women will suffer from depression at some time in their lives (Figure 13.3).[9] In the United States in 2019, over 19 million adults age 18 and older—7.8 percent of

Ask yourself: What factors might lead people living in different parts of the world to experience higher or lower levels of depression as a percentage of the population?

FIGURE 13.2. Sorrowing old man (at eternity's gate). This painting was done by Vincent van Gogh, who suffered from depression for most of his life and committed suicide in 1890.

all adults—experienced at least one major depressive episode in the past year, as did 15.7 percent of those age 12–17.[10]

According to the National Survey on Drug Use and Health,[11] the demographics of depression appear to be fairly straightforward—women experience it more than men, those who are younger more than those who are older, and Blacks and Asians have lower rates of depression than whites (Figure 13.4). Surveys that measure the prevalence of depression, however, are limited by how they define and diagnose depression, as well as by the confounding factors for which they control.

Over the course of a lifetime, women are 70 percent more likely to be diagnosed with major depression than men. Depression may have different symptoms, however, in men as opposed to women, which may lead to underdiagnosis in men. Women show sadness, guilt, and hopelessness, but depression in men may actually manifest as rage, aggression, irritability, risk taking, and substance abuse. When that difference is taken into consideration, the disparity between depression rates in men and women disappears.[12]

Depression is diagnosed more frequently in younger people than in those of middle age (i.e., ages 40–59).[13,14] The percentage of U.S. teens and young adults reporting mental distress, depression, and suicidal thoughts and actions has risen significantly in the past decade; in fact, past year prevalence of a major depressive episode in those age 12–17 is more than twice as high as in adults.[15,16] Some believe the significant increase

(a)

(b)

(c)

FIGURE 13.3. Celebrities with depression. (a) Brad Pitt, (b) Joseph Gordon-Levitt, and (c) Beyoncé Knowles have all suffered from depression. Many other celebrities have experienced depression including Christian Bale, Halle Berry, Johnny Depp and Harrison Ford.

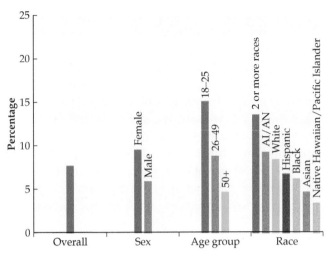

FIGURE 13.4. The demographics of depression. Prevalence of a major depressive episode in the past year among U.S. adults.

Source: (SAMHSA). (2020). Results from the 2019 national survey on drug use and health. *Rockville, MD: Center for Behavioral Health Statistics and Quality.*

Ask yourself: Why do you think rates of mental distress and depression have risen so greatly in teens and young adults?

symptoms.[17] Uncertain economic times and pressure to succeed may also play a role. Not only are young people being diagnosed more often with depression, but those with depression are more likely to use antidepressants than in the past.[18,19] Depression is even being diagnosed in preschool children; about 2.1 percent of preschoolers have been diagnosed with depression.[20]

Finally, when it comes to race, national surveys control for confounding factors associated with higher rates of depression, such as lack of health insurance, less education, and lower socioeconomic status, giving the result that Hispanics and whites have similar rates, and Blacks show significantly lower rates of depression. In the real world, however, these confounding factors cannot be simply "controlled away"; they have a profound effect on depression rates. It may be that these statistical adjustments affect the prevalence reports and Blacks and Hispanics actually have elevated rates of MDD relative to whites.[21] Another theory suggests that the specific coping behaviors chosen by certain groups raise or lower their reports of depression.[22]

in mental distress and depression have increased so greatly in teens may be due to increased exposure to social media. Adolescents are particularly concerned with peer status and approval, and social media exaggerates those images. One study showed the more time spent on social media, the greater the risk of depressive

Critical Evaluation

Why have depression rates increased?

The prevalence of depression has greatly increased, especially over the past 30 years. In fact, depression once was considered a rare condition. Among those born around World War I, the lifetime prevalence rate of major depression was only 1 percent. Why have rates skyrocketed?

Awareness. Have depression diagnoses increased simply because there is more awareness and less stigma surrounding the disease than in the past? People today are more open about depression, and are more likely to seek help than they were in the past. How have direct-to-consumer ads played a role in raising awareness of depression, and encouraging people to seek treatment?

Societal changes. How might feelings of isolation contribute to depression rates? Many people live far from their families and are not part of a close-knit neighborhood. There is also

great pressure to succeed financially and appear physically flawless. How might lifestyle choices, such as a lack of exercise and a diet high in processed foods exacerbate depression?

Overdiagnosis. Perhaps depression is overdiagnosed and we are medicalizing sadness. One study examined 5,639 patients who had been diagnosed with depression by a medical professional in the past 12 months. When assessed for depression using a structured interview, only 38.4 percent met the criteria for depression, despite the majority of participants being prescribed psychiatric medications. Among study participants age 65 or older, 86 percent did not meet the criteria.[23] Could overdiagnosis be due to a misunderstanding about what depression actually is? How might the fact that many diagnoses are made by one's primary care physician and not by a trained psychiatrist or psychologist influence diagnosis rates?

Availability of pharmaceutical treatments.
In the past, those suffering from severe depression had no options other than a stay in a mental institution. Today, a wide array of pharmaceutical choices is available to help alleviate depression. Are more people seeking help because it's perceived that there are easy fixes for depression?

Long-term effects of antidepressant drugs. Some evidence exists that antidepressant drugs may actually worsen symptoms and change what could be a one-time depressive event into a chronic, recurring illness. Many studies show that recovery times and outcomes for medicated patients are significantly worse than outcomes in patients who never took antidepressant drugs, and the longer the drug treatment, the higher the likelihood of relapse.[24,25,26,27,28] Is it that those with more severe depression are more likely to take antidepressant drugs? Or, might the use of antidepressant drugs produce changes in the brain that elevate the risk of recurrences?

Causes of Depression

There is no one single cause of depression. Biological, psychological, and social factors all play a role. Depression often co-occurs with other psychiatric problems. Over half of those with MDD also have an anxiety disorder, and depressed patients also have higher rates of alcohol and drug abuse. Depression also is associated with higher rates of cardiovascular disease, obesity, and smoking. With all of these **comorbidities**—one or more disorders present at the same time as a primary disorder—it is difficult to say whether depression caused the other disease, the other disease led to depression, or both disorders were due to yet another factor. Some biological factors that may influence the development of depression include genetics, neurochemistry, neuroanatomy, hormones, diet, and even the bacteria of the gut.

Genetics

Genetics are just one of the factors that underlie depression.[29] Children of depressed parents are four times more likely to have mood disorders than children of nondepressed parents.[30] Several genes have been implicated, but no single gene controls depression.[31,32]

Neurochemistry

The best known, but highly disputed, theory about the cause of depression is that it is due to low levels of **monoamines** in the brain—namely serotonin, dopamine, and norepinephrine. Because the most popular drugs currently used to treat depression affect the serotonergic system, we will take a closer look at the actions of this neurotransmitter at the synapse.

Figure 13.5 shows the actions of serotonin at the synapse. Serotonin is released from the presynaptic neuron, crosses the synapse, and binds to receptors on the postsynaptic neuron, where it initiates its effects. Serotonergic actions are halted by two main mechanisms: deactivation by the enzyme monoamine oxidase (MAO), and reuptake into the presynaptic neuron by the serotonin transporter (SERT). As we'll see later in the chapter, many antidepressants work by inhibiting these processes, which boosts the levels of serotonin at the synapse.

Presynaptic autoreceptors (Chapter 3) provide feedback to the presynaptic cell and help it to adjust for changing conditions. When serotonin is released from the presynaptic cell into the synapse, it not only binds to postsynaptic receptors, but also to presynaptic autoreceptors. These autoreceptors send a signal to the presynaptic cell, essentially saying, "Hey, you just released serotonin and it's here in the synapse. Ease up and don't release any more for a while."

The brain wants to maintain a stable internal environment and so will adjust the number of receptors based on the amount of neurotransmitter that is present. If more serotonin than normal is present in the synapse, the number of postsynaptic receptors decreases, a process called downregulation (Chapter 4).

Evidence in favor of the monoamine hypothesis of depression includes the fact that drugs (such as cocaine) that increase monoamine levels can elevate mood, and sometimes drugs that decrease these neurotransmitters can depress mood. Additionally, autopsies of suicide victims indicate that brain levels of these neurotransmitters may have been reduced.

There is also powerful evidence, however, suggesting that the monoamine theory is both simplistic and misguided, and that low levels of serotonin and other monoamines are not the only cause of depression.

Comorbidity: One or more disorders present at the same time as a primary disorder.

Monoamines: A group of structurally related neurotransmitters, including dopamine, norepinephrine, and serotonin.

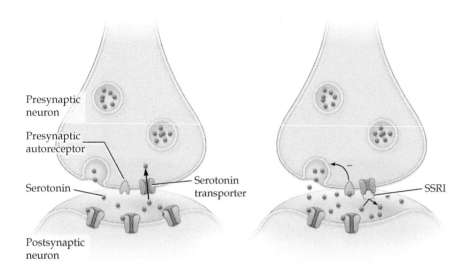

FIGURE 13.5. The actions of serotonin at the synapse. When serotonin is released into the synapse, homeostatic changes occur to adjust the number of receptors based on the amount of neurotransmitter that is present.

and the amount of hippocampal loss is correlated with the degree of impaired memory and depressed mood.

Contrary to what we once believed, existing neurons are sometimes able to repair themselves, and the brain is capable of making new neurons, especially in the frontal cortex, olfactory bulb, and hippocampus.[36] The production and growth of new neurons is called neurogenesis (Chapter 3). Things that decrease neurogenesis include stress, advancing age, cortisol, opioids, and glutamate.[37] On the other hand, learning, exercise, electroconvulsive therapy, and chronic administration of antidepressant drugs enhance neurogenesis and reverse hippocampal atrophy.[38,39,40,41]

- There is no proof that people with depression have lower monoamine levels than normal, and there is no correlation between serotonin metabolite levels and the severity of depression.[33]
- Antidepressants boost neurotransmitter levels within hours, but their mood-enhancing actions don't take effect for weeks. Some effective antidepressant treatments don't affect monoamines at all.
- Most antidepressant drugs raise synaptic levels of monoamines, but after a few weeks the receptors adjust for the elevated neurotransmitter levels, which would theoretically eliminate the antidepressant effect.

Neuroanatomy

Patients with major depressive disorder show some abnormalities in brain structures. MRI scans show smaller volumes of the basal ganglia (movement), thalamus (sensory processing), anterior cingulate cortex (helps govern impulse control and empathy), certain areas of the prefrontal cortex (decisions, reasoning, and emotional regulation), and the hippocampus (memory, emotions, and concentration).[34] They also show greater activity in the habenula, a part of the brain that is activated by disappointment and unexpected negative effects.[35]

The hippocampus of someone with long-term clinical depression can be as much as 20 percent smaller than that of someone who has never been depressed,

Overactive Stress Response

About 50 percent of depressed individuals display hyperactivity of the hypothalamic-pituitary-adrenal axis—the system that manages the body's response to stress. This can lead to a sustained elevation of the stress hormone cortisol, which can inhibit neurogenesis in the hippocampus.[42,43]

Inflammation and Immune Factors

Depression may occur as a response to infection,[44,45] chronic inflammation,[46,47] or problems with the brain's immune cells.[48] About one-third of those suffering from depression have higher levels of an inflammatory marker in their brains, and anti-inflammatory drugs may help improve the symptoms of depression.[49]

Diet

There is a correlation between obesity and the development of depression; obese individuals have a 20 percent elevated risk of depression.[50,51] But be careful not to confuse correlation and causation. It may be that obesity directly causes depression, perhaps by affecting the body's stress response or inflammation in the brain.[52] Or, maybe obesity indirectly leads to depression, due to the stigma against obesity in our society. On the other hand, perhaps it is depression that causes weight gain, due to either biological or behavioral changes. Finally, another factor, such as poverty or other health problems, may underlie both conditions.

Gut Bacteria

Although the wall of the gastrointestinal tract is normally impermeable to bacteria, about 35 percent of depressed subjects showed signs that gut bacteria had entered the bloodstream. Displaced gut bacteria can activate autoimmune responses and inflammation, which may play a role in depression.[53] In addition, the specific bacterial strains that are colonized in our gut may influence our emotions.[54,55,56]

Psychological Factors

Cognitive beliefs, interpersonal factors, and stressful life events may all play a role in the development of depression. For example, imagine that Jaime fails a math test. He's disappointed, but he realizes that although the test was hard, he knows he could have studied more than he did, and he vows to do better next time. Sarah fails the same test. She tells herself that she's stupid, that everyone sees her as a failure, and that she's going to flunk out of school and end up living in a van down by the river.

Psychologist Aaron Beck proposed that some people with depression develop a **negative cognitive triad** that involves an overly distorted and pessimistic view of themselves, of the world, and of the future.[57] People who are depressed put a negative slant on their experiences and memories, processing information in a distorted way and showing increased sensitivity to sad faces, greater memory for negative material, and reduced responsiveness to rewards as compared to healthy people.[58] Individuals with depression often blame themselves for negative events, which they believe will last a long time and affect most areas of their life; yet, they don't take credit for positive outcomes, which are looked at as short term and insignificant. They may also experience a sense of learned helplessness—the belief that no matter what they do, their efforts won't help their situation.

Interpersonal factors such as deficits in social skills or communication problems can influence one's emotional well-being, as can stressful life events, particularly ones that are significant, undesirable, and/or uncontrollable such as divorce, unemployment, or the death of a loved one. Eighty percent of people diagnosed with MDD report symptoms after a momentous life stress.[59]

Social Factors

Many social elements influence the development of depression as well, including poverty, adverse conditions at work, and a lack of social support. Physical, emotional, and sexual abuse as a child also can raise the probability of developing depression later in life.[60] In addition, the constant stress of prejudice may raise one's risk of depression; some members of the LGBTQ community have higher rates of depression, as do those in the immigrant and migrant populations.[61] Finally, drug and alcohol abuse is high among people with affective disorders, although this does not mean that having an affective disorder necessarily causes drug and alcohol use or that drug and alcohol use leads to affective disorders.

Symptoms of Depression

Major depressive disorder is characterized by a low mood that pervades all aspects of life. Those with depression have both psychological and physical signs that may manifest nearly every day, including

- Sadness, despair, depressed mood
- Feelings of inappropriate guilt, anxiety, low self-esteem, and worthlessness
- Lack of motivation, fatigue, or loss of energy
- Markedly diminished interest or pleasure in all, or almost all, activities
- Decreased cognitive functioning, diminished ability to think or concentrate
- Changes in appetite or weight
- Disrupted sleep patterns
- Agitated or sluggish motor activity
- Recurrent thoughts of death, suicidal ideation, or suicide attempts
- Physical symptoms such as fatigue, headache, or gastrointestinal problems

To be diagnosed with depression, a person must have at least five or more of the signs, and symptoms must persist continuously for at least two weeks. In addition, the changes must be severe enough that they cause distress or impair work, social, or personal functioning.

Depressive disorder can be mild, moderate, or severe, and the symptoms exist on a continuum. Depression may occur as a single episode, or there may be repeated and recurrent episodes over the years. These episodes may last 6–12 months or longer. A two-month interval of normal mood must occur for episodes to be considered separate from one another.[62]

Negative cognitive triad: A recurrent pattern of depressive thinking and distorted information processing, which gives someone negative thoughts about oneself, one's world, and one's future.

Ask yourself: Victorian culture valued women who were emotionally sensitive, socially unassertive, relaxed, melancholic, and melodramatic in response to perceived neglect.[64] Today's popularity of antidepressant drugs may emphasize our culture's preference for certain personality types—happy, energetic, assertive, and resilient. How much of depression is a constant, physical, measurable phenomenon, and how much of it is simply a deviation from society's expectations?

Although depression is more visible than in the past, it is still misunderstood and stigmatized. The comic in Figure 13.6 illustrates how it would be if we treated other diseases the way we treat depression.

Diagnosis of Depression

Ideally, depression is diagnosed by a psychologist or psychiatrist who considers the patient's self-reported symptoms and experiences, medical history, drug use, and social factors, as well as behavior reported by relatives or friends. They assess the presence and severity of depression with a questionnaire such as the Hamilton Rating Scale. A diagnosis of depression also depends on the context of the symptoms, and the norms of society. In the United States, sadness is less acceptable than in Eastern European countries, where mild levels of depressive symptoms are considered the norm.[63]

FIGURE 13.6. What if we treated every illness the way we treat mental illness? Mental illness is still misunderstood and stigmatized.

Prognosis of Depression

Depression is increasingly recognized as a chronic or recurrent illness.[65] Some people who have a depressive episode will recover, whether they are treated or not, but

FIGURE 13.7. Robin Williams. Comedian and actor Robin Williams committed suicide in 2014. He had been suffering from depression, had difficulties with both drugs and alcohol, and had been diagnosed with Lewy body dementia before his death.

most depressed patients will experience recurrences.[66] A variety of factors increase the risk of persistent or recurrent depression, including a prior history of depressed episodes, more severe depressive symptoms, co-occurrence of anxiety, and cigarette use or drug abuse.[67,68] Depression is associated with a number of physical ailments and a shorter life expectancy, which is in part due to suicide.

About 3.4 percent of people in the United States with MDD commit suicide. In fact, suicide is the 10th leading cause of death for Americans, and more people in the United States die from suicide than in car accidents. Suicide rates in the United States are at their highest rate in in 30 years (Figure 13.7).[69,70,71,72]

Antidepressant Treatments

Writer H.L. Mencken said, "For every complex problem there is an answer that is clear, simple, and wrong." Our belief that depression is easily treated with a pill illustrates his point. Although more people are receiving treatment than in the past, many millions of Americans are untreated for their depression. Men, racial minorities, and those with less education are especially unlikely to receive treatment for depression.[73]

History of Antidepressant Treatment

Thousands of years ago, mental illnesses were attributed to demonic possession and often were treated by priests, who sometimes cut holes in the afflicted person's head to release the evil spirits. In Ancient Greece, depression was thought to be due to an imbalance in body fluids and was treated with bloodletting. Early Christians considered melancholia to be a result of Satan's influence and God's anger, and they believed that depression represented the struggle against temptations and sins of the flesh. Depression was treated with exorcisms, drowning, and burning the afflicted at the stake.

By the eighteenth century, many thought that depression was an inherited, unalterable weakness of temperament, and depressed individuals were committed to institutions, often for life.[74] Mental patients were sometimes tied up, starved, and left to sit in their own waste.

In the twentieth century, depression began to be thought of as a disease and not a failure of character or weakness of will.[75] Sigmund Freud believed depression was due to unconscious emotional conflicts and that psychoanalysis was the best way to dig out these conflicts. By the mid-twentieth century, the idea that a chemical imbalance caused depression began to take hold.

Many of the current treatments for depression originally were created to treat other diseases, such as tuberculosis or psychosis, and their antidepressive actions were a happy side effect. Doctors did not know the mechanism by which these drugs exerted their antidepressant effects, but because they seemed to alleviate depression they began to be widely prescribed. Today, antidepressant drugs are the primary means to treat depression.

Prevalence of Antidepressant Drugs

There are more than 30 antidepressants available, and today, antidepressant drugs (ADDs) represent one of the three most common classes of medications prescribed in the United States.[76,77] In 1996, about 6 percent of the U.S. adult population, or 13 million people, were prescribed an antidepressant; by 2019, over 13 percent of the population, or about 30 million people reported using an antidepressant medication in the past month (Figure 13.8).[78]

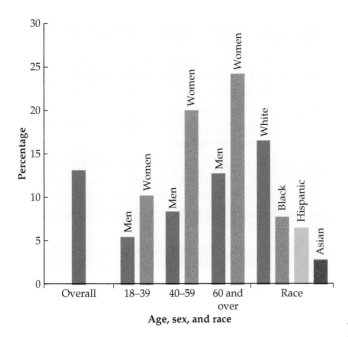

FIGURE 13.8. Percentage of adults in the U.S. who used an antidepressant medication in the past month, by age, sex, and race.

Source: Brody, D.J., & Gu, Q. (2020). Antidepressant use among adults: United States, 2015–2018. NCHS Data Brief, no 377. Hyattsville, MD: National Center for Health Statistics.

Why has the use of antidepressant drugs exploded over the last 30 years?

- Diagnoses of depression have increased greatly over the same time period.

- Many people on ADDs are taking them for an "off-label" use, which means that the drug is being used in a manner not specified by the Food and Drug Administration (FDA), perhaps in an untested age group, or to treat a disorder for which the drug hasn't been approved.
- Antidepressants are increasingly prescribed to patients to treat anxiety disorders, eating disorders, chronic pain, premenstrual syndrome, hot flashes, migraine headaches, and sexual compulsions, among other conditions.
- Direct-to-consumer marketing has led to an increased number of ADD prescriptions. In recent years, pharmaceutical companies have spent many billions of dollars each year on drug promotion, and a significant proportion is for ADD ads.

QUICK HIT

Three out of every four prescriptions for antidepressant drugs are written by family physicians rather than psychiatrists, and many of those who have been prescribed an ADD had no psychiatric diagnosis at all. When prescribing these drugs, one-half to two-thirds of physicians do not inform the patient about dosage, how long to take the drug, or possible side effects, and 80 percent of the time the patient's progress on the drug is not monitored with follow-up appointments.[79]

STRAIGHT DOPE	What to Do if You're Feeling Suicidal

Depression affects millions of people every year, and some even begin to feel that life isn't worth living. Suicidal thoughts mean your pain has temporarily exceeded your resources for coping with pain. If you are feeling suicidal:

- You need to
  - Get through this moment. Try to turn to other activities, and give yourself some distance. Say "I will wait 24 hours before I do anything."
  - Remove whatever can harm you from the immediate area. If there are guns, pills, or razors in the house—leave.
  - Try to reduce your pain. Reach out for help. Call friends and family, your physician, or a suicide prevention hotline.*
- Try to find ways to cope with the pain:
  - Learn to improve your coping resources.
  - Avoid drugs and alcohol. You may want to feel numb, but you won't make a rational decision while under the influence.

- Avoid being alone and doing things that make you feel worse.
- Know that
  - Your emptiness and despair may seem insurmountable and eternal, but solutions *do* exist and your pain *will* subside.
  - Pain is temporary, but suicide is forever. Suicide doesn't solve problems; it just hurts the people who love you.
  - Feelings and actions are different. You may feel like you don't want to live, but that doesn't mean you have to act on it.
  - People get through this—even people who are hurting as much as you are now.

* The National Suicide Prevention Hotline telephone number is 1-800-273-8255. The Crisis Text Line helps with concerns about anxiety, depression, and suicide. To reach them you can text the word "home" to 741741.

There are four different classes of antidepressant drugs: **monoamine oxidase inhibitors (MAOIs), tricyclic antidepressants (TCAs), selective serotonin reuptake inhibitors (SSRIs)**, and atypical/mixed action antidepressants. MAOIs such as isocarboxazid and selegiline were the first ADDs marketed. They work by inhibiting the enzyme that breaks down monoamine neurotransmitters. They are not widely used today because they are nonspecific and result in extensive side effects. TCAs such as imipramine, amitriptyline, and clomipramine were the second class of antidepressants developed. They raise levels of serotonin and norepinephrine by blocking their reuptake; they also block the postsynaptic effects of acetylcholine and histamine. SSRIs raise serotonin levels in the synapse by selectively blocking the reuptake of serotonin; because they have fewer side effects than older antidepressant

drugs, SSRIs such as fluoxetine, sertraline, and citalopram are more widely prescribed today. Atypical/mixed action ADDs such as bupropion, trazodone, and duloxetine also are gaining in popularity. Table 13.1 lists the most commonly prescribed antidepressant drugs in the United States, and Table 13.2 summarizes the effects of the four classes of ADDs.

Although the cellular effects of all four classes of these drugs begin immediately, it usually takes at least two to three weeks until depression symptoms ease.

Monoamine oxidase inhibitor (MAOI): A type of antidepressant drug that raises monoamine levels by inhibiting their enzymatic breakdown.

Tricyclic antidepressant (TCA): A type of antidepressant drug that raises serotonin and norepinephrine levels by blocking their reuptake.

Selective serotonin reuptake inhibitor (SSRI): A type of antidepressant drug that raises serotonin levels by blocking its reuptake.

TABLE 13.1. Most Commonly Prescribed Antidepressant Drugs in the United States in 2018

Generic Name	Trade Name	Type	Total Number of Prescriptions Dispensed in 2018
sertraline	Zoloft	SSRI	48,999,022
escitalopram	Lexapro	SSRI	37,927,469
trazodone	Desyrel	Atypical	34,665,828
bupropion	Wellbutrin	Atypical	34,372,232
fluoxetine	Prozac	SSRI	31,190,127
citalopram	Celexa	SSRI	28,011,615
duloxetine	Cymbalta	Atypical	26,032,770
venlafaxine	Effexor	Atypical	21,717,245
mirtazapine	Remeron	Atypical	13,539,039
paroxetine	Paxil	SSRI	12,874,006

Source: Grohol, J.M. (2019). Top 25 psychiatric medication prescriptions for 2018. PsychCentral. https://psychcentral.com/blog/top-25-psychiatric-medications-for-2018/

TABLE 13.2. Mechanism of Action of Antidepressant Drugs

Class	Examples	Mechanism of Action
MAOI	isocarboxazid (Marplan) selegiline (Eldepryl)	Inhibits the enzyme that breaks down serotonin, dopamine, norepinephrine, epinephrine, melatonin, and histamine
TCA	imipramine (Tofranil) amitriptyline (Elavil) clomipramine (Anafranil)	Blocks reuptake of serotonin and norepinephrine. Decreases levels of acetylcholine and histamine
SSRI	fluoxetine (Prozac) sertraline (Zoloft) citalopram (Celexa)	Blocks reuptake of serotonin
Atypical	bupropion (Wellbutrin) trazodone (Desyrel) duloxetine (Cymbalta)	Most block reuptake of serotonin and norepinephrine

Individual drugs show different degrees of efficacy due to the length of the half-life, the receptor selectivity, and the drug's effects on metabolic enzymes.[80] Today, SSRIs or atypical ADDs are usually the first drug of choice, with MAOIs only given to patients who are unresponsive to at least two other antidepressant drugs.

Pharmacokinetics of Antidepressant Drugs

Antidepressant drugs are well and rapidly absorbed through the gastrointestinal (GI) tract. They are very lipid-soluble and are highly bound to plasma proteins. They undergo significant first-pass metabolism, meaning they are largely metabolized before they reach the brain.

These drugs are metabolized by the cytochrome P450 (CYP450) system. Genetic differences in these enzymes will influence the rate of metabolism of ADDs. For example, people of Asian descent do not metabolize TCAs as quickly as whites, and must, therefore, take a lower dose.[81]

After being on an ADD for at least four weeks, patients who wish to discontinue its use must be slowly weaned off the medication. Stopping ADDs abruptly can cause **antidepressant discontinuation syndrome**. Symptoms include dizziness, nausea, insomnia, headaches, fatigue, and difficulty concentrating. Over half of those who attempt to come off antidepressants experience withdrawal effects, which can last for several weeks or more.[82] Additionally, abrupt discontinuation can cause depression to return. Paxil and Effexor are particularly difficult to discontinue. Fluoxetine has a longer half-life than other SSRIs and therefore has fewer problems associated with withdrawal.

Antidepressant Drug Interactions

Antidepressant drugs raise levels of monoamines; therefore, taking them with drugs or foods that also raise levels of these neurotransmitters can have serious effects:

- Many ADDs inhibit CYP450 enzymes, so the effects of alcohol, opioids, barbiturates, aspirin, and many other drugs are prolonged and intensified when a person is taking ADDs.

Antidepressant discontinuation syndrome: Flu-like symptoms and sensory disturbances associated with abrupt withdrawal from antidepressant medication.

Serotonin syndrome: A potentially life-threatening reaction that can occur when medications cause large amounts of serotonin to accumulate in the body.

Wine and cheese effect: The potentially fatal hypertensive crisis that can occur when people taking MAOIs ingest foods that raise tyramine levels.

- Substances that raise norepinephrine levels, including nasal sprays, cold medicines, anti-asthma drugs, amphetamine, or cocaine, can cause a dangerous interaction when taken with MAOIs and some other ADDs.
- Almost all ADDs raise levels of serotonin; mixing two or more different ADDs can lead to a potentially fatal condition called **serotonin syndrome**.

The MAOIs inhibit the normal metabolism of the amino acid tyramine, causing levels to rise. When foods with a high tyramine content are ingested—such as wine, cheese, unpasteurized milk and yogurt, yeast, bananas, avocado, raspberries, wine, soy sauce, and chocolate—tyramine levels increase excessively. When this happens, a potentially fatal hypertensive crisis referred to as the **wine and cheese effect** may occur, resulting in a heart attack or rupture of an aneurism.

Mechanism of Action of Antidepressant Drugs

The various classes of ADDs have distinct mechanisms of action, but all of them affect the amount of neurotransmitters at the synapse. MAOIs have a nonspecific mechanism of action; they inhibit MAO, the enzyme that breaks down monoamine neurotransmitters, thereby increasing the level of dopamine, norepinephrine, epinephrine, serotonin, melatonin, and histamine in the synapse.

The TCAs are fairly nonspecific. They block the reuptake of serotonin and norepinephrine, thus raising their levels in the synapse. They also lower synaptic effects of acetylcholine and histamine by blocking their postsynaptic receptors, an effect that accounts for most TCA side effects.

The SSRIs selectively block the reuptake of serotonin into the presynaptic neuron, making more serotonin available to postsynaptic receptors. Elevated serotonin accounts for most side effects.

Most atypical antidepressants block the reuptake of both serotonin and norepinephrine. These drugs differ from TCAs in their structure, and in that they do not have an effect on acetylcholine or histamine. Bupropion (Wellbutrin) is another atypical antidepressant. Wellbutrin inhibits the reuptake of norepinephrine and dopamine. In addition to its antidepressant effects, Wellbutrin has helped some people quit smoking.

Conventional wisdom accepts that depression is related to low serotonin levels; as such, many antidepressant treatments seek to address this presumed chemical imbalance. But MDD might be due to many other biological causes, and antidepressant drugs may exert their effects by rectifying these other biological factors, such as reduced brain volume and a hyperactive stress response.

Evidence exists that these drugs exert their antidepressant effects through their ability to increase both the growth and survival of newly formed neurons in the hippocampus. When this process is blocked, antidepressant drugs no longer produce antidepressant actions.[83] This may explain why antidepressant drugs take two to three weeks to work, even though they increase serotonin levels immediately. Serotonin increases proliferation of cells in the hippocampus, but it can take several weeks for the newly generated cells to develop, mature, and become functionally integrated into the brain.[84] In addition, antidepressant drugs can help normalize the levels of stress hormones.

Side Effects of Antidepressant Drugs

The side effects of ADDs can be quite distressing and can diminish the quality of life. Many ADDs (of all classes) produce dizziness, headache, dry mouth, GI disturbances and constipation, weight gain, sleep disturbances, and sexual dysfunction.

The MAOIs and TCAs also can cause drowsiness, fatigue, elevated body temperature, heart palpitations, and agitation. TCAs have a low therapeutic index—toxicity occurs at approximately 10 times the normal dose. This is especially troubling when one considers that these drugs are given to people who may have suicidal tendencies.

Because they have little to no effect on dopamine, norepinephrine, acetylcholine, or histamine, SSRIs tend to have fewer side effects than the older antidepressants, but they are by no means side-effect free. In addition to the common side effects seen with all ADDs, SSRIs also can cause apathy, sexual dysfunction, and an increased risk of suicide.

Between 36 and 70 percent of SSRI users develop sexual dysfunction, including decreased libido, erectile dysfunction, delayed orgasm, or anorgasmia (this percentage excludes patients with preexisting sexual dysfunction).[85] Sometimes, these sexual dysfunctions persist even after discontinuing SSRIs. Bupropion offers the lowest risk of sexual side effects.[86]

In 2004, the FDA reviewed 24 placebo-controlled trials among nearly 100,000 participants and concluded that antidepressant drugs doubled the risk of suicidal thoughts or behavior (from 2 to 4 percent) in children and adolescents.[87,88] Subsequently, the FDA mandated that a black box warning be put on the labels of antidepressants, indicating the increased risk of suicide in youth taking these medications. In 2007, that suicidality warning was extended to young adults age 18–24.

Within two years of the FDA advisory, there were significant reductions in antidepressant use among adolescents and young adults, and the number of suicide attempts *rose* by more than 20 percent in adolescents and by more than 33 percent in young adults.[89,90,91]

Other countries saw similar trends. In the Netherlands, the use of antidepressant drugs increased substantially between 1994 and 2008, and the suicide rate fell considerably over the same time period.[92] Between 2003 and 2005, there was a 22 percent drop in antidepressant prescriptions in patients under 18, and a 49 percent increase in suicides.[93]

Analyzing the relationship between antidepressant drug use and suicide risk is difficult, because there are so many confounding factors. Perhaps suicide rates are higher in those on ADDs because more severely depressed people—those who are at a higher risk of suicide due to their disease—are more likely to be put on antidepressant drugs. Are higher suicide rates of ADD users due to the medication or due to the depression itself? On the other hand, after the black box warning was issued, ADD prescriptions fell and suicide rates *rose*. But during this time frame, there was no increase in other treatments for depression, such as psychotherapy. Was this increase in suicide rates due to fewer people taking ADDs, or because they were now not receiving *any* help for their disease?

Efficacy of Antidepressant Drugs

Scientists have known for 50 years that ADDs are not a miracle cure for depression. Perhaps one-third of patients with major depression will experience full remission after their first round of pharmaceutical treatment; successive use of different ADDs will give relief to 20–25 percent more.[94] However, about 20–30 percent of those with MDD are resistant to all pharmacological treatments.

A number of meta-analyses found that although SSRIs are slightly more effective than placebo for severe depression, they are no more effective than placebo for mild to moderate depression.[95,96] Irving Kirsch and colleagues analyzed the data submitted to the FDA for the six most widely prescribed antidepressants. They found that the average difference between drug and placebo was less than two points on the Hamilton Depression Scale—a depressed person must have a drop of at least three points for it to be considered clinically significant. They also found that about 80 percent of any

Ask yourself: What if the benefits of antidepressant drugs are simply due to a placebo effect? If a drug works, should it be prescribed, even if its success is due to a placebo effect? Should doctors substitute placebos instead of antidepressants? Why or why not?

effectiveness attributed to the antidepressant drugs was actually a placebo effect.[97,98] When scientists reanalyzed the original data about the safety and efficacy of paroxetine (Paxil) in adolescents, they found that not only was paroxetine no more effective than placebo, but the drug also was significantly less safe.[99] In addition, a meta-analysis of studies involving almost 19,000 patients showed that published reports of five commonly used antidepressants also significantly under-reported aggressive behavior and suicidal thoughts.[100]

But antidepressant drugs do work in some people. In a meta-analysis of over 4,400 patients, 41 percent of patients who took an antidepressant drug but were (secretly) switched to a placebo relapsed, compared to an 18 percent relapse rate in those who remained on an antidepressant.[101]

So why is the "real world" efficacy of antidepressant drugs so much worse than we previously thought? One reason may be that when Prozac was undergoing its initial clinical trials, the drug was tested on severely depressed patients; however, those who take SSRIs today often only have mild to moderate depression.[102]

Another reason why antidepressant drugs may not be as effective as first thought might be the fact that patients are chosen very selectively in pharmaceutical industry–funded studies. Patients with coexisting illnesses or other health problems are typically not included in clinical trials, but in the real world, these people do have depression and might be less responsive to pharmacological treatment.

Additionally, drug companies do not publish all the relevant data in scientific journals. Studies that find ADDs to be effective are much more likely to be submitted for publication than those that find ADDs to be less or not effective. In fact, the pharmaceutical industry never published the results of about one-third of the drug trials they conducted, misleading doctors and consumers about the drugs' true effectiveness.[103] When scientists reviewed all the trials submitted to the FDA for 12 antidepressant drugs, both published and unpublished, they found that 97 percent of articles that showed a positive effect were published, but only 12 percent of articles that showed no effect were published.[104]

Finally, some journal articles about antidepressant drugs are not written by physicians and scientists conducting clinical trials, but instead are ghostwritten by pharmaceutical companies, who find doctors to claim authorship.[105] A 2016 meta-analysis of articles evaluating antidepressants found that 29 percent of the articles had authors who were employees of the company that manufactured the drug that was being assessed, and 79 percent had authors who had some other financial link to the drug manufacturer (received grants or speaking fees, for example). Additionally, articles by an author who was employed by the manufacturer of the drug under assessment were 22 times less likely than other analyses to include negative statements about the drug.[106]

QUICK HIT

Antidepressants can have negative effects on the environment. Some orally administered SSRIs are excreted unchanged in the urine, and enter the water supply. Sewage treatment plants are not equipped to filter the drugs, so it is likely that humans (especially those in urban areas) ingest a small amount.[107] So far, it is unknown whether these small amounts have an effect on humans, but they have been shown to affect other animals. For instance, low levels of antidepressants can trigger the expression of genes associated with brain development and aggressive behaviors in fish.[108]

Effect of Antidepressant Drug Use during Pregnancy

Up to 14 percent of pregnant women take antidepressants.[109] SSRI use during pregnancy is associated with an increased risk of spontaneous abortion, preterm birth, and low birth weight. It's important, however, not to confuse correlation and causation, because *untreated* maternal depression is also associated with these adverse pregnancy outcomes.[110] Additionally, untreated depression can result in worse prenatal care, poor nutrition, exposure to drugs or alcohol, and decreased bonding between mothers and infants.[111] One study found that depressed mothers who take ADDs during their pregnancy *reduce* the baby's risk of preterm birth.[112]

Other Treatments for Depression

In addition to antidepressants, there are other treatments for depression. These include hallucinogens, psychotherapy, electroconvulsive therapy (ECT), and transcranial direct current stimulation. Additional treatments include acupuncture, meditation, exercise, eating a healthy diet, art therapy, and animal interactions.[113,114, 115, 116,117]

Hallucinogens

A low dose of a form of the dissociative hallucinogen ketamine (Chapter 6) has been found to produce rapid relief in severe depression.[118] Esketamine (trade name Spravato) was approved by the FDA in 2019 for treatment-resistant MDD. Esketamine is the s-enantiomer of ketamine, one of two mirror image molecules that together make up ketamine. Unlike other ADDs, which can take weeks to work, esketamine's antidepressant effects can emerge within two hours and last for 3–10 days.[119] Because results occur so quickly, esketamine treatment is an option for suicidal patients as well as for those with depression who haven't been helped by other antidepressant drugs.[120]

In a randomized, placebo-controlled, double-blind study, 18 participants with MDD were given an intravenous infusion of a very low dose of ketamine—about one-tenth the amount used in anesthesia. By the next day, 71 percent of patients improved, 29 percent entered remission, and 35 percent maintained the response for at least a week.[121] In another study, when patients were given weekly or twice-weekly infusions for three weeks, half of those who responded improved so much they were no longer classified as depressed.[122]

Esketamine's mechanism of action is still being determined.[123] Esketamine and its metabolites may exert their antidepressant actions via their antagonistic effects on glutamate, which may be overproduced by the body as a result of chronic stress.[124] It may also alleviate depression by increasing the production of synapses and neurons in the hippocampus and the prefrontal cortex.[125, 126] Finally, esketamine may block activity in the habenula, an area of the brain that processes unexpected unpleasant events and is sometimes called the "disappointment circuit."[127]

Esketamine is given as a nasal spray and is to be taken in conjunction with an oral antidepressant. Since esketamine binds to NMDA receptors more tightly than ketamine does, it works at a significantly lower dose than ketamine, which helps to prevent ketamine's troubling side effects. Nevertheless, esketamine can only be administered in a supervised medical setting and the patient has to be monitored at the clinic for at least 2 hours after administration. Side effects include sedation, dissociation, wooziness, visual distortions, problems with attention and judgment, but most side effects are gone within a few hours. Esketamine is quite expensive, costing $590–885 per treatment session, or around $30,000 for the full 9 months of treatment.[128]

The hallucinogen psilocybin also has antidepressant properties.[129,130,131] Patients with moderate to severe, treatment-resistant depression showed a marked improvement in symptoms one week after receiving a dose of psilocybin, and three months later, half the patients were in complete remission.[132] The FDA has fast-tracked psilocybin testing as a potential breakthrough therapy for severe depression, and clinical trials regarding its efficacy and safety are currently underway. Psilocybin's antidepressant properties may be due to its anti-inflammatory effects, its effects on serotonin, its ability to increase neurogenesis in the hippocampus, or its ability to alter connectivity patterns within the brain.[133]

QUICK HIT

Some foods are thought to have antidepressant effects. Omega-3 fatty acids, as found in salmon and sardines, may reduce the risk of depression.[134] Curcumin, a substance found in the spice turmeric with anti-inflammatory properties, has a wide range of medicinal benefits and may be effective as an antidepressant.[135] Finally, polyphenols in dark chocolate enhance the growth of "good" gut bacteria that have anxiolytic and antidepressant properties.

Psychotherapies

Psychotherapies such as cognitive behavioral therapy (CBT) teach clients to change their negative beliefs and ways of thinking and behaving to more productive ones. A meta-analysis showed that 42–66 percent of patients no longer met the criteria for depression after going through CBT.[136] However, although pharmaceutical treatments often are covered by insurance, psychotherapy often is not.

Electroconvulsive Therapy

In the early twentieth century, a physician noted that psychotic patients who were also subject to epileptic seizures showed improvement immediately after each attack.[137] Today, about 1 million patients worldwide undergo **electroconvulsive therapy (ECT)** each year.[138] Before undergoing ECT, a patient is given anesthesia and a muscle relaxant. Electrodes are placed on each temple, and pulses of electricity are sent through the brain to induce a seizure. A patient typically receives 6–12 sessions over the course of two to four weeks. As a rule, ECT is used as a last resort in patients who are unresponsive to other treatments. ECT has a much

Electroconvulsive therapy (ECT): A medical procedure in which a small, carefully controlled amount of electricity is passed through the brain, intentionally triggering a brief seizure.

quicker effect than drugs, so it may be used in emergency situations, such as when someone is severely suicidal. The mechanism by which ECT exerts its antidepressant effects is unknown, but it may increase norepinephrine, dopamine, and serotonin functioning; encourage neurogenesis; and help to normalize the levels of stress hormones.[139] The most common side effects of ECT include headache, confusion, and memory loss.

Transcranial Direct Current Stimulation

To try to reduce the side effects of ECT, an experimental therapy known as **transcranial direct current stimulation** (tDCS) has been developed that gives patients a low-level charge—about 1/400th of that used in ECT—for about 20–30 minutes at a time while they are conscious.[140] Some studies suggest tDCS is a promising intervention, but it's efficacy is not yet proven.[141,142, 143,144]

Bipolar Disorder

Everyone has ups and downs. However, in **bipolar disorder (BD)**—an affective disorder associated with mood swings that range from manic highs to depressive lows—these peaks and valleys are more severe and can significantly impair one's life.

Transcranial direct current stimulation (tDCS): A procedure that uses a constant, low current to the brain to improve symptoms of depression.

Bipolar disorder (BD): An affective disorder associated with mood swings that range from manic highs to depressive lows.

Prevalence of Bipolar Disorder

Over the course of a lifetime, around 2.5 percent of American adults will have BD (Figure 13.9). Men and women are affected equally. Symptoms usually begin when people are in their late teens or early twenties, but more children and adolescents are being diagnosed with BD than in the past. Since 1994, reported diagnoses of pediatric and adolescent BD have risen at least 40-fold.[145,146]

Causes of Bipolar Disorder

As we saw with major depressive disorder (MDD), bipolar disorder (BD) is probably due to a combination of factors.[147] There is a strong genetic component to BD, although the specific chromosome has not been identified. In addition, the risk of BD is nearly 10 times higher in first-degree relatives of those affected compared to the general population.[148]

MRI studies show that patients with BD have reduced brain volumes, especially in the prefrontal cortex.[149] BD also may be associated with altered neurochemistry. Levels of serotonin, norepinephrine, dopamine, glutamate, and GABA may all be abnormal.

If someone inherits a BD gene, this does not necessarily mean that he or she will develop the disorder. Exposure to certain environmental events, however, may be more likely to trigger the disorder in those who have the genes. Being exposed to physical or emotional trauma during childhood may raise one's risk; 30–50 percent of adults diagnosed with BD report traumatic or abusive experiences in childhood. In addition, if a pregnant woman is exposed to the flu, the risk that her

(a)   (b)   (c)   (d)

FIGURE 13.9. Celebrities diagnosed with bipolar disorder. (a) Director Tim Burton, (b) musician John Mayer, and actors (c) Ben Stiller and (d) the late Carrie Fisher all were diagnosed with bipolar disorder.

child will develop BD increases nearly four-fold. This risk is slightly higher if the exposure occurs during the second or third trimester.[150] The reason for this is unknown, but infection with the influenza virus may reduce levels of a glycoprotein that regulates neuronal development.[151]

Personality may play a role as well. People with BD are more creative than those in the general population.[152,153,154] This may mean that BD makes it more likely that someone will be creative; that creativity causes the mood disorder; or that some third factor, such as a traumatic life experience, increases both.

Symptoms of Bipolar Disorder

Bipolar disorder, which used to be called "manic depression," is characterized by periods of high energy, inflated self-esteem, and impulsive actions alternating with periods of depression. During the **manic phase**, people with BD may be highly excited, euphoric, confident, and energized. They may be distractible, talk excessively, sleep very little, and have unrealistic goals and exaggerated beliefs in their abilities, talents, and intelligence. While in the manic phase, people with BD sometimes engage in pleasurable activities to such a great extent that the results are likely to be harmful—they may spend money recklessly, engage in unsafe and irresponsible sexual activities, drive wildly, or abuse drugs or alcohol. Individuals sometimes feel anxious, agitated, and angry at others. In its most severe form, BD causes marked impairment in one's occupation or social life, as well as psychotic features, such as delusions or hallucinations. Having three or more of these symptoms every day for at least a week may indicate a manic episode.

Hypomania is a less severe form of mania. Individuals in a hypomanic state may feel energized, productive, easily distracted, and have racing thoughts, but their symptoms may not be severe enough to cause impairment in their daily lives. Despite this, hypomania can still result in reckless behaviors that harm careers, relationships, or reputations. Hypomania can escalate to full-blown mania or be followed by a major depressive episode.[155]

During the depressed phase, a person with BD experiences many of the same symptoms as someone with MDD, but certain symptoms are more common in BD than in MDD.[156]

- BD is more likely to involve guilt, restlessness, and irritability.
- Individuals in the depressive stage of BD tend to move and speak slowly, sleep a lot, and gain weight.

- Those with BD are not helped by antidepressants; these drugs may even make BD worse by triggering a manic phase and causing rapid cycling between the mood states.

Bipolar disorder manifests itself differently in different people. Some people may be more prone to mania, while others have more depressive phases. Some experience mixed episodes—depression combined with anxiety, agitation, irritability, and racing thoughts. They may feel agitated or revved up while in despair. This combination of high energy and low mood makes for a particularly high risk of suicide. People with BD are 20–30 times more likely to attempt or commit suicide than those without the illness.[157] Between 20 and 50 percent of those suffering from BD will attempt suicide, and as many as 20 percent of those with BD eventually take their own lives.[158]

A **cycle** is the time it takes to go through one episode of mania or hypomania and one depressive episode. Episodes can be separated from each other by remission or can switch directly from (hypo)mania to depression (or vice versa). Most people cycle once every few years. About 10–15 percent of bipolar patients are rapid cyclers who have four or more episodes within a one-year span. Ultra-rapid cyclers have four episodes within a month. Some people even experience numerous cycles within a single day.

Treatment of Bipolar Disorder

Bipolar disorder is typically treated with drugs, but psychotherapy or ECT also may be used. Lithium, one of the most widely used drugs to treat BD, can help to normalize mood swings and has been shown to reduce the risk of suicide for patients with BD.[159]

Lithium is taken orally, completely absorbed in the GI tract, and distributed throughout the body. The drug is not metabolized, and it is excreted by the kidneys. Lithium typically takes one to two weeks to work.

Scientists do not fully understand how lithium works because its mechanisms are complex. Various studies show that lithium reduces excitatory neurotransmission, affects second messenger systems that control cell communication, protects neurons and

Manic phase: A phase of bipolar disorder characterized by periods of hyperactivity, insomnia, elation, inflated self-esteem, and sometimes delusions.

Hypomania: A less severe form of mania.

Cycle: The time it takes to go through one episode of mania or hypomania and one depressive episode.

reduces cell death, and may reverse neuronal abnormalities found in BD.[160,161]

Lithium is most effective in preventing or reducing the intensity of the manic episodes, in long-term maintenance of mood, and in preventing suicide. Lithium is only modestly effective in treating depression. The most common side effects include headache, dry mouth and thirst, gastrointestinal distress, sedation, confusion, and memory problems. Users also can experience blurry vision, ringing in the ears, and a metallic taste in the mouth, as well as hypothyroidism and abnormalities in movement. Because lithium has a very low therapeutic index—three to four times the effective dose can be toxic—users must carefully monitor their blood levels to avoid a toxic reaction. Toxic levels of lithium can lead to kidney failure, respiratory depression, seizures, coma, and death. If taken during the first trimester of pregnancy, lithium has a significant risk of causing cardiovascular problems in the fetus.

QUICK HIT

Lithium is a naturally occurring element present—in minute concentrations—in our drinking water. Communities that have higher levels of lithium in their drinking water show significantly lower levels of suicide, homicide, and rape than people whose water contained less lithium.[162,163] In addition, in the past, lithium often was added to drinks for alleged health-giving properties. Until 1950, 7Up soda—originally called Bib-Label Lithiated Lemon-Lime Soda—contained lithium.

Anticonvulsants and antipsychotics also provide some success in treating BD. Anticonvulsants such as carbamazepine (Tegretol), topiramate (Topamax), valproic acid (Depakote), and lamotrigine (Lamictal) may help control the symptoms of BD via their effects on GABA or glutamate. People taking these drugs need to monitor their liver function and white blood cell count. Antipsychotics such as chlorpromazine (Thorazine), gabapentin (Neurontin), and risperidone (Risperdal) are effective in controlling the acute manic stage. They act more quickly than lithium and are not as toxic. ECT may be used as a last resort in BD patients who are psychotic or suicidal and for whom drugs don't work.

Just as there are misgivings about the risk-to-benefit ratio of drugs that treat MDD, there are concerns about lithium and other drugs that treat BD. Since the

use of these drugs became the standard treatment, bipolar outcomes have worsened.[164,165] Nonpharmacological treatments, including interpersonal and social rhythm therapy (in which people improve their mood by understanding and working with their biological and social rhythms), CBT, and vocational rehabilitation also have been explored, but their effectiveness requires further study.

Schizophrenia

Schizophrenia is a chronic, severe, disabling mental disorder characterized by disturbances in thought, perception, language, emotional responsiveness, and behavior. The brain of a person with schizophrenia does not grow and develop normally, which leads to significant abnormalities in brain structure and function.[166,167] The word "schizophrenic" means "split mind," which has led to the misconception that those with schizophrenia have multiple personalities. Instead, the "split mind" refers to the way that people with schizophrenia are split off from reality and cannot distinguish what is real from what is not real.

Prevalence of Schizophrenia

About 0.5 percent of the world's population will suffer from schizophrenia during their lives (Figure 13.10), and 30 percent of them will spend a significant portion of their lives in mental hospitals.[168] Men are affected slightly more than women, tend to have symptoms at a younger age, and experience more severe symptoms.[169] Men first develop symptoms in their late teens and early twenties, while women first show signs in their late twenties and early thirties. Many people with schizophrenia have comorbid conditions, such as depression, anxiety disorders, and substance abuse disorders—the lifetime occurrence of substance use disorder among those with schizophrenia is almost 50 percent.

Causes of Schizophrenia

There is no single, easily identifiable cause of schizophrenia. Genes, structural abnormalities in the brain, neurochemical imbalances, and environmental factors may play a role in its development.

Genetics

If a person's parents or siblings have schizophrenia, he or she has a twelve-fold greater risk of developing the disorder, and individuals with afflicted second-degree relatives—grandparents, uncles, aunts, nieces

Schizophrenia: A severe mental disorder that makes it difficult to interpret reality, think clearly, manage emotions, and relate to others.

(a)   (b)   (c)   (d)

FIGURE 13.10. Famous people diagnosed with schizophrenia. Those with schizophrenia have included (a) novelist and poet Jack Kerouac; (b) Pink Floyd founding member Syd Barrett; (c) David Berkowitz, the Son of Sam killer who believed he was possessed by a demon who told him to kill; and (d) John Nash, a mathematician who won the Nobel Prize for economics.

or nephews—have a four-fold increased risk. Determining the importance of genetics in the causes of the disease, given that there are probably multiple genes involved, is difficult, as is separating the effects of genetics and environment. A consortium of scientists studied 37,000 people with schizophrenia, and they identified 108 different genetic locations potentially linked to the disorder.[170] Some of these affected genes may be related to abnormal neurotransmitter development,[171] signaling,[172] and maintenance of neural connections in the brain.[173] Because so many gene variants are related to the risk of schizophrenia, it is likely that we all carry at least some of these risky genes. Most likely, having many of the "schizophrenia genes" imparts a susceptibility to develop schizophrenia, and the disease itself is triggered by other factors.[174]

Structural Abnormalities in the Brain

Brain scans of those with schizophrenia show reduced volume in the temporal lobe, hippocampus, limbic system, basal ganglia, and frontal lobe, which may play a role in the memory impairment, language deficits, emotional deficiencies, motor abnormalities, and poor cognitive function seen with the disorder (Figure 13.11). There is some evidence that abnormal brain development begins in childhood, if not before.[175]

Neurochemical Abnormalities

Levels of dopamine and glutamate may be abnormal in schizophrenia. The most popular theory is that schizophrenia is due to atypical regulation of dopamine brain pathways, resulting in abnormal levels of dopamine. Drugs that block dopamine reduce many of

the positive symptoms of schizophrenia, and overdoses of dopamine-boosting drugs such as amphetamine can exacerbate or mimic psychotic symptoms. Glutamate levels may be high in people with schizophrenia.[176] The relationship of neurotransmitters and schizophrenia is summarized in Table 13.3 and Figure 13.12.

There is probably more to the story, however, than a simple imbalance in dopamine. Even if drugs that block dopamine receptors treat psychotic symptoms, this does not necessarily mean that schizophrenia is due to excess dopamine.[177] Dopamine metabolites in the cerebrospinal fluid of unmedicated individuals, as well as the autopsied brains of unmedicated individuals, are normal.[178] Antipsychotics have an immediate effect on dopamine receptors, but these drugs sometimes take many days to change behavior. Finally, atypical antipsychotics do not have strong antagonistic effects on dopamine and instead work on serotonin as well.

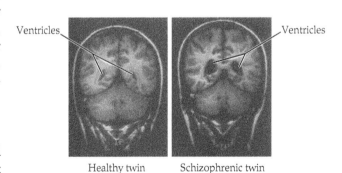

Ventricles   Ventricles

Healthy twin   Schizophrenic twin

FIGURE 13.11. Brain scans of those with schizophrenia. People with schizophrenia have enlarged ventricles (fluid-filled spaces in the brain), which is probably due to a loss of brain tissue.

TABLE 13.3. Neurochemical Abnormalities Associated with Schizophrenia

	Dopamine Pathway in the Brain	Function	Abnormalities Associated with Schizophrenia
Dopamine	Mesolimbic	Reinforcement and reward	Dopamine is hyperactive, which leads to the positive symptoms of schizophrenia.
	Mesocortical	Cognition	Dopamine is reduced, leading to problems with cognition and rational thought.
	Nigrostriatal	Movement	Dopamine is reduced, leading to abnormal movements.
	Tuberoinfundibular	Helps control prolactin levels	
Glutamate			Excessive release of glutamate damages cortical neurons and leads to hallucinations, cognitive defects, and out-of-body experiences.

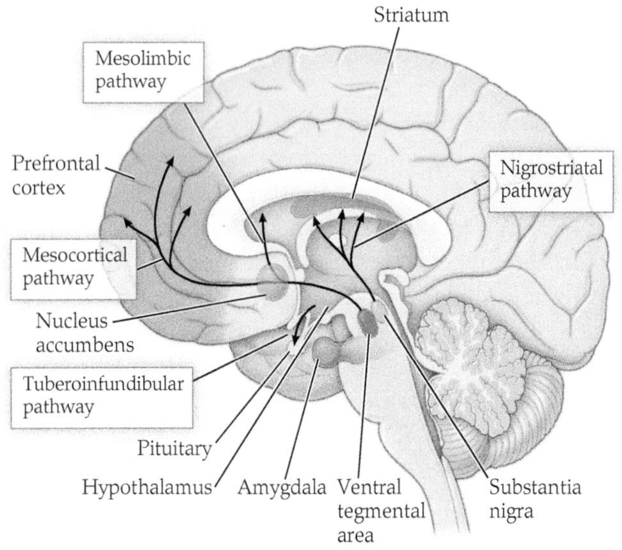

FIGURE 13.12. **Dopaminergic pathways of the brain.** Evidence suggests that dopamine pathways may be abnormal in schizophrenia.

Environmental Factors

Environmental risk factors play a major role in the development of schizophrenia,[179] and these risk factors can have an effect before a person is even born. Those who had a low birth weight, and those who experienced prenatal complications such as low prenatal blood flow, hypoxia, malnutrition, or infection have higher rates of schizophrenia.[180] Rh-positive babies (especially male babies) who are born to an Rh-negative mother are more prone to schizophrenia, possibly because the mother's immune system will produce a response against the fetus.[181] Finally, those with schizophrenia are disproportionately born in the late winter or early spring. It may be that preg-

nant mothers were more likely to contract a virus during a critical phase in the infant's development. This is supported by the fact that the incidence of schizophrenia rises in babies born a few months after flu epidemics. This seasonality effect is primarily seen in heavily populated urban areas, where viruses are more readily transmitted.[182]

Once born, social stressors such as childhood trauma, separation from families, being an immigrant, or being bullied or abused increase one's risk of schizophrenia, as does racial discrimination, social isolation, unemployment, and poor housing conditions. Drug use may play a role. Daily tobacco use is associated with an increased risk of psychosis,[183] and marijuana may raise the risk of schizophrenia in susceptible individuals (Chapter 9). Even owning a cat may raise one's risk for schizophrenia. *Toxoplasma gondii*, a parasite found in feline feces, has been linked to the development of mental disorders.[184]

Symptoms of Schizophrenia

Schizophrenia can be hard to diagnose because it is based on a cluster of several clinical symptoms that overlap with conditions such as BD or obsessive-compulsive disorder (OCD). Schizophrenia consists of "positive" symptoms (symptoms that most individuals do not normally experience), "negative" symptoms (the absence of normal behaviors), and cognitive impairments. These symptoms exist on a continuum and can range from mildly peculiar behavior, such as failing to brush one's teeth for a couple of days, to severely psychotic actions, such as wrapping oneself in tinfoil to prevent the aliens from transmitting signals to the brain.

Positive symptoms of schizophrenia include the following:

- *Delusions.* Bizarre, false beliefs that are not part of the person's culture and will remain even after other people prove the delusions are not true. These delusions may take many forms, including
  - Paranoid—irrational beliefs that one is being harmed, controlled, followed, or harassed
  - Grandiose—belief that one is an especially powerful or important person
  - Referential—belief that comments from news reports, passages from books, or song lyrics are personally directed
  - Somatic—a false belief that one's physical body is affected, usually by an outside source[185]
- *Hallucinations.* Bizarre, unreal perceptions of the environment. Schizophrenic hallucinations are usually auditory and may involve hearing voices that command or insult.
- *Disorganized thinking.* Illogical, unreasonable, confused, and disorganized thoughts. Schizophrenics often have vague, repetitive, disjointed speech. They may change topics midway through the sentence, speak in a way that conveys little real information, or use made-up words.
- *Abnormal motor behavior.* Schizophrenics may repeat certain motions over and over. Or, at the other extreme, they may experience catatonia and remain fixed in a single position for hours.

Positive symptoms may be more due to overexcitability of dopamine in the midbrain, given that they tend to respond well to drugs that block dopamine.

Negative symptoms of schizophrenia include

- *Flat affect.* Emotions are absent or inappropriate.
- *Poverty of speech.* Brief and empty replies to questions, even when forced to interact.
- *Low motivation* and lack of ability to begin and sustain planned activities.
- *Lack of pleasure* in everyday life.
- *Social withdrawal* from friends and family.
- *Reduced energy and activity* in everyday activities.
- *Neglect of basic personal hygiene* such as showering or brushing teeth.

Negative symptoms respond less well to medication, and may be more due to loss of brain tissue.

Cognitive impairments include

- *Poor executive functioning.* Schizophrenics find it hard to understand information and to use it to make rational decisions.
- *Problems with working memory* and the ability to use information immediately after learning it.

- *Trouble focusing or paying attention* to conversations and tasks.

Prognosis of Schizophrenia

Active psychosis has been ranked the most disabling mental condition.[186] The lifespan of a person with schizophrenia is 14–15 years shorter than average, due to physical health problems, poor social situations, and suicide.[187] These individuals are more likely to smoke, abuse drugs and alcohol, and lead a sedentary lifestyle, all of which may raise the risk for cardiovascular disease. Schizophrenia is also associated with long-term unemployment, poverty, and homelessness. Finally, those with schizophrenia are much more likely to die at their own hands; suicide rates are 38 times higher than in the general population.[188]

Treatments for Schizophrenia

Before 1950, there were no effective drugs for treating psychotic patients, who often spent the majority of their lives in mental hospitals, where they were maintained on high doses of barbiturates or given lobotomies. The first antipsychotic drugs were introduced in the 1950s, providing an easier and more cost-effective way to manage schizophrenia and other severe mental diseases. Patients became calmer and more controllable (Figure 13.13). Over the next 30 years, the resident population of mental hospitals in the United States declined by 80 percent. By the 1990s, patients were routinely stabilized on meds and rapidly discharged from institutions.[189]

There are three categories of antipsychotic drugs, which are summarized in Table 13.4.

Mechanism of Action of Antipsychotic Drugs

Typical antipsychotics—also known as **first-generation antipsychotics (FGAs)**—primarily block dopamine receptors, but they also block acetylcholine, norepinephrine, and histamine. Although these drugs have an immediate effect on receptors, their antipsychotic effects can take 10–14 days or more. By blocking dopamine receptors in the mesolimbic pathway, FGAs reduce schizophrenia's positive symptoms, such as delusions, hallucinations, paranoia, and agitation. But this also may block reward mechanisms, leaving patients apathetic, unable to feel pleasure, and lacking interest in social interactions, a state very similar to that of the

First-generation antipsychotic (FGA): Also called a "typical" antipsychotic or neuroleptic, this drug alleviates symptoms of schizophrenia by blocking dopamine receptors.

negative symptoms of schizophrenia.[190] Because typical antipsychotics also block dopamine receptors in the mesocortical pathway, where dopamine levels already may be low, this can worsen negative and cognitive symptoms.

Atypical antipsychotics—also called **second-generation antipsychotics (SGAs)**—block dopamine receptors as well, although to a lesser degree than FGAs. In addition, they block serotonin-2A receptors, which help to prevent motor side effects.[191] Unlike typical antipsychotics, SGAs may alleviate negative symptoms as well as positive.

Abilify (aripiprazole), a **third-generation antipsychotic**, has a unique mechanism of action. Abilify is a partial agonist at dopamine receptors, which means it readily binds to these receptors, but it produces less of an effect than dopamine itself. So in areas of the brain where dopamine may be overactive, Abilify binds to the dopamine receptors, but reduces the effect of dopamine for as long as it is bound, thus reducing positive symptoms of schizophrenia. In areas of the brain where there may be too little dopamine, such as the mesocortical pathway, Abilify binds and stimulates the receptors, thus reducing the negative symptoms. Abilify is also a partial agonist at serotonergic presyn-

Second-generation antipsychotic (SGA): An "atypical" antipsychotic; generally does not cause the same degree of motor side effects as do neuroleptics.

Third-generation antipsychotic: Aripiprazole is the only approved third-generation antipsychotic, and it acts as a partial agonist at dopamine receptors.

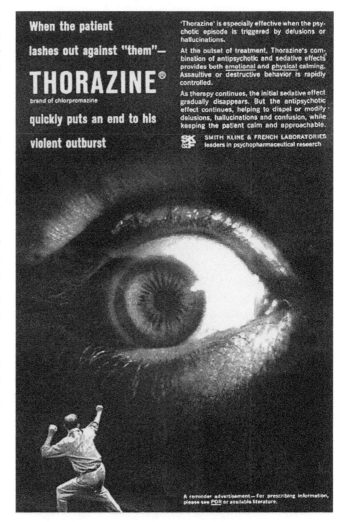

FIGURE 13.13. An ad for the antipsychotic Thorazine, circa 1960. After the introduction of antipsychotic drugs, fewer patients with schizophrenia needed to be held in mental hospitals.

TABLE 13.4.   Characteristics of Antipsychotic Drugs

	First Generation	**Second Generation**	**Third Generation**
Other Names	Typical antipsychotics, neuroleptics	Atypical antipsychotics	
Examples	Thorazine (chlorpromazine) Haldol (haloperidol) Stelazine (trifluoperazine) Loxitane (loxapine) Compazine (prochlorperazine)	Seroquel (quetiapine), Risperdal (risperidone), Geodon (ziprasidone), Zyprexa (olanzapine), Clozaril (clozapine)	Abilify (aripiprazole)
Main Mechanism of Action	Block dopamine receptors; also block norepinephrine, acetylcholine, and histamine receptors	Block dopamine and serotonin-2A receptors	Partial agonist at dopamine and serotonergic presynaptic autoreceptors, and antagonist at serotonin-2 receptors
Side Effects	Dry mouth, blurred vision, dizziness, weight gain, photosensitivity, motor effects, tardive dyskinesia	Weight gain, increased risk of type 2 diabetes	Fewer side effects than first generation

aptic autoreceptors, and an antagonist at serotonin-2 receptors, which may be responsible for its anxiolytic and antidepressant actions.

Side Effects Associated with Antipsychotic Drugs

Side effects of antipsychotics can be extremely unpleasant, as well as irreversible in some cases. The side effects of FGAs can be directly tied to the pathways affected by the drug (Table 13.5). Minor side effects include dry mouth, blurred vision, dizziness, extreme sensitivity to sunlight, and weight gain. The most concerning side effects of FGAs are neuroleptic malignant syndrome and movement disorders.

Neuroleptic malignant syndrome is a life-threatening reaction characterized by elevated body temperature, fast heart rate, muscle rigidity, instability of the autonomic nervous system, catatonia, stupor, and coma.[192] About 10–15 percent of people who develop neuroleptic malignant syndrome will die of it.

Some of the acute motor side effects that can occur include involuntary spasms of the face, mouth, and trunk; motor restlessness, manifested by pacing, rocking, or repetitive purposeless actions; and Parkinsonian symptoms, such as rigidity, tremor, slow movements, and shuffling gait.[193] These acute effects develop early in treatment in up to 90 percent of patients.[194]

Tardive dyskinesia (TD) occurs after several months or years on chronic neuroleptic treatment. TD affects about one-third of those on FGAs, and the rates increase with time; after 25 years of exposure, about 68 percent of users will develop TD.[195] TD is more likely to occur in females, as well as in those who develop psychosis after age 50. TD involves involuntary movements, such as facial grimacing, sucking and smacking

of the lips, and tongue protrusions, as well as flowing, dance-like movements of the limbs and trunk. About 20 percent of the time, these effects are irreversible. TD may occur because dopamine receptors in the nigrostriatal pathway increase in number after long-term use of dopamine-blocking agents.

Second-generation antipsychotics are less likely to induce motor disorders, although this side effect can still occur: about 13 percent of patients taking an SGA will eventually develop TD. The major problematic side effect of atypical antipsychotics is extreme weight gain and diabetes. Patients who take these drugs are 9–14 percent more likely to develop type 2 diabetes than patients who receive traditional FGAs. Other side effects of SGAs include sedation, constipation, seizure, and cardiovascular toxicities.

Because of these side effects, as well as the nature of the disease itself, compliance rates are low for antipsychotic drugs. Noncompliance rates in patients with schizophrenia are as high as 40–50 percent; in one study, 74 percent of patients with schizophrenia discontinued their drug over 18 months.[196]

Efficacy of Antipsychotic Drugs

About one-third of patients treated with antipsychotics will show excellent symptom reduction and may not require subsequent hospitalization; one-third will have significant improvement of symptoms, but may experience relapses that require hospitalization from time to time; and one-third exhibit lesser recovery and may

Tardive dyskinesia (TD): Involuntary movements, particularly of the face and jaw. "Tardive" means *tardy* or *late*; this symptom occurs after months or several years of antipsychotic drug use.

TABLE 13.5. Neurotransmitters Affected by First-Generation Antipsychotics and the Resultant Side Effects

Neurotransmitters Affected	Specific Neurotransmitter Pathway	Resultant Side Effects
Dopamine blockade	Mesolimbic pathway	Apathy, anhedonia, lack of motivation
	Mesocortical pathway	May worsen negative symptoms
	Nigrostriatal pathway	Motor side effects
	Tuberohypophyseal pathway	Men: breast enlargement, delayed ejaculation, reduced libido. Women: lactation, reduced libido, blocked ovulation, dysmenorrhea
Acetylcholine blockade	n/a	Dry mouth, dilated pupils, blurred vision, fast heart rate, constipation, difficulty urinating, cognitive and memory impairments
Norepinephrine blockade	n/a	Sedation, orthostatic hypotension, dizziness
Histamine blockade	n/a	Sedation, antiemetic, weight gain
Other/unknown	n/a	Sensitivity to sunlight, change in white blood cell count, liver function abnormalities, allergic reactions

spend a significant amount of time in a psychiatric hospital.[197] There is little to no difference in the efficacy of FGAs and SGAs and little evidence regarding any consistent and long-term benefits from their use beyond two to three years.[198,199]

Overprescription of Antipsychotic Drugs

Although the prevalence of bipolar disorder and schizophrenia have been stable in the U.S. adult population for years—at about 4 and 0.5 percent, respectively—rates of antipsychotic drug prescription are soaring. In 1995, there were 4.4 million prescriptions written for SGAs in the United States; by 2018, there were over 75 million prescriptions written for antipsychotics.[200,201,202] That rise was largely due to an increase in diagnosis as well as an increase in off-label use. Antipsychotics are now widely prescribed for conditions for which they have not been approved, such as very mild depression, everyday anxiety, insomnia, attention-deficit/hyperactivity disorder, and dementia.[203]

The rise in antipsychotic prescriptions is especially high in vulnerable populations, including children on Medicaid, foster-care children, and elderly nursing home residents.[204,205] Children covered by Medicaid and children in foster care receive antipsychotics at a rate four to four-and-a-half times higher than children whose parents have private insurance, and they are more likely to receive the drugs for less severe conditions than their middle-class counterparts.[206] In 2015, the U.S. Government Accountability Office released a study of older adults with dementia who spent more than 100 days in a nursing home, and found that about one-third of them were prescribed antipsychotic drugs to treat behavioral problems, even though studies have shown an increased risk of death for patients who take antipsychotics.[207]

As with antidepressants, there is some evidence that although antipsychotic drugs are effective in the short term, long-term use may actually worsen the course of schizophrenia in some people.[208] Long-term use of antipsychotics may exacerbate schizophrenia by causing the brain to become supersensitive to dopamine, which would require patients to stay on the drugs to prevent a relapse.[209]

Other Treatments for Schizophrenia

Psychotherapy, including cognitive therapy, group therapy, and social and vocational skills training, is helpful in alleviating symptoms of schizophrenia. Patients in cognitive therapy are encouraged to talk about their experiences, not only with their therapist, but with friends and family as well. They are reassured that hearing voices or feeling paranoid is something that many normal people have experienced from time to time, which reduces some of the anxiety that makes sufferers feel distressed and isolated.[210,211] (Indeed, a meta-analysis found that as many as 7.2 percent of the general population reported experiencing delusions and hallucinations at some time.[212])

Some evidence exists that a diet rich in omega-3-polyunsaturated fatty acids also may lower the risk of progression of the disease and reduce its symptoms.[213,214] And, because schizophrenia may result in part from inflammatory processes in the brain, the antibiotic minocycline also may alleviate symptoms.[215,216]

Anxiety Disorders

Anxiety is an important adaptation that helps us to perceive threats and deal with emergencies. But some people have uncontrollable anxiety that interferes with their day-to-day lives.

Prevalence of Anxiety Disorders

Approximately one-third of Americans will suffer from a significant anxiety disorder at some point in their lives.[217] Anxiety is the most common mental health concern on college campuses, far outpacing depression.[218] Anxiety disorders are characterized by excessive and persistent fear and anxiety. Fear is the emotional response to a real or perceived threat, and anxiety is the anticipation of a future threat.[219] Some people are anxious almost all the time, and others have situational anxiety. Anxiety and depression are linked: over one-half of patients with major depression also show signs of anxiety disorder, and as we discussed earlier in this chapter, stress may underlie the development of depression. Anxiety disorders are highly treatable; yet, only about one-third of those suffering from an anxiety disorder receive treatment.[220]

Causes of Anxiety Disorders

As with all mood disorders, a complex interaction of biology, personality, and environment underlie the development of anxiety disorders. Specifically,

- There may be a genetic component.[221]
- Neuroanatomical abnormalities may play a role. Anxiety is associated with increased blood flow to the amygdala, the part of the brain that orchestrates anxiety.[222]
- Connections between emotional centers of the brain and the prefrontal cortex may be irregular.

Normally, the prefrontal cortex provides inhibitory control over the more primitive fear responses of the amygdala, but those with anxiety disorders may have weaker neural connections.[223]

- Abnormalities in the basal ganglia may be involved.[224]
- GABA and serotonin levels may be low, and cortisol and norepinephrine levels may be high.

Symptoms and Types of Anxiety Disorders

There are several different types of anxiety disorders, including generalized anxiety disorder, panic disorder, social anxiety disorder, and various phobias. Most are characterized by sweating, elevated heart rate, and flushing; muscle tension, shakiness, and restlessness; apprehensiveness, fear, and anxiety; and impatience and insomnia.

Generalized anxiety disorder (GAD) is defined as excessive, uncontrollable, and often irrational worry even when there are no signs of trouble. This anxiety occurs almost every day for six months or more. In adults, the anxiety typically focuses on mundane issues such as health, money, relationships, or career, but these normal concerns are often amplified out of proportion. Women, those of lower socioeconomic status, and people who are divorced, separated, or widowed are more like to suffer from GAD. Symptoms include insomnia, fatigue, headaches, trembling, numbness in the hands and feet, dizziness, muscle tension, difficulty breathing, irritability, and an inability to relax and to concentrate.

A person suffering from **panic disorder** experiences severe episodes of anxiety and fear for no apparent reason. These feelings of terror can strike suddenly with no warning or discernable reason, or during situations that predispose an attack in a person, such as riding in an elevator or driving over a bridge. The pounding heart, dizziness, nausea, sweating, and pressure of a panic attack can make the sufferer feel like she or he is having a heart attack or dying.

A person suffering from **social anxiety disorder** feels very anxious about judgment from others or behavior that could be embarrassing or likely to be ridiculed. This is more than simple shyness or fear of public speaking; this intense anxiety may lead sufferers to avoid any social situation. Physical symptoms include heart palpitations, faintness, blushing, and profuse sweating.

Phobias are inappropriate or irrational intense fears of objects or situations and may lead those who suffer from them to avoid normal everyday activities or situations (Figure 13.14).

QUICK HIT

If it exists, someone is afraid of it. A phobia is an intense fear reaction to a specific object or situation. Some of the more unusual phobias include

- Anuptaphobia: Fear of staying single
- Coulrophobia: Fear of clowns
- Didaskaleinophobia: Fear of school
- Genuphobia: Fear of knees
- Hippopotomonstrosesquippedaliophobia: Fear of long words
- Panophobia—Fear of everything

Generalized anxiety disorder (GAD): An anxiety disorder characterized by persistent, uncontrollable, and irrational worry, usually about routine issues such as occupation, social relationships, health, or financial matters.

Panic disorder: An anxiety disorder characterized by sudden attacks of intense fear and anxiety associated with severe physical symptoms, even when there is no real dangerous or apparent cause.

Social anxiety disorder: An anxiety disorder in which a person has an excessive, unreasonable fear of social situations.

Phobia: An extreme or irrational fear of an object or situation.

FIGURE 13.14. **Some common phobias.** Do you have any of these phobias?

Treatment of Anxiety Disorders

Anxiety disorders are typically treated with both psychotherapy, such as CBT, exposure therapy, and relaxation techniques, and with drugs, such as benzodiazepines (Chapter 8).[225] Benzodiazepines also are used for acute anxiety attacks. Antidepressants often are prescribed to those with anxiety disorders, although because these drugs typically take weeks to work, they are not effective for acute anxiety attacks. Some find success with cannabis, especially high-CBD.[226] Acetaminophen (Tylenol), which dulls physical pain, may also alleviate emotional pain that is associated with anxiety.[227] The mechanism for this is unknown, but physical pain and emotional pain involve many of the same brain regions and neurochemicals. Acetaminophen may disarm some of the brain's initial emotional reactions to negative events and downplay their significance.

Trauma- and Stressor-Related Disorders

Once considered an anxiety disorder, the *Diagnostic and Statistical Manual of Mental Disorders, 5th edition* (DSM-5), now classifies **post-traumatic stress disorder (PTSD)** as a trauma- and stressor-related disorder. PTSD can follow exposure to a traumatic event such as sexual or physical assault, a serious accident, witness-

Post-traumatic Stress Disorder (PTSD): A condition of persistent mental and emotional stress triggered by experiencing or seeing a severe physical or psychological trauma.

ing a shocking or disturbing event, the unexpected death of a loved one, or a natural disaster. Victims of PTSD may relive the trauma in the form of nightmares and flashbacks. They may avoid places related to the incident and detach from others emotionally. They may be easily startled and irritable, and have difficulty sleeping and poor concentration.

Currently, PTSD is treated with a combination of psychotherapy and pharmacotherapy. The SSRIs Paxil and Zoloft are currently the only approved medications for PTSD, but the response rate to these drugs is only 20–22 percent greater than placebo. MDMA (Chapter 6), which enables patients to engage emotionally while revisiting traumatic experiences without being overwhelmed, may be particularly effective in the treatment of PTSD.[228]

Since 2004, there have been several randomized, double-blind, controlled clinical trials to investigate MDMA's safety and efficacy in treating PTSD. Individuals with PTSD receive either MDMA or a placebo during an 8-hour psychotherapy session. Compared to placebo, those who received MDMA during therapy show significant improvement, such that the majority no longer meet the diagnostic criteria for PTSD. For most patients, this improvement lasts for at least a year following the session and MDMA patients showed no drug-related serious adverse effects.[229,230,231,232,233] In 2016, the FDA approved Phase 3 clinical trials of MDMA, the final stage of testing before it can be submitted for approval as a prescription treatment for PTSD. In 2017, the FDA granted MDMA "Breakthrough Therapy" status, which means the FDA has agreed this treatment may have meaningful advantages over available medications for PTSD. Until it is approved,

---

however, supplying MDMA to a patient, even for therapeutic uses, carries a maximum prison term of 10 years.

The Future of Drugs Used to Treat Mental Illness

Although one out of every six Americans currently takes at least one psychiatric drug, and a significant proportion of the population is suffering from a psychiatric illness, funding for new, innovative medications is in serious decline. In 2013, the U.S. National Institutes of Health spent almost 13 times as much on cancer research as on depression research.[234] There is still a stigma against mental illnesses, and the public donates far less to support mental health research than it does to support cancer research. In part, this may be because campaigning for donations takes confidence, energy, and sociability, and the very nature of mood disorders makes it difficult for those with MDD and anxiety disorders to come forward and campaign for support.[235]

Some large pharmaceutical companies have decreased the size of their research programs, and others have closed their psychiatric laboratories entirely.[236] The reasons for this are two-fold. First of all, therapeutic development is difficult and risky. Drugs that affect the brain take about 18 years to go from preclinical experiments to approval, more than two years longer than average for other types of drugs, and the clinical trials for these drugs tend to be difficult and expensive.[237] Drugs may be tested on animals, but animal models are not an ideal representation of human diseases.

Secondly, the molecular and cellular mechanisms of these diseases are often unknown. When something goes wrong in a brain, as it does in mental illness, the only outward signs are symptoms. But symptoms are not perfect indicators. They are variable, context dependent, and based on (sometimes arbitrary) interpretation by patients and doctors.[238] In reality, the brain and mood are both incredibly complex. The chemical imbalance theory has boiled this complexity down to a single and oversimplified explanation that is easy to grasp and animate in a commercial, but which does not accurately represent the intricacy of the disorder. For the last few decades, pharmaceutical companies have simply produced new drugs that are slight variations on the same theme and are no more effective than pre-existing drugs.

The pharmaceutical companies do not see a feasible path to the discovery and development of new and effective treatments for mood disorders. We can only hope that scientists are able to learn the underlying causes of these diseases so that we can better treat the millions of people who suffer.

Chapter Summary

- **Psychological Disorders in Today's Society**
  » Mood fluctuations are normal, but sometimes emotions can become overwhelming, and unrealistic, and interfere with our daily lives.
  » About half of all Americans will meet the criteria for a mental health disorder during their lifetimes.
  » Although much more visible in the media than ever before, mental illness is still stigmatized.
- **Major Depressive Disorder**
  » MDD is a debilitating condition characterized by overwhelming sadness, feelings of worthlessness, and loss of interest in normally pleasurable activities. It is the most common disabling psychiatric illness in the adult population.
  » The prevalence of depression has greatly increased over the last few decades. Some reasons for this include greater awareness, less stigma, societal changes, overdiagnosis, increased availability of pharmaceutical treatments, and even long-term effects of the antidepressant drugs themselves.
  » There is no one single cause of depression.

  » Biological factors such as genetics, neurochemistry, neuroanatomy, hormones, diet, and even gut bacteria play a role.
  » Psychological factors such as cognitive beliefs, interpersonal factors, and stressful life events influence the onset of depression, as do social factors, such as poverty, adverse work conditions, trauma, drug use, and a lack of social support.
  » Antidepressant drugs (ADDs) are one of the most common classes of medications prescribed in the United States.
  » There are four different classes of ADDs—monoamine oxidase inhibitors (MAOIs), tricyclic antidepressants (TCAs), selective serotonin reuptake inhibitors (SSRIs), and atypical/mixed action antidepressants.
  » ADDs can interact with other drugs. Patients must be slowly weaned off ADDs to avoid antidepressant discontinuation syndrome.
  » The side effects associated with MAOIs and TCAs can be quite distressing. SSRIs tend to have fewer side effects than the older antidepressants, but they are by no means side-effect free.

» ADDs seem to increase the risk of suicidal thoughts or behavior in children and adolescents, but the exact relationship between ADDs and suicide is complex.

» A number of meta-analyses found that although SSRIs are slightly effective in treating severe depression, they are no more effective than placebo for mild to moderate depression.

» Other treatments for depression that have been explored include ketamine, psilocybin, psychotherapies, electroconvulsive therapy (ECT), and transcranial direct stimulation.

- **Bipolar Disorder**
  » About 2.5 percent of Americans will have bipolar disorder (BD) in their lifetimes. Men and women are equally affected.

  » BD is characterized by periods of mania/hypomania—high energy, confidence, and impulsive actions—alternating with periods of depression.

  » BD is probably due to a combination of biological, psychological, and environmental factors.

  » BD is typically treated with drugs such as lithium, anticonvulsants, and antipsychotics, but psychotherapy or electroconvulsive therapy may be used as well.

- **Schizophrenia**
  » Schizophrenia is a chronic, severe, disabling mental disorder characterized by disturbances in thought, perception, language, emotional responsiveness, and behavior.

  » About 0.5 percent of the world's population will suffer from schizophrenia during their lives. Men are affected slightly more than women.

  » Schizophrenia consists of "positive" symptoms, "negative" symptoms, and cognitive impairments.

  » Schizophrenics find it difficult to understand and process information, focus, pay attention, and make rational decisions.

  » Schizophrenia raises one's risk of long-term unemployment, poverty, homelessness, and shortened lifespan.

  » There are many underlying causes, including biological factors, such as genetics, structural abnormalities in the brain, and neurochemical imbalances; as well as environmental factors, such as prenatal complications, childhood traumas, or social isolation.

  » There are three categories of antipsychotic drugs used to treat schizophrenia.

  » First-generation antipsychotics (FGAs) also are called typical antipsychotics, or neuroleptics; they work by blocking dopamine receptors in the brain.

  » Second-generation antipsychotics (SGAs) also are called atypical antipsychotics; they block both dopamine and serotonin receptors.

  » Third-generation antipsychotics, such as Abilify, have a unique mechanism of action.

  » Many people with psychotic disorders don't respond to antipsychotic drugs.

  » There is little evidence regarding any consistent and long-term benefits from antipsychotic use beyond two to three years.

- **Anxiety Disorders**
  » About one-third of Americans will suffer from a significant anxiety disorder at some point in their lives.

  » Some common types of anxiety disorders include generalized anxiety disorder, panic attacks, social anxiety disorders, and phobias.

  » As with all mood disorders, anxiety disorders are due to a complex interaction of biology, personality, and environmental factors. They are typically treated with psychotherapy and pharmaceutics, such as benzodiazepines or SSRIs.

- **Trauma- and Stressor-Related Disorders**
  » PTSD is a condition of persistent mental and emotional stress triggered by experiencing or seeing a severe physical or psychological trauma.

  » The SSRIs Paxil and Zoloft are currently the only approved medications for PTSD, but MDMA is another potential treatment.

- **The Future of Drugs Used to Treat Mental Illness**
  » Although a significant proportion of the population suffers from psychiatric illness, funding for new, innovative medications is in serious decline, and many pharmaceutical companies have closed their psychiatric research laboratories.

Key Terms

Affective disorder (p.317)
Antidepressant discontinuation syndrome (p.328)
Bipolar disorder (BD) (p.332)
Comorbidity (p.321)
Cycle (p.333)
Electroconvulsive therapy (ECT) (p.331)
First-generation antipsychotic (FGA) (p.337)
Generalized anxiety disorder (GAD) (p.341)
Hypomania (p.333)

Major depressive disorder (MDD) (p.318)
Manic phase (p.333)
Monoamine oxidase inhibitor (MAOI) (p.327)
Monoamines (p.321)
Negative cognitive triad (p.323)
Panic disorder (p.341)
Phobia (p.341)
Post-traumatic stress disorder (PTSD) (p.342)
Schizophrenia (p.334)

Second-generation antipsychotic (SGA) (p.338)
Selective serotonin reuptake inhibitor (SSRI) (p.327)
Serotonin syndrome (p.328)
Social anxiety disorder (p.341)
Tardive dyskinesia (TD) (p.339)
Third-generation antipsychotic (p.338)
Transcranial direct current stimulation (tDCS) (p.332)
Tricyclic antidepressant (TCA) (p.327)
Wine and cheese effect (p.328)

Quiz Yourself!

1. True or false? About half of all Americans will meet the criteria for a mental health disorder during their lifetime.

2. List three reasons why the prevalence of depression has increased in the United States over the last few decades.

3. True or false? Major depressive disorder is typically diagnosed by a blood test.

4. Which is TRUE about depression?

    A. Depression is completely controlled by a gene on chromosome 17.

    B. Depression has been proven to be due to a chemical imbalance.

    C. Patients with major depressive disorder often have decreased neurogenesis and reduced volume of the hippocampus.

    D. Patients with depression show less response to stress than those who don't suffer from depression.

    E. Depression is solely due to social, environmental, and psychological factors.

5. Match the drug to its mechanism of action. One answer for each, and answers are only used once.

    1. Selectively blocks the reuptake of serotonin   A. MAOI

    2. Inhibits the enzyme that degrades dopamine, norepinephrine, serotonin, histamine, and melatonin   B. TCA

    3. Bupropion   C. SSRI

    4. Blocks the reuptake of both 5-HT and norepinephrine and also blocks the effects of acetylcholine and histamine   D. Atypical

    5. Proven to be the most effective antidepressant   E. None of these

6. True or false? Lithium is one of the safest drugs available and has a very high therapeutic index.

7. List at least three different types of anxiety disorders.

8. True or false? People with schizophrenia have multiple personalities.

9. Which of the following is NOT theorized to be an underlying risk factor for schizophrenia?

    A. Having a close relative with schizophrenia

    B. Enlarged volume of the frontal lobe

    C. Abnormal levels of dopamine

    D. Being born in the late winter or early spring

    E. Childhood traumas

10. _____ is a side effect of chronic neuroleptic treatment, characterized by involuntary movements, particularly of the face and jaw.

Additional Resources

Websites
21 comics that capture the frustrations of depression. https://imgur.com/gallery/UqbD7

Hyperbole and a half. See "adventures in depression" and "depression part 2" http://hyperboleandahalf.blogspot.com/

The Ten Minute Suicide Guide. Helpful thoughts for those contemplating suicide. http://www.cracked.com/article_15658_the-ten-minute-suicide-guide.html

Videos
The science of depression. https://www.youtube.com/watch?v=GOK1tKFFIQI

Articles
Do antidepressants work? https://aeon.co/essays/the-evidence-in-favour-of-antidepressants-is-terribly-flawed

Even when I'm psychotic, I'm still me. https://www.nytimes.com/2020/02/21/opinion/sunday/bipolar-disorder-psychosis.html

Books
Whitaker, R. (2010). *Anatomy of an epidemic*. New York: Broadway Paperbacks.

Learn more with this chapter's digital tools at www.oup.com/he/rosenthal2e.

CHAPTER

14 Performance-Enhancing Drugs

True or false?

1.
True or false? The typical anabolic steroid user is an educated man who is not active in organized sports.

2.
True or false? The sport of track and field first banned the use of performance-enhancing drugs by athletes in 1928.

3.
True or false? The United States consumes about over 80 percent of the world's ADHD drugs.

In our society, people often feel great pressure to achieve—both physically and academically—and may take drugs such as anabolic-androgenic steroids (AAS) to enhance their physical performance, and drugs such as Ritalin or Adderall to enhance their academic or mental performance. Although these drugs are used by millions of people—more males than females—AAS and drugs that treat attention-deficit/hyperactivity disorder can cause both physical and psychological damage.

Learning Objectives

- Define the terms *anabolic, androgenic, cycling, stacking,* and *pyramiding.*
- Summarize the effects and side effects of anabolic-androgenic steroids.
- Illustrate how the body regulates testosterone.
- Evaluate the effects of anabolic-androgenic steroids on aggression.
- List the symptoms of attention-deficit/ hyperactivity disorder (ADHD).
- Consider some possible causes underlying ADHD.
- Analyze some of the reasons for the increase in prevalence of ADHD diagnoses over the past few decades.
- Explain the mechanism of action of drugs used to treat ADHD.
- Describe the physiological and psychological effects of drugs used to treat ADHD.
- Assess the long-term effect of ADHD medications on academic achievement.

Anabolic-Androgenic Steroids

In the 1970s, physician Robert Goldman posed a question to elite athletes: "If you had a drug that would allow you to win every athletic competition you entered, but would kill you in 5 years, would you still take it?" More than half of the athletes polled said "yes."[1] This desire for victory even in the face of dreadful consequences is one factor underlying **doping**—the use of performance-enhancing drugs such as AAS—to improve athletic performance.

Anabolic-androgenic steroids have similar effects to testosterone. **Anabolic** substances encourage muscle growth, while **androgenic** ones promote male physiological characteristics. The term **steroid** describes a number of structurally similar substances with different functions, but not all steroids are anabolic-androgenic. For the purposes of this discussion, the term *steroid* will mean the synthetic forms of testosterone that are anabolic/ androgenic.

The goal of those who take steroids is usually to boost the anabolic effects while minimizing the androgenic effects, and chemical modifications are made to encourage this outcome. The physical risks of anabolic steroid use are well known, yet men and women still continue to take these drugs. There are numerous reasons for this.

Our society greatly values athletic superiority. Athletes are rewarded with admiration, fame, and financial rewards (Figure 14.1). The use of performance-enhancing drugs among top competitors is well-publicized. Athletes such as Lance Armstrong (cyclist), Ben Johnson (sprinter), Marion Jones (track), Maria Sharapova (tennis), and Alex Rodriguez (baseball player) lost titles, medals, and respect when they were shown to have used illegal performance-enhancing drugs. Much was made in the media about their dishonest methods, but this publicity also reinforced the idea that these drugs allow athletes to achieve athletic goals that are otherwise unobtainable.[2]

Others take steroids to increase muscle size or reduce body fat in order to feel more attractive. Television and movies (and even

Doping: The act of taking a drug to enhance one's athletic performance.

Anabolic: Related to the process of building tissue.

Androgenic: Related to the development or maintenance of male physiological characteristics.

Steroid: A type of lipid molecule with a multiple ring structure.

Anabolic-Androgenic Steroids

Type of drug: Performance-enhancing—physical

Chemical formula:
Testosterone: $C_{19}H_{28}O_2$

Routes of administration:
Intramuscular injection, oral, topical

Primary hormone affected:
Testosterone

Tolerance: Moderate

Physical dependence: Low to moderate

Psychological dependence:
Moderate

Withdrawal symptoms:
Depression, mood swings, fatigue, headache, insomnia, body dissatisfaction

Schedule: Schedule III

Slang: Juice, roids

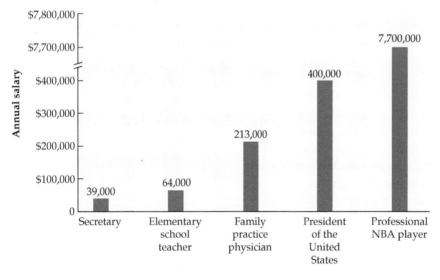

FIGURE 14.1. Average annual salary of chosen professions. The average professional National Basketball Association (NBA) player makes a secretary's annual salary in less than 2 days.

Source: Bureau of Labor Statistics. (2020). May 2019 national occupational employment and wage estimates United States. https://www.bls.gov/oes/current/oes_nat.htm#43-0000

(a highly toxic stimulant derived from the seeds of the *strychnos* tree) to help improve their performance.[3] The word "doping" comes from the Dutch word *doop*—a viscous opium juice used by the ancient Greeks.[4]

QUICK HIT

The world's first doping scandal occurred in 1876. The American professional long-distance walker Edward Weston challenged England's racewalking champion to a 24-hour, 115-mile marathon. Weston made it for the full 24 hours and 110 miles, while the English racewalking champion quit after 14 hours. Weston later admitted to having chewed coca leaves throughout the race. There was an outcry, but he kept his title.

action figures) may give people a false idea of the human form; just as we are constantly shown images of impossibly small women, the media image of the "ideal" male is getting larger (Figure 14.2).

History of Performance-Enhancing Drugs

The use of drugs to enhance athletic performance has occurred for millennia. During the first Olympic Games in Ancient Greece, athletes would eat bread soaked in opium, psychedelic mushrooms, or strychnine

In the early twentieth century, endurance athletes were known to use cocaine, low doses of strychnine, and other stimulants to improve their performance. In 1928, the governing body for the sport of track and field was the first international sporting federation to prohibit doping by athletes.

Synthetic AAS were developed in 1935. At the world weightlifting competition in Vienna in 1954, the Soviet team dominated, even though in the past the U.S. team routinely outscored the Soviets. When the American team physician took the Soviet team physician out for a few drinks, the Russian admitted that his team was using AAS. After the competition, the American physician began giving his weightlifters steroids.[5]

Throughout the 1950s, athletes began using amphetamines to increase endurance, and steroids to increase muscle mass and strength. Sadly, the increased use of performance-enhancing substances led to drug-related deaths among athletes. In 1960, Danish cyclist Knut Jensen died of amphetamine-induced heat stroke. He was the first athlete to die during Olympic competition due to doping. In 1967, British cyclist Tommy Simpson's death during the Tour de France was televised. Allegedly, his motto was, "If it takes 10 to kill you, take 9 and win." That year, the International Olympic Commit-

(a)

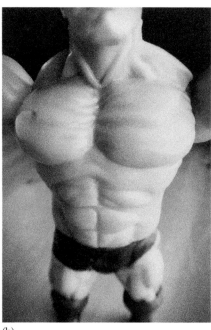

(b)

FIGURE 14.2. **The chest and bicep diameter of male action figures has expanded immensely.** In 1964, the G.I. Joe action figure (a) had a bicep circumference of 12.2 inches (if extrapolated to a 6-foot-tall man). By 1998, the G.I. Joe Extreme's biceps (b) had swelled to 26.8 inches.

tee (IOC) banned doping for Olympic athletes and, in 1968, implemented the first drug testing at the Olympic Games. During the 1988 Olympic Games, Canadian sprinter Ben Johnson won gold as he broke the world's record for the 100-meter dash. But after he tested positive for anabolic steroids, he was stripped of his medal and suspended from competing for two years. In 1991, Ben Johnson attempted a comeback. After winning a race in 1993, he again tested positive for steroids, and this time was banned for life from competitive running.

In 1990, the U.S. Congress passed the Anabolic Steroids Control Act, which reclassified 27 specific AAS as schedule III, and transferred their jurisdiction from the Food and Drug Administration (FDA) to the Drug Enforcement Agency (DEA). The act established that possession of AAS without a valid medical prescription was punishable by a minimum penalty of at least $1,000 and a maximum penalty of up to one year in prison. Those found guilty of possession with intent to sell could face up to five years in prison and sizable fines. Penalties are doubled for repeat offenses or sales to minors.

In 2000, tetrahydrogestrinone (THG, or "the clear") was developed and manufactured by the Bay Area Laboratory Co-Operative (BALCO). This synthetic performance-enhancing steroid was designed to escape detection during drug analysis. In 2003, a track coach called the U.S. anti-doping agency and reported that

many top athletes were using THG. He delivered a syringe of the drug, and said the source was Victor Conte, founder of BALCO labs. The lab was raided, and many steroids were found, along with a list of customers. Conte testified before a grand jury and named a long list of Olympic and professional athletes who had been his clients, including Major League Baseball star Barry Bonds and track star Marion Jones.

In 2007, Barry Bonds hit his 756th home run, breaking Hank Aaron's career record. He claimed before a grand jury that he didn't know the substances he used were steroids. It was later found that he did have knowledge, and he was indicted for perjury. That same year, Marion Jones admitted to using steroids during the 2000 Olympic Games. She was stripped of her medals, wiped from the Olympic record book, and sentenced to six months in prison.

Currently, all major sports bodies, including the Olympics, professional tennis, and Major League Baseball, as well as the National Football League (NFL), National Basketball Association (NBA), and National Hockey League (NHL), ban performance-enhancing drugs such as anabolic steroids; hormones such as growth hormone, corticotrophin, and erythropoietin; beta$_2$-agonists; and diuretics (Figure 14.3). The list of banned substances is constantly updated; in 2016, meldonium, which increases blood flow, was added to the

Ask yourself: *Saturday Night Live* once had a parody skit about the "All-Drug Olympics," in which competitors were not only allowed, but encouraged, to use any and all drugs. While this was obviously a joke, what are your thoughts about athletes using drugs? If some athletes use them, other athletes might feel compelled to use them in order to compete, so should there be separate games for those who use drugs? Should an athlete retain an athletic record achieved while using drugs? Should all professional athletes be tested? What about high school or college athletes? What do we gain, and what do we lose, when professional athletes use performance-enhancing drugs?

FIGURE 14.3. **Lance Armstrong.** In 2012, cycling star Lance Armstrong was stripped of seven Tour de France titles and barred for life from Olympic sports for doping. In 2013, he admitted to using performance-enhancing drugs.

list. Alcohol is prohibited only in certain sports, such as car racing, and beta-blockers are prohibited in sports where the absence of high pulse rate and tremor are advantageous, such as the biathlon and other shooting competitions. It is also against the rules to have blood transfusions before competition or chemically manipulate collected samples.

Prevalence of Performance-Enhancing Drug Use

Globally, 6.4 percent of men and 1.6 percent of women have reported ever using AAS.[6] The United States accounts for the largest number of steroid users worldwide; among Americans age 13–50, between 2.9 and 4 million have ever used steroids.[7, 8] In adults, about 50 times as many males as females use steroids.[9] However, the ratio of male to female steroid use is much lower among high school students—it is currently less than 1.5:1. The use of steroids in teenage girls is not limited to athletes; in fact, female high school students who use steroids are *less* likely to play school-sponsored team sports.[10]

According to the Youth Risk Behavior Surveillance Survey, steroid use by high school students has fluctuated over time (Figure 14.4).[11, 12] Although almost 90 percent of high school students disapprove of the use of steroids, just over 50 percent perceive them as being very harmful (down from a peak of 70 percent in 1992). About 19 percent of 12th grade students say steroids are fairly or very easy to obtain.[13]

About 2 percent of college men and 0.2 percent of college women reported steroid use in their lifetime.[14] Steroid use in adolescents and young adults may be part

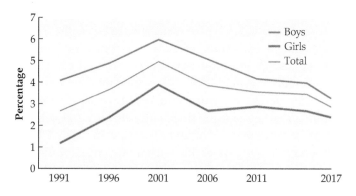

FIGURE 14.4. **Percentage of high school students who ever took anabolic-androgenic steroids without a doctor's prescription.** About 2.9% of high school students in used anabolic-androgenic steroids in 2017, down from a peak of 5% in 2001.

Source: Kann, L., McManus, T., Harris, W.L., Shanklin, S.L., & Flint, K.H., et al. (2018). Youth risk behavior surveillance—United States, 2017. MMWR, 67(8): 58–59.

of a pattern of high-risk behavior, given that it is positively associated with unsafe behaviors such as cigarette smoking, use of other illicit drugs, drinking and driving, and alcohol use disorder.[15]

Most media stories of steroid use deal with professional athletes and adolescents, but most steroid users are neither high school students nor active in competitive sports.[16, 17] Indeed, the typical steroid user is approximately 31 years old, white, highly educated, employed and earning an above-average income, and not active in organized sports. Adult users tend to be driven and motivated, and focused on goal attainment. Professional bodybuilding or sports participation is not a common motivating factor for adult steroid use; in fact, involvement in any organized sport is rare. Adult steroid users take the drug to increase their muscle mass and strength, decrease fat, and enhance their physical appearance. These users tend to research the drug carefully, plan their drug regimen, and closely monitor their diet; steroid use is less impulsive than other drug use, because it is the end result that is important to users, not the drug itself.[18]

Adult users may be more likely than nonusers to score high on measures of paranoia, narcissism, and antisocial personality traits, but it is difficult to tell whether these traits preceded steroid use, or if use itself raised the likelihood of these traits.[19] Users were significantly less confident about their body appearance before weight training and steroid use; body image disorders may be both a risk factor for steroid use and a consequence of it.[20] Some of those who abuse steroids can recall physical or sexual abuse in childhood and use steroids to increase muscle size; female weightlifters who had been raped were twice as likely to report use of steroids as those who had not been raped.[21]

Forms of Performance-Enhancing Drugs

There are many forms of performance-enhancing drugs, some of which increase strength, endurance, or aerobic capacity. These drugs include anabolic-androgenic steroids (AAS), central nervous system (CNS) stimulants, pain relievers, beta$_2$ agonists, beta-blockers, human growth hormone, creatine, as well as the process of blood doping. Their effects are summarized in Table 14.1.

TABLE 14.1. Performance-Enhancing Drugs and Their Effects

Category	Examples	Benefits	Side Effects
Anabolic-androgenic steroids	Androstenediol Androstenedione Testosterone	Increases muscle growth, strength, endurance	Adverse reproductive effects Weakens tendons Increases blood pressure Increases risk of heart attack and stroke Damages liver Impairs immune function Increases mood swings, anxiety
Stimulant	Amphetamine Cocaine Ephedrine Caffeine	Increases endurance and alertness Relieves fatigue Improves reaction time	Irregular heartbeat Irritability, nervousness, anxiety Decreases sleep and appetite
Pain relievers	Cortisone Opioids Local anesthetics	Allow athletes to play through the pain	Aside from the side effects of specific drugs themselves, can increase risk of career-ending injury
Blood doping	Erythropoietin Blood transfusions	Increases oxygen-carrying capacity of blood Increases endurance	Raises blood pressure and increases risk of heart attack, blood clots, and stroke
Beta$_2$ agonists	Albuterol	Dilates bronchi to increase oxygen delivery to lungs Oral or injected forms can build muscle	Nausea, cramps, headache
Beta-blockers	Atenolol Propranolol	Slows heart rate and blood pressure Decreases anxiety and can help in archery and shooting events	Makes physical exertion more difficult Increases sun sensitivity
Human growth hormone	Genotropin Humatrope	Increases muscle growth	Headaches, joint pain, raises blood pressure Increases risk of heart disease, diabetes, cancer May damage heart, liver, kidney

TABLE 14.2.   Anabolic-Androgenic Steroids Available by Prescription in the United States

Oral	Intramuscular Injection	Transdermal Patch
danazol (Danocrine)	nandrolone (Deca-Durabolin)	Testosterone
drostanolone (Masteron)	tetrahydrogestrinone (THG)	
methandrostenolone (Dianabol)	Many of the oral drugs are available in an IM formulation	
methyltestosterone (Android, Testred, Virilon)		
oxandrolone (Oxandrin)		
oxymetholone (Anadrol)		
stanozolol (Winstrol)		
boldenone (Equipoise)		

Anabolic-Androgenic Steroids (AAS)

There are more than 100 different types of AAS. Some of the formulations currently available in the United States are listed in Table 14.2. AAS are typically taken orally or by intramuscular (IM) injection, but there are also transdermal testosterone patches.

Androstenedione (Andro) is a naturally occurring metabolic precursor of testosterone. In 1998, Mark McGwire hit 70 home runs, far eclipsing the previous record for home runs in a single year. He admitted using the over-the-counter (OTC) supplement Andro, which already had been banned by the World Anti-Doping Agency, the IOC, and the NFL, but had not yet been banned by Major League Baseball. The following year, there was an enormous increase in the sales of Andro.[22] In 2004, the FDA banned the sale of Andro.

Dehydroepiandrosterone (DHEA) is produced by the adrenal glands and is an intermediary in the biosynthesis of androgens. It is a legal dietary supplement, but its use is banned in athletic competitions. Other testosterone drugs generally taken by older men (and sometimes older women) in order to increase sex drive are discussed in Chapter 16.

Most users obtain their steroids over the internet, where AAS are readily available and easy to purchase without a prescription.[23,24] Other sources include peers at their gym, physicians' prescriptions, or through the mail. They often are smuggled in from other countries, diverted from legitimate channels, synthesized in labs, or stolen from veterinary sources.

Central Nervous System Stimulants

Amphetamines, cocaine, ephedrine, and caffeine increase heart rate, aggression, and alertness, and have

Blood doping: A method of increasing the oxygen-carrying capacity of the blood in order to enhance athletic performance.

been used by athletes in endurance sports such as cycling, cross-country skiing, and marathons, as well as in sprinting, soccer, and football. They typically produce only a small improvement in performance, but at professional and Olympic levels, small differences can make the difference between winning and losing. Stimulants, however, increase the risk of anxiety, paranoia, and potentially life-threatening cardiovascular events. Stimulants are discussed in Chapter 5.

Pain Relievers

Cortisone, opioids (Chapter 7), and local anesthetics may be given to athletes who are injured during a game to allow them to continue playing. But pain is a sign from our bodies that damage has occurred; when athletes "play through the pain," they run the risk of career-ending injuries.

Blood Doping

The use of illicit products and methods to increase oxygen transport in the body is known as **blood doping**. Erythropoietin (EPO) is a hormone that controls red blood cell production. Because red blood cells carry oxygen through the body, increasing their production can improve an athlete's aerobic capacity and endurance. One danger of using EPO is that athletes, especially male athletes, already have a lot of red blood cells, so if they further increase their production, it can thicken the blood to a dangerous level, and increase the risk of myocardial infarction, blood clots, stroke, and pulmonary embolism. EPO has been blamed for the deaths of dozens of athletes since 1988.[25] Synthetic EPO can be distinguished in a lab test from naturally occurring EPO. Another method of blood doping is when athletes receive a blood transfusion one to seven days before a high-endurance event. Transfusions can now be detected by cell surface markers and breathing analyses.

Beta₂-Agonists and Beta-Blockers

Drugs that affect norepinephrine can influence athletic performance. Norepinephrine binds to both alpha and beta receptors. When inhaled, beta$_2$-agonists such as albuterol increase lung capacity by dilating the bronchi leading to the lungs. When taken orally or injected, beta$_2$-agonists may build muscle. Unfortunately, they also can cause nausea, cramps, headache, and palpitations. Beta-blockers, on the other hand, slow heart rate, lower blood pressure, and reduce anxiety and trembling, actions that are desired in archery and shooting events.

Human Growth Hormone

Human growth hormone (hGH) normally is released from the pituitary gland, and it leads to muscle gain and fat loss. Taking synthetic forms of HGH is expensive and dangerous, and it can cause severe headaches; vision problems; joint pain; enlargement of the jaw, forehead, hands, and feet; hypertension; heart disease; thyroid disorders; type 2 diabetes; and an increased risk of cancer.

Creatine

One of the most widely used substances among athletes is creatine. Made naturally in the kidney, creatine is considered a legal nutritional supplement and is not regulated by the FDA. Creatine may very slightly increase muscle size and strength by pulling water into muscles. Creatine also may boost levels of ATP, the chemical that powers muscle contractions, but only for very short bursts of energy. High levels of creatine may lead to muscle cramps, dehydration, water retention, kidney problems, and gastrointestinal distress.

Pharmacokinetics and Mechanism of Action of Anabolic-Androgenic Steroids

The remainder of this section deals specifically with AAS because they are the most well-known and commonly self-administered performance-enhancing drugs. As with all drugs, the route of administration and pattern of use of AAS can greatly influence their effects in the body. Those who use steroids manipulate these factors to try to obtain the optimum effect.

Routes of Administration

Anabolic-androgenic steroids can be administered orally, by intramuscular (IM) injection, or topically, as creams or gels either worn as skin patches or rubbed on the skin. Oral administration is the most convenient, but orally administered AAS undergo rapid first-pass metabolism by the liver, making the drugs less effective. Ninety-five percent of adult users said their preferred route of administration was by IM injection, which they favored due to health reasons (oral administration of steroids is especially toxic to the liver) and a belief in better outcomes.[26] Although almost all adult users deny sharing needles, younger users are much more likely to share the needles they use to inject steroids.[27]

Dosage and Pattern of Use

An average adult male produces 2.5–10 mg of testosterone each day. The appropriate medical dose for anabolic steroid replacement therapy is comparable. But those who abuse AAS in order to improve their appearance or athletic performance often self-administer doses 100 to 1000 times the therapeutic levels in adult men and proportionately even higher doses in women and adolescents.[28, 29]

AAS users often incorporate **cycling** in their pattern of use. Cycles of use are typically 4–18 weeks in duration followed by a period of abstinence that allows adverse side effects to subside, allows tolerance to decline, and reduces the chance of detection of banned substances. At the beginning of the cycle, users often start with low doses, which they slowly increase to a peak. At the second half of the cycle, the dose goes back down to zero, after which they enter the period of abstention. This pattern is called **pyramiding.** Steroid users believe this habit gives the body time to adjust to high doses and then recuperate, but there are no proven benefits to pyramiding.

Steroid users sometimes also **stack** their drugs—despite no scientific data indicating that this works—when they simultaneously take two or more types of steroids at the same time to increase the effects on

Cycling: A pattern of use of anabolic-androgenic steroids, in which a user takes steroids for 4–18 weeks, followed by an equal or longer period of abstinence.

Pyramiding: A pattern of use in which progressively increased doses of steroids are taken until a peak is reached mid cycle, and then reduced toward the end of the cycle.

Stacking: When a steroid user takes several types of steroids at the same time.

muscle size and potentially minimize the development of tolerance to any single agent.[30] Users may combine oral and injectable steroids, or may take other drugs, such as diuretics, anti-estrogens, or anti-acne medications, in order to combat the steroids' side effects.

Absorption, Distribution, Metabolism, and Elimination

Orally administered testosterone is rapidly absorbed into the bloodstream and is transported to the liver, where it is immediately metabolized, such that only a fraction of the dose is available in the active form before it reaches the systemic circulation. Once absorbed into the bloodstream, AAS circulate both freely and bound to a plasma protein called "sex hormone binding globulin." Only freely circulating unbound molecules, which represent perhaps 1 percent of the total, are free to leave the bloodstream and bind to receptor sites on muscles, bones, glands, and organs. When injected intramuscularly, some of the first-pass effect is diminished, and more steroid reaches the receptor sites. IM injection is preferred to intravenous injection, to allow for slower absorption and avoid sudden and extreme changes in the amount of steroid in the bloodstream. Topical administration, by creams and gels, provides inefficient absorption. Creams and gels can be sweated off during exercise, or rubbed off onto someone who comes in contact with the user's skin. Testosterone administered on transdermal patches is more efficient and can provide a steady dose that is absorbed into the bloodstream through the skin.

The liver metabolizes most forms of AAS very quickly. The cytochrome P450 enzymes of the liver are the major metabolizing system for steroids. There are genetic variations in these enzymes, which can lead to significant differences in the way that individuals metabolize steroids; for example, Swedes metabolize and eliminate testosterone at 16 times the rate of Koreans.[31] Water-soluble AAS are eliminated quickly, but highly fat-soluble compounds are metabolized slower and remain in the system for a longer time. Some injected steroids that have been suspended in oil can be detected in the body months after last use. After metabolism, about 90 percent of anabolic steroids are eliminated in the urine.

Mechanism of Action

In males, testosterone is normally produced in the testes; in women, the ovaries and adrenal glands are responsible. Males normally have about 7–10 times as much testosterone as women do. About 5–7 percent of testosterone

is converted by the enzyme 5-α-reductase into the more potent androgen dihydrotestosterone, a compound that causes acne, beard growth, and male-pattern baldness. A small amount of testosterone (less than 1 percent) is converted into the "female" hormone estradiol, a phenomenon that can explain some of the feminizing side effects of some AAS. Testosterone moves from the bloodstream into its target cells where it binds to androgen receptors. The receptors change shape in order to allow testosterone to move into the nucleus. There, it binds to DNA and guides the production of new proteins, such as in skeletal muscle.

Testosterone is normally regulated by negative feedback (Figure 14.5). The hypothalamus releases the hormone GnRH. This hormone travels to the anterior pituitary gland, and causes the gland to release the hormones FSH and LH. These hormones maintain the testes and cause it to release testosterone. Testosterone then travels throughout the body and produces many changes, including in the hypothalamus and pituitary gland, where it shuts off release of GnRH, FSH, and LH, thereby halting the release of testosterone from the testes. After a while, because the testosterone is no longer present to inhibit the hypothalamus, the cycle begins again. In this way, testosterone self-regulates its own release. However, when a person continually takes high doses of AAS, the hypothalamus and pituitary gland are constantly inhibited. Because FSH and LH are necessary for sperm production and maintenance of normal testicular function, chronic administration of AAS can lead to infertility, impotence, and shrinkage of the testes.

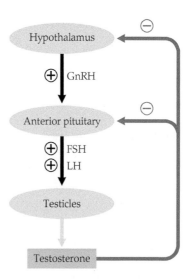

FIGURE 14.5. The regulation of testosterone. Testosterone self-regulates its own release, but when a person continually takes high doses of AAS, the hypothalamus and pituitary gland will remain inhibited, ultimately leading to infertility, impotence, and shrinkage of the testes.

Acute Effects of Anabolic-Androgenic Steroids

When individuals take AAS, several changes occur in the body. These effects depend on which drug is taken, as well as on the length of time and dosage. Some of the effects of steroids are anabolic—related to the synthesis of new proteins, such as in muscle cells; some are anti-catabolic—meaning that steroids inhibit the breakdown of complex molecules to release energy; and some effects are androgenic, or masculinizing. The major effects of AAS are summarized in Figure 14.6.

Physiological Effects

Some of the most common positive effects noted by AAS users include increased muscle mass, decreased fat, and improved athletic performance. The most common adverse effects include acne, more body hair, and increased aggressive behavior.[32] For a number of reasons, however, it is difficult to accurately determine the exact effects of AAS.[33]

Laboratory studies may underestimate the adverse effects of AAS. Typical doses are much higher in the field than in most laboratory studies; it would be unethical to administer the doses to research participants that users administer to themselves. Also, in the real world, users stack their drugs and pyramid their doses, but these practices are not usually done in the lab. In addition, laboratory studies use known products, but users in the real world often are buying their steroids on the black market and do not know the true composition of the drugs they are taking. Finally, adverse effects also may be overestimated. Case reports from real users can give a false impression, because these reports usually highlight the most severe adverse effects or complications.[34]

Musculoskeletal Effects

AAS increase skeletal muscle growth. The upper region of the body—the neck, shoulders, upper back, and upper arms—contain more androgen receptors than other parts of the body and are more susceptible to the effects of AAS.[35] These drugs increase muscle mass by boosting the production of proteins and by blocking muscle breakdown. AAS use also can cause tendons to weaken and increase the risk of tendon tears. When taken in adolescence, AAS can trigger bones to prematurely stop growing, and users may not grow as tall as they would otherwise.

Fat, Skin, and Hair

AAS decrease fat. Some forms of AAS are thought to work directly by affecting hormones that break down fat.[36] AAS also may indirectly decrease fat by raising the body's metabolic rate, given that skeletal muscle increases metabolic rate. AAS thicken the skin, increase pore size, and stimulate oil-producing sebaceous glands; users may develop acne, especially on the back and shoulders. Both males and females also can experience irreversible male-pattern baldness and a deeper voice.

Reproductive Effects

In males, AAS lead to reduced sperm production, testicular atrophy, enlarged prostate, and temporary

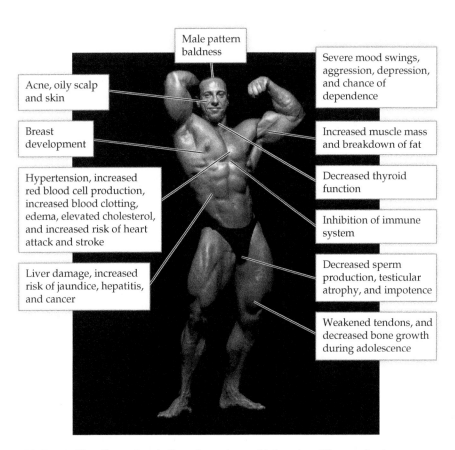

FIGURE 14.6. The effects of anabolic-androgenic steroids in males. Effects are for the most part the same in females, except females also experience menstrual irregularities, loss of breast tissue, permanent enlargement of the clitoris, and excessive growth of body and facial hair.

The following labels appear in the figure:

- Male pattern baldness
- Acne, oily scalp and skin
- Breast development
- Hypertension, increased red blood cell production, increased blood clotting, edema, elevated cholesterol, and increased risk of heart attack and stroke
- Liver damage, increased risk of jaundice, hepatitis, and cancer
- Severe mood swings, aggression, depression, and chance of dependence
- Increased muscle mass and breakdown of fat
- Decreased thyroid function
- Inhibition of immune system
- Decreased sperm production, testicular atrophy, and impotence
- Weakened tendons, and decreased bone growth during adolescence

infertility. Testicular size and sperm production usually return to normal four to seven months after stopping steroid use, but recovery depends on the doses taken and duration of AAS abuse. Small doses are said to increase libido, but larger doses can lead to impotence. Males can sometimes develop gynecomastia (enlarged breasts), because a small amount of testosterone is converted into estrogen. In its early stages, gynecomastia may spontaneously regress, but in later stages, it's often permanent and must be corrected surgically.[37] Some AAS users take the estrogen receptor blocker tamoxifen to try to prevent breast growth, but the scientific data do not support the effectiveness of this preventative measure. In females, AAS lead to reversible menstrual irregularities and loss of breast tissue, as well as permanent enlargement of the clitoris and excessive growth of body and facial hair.

Cardiovascular Effects

AAS increase red blood cell production and allow the tissues to access more oxygen from the blood.[38] They also increase blood clotting and can lead to hypertension and enlargement of the left ventricle of the heart. Users can retain sodium and water, resulting in edema (swelling). AAS reduce "good" cholesterol (HDL) while raising "bad" cholesterol (LDL), which increases the user's risk of atherosclerosis, blood clots, heart attack, and stroke.[39]

Liver

Steroids are very hard on the liver. Use can raise the risk of jaundice, hepatitis, peliosis hepatis (a vascular condition characterized by randomly distributed blood-filled cavities throughout the liver), and liver cancer. The use of orally administered AAS is particularly damaging to the liver.

Cognitive Effects

High doses of AAS increase cell death in neurons,[40] which raises the possibility of cognitive deficits. Long-term AAS users were found to perform significantly worse than nonusers on tests of visuospatial memory (such as recognizing patterns), and within the user group, the greater the lifetime use of AAS, the worse the visuospatial performance.[41]

Immunity

AAS reduce immune cell number and function, thereby inhibiting one's immune response. These effects may be profound and long-lasting, depending on the type used, dosing regimen, and extent and duration of AAS abuse.[42]

Athletic Performance

In the 1960s, there were many placebo-controlled studies to assess whether AAS were effective for gaining muscle mass. Most produced negative results, probably because these studies used dosages and durations far below those used by actual athletes in the field.[43] As a result, many scientists and physicians concluded that anabolic steroids were ineffective for athletic purposes. Some athletes began to hold medical professionals in contempt because they had firsthand knowledge of the effects of AAS on athletic performance. To this day, AAS users often distrust medical professionals on the subject and discount medical warnings about the possible physical and psychiatric dangers of these agents.[44]

> ## QUICK HIT
> Forty percent of AAS users in one survey reported they would trust information on steroids from their local drug dealer at least as much as information from any physician.[45]

So, how much does AAS use correspond to an actual improvement in athletic performance? Short answer: it depends. It depends on the type of steroids used, the dose and training regimen, and the type of athletic event. Steroids may help performance in sports that require strength and endurance. They also reduce recovery time after injury or exhaustion, which allows an athlete to train longer and harder (but also risk injury and permanent disability). Steroids also increase the proliferation of red blood cells, so they may increase one's endurance. Steroids have no real effect on aerobic capacity or accuracy, and they may actually hurt a person's flexibility.

Psychological Effects

Anabolic-androgenic steroids users initially report feelings of euphoria, well-being, increased energy, confidence, and sex drive. Eventually, some may experience severe mood swings, anxiety, heightened aggression, distractibility, forgetfulness, confusion, decreased sex drive, and even mania and delusions. Laboratory studies investigating the effects of AAS on mood are inconsistent. In some studies, users show some psychiatric effects or increased measures of manic or aggressive behaviors, but in other studies, participants experience no psychiatric changes.[46,47,48]

In order to evaluate the consequences of steroid use, some studies compare a group of real-world AAS users to placebo and control groups. Actual AAS users score statistically higher for aggression, anxiety, depression, obsessive-compulsiveness, hostility, phobia, and paranoia than nonusers.[49,50] These psychological effects were positively correlated with dose. To try to control for a genetic predisposition for these conditions, the authors looked at a small sample of identical twins, and AAS users had higher levels of these traits than their nonusing twins.[51]

Users of AAS sometimes experience an increase in paranoia and aggressive behaviors called "roid rage." But the link between AAS and aggression is complex and ambiguous. Some researchers have suggested that roid rage does not actually exist and is simply due to societal expectations.

Aside from the physical and psychological dangers, there are other risks that AAS users take. Most nonmedical AAS are obtained from illegitimate sources, and users can never be entirely sure what drug they are

Critical Evaluation

Does "roid rage" exist?

The extent, causes, and even the existence of "roid rage" are controversial. Use your critical thinking skills to evaluate the factors involved.

Definition. What is roid rage? Is it an increase in physically aggressive behaviors or emotional instability? Is roid rage brought on by events, or does it occur spontaneously?

Study design. Ethical considerations prohibit scientists from giving participants the much higher doses of AAS typically taken by real-world users. Also, participants with a history of aggression or psychiatric conditions are often excluded from these studies, or pulled from the study when they begin exhibiting troubling symptoms. In the real world, however, they may continue AAS use. How might we design a study to best test the effects of AAS, yet not expose participants to undue risks?

Controlling for other drugs. Laboratory experiments usually test one drug at a time, while steroid users often use multiple types of steroids together (stacking). It is also difficult to control what other drugs are being taken. Not only are people who use AAS more likely than nonusers to abuse alcohol and other drugs, but alcohol is strongly synergistic with AAS in producing impulsive violent behavior.[52] Do you think it's best to test these drugs alone to better understand their actions, or with other drugs, to better mimic typical use? What are some pros and cons of each approach?

Environmental factors. Some scientists believe that testosterone is related to social status and dominance rather than to aggression. Therefore, the environment in which AAS are taken

may play a role; perhaps in some cases the social situation necessitates an aggressive response while in others it does not.[53] Should AAS be tested under controlled laboratory conditions or observed in the "real world"?

Correlation and causation. Let's assume that a certain percentage of men who take AAS do show an increase in aggressive behavior while on the drug. Does this mean that steroids *cause* aggression? Or could it be that those who are already more naturally aggressive are more likely to take steroids?

Blind testing. Obviously, most steroid users are aware that they are taking steroids and are aware of the reported effects on aggression. Perhaps these steroid users aren't feeling any more aggression than they were before their drug use, but now they are free to express it. In a double-blind experiment, male participants were given either testosterone, placebo, or no treatment (control group) for one week. Their emotional state was assessed by themselves and by observers, both before and after treatment. After treatment, the group that scored highest on anger, irritation, and impulsivity was actually the placebo group.[54] In another study, in which women received testosterone and then played a game that assesses social dynamics, women who *thought* they received testosterone, regardless of whether they did or not, behaved more unfairly than those on placebo.[55] How would you design an experiment to determine whether roid rage was an actual physiological response to steroids, or if it was related to the cultural expectation of aggression?

taking. In addition, those who inject steroids face the risk of infection, and those who share needles greatly increase their risk. Finally, nonmedical use of these drugs is illegal, and users are subject to criminal prosecution.

Medical and Therapeutic Uses of Anabolic-Androgenic Steroids

AAS do have some legitimate therapeutic uses. They are used to replace male hormones in men who have androgen deficiency; to stimulate the bone marrow in the treatment of leukemia, kidney failure, and certain forms of aplastic anemia; to treat breast cancer and osteoporosis; and to treat severe muscle loss, such as after major trauma or HIV/AIDS. Steroids also are being investigated as a possible male contraceptive, although their results are not satisfactory as yet.[56] Finally, steroids are given to transgender men to aid their transition (Chapter 16).

Because all of these conditions come with different challenges and goals, the type of steroid given, as well as the ratio of androgenic to anabolic effects is important. Drugs with higher androgenic and lower anabolic effects are given to treat **hypogonadism** in males, while steroids higher in anabolic effects are used for anemia and osteoporosis, as well as to reverse protein loss following surgery or trauma.

Anabolic-Androgenic Steroid Tolerance and Dependence

In addition to the negative side effects seen with long-term AAS use, chronic users can experience tolerance and dependence. Tolerance to AAS begins to develop with the first dose. Because testosterone inhibits its own production, constant administration lowers the body's normal production of testosterone. Users may begin stacking and pyramiding in the hopes of increasing the effects. Withdrawal from steroids can cause depression, fatigue, headache, restlessness, insomnia, lack of energy, loss of appetite, and body dissatisfaction.

Because users often feel good when on steroids and bad when they go off, there is a risk of psychological dependence. About 30 percent of users become dependent; approximately 1 million Americans age 13–50 may have experienced AAS dependence.[57,58] Dependent users may continue to take steroids despite physical problems, mood swings, sizable financial outlay, and

negative effects on social relationships.[59] Dependence probably has physiological, psychological, and social underpinnings. AAS users may become "addicted" to maintaining the massive musculature they've achieved, and their self-esteem may plummet as their size diminishes. Additionally, since the use of AAS shuts down normal testosterone production, stopping use of exogenous steroids may lead to low testosterone levels. This may persist for months or even years, and lead to decreased energy, a loss of libido, and erectile dysfunction.[60] Dependence also is related to higher dosages; there is no evidence that medical use of AAS is addictive.

Prevention and Treatment of Anabolic-Androgenic Steroid Abuse

In order to prevent AAS abuse, some high schools and most professional sports organizations have instituted drug testing (Chapter 18). Sports officials test the blood and urine of athletes, but these tests are not perfect. First of all, not all athletes are tested. Also, athletes may try to cheat detection. Some methods include taking a drug that interferes with the metabolism of AAS; use of a substance that is not yet assayed or detected by the test, and carefully scheduling or limiting use of banned substances to keep levels below the threshold for detection.[61,62]

Some forms of steroids are detected by testing for elevated levels of testosterone in the body. A typical male has a 1:1 ratio of testosterone to epitestosterone. If a male athlete were to use some forms of AAS, his testosterone would increase but his epitestosterone would not. But some people do have higher than normal testosterone levels, so detection devices look for a ratio greater than 4:1. (Tests also look for higher than normal epitestosterone levels, which may indicate that an athlete has taken epitestosterone to mask his testosterone use.) This test is not ideal; there are racial differences in testosterone levels—Asians tend to have lower levels of testosterone than do Blacks or whites.

At the high school level, drug testing programs are heavily criticized for their cost and questionable success.[63] Over a three-year period, the drug testing program in Texas high schools cost $6 million and produced 0.5 percent positive or questionable results.

Everyone agrees that it would be better to prevent AAS use in high school students rather than simply punishing users. Adolescent athletes' intentions to use AAS are influenced by the social norms of their friends, teammates, and the expectations of their parents.[64,65] Programs that de-emphasize the benefits of use and highlight the adverse effects may help reduce use.[66]

Hypogonadism: A condition in which the male body does not make enough testosterone.

Attention-deficit/hyperactivity disorder (ADHD): A prolonged pattern of inattention and/or hyperactivity-impulsivity that negatively affects a person's development or functioning.

Athletes Training and Learning to Avoid Steroids (ATLAS) is an interactive, peer-led program designed to reduce the use of steroids among male high school athletes. The program includes information on both the positive and negative effects of steroids, healthy sports nutrition, drug-refusal role play, and demonstrations of strength training exercises as alternatives to the use of performance-enhancing drugs.

One year after completing the ATLAS program, students who had gone through ATLAS training were significantly less likely than those in the control group to use steroids or to intend to use them in the future, less likely to abuse alcohol and other drugs, less likely to drive under the influence of alcohol or to engage in other risky behaviors, and had improved body image.[67] Perhaps students trust the information because it is presented by peer leaders and facilitated by coaches, and because of the honest discussion of both the risks and benefits of performance-enhancing drugs.

The ATHENA program (Athletes Targeting Healthy Exercise and Nutrition Alternatives) is aimed at adolescent girls on sports teams. Girls who complete the program demonstrate decreased risky behaviors and reduced risk of using diet drugs, and have fewer injuries during the sports season.

Education about AAS may be having an impact. Remember Goldman's dilemma, wherein half of athletes queried would take a pill that would kill them if it would assure a gold medal? When athletes in 2012 were asked if they would take a drug guaranteeing Olympic success but that would result in their death in five years' time, only 6 percent answered in the affirmative.[68]

Treatment of steroid abuse usually consists of addressing the specific symptoms. Recovering users may take antidepressants, analgesics for joint pain, or other medications to restore the hormonal system. Psychological and behavioral therapy also can be beneficial.

Ask yourself: Given that it has been found to be less effective to teach youth about steroids by discussing only adverse effects and not mentioning positive effects as well, do you think we should take this approach when teaching students about recreational drugs, rather than having a "just say no" approach? Why or why not?

Drugs to Treat Attention-Deficit/Hyperactivity Disorder

Amphetamine is widely recognized as one of the most addictive and dangerous drugs. Yet, amphetamines and other structurally related drugs are routinely given to millions of American children every day to treat **attention-deficit/hyperactivity disorder (ADHD)**.

Symptoms and Diagnosis of ADHD

Attention-deficit/hyperactivity disorder is a chronic behavioral disorder in which a person shows developmentally inappropriate levels of inattention, impulsiveness, or hyperactivity. Previously considered a disorder of childhood, recent findings suggest that ADHD persists into adolescence in as many as 65 percent and into adulthood in almost 30 percent of those who were diagnosed as children.[69,70] In the U.S., the annual societal costs of ADHD, including healthcare, education, and reduced family productivity, is estimated to range from $38–72 billion.[71]

There are no definitive tests to diagnose ADHD. Many doctors rely on the Vanderbilt Assessment Scale, a questionnaire based on the diagnostic criteria in the DSM-5, in which parents and teachers rate a child on a scale of 0–3 for various symptoms indicative of inattention, impulsiveness, and hyperactivity (Figure 14.7).[72]

FIGURE 14.7. ADHD. Those with ADHD may have trouble focusing, but may conversely be able to immerse themselves completely in a subject that interests them.

Drugs to Treat ADHD

Type of drug:
Performance-enhancing—
mental focus

Chemical formula:
- Methylphenidate: $C_{14}H_{19}NO_2$
- Amphetamine/
  Dextroamphetamine: $C_9H_{13}N$

Routes of administration: Oral,
insufflation

Duration:
Ritalin: 2–4 hours, Vyvanse:
10–12 hours, Concerta: 8–12
hours

**Main neurotransmitters
affected:** Dopamine,
norepinephrine

Tolerance: Low to moderate

Physical dependence: Low

Psychological dependence:
Moderate

Withdrawal symptoms:
Agitation, depression, fatigue,
foggy thinking, anxiety,
concentration problems, sleep
and appetite changes

Schedule: Schedule II

Slang: Addies, Diet Coke,
Smarties, Rid

Inattention

- Often fails to pay close attention to details or makes careless mistakes.
- Often has trouble sustaining attention.
- Often does not appear to listen when spoken to directly.
- Often loses focus and does not follow through on instructions and fails to finish schoolwork, chores, or duties in the workplace.
- Often has trouble with organization.
- Often avoids or dislikes tasks that require sustained mental effort.
- Often loses things that are necessary for tasks and activities.
- Often easily distracted.
- Often is forgetful in daily activities.

Hyperactivity-Impulsivity

- Often squirms in chair or fidgets with hands or feet.
- Often has difficulty remaining seated in situations when remaining seated is expected.
- Often runs about or climbs when not appropriate (in children) or extreme restlessness (in adults).
- Often unable to engage in quiet leisure activities.
- Often "on the go," or acting as if "driven by a motor."
- Often talks excessively.

- Often blurts out an answer before a question has been completed.
- Often has trouble waiting his/her turn.
- Often interrupts others or butts into conversations or games.

To be officially diagnosed, there must be a persistent pattern of inattention and/or hyperactivity-impulsivity that interferes with social, academic, or occupational development or functioning. Children up to age 16 must show six or more symptoms of inattention, and/or six or more symptoms of impulsivity-hyperactivity; those over age 16 can be diagnosed if they have five or more symptoms.[73] In addition, the following criteria must be met for diagnosis:

- Several symptoms were present before the age of 12.
- Several symptoms are present in two or more settings (such as at school, home, or work; with friends or relatives; or in other activities).
- There is clear evidence that the symptoms interfere with the quality of school, work, or social functioning.
- These symptoms are not due to another mental disorder such as depression, anxiety, or substance abuse.

A diagnosis of childhood ADHD usually starts with observations by parents and elementary school teachers, who have the opportunity to observe children for hours a day and to see how their behavior compares with others in their age group. The official diagnosis of ADHD is usually made by pediatricians or other primary care physicians. One-third of these diagnostic visits with pediatricians last less than ten minutes, significantly less than the time required for a psychosocial evaluation, and often do not include the recommended follow-up care.[74,75,76]

Adolescents are sometimes harder to diagnose than younger children. They often have several teachers, each of whom is responsible for more than 100 students and may only see students for a small portion of the school day. Adolescents also typically spend less time with their parents, and symptoms may go unnoticed. Adults often notice characteristic behaviors in themselves and sometimes take online quizzes to assess their symptoms. These quizzes often are sponsored by drug companies and encourage users to "talk to their doctors about ADHD."

ADHD is a subjective diagnosis that is open to interpretation based on symptoms and how one's behavior appears in certain contexts. Imagine Billy. He is eight years old. Billy is distracted in class and doesn't always follow through on instructions. He doesn't wait his turn and often blurts out answers. He frequently fails to bring his homework to class. Billy may, in fact, have ADHD. On the other hand, perhaps there is discord at home, and Billy is acting out in response to that. Or perhaps all is fine at home, but Billy's parents don't believe in stifling a child's inclinations and they encourage him to act out. Or maybe Billy has problems processing auditory information—he may hear the teacher's instructions, but they may get scrambled in his brain, so he takes out the wrong book, can't follow along, talks to his friend for help, and eventually just looks out the window.[77] ADHD medications may help Billy if he truly has ADHD, but giving him a stimulant—although it might address his symptoms—will not address the underlying causes if his behaviors are not due to ADHD.

Prevalence of ADHD
Over 9 percent of school-age kids in the United States—some 6.1 million children—have received a medical diagnosis of ADHD.[78] This represents a greater than 1,100-percent increase since 1988. Most children with a current ADHD diagnosis have a co-occurring condition, such as behavioral or conduct problems, anxiety, or depression.[79] Almost two-thirds of those with a current diagnosis receive prescriptions for ADHD medications. About 4.4 percent of adults in the U.S. have a diagnosis of ADHD.

Sex/Gender
Males are diagnosed at about two to three times the rate of females. Almost 13 percent of school-age boys and 5.6 percent of school-age girls have been diagnosed.[80] This may be because boys are more prone to the underlying biological or psychological causes, or it may be a matter of overdiagnosis in boys or underdiagnosis in girls. Parents and teachers may be more likely to ascribe a young boy's hyperactive or rambunctious behavior to ADHD but less likely to recognize a girl's subtler and less disruptive symptoms of inattentiveness.[81] By high school, the gender gap has closed a bit: 19 percent of boys and 10 percent of girls age 14–17 have been diagnosed with ADHD,[82] and by adulthood, men and women receive ADHD diagnoses in relatively equal proportions.

Race and Socioeconomic Status
Rates are still highest in middle- to upper-middle-class white boys, but ADHD is also highly diagnosed in Blacks and Hispanics and those of lower socioeconomic status. Between 2001 and 2010, diagnosis rates rose nearly 70 percent in Black children and 60 percent among Hispanic children. Among Black girls, rates jumped 90 percent.[83] Children living below the poverty line and those covered by Medicaid now have a significantly higher risk of being diagnosed with ADHD.

Professors Stephen Hinshaw and Richard Scheffler have an intriguing explanation for this phenomenon.[84] Southern states—Arkansas, Kentucky, Louisiana, and North and South Carolina—show about 23 percent of school-age boys, especially those in poorer areas of the state, receiving an ADHD diagnosis, while California, Colorado, and Nevada have diagnosis rates below 10 percent (Figure 14.8).[85] Hinshaw and Scheffler investigated racial and ethnic variations, access to physicians, cultural differences, and other factors to explain this difference, but none of these factors explained the discrepancy. Then they considered school funding. In 2002, the No Child Left Behind Act went into effect. As a result, schools started receiving funding if students scored better on standardized math and reading tests. If a child is diagnosed with ADHD, the school can receive extra funds to tutor these children, or put them in smaller classes. Schools also can remove students diagnosed with ADHD from the test pool used to assess the school. Hinshaw and Scheffler found that after a state passed laws tying its schools' funding to their standardized test scores, ADHD diagnoses in that state increased not long afterward.[86]

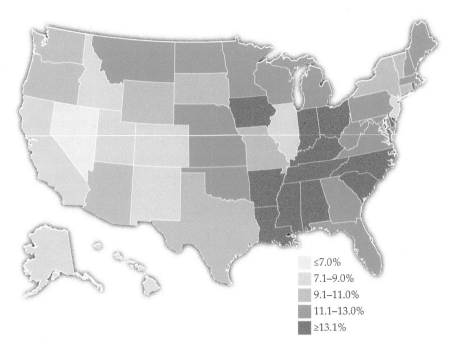

≤7.0%

7.1–9.0%

9.1–11.0%

11.1–13.0%

≥13.1%

FIGURE 14.8. ADHD diagnoses in children, by state. Children in southern states are diagnosed with ADHD at a significantly higher rate than those living in western states, a phenomenon that might be tied to school funding.

Source: Hinshaw, S., & Scheffler, R. (2014). The ADHD Explosion: Myths, medication, money, and today's push for performance. New York: Oxford University Press.

Why the Increase in Prevalence?

Since 1988, the ADHD diagnosis rate has increased more than 11-fold. The rise in diagnoses has been so large and so precipitous that it can't solely be due to neurological changes. Some possible explanations for this phenomenon include the following:

• Medicalization of problems. There is a growing tendency in our society to medicalize problems that, in the past, were attributed to behavioral issues or personality traits. Our great-grandparents might have shaken their heads and said "boys will be boys" when six-year-old Johnny didn't want to stay in his seat and turned in messy homework, but today, we are much more likely to ascribe such behavior to a psychological disorder. Another reason we are prone to medicalize conditions is financial—for conditions to be covered by insurance, they need to be labeled with a recognized condition.

• Direct-to-consumer ads. We are bombarded with direct-to-consumer ads that show us how medication can improve a child's life, and how loving parents want to give their children every possible advantage. A magazine ad for Concerta showed a grateful mother praising the drug, because it resulted in "better test scores at school, more chores done at home, an independence I try to encourage, a smile I can always count on."[90] The FDA has formally reprimanded the manufacturers of every ADHD drug for false, misleading, or exaggerated claims.

• Electronic devices. Many of us stare at screens for most of our waking lives—smart phones, tablets, videos, and TV, all with colorful, rapidly changing images. These images, shown to a developing brain, may potentially change the way we process information. Also, when a child who was raised on these images is put in school, and is dismayed to find that the teacher does not change color and leap across the room with stars coming out of her ears, he or she can grow bored.

Age

ADHD begins in childhood. Most people with ADHD are diagnosed in elementary school, but in some cases, the disorder is not diagnosed until later in life. Often, ADHD does not cease once a child enters puberty. As many as 65 percent of children diagnosed will have symptoms persist into adolescence, although the way the symptoms manifest often changes. Hyperactivity becomes less visible; academic problems may become more of a problem, as the adolescent's cognitive and organizational demands increase; and problems with peers and socialization may become more obvious.[87] Almost one-third of the time, childhood ADHD persists into adulthood, with estimates that about 4.4 percent of the adult population has ADHD.

QUICK HIT

More than 10,000 toddlers in the United States—those under three years of age—are being medicated for ADHD, outside of established pediatric guidelines.[88] Toddlers covered by Medicaid are particularly prone to being put on these medications. The American Academy of Pediatrics standard practice guidelines for ADHD do not address diagnosis in children three years old and younger, because behaviors such as hyperactivity and impulsiveness are considered developmentally appropriate for that age.[89]

STRAIGHT DOPE
A Possible Evolutionary Advantage of ADHD

Having ADHD may be so common because it was evolutionarily adaptive. As hunters, humans needed to adjust to an ever-changing environment where dangers were unpredictable. Having a rapidly shifting but intense attention span and a taste for novelty might have allowed our ancestors to venture out to find a new source of food, and also be especially quick to notice the irate wooly mammoth barreling down on them, thus increasing their chance of survival. To investigate this hypothesis, scientists examined the frequency of a genetic variant of the dopamine receptor in two groups of a tribe in Kenya, some of whom were nomadic, and others who split off and settled in one location. The genetic variant, which is linked to ADHD,

makes the dopamine receptor less responsive than normal. The nomadic men who had the less responsive dopamine receptors were better nourished than nomadic men without the genetic variation. In the settlers, the opposite was true—those with less responsive dopamine receptors were more underweight compared with those without the variation. Alas, this gene may no longer provide adaptive benefits in our sedentary world.

Source: Eisenberg, D.T.A., Campbell, B., Gray, P.B., & Sorenson, M.D. (2008). Dopamine receptor genetic polymorphisms and body composition in undernourished pastoralists: An exploration of nutrition indices among nomadic and recently settled Ariaal men of northern Kenya. BMC Evolutionary Biology, 8: 173.

Ask yourself: Why do you think ADHD is diagnosed so much more frequently today than in the past?

- *Changes in schooling.* We require younger and younger children to be in increasingly structured and demanding academic environments. Elementary schools give more homework, and provide less time for recess, gym, and music than, in the past. It is also significantly harder to get into a good college and to land a job after graduation than it was 30 years ago. Some students in high school and college may seek out an ADHD diagnosis to allow them access to tutors and increased time on standardized tests. Others take ADHD drugs—sometimes called "steroids for school"—to help improve their academic performance.

The main factor, however, underlying the apparent rise in prevalence may be overdiagnosis. A meta-analysis of hundreds of studies found that when standard diagnostic criteria are used, the true prevalence of ADHD stayed steady between 1985 and 2012.[91] In 2013, the new edition of the Diagnostic and Statistical Manual was released. DSM-5 changed the diagnostic criteria for ADHD, such that symptoms had to be present by age 12 rather than age 7, which increased the window for diagnosis. It may be relevant to note that over three-quarters of the DSM-5 working group members for the ADHD section had ties to the pharmaceutical industry.[92]

In one study, researchers sent hypothetical descriptions of children to 1,000 mental health professionals. Some of the vignettes included several symptoms of ADHD, but did not qualify as an ADHD diagnosis. Still, almost 17 percent of the therapists diagnosed those children with ADHD, and these errors were especially frequent for boys, possibly because therapists are more likely to diagnose boys with ADHD.[93]

Causes of ADHD

We don't know the exact causes of ADHD. Genetic, biological, and environmental factors contribute to its development. First-degree relatives of those with ADHD are two to eight times more likely than unrelated individuals to have the disorder.[94] Adoption and twin studies suggest that ADHD is a highly heritable condition.[95,96,97,98] ADHD is most likely due to a complex interaction involving numerous genes. Some of the genes thought to be involved control dopamine and serotonin transport in the brain.[99]

There are neuroanatomical differences in those with ADHD. People with ADHD have significantly reduced brain volume in the frontal lobe, hippocampus, basal ganglia, amygdala, and cerebellar areas that are involved with attention.[100,101] These brain circuits are rich in norepinephrine and dopamine, but the precise role of dopamine in ADHD is unclear.

Positron emission tomography (PET) scans of never-medicated ADHD patients show low levels of dopamine receptors in the frontal lobe and in reward centers of the brain (Figure 14.9).[102,103] This may make normally interesting activities seem dull, and repetitive and routine tasks seem especially unrewarding. This finding, however,

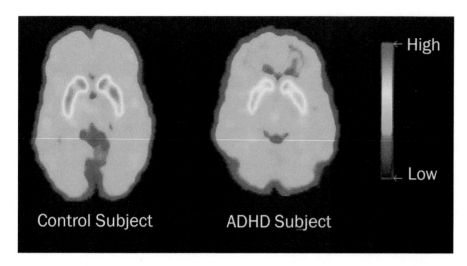

FIGURE 14.9. Brain scans of individuals with ADHD. Compared to controls, individuals with ADHD have lower levels of dopamine transporters in the nucleus accumbens, as seen by the less vibrant comma-shaped yellow bands on the right.

Source: Volkow, N.D., Wang, G-J., Kollins, S.H., Wigal, T.L., & Newcorn, J.H., et al. (2009). Evaluating dopamine reward pathway in ADHD: Clinical implications. JAMA, 302(10): 1084–91.

is not as clear cut as it seems. Like so many conditions, symptoms of ADHD lie along a continuum; the relationship between dopamine levels, attention, and response to ADHD drugs is complex; and any possible defects in dopamine alone do not seem to account for an ADHD diagnosis.[104]

Sleep disorders such as insomnia and sleep apnea may also underlie ADHD.[105,106,107,108] Sleep-deprived adults seem drowsy and sluggish, but sleep-deprived children often become wired, moody, and stubborn, and have trouble focusing and sitting still. Unfortunately, many of the stimulant drugs used to treat ADHD may exacerbate this problem and further reduce sleep.

Environmental factors also influence the development of ADHD. Exposure to domestic violence, chaotic living situations, secondhand smoke, and a lack of social support from friends or relatives may increase ADHD behaviors.[109,110] Children whose mothers smoked while pregnant, who abused alcohol or other drugs, used acetaminophen, or who did not breastfeed them have higher rates of ADHD.[111,112] Premature babies who were given corticosteroids to help their breathing also have higher rates.[113]

Even your birthdate can affect your chance of being diagnosed with ADHD. No, it's not related to your astrological sign, but rather to how old you are in relation to others in your class.[114,115,116] Most states have a cutoff date for when a student may enter a grade. Imagine two boys—Jason and Jeremy—both entering kindergarten. Their school's cut-off date is September 1. Jason is born in August; he makes the cut-off and enters kindergarten when he is 5 years and 1 month old. Jeremy, born in September, does not make the cut, so he will enter next year, when he is 5 years and 11 months old. Jason—who is one of the youngest and least developmentally mature students in the class— will be significantly more likely to be diagnosed with ADHD than Jeremy, who is almost a full year older than others in his class. If ADHD were solely a neurological disorder, then a child's age shouldn't affect the likelihood of diagnosis, but numerous studies found that elementary school children who were among the youngest in their grade were 34–70 percent more likely to be diagnosed with ADHD than their older peers in the same grade.[117,118,119]

Consequences of ADHD

Attention-deficit/hyperactivity disorder can cause problems in many areas of life. People with ADHD may have trouble keeping up with school or work assignments, managing finances, or following rules. These characteristics also can have a negative effect on one's relationships. ADHD is also associated with a variety of physical and mental health problems.

Those with untreated ADHD often function below their ability. In school, they are three times as likely to fail a grade and be held back and eight times more likely to be expelled.[120] They are less likely to graduate high school or college. At work, undiagnosed or untreated sufferers have lower performance ratings, lower occupational status, and higher job turnover.[121,122]

Adolescents and adults with untreated ADHD have more driving violations, motor vehicle accidents, and suspended licenses.[123] They also have an increased risk of adult criminal activity and incarceration.[124]

People with untreated ADHD also have an increased risk of having comorbid disorders, including anxiety, depression, and conduct disorders; in fact, only 37.5 percent of adults who had been diagnosed with ADHD as children were free of other psychiatric disorders in their late twenties.[125] Adults who had been diagnosed with childhood ADHD had a mortality rate due to suicide nearly five times as high as a control population of the same age.[126,127,128] They also have poorer social relationships and higher rates of alcohol and substance abuse.[129,130,131] Young women who had been diagnosed with ADHD during childhood are more likely to become involved with violent partners and have four times the rates of unplanned pregnancies as women without ADHD.[132]

ADHD may even affect later obesity—adult men who had childhood ADHD showed almost twice the obesity rates compared with men who did not have ADHD in childhood.[133,134] The reasons for this are unclear. A common genetic factor may underlie both ADHD and obesity; perhaps increased impulsivity drives individuals to overeat; or a third factor, such as insomnia, may underlie both conditions. Although ADHD is associated with some negative consequences, early and accurate diagnosis, followed by appropriate treatment, can dramatically improve these long-term outcomes.

Pharmacological Treatments for ADHD
Almost two-thirds of those who are diagnosed with ADHD in the United States are prescribed stimulant drugs (Figure 14.10). Since the 1980s, the use of drugs to treat ADHD has increased 20-fold[135]; today, the United States consumes over 80 percent of the world's ADHD drugs. Over five percent of those age 12 and older—some 14.3 million people—and 6.6 percent of those age 12–17 used a prescription medication for ADHD in 2019.[136] It is hard to know the exact preva-

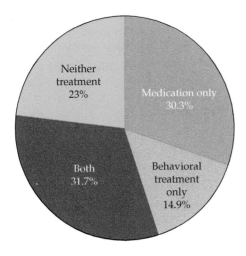

FIGURE 14.10. Treatments received in children with current ADHD, by percentage. 62% of children with a current diagnosis of ADHD receive medication. Of those who receive no treatment, half have no health insurance.

Source: Danielson, M.L., Bitsko, R.H., Ghandour, R.M., Holbrook, J.R., & Hogan, M.D., et al. (2018). Prevalence of parent-reported ADHD diagnosis and associated treatment among U.S. children and adolescents, 2016. Journal of Clinical Child and Adolescent Psychology, 47(2): 199–212.

lence, but various studies have estimated that up to one-third of college students try to improve their academic performance by taking stimulant pills. These students should understand that because these drugs are classified as schedule II (the same category as cocaine), giving or accepting even one Adderall without a prescription is a federal crime.[137]

The most common ADHD drugs are stimulants such as methylphenidate and amphetamine (Figure 14.11). Ritalin, Concerta, and Focalin are the most common brands of methylphenidate and Adderall, Dexedrine, and Vyvanse are commonly administered amphetamines (Table 14.3). In recent years, non-stimulant alpha-2 agonists such as clonidine and guanfacine have increased in popularity.

Pharmacokinetics of ADHD Drugs
Stimulant drugs to treat ADHD are administered orally and are well absorbed in the gastrointestinal tract. They are available as immediate release, which has its peak action within two to four hours; sustained release, active for three to eight hours; and extended release, which works for eight to twelve hours. Typically, children begin with a low dose, but the dose may be increased gradually depending on the child's response as judged by parents, teachers, and the physician. Some users abuse these medications by crushing the tablets and snorting the powder, which gives a much faster onset of action, and is more dangerous and addictive.

Mechanism of Action of ADHD Drugs
Attention-deficit/hyperactivity disorder may be caused, in part, by reduced dopamine and norepinephrine activity in the brain. Both methylphenidate and amphetamine increase dopamine and norepinephrine levels in the nucleus accumbens, striatum, and other areas.[140] Methylphenidate works mostly by blocking reuptake of dopamine, norepinephrine, and serotonin; amphetamines block reuptake of these neurotransmitters but also increase release of dopamine.[141]

It may seem counterintuitive that a drug that increases norepinephrine—one of the neurotransmitters

TABLE 14.3.   Top-Earning ADHD Drugs in the United States, 2018

Drug	Amount earned for manufacturer	Number of prescriptions
Adderall (dextroamphetamine)	$1.914 billion	33,807,381
Concerta (methylphenidate)	$2.176 billion	15,104,867
Kapvay (clonidine)	$171 million	15,058,561
Vyvanse (lisdexamfetamine)	$3.594 billion	11,569,232

Source: Grohol, J.M. (2019). Top 25 psychiatric medications for 2018. https://psychcentral.com/blog/top-25-psychiatric-medications-for-2018/

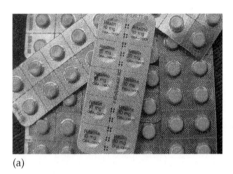
(a)

(b)

FIGURE 14.11. Concerta (a) and Adderall (b) are two commonly prescribed drugs for Attention-Deficit/Hyperactivity Disorder. In 2015, ADHD medication accounted for almost $13 billion in sales in the United States.

• Headache
• Dizziness
• Dilated pupils

• Increased focus and attention
• Insomnia
• Decreased appetite
• Dry mouth

• Increased heart rate and blood pressure

• Stomachache
• Nausea

• Potential for moodiness, anxiety, irritability, and bizarre behaviors
• Dependence can develop

FIGURE 14.12. Acute effects of ADHD medications.

of the sympathetic nervous system—can be used to treat hyperactivity. These drugs boost levels of norepinephrine located in an area of the brain called the locus coeruleus, which helps focus attention and filter out extraneous stimuli.

Alpha-2 agonists such as clonidine and guanfacine are also given for ADHD, typically in conjunction with stimulant medications. These non-stimulant drugs increase norepinephrine in the locus coeruleus, and can help ADHD symptoms such as hyperactivity, impulsivity, and insomnia.

Physiological and Psychological Effects of ADHD Drugs

The physiological and psychological effects of stimulant drugs used to treat ADHD are similar to those of amphetamine and cocaine (Chapter 5). Users experience increased focus, alertness, arousal, and elevations in heart rate and blood pressure (Figure 14.12). Some studies suggest that those who treat their ADHD with medication improve their test scores and grades (although the magnitude of these effects and how long they last is uncertain). Treatment may help social acceptance among peers, and may make life easier for parents and teachers. One study suggested that children who took ADHD meds were less likely to abuse alcohol or drugs later in life,[142] but more recent studies do not show that to be true.[143]

Some common side effects include headache, dizziness, stomachache, nausea, loss of appetite, and insomnia. The appetite suppression and insomnia are particularly concerning, because these drugs are most commonly given to children, who need adequate food and sleep for proper growth and development. These drugs can also cause agitation, irritability, heart palpitations and rapid heart rate, and in some cases can raise the risk of psychotic behavior or worsen existing psychosis.

The human brain is a work in progress and is constantly changing, growing, and adapting, especially during childhood and adolescence. Giving powerful psychoactive drugs to children as young as two or three years old may have long-term effects on the brain.

Overdose can cause a wide array of symptoms, including teeth grinding, obsessive-compulsive repetitive behaviors, aggressiveness, paranoia, confusion, and hallucinations.[144] The dose required to produce these effects varies, depending on the user's size and pattern of use. These physiological and psychological effects usually resolve within hours or days, but in some cases have lasted for weeks or longer.[145]

Although fairly rare, there are cases of sudden death and serious cardiovascular events in those on prescribed doses of methylphenidate and amphetamines.[146] The former commissioner of the FDA stated that adverse event reports received by the FDA probably represent only about 1 percent of the actual number of adverse events.[147] Dangerous effects increase sharply if one crushes the pills and snorts them.

Finally, medicating ADHD may have a societal impact. Some people are concerned that overdiagnosing ADHD gives millions of children the idea that there is something "wrong" with their brains, and that too readily prescribing Ritalin teaches children that all of life's problems can be solved with a pill.[148]

Effectiveness of ADHD Drugs

Every day, millions of children are given drugs to treat ADHD, but how effective are they? These drugs enhance focus and increase the ability to concentrate, but are they associated with significant, real-world improvements in grades, learning, and academic achievement?

Many studies have documented that ADHD medications have significant short-term impact on quiz scores, classwork productivity, and other objective measures of academic functioning.[149,150] But it is less clear whether long-term medication improves behavioral problems, relationships with peers, or grades.

Some studies suggest that long-term use of drugs to treat ADHD is associated with improvements in test scores and grades, although the extent of these improvements is small and the degree to which these improvements translate to "real-world" success is questionable.[151]

Other studies show that these drugs have no long-term benefits on behavioral problems, social interactions, or academic performance.[152] In one study, 579 children with attention problems, 7–10 years of age, were randomly assigned to receive one of four treatment conditions—ADHD medication, cognitive behavioral therapy, medication plus therapy, or no treatment. After 14 months, the medication group and the medication-plus-therapy group showed fewer symptoms than the other groups, but after three years, these positive effects were gone, and there was no evidence that medication produced any lasting benefits.[153]

Drugs may even worsen the outcomes. In a Canadian study, children who began taking methylphenidate actually did worse at school, had more emotional or relational problems, and were more likely to drop out than those with similar levels of symptoms who did not receive drugs.[154]

So what is going on? Unfortunately, it is particularly hard to analyze these data in a meaningful way.

Nonpharmaceutical Treatments for ADHD

Methylphenidate and amphetamines can improve focus and memory retention, but good study habits are more effective than drugs in improving academic performance.[157] Cognitive behavioral therapy can reduce impulsivity and reinforce positive long-term habits. Indeed, studies show that behavioral therapy, either alone or in combination with drugs, is more effective than medication alone.[158] Mindfulness training—teaching someone to become aware of all incoming thoughts, but not to react to all of them—improved mental performance in adults as well as medication.[159] Children with ADHD show better results when they are first treated with behavioral approaches, such as social skills, rewarding good behavior, and classroom monitoring, than when they immediately start on medication.[160]

Changing one's diet may reduce ADHD symptoms. The Feingold diet, introduced in the 1970s, suggested that food additives, such as artificial colors and flavors, were associated with ADHD. Others believe that hyperactivity in children can result from food allergies and sensitivities. Omega-3 fatty acids (found in walnuts, flaxseed, and salmon) and omega-6 fatty acids (in canola and flax) can reduce hyperactivity and other ADHD symptoms.[161,162] The effects of diet on ADHD are controversial, but eating a healthful diet of nonprocessed foods would be beneficial for everyone.

Exercise also plays a role. In the 1970s, 43 percent of schools in the United States offered daily physical education; today, that number has fallen to 3.8 percent of elementary schools.[163] Many recent studies show that kids who take part in regular physical activity programs before school show significant enhancement of academic performance.[164,165,166]

Critical Evaluation

Does long-term use of ADHD medications lead to academic improvement?

One of the primary reasons that children and adolescents take ADHD drugs is to improve academic performance. But how effective are these drugs in boosting academic success? Use your critical thinking skills to analyze the issues involved.

Study design. A double-blind, randomized, controlled trial is the gold standard of research studies. Many parents, however, do not like the idea of randomly assigning their children to a drug protocol. Also, if a randomized study were performed, would it be ethical to force participants to remain in randomly assigned treatment groups for extended periods of time? How might this make it difficult to obtain long-term data?

Just because someone has been prescribed medication, it doesn't mean he or she is taking it as directed. What if users grow tolerant to the drug's effects, or perhaps the dosage becomes inadequate as they grow? What if they simply refuse to take the drug at all? How can we best evaluate actual medication use?

Analyzing results. How do we measure success? If the child's symptoms disappear? If his or her test scores improve? If he or she gets into college?

How much improvement must there be to signify success? Is statistical significance enough, or must there be real-world improvement? How long must the improvement last—one year? Five years? Ten years?

Reliability of published results. How should we account for bias? Many researchers who write articles citing the benefits of ADHD medications receive financial support from the pharmaceutical companies that produce the drugs. Does this necessarily mean that we should discount their findings? To what degree should their involvement be taken into consideration?

Other factors. How does one know if results are due to drugs or to a different factor? It is important not to confuse correlation and causation. If the test scores of a population of ADHD students on medication go up (or down), it's not necessarily caused by the drugs. There may be inherent differences in home life, personality, socioeconomic status, or other factors between those who take drugs for ADHD and those who do not.

What impact, if any, might teachers' attitudes toward the student have on that student? In one study, when teachers were aware that children had been put on ADHD meds, they rated their academic performance as greatly improved, even though objective measurements showed the quality of their work had not changed.[155] Instead, what *did* change was the students' manageability in the classroom.

What about the placebo effect? In those who don't have ADHD, any possible effect of these drugs on test scores may be due to expectations rather than pharmacology; in a study of college students without ADHD, participants who *believed* that they received Adderall (but actually received a placebo) scored higher on memory and attention tests compared with other participants who believed they got a placebo, even though they actually received Adderall.[156]

Weighing the benefits and risks. How do you weigh the relative importance of academic success, physical health, manageability of classrooms, parental desires, and economic realities to ascertain the best choice for the student?

Chapter Summary

- **Anabolic-Androgenic Steroids (AAS)**
  - » AAS have similar effects to testosterone. Anabolic substances encourage muscle growth, while androgenic ones promote male physiological characteristics.
  - » People usually take AAS to increase muscle size, reduce body fat, feel more attractive, or improve athletic performance.
  - » The use of drugs to enhance athletic performance has occurred for millennia. After several drug-related deaths, the International Olympic Committee (IOC) began banning substances and drug testing athletes. Currently, all major sports ban the use of performance-enhancing drugs.
  - » As many as 4 million Americans have used nonmedical AAS. They are used significantly more often by men than women. The typical user is over 30 years of age, white, educated, employed, and not active in organized sports.

» In addition to AAS, there are many other types of performance-enhancing drugs.
  » CNS stimulants increase heart rate, alertness, and endurance.
  » Pain relievers help one play through the pain.
  » Blood doping increases oxygen transport in the body to improve aerobic capacity and endurance.
  » Beta$_2$-agonists increase lung capacity, and beta-blockers reduce anxiety.
  » Human growth hormone encourages the growth of skeletal muscle and the loss of adipose.
  » Creatine may very slightly increase muscle size and slightly boost ATP levels.
» AAS can be administered orally, by IM injection, or topically.
» Those who abuse AAS often take 100 times the recommended medical dose, or even more.
» Users often cycle their use, by taking steroids for 4–18 weeks, followed by a period of abstinence. They often take several types of AAS at the same time, progressively increase their dose until a peak is reached mid-cycle, and then reduce it.
» Testosterone normally self-regulates its own release, such that it travels to the brain to shut itself off. When a person continually takes high doses of AAS, release of FSH and LH from the pituitary gland will be constantly inhibited.
» AAS increase skeletal muscle mass, especially in the upper body. Due to their inhibitory effects on the pituitary gland, constant administration can lead to reduced sperm production, impotence, and testicle shrinkage in men, and clitoral enlargement and menstrual irregularities in women.
» AAS decrease fat, thicken the skin, and promote male-pattern baldness. They can lead to hypertension, enlargement of the heart, and elevation of "bad" cholesterol. AAS are very hard on the liver and inhibit the immune system.
» AAS users initially report feelings of euphoria and well-being, and increased energy, confidence, and sex drive. Eventually, some may experience severe mood swings, heightened aggression, forgetfulness, confusion, decreased sex drive, and even delusions. The effect of AAS on aggression is controversial.
» AAS are approved to treat androgen deficiency, some forms of anemia, breast cancer, and osteoporosis.

» Tolerance begins with the first dose of AAS. Withdrawal can cause depression, mood swings, fatigue, insomnia, and body dissatisfaction. There is a risk of psychological dependence associated with AAS, and there are approximately 1 million Americans who have experienced AAS dependence in their lifetime.
» Treatment of steroid abuse usually consists of addressing the specific symptoms.
» ATLAS and ATHENA are peer-led, gender-specific, interactive programs that provide information on both the positive and negative effects of steroids, healthy sports nutrition, and alternatives to performance-enhancing drugs.

• **Drugs to Treat Attention-Deficit/Hyperactivity Disorder (ADHD)**
» ADHD is a chronic behavioral disorder in which a person shows developmentally inappropriate levels of inattention, impulsiveness, or hyperactivity. There are no definitive tests to diagnose ADHD, and its diagnosis is open to interpretation of one's symptoms in a certain context.
» Over 9 percent of school-age kids in the United States have received a medical diagnosis of ADHD, which represents a greater than 1,100-percent increase since 1988.
» Some possible explanations for the increase in ADHD diagnoses include overdiagnosis, an increasing tendency to medicalize issues, direct-to-consumer ads, use of electronic devices, and changes in academic environments.
» ADHD is probably caused by a combination of biological and environmental factors and, if left untreated, can lead to problems in many areas of life.
» Most people diagnosed with ADHD in the United States are prescribed stimulant drugs, and use of these drugs has risen 20-fold since the 1980s.
» ADHD drugs increase dopamine and norepinephrine levels in areas of the brain related to attention.
» ADHD drugs have significant short-term effects on quiz scores and classwork productivity, but their long-term effects on academic achievement are less clear.
» ADHD drugs have both positive and negative effects. Nonpharmacological treatments for ADHD can also be considered.

Key Terms

Quiz Yourself!

1. True or false? Anabolic-androgenic steroids (AAS) are classified as schedule IV.

2. True or false? Most of those who use AAS prefer IM injection rather than oral administration.

3. Which of the following are NOT effects of AAS?

    A. Increased skeletal muscle growth

    B. Increased sperm production

    C. Decreased fat

    D. Increased acne

    E. Increased blood pressure

    F. Improved immune function

    G. Increased male-pattern baldness

    H. Increased height and growth if taken during adolescence

4. Match the performance-enhancing drug to its mechanism of action.

    1. Anabolic-androgenic steroids
    A. Increases endurance

    2. CNS stimulants
    B. Increases oxygen-carrying capacity of the body

    3. Blood doping
    C. Dilates the bronchi of the lung

    4. Pain relievers
    D. Increases testosterone levels promoting muscle growth

    5. Beta$_2$-agonists
    E. Allows one to continue playing through the pain

5. True or false? About three times as many adult males as adult females use AAS.

6. True or false? AAS have been proven to cause an increase in aggression in humans.

7. Name two approved medical uses of AAS.

8. What are some reasons for the increase in ADHD diagnoses over the past few decades?

9. Billy and Bobby are both first graders. Billy is 6 years and 1 month old, and Bobby is 6 years and 10 months old. Who is more likely to be diagnosed with ADHD?

10. True or false? ADHD drugs work by boosting levels of GABA in the brain.

Additional Resources

Websites

ATLAS. https://youth.gov/content/athletes-training-and-learning-avoid-steroids-atlas

Videos

Take your pills. 2018. 87 minutes. Available on Netflix.

Books

Schwarz, A. (2016). *ADHD nation. Children, doctors, big pharma, and the making of an American epidemic.* New York: Scribner.

Learn more with this chapter's digital tools at www.oup.com/he/rosenthal2e.

Over-the-Counter Drugs

True or false?

1.
True or false? Acetaminophen is responsible for more poisonings than any other drug.

2.
True or false? People can become dependent on decongestants.

3.
True or false? Chocolate has been found to be a more effective cough suppressant than codeine.

Answers: 1. F (It is second; alcohol is number one), 2. T, 3. T

....

Learning Objectives

- Specify some differences between OTC drugs and prescription drugs.

- List some common OTC drugs.

- Describe some of the risks inherent with unsupervised use of OTC drugs.

- Evaluate the pros and cons of the ease of OTC drug availability.

- Explain the mechanism of action of non-narcotic analgesics and the role of prostaglandins in the body.

- Differentiate among the various forms of non-narcotic analgesics.

- Understand why using cough and cold medications may actually delay healing.

- Specify the actions of some common ingredients found in cough and cold medications.

- Distinguish among the various medications that treat gastrointestinal ailments.

- Assess the value of using drugs to aid weight loss.

Over-the-counter drug (OTC): Medication that is available to the consumer without a prescription.

Throughout this book, we have discussed many types of drugs. Some, such as cocaine, heroin, and LSD, are illegal and available for recreational use only from illicit sources. Others, such as tobacco and alcohol, are legal but regulated, and available for purchase if one is of age. Still other drugs, such as antidepressants or Ritalin, require a doctor's prescription. In this chapter, we will discuss over-the-counter (OTC) drugs, which are legally available to consumers without a prescription. Over 80 percent of adults use OTC meds as their first response to minor ailments.[1] Users of OTC drugs often diagnose themselves and select an OTC product to relieve their symptoms, so the use of these drugs is typically not supervised by a healthcare professional. Therefore, consumers are personally responsible for monitoring the proper use, appropriate dosage, and potential interactions of OTC drugs. But it is important to remember that OTC drugs are just that—drugs—and as such can be misused, abused, or even potentially lethal.

OTC Drugs: Regulation and Dangers

There are over 100,000 **over-the-counter (OTC)** drugs and drug products available today. These products include more than 1,000 active ingredients and cover more than 80 therapeutic categories (Figure 15.1), including[2,3]

- Pain relief
- Cough, cold, and allergy treatment
- Heartburn, constipation, and diarrhea
- Weight loss
- Sleep aids
- Treatment of minor infections

The typical American consumer makes 26 trips a year to a drugstore or supermarket to purchase OTC products, as compared to an average of three annual visits to a physician.[4] And, on average, in 2019, households in the United States spend about $338 per year on OTC products, for a total of almost $36 billion.[5]

Today, OTC drugs are regulated by the Food and Drug Administration (FDA), which approves the acceptable ingredients, doses, formulations, and labeling, but it hasn't always been so. In the past, patent medicines—compounds that were sold without prescription as medical cures—were unregulated and unlabeled.

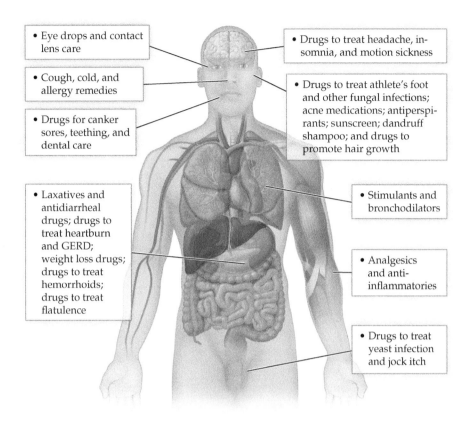

- Eye drops and contact lens care
- Cough, cold, and allergy remedies
- Drugs for canker sores, teething, and dental care
- Laxatives and antidiarrheal drugs; drugs to treat heartburn and GERD; weight loss drugs; drugs to treat hemorrhoids; drugs to treat flatulence

- Drugs to treat headache, insomnia, and motion sickness
- Drugs to treat athlete's foot and other fungal infections; acne medications; antiperspirants; sunscreen; dandruff shampoo; and drugs to promote hair growth
- Stimulants and bronchodilators
- Analgesics and anti-inflammatories
- Drugs to treat yeast infection and jock itch

FIGURE 15.1. OTC drugs. OTC drugs are used to treat conditions that affect the whole body.

History of Over-the-Counter Regulations

In 1906, the passage of the Pure Food and Drug Act required manufacturers to list a drug's ingredients on the label. This was the first law to allow the government some oversight of the drug marketplace. This surveillance continued with the passage of the Food, Drug, and Cosmetics Act of 1938 following a tragic event.

In 1937, the antibiotic sulfanilamide was very much in demand for the treatment of streptococcal infections. Harold Watkins, a chemist at the Massengill Company, dissolved sulfanilamide in diethylene glycol. He added water and some pink raspberry flavor and branded the concoction "Elixir Sulfanilamide." Without checking for toxicity or performing clinical trials, Massengill's salesmen rushed to sell it to doctors and pharmacies across the country. Things soon went horribly wrong. Diethylene glycol is toxic, and over one hundred people died in excruciating pain. Watkins committed suicide while awaiting trial.[6]

The Food, Drug, and Cosmetics Act gave the FDA more authority and responsibility, and greatly increased the accountability of drug companies regarding the safety of drugs, food, cosmetics, and medical devices. Under the new law, drug companies were required to label products with adequate directions for safe use, and to determine if drugs should be sold over the counter or by prescription. The act also required pharmaceutical companies to show that newly developed prescription drugs were both safe and effective before they could be marketed. The Kefauver-Harris Amendment of 1962 extended this regulation to nonprescription drugs.

Such regulation, however, was easier said than done. At the time the Amendment was passed, there were over 300,000 different OTC medications already being marketed, so the FDA decided they would review each active ingredient, rather than each individual product. They divided the existing OTC drugs into different categories, including analgesics, cough and cold remedies, and sleep aids, and appointed an advisory panel to review each category. The FDA ruled that although new products would have to be evaluated before being approved for sale, any existing OTC drugs could remain on the market until they were evaluated for safety and effectiveness. According to the FDA,[7] *safety* means "a low incidence of adverse reactions or significant side effects under adequate directions for use and warnings against unsafe use as well as low potential for harm which may result from abuse," and *effectiveness* is defined as "a reasonable expectation that, in a significant proportion of the target population, the pharmacological effect of the drug, when used under adequate directions for use and warnings against unsafe use, will provide clinically significant relief of the type claimed."

Today, the FDA regulates both prescription and OTC drugs. The dose and potency of the active ingredients in OTC drugs must typically show a greater margin of safety than that required of prescription drugs. The active ingredients are continually evaluated for safety and effectiveness. This means that sometimes drugs (such as phenylpropanolamine, the active ingredient in the diet aid Dexatrim) are removed from the marketplace, and other drugs previously available only by prescription are made available OTC (Table 15.1).

TABLE 15.1.   Previously Prescription Drugs Now Available OTC

Drug	Use
Actifed (chlorpheniramine, phenylephrine)	Decongestant
Advil, Motrin (ibuprofen)	Analgesic, anti-inflammatory
Aleve (naproxen)	Analgesic, anti-inflammatory
Allegra (fexofenadine)	Allergy
Alli (orlistat)	Weight loss
Benadryl (diphenhydramine)	Antihistamine
Claritin D (loratadine and pseudoephedrine)	Allergy, cold medicine
Cortaid (hydrocortisone)	Anti-inflammatory
Dimetapp (brompheniramine, phenylephrine)	Antihistamine, cold medicine
Dramamine (dimenhydrinate)	Motion sickness
Flonase (fluticasone)	Allergy
Imodium (loperamide)	Antidiarrheal
Monistat (miconazole)	Antifungal, yeast infections
Nexium (esomeprazole)	Reduce acid secretion in the stomach
Nicotrol (nicotine)	Smoking cessation
Pepcid AC, Tagamet (cimetidine)	Heartburn
Plan B (levonorgestrel)	Emergency contraception
Prilosec (omeprazole)	Reduce acid secretion in the stomach
Rogaine (minoxidil)	Hair growth
Sominex (diphenhydramine)	Sleep aid
Voltaren (diclofenac)	Anti-inflammatory
Zyrtec (cetirizine)	Allergy

It's not just the drugs that are regulated by the FDA, the labels and even the bottles themselves must adhere to certain standards. In 1999, the FDA standardized the required drug facts label. The following information must appear, in this order, on OTC drug labels (Figure 15.2)[8]:

- The product's active ingredients, and the amount in each dose
- The purpose and uses of the product
- Specific warnings regarding the product's use, side effects that may occur, and substances or activities to avoid
- Directions as to the product's use, including when, how, how much, and how often to take the drug
- The product's inactive ingredients

In addition, some containers are made to be child-resistant (meaning that most five-year-olds would not be able to open them within five minutes) and tamper-resistant.

Dangers of Over-the-Counter Drugs and Self-Care

Over-the-counter drugs may seem harmless, but there are dangers inherent in their use. In addition to making a correct diagnosis and using the appropriate drug, patients must be sure to take the appropriate dosage for the required length of time, administer the drug as directed, and store it properly. OTC drugs have an expiration date and become less effective over time. For example, over time, aspirin develops a hard, external shell that increases the breakdown of its active ingredient into salicylic acid and acetic acid. Moisture and heat also increase the speed of decomposition. If aspirin smells like vinegar, it should be discarded.

Drug interactions are another concern. OTC drugs can interact with prescription drugs, alcohol, birth control pills, or even food.

- NSAIDs (nonsteroidal anti-inflammatory drugs such as aspirin, ibuprofen, and naproxen) may interact with alcohol, warfarin (blood thinner),

FIGURE 15.2. Drug labels. The FDA requires uniform standards for OTC drug labels.

and MAO inhibitors (antidepressants); and dextromethorphan (a cough suppressant) may interact with alcohol, grapefruit juice, and with other drugs that treat allergy, cough, and cold.

- Antacids should not be taken with NSAIDs, and Prilosec (a proton pump inhibitor used for treatment of gastrointestinal [GI] ailments) interacts with the SSRI Celexa.
- The herbal supplement St. John's wort may decrease the effectiveness of the birth control pill, and kava (an herbal remedy sometimes used to treat depression and anxiety) interacts with many drugs, including buprenorphine (a synthetic opioid used to treat opioid addiction), Abilify (a third-generation antipsychotic), and drugs that treat allergy, cough, and cold.

Some users may have a response to, or even be allergic to, active or inactive ingredients in the medication. For example, lactose, an inert filler in many capsules and tablets, can cause diarrhea, dehydration, and cramping.[9]

Finally, some OTC medications can cause dependence. Overuse of nasal decongestant spray, antacids, or even Chapstick can lead to a rebound phenomenon that necessitates frequent use of the product.

SSRIs, and diuretics (covered in more detail in Table 15.2).

- Decongestants can cause a dangerous reaction when combined with tricyclic antidepressants or caffeine; antihistamines (used to combat allergies) can interact with sedatives, attention-deficit/hyperactivity disorder (ADHD) drugs,

TABLE 15.2. Drugs that Interact with OTC Pain Medications

Food or Drug	When Taken with	Can Produce
Warfarin or other drugs that prevent clotting	Aspirin or other NSAIDs	Hemorrhage/increased bleeding
Garlic, ginkgo, fish oil, and other natural substances that have COX2 inhibiting properties	Aspirin or other NSAIDs, acetaminophen	Increased erosion of stomach lining
Products containing calcium, aluminum, magnesium (such as antacids)	Aspirin or other NSAIDs	Increased NSAID elimination, so decreased levels of NSAIDs in the blood
More than two drinks a day of alcohol	Aspirin, acetaminophen	Increased risk of internal bleed, GI bleed, Increased risk of liver damage
Ibuprofen, naproxen	Aspirin	Reduced heart-protective properties of aspirin, Exacerbates erosion of stomach lining
Diuretics	NSAIDs	Decreased efficacy of diuretics
SSRI	NSAIDs	Decreased efficacy of SSRI

STRAIGHT DOPE

The Chicago Tylenol Murders

On September 29, 1982, in a suburb of Chicago, 12-year-old Mary Kellerman woke up with a sore throat, and her parents gave her a Tylenol to soothe her pain. She died within hours. Later that morning, in a town a few miles away, a 27-year-old postal worker named Adam Janus also died suddenly, and his family gathered at his home. Adam's brother Stanley and sister-in-law Theresa had headaches, so they each took a Tylenol from the same bottle Adam had used earlier in the day. Stanley and Theresa died soon after. Over the next few days, three more people in the Chicago area died.

Investigators discovered that all of the deceased had taken Tylenol shortly before they died, and it was soon found that the Tylenol capsules in random bottles spread throughout the Chicago area had been laced with cyanide. The tampered bottles came from different factories. Investigators believe that the culprit purchased bottles from various supermarkets, added cyanide to the capsules, returned to the stores, and placed the bottles back on the shelves.

Johnson & Johnson immediately ordered a nationwide recall of Tylenol products estimated to encompass over 31 million bottles, at a retail value of over $100 million (Figure 15.3). The event became the impetus for putting tamper-resistant seals on bottles of OTC drugs. As a result, pharmaceutical companies also changed the formulation of many drugs from capsules, which can be easier to tamper with, to solid tablets.

No suspect was ever charged or convicted.

FIGURE 15.3. The Chicago Tylenol murders. In 1982, seven people died after taking Tylenol that had been laced with cyanide.

Critical Evaluation

Should OTC drugs be more or less available than they currently are?

Ninety-three percent of Americans prefer to treat minor ailments and illnesses with OTC drugs before seeing a doctor.[10] But should OTC drugs be the first line of defense? Do their benefits outweigh their risks? Use your critical thinking skills to evaluate some of the issues involved.

Effectiveness. Many OTC drugs alleviate symptoms rather than cure the underlying cause. How effective are OTC drugs? Should it matter if a drug actually cures the problem?

Risks versus benefits. OTC meds give people 24-hour access to affordable health care. Without OTC medications, 60 million Americans would not seek treatment for illnesses.[11] On the other hand, consumers are not physicians. OTC medications require consumers to self-diagnose, choose the proper medication at the right dose, and avoid drug interactions. Consumers also may not be aware of the dangers of overdose and side effects that can occur with any drug. How should we weigh the risks and benefits of OTC drugs?

Economic considerations. Americans spend almost $36 billion a year on OTC products. But what are the savings? The Consumer Healthcare Products Association estimates that every dollar spent by American consumers on OTC drugs saves the health care system over $7.[12] OTC drugs are thought to save $95 billion a year in clinical office visit fees and $52 billion a year in drug costs, because OTC drugs are typically less expensive than prescription drugs. In addition, OTC drugs can reduce losses in workplace productivity, because people are less likely to call in sick or take time off work to visit their doctors, a savings of perhaps $34 billion per year.[13] How much should convenience and cost be considered when talking about health?

Autonomy. OTC drugs may give individuals more independence and control over their health than they would have if they had to rely solely on physicians for all medical concerns. Should a pharmacist be available to confer with patients about their OTC drug choices? If so, should they be legally responsible if the patients have a bad reaction?

Social considerations. There is an old saying: "A headache is not a sign that your body is low on aspirin." OTC drugs are easily available 24 hours a day—they are accessible in the middle of the night to reduce a fever, and they are easy to pop in a restaurant to relieve heartburn. Does the availability of OTC drugs make us believe that pills are the answer to our problems and discourage us from seeking out and dealing with the underlying causes?

Non-Narcotic Analgesics

At one time or another, everyone feels pain. For severe, chronic pain, some people may take opioids (Chapter 7), but their side effects and potential for addiction make them less than ideal. For mild to moderate pain, millions of people turn to non-narcotic, nonsteroidal analgesics, such as aspirin, acetaminophen, ibuprofen, naproxen, and diclofenac. Of these, aspirin, ibuprofen, naproxen, and diclofenac are classified as **NSAID**s—nonsteroidal anti-inflammatory drugs. Acetaminophen does not reduce inflammation, so it is not an NSAID.

History of Non-Narcotic Analgesics

Ancient Egyptians and Greeks used the bark from willow trees to treat a variety of ailments. Hippocrates (440–377 BCE) recommended using willow bark extract to treat pain, gout, and other conditions, and American Indians drank willow bark tea to reduce fever.[14] In the mid-nineteenth century, willow bark's active ingredient—salicylic acid—was isolated, identified, and synthesized. Salicylic acid treated pain, but it was very hard on the digestive system.

The conventional wisdom about aspirin's discovery is that Felix Hoffmann, a chemist at the Bayer Company in Germany, created aspirin in 1897. As the story goes, Hoffmann's father suffered from rheumatism and used salicylic acid for treatment, which caused gastric distress, forcing him to discontinue its use. Earlier that year, Hoffmann had added two acetyl groups to morphine and invented heroin. He decided to use the same method by sticking an acetyl group on to salicylic acid, creating acetylsalicylic acid. Hoffman gave some to his father, and it worked well in relieving pain without causing severe stomach upset. Two years later, the Bayer Company began to market acetylsalicylic acid as Aspirin.

This story, however, may not be entirely accurate. It is true that Hoffmann was the technician that added the acetyl groups, but he did so under the direction and supervision of Arthur Eichengrün, a German Jew. Another of Hoffmann's supervisors, Heinrich Dreser, was much more interested in the potential clinical effects of heroin, but Eichengrün was convinced that acetylsalicylic acid had potential benefits. Therefore, he tested the drug on himself and smuggled some samples to doctors, who all reported positive responses. Aspirin was launched two years later, in 1899, despite pushback from Dreser, who thought the product was worthless.

It wasn't until 1934 that Heinrich Dreser published a paper giving himself and Hoffmann full credit for aspirin's invention and development. The year is significant—in 1934, the Nazis had come to power in Germany, and Jews were being forced out of professions. Indeed, Eichengrün was later interned in a concentration camp, and he was not able to write about his role in aspirin's development until after the war.[15] The laboratory records from the Bayer Company support Eichengrün's claim.

Bayer Aspirin has been available without prescription since 1915. Since then, pharmaceutical companies have developed several other non-narcotic analgesics. Acetaminophen (e.g., Paracetamol and Tylenol) was discovered in 1877 and has been available OTC since 1955. Ibuprofen (e.g., Advil) was launched in the United States in 1974 and has been available without prescription since 1984; naproxen (e.g., Aleve) has been approved since 1994 for OTC use; and diclofenac (e.g., Voltaren) was approved for OTC use in 2020.

Prevalence of Non-Narcotic Analgesic Use

Over-the-counter pain medications are among the most commonly used drugs in the world. In the United States, about 43 million adults take aspirin at least three times per week.[16] Even more use acetaminophen; more than 60 million Americans—about one-quarter of adults—use acetaminophen at least once a week.[17] More than 30 million people around the world and

Ask yourself: Do you think of OTC drugs as less dangerous than some of the other drugs covered in this book? Why or why not?

NSAID: A nonsteroidal anti-inflammatory drug such as aspirin, ibuprofen, or naproxen that is often used to treat mild to moderate pain, as well as inflammation.

17 million people in the United States use non-narcotic analgesics on a daily basis.[18,19]

Pharmacokinetics of Non-Narcotic Analgesics

The clinical dose depends on the type of analgesic used, but typically varies from 200–650 mg. These drugs are well absorbed in the stomach, but taking them with food or antacids may in some cases slow or reduce their absorption into the bloodstream. Most give pain relief for four to six hours, but naproxen is more potent than other non-narcotic analgesics and is typically taken every 12 hours.

Mechanism of Action of Non-Narcotic Analgesics

Aspirin was used for decades before anyone began to understand its mechanism of action. In 1971, John R. Vane discovered that aspirin works by blocking the synthesis of prostaglandins. For this discovery, Vane was awarded the Nobel Prize for medicine in 1982.[20]

Prostaglandins

Prostaglandins are substances found throughout the body. Some are produced and released when cells are damaged or injured. They have diverse effects—some transmit signals of pain to the brain; others regulate body temperature in the hypothalamus; some promote the aggregation of blood platelets that is part of the normal clotting process; and still others are involved in inflammation.

COX1 and COX2

Nonsteroidal anti-inflammatory drugs and non-narcotic analgesics inhibit an enzyme called cyclooxygenase (COX), which is involved in the synthesis of prostaglandins. There are two forms of COX that are known to play a role in the regulation of prostaglandins.

COX1 is involved with the normal production of prostaglandins that play a role in many physiological actions, including maintaining normal kidney function, regulating platelets for normal blood clotting, and protecting the lining of the stomach from acid.[21]

COX2 turns on in response to inflammation, leading to increased production of prostaglandins that mediate inflammation, fever, and pain.

Most NSAIDs decrease the production of prostaglandins by inhibiting both COX1 and COX2. Inhibition of COX2 leads to a reduction in pain, inflammation, fever, and a greater risk of cardiovascular side effects; reduction of COX1 can interfere with blood clotting and inhibit the protective mucus layer in the GI tract.

Ibuprofen and naproxen inhibit COX1 and COX2 reversibly, while aspirin irreversibly inhibits these enzymes. Acetaminophen is not generally considered to be a true NSAID, because it does not have significant anti-inflammatory effects. Its exact mechanism of action is unknown, but evidence suggests that part of its analgesic effects is due to activating the endocannabinoid system (Chapter 9).[22,23,24]

Acute Effects and Medical Benefits of Non-Narcotic Analgesics at Low and Moderate Doses

The main therapeutic effects of non-narcotic analgesics are reduction of pain, alleviation of fever, and reduction in inflammation. Some people take a daily low dose of aspirin to inhibit blood clotting. Aspirin and other NSAIDs may have other medical benefits as well.

Analgesia

These drugs are effective for reducing mild to moderate pain without sedation or the risk of addiction. They work better for dull pains such as headaches, muscle aches, or soreness due to inflammation (such as with arthritis) than for sharp pain, stomach pain, sore throat, or toothache. Acetaminophen is about as good a pain reliever as aspirin, and ibuprofen and naproxen are slightly more effective than aspirin. NSAIDs may help alleviate the pain of mild migraine headaches, but for severe migraine pain, medications that contain serotonin or caffeine (Chapter 11) are more effective.

Antipyretic

These drugs can reduce body temperature when a patient has a fever. They do so by blocking the synthesis of a specific prostaglandin that works in the hypothalamus. This prostaglandin normally decreases heat loss by inhibiting perspiration and constricting peripheral blood vessels. When these drugs block the prostaglandin, a person will sweat more and lose heat, thus cooling the body and reducing fever.

Reducing an elevated body temperature, however, is not always wise. Fever is an attempt by the body to destroy invading viruses and bacteria, so lowering fever may be counterproductive. If one's body temperature is at or below 102°F, it might be better left unmedicated, but that decision should be made after consultation with a healthcare professional.

Anti-inflammatory

Inflammation is a condition in which a part of the body becomes swollen, red, warm, and often painful, due to the body's immune response. When caused by an infection or injury, the acute inflammatory response can help wounds heal. But sometimes inflammation itself becomes self-perpetuating, leading to a chronic inflammatory response. And sometimes, a person's body initiates an immune response against its own cells. By inhibiting the COX2 prostaglandin pathway, NSAIDs can help reduce the swelling and pain associated with inflammation.

Anticoagulant

Inhibition of COX1 will prolong bleeding time, because prostaglandins are necessary for platelets to aggregate and allow blood to clot. People at risk of heart attack or stroke are sometimes advised to take a low-dose daily aspirin in order to prevent small clots from forming and blocking the arteries around the heart or in the brain. Because it irreversibly inhibits COX1 and COX2, aspirin has the strongest anticoagulating effects, followed by ibuprofen and naproxen. Acetaminophen does not inhibit platelet aggregation and has no anticlotting effects, so it can be used by hemophiliacs and others in whom failure of blood clotting is a concern.

Cardioprotective Effects

A daily low dose of aspirin (but *not* other NSAIDs) may reduce risk of heart attack and stroke in those who already have experienced these events. Aspirin reduces platelet aggregation, so it lowers the chance of arteries becoming blocked.

Cancer

A daily low dose of aspirin may reduce the risk of developing cancer,[25,26] help reduce metastasis (the spread of cancer cells throughout the body),[27] and reduce the long-term risk of death due to cancer.[28,29] Aspirin may

lower the risk of several common cancers, including colorectal, breast, prostate, and endometrial cancer.

Alzheimer's Disease

Nonsteroidal anti-inflammatory drugs may help prevent Alzheimer's disease, but the evidence is controversial. Observational studies show that those who use NSAIDs seem to have a lower risk of developing Alzheimer's disease.[30,31,32,33] A study of almost 7,000 middle-aged and elderly individuals in the Netherlands found that compared with nonusers, those who had taken NSAIDs daily for at least two years had a lower likelihood of developing Alzheimer's disease, and the longer they had taken NSAIDs, the lower their risk.[34] Randomized trials, however, have found that NSAIDs are not effective in treating patients who already have been diagnosed with Alzheimer's disease or in preventing the onset of dementia.[35] If these drugs do have a protective role, it might be through their anti-inflammatory effects.[36]

Adverse Effects of Non-Narcotic Analgesics

Despite their obvious benefits in certain situations, OTC pain medications may not be the benign substances we think they are. These drugs are estimated to cause at least 16,000 deaths and 100,000 emergency room (ER) visits each year.[37] Acetaminophen is particularly problematic; after alcohol, acetaminophen accounts for the most poisonings of any drug.[38] Aside from risks associated with overdose, extensive use of non-narcotic analgesics can lead to liver damage, kidney damage, enhanced risk of heart attack or stroke, and other potentially fatal conditions. Other side effects, such as gastric upset and decreased blood clotting, are more common.

Talk with your doctor before taking non-narcotic analgesics if you are

- Allergic
- Over 50 years of age
- Pregnant or nursing
- Scheduled for surgery
- Have three or more alcoholic drinks every day
- Have bleeding problems such as hemophilia or are on drugs that thin the blood
- Have irritable bowel syndrome; gout; heart, liver, or kidney disease; peptic ulcer; or gastritis

Side Effects Associated with Non-Narcotic Analgesics

Several side effects can occur with the use of OTC pain medications: some common (GI distress and decreased blood clotting); some less common (cardiovascular problems, asthma exacerbation, and ringing in the ears); and some extremely rare (kidney failure and Stevens-Johnson syndrome). Still other side effects are specific to particular NSAIDs. Aspirin can lead to Reye's syndrome, and acetaminophen is associated with an increased risk of liver failure, blunted emotions, and snake death. About one-half of NSAID users are not aware of the drug's potential side effects.[39]

GI Distress and Decreased Blood Clotting

Because prostaglandins play a role in maintaining the protective mucus layer in the GI tract, many NSAID users experience GI problems. Gastric distress can range from a mild stomachache and heartburn to severe ulcerations and bleeding.

QUICK HIT

One day in 2013, two thousand dead mice, each pumped full of acetaminophen and attached to tiny parachutes, wafted down from helicopters to land on the small U.S. territory of Guam. The reason? Guam was overrun with millions of brown tree snakes—as many as 13,000 per square mile. These snakes, which can grow up to eight feet long, have not only wiped out most of Guam's native forest birds, but they cause numerous power outages each year because they get tangled in electrical lines. But it turns out that these snakes are extremely sensitive to acetaminophen. About 80 mg—one-sixth of a standard pill—is a lethal dose. As the drug-laden mice fell from the sky, the little parachutes got caught in the trees, the tree snakes ate the mice, and the venomous reptile population in Guam slowly decreased (Figure 15.4).[40,41]

Nonsteroidal anti-inflammatory drugs block the production of prostaglandins that are involved in platelet aggregation, so users' ability to clot is impaired. Aspirin

FIGURE 15.4. Tylenol is toxic to snakes. In 2013, 2000 dead mice stuffed with acetaminophen were airlifted down to try to eradicate the snake population in Guam.

does this irreversibly; a single 40-mg dose of aspirin will inhibit platelet function for the life of the platelet (8–11 days) and double the normal bleeding time for about a week.[42] Ibuprofen and naproxen block progesterone reversibly, so their duration of action depends on the specific dose taken, as well as other factors.[43] Patients with hemophilia or bleeding gastric ulcers should speak to their doctor before using NSAIDs. Acetaminophen causes significantly less GI distress and clotting effects, which is one of the reasons it is the leading form of OTC pain reliever in the United States.[44]

Cardiovascular Problems

Although a daily low-dose aspirin can lower the risk of heart attack and stroke in someone who already has experienced one of these events, the other non-narcotic analgesics actually *increase* one's risk of these cardiovascular conditions, and the risk increases with higher doses and longer use. When taken four to five times a week, these drugs may also raise the risk of hypertension.[45]

Allergy

Some people are allergic to aspirin, and others have a sensitivity such that they cannot metabolize even small amounts, resulting in an overdose. If someone is allergic or sensitive to aspirin, they may also have a reaction to the other non-narcotic analgesics. The symptoms of aspirin allergy include rash or hives; runny nose, red eyes, and swelling of the lips, tongue, and face; headache, coughing, and shortness of breath; muscle weakness; stomach pain; and dizziness or disorientation.

Asthma Exacerbation

In up to 20 percent of those with asthma, NSAIDs can worsen asthma symptoms, sometimes fatally.[46] Use can trigger an immune response that constricts the airway. This effect is not seen with acetaminophen.

Ringing in the Ears

Most NSAIDs can cause temporary ringing in the ears and hearing loss, possibly due to vasoconstriction in the inner ear.[47] This effect is usually completely reversed within two to three days after withdrawal from the drug.

Kidney Failure

Normal kidney function is mediated by prostaglandins, so in rare cases, the use of NSAIDs can impair the kidney's blood supply, interfere with normal processes, and increase the risk of kidney failure. Some degree of kidney damage occurs in approximately 1–5 percent of all patients using NSAIDs, but because their use is so ubiquitous, many people may be at risk. Luckily, the damage is usually short-term and reversible upon drug withdrawal. Patients with other risk factors, such as diabetes and renal dysfunction, or those who are elderly, should discuss NSAID use with their physician.[48]

Stevens-Johnson Syndrome

Stevens-Johnson syndrome (SJS) is an extremely rare disorder of the skin and mucous membranes.[49] The disorder begins with flu-like symptoms, then the face and tongue swell, and a painful, reddish rash spreads across the skin and mucous membranes. The rash forms blisters, and the top layer of the skin dies and falls off. Recovery can take weeks to months. SJS can lead to blindness, permanent skin damage, internal organ damage or failure, or death; SJS is fatal up to 40 percent of the time. SJS usually occurs due to an immune reaction triggered by an infection or medication, such as acetaminophen, aspirin, or other NSAIDs; penicillin; anti-gout medications; or antipsychotics.

Reye's Syndrome

Reye's (pronounced "rise") syndrome is an extremely rare condition that occurs almost exclusively in children who were given aspirin when they had chicken pox or the flu. Symptoms include severe vomiting, lethargy, disorientation, personality changes, and sometimes coma, brain damage, and death. This condition is fatal about 25–30 percent of the time. The exact cause of Reye's syndrome is unknown. This condition also occurs in the absence of aspirin use, although aspirin can increase the risk as much as 25 times. Reye's syndrome may occur due to damage to the energy-producing cells in the liver, which may be exacerbated by aspirin.[50]

Liver Failure

Acetaminophen use is the leading cause of acute liver failure.[51] Each year, hundreds of people in the United States die because of liver failure from unintentional overdoses of acetaminophen, which can occur with two to three times the recommended dose within two days. The risk of liver failure increases when acetaminophen is taken with alcohol, and those with hepatitis or cirrhosis of the liver should use it only with caution.

Loss of Empathy and Blunted Emotions

Some areas of the brain are involved in processing both physical and emotional pain. Compared with those who took a placebo, participants who took acetaminophen for three weeks evaluated unpleasant stimuli less negatively, and expressed fewer hurt feelings in social relationships.[52] Unfortunately, acetaminophen use also is associated with dampened positive emotions and reduced empathy for others.[53]

Use During Pregnancy

If a woman takes aspirin while she is pregnant, the risk of heart problems in the fetus may increase. Ibuprofen and naproxen use can increase the risk of miscarriage. Only acetaminophen appears to be safe during pregnancy,[54] although recent studies have found that use of acetaminophen during pregnancy is associated with a higher risk of ADHD and autism spectrum disorder in children.[55,56] Up to 70 percent of pregnant women in the U.S. have reported taking acetaminophen during pregnancy. Pregnant women should check with their physician before taking any medications.

Drug Interactions

Over-the-counter pain medications will interact with other substances. Some drug interactions are summarized in Table 15.2.

Overdose

Overdoses of non-narcotic analgesics account for hundreds, if not thousands, of deaths each year. In fact, acetaminophen is one of the leading causes of poisoning, and accounts for over 100,000 calls to poison control centers, approximately 56,000 ER visits, 2,600 hospitalizations, and about 500 deaths each year.[57,58] The therapeutic index for aspirin is about 199, for ibuprofen perhaps 150, and about 15 for acetaminophen, although liver toxicity can occur with significantly lower doses.[59] Overdose also can occur if a person takes multiple products containing one of these drugs without knowing it. Given that more than 600 prescription drugs and OTC medications contain acetaminophen, this can occur fairly easily.[60]

An overdose can be either acute, in which a person accidentally or intentionally takes a very large dose at one time, or chronic, in which a regular daily dose builds up in the system over time, sometimes due to compromised kidney function. Overdose symptoms include sweating, thirst, headache, dizziness, mental confusion, upset stomach, hyperventilation, ringing in the ears, and hearing loss. Seizures, coma, and death can occur. Overdoses may be treated with activated charcoal to slow and prevent absorption into the bloodstream, and with dialysis if necessary.

Non-narcotic analgesics have many benefits, but many potential risks as well. Information about the four major types is summarized in Table 15.3.

TABLE 15.3. Comparison of OTC Non-Narcotic Analgesic Drugs

		Aspirin	Acetaminophen	Ibuprofen	Naproxen
Examples		Bayer Aspirin Excedrin	Tylenol Paracetamol	Advil Motrin	Aleve Naprosyn
Chemical name and formula		Acetylsalicylic acid $C_9H_8O_4$	Paracetamol $C_8H_9NO_2$	Isobutylphenyl-propionic acid $C_{13}H_{18}O_2$	Methoxynaphthalen-2-yl propionic acid $C_{14}H_{14}O_3$
Dose*		• 325 mg/tablet • Typical adult dose for pain is 325–650 mg every 4 hours • Maximum dose 4,000 mg/day	• 325 mg/tablet (Extra strength 500 mg/tablet) • Typical adult dose for pain is 325–650 mg every 4 hours • Maximum dose 3,000 mg/day	• 200 mg/tablet • Typical adult dose for pain is 200–400 mg every 4–6 hours • Maximum dose 1,200 mg/day	• 220 mg/tablet • Typical adult dose for pain is 550 mg every 12 hours • Maximum dose 1,000 mg/day
Mechanism of action		Irreversibly inhibits COX1 and COX2 to block production of prostaglandins; may affect COX1 more than the other analgesics	Uncertain mechanism; may reversibly inhibit COX2 or affect serotonin or endocannabinoids	Reversibly inhibits COX1 and COX2	Reversibly inhibits COX1 and COX2
Uses	**Reduces pain**	✓	✓	✓✓	✓✓
	Reduces fever	✓	✓	✓	✓
	Anti-inflammatory	✓		✓	✓
	Inhibits blood clot formation	✓✓		✓	✓
	Other benefits	• May reduce risk of heart attack and stroke • May help reduce risk of some types of cancer • May help prevent Alzheimer's disease • May help reduce risk of retinopathy and cataracts		• May help reduce risk of some types of cancer	
Adverse effects	**GI distress**	Moderate-high	Lowest	Moderate	Moderate-high
	Prolongs bleeding time	✓✓		✓	✓
	Risk of heart attack	Low dose reduces risk of heart attack and stroke	Chronic use may increase risk, but not as much as ibuprofen	Chronic use may increase risk	Chronic use may increase risk, but not as much as ibuprofen
	Kidney damage	Low dose doesn't seem to increase risk	Lowest risk of kidney damage	Use may increase risk	Use may increase risk
	Other risks	• Can cause allergic reaction • Risk of kidney damage • Ringing in ears • Can exacerbate asthma • Extremely rare risk of Stevens-Johnson syndrome • Risk of Reye's syndrome in children and adolescents	• Can cause allergic reaction, but it's extremely rare • Risk of kidney damage, but lower than with NSAIDs • Ringing in the ears • Extremely rare risk of Stevens-Johnson syndrome • Liver damage/failure • Can reduce empathy for others • Will kill your pet snake	• Can cause allergic reaction • Risk of kidney damage • Ringing in ears • Can exacerbate asthma • Photosensitivity • Extremely rare risk of Stevens-Johnson syndrome	• Can cause allergic reaction • Risk of kidney damage • Ringing in ears • Can exacerbate asthma • Extremely rare risk of Stevens-Johnson syndrome

	Aspirin	Acetaminophen	Ibuprofen	Naproxen
Use during pregnancy	May cause damage to the fetus's heart	Considered safe during pregnancy, but use is correlated with increased risk of ADHD and autism spectrum disorder	May increase risk of miscarriage	May increase risk of miscarriage
Overall advantages	• Good for pain, fever, inflammation • Can reduce risk of another heart attack or stroke in those who have already had one	• Good for pain and fever • Less stomach upset, ulcers than other OTC pain meds • Less bruising, bleeding than others, does not interfere with clotting process • Less risk of kidney damage • Safer during pregnancy • Can usually take if allergic to aspirin • Safer for those with asthma	• Good for pain, fever, inflammation • Best for menstrual cramps • Less stomach upset than aspirin, even less if taken with milk or food	• Good for pain, fever, inflammation • Lasts longer than other non-narcotic pain relievers • Less stomach upset than aspirin • Lower risk of cardiovascular complications than ibuprofen
Overall disadvantages	• Can cause stomach upset, so best to take with food • Risk of Reye's syndrome in those under 19 • Prolongs bleeding time	• Not effective against inflammation • Not as effective against pain as ibuprofen and naproxen • Common poisoning agent • Potential for liver damage, especially with alcohol use	• Can cause stomach upset, so best to take with food • Increased risk of heart attack, stroke, blood clots	• Can cause stomach upset, so best to take with food • Increased risk of heart attack, stroke, blood clots

The appropriate dose depends on the desired effect. For example, an appropriate dose of aspirin to alleviate pain might be 325–650 mg every four to six hours, but a daily dose of only 40–80 mg is necessary to inhibit platelet aggregation. The doses given here are to treat mild to moderate pain. It is best to consult with a medical professional before taking any non-narcotic analgesic drugs.

Cough, Cold, and Allergy Products

The "common cold" doesn't feel so common when you are coughing and sneezing and hacking your way through miserable days and sleepless nights. In response, every year, Americans spend almost $9 billion dollars on OTC drugs to treat cold symptoms.[61]

But what is a cold? More than one hundred individual viruses can cause a cold. The most common viruses invade the upper respiratory tract and irritate the cells there. After infection, it usually takes two to three days until symptoms appear. The body responds to the infection with an immune response and some nervous system reflexes, which causes the symptoms. Cell irritation leads to an inflammatory response, which makes the membranes of the nose, mouth, and throat swollen and sore. As a means of defense, your mucous membranes will release fluid, causing a runny nose, watery

Ask yourself: Given the potential for adverse effects, how could we make people more aware of the potential negative effects of non-narcotic analgesics?

eyes, and postnasal drip. Cell irritation also activates cough and sneeze reflexes.

There is a saying: "A cold will be gone in a week with treatment, or in seven days without." To date, modern medicine has no cure for the common cold; indeed, it has no cure for any virus (except Hepatitis C). OTC cough and cold medications simply mask the symptoms and may actually delay healing. This is because your body produces these symptoms in an attempt to clear your body of the virus. A cough helps to clear the airway; mucus tries to trap the invading microorganisms; and a fever is your body's attempt to burn the virus out. Nevertheless, millions of people routinely take OTC medications to treat their cold symptoms.

TABLE 15.4. Common Ingredients in Cough and Cold Medications

Type of Drug	Function	Common Active Ingredient	Common Brand Names
Antitussive agent	Cough suppressant	Codeine Dextromethorphan	Robitussin, Robitussin AC, Dimetapp
Expectorant	Reduces thickness of mucus in throat, increases mucus secretion, and makes it easier to expel	Acetylcysteine Guaifenesin	Fluimucil, Mucinex
Decongestant	Reduces swelling in blocked nasal passages	Pseudoephedrine Phenylephrine Oxymetazoline	Sudafed, Sinutab, Afrin, Dristan
Antihistamine	Relieves sneezing, teary eyes, runny nose, and itching	Diphenhydramine Chlorpheniramine	Benadryl, Contac 12 Hour
Analgesic	Relieves headache and reduces sinus pain	Acetaminophen	Tylenol
Antipyretic	Relieves fever	Acetaminophen	Tylenol

Components of Cough and Cold Medications

There are many symptoms of a cold, so most cough and cold medications contain a variety of active ingredients to address a cold's numerous symptoms. These ingredients can include cough suppressants, expectorants, decongestants, antihistamines, analgesics, and antipyretics (Table 15.4).

Cough Suppressants and Expectorants

A cough can be productive—one that removes mucous secretions or foreign matter—or nonproductive—a dry cough that will irritate the throat. Cough medicines often contain antitussives and/or expectorants.

Antitussives are drugs that suppress or prevent coughing. They act in the medulla and raise the threshold for the stimulus to produce a cough. Two common antitussive drugs are codeine and dextromethorphan (Chapter 7). Codeine is an opioid that alleviates cough within 15–30 minutes and provides relief for up to six hours. Its sale is regulated because of the potential for addiction. Dextromethorphan is a non-narcotic cough suppressant found in Robitussin, NyQuil, Dimetapp, Theraflu, Vicks, and other medications. Dextromethorphan has a lower

Antitussive: A drug that suppresses or prevents coughing.

Expectorant: An agent that facilitates expulsion of phlegm from the throat or airways.

Robotripping: The slang term for recreational use of dextromethorphan, the active ingredient in cough suppressants such as Robitussin.

potential for dependency than codeine, although it is sometimes used recreationally for its sedative and dissociative properties.

Expectorants are substances that increase and thin mucous secretions and make a cough more productive. This can help remove mucus and foreign matter from the throat. Two common expectorants are guaifenesin and acetylcysteine.

Cough medicines can cause stomach upset, nausea, and vomiting. Low doses of dextromethorphan cause drowsiness, but at higher doses, the drug acts as a stimulant. Sometimes people use dextromethorphan recreationally, a phenomenon known as "**robotripping**." Recreational users take doses at least 10 times higher than therapeutic. Those who consume 3–10 times the recommended dose may feel euphoria, intoxication, increased energy and confidence, and may feel some slight perceptual effects. At 15–75 times the therapeutic dose, users can experience hallucinations, distorted bodily perceptions, and feelings of dissociation. Dextromethorphan has pharmacological properties similar to (but distinct from) PCP (Chapter 6).

There is no good evidence for the effectiveness of OTC cough medicines.[62] In fact, sucking on hard candies may be just as effective at relieving throat irritation. Honey may also reduce the frequency and severity of the cough as effectively as dextromethorphan, but without its side effects and at a fraction of the cost.[63] Finally, chocolate has been found to be a more effective cough suppressant than codeine, perhaps due to the theobromine (Chapter 11).[64,65]

Decongestants

Decongestants improve airflow by constricting swollen blood vessels in the nose. They come in many forms—nasal sprays, nose drops, liquids, and pills—as well as many formulations—pseudoephedrine (Sudafed), phenylephrine (Neo-Synephrine, Suphedrin), and oxymetazoline (Afrin, Dristan).

Use of pseudoephedrine can cause dry mouth, dizziness, headache, tremor, rapid heartbeat, nausea and vomiting, difficulty urinating, anxiety, and insomnia. The instructions on nasal spray packages indicate they should not be used for more than three consecutive days. If used for longer than recommended, withdrawal to the vasoconstricting effects can occur and lead to a rebound effect, wherein nasal congestion becomes worse than it was originally, causing people to become dependent on the product.[66]

Antihistamines

Histamine regulates many processes throughout the body; for this reason, many drugs—including cough syrup, decongestants, allergy meds, motion sickness drugs, heartburn treatments, and sleep aids—contain **antihistamines**.

There are four known types of histamine receptors. Among other effects, these receptors are responsible for affecting

- H_1 receptors: Inflammatory processes, sleep, itch, bronchoconstriction, and vasodilation
- H_2 receptors: Stimulating acid secretion into the stomach
- H_3 receptors: Influencing neurotransmitter release in the central nervous system (CNS)
- H_4 receptors: Immune response

Many cold and allergy medications contain antihistamines. Allergic reactions increase histamine levels, which makes capillaries more permeable. Fluid then escapes from the blood vessels, causing congestion, runny nose, and watery eyes. Blocking H_1 receptors can alleviate some of the annoying symptoms associated with allergy (their effectiveness in treating colds is not as well established). H_1 blockers also are used to treat insomnia and motion sickness.

Diphenhydramine (Benadryl), fexofenadine (Allegra), and loratadine (Claritin) all block H_1 histamine receptors. Side effects of antihistamines include drowsiness, dry mouth, weakness, and constipation. Some people have an allergic reaction to these drugs and may experience headache, dizziness, blurred vision, hives, and an inability to urinate.

Ask yourself: Due to its potential for recreational use and abuse, some retailers in the United States have moved dextromethorphan-containing products behind the pharmacist's counter. Do you think dextromethorphan should be available OTC? Why or why not?

OTC Drugs to Treat Gastrointestinal Ailments

As a result of our dietary choices and sedentary lifestyle, many people experience heartburn, indigestion, diarrhea, and constipation, and often will turn to OTC drugs to alleviate their symptoms. In 2020, Americans spent almost $4.5 billion on OTC drugs to treat GI ailments.[67]

Drugs to Treat Heartburn, Gastric Reflux, and Peptic Ulcer

Your stomach normally produces hydrochloric acid (HCl), which helps with digestion. When the normal protective properties of the stomach are compromised, however, this powerful acid can irritate and even erode the lining of the stomach or esophagus, leading to heartburn, reflux, or ulcer.

Heartburn, also called acid indigestion, is a burning sensation in the upper abdomen or middle of the chest. Heartburn is a common condition and can be due to overeating; eating too fast; consuming acidic foods, alcohol, tobacco, or caffeine; or lying down after a meal. Heartburn often occurs an hour or two after eating, when the stomach contents have passed into the small intestine, and the HCl remains and irritates the lining of the stomach. When heartburn is chronic or intense, it may be a symptom of gastroesophageal reflux disease.

As many as 28 percent of the adult U.S. population suffers from **gastroesophageal reflux disease (GERD)**.[68] Those with GERD suffer frequent heartburn and regurgitation of stomach acids into the back of the

Decongestant: Medication that improves airflow by constricting swollen blood vessels in the nose; comes in many forms, including nasal sprays, nose drops, liquids, and pills.

Antihistamine: Medication that blocks histamine receptors; found in many cold and allergy products.

Heartburn: Indigestion leading to a short-term burning sensation in the upper abdomen.

Gastroesophageal reflux disease (GERD): A chronic sensation of heartburn, often due to the failure of the valve between the stomach and esophagus.

Ask yourself: The United States has the highest prevalence of GERD in the world. Why do you think this is? Is it due to our diet? Stress? The type of gut bacteria? Or is it simply increased awareness or overdiagnosis?

throat. The pain associated with reflux can be so bad that it can be mistaken for a heart attack. One cause of GERD may be that the valve between the stomach and the esophagus does not close properly, which allows HCl to move back up into the esophagus toward the mouth. Obesity increases the risk, because obesity increases the pressure between the stomach and esophagus. The type of foods eaten also may influence the reflex—acidic, spicy, or fatty foods worsen the condition, as can the type of gut bacteria present. GERD may also be due to an inflammatory reaction.[69]

A **peptic ulcer** is a break in the protective lining of the stomach, lower esophagus, or small intestine. Ulcers cause intense, burning pain and, if untreated, can lead to potentially life-threatening bleeding or perforations. Peptic ulcers often are caused by the bacteria *Helicobacter pylori*, but stress or the use of NSAIDs, tobacco, and alcohol increases one's risk. Peptic ulcer is usually treated with antibiotics, as well as drugs to neutralize the stomach acid. Some drugs that reduce stomach acid include antacids, H_2 blockers, and proton pump inhibitors.

Peptic ulcer: A break in the protective lining of the stomach, often due to the bacteria *H. pylori*.

Antacids

Antacids such as Alka-Seltzer, Rolaids, and Tums contain alkaline ions to give fast—yet short-term—relief of heartburn by neutralizing the acids in the stomach. Some antacids (like Alka-Seltzer) have high sodium levels, which can raise blood pressure. Rolaids and Tums contain calcium carbonate, so they do not raise blood pressure but can produce a rebound effect in which stomach acidity actually increases after the antacid's effects wear off. Antacids also can cause constipation. These drugs should not be used for more than two weeks at a time, and a physician should be contacted if the heartburn persists.

H_2 Blockers

Histamine is necessary for HCl to be secreted into the stomach. Drugs such as Tagamet and Zantac that block H_2 receptors can reduce the symptoms of heartburn, GERD, and peptic ulcer. H_2 receptors are found mostly in the stomach, so the incidence of side effects is fairly low.

Proton Pump Inhibitors

Drugs such as omeprazole (Prilosec), lansoprazole (Prevacid), and esomeprazole (Nexium) irreversibly inhibit the protein that secretes H^+ ions into the stomach, a process that is necessary for gastric HCl secretion. These drugs are the most potent inhibitors of stomach HCl available. Because gastric HCl plays an important role in digestion, taking these drugs may interfere with the absorption of calcium and magnesium, and possibly iron and vitamin B_{12}. High doses, or long-term use, may increase the risk of bone fractures. The FDA recommends these drugs only for short-term use—no more than three 14-day treatment courses within a single year.[70]

> **STRAIGHT DOPE**
>
> ## COVID-19 and Drugs to Treat GI Disorders
>
> COVID-19 has had a devastating effect on the world and has highlighted the need for reliable scientific data, as well as for a population that can critically evaluate the available information. Drugs that treat GI disorders were pulled into the fray in 2020. Some studies reported that proton pump inhibitors were correlated with higher COVID-19 infection rates and risk of death in those hospitalized with the virus. But remember not to confuse correlation with causation. Is this phenomenon related to the drug or to gastric reflux? To inflammation or obesity? Or to some other factor, such as a reduced diversity of gut bacteria? On the other hand, some studies have suggested that the H_2 blocker ranitidine (Zantac) may suppress replication of the virus, leading to decreased viral loads. But many of these studies are done in vitro or in animals, and have not been through clinical controlled trials. The take-home message is to use your critical thinking skills and be measured in your interpretation of the data.
>
> *Sources: Yuan, S., Wang, R., Chan, J. F-W., Zhang, A.J., & Cheng, T., et al. (2020). Metallodrug ranitidine bismuth citrate suppresses SARS-CoV-2 replication and relieves virus-associated pneumonia in Syrian hamsters. Nature Microbiology, 5: 1439–48.*
>
> *Almario, C.V., Chey, W.D., Spiegel, B.M.R. (2020). Increased risk of COVID-19 among users of proton pump inhibitors. American Journal of Gastroenterology, 10.14309/ajg.0000000000000798.*

Drugs to Treat Diarrhea

Most of the time, diarrhea does not require treatment. Although diarrhea usually stops on its own, antidiarrheal medications can help with the cramping and inconvenience of frequent bowel movements. If diarrhea is a result of a parasitic or bacterial infection, however, antibiotics may be in order, and antidiarrheal medication may actually make the situation worse, because diarrhea is the body's response to try to clear the invading organism from the system.

Loperamide (Imodium) mostly acts on opioid receptors found in the large intestine. Loperamide reduces secretions and slows movements of the intestine, giving the body more time to absorb water from the intestine back into the bloodstream. Although it is an opioid, loperamide does not cross the blood–brain barrier to affect the CNS. Bismuth subsalicylate (Pepto-Bismol, Kaopectate) reduces inflammation and may prevent the absorption of bacterial toxins that can cause diarrhea.

Side effects of antidiarrheal drugs include constipation and abdominal pain. Bismuth subsalicylates also may cause blackened stool and/or tongue and ringing in the ears. If you have diarrhea, be sure to replace any lost fluids and electrolytes to prevent dehydration.

Laxatives

Constipation is defined as stool frequency of less than three bowel movements per week, although patients usually define it as any form of difficult defecation—hard stool, straining, or having the urge to go but not being able to move one's bowels.[71] Constipation can occur due to a number of factors, including not eating enough fiber or drinking enough water, stress, or certain drugs, toxins, or diseases.[72] Chronic constipation affects up to 27 percent of the population,[73] and in 2019, Americans purchased over $1.5 billion worth of laxatives.[74]

QUICK HIT

Singer Elvis Presley died on the toilet. Some believe he had a heart attack due to the decreased blood flow to his heart caused by straining to defecate. Elvis had been a long-time user of opioids, which are known to cause constipation.[75]

Laxatives are used to treat and prevent constipation, by loosening stool and increasing bowel movements. Types of laxatives include fiber and bulk-forming agents, stool softeners, lubricants, hyperosmotic agents, and stimulant laxatives.

Dietary Fiber and Bulk-Forming Laxatives

High-fiber foods such as bran, beans, fruits, and whole grains, as well as bulk-forming drugs such as Metamucil and Citrucel, are the gentlest forms of laxatives, and can be used for long-term maintenance of regular bowel movements. These add bulk and water so the stool can pass more easily through the intestines.

Stool Softeners

Straining to defecate can increase the pressure in the chest and temporarily reduce blood flow to the heart, which can be dangerous in the elderly or in those with heart problems. The elderly are disproportionately affected by constipation, so they often take stool softeners to prevent straining when trying to defecate. Stool softeners such as Colace work on the surface of the stool to allow additional water and fats to be incorporated into the stool so that it moves through the GI tract more easily.[76]

Lubricants

Mineral oil and other lubricants coat the surface of the stool with slippery lipids. This slows the absorption of water in the large intestine and allows the stool to slide more easily through the intestine.

Hyperosmotic Agents

Saline and other hyperosmotic agents attract and retain water in the intestine, which stretches the intestine and stimulates evacuation of the bowel. Hyperosmotic agents include MiraLAX, Milk of Magnesia, and Epsom salts.

Stimulant Laxatives

Drugs such as senna and bisacodyl (Dulcolax) are the most powerful of the laxatives. They promote the accumulation of water and electrolytes in the colon, and stimulate movement in the intestine. These drugs should be used with caution, because they can cause dependence in users. Stimulant laxatives can damage the folds of the intestine and make users less able to move feces through the colon on their own.

Side effects of laxatives include diarrhea, flatulence, abdominal cramping, and discomfort. Abuse or overuse can lead to dehydration, hypotension, elevated heart rate, as well as potentially fatal imbalances in pH and electrolytes.

OTC Weight Loss Aids

The World Health Organization reports worldwide obesity has nearly tripled since 1975. Globally, 39 percent of adults are overweight (more than 1.9 billion adults) and

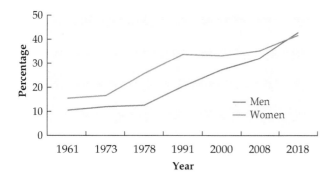

FIGURE 15.5. **Obesity in the United States, 1961–2018.** The percentage of adult men and women who are obese has soared in the past 60 years.

Sources: Hales, C.M., Carroll, M.D., & Fryar, C.D., et al. (2020). Prevalence of obesity and severe obesity among adults: United States, 2017–2018. NCHS Data Brief No. 360.

Fryar, C.D., Carroll, M.D., & Ogden, C.L. (2018). Prevalence of overweight, obesity, and severe obesity among adults age 20 and over: United States, 1960–1962 through 2015–2016.

13 percent, or over 650 million, are obese.[77] In the United States, almost 71 percent of adults age 20 and older are overweight and over 42 percent are obese, as are over 20 percent of those age 12-19, 18.4 percent of those age 6–11 years and 13.4 percent of those age 2–5.[78] Although rates of obesity and overweight have been increasing in prevalence for over one hundred years, they have jumped significantly since the mid-1990s, when the rates were about 27 percent (Figure 15.5). Part of the jump can be traced to 1998, when the National Institutes of Health (NIH) lowered the cutoff for classifying a person as overweight, meaning that overnight, 25 million Americans became "fat" without gaining a pound. There is, however, no doubt that Americans are also getting heavier. By 2030, it is estimated that nearly 1 in 2 adults will be obese.[79]

Although most Americans are overweight, there is still a strong stigma against obesity. Individuals who are overweight experience discrimination in social situations, at school, at work, in health care, and even in jury selection and adoption proceedings.[80,81,82,83]

Many people naively believe that weight control is simply a matter of "calories in equals calories out," but the reality is much more complex. Weight and metabolism are controlled by an intricate interaction of biological, environmental, social, and behavioral factors.

As we've been told again and again, obesity kills. Obesity is associated with higher rates of type 2 diabetes, heart attack, hypertension, sleep apnea, gallstones, and cancer. But we must be careful not to confuse correlation and causation. These health issues may not be due to a person's weight, but rather to stress, poverty, a lack of health care or exercise, or the type of food eaten, all of which are correlated with obesity.

QUICK HIT

To the dismay of diet-drug dispensaries, there is a phenomenon called "the obesity paradox." In a meta-analysis of 97 studies that included 2.88 million people, those who were considered overweight or moderately obese according to the body mass index (BMI) were 6 percent *less* likely to die than were those of normal weight, and the benefits to being overweight increased with age.[84]

Many people want a magic pill that will provide them with a quick fix when it comes to weight loss. Spoiler alert: As of yet, there is no magic pill. Diet drugs do not lead to lasting weight loss, and have significant adverse effects.[85,86,87] Nonetheless, the weight loss industry in the U.S. is worth $72 billion per year.[88] Currently, more than 17,000 diet plans, products, programs, and pills aim to help people achieve their dream body. Although millions of Americans are overweight or obese, only 3 percent of those trying to lose weight reported that they took prescription weight loss medication.[89] This history of weight loss drugs shows a disturbing pattern: A new "miracle" diet pill is released, often over the objections of healthcare professionals who have evaluated the drug. The drug is wildly popular and highly prescribed. People on the drug not only have limited success, but have negative—and sometimes fatal—reactions to the drug, and the drug is pulled from the market. Currently, only a few prescription drugs are approved for weight loss; the latest—Wegovy (semaglutide)—was approved in 2021.

In the past, phenylpropanolamine and ephedra were available OTC for weight loss, but they were pulled from the market due to dangerous side effects and deaths.[90] The pancreatic lipase inhibitor orlistat—marketed as the OTC drug Alli—is the only antiobesity medication currently approved by the FDA for OTC availability. Taken before each meal, orlistat decreases the intestines' ability to absorb fat by about 25–33 percent, depending on the dose. Over the course of a year, those who take orlistat in addition to diet and exercise lose about 8–12 pounds more a year than those not taking the drug. Orlistat helps weight loss by blocking lipase, the enzyme that breaks down triglycerides in the intestine. Because the fats are not broken down, they are not absorbed into the bloodstream and are excreted undigested.

There are some unpleasant side effects associated with orlistat. If fats are consumed, they remain in the intestine, where they pull in water, leading to flatulence, diarrhea, cramping, oily stool, and anal leakage. The manufacturers admit that part of the drug's success is due to aversion therapy—users learn to associate eating fatty foods with distasteful side effects and begin to

Ask yourself: How do you weigh the (usually) short-term benefits against the (often) long-term risks of diet drugs? Due to society's stigma against obesity, there is strong pressure to find a "quick fix" for weight loss. Should the government ban the use of diet drugs, which have been proven to be ineffective, or do people have the right to take these drugs, even if they are ineffective and often dangerous?

avoid consuming fats, including healthy omega-3 fatty acids.[91] As the fats are washed out of the body, they also carry fat-soluble vitamins A, D, E, and K with them.

OTC Sleep Aids

At least 20 percent of the U.S. population experiences insomnia at some point in time, and millions of these sufferers turn to OTC sleep aids. Over 58 million were sold in 2020 alone.[92] Some prescription sleep medications, such as benzodiazepines and Z drugs, are discussed in Chapter 8. OTC drugs to treat insomnia include melatonin, antihistamines, and herbal remedies.

Melatonin is a hormone produced by the brain's pineal gland. It is synthesized in the dark, and helps to regulate the body's biological clock. Melatonin is classified as a dietary supplement, and as such is not regulated by the FDA. Higher doses may help reduce jet lag, but lower doses (less than 1 mg) are better at treating in-

somnia.[93] Melatonin levels can be increased naturally by meditating, avoiding computer and TV screens too close to bedtime, and eating cherries, walnuts, and red grapes.

Antihistamines such as diphenhydramine (Benadryl, ZzzQuil, Tylenol PM, and Nytol) and doxylamine succinate (Unisom, NyQuil) also are used as sleep aids, due to their sedating properties.

Herbal remedies such as valerian root and kava also are sometimes used to combat insomnia. However, the evidence supporting the efficacy of these dietary supplements is weak or nonexistent.

Dietary Supplements

Dietary supplement use is at an all-time high. In 2018, 77 percent of Americans reported consuming dietary supplements.[94] Herbal medications and dietary supplements exist in a gray area of regulation. Prescription and OTC drugs are overseen by the FDA, and their active ingredients, dosages, and side effects are clearly labeled, but dietary supplements are not overseen by the FDA. The Dietary Supplement Health and Education Act of 1994 (DSHEA) reduced the authority of the FDA to regulate these products. Dietary supplements include vitamins, minerals, amino acids, herbs, herbal extracts and concentrates, and even some hormones.

Dietary supplements cannot legally claim to diagnose, prevent, treat, or cure disorders, but they can state that the supplement has beneficial physical or psychological effects, although sellers do not actually have to prove these claims. Also, these products can be sold without clearly labeling the active ingredient, how much is in each tablet, the safe dosage, or potential adverse effects (Figure 15.6). In fact, dietary supplements are not required to undergo testing for safety and efficacy.

The FDA can only ban a supplement if it has been proven to be dangerous; as a result, unsafe supplements can be freely sold until the FDA has gathered enough data to prove that the product presents a significant risk. Figure 15.7 summarizes the scientific evidence for the efficacy of some popular dietary supplements.

FIGURE 15.6. GNC. GNC sells vitamins, herbs, and dietary supplements, but most of their products are not regulated by the FDA for safety or efficacy.

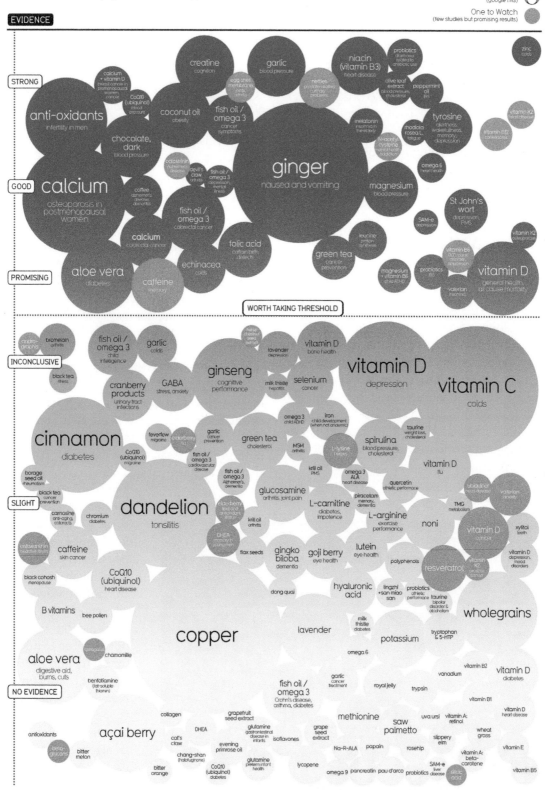

FIGURE 15.7. The efficacy of some popular dietary supplements. While many dietary supplements may claim to have health benefits, the scientific evidence may be lacking for some. This graphic summarizes the existing evidence for a variety of supplements. The larger circles indicate the more popular supplements, and the higher on the Y-axis the supplement appears, the more clinical evidence there is for its efficacy.

TABLE 15.5. Common Dietary Supplements

Dietary Supplement	Common Uses	Cautions
Ginkgo biloba	Used to improve memory or cognition	Can increase bleeding in those who are taking warfarin or aspirin
Ginseng	Used for energy	Dangerous if one has a blood clotting disorder; will increase blood pressure and reduce the effectiveness of antihypertensive agents
Glucosamine	Stimulates growth of cartilage May help reduce inflammation	May exacerbate diabetes
Honey	Softens the cough	Dangerous in children less than one year old; linked to infantile botulism
Kava	Used for depression and anxiety	Many adverse drug interactions
Melatonin	Can help reset circadian rhythm and help with sleep	Can cause some stomach upset
St. John's wort	Antidepressant Antiviral	Can cause GI upset, dizziness, and photosensitivity; should not be taken by women on birth control pills
Valerian root	Sedative actions Treats insomnia	Should not be used in children, or in those with impaired liver function

If you choose to take dietary supplements, the FDA recommends[95]

- Using noncommercial sites such as the FDA, USDA, or NIH rather than the manufacturer's pages when searching for information online.
- Watching out for suspicious statements, such as "totally safe," "cure," "no side effects."
- Obtaining the supplements from a reputable source, and understanding the potential consequences of taking physiologically active substances.
- Letting your healthcare provider know you are taking the supplement.
- Remembering that just because a product is "natural" doesn't mean it is safe. Arsenic and strychnine are also natural.

Ask yourself: Have you ever used alternate therapies—changing your diet, acupuncture, meditation, biofeedback, aromatherapy, massage, etc.—instead of taking an OTC drug or dietary supplement? Why or why not? Did the alternate therapy work?

Some common dietary supplements are found in Table 15.5. Many (if not most) of the purported advantages of these supplements are either untested, inconclusive, or false.

Chapter Summary

- **OTC Drugs: Regulation and Dangers**
  - » Over-the-counter (OTC) drugs are legally available to consumers without a prescription.
  - » Users of OTC drugs often diagnose themselves and select an OTC product to relieve their symptoms, so the use of these drugs is typically not supervised by a health care professional.
  - » There are over 100,000 OTC drugs and drug products available today.
  - » The FDA regulates OTC drugs and approves the acceptable ingredients, doses, formulations, and labeling. The dose and potency of the active ingredients in OTC drugs

must typically show a greater margin of safety than that required of prescription drugs.
  - » There are both advantages and disadvantages to the ease of access to OTC drugs.
- **Non-Narcotic Analgesics**
  - » Non-narcotic analgesics include aspirin, acetaminophen, ibuprofen, and naproxen. Of these, aspirin, ibuprofen, and naproxen are classified as NSAIDs—nonsteroidal anti-inflammatory drugs.
  - » The active ingredient in aspirin comes from the bark of willow trees. The Bayer Company in Germany was the first to market acetylsalicylic acid (aspirin).

» The clinical dose depends on the type of analgesic used, but typically varies from 200–650 mg.
» Non-narcotic analgesics work by blocking the synthesis of prostaglandins, substances found throughout the body whose functions include pain, temperature control, blood clotting, and inflammation.
» These drugs work by inhibiting enzymes called cyclooxygenase (COX). Ibuprofen and naproxen inhibit COX enzymes reversibly, while aspirin irreversibly inhibits these enzymes. The exact mechanism of action of acetaminophen is unknown.
» The main therapeutic effects of non-narcotic analgesics are reduction of pain, alleviation of fever, and reduction of inflammation.
» Acetaminophen has few to no anti-inflammatory effects, and as such is not classified as an NSAID.
» Aspirin, ibuprofen, and naproxen inhibit platelet aggregation and reduce blood clotting.
» There is some evidence that non-narcotic analgesics may have other medical benefits.
» OTC pain medications have adverse effects and are estimated to cause at least 16,000 deaths and 100,000 ER visits each year.
» Gastric upset and decreased blood clotting are risks associated with NSAID use. Other dangers include the risk of overdose, liver and kidney damage, enhanced risk of heart attack or stroke, and other potentially fatal conditions.
» Pregnant women should avoid using NSAIDs.
» Overdoses of non-narcotic analgesics account for hundreds, if not thousands, of deaths each year. In fact, acetaminophen is one of the leading causes of poisoning in the United States.

- **Cough, Cold, and Allergy Products**
» More than 100 individual viruses can cause a cold.
» Infection leads to an immune response that causes the symptoms of runny nose, sore throat, watery eyes, coughing, and sneezing.
» Because cough, cold, and allergy products simply mask the symptoms, they may actually delay healing.
» Cough and cold medications include cough suppressants, expectorants, decongestants, antihistamines, analgesics, and antipyretics.

- **OTC Drugs to Treat Gastrointestinal (GI) Ailments**
» GI ailments include heartburn, indigestion, diarrhea, and constipation.

» Drugs to treat heartburn, gastric reflux, and peptic ulcer neutralize the acid in the stomach.
» Antacids are bases that give short-term relief by neutralizing the acids in the stomach.
» H_2 blockers reduce secretion of HCl into the stomach.
» Proton pump inhibitors are the most potent and irreversibly inhibit the protein that secretes H^+ ions into the stomach, a process that is necessary for gastric HCl secretion.
» Drugs to treat diarrhea include loperamide, which reduces secretions and slows movement in the intestine by acting on opioid receptors, and bismuth subsalicylate, which reduces inflammation and may prevent the absorption of bacterial toxins that can cause diarrhea.
» Different types of laxatives include fiber and bulk-forming agents, stool softeners, lubricants, hyperosmotic agents, and stimulant laxatives.

- **OTC Weight Loss Aids**
» Even though almost 71 percent of adults in the United States are overweight, there is still a great stigma against obesity. Overweight people experience discrimination in social situations, at school, at work, in health care, and even in jury selection and adoption proceedings.
» Currently, there is only one OTC drug approved for weight loss. Orlistat (trade name Alli) decreases the intestine's ability to absorb fat. Because the fats are not broken down and absorbed into the bloodstream, they are excreted undigested. If fats are consumed, they remain in the intestine, where they pull in water, leading to flatulence, diarrhea, cramping, oily stool, and anal leakage.

- **OTC Sleep Aids**
» At least 20 percent of the U.S. population experiences insomnia at some point in time, and millions of these sufferers turn to OTC sleep aids.
» OTC drugs used to treat insomnia include melatonin and antihistamines.

- **Dietary Supplements**
» Dietary supplements include vitamins, minerals, amino acids, herbs, herbal extracts and concentrates, and some hormones.
» The FDA does not regulate these products, which can be sold without clearly labeling the active ingredient, or identifying how much is in each tablet, the safe dosage, or potential adverse effects.

Key Terms

Antihistamine (p.385)
Antitussive (p.384)
Decongestant (p.385)
Expectorant (p.384)

Gastroesophageal reflux disease (GERD) (p.385)
Heartburn (p.385)
NSAID (p.377)

Over-the-counter drug (OTC) (p.372)
Peptic ulcer (p.386)
Robotripping (p.384)

Quiz Yourself!

1. True or false? The FDA regulates prescription drugs but not OTC drugs.

2. Name three drugs that were previously available only by prescription but are now available OTC.

3. Which of the following is NOT required to appear on an OTC drug label?

   A. The active ingredients
   B. The inactive ingredients
   C. The year the drug was first approved by the FDA
   D. The dosage
   E. Possible side effects

4. Which of the following is NOT a typical effect of NSAIDs?

   A. Reduces fever
   B. Reduces pain
   C. Promotes blood clotting
   D. Reduces inflammation

5. True or false? Those who take cold medicines to treat their cold recover an average of three days sooner than those who take no medications.

6. True or false? Antacids such as Rolaids and proton pump inhibitors such as Prilosec reduce acid in the stomach by the same mechanism; the only difference is the dosage.

7. True or false? Those who are overweight or moderately obese on the BMI are *less* likely to die than those of normal weight.

8. Match the following questions about OTC non-narcotic pain relievers. Answers may be used once, more than once, or not at all.

   1. _____ Not classified as an NSAID
   2. _____ Reduces pain
   3. _____ May help reduce risk of heart attack
   4. _____ Irreversibly inhibits COX1 and COX2
   5. _____ Does not reduce inflammation
   6. _____ Free of adverse effects
   7. _____ Considered most potent in alleviating pain
   8. _____ Associated with Reye's syndrome
   9. _____ Considered safest during pregnancy
   10. _____ Trade name Advil
   11. _____ Reduces fever

   A. Aspirin
   B. Acetaminophen
   C. Ibuprofen
   D. Naproxen
   E. All of the above
   F. None of the above

9. True or false? Dietary supplements such as herbs and vitamins can be sold without clearly labeling the active ingredient, how much is in each tablet, the safe dosage, or potential adverse effects.

10. Which is the INCORRECT association?

    A. NSAID—ibuprofen
    B. Laxative—dextromethorphan
    C. Decongestant—pseudoephedrine
    D. Sleep aid—antihistamine

Additional Resources

Websites
What are OTC drugs and how are they approved?
https://www.fda.gov/drugs/how-drugs-are-developed-and-approved/over-counter-otc-nonprescription-drugs

Videos
WebMD videos about OTC drugs

https://www.webmd.com/pain-management/video/side-effects-interactions-of-drugs

Books
Griffith, H.W. (2017). *Complete guide to prescription and nonprescription drugs 2018–2019.* New York: Tarcher Perigee Press.

Learn more with this chapter's digital tools at www.oup.com/he/rosenthal2e.

CHAPTER

16 Sex and Reproductive Drugs

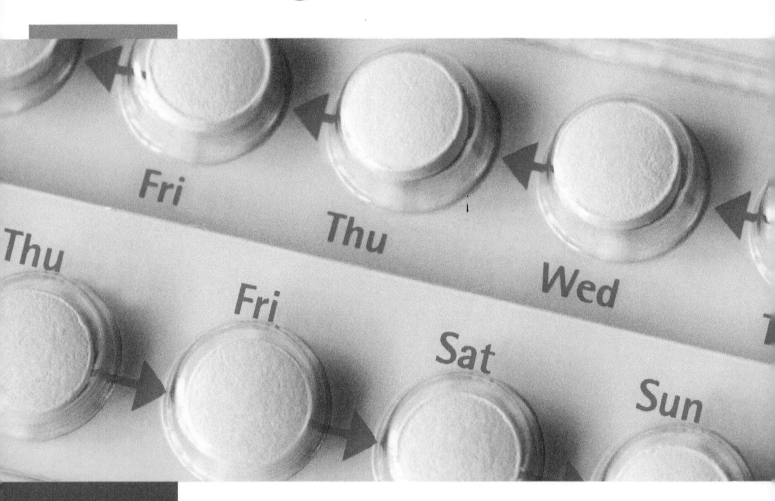

True or false?

1.
True or false? The use of contraceptives was illegal for unmarried people in the United States until 1972.

2.
True or false? The contraceptive implant Nexplanon is more effective in preventing pregnancy than is sterilization.

3.
True or false? A pharmacist can legally refuse to fill your prescription for birth control pills.

Most drug textbooks do not include a chapter about drugs that affect the reproductive system, but your author thinks this is vital. Although no one would question including a chapter about heroin or LSD, it is much more likely that you can name 10 friends who have taken "the Pill" or received the human papillomavirus (HPV) vaccine than you could name 10 friends who use heroin. There are many drugs that affect the reproductive system, including hormonal contraceptives, fertility drugs, hormone replacement therapy, Viagra, aphrodisiacs, and the HPV vaccine. Not only are these some of the most widely used drugs in the United States, but they also affect some experiences that lie at the very core of our existence, such as parenthood, sexual response, and desire.

Learning Objectives

- List some forms of hormonal contraceptives.
- Summarize the effects of estrogen and progesterone on the female body.
- Outline the mechanism of action of hormonal contraceptives.
- Identify the advantages and disadvantages of the various forms of hormonal contraceptives.
- Explain how emergency contraception works.
- Compare and contrast the mechanism of action of hormonal contraceptives and fertility drugs.
- Describe some of the physical and emotional changes associated with menopause.
- List some pharmacological treatments for erectile dysfunction and hypoactive sexual desire disorder, their mechanism of action, and their side effects.
- Illustrate some of the ways that drugs can enhance or reduce a person's libido.
- Define *human papillomavirus* (HPV).
- Evaluate the risks and benefits of the HPV vaccine.

Hormonal Contraceptives

Why do college students have sex? Although this may seem like an obvious question, there are several possible motives. Students were asked to rank a list of eight possible reasons for engaging in intercourse, including the following: to feel pleasure, to feel valued by and to express value for one's partner, as a means of stress relief, to nurture a partner, and to enhance feelings of power. Not surprisingly, "having a baby" was by far the least common response.[1] In another survey, researchers questioned nearly 2,000 people age 17–52 and compiled a list of all the reasons why people have sex.[2] They found 237 separate reasons, including "I was attracted to the person," "It feels good," "I was in love," "I wanted to burn calories," "I was bored," and the inexplicable "I wanted to change the topic of conversation." Of the reasons why men and women have sex, "I wanted to have a child" was not in the top 50. Throughout history, humans have looked for ways to separate the pleasurable act of intercourse from its sometimes inconvenient consequence of childbirth.

A typical woman is fertile for almost 39 years of her life. If she chooses to give birth to only two children, she will need to spend 89 percent of her fertile life—about three decades—using birth control.[3] Many women choose to use hormonal methods of contraception to prevent pregnancy.

Many methods of birth control—including oral contraceptives, the patch, the ring, the Depo-Provera shot, and the Nexplanon implant—work by affecting a woman's hormones (Table 16.1). Ninety-nine percent of women age 15–44 in the United States who have ever had sexual intercourse with a male have used at least one contraceptive method at some point in their lives.[4]

TABLE 16.1. Current Contraceptive Use Among U.S. Women Age 15–49

	Method	Year Approved by FDA	Number of Users	Percent of All Women Age 15–44	Percent of All Female Contraceptive Users
Hormonal methods and IUD	The Pill	1960	9,097,200	12.6%	19.4%
	Long-Acting Reversible Contraceptives	IUD: 1988, 2000, 2013 Nexplanon: 2006	7,436,600	10.3%	15.8%
	Other hormonal methods	Depo-Provera: 1992 NuvaRing: 2001 Contraceptive patch: 2002	2,310,400	3.2%	5%
Non-hormonal methods	Female sterilization		13,429,200	18.6%	28.6%
	Male sterilization		4,259,800	5.9%	9.1%
	Male condoms		6,281,400	8.7%	13.4%
	Other		4,043,200	5.6%	8.6%
No contraceptive use			25,342,200	35.1%	

Source: Daniels, K., & Abma, J.C. (2018). Current contraceptive status among women aged 15–49: United States, 2015–2017. NCHS Data Brief no. 327. *https://www.cdc.gov/nchs/data/databriefs/db327-h.pdf*

QUICK HIT

The Pill is the second most commonly used form of contraception in the United States (female sterilization is first). Worldwide, about 151 million women age 15–49 currently use oral contraceptives.[5,6]

Oral Contraceptives

Oral contraceptives ("the Pill") are various combinations of the **hormones** estrogen and progesterone. Estrogen and progesterone occur in both men and women, but they are present in much higher concentrations in women. **Estrogen** is a generic term for a group of female sex hormones that affect secondary sexual characteristics and regulate the menstrual cycle. **Progesterone** is secreted by the ovaries and plays an essential role in the maintenance of pregnancy. The effects of estrogen and progesterone are summarized in Figure 16.1.

History of the Birth Control Pill

For as long as women have been having babies, women have been trying to prevent themselves from

Hormone: A chemical substance that is produced in one organ and is carried through the bloodstream to affect another part of the body.

Estrogen: A group of steroid hormones that affect female secondary sexual characteristics and regulate the menstrual cycle.

Progesterone: A hormone involved in the maintenance of pregnancy.

having babies. The earliest oral contraceptives came from fruits and plants, including pennyroyal, willow, juniper, Queen Anne's lace, pomegranates, and yams. Some of these contain substances that may provide protection against pregnancy, although the dosages are hard to estimate and their potency is inconsistent.

In part due to the Biblical command to "be fruitful and multiply," contraception was discouraged by all Christian faiths for many years. Contraception was, however, legal in the United States until the Comstock Act was passed in 1873. This law made it illegal to possess contraceptive devices, as well as reproductive health–related educational materials, because they were classified as obscene. Furthermore, physicians were not allowed to provide their patients with any information that might help them prevent pregnancy or sexually transmitted diseases.

Margaret Sanger, who worked as an obstetric nurse in New York in the early twentieth century, was troubled by the difficult conditions and suffering of women who had no power to control their fertility. She led the movement for the distribution of information about sexuality and contraception. For decades, she fought for open access to information about contraception, and her efforts led to the eventual weakening of the Comstock laws.[7]

Sanger led the search to develop a simple and foolproof method of birth control. In 1951, Sanger, then 72 years old, met biologist Gregory Pincus at a dinner party and persuaded him to work on the development of an oral contraceptive pill. Early studies of estrogen and progesterone showed that they could be used to inhibit fertility. However, it took 80,000 pig ovaries to produce just 12 mg of estradiol, and a gram of progesterone cost more than a car.[8,9] Obviously, a synthetic form of hormone would be needed.

In the 1940s, Russell Marker (who also invented the octane rating for gasoline) found a way to produce synthetic progesterone from Mexican yams. Pincus tested the effects of progesterone on rats and rabbits, and found that it eliminated ovulation and pregnancy. Excited, he informed Planned Parenthood of his findings and requested more funding. The organization, deciding Pincus's work was too risky, chose not to continue funding his research, and the project stagnated. In 1953, Katharine McCormick, one of the first female graduates of MIT, and the heir to the International Harvester fortune, agreed to fund Pincus's work (Figure 16.2). It took $2 million to develop and test the oral contraceptive, which was provided almost entirely by Katharine McCormick.

The following year, Pincus teamed up with gynecologist John Rock. They conducted the first human trials of the Pill under the guise of a fertility study. In 1956, they ran large-scale clinical trials in Puerto Rico, where there were no anticontraception laws. In 1957, the Pill was approved by the Food and Drug Administration (FDA)—not as a contraceptive, but to treat severe menstrual disorders. Over the next few years, an unusually large number of women reported severe menstrual disorders.[10] The FDA approved Enovid, the world's first birth control pill (BCP), in 1960. The Pill's popularity rose quickly (Figure 16.3).

The use of contraceptives remained illegal in the United States until 1965, when the Supreme Court ruled that married couples' access to contraception was protected by their constitutional right to marital

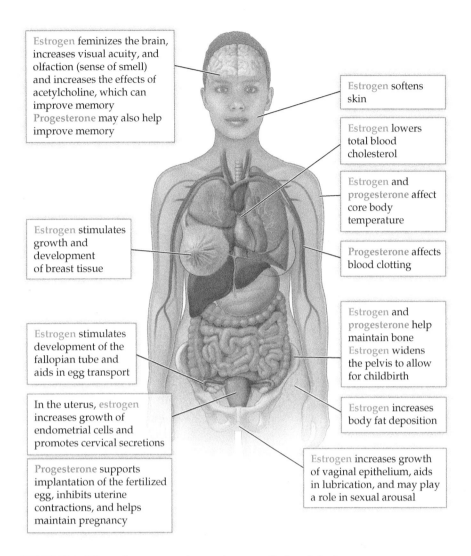

FIGURE 16.1. Effects of estrogen and progesterone on the female body.

privacy. Unmarried couples would be awarded the same right in 1972. Today, although contraception is legal, many state and federal policies limit women's access to contraceptive information and services.[11]

Mechanism of Action of Oral Contraceptives

Oral contraceptives are chemicals that are taken by mouth to inhibit normal fertility. They typically contain varying levels of synthetic estrogen and progesterone-like compounds called **progestins**. To understand how these hormones help prevent pregnancy, let's review the normal hormonal cycle in fertile women.

The hypothalamus releases the hormone GnRH, which travels to the anterior pituitary gland, causing

Progestin: Synthetic progesterone-like compound.

(a)

(b)

(c)

FIGURE 16.2. The development of the birth control pill. (a) Margaret Sanger, the activist; (b) Gregory Pincus, the scientist; and (c) Katharine McCormick, the financial backer were instrumental in the development of the Pill.

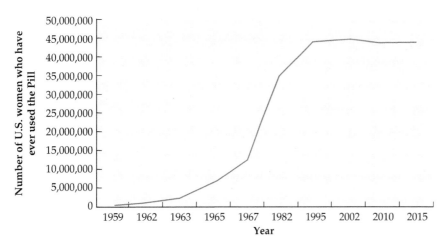

FIGURE 16.3. Number of U.S. women who had ever used the Pill, by year. The rate has decreased slightly over recent years as more hormonal contraceptive options, such as Depo-Provera and Implanon, become available.

Sources: Nikolchev, A. (2010). A brief history of the birth control pill. https://www.pbs.org/wnet/need-to-know/health/a-brief-history-of-the-birth-control-pill/480/

Daniels, K., Mosher, W.D., & Jones, J. (2013). Contraceptive methods women have ever used: United States, 1982–2010. National Health Statistics Reports, no 62. Hyattsville, MD: National Center for Health Statistics

Daniels, K., Daugherty, J., Jones, J., & Mosher, W. (2015). Current contraceptive use and variation by selected characteristics among women aged 15–44: United States, 2011–2013. National Health Statistics Reports, 86. Washington, DC: NCHS

Tyrer, L. (1999). Introduction of the pill and its impact. Contraception, 59(suppl 1): 11S–16S.

Follicle stimulating hormone (FSH): A hormone that stimulates the development of eggs during a woman's ovulatory cycle.

Luteinizing hormone (LH): A hormone that stimulates ovulation in females.

Ovulation: The release of the egg from the ovary into the fallopian tube.

the secretion of two hormones: **follicle stimulating hormone (FSH)** and **luteinizing hormone (LH)**. FSH and LH travel through the bloodstream to the ovaries. Once there:

- FSH stimulates the follicles, or immature eggs, to finish developing.
- LH causes **ovulation** (the mature egg to be released from the ovary into the fallopian tube).
- FSH and LH also promote the production and release of estrogen and progesterone from the ovaries.
- Estrogen and progesterone are released into the bloodstream, and have widespread effects on the body. They travel to the hypothalamus and pituitary gland to temporarily halt production of GnRH, FSH, and LH, thus regulating their own production (Figure 16.4).

The estrogen in the Pill inhibits the pituitary gland from releasing FSH, so no eggs develop.

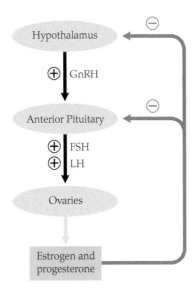

FIGURE 16.4. The regulation of estrogen and progesterone in the female body. The hypothalamus releases the hormone GnRH, which travels to the anterior pituitary, which releases LH and FSH. These hormones travel to the ovaries, which release estrogen and progesterone, which then temporarily shut down the release of GnRH, FSH, and LH from the hypothalamus and pituitary.

Progestins block the secretion of LH, thus preventing ovulation. Progestins also thicken the cervical mucus and increase its acidity. Not only does the thickened mucus make it more difficult for sperm to enter the uterus, but it actually causes changes that inhibit the sperm's ability to penetrate and fertilize an egg.

Use of Oral Contraceptives

Oral contraceptives are used by millions of women each day, but to ensure their effectiveness, they must be used correctly. BCPs are often numbered or named for the days of the week (Figure 16.5). A woman takes one BCP for 21 days and then either takes no pill or a placebo for the next seven days. During these days, the sudden drop in hormone levels causes a "pill period," which is not due to the shedding of the endometrium, but rather is the body's response to the withdrawal of the hormone-containing pills.

Most BCPs must be taken every day for 21 days in a row, preferably at the same time each day. If a woman forgets to take a pill, she should take it as soon as she remembers, even if she ends up having two pills in one day. If she forgets to take more than one pill, she should continue taking the rest of the packet, but should use additional forms of birth control, such as condoms, to prevent pregnancy during that cycle.

Some women, anticipating a vacation or other event, choose to skip the pill-free week entirely, thus eliminating their menstrual period for that month. Certain oral contraceptives are specifically designed to be taken continually, which eliminates a woman's period for months or even years at a time, if she chooses. Although some women enjoy the freedom from menstruation, the easing of menstrual cramps and mood swings, and alleviation of the symptoms of endometriosis, others are uncomfortable without the monthly proof that they're not pregnant. Also, no-period oral contraceptives can cause spotting, and long-term effects of these drugs are not yet fully known.

Advantages and Disadvantages of Oral Contraceptives

Oral contraceptives are a simple, safe, and effective method of birth control. With perfect use, the Pill's failure rate is only three out of every thousand women.[12] BCPs do not reduce sexual sensations or interfere with sexual spontaneity. And when a woman decides she is ready to try to get pregnant, she simply stops taking the Pill, and fertility typically returns within one to three months.[13]

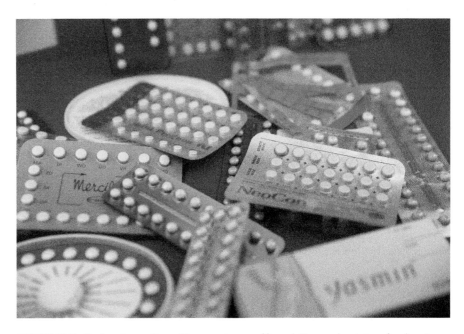

FIGURE 16.5. Oral contraceptives. There are dozens of formulations and varieties of oral contraceptive pills. With many pills, a woman takes one BCP for 21 days, and then either takes no pill or a placebo for the next 7 days.

Additionally, the Pill can provide a number of noncontraceptive benefits:

- Women on the Pill usually have lighter, less painful, and more regular periods, and less severe premenstrual syndrome (PMS).
- The Pill can help alleviate the anemia that may occur due to a heavy flow.
- Some women see an improvement in their acne while on the Pill.
- Oral contraceptives may help to control symptoms of polycystic ovarian syndrome and endometriosis.
- If pregnancy does occur when a woman is on the Pill, she has a lower risk of ectopic pregnancy.[14]
- The Pill may also reduce the risk of pelvic inflammatory disease, ovarian cysts, and even reduce a woman's risk of getting ovarian and endometrial cancers.[15]

In one long-term study, scientists followed over 46,000 women for almost 40 years. They found that women who used oral contraceptives had a lower risk of dying prematurely from any cause, including heart disease and cancer.[16]

QUICK HIT

Because of the Pill's noncontraceptive benefits, many women take oral contraceptives exclusively for noncontraceptive reasons; in fact, 9 percent of Pill users—some 819,000 women—have never had intercourse.[17]

Despite its advantages, the Pill isn't perfect. There are also disadvantages that women must be aware of:

- BCPs must be taken every day, even when a woman is not sexually active.
- Most women don't always take the Pill correctly every time.
- Many women occasionally forget to take a pill.
- Several drugs and foods can interfere with the Pill's efficacy.
- Oral contraceptives are only available by prescription.
- Some women are uncomfortable with the fact that the Pill interferes with a normal hormonal cycle.

In one study, in which users kept a diary recording their BCP usage, and their actual usage was monitored electronically, the average number of pills missed per month was 4.7, although participants only recorded missing one pill per month.[18] Taking this into consideration, with typical use, approximately 7 percent of

women may become pregnant each year while using oral contraceptives.[19]

Drug Interactions with Oral Contraceptives

Some drugs, including phenobarbital, phenytoin, St. John's wort, and the antibiotic rifampin decrease the effectiveness of oral contraceptives. Although many people believe that oral contraceptives are ineffective with all antibiotics, with the exception of rifampin, there is a lack of scientific evidence supporting the idea that commonly prescribed antibiotics reduce the Pill's effectiveness.[20,21] Some individual patients, however, do seem to show large decreases in blood concentrations of estrogen when taking antibiotics.[22]

Due to their actions on the cytochrome P450 system, oral contraceptives can increase the toxicity of benzodiazepines, beta-blockers, caffeine, prednisone-like drugs, and tricyclic antidepressants, and decrease the effectiveness of acetaminophen (Tylenol). Women who smoke cigarettes should be especially cautious, because women who are on the Pill and who also smoke have a significantly increased risk of heart attack and stroke.[23]

Adverse Effects of Oral Contraceptives

Oral contraceptives are quite safe—in fact, in the United States, a woman stands twice the risk of death by childbirth than she does by using oral contraceptives! Many of the perceptions of the dangers of birth control pills are based on Enovid, the first birth control pill, which contained up to seven times the dose of estrogen and up to 200 times the dose of progestin that is used in today's oral contraceptives.[24] Oral contraceptives are associated, however, with some side effects, both minor and major.

Common temporary side effects of oral contraceptives include breast tenderness, minor depression, headache, nausea, slight weight gain, and a change in skin pigmentation. Oral contraceptives elevate levels of sex hormone binding globulin (SHBG), a substance that binds testosterone.[25] When testosterone—the main hormone that affects sexual desire—is bound to SHBG, it is rendered biologically inactive, because it cannot attach to receptors in the body. SHBG levels may remain elevated for months after oral contraceptives have been discontinued, which may lead to a prolonged loss of sexual interest.[26]

More serious, but less common, adverse effects of oral contraceptives include an increased risk of blood clots, deep vein thrombosis, pulmonary embolism, heart attack, and stroke, although the risk remains very small.

The Pill and Attraction

Taking the Pill may affect which types of men a woman is attracted to. The human leukocyte antigens (HLAs; also called the major histocompatibility complex) are a series of genes that help an organism recognize its own healthy cells and reject invading parasitic organisms; as such, it is important to have a mix of HLA types, so a body is able to fight various diseases. Because there are so many HLA proteins, no individual carries a complete set, and it is advantageous to pick a partner with different HLA genes, so as to give one's offspring the ability to recognize and destroy a wide variety of invading organisms.

The HLA also influences both body odors and body odor perception. Women who are not on the Pill rate the body odor from men with HLAs that are different from their own as more pleasant than odors of men with similar HLAs. But when women are on oral contraceptives, they prefer the smell of men with HLAs similar to their own. A number of studies have found that women who are taking oral contraceptives when they meet their partners are less attracted to them and less sexually satisfied during their subsequent relationship compared with women who were not on the Pill when first meeting their mates. In fact, the more HLA alleles the couples shared, the more women's responsiveness to their partners decreased, their number of extramarital partners increased, and their attraction to men other than their primary partner increased.

Sources:

Rosenthal, M.S. (2013). Human sexuality from cells to society. Belmont, CA: Wadsworth Publishing/Cengage Learning.

Wedekind, C., Seebeck, T., Bettens, F., & Paepke, A.J. (1995). MHC-dependent mate preferences in humans. Proceedings of the Royal Society B: Biological Sciences, 260(1359): 245–49.

Roberts, S.C., Gosling, L.M., Carter, V., & Petrie, M. (2008). MHC-correlated odor preferences in humans and the use of oral contraceptives. Proceedings of the Royal Society B, 275(1652): 2715–22.

Garver-Apgar, C.E., Gangestad, S.W., Thornhill, R., Miller, R.D., & Olp, J.J. (2006). Major histocompatibility complex alleles, sexual responsivity, and unfaithfulness in romantic couples. Psychological Science, 17(10): 830–35.

Each year the use of the Pill results in blood clots in an additional 10 women out of 100,000, and about four additional strokes per 100,000 women.[27,28,29] To be safe, women who have circulatory problems or a history of heart attack, stroke, breast cancer, or blood clots should not take the Pill. Women over 35 years of age, as well as those who smoke, should be particularly aware of these risks.

A study of over 1 million women in Denmark found that those who used the Pill during adolescence had a higher risk of depression later in life.[30] After controlling for age of menarche, age at first sex, current relationship status, socioeconomic status, and ethnicity, they found that the risk of depression was 6 percent in those who never used the Pill, 9 percent in those who started using oral contraceptives as adults, and 16 percent in those who used oral contraceptives as a teenager. It may be that during puberty, levels of estrogen and progesterone change brain development, which can affect future emotional processing and mood.

The relationship between oral contraceptives and breast cancer is not entirely clear. Some studies suggest that oral contraceptive use is correlated with a higher risk of breast cancer,[31,32] while other studies suggest that the newer formulations are not associated with an increased risk.[33,34,35]

The Pill is not associated with any birth defects, even if a woman becomes pregnant while on the Pill. A woman should, however, discontinue the use of oral contraceptives as soon as she discovers she is pregnant.

Other Forms of Hormonal Contraceptives

Hormonal contraception does not have to be administered orally. Contraceptive hormones can access the bloodstream through the skin (the patch), across the mucosal membrane of the vagina (the ring), as a subcutaneous implant (Nexplanon), or as an intramuscular injection (Depo-Provera) (Figure 16.6). Like the Pill, these hormonal contraceptives also contain progestins (and sometimes estrogen) to prevent ovulation and thicken the cervical mucus (Table 16.2).

The Patch and the Ring

Xulane is a matchbook-sized patch that is placed on the skin of the buttocks, stomach, upper outer arm, or upper torso, which protects a woman from pregnancy for a week at a time. A new patch is put on each week for three weeks in a row, and then the fourth week the user does not wear the patch. Replacement patches should be placed in a location different from the one just used, and they should never be placed on the breast.

NuvaRing is a small, flexible ring that is inserted into the vagina (as far as possible) once a month. There is no danger of the ring being pushed up too far or getting lost. Vaginal muscles keep the ring in place, even during exercise or sex. If the ring is accidentally

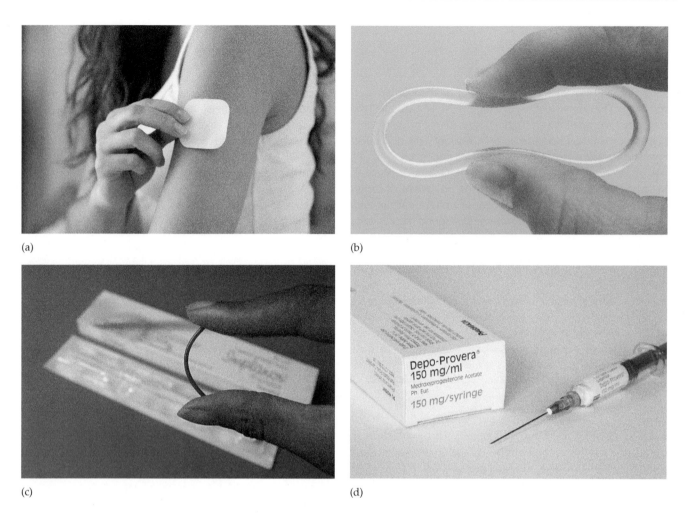

(a)

(b)

(c)

(d)

FIGURE 16.6. Other varieties of hormonal contraceptives. (a) The Ortho-Evra patch, (b) the NuvaRing, (c) Nexplanon, and (d) Depo-Provera.

TABLE 16.2. Summary of Contraceptive Methods

Type of Hormonal Contraceptive	Mechanism of Action	For Every 100 Women, How Many Will Have an Unplanned Pregnancy in 1 Year?		Noncontraceptive Risks	Noncontraceptive Benefits
		Perfect use	Typical use		
Oral contraceptive	Prevents ovulation, thickens cervical mucus, may decrease mobility of fallopian tubes	0.3	7	Menstrual irregularities, breast tenderness, headache, minor depression, loss of sexual desire, slightly increased risk of blood clots, stroke, and heart attack	Lighter flow and less risk of anemia; protection against pelvic inflammatory disease, ovarian cysts, and some forms of cancer
Patch		0.3	7		
Ring		0.3	7		
Implant		0.05–0.1	0.05–0.1		
Injectable		0.2	4	Same as oral contraceptive plus weight gain	

Sources: Daniels, K., Daugherty, J., Jones, J., & Mosher, W. (2015). Current contraceptive use and variation by selected characteristics among women aged 15–44: United States, 2011–2013. National Health Statistics Reports, 86. Washington, DC: NCHS.

Trussell, J. (2018). Contraceptive efficacy. In R.A. Hatcher, J. Trussell, F. Stewart, A. Nelson, W. Cates, F. Guest, & D. Kowal (Eds.), Contraceptive technology (21st ed.). New York: Managing Contraception LLC.

Rosenthal, M.S. (2013). Human sexuality from cells to society. Belmont, CA: Wadsworth Publishing/Cengage Learning.

expelled, the user can rinse it off in cool water and re-insert as soon as possible. The ring is left in for three weeks, and then taken out for one week, before a new ring is inserted.

Because these methods stay in place for a week or more at a time, the patch and the ring may have less chance of user error than daily oral contraceptives. Their failure rate increases if the woman uses them incorrectly, or if they become displaced and are not replaced in a timely manner.

Advantages, disadvantages, and side effects of these methods are similar to those of oral contraceptives, although the patch and the ring do not seem to increase formation of SHBG, which may mean women are less likely to experience a decrease in sex drive. Women on the Xulane patch should be aware that they may be exposed to as much as 60 percent more estrogen than on oral contraceptives, which can increase the risk of blood clots.[36]

Nexplanon

Nexplanon is a thin, flexible, progestin-containing plastic rod about the size of a matchstick. When this long-acting reversible contraceptive is inserted on the inside of a woman's upper arm, it gives continuous contraceptive protection for up to three years. Available since 2006, the contraceptive implant is the most effective method of birth control on the market today (in fact, it is even more effective in preventing pregnancy than sterilization!).[37] In a three-year study of over 2,300 women, not one pregnancy was reported to have occurred in over 73,000 monthly cycles.[38,39,40] Overall, Nexplanon's failure rate is 0.05–0.1 percent, meaning that fewer than 1 in 1,000 women using the rod will become pregnant over the course of a year.

Insertion and removal of Nexplanon takes only a few minutes, but it must be done by a healthcare professional. Because the implant only contains progestin, the method can be used by women who are breastfeeding and by other women who cannot take estrogen. Nexplanon may cause irregular bleeding, especially in the first 6–12 months of use. Some women have heavier periods, and some have mid-cycle spotting, but for most women, periods become fewer and lighter: after a year, one-third of women will stop having periods completely.

Depo-Provera

Depo-Provera (depot medroxyprogesterone acetate, or DMPA) is an injection given every three months into the muscles of the arm or buttock. Because the injection contains only progestin, women who cannot take estrogen can use DMPA. Side effects resemble those of the other forms of hormonal contraception; however, if a woman experiences negative side effects, she cannot immediately discontinue Depo-Provera, given that the drug remains in her system for up to 16 weeks.

Irregular bleeding is the most common side effect associated with DMPA. In most women, periods become fewer and lighter: 50 percent of women will stop having their periods entirely after a year of use, and 80 percent will stop after five years of use.[41] Weight gain is also more significant with Depo-Provera than with the other forms of hormonal contraception, especially in overweight women.[42,43,44] Adolescent girls who were obese before starting Depo-Provera gained significantly more weight—an average of 20 pounds in 18 months—compared with obese girls taking the Pill or those who were not on hormonal contraceptives.[45] Girls who were not obese also gained more weight on DMPA than girls on oral contraceptives or girls in the control group, an average of nine pounds in 18 months.[46] In addition, it may take a few months more for fertility to return after discontinuing DMPA compared with other hormonal contraceptives.[47]

Emergency Contraception

No contraceptive method is perfect; about half of unintended pregnancies occur among women who are using contraception.[48] Additionally, women may be forced into having unprotected sex. Emergency contraception is designed to prevent a pregnancy after unprotected vaginal intercourse has already occurred.

Emergency contraceptive pills (ECPs), such as Plan B or Ella, typically contain progesterone, albeit in higher doses than is found in BCPs. Plan B was first approved in 1999, and it has been available over-the-counter for all ages since 2013 (a prescription is still required for Ella). As a result, more women have access to emergency contraception; in 2002, 4 percent of sexually active women in the United States had ever used emergency contraception, 11 percent by 2010, and by 2015, 20 percent of American women who have ever had sexual intercourse with a man had used emergency contraception at least once.[49] However, *refusal statutes* in some states (see definition on p. 405) may still prevent women from easily obtaining ECP.

Emergency contraceptive pills are most effective if taken as soon as possible after unprotected intercourse—within 72 hours is best—given that these

Ask yourself: The earlier a woman takes an ECP, the more effective it is—requiring a doctor's prescription would delay the time until a woman could take the medication. If no prescription is required, however, women are less likely to be counseled by a physician as to the medication's proper use, or monitored afterward. In addition, OTC pills are available to sexually active adolescents, who are at a high risk of new diagnoses of chlamydia, gonorrhea, and other sexually transmitted infections—in other words, a population that most needs to be examined and counseled. Do you think ECPs should be available over the counter for all ages? Why or why not?

drugs prevent fertilization and are not effective if ovulation already has occurred.[50]

Mechanism of Action of Emergency Contraceptive Pills

ECPs prevent fertilization by delaying or inhibiting ovulation.[51,52] If they are taken after the sperm has already penetrated the egg, ECPs do not interfere with implantation.[53]

FIGURE 16.7. Hobby Lobby. The owners of Hobby Lobby fought to prevent their insurance from covering certain forms of contraception for their employees. Incidentally, Hobby Lobby has invested millions of dollars in the manufacturers of contraception, including some forms that were specifically named in their complaint.

Emergency contraceptive pills are *not* abortion pills. If a woman is already pregnant when she takes ECPs (which is not recommended), her fetus will not be harmed.[54] Susan Wood, past assistant commissioner of women's health at the FDA said, "The only connection this pill has with abortion is that is has the potential to prevent the need for one." [55]

Advantages and Disadvantages of Emergency Contraceptive Pills

Emergency contraceptive pills reduce a woman's chance of pregnancy. They are effective, easy to use, and safe—no deaths or serious complications have been linked to their use.[56] Given the short duration of exposure, ECPs can even be used by women who have been advised not to use oral contraceptives as their method of birth control. However, Plan B is less effective in women who weigh over 145 pounds or with a BMI over 26 and ineffective in women over 176 pounds (the average American woman weighs 169 pounds).[57,58,59] In addition, Ella is less effective in women with a BMI over 30 or weight over 187. After taking ECPs, some women experience nausea, breast tenderness, headache, or a change in the timing or flow of their next menstrual period.

Hormonal Contraceptives and Society

The Pill changed the world. With the availability of a safe, reversible, female-controlled, highly effective, and easy-to-use contraceptive, women—for the first time in history—could have sex without the imminent and very real likelihood of pregnancy. Due to the Pill, more women could pursue careers, control their sexuality, and plan their families. The Pill also may have boosted the economy; when individuals delay the start of families or have fewer children, they tend to be better able to support their children financially and to help them succeed.[60] Some people, however, criticized the changes in sexual mores that were correlated to the introduction of the Pill.

Today, some religions, including the Roman Catholic Church, a few Protestant denominations, and many Hindus, condemn the use of contraception. The clash

Ask yourself: Do you think businesses should be allowed to choose whether their insurance plans cover contraception? Should certain institutions be allowed to simply opt out of the country's laws because of their moral objections? By what criteria should we determine which moral objections are valid, or which laws we can disregard? Under what circumstances, if any, should the government be able to force a person to act in ways that violate his or her religious beliefs?

between religion and contraception made the news in 2014 with the U.S. Supreme Court decision of *Burwell v. Hobby Lobby Stores* (Figure 16.7). The Affordable Care Act required employer-provided insurance to cover medically authorized forms of contraception. The owners of Hobby Lobby objected based on religious grounds. In 2012, they filed a lawsuit against the U.S. government, and in 2014, the Supreme Court ruled 5-to-4 that Hobby Lobby can choose to be exempt from the law based on religious preferences. In 2020, a similar ruling allows any employer with a sincere moral or religious objection to opt out of covering contraceptives in employee health plans.

After the *Roe v. Wade* decision in 1973, most states passed laws protecting medical professionals who choose not to perform abortions based on their religious, moral, or personal values. These **refusal statutes** have been expanded to include many other medical procedures, such as physician-assisted suicide (which is currently legal in eight states and the District of Colombia), sterilization, and in vitro fertilization procedures. The millions of women in the United States who use prescription methods of birth control or take emergency contraception should be aware that in 12 states, pharmacists or other healthcare providers could refuse to provide contraceptive services or fill prescriptions if they do not personally believe in the use of contraceptives.[61]

Medical-professional refusal rights lead to thorny ethical dilemmas. On one hand, when they are licensed in their respective fields, health care professionals have agreed to serve a patient's physical and psychological needs. On the other hand, do people lose the right to act on their moral and religious beliefs when they enter health care? Whose well-being comes first—the patient's or the healthcare provider's? Where do provider rights end and patient rights begin?

Ask yourself: Who should make the final decision about health-related issues—the patient or the caregiver? Should scientific factors be considered in this decision, or the moral or religious beliefs of the caregivers?

Contraception for Men

Many a woman, after paying for a prescription and riding the emotional hormonal roller coaster that the Pill can sometimes cause, has wondered why most forms of reversible birth control are the responsibility of the woman. The short answer is: Life isn't fair.

Male methods of birth control—condoms, withdrawal, and vasectomy—account for just over a quarter of contraceptive practice worldwide.[62] The current lack of male-oriented chemical contraception (in other words, a "male pill") may be due to the physical realities of the male and female body. Men produce 1,300 sperm every *second*, while women release one egg each month. Therefore, a male pill would involve completely suppressing production of the millions of sperm that are produced daily, while in women, it involves preventing the development or fertilization of (usually) one egg per month. Of course, the lack of male contraception also may be because women are the ones who get pregnant. In women, the risk of side effects from contraception is offset by the benefit of avoiding an unintended pregnancy, which men do not face. Therefore, the side effects of a male contraceptive may be harder to justify.[63] Political realities factor in as well—due to some well-publicized drug recalls and our litigious society, pharmaceutical companies and the FDA are more risk-averse than they were in the past, and may be less likely to develop and approve new drugs that are designed to be used by basically healthy individuals.[64]

Nevertheless, several male contraceptive agents have recently entered clinical trials, some hormonal and some non-hormonal. Studies suggest that over 50 percent of men would be interested in using a reversible method of birth control if one were available and many women would be willing to rely on their partner to use a contraceptive.[65]

When testosterone is administered in high enough doses to suppress sperm production, it often also decreases many other things, including libido, levels of "good" cholesterol, the ability to get and maintain an

Refusal statute: Law that protects healthcare professionals from providing services to which they have strong religious or moral objections.

Ask yourself: Women, would you trust your male partner to take a contraceptive pill? Men, would you take a contraceptive pill if one were available with limited side effects? Why or why not?

erection, muscle mass, and mood. The challenge is to find the right formulation that suppresses spermatogenesis, minimizes side effects, and is also easy to administer. Two hormonal methods currently undergoing clinical trials include NES/T and DMAU. NES/T is a gel that is applied to a man's arms and shoulders. It contains testosterone as well as Nestorone, a progestin. Combining testosterone with a progestin increases the rate and extent of the suppression of spermatogenesis. Scientists are also working on a male hormonal contraceptive pill. However, orally-administered testosterone is not only more toxic to the liver, but is cleared from the body rapidly enough such that multiple doses throughout the day would be necessary to effectively suppress sperm production. To that end, dimethandrolone undecanoate (DMAU) contains testosterone, progestin, as well as a long-chain fatty acid that slows the breakdown of testosterone and can allow for an effective, once-daily pill.[66]

In order to try to minimize side effects, non-hormonal methods are also being tested. Some of these work by targeting proteins that affect sperm production or function. CatSper is a calcium ion channel that is specific to sperm and is essential for sperm movement and male fertility.[67] Affecting this channel means the sperm won't be able to swim to reach the egg. A substance called ouabain also prevents sperm motility. Ouabain affects a sperm-specific form of the sodium-potassium pump, thus immobilizing the sperm and preventing fertilization.[68,69]

Gamendazole interrupts sperm maturation, making them nonfunctional.[70] Gamendazole blocks the production of retinoic acid, which is important for sperm production. Unfortunately, it also blocks testicular aldehyde dehydrogenase, so if a person consumes alcohol while taking the drug, he'll experience unpleasant side effects, such as reddening of the skin, rapid heart rate, and nausea.

Fertility Drugs

At one point in your life, you may be concerned with preventing pregnancy, but at another time, you or your partner may *want* to get pregnant and find you are

Fertility drug: A drug given to a woman to improve her fertility.

having difficulty. **Fertility drugs** are medications used to enhance fertility in women. (If low hormone levels underlie a man's infertility, testosterone supplements are available to increase the number of viable sperm; otherwise, all fertility drugs are used by women.)

How an Egg Is Fertilized

Before discussing these drugs, let's briefly cover how pregnancy occurs. In the middle of her monthly cycle, a woman's levels of LH sharply increase, which causes her to release an egg from the ovary into the fallopian tube. If a sperm penetrates the egg, the fertilized egg (now called a "zygote") travels down the fallopian tube, where it implants in the endometrial lining of the uterus. If all goes as planned (which, more often than not, it doesn't; two-thirds to three-quarters of fertilized eggs do not result in live births), nine months later a baby will be born.

Women usually release only one egg at a time. If a woman releases two eggs, and each egg is fertilized by a sperm, this results in fraternal twins. If a woman releases one egg that is fertilized by a sperm, but the fertilized egg splits into two separate entities very early in development, this results in identical twins.

The average ejaculate contains about 250 million sperm, but fertilization occurs when only one sperm penetrates an egg. Why, then, do men release so many? It's a perilous journey from the vagina to the egg, and very few sperm make it all the way. Because the vagina is acidic, many sperm die instantly once ejaculated into the vagina. Still others flow out of the vagina due to gravity. The ones that survive have a long swim ahead of them—they have to travel 2,000 times their own length (which would be comparable to a 6-foot-tall man swimming 2.25 miles). The sperm need to swim from the vagina through the cervix, which is blocked by mucus. Those that get through the cervical mucus then need to travel the length of the uterus, before entering the fallopian tube. Remember, though, there are two fallopian tubes, and a woman only ovulates into one each month. Perhaps because they refuse to stop to ask for directions, half the sperm pick the wrong fallopian tube. By the time they reach the fallopian tube that contains the egg, fewer than 200 sperm have successfully made the journey. Once the remaining sperm reach the egg, they encounter a jelly-like "shell." The head of each sperm contains an enzyme that helps to break through the shell, but it takes the combined enzymes of between 20 and 200 sperm to break through the shell to allow one lucky sperm to fertilize the egg. Once the egg is fertilized, it causes an electrical change in the egg's cell membrane to prevent any other sperm from entering.

Infertility

Infertility is a decreased ability to reproduce (in contrast to *sterility*, which is a complete inability to reproduce—for instance, if a woman has had her uterus removed). Doctors often define infertility as a failure to conceive despite having had regular unprotected intercourse for a year (although a physician may begin infertility treatments sooner, depending on the age of the couple).

Unfortunately, infertility is increasingly common in the United States. Up to 15 percent of American couples have fertility problems.[71] Sometimes infertility is due to issues in the male, such as having a low sperm count, or sperm that are abnormally shaped or can't swim long enough. Sometimes infertility is due to issues in the female, such as having an abnormally shaped uterus or blocked fallopian tubes, low levels of progesterone, or problems with ovulation. Irregular or infrequent ovulation can be addressed with fertility drugs.

Drugs to Treat Infertility

Fertility drugs typically stimulate the production and release of eggs, increasing the odds that a sperm will encounter an egg to fertilize. These drugs can be taken on their own, or used in conjunction with assisted reproductive technologies such as in vitro fertilization (in which a woman's eggs and a man's sperm are typically combined outside the woman's body in a Petri dish, and after a day or two, the embryo is implanted in the uterus).

There are different types of fertility drugs, but all increase the production and release of eggs. Some drugs, such as Lupron, stimulate the hypothalamic hormone GnRH, which increases the release of FSH and LH, the hormones responsible for the development and release of eggs from the ovary. Other drugs, such as Pergonal or other menotropins, consist of FSH and LH.

The most common fertility drugs, including Clomid and Serophene, temporarily block estrogen receptors in the hypothalamus, pituitary gland, and reproductive tract. Remember that estrogen feeds back to temporarily shut off the hypothalamus and pituitary gland, thus inhibiting FSH and LH (which is how BCPs work; recall Figure 16.4). Fertility pills have the opposite effect. They block estrogen, which inhibits the negative feedback signal. The hypothalamus and anterior pituitary get the message that there is *no* estrogen, and so the pituitary gland boosts release of FSH and LH.

Clomid is usually taken orally for five days, starting on days 3, 4, or 5 of the menstrual cycle, and ovulation usually occurs about a week after the last dose. Women on fertility drugs need to properly time their intercourse in relationship to ovulation. Women can monitor their ovulation with body temperature graphs or with store-bought ovulation indicators. The success rate of fertility drugs is about 25 percent, but success depends on many factors, including the age of the woman and the cause of infertility.[72,73,74]

Side effects of Clomid include bloating, stomach upset, breast tenderness, hot flashes, blurred vision or light sensitivity, dizziness, and headache. In rare cases, a woman might experience ovarian hyperstimulation syndrome, a life-threatening condition whose symptoms include swelling in many areas of the body, including hands, legs, and abdomen; shortness of breath; and nausea and vomiting. Because fertility drugs cause the release of multiple eggs, they increase the risk of multiple births—twins, triplets, etc. Multiple births are riskier, both for the babies and the mother.[75]

Hormone Replacement Therapy

Over time, both men and women experience a decline in their libido and fertility. In order to reverse and alleviate some of the changes associated with aging, some women and men turn to **hormone replacement therapy (HRT)**, the replacement of naturally occurring reproductive hormones with (usually) synthetic equivalents. Women may take estrogen and progesterone to alleviate the symptoms of menopause, men sometimes take testosterone to boost libido, and transmen and transwomen sometimes take hormones so their body better matches their gender identity.

Infertility: A reduced ability to reproduce, often defined as a failure to get pregnant after a year or more of regular, unprotected sexual intercourse.

Hormone replacement therapy (HRT): The use of synthetic or natural reproductive hormones to alleviate symptoms associated with aging.

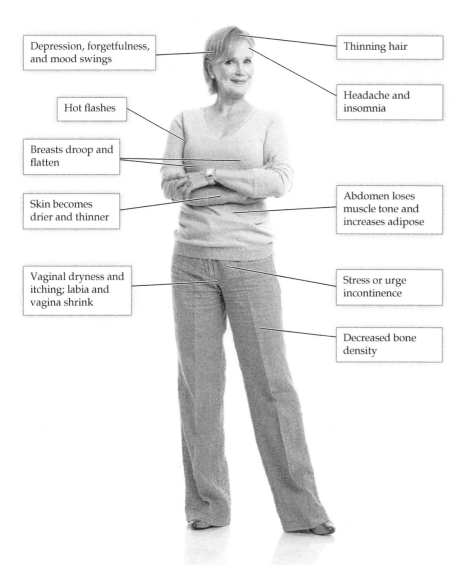

Depression, forgetfulness, and mood swings

Hot flashes

Breasts droop and flatten

Skin becomes drier and thinner

Vaginal dryness and itching; labia and vagina shrink

Thinning hair

Headache and insomnia

Abdomen loses muscle tone and increases adipose

Stress or urge incontinence

Decreased bone density

FIGURE 16.8. Signs of menopause.

Hormone Replacement Therapy in Women

By the time she's in her forties, a woman's ovaries begin to lose their capacity to respond to FSH and LH, so fewer eggs develop, and the production of estrogen and progesterone gradually diminishes. This process of hormonal decline generally lasts for anywhere from a few months to as long as 10 years. This transitional period ends with **menopause**, the cessation of menstruation. A woman is considered to have gone through menopause when she has had no periods for 12 consecutive months.

Menopause: The time in a woman's life when her menstrual cycle no longer occurs.

Menopause, and the preceding years, are associated with both physical and emotional changes (Figure 16.8). As estrogen levels decrease, the labia majora and breasts shrink, the vagina has less lubrication, body fat may redistribute from the thighs and buttocks to the abdomen, bone density diminishes, and hot flashes—sudden, intense feelings of warmth—can occur. Women going through menopause also may experience depression, anxiety, forgetfulness, irritability, and mood swings. These effects are largely due to estrogen's direct effects on mood, but they also may be due to subjective factors, such as culturally shaped expectations, changes in social roles, and concerns about female aging.[76] In Western society, postmenopausal women are often ignored or derided. In societies in which older women are respected and have high status, such as the Hmong women of Laos, women tend to have no negative physical or psychological symptoms associated with menopause.[77]

To reduce the uncomfortable symptoms of menopause, some women turn to HRT. The use of HRT has a long and complex history.

For decades, scientists observed that postmenopausal women and women whose ovaries had been removed were more likely to have coronary heart disease. Giving estrogen and progesterone to postmenopausal women was thought to reduce a woman's chance of getting heart disease, osteoporosis, colon cancer, and Alzheimer's disease, and to reduce the unpleasant symptoms of menopause.[78,79,80] By the early 1990s, up to 25 percent of American women over the age of 50 took estrogen or progesterone for menopausal symptoms.[81] Since so many women were routinely put on HRT, many studies were initiated to investigate the long-term risks and benefits of HRT.[82] The Women's Health Initiative followed over 161,000 postmenopausal women age 50–79 in both clinical and observational trials.

Ask yourself: Is menopause a normal stage of life, or an endocrine deficiency disease that needs to be treated with hormone therapy?

Ask yourself: What similarities and differences do you see with testosterone replacement therapy for older men and HRT for older women? Is "low T" a new disease or simply a new stage of life?

For years after the trials, women were given confusing and contradictory advice based on the findings, because a woman's age, specific risk factors, and number of years since menopause seem to have a powerful effect on whether HRT is a safe choice.

QUICK HIT

Premarin, the most commonly prescribed form of estrogen in HRT, is named for its source: PREgnant MARe urINe.

Today, most doctors agree that it is safe for a woman to take hormone therapy up to age 59 and within 10 years of menopause to deal with menopausal symptoms such as moderate to severe hot flashes and vaginal dryness. Women can take either estrogen alone (if they have had a hysterectomy) or estrogen plus a progestin (to prevent increased growth of the cells of the endometrium). The hormones can be administered orally, as a transdermal patch, or by vaginal creams, gels, or rings. If a woman uses HRT, it's recommended that she take the lowest possible dosage for the shortest possible length of time to address her symptoms. HRT may not be recommended for women with uncontrolled hypertension; unexplained vaginal bleeding; a history of blood clots, stroke, heart disease, liver disease, gall bladder disease, breast cancer, or uterine cancer; or if she is pregnant.[83]

It's important to remember that HRT is not one-size-fits-all, because every woman has different symptoms, needs, and risk factors. Menopausal women considering HRT should carefully weigh its risks and benefits and discuss this therapy with their physicians. Nonpharmacological treatments can also be considered. Soy and the flowering plant black cohosh may help alleviate some symptoms of menopause. Over-the-counter lubricants can battle vaginal dryness. To avoid hot flashes, women can avoid spicy foods and caffeine and incorporate stress-relieving activities into their day. And, finally, exercise can protect the heart, increase bone density, improve mood, and lower stress.

Hormone Replacement Therapy in Men

Testosterone is the main hormone that controls libido in both men and women. Testosterone levels are highest in adolescent and young adult males, and begin to decline about 1 percent each year after age 30. Low levels of testosterone ("low T") are associated with a loss of libido, erectile dysfunction, depression, low self-confidence, decreased concentration and memory, lethargy, reduced bone density, and loss of muscle mass and strength. These symptoms are known collectively as ADAM (androgen deficiency of the aging male) or **andropause**.

In recent years, it has become common for men to seek a pharmacological solution for this normal hormonal change. Since 2000, annual prescriptions for testosterone replacement therapies have increased four-fold.[84,85] Many physicians write prescriptions for their patients without first measuring the patient's baseline levels of testosterone or monitoring their levels afterward.[86]

As we know from Chapter 14, men (usually young men) who take high doses of anabolic steroids face an increased risk of stroke, heart attack, and shrunken testicles. But what about older men taking prescription testosterone to boost their naturally diminishing levels of the hormone? Overall, the risks outweigh the benefits. In older men with low testosterone, HRT improved bone density and boosted red blood cell count in anemic men, but did not improve cognition or memory, and significantly increased the risk of heart attack and stroke.[87,88,89,90,91] In one study, within three months, prescription testosterone doubled the rate of heart attacks in men 65 and older, and raised the risk two to three times in younger men who had a history of heart disease.[92]

Hormone Replacement Therapy for Transgender Individuals

Transgender individuals sometimes take hormones so that their bodies more closely align with their gender identity. Transmen—those who were assigned as female at birth but who identify as male—may undergo testosterone therapy, and transwomen—those who were assigned male at birth but who identify as female—may take estrogen. The aim is to achieve hormone levels seen in the normal range for the target

---

Andropause: A collection of symptoms, including a reduced sexual desire, fatigue, and mood changes, experienced by some middle-aged men and attributed to a gradual decline in testosterone levels.

gender, but the end result should be tailored to the individual's needs and goals.

Transmen may undergo testosterone therapy in order to suppress female secondary sexual characteristics and masculinize the body. The most commonly used formulations are intramuscular or subcutaneous injections, administered weekly. Implants, gels, and patches may also be used. Within three months of initiating androgen therapy, the menstrual cycle should cease, facial and body hair grows, fat distribution on the body changes, and muscle mass and libido increase. Later, the testosterone may thicken the vocal cords to deepen the voice, and the clitoris may increase in size.[93]

Transwomen may choose to take estrogen as well as some anti-androgen drugs. These drugs can increase body fat and change its distribution around the body, induce growth of breasts, slow the growth of body hair, facial hair, and muscles, and shrink the testicles. Timing varies, but this may take up to 18–24 months to occur.[94] Transwomen over age 50 may use a lower dose of estrogen or anti-androgen drugs only, to more closely mimic the hormonal changes that happen with menopause.

Gender affirming hormone therapy can have a positive effect on a transgender person's quality of life and psychological functioning.[95]

Viagra and Other Drugs to Treat Erectile Dysfunction

Many men, at some point in their lives, have difficulty maintaining an erection sufficient for sexual activity. When impotence becomes persistent, however, it may be classified as **erectile dysfunction (ED)**. ED may have physiological, psychological, or situational causes. It is estimated that as many as 322 million men worldwide will be affected by ED by 2025.[96] ED affects millions of men in the United States between the ages of 40 and 70, and the incidence increases with age.[97,98] ED is by no means limited to older men; one in four patients seeking medical help for new onset of ED is under the age of 40.[99] ED can hurt a man's self-esteem and damage his relationship with his partner. Treatments for ED include psychological, surgical, or mechanical approaches, but pharmacological treatments, such as Viagra, Cialis, and Levitra, are the most popular.

Erectile dysfunction (ED): The persistent inability of a man to achieve or sustain an erection.

Viagra (Figure 16.9) was originally developed as a drug to lower blood pressure and treat cardiovascular ailments. At the end of the clinical trials, the male participants did not want to give their drug samples back; further questioning of the participants revealed Viagra's effectiveness in helping to maintain erections. Viagra was released in the United States on March 27, 1998, and within three months, over three million prescriptions had been issued, making it the fastest-selling drug at that time. Other popular ED drugs include Cialis, Levitra, and Stendra.

Mechanism of Action of Drugs to Treat Erectile Dysfunction

To understand how Viagra and other drugs treat ED, let's first briefly discuss how erections occur. During an erection, the erectile tissue in the penis releases nitric oxide, which elevates levels of a substance called cyclic GMP (cGMP). Cyclic GMP relaxes the smooth muscle of the penis, allowing blood to flow in. To end the erection, an enzyme called phosphodiesterase-5 (PDE-5) breaks down cGMP. Viagra and other ED drugs inhibit PDE-5, thus facilitating cGMP's effect on erection.

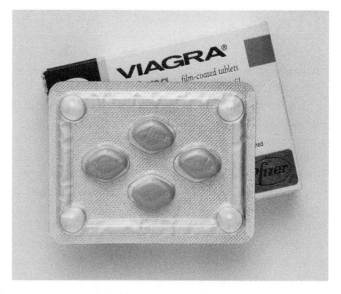

FIGURE 16.9. Viagra. Viagra treats erectile dysfunction.

Ask yourself: The Pill is not always covered by insurance, but drugs to treat ED usually are. Why do you think that is? Should Viagra and other drugs that treat ED be covered by insurance? Why or why not?

PDE-5 inhibitors do not produce a spontaneous erection; they only prolong an erection that occurs due to sexual stimulation. Viagra, Cialis, Levitra, and Stendra share the same mechanism of action but have minor differences in their potency, time of onset, duration of action, and side effects.[101]

As is so often the case, nonpharmacological options should be considered. ED may be a symptom of stress or fatigue, and a man can try to address those conditions rather than just treating the symptom of impotence. ED can also be due to poor circulation related to diabetes or other conditions. A healthy diet and moderate exercise may help blood flow to all areas of the body, including the penis. Finally, men should have realistic expectations. Erections simply will not be the same at age 50 as they were at age 20.

Side Effects and Drug Interactions of Erectile Dysfunction Drugs

Common side effects of PDE-5-inhibiting drugs include headache, facial flushing, dizziness, nasal congestion, back pain, muscle ache, and indigestion. Some men experience visual disturbances, including temporary increased brightness, or a blue haze. These effects, which may last for a few minutes to a few hours, occur because PDE-6, an enzyme in the retina, is also partially inhibited by sildenafil. Men who take Viagra may also double their chances of sudden hearing impairment.[102]

Sildenafil was invented to treat hypertension; as such, ED drugs should never be taken along with nitroglycerin or other nitrate-containing drugs, which dilate blood vessels. Together, these drugs can result in low blood pressure and loss of consciousness. Some antibiotics, antiseizure medications, and blood thinners also interact with these drugs. Sildenafil might not be safe in men who have heart problems, a history of stroke, high or low blood pressure, eye problems, or liver or kidney disease.

Some men who are not experiencing ED take sildenafil and ecstasy (MDMA) together, a combination called "sextacy." The use of sildenafil in young men without ED can lead to priapism, a sustained and painful erection, and the combination of sildenafil with MDMA can significantly raise a man's risk of heart attack and other cardiovascular dangers.

Drugs to Treat Hypoactive Sexual Desire Disorder in Women

Women also may encounter problems with sexual arousal. They may be slow to lubricate or have trouble becoming sexually excited in response to sexual stimulation. Does Viagra help women? All evidence points to "no." Women's sexual arousal is not as closely tied to their physical responses as it is in men (Figure 16.10). In men, physical arousal often leads to sexual desire, but in women, arousal and desire may be disconnected.[103,104] Rather than a lack of clitoral erection, psychological states such as anxiety, fatigue, or relationship issues are more likely to underlie a woman's lack of arousal. So, a PDE-5 inhibitor may increase a woman's vaginal blood flow, but it will not necessarily affect her desire to have sex. The most common sexual disorder in women in the U.S. in hypoactive sexual desire.

There are two FDA approved medications to treat female sexual dysfunction. Flibanserin (fly-BAN-sir-in; brand name Addyi [pronounced ADD-ee]) was approved in 2015 for the treatment of low sexual desire; and bremelanotide (brand name Vyleesi) [pronounced

(a)

(b)

FIGURE 16.10. Gender differences in sexual arousal. Sexual arousal is different in (a) men and (b) women.

TABLE 16.3.   Comparison of sildenafil, flibanserin, and bremelanotide

	Sildenafil (Viagra)	Flibanserin (Addyi)	Bremelanotide (Vyleesi)
Mechanism of action	Inhibits PDE-5 to increase blood flow to the penis	Works in the brain to lower serotonin and raise dopamine and norepinephrine	Affects melanocortin receptors in the brain
Use	Tablet, taken as needed, before sexual activity. Begins working in minutes	Tablet taken every night. May take 4–8 weeks to take effect	Injection under the skin of the abdomen or thigh before anticipated sexual activity
Efficacy	Success rate around 70%. Performs about 50% better than placebo	Success rate 8–13%. Women report an average of 0.5 more satisfying sexual events per month compared to placebo	About 25% had a small increase in sexual desire score. No difference in number of satisfying sexual events compared to control group
Side effects	Relatively minor, affect about 15% of men	Sedation, nausea, dizziness, low blood pressure, and sudden loss of consciousness, which can occur at any time. Side effects are seen in up to 20% of women	Nausea (40%), vomiting, flushing (21%), headache (12%), darkening of skin (which is rarely, but sometimes permanent)

Ask yourself: There are fewer drugs to treat sexual dysfunction for women than there are for men (most are drugs to treat erectile dysfunction), and the drugs for women have much lower efficacy and much greater risk of side effects. Does this reflect societal views on male and female sexuality or just the complexity of desire?

vie-LEE-see], approved in 2019. Although these drugs are sometimes called "female Viagra," there are significant differences between them (Table 16.3).

Flibanserin was first developed as an antidepressant, but it failed in clinical trials and was not approved by the FDA. The makers of flibanserin took another route, and submitted it as a drug to increase sexual desire in women. Advisory committees to the FDA voted it down twice, due to concerns over low efficacy and a high incidence of adverse effects. In 2015, the manufacturers led a huge marketing campaign claiming that the FDA was sexist for not approving the drug, and the FDA approved the use of flibanserin by a vote of 0:18:6 (0 votes for outright approval, 6 votes against approval, and 18 votes that agreed to approval if conditions and steps were taken to limit the risks of the drug).

Flibanserin is a daily pill that works in the brain to lower serotonin and raise dopamine and norepinephrine levels. Women who use flibanserin have an average of about 0.5 more satisfying sexual events per month

compared to placebo.[105,106] About 20 percent of women using flibanserin will suffer side effects, including sedation, sleepiness, nausea, dizziness, low blood pressure, and a sudden loss of consciousness, which can occur at any time. Drinking alcohol significantly exacerbates these side effects.

Bremelanotide is an injection taken at least 45 minutes before anticipated sexual activity. About 25 percent of women taking bremelanotide reported a slight increase in their sexual desire score, compared to 17 percent of women on placebo. There was no difference between the treatment and control groups with the number of satisfying sexual events.[107] Common side effects include nausea, vomiting, flushing, increased blood pressure, and headache. About 1 percent have darkening of the skin of the face, breasts, and gums, which is permanent in about half the patients.

Aphrodisiacs and Anaphrodisiacs

Aphrodisiacs, named for Aphrodite, the Greek goddess of love and desire, are substances that are thought to arouse or increase sexual response. Viagra is not considered an aphrodisiac, because it helps to maintain erections but does not necessarily enhance arousal. Drugs may enhance a person's libido in several ways. They may improve mood, alleviate stress, or reduce inhibitions. Healthcare professionals and those who study human sexuality generally agree that there are no

Aphrodisiac: A substance that is thought to arouse or increase sexual response.

Ask yourself: Do you think aphrodisiacs exist? What effect would a substance need to have to be considered an aphrodisiac?

true aphrodisiacs; however, a substance with no actual physiological effects may still influence a person's arousal if the user *believes* that it will work. Our state of mind has a powerful influence over sexual arousal.

QUICK HIT

In the past, a substance called "Spanish fly" was believed to be an aphrodisiac. Spanish fly is actually the dried remains of a certain family of beetles, whose bodies contain the potentially fatal irritant cantharidin. When cantharidin is excreted by the kidney, it irritates the lining of the urethra, which increases blood flow to the region, and may result in a painful and long-lasting erection. Ingestion of this substance is also associated, however, with a burning sensation in the mouth and throat, pain, fever, cramps, vomiting, diarrhea, bloody discharge, and potential kidney failure. If you were to meet someone who had taken Spanish fly, noticed their erection, and assumed that they were in the mood for sex, they would probably indicate their disinterest by vomiting on your shoes.[108]

Herbs and Plants

Many substances from herbs and plants, including the bark and roots of the South American *Muira puama* tree; yohimbine, the active ingredient from the bark of a tree that grows in western Africa; and *maca*, a root from a mustard plant, are reported to have aphrodisiac properties.[109] These drugs may have some effect, perhaps by affecting hormone levels or vasodilating blood vessels to the genitals. It is important to remember that herbal remedies are not subject to FDA oversight. Their potency and purity are inconsistent, and any claims of effectiveness are usually not scientifically evaluated (Chapter 15).

Alcohol and Other Drugs

William Shakespeare described alcohol as "provoking the desire, but taking away the performance." In some people, small amounts of alcohol lower inhibitions, anxiety, and judgments, which may lead to enhanced arousal and more sexual encounters. This phenomenon is even seen in fruit flies: chronic alcohol exposure caused male fruit flies to become hypersexual. They increased their courtship behavior and even tried to mate with other male flies.[110] As Shakespeare knew 400 years ago, however, alcohol impairs sexual functioning. Alcohol increases the chance of impotence, reduces

vaginal blood flow and lubrication, and makes orgasm harder to achieve. (Even intoxicated fruit flies feel the effects—they exhibit enhanced sexual arousal, but reduced sexual performance.)

Images in the media associate alcohol with sexual undertones, and suggest that alcohol will help create romantic or sexually charged encounters. This association is so ingrained that the mere thought of alcohol can influence a person's sex drive. In one study, male college students filled out a questionnaire that measured their beliefs about how alcohol affected their sexual arousal. They then watched a computer screen on which words were flashed at a speed too quick for conscious awareness. One group of men saw alcohol-related words (such as "beer," "whiskey," or "drunk"), while the control group were flashed non-alcohol-related words (such as "coffee," "lemonade," or "water"). Finally, the men viewed photographs of young women and assessed their attractiveness. The men whose scores on the questionnaire indicated that they expected alcohol to boost their libido rated the photos of women more favorably if they had previously been subliminally exposed to alcohol-related words. Those who expected alcohol to hurt sexual desire rated the girls as less attractive after exposure to alcohol cue words.[111]

In earlier chapters, we discussed the effects that many illicit drugs have on sexual desire.

- Amyl nitrates ("poppers") were a popular drug in gay bars and discos during the 1970s and 1980s. Poppers cause a "head rush" by dilating the blood vessels in the head, facilitate erection through vasodilation in the genitals, and relax the anal sphincter (Chapter 8).
- MDMA (ecstasy or Molly) does not improve sexual functioning, but some find it enhances empathy and bonding (Chapter 6).
- Cocaine and amphetamines may enhance sexual desire initially, but long-term use can lead to sexual dysfunction, impotence, and difficulty achieving orgasm (Chapter 5).[112,113]
- Some people find that cannabis enhances and prolongs orgasm, but its arousing effects are most likely due to increased awareness of bodily sensations and diminished time perception (Chapter 9).

Anaphrodisiacs

A number of substances, called **anaphrodisiacs**, inhibit sexual response. Antidepressants such as Celexa

Anaphrodisiac: A substance that diminishes sexual response.

GARDASIL

The **human papillomavirus (HPV)** is the world's most common sexually transmitted virus. By age 50, up to 80 percent of sexually active Americans will have had an HPV infection sometime in their lives. HPV can be transmitted by oral, anal, and vaginal sex, as well as skin-to-skin contact during sex with an infected partner.

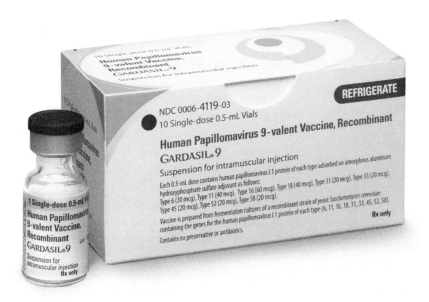

FIGURE 16.11. **Gardasil.** Gardasil-9 protects against 9 strains of the human papillomavirus (HPV).

There are more than 150 strains of HPV, most of which are harmless and cause no symptoms at all. More than 40 types of the virus are sexually transmitted and can infect the genitals. Low-risk strains of HPV cause genital warts—painless, itchy bumps on the genitals. High-risk strains can lead, in rare cases, to development of cancers of the cervix, vagina, penis, anus, mouth, or throat. Women with HPV are 10 times more likely to develop cervical cancer than women without, and cervical cancer causes the death of almost a quarter of a million women each year worldwide. It is important to note that most high-risk HPV infections *don't* progress to cancer; only about 1 in 1,000 women with HPV develops cervical cancer. Men likewise can get genital cancers from HPV infection, although penile and anal cancers are rare. HPV also can cause other cancers—men and women infected with HPV are 32 times more likely to develop cancers of the mouth and throat than those without the virus. Although there is no cure for HPV, most people clear the infection on their own.

From their introduction in 2006 until 2020, more than 120 million doses of HPV vaccines were distributed in the United States.[115] **Gardasil-9** (Figure 16.11) is the only HPV vaccine currently available for use in the United States. This vaccine is designed to protect against the two strains of HPV that cause 66 percent of cervical cancers, five additional cancer-causing strains, as well as two strains of HPV that cause 90 percent of genital warts.[116] These vaccines are approved for women and men age 9–45. The vaccine is

alter synaptic levels of serotonin, a substance involved in modulating sexual desire. Antidepressants may delay or increase the difficulty in achieving erection and orgasm, and in some cases, these effects can last after the patient has discontinued the drug (Chapter 13). Opioids such as codeine, heroin, and OxyContin also diminish sexual function and make it more difficult to achieve orgasm (Chapter 7). Nicotine constricts blood vessels, which can impair the ability of the genitals to become engorged with blood during excitement (Chapter 10). People's sex drives may even be affected by drugs that their mothers took before they were born. Aspirin blocks prostaglandin production, which is thought to be necessary to masculinize the brain (Chapter 15). When baby male mice were exposed to low doses of aspirin, either through the womb or through nursing, they showed lower-than-normal sex drives as adults.[114]

Human papillomavirus (HPV): A group of over 150 related viruses, some of which can infect the genitals.

Gardasil-9: A vaccine that protects against infection with certain types of the human papillomavirus (HPV).

Critical Evaluation

Should the HPV vaccine be required for enrollment in schools?

Vaccines against mumps, measles, polio, and other diseases are required in many states for students to enroll in school, unless there are medical, religious, or philosophical exemptions granted. Should the HPV vaccine be required as well? What factors should be considered in making your decision?

Weighing the benefits versus the risks of the vaccine. How do you compare an estimate of potentially fewer cancer cases in the future (which, after all, haven't occurred) with actual side effects (which may or may not be directly due to the vaccine)? What makes a side effect too serious to justify the vaccine's use? How many people must experience a negative side effect to make the benefits no longer worth the risks?

Evaluating the effectiveness of the vaccine. Gardasil does not protect against all high-risk strains of HPV. In addition, the long-term efficacy of Gardasil is unknown. The vaccine protects against HPV for at least 10 years, but it might not give indefinite protection. We don't know if or when users would need a booster shot in order to remain protected against the virus. Should a vaccine be discarded because it is not 100 percent effective?

Economic considerations. Cervical cancer is a slow-growing cancer, and an annual Pap test (which tests the cells of the cervix for potentially cancerous cells) easily detects precancerous changes. Testing for the presence of HPV also serves as a screening mechanism. Without routine screening, about 1 percent of women with high-risk HPV will develop cervical cancer. In fact, women age 18–64 who have not had a Pap test in the past three years account for the majority of cervical cancer diagnoses.[121] Instead of paying to provide an HPV vaccine, would a better use of the money be to provide regular cervical exams or HPV screening for all women? If the vaccine were mandatory, women of a lower socioeconomic status would receive the vaccination for free. These women are most likely to not have a yearly Pap test, so might a vaccine, therefore, be particularly helpful for them?

Balancing personal freedoms against public safety. Some conservative religious groups have opposed these vaccines, because they believe they will make girls more promiscuous. (No evidence supports this idea.) How do you weigh the risks of Gardasil and the social implications of mandatory vaccination against the benefit of reducing the incidence of a life-threatening cancer?

approved for such a young age because an HPV vaccine is only effective if it is administered before one is exposed to the HPV.

About 44,000 new cancers attributable to HPV occur each year in the United States.[117] In the ten years following the introduction of the vaccine in 2006, the HPV infection rate among teen girls in the United States fell by 64 percent, and cervical cancer rates are 29 percent lower in females age 15–29.[118,119] Because of the vaccine, there are fewer people infected with the virus, so fewer people can spread the virus, which should result in fewer cases of cancer.

The most frequently reported side effects of Gardasil are pain and swelling at the site of injection, dizziness, nausea, headache, and fever. Some individuals faint after receiving the injection, but that is most likely due to fear of needles, rather than some factor in the vaccine.

The Centers for Disease Control and Prevention (CDC) and the FDA collect and investigate data about adverse effects following the administration of vaccines via a program called VAERS (the Vaccine Adverse Event Reporting System). Since Gardasil-9 has been introduced, VAERS has received approximately 7,200 adverse event reports occurring in those receiving HPV vaccines; this represents about 0.025 percent of the HPV vaccine doses. Of the adverse event reports, 3 percent were classified as "serious." In these relatively few instances of serious adverse reactions to the vaccine, no common pattern suggested that Gardasil was the cause, and scientists at the CDC and FDA have concluded that the HPV vaccine is safe.[120]

Chapter Summary

- **Hormonal Contraceptives**
  » Oral contraceptives, the patch, the ring, the Depo-Provera shot, and the Nexplanon implant work by affecting a woman's hormones.
  » Oral contraceptives are various combinations of the hormones estrogen and progesterone. The hormones in oral contraceptives travel through the bloodstream to the brain to shut off the release of the hormones FSH and LH, thus preventing maturation and ovulation of the egg.
  » Typically, a woman takes one birth control pill for 21 days, and then takes either no pill or a placebo for the next seven days. With perfect use, the Pill's failure rate is only three out of every thousand women. Many women, however, don't always take the Pill correctly, so with typical use, approximately 7 percent of women become pregnant each year while on the Pill.
  » The contraceptive patch is placed on the skin and protects a woman from pregnancy for a week at a time.
  » The ring is inserted into the vagina for contraceptive effects that last for three weeks.
  » The Nexplanon rod is inserted on the inside of the upper arm and gives continuous contraceptive protection for up to three years.
  » Depo-Provera is a hormonal contraceptive injection given every three months.
  » Emergency contraceptive pills prevent fertilization of the egg; they do not cause an abortion.
  » New forms of reversible contraceptives for men are under investigation.
- **Fertility Drugs**
  » Infertility is a reduced ability to reproduce.
  » Fertility drugs are used to enhance fertility in women.
  » Fertility drugs typically stimulate the production and release of eggs, increasing the odds that a sperm can encounter an egg to fertilize.
- **Hormone Replacement Therapy**
  » Both men and women experience hormonal changes as they age.
  » As a woman's estrogen levels decrease during menopause, there are both physical and emotional changes.
  » To reduce the uncomfortable symptoms of menopause, some women turn to hormone replacement therapy (HRT), the replacement of naturally occurring estrogen and progesterone with (usually) synthetic equivalents.
  » Men going through andropause sometimes take replacement testosterone to reverse changes in their body and their libido.
  » Transgender individuals may use hormones so their bodies more closely align with their gender identity.
- **Viagra and Other Drugs to Treat Erectile Dysfunction**
  » Many men have difficulty in maintaining an erection at some time in their lives.
  » Viagra and other drugs are commonly prescribed to treat erectile dysfunction.
- **Drugs to Treat Hypoactive Sexual Desire Disorder in Women**
  » There are two FDA approved medications to treat female hypoactive sexual dysfunction. Both have relatively low efficacy rates and significant side effects.
- **Aphrodisiacs and Anaphrodisiacs**
  » Aphrodisiacs are substances that are thought to arouse or increase sexual response.
  » Healthcare professionals generally agree that there are no true aphrodisiacs, although some substances may affect arousal by increasing blood flow to the genitals, reducing inhibitions, or acting as a placebo.
  » Anaphrodisiacs such as antidepressants, opioids, and nicotine may inhibit sexual response.
- **Gardasil**
  » The human papillomavirus (HPV) is the world's most common sexually transmitted virus.
  » More than 40 strains of HPV are sexually transmitted and can cause genital warts or even lead to the development of cancer.
  » Gardasil-9 is a vaccine that protects against nine strains of HPV and gives some protection against many forms of cancer, as well as against genital warts.
  » Gardasil-9 is approved for use in those age 9–45.
  » Gardasil-9 is only effective if it is administered before one is exposed to HPV.

Key Terms

Anaphrodisiac (p.413)
Andropause (p.409)
Aphrodisiac (p.412)
Erectile dysfunction (p.410)
Estrogen (p.396)
Fertility drug (p.406)

Follicle stimulating hormone (FSH) (p.398)
Gardasil-9 (p.414)
Hormone (p.396)
Hormone replacement therapy (HRT) (p.407)
Human papillomavirus (HPV) (p.414)

Infertility (p.407)
Luteinizing hormone (LH) (p.398)
Menopause (p.408)
Ovulation (p.398)
Progesterone (p.396)
Progestin (p.397)
Refusal statute (p.405)

Quiz Yourself!

1. In what year did the FDA approve the world's first birth control pill?

2. Which of the following is TRUE about the mechanism of action of hormonal contraceptives?
   A. They work by increasing levels of FSH and LH.
   B. They increase a woman's risk of ovarian cancer.
   C. They prevent ovulation.
   D. The pill is not safe for women over 27 years of age.

3. True or false? The Nexplanon rod is the most effective method of birth control on the market today.

4. Name three common side effects of oral contraceptives.

5. True or false? Emergency contraception causes an abortion.

6. True or false? Hormone replacement therapy has been proven to be a safe and effective method of reducing a woman's risk of heart disease and breast cancer in menopausal women of any age.

7. True or false? Viagra lowers blood pressure.

8. Which of the following is FALSE?
   A. Viagra is an aphrodisiac.
   B. Testosterone increases a man's risk of heart attack and stroke.
   C. Images in the media associate alcohol with sex and romance.
   D. Antidepressants may delay or increase the difficulty in achieving erection and orgasm.

9. Matching:
   1. _____ Placed in the vagina for three weeks at a time
   2. _____ Available over the counter for women of all ages
   3. _____ A rod placed under the skin of the upper arm
   4. _____ The second most commonly used form of contraception in United States
   5. _____ Placed on the skin of the buttock or hip for one week at a time
   6. _____ A hormonal shot given every three months
   A. Oral contraceptives
   B. The patch
   C. The ring
   D. Depo-Provera
   E. Nexplanon
   F. Emergency contraceptive pills

10. Which of the following is true about HPV and Gardasil?
   A. About 10 percent of women infected with the human papillomavirus (HPV) will develop cervical cancer.
   B. Gardasil protects completely against genital warts and cervical cancer.
   C. Since Gardasil was first administered in 2006, HPV has been essentially eradicated in the United States.
   D. Gardasil is only effective if it is administered before one is exposed to HPV.

Additional Resources

Websites
Planned Parenthood provides reproductive health services. They work to improve women's health and safety, provide resources for the prevention of unintended pregnancies and sexually transmitted infections, and advance the right and ability of individuals and families to make informed and responsible choices. https://www.plannedparenthood.org

A brief history of the birth control pill. https://www.pbs.org/wnet/need-to-know/health/a-brief-history-of-the-birth-control-pill/480/

Learn more with this chapter's digital tools at www.oup.com/he/rosenthal2e.

Videos
Basics of the female reproductive tract, hormones, fertilization, and mechanism of action of oral contraceptives. https://www.youtube.com/watch?v=lCYqLtmo670

Books
Rosenthal, M.S. (2013). *Human sexuality from cells to society.* Belmont, CA: Wadsworth Publishing/Cengage Learning

17 Problematic Drug Use and Addiction

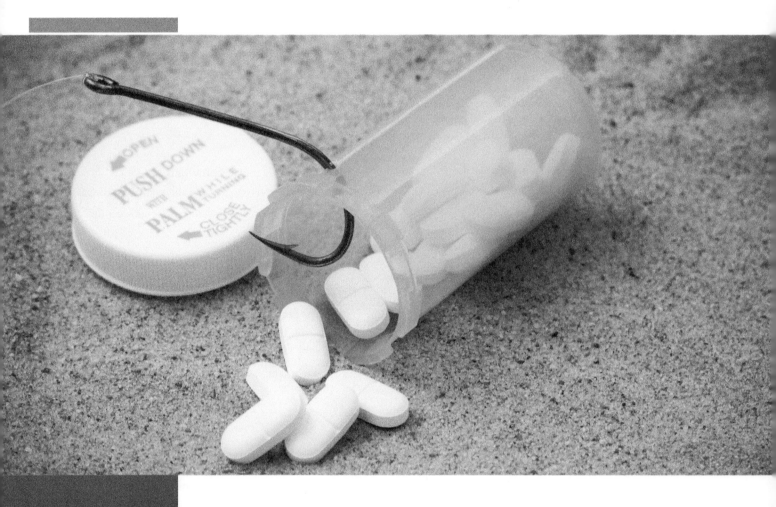

True or false?

1.
True or false? Regular drug use usually leads to addiction.

2.
True or false? When someone goes through withdrawal, it means he or she is addicted to a drug.

3.
True or false? Less than 10 percent of American medical schools, nursing programs, and pharmacy schools have a course on addiction.

Drug addiction is complex and mysterious. Although more than 88 percent of the population of the United States uses at least one potentially addictive drug daily, most people do not become addicted, and among those who do, most stop problematic drug use on their own.[1,2,3] Although many of those in recovery require total abstinence, some are able to manage their alcohol and drug use.[4,5,6]

How do you know if you or someone you know has a problem with alcohol or other drugs? Is it simply a matter of the amount of drug consumed, or are the frequency and pattern of use also important? Perhaps it's not how much or how often a person uses drugs, but the consequences of their use, including physical costs, such as tolerance, withdrawal, or damage to the brain and body; psychological consequences, such as stress or depression; or social ramifications, such as problems at work, with the legal justice system, or with friends and family. Or, perhaps it is not the quantity or the consequences of drug use, but rather a loss of control over its use.

Regardless of the definition, drug addiction ravages not only the individuals caught in its grip, but also their friends, family, and society in general. In this chapter, we will consider the myths and realities of drug dependence and addiction.

....

Learning Objectives

- Differentiate between physical and psychological dependence.
- Describe some factors that are used to measure a drug's addictive potential.
- Compare drug addiction rates by sex/gender, race, and age.
- Summarize some of the important characteristics of addiction.
- Evaluate the implications of classifying addiction as a disease or as a choice.
- List some biological factors that influence addiction.
- Clarify dopamine's role in addiction and motivation.
- Describe ways to recognize, diagnose, and assess addiction.
- Identify some biological, psychological, interpersonal, social, and environmental factors that underlie addiction.
- Consider the way one's personal characteristics, as well as societal views of a drug, influence our opinions about addiction.

Definitions of Dependence and Addiction

Drug addiction is devastating to individuals, families, and societies. Tobacco, alcohol, and illicit drug use is responsible for one in every five deaths around the world—an estimated 11.8 million deaths each year.[7] The death rate alone doesn't fully capture the health consequences of substance use disorder. There are other physical risks, such as damage to organ systems, increased chance of injury, and higher rates of suicide; psychosocial harm to one's relationships and community; and economic costs, both on a personal and societal level.

But what differentiates drug use from drug abuse? Dependence from addiction? These words often are used interchangeably and inconsistently, and our values, goals, and beliefs about drugs influence how we use the words. Government agencies might use the words one way when pursuing a political agenda,

Drug Addiction vs. Drug Dependence

"My name is Jenny, and I'm a grad student in my twenties. Two years ago, three discs in my lower back spontaneously ruptured, which led to chronic pain, requiring management with several long-term opioid medications and physical therapy. Being on the drugs has allowed me to manage the pain to the point of allowing me to get back to school and perform my daily tasks (vacuuming, laundry, etc.) with much less severe side effects.

"Last year I became extremely sick and was hospitalized. I couldn't keep anything down for almost two weeks, and thus I went through full-blown withdrawal. This occurred during my first two months of grad school. It was the most miserable time of my life aside from the original back injury. Withdrawal is the most painful, sickening, anxiety-inducing, physically taxing event a human body can experience, in my opinion. During this time, I tried to maintain a professional demeanor and attitude while suffering in complete agony. I was constantly having chills, sweating through my clothes even in a cold room, shaking, throwing up, having diarrhea, constantly flooded with anxiety, and horrified that someone would notice these obvious symptoms and report me. Finally, around week 6 I decided to return to my pain management doctor, who put me back on opioids. I was devastated to be back depending on narcotics, especially after conquering withdrawal, but I had exhausted all other options and my quality of life had become vastly compromised once again so I really didn't have a choice.

"I'm now on opioid medications, and I'm able to perform my duties at work and impress my supervisors with my talent in the field. I have been on the medications so long that I do not feel any euphoria anymore (it went away after about two weeks on each opioid) and my mental status and judgment are not impaired whatsoever.

"It is clear to me that I am physically dependent on narcotics. It is devastating to admit something like that. I feel guilty every time I fill a prescription, or take a pill in class, or calculate at what time to take a pill so I don't have to take one at work. Due to the nature of my profession, I am constantly drug tested. I feel like a criminal sometimes despite not doing anything wrong. With all the changes in healthcare management these days I live in fear that my access to the medications that gave me my life back will be taken away. I am very conflicted; I know in my heart I need the meds to live a normal life, but society makes me feel like I am doing something wrong, that I haven't done everything possible to improve my health on my own. I'm afraid of what will happen when I graduate and go to get a job and have to take a drug test. My entire life, especially my feeling of self-worth, is affected every single day and I hope someday things will change and I can have a much more normal life again."

What do you think of Jenny's experience? Would you consider her to be addicted to opioids, or is she dependent on them to treat the disease of chronic pain? Does your answer depend on her experience of withdrawal, her reason for using the drug, or whether her drug use improves or hinders her ability to function in the world?

---

while scientists, social workers, and attorneys might use them another way.

The differentiation between "drug use" and "drug abuse" is particularly political. Although most Americans use the addictive psychoactive substance caffeine every day, we are not overly concerned with caffeine addiction. A two-pack-a-day smoker is not usually called a "nicotine addict," but a person who occasionally uses heroin often is considered a heroin addict. Also, people may make a different moral judgment about a person who uses OxyContin to deal with the pain of cancer versus someone who uses it to deal with emotional pain. Use alone of any drug does not constitute abuse or addiction.

And what about the difference between dependence and addiction? A person with type 1 diabetes is physically dependent on insulin, yet is not considered to be addicted to it. Patients with diabetes do not typically rob a 7-Eleven to get money to buy insulin . . . but if one did, we'd probably be more understanding. Traditional models of addiction assume that an individual will develop both physical and psychological dependence, although many commonly abused drugs do not fit this narrow parameter. Recent concepts of addiction focus more on behavior and psychological craving for the drug.

Physical dependence reflects the changes that occur when the body and brain adapt to the presence of a drug, requiring increasingly higher amounts of the substance to achieve the desired effect (tolerance) and producing drug-specific symptoms when drug use is terminated (withdrawal). Although it often accompanies addiction, physical dependence alone does not constitute addiction. Cocaine is extremely addictive, yet cessation leads to little physical withdrawal. On the other hand, antidepressants are not considered addictive substances even though a person who abruptly stops taking an antidepressant such as an SSRI will experience withdrawal symptoms.

Physical dependence: Physical adaptations to drug use, including tolerance and withdrawal.

Psychological dependence is the state of strongly craving a drug. People may be psychologically dependent on a drug if they compulsively use it for its positive effects or to experience relief from stress or emotional discomfort. Psychological dependence can be even more powerful than physical dependence. It is not unusual for someone to crave a cigarette years after he or she has quit—long after the physical withdrawal symptoms have passed.

Addiction is more complex than physical or psychological dependence. For this reason, this text generally uses the term *addiction* in order to be precise and consistent. We define **addiction** as the compulsive use of and preoccupation with a substance such that it causes physical, psychological, and/or social harm to the user. We will also sometimes use the term "substance use disorder" (SUD). Substance use disorders include the misuse, dependence, and addiction to alcohol, legal, and/or illegal drugs. Some consider the use of the word "disorder" to be problematic, as it is affiliated with stigmatized conditions such as mental health disorders, but others consider the word "addiction" to be unsatisfactory and stigmatizing. Know that both terms are used with the utmost compassion and respect.

Ask yourself: Which term do you prefer—drug dependence, drug addiction, or substance use disorder? What are the social or political ramifications of using one term instead of another?

QUICK HIT

The word *addiction* comes from the Latin term *addicere*, meaning "to assign, surrender, or enslave." It was generally used in a legal sense and could refer to money, goods, or people that were sentenced to belong to someone. The word was revived in the 1500s to mean someone was "bound and devoted" to something. The Victorians compared the conduct of opium addicts to that of debtors, and they became known as addicts.

So which drugs are the most addictive? That's a difficult question to answer, because many factors need to be considered. Should we measure addiction by the **capture ratio**—the percent of those who try a drug and become habitual users? By that measure, nicotine nears the top of the scale (Figure 17.1). But the capture ratio is influenced by a drug's legal status, given that an illegal drug's potential penalties may decrease its capture ratio. Perhaps we should measure addiction by the number of people who seek treatment for addiction

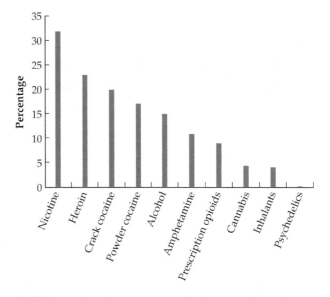

FIGURE 17.1. Some drugs are more addictive than others. The capture ratio is the percentage of users who become addicted to a drug. This figure shows the lifetime rates of addiction among persons who use specific substances.

Sources: Rose, M.E., & Cherpitel, C.J. (2011) Alcohol: Its history, pharmacology, and treatment. *Center City, Minnesota: Hazelden.*

Substance Abuse and Mental Health Services Administration (SAMHSA). (2020). Results from the 2019 national survey on drug use and health. *Rockville, MD: Center for Behavioral Health Statistics and Quality.*

to a drug? By that measure, alcohol would appear to be the most addictive; in fact, more than four times as many people seek treatment for alcohol addiction than for cocaine addiction. But might that be a factor of how common and accepted alcohol is in our society? Other measures of addiction evaluate withdrawal, tolerance, a drug's reinforcing qualities, and the degree of intoxication that occurs. For decades, scientists have tried to systematically rate the addiction potential of various drugs. Although their ratings differ in some ways, heroin routinely tops the chart as the most addictive drug. Cocaine, nicotine, and alcohol fall below heroin on the scale, and marijuana and hallucinogens are among the least addictive (Table 17.1).[8,9,10,11]

Ask yourself: What do you think is the best way to measure the addictive potential of a drug? Why?

Psychological dependence: An emotional need for a drug that has no underlying physical foundation.

Addiction: The compulsive use of and preoccupation with a substance such that it causes physical, psychological, and/or social harm to the user.

Capture ratio: The number of people who try a drug divided by the number who become regular or habitual users.

	Substance	Average Score*	Average of Both Researchers
Henningfield Ratings	Heroin	1.8	Heroin: 1.9
	Alcohol	2.4	
	Cocaine	3	Alcohol: 2.5
	Nicotine	3	
	Caffeine	5.4	Cocaine: 2.6
	Marijuana	5.4	
Benowitz Ratings	Heroin	2	Nicotine: 3.3
	Alcohol	2.6	
	Cocaine	2.2	Caffeine: 4.9
	Nicotine	3.6	
	Caffeine	4.4	Marijuana: 5.3
	Marijuana	5.2	

TABLE 17.1. Relative Addictiveness of Substances

* Scores were determined based on a measurement of withdrawal, tolerance, reinforcement, dependence, and intoxication; 1 is the most serious and 6 is the least.

Prevalence of Addiction

In Chapter 1, we discussed the prevalence of alcohol and other drug (AOD) use in the United States and around the world. In this chapter, we will focus on rates of drug addiction. Addiction affects men and women of all ages, races, and occupations. Globally, it is estimated that over 2 percent of the world population, some 164 million people, have alcohol or drug use disorder.[12] Drug use isn't consistent across all nations. There are two clear outliers: Russia has the highest rates of alcoholism, and the U.S. has the highest prevalence of addiction to other drugs.

In 2019, 7.4 percent of those age 12 and older in the United States—over 20 million persons—were considered to have substance dependence or abuse (Figure 17.2).[13] Of these, about 14.5 million were addicted to alcohol, 8.3 million to illicit drugs, and 2.4 million were diagnosed with dependence to both alcohol and illicit drugs (Figure 17.3). In the United States alone, addiction to alcohol, nicotine, and illicit drugs is estimated to have cost over half a trillion dollars, when considering healthcare expenses, lost productivity, and legal costs.

Millions of Americans suffer from alcohol use disorder (AUD). The National Survey on Drug Use and Health reports that in 2019, 5.3 percent of those over the age of 12 reported AUD in the past year. But some

feel this survey greatly underestimates the actual scope of AUD and that rates may be as high as 14 percent.[14]

Ask yourself: One study found that college students who binge drink are more positive about their social experience than those who do not.[17] Does this mean that binge drinking *causes* happiness? Or, may there be other factors at work that account for this finding?

Problematic drinking often manifests as binge drinking and/or heavy drinking. As discussed in Chapter 12, most studies in the United States define binge drinking as consuming five or more drinks on the same occasion on at least one day in the past month for a male, and four or more drinks for a female; almost a quarter of Americans age 12 and older (and about one-third of college students) report binge drinking in the past month.[15] In addition, almost 6 percent of the population age 12 and older—some 16 million people—reported heavy drinking,[16] defined as drinking five or more drinks on the same occasion on five or more days in the past month.

Addiction and Race

Addiction is an equal opportunity disorder. Due to both biological and social factors, however, there are some racial differences in rates of alcohol and drug addiction. As seen in Figure 17.4, American Indians/Alaska Natives and those who are 2 or more races are the most affected by addiction.

Addiction and Age

Addiction rates vary by age. The highest rates of substance dependence were found in those age 18–25, followed by adults age 26 and older, and by youth age 12–17 (Figure 17.4).[18] Rates of alcohol and drug abuse among youth have been steadily falling since 2002, when 8.9 percent of this population showed drug or alcohol dependence.[19]

Lowest addiction rates are seen in those over the age of 50, but substance abuse among adults age 50 and older—particularly of alcohol and prescription drugs—is one of the fastest growing health problems in the United States. The drug problem among seniors may be related to the fact that some baby boomers have a history with mind-altering substances, and they are now growing older in an era of widespread opioid painkiller availability.[20] An estimated 4.5 million Americans over

FIGURE 17.2. Addiction can affect anyone. Celebrities who have struggled with alcohol and/or drug addiction include (a) Robert Downey Jr., (b) Drew Barrymore, (c) Lindsay Lohan, (d) Daniel Radcliffe, (e) Samuel L. Jackson, and (f) Zac Efron.

the age of 50 are addicted to drugs or alcohol, yet the problem is still underdiagnosed and undertreated.[21]

Substance abuse may be hard to diagnose in the elderly, given that its symptoms can mimic other medical and behavioral conditions common among this population, such as dementia, depression, and diabetes. Additionally, older people may feel a stronger stigma against drug use and misuse, and they may be more reluctant to seek help for what they consider to be a private matter.[22,23] Finally, family members may be hesitant to encourage their elderly loved ones to seek treatment, because they may feel that treatment wouldn't matter much at this stage. Unfortunately, drug abuse may be particularly harmful in this population. Elderly people

are more likely to have diminished liver and kidney function, which can interfere with the metabolism of the drugs; in addition, they may be concurrently taking a number of prescription medications, which may interact negatively with the abused substance. Finally, the effects of some drugs of abuse are cumulative, and a lifetime of drug abuse may lead to significantly diminished health.

Addiction and Gender

Men are more likely than women to be diagnosed with substance abuse or dependence. Rates of substance dependence among adolescent men and women are similar, but in those over age 18, men are 70 percent more

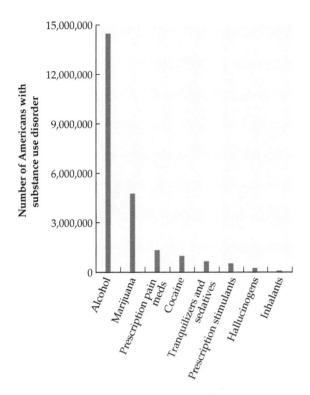

FIGURE 17.3. Past year drug or alcohol abuse or dependence in Americans age 12 and older. Although other drugs are considered more addictive, there are more Americans—almost 15 million—who are dependent on alcohol, largely because it is so widely used.

Source: (SAMHSA). (2020). Results from the 2019 national survey on drug use and health. Rockville, MD: Center for Behavioral Health Statistics and Quality

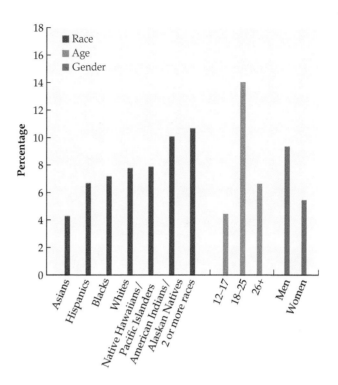

FIGURE 17.4. Past year substance use disorder by race, age, and gender. Addiction affects men and women of all races and ages.

Source: (SAMHSA). (2020). Results from the 2019 national survey on drug use and health. Rockville, MD: Center for Behavioral Health Statistics and Quality

likely to be classified as being dependent on drugs or alcohol than women (Figure 17.4).[24]

There are also differences in how men and women enter onto the path that can lead to addiction. Men are more likely to take drugs and alcohol as part of a pattern of risky behavior, or to enhance their behavior in social situations. Women, on the other hand, are more likely than men to begin taking drugs as self-medication to reduce stress, decrease feelings of social isolation, or alleviate depression.[25]

Many men and women with drug and alcohol dependence have been co-diagnosed with a psychiatric disorder. Women are more likely to be diagnosed with depression, anxiety, and phobias, and men have higher rates of attention-deficit/hyperactivity disorder (ADHD) and antisocial personality disorder.[26] In women, depression usually comes first and drug abuse follows, but in men, depression and other psychiatric disorders are more often secondary to the substance

Spontaneous remission: The reversal of a disease or condition—in this case, alcohol or drug addiction—without formal treatment.

abuse diagnosis.[27] In women, the progression from first use to the appearance of substance-related problems is significantly faster than it is in men.

Recognition, Diagnosis, and Assessment

Conventional wisdom notwithstanding, most people who use alcohol and drugs do not become addicted. And most of those who do become dependent at some point in their lives quit on their own, without formal treatment or relapse. But unlike those in formal treatment programs, from which it is fairly easy to obtain data, we have very little information about those who quit on their own, which is known as **spontaneous remission**.

Many with alcohol or drug addiction "mature out" of drug use—they reach a new stage of their lives, and stop using.[28,29,30] Some users stop problematic AOD use when the costs outweighed the benefits, and in others, the change is triggered by a major event—either negative, such as an arrest for driving under the influence (DUI) or a drug-related health problem—or positive, such as a marriage, new baby, or new job.[31,32]

For some, however, addiction can develop slowly and insidiously. Addiction almost always begins with experimental, casual, or social drug use. A drug's euphoric effects may be reinforcing, but its negative consequences can discourage use, and in most people, the cycle stops here. But in others, biological, psychological, and environmental factors increase the likelihood that drug use will escalate toward compulsive use and dependence, often manifesting as a cycle of tolerance and elevated use, withdrawal, and relapse (Figure 17.5).[33]

As a user moves toward dependency, drug use may become a big part of his or her social identity. The user may be increasingly more likely to use the drug for a specific purpose, such as dealing with anxiety or anger, or alleviating boredom or loneliness. At this stage, some signs of dependency begin to appear—he or she may drift away from old friends and spend more time with those who also use the drug freely; in fact, the main form of socializing may now involve the drug.[34]

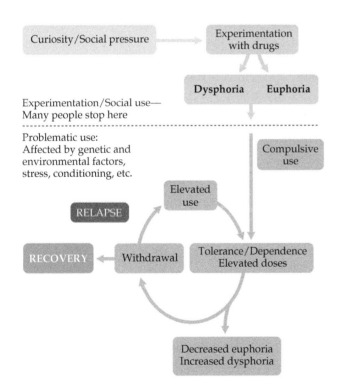

FIGURE 17.5. **The cycle of drug addiction.** Some people experiment with drugs but never progress to addiction. When use becomes problematic, behavior can cycle from tolerance, to withdrawal, to relapse and elevated use.

When someone with a substance use disorder is maintaining, he or she shows relatively stable drug use, getting high regularly but often feeling confident in his or her ability to maintain the habit. As tolerance develops, the user may need increasingly elevated doses. When cycling deeper into dependence, he or she may become preoccupied with the drug and experience more negative consequences because of its use. The person struggling with problematic drug use may attempt to stop using, which can culminate in either recovery or relapse.

Drug addiction often is considered a condition characterized by an overwhelming desire to take drugs, even when use leads to negative consequences; preoccupation with the drug, increased use, and loss of control over drug intake; and negative emotional states when denied access to drugs.[35] There are several components common to addiction[36]:

- *Preoccupation.* When a substance or behavior becomes the most important activity in a person's life and dominates his or her thoughts, feelings, and actions.
- *Mood modification.* When the activity causes a change in a person's mood—be it an energizing high or a relaxing numbness. The drug or activity may cause different moods at different times—a person's first cigarette of the day might energize her, but her after-dinner smoke may help her relax.
- *Tolerance.* When increasing amounts of the substance are required to achieve the former effects, such as when a drinker once felt the effects after four drinks but now requires eight.
- *Withdrawal.* The often-unpleasant effects the user experiences when drug use is reduced or discontinued. These effects are often the opposite of the effects initially caused by the drug.
- *Conflict.* The person may experience conflicts between himself and those around him, or conflicts with himself, regarding his use.
- *Relapse.* Sometimes a person can revert to earlier patterns of abuse even after years of abstinence or controlled use.

Before undergoing treatment for addiction, a person must first recognize that he or she has a problem. This can be difficult, because many users may erroneously believe that AODs are the solution, rather than the source, of their problems. The wake-up call that it is time to seek help for their substance abuse may come from the individual, or from their loved ones, coworkers, or the criminal justice system.

The fifth edition of the *Diagnostic and Statistical Manual of Mental Disorders*—the American Psychiatric Association's diagnostic reference guide—was released in 2013.[40] The DSM-5 considers "substance abuse disorders" as a continuum ranging from mild to moderate to severe based on the number of criteria that are met within a 12-month period.[41] The DSM-5 also divides substance use disorders into nine types—alcohol, caffeine, cannabis, hallucinogens, inhalants, opioids, sedative/hypnotics, stimulants, and tobacco. Regardless of which substance is abused, a diagnosis of substance use disorder depends on the user's behavior. There are

a total of 11 criteria; mild substance use disorder is diagnosed based on the presence of two to three criteria, moderate requires four to five criteria, and substance use is considered severe with the presence of six or more criteria. The 11 criteria are clustered into four groups, as seen in Table 17.2.

Once a substance use problem has been identified, the Addiction Severity Index (ASI) can assess its magnitude. The ASI is an hour-long, semi-structured interview used to gather information about recent and lifetime problems in six key areas of the user's life:

- Medical status
- Employment and support
- Alcohol and other drug use
- Legal circumstances
- Family and social relationships
- Psychiatric status

Problems are rated on a 10-point scale; scores can help to identify and prioritize problem areas, and higher scores indicate a greater need for treatment.

Although there are diagnostic criteria, as well as many biological factors underlying addiction, less than 10 percent of American medical schools, nursing programs, and pharmacy schools have a course on addiction. We would be appalled if our doctor were to say, "Sorry, I didn't learn about type 1 diabetes in med school." Yet, while there are 1.6 million Americans with type 1 diabetes, there are over 20 million with substance abuse problems. Perhaps addiction is so under-represented in medical schools because its classification as a disease is inconsistent.

TABLE 17.2.   Criteria for Substance Abuse Disorder from DSM-5

Impaired Control	Substance often taken over a longer period of time or in larger amounts than was intended
	Unsuccessful efforts to stop, reduce, or control use
	A great deal of time spent to obtain, use, or recover from use of the substance
	Overwhelming cravings or desire for the substance
Social Impairment	Use may lead to failure to fulfill major obligations
	Use continues despite persistent or recurrent interpersonal or social problems caused or exacerbated by use
	Important occupational, social, or recreational activities are given up or reduced due to substance use
Risky Use	Recurrent use in physically dangerous situations
	Continued use despite physical or psychological problems that are caused or exacerbated by substance use
Pharmacological Dependence	Tolerance to the effects of the substance
	Withdrawal symptoms when not using or using less

Alcohol Abuse Assessment Tests

How do you know if you or someone you love has a problem with alcohol? The CAGE screening test is one of the oldest and most popular.

- C: Have you ever felt the need to **C**ut down on your drinking?
- A: Have you ever felt **A**nnoyed by someone criticizing your drinking?
- G: Have you ever felt **G**uilty about your drinking?
- E: Have you ever felt the need for an **E**ye opener (drink at the beginning of the day)?

Two or more positive responses may indicate some degree of alcohol problem. The CAGE test is short and easy, but it is more accurate for white, middle-age men than it is for older individuals, women, and minorities. This may be due to cultural and gender differences in the perceptions of drinking and its consequences.

The AUDIT—Alcohol Use Disorders Identification Test—was developed by the World Health Organization in 1982. It takes longer to administer and is more difficult to score, but it is more accurate for women and people of different races or ethnic backgrounds.

1. **How often do you have a drink containing alcohol?**

(0) Never (skip to questions 9 and 10)
(1) Monthly or less
(2) 2–4 times a month
(3) 2–4 times a week
(4) 4 or more times a week

2. **How many drinks containing alcohol do you have on a typical day when you are drinking?**

(0) 1 or 2
(1) 3 or 4
(2) 5 or 6
(3) 7, 8, or 9
(4) 10 or more

3. **How often do you have six or more drinks on one occasion?**

(0) Never
(1) Less than monthly
(2) Monthly
(3) Weekly
(4) Daily or almost daily
(5) (Skip to questions 9 and 10 if total score for questions 2 and 3 = 0)

4. **How often during the last year have you found that you were not able to stop drinking once you had started?**

(0) Never
(1) Less than monthly
(2) Monthly
(3) Weekly
(4) Daily or almost daily

5. **How often during the last year have you failed to do what was normally expected from you because of drinking?**

(0) Never
(1) Less than monthly
(2) Monthly
(3) Weekly
(4) Daily or almost daily

6. **How often during the last year have you needed an alcoholic drink first thing in the morning to get yourself going after a heavy drinking session?**

(0) Never
(1) Less than monthly
(2) Monthly
(3) Weekly
(4) Daily or almost daily

7. **How often during the last year have you had a feeling of guilt or remorse after drinking?**

(0) Never
(1) Less than monthly
(2) Monthly
(3) Weekly
(4) Daily or almost daily

8. **How often during the last year have you been unable to remember what happened the night before because you had been drinking?**

(0) Never
(1) Less than monthly
(2) Monthly
(3) Weekly
(4) Daily or almost daily

9. **Have you or someone else been injured as a result of your drinking?**

(0) No
(1) Yes, but not in the last year
(2) Yes, during the last year

10. **Has a relative, friend, doctor, or another health worker been concerned about your drinking or suggested you cut down?**

(0) No
(1) Yes, but not in the last year
(2) Yes, during the last year

Add up the points associated with your answers above. A total score of 8 or more indicates harmful drinking behavior. An actual diagnosis for an alcohol use disorder should be made by a health professional trained in addiction.

Source: Babor, T.F., Higgins-Biddle, J.C., Saunders, J.B., & Monteiro, M.G. (2001). AUDIT: The alcohol use disorders identification test. Guidelines for use in primary care (2nd ed.). Geneva, Switzerland: World Health Organization.

Critical Evaluation

Is addiction a disease?

Some people define addiction as a chronic, recurrent disease, while others believe it to be a choice. How we classify addiction has legal, medical, and social implications. Use your critical thinking skills to evaluate some of the factors involved.

Definition of disease. What is a disease? Conditions that we consider to be diseases can change over time, in part due to shifting expectations of health, and in part due to evolving societal views.[42] For example, until the 1970s, homosexuality was classified as a disease, and gays and lesbians were sometimes subject to chemical or surgical "treatments" to try to cure them. So, what is a disease? Is it a deviation from the norm? If so, is the deviation biological, behavioral, or both? Is it a condition that causes impairment? What if the "sufferer" is not bothered by the condition? How might our definition of "disease" influence how we view addiction?

Genetic basis. Those who believe that addiction is a disease argue that people with addiction have a genetic predisposition to it, and their genes make them particularly vulnerable to drug abuse. Yet, does a genetic basis mean a person has no choice in behaviors and use is involuntary? Very few persons inject drugs right in front of police officers, regardless of whether they are addicted, suggesting that free will is not completely eliminated.[43] On the other hand, many people make choices that increase their risk of disease, but this does not mean they do not have a disease. For example, a person can have a genetic predisposition for type 2 diabetes and lifestyle choices can increase or decrease the likelihood of developing the disease. Nature and nurture are greatly entwined. Must it be one or the other?

Treatment. Should the way we categorize addiction influence the way we treat it? If addiction is a disease, should insurance cover the cost of treatment? If addiction is a choice, should the person bear the cost of treatment? Should insurance cover a smoker with emphysema or cancer? Should a runner be treated for a torn ligament? How should we weigh the costs to society to have taxpayer dollars cover addiction treatment, versus the cost to society to *not* cover treatment?

Stigma. If addiction is classified as a disease, is there an increased stigma because the person has an illness? Or, is the stigma less because it is not considered a person's "fault?" How much should these factors play into our classification?

Factors Underlying Drug Abuse and Addiction

As mentioned in the previous section, only a small percentage of those who use drugs progress to a state of dependence.[44] Why do some people become addicted and others do not? Multiple variables affect a person's onset and continuation of drug abuse and addiction.

In the past, drug use was considered to be a moral failing; many believed that people abused drugs because they chose to do so, or because there was something lacking in their character. In the mid-twentieth century, the disease model of addiction—the idea that addiction is a chronic, progressive, and irreversible disease over which the sufferer has no control—gained traction. Today, most people recognize that substance abuse and dependence is a complex, multifaceted condition, involving a combination of biological, psychological, and societal factors. Drug use may be influenced by individual factors, environmental conditions, and characteristics of the drug itself.

Biological Factors

Drug addiction is influenced by biological factors. Neuroanatomical, neurochemical, and genetic influences interact in complex ways to play a role in addiction.

Neuroanatomy

Drug addiction can be conceptualized as a cycle of 3 states: binge/intoxication, withdrawal/negative affect, and preoccupation/anticipation/craving.[45] These stages are each associated with dysregulation in brain circuits and neurotransmitter systems that control reward, stress, and executive function.

Those who are addicted to drugs—and those who may be genetically predisposed to one day develop an addiction—have unique responses in certain parts of their brain. Those who have a history of drug addiction tend to show differences in the areas of the brain involved in pleasure, impulse control, and memory. They show the following features:

- A functional deficiency of the dopaminergic neurons projecting to "pleasure centers" of the brain—leading to diminished subjective feelings of intoxication or pleasure.[46]
- Changes in parts of the prefrontal cortex, which may influence impulse control and cravings.[47,48]
- Sensitization in the hippocampus, amplifying the learned responses to drug cues and situations.[49]

Ventral Tegmental Area (VTA)/Nucleus accumbens (NAc) In the 1950s, Peter Milner and James Olds implanted electrodes into the limbic system of rats. If rats entered a certain section of the cage, an electrical current would stimulate their brains. Rats quickly showed a strong preference for that corner of the cage. When Milner and Olds allowed the rats to press a bar to control the electrical stimulation, the rats would press it hundreds of times an hour. The brain region soon became known as the "pleasure center," although later research showed this designation to be an oversimplification.[50] This pathway (Figure 17.6), which connects the VTA of the midbrain, the NAc, the limbic system, and the frontal cortex, produces and releases dopamine whenever a person engages in rewarding behaviors, and it plays a powerful role in pleasure, motivation, and addiction.

QUICK HIT

The reward areas of the brain also are involved in compulsive behaviors related to pleasurable activities such as food, sex, gambling, shopping. . . and Instagram. One study found that posting about oneself online is as rewarding to the brain as sex or eating.[51]

Prefrontal Cortex. The prefrontal cortex controls many things, including the ability to regulate emotions, suppress urges, and make decisions.

With long-term drug use, normal baseline activity of the orbitofrontal cortex shows reduced activity, which may allow impulsive behaviors to override rational decisions.[52] However, activity in the dorsolateral prefrontal cortex, an area that regulates cue-related cravings, may be increased.[53]

Amygdala. The amygdala, which is involved with feelings of fear, rage, and stress, may also play a key role in the transition from drug use to drug addiction.[54] Excessive drug taking can activate areas of the amygdala, accompanied by feelings of anxiety.[55] The amygdala may also be involved in learned associations that occur during the process of drug addiction and relapse.

Hippocampus. The hippocampus, involved in learning and memory, may play a role in addiction. When people begin using drugs, the action (finding and taking drugs) leads to a particular outcome (feeling good). The user learns to associate the positive feelings produced by the drugs with the drug paraphernalia used and with the environment in which it occurs. Over time, these drug cues produce greater responses in the reward pathways

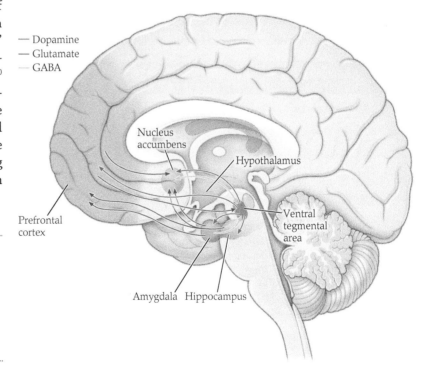

— Dopamine
— Glutamate
— GABA

Nucleus accumbens
Hypothalamus
Prefrontal cortex
Ventral tegmental area
Amygdala   Hippocampus

FIGURE 17.6. The mesolimbic dopaminergic pathway plays a powerful role in addiction. If this pathway is cut or destroyed, animals no longer show addictive behaviors. The amygdala is involved in drug withdrawal and the negative emotional characteristics of drug use. The hippocampus is part of the circuit that controls memories of and conditioned responses to drug experiences, and the prefrontal cortex coordinates all the incoming information and helps plan activities and inhibit certain behaviors.

than the drugs themselves. This associative learning is mediated, in part, by the hippocampus, which becomes sensitized, and drug seeking becomes compulsive.[56,57] The hippocampus also sends excitatory signals to the frontal lobe, enhancing the powerful cravings elicited by drug cues. Researchers have been investigating ways to decrease relapse in those recovering from drug addiction by weakening their memories of drug taking and breaking this conditioned response.[58]

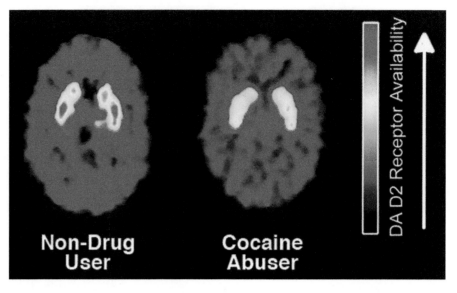

FIGURE 17.7. Subjects who are addicted to cocaine and other drugs have fewer dopamine receptors in the reward centers of the brain. The red areas on the left indicate a greater number of dopamine receptors in nonusers.

Neurochemistry

The neurochemistry of addiction is complex and involves multiple neurotransmitters (Table 17.3)

Dopamine is considered to be one of the primary neurotransmitters of reward and motivation (Figure 17.7). As far as we know, all drugs of abuse increase dopamine transmission in the VTA/NAc, amygdala, hippocampus, and prefrontal cortex circuit.

TABLE 17.3.	Neurotransmitters involved in drug addiction
Stage in drug addiction	**Neurochemical changes in the brain**
Binge/intoxication	Increased levels of: Glutamate Dopamine Serotonin GABA Acetylcholine
Withdrawal/negative affect	Increased levels of: CRF Dynorphin Norepinephrine Decreased levels of Dopamine Serotonin Opioids Endocannabinoids Oxytocin
Preoccupation/anticipation/craving	Increased levels of: Dopamine Glutamate Serotonin CRF

Source: Koob, G.F., & Volkow, N.D. (2016). Neurobiology of addiction: A neurocircuitry analysis. Lancet Psychiatry, 3(8): 760–73.

Some drugs, like amphetamine and nicotine, directly increase release, while others do it indirectly. Long-term, chronic exposure to addictive drugs changes these dopaminergic pathways so that they are less responsive to rewarding stimulation.

In addition, there may be a difference in the brains of those who are predisposed to addiction—perhaps due to genetic factors—that causes them to have lower levels of dopamine receptors, such that they need a drug to artificially raise their dopamine levels up to other people's normal levels.[59]

Scientists once believed that dopaminergic mesolimbic pathways were involved solely with pleasure, but scientists now believe that dopamine's role is more complex. People often experience *less* pleasure with chronic drug use, even as they exert more effort to attain it.[60] The complex role of dopamine in the mesolimbic pathways may help to explain this phenomenon.

Imagine that you destroy the dopamine fibers in a rat's brain, and the rat no longer follows a maze to obtain food. What should you deduce from that finding? You could say that the rat no longer experiences pleasure, so it doesn't seek out food. Or, perhaps the rat would like the food if it were placed in front of him, but he has no motivation to run the maze. Maybe he is motivated and takes pleasure in the food, but the lack of dopamine means he can't walk. Or maybe dopamine affects his sense of smell or his hunger. Obviously, further studies would need to be done to tease out the best interpretation. Science is not a collection of facts; it is a process of learning. We are still learning about the exact role that dopamine plays in the brain.

We now know that it is an oversimplification to say that the stimulation of these pathways causes pleasure. High dopamine activity is not always associated with pleasure. Schizophrenics—who have high dopamine levels—do not experience more pleasure than other people, and soldiers with post-traumatic stress disorder (PTSD) show increased dopamine activity when they hear recorded sounds of combat.[61] Additionally, dopaminergic neurons in the NAc will often discharge in *anticipation* of reward, not during the actual reward, when the most pleasure is presumably experienced.[62] Instead of simply controlling pleasure, dopamine seems to be involved in the *motivational processes* behind attaining goals—how hard you will work for your goal, and how long you will focus on the task.

Dr. John Salamone artificially raises and lowers dopamine levels in animals, and then allows them to choose between two rewards—a less desirable reward that is easy to obtain, and a more desirable reward for which they must work harder. Animals with reduced dopamine levels are much more likely to opt for the easy, low-value reward, but animals with normal dopamine levels will exert more effort for a higher-value reward.[63,64] This doesn't mean that dopamine isn't involved in pleasure and reward; simply that pleasure is not its *only* function.

This deeper understanding of the role of dopamine may help clarify the difference between "liking" and "wanting" with regards to drug addiction. Those addicted to drugs might want the drug, but they don't always like it. They may report that they are deeply unhappy, their life is a mess, and they don't even particularly enjoy taking the drug anymore, even as they compulsively seek it out.[65] Low dopamine levels in the midbrain may diminish the sense of pleasure experienced by those addicted to drugs but sensitize the areas that control motivation.

Other neurotransmitters, including GABA, glutamate, serotonin, dynorphin (an opioid peptide involved in analgesia, addiction, and mood), endocannabinoids, and corticotropin-releasing hormone (CRF) also play a role in addiction. GABA normally inhibits dopamine release in the mesolimbic pathway. Drugs such as heroin and alcohol inhibit GABA, thus indirectly raising dopamine levels in the reward pathways (Figure 17.6; see also figures in Chapter 7 [Figure 7.13] and Chapter 12 [Figure 12.10]).

Glutamate, a neurotransmitter involved in learning and memory, also plays an important role. Fibers that run from the prefrontal cortex to the VTA and NAc, and from the hippocampus and amygdala back to the prefrontal cortex, are mostly glutamatergic. Glutamate not only activates dopamine in the NAc, but it also makes the hippocampus and frontal lobe hypersensitive to drug cues, which might underlie the impulsivity and compulsivity involved in drug abuse (Figure 17.6).[66,67]

Some addicts have a genetic variant of the serotonin transporter, which leads to low levels of serotonin. This is associated with impulsive aggression, compulsive behavior, anxiety, negative mood states, and low response to alcohol intake, which are all associated with behavior patterns relevant for alcohol dependence.[68,69]

Some neurochemical circuits controlling reward and stress are abnormal in those who suffer from alcohol addiction. CRF is a neurotransmitter and hormone involved in the stress response. Increased activity in the CRF system is partially responsible for the anxiety and enhanced drinking seen during alcohol withdrawal.[70,71]

Genetic Factors Underlying Addiction

An individual's risk of drug addiction increases if he or she has a parent or sibling who is dependent on drugs or alcohol.[72] But addiction is a complex phenomenon, and there is no single "addiction gene" that controls it. Multiple genes and environmental factors interact to affect a person's susceptibility to drug addiction. In recent years, scientists have made significant progress in identifying genes that increase a person's susceptibility to addiction. Regions on chromosomes 4, 5, 9–11, and 17 are of particular interest.[73] Family studies of addiction suggest that perhaps 40–60 percent of one's predisposition to addiction can be attributed to genes.[74]

Twin studies can provide information about how heritable a trait is. Researchers can look at the concordance rate—the likelihood that a pair of individuals will both have a certain characteristic. Because identical twins share virtually 100 percent of genes, and fraternal twins share 50 percent, if a condition were entirely genetic, the concordance rate for identical twins would be at or close to 100 percent. Concordance rates for drug use, abuse, and dependence are often significantly higher for identical twins than fraternal twins.[75,76,77,78] The concordance rates for identical twins ranges from 58–71 percent, while concordance rates for fraternal twins are about 28–39 percent. Therefore, genetics are partially, but not entirely, responsible for drug and alcohol dependence. The role of genetic influences can vary across populations; heritability depends on sex, age, and culture.[79] Genetic factors for drug abuse seem to be stronger in males than in females.[80,81] The impact of genetic factors also seems to differ for specific drugs—in males, heroin and cocaine have some of the highest heritability, and hallucinogens and marijuana have the lowest.[82,83]

Addiction runs in families, but it is important to remember that "familial" and "genetic" are not the same thing. Members of the same family may speak the same language, but that doesn't mean that there is a gene that controls whether a person speaks English or Spanish. For this reason, adoption studies can be very helpful. Adoption studies compare the presence of a trait among family members who are biologically related and those who are adopted. Adopted siblings share the same family environment, but they don't share genes. Some classic studies done in the 1970s found that adult children of alcoholic birth parents raised by nonalcoholic adoptive parents had significantly higher rates of alcoholism compared with biological children of nonalcoholic parents.[84,85,86] Being raised by alcoholic parents, however, didn't further increase the likelihood of developing alcoholism—children who were raised by their alcoholic birth parents didn't have higher rates of alcoholism compared with those who were adopted away from alcoholic birth parents.

How would a gene affect one's susceptibility to drug addiction? Some specific genes suspected to play a role in addiction include those that code for metabolic enzymes, hormone secretion, or neurotransmitters such as dopamine, serotonin, GABA, and glutamate.[87,88] Even personality traits can be genetically controlled. Levels of a serotonin transporter are correlated with how resilient a person is,[89] and one serotonin transporter gene seems to be involved in how susceptible a person is to peer pressure.[90]

Genetic factors play an important role in the development of addiction, but like other complex diseases such as diabetes and cancer, drug addiction is strongly influenced by lifestyle and environment.[91] **Epigenetic** factors—those inherited modifications in gene expression caused by environmental factors—also play an important role in the development and maintenance of drug addiction and may be one of the missing links between environmental stimuli and genetic inheritance.

Almost all the cells in our body contain DNA, the blueprint for producing proteins. But not all genes are expressed in every cell of the body. Skin cells require different proteins than do liver cells or brain cells. The DNA sequence itself does not change, but a variety of factors including diet, stress, and environmental toxins allow some genes to be turned on and expressed, and other genes to be shut off, and these modifications can be passed down for generations. Many drugs of abuse can cause changes in the expression of genes and, in this way, may influence drug use in generations to come.[92,93]

QUICK HIT

Even the uterine environment may influence a person's predisposition to drug and alcohol use. Alcohol may taste sweeter if you are exposed to it before birth. Alcohol's taste is a mixture of sweet and bitter, but prenatal exposure seems to reduce the perceived bitterness of alcohol, making it seem sweeter.[94] Prenatal alcohol exposure may also disrupt brain development in the fetus that could predispose a person to problematic alcohol use later in life.

Psychological and Interpersonal Factors

Psychological and interpersonal factors also affect the likelihood of addiction. No single personality trait can adequately characterize people with alcohol or drug problems, or predict who will develop such problems. But certain personality traits are associated with a higher risk of alcohol or drug addiction. Impulsiveness, rebelliousness, and sensation-seeking can raise one's risk, as can insecurity, poor self-esteem, and a lack of resilience.[95,96,97]

Some drug abusers are especially reluctant to endure negative emotions such as anxiety, depression, anger, or frustration, and might favor different drugs to cope with their painful emotional states. For example, one person may use opioids to help deal with anger or anxiety, another might choose stimulants to help raise his energy level or mood, and yet another might seek out alcohol or benzodiazepines to numb overwhelming emotions. The common element is that the drug often serves as an antidote to disordered emotions.[98] This can lead to a cycle of drug abuse and addiction (Figure 17.8).

Many of those who suffer from addiction also have other psychiatric disorders such as schizophrenia, major depressive disorder or bipolar disorder, and anxiety disorders (Figure 17.9).[99] Drugs may be a coping mechanism for those suffering from these disorders to deal with their grief, stress, and anxiety, although the drug use and abuse is much more likely to worsen outcomes than it is to help.

Peer influences and role models are among the most powerful factors influencing whether a person begins using and abusing drugs. Associating with drug-using peers increases the chance that a person will try drugs, and that he or she will continue to abuse drugs. This is especially true during adolescence.

Epigenetics: Inherited modifications in gene expression caused by external or environmental factors.

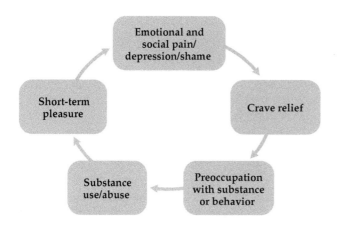

FIGURE 17.8. Cycle of drug abuse and addiction. Using drugs to cope with difficult emotions can lead to an endless cycle of abuse.

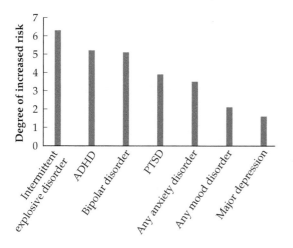

FIGURE 17.9. Increased risk of developing a SUD in individuals with a given mental health disorder, relative to those without. Someone with ADHD is 5.2 times as likely to develop substance abuse disorder compared to one without.

Source: Ritchie, H. (2019). Mental health disorders as risk factors for substance use. Accessed on September 11, 2020, from https://ourworldindata.org/mental-health-disorders-as-risk-for-substance-use

Growing up in a family with a parent or sibling who abuses drugs raises a person's risk of drug addiction. This may be due to genetic factors, because they learn to use drugs as a coping mechanism, or due to abuse and neglect associated with their upbringing.[100] Dysfunctional family dynamics, such as poor communication, neglect, trauma, or emotional or physical abuse, also raise a person's risk of addiction.[101]

Social isolation and loneliness may play powerful roles. Drug-dependent people often have poor interpersonal skills. They are also less likely to belong to a religious or community organization.

With all of these factors, it is important not to confuse correlation and causation. It can be hard to determine whether factors such as depression, impulsiveness, and poor social skills *cause* drug use, are caused *by* drug use, or if these factors and drug use are both caused by a separate element.

Adolescents and Drug Abuse

Adolescents may be particularly at risk of drug use and abuse because they are in a period of their lives when they want to rebel, show their independence from their parents, and take risks. They also want to gain acceptance from peers, develop a sense of identity, and seek fun. At the same time, the rational, decision-making areas of their brains are not fully developed.[102,103]

Peer influences and role models are among the most powerful factors affecting whether a person begins using and abusing drugs; this especially affects adolescents.[104] When an adolescent's peers use drugs, it may lead him or her to think, "Everyone is doing it." Indeed, believing that alcohol or drug (AOD) use is more widespread than it actually is raises a teen's risk of abuse or dependence. Adolescent exposure to alcohol, tobacco, and drugs of abuse leads to a significantly higher likelihood of drug addiction and drug-related problems in adulthood.[105,106] For example, if person begins drinking before age 15, he or she is more than five times as likely to develop alcohol dependence as someone who started drinking at age 21.[107,108]

Compared to nonusing teens, adolescents who use drugs are more rebellious, independent, and resistant to authority, and have lower self-esteem. They may have poor interpersonal skills, academic failures, a lack of commitment to school, and little involvement in community or religious organizations.

Family dynamics are also vitally important. Teens who are raised in a household with inconsistent parental discipline, permissiveness, unclear limits to behavior, poor communication, or family conflicts, or with family members who abuse AODs and who are permissive of AOD use, are at higher risk of developing dependence.

Perhaps more for adolescents than for adults, the availability of AODs in a community plays a role in use, abuse, and dependence. Increased availability—as exhibited by lower cost, less enforcement of laws regarding AODs, and a stronger media presence—manifests in increased alcohol and drug use and abuse. Stress, boredom, and access to spending money also raise a teenager's risk of substance abuse.[109]

Social and Environmental Factors

Remember Rat Park (Chapter 7)? When animals were left alone in their cages, with no social, creative, or intellectual stimulation, they would quickly become addicted to opioids. But in Rat Park—a large, lush

STRAIGHT
DOPE

COVID-19 and Substance Use Disorders

In early 2020, the SARS-CoV-2 virus, otherwise known as COVID-19, spread throughout the world, causing overwhelming physical and psychosocial devastation. This airborne virus spreads easily and has the potential to cause extensive damage to several organs of the body. Many people sheltered at home and physically distanced from others for months on end to avoid infection and reduce transmission.

The COVID-19 pandemic is associated with a significant increase in substance use. According to the CDC, as of June 2020, 13 percent of Americans surveyed reported starting or increasing drug or alcohol use to cope with the stress or emotions related to COVID-19.[111] COVID is also associated with a significant increase in anxiety and depression, which are risk factors for substance use disorder.

Social distancing and isolation are difficult for most people, but may be especially challenging to those battling substance use disorders.[112] Those with SUDs may be particularly vulnerable to contract the virus and may suffer a greater physical burden if they do, because of preexisting damage to the heart and lung, compromised immunity, and inadequate health care behavior. In addition, for those in recovery, self-quarantine may disrupt access to medications and other support services.[113] Also, as many hospitals are full to capacity with COVID-19 cases, those seeking medical treatment for drug-related issues may be less likely to receive the assistance they need.

enclosure full of food, toys, and many rats of both sexes—animals avoided the morphine-laced water, even when it was made to taste sweet. And already-addicted rats could get off drugs significantly more easily in the park than in a cage.

Social and environmental factors powerfully affect addiction. Drug addiction is often heavily concentrated in the poorest communities. Poverty, racism, and occupational stress are associated with higher rates of addiction, as are communities that have reduced opportunities for employment, education, and cultural outlets.

A person's likelihood to become addicted to drugs is, in part, affected by the availability of the drug. The number of bars in the area, how diligent storeowners are in checking the customer's age for purchases of tobacco and alcohol, and the availability of illicit drugs influence the development of addiction in adolescents. The cost plays a role as well. As the price of alcohol increases, excessive drinking decreases; a 10 percent increase in alcohol prices results in a 3–10 percent decrease in alcohol consumption.[110]

Finally, the media—movies, television, radio, magazines, and newspapers—impact our perception and use of alcohol, tobacco, and other drugs. Studies have shown that media exposure to tobacco,[114] alcohol,[115,116,117] and illegal drugs[118] is linked to use. Portrayals of use are often glamorized, so organizations such as the Entertainment Industries Council promote accurate depictions of the physical and emotional costs of substance abuse, addiction, and mental health in film, television, and music (Figure 17.10).

(a)

(b)

(c)

FIGURE 17.10. Depictions of substance abuse in the media. Depictions of substance abuse in the media. Some portrayals of substance abuse in movies, television, and music include (a) the movie *Requiem for a Dream*, (b) the television show *Euphoria*, and (c) the song "Starting Over" by Macklemore.

Ask yourself: What do you think are the most significant factors influencing addiction to drugs/maintaining compulsive drug use? Why?

Societal Views on Drug Addiction

How does society view addiction? In one random sample survey of over 700 adults, respondents were asked about their attitudes regarding addiction and mental illness.[119] The results found widespread negative feelings about those with drug addiction.

Figure 17.11 shows that people in this survey viewed addiction extremely negatively. Not only do most people not want someone with a substance abuse disorder to marry into their family or work at their place of business, but they also feel that treatment is ineffective, and that discriminating against those with a substance abuse disorder is not a problem.

Other studies back this up. In another study, survey participants read vignettes about a person with either a physical disability, mental illness, or alcohol or drug dependency, and were asked if the person in question should be avoided, blamed, or if they considered them to be dangerous.[120] Respondents labeled those with drug addiction as more personally responsible for their condition, and more dangerous, compared to individuals labeled with mental illness (who were viewed more negatively than those with physical disabilities). Such beliefs can lead to avoidance of and less support for those suffering from addiction.

Attitudes about addiction can depend on many factors, including a person's sex/gender, profession, personal experience with drugs, the drug in question, and even the way the survey is written.

Attitudes about Addiction Based on Gender

Scientists presented vignettes about people seeking help for an addiction problem to a group of students.[121] The stories varied the drug user's gender and which drug was used—alcohol, marijuana, crack, or heroin. They had the participants rate the hypothetical drug users on their levels of either internal or external responsibility. Internal responsibility included such beliefs as "he/she (the drug user) could have fought the circumstances that led to his/her addiction, but he/she didn't try," "he/she puts pleasure first," and "he/she lacks willpower." External responsibility was rated with such statements as "he/she didn't realize how addictive the substance was until he/she was already addicted," and "he/she didn't realize how deeply dependent he/she was until it was too late." A higher internal–external ratio represents a belief in higher personal responsibility for addiction. Beliefs about a user's personal responsibility depended on the drug used, whether the reader had personal experience with the drug, as well as on the gender of the reader.

- Participants attributed greater personal responsibility for problems with marijuana use compared to alcohol, heroin, and cocaine, perhaps because they believed marijuana was less addictive than those other drugs.[122]
- Participants attributed less personal responsibility to the users if the participant or someone close to them had experience with excessive AOD use.[123] Male participants attributed more

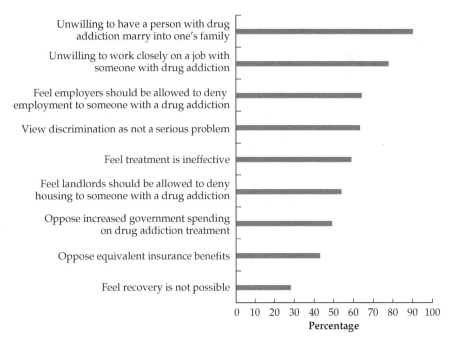

FIGURE 17.11. Attitudes about drug addiction. Many respondents had a very negative view of drug addiction compared to mental illness.

Source: Barry, C.L., McGinty, E.E., Pescosolido, B.A., & Goldman, H.H. (2014). Stigma, discrimination, treatment, effectiveness, and policy: Public views about drug addiction and mental illness. Psychiatric Services, 65(10): 1269–72.

personal responsibility for men with substance abuse disorders than for women. When judging users with alcohol dependence in particular, both men and women believed that men who were alcohol dependent had more personal responsibility for their addiction than female users did.[124]

Attitudes about Addiction Based on Occupation

A person's occupation can also affect attitudes about drug addiction. Instructors who taught substance abuse and addiction courses completed an addiction belief inventory in which they had to rate their views about addiction, including the following[125]:

- whether the addicted person could control use;
- whether addiction is a chronic disease that does not get better;
- whether addiction is inherited and predetermined for some people;
- whether recovery is possible and, if so, by what means;
- the degree to which those with substance use disorder are responsible for their actions and for their own recovery;
- the extent to which AODs are used to cope with difficult situations and personal problems; and
- whether using AODs is a choice and a sign of personal or moral weakness.

Researchers found that addiction educators, especially those who do research in the field, strongly believe that addiction is a coping mechanism for dealing with stressful life situations or psychiatric issues. Most do not characterize addiction as a moral failure. Also, the longer one has been an addiction educator, and the higher his or her academic degree, the less an addiction educator supports the idea that addiction is a disease and that people are genetically predisposed to be addicts from birth.

Why Do People's Beliefs about Addiction Matter?

You might be wondering why a person's beliefs about addiction are important. The reason is that attitudes influence policies and decisions, from the governmental level down to the personal level.[126] At the governmental level, views about addiction can determine how and where resources are allocated—toward treatment programs, prevention, or the criminal justice system. Attitudes about addiction may influence the way that judges and juries make decisions when

substance abuse has played a role in a crime. Physicians and other healthcare providers may suggest different treatments, depending on their views—or they may even refuse to treat someone who struggles with addiction. In fact, health professionals often have very negative attitudes about those with active substance use disorder, describing them as "difficult" and "annoying," although they hold less harsh views about those in recovery.[127]

Attitudes about addiction may affect one's personal and professional interactions. One study showed that many people believe that employers and landlords should be allowed to discriminate against those struggling with substance abuse.[128] Indeed, many of those who recognize that they have a substance abuse disorder do not seek treatment because they are afraid of the possible negative effects on their jobs or the response from their communities.[129] Finally, a person's attitudes about addiction also can influence decisions about treatments for themselves or for loved ones.

What are *your* views about addiction and those who suffer from it? Do your attitudes depend upon the sex, age, race, occupation, or socioeconomic status of the user? Do they depend on which drug is used? As an example, let's consider America's most widely used recreational drug—alcohol.

Attitudes about Problematic Drinking and Other Compulsive Behaviors

What constitutes problematic drinking? How much is "too much" alcohol? Millions of Americans have behavior that could be classified as heavy drinking, but excessive drinking is not the same thing as addiction. A government survey of over 138,000 people found that 90 percent of heavy drinkers did not meet the criteria for alcohol dependence.[130]

What then are the limits of "social drinking?" On the TV show *Mad Men*, the advertising executives drink enormous amounts of alcohol all day, and most of the time it's not considered to be an issue. Of course, that was during a different era. But still, does the amount of alcohol that constitutes problematic drinking depend on a person's job? Gender? Age? Race? Tolerance level? Or on the historical era in which he or she lives? Perhaps the definition should consider the effect to which alcohol interferes with a person's health, family, social, and work life.[131]

The actual harm—physical or otherwise—caused by the drug may not be one of the primary factors underlying our attitude about a drug. For example, there is much greater stigma against heroin use than alcohol

TABLE 17.4.   Comparison of the Long-Term Effects of Alcohol and Heroin

	Alcohol	Heroin
Schedule	Legal and unscheduled	Schedule I
Prevalence of Use and Abuse	About 140 million current users in the United States. Some 6.8% of men and 3.9% of women in the United States meet the criteria for alcohol dependence or abuse.	Between 700,000 and 1 million people in the United States use heroin occasionally, and about 431,000 are current users. Addiction typically takes 5 to 18 months to develop. Addiction may be strongly determined by environment.
Chronic Effects	Long-term heavy drinking can lead to brain damage, cardiomyopathy, endocrine disorders, impotence, diminished immune function, gastritis, liver disease, and cancer.	Long-term chronic heroin use leads to impotence and constipation. No major malformations or tissue damage occurs as a direct result of chronic opioid use. Most danger comes from overdose and shared needles.
Therapeutic Index	5–10	6
Withdrawal	More severe and dangerous than opioid withdrawal. Withdrawal may be fatal. In untreated advanced cases, as many as 1 in 7 die of withdrawal.	Miserable but not life-threatening.
Use in Pregnant Women	Fetal alcohol syndrome. Cognitive and behavioral impairments, pattern of abnormal features of head and face, coordination problems. Effects last a lifetime.	Neonatal abstinence syndrome. Increased irritability, gastrointestinal distress, respiratory distress, seizures, low birth weight, neurobehavioral abnormalities, higher risk of sudden infant death syndrome. Symptoms typically last up to 6 months.
Cost to Society	Alcohol abuse and alcohol use disorders cost the United States approximately $249 billion each year.	Heroin abuse costs the United States $19.6 to $33.4 billion each year.
Deaths in United States	93,000 per year	15,000 per year

use, but heavy chronic alcohol use is actually harder on the body than is chronic use of heroin (assuming the heroin is of a known dosage and sterile techniques are used to administer the drug) (see Chapter 7). Table 17.4 compares the long-term effects of heavy alcohol use with chronic heroin abuse.

Ask yourself: What is responsible drinking? Being able to remain in control of one's behavior and stop at specified times or number of drinks? Drinking that doesn't jeopardize one's health, life, occupational status, relationships, or legal status? Drinking that doesn't harm others? Do you know anyone who drinks irresponsibly? What is it that makes you consider the behavior irresponsible?

When discussing addiction, should we consider only drugs and alcohol? Do you believe that people can become addicted to sex, food, gambling, shopping, video games, or other activities? Are problematic behaviors a true addiction, or just bad habits? This is a topic of hot debate among those in the field. Some are "purists" who believe that only substances such as alcohol or drugs can cause true

addiction because they lead to tolerance and withdrawal. But others have a broader definition, and may consider something an addiction if the behavior fits the criteria of compulsion, preoccupation, and resulting harm.

Many other questions muddy the waters further. "Normal" and "deviance" are socially relative, ambiguous terms that vary greatly from place to place, time to time, and person to person. What, for instance, is a "normal" amount of sex? Does it depend on a person's age or gender? In one study of men and women who self-identified as sex addicts, men reported an average of 59 sexual partners over the previous five years, while women reported an average of eight partners during the same time period.[132] If these behaviors can be considered addictions, do we need to change our treatment approach? As we'll see in Chapter 18, most AOD treatment programs in the United States require lifelong abstinence as a goal. This is clearly an unattainable goal for food addictions, and probably unrealistic for shopping, sex, and internet addictions as well.

Ask yourself: Do you think the term *addiction* should be reserved for only AODs, or should it be applied to problematic behaviors as well? Why do you think so?

Chapter Summary

- **Definitions of Dependence and Addiction**
  - » Drug addiction is devastating to individuals, families, and societies.
  - » It can be difficult to differentiate between drug use and abuse.
  - » Drug dependence often has both physical and psychological components. Physical dependence reflects the changes that occur when the body and brain adapt to the presence of a drug, and psychological dependence is the state of strongly craving a drug.
  - » Drug dependence and addiction are not the same thing. Drug addiction is often considered a condition characterized by a compulsion to seek and take drugs even in the face of negative consequences, loss of control over drug intake, and the emergence of a negative emotional state when denied access to drugs.
  - » Addiction is sometimes referred to as "substance use disorder."
  - » It is difficult to measure which drugs are most addictive, because there are many factors that need to be considered.
  - » When scientists evaluated drug withdrawal, tolerance, reinforcement, dependence, and intoxication, heroin was assessed as the most addictive drug, followed by alcohol, cocaine, and nicotine. Caffeine, hallucinogens, and marijuana are among the least addictive drugs.
- **Prevalence of Addiction**
  - » In the United States, over 7 percent of individuals age 12 and older are classified with substance dependence or abuse.
  - » Of those age 12 and older, about one-quarter report binge drinking, and 6 percent reported heavy drinking in the past month. Those who are 2 or more races are the most at risk of addiction, and Asians are least at risk.
  - » Addiction rates are highest in those age 18–25, followed by those age 26 and older. Rates of alcohol and drug abuse among youth have been falling since 2002, while rates are rising among adults 50 years of age and older.
  - » Men are more likely than women to be diagnosed with addiction. Men are more likely to begin abusing AODs as part of a pattern of risky behavior, while women are more likely to use drugs to try to reduce stress, anxiety, loneliness, or depression.
- **Recognition, Diagnosis, and Assessment**
  - » Most people who use alcohol and drugs do not become addicted, and most of those who do become dependent at some point in their lives quit on their own.
  - » Scientists have comparatively little data about spontaneous remission.
  - » People may escalate from casual toward compulsive use, manifested by a cycle of elevated tolerance, increased doses, withdrawal, and relapse.
  - » Before treatment, a person must first recognize that he or she has a problem with addiction.
  - » Substance abuse disorder is diagnosed based on the presence of certain criteria listed in the fifth edition

of the *Diagnostic and Statistical Manual of Mental Disorders* (DSM-5). The DSM-5 characterizes substance use disorder as mild, moderate, or severe, based on the number of symptoms the individual displays.
  - » Once a substance use problem has been identified, the Addiction Severity Index (ASI) can assess its magnitude.
  - » Some people consider addiction to be a chronic disease, while others consider it to be a choice. How we classify addiction has far-reaching implications.
- **Factors Underlying Drug Abuse and Addiction**
  - » Although many people use drugs, only a small percentage will progress to a state of addiction.
  - » Biological, psychological, and environmental variables affect a person's onset and continuation of drug abuse and addiction.
  - » Neuroanatomical, neurochemical, and genetic factors contribute to addiction.
  - » Some key brain areas involved in addiction include the ventral tegmental area and nucleus accumbens, the prefrontal cortex, amygdala, and the hippocampus.
  - » The neurochemistry of addiction is complex and involves multiple neurotransmitters. Dopaminergic pathways in the midbrain play a major role in addiction and motivation. Other neurotransmitters also play a role.
  - » Genetic factors influence one's susceptibility to addiction, although there is no single "addiction gene"; instead, multiple genes and environmental factors interact to affect a person's susceptibility to drug addiction.
  - » Psychological and interpersonal factors also affect the likelihood of addiction.
  - » Certain personality traits such as impulsiveness, rebelliousness, insecurity, and poor self-esteem are associated with a higher risk of drug addiction. Adolescents may be particularly at risk of drug use and abuse.
  - » Peer influences and family dynamics are also powerful factors influencing whether a person begins using and abusing drugs.
  - » Social and environmental factors powerfully affect addiction.
  - » Poverty, racism, and occupational stress are associated with higher rates of addiction, and rates are higher in those who live in communities with fewer educational or occupational opportunities and higher availability of alcohol and drugs.
- **Societal Views on Drug Addiction**
  - » Many people hold negative views about those with drug addiction.
  - » Attitudes about addiction depend on many factors, including a person's sex/gender, profession, personal experience with drugs, and the drug in question.
  - » People's beliefs about addiction are important, because attitudes can influence policies and decisions from the governmental level to the personal level.
  - » The question of whether problematic behaviors such as compulsive sex, eating, gambling, shopping, or other activities can be considered true addictions is controversial.

Key Terms

Addiction (p.421)
Capture ratio (p.421)

Epigenetics (p.432)
Physical dependence (p.420)

Psychological dependence (p.421)
Spontaneous remission (p.424)

Quiz Yourself!

1. True or false? If a person is physically dependent on a drug, this means the person is addicted to the drug.

2. Rate the following drugs from MOST addictive to LEAST addictive: alcohol, caffeine, heroin, marijuana.

3. Which of the following is true regarding the demographics of drug addiction?

   (A) Drug addiction rates in those over 50 are decreasing.
   (B) Blacks have the highest rates of substance abuse of any race.
   (C) Drug addiction rates are highest among those age 18–25.
   (D) Women have higher rates of drug addiction than men have.

4. Name three components characteristic of addiction.

5. Which of the following brain regions is NOT thought to play a direct role in addiction?

   (A) Nucleus accumbens
   (B) Prefrontal cortex
   (C) Hippocampus
   (D) Parietal lobe

6. True or false? Alcohol abuse disorder is genetically determined by a single gene on chromosome 2.

7. True or false? Peer influences are among the most powerful factors influencing adolescent drug use.

8. Name three factors that raise a teenager's risk of substance abuse.

9. True or false? Most heavy drinkers are addicted to alcohol.

10. True or false? Our attitudes about drugs are directly correlated with how dangerous they are.

Additional Resources

Websites
The Addiction Project. https://www.hbo.com/documentaries/addiction
Self-help tools to deal with addiction. http://www.helpguide.org/topics/addiction.htm
Global demographics of drug use. https://ourworldindata.org/drug-use#citation

Videos
Great animation about addiction. http://www.hykade.de/(Go to "films" and then to "nuggets.")

Movies
Requiem for a Dream. (2000) (102 minutes). Brilliant and emotionally shattering film that shows the devastating effects of addiction.

Books
Knapp, C. (1997). *Drinking: A Love Story*. New York: Dial Press.

Learn more with this chapter's digital tools at www.oup.com/he/rosenthal2e.

18

Prevention and Treatment of Drug Use and Abuse

True or false?

1.
True or false? Some anti-drug ad campaigns actually increase drug use.

2.
True or false? Most people who become dependent on alcohol or other drugs cannot quit without a formal treatment program.

3.
True or false? To recover from addiction, lifelong abstinence is the only available option.

Millions of people are dependent on alcohol and other drugs (AODs). Substance abuse costs the United States more than half a trillion dollars each year, as well as exerting a devastating personal burden on the individuals who are addicted, their families, friends, and coworkers.[1] Alcohol and drug abuse leads to hundreds of thousands of deaths and over $700 billion a year in costs due to crime, health care, and reduced productivity.[2]

Because drugs can be so destructive, the government employs various methods and programs to try to alleviate drug-related harm. The national policy to control drug use has three priorities:

- Stop drug use before it starts.
- Provide treatment programs for those who are abusing or who are dependent on drugs.
- Disrupt the supply of drugs and impose harsh penalties for drug trafficking.

This chapter discusses various types of programs designed to help prevent drug use and abuse, including school-based educational programs, advertising and media campaigns, and drug testing. This chapter also describes various methods of treatment for when prevention fails.

Learning Objectives

- Describe various types of prevention programs.
- Identify characteristics of successful and unsuccessful school-based drug prevention programs.
- Weigh the success of advertising campaigns to prevent drug use.
- Compare and contrast the five primary types of drug tests.
- Trace the stages of recovery.
- Summarize the pharmacological and psychosocial treatments for addiction.
- Compare and contrast the principles behind 12-Step programs and secular self-help treatment programs.
- Evaluate whether total abstinence is the only solution for drug or alcohol abuse.
- List the characteristics of effective addiction treatments.
- Explain some factors that underlie the probability of relapse.

Types of Prevention

From past chapters, we know that reducing the availability of drugs and enforcing harsh drug laws have not prevented drug use. In addition, as we will see later in this chapter, it can take years for drug users (especially for users of alcohol and tobacco) to quit successfully, and most eventually will relapse.[3] The best way to avoid drug use and addiction is to prevent someone from starting rather than trying to get them to stop. Prevention of substance abuse has traditionally been classified as primary, secondary, and tertiary prevention, but drug prevention programs also can be categorized according to the intended target population. This method categorizes prevention programs as universal, selective, and indicated.[4,5]

Primary Prevention

Primary prevention is directed at those who have had little to no personal experience with drugs; the goal is to prevent drug use and abuse from starting. Primary prevention programs, such as the school-based program LifeSkills Training, are typically used in elementary and middle schools. Common approaches include providing information about drugs and building drug-resistance skills.

Secondary Prevention

Secondary prevention aims to minimize the damage in a population that already has had some experience with drugs. The goals are to limit the extent of abuse, prevent drug use from spreading to substances beyond those that already are being used, alter attitudes and behaviors about drugs, and stress healthy and responsible lifestyles. These programs are more typically offered in high schools or college environments.

Tertiary Prevention

Tertiary prevention is geared to those who are already heavy drug users. The goals are to assess and diagnose, refer into treatment, terminate use of the substance, and prevent relapse. Tertiary prevention of drug use is discussed later in this chapter.

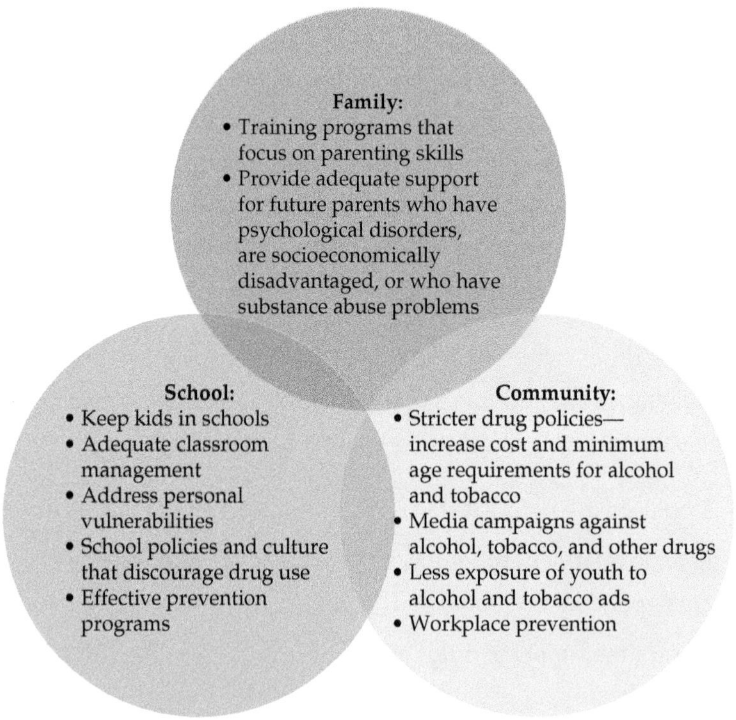

Family:
- Training programs that focus on parenting skills
- Provide adequate support for future parents who have psychological disorders, are socioeconomically disadvantaged, or who have substance abuse problems

School:
- Keep kids in schools
- Adequate classroom management
- Address personal vulnerabilities
- School policies and culture that discourage drug use
- Effective prevention programs

Community:
- Stricter drug policies—increase cost and minimum age requirements for alcohol and tobacco
- Media campaigns against alcohol, tobacco, and other drugs
- Less exposure of youth to alcohol and tobacco ads
- Workplace prevention

FIGURE 18.1. A multidisciplinary approach is often the best way to prevent drug addiction. Preventing drug use and abuse is most effective when the family, schools, and community are involved.

Universal Prevention

Universal prevention programs are designed to preclude the development of drug use and abuse and are delivered to the general population. A national media campaign to discourage tobacco use is one example of a universal prevention program.

Selective Prevention

Selective prevention programs are targeted to individuals of the general population who are thought to be at a higher risk of developing AOD dependence, due to biological, psychological, social, or environmental factors. Children of those who suffer from alcohol use disorders or students doing poorly in school might be targeted for selective prevention programs. Although it can be difficult to identify, recruit, and attract high-risk youth, the content of selective prevention programs can be tailored to the specific risks of those in the group. Some programs specifically target children of substance abusers, while others may focus on students who test high on personality characteristics such as anxiety, impulsivity, and risk-taking.[6,7]

Indicated Prevention

Indicated prevention programs are for individuals who show early danger signs of abuse, but have not yet been diagnosed with drug addiction. These programs might focus on children who begin alcohol or tobacco use at a young age, or an adult who has received his first DUI (driving under the influence) arrest. One indicated program, Project Towards No Drug Abuse (Project TND), targets at-risk high school students. The interactive program focuses on students' attitudes, beliefs, and expectations about drugs; communication and coping skills; and healthy decision-making.

As we saw in Chapter 17, the development and maintenance of drug addiction is a complex, multifaceted condition that involves biological, psychosocial, and environmental factors. As such, a multidisciplinary approach is often the best way to prevent drug addiction from happening (Figure 18.1). Some approaches to prevent drug use include school-based campaigns, family and community involvement, advertising campaigns, and drug testing.

Ask yourself: Of the three key participants in prevention programs—schools, family, and community—do you think there's one that has the most impact? If so, which one, and why?

School-Based Prevention Campaigns

The school system is an opportune setting to educate young people about drugs and to enhance the skills they need to avoid beginning a cycle of dependence. Prevention methods should be research-based and effective. Unfortunately, after a long journey of trial and error, there have still been more failures than successes.

Ineffective K–12 School-Based Methods of Drug Abuse Prevention

Some school-based methods found to be ineffective in preventing drug use include lecturing about drug facts, scare tactics, presentations by former addicts or police officers, and only addressing students' self-esteem or values.[8]

Cognitive Approaches and Scare Tactics

Drug prevention programs in the 1970s and 1980s were driven by the assumption that if students had accurate information about drugs—especially about their harmful effects—they would make a rational choice not to use them. In these programs, police officers would go to schools and discuss how alcohol or drugs exert their effects in the body. They would bring in pills, joints, and other drugs to show students what the substances looked like, so students would know what to avoid. Most of the presentation focused on horror stories about the frightening physical and legal ramifications of drug use.

Unfortunately, cognitive and scare tactics not only did not deter drug use, they actually may have increased it[9]:

- The *mere exposure effect* suggests that the more we're exposed to something, the more we like it.
- Demonstrating the drugs aroused the students' curiosity and taught them of the existence of some substances that they might not have known of otherwise.
- Many students who had previous pleasant experiences with drugs learned to distrust everything in the officers' message and to disbelieve the reality of AOD's harmful effects.

- Adolescents often *want* to take risks and rebel, so trying to scare them actually may have increased drug use.
- This approach assumes that drug use is a conscious, rational decision, and that it can be stopped or prevented based on information alone.

Affective Programs

As cognitive and scare tactics were found to be ineffective, prevention programs shifted their approach to affective programs focused on the feelings, emotions, attitudes, and values that may underlie drug use. These programs often did not directly mention alcohol, tobacco, and other drugs at all. Affective programs assumed that adolescents begin to use drugs due to a lack of personal and social skills. These programs identified low self-esteem, negative self-awareness, and poor communication and interpersonal skills as risk factors for drug use. They then taught the students to recognize their feelings and express them, and to analyze and clarify their values.[10] Although sometimes helpful in boosting self-esteem, these programs did not prevent drug use.[11]

Presentations by Law Enforcement

The DARE program—Drug Abuse Resistance Education—was created in 1981 by Daryl Gates of the Los Angeles Police Department. Over a 17-week program, police officers would go to elementary school classrooms and teach students about drugs and personal safety (Figure 18.2). Students would write essays

FIGURE 18.2. DARE. Although it was very popular, the DARE program has been shown to be ineffective in preventing drug use.

critical of drug use and publicly pledge their opposition to drug use. Hundreds of millions of dollars were dedicated to the program, which quickly spread to 70 percent of schools in the United States and more than 50 nations worldwide. One factor underlying DARE's popularity was that parents liked it, perhaps because they were intimidated by having to give "the drug talk" to their children.[12] Unfortunately, the program did not work.[13] Some students who went through the DARE program showed higher drug use compared with students who never went through the program, and by other metrics there was no difference in drug use.[14] In 2009, DARE partnered with the creators of Keepin' It REAL (KiR; discussed below) to adapt the KiR program to be administered by DARE workers. Keepin' It REAL DARE employs more elements shown to be effective in preventing drug use, but the adaptation has only been tested on a narrow audience and may not be appropriate or effective for DARE's larger audience.[15,16]

QUICK HIT

Daryl Gates, the founder of the DARE program, testified to the Senate judiciary committee that casual drug users were guilty of "treason" and should be "taken out and shot."[17]

Effective School-Based Methods of Drug Abuse Prevention

The United Nations Office on Drugs and Crime (UNODC) has summarized all currently available scientific evidence regarding drug abuse prevention and has identified the major features of effective programs.[18] The best school-based prevention programs provide students with both information and life skills, through an effective methodology:

- They are structured, interactive sessions given once a week over the course of a school term, with booster sessions presented over subsequent years.
- They are delivered by trained facilitators and peer counselors.
- They provide opportunities to learn and practice personal and social skills, such as decision making, coping strategies, and avoiding peer pressure.

Social influence model: A multifaceted approach to drug prevention that includes information, drug-resistance skills, and the involvement of parents and community members.

Media literacy: The ability to understand, analyze, and evaluate media.

- They dispel misconceptions about the prevalence of drug use and present the realities of its effects.
- They include many shareholders—students, teachers, facilitators, administrators, parents, and community members.

Programs that use these methods are sometimes called the **social influence model** of drug prevention, which is based on the hypothesis that young people use drugs because they have difficulty resisting peer and media influences that encourage drug use. This model retains some aspects from the cognitive and affective approaches, but it goes beyond them, combining many of the tactics from more effective approaches.[19,20,21,22,23]

Information

Drug prevention programs are most effective when they provide straightforward and honest information about drugs. This enables students to directly connect the life skills they learn with AOD use in order to make better decisions. These programs also can suggest recreational, cultural, and athletic alternatives to drug use.

Effective programs correct misperceptions about the prevalence of use. Many youth believe that AOD use is more widespread than it actually is, which may encourage them to use the drugs in order to fit in with their peers.

Giving accurate information about potential harmful effects also can decrease use. Rumors of the purported benefits of using a drug usually spread much faster than information about its potentially negative consequences.[24] It can take longer for evidence of adverse consequences to accumulate and be disseminated. Prevention also needs to occur drug by drug, because young people often hold drug-specific beliefs and will not necessarily generalize the adverse consequences of using one drug to the use of others.[25]

Media Literacy Campaigns

We in modern society are continually bombarded with information from companies trying to convince us to purchase their products. Because alcohol and tobacco company ads promoting the use of their products have been shown to increase use, some school-based programs combat this by teaching students about media literacy. **Media literacy** is the ability to understand, analyze, and critically evaluate messages from ads, television shows, or movies, in order to be less influenced by these messages. Media literacy helps viewers to recognize that the authors of these ads, shows, and films[26]

- often have political or financial motives;
- target their message to specific audiences, such as minorities or adolescents;
- try to link the use of the product to romance, love, good looks, and power; and
- make the product look as attractive as possible, while leaving out important (negative) information.

Many studies suggest that higher media literacy is correlated with a reduced intent to use tobacco or other drugs.[27,28,29,30,31,32] One study, however, found that media literacy campaigns actually *increased* a participant's expectations of future smoking.[33] This effect may be due to an increased curiosity about smoking, or a fatalistic sense of inevitability when learning about the techniques of the advertising industry. Another potential problem with media literacy campaigns is that they assume that people's behaviors are a result of careful analysis and reasoned choices, which is not always the case.

Skills

Effective programs encourage skills and abilities such as decision making, problem solving, and assertiveness, as well as improve social skills and communication. They teach strategies to cope with anxiety and stress, and encourage students to learn how to recognize and resist pressure from peers and the media. These programs help adolescents to recognize high-risk situations where they may be pressured to drink, smoke, or use drugs, and discuss ways for the youth to effectively deal with or avoid these situations. Program leaders guide them in what to say and how to respond most effectively.[34] To do this successfully, these programs must provide opportunities to reinforce these skills.

Methods

Drug prevention programs work best when they are active, participatory learning experiences that include role-playing and the opportunity to practice drug-resistance skills (Figure 18.3). The messages learned and the skills acquired need to be reinforced over time—many sessions repeated over several years are

most effective. Effective programs have a substantial amount of interaction between instructors and students, and peer leaders serve a pivotal role. Ideally, group leaders should be honest, respectful, nonjudgmental, and knowledgeable. Encouraging students to make a public commitment not to use drugs has shown some degree of success, as has reinforcing drug-free behaviors with recognition, praise, and rewards.

One successful school-based drug prevention program is Keepin' It REAL (KiR). Developed in the late 1980s by researchers at Penn State University, KiR identified the strategies that adolescents use to offer and to resist offers of AOD, as well as the underlying cognitive processes by which decisions about AOD were made. This information was then translated into prevention programs to teach adolescents resistance skills.[35] These resistance strategies included Refuse, Explain, Avoid, and Leave (REAL). The KiR program is interactive and culturally sensitive.[36] Middle school students who go through program were found to have tried AOD less than those in a control group, used a wider variety of strategies to stay sober, and were more likely to maintain anti-drug attitudes over time.[37]

Another successful program is the LifeSkills Training program (LST), an evidence-based substance abuse

Ask yourself: What do you think is the best way to measure the success of school-based drug prevention programs?

FIGURE 18.3. School-based drug prevention programs. These programs work best when they are interactive and give students a chance to practice the skills they are learning.

prevention program shown to be effective in preventing tobacco, alcohol, and illicit and prescription drug misuse.[38,39] The program typically is delivered in 15 class sessions (each session is 40–45 minutes long) in the seventh grade, with 10 booster classes in eighth grade and five in ninth grade. Many studies have shown that LST reduces the use of alcohol, tobacco, and marijuana, even in long-range follow-up surveys over a six-year period.[40] The program appears to be effective in middle school and high school students, white middle-class students and ethnic minorities, and students in the inner city, suburbs, and in rural populations.[41,42,43]

Family and Community Involvement

Drug use is reduced in families with supportive parents, who communicate, manage family conflicts, set clear and consistent expectations, and have high expectations for their children. The most effective drug prevention programs involve families in a variety of ways.

Some programs are presented to parents alone, without children present. These may focus on parenting skills, rule setting, training parents to recognize risky behavior in children, and techniques to monitor their children's activities. Other programs include both parents and children, and seek to strengthen parent–child bonds, improve family functioning, and enhance communication.[44]

Programs are more successful when there are collaborative efforts between schools, parents, civic organizations, law enforcement officials, religious organizations, businesses, and the local media. Community involvement in drug prevention programs may be manifested as stricter enforcement of local laws regarding the availability of tobacco, alcohol, and drugs; increased law enforcement and sobriety checkpoints; fewer billboards advertising alcohol, tobacco, and

drugs; and the availability of non-drug-related recreational, cultural, or athletic opportunities. Raising the cost of legal drugs via tax increases have proven effective. For every 10 percent increase in cigarette price, cigarette consumption falls by 3–5 percent overall, and by 6–7 percent among youth.[45] In general, states with the lowest taxes on cigarettes (and lowest overall prices) have the highest rates of smoking.[46]

Alcohol and Drug Prevention Programs at Colleges and Universities

Prevention programs are not limited to elementary and high schools. During college, undergraduate students are at risk of either starting or continuing to use alcohol and illicit drugs, due to their widespread availability, reduced parental supervision and monitoring, perceptions of the acceptability and prevalence of drug use, and relatively low perceived risk of consequences associated with drug use.[47] Colleges and universities have implemented many programs to try to minimize the damage caused by irresponsible alcohol and drug consumption. Many of these programs focus on identifying at-risk students, providing peer mentoring and monitoring drug use, changing attitudes and beliefs about AODs, providing safer options for students, offering counseling for students in need, and reducing the availability of alcohol.[48]

Even though the majority of college students are underage, alcohol is the drug of choice on most college campuses and is the drug that contributes to the most physical, psychological, and academic problems. Some educational programs on college campuses increase student awareness of the negative consequences of heavy drinking and teach strategies for changing drinking behavior.[49] Interviewers use a questionnaire to assess student alcohol use. When at-risk students are

---

STRAIGHT DOPE | **Iceland Lowers Teen Drug and Alcohol Use**

Teens in Iceland have the lowest drug and alcohol use in Europe. But it wasn't always that way. Between 1998 and 2016, the percentage of 15- and 16-year-olds who had been drunk in the previous month fell from 42 to 5 percent; the percentage of teens who had ever used marijuana fell from 17 to 7 percent; and tobacco use plummeted from 23 to 3 percent. What brought about the changes? One possible explanation is that Iceland initiated a program that increased funding to give teens greater access to activities—such as martial arts, meditation, and music—that are alternatives to AODs. Some

teens chose activities that helped reduce anxiety, while others preferred pastimes that gave them a rush. Similar to the fact that rats are loath to use morphine when presented with toys and social opportunities (Chapter 7), increased access to organized recreational opportunities might prevent AOD use in teens.

Source: Young, E. (2017). Iceland knows how to stop teen substance abuse but the rest of the world isn't listening. Mosaic. https://mosaicscience.com/story/iceland-prevent-teen-substance-abuse

identified, they are provided with information about alcohol's negative consequences, offered nonjudgmental feedback on how their drinking behavior compares to others, provided information to alter their expectations about alcohol, and taught cognitive behavioral skills to support safer habits.[50]

Many universities have programs in place to improve available safe options, such as alcohol-free or drug-free dorms or activities and safe-ride programs for those who are too drunk to drive. Making alcohol harder to obtain also reduces drinking. Some colleges have worked with their communities to raise alcohol prices, limit the number of places a student can go to purchase alcohol, more closely regulate happy hours and alcohol sales, and more effectively enforce minimum legal drinking age laws. In fact, minimum legal drinking age laws (Chapter 2) may be the single most effective method to combat alcohol use and its adverse consequences among young people.[51]

Advertising Campaigns to Prevent Drug Use

As discussed in the *Thinking Critically about Drugs* section at the beginning of this book, as well as in Chapter 10, there is a positive relationship between alcohol and tobacco advertising and increased use. But ads can also be used to *prevent* such use.

Anti-Drug Ads

In 2017, President Donald Trump declared the opioid drug crisis to be a national health emergency. Although he committed no funds for treatment facilities, he said the government would produce "really tough, really big, really great advertising" intended to prevent Americans from using opioids. "This was an idea that I had, where if we can teach young people not to take drugs. It's really, really easy not to take them."[52] However, this was not a new idea. In 1997, the U.S. government embarked on the first federally funded media campaign to reduce drug use in adolescents. Since the inception of the National Youth Anti-Drug Media campaign, the federal government has spent more than $1.4 billion on televised ads designed to dissuade teens from using marijuana, inhalants, and other illegal drugs.[53,54]

This social marketing campaign aimed anti-drug messages at 9- to 18-year-olds. The expectation was that an American youth would see an average of 2.5 ads per week.[55] These ads had three goals: to educate

the youth of America and to enable them to say no to illegal drugs, to prevent the start of drug use, and to convince those who used drugs only occasionally to stop. These anti-drug ads used a variety of techniques. Some presented resistance skills and tried to instill the confidence to reject drugs; some presented positive alternatives to drug use; others focused on the negative consequences of drug use.[56]

So how effective were these ads? The National Institute of Drug Abuse (NIDA) contracted Westat, a health research survey company, to study the effectiveness of the ads in the National Anti-Drug Media campaign shown between November 1999 and June 2004. These ads were part of the *What's Your Anti-Drug?* campaign. The campaign included ads showing teenagers doing healthy activities. Other ads demonstrated the potentially catastrophic consequences of smoking marijuana. In one ad, a pot-smoking teen hits a child riding a bike; in another, a stoned teen accidentally shoots his friend in the head.

Unfortunately, the study found that these ads actually *increased* the likeliness that adolescents will smoke marijuana. More exposure to the ads led to higher rates of first-time drug use among 14- to 16-year-olds, as well as increased perceptions that others use marijuana.[57] It is important to critically evaluate these results—Westat's study did not include a control group and relied on teens' self-reported exposure to ads—but the finding was troubling nevertheless. NIDA and the White House Drug Office sat on the report for a year and a half and spent an additional $220 million in anti-marijuana ads. When they finally released the report, they said its findings should be ignored, because the data were more than two years old.[58] The Government Accountability Office (GAO) called the anti-drug ad campaign a failure and urged Congress to stop funding it. A spokesman for the Office of National Drug Control Policy stated that the GAO report was "irrelevant to us."[59]

A systematic evaluation of the effectiveness of these ads and public service announcements (PSAs) has also not been promising. The authors of the systematic evaluation analyzed several randomized trials showing the relationship of PSA exposure to the viewer's intention to use illicit drugs. Most of the anti-drug PSAs had no significant effect on drug use; two randomized trials found evidence that PSAs increased the viewer's intention to use illicit drugs; and only one study found that viewing a PSA decreased one's intention to use drugs.[60]

Newer ad campaigns such as *Above the Influence* (Figure 18.4) may be more effective than past campaigns. More recent commercials focus on autonomy

FIGURE 18.4. Above the Influence ads. These ads tap into many teens' desires to be independent and in control of many aspects of their lives.

and aspirations rather than on unrealistic worst-case scenarios associated with drug use.[61] One newer ad campaign (Figure 18.5) uses the image of a frying egg from a 30-year-old drug education campaign (one of the most famous PSA campaigns of all time). The ad encourages parents to seek out the Partnership for Drug Free Kids' website to help them answer their children's questions about drugs.

Anti-Tobacco Ads

The American Legacy Foundation launched the TRUTH anti-smoking campaign in 2000. This was the first national anti-smoking campaign to discourage tobacco use among youth, with an annual funding of $100 million per year

FIGURE 18.5. Anti-drug campaigns. One newer anti-drug campaign is aimed at parents and encourages them to answer their children's questions about drugs.

Ask yourself: In a "real world" setting, it can be difficult to accurately ascertain how effective ad campaigns are in reducing drug use. How would *you* design a study to determine the effectiveness of these ads?

from February 2000 to 2002. These ads didn't just tell young people not to smoke. The campaign used graphic images, highlighted health consequences, deglamorized the social appeal, countered perceptions that smoking is widespread among youth, and exposed the tobacco industry's marketing practices and denial of tobacco's addictive and deleterious health effects. Significantly fewer young people smoke today than in the past, and researchers attribute much of the decline to this campaign. Researchers also have found that more effective anti-smoking ads contain strong messages about the destructive health consequences of tobacco instead of trying to be humorous or emotionally neutral.[62] From 1999–2002, smoking among eighth, tenth, and twelfth graders declined from 25.3 to 18 percent. The TRUTH campaign accounted for approximately 22 percent of this decline, or roughly 300,000 fewer youth smokers.[63]

Cigarette use has declined, but the use of e-cigarettes has risen in recent years, and anti-vaping ads aimed at teens have hit the airwaves. Many of these ads give teens the perception that vaping is widespread, rebellious, and cool, and that even though all their friends might be doing it, they shouldn't. Unsurprisingly, the message may have backfired; vaping rates have increased significantly since the release of these messages. Even if the ads themselves don't directly cause teens to vape, marketing against a product increases awareness of its existence, which may make people more likely to try it.[64]

Drug Testing

Another method that both schools and workplaces are using to prevent drug abuse is drug testing. In 1988, President Ronald Reagan signed the Drug Free Workplace Act, which required all federal grantees and some federal contractors to establish drug-free workplaces, including programs for drug education, awareness, and testing. Today, almost all federal agencies and some major corporations have drug-monitoring programs in place, and **drug testing** is required for many people seeking employment, welfare, or adoption of a baby. Individuals can legally refuse a drug screen, but they risk

losing their job or benefits if they do. And if one is fired for refusing to take a drug test, it is almost impossible to get unemployment benefits.

Who Is Subject to Drug Tests?

Many job postings don't disclose if they require drug testing for employment. Although over half of American companies report drug testing, less than 1.5 percent of job postings in the U.S. mention that they require pre-employment drug tests, and even fewer—0.66 percent—mention that they require regular drug screenings during employment. Industries most likely to require pre-employment drug tests are government, health care and hospitals, manufacturing, automotive, transportation, private security, aerospace and defense, construction, information technology, and education.[65] Federal employees, law enforcement agents, transportation workers, and those in the military are subject to random drug testing. In 1996, 81 percent of American companies drug tested their employees, but today, that is down to about 56 percent, largely because recent studies have found that drug testing did not reduce workplace absenteeism.[66,67]

Professional athletes are tested for the presence of performance enhancing drugs, and about 20 percent of private and public secondary schools in the United States have some form of student drug testing. Some schools require drug tests of all students who participate in sports or extracurricular activities; others only test students they have reason to suspect are abusing drugs; and still others have mandatory random testing.[68,69] After comparing over 94,000 students from schools that did some type of drug testing with those from schools that did not, drug testing in schools was not found to be associated with any decrease in drug use.[70,71]

QUICK HIT

Although federal employees are subject to random drug testing, members of the U.S. Congress are not.

Many states have initiated programs that require those who receive welfare to undergo a drug test. Although universal drug screening for applicants of TANF (Temporary Assistance for Needy Families) was ruled unconstitutional in 2014, in 2020, some 13 states

Drug testing: An analysis of a biological specimen to test for the presence of specified drugs.

require drug screening of TANF applicants or beneficiaries with a "reasonable suspicion" of drug misuse.[72] Proponents claim it will save the state money by getting drug users off public assistance. Although the tests have cost hundreds of thousands of dollars, only a handful of drug users have been identified through these programs; often, the staffing and administration of the drug tests cost the state more than would have been paid out in aid to the applicants who failed the tests.[73,74] In fact, TANF applicants actually test positive for drug use at a lower rate than the general population.

When Do Drug Tests Typically Occur?

Drug testing typically occurs under the following conditions:

- *Pre-employment:* After one has applied for a job, a job offer may be conditional upon passing a drug screen (Figure 18.6).
- *Reasonable suspicion:* A drug test may be required if someone is suspected of using a prohibited drug, either due to direct observation of drug use, physical symptoms of drug use, abnormal or erratic behavior, absenteeism, or deterioration of one's productivity at work.
- *Post-incident:* If an accident or injury occurs at work, drug testing can help to determine whether drugs or alcohol were a factor.
- *Periodic:* Periodic testing is usually scheduled in advance and uniformly administered.
- *Random:* Some organizations give random drug tests. In a truly random test, there is an equal probability that any employee from the group of workers subject to testing will be selected without warning.
- *Return to duty:* When someone who has previously tested positive is returning to work after completing the required treatment, he or she may be asked to complete a one-time, announced drug test.

QUICK HIT

Quest Diagnostics reported that about 4.5 percent of all drug tests performed in 2019 were positive.[75] Of those who tested positive, pre-employment testing gave the lowest positivity rate—around 5 percent, while those who were tested for cause or reasonable suspicion showed the highest rates of positive tests—about 36 percent.[76] In 2019, drug use among American employees, as measured by the percentage of employees who tested positive in urine drug tests, was at a 16-year high, largely due to testing positive for the use of cannabis.[77]

Immunoassay: A procedure for detecting specific substances based on the principles of antigen-antibody reactions.

FIGURE 18.6. Drug testing. Many workplaces require pre-employment drug testing.

What Process Is Used for Drug Testing?

Drug testing involves evaluating a person's urine, blood, or other biological substances to determine if the person has been using drugs. Most drug tests involve a two-step process. Typically, the sample is first screened using immunoassay. Quick and inexpensive, **immunoassay** measures the metabolites of drugs. Immunoassays are not very accurate, however, and might not distinguish between drug metabolites and closely similar structures. If no drugs are detected, the results are reported as negative and no further action occurs. If drugs are detected, an individual might be asked to speak to a medical review officer, who would ask if there might be an explanation for the positive test other than illegal drug use.

Often, the officer would then order a second drug test. **Gas chromatography/mass spectrometry (GC/MS)** is used as a confirmation test. GC/MS is more time-consuming and expensive, but it is also more precise and specific—for example, it can distinguish between cold medicines and amphetamines. During credible drug tests, strict chain-of-custody practices are followed to prevent a sample from being compromised.

For Which Drugs Are Tests Run?

When drug testing began in the late 1980s, federal guidelines required the testing of five specific drug groups. These drug groups, called the **SAMHSA-5**, include amphetamines, cannabinoids, cocaine, opioids, and PCP. These drugs do not necessarily account for current drug usage patterns, so employers can choose to test for other drugs, such as benzodiazepines, MDMA, and commonly abused prescription opioids. Alcohol—the drug most associated with accidents, absenteeism, and reduced workplace productivity—is not included in the SAMHSA-5 and often is not included in testing.

The levels of the drug or its metabolite that constitute a positive test differ for each drug. Generally, if a drug is detected, the follow-up GC/MS confirmation test requires a lower level of drug to trigger a positive test.

How Long after Using a Drug Will Someone Test Positive?

Detection times for a drug can be difficult to pinpoint, given that it depends on many factors, including the exact strain or formulation of the drug, dose, frequency and duration of use, route of administration, individual differences in metabolism, tolerance to the drug, whether the test measures the drug itself or a metabolite, and other factors. Detection times also depend on the test used. In general, detection times are longest with a hair test, followed by urine, saliva, and, finally, blood tests.

Marijuana is fat soluble, and its metabolites remain in the body longer than most other drugs. Because of this, as well as the fact that the number of marijuana users is far greater than the number of cocaine or heroin users, most people who test positive on drug tests are caught for marijuana. Approximate detection times for various drugs can be found in Table 18.1.[78,79]

What Types of Drug Tests Are Used?

Many biological substances can be tested to ascertain drug use. The five primary types of drug tests are urine, saliva, hair, sweat, and blood, but breath can be used as well to determine the presence of alcohol.

Urine

Urine is the most common test, because it is the least expensive of the test methods and it is easy to collect the sample. Urine tests typically detect drug use within the past week but do not detect drug use immediately; it usually takes six to eight hours after consumption for a drug to be metabolized and excreted.

Drug abusers have tried many methods to "beat" a urine drug test. Drug users may try to drink large quantities of fluids before a urine drug test in order to dilute their urine so drug metabolites won't register. But testing labs are aware of this, and if a urine sample shows up as too diluted, the lab will reject the sample and the subject will be retested. Some may try to adulterate their sample with compounds that interfere with mechanisms the screening tests use to detect drug metabolites. But this often produces a characteristic change in the sample, causing it to be flagged. Users may also simply submit someone else's urine sample as their own. To prevent this, some organizations require the subjects to be directly observed when providing the urine sample. Labs will also test the sample's temperature to make sure it has not been adulterated.

Saliva

Saliva is becoming a popular testing option in some situations. A toothbrush-like swab, with pads instead of bristles, is placed between the lower cheek and gum for about two minutes. Saliva tests are convenient, easy, safe, and less invasive than other forms of drug testing. This method is also less prone to a user's efforts to beat the drug test. A little more expensive than urine testing, saliva testing is still less expensive than testing hair or blood. Some drugs, like MDMA, inhibit salivary secretions, which may make collection difficult. Salivary tests, like blood tests, typically only measure drugs used in the past 24 hours, so they are more commonly being used to measure recent drug use, such as with motor vehicle or workplace accidents.

Hair

Hair tests can be used to evaluate long-term patterns of drug use. Drugs are incorporated into the hair shaft from the bloodstream. About 10 days after use, the affected hair grows from the follicle to emerge

Gas chromatography/mass spectrometry (GC/MS): A technique to analyze and quantify the different specific substances in a test sample.

SAMHSA-5: Also called the NIDA-5; the five groups of drugs—amphetamines, cannabinoids, cocaine, opioids, and PCP—that are most commonly tested for in a urine drug test.

TABLE 18.1.   Detection Levels for Drug Testing

Drug	Levels that Constitute a Positive Test	Detection Periods			
		Blood	Saliva	Urine	Hair
Alcohol	• 0.02% (20 mg/dL) ethanol or 250 ng/mL ethyl glucuronide (EtG), an ethanol metabolite	1–24 hours	1–12 hours	1–24 hours, up to 80 hours for metabolite	Up to 90 days
Amphetamines	• First test: 1,000 ng/mL • Confirmation: 500 ng/mL	12 hours–2 days	1–2 days	1–3 days	Up to 90 days
Barbiturates	• 200 ng/mL for many barbiturates but depends on the specific drug	1–2 days	1–2 days	Short-acting 1–4 days, long acting 2–3 weeks	Up to 90 days
Benzodiazepines	• 200 ng/mL for many benzodiazepines but depends on the specific drug	6–48 hours	6–48 hours	Short-term use 1–7 days, chronic use for over a year, 4–6 weeks	?
Cannabis — Smoked/ single use	• First test: 50 ng/mL • Confirmation: 15 ng/mL	1–3 days	12–24 hours	1–5 days	Up to 90 days
Cannabis — Smoked/ regular use		1–2 weeks	12–24 hours	15–50 days	Up to 90 days
Cannabis — Oral/single use		2–7 days	?	?	Up to 90 days
Cocaine	• First test: 300 ng/mL • Confirmation: 150 ng/mL	1–2 days	1–2 days	2–4 days	Up to 90 days
Codeine/ morphine	• First test and confirmation: 2,000 ng/mL	?	12–36 hours	2–4 days	Up to 90 days
Heroin	• First test and confirmation: 2,000 ng/mL	20 hours	30 minutes–8 hours	1–3 days	Up to 90 days
MDMA	• First test: 500 ng/mL • Confirmation: 250 ng/mL	1–2	1–2 days	1–3 days	Up to 90 days
Metham-phetamine	• First test: 1,000 ng/mL • Confirmation: 500 ng/mL	1–2 days	1–3 days	2–6 days	Up to 90 days
PCP	• First test and confirmation: 25 ng/mL	1–3 days	3 days	2–7 days for single use, up to 30 days in chronic users	Up to 90 days

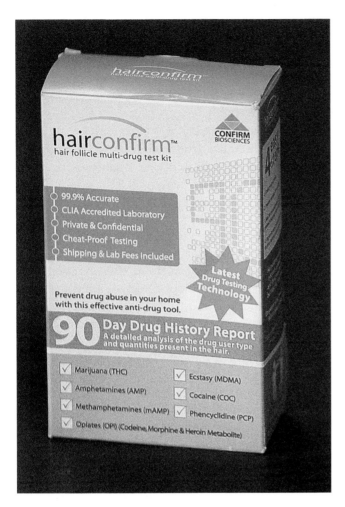

FIGURE 18.7. Hair drug testing. In hair drug testing, a sample of about 90–120 hair fibers is taken; each piece is cut about 1.5 inches from the root. If a subject doesn't have hair on his or her head, body hair can be used.

above the scalp. In a hair drug test, a one-and-a-half-inch sample of about 100 strands of hair is cut as close to the scalp as possible (Figure 18.7). Because most people's hair grows about half an inch per month, this will show drug use for the past 90 days. If a person has no hair on his head, body hair, fingernails, or toenails can be used. Bleaching or dyeing one's hair won't change the results, because the drugs are incorporated into the hair shaft itself. Some drugs, like cocaine, migrate along the shaft and will show use at an undetermined time in the testing period. For other drugs, like opioids, it's sometimes possible to pinpoint exactly when drug use occurred and whether it has been discontinued.

Hair tests are more expensive than urine or saliva tests and may not be as accurate. Environmental factors, such as exposure to marijuana smoke, shampoo, hair treatments, and air pollution may potentially influence the results. However, the lab usually washes the hair sample to remove some contaminants, and external exposure to a drug can sometimes be differentiated from actual use due to the presence of drug metabolites.

QUICK HIT

Even a seemingly impartial drug test is influenced by race. African Americans, Hispanics, and Asians may be more likely to test positive to a hair test than Caucasians. Darker hair has more melanin, which more strongly incorporates and retains drugs. A dark-haired person is 10–50 times more likely to test positive on a hair drug test than a lighter-haired person who used the same amount of drug.[80,81]

Sweat

Sweat tests are not very common. They are mostly used by the criminal justice system and by Child Protective Services to monitor drug use over long periods of time. Drugs and their metabolites can collect in sweat, which is captured in a waterproof adhesive pad about the size of a playing card. The patch is worn for about a week or two, then removed and sent for analysis. Sweat patches are more expensive than urine tests, and considered more intrusive, because they must be worn for an extended period of time. Security features keep them from being removed and reapplied.

Blood

Blood tests are the most expensive and intrusive, but also the most accurate. They are the least common form of drug test, due to their cost, invasiveness, and ability to test only recent drug use. Blood drug tests are usually done for clinical and diagnostic purposes, or in hospital emergency rooms (ER) with a drug overdose. Blood tests can be performed on those who can't willingly submit a urine sample, such as those who are severely intoxicated, comatose, or dead.

How Accurate Are Drug Tests?

Drug tests are not 100 percent accurate. In addition, they can't determine exactly how much of a drug was used or precisely when it was used. They also don't measure the impairment of a person—a chronic user who has grown tolerant to a drug might not be as impaired by drug use as someone who does not use as often.

To ensure that a drug test is accurate, it must be conducted properly, testing procedures must be standardized, and the accuracy of the certified labs must be confirmed. Unfortunately, federally certified labs may not be entirely accurate. In 2007, the U.S. Government Accountability Office studied 23 labs, all of which were federally certified by the U.S. Department of Health and Human Services. The GAO found that none of these labs consistently followed federally mandated procedures for lab accuracy.[82] Unfortunately, drug testing can result in both false positives and false negatives.

A **false positive** occurs when a test indicates that a drug is present when none was used. This may occur if a food or a medically prescribed drug is identified as an illicit substance. For example, antihistamines can give a false positive for methadone, decongestants and Wellbutrin may flag as amphetamines, and eating as little as one teaspoon of poppy seeds can result in a positive drug test for opioids. After testing positive, the applicant will usually take a more accurate GC/MS confirmation test, which can differentiate between these illicit drugs and other substances. Through technological advances, drug-testing laboratories have greatly reduced the incidence of false-positive tests, although they still occur in 5–10 percent of drug tests.

In a **false negative**, a drug user may be under the influence of a drug at the time the test is given, but the test will still show up as negative. This may depend on the type of test given—it takes several hours for some drug metabolites to appear in urine, and hair tests will not show the presence of a drug for 10–14 days. This also may depend on the drug used; most standard drug tests have a substantial false-negative rate for oxycodone, fentanyl, and other opioids. False negatives may occur in 10–15 percent of cases.

How Effective Are Drug Tests?

Drug testing is expensive. One must consider the cost of the tests, as well as the cost of the time and manpower spent taking the tests. Do the results justify the expense? To try to answer this question, we need to ask why organizations perform drug tests. Is it to make the workplace safer? To prevent waste associated with drug use? To discourage drug use? Let's consider each of these reasons.

Workplace Safety

Drug users can be a safety hazard to themselves, their coworkers, and the public. By law, many transportation workers—pilots, bus drivers, and truck drivers, to name a few—are subject to random drug tests. Following the implementation of drug testing, Southern Pacific Railroad experienced a 71 percent drop in accidents that resulted in injuries.[83] But what about other professions?

Should surgeons and other healthcare professionals be subject to drug tests? Factory workers? Grocery store baggers? In some way, almost every worker's actions will have an effect on the public, so by what criteria should we determine who should be tested?

Workplace Productivity

We often are told that drug testing increases workplace productivity and profitability. A frequently repeated statistic states that drug users are 2.5 times more likely to be absent from work for eight days or more, 3.6 times more likely to be involved in a workplace accident, and 5 times more likely to file a worker's compensation claim. These claims are often made without citation. Actually, these statistics were first made in 1972 at a luncheon to encourage the adoption of employee assistance programs for workers with "medical-behavioral problems." No data or sources were given at the time, and since then, the suspicious data have been misrepresented and reprinted as being about illicit drug users.[84,85]

An analysis by the Rand Corporation found that there is an association between alcohol and drug use and workplace injury, but substance abuse itself only caused a small proportion of the injuries. Instead, it appears that problematic substance use is just one of a group of behaviors exhibited by certain individuals, who also have a higher absenteeism rate, take greater work-related risks, and show fewer safety precautions, and who, therefore, suffer more work-related injuries.[86]

Alcohol and drugs may reduce workplace productivity, but there is no evidence that drug *testing* increases it.[87] But even if it did, would this justify violating one's personal freedom? Parents of young children are also more likely to leave early and take more personal time. Would it be acceptable for an employer to refuse to hire workers who have children? Those with certain illnesses may also take more sick time. Cigarette smokers file more insurance claims and take "smoking breaks" during the day. Yet, for most professions, cigarette use is not tested for or prohibited. What is the line between economic expediency and a worker's personal freedoms?

Prevention of Drug Use

So how effective is drug testing in preventing use? Evidence is mixed. Some evidence suggests that drug testing deters drug use. One study looked at 36 high schools

False positive: A test result that incorrectly indicates that a drug is present.

False negative: A test result that does not detect a drug that is present.

that performed random drug tests, and found that students at these schools reported less substance use than comparable students in high schools without mandatory random testing.[88] However, another study that analyzed data from 497 high schools and 225 middle schools around the country found no significant difference in the rates of drug use in schools that have drug testing and schools that do not.[89] The UNODC committee that set the international standards on drug use prevention found that random drug tests in schools did not significantly deter drug use.[90] When considering this contradictory information, be sure to think about the many confounding factors. Perhaps schools with more of a drug problem are more likely to implement random drug testing. Or, perhaps the way the program is implemented determines its success. Also remember that estimates of drug use are often obtained by questionnaire, and both students and administrators may lie.

Overall, the percentage of positive drug tests has fallen significantly since the late 1980s. This may mean that drug testing deters drug use. Or, it may be that drug use overall has decreased since the late 1980s. Also, the early days of drug testing were mostly "for cause or suspicion," so they showed a higher percentage of positive tests. Today, more prescreening and random tests take place, so the percentage of positives has fallen.

The issue of drug testing raises many questions:

- How do we analyze the costs and benefits of drug testing? What percentage of tests should be positive to justify testing?
- What about issues of privacy? Should insurance companies have access to the results? Is drug testing a violation of the Fourth Amendment—a person's freedom from unreasonable search and seizure? If a person loses his or her job because of drug testing, is it a violation of that person's right to not testify against themselves as guaranteed by the Fifth Amendment?
- Most workers who use illicit drugs don't use them at work. But metabolites may still show up in the test long after the effects of the drug are gone.

Does a company have the right to control what you do when you're not at work? If yes, does that mean that people who enter certain professions have less right to privacy than others?

- And, finally, how do we balance our desire for public safety with our desire for personal freedom?

Ask yourself: How would you summarize your views on drug testing?

Prevalence of Treatment for Alcohol and Drug Addiction

Unfortunately, prevention of problematic AOD use is not always effective, and millions of people suffer from addiction (Chapter 17). In 2019, some 20.4 million people aged 12 and older—7.4 percent of that population—were classified with substance use disorder, and over 4.1 million received treatment.[91] Of these, 2.3 million were treated for abuse of illicit drugs and 2.5 million for alcohol dependence, and almost 1.2 million received treatment for abuse of both illicit drugs and alcohol. (The estimates by substance do not add up to the total number who received treatment because that figure of 4.1 million includes those who received treatment but did not specify for which substance.[92]) Most of those who were treated received their treatment from a self-help group or a rehabilitation facility (Figure 18.8).[93]

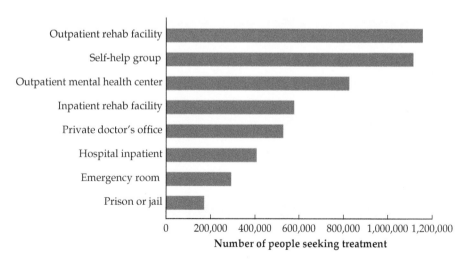

FIGURE 18.8. Location where substance use treatment was received. Most of those who seek treatment for AOD dependency go to outpatient rehab facilities or self-help groups.

Source: (SAMHSA). (2020). Results from the 2018 national survey on drug use and health. *Rockville, MD: Center for Behavioral Health Statistics and Quality.*

Although millions of people received treatment for an illicit drug problem, approximately 88 percent of those who needed treatment at a specialty facility did not receive it.[94] Among those who needed treatment but did not receive it, only 4.3 percent believed that they did, in fact, need to be treated for an AOD problem. Of those who were untreated and recognized their need for treatment, 71 percent made no effort to obtain treatment.[95] Of those who made an effort, some decided they were not ready to stop using, some had no health coverage and could not afford the cost, and others were concerned that seeking treatment might have a negative effect on their job or social interactions.

The Stages of Recovery

Those with substance abuse disorders may take different paths on the way to recovery. Some enter treatment of their own volition, while others are forced into treatment by their families or by the court system. Treatment does not need to be voluntary to be effective—those struggling with substance abuse who enter treatment voluntarily actually have lower success rates, mostly because those who are compelled to be there stay longer, which relates to longer periods of abstinence.[96]

A person goes through various stages on the way to recovery (Figure 18.9)[97,98]:

- During the *precontemplation* stage, the person struggling with drugs may not believe that he or she has a problem and may just think that other people are overreacting to the situation.

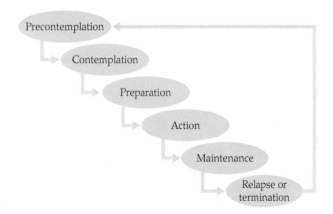

FIGURE 18.9. The stages of recovery. These stages apply to more than AOD dependence. You may have experienced these if you have struggled with a diet or exercise plan, a decision to be more organized, or an effort to be financially responsible.

- During *contemplation*, the person may be willing to admit to a problem and be open to the idea of addressing it, but has not yet made a commitment to change.
- *Preparation* involves setting a date for action, developing a strategy, and perhaps making a declaration to others about the plan.
- During *action,* the user takes steps to modify his or her behavior, environment, and/or relationships in order to overcome the problem. He or she may feel ambiguous about this change, and there is a high risk of relapse.
- One achieves *maintenance* after being alcohol or drug free for at least six months, often developing new skills and strategies and making changes in the environment to reduce the risk of relapse.
- The *termination* stage is reached when the temptation no longer exists. At this point, some consider the problem solved, but others believe that addiction is a lifelong condition that can never be entirely cured. If a person with a substance abuse disorder relapses, he or she may begin the cycle all over again.

Methods of Treatment

The first step in treating addiction is often **medical detoxification**, in which a user goes through physical withdrawal from the drug, and the body and brain readapt to its absence. Withdrawal from some drugs, such as alcohol, can be life-threatening, and so medical detoxification often needs to be done in a hospital setting. Medical professionals used to believe that detoxification was all a patient needed to stop using drugs.[99] We now recognize that because biological, psychological, and social factors underlie the development of addiction, a multifaceted treatment approach is often the most effective. Treatments can include a variety of pharmacological and psychosocial options.

Pharmacological Treatments for Addiction

Sometimes, medications are used to help people in their recovery. Medications are usually used by persons early in sobriety or to complement other approaches; they are typically not intended to be the sole treatment for alcohol or drug addiction.[100] Pharmacological treatments can be used to reduce the intoxicating effects of the drug, to ease withdrawal symptoms,

Medical detoxification: A process that systematically and safely withdraws people from drugs under the care of a physician.

TABLE 18.2. Pharmacological Treatments for Addiction

Therapeutic Drug	Drug of Abuse for Which It Is Typically Used	Mechanism of Action
methadone (Dolophine)	Opioids	Opioid agonist Decreases intoxication and lessens withdrawal symptoms
clonidine (Catapres)	Opioids	Alpha$_2$-adrenergic agonist Suppresses symptoms of opioid withdrawal
buprenorphine (Subutex, Suboxone)	Opioids	Partial agonist at opioid receptors Decreases intoxication and lessens withdrawal symptoms
naltrexone (ReVia)	Opioids Alcohol	Opioid antagonist Decreases intoxication from opioids and lessens binge drinking in alcoholics
LSD	Alcohol	Works at serotonin receptors Prevents relapse
ondansetron (Zofran)	Alcohol	Serotonin antagonist Lessens withdrawal symptoms, reduces cravings
disulfiram (Antabuse)	Alcohol	Inhibits acetaldehyde dehydrogenase Decreases intoxication and increases the aversive effects of alcohol
acamprosate (Campral)	Alcohol	Glutamate antagonist and GABA agonist Decreases intoxication and lessens cravings and withdrawal symptoms
oxytocin	Alcohol	Blocks development of tolerance Decreases withdrawal symptoms
Nicotine replacement	Nicotine	Acetylcholine agonist Eases withdrawal symptoms
varenicline (Chantix)	Nicotine Alcohol	Partial agonist at nicotinic receptors Reduces the pleasurable effects of nicotine, decreases cravings, and lessens withdrawal symptoms
bupropion (Zyban)	Nicotine	Blocks reuptake of norepinephrine and dopamine Reduces cravings
psilocybin	Nicotine	Serotonin 2$_A$ agonist Facilitates quitting and abstaining

or to reduce cravings. The most common therapeutic agents help with tobacco, alcohol, and opioid dependence (Table 18.2).

Medications to Help with Nicotine Addiction

Nicotine replacement therapies reduce the user's withdrawal symptoms. Although nicotine itself is toxic, replacement therapies provide safer routes of administration, without the tar and carbon monoxide. Nicotine is available in patches, gum, nasal sprays, inhalers, and electronic cigarettes (Chapter 10).

The antidepressant bupropion (Zyban) has been found to help people quit smoking. It raises synaptic levels of dopamine and norepinephrine by blocking their reuptake. Varenicline (Chantix) is a partial nicotinic agonist. This means it only partially binds to nicotinic acetylcholine receptors, so it provides sufficient stimulation to reduce withdrawal but eliminates the

high and the cravings. Varenicline may also help reduce alcohol consumption.[101]

Hallucinogenic drugs may aid smokers to quit and to continue to abstain. Studies have found that when subjects were given moderate to high doses of psilocybin during a cognitive behavioral therapy (CBT) session for smoking cessation, they were significantly more likely to have maintained their abstention months later compared with those who received only CBT.[102]

Medications to Help with Alcohol Addiction

Disulfiram (Antabuse) is designed to make alcohol ingestion unpleasant (Chapter 12). Taken once a day, the disulfiram pill inhibits the enzyme aldehyde dehydrogenase; consequently, drinking will result in a pounding headache, flushing, rapid heart rate, sweating, shortness of breath, and nausea and vomiting. As little as a quarter of an ounce of ethanol within a few days can cause this reaction, and alcohol-containing substances, such as mouthwash and cough syrup, can also cause this toxic reaction. Perhaps unsurprisingly, compliance rates may be low, but disulfiram has had some success in those who are highly motivated to stop drinking.

The serotonin antagonist ondansetron (Zofran) increases abstinence in some people with alcohol use disorders. Its mechanism of action may be related to the finding that some people with more severe drinking problems have been found to have variations in genes that code for serotonin transporters. Zofran's effectiveness depends on the genetic makeup of individuals who receive it.[103]

Acamprosate (Campral) restores the balance between excitatory (glutamate) and inhibitory (GABA) neurotransmission following chronic alcohol consumption and withdrawal.[104] When chronically administered, alcohol antagonizes glutamate and enhances GABA, which produces hypoexcitability. Withdrawal from alcohol produces the opposite effect. Campral restores the disrupted brain neurochemistry that is a consequence of alcohol withdrawal. By antagonizing glutamate and stimulating GABA, acamprosate has been found to be more effective than placebo in preventing alcohol relapse.[105,106] It also seems to reduce cravings and lessen alcohol's intoxicating effects.

A single dose of a hallucinogenic drug such as LSD, psilocybin, or MDMA has been shown to have a significant beneficial effect in reducing alcohol relapse for up to a year after administration.[107,108] Hallucinogens' effectiveness compares well with naltrexone, acamprosate, and disulfiram. Researchers noted that following their psychedelic treatment, many patients found significant insights into their problems, became more self-accepting, and adopted a more positive, optimistic view of their capacity to deal with future problems. LSD, psilocybin, and MDMA remain schedule I drugs, and because of this will most likely not be considered for treatment any time in the near future (Chapter 6).

Oxytocin also may help treat alcohol use disorders. Oxytocin blocks the development of tolerance and decreases withdrawal symptoms. This may occur because oxytocin blocks the GABA receptor subunit, preventing alcohol from binding.[109] Alcohol-dependent volunteers who received daily doses of an oxytocin nasal spray had fewer alcohol cravings and milder withdrawal symptoms than a placebo group.[110] Oxytocin administration may lower the likelihood of relapse due to the desire to alleviate unpleasant withdrawal symptoms.

The opioid antagonist naltrexone also has shown success in reducing alcohol cravings by blocking alcohol-induced endorphin release, thereby decreasing the rewarding feelings one usually gets from alcohol.[111] Naltrexone also seems to decrease alcohol's intoxicating effects and reduce relapse rates after treatment, but its primary use is with opioid addiction.

Medications to Help with Opioid Addiction

Naltrexone (ReVia) is an opioid antagonist that helps patients overcome opioid addiction by blocking the drug's euphoric effects and putting the user immediately into withdrawal. Naltrexone should not be confused with naloxone. Naltrexone is longer acting, so it is better at treating long-term dependence, while short-acting naloxone is used in emergency cases of opioid overdose (Chapter 7). Naltrexone can cause nausea and liver toxicity when taken daily. Also, naltrexone has poor patient compliance; patients must be highly motivated to quit. If a patient stops using naltrexone and returns to opioid use, he or she runs the risk of overdose because of lost tolerance to the drug.

Methadone is an orally administered opioid agonist that has a relatively slow onset of action and a long half-life. As a result, methadone does not produce the rush of euphoria seen with faster-acting opioids. Methadone can be taken once a day to reduce cravings and prevent withdrawal (Figure 18.10). Methadone is still an addictive drug, however, and can be fatal in overdose.

Buprenorphine (Subutex) is safer and more effective than methadone. Buprenorphine is a long-lasting partial agonist at opioid receptors. As it binds to opioid receptors, the buprenorphine prevents withdrawal, and it effectively stops other opioids from binding and producing euphoric effects. But because buprenorphine only *partially* binds to the receptor, it produces limited opioid effects, so users do not get high and do not become dependent, and overdose is rare. Subutex and Suboxone (buprenorphine plus naloxone) are approved for office-based treatment of addiction. Treating opioid-dependent patients in the ER with Suboxone significantly decreased opioid use and increased the percentage of those in treatment 30 days after the ER visit compared to those who were just referred to a treatment program.[112]

Immunopharmacotherapy

A drug "vaccine" would entail stimulating the production of drug-specific antibodies. If a person used that drug of abuse, the antibodies would bind to the drug in the blood and prevent it from crossing the blood–brain barrier into the central nervous system, thus suppressing its addictive qualities.[113,114,115] There are several reasons, however,

and group therapy sessions, inpatient or outpatient treatment programs, behavioral approaches, or self-help groups such as Alcoholics Anonymous or Narcotics Anonymous. Unfortunately, although many people believe that addiction is a disease, the field of addiction treatment is not held to the rigorous scientific standards of other medical fields. Less than 0.05 percent of doctors in the United States identify as addiction specialists.[118] Many substance abuse counselors are not medical professionals and have only a high school diploma or general equivalency degree (GED). In fact, counselors in 14 states are not required to be licensed or, indeed, to have any coursework in addiction treatment.[119]

The best treatment program depends on the unique needs of the individual. Typically, those who have experienced more long-term and severe substance abuse will require longer and more intense treatment. Given that addiction is due to biological, psychological, and social factors, a multifaceted approach is usually more effective. Plans also should be made for what will happen after treatment is completed.

Inpatient Programs

Inpatient treatment centers include hospitals, clinics, and chemical dependence centers. Rehab programs may last 30–90 days, but the average length of stay is 26–28 days, during which residents are under 24-hour-a-day supervised care at the treatment facility and undergo intensive daily treatment. Medical professionals assist the detox process, and individual and group therapy sessions address underlying psychosocial issues (Figure 18.11). Moreover, residents are removed from distractions that might impede the recovery process, and they are away from familiar triggers and drug cues. Inpatient programs can cost from as little as $7,500 per month to as much as $120,000 per month for high-end luxury programs. The average cost ranges from $15,000 to $30,000 per month.

When choosing the most effective treatment program, there are several questions to consider:

- Is the program accredited and run by licensed, well-trained professionals?
- Is the facility clean, organized, and well run?
- Does the program use effective treatments backed by scientific evidence?
- Does the program consider and address the full range of needs of the individual—medical, psychological, family, social, legal, and vocational—and is it appropriate for the person's age, sex/gender, ethnicity, culture, and particular drug use?

FIGURE 18.10. **A woman awaits patients at a methadone clinic.** Methadone can be taken once a day to reduce cravings and prevent withdrawal.

why it is difficult to create a vaccine that targets specific drugs. Drug molecules are tiny—much smaller than those of a virus or bacterium that might typically trigger an immune response. Also, a drug may have active metabolites that must also be controlled by the vaccine. The chemists working on developing a heroin vaccine had to create a multitarget vaccine "cocktail" with three components: a large protein that carries drug-like molecules into the body, a molecule designed to make the body's immune system respond to heroin as well as to its psychoactive metabolites, and an agent that stimulates the body's immune cells to destroy invaders.[116,117] Progress has been made in creating vaccines for cocaine, nicotine, methamphetamine, PCP, and heroin.

Psychosocial Therapeutic Treatments for Addiction

Those who are dependent on drugs and alcohol may pursue psychosocial treatments, including individual

FIGURE 18.11. **Group therapy.** Group therapy is a part of many inpatient addiction programs.

- Does the program accept insurance?
- Does the program provide aftercare, such as referrals to other recovery services or support groups in the community?

Those recovering from addiction to drugs or alcohol who move directly from an inpatient treatment facility into their old lives, with its habits and temptations, have a strong likelihood of relapse. **Sober living homes** are a way to bridge the gap from total immersion and supervision in a rehab center to the unrestricted environment of the "real world." Sober living homes, also called "halfway houses," provide an abstinent environment with less supervision and more responsibilities than the rehab facility, but more structure and peer support than can typically be found in a patient's home. Residents must remain sober, pay rent and other fees, do their share of household chores, and attend house meetings. Sober living homes strongly encourage involvement in 12-Step groups and provide social support for recovery. They are self-sustaining, because the residents themselves pay the costs. Those recovering from addiction who passed through some kind of structured sober house were significantly less likely to face relapse, arrest, and homelessness compared with those who went straight home from rehab.[120,121] Not all sober houses are the same; residents have better outcomes in houses that are part of a larger organization or group of houses, are affiliated with a treatment program, and that require 30 days sobriety prior to entry.[122]

Outpatient Programs

Those who either do not need the intensity of an inpatient program, who can't afford the time or expense, or who are employed or have extensive family or community support may consider outpatient options. These include intensive outpatient programs and individual, group, and family counseling.

In an intensive outpatient program, patients spend considerable time in comprehensive therapy sessions during the day—perhaps two to four hours a day for three days a week—but reside in their own homes at night. Sometimes these programs can be arranged around one's work or school schedule. Outpatient programs are less expensive, less disruptive, less stigmatized, and help the patient to concentrate on adjusting to a drug-free life while still living and functioning in the real world.

Counseling can provide emotional support and address psychological and social problems that may be associated with dependence. It works best in conjunction with other forms of treatment or as aftercare support. Individual, group, and/or family counseling help the individuals identify causes of drug use, repair relationships, and learn non-drug-related coping mechanisms. **Cognitive behavioral therapy (CBT)** has been shown to be effective in treating alcohol and drug addiction.[123,124,125] CBT can help address issues obstructing recovery, teach the patients non-drug-related reinforcing activities, help them develop effective coping strategies, and teach them to identify and prevent high-risk situations.[126] Indeed, a meta-analysis of treatment options found that psychological treatments that focus on empathy, empowerment, and motivation to change are more effective than "traditional" approaches that emphasize punishment, interventions, or a user's powerlessness over addiction.[127]

Sober living home: A therapeutic residential facility that may be used to bridge the gap between an inpatient rehab facility and a return to former lives.

Cognitive behavioral therapy (CBT): An action-oriented form of therapy that focuses on changing maladaptive thought patterns and behaviors.

Behavioral Approaches

Contingency management (CM) and the **community reinforcement** approach (CR) are two of the most successful treatments for substance use disorders.[128,129]

Contingency management is a behavioral approach that rewards those in recovery with money and prizes for staying abstinent. It helps those in recovery appreciate non-substance-related rewards, which not only encourages abstinence, but help to boost self-confidence. Participants come to the clinic twice a week to provide a urine sample. If their sample is clean, they can draw a slip of paper out of a fishbowl. Some papers might be vouchers for cash, goods, or services that are consistent with a drug-free lifestyle; others may be encouraging messages. Often, the prizes increase in value as the number of consecutive drug-free urine samples increases.[130] A meta-analysis of 50 randomized controlled clinical trials found that CM plus CR had more abstinent patients at the end of treatment compared to CBT, 12-Step programs, and other treatment options.[131] Unfortunately, it can be hard to find CM programs. While there are a few pilot programs, no public or private insurer currently pays for them. CM is used mostly by the Department of Veterans Affairs, where it has a good success rate.[132]

Community reinforcement is a multi-layered intervention that helps people change their lifestyles such that healthy, drug-free living is rewarding, and clients become more involved in non-drug-related, pleasurable activities. CR focuses on helping the client analyze their reasons for substance use as well as the positive and negative consequences of use; providing coping skills training; and helping the participant find pleasure in their social, familial, recreational, and occupational life.[133]

Self-Help Groups

Self-help groups are nonprofessional organizations that are peer-operated by people who share the same

Contingency management: A behavioral therapy that uses incentives and rewards to encourage a person to remain abstinent from alcohol or other drugs.

Community reinforcement: A behavioral therapy that helps people change their lifestyle such that healthy, drug-free living becomes rewarding.

Alcoholics Anonymous (AA): An international organization whose purpose is to help those with alcohol use disorders to stay sober.

Narcotics Anonymous (NA): A nonprofit organization for people with substance abuse issues.

addictive disorder. Attendance is free, and members can attend indefinitely if they wish.[134] During the COVID-19 pandemic, some support groups held online meetings, so those struggling with addiction could still maintain the social contact and support so important for those in recovery. **Alcoholics Anonymous (AA)** is one of the most popular self-help programs (Figure 18.12). As of January 2019, there are over 2 million AA members belonging to over 118,000 groups. **Narcotics Anonymous (NA)** uses the same 12-Step program principles as AA, but it is open to all who suffer from drug addiction.

On June 10, 1935, after 19 years of alcoholism, Bill Wilson took his last drink. He joined with Dr. Bob Smith to help others to attain sobriety. In 1939, they published a manifesto—*Alcoholics Anonymous*—also known as "the Big Book," which created a spiritual toolkit by which alcoholics might reform themselves via a 12-Step program.[135] Bill W. and Dr. Bob (as they are known) created the 12 Steps as a set of guiding principles to help others on their journey to recovery (Figure 18.13).

QUICK HIT

Bill W. decided on having 12 Steps because, in the Christian Bible, there are 12 apostles. The book *Alcoholics Anonymous* was referred to as "the Big Book" because the printers of the first edition were instructed to use the thickest paper available so it would seem worth the price to the generally financially strapped alcoholics to whom it was targeted.[136]

Alcoholics Anonymous seeks to change the mindset of those who suffer from alcohol use disorders, not just their way of drinking. AA endorses the disease model of alcohol use disorders. They believe that the disorder is a chronic and progressive disease that can never be cured, and that total abstinence is the only solution. Although 12-Step group members rely on a higher power to aid their journey, they also are encouraged to take responsibility for their own recovery by "working the steps." New members are advised to pair with a sponsor—one who has successfully completed the 12 Steps—as a source of support and accountability.

Neither AA nor NA charge dues; they are self-supported by personal contributions. The only requirement for membership is a desire to stop abusing drugs and alcohol. There are various types of meetings, so those with substance abuse issues can find a meeting that suits them best, such as closed (members only), open (where anyone is welcome to attend), smoking,

FIGURE 18.12. Alcoholics Anonymous. The number of sobriety chips a person has indicates the amount of time a person has been sober.

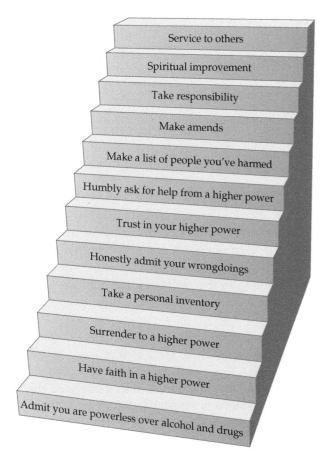

Service to others

Spiritual improvement

Take responsibility

Make amends

Make a list of people you've harmed

Humbly ask for help from a higher power

Trust in your higher power

Honestly admit your wrongdoings

Take a personal inventory

Surrender to a higher power

Have faith in a higher power

Admit you are powerless over alcohol and drugs

FIGURE 18.13. The 12 Steps. The 12-Step program of recovery is sometimes described as "a simple program for complicated people." The program instructs followers not to use regardless of what happens, to attend meetings, to ask for help, to find a sponsor, to join a group, and to become active.

nonsmoking, men only, women only, LGBTQ, newcomers, old-timers, and veterans.

Alcoholics Anonymous is the most popular of the self-help groups, but it is difficult to accurately determine its success rate. AA is, by definition, anonymous, so there is no official record of who attends, who drops out, and what their outcomes are. AA claims that 75 percent of those who are committed to the program stop drinking. Some studies suggest that abstinence rates are higher among those who attend AA or other 12-Step programs compared with those who use other interventions (such as CBT).[137] Those with higher levels of involvement (reading AA literature, participating as sponsors, applying the 12 Steps to daily life) are more likely to remain abstinent. Those who attended at least 50 AA meetings a year were more than twice as likely to be abstinent one year later compared with those who attended 1–19 meetings a year, and three times as likely to be abstinent compared to those who had attended no meetings in the past year.[138]

However, because it's not a random sample that attends AA, it's hard to determine whether attendance at self-help program meetings itself increases abstinence, or if it is that people who attend more meetings are more motivated in their sobriety. Some studies have tried to randomly assign recovering outpatients to different treatment protocols, or to use innovative statistical techniques to tease out the real effects, and they have found that AA attendance itself was indeed related to increased days of abstinence.[139,140]

So, what is the mechanism by which AA might increase abstinence? It may be because these programs give users sober role models and social opportunities to help them believe that they can achieve sobriety. AA might also work because it encourages its members to participate in rewarding educational, social, spiritual, and recreational alcohol-free pursuits. Or, perhaps these groups are effective because meetings provide an opportunity to help members talk about feelings, build self-efficacy and effective coping skills, and change their attitudes.[141,142]

Conversely, other studies suggest that AA greatly overestimates its success rates and that some supporting studies are fraught with design flaws, such as a lack of control groups. Lance Dodes, a professor of psychiatry at Harvard Medical School, analyzed the data and found that AA's success rate is closer to 5–8 percent.[143] AA's "Big Book" explains failures thus: "Those who do not recover are people who cannot or will not completely give themselves to this simple program, usually men and women who are constitutionally incapable of being honest with themselves." This puts blame for failure firmly in the hands of those with a substance abuse problem, and assumes that they failed the program, rather than that the program failed them.[144]

Secular Recovery Programs

For those who are uncomfortable with the spiritual foundations of AA, there are a number of secular recovery programs. These are based on the idea that the key to maintaining sobriety comes not from a higher power, but from within. Members reject the idea that they are powerless; these programs place a major emphasis on self-reliance, personal empowerment, and self-determination. Also, spirituality-based recovery programs emphasize *wisdom*, in the form of experience, a search for meaning, and self-transcendence through connection to a greater whole. Secular-based programs, however, emphasize *knowledge*, through scientific evidence, understanding of one's problem, and strength from personal competence.[145]

Secular programs differ from spirituality-based programs in other ways.[146] They discourage the labels of "alcoholic" and "addict," and they support the concept of complete recovery and time-limited involvement in the program. Secular programs more commonly meet in homes and religiously neutral sites and allow volunteer professionals who are not necessarily in recovery to facilitate and speak at the meetings. They don't have formal sponsorship; instead, personal independence is encouraged. Crosstalk—direct feedback and advice— is allowed at secular recovery meetings. Some secular programs include the Secular Organizations for Sobriety (SOS), Rational Recovery, SMART recovery, Women for Sobriety, and Moderation Management. Moderation Management does not believe that drinkers are powerless, or that abstinence is the only solution for drug or alcohol abuse. Instead, the program encourages personal responsibility for drinking, and it offers its members the goal of reducing and controlling their drinking.[147,148,149]

Most treatment programs in the United States follow the 12-Step approach, and have lifelong abstinence as their goal. But is this always the best approach?

Ask yourself: How would you deal with a person who you felt had a drug problem but who told you that she or he could control the use?

Characteristics of Effective Addiction Treatments

Over years of trial and error, of success and failure, NIDA has compiled its *Principles of Drug Addiction Treatment* to summarize our current understanding of the best ways to treat addiction.[156]

- *Addiction is a complex but treatable condition that affects brain function and behavior.* The neurological deviations may, in part, explain why the risk of relapse is so high.
- *No single treatment is appropriate for all individuals.* Much depends on which drug is used and on the person's particular needs.
- *Treatment needs to be readily available and accessible.* The earlier treatment is offered, the higher the likelihood of success.
- *Effective treatment must address issues other than drug use.* A person's medical, psychological, social, occupational, and legal problems must be addressed. Also, effective treatment needs to take an individual's age, sex/gender, race, and other factors into consideration.
- *It is important that treatment lasts for an adequate time.* The appropriate duration depends on the individual patient's situation.
- *Behavioral therapies are the most commonly used type of drug abuse treatment.* This can include individual, family, or group counseling, and can address motivations and problem-solving skills, as well as facilitate building stronger interpersonal relationships.
- *Medications can be an important element for some patients.* They are best combined with counseling and other behavioral therapies.
- *An effective treatment program will continually assess an individual's treatment plan.* Treatment should be adjusted as necessary to meet changing needs.
- *Any comorbid psychiatric conditions must be addressed.* Many individuals addicted to drugs also have other mental disorders, such as depression.

Critical Evaluation

Is total abstinence the only solution for drug or alcohol abuse?

The prevailing conventional wisdom in the United States is that those with substance abuse disorders must have lifelong abstinence as their goal. Use your critical thinking skills to evaluate this theory.

Is something as complex as substance abuse disorder best treated with an all-or-none approach? Is everyone who has a problem with AODs an addict, or can problematic drug use sometimes be due to a temporary or modifiable situation? Might the fact that AA and many other treatment programs are based on lifelong abstinence as the only path to success prevent some people from seeking to control their problematic use because they don't want to stop completely?

What is success? Is it measured by abstinence or by an improvement in one's quality of life? What is failure? If someone hasn't had a drink for 10 years and then has one glass of champagne at a wedding, have they failed? Or have they successfully managed to control their drinking and stop at one? If one drink is as bad as 100, might that person say, "Oh well, I blew it. Might as well get wasted for the next month." On the other hand, does abstinence allow people to avoid taking that first step on the slippery slope toward abuse?

How does abstinence fit with the disease model of addiction? Does it support it, by recognizing that the brain of someone with a substance abuse disorder is wired differently and can't handle moderate use? Or does it punish the user for relapsing? For example, even though a doctor would not stop treating a patient with diabetes if he ate a cookie, many rehab facilities expel clients who relapse.

Does one solution fit all? All users are different. They use for different reasons and have different responses to drugs. In diagnosing substance abuse disorders, the fifth edition of the *Diagnostic and Statistical Manual of Mental Disorders* (DSM-5) uses a continuum from mild to severe. About 15 percent of those with alcohol use disorders are on the severe end of the spectrum.[150] Perhaps abstinence is needed for some problematic users but not all. As one study showed, 90 percent of those classified as heavy drinkers don't have a substance abuse disorder.[151]

Beliefs of substance abuse counselors. About 50 percent of substance abuse counselors—twice as many as in the 1990s—now find it acceptable for at least some of their clients to drink occasionally.[152] These are the men and women who work with substance abusers every day and see what works and what doesn't work. On the other hand, most counselors are not health professionals; indeed, many have little to no training in addiction. How much should the opinions of substance abuse counselors be taken into consideration?

How effective is abstinence compared to moderation? Most people who have a problem with substance abuse learn to stop or manage their drug use on their own without treatment.[153,154,155] But these people do not enter "the system" of rehab or other treatment programs, so we have little data on them. How can we better learn about the relative success of abstinence and moderation programs?

- *Medically assisted drug detoxification is only the first state of treatment.* By itself, it is not effective for long-term improvement of problematic drug use.
- *Treatment does not need to be voluntary to be effective.* Patients who enter treatment because their family, workplace, or the criminal justice system requires it can actually have higher success rates than those who enter voluntarily.[157]
- *Relapses occur, so drug use must be monitored continually during treatment.* Knowing they are being monitored can help patients avoid relapse.
- *Treatment programs should test to see if the patient has infectious diseases such as hepatitis B and C,*

HIV/AIDS, and tuberculosis. These patients should receive risk-reduction counseling and treatment, if necessary.

Drug addiction often requires a combination of treatments. One course of treatment is often insufficient, given that many users will relapse on their journey toward a healthier lifestyle. When designing a treatment, it is important to consider the individual's goals—does he or she desire total abstinence or responsible use? What health concerns or psychological challenges is she or he facing? How might these goals change over the course of the treatment?

Relapse

Most drug treatment centers, websites, and addiction counselors assert that addiction is a chronic relapsing disease, remission is at best a temporary state, and most people who try to quit using drugs will eventually relapse. But it is important to remember that most data on addiction come from those whose lives became unmanageable, and who entered into a formal treatment program after trying and failing to quit numerous times over the years. Data about those who become dependent on drugs and are able to quit on their own generally do not make it into the studies.

Rates of relapse for those trying to recover from substance abuse range from 40–80 percent. The reason for such a wide range is that these figures depend on the population studied, the drug, the type of treatment program, and how relapse is defined.[158] Remission rates are markedly different for legal and illegal drugs and for different racial/ethnic groups (mostly due to social and socioeconomic factors).

The drug of choice can influence the likelihood of relapse. When considering how long it took an average of two-thirds of the users of a particular drug to quit, national surveys indicate that it takes an average of seven years for cocaine users and nine years for marijuana users to quit. (Although marijuana is not as addictive as other drugs, it is possible to become dependent—see Chapter 9.) Cigarette smokers and those suffering from alcohol use disorders don't give up their drugs as easily—it takes an average of 27 years for two-thirds of those with alcohol use disorders to quit or significantly cut down on their drinking, and 49 years for tobacco users to quit smoking (Figure 18.14).[159] This might be, in part, because alcohol and tobacco can be legally purchased on any corner, and users are constantly bombarded with ads glamorizing their use.

Factors that increase a person's risk of relapse include having less education, a lower likelihood of employment, fewer positive life events, less family and social support, more frequent and heavier AOD consumption, and more drug-related psychological and social problems.[160] Relapse may be triggered by re-exposure to the drug or to the people or environments associated with the drug. Both negative moods ("I had a hard day—I just need to take a Xanax") and positive moods ("Let's celebrate with a drink!") also can increase the risk of relapse.

Biological factors also may be involved. In one study, patients watched relaxing scenarios while in an fMRI scanner. Participants who showed abnormal

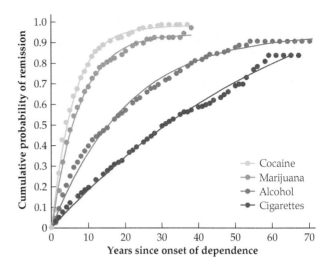

FIGURE 18.14. **Average number of years it takes someone who is dependent on these drugs to quit cocaine, marijuana, alcohol, and cigarettes.** It takes users significantly longer to quit alcohol and tobacco than it does to quit cocaine or marijuana.

Source: Bower, B. (2014). The addiction paradox. Science News, 185(6).

activity in the prefrontal cortex—an area related to the ability to regulate emotion, suppress urges, and make decisions—were 8.5 times as likely to relapse compared to those with normal brain patterns or to healthy controls.[161]

There are a number of mistaken beliefs about relapse,[162] some of which are listed here.

- *Mistaken Belief #1: A person has recovered from substance abuse as long as he or she is not using.* Drug addiction isn't only about the drug; it's about the emotions, attitudes, and behaviors that underlie the drug use. Abstinence itself is not recovery; it is only a prerequisite to recovery.
- *Mistaken Belief #2: Relapse occurs quickly and unexpectedly.* Actually, the process underlying relapse begins long before a person resumes drug use. Perhaps the person does not believe that she or he can live a life without alcohol or drugs, or maybe she or he has not learned any coping skills or techniques. Then, when the person who is recovering from addiction is exposed to drug cues or to stressful situations, alcohol or drugs can seem like the only solution.
- *Mistaken Belief #3: A person relapses because he or she has stopped going to self-help meetings or has dropped out of treatment.* Most people stop their treatment because they are already in the process of relapse. They believe that participating in a recovery program is unimportant, and they begin to return to addictive thinking and denial about their drinking or drug use. Discontinuing treatment and/or attendance at self-help programs

Journeys to Recovery

Eight people in recovery were interviewed about their journey. Here are their responses.

- How many years sober are you?
  - Bob, age 62
    - Two years sober. I drank alcohol for 45 years. The last six years of my drinking I drank every waking hour. When I was 16, I became a heroin addict* for one year. When I was 28, I went on a five-year cocaine binge. Then again when I was 52. I also was an opiate addict from 52 to 57. I never stopped drinking until I was 59.
  - Evan, age 39
    - 10 years
  - Jenny, age 24
    - I'm not currently sober.
  - Hilary, age 50
    - The last time I drank was 11 years ago.
  - Jesse, age 60
    - 27 years sober
  - Julie, age 52
    - I planned this summer to have a drink and see if I could do it and if not, I would go right back to AA. Well, that was three months ago and I'm doing fine. Don't drink much, enjoy it and have no obsession with it. I know I'm not the norm and I know things could change, but I'm very willing to quit again if I have to.
  - Liz, age 28
    - 3 years sober
  - Sarah, age 47
    - Four years and some months
- What's the one thing you want others to know about addiction?
  - Sarah, 47
    - There is hope. People die. It is an illness of the mind and body.
  - Bob, 62
    - Addictions are only symptoms of much more deep-seated issues that the addict or alcoholic is usually unaware of. The drug chemically alters the brain to make the addict or alcoholic believe they need whatever substance they're addicted to, thus creating an uncontrollably strong obsession. It's almost like a perpetual motion machine that requires fuel—the drug. The more fuel you give it, the more it requires.
  - Evan, 39
    - Addiction does not discriminate. I have met addicts from all walks of life, from the young person that started a social drinker to the old person that started taking pain meds for a broken hip. It does not limit itself to any

social class, age group, lifestyle, ethnicity, or any other category you can think of.

- Jesse, 60
  - That it sucks, that it can kill you, and that it's always a part of your life. Having said that, it's also the best thing that ever happened to me because it forced me to change my life in a dramatic way, which led to my living a life I could never have imagined for myself.
- Jenny, 24
  - I want people to know it is easy to get caught up in drugs. You can find yourself counting every pill trying to see how many extra you can get away with taking before filling your prescription early, or stealing money and valuables to afford more meth, or begging on the street for money to buy alcohol. The most shocking part is that you could be right around the corner from that life and not even realize it. Just a small step into addictive substances, just a line, just a toke, just a shot, just a hit, just a sip, can end your entire future and eventually your life. So before going down that road, think about it. Consider your options. Consider your loved ones, your quality of life, your future, your kids, your family, your career, and most of all your love for yourself and God's love for you.
- What's the one thing you want others to know about recovery?
  - Jesse, 60
    - Recovery is ongoing. It's never over. I won't ever be "cured." I can destroy everything I've been given in sobriety by drinking again.
- Bob, 62
  - The obsession does go away—if it didn't, there could never be a real recovery. But it won't go away until the addict develops self-love and love for others, and is no longer spiritually bankrupt. He must develop assets, through good deeds, by making amends for his past, by truly being happy in life. These assets help him develop the self-love necessary to alleviate the obsession of his addiction.
- Evan, 39
  - Recovery is possible, but the desire for recovery needs to come from the alcoholic/addict, not loved ones, or job pressures, or a piano hanging over his/her head. Only then will there be the willingness to do what is needed to get sober and remain sober. The good news is that if this willingness is found, life can be amazing for all of those involved. Those same traits that allow us to focus on alcohol and drugs to such a strong degree can also be used to focus on the positive things in our lives.
- What's been the hardest part of your journey?

- Liz, 28
  - It can feel lonely. Drugs are so normalized in our society—Xanax and Adderall and alcohol—and everyone takes something.
- Evan, 39
  - Learning to live. When a person spends a large part of their lives drinking/drugging, many other life skills and coping skills are neglected. Also, emotions that have been deadened by substances suddenly come screaming back. It took a lot of work and patience to get caught up, rediscover myself, and find some peace of mind. This is where 12-Step programs can be very helpful.
- Sarah, 47
  - Early sobriety was tough. All of my emotions had been mitigated by alcohol and I found myself easily overwhelmed. I didn't feel comfortable anywhere with anyone and I really needed a lot of support. Fortunately, I had people in my life who helped me with patience and love. The best thing about recovery is that you keep it by giving it away and that has saved me over and over.
- Jenny, 24
  - Withdrawal is hell. Never try to go through withdrawal on your own because you can potentially die from it, and besides that, it's the most horrible thing you could ever experience in your life.
- Jesse, 60
  - The hardest part is looking back and thinking about the people I hurt, either through sins of commission or omission.
- Drinking/drugging makes you part of a society. So does being sober. Did/do you feel less isolated when you were using or now when you're sober?
  - Liz, 28
    - Being back in college sober is interesting. My drinking friends don't invite me out anymore.
  - Sarah, 47
    - When I was finally done with drinking my life was the size of a postage stamp. It just kept getting smaller and smaller and I could not seem to do anything to stop it. I spent years renegotiating the rules of my life so that I could "function." I left little pieces of myself all over the sidewalk. [My drinking] was shrouded in secrecy (although not as much as I had thought). I had to keep my friends and family at a distance and really had no close, honest relationships.
  - Bob, 62
    - The first 35 years of my drinking I felt like an accepted member of society with friends and family. Even though I knew I drank more than everyone else and more incidents related to my drinking, I still felt like I was accepted and liked by all. When my drinking kept increasing, the negative incidents did as well. My friends and family wanted less and less to do with me. It really got to the point where I was totally alone. Just me and the booze.
- Jesse, 60
  - At first when I drank, I loved the companionship. In college, I was the life of the party. At my blue-collar job in Chicago, I got to hang with working-class heroes, and I felt like I was part of the real world. However, by the end of my long drinking career, I preferred to drink alone in my apartment. I hated being around anyone.
- Any other thoughts you'd like to share?
  - Sarah, 47
    - We hear the shocking and horrific stories of young people killing themselves with alcohol in many ways, but I think the real tragedy is the loss of potential. All the time and energy that it takes to acquire, consume, and recover from drinking results in less dramatic, but nonetheless heartbreaking losses.
- Jesse, 60
  - I learned that addiction is incredibly powerful. In the case of alcohol, when I first started drinking, it was the single most miraculous experience I'd ever had. I was 18 at the time, and suddenly here was this potion that removed my depression, helped me be comfortable around other people, and, for the first 10 years or so, was often exhilarating. I mean rolling down hills, sliding in mud kind of exhilarating. Unfortunately, for every big night I had, there was another night where I sat in my dorm room and cried. I loved the melancholy part as well. I loved being drunk and sad. If you're an alcoholic (or addict), what you don't realize early on is that the depression part, that soul sinking, bottomless fall into the bottle part, becomes the norm at the end of one's career. My final word: When I first stopped drinking, I was told I had a disease. And I took comfort in the fact that it was genetic, hereditary, and just had to do with being born into my particular body. There were alcoholics aplenty clamoring around my family tree, and many of them fell to their deaths. For years I've tried to make sense of this "disease" concept, and what I've realized is that it just doesn't matter. If it's bone-deep, if it's been passed down to me by my parents, so be it. If it's a combination of genetics and lived experience, so be it. It just doesn't matter. The only real wisdom I own is the very valuable, life-saving understanding that if I drink, I lose everything: my wife, my job—my life. So, what the hell does it matter if it's a disease, a predilection, a choice, a spiritual failure, a moral shortcoming? It'll kill me just as dead no matter how I (or anyone else) define it.

---

* I have avoided the use of the term addict to describe those with problematic drug use. Many people have challenges in their lives, but are not defined by them—we don't say, "This is my friend, the leukemia." Having a substance use disorder does not define someone; it is only one aspect of his or her life. However, these are the words of those who have personally struggled with addiction, and I have honored how they choose to define themselves.

is often the result of the relapse process rather than the cause.

- *Mistaken Belief #4: If a person had enough willpower and self-discipline, he or she wouldn't relapse.* Relapse is not as simple as a lack of self-discipline; it occurs because there are problems or conditions that are not being effectively managed or treated. There is something the person needs to do, learn, or stop. Additionally, most people who relapse are not consciously aware of the warning signs of relapse as they occur. It is only when they look back later that they can see what was going on.
- *Mistaken Belief #5: Those who relapse repeatedly are constitutionally incapable of recovery.*

Those who repeatedly relapse have not yet completely learned how to manage their dependence. This does not mean that they are not motivated to recover, or that the treatment failed, or that they will never recover. Each relapse, if properly dealt with, can become a learning experience that makes the patient less likely to relapse in the future.

Ask yourself: What is the goal of treatment? Is it complete abstinence? Harm reduction? Does it depend on the drug used or individual situation?

Chapter Summary

- **Introduction**
  - » The best way to avoid drug abuse and addiction is to prevent someone from starting drugs rather than to try to get them to stop.
  - » Some methods of prevention include school-based programs, media campaigns, and drug testing.
- **Types of Prevention**
  - » Prevention of substance abuse can be classified as primary, secondary, and tertiary, based on the degree of alcohol and other drug experience the participant has already experienced.
  - » Drug prevention programs also can be categorized according to the intended target population, including universal, selective, or indicated.
  - » Programs to prevent drug use include school-based campaigns that include family and community involvement, advertising campaigns, and drug testing.
- **School-Based Prevention Campaigns**
  - » Some ineffective school-based methods of drug use prevention include cognitive approaches, scare tactics, and affective programs.
  - » The DARE program has been unsuccessful in the past, but its revised version has shown some success.
  - » The social influence model is a more effective method of drug use prevention. It provides honest and straightforward information about drugs that enables students to use the life skills they learn in order to make better decisions.
  - » Drug use prevention programs work best when they are active, participatory learning experiences that use peer counselors and family and community involvement, and include role-playing and the opportunity to practice drug-resistance skills.
  - » The LifeSkills Training program (LST) and Keepin' It REAL are two of the more successful school-based prevention programs.

- » Media literacy teaches viewers to understand, analyze, and critically evaluate messages from ads, television, and movies.
- » Prevention programs are not limited to elementary and high schools. Colleges and universities have implemented many programs to try to minimize the damage caused by irresponsible alcohol consumption.
- **Advertising Campaigns to Prevent Drug Use**
  - » Advertising campaigns, including anti-drug ads and anti-tobacco ads, have been used to prevent drug use. Their success has been inconsistent.
- **Drug Testing**
  - » Almost all federal agencies and many major corporations have drug-testing programs in place for those seeking employment, welfare, or adoption of a baby.
  - » Drug testing involves evaluating a person's urine, blood, or other biological substances to determine whether drugs have been used.
  - » Federal guidelines require testing for amphetamines, cannabinoids, cocaine, opioids, and PCP—a combination known as the "SAMHSA5."
  - » Detection times depend upon the drug, its frequency and duration of use, route of administration, individual differences in metabolism, tolerance to the drug, whether the test measures the drug itself or a metabolite, and other factors.
  - » The five primary types of drug tests are urine, saliva, hair, sweat, and blood.
  - » The effectiveness of drug testing in increasing workplace productivity is controversial.
- **Prevalence of Treatment for Alcohol and Drug Addiction**
  - » In 2019, 7.4 percent of those age 12 and older were classified with substance abuse or dependence, but only about 10 percent received treatment.

» Most of those who seek treatment for alcohol or other drug (AOD) dependence go to self-help groups or outpatient rehabilitation facilities.

- **The Stages of Recovery**
  » Those with substance abuse disorders may take different paths on the way to recovery, but many go through a series of stages, including precontemplation, contemplation, preparation, action, maintenance, and then either relapse or termination.

- **Methods of Treatment**
  » Drug addiction is a complex, multifaceted condition. As such, it often requires a combination of treatments.
  » Some users must go through medical detoxification.
  » Pharmacological treatments can help people in their recovery, but they are not intended to be the sole treatment for addiction.
  » Psychosocial treatments include individual and group therapy sessions, inpatient or outpatient treatment programs, behavioral approaches, or self-help groups such as Alcoholics Anonymous (AA) or Narcotics Anonymous (NA).
  » Although many people believe that addiction is a disease, the field of addiction treatment is not held to the rigorous scientific standards of other medical fields.
  » Inpatient treatment centers include hospitals, clinics, and chemical dependence centers where residents live while undergoing intensive treatment during the day. After leaving an inpatient facility, some choose to stay temporarily at sober living houses.

» Those who don't need the intensity of an inpatient program, or whose circumstances are incompatible with a stay, might consider outpatient programs or therapy. Cognitive behavioral therapy (CBT) has been shown to be effective in treating substance abuse disorder.

» Self-help groups, such as AA or NA, are nonprofessional organizations that are peer-operated by people who share the same addictive disorder. Members of AA follow a 12-Step program of recovery. AA's effectiveness is unclear.

» Other self-help groups are based on the idea that the key to maintaining sobriety comes not from a higher power, but from within.

» Most treatment programs in the United States follow the 12-Step approach, but there is disagreement over whether lifelong abstinence is the only solution for drug or alcohol abuse.

- **Characteristics of Effective Addiction Treatments**
  » The National Institute on Drug Abuse (NIDA) has compiled 13 points that summarize current understanding of the best way to treat addiction.

- **Relapse**
  » For some, addiction is a chronic and relapsing condition, and many addicts may relapse.
  » Individuals with less education, lower likelihood of employment, fewer positive life events, less family and social support, more frequent and heavier AOD consumption, and more drug-related psychological and social problems are more likely to relapse.

Key Terms

Alcoholics Anonymous (AA)(p.461)
Cognitive behavioral therapy (CBT) (p.460)
Community reinforcement (p.461)
Contingency management (p.461)
Drug testing (p.449)

False negative (p.454)
False positive (p.454)
Gas chromatography/mass spectrometry (GC/MS) (p.451)
Immunoassay (p.450)
Media literacy (p.444)

Medical detoxification (p.456)
Narcotics Anonymous (NA) (p.461)
Sober living home (p.460)
Social influence model (p.444)
SAMHSA-5 (p.451)

Quiz Yourself!

1. Which of these is NOT one of the priorities of national policy to control drug use?

   A. Stop drug use before it starts

   B. Provide treatment programs for those who are dependent on drugs

   C. Implement widespread drug education programs that include information about the mechanism of action and effects of alcohol, tobacco, and other drugs

   D. Disrupt the supply of drugs

2. Which of these would be most effective for a seventh grader who has had little to no personal experience with drugs?

   A. Primary prevention program

   B. Secondary prevention program

   C. Tertiary prevention program

   D. Selective prevention program

3. Match the type of school-based drug prevention program to its description.

    1. Focuses on the feelings, emotions, and attitudes that underlie drug use
    2. Present horror stories and frightening physical and legal ramifications of drug use
    3. Provide information and drug-resistance skills, and use peer counselors, parents, and community members
    4. Give accurate information about drugs so students will make a rational choice not to use them

    A. Cognitive approaches
    B. Scare tactics
    C. Affective programs
    D. Social influence model

4. True or false? Most prevention programs at colleges and universities focus on preventing the use of marijuana.

5. List three conditions during which a drug test typically occurs.

6. Match the type of drug test to its description. Answers are used only once.

    1. Urine   A. Shows drug use for past 90 days
    2. Saliva B. Most common and least expensive drug test
    3. Hair   C. Most expensive, most accurate, and least commonly performed drug test
    4. Blood   D. Used mostly by the criminal justice system to monitor drug use over long periods of time
    5. Sweat   E. Easy, noninvasive, measures drug use in past 24 hours

7. Match the following terms in the process of recovery. One answer per blank; each answer is used once.

    1. Action   A. Users may not believe they have a problem
    2. Contemplation   B. User is AOD-free for at least 6 months
    3. Maintenance   C. The temptation to use no longer exists
    4. Precontemplation D. The user has set a date and made a plan of action
    5. Preparation   E. Users are willing to admit they have a problem
    6. Termination   F. Users are taking steps to modify their behavior

8. True or false? The federal guidelines for treatment of substance abuse require counselors to have at least a bachelor's degree plus a 30-hour course of training.

9. Match the pharmacological treatment to the drug of abuse for which it is typically used.

    1. Acamprosate   A. Opioids
    2. Buprenorphine   B. Alcohol
    3. Disulfiram   C. Tobacco
    4. Methadone
    5. Bupropion

10. Billy has been addicted to alcohol for 30 years. He has been drinking heavily since he was 16 years old. After his third DUI, he was ordered to enter treatment for his drinking. Put the following potential treatments for Billy in chronological order:

    Sober living home
    Medical detoxification
    Self-help program such as AA
    Inpatient facility

11. Which of these takes longest on average for two out of three users to quit?

    A. Alcohol
    B. Cocaine
    C. Marijuana
    D. Tobacco

12. True or false? Those who relapse repeatedly are constitutionally incapable of recovery.

Additional Resources

Websites

Partnership for Drug Free Kids https://drugfree.org/

Drug testing FAQs. https://www.drugs.com/article/drug-testing.html

NIDA's page on drug testing. https://www.drugabuse.gov/related-topics/drug-testing

NIDA's page on school-based prevention programs. https://www.drugabuse.gov/publications/preventing-drug-abuse-among-children-adolescents/chapter-4-examples-research-based-drug-abuse-prevention-progr-0

Videos

How accurate are drug tests? https://www.youtube.com/watch?v=3z-xjfdJWAI

Movies

28 Days. (2000). (103 minutes). Sandra Bullock stars in a film about a woman forced to enter a drug and alcohol rehab center.

Books

Alcoholics Anonymous. (2014). *Alcoholics Anonymous: Big book reference edition for addiction treatment.*

Learn more with this chapter's digital tools at www.oup.com/he/rosenthal2e.

Appendix

Drugs

Generic Name	Trade Name	Street Name	Type of Drug	Uses
Acamprosate	Campral		Glutamate antagonist and GABA agonist	Alcohol addiction
Acetaminophen	Tylenol		Non-narcotic analgesic	Analgesia, fever reduction
Acetylcysteine	Mucomyst, Fluimucil		Expectorant	Cough medicine
Albuterol	Ventolin		Stimulant	Bronchodilator
Alcohol		Booze, sauce, hooch	Depressant	Intoxicant
Alprazolam	Xanax	Bars, footballs, zannies	Benzodiazepine sedative/hypnotic	Anxiolytic, antidepressant, anticonvulsant, sleep aid, chronic alcohol withdrawal, muscle relaxant, pre-anesthetic sedation, status epilepticus
Amanita muscaria			Dissociative hallucinogen	Hallucinogen, religious rituals
Amobarbital	Amytal	Bluebirds	Barbiturate sedative/hypnotic	Sleep aid, emergency management of seizures, pre-anesthetic sedative
Amphetamine, dextroamphetamine	Adderall, Dexedrine, Vyvanse	Speed, bennies, uppers, addies, smarties	Stimulant	ADHD, weight loss, narcolepsy
Amitriptyline	Elavil		Tricyclic antidepressant	Antidepressant
Amyl nitrite	Amyl nitrite	Poppers, rush	Vasodilator	Angina, heart disease
Androstenedione	Androvax (veterinary use)	Andro	Anabolic steroid	Athletic performance-enhancing
Aripiprazole	Abilify		Third generation antipsychotic	Schizophrenia
Aspirin, acetylsalicylic acid	Bayer Aspirin, Excedrin		NSAID	Analgesia, fever reduction, anti-inflammatory, anticlotting
Atenolol	Tenormin		Beta blocker	Slows heart rate and lowers blood pressure
Atropa belladonna, (atropine)	Atreza		Deliriant hallucinogen	Hallucinogen, ophthalmic use, surgical use, Parkinson's disease
Avanafil	Stendra		PDE-5 inhibitor	Erectile dysfunction
Ayahuasca		Yage	Psychedelic hallucinogen	Hallucinogen, religious rituals
Bisacodyl	Dulcolax	Colon blow	Stimulant laxative	Laxative
Bismuth subsalicylate	Pepto Bismol, Kaopectate		Antacid	Heartburn, nausea, upset stomach, diarrhea
Boldenone	Equipoise		Anabolic steroid	Athletic performance-enhancing

Generic Name	Trade Name	Street Name	Type of Drug	Uses
Bremelanotide	Vyleesi		Melanocortin agonist	Treat hypoactive sexual desire disorder in women
Bufotonine			Psychedelic hallucinogen	Hallucinogen
Buprenorphine	Subutex, Suboxone	Bupe, subs	Opioid	Opioid addiction
Bupropion	Zyban, Wellbutrin		Atypical antidepressant	Antidepressant, smoking cessation
Caffeine			Stimulant	Stimulant, headache
Calcium bicarbonate	Tums, Rolaids		Antacid	Heartburn
Cannabis		Marijuana, pot, weed, grass	Cannabinoid	Analgesic, anti-emetic, appetite enhancer, recreational use
Carbamazepine	Tegretol		Anticonvulsant	Analgesic, anticonvulsant, bipolar disorder
Carfentanil	WildNil		Opioid	Animal tranquilizer
Cathinone		Khat	Stimulant	Stimulant
Cetirizine	Zyrtec		Antihistamine	Allergy
Chloral hydrate			Sedative/hypnotic	Sedative, opioid and alcohol withdrawal
Chlordiazepoxide	Librium	Downers, tranqs, bennies, benzos	Benzodiazepine sedative/hypnotic	Anxiolytic, anticonvulsant, chronic alcohol withdrawal, muscle relaxant, pre-anesthetic sedation, status epilepticus
Chlorpheniramine	Chlor-Trimeton, Contac 12 hour		Antihistamine	Cold medicine, allergy
Chlorpromazine	Thorazine		Typical antipsychotic	Bipolar disorder, schizophrenia
Cimetidine	Tagamet, Pepcid		H_2 blocker	Heartburn, GERD, peptic ulcer
Citalopram	Celexa		SSRI antidepressant	Antidepressant
Clomifene	Clomid, Serophene		Estrogen antagonist	Infertility
Clomipramine	Anafranil		Tricyclic antidepressant	Antidepressant
Clonazepam	Klonopin	Pin, super valium	Benzodiazepine sedative/hypnotic	Anxiolytic, antidepressant, Anticonvulsant, sleep aid, chronic alcohol withdrawal, muscle relaxant, pre-anesthetic sedation, status epilepticus
Clozapine	Clozaril		Atypical antipsychotic	Schizophrenia
Cocaine	Cocaine hydrochloride	Coke, blow, nose candy	Stimulant	Local anesthetic, stimulant
Codeine	Codeine sulfate	Schoolboy	Opioid	Analgesia, cough suppressant
Danazol	Danocrine		Anabolic steroid	Athletic performance-enhancing
Datura			Deliriant hallucinogen	Parkinson's disease
Dehydroepiandrosterone	DHEA, Deandros		Anabolic steroid	Athletic performance-enhancing

Generic Name	Trade Name	Street Name	Type of Drug	Uses
Deprenyl	Selegiline		MAO-I antidepressant	Antidepressant
Desvenlafaxine	Pristiq		Atypical antidepressant	Antidepressant
Desyrel	Trazadone		Atypical antidepressant	Antidepressant
Dextromethorphan	Robitussin, NyQuil, Dimetapp, Theraflu		Antitussive	Cough suppressant
Diazepam	Valium	V, tranqs, benzos	Benzodiazepine sedative/ hypnotic	Anxiolytic, anticonvulsant, chronic alcohol withdrawal, muscle relaxant, pre-anesthetic sedation, status epilepticus
Diclofenac	Voltaren, Cataflam		NSAID	Analgesia, fever reduction, anti-inflammatory, anticlotting
Diphenhydramine	Benadryl, ZzzQuil, Sominex, others		Antihistamine	Cold medicine, hives, sleep aid, allergy, motion sickness
Disulfiram	Antabuse		Acetaldehyde dehydrogenase inhibitor	Alcohol addiction
DMT		Businessman's high	Psychedelic hallucinogen	Hallucinogen, religious rituals
Docusate	Colace		Stool softener	Laxative
Doxylamine succinate	Unisom, NyQuil		Antihistamine	Sleep aid
Dronabinol (synthetic THC)	Marinol		Synthetic cannabinoid	Analgesia, anti-emetic, increase appetite
Drostanolone	Masteron		Anabolic/androgenic steroid	Athletic performance-enhancing
Duloxetine	Cymbalta		Atypical antidepressant	Antidepressant
Ephedrine	Primatene		Stimulant	Bronchodilator, weight loss
Escitalopram	Lexapro		SSRI antidepressant	Antidepressant
Esketamine	Spravato		NMDA receptor antagonist	Antidepressant
Esomeprazole	Nexium		Proton pump inhibitor	GERD
Estrogens, conjugated (sodium estrone sulfate, sodium equilin sulfate)	Premarin		Sex steroid/ Estrogen	Hormone replacement therapy in females, alleviate symptoms of menopause
Ether	Ether		Sedative/ hypnotic	Sedative, anesthetic
Ethinyl estradiol plus etonogestrel	NuvaRing	The ring	Sex steroids/ Estrogen and progestin	Hormonal contraceptive
Ethinyl estradiol plus norgestimate	Ortho Cyclen, Ortho Tri-Cyclen, many others	The pill	Sex steroids/ Estrogen and progestin	Hormonal contraceptive
Ethinyl estradiol plus norelgestromin	Xulane	The patch	Sex steroids/ Estrogen and progestin	Hormonal contraceptive
Etonogestrel	Nexplanon		Synthetic sex steroid/ Progestin	Hormonal contraceptive
Etorphine	M99, Immobilon		Opioid	Veterinary use only
Fentanyl	Sublimaze, Actiq	China white, China girl, apache, murder 8	Opioid	Analgesia

Generic Name	Trade Name	Street Name	Type of Drug	Uses
Fexofenadine	Allegra		Antihistamine	Allergy
Flibanserin	Addyi		Serotonin 1A agonist/serotonin 2A antagonist	Treat hypoactive sexual desire disorder in women
Flunitrazepam	Rohypnol	Roofies	Benzodiazepine sedative/hypnotic	Sleep aid, pre-anesthetic sedative
Fluoxetine	Prozac		SSRI antidepressant	Antidepressant
Flurazepam	Dalmane	Downers, tranqs, bennies, benzos	Benzodiazepine sedative/hypnotic	Anxiolytic, anticonvulsant, chronic alcohol withdrawal, muscle relaxant, pre-anesthetic sedation, status epilepticus
Gabapentin	Neurontin		Anticonvulsant	Analgesic, anticonvulsant, restless leg syndrome, bipolar disorder, schizophrenia
Gamendazole			Indazole carboxylic acid derivative	Male contraception
Gamma hydroxybutyrate (GHB)	Xyrem	Grievous bodily harm, Georgia home boy	Sedative/ hypnotic	Narcolepsy
Guaifenesin	Mucinex		Expectorant	Cough medicine
Haloperidol	Haldol		Typical antipsychotic	Schizophrenia
Heroin		H, snow, horse, scag, junk	Opioid	Analgesia, euphoriant
Hydrocortisone	Cortaid		Corticosteroid	Anti-inflammatory
Hydrocodone	Vicodin, Lortab	Vikes, hydro	Opioid	Analgesia
Hydromorphone	Dilaudid	Dillies	Opioid	Analgesia
Ibogaine				Hallucinogen, religious rituals, possible use to treat drug addiction
Ibuprofen	Advil, Motrin		NSAID	Analgesia, fever reduction, anti-inflammatory, anticlotting
Imipramine	Tofranil		Tricyclic antidepressant	Antidepressant
Isocarboxazid	Marplan		MAO-I antidepressant	Antidepressant
Ketamine	Ketalar	Special K	Dissociative hallucinogen	Hallucinogen, anesthetic, possible treatment for depression
Lamotrigine	Lamictal		Anticonvulsant	Analgesia, anticonvulsant, bipolar disorder
Lansoprazole	Prevacid		Proton pump inhibitor	GERD
Laudanum			Opioid/ alcohol	Analgesic, cough suppressant
Leuprorelin	Lupron		GnRH stimulator	Cancer treatment, infertility
Levonorgestrel	Plan B, Mirena		Synthetic sex hormone	Emergency contraceptive
Lithium salts	Camcolit, Lithobid		Mood stabilizer	Bipolar disorder
Loperamide	Imodium		Opioid	Diarrhea
Loratadine	Claritin		Antihistamine	Allergy

Generic Name	Trade Name	Street Name	Type of Drug	Uses
Lorazepam	Ativan	Control, silence	Benzodiazepine sedative/hypnotic	Anxiolytic, antidepressant, anticonvulsant, sleep aid, chronic alcohol withdrawal, muscle relaxant, pre-anesthetic sedation, status epilepticus
Loxapine	Loxitane		Typical antipsychotic	Schizophrenia
Lysergic acid diethylamide (LSD)	Delysid (no longer available)	Acid, blotter, windowpane, Lucy in the sky with diamonds	Psychedelic hallucinogen	Hallucinogen, cluster headaches, possible treatment for depression and addiction
Macrogol	MiraLAX		Hyperosmotic agent	Laxative
Magnesium hydroxide	Milk of Magnesia		Hyperosmotic agent	Laxative
Mandrake			Deliriant hallucinogen	Hallucinogen
MDMA		Ecstasy, X, rave, love drug, Molly	Stimulant and hallucinogen	Hallucinogen, stimulant, possible treatment for PTSD
Medroxyprogesterone acetate	Depo-Provera	The shot	Synthetic sex hormone/Progestin	Hormonal contraceptive
Melatonin	Melatonin		Pineal hormone	Sleep aid, jet lag
Menotropin	Pergonal		Gonadotropin hormone	Infertility
Meperidine	Demerol	Doctors	Opioid	Analgesia, cough suppressant
Mephedrone		Bath salts, M-cat, meow meow	Stimulant	Stimulant, euphoriant
Mescaline		Mesc, buttons	Psychedelic hallucinogen	Hallucinogen, religious rituals
Mestranol and norethindrone	Ortho-Novum, Norinyl, and many others	The Pill	Sex hormones/ Estrogen and progestin	Hormonal contraceptive
Methadone	Dolophine	Dollies	Opioid	Analgesia, treat opioid addiction
Methamphetamine	Desoxyn	Meth, crystal	Stimulant	ADHD, weight loss, narcolepsy
Methandrostenolone	Dianabol		Anabolic/androgenic steroid	Athletic performance-enhancing
Methaqualone	Quaaludes	Ludes	Sedative/hypnotic	CNS depressant
Methcathinone		Cat	Stimulant	Stimulant
Methyl cellulose	Citrucel		Dietary fiber	Laxative
Methylphenidate	Ritalin, Concerta, Focalin	Diet coke, rid, smarties	Stimulant	ADHD
Methyltestosterone	Android, Virilon		Anabolic/androgenic steroid	Athletic performance-enhancing
Miconazole	Monistat		Antifungal	Yeast infections
Midazolam	Versed		Benzodiazepine sedative/hypnotic	Anxiolytic, anticonvulsant, sleep aid, muscle relaxant, pre-anesthetic sedation
Minoxidil	Rogaine		Antihypertensive	Hair growth

Generic Name	Trade Name	Street Name	Type of Drug	Uses
Morning glory seeds			Psychedelic hallucinogen	Hallucinogen
Morphine	MS-Contin	Morpho, Miss Emma	Opioid	Analgesia, cough suppressant
Nabiximols (THC + cannabidiol)	Sativex		Cannabinoid	Analgesia, anti-emetic, appetite enhancer
Naloxone	Narcan		Opioid antagonist	Reverse effects of opioid overdose
Naltrexone	Revia, Vivitrol		Opioid antagonist	Opioid and alcohol addiction
Nandrolone	Deca-Durabolin		Anabolic/androgenic steroid	Athletic performance-enhancing
Naproxen	Aleve, Naprosyn		NSAID	Analgesia, fever reduction, anti-inflammatory, anticlotting
Nicotine	Found in cigarettes, cigars, pipes, dip, and vape; also, Nicotrol, Nicorette		Stimulant	Nicotrol and Nicorette for smoking cessation
Nitrous oxide		Nitrous, laughing gas, whippets	Sedative/ hypnotic	Anesthetic and analgesic in dental procedures
Olanzapine	Zyprexa		Atypical antipsychotic	Schizophrenia
Omeprazole	Prilosec		Proton pump inhibitor	GERD
Ondansetron	Zofran		Serotonin antagonist	Alcohol addiction
Opium	Opium	Buddha, joy plant	Opioid	Analgesia, cough suppressant
Orlistat	Alli		Pancreatic lipase inhibitor	Weight loss
Oxyandrolone	Oxandrin		Anabolic steroid	Athletic performance-enhancing, osteoporosis
Oxycodone HCl	Percodan, Percocet, OxyContin	Oxy, O's, OC, roxies, percs, hillbilly heroin	Opioid	Analgesia
Oxymetazoline	Afrin, Dristan		Decongestant	Decongestant
Paroxetine	Paxil		SSRI antidepressant	Antidepressant
Pentobarbital	Nembutal	Yellow jackets	Barbiturate sedative/ hypnotic	Sleep aid, emergency management of seizures, pre-anesthetic sedative
Peyote		Buttons	Psychedelic hallucinogen	Hallucinogen, religious rituals
Phencyclidine	Sernyl (no longer available)	PCP, Angel dust	Dissociative hallucinogen	Hallucinogen
Phenobarbital	Luminal	Goofballs, purple hearts	Barbiturate sedative/ hypnotic	Anticonvulsant Anxiolytic
Phenylephrine	Neo-synephrine, Actifed		Decongestant	Decongestant
Phenylpropanolamine	Dexatrim, Acutrim		Stimulant	Weight loss, decongestant
Phenytoin	Dilantin		Anticonvulsant	Antiseizure
Prochlorperazine	Compazine		Typical antipsychotic	Schizophrenia
Propofol	Diprivan	Milk of amnesia	Sedative/hypnotic	Fast-acting anesthetic
Propranolol	Hemangeol		Beta blocker	Slows heart rate and lowers blood pressure
Pseudoephedrine	Sudafed, Sinutab		Decongestant	Decongestant

Generic Name	Trade Name	Street Name	Type of Drug	Uses
Psilocybin		Shrooms	Psychedelic hallucinogen	Hallucinogen, religious rituals, cluster headaches, possible treatment for depression
Psyllium	Metamucil		Dietary fiber	Laxative
Quetiapine	Seroquel		Atypical antipsychotic	Schizophrenia
Ranitidine	Zantac		H_2 blocker	Heartburn, GERD, peptic ulcer
Recombinant human papillomavirus vaccine	Gardasil		HPV vaccine	HPV vaccine
Risperidone	Risperdal		Atypical antipsychotic	Bipolar disorder, schizophrenia
Salvia		Magic mint	Dissociative hallucinogen	Hallucinogen, religious ceremonies
Scopolamine	Transderm Scop		Deliriant hallucinogen	Motion sickness, surgical use
Secobarbital	Seconal	Reds	Barbiturate sedative/hypnotic	Sleep aid, emergency management of seizures, pre-anesthetic sedative
Selegiline	Eldepryl		MAO-I antidepressant	Antidepressant
Sertraline	Zoloft		SSRI antidepressant	Antidepressant
Sildenafil	Viagra		PDE-5 inhibitor	Erectile dysfunction
Sodium bicarbonate	Alka-Seltzer		Antacid	Heartburn
Spice (synthetic cannabinoids)		K2	Synthetic cannabinoid	Euphoriant, recreational use
Stanozolol	Winstrol		Anabolic steroid	Athletic performance-enhancing
Tadalafil	Cialis		PDE-5 inhibitor	Erectile dysfunction
Temazepam	Restoril	Rugby balls, tems	Benzodiazepine sedative/hypnotic	Anxiolytic, antidepressant, anticonvulsant, sleep aid, chronic alcohol withdrawal, muscle relaxant, pre-anesthetic sedation, status epilepticus
Testosterone	AndroGel, Depo-Testosterone		Sex hormone/Testosterone	Breast cancer, hormone replacement therapy in males, athletic performance-enhancing
Tetracycline			Antibiotic	Antibiotic
Tetrahydrogestrinone		THG, the clear	Anabolic/androgenic steroid	Athletic performance-enhancing
Thiopental	Pentothal	Downers	Barbiturate sedative/hypnotic	Rapid surgical anesthesia
Topiramate	Topamax		Anticonvulsant	Anticonvulsant, migraines, weight loss, bipolar disorder
Tramadol	Ultram	Chill pills, ultra	Opioid	Analgesia
Trazodone	Desyrel		Atypical antidepressant	Antidepressant

Generic Name	Trade Name	Street Name	Type of Drug	Uses
Triazolam	Halcion	Up Johns	Benzodiazepine sedative/hypnotic	Anxiolytic, anticonvulsant, sleep aid, muscle relaxant, pre-anesthetic sedation
Trifluoperazine	Stelazine		Typical antipsychotic	Schizophrenia
Valproic acid	Depakote		Anticonvulsant	Anticonvulsant, migraines, bipolar disorder
Vardenafil	Levitra		PDE-5 inhibitor	Erectile dysfunction
Varenicline	Chantix		Smoking cessation	Smoking cessation
Venlafaxine	Effexor		Atypical antidepressant	Antidepressant
Warfarin	Coumadin		Blood thinner	Blood clots, prevent stroke
Yohimbine	Yohimbine		Adrenergic receptor agonist	Erectile dysfunction
Ziprasidone	Geodon		Atypical antipsychotic	Schizophrenia

Answers to the Quiz Yourself! Questions

1. C
2. False. External validity is a measure of how generalizable the study is.
3. A. Drinking vodka
   B. Attitudes toward women
   C. Drinking club soda
4. True
5. 1. E, 2. A, 3. D, 4. H, 5. I, 6. B, 7. J, 8. F, 9. C, 10. G
6. E

CHAPTER 1

1. False
2. True
3. C
4. Alcohol, tobacco, marijuana, nonmedical use of prescription drugs, cocaine
5. To feel pleasure, to avoid pain, to change one's state of consciousness, to enhance spiritual experiences, to facilitate social interactions, to alter the body
6. False
7. B, B, A, C, B
8. C, A, D, B
9. C
10. Animal testing, IND application, clinical trials, NDA application, FDA review, FDA approval, and post-marketing analysis

CHAPTER 2

1. Controlled Substances Act, 1970
2. False. There were eight times as many.
3. False
4. True
5. 0.08
6. D
7. B
8. False. 11 percent.
9. D
10. False
11. 1. B, 2. D, 3. A, 4. E, 5. C

CHAPTER 3

1. a. dendrites, b. axon (or node of Ranvier), c. myelin, d. axon terminal, e. nucleus, f. cell body (soma)
2. Synapse
3. B
4. Brain and spinal cord
5. F
6. 1. F, 2. C, 3. D, 4. B, 5. G, 6. A
7. False. The cerebrum contains the cerebral cortex, hippocampus, and basal ganglia.
8. E
9. False
10. B

CHAPTER 4

1. Advantages and disadvantages:
   - Oral
     - Advantages: Easy, safe, compact, economical, self-administered
     - Disadvantages: Slow and highly variable absorption, first-pass effect, not good in emergencies, not appropriate for nausea and vomiting, can't be taken by everyone
   - Intravenous
     - Advantages: Fast, accurate blood concentration
     - Disadvantages: Expensive, painful, requires sterile equipment and training, can't readily be reversed
   - Transdermal
     - Advantages: Easy to administer, noninvasive, slow and continuous drug delivery
     - Disadvantages: Not appropriate for all drugs, hard to control accuracy of dose, may irritate skin
2. CYP450
3. C
4. 1. A, 2. A, 3. A, 4. B
5. False

6. False
7. A is fentanyl, B is morphine, C is aspirin.
8. 100
9. Downregulation
10. True

CHAPTER 5

1. True
2. True
3. Smoked, injected, snorted, oral
4. It blocks reuptake.
5. False
6. False
7. Methamphetamine
8. D
9. ADHD, narcolepsy, and short-term weight loss
10. False

CHAPTER 6

1. Answers may include morning glory seeds, peyote cactus, psilocybin mushrooms, nutmeg, deadly nightshade, datura, henbane, mandrake, salvia, roots of the iboga tree
2. True
3. True
4. C
5. False
6. False
7. 1. D, 2. D, 3. B (C is acceptable as well), 4. D, 5. A, 6. C
8. B
9. Synesthesia
10. A

CHAPTER 7

1. False. Gone up five-fold.
2. B
3. Codeine, morphine, OxyContin, heroin, carfentanil
4. Isolation of morphine, development of hypodermic syringe, importation of Chinese laborers, war, popularity of patent medicines
5. True
6. C

7. False
8. False
9. Although caged and isolated rats quickly become addicted to opioids, when rats have access to toys, space, and other rats, they do not become addicted. This suggests that social and environmental factors play a role in the development of addiction.
10. D
11. Extra credit: Sol Snyder and Candace Pert

CHAPTER 8

1. True
2. A
3. C
4. Frequency, duration of time
5. D
6. False. They are metabolized too slowly, and their effects can linger for days or even weeks.
7. True
8. False
9. Volatile substances—glue, paint thinner, spray paint; anesthetics—ether and nitrous oxide; and nitrites—amyl nitrite
10. Quaaludes

CHAPTER 9

1. a. Female
   b. Marijuana
2. False
3. True
4. B
5. Phytocannabinoid: THC, CBD, CBN, THCV, CBG, others
   Endocannabinoid: Anandamide, 2-AG
6. Confusing correlation and causation
7. False
8. D
9. False
10. Consider the following: What is "moderate" use of marijuana? How can you know for sure how much participants smoked? How do you know what the potency of the marijuana was? How long had both groups been smoking, and was it long enough for cancer to develop? What other differences exist

between the two groups, including drug use, exercise, diet, age, other health issues, stress levels, socioeconomic status, etc.? Finally, do lower rates of cancer imply a cure?

CHAPTER 10

1. True
2. False. About 21.1 percent.
3. B
4. D
5. Raises heart rate and blood pressure; CO decreases the ability of blood to carry oxygen to the tissues; Increases blood clotting and constricts blood vessels of skin, hands, and feet.
6. 21
7. False. 50 percent.
8. Whether the author was affiliated with the tobacco industry
9. Nicotine replacement, pharmaceutical treatments that don't replace nicotine, counseling, stress management. behavior modification, media literacy, and pictorial cigarette pack warnings
10. False. The FDA had not yet evaluated e-cigarettes

CHAPTER 11

1. False. Those age 50–64.
2. False
3. False
4. Theobromine
5. The amount of caffeine in a cup of coffee depends on the type of beans used, how they were roasted, how the coffee was brewed, and the size of the cup.
6. You should consider the way the study was designed (survey or empirical study); how accurate the subjects' assessments of their caffeine intake are; what substance was consumed, how much, and how often; how caffeine-consuming subjects differ from non-caffeine drinkers; and how other factors—social, psychological, dietary, or economic—may influence the results.
7. a. The man
    b. The pregnant woman
    c. The Asian man
    d. The woman on SSRIs
    e. The nonsmoking man
8. False. It binds and blocks adenosine receptors.

9. B
10. 100

CHAPTER 12

1. 18th and 21st
2. A
3. False
4. A, C, D, E
5. True
6. False
7. GABA, DA, GLU, opioids, serotonin, endocannabinoids
8. C
9. 5–10
10. False

CHAPTER 13

1. True
2. Greater awareness, less stigma, societal changes, overdiagnosis, greater availability of pharmaceutical treatments, long-term effects of antidepressants themselves
3. False
4. C
5. 1. C, 2. A, 3. D, 4. B, 5. E
6. False
7. Generalized anxiety disorder, panic attacks, social anxiety disorders, phobias
8. False
9. B
10. Tardive dyskinesia

CHAPTER 14

1. False. Schedule III.
2. True
3. B, F, H
4. 1. D, 2. A, 3. B, 4. E, 5. C
5. False. Up to 50 times more.
6. False
7. Androgen deficiency, stimulates bone marrow, treats breast cancer and osteoporosis, treats severe muscle loss
8. Overdiagnosis, increasing tendency to medicalize issues, direct-to-consumer ads, electronic devices, changes in academic environments
9. Billy
10. False. Norepinephrine and dopamine.

CHAPTER 15

1. False
2. Answers may include: Actifed, Advil, Allegra, Aleve, Alli, Benadryl, Claritin, Cortaid, Dimetapp, Dramamine, Flonase, Imodium, Monistat, Motrin, Nexium, Nicotrol, Pepcid, Plan B, Prilosec, Rogaine, Sominex, Voltaren, Zyrtec.
3. C
4. C
5. False
6. False
7. True
8. 1. B, 2. E, 3. A, 4. A, 5. B, 6. F, 7. D, 8. A, 9. B, 10. C, 11. E
9. True
10. B

CHAPTER 16

1. 1960
2. C
3. True
4. Breast tenderness, minor depression, headache, nausea, slight weight gain, a change in skin pigmentation, and elevation of sex hormone binding globulin that may reduce libido
5. False
6. False
7. True
8. A
9. 1. C, 2. F, 3. E, 4. A, 5. B, 6. D
10. D

CHAPTER 17

1. False
2. Heroin, alcohol, caffeine, marijuana

3. C
4. Preoccupation with the drug, mood changes, tolerance, withdrawal, conflict, relapse
5. D
6. False
7. True
8. Use of AOD by peers or family members; personality traits such as rebelliousness, resistance to authority, and lower self-esteem; poor interpersonal skills; academic failures; little involvement in community or religious organizations; suboptimal family dynamics; increased availability of AOD; stress; boredom; more spending money
9. False
10. False

CHAPTER 18

1. C
2. A
3. C, B, D, A
4. False
5. Pre-employment, reasonable suspicion, post-incident, periodic, random, or after a return to duty.
6. 1. B, 2. E, 3. A, 4. C, 5. D
7. 1. F, 2. E, 3. B, 4. A, 5. D, 6. C
8. False
9. 1. B, 2. A, 3. B, 4. A, 5. C
10. Medical detoxification, inpatient facility, sober-living home. He may attend a self-help program in the facility while he is in the sober-living home and immediately afterward.
11. D
12. False

Glossary

A

absorption: The process and mechanisms by which drugs pass from the outside world into the bloodstream.

acetylcholine: The first neurotransmitter to be discovered and the most common neurotransmitter in the body.

action potential: The short-term change in electrical potential between the inside and outside of a neuron that leads to transmission of nerve signals.

acute tolerance: Tolerance that occurs within a single exposure to a drug.

addiction: The compulsive use of and preoccupation with a substance such that it causes physical, psychological, and/or social harm to the user.

additive effects: The combined effect of drugs is equal to the sum of each drug's effect alone.

affective disorder: Mood disorder such as depression or anxiety, characterized by abnormalities in mood, behavior, sleep, and neurochemical equilibrium.

affinity: How well a drug binds to its target.

agonist: A chemical or drug that mimics the effects of a neurotransmitter.

alcohol dehydrogenase (ADH): An enzyme that metabolizes ethanol into acetaldehyde.

alcoholic cirrhosis: A chronic liver condition characterized by replacement of liver cells with scar tissue, leading to loss of liver function.

alcoholic hepatitis: Inflammation of the liver due to excessive alcohol intake.

Alcoholics Anonymous (AA): An international organization whose purpose is to help those with alcohol use disorders to stay sober.

aldehyde dehydrogenase (ALDH): The enzyme that breaks down acetaldehyde.

allosteric modulators: Substances that bind to alternate sites and influence the binding of agonists to the main receptor site.

alkaloid: A nitrogen-containing compound of fungal or plant origin that produces physiological effects in humans.

amotivational syndrome: A condition of apathy, loss of motivation, and unwillingness to work associated with prolonged heavy use of marijuana.

AMPA receptors: The most common type of glutamate receptor.

anabolic: Related to the process of building tissue.

anaphrodisiac: A substance that diminishes sexual response.

androgenic: Related to the development or maintenance of male physiological characteristics.

andropause: A collection of symptoms, including a reduced sexual desire, fatigue, and mood changes, experienced by some middle-aged men and attributed to a gradual decline in testosterone levels.

antagonism: The combined effect of drugs is less than the sum of each drug's effect alone.

antagonist: A chemical or drug that blocks a receptor and inhibits the effects of a neurotransmitter.

antidepressant discontinuation syndrome: Flu-like symptoms and sensory disturbances associated with abrupt withdrawal from antidepressant medication.

antihistamine: Medication that blocks histamine receptors; found in many cold and allergy products.

antitussive: A drug that suppresses or prevents coughing.

anxiolytic: A drug used to reduce anxiety.

aphrodisiac: A substance that is thought to arouse or increase sexual response.

area postrema: The vomiting center of the brain.

attention-deficit/hyperactivity disorder (ADHD): A prolonged pattern of inattention and/ or hyperactivity-impulsivity that negatively affects a person's development or functioning.

autonomic nervous system (ANS): Part of the PNS, the ANS consists of nerves that go to and from smooth muscle, heart muscle, and glands.

axon: The long, wire-like part of a neuron along which electrical impulses are conducted away from the cell body.

axon terminal: The end of the axon, which contains vesicles of neurotransmitter.

B

bad trip: A disturbing and frightening psychological experience associated with the use of a psychedelic drug.

barbiturates: A group of sedative/hypnotic drugs used mainly for anesthesia and treatment of seizure disorders.

basal ganglia: A group of connected nuclei that influence muscle movement, emotions, and mood.

behavioral tolerance: Tolerance that occurs when people learn to "handle themselves" while on a drug by developing resistance to the drug's effects.

benzodiazepines (BZDs): A group of sedative/hypnotic drugs used mainly as antianxiety agents, sleep inducers, and muscle relaxants.

binge drinking: The consumption of five or more drinks on the same occasion on at least one day in the past month for a male, and four or more drinks for a female.

bioavailability: The degree to which the original drug dose reaches its site of action.

biotransformation (metabolism): The biochemical modification(s) made by an organism on a chemical compound in order to make it easier to be excreted by the body.

bipolar disorder (BD): An affective disorder associated with mood swings that range from manic highs to depressive lows.

blackout: An inability to recall events that occurred while drinking, even with no loss of consciousness.

blinded study: A research design in which the investigator or participant (or both) is unaware whether the participant is in the experimental group or the control group.

blood alcohol content (BAC): The percentage of alcohol in the blood.

blood–brain barrier (BBB): The specialized capillaries that carry blood to the CNS, blocking the entry of certain substances.

blood doping: A method of increasing the oxygen-carrying capacity of the blood in order to enhance athletic performance.

bong: A filtration device generally used for smoking marijuana.

bootlegger: Someone who illegally distills or sells liquor.

brainstem: Part of the brain that includes the medulla oblongata, pons, and midbrain and controls basic vegetative processes and other automatic activities of the body.

brand or trade name: A proprietary trademarked name that a company gives a drug.

SAMHSA-5: Also called the NIDA-5; the five groups of drugs—amphetamines, cannabinoids, cocaine, opioids, and PCP—that are most commonly tested for in a urine drug test.

buccal administration: The administration of drugs across the mucous membrane of the cheek.

C

caffeinism: A toxic condition due to excessive caffeine consumption.

cannabinoid: A diverse group of physiologically active compounds found in cannabis and the human body that bind to cannabinoid receptors.

cannabis: A tall plant with serrated leaves. Also refers to any of the preparations or chemicals derived from the plant. Both marijuana and hemp are cannabis but have different amounts of psychoactive chemicals.

cannabis indica: A shorter, bushier cannabis plant that grows in cooler climates.

cannabis sativa: A tall, slender plant with light green serrated leaves that grows in warm climates.

capture ratio: The number of people who try a drug divided by the number who become regular or habitual users.

cardiac arrest: The normal electrical rhythm of the heart fails, preventing the heart from pumping blood to the body, which can lead to sudden death.

cardiovascular disease: Also called heart disease, this is a broad term that includes a range of diseases that affect the heart, including coronary heart disease and ischemic stroke.

catalepsy: A medical condition characterized by a trance-like stare, rigidity, and diminished responsiveness.

catecholamine: Neurotransmitters, including dopamine, norepinephrine, and epinephrine, all of which have a similar structure and function.

causation: When one variable causes the other.

CBD: Cannabidiol is a biologically active, yet intoxicating compound in cannabis.

cellular tolerance: Exposure to more or less neurotransmitter than usual can change the number of available receptors for that neurotransmitter, a process which can lead to cellular tolerance.

central nervous system (CNS): The brain and spinal cord.

cerebral cortex: The outermost portion of the brain hemispheres; cortex translates to "bark."

cerebrum: Part of the forebrain containing the cerebral cortex, basal ganglia, and hippocampus.

chewing tobacco: A form of smokeless tobacco that is sold in packets of sweetened, loose tobacco leaves that are sometimes fashioned into long strands or twists.

chronic obstructive pulmonary disease (COPD): A group of lung diseases that obstruct airflow and make breathing difficult. COPD includes emphysema and chronic bronchitis.

cognitive behavioral therapy (CBT): An action-oriented form of therapy that focuses on changing maladaptive thought patterns and behaviors.

community reinforcement: A behavioral therapy that helps people change their lifestyle such that healthy, drug-free living becomes rewarding.

comorbidity: One or more disorders present at the same time as a primary disorder.

confidentiality: How a patient's relevant information from the study will be kept private.

confirmation bias: The tendency to interpret evidence as confirmation of one's preexisting beliefs.

confounding factor: A variable that is not the focus of the experiment, but which changes along with the independent variable, making it difficult to determine causal factors underlying the result.

conspiracy: An agreement between two or more people to violate the federal drug laws.

contingency management: A behavioral therapy that uses incentives and rewards to encourage a person to remain abstinent from alcohol or other drugs.

control group: The group of participants who are not exposed to the independent variable.

Controlled Substances Act (CSA): The federal policy under which the manufacture, importation, distribution, possession, and use of certain substances is regulated.

convenience sample: A sample that is not necessarily representative of the population, but that is easily accessible to the researcher.

corpus callosum: A band of nerve fibers that connect the left and right hemispheres of the brain.

correlation: A complementary, parallel, or reciprocal relationship between two variables.

crack: A potent, smokable form of cocaine.

craving: A powerful desire to use a drug.

cross-sectional: Surveys that obtain data from respondents at one point in time; cannot be used to examine trends over a longer period of time.

cross tolerance: Resistance to the effects of a drug as a result of tolerance previously developed to a pharmacologically similar compound.

cycle: The time it takes to go through one episode of mania or hypomania and one depressive episode.

cycling: A pattern of use of anabolic-androgenic steroids, in which a user takes steroids for 4–18 weeks, followed by an equal or longer period of abstinence.

cytochrome P450 (CYP450): A superfamily of enzymes that play a role in many activities, including metabolism of drugs and toxins.

D

dab: A highly concentrated THC which is vaporized on a heated metal plate.

decriminalization: To remove or reduce the criminal and/or monetary penalties associated with an action, although the underlying law remains.

decongestant: Medication that improves airflow by constricting swollen blood vessels in the nose; comes in many forms, including nasal sprays, nose drops, liquids, and pills.

deliriants: Drugs that produce a vivid perceptual experience. These include hallucinogens such as

LSD and psilocybin that are structurally similar to serotonin, as well as substances such as peyote, mescaline, and MDMA that structurally resemble dopamine.

delirium tremens (DTs): A severe withdrawal symptom experienced by some chronic alcoholics, involving convulsions, disorientation, anxiety, and hallucinations.

dendrites: The branched outgrowths from the soma, they are the main receptive surface of the neuron.

dependent variable: The variable that is observed and measured and that may change as a result of manipulations to the independent variable.

depolarization: When the charge across the neuron is reversed; in a neuron, depolarization refers to the inside of a neuron becoming more positively charged compared with the outside.

direct-to-consumer (DTC) advertising: A form of marketing promotion used by pharmaceutical companies aimed at patients rather than healthcare professionals.

dissociatives: Drugs that produce analgesia, amnesia, catalepsy, and a sense of detachment. These include PCP and ketamine.

distillation: A process that concentrates the alcohol in a beverage.

distribution: The transport of drugs to their site(s) of action in the body.

diterpenes: Chemical compounds with anti-inflammatory and antimicrobial properties.

doping: The act of taking a drug to enhance one's athletic performance.

dose-response curve: A measure of a drug's effectiveness as a function of the dose administered.

double-blinded study: An experimental procedure in which neither the investigator nor the participants know who is in the experimental group and who is in the control group.

downregulation: The process by which a cell decreases the number of receptors in response to an increased amount of neurotransmitter in the synapse.

drug: Any chemical entity or mixture, other than those required for the maintenance of normal health (such as food), which alters biological function or structure when administered.

drug action: The molecular changes produced by a drug when it binds to a receptor, and the physiological or psychological changes that occur as a result.

drug depot: An area of the body in which a drug can be accumulated or stored.

drug mule: A person who transports illegal drugs by swallowing them or concealing them in a body cavity.

drug schedules: The five categories that drugs are classified into based upon the drug's accepted medical use and its potential for abuse and addiction.

drug testing: An analysis of a biological specimen to test for the presence of specified drugs.

E

efficacy: The maximum effect that can be produced by a drug; the peak of the dose-response curve.

egocentrism: The practice of regarding one's own experiences or opinions as most important.

electroconvulsive therapy (ECT): A medical procedure in which a small, carefully controlled amount of electricity is passed through the brain, intentionally triggering a brief seizure.

elimination: The process of substances leaving the body, usually through urine, breath, digestion, and sweat.

endocannabinoids: Endogenous substances such as anandamide and 2-AG that bind to the body's cannabinoid receptors.

endocannabinoid system (ECS): A widespread physiological system involved in maintaining homeostasis in the body.

endogenous: Produced or originated from within an organism.

endorphin: A morphine-like substance originating from within the body that blocks pain transmission. Endorphins got their name by combining "endogenous," meaning "from within the body," and "morphine."

ENDS: Electronic nicotine delivery systems, such as e-cigarettes and vaporizers.

ensemble effect: Also called the "entourage effect," the compounds in cannabis interact synergistically to magnify the therapeutic effects of the plant's individual components, such that the whole is greater than the sum of its parts.

epigenetics: Inherited modifications in gene expression caused by external or environmental factors.

epilepsy: A neurological disorder characterized by a predisposition to experience seizures.

erectile dysfunction (ED): The persistent inability of a man to achieve or sustain an erection.

ergot: A family of fungi that grows on rye and barley and produces alkaloids when consumed, which may result in hallucinatory effects.

estrogen: A group of steroid hormones that affect female secondary sexual characteristics and regulate the menstrual cycle.

expectancy effect: An effect that may occur when a research participant's expectation of a certain result affects the outcome of the experiment.

expectorant: An agent that facilitates expulsion of phlegm from the throat or airways.

experiment: A controlled test or investigation, designed to examine the validity of a hypothesis. Also, the act of conducting an investigation.

external validity: The degree to which the findings can be applied in other settings.

F

fallacy of insufficient evidence: An argument that does not provide sufficient evidence to support the conclusion.

fallacy of relevance: An argument that is irrelevant to the matter at hand.

false negative: A test result that does not detect a drug that is present.

false positive: A test result that incorrectly indicates that a drug is present.

fat-soluble: Also called lipid-soluble, this refers to substances that dissolve in fats or oils.

fatty liver: A reversible condition in which large vacuoles of fat accumulate in the liver.

felony: A serious crime, typically punishable by at least a year in prison.

fermentation: Production of alcohol from sugars through the action of yeast.

fertility drug: A drug given to a woman to improve her fertility.

fetal alcohol syndrome (FAS): A collection of physical and behavioral abnormalities associated with prenatal alcohol exposure.

first generation antipsychotic (FGA): Also called a "typical" antipsychotic or neuroleptic, this drug alleviates symptoms of schizophrenia by blocking dopamine receptors.

first-order kinetics: The rate of the drug's metabolism is proportional to the concentration of the drug.

first-pass effect: The phenomenon by which orally administered drugs are metabolized by liver enzymes before they reach the general circulation, which usually reduces their bioavailability.

flashback: A phenomenon in which an individual re-experiences perceptual elements of a psychedelic episode long after the effects of LSD have worn off.

flavonoids: Components of plants that give color to plants and have antioxidant and anti-inflammatory effects.

flavanol: A type of polyphenol found in tea and chocolate, which is thought to have antioxidant, anti-inflammatory, and anticarcinogenic properties.

follicle stimulating hormone (FSH): A hormone that stimulates the development of eggs during a woman's ovulatory cycle.

formication: The delusion that insects are crawling on or under one's skin; usually associated with high doses of cocaine or amphetamines.

frontal lobe: The part of the cerebrum responsible for planning, programming, speech, and initiating voluntary movements.

full agonist: A substance that binds to and activates a receptor, producing a maximal response.

G

GABA: Gamma-aminobutyric acid is the major inhibitory neurotransmitter of the brain.

Gardasil-9: A vaccine that protects against infection with certain types of the human papillomavirus (HPV).

gas chromatography/mass spectrometry (GC/MS): A technique to analyze and quantify the different specific substances in a test sample.

gastroesophageal reflux disease (GERD): A chronic sensation of heartburn, often due to the failure of the valve between the stomach and esophagus.

gateway drug: A drug whose use is thought to lead to the use of a harder drug.

generalizable: The degree to which the results of the study represent the results that would be obtained from the entire population.

generalized anxiety disorder (GAD): An anxiety disorder characterized by persistent, uncontrollable, and irrational worry, usually about routine issues such as occupation, social relationships, health, or financial matters.

generic name: The nonproprietary drug name that is in general public use. It is not subject to trademark rights.

glutamate: The major excitatory neurotransmitter in the central nervous system.

H

half-life: The time it takes for the amount of drug in the body to be reduced by 50 percent.

hallucinate: An experience involving the perception of something that may not actually be present.

hallucinogen: From the Latin *alucinare*, meaning "to wander in mind, to idle, or prate," a hallucinogen is a drug that distorts one's perceptions of reality.

Harrison Narcotics Act: Signed into law in 1914, this act regulated and taxed the production, distribution, and prescription of opium, morphine, and cocaine.

heartburn: Indigestion leading to a short-term burning sensation in the upper abdomen.

hemp: A cannabis plant with low THC content primarily grown for industrial or food use. Hemp is nonpsychoactive.

homeostasis: The state of maintaining steady and stable physiological conditions despite fluctuations in the external environment.

hormone: A chemical substance that is produced in one organ and is carried through the bloodstream to affect another part of the body.

hormone replacement therapy (HRT): The use of synthetic or natural reproductive hormones to alleviate symptoms associated with aging.

huffing: Using inhalants in order to get high. Also, the act of soaking a rag or handkerchief with the chemical and then deeply inhaling the cloth.

human papillomavirus (HPV): A group of over 150 related viruses, some of which can infect the genitals.

hypnotic: A sleep-inducing drug.

hypogonadism: A condition in which the male body does not make enough testosterone.

hypomania: A less severe form of mania.

hyponatremia: Low sodium concentration in the blood.

hypothalamus: Part of the limbic system, it integrates and controls the autonomic nervous system, and helps regulate blood pressure, heart rate, respiratory rate, body temperature, and pupil diameter, as well as emotions, food intake, water balance, and sleep; it is also involved with such drives as pleasure and addiction.

hypothesis: A proposed explanation for facts or observations.

I

ice: A potent, smokable form of methamphetamine.

illegal: Restricted at some level of government or authority—national, state, county, or in the individual institution, school, or work site.

illicit: Forbidden by laws, rules, or customs. Illicit drugs are not necessarily illegal; they are illicit when taken outside of their regulated or medically prescribed use.

illusion: A perceptual alteration, in which an actual object is seen in a distorted form.

immunoassay: A procedure for detecting specific substances based on the principles of antigen-antibody reactions.

implied consent: Any person who operates a motor vehicle on a public road has, by that action, consented to a chemical test to determine his or her blood alcohol concentration.

independent variable: The variable that is manipulated in an experiment.

infertility: A reduced ability to reproduce, often defined as a failure to get pregnant after a year or more of regular, unprotected sexual intercourse.

informed consent: The process by which a study participant is informed of any risks, benefits, or other ramifications when participating in a study.

inhalants: Volatile substances, anesthetics, or nitrites that produce inhalable vapors that can have mind-altering effects.

innervate: To supply a part of the body with nerves, or to stimulate an area by a nerve.

insomnia: Difficulty falling asleep or staying asleep.

insula: The fifth lobe of the cerebrum that receives and responds to internal sensations and translates these into a conscious, subjective experience.

interdiction: The action of intercepting and preventing access to a prohibited substance.

internal validity: The degree to which an experiment avoids confounding factors.

intramuscular (IM) injection: The administration of drugs by injecting them into a muscle.

intravenous (IV) injection: The administration of drugs by injecting them into a vein.

inverse agonists: Substances that bind to the main receptor site and produce the opposite effect that an agonist does.

ionotropic receptor: A type of receptor that is also an ion channel; when a substance binds, the receptor quickly opens, and an ion such as sodium or chloride rushes into the cell.

J

joint: A hand-rolled marijuana cigarette.

K

Korsakoff's syndrome: A syndrome of severe mental impairment that features loss of coordination, disorientation, and a tendency to make up stories to cover memory loss of recent events.

L

legalization: Removal of criminal penalties. Legalization allows for full taxation and regulation. Alcohol and tobacco are two examples of legal drugs.

ligand: From the Latin word *ligare*, meaning "that which binds," a ligand is any man-made or natural substance, such as a drug or neurotransmitter, which binds to a receptor.

limbic system: Involved in the control of emotions and memory, this entity includes the hypothalamus, hippocampus, and amygdala, among other areas.

longitudinal study: The same group of participants is observed, measured, or tested over time.

luteinizing hormone (LH): A hormone that stimulates ovulation in females.

M

margin of safety: An index of a drug's effectiveness and safety; LD1/ED99.

marijuana: A slang term for cannabis that contains enough psychoactive compounds to have an intoxicating effect. Also refers to the leaves and flowers of the female cannabis plant that are dried and shredded.

major depressive disorder (MDD): Also known as depression, or unipolar depression, MDD is an affective disorder characterized by overwhelming sadness, feelings of worthlessness, and a loss of interest in normally pleasurable activities.

manic phase: A phase of bipolar disorder characterized by periods of hyperactivity, insomnia, elation, inflated self-esteem, and sometimes delusions.

Master Settlement Agreement (MSA): A legal agreement between the four largest tobacco companies and 46 of the United States.

media literacy: The ability to understand, analyze, and evaluate media.

medical detoxification: A process that systematically and safely withdraws people from drugs under the care of a physician.

medulla oblongata: Part of the brainstem that controls basic vegetative processes such as heart rate, blood vessel diameter, respiratory rate, coughing, swallowing, and sneezing.

menopause: The time in a woman's life when her menstrual cycle no longer occurs.

metabolic tolerance: Tolerance that occurs when the body speeds up the metabolism of a drug by increasing the production of certain liver enzymes.

metabolism (biotransformation): The biochemical modification(s) made by an organism on a chemical compound in order to make it easier to be excreted by the body.

metabolites: Chemical products of metabolism.

metabotropic receptor: A type of receptor that is separate from an ion channel; if a substance binds to the receptor, a series of events may open a separate ion channel or cause another change in the cell, but it happens relatively slowly.

microdose: A sub-hallucinogenic dose of LSD or psilocybin often taken for therapeutic purposes.

misdemeanor: A lesser crime punishable by no more than one year in prison.

monoamine oxidase inhibitor (MAOI): A type of antidepressant drug that raises monoamine levels by inhibiting their enzymatic breakdown.

monoamines: A group of structurally related neurotransmitters, including dopamine, norepinephrine, and serotonin.

motor neuron: A nerve cell that sends instructions from the brain and spinal cord out to nerves, muscles, and glands.

myelin: A white fatty material that encloses and insulates some axons and speeds neurotransmission.

myocardial infarction: Also called a heart attack, a myocardial infarction is when the arteries supplying blood to the heart become blocked, and the heart muscle is starved of oxygen. During a heart attack, the heart continues to pump blood throughout the body.

N

narcotic: From the Greek word *narke*, meaning "numbness" or "stupor" (which gives rise to the word "stupid"), a narcotic is a drug that relieves pain, induces sleep, and reduces sensibility.

Narcotics Anonymous (NA): A nonprofit organization for people with substance abuse issues.

needle exchange program (NEP): An intervention program that provides clean needles to IV drug users in return for used syringes, which are destroyed.

negative cognitive triad: A recurrent pattern of depressive thinking and distorted information processing, which gives someone negative thoughts about oneself, one's world, and one's future.

neonatal abstinence syndrome: A group of conditions that occur when a baby withdraws from opioid drugs he or she was exposed to as a fetus.

neurogenesis: The production of new neurons.

neuroglia: Nerve cells that support neurons and aid in neurotransmission.

neuromuscular junction (NMJ): The site at which motor neurons from the somatic nervous system influence skeletal muscles.

neuron: A nerve cell that receives and sends signals within the body.

neurotoxic: Something that damages nervous tissue.

neurotransmitter: A chemical substance released from a neuron that binds to a receptor and affects another cell.

NMDA receptors: N-Methyl-D-aspartate is an important class of glutamate receptors that are involved in memory.

nociceptor: A sensory receptor for painful stimuli.

node of Ranvier: A gap in the myelin sheath of an axon, where action potentials are propagated.

NSAID: A nonsteroidal anti-inflammatory drug such as aspirin, ibuprofen, or naproxen that is often used to treat mild to moderate pain, as well as inflammation.

nucleus: The part of a cell that contains genes that code for proteins.

nucleus accumbens: An area in the basal ganglia that plays an important role in reward, pleasure, and addiction.

O

observer effect: The effect that the presence of the observer has on a participant's behavior.

occipital lobe: The part of the cerebrum where visual images are sent.

opiate: A drug derived from opium.

opioid: Any natural, synthetic, or endogenous substance that binds to the opioid receptor.

opioid triad: The symptoms of coma, depressed respiration, and pinpoint pupils, which are indicative of opioid poisoning.

orexin: A neurotransmitter that promotes appetite and wakefulness.

over-the-counter drug (OTC): Medication that is available to the consumer without a prescription.

ovulation: The release of the egg from the ovary into the fallopian tube.

P

panic disorder: An anxiety disorder characterized by sudden attacks of intense fear and anxiety associated with severe physical symptoms, even when there is no real dangerous or apparent cause.

parasympathetic nervous system: Part of the PNS, the parasympathetic nervous system regulates restful, "business as usual" impulses.

parietal lobe: The part of the cerebrum that contains the primary somatosensory area of the cortex, where sensations such as pain, temperature, and touch are processed.

partial agonist: A chemical that binds to and activates a receptor, but not as completely as a full agonist.

peer review process: The means by which experts in the field check the quality of a research study.

peptic ulcer: A break in the protective lining of the stomach, often due to the bacteria *H. pylori*.

periaqueductal gray: An area of the midbrain involved in pain control.

peripheral nervous system (PNS): All the nerves going to and from the brain and spinal cord.

pharmacodynamics: The branch of pharmacology concerned with the actions of an administered drug on an organism.

pharmacokinetics: The branch of pharmacology concerned with the actions of a body on an administered drug.

pharmacology: The scientific study of the actions of drugs and their effects on a living organism.

phobia: An extreme or irrational fear of an object or situation.

physical dependence: Physical adaptations to drug use, including tolerance and withdrawal.

phytocannabinoids: Naturally-occurring plant compounds, such as THC and CBD, which bind to the body's cannabinoid receptors.

pineal gland: One of our biological clocks that produces a substance called melatonin, which is involved in sleep and depression.

pituitary gland: Sometimes called the master gland, it releases many important hormones.

placebo: A substance or procedure that has no therapeutic effect and may be used as a control in experimental research designs or to reinforce a patient's expectation of recovery.

placebo effect: When a placebo treatment produces a perceived or actual improvement in a medical condition.

plasma proteins: Proteins found in the blood that serve many functions, including transport of some substances.

polyphenols: A class of compounds found in fruits, vegetables, cocoa, teas, and other plants, which are thought to have antioxidant, anti-inflammatory, and anticarcinogenic properties. There are many different subclasses of polyphenols, including flavanols.

pons: Part of the brainstem that contains respiratory nuclei that help smooth out breathing patterns; it is also important in sleep and arousal.

population: The group of individuals being studied.

possession: The crime of having illegal or nonprescribed controlled substances under one's control.

post-traumatic stress disorder (PTSD): A condition of persistent mental and emotional stress triggered by experiencing or seeing a severe physical or psychological trauma.

potency: The minimum dose of a drug that yields its desired effect.

prefrontal cortex: The part of the cerebrum responsible for reasoning, judgments, and decision making.

presynaptic autoreceptor: A type of receptor located on the presynaptic membrane, which detects the presence of neurotransmitter in the synapse and sends a signal to inhibit synthesis or release of that neurotransmitter.

primary source: The original publication of a scientist's data, results, and theories.

progesterone: A hormone involved in the maintenance of pregnancy.

progestin: Synthetic progesterone-like compound.

proof: The proportion of alcohol in a beverage, by volume.

psychedelics: Drugs that produce a vivid perceptual experience. These include hallucinogens such as LSD and psilocybin that are structurally similar to serotonin, as well as substances such as peyote, mescaline, and MDMA that structurally resemble dopamine.

psychoactive: A substance that affects the mind. Psychoactive substances often produce feelings of euphoria or altered perception.

psychological dependence: An emotional need for a drug that has no underlying physical foundation.

purposive nonprobability sample: A sample in which participants are selected because they reflect a specific purpose of the study.

pyramiding: A pattern of use in which progressively increased doses of steroids are taken until a peak is reached mid cycle, and then reduced toward the end of the cycle.

Q

R

receptor: A protein molecule located on or in a cell, which responds specifically to a particular neurotransmitter, hormone, or drug.

recreational drugs: Drugs that are taken for nonmedical purposes.

refusal statute: Law that protects healthcare professionals from providing services to which they have strong religious or moral objections.

representative sample: A sample that has similar characteristics (such as age, gender, ethnicity, education) as the population from which it was drawn.

research methods: A systematic approach to gathering information and evaluating the findings.

reticular formation: A network of nuclei involved in mediating levels of arousal and attention.

reuptake: The process by which a presynaptic neuron reabsorbs a neurotransmitter that it has released.

reverse tolerance: Also called sensitization or kindling, this is when repeated use of a drug causes increased sensitivity to its effects.

robotripping: The slang term for recreational use of dextromethorphan, the active ingredient in cough suppressants such as Robitussin.

route of administration (ROA): The method by which a drug is taken into the body.

rumrunner: Someone who illegally smuggles liquor across a border.

S

sample: A subset of individuals in the population.

sampling bias: The tendency for some members of the population to be over-represented and others to be excluded from a sample.

schizophrenia: A severe mental disorder that makes it difficult to interpret reality, think clearly, manage emotions, and relate to others.

second-generation antipsychotic (SGA): An "atypical" antipsychotic; generally, does not cause the same degree of motor side effects as do neuroleptics.

secondhand smoke (SHS): Also called passive smoke or environmental tobacco smoke, secondhand smoke is a combination of mainstream smoke and sidestream smoke.

sedative: A drug taken to promote relaxation and calm.

selective serotonin reuptake inhibitor (SSRI): A type of antidepressant drug that raises serotonin levels by blocking its reuptake.

select tolerance: When the body develops tolerance to different aspects of the drug at different rates.

self-selection sample: A sample in which participants volunteer to take part in the study.

sensory neuron: A nerve cell that carries information into the brain and spinal cord.

serotonin: A neurotransmitter found throughout the brain and body, involved in many functions, including mood, sleep, appetite, and visual perception.

serotonin syndrome: A potentially life-threatening reaction that can occur when medications cause large amounts of serotonin to accumulate in the body.

set: The effect of a person's expectations on drug effect.

setting: The physical, social, and cultural environment in which a drug is used.

shatter: An extract of the cannabis plant in concentrate form.

side effects: Pharmacological actions that occur in addition to the main drug action.

simple random sample: A sample in which each member of the population has an equal probability of participating.

single-blinded study: An experimental procedure in which the participants do not know whether they have received the treatment being tested.

snuff: A form of finely ground and powdered smokeless tobacco that is snorted into the nose or inserted between the gum and lip.

sober living home: A therapeutic residential facility that may be used to bridge the gap between an inpatient rehab facility and a return to former lives.

social anxiety disorder: An anxiety disorder in which a person has an excessive, unreasonable fear of social situations.

social influence model: A multifaceted approach to drug prevention that includes information, drug-resistance skills, and the involvement of parents and community members.

soma: The cell body of a neuron.

somatic nervous system: Part of the PNS, the somatic nervous system consists of nerves that carry sensory information into the CNS, as well as nerves that carry motor signals from the CNS to skeletal muscle cells.

speakeasy: Illegal and clandestine nightclub and drinking spot.

spinal cord: A longitudinal system of neurons and supporting tissue that carries signals between the brain and the peripheral nervous system.

spontaneous remission: The reversal of a disease or condition—in this case, alcohol or drug addiction—without formal treatment.

stacking: When a steroid user takes several types of steroids at the same time

steroid: A type of lipid molecule with a multiple ring structure.

stratified random sample: A sample in which the population is divided into subgroups of certain characteristics and a random sample from each group is taken in a number proportional to what is seen in the larger population.

subcutaneous (SubQ) injection: The administration of drugs by injecting them directly underneath the skin.

sublingual administration: The administration of drugs under the tongue.

substantia nigra: Part of the midbrain that plays an important role in movement.

sudden sniffing death syndrome: Sudden death due to cardiac arrhythmias after using inhalants.

sympathetic nervous system: Part of the PNS, the sympathetic nervous system regulates "fight or flight" impulses.

sympathomimetic: A substance whose actions mimic those of the sympathetic nervous system.

synapse: The gap between two nerve cells.

synergistic: The combined effect of drugs is greater than the sum of each drug's effect alone.

synesthesia: When stimulation of one sense leads to sensations in a different sense.

T

Tar: The particulate matter generated by burning tobacco.

tardive dyskinesia (TD): Involuntary movements, particularly of the face and jaw. "Tardive" means *tardy* or *late*; this symptom occurs after months or several years of antipsychotic drug use.

tectum: Part of the midbrain that contains nuclei that control eye movements, pupillary response to light, and reactions to moving stimuli, as well as auditory reflexes.

tegmentum: A neural network in the midbrain that is involved in many reflexive and homeostatic pathways.

temperance movement: A social program urging restrictions or prohibitions on the use of alcoholic beverages.

temporal lobe: The part of the cerebrum that processes hearing, memory, and integration of sensory functions.

terpenes: Aromatic oils that occur in plants and have physiological effects in humans.

thalamus: Part of the forebrain that serves as the relay station of the brain; it sorts many sensory signals and sends them to the appropriate areas of the cortex.

THC: Delta-9-tetrahydrocannabinol, the primary psychoactive substance in cannabis.

therapeutic index: A measure of a drug's safety given as the ratio of the average lethal dose of a drug divided by the therapeutic dose; LD50/ED50.

third-generation antipsychotic: Aripiprazole is the only approved third-generation antipsychotic, and it acts as a partial agonist at dopamine receptors.

tolerance: A phenomenon whereby chronic use of a drug can decrease the drug's effects.

trafficking: The unauthorized manufacture, distribution, or sale of any controlled substance.

transcranial direct current stimulation (tDCS): A procedure that uses a constant, low current to the brain to improve symptoms of depression.

transdermal administration: The administration of drugs to the skin as creams or patches.

tricyclic antidepressant (TCA): A type of antidepressant drug that raises serotonin and norepinephrine levels by blocking their reuptake.

trigonelline: A substance found in many plants, including potatoes, hemp, and coffee, which may have hypoglycemic, antiviral, antibacterial, anticarcinogenic, and neuroprotective properties.

U

ultra-rapid opioid detoxification (UROD): A detoxification procedure in which a person who is addicted to opioids quickly goes through opioid withdrawal while under anesthesia.

upregulation: The process by which a cell increases the number of receptors in response to less neurotransmitter in the synapse.

V

validity: An indication of how reliable the research is.

vaping: The process of inhaling and exhaling the vapor produced by an electronic cigarette or similar device. The electronic cigarette itself is sometimes called a vape.

vaporizer: An electronic device used to vaporize substances such as THC or nicotine, which are then inhaled.

variable: Anything that can vary or change, such as an attitude or a behavior.

ventral tegmental area (VTA): An area of the midbrain involved in addiction, reward, and rational processing.

vesicle: A small sac in the axon terminal that contains neurotransmitter molecules.

volunteer bias: The tendency for those who volunteer for research to be different in some way from those who refuse to participate

W

war on drugs: The U.S. government's campaign to reduce the importation, manufacture, sale, and use of illegal drugs.

water-soluble: Substances that dissolve in water.

Wernicke's encephalopathy: A neurological disorder caused by a deficiency of thiamine, characterized by mental confusion, abnormal eye movements, and an unsteady gait.

wine and cheese effect: The potentially fatal hypertensive crisis that can occur when people taking MAOIs ingest foods that raise tyramine levels.

withdrawal: The physical symptoms that occur upon abrupt discontinuation of a chronically used drug.

X

Y

Z

Z drugs: Nonbenzodiazepine hypnotic drugs such as Ambien, Lunesta, and Sonata, often used to treat insomnia.

Zero-order kinetics: The rate of the drug's metabolism is constant over time and independent of the concentration of the drug.

Endnotes

CHAPTER 0

[1] Rosenthal, M.S. (2013). *Human sexuality from cells to society*. Belmont, CA: Wadsworth Publishing/Cengage Learning.

[2] McLeod, S.A. (2014). Sampling methods. Accessed on November 6, 2015, from www.simplypsychology.org/sampling.html

[3] Myers, A., & Hansen, C. (2012). *Experimental psychology* (7th ed.). Belmont, CA: Wadsworth Cengage.

[4] Ibid.

[5] Ibid.

[6] Caulkins, J.P., Hawken, A., Kilmer, B., & Kleiman, M.A.R. (2016). *Marijuana legalization: What everyone needs to know* (2nd ed.). New York: Oxford University Press.

[7] Rosenthal, M.S. (2013). *Human sexuality from cells to society*. Belmont, CA: Wadsworth Publishing/Cengage Learning.

[8] Ibid.

[9] Myers, A., & Hansen, C. (2012). *Experimental psychology* (7th ed.). Belmont, CA: Wadsworth Cengage.

[10] Spunt, B. (2011). What is a confounding variable? *Psychology in Action.* https://psychology-inaction.squarespace.com/search?q=what+is+a+confounding+variable

[11] Lawlor, D.A., Smith, G.D., & Ebrahim, S. (2004). Socioeconomic position and hormone replacement therapy use: Explaining the discrepancy in evidence from observational and randomized controlled trials. *American Journal of Public Health, 94*(12): 2149–54.

[12] Myers, A., & Hansen, C. (2012). *Experimental psychology* (7th ed.). Belmont, CA: Wadsworth Cengage.

[13] Rosenthal, M.S. (2013). *Human sexuality from cells to society*. Belmont, CA: Wadsworth Publishing/Cengage Learning.

[14] Dunn, A.G., Arachi, D., Hudgins, J., Tsafnat, G., Coiera, E., et al. (2014). Financial conflicts of interest and conclusions about neuraminidase inhibitors for influenza. *Annals of Internal Medicine, 161*(7): 513.

[15] Elliot, M.L., Knodt, A.R., Ireland, D., Morris, M.L., & Poulton, R., et al. (2020). What is the test-retest reliability of common task-functional MRI measures? New empirical evidence and a meta-analysis. *Psychological Science, 31*(7): 792–806.

[16] Bennett, C.M., Baird, A.A., Miller, M.B., & Wolford, G.L. (2010). Neural correlates of interspecies perspective taking in the post-mortem Atlantic salmon: An argument for proper multiple comparisons correction. *Journal of Serendipitous and Unexpected Results, 1*(1): 1–5.

[17] Bassham, G., Irwin, W., Nardone, H., & Wallace, J.M. (2010). *Critical thinking: A student's introduction* (4th ed.). New York: McGraw Hill.

[18] Browne, M.N., & Keeley, S. (2014). *Asking the right questions: A guide to critical thinking* (11th ed.). Saddle River, NJ: Prentice Hall.

[19] Lee, J. (2000). *The scientific endeavor: A primer on scientific principles and practice*. New York: Addison Wesley Longman.

[20] Way, T. (2012). Dihydrogen monoxide research division. Accessed on November 10, 2012, from http://dhmo.org/

[21] Ibid.

[22] Rector, L.H. (2008). Comparison of Wikipedia and other encyclopedias for accuracy, breadth, and depth in historical articles. *Reference Services Review, 36*(1): 7–22.

[23] Lavsa, S.M., Corman, S.L., Culley, C.M., & Pummer, T.L., (2011). Reliability of Wikipedia as a medication information source for pharmacy students. *Currents in Pharmacy Teaching and Learning, 3*(2): 154–58.

[24] Kapoun, J. (July/August 1998). Teaching undergrads WEB evaluation: A guide for library instruction. *College and Research Libraries News, 59*(7): 522–23.

[25] Browne, M.N., & Keeley, S. (2014). *Asking the right questions: A guide to critical thinking* (11th ed.). Saddle River, NJ: Prentice Hall.

[26] Rosenthal, M.S. (2013). *Human sexuality from cells to society*. Belmont, CA: Wadsworth Publishing/Cengage Learning.

[27] Browne, M.N., & Keeley, S. (2014). *Asking the right questions: A guide to critical thinking* (11th ed.). Saddle River, NJ: Prentice Hall.

[28] Ibid.

[29] Rosenthal, M.S. (2013). *Human sexuality from cells to society*. Belmont, CA: Wadsworth Publishing/Cengage Learning.

[30] Browne, M.N., & Keeley, S. (2014). *Asking the right questions: A guide to critical thinking* (11th ed.). Saddle River, NJ: Prentice Hall.

[31] Rosenthal, M.S. (2013). *Human sexuality from cells to society*. Belmont, CA: Wadsworth Publishing/Cengage Learning.

[32] Bolton, P. (2010). Statistical literacy guide. Accessed on December 16, 2016, from https://researchbriefings.files.parliament.uk/documents/SN04944/SN04944.pdf

[33] Gigerenzer, G. (2015). *Simply rational: Decision making in the real world*. New York: Oxford University Press.

[34] Koordeman, R., Anschutz, D.J., & Engels, R.C. (2012). Alcohol portrayals in movies, music videos, and soap operas and alcohol use of young people: Current status and future challenges. *Alcohol and Alcoholism, 47*(5): 612–23.

[35] Stephens, R.P. (2011). Addiction to melodrama. *Substance Use and Misuse, 46*(7): 859–71.

[36] Roberts, D.F., & Christensen, P.G. (2000). Here's looking at you, kid: Alcohol, drugs and tobacco in entertainment media. *Kaiser Family Foundation.* http://www.issuelab.org/resources/6906/6906.pdf

[37] Russell, C.A., & Russell, D.W. (2009). Alcohol messages in prime-time television series. *Journal of Consumer Affairs, 43*(1): 108–28.

[38] Roberts, D.F., & Christensen, P.G. (2000). Here's looking at you, kid: Alcohol, drugs and tobacco in entertainment media. *Kaiser Family Foundation.* http://www.issuelab.org/resources/6906/6906.pdf

[39] Russell, C.A., & Russell, D.W. (2009). Alcohol messages in prime-time television series. *Journal of Consumer Affairs, 43*(1): 108–28.

[40] Montagne, M. (2011). Drugs and the media: An introduction. *Substance Use and Misuse, 46*: 849–51.

[41] Primack, B.A., Dalton, M.A., Carroll, M.V., Agarwal, A.A., & Fine, M.J. (2008). Content analysis of tobacco, alcohol, and other drugs in popular music. *Archives of Pediatric and Adolescent Medicine, 162*(2): 169–75.

[42] Siegel, M., Johnson, R.M., Tyagi, K., Power, J., Lohsen, M.C., Ayers, A.J., & Jernigan, D.H. (2013). Alcohol brand references in U.S. popular music, 2009–2011. *Substance Use and Misuse, 48*(14): 1475–84.

43 Roberts, D.F., & Christenson, P.G. (2000). Here's looking at you, kid: Alcohol, drugs and tobacco in entertainment media. *Kaiser Family Foundation.* http://www.issuelab.org/resources/6906/6906.pdf

44 Montagne, M. (2011). Drugs and the media: An introduction. *Substance Use and Misuse, 46:* 849–51.

45 Sargent, J.D., Beach, M., Adachi-Mejia, A., et al. (2005). Exposure to movie smoking: Its relation to smoking initiation among U.S. adolescents. *Pediatrics, 116(5):* 1183–91.

46 Koordeman, R., Anschutz, D.J., & Engels, R.C. (2012). Alcohol portrayals in movies, music videos, and soap operas and alcohol use of young people: Current status and future challenges. *Alcohol and Alcoholism, 47(5):* 612–23.

47 Engels, R.C.M.E., Hermans, R., van Baaren, R.B., Hollenstein, T., & Bot, S.M. (2009). Alcohol portrayal on television affects actual drinking behavior. *Alcohol and Alcoholism, 44(3):* 244–49.

48 Snyder, L.B., Milici, F.F., Slater, M., Sun, H., & Strizhakova, Y. (2006). Effects of alcohol advertising exposure on drinking among youth. *Archives of Pediatric and Adolescent Medicine, 160:* 18–24.

49 Primack, B.A., Douglas, E., & Kraemer, K. (2010). Exposure to cannabis in popular music and cannabis use among adolescents. *Addiction, 105:* 515–23.

50 Wilcox, G.B. Kang, E.Y., & Chilek, L.A. (2015). Beer, wine, or spirits? Advertising's impact on four decades of category sales. *International Journal of Advertising, 34(4):* 641–47.

51 Jernigan, D. (2008). Intoxicating brands: Alcohol advertising and youth. *Multinational Monitor, 30(1):* 1–6.

52 Mart, S.M. (2011). Alcohol marketing in the 21st century: New methods, old problems. *Substance Use and Misuse, 46:* 889–92.

53 Anderson, P., de Bruijn, A., Angus, K., Gordon, R., & Hastings, G. (2009). Impact of alcohol advertising and media exposure on adolescent alcohol use: A systematic review of longitudinal studies. *Alcohol and Alcoholism, 44(3):* 229–43.

54 Jernigan, D. (2008). Intoxicating brands: Alcohol advertising and youth. *Multinational Monitor, 30(1):* 1–6.

55 Chen, M.J., Grube, J.W., Bersamin, M., Waiters, E., & Keefe, D.B. (2005). Alcohol advertising: What makes it attractive to youth? *Journal of Health Communication, 10:* 553–65.

56 Jernigan, D. (2008). Intoxicating brands: Alcohol advertising and youth. *Multinational Monitor, 30(1):* 1–6.

57 Schwartz, L.M., & Woloshin, S. (2019). Medical marketing in the United States, 1997–2016. *JAMA, 321(1):* 80–96.

58 ProCon.org. (2019). Should prescription drugs be advertised directly to consumers? Accessed on October 9, 2019 from https://prescriptiondrugs.procon.org/

59 Eberling, M. (2008). Beyond advertising: The pharmaceutical industry's hidden marketing tactics. *PR Watch.* Accessed on October 20, 2012, from http://www.prwatch.org/node/7026

60 Robinson, A.R., Hohmann, K.B., Rifkin, J.I., Topp, D., Gilroy, C., et al. (2004). Direct-to-consumer pharmaceutical advertising. *Archives of Internal Medicine, 164:* 427–32.

61 Lurie, P. (2008). DTC advertising harms patients and should be tightly regulated. In R. Goldberg (Ed.), *Taking sides: Clashing views in drugs and society* (10th ed.) (pp. 283–301). Dubuque, IA: McGraw Hill/Dushkin.

62 Mintzes, B., Barer, M.L., Kravitz, R.L., Kazanjian, A., Bassett, K., et al. (2002). Influence of direct-to-consumer pharmaceutical advertising and patient's requests on prescribing decisions: Two site cross section survey. *BMJ, 324:* 278–79.

CHAPTER 1

1 Gahlinger, P. (2004). *Illegal drugs: A complete guide to their history, chemistry, use, and abuse.* New York: Plume.

2 Julien, R.M. (2001). *A primer of drug action.* New York: Worth Publishers.

3 Weil, A., & Rosen, W. (2004). *From chocolate to morphine: Everything you need to know about mind altering drugs.* Boston: Houghton Mifflin.

4 World Health Organization (WHO). (1981). Nomenclature and classification of drugs and alcohol-related problems: A WHO memorandum. *Bulletin of the World Health Organization, 59:* 225–42.

5 Weil, A., & Rosen, W. (2004). *From chocolate to morphine: Everything you need to know about mind altering drugs* (p. 29). Boston: Houghton Mifflin.

6 United Nations Office on Drugs and Crime. (2021). World Drug Report 2021 (United Nations publication, Sales No. E.21.XI.8). https://www.unodc.org/res/wdr2021/field/WDR21_Booklet_1.pdf.

7 Degenhardt, L., Chiu, W-T., Sampson, N., Kessler, R.C., Anthony, J.C., et al. (2008). Toward a global view of alcohol, tobacco, cannabis, and cocaine use: Findings from the WHO World Mental Health surveys. *PLoS Medicine, 5(7):* 1053–67.

8 United Nations Office on Drugs and Crime. (2020). World drug report, 2020. United Nations publication, sales no. E.20.XI.6. https://wdr.unodc.org/wdr2020/en/index.html

9 SAMHSA. (2020). *Results from the 2019 National Survey on Drug Use and Health: Detailed Tables.* Rockville, MD: Center for Behavioral Health Statistics and Quality.

10 United Nations Office on Drugs and Crime. (2020). World drug report, 2020. United Nations publication, sales no. E.20.XI.6. https://wdr.unodc.org/wdr2020/en/index.html

11 Centers for Disease Control and Prevention. (2020). Deaths and mortality. Accessed on October 2, 2020, from http://www.cdc.gov/nchs/deaths.htm

12 Goodnough, A. (2021). Overdose deaths have surged during the pandemic, CDC data shows. Accessed on June 1, 2021, from https://www.nytimes.com/2021/04/14/health/overdose-deaths-fentanyl-opiods-coronaviurs-pandemic.html

13 Centers for Disease Control and Prevention. (2020). Drug overdose deaths in the United States, 1999-2018. NCHS Data Brief, no 356. Hyattsville, MD: National Center for Health Statistics.

14 Kounang, N. (2017). U.S. heroin deaths jump 533 percent since 2002, report says. *CNN.com.* Accessed on December 14, 2017 from http://www.cnn.com/2017/09/08/health/heroin-deaths-samhsa-report/index.html

15 Ahmad, F.B., Rossen, L.M., & Sutton, P. (2020). Provisional drug overdose death counts. *National Center for Health Statistics.* Accessed on October 10, 2020 from https://www.cdc.gov/nchs/nvss/vsrr/drug-overdose-data.htm

16 Katz, J. (2017). Drug deaths in America are rising faster than ever. *The New York Times.* Accessed on June 27, 2017, from https://www.nytimes.com/interactive/2017/06/05/upshot/opioid-epidemic-drug-overdose-deaths-are-rising-faster-than-ever.html

17 Substance Abuse and Mental Health Services Administration (SAMHSA). (2020). *Results from the 2019 National Survey on Drug Use and Health: Detailed Tables.* Rockville, MD: Center for Behavioral Health Statistics and Quality.

18 Czeisler, M.E., Lane, R.I., & Petrosky, E., et al. (2020). Mental health, substance use, and suicidal ideation during the COVID-19 pandemic—United States, June 24–30, 2020. *MMWR, 69:* 1049–57.

19 Kann, L., Kinchen, S., Shanklin, S.L., McManus, T., & Harris, W.A., et al. (2019). Youth risk behavior surveillance—United States, 2017. *MMWR, 67(8):* 1–479.

20 Johnston, L.D., Meich, R.A., O'Malley, P.M. Bachman, J.G., & Schulenberg, J.E., et al. (2019). *Monitoring the*

Future: National survey results on drug use: Overview of key findings, 2018 overview. Ann Arbor: Institute for Social Research, The University of Michigan.

21 SAMHSA. (2020). *Results from the 2019 National Survey on Drug Use and Health: Detailed Tables*. Rockville, MD: Center for Behavioral Health Statistics and Quality.

22 Ibid.

23 Ibid.

24 Ibid.

25 Hagen, S. (2019). Nearly one in two Americans takes prescription drugs: Survey. *Bloomberg News*. Accessed on September 28, 2019 from https://www.bloomberg.com/news/articles/2019-05-08/nearly-one-in-two-americans-takes-prescription-drugs-survey.

26 Kirzinger, A., Neuman, T., Cubanski, J., & Brodie, M. (2019). Data note: Prescription drugs and older adults. *Kaiser Family Foundation*. Accessed on October 3, 2019 from https://www.kff.org/health-reform/issue-brief/data-note-prescription-drugs-and-older-adults/.

27 Hagen, S. (2019). Nearly one in two Americans takes prescription drugs: Survey. *Bloomberg News*. Accessed on September 28, 2019 from https://www.bloomberg.com/news/articles/2019-05-08/nearly-one-in-two-americans-takes-prescription-drugs-survey.

28 Light, D.W., Lexchin, J., & Darrow, J.J. (2013). Institutional corruption of pharmaceuticals and the myth of safe and effective drugs. *Journal of Law and Medical Ethics, 41*(3): 590–600.

29 Centers for Disease Control and Prevention. (2020). Drug overdose deaths in the United States, 1999–2018. NCHS Data Brief, no 356. Hyattsville, MD: National Center for Health Statistics.

30 Behavioral Health Coordinating Committee Prescription Drug Abuse Subcommittee. (2015). Addressing prescription drug abuse in the United States. Washington, DC: Health and Human Services. Accessed on January 21, 2016, from http://www.cdc.gov/drugoverdose/pdf/hhs_prescription_drug_abuse_report_09.2013.pdf

31 Johnston, L.D., O'Malley, P.M., Meich, R.A., Bachman, J.G., & Schulenberg, J.E. (2014). *Monitoring the Future national results on adolescent drug use: Overview of key findings, 2013*. Ann Arbor: Institute for Social Research, The University of Michigan.

32 Gahlinger, P. (2004). *Illegal drugs: A complete guide to their history, chemistry, use, and abuse*. New York: Plume.

33 Johnston, L.D., O'Malley, P.M., Meich, R.A., Bachman, J.G., & Schulenberg, J.E. (2014). *Monitoring the Future national results on adolescent drug use: Overview of key findings, 2013*. Ann Arbor: Institute for Social Research, The University of Michigan.

34 Grim, R. (2009). *This is your country on drugs: The secret history of getting high in America*. Hoboken, NJ: John Wiley and Sons.

35 Ibid.

36 Whitman, S.H. (2012). *Edgar Poe and his critics* (p. 74). Charleston, SC: Nabu Press.

37 Griffiths, R.R., Richards, W.A., McCann, U., & Jesse, R. (2006). Psilocybin can occasion mystical experiences having substantial and sustained personal meaning and spiritual significance. *Psychopharmacology, 187*: 268–83.

38 Nation, M., & Heflinger, C.A. (2006). Risk factors for serious alcohol and drug use: The role of psychosocial variables in predicting the frequency of substance use among adolescents. *American Journal of Drug and Alcohol Abuse, 32*: 415–33.

39 NIDA. (2017). Trends & Statistics. Retrieved on September 30, 2019 from https://www.drugabuse.gov/related-topics/trends-statistics/

40 Jogalekar, A. (2014, January 7). Why drug discovery is hard: Part 2. *Scientific American*.

41 Ibid.

42 Weil, A., & Rosen W. (2004). *From chocolate to morphine: Everything you need to know about mind altering drugs*. Boston: Houghton Mifflin.

43 Gahlinger, P. (2004). *Illegal drugs: A complete guide to their history, chemistry, use, and abuse*. New York: Plume.

44 Ibid.

45 Holland, J. (2001). The legal status of MDMA around the world. In J. Holland (Ed.), *Ecstasy: The complete guide (pp. 147–48)*. Rochester, VT: Park Street Press.

46 Maisto, S.A., Galizio, M., & Connors, G.J. (2011). *Drug use and abuse*. New York: Wadsworth Cengage Learning.

47 U.S. Food and Drug Administration (FDA). (2014). Fast track. Accessed on November 6, 2015, from www.fda.gov/forpatients/approvals/fast/ucm405399.htm

48 Maisto, S.A., Galizio, M., & Connors, G.J. (2011). *Drug use and abuse*. New York: Wadsworth Cengage Learning.

49 Stanley, T.H. (2000). Anesthesia for the 21st century. *Baylor University Medical Center Proceedings, 13*(1): 7–10.

50 DiMasi, J.A., Grabowski, H.G., & Hansen, R.W. (2016). Innovation in the pharmaceutical industry: New estimates of R&D costs. *Journal of Health Economics, 47*: 20–33.

51 PhRMA. (2019). Industry profile 2019. Accessed on September 30, 2019 from https://www.phrma.org/Report/Industry-Profile-2019

52 U.S. Food and Drug Administration (FDA). (2014). Fast track. Accessed on November 6, 2015, from www.fda.gov/forpatients/approvals/fast/ucm405399.htm

53 Maisto, S.A., Galizio, M., & Connors, G.J. (2011). *Drug use and abuse*. New York: Wadsworth Cengage Learning.

54 Ventola, C.L. (2011). Direct-to-consumer pharmaceutical advertising. *Pharmacy and Therapeutics, 36*(10): 669–74.

55 Belloni, A., Morgan, D., & Paris, V. (2016). Pharmaceutical expenditure and policies: Past trends and future challenges. *OECD Health Working Papers*. DOI: 10.1787/5jm0q1f4cdq7-en.

56 Kamal, R., Cox, C., & McDermott, D. (2019). What are the recent and forecasted trends in prescription drug spending? *Health System Tracker*. Accessed on October 3, 2019 from https://www.healthsystemtracker.org/chart-collection/recent-forecasted-trends-prescription-drug-spending/#item-most-people-taking-rx-drugs-say-they-can-afford-their-treatment-but-about-1-in-4-have-a-difficult-time-affording-their-medicine_2019.

57 Ibid.

58 Commins, J. (2019). Final rule requires drug price disclosures in TV ads. Accessed on June 21, 2019 from https://www.healthleadersmedia.com/final-rule-requires-drug-price-disclosures-tv-ads

59 Kaiser Family Foundation. (2019). Poll: Nearly 1 in 4 Americans taking prescription drugs say it's difficult to afford their medicines, including larger shares among those with health issues, with low incomes, and nearing Medicare age. Accessed on September 30, 2019 from https://www.kff.org/health-costs/press-release/poll-nearly-1-in-4-americans-taking-prescription-drugs-say-its-difficult-to-afford-medicines-including-larger-shares-with-low-incomes/

60 Saul, S. (2008). Pfizer to end Lipitor ads by Jarvik. *The New York Times*. Accessed on March 1, 2017, from http://www.nytimes.com/2008/02/26/business/26pfizer.html

61 Applequist, J., & Ball, J.G. (2018). An updated analysis of direct-to-consumer television advertisements for prescription drugs. *Annals of Family Medicine, 16*(3): 211–16.

62 Ibid.

63 Goldberg, R. (2012). Do consumers benefit when prescription drugs are advertised? In R. Goldberg (Ed.), *Taking sides: Clashing views in drugs and society* (10th ed.) (pp. 283–301). Dubuque, IA: McGraw-Hill/Dushkin.

64 Royne, M.B., & Myers, S.D. (2008). Recognizing consumer issues in DTC pharmaceutical advertising. *The Journal of Consumer Affairs, 42*(1): 60–80.

65 Robinson, A.R., Hohmann, K.B., Rifkin, J.I., Topp, D., Gilroy, C.M., et al. (2004). Direct-to-consumer pharmaceutical advertising: Physician and public opinion and potential effects on the physician-patient relationship. *Archives of Internal Medicine, 164*(4): 427–32.

66 Ibid.

67 Friedman, R.A. (2016). What drug ads don't say. *The New York Times.* Accessed on April 26, 2016, from http://www.nytimes.com/2016/04/24/opinion/sunday/what-drug-ads-dont-say.html?_r=0

CHAPTER 2

1 Lee, M.A. (2012). *Smoke signals: A social history of marijuana—Medical, recreational, and scientific.* New York: Scribner.

2 Legal Information Institute. (2015). Accessed on March 17, 2015, from https://www.law.cornell.edu/wex/forfeiture

3 Lee, M.A. (2012). *Smoke signals: A social history of marijuana—Medical, recreational, and scientific.* New York: Scribner.

4 Fellner, J. (2013). Race and drugs. *Oxford Handbooks Online.* New York: Oxford University Press.

5 The Sentencing Project. (2020). Trends in U.S. Corrections. Accessed on November 5, 2020 from https://www.sentencingproject.org/publications/trends-in-u-s-corrections/

6 Substance Abuse and Mental Health Services Administration (SAMHSA). (2020). *Results from the 2019 national survey on drug use and health.* Rockville, MD: Center for Behavioral Health Statistics and Quality

7 FBI. (2020). Crime in the United States, 2019. *FBI Uniform Crime Report.* Washington, DC: U.S. Department of Justice.

8 McBride, D.C., VanderWaal, C.J., & Terry-McElrath, Y.M. (2003). *The drugs-crime wars: Past, present, and future directions in theory, policy, and program interventions. Towards a drugs and crime research agenda for the 21st century.* Washington, DC: National Institute of Justice.

9 Elderbroom, B., & Durnan, J. (2018). State drug law reforms to reduce felony convictions and increase second chances. *Urban Institute.* Accessed on October 13, 2019 from https://www.urban.org/sites/default/files/publication/99077/reclassified_state_drug_law_reforms_to_reduce_felony_convictions_and_increase_second_chances.pdf

10 PEW Research Center. (2014). Feds may be rethinking the drug war, but states have been leading the way. Accessed on August 3, 2015, from http://www.pewresearch.org/fact-tank/2014/04/02/feds-may-be-rethinking-the-drug-war-but-states-have-been-leading-the-way/

11 Degenhardt, L., Chiu, W-T., Sampson, N., Kessler, R.C., Anthony, J.C., et al. (2008). Toward a global view of alcohol, tobacco, cannabis, and cocaine use: Findings from the WHO world mental health surveys. *PLoS Medicine, 5*(7): 1053–67.

12 United Nations Office on Drugs and Crime. (2019). World Drug Report. Accessed on September 20, 2019 from https://wdr.unodc.org/wdr2019/

13 International Comparators. (2014). Accessed on May 12, 2015,from https://www.gov.uk/government/publications/drugs-international-comparators

14 Travis, A. (2014, October 29). Eleven countries studied, one inescapable conclusion—The drug laws don't work. *The Guardian.* https://www.theguardian.com/society/2014/oct/30/drug-laws-international-study-tough-policy-use-problem

15 EMCDDA. (2019). European drug report, 2019. Accessed on October 14, 2019, from http://www.emcdda.europa.eu/emcdda-home-page_en

16 International Comparators. (2014). Accessed on May 12, 2015,from https://www.gov.uk/government/publications/drugs-international-comparators

17 Jelsma, M. (2011). *The development of international drug control: Lessons learned and strategic challenges for the future.* Geneva: Global Commission on Drug Policies.

18 Justice Policy Institute. (2008). Substance abuse treatment and public safety. Accessed on August 3, 2015, from http://www.justicepolicy.org/images/upload/08_01_rep_drugtx_ac-ps.pdf

19 McVay, D., Schiraldi, V., & Ziedenberg, J. (2004). *Treatment or incarceration? National and state findings on the efficacy and cost savings of drug treatment versus imprisonment.* Washington, DC: Justice Policy Institute.

20 Justice Policy Institute. (2008). Substance abuse treatment and public safety. Accessed on August 3, 2015, from http://www.justicepolicy.org/images/upload/08_01_rep_drugtx_ac-ps.pdf

21 McVay, D., Schiraldi, V., & Ziedenberg, J. (2004). *Treatment or incarceration? National and state findings on the efficacy and cost savings of drug treatment versus imprisonment.* Washington, DC: Justice Policy Institute.

22 Boire, R.G. (2007). Life sentences: The collateral sanctions associated with marijuana offenses. http://www.mpp.org/assets/pdfs/library/The-Collateral-Sanctions-Associated-with-Marijuana-Offenses.pdf

23 Ibid.

24 Ibid.

25 The Sentencing Project. (2020). Trends in U.S. Corrections. Accessed on November 5, 2020 from https://www.sentencingproject.org/wp-content/uploads/2020/08/Trends-in-US-Corrections.pdf

26 Ibid

27 SAMHSA. (2020). *Results from the 2019 national survey on drug use and health. HHS Publication no PEP19-5068.* Rockville, MD: Center for Behavioral Health Statistics and Quality

28 The Sentencing Project. (2020). Trends in U.S. Corrections. Accessed on November 5, 2020 from https://www.sentencingproject.org/wp-content/uploads/2020/08/Trends-in-US-Corrections.pdf

29 FBI. (2010). Crime in the United States, 2019: Crime in the United States. *FBI Uniform Crime Report.* Washington, DC: U.S. Department of Justice.

30 Ibid.

31 Vera Institute. (2017). Prison spending in 2015. Accessed on October 18, 2019 from https://www.vera.org/publications/price-of-prisons-2015-state-spending-trends/price-of-prisons-2015-state-spending-trends/price-of-prisons-2015-state-spending-trends-prison-spending

32 Federal Register. (2018). Annual determination of average cost of incarceration. Accessed on October 18, 2019 from https://www.vera.org/publications/price-of-prisons-2015-state-spending-trends/price-of-prisons-2015-state-spending-trends/price-of-prisons-2015-state-spending-trends-prison-spending

33 Buchheit, P. (2012). Five misconceptions about our tattered safety net. *Common Dreams.* http://www.commondreams.org/views/2012/11/12/five-misconceptions-about-our-tattered-safety-net

34 Jelsma, M. (2011). *The development of international drug control: Lessons learned and strategic challenges for the future.* Geneva: Global Commission on Drug Policies.

35 Bowe, R. (2004). The drug war on the Amazon. *E: The Environmental Magazine.* Accessed on August 2, 2015, from http://www.emagazine.com/magazine-archive/the-drug-war-on-the-amazon

36 Global Commission on Drug Policy. (2011). *War on drugs: Report of the Global Commission on Drug Policy.* http://www.globalcommissionondrugs.org/wp-content/themes/gcdp_v1/pdf/Global_Commission_Report_English.pdf

37 Drug Enforcement Agency. (2015). Office of Diversion Control. Title 21 United States Code Controlled Substances Act. Accessed on August 12, 2015, from http://www.deadiversion.usdoj.gov/21cfr/21usc/811.htm

38 Gahlinger, P. (2004). *Illegal drugs: A complete guide to their history, chemistry, use, and abuse.* New York: Plume.

39 Lachenmeier, D.W., & Rehm, J. (2015). Comparative risk assessment of alcohol, tobacco, cannabis and other illicit drugs using the margin of exposure approach. *Scientific Reports, 5:* 8126.

40 Nutt, D.J., King, L.A., & Phillips, L.D. (2010). Drug harms in the UK: A multicriteria decision analysis. *Lancet, 376*(9752): 1558–65.

41 Pew Research Center (2014). America's new drug policy landscape. Accessed on February 18, 2015, from http://www.people-press.org/2014/04/02/americas-new-drug-policy-landscape/

42 Ibid.

43 McCartt, A.T., & Kirley, B.B. (2006). Minimum purchase age laws: How effective are they in reducing alcohol-impaired driving? *Transportation Research Circular, E-C123:* 84–96.

44 Ibid.

45 Ibid.

46 Ibid.

47 Lacey, J.H., Kelley-Baker, T., Furr-Holden, D., Voas, R.B., Romano, E., et al. (2009). *2007 National roadside survey of alcohol and drug use by drivers: Alcohol results.* Washington, DC: Office of Behavioral Safety Research, National Highway Traffic Safety Administration.

48 McCartt, A.T., & Kirley, B.B. (2006). Minimum purchase age laws: How effective are they in reducing alcohol-impaired driving? *Transportation Research Circular, E-C123:* 84–96.

49 Johnston, L.D., Miech, R.A., O'Malley, P.M., Bachman, J.G., & Schulenberg, J.E., et al. (2020). Monitoring the future: National survey results on drug use 1975–2019. Institute for Social Research: The University of Michigan.

50 Substance Abuse and Mental Health Services Administration (SAMHSA). (2020). *Results from the 2019 survey on drug use and health.* Rockville, MD: Center for Behavioral Health Statistics and Quality.

51 Ibid.

52 Centers for Disease Control and Prevention (CDC). (2017). Impaired driving: Get the facts. Accessed on March 2, 2017, from https://www.cdc.gov/motorvehiclesafety/impaired_driving/impaired-drv_factsheet.html

53 MMWR. (2011). Vital signs: Alcohol-impaired driving among adults—United States, 2010. *Morbidity and Mortality Weekly Report, 60*(39): 1351–56.

54 Underwood, J.M., Brener, N., Thornton, J., Harris, W.A., & Bryan, L.N., et al. (2020). Overview and methods for the Youth Risk Behavior Surveillance System—United States, 2019. *MMWR, 69*(1): 1–88.

55 CDC. (2020). Impaired driving. Accessed on November 5, 2020 from https://www.cdc.gov/motorvehiclesafety/impaired_driving/index.html

56 FBI. (2018). Crime in the United States, 2017. *FBI Uniform Crime Report.* Washington, DC: U.S. Department of Justice.

57 MMWR. (2011). Vital signs: Alcohol-impaired driving among adults—United States, 2010. *Morbidity and Mortality Weekly Report, 60*(39): 1351–56.

58 Zador, P.L. (1991). Alcohol related relative risk of fatal driver injuries in relation to driver age and sex. *Journal of Studies on Alcohol, 52*(4): 302–10.

59 SAMHSA. (2020). *Results from the 2019 national survey on drug use and health.* Rockville, MD: Center for Behavioral Health Statistics and Quality

60 Substance Abuse and Mental Health Data Archives. 2011. http://www.icpsr.umich.edu/quicktables/quickconfig.do?34481-0001_all

61 Substance Abuse and Mental Health Services Administration (SAMHSA). (2014). *Results from the 2013 national survey on drug use and health: summary of national findings.* NSDUH Series H-41, HHS Publication (SMA) 11-4658. Rockville, MD: Substance Abuse and Mental Health Services Administration.

62 SAMHSA. (2020). *Results from the 2019 national survey on drug use and health.* Rockville, MD: Center for Behavioral Health Statistics and Quality

63 Ibid.

64 Lester, B.M., Andreozzi, L., & Appiah, L. (2004). Substance use during pregnancy: Time for policy to catch up with research. *Harm Reduction Journal, 1*(5): 13.

65 Brown, E.N. (2014). Pregnant women increasingly face criminal prosecution for positive drug tests. *Reason.* Accessed on March 13, 2015, from http://reason.com/archives/2014/05/16/prosecuting-pregnant-women-for-drug-use

66 Kunins, H.V., Chazotte, C., & Arnsten, J.H. (2007). The effects of race on provider decisions to test for illicit drug use in the peripartum setting. *Journal of Women's Health, 16*(2): 245–55.

67 Rosenthal, M.S. (2013). *Human sexuality from cells to society.* Belmont, CA: Wadsworth Publishing/Cengage Learning.

CHAPTER 3

1 Litvina, L. (2010). Adult neurogenesis under stress. *Mind Matters: The Wesleyan Journal of Psychology, 5:* 51–60.

2 Snyder, J.S., Soumier, A., Brewer, M., Pickel, J., & Cameron, H.A. (2011). Adult hippocampal neurogenesis buffers stress responses and depressive behavior. *Nature, 476*(7361): 458–56.

3 Palaniyappan, L., Marques, T.R., Taylor, H., Handley, R., Mondelli, V., et al. (2013). Cortical folding defects as markers of poor treatment response in first-episode psychosis. *JAMA Psychiatry, 70*(10): 1031–40.

4 Dully, H., & Fleming, C. (2007). *My lobotomy* (pp. 77–78). New York: Crown Publisher.

5 Falk, D. (2009). New information about Albert Einstein's brain. *Frontiers in Evolutionary Neuroscience, 1*(3). https://doi.org/10.3389/neuro.18.003.2009

6 Naqvi, N.H., Rudrauf, D., Damasio, H., & Bechara, A. (2007). Damage to the insula disrupts addiction to cigarette smoking. *Science, 315*(5811): 531–34.

7 Bear, M.F., Connors, B.W., & Paradiso, M.A. (2012). *Neuroscience: Exploring the brain* (3rd ed.). Philadelphia: Lippincott Williams & Wilkins.

8 Bargu, S., Silver M.W., Ohman, M.D., Benitez-Nelson, C.R., & Garrison, D.L. (2012). Mystery behind Hitchcock's birds. *Nature Geoscience, (5)*2–3.

9 Nichols, D.E., & Nichols, D.D. (2008). Serotonin receptors. *Chemical Reviews, 108:* 1614–41.

10 Meyer, J.S., & Quenzer, L.F. (2005). *Psychopharmacology: Drugs, the brain and behavior.* Sunderland, MA: Sinauer Associates, Inc.

CHAPTER 4

1 Buxton, I.L.O., & Benet, L.Z. (2011). Pharmacokinetics: The dynamics of drug absorption, distribution, metabolism, and elimination. In L.L. Brunton, B.A. Chabner, & B.C. Knollman, (Eds.), *Goodman & Gilman's The pharmacological basis of therapeutics* (12th ed.). New York: McGraw Hill.

2 Fox, A.W. (2011). Pharmaceutics. In L.D. Edwards, A.W. Fox, & P.D. Stonier (Eds.), *Principles and practice of pharmaceutical medicine* (3rd ed.) (p. 64). Hoboken, NJ: Wiley-Blackwell.

3 Hogshire, J. (1999). *Pills-a-go-go: A fiendish investigation into pill marketing, art, history and consumption.* Venice, CA: Feral House.

4 Dhar, S., Seth, J., & Parikh, D. (2014). Systemic side-effects of topical corticosteroids. *Indian Journal of Dermatology, 59*(5): 460–64.

5 Prausnitz, M.R., & Langer, R. (2008). Transdermal drug delivery. *Natural Biotechnology, 26*(11): 1261–68.

6 Blackburn, J. (2010). A review of medication dosage forms, drug administration, pharmacokinetics, and abbreviations: A knowledge-based course for technicians. *Texas Tech University School of Pharmacy.* Accessed on August 16, 2012, from www.jdeducation.com

7 Alexander, N.J., Baker, E., Kaptein, M., Karck, U., Miller, L., & Zampaglione, E. (2004). Why consider vaginal drug administration? *Fertility and Sterility: 82*(1): 1–12.

8 Shojaei, A.H. (1998). Buccal mucosa as a route for systemic drug delivery: A review. *The Journal of Pharmacy and Pharmaceutical Sciences, 1*(1): 15–30.

9 Harper, D. (2015). Online etymology dictionary: Drug. Accessed on May 15, 2015, from www.etymonline.com/index.php?term=drug

10 Meyer, J.S., & Quenzer, L.F. (2013). *Psychopharmacology: Drugs, the brain and behavior* (2nd ed.). Sunderland, MA: Sinauer Associates.

11 Guengerich, F.P. (2008). Cytochrome p450 and chemical toxicology. *Chemical Research in Toxicology, 21*(1): 70–83.

12 Woll, S., Kim, S.H., Greten, H.J., & Efferth, T. (2013). Animal plant warfare and secondary metabolite evolution. *Natural Products and Bioprospecting, 3*(1): 1–7.

13 Levinthal, C.F. (2005). *Drugs, behavior and modern society* (4th ed.). New York: Pearson.

14 De la Torre, R., Yubero-Lahoz, S., Pardo-Lozano, R., & Farre, M. (2012). MDMA, methamphetamine, and CYP2D6 pharmacogenetics: What is clinically relevant? *Frontiers in Genetics, 3*: 235.

15 Bradford, L.D. (2008). Race, genetics, metabolism: Drug therapy and clinical trials. *MIWatch.org.* Accessed on September 28, 2016, from http://www.miwatch.org/2008/04/race_genetics_metabolism_drug_1.html

16 Han, C., & Pae, C-U. (2013). Do we need to consider ethno-cultural variation in the use of atypical antipsychotics for Asian patients with major depressive disorder? *CNS Drugs, 27*: 47–51.

17 Perez-Stable, E.J., Herrera, B., Jacob, P., & Benowitz, N.L. (1998). Nicotine metabolism and intake in black and white smokers. *JAMA, 280*(2): 152–56.

18 Mwenifumbo, J.C., Koudsi, N.A., Ho, M.K., Zhou, Q., Hoffmann, E.W., et al. (2008). Novel and established CYP2A6 alleles impair in vivo nicotine metabolism in a population of black African descent. *Human Mutation Variation, Informatics, and Disease, 29*(5): 679–88.

19 Flockhart Table. (2016). University of Indiana. Accessed on September 30, 2016, from http://medicine.iupui.edu/clinpharm/ddis/main-table/

20 Ibid.

21 Weathermon, R., & Crabb, D.W. (1999). Alcohol and medication interactions. *Alcohol Research and Health, 23*(1): 40–54.

22 Gibson, G.G., & Skett, P. (2001). *Introduction to drug metabolism* (3rd ed.). Hampshire, UK: Cengage Learning.

23 Ibid.

24 Mudhoo, A., Sharma, S.J., Garg, V.K., & Tseng, C-H. (2011). Arsenic: An overview of applications, health, and environmental concerns and removal processes. *Critical Reviews in Environmental Science and Technology, 41*(5): 435–519.

25 Pert, C.B. (1997). *Molecules of emotion.* New York: Scribner.

26 Advokat, C.D., Comaty, J.E., & Julien, R.M. (2014). *Julien's primer of drug action* (13th ed.). New York: Worth Publishers.

27 Schacter, S., & Singer, J. (1962). Cognitive, social and physiological determinants of emotional states. *Psychological Review, 69*: 379–99.

28 Mosely, J.B., O'Malley, K., Petersen, N.J., Menke, T.J., Brody, B.A., et al. (2002). A controlled trial of arthroscopic surgery for osteoarthritis of the knee. *New England Journal of Medicine, 347*(2): 81–88.

29 Wager, T.D., & Roy, M. (2010). Separate mechanisms for placebo and opiate analgesia? *Pain, 150*(1): 8–9.

30 Benedetti, F. (2002). How the doctor's words affect the patient's brain. *Evaluation and the Health Professions, 25*(4): 369–86.

31 Furmark, T., Appel, L., Henningsson, S., Åhs, F., Faria, V., et al. (2008). A link between serotonin-related gene polymorphisms, amygdala activity, and placebo-induced relief from social anxiety. *The Journal of Neuroscience, 28* (49): 13066–74.

32 Schweinhardt, P., Seminowicz, D.A., Jaeger, E., Duncan, G.H., & Bushnell, M.C. (2009). The anatomy of the mesolimbic reward system: A link between personality and the placebo analgesic response. *The Journal of Neuroscience, 29*(15): 4882–87.

33 Ibid.

34 Waber, R.L., Shiv, B., Carmon, Z, & Ariely, D. (2008). Commercial features of placebo and therapeutic efficacy. *JAMA, 299*(9): 1016–17.

35 Koteles, F., Komso, I., & Bardos, G. (2010). The effect of perceptual characteristics of tablets upon patient's choice. *Clinical and Experimental Medical Journal, 4*(10): 99–104.

36 Ibid.

37 Meynen, G., & Swaab, D. (2011). Why medication in involuntary treatment may be less effective: The placebo/nocebo effect. *Medical Hypotheses, 77*: 993–95.

38 Benedetti, F. (2002). How the doctor's words affect the patient's brain. *Evaluation and the Health Professions, 25*(4): 369–86.

39 Ibid.

40 Ibid.

41 Kaptchuk, T.J., Friedlander, E., Kelley, J.M., Sanchez, M.N., Kokkotou, E., Singer, J.P., Kowalczykowski, M., Miller, F.G., Kirsch, I., & Lembo. A.J. (2010). Placebo without deception: A randomized controlled trial in irritable bowel syndrome. *PLoS ONE, 5*(12): e15591.

42 Breidart, M., & Hofbauer, K. (2009). Placebo: Misunderstandings and prejudices. *Deutsches Arzteblatt International, 106*(46): 751–55.

43 Tilburt, J.C., Emanuel, E.J., Kaptchuk, T.J., Curlin, F.A., & Miller, F.G. (2008). *British Medical Journal, 337*: a1938.

44 Cami, A., Arnold, A., Manzi, S., & Reis, B. (2011). Predicting adverse drug events using pharmacological network models. *Science Translational Medicine, 3*(114): 114.

45 Erickson, M.A. & Penning, T.M. (2018). Drug toxicity and poisoning. In L.L. Brunton, R. Hilal-Dandan, & B.C. Knollman (Eds.), *Goodman & Gilman's The pharmacological basis of therapeutics* (13th ed.) (pp. 55–64). New York: McGraw-Hill.

46 Fearnow, B. (2013). Study: 70% of Americans on prescription drugs. Accessed on September 28, 2016, from http://atlanta.cbslocal.com/2013/06/19/study-70-percent-of-americans-on-prescription-drugs-one-fifth-take-5-or-more/

47 Vogel-Sprott, M. (1997). Is behavioral tolerance learned? *Alcohol Health and Research World, 21*(3): 161–76.

48 Wenger, J.R., Tiffany, T.M., Bombardier, C., Nicholls, K., & Woods, S.C. (1981). Ethanol tolerance in the rat is learned. *Science, 213*(4507): 575–77.

CHAPTER 5

1 Thoumi, F.E. (2003). *Illegal drugs, economy, and society in the Andes.* Baltimore: Johns Hopkins University Press.

2 Hecht, A. (2011). *Understanding drugs: Cocaine and crack.* New York: Chelsea House.

3 Musto, D.F. (1991). Opium, cocaine, and marijuana in American history. *Scientific American, 265*(1): 20–27.

4 Hecht, A. (2011). *Understanding drugs: Cocaine and crack*. New York: Chelsea House.

5 Spillane, J.F. (2000). *Cocaine: From medical marvel to modern menace in the United States, 1884–1920*. Baltimore: Johns Hopkins University Press.

6 Ibid.

7 Eberle, E.G., & Gordon, F.T. (1903). *Report of committee on the acquirement of drug habits*. American Journal of Pharmacy, October: 474.

8 Gahlinger, P. (2004). *Illegal drugs: A complete guide to their history, chemistry, use, and abuse*. New York: Plume

9 Streatfeild, D. (2003). *Cocaine: An unauthorized biography*. New York: Picador.

10 Office of National Drug Control Policy (ONDCP). (1995). Fact sheet: Drug use trends. http://www.druglibrary.org/schaffer/govpubs/fsduse.pdf

11 Vagins, D.J., & McCurdy, J. (2006). *Cracks in the system: Twenty years of the unjust federal crack cocaine law*. Washington DC: American Civil Liberties Union.

12 Ibid.

13 Ibid.

14 United Nations Office on Drugs and Crime. (2020). *World drug report, 2020*. United Nations publication, sales no. E.20.XI.6. https://wdr.unodc.org/wdr2020/en/index.html

15 Ibid.

16 SAMHSA. (2020). *Results from the 2019 National Survey on Drug Use and Health: Detailed Tables*. Rockville, MD: Center for Behavioral Health Statistics and Quality.

17 Ibid.

18 Ibid.

19 DEA. (2019). *National drug threat assessment*. Accessed on October 10, 2020 from https://www.dea.gov/sites/default/files/2020-01/2019-NDTA-final-01-14-2020_Low_Web-DIR-007-20_2019.pdf

20 SAMHSA. (2020). *Results from the 2019 National Survey on Drug Use and Health: Detailed Tables*. Rockville, MD: Center for Behavioral Health Statistics and Quality.

21 Ibid.

22 Meich, R.A., Johnston, L.D., O'Malley, P.M., Bachman, J.G., & Schulenberg, J.E., et al. (2021). *Monitoring the Future: National survey results on drug use 1975-2020*. Ann Arbor: Institute for Social Research, The University of Michigan.

23 Eaton, D. K., Kann, L., Kinchen, S., Shanklin, S., Flint, K.H., et al. (2012, June 8). Youth risk behavior surveillance—United States, 2011. *MMWR*, 61(4): 1–162.

24 Gahlinger, P. (2004*). Illegal drugs: A complete guide to their history, chemistry, use, and abuse*. New York: Plume

25 United Nations Office on Drugs and Crime. (2019). *World drug report, 2019*. United Nations publication, sales no. E.19.XI.9. http://www.unodc.org/wdr2019/

26 Casale, J.F., & Klein, R.F.X. (1993). Illicit production of cocaine. *Forensic Science Review*, 5: 95–107.

27 United Nations Office on Drugs and Crime. (2019). *World drug report, 2019*. United Nations publication, sales no. E.19.XI.9. http://www.unodc.org/wdr2019/

28 Ibid.

29 Drug abuse.com (2015). Dangerous additives: What's really in your cocaine? Accessed on October 5, 2016, from http://drugabuse.com/dangerous-additives-whats-really-in-your-cocaine/

30 Mateo, Y., Budygin, E.A., John, C.E., & Jones, S.R. (2004). Role of serotonin in cocaine effects in mice with reduced dopamine transporter function. PNAS, 101(1): 372–77.

31 Engblom, D., Bilbao, A., Sanchis-Segura, C., Dahan, L. Perreau-Lenz, S., et al. (2008). Glutamate receptors on dopamine neurons control the persistence of cocaine seeking. *Neuron*, 59: 497–508.

32 Kufahl, P., Li, Z., Risinger, R., Rainey, C., & Piacentine, L. (2008). Expectation modulates human brain responses to acute cocaine: A functional magnetic resonance imaging study. *Biological Psychiatry*, 63: 222–30.

33 Simon, S.L., Domier, C.P., Sim, T., Richardson, K., Rawson, R.A., et al. (2002). Cognitive performance of current methamphetamine and cocaine abusers. *Journal of Addictive Diseases*, 21(1): 61–74.

34 Burnett, L.B. (2012). Cocaine toxicity in emergency medicine. Accessed on January 14, 2013, from http://emedicine.medscape.com/article/813959-overview

35 Ibid.

36 Ibid.

37 Hecht, A. (2011). *Understanding drugs: Cocaine and crack*. New York: Chelsea House.

38 Ibid.

39 Gable, R.S. (2006). The toxicity of recreational drugs. *American Scientist*, 94: 206–8.

40 Goodnough, A. (2019). A new drug scourge: Deaths involving meth are rising fast. *The New York Times*. Accessed on October 10, 2020 from https://www.nytimes.com/2019/12/17/health/meth-deaths-opioids.html

41 Nolan, M.L., Shamasunder, S., Colon-Berezin, C., Kunins, H.V., & Paone, D. (2019). Increased presence of fentanyl in cocaine-involved fatal overdoses: Implications for prevention. *Journal of Urban Health*, 96(1): 49–54.

42 Hedegaard, J., Minino, A.M., & Warner, M. (2021). *Co-involvement of opioids in drug overdose deaths involving cocaine and psychostimulants*. NCHS Data Brief, no 406. Hyattsville, MD: National Center for Health Statistics.

43 Centers for Disease Control and Prevention. (2020). *Drug overdose deaths in the United States, 1999–2018*. NCHS Data Brief, no 356. Hyattsville, MD: National Center for Health Statistics.

44 Burnett, L.B. (2012). Cocaine toxicity in emergency medicine. Accessed on January 14, 2013, from http://emedicine.medscape.com/article/813959-overview

45 Ibid.

46 Hecht, A. (2011). *Understanding drugs: Cocaine and crack*. New York: Chelsea House.

47 Mendelson, J.E., Tolliver, B.K., Delucchi, K.L., Baggott, M.J., Flower, K., et al. (2010). Capsaicin, an active ingredient in pepper sprays, increases the lethality of cocaine. *Forensic Toxicology*, 28: 33–37.

48 Gawin, F.H., & Kleber, H.C. (1986). Abstinence symptomatology and psychiatric diagnosis in cocaine abuses. *Archives of General Psychiatry*, 43: 107–13.

49 Coffey, S.F., Dansky, B.S., Carrigan, M.H., & Brady, K.T. (2000). Acute and protracted cocaine abstinence in an outpatient population: A prospective study of mood, sleep, and withdrawal symptoms. *Drug and Alcohol Dependence*, 59: 277–86.

50 Walsh, S.L., Stoops, W.W., Moody, D.E., Lin, S-N., & Bigelow, G.E. (2009). Repeated dosing with oral cocaine in humans: Assessment of direct effects, withdrawal, and pharmacokinetics. *Experimental and Clinical Psychopharmacology*, 17(4): 205–16.

51 Ersche, K.D., Jones, P.S., Williams, G.B., Robbins, T.W., & Bullmore, E.T. (2012). Cocaine dependence: A fast-track for brain ageing? *Molecular Psychiatry*, 18(2): 134–35.

52 Ibid.

53 D'Cruz, D. (2000). Autoimmune diseases associated with drugs, chemicals and environmental factors. *Toxicology Letters*, 112–113: 421–32.

54 Hess, E.V. (2002). Environmental chemicals and autoimmune disease: cause and effect. *Toxicology*, 181–182: 65–70.

55 Johnson, K. (2012). Levamisole-laced cocaine may unmask autoimmune process. Medscape Medical News. Accessed on September 6, 2015, from http://www.medscape.com/viewarticle/760831

56 Juang, D., Braverman, A.C., & Eagle, K. (2008). Aortic dissection. *Circulation*, 118: e507–10.

57 Okie, S. (2009). The epidemic that wasn't. *The New York Times*. Accessed on January 14, 2013, from http://www.nytimes.com/2009/01/27/health/27coca.html?pagewanted=all&_r=0.

58 Frank, D.A., Augustyn, M., Knight, W.G., Pell, T., & Zuckerman, B. (2001). Growth, development, and behavior in early childhood following prenatal cocaine exposure: A systematic review. *JAMA*, 285(12): 1613–25.

59 Behnke, M., Smith, V.C., the Committee on Substance Abuse, and the Committee of Fetus and Newborn. (2013). Prenatal substance abuse: Short-and long-term effects on the exposed fetus. *Pediatrics*, 3: e1009–24.

60 Addis, A., Moretti, M.E., Ahmed Syed, F., Einarson, T.R., & Koren, G. (2001). Fetal effects of cocaine: An updated meta-analysis. *Reproductive Toxicology*, 15(4): 341–69.

61 Okie, S. (2009). The epidemic that wasn't. *The New York Times*. Accessed on January 14, 2013, from http://www.nytimes.com/2009/01/27/health/27coca.html?pagewanted=all&_r=0.

62 Kalant, H. (2010). What neurobiology cannot tell us about addiction. *Addiction*, 105(5): 780–89.

63 Centers for Disease Control and Prevention. (2020). *Drug overdose deaths in the United States, 1999–2018*. NCHS Data Brief, no 356. Hyattsville, MD: National Center for Health Statistics.

64 Cohen S. (1985). Reinforcement and rapid delivery systems: understanding adverse consequences of cocaine. *NIDA Res Monograph*, 61: 151–57.

65 Bozarth, M.A., & Wise, R.A. (1985). Toxicity associated with long-term intravenous heroin and cocaine self-administration in the rat. *JAMA*, 254(1): 81–83.

66 Kosten, T.R., Wu, G., Huang, W., Harding, M.J., Harnon, S.C., Lappalainen, J., & Neilsen, D.A. (2012). Pharmacogenetic randomized trial for cocaine abuse: Disulfiram and dopamine β-hydroxylase. *Biological Psychiatry*, 73(3): 219–24.

67 Mash, D.C., Kovera, C.A., Pablo, J., Tyndale, R.F., & Ervin, F.D., et al. (2000). Igobaine: Complex pharmacokinetics, concerns for safety, and preliminary efficacy measures. *Annals of the New York Academy of Sciences*, 914: 394–401.

68 Cappendijk, S.L.T., & Dzolijic, M.R. (1993). Inhibitor effects of ibogaine on cocaine self-administration in rats. *European Journal of Pharmacology*, 241(2–3): 261–65.

69 Shorter, D., & Kosten, T.R. (2011). Novel pharmacotherapeutic treatments for cocaine addiction. *BMC Medicine*, 9: 119.

70 Mash, D.C., Kovera, C.A., Pablo, J., Tyndale, R.F., & Ervin, F.D., et al. (2000). Ibogaine: Complex pharmacokinetics, concerns for safety, and preliminary efficacy measures. *Annals of the New York Academy of Sciences*, 914: 394–401.

71 Mash, D.C. (2010). The ibogaine therapy for substance abuse disorders. In D. Brizer, R. Castaneda (Eds.), *Clinical addiction psychiatry*. Cambridge: Cambridge University Press.

72 Mash, D.C., Duque, L., Page, B., & Allen-Ferdinand, K. (2018). Ibogaine detoxification transitions opioid and cocaine abusers between dependence and abstinence: Clinical observations and treatment outcomes. *Frontiers in Pharmacology*, 9: 529.

73 Martell, B.A., Orson, F.M., Poling, J., Mitchell, E., & Rossen, R.D., et al. (2009). Cocaine vaccine for the treatment of cocaine dependence in methadone-maintained patients: A randomized double-blind placebo-controlled efficacy trial. *Archives of General Psychiatry*, 66(10): 1116–23.

74 Ibid.

75 Li, Y., Kong, Q., Yue, J., Gou, X., & Xu, M, et al. (2019). Genome-edited skin epidermal stem cells protect mice from cocaine-seeking behavior and cocaine overdose. *Nature Biomedical Engineering*, 3: 105–13.

76 United Nations Office on Drugs and Crime. (2020). *World drug report, 2020*. United Nations publication, sales no. E.20.XI.6. https://wdr.unodc.org/wdr2020/en/index.html

77 Ibid.

78 Lee, M.R. (2011). The history of Ephedra (ma-huang). *The Journal of the Royal College of Physicians of Edinburgh*, 41(1): 78–84.

79 Farren, M. (2010). *Speed speed speedfreak: A fast history of amphetamine*. Port Townsend, WA: Feral House.

80 Rasmussen, N. (2008). America's first amphetamine epidemic 1929–1971. *American Journal of Public Health*, 98(8): 974–85.

81 Farren, M. (2010). *Speed speed speedfreak: A fast history of amphetamine*. Port Townsend, WA: Feral House.

82 Gahlinger, P. (2004). *Illegal drugs: A complete guide to their history, chemistry, use, and abuse*. New York: Plume.

83 SAMHSA. (2020). *Results from the 2019 National Survey on Drug Use and Health: Detailed Tables*. Rockville, MD: Center for Behavioral Health Statistics and Quality.

84 Ibid.

85 Ibid.

86 Ibid.

87 Borders, T.F., Booth, B.M., Han, X., Wright, P., & Leukefeld, C., et al. (2008). Longitudinal changes in methamphetamine and cocaine use in untreated rural stimulant users: Racial differences and the impact of methamphetamine legislation. *Addiction*, 103: 800–808.

88 SAMHSA. (2020). *Results from the 2019 National Survey on Drug Use and Health: Detailed Tables*. Rockville, MD: Center for Behavioral Health Statistics and Quality.

89 Cunningham, J.K., & Liu, L-M. (2005). Impacts of federal precursor chemical regulations on methamphetamine arrests. *Addiction*, 100: 479–88.

90 DEA. (2019). *National drug threat assessment*. Accessed on October 10, 2020 from https://www.dea.gov/sites/default/files/2020–01/2019-NDTA-final-01-14-2020_Low_Web-DIR-007-20_2019.pdf

91 Farren, M. (2010). *Speed speed speedfreak: A fast history of amphetamine*. Port Townsend, WA: Feral House.

92 Cunningham, J.K., & Liu, L-M. (2005). Impacts of federal precursor chemical regulations on methamphetamine arrests. *Addiction*, 100: 479–88.

93 DEA. (2019). *National drug threat assessment*. Accessed on October 10, 2020 from https://www.dea.gov/sites/default/files/2020–01/2019-NDTA-final-01-14-2020_Low_Web-DIR-007-20_2019.pdf

94 United Nations Office on Drugs and Crime. (2020). *World drug report, 2020*. United Nations publication, sales no. E.20.XI.6. https://wdr.unodc.org/wdr2020/en/index.html

95 Ellinwood, E.H., King, G., & Lee, T.H. (2002). Chronic amphetamine use and abuse. In K.L. Davis, D. Charney, J.T. Coyle, and C. Nemeroff (Eds.), *Neuropsychopharmacology: The fifth generation of progress*. Philadelphia: Lippincott Williams & Wilkins.

96 Rudnick, G., & Clark, J. (1993). From synapse to vesicle: The reuptake and storage of biogenic amine neurotransmitters. *Biochimica et Biophysica Acta*, 1144: 249–63.

97 Fleckenstein, A.E., Volz, T.J., Riddle, E.L., Gibb, J.W., & Hanson, G.R. (2007). New insights into the mechanism of action of amphetamines. *Annual Review of Pharmacology and Toxicology*, 47: 681–98.

98 Rothman, R.B., Baumann, M.H., Dersch, C.M., Romero, D.V., Rice, K.C., et al. (2001). Amphetamine-type central nervous system stimulants release norepinephrine more potently than they release dopamine and serotonin. *Synapse*, 39: 32–41.

99 Hedegaard, J., Minino, A.M., & Warner, M. (2021). *Co-involvement of opioids in drug overdose deaths involving cocaine and psychostimulants*. NCHS Data Brief, no 406. Hyattsville, MD: National Center for Health Statistics.

100 Ellinwood, E.H., King, G., & Lee, T.H. (2002). Chronic amphetamine use and abuse. In K.L. Davis, D. Charney, J.T. Coyle, & C. Nemeroff (Eds.), *Neuropsychopharmacology: The fifth generation of progress*. Philadelphia: Lippincott Williams & Wilkins.

101 McCann, U.D., Wong, D.F., Yokoi, F., Villemagne, V., Dannals, R.F. et al. (1998). Reduced striatal dopamine transporter density in abstinent methamphetamine and methcathinone users: Evidence from positron

emission tomography studies with [11C]WIN-35,428. *The Journal of Neuroscience*, 18(20): 8417–22.

102 Volkow, N.D., Chang, L., Wang, G.J., Fowler, J.S., Neonido-Yee, M., et al. (2001). Association of dopamine transporter reduction with psychomotor impairment in methamphetamine abusers. *American Journal of Psychiatry*, 158(3): 377–82.

103 Volkow, N.D., Chang, L., Wang, G-J., Fowler, J.S., Franceschi, D., Sedler, M., et al. (2001). Loss of dopamine transporters in methamphetamine abusers recovers with protracted abstinence. *Journal of Neuroscience*, 21(23): 9414–18.

104 Yuan, J., Hatzidimitriou, G., Suthar, P., Mueller, M., McCann, U., & Ricaurte, G. (2006). Relationship between temperature, dopaminergic neurotoxicity, and plasma drug concentrations in methamphetamine-treated squirrel monkeys. *The Journal of Pharmacology and Experimental Therapeutics*, 316: 1210–18.

105 Borders, T.F., Booth, B.M., Han, X., Wright, P., & Leukefeld, C., et al. (2008). Longitudinal changes in methamphetamine and cocaine use in untreated rural stimulant users: Racial differences and the impact of methamphetamine legislation. *Addiction*, 103: 800–808.

106 SAMHSA. (2020). *Results from the 2019 National Survey on Drug Use and Health: Detailed Tables*. Rockville, MD: Center for Behavioral Health Statistics and Quality.

107 Gahlinger, P. (2004). *Illegal drugs: A complete guide to their history, chemistry, use, and abuse*. New York: Plume.

108 Pinger, R.R., Payne, W.A., Hahn, D.B., & Hahn, E.J. (1998). *Drugs: Issues for today (3rd ed.)*. Boston: McGraw-Hill.

109 Gahlinger, P. (2004). *Illegal drugs: A complete guide to their history, chemistry, use, and abuse*. New York: Plume.

110 Prosser, J.M., & Nelson, L.S. (2012). *The toxicology of bath salts: A review of synthetic cathinones*. Journal of Medical Toxicology. 8(1): 33–42.

111 Ross, E.A., Watson, M., & Goldberger, B. (2011). "Bath salts" intoxication. *New England Journal of Medicine*, 305(10): 967–68.

112 Prosser, J.M., & Nelson, L.S. (2012). The toxicology of bath salts: A review of synthetic cathinones. *Journal of Medical Toxicology*. 8(1): 33–42.

113 Ross, E.A., Watson, M., & Goldberger, B. (2011). "Bath salts" intoxication. *New England Journal of Medicine*, 305(10): 967–68.

CHAPTER 6

1 Nichols, D.E. (2004). Hallucinogens. *Pharmacology and Therapeutics*, 101(2): 131–81.

2 Weil, A., & Rosen W. (2004). *From chocolate to morphine: Everything you need to know about mind-altering drugs*. Boston: Houghton Mifflin.

3 Woolf (2000). Witchcraft of mycotoxin? The Salem witch trials. *Clinical Toxicology*, 38(4): 457–60.

4 Caporael, L.R. (1976). Ergotism: The Satan loosed in Salem? *Science, 192*(4234): 21–26. Doblin, R. (1991). Pahnke's "Good Friday Experiment": A long-term follow-up and methodological critique. *The Journal of Transpersonal Psychology, 23*(1): 1–28.

5 Matossian, M.K. (1982). Ergot and the Salem witchcraft affair. *American Scientists, 70*(4): 355–57.

6 Spanos, N.P., & Gottlieb, J. (1976). Ergotism and the Salem village witch trials. *Science, 194*(4272): 1390–94.

7 Woolf, A. (2000). Witchcraft of mycotoxin? The Salem witch trials. *Clinical Toxicology*, 38(4): 457–60.

8 Lee, M.A., & Shlain, B. (1994): *Acid dreams: The complete social history of LSD: The CIA, the sixties, and beyond*. New York: Grove Press.

9 Ibid.

10 Hofmann, A. (2009). *LSD My problem child: Reflections on sacred drugs, mysticism, and science* (4th ed.) (pp. 48–50). Santa Cruz: Multidisciplinary Association for Psychedelic Studies.

11 Ibid.

12 Disbennett, B.M. (2014). An analysis of CIA and military testing on LSD on non-consenting service members and recovery through the VA disability program. *Tennessee Journal of Race, Gender, and Social Justice, 3*(2): 173–202.

13 Ibid.

14 Lee, M.A., & Shlain, B. (1994): *Acid dreams: The complete social history of LSD: The CIA, the sixties, and beyond*. New York: Grove Press.

15 Ibid.

16 Gahlinger, P. (2004). *Illegal drugs: A complete guide to their history, chemistry, use, and abuse*. New York: Plume.

17 Lee, M.A., & Shlain, B. (1994): *Acid dreams: The complete social history of LSD: The CIA, the sixties, and beyond*. New York: Grove Press.

18 Greenfield, R. (2006). *Timothy Leary: A biography*. New York: Harcourt Books.

19 Ibid.

20 Lee, M.A., & Shlain, B. (1994): *Acid dreams: The complete social history of LSD: The CIA, the sixties, and beyond*. New York: Grove Press.

21 Ibid.

22 Holland, J. (2001). The history of MDMA. In J. Holland (Ed.), *Ecstasy: The complete guide*. Rochester, VT: Park Street Press p. 11–21.

23 Iversen, L. (2008). *Speed, Ecstasy, Ritalin: The science of amphetamines*. New York: Oxford University Press.

24 Ibid.

25 Farren, M. (2010). *Speed speed speedfreak: A fast history of amphetamine*. Port Townsend, WA: Feral House.

26 Holland, J. (2001). The history of MDMA. In J. Holland (Ed.), *Ecstasy: The complete guide*. Rochester, VT: Park Street Press p. 11–21.

27 Holland, J. (2001). The legal status of MDMA around the world. In J. Holland (Ed.), *Ecstasy: the complete guide*. Rochester, VT: Park Street Press p. 11-21.

28 Center for Substance Abuse Research. (2013). Ketamine. Accessed on February 1, 2016, from http://www.cesar.umd.edu/cesar/drugs/ketamine.asp

29 National Highway Traffic Safety Association. (2004). Ketamine. Accessed on February 1, 2016, from http://www.nhtsa.gov/people/injury/research/job185drugs/ketamine.htm

30 Grim, R. (2009). *This is your country on drugs: The secret history of getting high in America*. Hoboken, NJ: John Wiley and Sons.

31 Substance Abuse and Mental Health Services Administration (SAMHSA). (2020). Results from the 2019 survey on drug use and health: Detailed tables. Rockville, MD: Center for Behavioral Health Statistics and Quality.

32 Yockey, R.A., Vidourek, R.A., & King, K.A. (2020). Trends in LSD use among US adults: 2015-2018. *Drug and Alcohol Dependence, 212*: 108071.

33 Ibid.

34 Substance Abuse and Mental Health Services Administration (SAMHSA). (2020). Results from the 2019 survey on drug use and health: Detailed tables. Rockville, MD: Center for Behavioral Health Statistics and Quality.

35 Ibid.

36 Ibid.

37 Ibid.

38 Gahlinger, P. (2004). *Illegal drugs: A complete guide to their history, chemistry, use, and abuse*. New York: Plume.

39 Ibid.

40 Shanon, B. (2008). Biblical entheogens: A speculative hypothesis. *Time and Mind: The Journal of Archaeology Consciousness and Culture, 1*(1): 51–74.

41 Ibid.

42 Alper, K.R., Lotsof, H.S., & Kaplan, C.D. (2008). The ibogaine medical subculture. *Journal of Ethnopharmacology, 115*(1): 9–24.

43 Garg, A., Hippargi, R., & Gandhare, A. (2008). Toad skin secretions: Potent source of pharmacologically and therapeutically significant compounds. *The Internet Journal of Pharmacology, 5*(2): 17.

44 Mithoefer, M.C., Wagner, M.T., Mithoefer, A.T., Jerome, L., & Doblin, R. (2010). The safety and efficacy of 3,4-methylenedioxymethamphetamine-assisted psychotherapy in subjects with chronic, treatment-resistant posttraumatic stress disorder: The first randomized controlled pilot study. *Journal of Psychopharmacology, 25*(4): 439–52.

45 Mithoefer, M.C., Wagner, M.T., Mithoefer, A.T., Jerome, L., Martin, S.F., Yazar-Klosinski, B., Michel, Y., Brewerton, T.D., & Doblin, R. (2012). Durability of improvement in posttraumatic stress disorder symptoms and absence of harmful effects of drug dependency after 3,4-methylenedioxymethamphetamine-assisted psychotherapy: A prospective long-term follow-up study. *Journal of Psychopharmacology, 27*(1): 28–39.

46 Havocscope. (2016). Ecstasy pills prices. Accessed on February 1, 2016, from http://www.havocscope.com/black-market-prices/ecstasy-prices/

47 Global drug survey 2016. (2016). Accessed on October 6, 2016, from www.globaldrugsurvey.com

48 Kroll, D. (2012). Why do witches ride broomsticks? Hallucinogens. *Forbes Online*. Accessed on April 12, 2014, from http://www.forbes.com/sites/davidkroll/2012/10/31/witches-broomsticks-and-flying-heres-why/

49 Freye, E. (2010). Toxicity of *Datura stramonium*. In E. Freye & J.V. Levy, (Eds.), *Pharmacology and abuse of cocaine, amphetamine, ecstasy, and related designer drugs* (pp. 217–219). New York: Springer.

50 Wasson, R.G. (1972). *Soma: Divine mushroom of immortality*. New York: Harcourt Brace Jovanovich.

51 Ibid.

52 O'Brien, C.P. (2011). Drug addiction and drug abuse. In L.L. Brunton, B.A. Chabner, & B.C. Knollman, (Eds.), *Goodman & Gilman's The pharmacological basis of therapeutics* (12th ed.). New York: McGraw Hill.

53 Pahnke, W. (1963). Drugs and mysticism: An analysis of the relationship between psychedelic drugs and the mystical consciousness [dissertation]. Cambridge, MA: Harvard University.

54 Doblin, R. (1991). Pahnke's "Good Friday Experiment": A long-term follow-up and methodological critique. *The Journal of Transpersonal Psychology, 23*(1): 1–28.

55 Disbennett, B.M. (2014). An analysis of CIA and military testing on LSD on non-consenting service members and recovery through the VA disability program. *Tennessee Journal of Race, Gender, and Social Justice, 3*(2): 173–202.

56 *Employment Division, Department of Human Resources of Oregon* v. *Smith*, 494 U.S. 872.

57 Carhart-Harris, R.L., Muthukumaraswamy, S., Roseman, L., Kaelen, M., Droog, W., et al. (2016). Neural correlates of the LSD experience revealed by multimodal neuroimaging. *PNAS, 113*(17): 4853–58.

58 Lord, L-D., Expert, P., Atasoy, S., Roseman, L., & Rapuano, K., et al. (2018). Altered trajectories in the dynamical repertoire of functional network states under psilocybin. *bioRxiv*. Accessed on November 14, 2019 from https://www.biorxiv.org/content/10.1101/376491v1

59 Preller, K.H., Razi, A., Zeidman, P., Stampfli, P., & Friston, K.J., et al. (2019). Effective connectivity changes in LSD-induced altered states of consciousness in humans. *PNAS, 116*(7): 2743-48.

60 Johnson, M.W., Garcia-Romeu, A., & Griffiths, R.R. (2017). Long-term follow-up of psilocybin-facilitated smoking cessation. *American Journal of Drug and Alcohol Abuse, 43*(1): 55-60.

61 Tagliazucchi, E., Roseman, L., Kaelen, M., Orban, C., Muthukumaraswamy, S.D., et al. (2016). Increased global functional connectivity correlates with LSD-induced ego dissolution. *Current Biology, 26*(8): 1043–50.

62 Carhart-Harris, R.L., Erritzoe, D., Williams, T., Stone, J.M., Reed, L.J., et al. (2012). Neural correlates of the psychedelic state as determined by fMRI studies with psilocybin. *PNAS, 109*(6): 2138–43.

63 Ibid.

64 Morton, J. (2005). Ecstasy: Pharmacology and neurotoxicity. *Current Opinion in Pharmacology, 5*: 79–86.

65 Malberg, J.E., & Bonson, K.R. (2001). How MDMA works in the brain. In J. Holland (Ed.), *Ecstasy: The complete guide*. Rochester, VT: Park Street Press p. 11–21.

66 Mithoefer, M.C., Wagner, M.T., Mithoefer, A.T., Jerome, L., & Doblin, R. (2010). The safety and efficacy of 3,4-methylenedioxymethamphetamine-assisted psychotherapy in subjects with chronic, treatment-resistant posttraumatic stress disorder: The first randomized controlled pilot study. *Journal of Psychopharmacology, 25*(4): 439–52.

67 jects with chronic, treatment-resistant posttraumatic stress disorder: The first randomized controlled pilot study. *Journal of Psychopharmacology, 25*(4): 439–52.-methylenedioxymethamphetamine ("ecstasy"). *Neuroscience, 146*(2): 509–14.

68 Wardle, M.C., & de Wit, H. (2014). MDMA alters emotional processing and facilitates positive social interaction. *Psychopharmacology, 231*: 4219–29.

69 Skomorowsky, A. (2015). How molly works in the brain. *Scientific American*. Accessed on September 13, 2015, from http://www.scientificamerican.com/article/how-molly-works-in-the-brain/

70 Willmore-Fordham, C., Krall, D.M., McCurdy, C.R., & Kinder, D.H. (2007). The hallucinogen derived from *Salvia divinorum*, salvinorin A, has κ-opioid agonist discriminative stimulus effects in rats. *Neuropharmacology, 53*: 481–86.

71 Zanos, P. & Gould, T.D. (2018). Mechanisms of ketamine action as an antidepressant. *Molecular Psychiatry, 23*(4): 801-11.

72 Bravo, G.L. (2001). What does MDMA feel like? In J. Holland (Ed.), *Ecstasy: The complete guide*. Rochester, VT: Park Street Press p. 11-21.

73 Holze, F., Vizeli, P., Muller, F., Ley, L., & Duerig, R., et al. (2020). Distinct acute effects of LSD, MDMA, and D-amphetamine in healthy subjects. *Neuropsychopharmacology, 45*: 462-71.

74 Hofmann, A. (2009). *LSD My problem child: Reflections on sacred drugs, mysticism, and science* (4th ed.) (pp. 48–50). Santa Cruz: Multidisciplinary Association for Psychedelic Studies.

75 Weil, A., & Rosen W. (2004). *From chocolate to morphine: Everything you need to know about mind-altering drugs*. Boston: Houghton Mifflin.

76 Nichols, D.E. (2004). Hallucinogens. *Pharmacology and Therapeutics, 101*(2): 131–81.

77 Levinthal, C.F. (2005). *Drugs, behavior and modern society* (4th ed.). New York: Pearson.

78 O'Brien, C.P. (2011). Drug addiction and drug abuse. In L.L. Brunton, B.A. Chabner, & B.C. Knollman, (Eds.), *Goodman & Gilman's The pharmacological basis of therapeutics* (12th ed.). New York: McGraw Hill.

79 Disbennett, B.M. (2014). An analysis of CIA and military testing on LSD on non-consenting service members and recovery through the VA disability program. *Tennessee Journal of Race, Gender, and Social Justice, 3*(2): 173–202.

80 Nichols, D.E. (2004). Hallucinogens. *Pharmacology and Therapeutics, 101*(2): 131–81.

81 Disbennett, B.M. (2014). An analysis of CIA and military testing on LSD on non-consenting service members and recovery through the VA disability program. *Tennessee Journal of Race, Gender, and Social Justice, 3*(2): 173–202.

82 Gable, R.S. (2006). The toxicity of recreational drugs. *American Scientist, 94*: 206–208.

83 Soleimani, A.S., Mehdizadeh, M., Hamedi, S.S., Artimani, T., & Joghataei, M.T. (2015). Sex differences in MDMA-induced toxicity in Sprague-Dawley rats. *Functional Neurology, 30*(2): 131–37.

84 Di Iorio, C.R., Watkins, T.J., Dietrich, M.S., Cao, A., Blackford, J.U., et al. (2011). Evidence for chronically altered serotonin function in the cerebral cortex of female 3,4-methylenedioxymethamphetamine polydrug users. *Archives of General Psychiatry, 69*(4): 399–409.

85 Liechti, M.E., Gamma, A., & Vollenweider, F.X. (2001). Gender differences in the subjective effects of MDMA. *Psychopharmacology, 154*: 161–68.

86 Global drug survey 2016. (2016). Accessed on October 6, 2016, from www.globaldrugsurvey.com

87 Gable, R.S. (2006). The toxicity of recreational drugs. *American Scientist, 94*: 206–208.

88 Morton, J. (2005). Ecstasy: Pharmacology and neurotoxicity. *Current Opinion in Pharmacology, 5*: 79–86.

89 Henry J.A., & Rella, J.G. (2001). Medical risks associated with MDMA use. In J. Holland (Ed.), *Ecstasy: The complete guide.* Rochester, VT: Park Street Press p. 11-21.

90 Van Dijken, G.D., Blom, R.E., Hene, R.J., & Boer, W.J. (2013). High incidence of mild hyponatraemia in females using ecstasy at a rave party. *Nephrology, Dialysis, and Transplant, 28*: 2277–83.

91 Ibid.

92 Ibid.

93 Weil, A., & Rosen W. (2004). *From chocolate to morphine: Everything you need to know about mind-altering drugs.* Boston: Houghton Mifflin.

94 Disbennett, B.M. (2014). An analysis of CIA and military testing on LSD on non-consenting service members and recovery through the VA disability program. *Tennessee Journal of Race, Gender, and Social Justice, 3*(2): 173–202.

95 Kuhn, C., Swartzwelder, S., & Wilson, W. (2008). *Buzzed: The straight facts about the most used and abused drugs from alcohol to ecstasy* (3rd ed.). New York: W.W. Norton & Company.

96 Patel, P.M., Patel, H.H., & Roth, D.M. (2011). General anesthetics. In L.L. Brunton, B.A. Chabner, & B.C. Knollman, (Eds.), *Goodman & Gilman's The pharmacological basis of therapeutics* (12th ed.). New York: McGraw Hill.

97 Malberg, J.E., & Bonson, K.R. (2001). How MDMA works in the brain. In J. Holland (Ed.), *Ecstasy: The complete guide.* Rochester, VT: Park Street Press. p. 11–21

98 Farre, M., Abanades, S., Roset, P.N., Peiro, A.M., Torrens, M., et al. (2007). Pharmacological interaction between 3,4-methylenedioxymethamphetamine (Ecstasy) and paroxetine: Pharmacological effects and pharmacokinetics. Journal of Phar*macology and Experimental Therapeutics, 323*(3): 954–62.

99 Nichols, D.E. (2004). Hallucinogens. *Pharmacology and Therapeutics, 101*(2): 131–81.

100 Ibid.

101 Sewell, R.A., Halpern, J.H., & Pope, H.G. (2006). Response of cluster headache to psilocybin and LSD. *Neurology, 66*: 1920–22.

102 Andersson, M., Persson, M., & Kjellgren, A. (2017). Psychoactive substances as a last resort—a qualitative study of self-treatment of migraine and cluster headaches. *Harm Reduction Journal,* 14(60): doi: 10.1186/s12954-017-0186-6.

103 Karst, M., Halpern, J.H., Bernateck, M., & Passie, T. (2010). The non-hallucinogen 2-bromo-lysergic acid diethylamide as preventative treatment for cluster headache: An open, non-randomized case series. *Cephalalgia, 30*(9): 1140–44.

104 Grob, C.S., Danforth, A.L., Chopra, G.S., Hagerty, M., McKay, C.R., et al. (2011). Pilot study of psilocybin treatment for anxiety in patients with advanced-stage cancer. *Archives of General Psychiatry, 68*(1): 71–78.

105 Gasser, P., Holstein, D., Michel, Y., Doblin, R., Yazar-Klosinski, B., Passle, T., & Brenneisen, R. (2014). Safety and efficacy of lysergic acid diethylamide-assisted

psychotherapy for anxiety associated with life-threatening diseases. *Journal of Nervous and Mental Diseases, 202*(7): 513–20.

106 Griffiths, R.R., Johnson, M.W., Carducci, M.A., Umbricht, A., & Richards, W.A., et al. (2016). Psilocybin produces substantial and sustained decreases in depression and anxiety in patients with life-threatening cancer: A randomized double-blind trial. *Journal of Psychopharmacology, 30*(12): 1181-97.

107 Gasser, P., Holstein, D., Michel, Y., Doblin, R., Yazar-Klosinski, B., Passle, T., & Brenneisen, R. (2014). Safety and efficacy of lysergic acid diethylamide-assisted psychotherapy for anxiety associated with life-threatening diseases. *Journal of Nervous and Mental Diseases, 202*(7): 513–20.

108 Nichols, D.E. (2004). Hallucinogens. *Pharmacology and Therapeutics, 101*(2): 131–81.

109 Disbennett, B.M. (2014). An analysis of CIA and military testing on LSD on non-consenting service members and recovery through the VA disability program. *Tennessee Journal of Race, Gender, and Social Justice, 3*(2): 173–202.

110 Vollenweider, F.X., & Kometer, M. (2010). The neurobiology of psychedelic drugs: Implications for the treatment of mood disorder. *Nature Reviews Neuroscience, 11*(9): 642–51.

111 Li, J-H., Vicknasingham, B., Cheung, Y-W., Zhou, W., Nurhidayat, A.W., et al. (2011). To use or not to use: An update on licit and illicit ketamine use. *Substance Abuse and Rehabilitation, 2*: 11–20.

112 Carhart-Harris, R.L., Bolstridge, M., Rucker, J., Day, C.M.J., & Erritzoe, D. (2016). Psilocybin with psychological support for treatment-resistant depression: An open-label feasibility study. *Lancet Psychiatry, 3*(7): 619–27.

113 Carhart-Harris, R.L., Roseman, L., Bolstridge, M, et al. (2017). Psilocybin for treatment-resistant depression: fMRI-measured brain mechanisms. *Scientific Reports, 7*: 13187.

114 Griffiths, R.R., Johnson, M.W., Carducci, M.A., Umbricht, A., & Richards, W.A., et al. (2016). Psilocybin produces substantial and sustained decreases in depression and anxiety in patients with life-threatening cancer: A randomized double-blind trial. *Journal of Psychopharmacology, 30*(12): 1181-97.

115 Johnson, M.W., Garcia-Romeu, A., & Griffiths, R.R. (2017). Long-term follow-up of psilocybin-facilitated smoking cessation. *American Journal of Drug and Alcohol Abuse, 43*(1): 55-60.

116 Davis, A.K., Barrett, F.S., May, D.G., Cosimano, MP., & Sepeda, N.D., et al. (2021). Effects of psilocybin assisted therapy on major depressive disorder: A randomized clinical trial. *JAMA Psychiatry, 78*(5): 481-89.

117 Mithoefer, M.C., Wagner, M.T., Mithoefer, A.T., Jerome, L., & Doblin, R. (2010). The safety and efficacy of 3,4-methylenedioxymethamphetamine-assisted psychotherapy in subjects with chronic, treatment-resistant posttraumatic stress disorder: The first randomized controlled pilot study. *Journal of Psychopharmacology, 25*(4): 439-52.

118 Mithoefer, M.C., Wagner, M.T., Mithoefer, A.T., Jerome, L., Martin, S.F., Yazar-Klosinski, B., Michel, Y., Brewerton, T.D., & Doblin, R. (2012). Durability of improvement in posttraumatic stress disorder symptoms and absence of harmful effects of drug dependency after 3,4-methylenedioxymethamphetamine-assisted psychotherapy: A prospective long-term follow-up study. *Journal of Psychopharmacology, 27*(1): 28–39.

119 Mithoefer, M.C., Feduccia, A.A., Jerome, L., Mithoefer, A., & Wager, M., et al. (2019). MDMA-assisted psychotherapy for treatment of PTSD: Study design and rationale for phase 3 trials based on pooled

analysis of six phase 2 randomized controlled trials. *Psychopharmacology,236*(9): 2735-45.

[120] Ot'alora G., M., Grigsby J., Poulter, B., Van Derveer, J.W., & Giron, S.G., et al. (2018). 3,4-methylenedioxymethamphetamine-assisted psychotherapy for treatment of chronic posttraumatic stress disorder: A randomized phase 2 controlled trial. *Journal of Psychopharmacology, 32*(12): 1295-1307.

[121] Johnson, M.W., Garcia-Romeu, A., Cosimano, M.P., & Griffiths, R.R. (2014). Pilot study of the 5HT-$_{2A}$R agonist psilocybin in the treatment of tobacco addiction. *Journal of Psychopharmacology, 28*: 983–92.

[122] Garcia-Romeu, A., Griffiths, R.R., & Johnson, M.W. (2014). Psilocybin-occasioned mystical experiences in the treatment of tobacco addiction. *Current Drug Abuse Reviews, 7*(93): 157–64.

[123] Johnson, M.W., Garcia-Romeu, A., & Griffiths, R.R. (2017). Long-term follow-up of psilocybin-facilitated smoking cessation. *American Journal of Drug and Alcohol Abuse, 43*(1): 55-60.

[124] Sessa, B. (2017). Why MDMA therapy for alcohol use disorder? And why now? *Neuropharmacology, 142*: 83-88.

[125] Garcia-Romeu, A., Griffiths, R.R., & Johnson, M.W. (2014). Psilocybin-occasioned mystical experiences in the treatment of tobacco addiction. *Current Drug Abuse Reviews, 7*(93): 157–64.

[126] Johnson, M.W., Garcia-Romeu, A., & Griffiths, R.R. (2017). Long-term follow-up of psilocybin-facilitated smoking cessation. *American Journal of Drug and Alcohol Abuse, 43*(1): 55-60.

[127] Mash, D.C., Kovera, C.A., Pablo, J., Tyndale, R.F., Ervin, F.D., Williams, I.C., Singleton, E.G., & Mayor, M. (2000). Igobaine: Complex pharmacokinetics, concerns for safety, and preliminary efficacy measures. *Annals of the New York Academy of Sciences, 914*: 394–401.

[128] Vastag, B. (2005). Ibogaine therapy: A "vast, uncontrolled experiment." *Science, 308*(5720): 345–56.

[129] Belgers, M., Leenaars, M., Homberg, J.R., Ritskes-Hoitinga, M., Schellekens, A., et al. (2016). Ibogaine and addiction in the animal model, a systematic review and meta-analysis. *Translational Psychiatry, 6*: e826.

[130] Krebs, T.S., & Johansen, P-O. (2012). Lysergic acid diethylamide (LSD) for alcoholism: Meta-analysis of randomized controlled trials. *Journal of Psychopharmacology, 26*(7): 994–1002.

[131] Das, R.K., Gale, G., Walsh, K., Hennessy, V.E., & Iskander, G., et al. (2019). Ketamine can reduce harmful drinking by pharmacologically rewriting drinking memories. *Nature Communications, 10*(5187): doi: 10.1038/s41467-019-13162-w.

[132] Lopez, G., & Zarracina, J. (2016). The fascinating, strange medical potential of psychedelic drugs, explained in 50+ studies. *Vox.* Accessed on July 15, 2016, from http://www.vox.com/2016/6/27/11544250/psychedelic-drugs-lsd-psilocybin-effects.

[133] Pontes, J., Duarte, J.A., de Pinho, P.G., Soares, M.E., Fernandes, E., et al. (2008). Chronic exposure to ethanol exacerbates MDMA-induced hyperthermia and exposes liver to severe MDMA-induced toxicity in CD1 mice. *Toxicology, 252*(1–3): 64–71.

[134] Li, J-H., Vicknasingham, B., Cheung, Y-W., Zhou, W., Nurhidayat, A.W., et al. (2011). To use or not to use: An update on licit and illicit ketamine use. *Substance Abuse and Rehabilitation, 2*: 11–20.

[135] Hoffer, A., & Osmond, J. (1967). *The hallucinogens.* New York: Academic Press.

[136] Boot, B.P., McGregor, I.S., & Hall, W. (2000). MDMA (Ecstasy) neurotoxicity: Assessing and communicating the risks. *The Lancet, 355*: 1818–21.

[137] Pontes, J., Duarte, J.A., de Pinho, P.G., Soares, M.E., Fernandes, E., et al. (2008). Chronic exposure to ethanol exacerbates MDMA-induced hyperthermia and

exposes liver to severe MDMA-induced toxicity in CD1 mice. *Toxicology, 252*(1–3): 64–71.

[138] McCardle, K., Luebbers, S., Carter, J.D., Croft, R.J., & Stough, C. (2004). Chronic MDMA (Ecstasy) use, cognition and mood. *Psychopharmacology, 173*(3–4): 434–39.

[139] MacInnes, N., Handley, S.L., & Harding, G.F.A. (2001). Former chronic methylenedioxymethamphetamine (MDMA or ecstasy) users report mild depressive symptoms. *Journal of Psychopharmacology, 15*(3): 181–86.

[140] Guillot, C., & Greenway, D. (2006). Recreational ecstasy use and depression. *Journal of Psychopharmacology, 20*(3): 411–16.

[141] Falck, R.S., Wang, J., & Carlson, R.G. (2008). Depressive symptomatology in young adults with a history of MDMA use: A longitudinal analysis. *Journal of Psychopharmacology, 22*(1): 47–54.

[142] Roiser, J.P., & Sahakian, B.J. (2004). Relationship between ecstasy use and depression: A study controlling for poly-drug use. *Psychopharmacology, 173*(3–4): 411–47.

[143] Baggott, M., & Mendelson, J. (2001). Does MDMA cause brain damage? In J. Holland (Ed.), *Ecstasy: The complete guide.* Rochester, VT: Park Street Press.

[144] McCann, U.D., Szabo, Z., Seckin, E., Rosenblatt, P, Mathews, W.B., et al. (2005). Quantitative PET studies of the serotonin transporter in MDMA users and controls using [^{11}C]McN5652 and [^{11}C]DASB. *Neuropsychopharmacology, 30*: 1741–50.

[145] Ricaurte, G.A., & McCann, U.D. (2000). (+) 3,4-Methylenedioxymethamphetamine ("ecstasy")-induced serotonin neurotoxicity: Studies in animals. *Neuropsychobiology, 42*: 5–10.

[146] Verrico, C.D., Miller, G.M., & Madras, B.K. (2007). MDMA (Ecstasy) and human DA, NE, and serotonin transporters: Implications for MDMA-induced neurotoxicity and treatment. *Psychopharmacology, 189*: 489–503.

[147] Baggott, M., & Mendelson, J. (2001). Does MDMA cause brain damage? In J. Holland (Ed.), *Ecstasy: The complete guide.* Rochester, VT: Park Street Press p. 11–21.

[148] Erritzoe, D., Frokjaer, V.G., Holst, K.K., Christofferson, M., Johansen, J.J., et al. (2011). In vivo imaging of cerebral serotonin transporter and serotonin 2A receptor binding in 3,4-methylenedioxymethamphetamine (MDMA or "Ecstasy") and hallucinogen users. *JAMA Psychiatry, 68*(6): 562–76.

[149] Wagner, D., Becker, B., Koester, P., Gouzoulis-Mayfrank E., & Daumann, J. (2012). A prospective study of learning, memory, and executive function in new MDMA users. *Addiction, 108*: 136–45.

[150] Halpern, J.H., Sherwood, A.R., Hudson, J.I., Gruber, S., Kozin, D., & Pope, H.G. (2010). *Addiction.* 2011 Apr;106(4): 777-86. doi: 10.1111/j.1360-0443.2010.03252.x. Epub 2011 Feb 15

[151] Morton, J. (2005). Ecstasy: Pharmacology and neurotoxicity. *Current Opinion in Pharmacology, 5*: 79–86.

[152] Halpern, J.H., Pope, H.G., Sherwood, A.R., Hudson, B.S., & Yurgelun-Todd, D. (2004). Residual neuropsychological effects of illicit 3,4-methylenedioxymethamphetamine (MDMA) in individuals with minimal exposure to other drugs. *Drug and Alcohol Dependency, 75* (2): 135–47.

[153] Di Iorio, C.R., Watkins, T.J., Dietrich, M.S., Cao, A., Blackford, J.U., et al. (2011). Evidence for chronically altered serotonin function in the cerebral cortex of female 3.4-methylenedioxymethamphetamine polydrug users. *Archives of General Psychiatry, 69*(4): 399–409.

[154] McCann, U.D., Szabo, Z., Seckin, E., Rosenblatt, P, Mathews, W.B., et al. (2005). Quantitative PET studies of the serotonin transporter in MDMA users and zcontrols using [^{11}C]McN5652 and [^{11}C]DASB. *Neuropsychopharmacology, 30*: 1741–50.

[155] Selvaraj, S., Hoshi, R., Bhagwagar, Z., Murthy, N.V., Hinz, R., & Cowen, P. (2009). Brain serotonin transporter binding in former users of MDMA. *British Journal of Psychiatry, 194*: 355–59.

156 Ricaurte, G.A., Hatzidimitriou, G., Cord, B.J., & McCann, U.D. (2002). Severe dopaminergic neurotoxicity in primates after a common recreational dose regimen of MDMA ("ecstasy"). *Science, 297*(5590): 2260-63.

157 Ibid.

158 Li, J-H., Vicknasingham, B., Cheung, Y-W., Zhou, W., Nurhidayat, A.W., et al. (2011). To use or not to use: An update on licit and illicit ketamine use. *Substance Abuse and Rehabilitation, 2*: 11-20.

159 Johnson, M.W., Griffiths, R.R., Hendricks, P.S., & Henningfield, J.E. (2018). The abuse potential of medical psilocybin according to the 8 factors of the Controlled Substances Act. *Neuropharmacology, 142*: 143-66.

160 Gorelick, D.A. & Balster, R.L. (2002). Phencyclidine. In K.L. Davis, D. Charney, J.T. Coyle, and C. Nemeroff (Eds.), *Neuropsychopharmacology: The fourth generation of progress*. Philadelphia: Lippincott Williams & Wilkins.

CHAPTER 7

1 Batmanabane, G. (2014). Why patients in pain cannot get "God's own medicine?" *Journal of Pharmacology and Pharmacotherapy, 5*(2): 81–82.

2 Gahlinger, P. (2004). *Illegal drugs: A complete guide to their history, chemistry, use, and abuse*. New York: Plume.

3 Weil, A., & Rosen W. (2004). *From chocolate to morphine: Everything you need to know about mind-altering drugs*. Boston: Houghton Mifflin.

4 Gahlinger, P. (2004). *Illegal drugs: A complete guide to their history, chemistry, use, and abuse*. New York: Plume.

5 Courtwright, D.T. (2001). *Dark paradise: A history of opiate addiction in America*. Cambridge, MA: Harvard University Press.

6 Gahlinger, P. (2004). *Illegal drugs: A complete guide to their history, chemistry, use, and abuse*. New York: Plume.

7 Grim, R. (2009). *This is your country on drugs: The secret history of getting high in America*. Hoboken, NJ: John Wiley and Sons.

8 Hodgson, B. (2004). *Opium: A portrait of the heavenly demon*. San Francisco: Chronicle Books.

9 Courtwright, D.T. (2001). *Dark paradise: A history of opiate addiction in America*. Cambridge, MA: Harvard University Press.

10 Ibid.

11 Marion, N.E., & Oliver, W.M. (2014). *Drugs in American society: An encyclopedia of history, politics, culture, and the law*. Santa Barbara, CA: ABC-CLIO.

12 Grim, R. (2009). *This is your country on drugs: The secret history of getting high in America*. Hoboken, NJ: John Wiley and Sons.

13 Levinthal, C.F. (2005). *Drugs, behavior and modern society* (4th ed.). New York: Pearson.

14 Courtwright, D.T. (2001). *Dark paradise: A history of opiate addiction in America*. Cambridge, MA: Harvard University Press.

15 Public Broadcasting System (PBS). (1998). Opium throughout history. Accessed on June 18, 2013, from http://www.pbs.org/wgbh/pages/frontline/shows/heroin/etc/history.html

16 Robins, L.N., Helzer, J.E., Hesselbrock, M., & Wish, E. (2010). Vietnam veterans three years after Vietnam: How our study changed our view of heroin. *American Journal on Addiction, 19*: 203–11.

17 Robins, L.N. (1993). Vietnam veterans' rapid recovery from heroin addiction: A fluke or normal expectation? *Addiction, 88*: 1041–54.

18 Ibid.

19 Ibid.

20 United Nations Office on Drugs and Crime. (2019). World drug report, 2019. United Nations publication, sales no. E.19.XI.8. Accessed from https://wdr.unodc.org/wdr2019/prelaunch/WDR19_Booklet_3_DEPRESSANTS.pdf

21 UNODC. (2019). Heroin and cocaine prices in Europe and USA. Accessed on December 6, 2019 from https://dataunodc.un.org/drugs/heroin_and_cocaine_prices_in_eu_and_usa-2017

22 UNODC. (2019). Retail and wholesale drug prices. Accessed on December 6, 2019 from https://dataunodc.un.org/drugs/prices-2017

23 Substance Abuse and Mental Health Services Administration (SAMHSA). (2020). Results from the 2019 National Survey on Drug Use and Health: Detailed tables. Rockville, MD: Center for Behavioral Health Statistics and Quality.

24 Davenport, S., Weaver, A., & Caverly, M. (2019). Economic impact of non-medical opioid use in the United States. *Society of Actuaries*. Accessed on January 12, 2020, from https://www.soa.org/globalassets/assets/files/resources/research-report/2019/econ-impact-non-medical-opioid-use.pdf

25 Manchikanti, L., Helm, S., Fellows, B., Janata, J.W., Pampati, V., Grider, J.S., & Boswell, M.V. (2012). Opioid epidemic in the United States. *Pain Physician, 15*: ES9–38.

26 Gusovsky, D. (2016). Americans consume vast majority of world's opioids. *CNBC*. Accessed on July 12, 2017, from http://www.cnbc.com/2016/04/27/americans-consume-almost-all-of-the-global-opioid-supply.html

27 Ladha, K.S., Neuman, M.D., Broms, G., Bethell, J., & Bateman, B.T., et al. (2019). Opioid prescribing after surgery in the United States, Canada, and Sweden. *JAMA Network Open, 2*(9): e1910734.

28 Krebs, E.E., Gravely, A., Nugent, S., Jensen, A.C., & DeRonne, B., et al. (2018). Effect of opioid vs nonopioid medications on pain-related function in patients with chronic back pain or hip or knee osteoarthritis pain: The SPACE randomized clinical trial. *JAMA, 319*(9): 872–82.

29 Substance Abuse and Mental Health Services Administration (SAMHSA). (2020). Results from the 2019 National Survey on Drug Use and Health: Detailed tables. Rockville, MD: Center for Behavioral Health Statistics and Quality.

30 Ibid.

31 Young, A.M., Havens, J.R., & Leukefeld, C.G. (2010). Route of administration for illicit prescription opioids: A comparison of rural and urban drug users. *Harm Reduction Journal, 7*: 24.

32 Spiller, H., Lorenz, D.J., Bailey, E.J., & Dart, R.C. (2009). Epidemiological trends in abuse and misuse of prescription opioids. *Journal of Addictive Diseases, 28*: 130–36.

33 Keyes, K.M., Cerda, M., Brady, J.E., Havens, J.R., & Galea, S. (2014). Understanding the rural-urban differences in nonmedical prescription opioid use and abuse in the United States. *American Journal of Public Health, 104*(2): e52–59.

34 Spiller, H., Lorenz, D.J., Bailey, E.J., & Dart, R.C. (2009). Epidemiological trends in abuse and misuse of prescription opioids. *Journal of Addictive Diseases, 28*: 130–36.

35 Substance Abuse and Mental Health Services Administration (SAMHSA). (2020). Results from the 2019 National Survey on Drug Use and Health: Detailed tables. Rockville, MD: Center for Behavioral Health Statistics and Quality.

36 Casteel, K. (2017). Data on drug use is disappearing just when we need it most. *FiveThirtyEight*. Accessed on December 16, 2017, from https://fivethirtyeight.com/features/data-on-drug-use-is-disappearing-just-when-we-need-it-most/

37 American Society of Addiction Medicine. (2016). Opioid addiction. Accessed on January 20, 2016, from http://www.asam.org/docs/default-source/advocacy/opioid-addiction-disease-facts-figures.pdf

38 Lipari, R.N., & Hughes, A. (2015). Trends in heroin use in the United States: 2002–2013. *SAMHSA: The CBHSQ Report*. Accessed on January 20, 2016, from http://www.samhsa.gov/data/sites/default/files/report_1943/ShortReport-1943.html

[39] Cicero, T.J., Ellis, M.S., Surratt, H.L., & Kurtz, S.P. (2014). The changing face of heroin use in the United States: A retrospective analysis of the past 50 years. *JAMA Psychiatry, 71*(7): 821–26.

[40] Hodgson, B. (2004). *Opium: A portrait of the heavenly demon.* San Francisco: Chronicle Books.

[41] QuintilesIMS. (2016). Medicine use and spending in the U.S. Accessed on March 7, 2017, from https://morningconsult.com/wp-content/uploads/2016/04/IMS-Institute-US-Drug-Spending-2015.pdf

[42] Sanders, L. (2016). Fentanyl's death toll is rising. *ScienceNews, 190*(5): 14.

[43] Burns, G., DeRienz, R.T., Baker, D.D., Casavant, M., & Spiller, H.A. (2016). Could chest wall rigidity be a factor in rapid death from illicit fentanyl abuse? *Clinical Toxicology, 54*(5): 420–23.

[44] Young, A.M., Havens, J.R., & Leukefeld, C.G. (2010). Route of administration for illicit prescription opioids: A comparison of rural and urban drug users. *Harm Reduction Journal,7:* 24.

[45] Stoeber, M., Jullie, D., Lobingier, B.T., Laeremans, T., & Steyaert, J. et al. (2018). A genetically encoded biosensor reveals location bias of opioid drug action. *Neuron, 98*(5): 963–76.

[46] Yalsh, T.L., & Wallace, M.S. (2011). Opioid analgesics and antagonists. In L. Brunton, B. Chabner, & B. Knollman (Eds.), *Goodman & Gilman's The pharmacological basis of therapeutics* (12th ed.). New York: McGraw Hill.

[47] Patrick, S.W., Schumacher, R.E., Benneyworth, B.D., Krans, E.E., McAllister, J.M., & Davis, M.M. (2012). Neonatal abstinence syndrome and associated health care expenditures. *JAMA, 307*(8): 1934–40.

[48] Ko, J.Y., Patrick S.W., Tong, V.T., Patel, R., Lind, J.M., et al. (2016). Incidence of neonatal abstinence syndrome—28 states, 1999–2013. *Morbidity and Mortality Weekly Report, 65*(31): 799–802.

[49] Volkow, N.D. (2014). America's addiction to opioids: Heroin and prescription drug abuse. Presented at the *Senate Caucus on International Narcotics Control Hearing,* May 14, 2014. Accessed on October 13, 2016, from https://www.drugabuse.gov/about-nida/legislative-activities/testimony-to-congress/2016/americas-addiction-to-opioids-heroin-prescription-drug-abuse.

[50] Jilani, S.M., Frey, M.T., Pepin, D., Jewell, T., & Jordan, M., et al. (2019). Evaluation of state-mandated reporting of neonatal abstinence syndrome—six states, 2013–2017. *MMWR, 68*(1): 6–10.

[51] Rosen, M. (2017). For babies exposed to opioids in the womb, parents may be the best medicine. *ScienceNews, 191*(11): 15–25.

[52] Ibid.

[53] Ibid.

[54] Logan, B.A., Brown, M.S., & Hayes, M.J. (2013). Neonatal abstinence syndrome: Treatment and pediatric outcomes. *Clinical Obstetrics and Gynecology, 56*(1): 186–92.

[55] Oei, J.L., Melhuish, E., Uebel, H., Azzam, N., & Breen, C., et al. (2017). Neonatal abstinence syndrome and high school performance. *Pediatrics, 139*(2): e20162651.

[56] Centers for Disease Control and Prevention. (2015). Deaths from prescription opioid overdose. Accessed on January 20, 2016, from http://www.cdc.gov/drugoverdose/data/overdose.html

[57] Centers for Disease Control and Prevention. (2020). Drug overdose deaths in the United States, 1999–2018. NCHS Data Brief, no 356. Hyattsville, MD: National Center for Health Statistics.

[58] Gomes, T., Tadrous, M., & Mamdani, M.M. (2018). The burden of opioid-related mortality in the United States. *JAMA Network Open, 1*(2): e180217.

[59] Centers for Disease Control and Prevention. (2020). Drug overdose deaths in the United States, 1999–2018. NCHS Data Brief, no 356. Hyattsville, MD: National Center for Health Statistics.

[60] CDC. (2018). Understanding the epidemic. Accessed on December 4, 2019 from https://www.cdc.gov/drugoverdose/epidemic/index.html.

[61] Hernandez, I., He M., & Brooks, M.M. et al. (2018). Exposure-response association between concurrent opioid and benzodiazepine use and risk of opioid-related overdose in Medicare Part D beneficiaries. *JAMA Network Open, 1*(2): e180919.

[62] Centers for Disease Control and Prevention. (2020). Drug overdose deaths in the United States, 1999–2018. NCHS Data Brief, no 356. Hyattsville, MD: National Center for Health Statistics.

[63] American Society of Addiction Medicine. (2016). Opioid addiction. Accessed on January 20, 2016 from http://www.asam.org/docs/default-source/advocacy/opioid-addiction-disease-facts-figures.pdf

[64] Coffin, P.O., & Sullivan, S.D. (2013). Cost-effectiveness of distributing naloxone to heroin users for lay overdose reversal. *Annals of Internal Medicine, 158*(1): 1–9.

[65] Seal, K.H., Thawley, R., Gee, L., Bamberger, J., Kral, A.H., Ciccarone, D., Downing, M., & Edlin, B.R. (2005). Naloxone distribution and cardiopulmonary resuscitation training for injection drug users to prevent hero in overdose death: A pilot study. *Journal of Urban Health, 82*(2): 308.

[66] Walley, A.Y., Xuan, Z., Hackman, H.H., Quinn, E., & Doe-Simkins, M., et al. (2013). Opioid overdose rates and implementation of overdose education and nasal naloxone distribution in Massachusetts: Interrupted time series analysis. *BMJ, 246:* f174.

[67] Stanley, T.H. (2000). Anesthesia for the 21st century. *Baylor University Medical Center Proceedings, 13*(1): 7–10.

[68] Dahlhamer, J., Lucas, J., Zelaya, Cl., Nahin, R., & Mackey, S., et al. (2018). Prevalence of chronic pain and high-impact chronic pain among adults—United States, 2016. *MMWR, 67*(36): 1001–06.

[69] Manchikanti, L., Helm, S., Fellows, B., Janata, J.W., Pampati, V., Grider, J.S., & Boswell, M.V. (2012). Opioid epidemic in the United States. *Pain Physician, 15:* ES9–38.

[70] Szalavitz, M. (2016). Opioid addiction is a huge problem, but pain prescriptions are not the cause. *Scientific American,* Accessed on October 14, 2016 from https://blogs.scientificamerican.com/mind-guest-blog/opioid-addiction-is-a-huge-problem-but-pain-prescriptions-are-not-the-cause/

[71] Brookoff, D. (1997). Interstitial cystitis and pain management. Accessed on January 22, 2016, from http://www.ic-network.com/handbook/brookoff.pdf

[72] Hamers, L. (2017). The opioid epidemic spurs a search for new, safer painkillers. *ScienceNews, 191*(11): 22.

[73] Ding, H., Kiguchi, N., Yasuda, D., Daga, P.R., & Polgar, W.E., et al. (2018). A bifunctional nociception and mu opioid receptor agonist is analgesic without opioid side effects in nonhuman primates. *Science Translational Medicine, 10*(456): 3483.

[74] Tuttle, A.H, Tohyama, S., Ramsay, T., Kimmelman, J., Schweinhardt, P., et al. (2015). Increasing placebo responses over time in United States clinical trials of neuropathic pain. *Pain, 156*(12): 2616–26.

[75] Christie, M.J. (2008). Cellular neuroadaptations to chronic opioids: Tolerance, withdrawal and addiction. *British Journal of Pharmacology, 154*(2): 384–96.

[76] Siegel, S. (1976). Morphine analgesic tolerance: Its situation specificity supports a Pavlovian conditioning model. *Science, 193*(4250): 323–25.

[77] Siegel, S., Hinson, R.E., Krank, M.D., & McCully, J. (1982). Heroin "overdose" death: contribution of drug-associated environmental cues. *Science, 216*(4544): 436–37.

[78] Trujillo, K.A. (2000). Are NMDA receptors involved in opiate-induced neural and behavioral plasticity? *Psychopharmacology, 151:* 121–41.

[79] Goode, E. (2011). *Drugs in American society* (5th ed.). NY: McGraw Hill.

80 Gahlinger, P. (2004). *Illegal drugs: A complete guide to their history, chemistry, use, and abuse.* New York: Plume.

81 Grace, P.M., Strand, K.A., Galer, E.L., Urban, D.J., Wang, X, et al. (2016). Morphine paradoxically prolongs neuropathic pain in rats by amplifying spinal NLRP3 inflammasome activation. *Proceedings of the National Academy of Science, 113*(24): E3441–50.

82 Brauser, D. (2014). Fentanyl-laced heroin deaths on the rise once again. Accessed on February 19, 2016, from http://www.medscape.com/viewarticle/837417

83 Hser, Y-I., Hoffman, V., Grella, C.E., & Anglin, D. (2001). A 33-year follow-up of narcotics addicts. *Archives of General Psychiatry, 58*: 503–08.

84 Minozzi, S., Amato, L., & Davoli, M. (2013). Development of dependence following treatment with opioid analgesics for pain relief: A systematic review. *Addiction, 108*(4): 688–98.

85 Porter, J., & Jick, J. (1980). Addiction rare in patients treated with narcotics. *New England Journal of Medicine, 302*(2): 123.

86 American Society of Addiction Medicine. (2016). Opioid addiction. Accessed on January 20, 2016, from http://www.asam.org/docs/default-source/advocacy/opioid-addiction-disease-facts-figures.pdf

87 Weil, A., & Rosen W. (2004). *From chocolate to morphine: Everything you need to know about mind-altering drugs.* Boston: Houghton Mifflin.

88 Robins, L.N., Helzer, J.E., Hesselbrock, M., & Wish, E. (2010). Vietnam veterans three years after Vietnam: How our study changed our view of heroin. *American Journal on Addiction, 19*: 203–11.

89 Alexander, B.K., Coambs, R.B., & Hadaway, P.F. (1978). The effect of housing and gender on morphine self-administration in rats. *Psychopharmacology, 58*: 175–79.

90 MacBride, K. (2017). This 38-year-old study is still spreading bad ideas about addiction. *The Outline.* Accessed on October 20, 2020, from https://theoutline.com/post/2205/this-38-year-old-study-is-still-spreading-bad-ideas-about-addiction?zd=1&zi=wjnd4loo

91 Hutchinson, M.R., Northcutt, A.L., Hiranita, T., Wang, X., Lewis, S.S., Thomas, J., et al. (2012). Opioid activation of toll-like receptor 4 contributes to drug reinforcement. *Journal of Neuroscience, 32*: 33.

92 Volkow, N.D. (2014). America's addiction to opioids: Heroin and prescription drug abuse. Presented at the *Senate Caucus on International Narcotics Control Hearing*, May 14, 2014. Accessed on October 13, 2016, from https://www.drugabuse.gov/about-nida/legislative-activities/testimony-to-congress/2016/americas-addiction-to-opioids-heroin-prescription-drug-abuse

93 Srivastava, A.B., & Gold, M.S. (2018). Naltrexone: A history and future directions. *Cerebrum, Sept.–Oct.:* cer 13–18.

94 Simon, D.L. (1997). Rapid opioid detoxification using opioid antagonists: History, theory, and the state of the art. *Journal of Addictive Diseases, 16*(1): 103–22.

95 Gowing, L., Ali, R., & White, J.M. (2010). Opioid antagonists under heavy sedation or anaesthesia for opioid withdrawal. *Cochrane Database of Systematic Reviews, 1:* CD002022.

96 Nasr, D.A., Omran, H.A., Hakim, S.M., & Mansour, W.A. (2011). Ultra-rapid opioid detoxification using dexmedetomidine under general anesthesia. *Journal of Opioid Management, 7*(5): 337–44.

97 Singh, J., & Basu, D. (2004). Ultra-rapid opioid detoxification: Current status and controversies. *Journal of Postgraduate Medicine, 50*(3): 227–32.

98 Salimi, A., Safari, F., Mohajerani, S.A., Hashemian, M., Kolahi, A.A., & Mottaghi, D. (2014). Long-term relapse of ultra-rapid opioid detoxification. *Journal of Addictive Diseases, 33*(1): 33–40.

99 Forozeshfard, M., Zoroufchi, B.H., Zafarghandi, M.B.S., Bandari, R., & Foroutan, B. (2014). Six-month follow-up study of ultrarapid opiate detoxification with naltrexone. *International Journal of High-Risk Behaviors and Addiction, 3*(4): e20944.

100 Singh, J., & Basu, D. (2004). Ultra-rapid opioid detoxification: Current status and controversies. *Journal of Postgraduate Medicine, 50*(3): 227–32.

101 CDC. (2013). Deaths and severe adverse events associated with anesthesia-assisted rapid opioid detoxification—New York City, 2012. *MMWR, 62*(38): 777–80.

102 Weiss, R.D., Potter, J.S., Fiellin, D.A., et al. (2011). Adjunctive counseling during brief and extended buprenorphine-naloxone treatment for prescription opioid dependence. *Archives of General Psychiatry, 68*(12): 1238–46.

103 Maddux, J.F., & Desmond, D.P. (1997). Outcomes of methadone maintenance 1 year after admission. *Journal of Drug Issues, 27*(2): 225–38.

104 Pierce, M., Bird, S.M., Hickman, M., Marsden, J., Dunn, G., et al. (2016). Impact of treatment for opioid dependence on fatal drug-related poisoning: A national cohort study in England. *Addiction, 111*(2): 298–308.

105 Ibid.

106 Institute for Clinical and Economic Review. (2014). Management of patients with opioid dependency: A review of clinical, delivery system, and policy options. Accessed on September 24, 2015, from http://cepac.icer-review.org/wp-content/uploads/2014/04/CEPAC-Opioid-Dependence-Final-Report-For-Posting-July-211.pdf

107 Volkow, N.D. (2014). America's addiction to opioids: Heroin and prescription drug abuse. Presented at the Senate Caucus on International Narcotics Control Hearing, May 14, 2014. Accessed on October 13, 2016, from https://www.drugabuse.gov/about-nida/legislative-activities/testimony-to-congress/2016/americas-addiction-to-opioids-heroin-prescription-drug-abuse

108 Thomas, C.P., Fullerton, C.A., Kim, M., Montejano, L., Lyman, D.R., et al. (2013). Medication-assisted treatment with buprenorphine: Assessing the evidence. *Psychiatric Services, 65*(2): 158–70.

109 NCAAD. (2016). FDA panel recommends approval of buprenorphine implant to treat addiction. Accessed on February 19, 2016, from https://www.ncadd.org/blogs/in-the-news/fda-panel-recommends-approval-of-buprenorphine-implant-to-treat-addiction

110 Oviedo-Joekes, E., Brissette, S., Marsh, D.C., Lauzon, P., Guh, D., Anis, A., & Schechter, M.T. (2009). Diacetylmorphine versus methadone for the treatment of opioid addiction. *New England Journal of Medicine, 361*(7): 777–86.

111 Rehm, J., Frick, U., Hartwig, C., Gutzwiller, F., Gschwent, P., & Uchtenhagen, A. (2005). Mortality in heroin-assisted treatment in Switzerland, 1994–2000. *Drug and Alcohol Dependence, 79*: 137–43.

112 Nosyk, B., Guh, D.P., Bansback, N.J., Oviedo-Joekes, E., Brissett, S., Marsh, D.C., Meikleham, E., Schechter, M.T., & Anis, A.H. (2012). Cost-effectiveness of diacetylmorphine versus methadone for chronic opioid dependence refractory to treatment. *Canadian Medical Association Journal, 184*(6): E317–28.

113 Patel, K. (2007). Research note: Drug consumption rooms and needle and syringe exchange programs. *Journal of Drug Issues, 37*: 737–47.

114 Hurley, S.F., Jolley, D.J., & Kaldor, J.M. (1997). Effectiveness of needle-exchange programmes for prevention of HIV infection. *Lancet, 349*(9068): 1797–800.

115 Patel, K. (2007). Research note: Drug consumption rooms and needle and syringe exchange programs. *Journal of Drug Issues, 37*: 737–47.

116 Drugs.com. (2020). Truvada prices, coupons, and patient assistance programs. Accessed on October 23, 2020, from. https://www.drugs.com/price-guide/truvada

117 Solem, C.T., Snedecor, S.J., Khachatrya, A., Nedrow, K., & Tawadrous, M., et al. (2014). Cost of treatment in a

U.S. commercially insured, HIV-1-infected population. *PLoS ONE, 9*(5): e98152.

[118] WHO. (2020). People who inject drugs. Accessed on October 23, 2020, from https://www.who.int/hiv/topics/idu/en/

[119] Palmateer, N., Kimber, J., Hickman, M., Hutchinson, S., Rhodes, T., & Goldberg, D. (2010). Evidence for the effectiveness of sterile injecting equipment provision in preventing hepatitis C and human immunodeficiency virus transmission among injecting drug users: A review of reviews. *Addiction, 105*: 844–59.

CHAPTER 8

[1] Arkowitz, J., & Lilienfeld, S.O. (2013). Can herbs ease anxiety and depression? *Scientific American Mind, 24*(3): 72–73.

[2] Chung, T., Hoffer, F.A., Connor, L., Zurakowski, D., & Burrows, P.E. (2000). The use of oral pentobarbital sodium (Nembutal) versus oral chloral hydrate in infants undergoing CT and MR imaging—A pilot study. *Pediatric Radiology, 30*(5): 332–35.

[3] Agnew, J. (2013). *Alcohol and opium in the Old West: Use, abuse and influence.* Jefferson, NC: McFarland & Company.

[4] Pepling, R. (2005). Phenobarbital. *Chemical and Engineering News, 83*(25).

[5] Lopez-Munoz, F., Ucha-Udabe, R., & Alamo, C. (2005). The history of barbiturates a century after their clinical introduction. *Neuropsychiatric Disease and Treatment, 1*(4): 329–43.

[6] Ibid.

[7] Bachhuber, M.A., Hennessy, S., Cunningham, C.O., & Starrels, J.L. (2016). Increasing benzodiazepine prescriptions and overdose mortality in the United States, 1996–2013. *American Journal of Public Health, 106*(4): 686–88.

[8] Lembke, A., Papac, J., & Humphreys, K. (2018). Our other prescription drug problem. *New England Journal of Medicine, 378*: 693–95.

[9] Substance Abuse and Mental Health Services Administration (SAMHSA). (2020). *Results from the 2019 National Survey on Drug Use and Health: Detailed tables.* Rockville. *HHS Publication no PEP19-5068.* Rockville, MD: Center for Behavioral Health Statistics and Quality.

[10] Ibid.

[11] Ilomaki, J., Paljarvi, T., Korhonen, M.J., Enlund, H., Alderman, C.P., et al. (2013). Prevalence of concomitant use of alcohol and sedative-hypnotic drugs in middle- and older aged persons: A systematic review. *Annals of Pharmacotherapy, 47*: 257–68.

[12] Olfson, M., King, M., & Schoenbaum, M. (2015). Benzodiazepine use in the United States. *JAMA Psychiatry, 72*(2): 136–42.

[13] Lembke, A., Papac, J., & Humphreys, K. (2018). Our other prescription drug problem. *New England Journal of Medicine, 378*: 693.

[14] Zhu, S., Noviello, C.M., Teng, J., Walsh, R.M., & Jim, J.J., et al. (2018). Structure of a human synaptic $GABA_A$ receptor. *Nature, 559*(7712):67–72.

[15] Belelli, D., & Lambert, J.J. (2005). Neurosteroids: Endogenous regulators of the $GABA_A$ receptor. *Nature Reviews Neuroscience, 6*: 565–75.

[16] Licata, S.C., & Rowlett, J.K. (2008). Abuse and dependence liability of benzodiazepine-type drugs: $GABA_A$ receptor modulation and beyond. *Pharmacology, Biochemistry, and Behavior, 90*(1): 74–89.

[17] Ibid.

[18] Christian, C.A., Herbert, A.G., Holt, R.L., Peng, K., Sherwood, K.D., et al. (2013). Endogenous positive allosteric modulation of GABA(A) receptors by diazepam binding inhibitor. *Neuron, 78*(6): 1063–74.

[19] Substance Abuse and Mental Health Services Administration (SAMHSA). (2012). *The DAWN Report: Highlights of the 2010 Drug Abuse Warning Network (DAWN) findings on drug-related emergency department visits.* Rockville, MD: Center for Behavioral Health Statistics and Quality.

[20] Kripke, D.F., Langer, R.D., & Kline, L.E. (2012). Hypnotics' association with mortality or cancer: a matched cohort study. *BMJ Open, 2*: e000850.

[21] Weich, S., Pearce, H.L., Croft, P., Singh, S., Crome, I., Bashford, J., & Frisher, M. (2014). Effect of anxiolytic and hypnotic drug prescriptions on mortality hazards: Retrospective cohort study. *British Medical Journal, 348*: g1996. DOI: https://doi.org/10.1136/bmj.g1996

[22] Barker, M.J., Greenwood, K.M., Jackson, M., & Crowe, S.F. (2004). Cognitive effects of long-term benzodiazepine use: A meta-analysis. *CNS Drugs, 18*(1): 37–48.

[23] Ban, L., West, J., Gibson, J.E., Fiaschi, L., & Sokal, R., et al. (2014). First trimester exposure to anxiolytic and hypnotic drugs and the risks of major congenital anomalies: A United Kingdom population-based cohort study. *PLoS One, 9*(6): e100996.

[24] Bercovici, E. (2005). Prenatal and perinatal effects of psychotropic drugs on neuro-cognitive development in the fetus. *Journal on Developmental Disabilities, 11*(2): 1–20.

[25] Ibid.

[26] American College of Obstetricians and Gynecologists (ACOG). (2009). Use of psychiatric medications during pregnancy and lactation. *ACOG Practice Bulletin, VII*(3): 385–400.

[27] Iqbal, M.M., Sobhan, T., & Ryals, T. (2002). Effects of commonly used benzodiazepines on the fetus, the neonate, and the nursing infant. *Psychiatric Services, 54*(1): 39–49.

[28] Sheehy, O., Zhao, J.-P., & Berard, A. (2019). Association between incident exposure to benzodiazepines in early pregnancy and risk of spontaneous abortion. *JAMA Psychiatry, 76*(9): 948–57.

[29] Enato, E., Moretti, M., & Koren, G. (2011). The fetal safety of benzodiazepines: An updated meta-analysis. *Journal of Obstetrics and Gynecology Canada, 33*(1): 46–48.

[30] Ban, L., West, J., Gibson, J.E., Fiaschi, L., & Sokal, R. et al. (2014). First trimester exposure to anxiolytic and hypnotic drugs and the risks of major congenital anomalies: A United Kingdom population-based cohort study. *PLoS One, 9*(6): e100996.

[31] Yonkers, K.A., Gilstad-Hayden, K., Forray, A., & Lipkind, H.S. (2017). Association of panic disorder, generalized anxiety disorder, and benzodiazepine treatment during pregnancy with risk of adverse birth outcomes. *JAMA Psychiatry, 74*(11): 1145–52.

[32] Bercovici, E. (2005). Prenatal and perinatal effects of psychotropic drugs on neuro-cognitive development in the fetus. *Journal on Developmental Disabilities, 11*(2): 1–20.

[33] Ibid.

[34] Hernandez, I., He M., Brooks, M.M., & Zhang, Y. (2018). Exposure-response association between concurrent opioid and benzodiazepine use and risk of opioid-related overdose in Medicare Part D beneficiaries. *JAMA Network Open, 1*(2)e180919.

[35] Lembke, A., Papac, J., & Humphreys, K. (2018). Our other prescription drug problem. *New England Journal of Medicine, 378*: 693.

[36] NIDA. (2021). Overdose death rates. Accessed on June 28, 2021, from https://www.drugabuse.gov/drug-topics/trends-statistics/overdose-death-rates

[37] Ibid.

[38] Bachhuber, M.A., Hennessy, S., Cunningham, C.O., & Starrels, J.L. (2016). Increasing benzodiazepine prescriptions and overdose mortality in the United States, 1996–2013. *American Journal of Public Health, 106*(4): 686–88.

[39] Lembke, A., Papac, J., & Humphreys, K. (2018). Our other prescription drug problem. *New England Journal of Medicine, 378*: 693.

[40] American Academy of Pediatrics (AAP). (2014). Let them sleep: AAP recommends delaying start times of middle and high schools to combat teen sleep deprivation. Accessed on September 11, 2014, from http://www.aap.org/en-us/about-the-aap/aap-press-room/Pages/Let-Them-Sleep-AAP-Recommends-Delaying-Start-Times-of-Middle-and-High-Schools-to-Combat-Teen-Sleep-Deprivation.aspx

[41] Ram, S., Seirawan, J., Kumar, S.J.S., & Clark, G.T. (2010). Prevalence and impact of sleep disorders and sleep habits in the United States. *Sleep and Breathing, 4*(1): 63–70.

[42] Garrison, M.M. (2015). The feedback whirlpool of early childhood sleep and behavior problems. *JAMA Pediatrics, 169*(6): 525–56.

[43] Risk, C.G., & Winzer, J.A. (2004). Impact of continuous positive airway pressure treatment on attention deficit in obstructive sleep apnea. *Chest Journal, 126*(4):1593–1602.

[44] Chang, P.P., Ford, D.E., Mead, L.A., Cooper-Patrick, L., & Klag, M.J. (1997). Insomnia in young men and subsequent depression: The Johns Hopkins Precursors Study. *American Journal of Epidemiology, 146*(2): 105–14.

[45] Baglioni, C., Battagliese, G., Feige, B., Spiegelhalder, K., Nissen, C., et al. (2011). Insomnia as a predictor of depression: A meta-analytic evaluation of longitudinal epidemiological studies. *Journal of Affective Disorders, 135*(1–3): 10–19.

[46] Jansson-Frojmark, M., & Lindblom, K. (2008). A bidirectional relationship between anxiety and depression, and insomnia? A prospective study in the general population. *Journal of Psychosomatic Research, 64*(4): 443–49.

[47] Buysse, D.J., Angst, J., Gamma, A., Jdacic, V., Eich, D., et al. (2008). Prevalence, course, and comorbidity of insomnia and depression in young adults. *Sleep, 31*(4): 473–80.

[48] Keenan, S., & Hirshkowitz, M. (2011). Monitoring and staging human sleep. In M.H. Kryger, T. Roth, & W.C. Dement (Eds.), *Principles and practice of sleep medicine,* 5th edition, (pp 1602–1609). St. Louis: Elsevier Saunders.

[49] Substance Abuse and Mental Health Services Administration (SAMHSA). (2012). *The DAWN Report: Highlights of the 2010 Drug Abuse Warning Network (DAWN) findings on drug-related emergency department visits.* Rockville, MD: Center for Behavioral Health Statistics and Quality.

[50] Substance Abuse and Mental Health Services Administration (SAMHSA). (2013). *The DAWN Report: Emergency department visits for adverse reactions involving the insomnia medication Zolpidem.* Accessed on September 11, 2014, from http://www.samhsa.gov/data/2k13/DAWN079/sr079-Zolpidem.htm

[51] Gustavsen, I., Bramness, J.G., Skurtveit, S., Engeland, A., Neutel, I, & Morland, J. (2008). Road traffic accident risk related to prescriptions of the hypnotics zopiclone, zolpidem, flunitrazepam, and nitrazepam. *Sleep Medicine, 9*(8): 818–22.

[52] U.S. Food and Drug Administration (FDA). (2013). FDA Drug Safety Communication: Risk of next-morning impairment after use of insomnia drugs; FDA requires lower recommended doses for certain drugs containing zolpidem (Ambien, Ambien CR, Edluar, and Zolpimist). Accessed on December 19, 2013, from http://www.fda.gov/downloads/Drugs/DrugSafety/UCM335007.pdf

[53] Kotz, D. (2014). Research lacking on gender differences in disease, study finds. Accessed on December 17, 2016 from https://www.bostonglobe.com/lifestyle/health-wellness/2014/03/03/research-lacking-gender-differences-disease-study-finds/HV1QWeYEm8J1Lu6KTrIW1H/story.html

[54] Greenblatt, D.J., Harmatz, J.S., Singh, N.N., et al. (2013). Gender differences in pharmacokinetics and pharmacodynamics of zolpidem following sublingual administration. *Clinical Pharmacology, 54*(3): 282–90.

[55] Saul, S. (2007). FDA warns of sleeping pill's strange effects. *The New York Times.* Accessed on December 19, 2013, from http://www.nytimes.com/2007/03/15/business/15drug.ready.html?pagewanted=all&_r=0

[56] Citrome, L. (2014). Suvorexant for insomnia: A systematic review of the efficacy and safety profile for this newly approved hypnotic—What is the number needed to treat, number needed to harm, and likelihood to be helped or harmed? *International Journal of Clinical Practice, 689*(12): 1429–41.

[57] Ku, S.-W., Lee, U., Noh, G.-J., & Mashour, G.A. (2011). Preferential inhibition of frontal to parietal feedback connectivity is a neurophysiologic correlate of general anesthesia in surgical patients. *PLoS ONE, 6*(10): e25155.

[58] Weich, S., Pearce, H.L., Croft, P., Singh, S., Crome, I., Bashford, J., & Frisher, M. (2014). Effect of anxiolytic and hypnotic drug prescriptions on mortality hazards: Retrospective cohort study. *British Medical Journal, 348*: g1996. DOI: https://doi.org/10.1136/bmj.g1996

[59] Kate, N.S., Pawar, S.S., Parkar, S.R., & Sawant, N.S. (2015). Adverse drug reactions due to antipsychotics and sedative-hypnotics in the elderly. *Journal of Geriatric Mental Health, 2*: 16–29.

[60] McKim, W.A., & Hancock, S.D. (2012). *Drugs and behavior: An introduction to behavioral pharmacology* (7th ed.). New York: Pearson.

[61] Licata, S.C., & Rowlett, J.K. (2008). Abuse and dependence liability of benzodiazepine-type drugs: $GABA_A$ receptor modulation and beyond. *Pharmacology, Biochemistry, and Behavior, 90*(1): 74–89.

[62] Substance Abuse and Mental Health Services Administration (SAMHSA). (2020). *Results from the 2019 National Survey on Drug Use and Health: Detailed tables. HHS Publication no PEP19-5068.* Rockville, MD: Center for Behavioral Health Statistics and Quality

[63] Barceloux, D.G. (2012). Gamma hydroxybutyrate and related drugs. *Medical toxicology of drug abuse: Synthesized chemicals and psychoactive plants.* Hoboken, NJ: John Wiley & Sons.

[64] Johnston, L.D., O'Malley, P.M., Meich, R.A., Bachman, J.G., & Schulenberg, J.E. (2014). *Monitoring the Future national results on adolescent drug use: Overview of key findings, 2013.* Ann Arbor: Institute for Social Research, The University of Michigan.

[65] Gahlinger, P. (2004). *Illegal drugs: A complete guide to their history, chemistry, use, and abuse.* New York: Plume.

[66] CNN. (2007). Toy contaminated with "date rape" drug pulled. Accessed on March 4, 2016, from http://www.cnn.com/2007/US/11/08/toy.recall/index.html?eref=yahoo

[67] Caputo, F., Vignoli, T., Maremmani, I., Bernardi, M., & Zoli, G. (2009). Gamma hydroxybutyric acid (GHB) for the treatment of alcohol dependence: A review. *International Journal of Environmental Research and Public Health, 6*(6): 1917–29.

[68] Leone, M.A., Vigna-Taglianti, F., Avanzi, G., Brambilla, R., & Faggiano, F. (2010). Gamma hydroxyl butyric acid (GHB) for the treatment of alcohol withdrawal and prevention of relapses. *Cochrane Database of Systematic Reviews, 2*: CD006266.

[69] Herran-Arita, A.K., Kornum, B.R., Mahlios, J., Jiang, W., Lin, L., et al. (2013). CD4+ T cell autoimmunity to hypocretin/orexin and cross-reactivity to a 2009 H1N1 influenza A epitope in narcolepsy. *Science Translational Medicine, 5*(216): 216.

[70] Hammer, H., Bader, B.M., Ehnert, C., Bundgaard, C., & Bunch, L., et al. (2015). A multifaceted $GABA_A$ receptor modulator: Functional properties and mechanism of action of the sedative-hypnotic and recreational drug methaqualone (Quaalude). *Molecular Pharmacology, 88*(2): 401–20.

[71] Yan, H., McLaughlin, E.C., & Ford, D. (2015). Bill Cosby admitted to getting Quaaludes to give to women. Accessed on October 15, 2015, from http://www.cnn.com/2015/07/07/us/bill-cosby-quaaludes-sexual-assault-allegations/

72 Patel, S., Wohlfeil, E.R., Rademacher, D.J., Carrier, E.J., & Perry, L, J. et al. (2003). The general anesthetic propofol increases brain N-arachidonylethanolamine (anandamide) content and inhibits fatty acid amid hydrolase. *British Journal of Pharmacology, 139*(5): 1005–13.

73 Stocks, G. (2011). Abuse of propofol by anesthesia providers: The case for re-classification as a controlled substance. *Journal of Addictions Nursing, 22*(1–2): 57–62.

74 Earley, P.H., & Finver, T. (2013). Addiction to propofol: A study of 22 treatment cases. *Journal of Addiction Medicine, 7*(3): 169–76.

75 Mashour, G. (2008). *In vino veritas: Anesthesia and mystical truth.* Accessed on December 2, 2013, from http://www.csahq.org/pdf/bulletin/mashour_57_1.pdf

76 Patel, P.M., Patel, H.H., & Roth, D.M. (2011). General anesthetics and therapeutic gases. In L.L. Brunton, B.A. Chabner, & B.C. Knollman, (Eds.), *Goodman & Gilman's The pharmacological basis of therapeutics* (12th ed.). New York: McGraw Hill.

77 Ibid.

78 Menhard, F.R. (2004). *The facts about inhalants.* Salt Lake City: Benchmark Books.

79 Substance Abuse and Mental Health Services Administration (SAMHSA). (2020). *Results from the 2019 National Survey on Drug Use and Health: Detailed tables.* Rockville, MD: Center for Behavioral Health Statistics and Quality.

80 Johnston, L.D., Meich, R.A., O'Malley, P.M., Bachman, J.G., & Schulenberg, J.E., et al. (2020). *Monitoring the Future: National survey results on drug use, 1975–2019.* Ann Arbor: Institute for Social Research, The University of Michigan.

81 Substance Abuse and Mental Health Services Administration (SAMHSA). (2020). *Results from the 2019 National Survey on Drug Use and Health: Detailed tables.* Rockville. *HHS Publication no PEP19-5068.* Rockville, MD: Center for Behavioral Health Statistics and Quality.

82 Howard, M.O., Bowen, S.E., Garland, E.L., Perron, B.E., & Baughn, M.G. (2011). Inhalant use and inhalant use disorders in the United States. *Addiction Science and Clinical Practice, 6*(1): 318–31.

83 Lipari, R.N. (2017). Understanding adolescent inhalant use. The CBHSQ Report, SAMHSA. Accessed on February 3, 2020, from https://www.samhsa.gov/data/sites/default/files/report_3095/ShortReport-3095.html

84 Johnston, L.D., Miech, R.A., O'Malley, P.M., Bachman, J.G., & Schulenberg, J.E., et al. (2020). Monitoring the future: National survey results on drug use 1975–2019.

85 Kann, L., McManus, T., Harris, W.A., Shanklin, S.L., & Flint, K.H., et al. (2019). Youth Risk Behavior Surveillance—United States, 2017. *MMWR, 67*(8).

86 Lowry, T.P. (1982). The inhalable nitrites may be the nearest thing to a true aphrodisiac. *Journal of Psychoactive Drugs, 14*(2): 77–79.

87 Howard, M.O., Bowen, S.E., Garland, E.L., Perron, B.E., & Baughn, M.G. (2011). Inhalant use and inhalant use disorders in the United States. *Addiction Science and Clinical Practice, 6*(1): 318–31.

88 Balster, R.L. (1998). Neural basis of inhalant abuse. *Drug and Alcohol Dependence, 51*(1–2): 207–14.

89 Levinthal, C.F. (2013). *Drugs, behavior and modern society* (8th ed.). New York: Pearson.

90 Ibid.

91 Kuhn, C., Swartzwelder, S., & Wilson, W. (2008). *Buzzed: The straight facts about the most used and abused drugs from alcohol to ecstasy* (3rd ed.). New York: W.W. Norton and Company.

92 Gahlinger, P. (2004). *Illegal drugs: A complete guide to their history, chemistry, use, and abuse.* New York: Plume.

93 Lowry, T.P. (1982). The inhalable nitrites may be the nearest thing to a true aphrodisiac. *Journal of Psychoactive Drugs, 14*(2): 77–79.

94 Mathias, R. (2002). Chronic solvent abusers have more brain abnormalities and cognitive impairments than cocaine abusers. *NIDA Notes, 17*(4). Accessed on November 21, 2013, from http://archives.drugabuse.gov/NIDA_Notes/NNVol17N4/Chronic.html

95 Howard, M.O., Bowen, S.E., Garland, E.L., Perron, B.E., & Baughn, M.G. (2011). Inhalant use and inhalant use disorders in the United States. *Addiction Science and Clinical Practice, 6*(1): 318–31.

96 Mathias, R. (2002). Chronic solvent abusers have more brain abnormalities and cognitive impairments than cocaine abusers. *NIDA Notes, 17*(4). Accessed on November 21, 2013, from http://archives.drugabuse.gov/NIDA_Notes/NNVol17N4/Chronic.html

97 Rosenberg, N.L., Grigsby, J., Dreisbach, J., Busenbark, D., & Grigsby, P. (2002). Neuropsychologic impairment and MRI abnormalities associated with chronic solvent abuse. *Clinical Toxicology, 40*(1): 21–34.

98 Ibid.

99 Ibid.

100 Ibid.

101 Mathias, R. (2002). Chronic solvent abusers have more brain abnormalities and cognitive impairments than cocaine abusers. *NIDA Notes, 17*(4). Accessed on November 21, 2013, from http://archives.drugabuse.gov/NIDA_Notes/NNVol17N4/Chronic.html

CHAPTER 9

1 Childers, S.R., & Breivogel, C.S. (1998). Cannabis and endogenous cannabinoid systems. *Drug and Alcohol Dependence, 51*(1–2): 173–87.

2 Kuhn, C., Swartzwelder, S., & Wilson, W. (2008). *Buzzed: The straight facts about the most used and abused drugs from alcohol to ecstasy* (3rd ed.). New York: W.W. Norton & Company.

3 Lee, M.A. (2012). *Smoke signals: A social history of marijuana—Medical, recreational, and scientific.* New York: Scribner.

4 Ibid.

5 National Geographic. (October 25, 2019). Marijuana throughout history. *National Geographic.*

6 Lee, M.A. (2012). *Smoke signals: A social history of marijuana—Medical, recreational, and scientific.* New York: Scribner.

7 Ibid.

8 Public Broadcasting System. (2014). Busted—America's war on marijuana. Accessed on March 7, 2016, from http://www.pbs.org/wgbh/pages/frontline/shows/dope/etc/cron.html

9 Lee, M.A. (2012). *Smoke signals: A social history of marijuana—Medical, recreational, and scientific.* New York: Scribner.

10 Ibid.

11 Ibid.

12 Caulkins, J.P., Kilmer, B., & Kleiman, M.A.R. (2016). *Marijuana legalization: What everyone needs to know* (2nd ed.). New York: Oxford University Press.

13 Marihuana Tax Act of 1937. Pub. 238, 75th Congress, 50 Stat. 551.Text found at http://www.druglibrary.org/schaffer/hemp/taxact/mjtaxact.htm

14 Schlosser, E. (2003). *Reefer madness: Sex, drugs, and the cheap labor in the American black market.* Boston: Houghton Mifflin.

15 Kushner, H.I. (2011). Historical perspectives of addiction. In B.A. Johnson (Ed.), *Addiction medicine: Science and practice, Volume 1* (pp. 75–93). New York: Springer. pp 75–93.

16 Ibid.

17 Lee, M.A. (2012). *Smoke signals: A social history of marijuana—Medical, recreational, and scientific.* New York: Scribner.

18 Nixon, R. (1971, May 26). Recorded conversation in Oval Office between R Nixon and HR Haldeman. https://www.csdp.org/research/nixonpot.txt

19 Lee, M.A. (2012). *Smoke signals: A social history of marijuana—Medical, recreational, and scientific.* New York: Scribner.

[20] Carter, J. (1977). Drug abuse message to the Congress, August 2, 1977. Accessed on March 9, 2016, from http://www.presidency.ucsb.edu/ws/?pid=7908

[21] Lee, M.A. (2012). *Smoke signals: A social history of marijuana—Medical, recreational, and scientific.* New York: Scribner.

[22] Blumenson, E., & Nilsen, E. (2010). Liberty lost: The moral case for marijuana law reform. *Indiana Law Journal, 85*(1): 1–23.

[23] Lee, M.A. (2012). *Smoke signals: A social history of marijuana—Medical, recreational, and scientific.* New York: Scribner.

[24] Ibid.

[25] World Drug Report. (2020). *Drug use and health consequences.* New York: United Nations Publications.

[26] Ibid.

[27] Lee, M.A. (2012). *Smoke signals: A social history of marijuana—Medical, recreational, and scientific.* New York: Scribner.

[28] Substance Abuse and Mental Health Services Administration (SAMHSA). (2020). *Results from the 2019 national survey on drug use and health.* Rockville, MD: Center for Behavioral Health Statistics and Quality.

[29] Substance Abuse and Mental Health Services Administration (SAMHSA). (2016). 2015 *Survey on drug use and health: Detailed tables.* Rockville, MD: Center for Behavioral Health Statistics and Quality.

[30] Substance Abuse and Mental Health Services Administration (SAMHSA). (2020). *Results from the 2019 national survey on drug use and health.* Rockville, MD: Center for Behavioral Health Statistics and Quality.

[31] Ibid.

[32] Ibid.

[33] Ibid.

[34] American Civil Liberties Union. (2020). *A tale of two countries: Racially targeted arrests in the era of marijuana reform.* Accessed on April 20, 2020, from https://www.aclu.org/report/tale-two-countries-racially-targeted-arrests-era-marijuana-reform

[35] Ibid.

[36] Richmond-Rakerd, L.S., Slutske, W.S., & Wood, P.K. (2017). Age of initiation and substance use progression: A multivariate latent growth analysis. *Psychology of Addictive Behaviors, 31*(6): 664–75.

[37] Johnston, L.D., Meich, R.A., O'Malley, P.M. Bachman, J.G., & Schulenberg, J.E., et al. (2020). *Monitoring the Future: National survey results on drug use 1975–2019.* Ann Arbor: Institute for Social Research, The University of Michigan.

[38] Ibid.

[39] Johnson, L.D., O'Malley, P.M., & Bachman, J.G. (1996). *National survey results on drug use from the Monitoring the Future study, 1975–1995.* Ann Arbor: Institute for Social Research, The University of Michigan.

[40] 2018 Cannabis Price Index. Retrieved on March 7, 2020, from http://weedindex.io/#fullstudy

[41] Drug Enforcement Agency. (2016). Drug scheduling. Accessed on March 7, 2016, from http://www.dea.gov/druginfo/ds.shtml

[42] FBI. (2020). Crime in the United States, 2019: Drug abuse violations. *FBI Uniform Crime Report.* Washington, DC: US Dept. of Justice.

[43] Ibid.

[44] American Civil Liberties Union. (2013). *The war on marijuana in black and white.* Accessed on September 26, 2014, from http://www.aclu.org/files/assets/aclu-thewar on-marijuana-rel2.pdf

[45] Ibid.

[46] Lee, M.A. (2012). *Smoke signals: A social history of marijuana—Medical, recreational, and scientific.* New York: Scribner.

[47] Reinarman, C., Cohen, P.D.A., & Kaal, H.L. (2004). The limited relevance of drug policy: Cannabis in Amsterdam and San Francisco. *American Journal of Public Health, 94*(5): 836–42.

[48] Gallup. (2020). Support for legal marijuana inches up to new high of 68 percent. Accessed on November 9, 2020, from https://news.gallup.com/poll/323582/support-legal-marijuana-inches-new-high.aspx

[49] Pew Research Center (2019). Two-thirds of Americans support marijuana legalization. Accessed on March 9, 2020, from https://www.pewresearch.org/fact-tank/2019/11/14/americans-support-marijuana-legalization/

[50] Pew Research Center. (2013). Majority now supports legalizing marijuana. Accessed on June 7, 2014, from http://www.people-press.org/files/legacy-pdf/4-4-13 percent20Marijuana percent20Release.pdf

[51] Lee, M.A. (2012). *Smoke signals: A social history of marijuana—Medical, recreational, and scientific.* New York: Scribner.

[52] Ibid.

[53] Caulkins, J.P., Hawken, A., Kilmer, B., & Kleiman, M.A.R. (2016). *Marijuana legalization: What everyone needs to know* (2nd ed.). New York: Oxford University Press.

[54] Ibid.

[55] Lee, M.A. (2012). *Smoke signals: A social history of marijuana—Medical, recreational, and scientific.* New York: Scribner.

[56] National Geographic. (October 25, 2019). Marijuana throughout history. *National Geographic.*

[57] Grotenhermen, F. (2006). Cannabinoids and the endocannabinoid system. *Cannabinoids, 1*(1): 10–14.

[58] Alger, B.E. (2013). Getting high on the endocannabinoid system. *Cerebrum* (November–December): 14.

[59] Russo, E.B., Burnett, A., Hall, B., & Parker, K.K. (2005). Agonistic properties of cannabidiol and 5-HT1a receptors. *Neurochemical Research, 30*(8): 1037–43.

[60] Russo, E., & Guy, G.W. (2006). A tale of two cannabinoids: The therapeutic rationale for combining tetrahydrocannabinol and cannabidiol. *Medical Hypotheses, 66*: 234–46.

[61] National Drug Control Strategy. (2014). Accessed on October 9, 2015, from https://www.whitehouse.gov/sites/default/files/ondcp/policy-and-research/ndcs_data_supplement_2014.pdf

[62] Lee, M.A. (2012). *Smoke signals: A social history of marijuana—Medical, recreational, and scientific.* New York: Scribner.

[63] Ibid.

[64] Spaderna, M., Addy, P.H., & D'Souza, C. (2013). Spicing things up: Synthetic cannabinoids. *Psychopharmacology, 228*(4): 525–40.

[65] Ibid.

[66] Ibid.

[67] Maron, D.F. (2015). Fake week, real crisis. *Scientific American, 313*(5): 23.

[68] Global drug survey 2016. (2016). Accessed on October 6, 2016, from www.globaldrugsurvey.com

[69] Duffy, B., Li, L., Lu, S., Durocher, L., & Dittmar, M., et al. (2020). Analysis of cannabinoid-containing fluids in illicit vaping cartridges recovered from pulmonary injury patients: Identification of vitamin E acetate as a major diluent. *Toxics, 8*(1): 8.

[70] Alger, B.E. (2013). Getting high on the endocannabinoid system. *Cerebrum* (November–December): 14.

[71] Caulkins, J.P., Kilmer, B., & Kleiman, M.A.R. (2016). *Marijuana legalization: What everyone needs to know* (2nd ed.). New York: Oxford University Press.

[72] Ridgeway, G., & Kilmer, B. (2016). Bayesian inference for the distribution of grams of marijuana in a joint. *Drug and Alcohol Dependence, 165*: 175–80.

[73] Devane, W.A., Dysarz, F.A., Johnson, M.R., Melvin, L.S., & Howlett, A.C. (1988). Determination and characterization of a cannabinoid receptor in rat brain. *Molecular Pharmacology, 34*(5): 605–13.

[74] Matsuda, L.A., Lolait, S.J., Brownstein, M.J., Young, A.C., & Bonner, T.I. (1990). Structure of a cannabinoid

receptor and functional expression of the cloned cDNA. *Nature, 346*(6284): 561–64.

75 Martin, B.R. (2002). Marijuana. In K.L. Davis, D. Charney, J.T. Coyle, & C. Nemeroff (Eds.), *Neuropsychopharmacology: The fifth generation of progress.* Philadelphia: Lippincott Williams & Wilkins.

76 Nicoll, R.A., & Alger, B.E. (2004). The brain's own marijuana. *Scientific American, 219:* 68–74.

77 Guzman, M. (2003). Cannabinoids: Potential anticancer agents. *Nature Reviews Cancer, 3:* 745–55.

78 Grant, I., Gonzalez, R., Carey, C.L., Natarajan, L., & Wolfson, T. (2003). Non-acute (residual) neurocognitive effects of cannabis use: A meta-analytic study. *Journal of the International Neuropsychological Society,* 9(5): 679–89.

79 Mechoulam, R., Panikashvili, D., & Shohami, E. (2002). Cannabinoids and brain injury: therapeutic implications. *TRENDS in Molecular Medicine,* 8(2): 58–61.

80 Vandrey, R., Umbricht, A., & Strain, E.C. (2011). Increased blood pressure following abrupt cessation of daily cannabis use. *Journal of Addiction Medicine,* 5(1): 16–20.

81 Koch, M., Varela, L., Kim, J.G., Kim, J.D., & Hernandez-Nuno, F., et al. (2015). Hypothalamic POMC neurons promote cannabinoid-induced feeding. *Nature, 519:* 45–50.

82 Alger, B.E. (2013). Getting high on the endocannabinoid system. *Cerebrum* (November–December).

83 Tanasescu, R., & Constantinescu, C.S. (2010). Cannabinoids and the immune system: An overview. *Immunobiology,* 215(8): 588–97.

84 Lee, M.A. (2012). *Smoke signals: A social history of marijuana—Medical, recreational, and scientific.* New York: Scribner.

85 Schmid, P.C., Paria, B.C., Krebsbach, R.J., Schmid, H.H., & Dey, S.K. (1997). Changes in anandamide levels in mouse uterus are associated with uterine receptivity for embryo implantation. *Proceedings of the National Academy of Sciences,* 94(8): 4188–92.

86 Schuel, H. (2006). Tuning the oviduct to the anandamide tone. *The Journal of Clinical Investigation,* 116(8): 2087–90.

87 Shamloul, R., & Bella, A.J. (2011). Impact of cannabis use on male sexual health. *Journal of Sexual Medicine,* 8: 971–75.

88 Sun, A.J., & Eisenberg, M.L. (2017). Association between marijuana use and sexual frequency in the United States: A population-based study. *Journal of Sex Medicine,* 14: 1342–47.

89 Shamloul, R., & Bella, A.J. (2011). Impact of cannabis use on male sexual health. *Journal of Sexual Medicine,* 8: 971–75.

90 Ibid.

91 Morgan, C.J.A., Schafer, G., Freeman, T.P., & Curran, H.V. (2010). Impact of cannabidiol on the acute memory and psychotomimetic effects of smoked cannabis: Naturalistic study. *British Journal of Psychiatry,* 197(4): 285–90.

92 Young, F. (1988). In the matter of marijuana rescheduling petition. Docket #86–22. US Department of Justice to the Drug Enforcement Administration. September 6, 1988. http://medicalmarijuana.procon.org/sourcefiles/Young1988.pdf

93 Ibid.

94 Gable, R.S. (2006). The toxicity of recreational drugs. *American Scientist, 94:* 206–208.

95 Greenson, T. (2013). What are you smoking? Study finds pesticides transfer to marijuana smoke. Accessed on April 14, 2014, from http://www.times-standard.com/local/news/ci_24628828/what-are-you-smoking-study-finds-pesticides-transfer

96 Advokat, C.D., Comaty, J.E., & Julien, R.M. (2014). *Julien's primer of drug action* (13th ed.). New York: Worth Publishers.

97 National Academies of Sciences, Engineering, and Medicine. (2017). *The health effects of cannabis and cannabinoids.* Washington, DC: National Academies Press.

98 Bechtold, J., Simpson, T., White, H.R., & Pardini, D. (2015). Chronic adolescent marijuana use as a risk factor for physical and mental health problems in young adult men. *Psychology of Addictive Behaviors,* 29(3): 552–63.

99 National Academies of Sciences, Engineering, and Medicine. (2017). *The health effects of cannabis and cannabinoids.* Washington, DC: National Academies Press.

100 Pletcher, M.J., Vittinghoff, E., Kalhan, R., Richman, J., Safford, M., Sidney, S., Lin, F., & Kertesz, S. (2012). Association between marijuana exposure and pulmonary function over 20 years. *JAMA,* 307(2): 173–81.

101 National Academies of Sciences, Engineering, and Medicine. (2017). *The health effects of cannabis and cannabinoids.* Washington, DC: National Academies Press.

102 Sidney, S., Beck, J.E., & Friedman, G.D. (1997). Marijuana use and mortality. *American Journal of Public Health,* 87: 585–90.

103 National Academies of Sciences, Engineering, and Medicine. (2017). *The health effects of cannabis and cannabinoids.* Washington, DC: National Academies Press.

104 Pacher, P., Batkai, S., & Kunos, G. (2006). The endocannabinoid system as an emerging target of pharmacotherapy. *Pharmacological Reviews,* 58: 389–462.

105 Burkman, L.J., Bodziak, M.L., Schuel, H., Palaszewski, D., & Gurunatha, R. (2003). Marijuana (MJ) impacts sperm function both in vivo and in vitro: Semen analysis from men smoking marijuana. American Society of Reproductive Medicine, San Antonia, Texas. October 13, 2003. http://www.ukcia.org/research/MarijuanaImpactsSpermFunction.pdf

106 Martin, B.R. (2002). Marijuana. In K.L. Davis, D. Charney, J.T. Coyle, & C. Nemeroff (Eds.), *Neuropsychopharmacology: The fifth generation of progress.* Philadelphia: Lippincott Williams & Wilkins.

107 Young-Wolff, K.C., Tucker, L-Y., Alexeeff, S., Armstrong, M.A., & Conway, A., et al. (2017). Trends in self-reported and biochemically tested marijuana use among pregnant females in California from 2009–2016. *JAMA,* 318(24): 2490–91.

108 Young-Wolff, K.C., Sarovar, V., Tucker, L-Y, Avalos, L.A., & Conway, A., et al. (2018). Association of nausea and vomiting in pregnancy with prenatal marijuana use. *JAMA,* 178(10): 1423–24.

109 National Academies of Sciences, Engineering, and Medicine. (2017). *The health effects of cannabis and cannabinoids.* Washington, DC: National Academies Press.

110 Brown, H.L., & Graves, C.R. (2013). Smoking and marijuana use in pregnancy. *Clinical Obstetrics and Gynecology,* 56(1): 107–13.

111 Dreher, M.C., Nugent, K., & Hudgins, R. (1994). Prenatal marijuana exposure and neonatal outcomes in Jamaica: An ethnographic study. *Pediatrics,* 93(2): 254–60.

112 Castle, D.J. (2013). Cannabis and psychosis: What causes what? *Medical Reports,* 5: 1.

113 Martin, B.R. (2002). Marijuana. In K.L. Davis, D. Charney, J.T. Coyle, & C. Nemeroff (Eds.), *Neuropsychopharmacology: The fifth generation of progress.* Philadelphia: Lippincott Williams & Wilkins.

114 National Academies of Sciences, Engineering, and Medicine. (2017). *The health effects of cannabis and cannabinoids.* Washington, DC: National Academies Press.

115 Di Forti, M., Quattrone, D., Freeman, T.P., Tripoli, G., & Gayer-Anderson, C., et al. (2019). The contribution of cannabis use to variation in the incidence of psychotic disorder across Europe (EU-GEI): A multicenter case-control study. *The Lancet Psychiatry,* 6(5): P427-36.

116 Andreasson, S., Allebeck, P., Engstrom, A., & Rydberg, U. (1987). Cannabis and schizophrenia: A longitudinal study of Swedish conscripts. *Lancet,* 2(8574): 1483–86.

[117] Zammit, S., Allebeck, P., Andreasson, S., Lundberg, I., & Lewis, G. (2002). Self-reported cannabis use as a risk factor for schizophrenia in Swedish conscripts of 1969: historical cohort study. *BMJ, 325:* 1199–03.

[118] Castle, D.J. (2013). Cannabis and psychosis: What causes what? *Medical Reports, 5:*1.

[119] Schiffman, J., Nakamura, B., Earleywine, M., & LaBrie, J. (2005). Symptoms of schizotypy precede cannabis use. *Psychiatry Research, 134*(1): 37–42.

[120] Frisher, M., Crome, I., Martino, O., & Croft, P. (2009). Assessing the impact of cannabis use on trends in diagnosed schizophrenia in the United Kingdom from 1996 to 2005. *Schizophrenia Research, 113*(2–3): 123–28.

[121] Iversen, L. (2003). Cannabis and the brain. *Brain, 126:* 1252–70.

[122] Bechtold, J., Simpson, T., White, H.R., & Pardini, D. (2015). Chronic adolescent marijuana use as a risk factor for physical and mental health problems in young adult men. *Psychology of Addictive Behaviors, 29*(3): 552–63.

[123] Fields, R.D. (2017). Link between adolescent pot smoking and psychosis strengthens. *Scientific American.* Accessed on December 16, 2017, from https://www.scientificamerican.com/article/link-between-adolescent-pot-smoking-and-psychosis-strengthens/

[124] National Academies of Sciences, Engineering, and Medicine. (2017). *The health effects of cannabis and cannabinoids.* Washington, DC: National Academies Press.

[125] Martin, B.R. (2002). Marijuana. In K.L. Davis, D. Charney, J.T. Coyle, & C. Nemeroff (Eds.), *Neuropsychopharmacology: The fifth generation of progress.* Philadelphia: Lippincott Williams & Wilkins.

[126] National Academies of Sciences, Engineering, and Medicine. (2017). *The health effects of cannabis and cannabinoids.* Washington, DC: National Academies Press.

[127] Solowij, N., Stephens, R.S., Roffman, R.A., Babor, T., Kaden, R., et al. (2002). Cognitive functioning of long-term heavy cannabis users seeking treatment. *JAMA, 287*(9): 1123–31.

[128] Grant, I., Gonzalez, R., Carey, C.L., Natarajan, L., & Wolfson, T. (2003). Non-acute (residual) neurocognitive effects of cannabis use: A meta-analytic study. *Journal of the International Neuropsychological Society, 9*(5): 679–89.

[129] Fried, P., Watkinson, B., James, D., & Gray, R. (2002). Current and former marijuana use: Preliminary findings of a longitudinal study of effects on IQ in young adults. *CMAJ, 166:* 887–91.

[130] Bilkei-Gorzo, Z., Albayram, O., Draffehn, A., Michel, K., Piyanova, A., et al. (2017). A chronic low dose of delta9-tetrahydrocannabinol (THC) restores cognitive function in old mice. *Nature Medicine, 23*(6): 782–87.

[131] Iversen, L. (2003). Cannabis and the brain. *Brain, 126:* 1252–70.

[132] Jackson, N.J., Isen, J.D., Khoddam, R., Irons, D., & Tuvlad, C., et al. (2016). Impact of adolescent marijuana use on intelligence: Results from two longitudinal twin studies. *PNAS, 113*(5): E500–8.

[133] D'Souza, D.C., Ranganathan, M., Braley, G., Gueorguiea, R., Zimolo, Z., et al. (2008). Blunted psychotomimetic and amnestic effects of delta-9-tetrahydrocannabinol in frequent users of cannabis. *Neuropsychopharmacology, 33:* 2505–16.

[134] Ramaekers, J.G., Kauert, G., Theunissen, E.L., Toennes, S.W., & Moeller, M.R. (2009). Neurocognitive performance during acute THC intoxication in heavy and occasional cannabis users. *Journal of Psychopharmacology, 23*(3): 266–77.

[135] Meier, M.H., Caspi, A. Ambler, A., Harrington, J., Houts, R., et al. (2012). Persistent cannabis users show neuropsychological decline from childhood to midlife. *PNAS, 109*(40): E2657–64.

[136] Meier, M.H., Caspi, A., Danese, A., Fisher, H.L., & Houts, R., et al. (2017). Associations between adolescent cannabis use and neuropsychological decline: A longitudinal co-twin control study. *Addiction, 113*(2): 257–65.

[137] Han, J., Jesner, P., Metna-Laurent, M., Duan, T., Xu, L., et al., (2012). Acute cannabinoids impair working memory through astroglial CB1 receptor modulation of hippocampal LTD. *Cell, 148:* 1039–50.

[138] Joy, J.E., Watson, S.J., & Benson, J.A. (1999). *Marijuana and medicine: Assessing the science base.* Washington, DC: National Academy Press.

[139] Hartman, R.L., Brown, T.L., Milavetz, G., Spurgin, A., Gorelick, D.A., et al. (2015). Controlled cannabis vaporizer administration: Blood and plasma cannabinoids with and without alcohol. *Clinical Chemistry, 61*(6): 850–69.

[140] Pacher, P., Batkai, S., & Kunos, G. (2006). The endocannabinoid system as an emerging target of pharmacotherapy. *Pharmacological Reviews, 58:* 389–462.

[141] Cheetham, A., Allen, M.B., Whittle, S., Simmons, J.G., & Yucel, M., et al. (2012). Orbitofrontal volumes in early adolescence predict initiation of cannabis use: A 4-year longitudinal and prospective study. *Biological Psychiatry, 71*(8): 684–92.

[142] Schweinsburg, A.D., Brown, S.A., & Tapert, S.F. (2008). The influence of marijuana use on neurocognitive functioning in adolescents. *Current Drug Abuse Reviews, 1*(1): 99–111.

[143] Grinspoon, L., & Bakalar, J.B. (1995). Marihuana as medicine: A plea for reconsideration. *JAMA, 273*(23): 1876.

[144] Asbridge, M., & Hayden, J.A. (2012). Acute cannabis consumption and motor vehicle collision risk: Systematic review of observational studies and meta-analysis. *British Medical Journal, 344:* E536.

[145] Dahlgren, M.K., Sagar, K.A., Smith, R.T., Lambros, A.M., & Kuppe, M.K., et al. (2020). Recreational cannabis use impairs driving performance in the absence of acute intoxication. *Drug and Alcohol Dependence, 208:* 107771.

[146] Rogeberg, O., & Elvik, R. (2016). The effects of cannabis intoxication on motor vehicle collision revisited and revised: Cannabis and motor vehicle collision risk. *Addiction, 111:* 1348–59.

[147] Rogeberg, O. (2019). A meta-analysis of the crash risk of cannabis-positive drivers in culpability studies—Avoiding interpretational bias. *Accident, Analysis, and Prevention, 123:* 69–78.

[148] Brands, B., Mann, R.E., Wickens, C.M. Sproule, B., & Stoduto, G., et al. (2019). Acute and residual effects of smoked cannabis: Impact on driving speed and lateral control, heart rate, and self-reported drug effects. *Drug and Alcohol Dependence, 205:* 107641.

[149] Brown, T., Banz, B., & Li, K., Camenga, D., & Vaca, F., et al. (2019). Variability of baseline vehicle control among sober young adult cannabis users: A simulator-based exploratory study. *Traffic Injury Prevention, 20*(2): S145-48.

[150] Anderson, D.M., Hansen, B., & Rees, D.I. (2013). Medical marijuana laws, traffic fatalities, and alcohol consumption. *Journal of Law and Economics, 56*(2): 333–69.

[151] Henry, K.L, Schmidt, E.A., & Caldwell, L.L. (2007). Deterioration of academic achievement and marijuana use onset among rural adolescents. *Health Education Research, 22:* 372–84.

[152] Lynskey, M., & Hall, W. (2000). The effects of adolescent cannabis use on educational attainment: A review. *Addiction, 95:* 1621–30.

[153] National Academies of Sciences, Engineering, and Medicine. (2017). *The health effects of cannabis and cannabinoids.* Washington, DC: National Academies Press.

[154] National Academy of Sciences, Engineering, and Medicine. (2017). *The health effects of cannabis and cannabinoids: The current state of evidence and recommendations*

for research. Washington, DC. The National Academies Press.

155 Golub, A., & Johnson, B.D. (2001). Variation in youthful risks of progression from alcohol and tobacco to marijuana and to hard drugs across generations. *American Journal of Public Health, 91*(2): 225–32.

156 Caulkins, J.P., Kilmer, B., & Kleiman, M.A.R. (2016). *Marijuana legalization: What everyone needs to know* (2nd ed.). New York: Oxford University Press.

157 Nutt, D. (2013). The potential of LSD, heroin, marijuana and other controlled substances in brain research. *Scientific American.* Accessed on January 21, 2014, from http://blogs.scientificamerican.com/guest-blog/2013/11/27/the-potential-of-lsd-heroin-marijuana-and-other-controlled-substances-in-brain-research/

158 National Academies of Sciences, Engineering, and Medicine. (2017). *The health effects of cannabis and cannabinoids*. Washington, DC: National Academies Press.

159 Ibid.

160 Yanes, J.A., McKinnell, Z.E., Reid, M.A., Busler, J.N., & Michel, J.S., et al. (2019). Effects of cannabinoid administration for pain: A meta-analysis and meta-regression. *Experimental Clinical Psychopharmacology, 27*(4): 370–82.

161 Finnerup, N.B., Attal, N., Haroutounian, S., McNicol, E., & Baron, R., et al. (2015). Pharmacotherapy for neuropathic pain in adults: A systematic review and meta-analysis. *Lancet Neurology, 14*(2): 162–73.

162 Elikottil, J., Gupta, P., & Gupta, K. (2009). The analgesic potential of cannabinoids. *Journal of Opioid Management, 5*(6): 341–57.

163 Ibid.

164 Hill, K.P., Palastro, M.D., Johnson, B., & Ditre, J.W. (2017). Cannabis and pain: A clinical review. *Cannabis and Cannabinoid Research, 2*(1): 96–104.

165 Alger, B.E. (2013). Getting high on the endocannabinoid system. *Cerebrum* (November–December): 14

166 Dietrich, A., & McDaniel, W.F. (2004). Endocannabinoids and exercise. *British Journal of Sports Medicine, 38*: 536–41.

167 Fuss, J., Steinle, J., Bindila, L., Auer, M.K., & Kirchherr, H. (2015). A runner's high depends on cannabinoid receptors in mice. *PNAS, 112*(42): 13105–08.

168 Bushlin, I., Rozenfeld, R., & Devi, L.A. (2010). Cannabinoid-opioid interactions during neuropathic pain and analgesia. *Current Opinion in Pharmacology, 10*(1): 80–86.

169 McPartland, J.M. (2013). Care and feeding of the endocannabinoid system. *O'Shaughnessy's, Winter/Spring*: 5–6.

170 Epilepsy Research UK. (2016). Third phase trial completed for cannabidiol epilepsy treatment. Accessed on December 21, 2017, from https://www.epilepsyresearch.org.uk/third-phase-trial-completed-for-cannabidiol-epilepsy-treatment/

171 Devinsky, O., Marsh, E., Friedman, Thiele, E., Laux, L., et al. (2015). Cannabidiol in patients with treatment-resistant epilepsy: An open-label interventional trial. *Lancet, 15*(3): 270–78.

172 Press, C.A., Knupp, K.G., & Chapman, K.E. (2015). Parental reporting of response to oral cannabis extracts for treatment of refractory epilepsy. *Epilepsy Behavior, 45*: 49–52.

173 Devinsky, O., Marsh, E., Friedman, Thiele, E., & Laux, L., et al. (2015). Cannabidiol in patients with treatment-resistant epilepsy: An open-label interventional trial. *Lancet,* DOI: 10.1016/S1474-4422(15)00379-78.

174 Devinsky, O., Cross, J.H., Laux, L., Marsh, E., Miller, I., et al. (2017). Trial of cannabidiol for drug-resistant seizures in the Dravet syndrome. *New England Journal of Medicine, 376*: 2011–20.

175 Iversen, L. (2003). Cannabis and the brain. *Brain, 126*: 1252–70.

176 National Academies of Sciences, Engineering, and Medicine. (2017). *The health effects of cannabis and cannabinoids*. Washington, DC: National Academies Press.

177 Schleider, L.B.-L., Mechoulam, R., Lederman, V., Hilou, M., Lencovsky, O., et al. (2018). Prospective analysis of safety and efficacy of medical cannabis in large unselected population of patients with cancer. *European Journal of Internal Medicine, 49*: 37–43.

178 National Academies of Sciences, Engineering, and Medicine. (2017). *The health effects of cannabis and cannabinoids*. Washington, DC: National Academies Press.

179 Chen, A.L.C., Chen, T.J.H., Braverman, E.R., Acuri, V., Kerner, M., et al. (2008). Hypothesizing that marijuana smokers are at a significantly lower risk of carcinogenicity relative to tobacco-non-marijuana smokers: Evidenced based on statistical reevaluation of current literature. *Journal of Psychoactive Drugs, 40*(3): 263–72.

180 Munson, A.E., Harris, L.S., Friedman, M.A., Dewey, W.L., & Carchman, R.A. (1975). Antineoplastic activity of cannabinoids. *Journal of the National Cancer Institute, 55*(3): 597–602.

181 McAllister, S.D., Murase, R., Christian, R.T., Lau, D., Zielinski, A.J., et al. (2011). Pathways mediating the effects of cannabidiol on the reduction of breast cancer cell proliferation, invasion and metastasis. *Breast Cancer Research and Treatment, 129*(10): 37–47.

182 Casanova, M.L., Blazquez, C., Martinez-Palacio, J., Villanueva, C., Fernandez-Acenero, M.J. Guzman, M., et al. (2003). Inhibition of skin tumor growth and angiogenesis in vivo by activation of cannabinoid receptors. *Journal of Clinical Investigations, 111*(1): 43–50.

183 Guzman, M. (2006). A pilot clinical study of delta(9)-tetrahydrocannabinol in patients with recurrent glioblastoma multiforme. *British Journal of Cancer, 95*: 197–203.

184 Dumitru, C.A., Sandalcioglu, I.E., & Karsak, M. (2019). Cannabinoids in glioblastoma therapy: New applications for old drugs. *Frontiers in Molecular Neuroscience, 11*: 159.

185 Liang, C., McClean, M.D., Marsit, C., Christensen, B., Peters, E. Nelson, J.J., & Kelsey, K.T. (2009). A population-based case control study of marijuana use and head and neck squamous cell carcinoma. *Cancer Prevention Research, 2*(8): 759–68.

186 Hermanson, D.J., & Marnett, L.J. (2011). Cannabinoids, endocannabinoids and cancer. *Cancer Metastasis Review, 30*(3–4): 599–612.

187 Sledzinski, P., Zeyland, J., & Slomski, R., et al. (2018). The current state and future perspectives of cannabinoids in cancer biology. *Cancer Medicine, 7*(3): 765–75.

188 Pacher, P., Batkai, S., & Kunos, G. (2006). The endocannabinoid system as an emerging target of pharmacotherapy. *Pharmacological Reviews, 58*: 389–462.

189 Hashibe, M., Strait, K., Tashkin, D.P., Morgenstern, H., Greenland, S., & Zhang, Z-F. (2005). Epidemiologic review of marijuana use and cancer risk. *Alcohol, 35*: 265–75.

190 National Academies of Sciences, Engineering, and Medicine. (2017). *The health effects of cannabis and cannabinoids*. Washington, DC: National Academies Press.

191 Mechoulam, R., Panikashvili, D., & Shohami, E. (2002). Cannabinoids and brain injury: therapeutic implications. *TRENDS in Molecular Medicine, 8*(2): 58–61.

192 Ibid.

193 Pacher, P., Batkai, S., & Kunos, G. (2006). The endocannabinoid system as an emerging target of pharmacotherapy. *Pharmacological Reviews, 58*: 389–462.

194 Consroe, P., Musty, R., Rein, J., Tillery, W., & Pertwee, R. (1997). The perceived effects of smoked cannabis on patients with multiple sclerosis. *European Neurology, 38*(1): 44–48.

195 Corey-Bloom, J., Wolfson, T., Gamst, A., Jim, S., Marcotte, T.D., Bentley, J., & Gouaux, B. (2012). Smoked cannabis for spasticity in multiple sclerosis:

A randomized, placebo-controlled trial. *CMAJ, 184*(10): 1143–50.

[196] National Academies of Sciences, Engineering, and Medicine. (2017). *The health effects of cannabis and cannabinoids*. Washington, DC: National Academies Press.

[197] Eubanks, L.M., Rogers, C.J., Beuscher, A.E., Koob, G.F., Dickerson, T.J., & Janda, K.D. (2006). A molecular link between the active component of marijuana and Alzheimer's disease pathology. *Molecular Pharmacology, 3*(6): 773–77.

[198] Ramirez, B.G., Blazquez, C., del Pulgar T.G., Guzman, M., & de Ceballos, M.L. (2005). Prevention of Alzheimer's disease pathology by cannabinoids: Neuroprotection mediated by blockade of microglial activation. *The Journal of Neuroscience, 25*(8): 1904–13.

[199] National Academies of Sciences, Engineering, and Medicine. (2017). *The health effects of cannabis and cannabinoids*. Washington, DC: National Academies Press.

[200] Bilkei-Gorzo, Z., Albayram, O., Draffehn, A., Michel, K., Piyanova, A., et al. (2017). A chronic low dose of delta9-tetrahydrocannabinol (THC) restores cognitive function in old mice. *Nature Medicine, 23*(6): 782–87.

[201] Penner, E.A., Buettner, J., & Mittleman, M.A. (2013). The impact of marijuana use on glucose, insulin, and insulin resistance among US adults. *American Journal of Medicine, 126*(7): 583–89.

[202] Rajavashisth, T.B., Shaheen, M., Norris, K.C., Pan, D., Sinha, S.K., Ortega, J., & Friedman, T.C. (2012). Decreased prevalence of diabetes in marijuana users: cross-sectional data from the National Health and Nutrition Examination Survey (NHANES) III. *BMJ Open, 2*(1): 1–9.

[203] McPartland, J.M., (2013). Care and feeding of the endocannabinoid system. *O'Shaughnessy's. Winter/Spring*:5–6.

[204] Campos, A.C., Moreira, F.A., Gomes, F.V., Del Bel, E.A., & Guimaraes, F.S. (2012). Multiple mechanisms involved in the large-spectrum therapeutic potential of cannabidiol in psychiatric disorders. *Philosophical Transactions of the Royal Society B, 367*: 3364–78.

[205] Jiang, W., Zhang, Y., Xiao, L., Van Cleemput, J., Ji, S.P., et al. (2005). Cannabinoids promote embryonic and adult hippocampus neurogenesis and produce anxiolytic and antidepressant like effects. *Journal of Clinical Investigations, 115*(11): 3104–16.

[206] Serra, G., & Fratta, W. (2007). A possible role for the endocannabinoid system in the neurobiology of depression. *Clinical Practice and Epidemiology in Mental Health, 3*: 25.

[207] Denson, T.F., & Earleywine, M. (2006). Decreased depression in marijuana users. *Addictive Behaviors, 31*: 738–42.

[208] Cuttler, C., Spradlin, A., & McLaughlin, R.J. (2018). A naturalistic examination of the perceived effects of cannabis on negative affect. *Journal of Affective Disorders, 235*(1): 198–205.

[209] Lee, M.A. (2012). *Smoke signals: A social history of marijuana—Medical, recreational, and scientific*. New York: Scribner.

[210] Lenza, M. (2007). Toking their way sober: Alcoholics and marijuana as folk medicine. *Contemporary Justice Review, 10*(3): 307–22.

[211] Peters, D.C. (2013). Patients and caregivers report using medical marijuana to decrease prescription narcotics use. *Humboldt Journal of Social Relations, 35*: 24–40.

[212] Vigil, J.M., Stith, S.S., Adams, I.M., & Reeve, A.P. (2017). Associations between medical cannabis and prescription opioid use in chronic pain patients: A preliminary cohort study. *PLoS ONE, 129*(11): e0187795.

[213] Bradford, A.C., & Bradford, W.D. (2016). Medical marijuana laws reduce prescription medication use in Medicare Part D. *Health Affairs, 35*(7): 1230–36.

[214] Reiman, A., Welty, M., & Solomon, P. (2017). Cannabis as a substitute for opioid-based pain medication: Patient self report. *Cannabis and Cannabinoid Research, 2*(1):160–66.

[215] Boehnke, K.F., Litina, E., & Clauw, D.J. (2016). Medical cannabis use is associated with decreased opiate medication use in a retrospective cross-sectional survey of patients with chronic pain. *Journal of Pain, 17*(6):739–44.

[216] Purcell, C., Davis, A., Moolman, N., & Taylor, S.M. (2019). Reduction of benzodiazepine use in patients prescribed medical cannabis. *Cannabis and Cannabinoid Research, 4*(3): 214–18.

[217] Lucas, P., & Walsh, Z. (2017). Medical cannabis access, use, and substitution for prescription opioids and other substances: A survey of authorized medical cannabis patients. *International Journal of Drug Policy, 42*:30–35.

[218] Kruger, D.J., & J.S. Kruger. (2019). Medical cannabis users' comparisons between medical cannabis and mainstream medicine. *Journal of Psychoactive Drugs, 51*(1):31–36.

[219] Corroon, J.M., Mischley, L.K., & Sexton, M. (2017). Cannabis as a substitute for prescription drugs—a cross-sectional study. Journal of Pain Research, 10:989–98.

[220] Bradford, A.C., & Bradford, W.D. (2016). Medical marijuana laws reduce prescription medication use in Medicare Part D. *Health Affairs, 35*(7): 1230–36.

[221] Lucas, P., & Walsh, Z. (2017). Medical cannabis access, use, and substitution for prescription opioids and other substances: A survey of authorized medical cannabis patients. *International Journal of Drug Policy, 42*:30–35.

[222] Kruger, D.J., & J.S. Kruger. (2019). Medical cannabis users' comparisons between medical cannabis and mainstream medicine. *Journal of Psychoactive Drugs, 51*(1):31–36.

[223] Bechtold, J., Simpson, T., White, H.R., & Pardini, D. (2015). Chronic adolescent marijuana use as a risk factor for physical and mental health problems in young adult men. *Psychology of Addictive Behaviors, 29*(3): 552–63.

[224] Joy, J.E., Watson, S.J., & Benson, J.A. (1999). *Marijuana and medicine: Assessing the science base*. Washington, DC: National Academy Press.

[225] Tanda, G., & Goldberg, S.R. (2003). Cannabinoids: Reward, dependence and underlying neurochemical mechanisms—A review of recent preclinical data. *Psychopharmacology, 169*: 115–34.

[226] Ibid.

[227] Cressey, D. (2015). The cannabis experiment. *Nature, 524*: 280–83.

[228] Caulkins, J.P., Kilmer, B., & Kleiman, M.A.R. (2016). *Marijuana legalization: What everyone needs to know* (2nd ed.). New York: Oxford University Press.

[229] National Academies of Sciences, Engineering, and Medicine. (2017). *The health effects of cannabis and cannabinoids*. Washington, DC: National Academies Press.

[230] Budney, A.J., Roffman, R., Stephens, R.S., & Walker, D. (2007). Marijuana dependence and its treatment. *Addiction Science and Clinical Practice, 4*(1): 4–16.

[231] Substance Abuse and Mental Health Services Administration (SAMHSA). (2020). *Results from the 2019 national survey on drug use and health*. Rockville, MD: Center for Behavioral Health Statistics and Quality.

[232] Ibid.

[233] Ibid.

[234] Lee, M.A. (2012). *Smoke signals: A social history of marijuana—medical, recreational, and scientific*. New York: Scribner.

[235] Budney, A.J., Roffman, R., Stephens, R.S., & Walker, D. (2007). Marijuana dependence and its treatment. *Addiction Science and Clinical Practice, 4*(1): 4–16.

[236] Tanda, G., & Goldberg, S.R. (2003). Cannabinoids: Reward, dependence and underlying neurochemical mechanisms—A review of recent preclinical data. *Psychopharmacology, 169*: 115–34.

[237] Anthony, J.V., Warner, L.A., & Kessler, R.C. (1994). Comparative epidemiology of dependence on tobacco,

alcohol, controlled substances and inhalants: Basic findings from the National Comorbidity Survey. *Experimental and Clinical Psychopharmacology, 2*: 244–68.

[238] Ibid.

[239] Budney, A.J., Roffman, R., Stephens, R.S., & Walker, D. (2007). Marijuana dependence and its treatment. *Addiction Science and Clinical Practice, 4*(1): 4–16.

[240] Budney, A.J., Roffman, R., Stephens, R.S., & Walker, D. (2007). Marijuana dependence and its treatment. *Addiction Science and Clinical Practice, 4*(1): 4–16.

CHAPTER 10

[1] Faulkner, J.M. (1933). Nicotine poisoning by absorption through the skin. *JAMA, 100*(21):1664–65.

[2] Travell, J. (1960). Absorption of nicotine from various sites. *Annals of the New York Academy of Sciences, 90*: 13–30.

[3] Martin, T. (2020). Smoking statistics from around the world. Accessed on May 1, 2020, from https://www.verywellmind.com/global-smoking-statistics-2824393

[4] Naff, C.F. (2007). *Nicotine and tobacco*. San Diego, CA: Reference Point Press.

[5] Wagner, H.L. (2003). *Nicotine*. Philadelphia: Chelsea House Publishers.

[6] Ibid.

[7] Gately, I. (2001). *Tobacco: A cultural history of how an exotic plant seduced civilization*. New York: Grove Press.

[8] Ibid.

[9] Wagner, H.L. (2003). *Nicotine*. Philadelphia: Chelsea House Publishers.

[10] Gately, I. (2001). *Tobacco: A cultural history of how an exotic plant seduced civilization*. New York: Grove Press.

[11] Wagner, H.L. (2003). *Nicotine*. Philadelphia: Chelsea House Publishers.

[12] Gately, I. (2001). *Tobacco: A cultural history of how an exotic plant seduced civilization*. New York: Grove Press.

[13] Ibid.

[14] Wagner, H.L. (2003). *Nicotine*. Philadelphia: Chelsea House Publishers.

[15] Ibid.

[16] Gately, I. (2001). *Tobacco: A cultural history of how an exotic plant seduced civilization*. New York: Grove Press.

[17] Ibid.

[18] Capehart, T.C. (2001). *Trends in the cigarette industry after the Master Settlement Agreement*. Washington, DC: U.S. Department of Agriculture, Economic Research Service.

[19] U.S. Department of Health and Human Services. (2014). *The health consequences of smoking—50 years of progress: A report of the Surgeon General*. Atlanta, GA: Centers for Disease Control and Prevention.

[20] OpenSecrets.org. (2020). Center for Responsive Politics. Accessed on May 4, 2020, from http://www.opensecrets.org/industries/lobbying.php?cycle=2020&ind=A02

[21] Drope, J., Schluger, N., Cahn, Z., Drope, J., & Hamill, S., et al. (2018). The Tobacco Atlas, 6th edition. Atlanta: American Cancer Society and Vital Strategies.

[22] World Health Organization. (2020). Prevalence of tobacco smoking. Accessed on May 1, 2020, from https://www.who.int/gho/tobacco/use/en/

[23] Eriksen, M., Mackay, J., Schluger, N., Gomeshtapeh, F.I., & Drope, J. (2015). *The tobacco atlas* (5th ed.). Atlanta, GA: American Cancer Society.

[24] Roberts, M. (2014). Smoker numbers edge close to one billion. *BBC Online*. Accessed on October 22, 2015, from http://www.bbc.com/news/health-25635121

[25] Substance Abuse and Mental Health Services Administration (SAMHSA). (2020). *Results from the 2019 National Survey on Drug Use and Health*. Rockville, MD: Center for Behavioral Health Statistics and Quality.

[26] Ibid.

[27] Mirbolouk, M., Charkhchi, P., Kianoush, S., Uddin, I., & Orimoloye, O.A., et al. (2018). Prevalence and distribution of e-cigarette use among U.S. adults: Behavioral risk factor surveillance system, 2016. *Annals of Internal Medicine, 169*(7): 429–38.

[28] Ibid.

[29] Truth Initiative. (2019). Accessed on May 1, 2020, from https://truthinitiative.org/sites/default/files/media/files/2020/02/Truth_E-Cigarette_FactSheet 202019_Update_010920.pdf

[30] Wang, T.W., Asman, K., Gentzke, A.S., Cullen, K.A., & Holder-Hayes, E., et al. (2018). Tobacco product use among adults—United States, 2017. *MMWR, 67*: 1225–32.

[31] Substance Abuse and Mental Health Services Administration (SAMHSA). (2014). *Results from the 2013 National Survey on Drug Use and Health: Summary of national findings*. NSDUH Series H-41, HHS Publication no (SMA) 11-4658. Rockville, MD: Substance Abuse and Mental Health Services Administration.

[32] Substance Abuse and Mental Health Services Administration (SAMHSA). (2020). *Results from the 2019 national survey on drug use and health*. Rockville, MD: Center for Behavioral Health Statistics and Quality.

[33] Ibid.

[34] Johnston, L.D., Miech, R.A., O'Malley, P.M., Bachman, J.G., & Schulenberg, J.E., et al. (2020). Monitoring the future: National survey results on drug use 1975–2019. Ann Arbor: Institute for Social Research, The University of Michigan.

[35] Schnohr, C.W., Kreiner, S., Rasmussen, M., Due, P., Currie, C., & Diderichsen, F. (2008). The role of national policies intended to regulate adolescent smoking in explaining the prevalence of daily smoking: A study of adolescents from 27 European countries. *Addiction, 103*: 824–31.

[36] Johnston, L.D., Miech, R.A., O'Malley, P.M., Bachman, J.G., & Schulenberg, J.E et al. (2020). Monitoring the future: National survey results on drug use 1975–2019. Ann Arbor: Institute for Social Research, The University of Michigan.

[37] Naff, C.F. (2007). *Nicotine and tobacco*. San Diego, CA: Reference Point Press.

[38] Anda, R.F., Croft, J.B., Felitti, V.J., Nordenberg, D., Giles, W.H, Williamson, D.F., & Giovino, G.A. (1999). Adverse childhood experiences and smoking during adolescence and adulthood. *JAMA, 282*(17): 1652–58.

[39] Wagner, H.L. (2003). *Nicotine*. Philadelphia: Chelsea House Publishers.

[40] Centers for Disease Control and Prevention. (2017). Tobacco use in top-grossing movies—United States, 2010–2016. *MMWR, 66*(26): 681–86.

[41] Belluzzi, J.D., Lee, A.G., Oliff, H.S., & Leslie, F.M. (2004). Age-dependent effects of nicotine on locomotor activity and conditioned place preference in rats. *Psychopharmacology, 174*: 389–95.

[42] Levin, E.D., Rezvani, A.H., Montoya, D., Rose, J.E., & Swartzwelder, H.S. (2003). Adolescent-onset nicotine self-administration modeled in female rats. *Psychopharmacology, 169*: 141–49.

[43] Kandel, E.R., & Kandel, D.B. (2014). A molecular basis for nicotine as a gateway drug. *New England Journal of Medicine, 371*(10: 932–43.

[44] Perkins, K.A., Karelitz, J.L., & Boldry, M.C. (2017). Nicotine acutely enhances reinforcement from non-drug rewards in humans. *Frontiers in Psychiatry, 8*: 65.

[45] Tobacco Free Kids. (2020). The global cigarette industry. Accessed on May 2, 2020, from https://www.tobaccofreekids.org/assets/global/pdfs/en/Global_Cigarette_Industry_pdf.pdf

[46] Hirsig, R.J. (2009). *Cigarette taxes, prices, and sales*. Sacramento, CA: State Board of Equalization. Accessed on March 4, 2013, from http://www.boe.ca.gov/news/cigarette_price_effects_d2.pdf

[47] Fair Reporters. (2015). Prices of cigarettes by state. Accessed on October 22, 2015, from *fairreporters.net/health/prices-of-cigarettes-by-state/*

[48] Eriksen, M., Mackay, J., & Ross, H. (2012). *The tobacco atlas* (4th ed.). Atlanta, GA: American Cancer Society.

[49] Thomas, K & Kaplan, S. (2019). E-cigarettes went unchecked in 10 years of federal inaction. *The New York Times*. Accessed on April 29, 2020, from https://www.nytimes.com/2019/10/14/health/vaping-e-cigarettes-fda.html

[50] FDA. (2019). How could lowering nicotine levels in cigarettes change the future of public health? Accessed on April 29, 2020, from https://www.fda.gov/tobacco-products/public-health-education/how-could-lowering-nicotine-levels-cigarettes-change-future-public-health#reference.

[51] Apelberg, B.J., Feirman, S.P., Salazar, E., Ambrosse, B.K., & Paredes, A., et al. (2018). Potential public health effects of reducing nicotine levels in cigarettes in the United States. *New England Journal of Medicine, 378*: 1725–33.

[52] Thomas, K & Kaplan, S. (2019). E-cigarettes went unchecked in 10 years of federal inaction. *The New York Times*. Accessed on April 29, 2020, from https://www.nytimes.com/2019/10/14/health/vaping-e-cigarettes-fda.html

[53] CDC. (2019). Economic trends in tobacco. Accessed on May 2, 2020, from https://www.cdc.gov/tobacco/data_statistics/fact_sheets/economics/econ_facts/index.htm

[54] Gilpin, E.A., Pierce, J.P., & Rosebrook, B. (1997). Are adolescents receptive to current sales promotion practices of the tobacco industry? *Preventive Medicine, 26*: 14–21.

[55] CDC. (2019). Economic trends in tobacco. Accessed on May 2, 2020, from https://www.cdc.gov/tobacco/data_statistics/fact_sheets/economics/econ_facts/index.htm

[56] Loukas, A., Paddock, E.M., Li, X, Harrell, M.B., & Pasch, K.E., et al. (2019). Electronic nicotine delivery systems marketing and initiation among youth and young adults. *Pediatrics, 144*(3): e20183601.

[57] Gilpin, E.A., Pierce, J.P., & Rosebrook, B. (1997). Are adolescents receptive to current sales promotion practices of the tobacco industry? *Preventive Medicine, 26*: 14–21.

[58] Pierce, J.P., Gilpin, E., Burns, D.M., Whalen, E., Rosebrook, B., Shopland, D., & Johnson, M. (1991). Does tobacco advertising target young people to start smoking? Evidence from California. *JAMA, 11*(22): 3154–58.

[59] Henriksen, L., Schleicher, N.C., Feighergy, E.C., & Fortmann, S.P. (2010). A longitudinal study of exposure to retail advertising and smoking initiation. *Pediatrics, 126*(2): 232–38.

[60] Yerger, V.B., Przewoznik, J., & Malone, R.E. (2007). Racialized geography, corporate activity, and health disparity: Tobacco industry targeting of inner cities. *Journal of Health Care for the Poor and Underserved, 18*(4): 10–38.

[61] Wagner, H.L. (2003). *Nicotine*. Philadelphia: Chelsea House Publishers.

[62] Naff, C.F. (2007). *Nicotine and tobacco*. San Diego, CA: Reference Point Press.

[63] DiFranza, J.R., Richards, J.W., Paulman, P.M., Wolf-Gillespie, N., Fletcher, C., Jaffe, R.D., & Murray, D. (1991). RJR Nabisco's cartoon camel promotes Camel cigarettes to children. *JAMA, 266*(22): 3149–53.

[64] Fischer, P.M., Schwartz, M.P., Richards, J.W., Goldstein, A.O., & Rojas, T.H. (1991). Brand logo recognition by children aged 3 to 6 years: Mickey Mouse and Old Joe the Camel. *JAMA, 266*(22): 3145–48.

[65] Henriksen, L., Dauphine, A.L., Wang, Y., & Fortmann, S.P. (2006). Industry sponsored anti-smoking ads and adolescent reactance: Test of a boomerang effect. *Tobacco Control, 15*(1): 13–18.

[66] Farrelly, M.C., Davis, K.C., Haviland, L., Messeri, P., & Healton, C.G. (2005). Evidence of a dose-response relationship between "truth" antismoking ads and youth smoking prevalence. *American Journal of Public Health, 95*(3): 425–31.

[67] Holtgrave, D.R., Wunderink, K.A., Vallone, D.M., & Healton, C.G. (2009). Cost-utility analysis of the National Truth Campaign to prevent youth smoking. *American Journal of Preventive Medicine, 36*(5): 385–88.

[68] Tynan, M.A., Polansky, J.R., Driscoll, D., Garcia, C., & Glantz, S.A. (2019). Tobacco use in top-grossing movies—United States, 2010–2018. *MMWR, 68*(43): 974–78.

[69] Ibid.

[70] Wagner, H.L. (2003). *Nicotine*. Philadelphia: Chelsea House Publishers.

[71] Sargent, J.D., Beach, M.L., Dalton, M.A., Mott, L.A., Tickle, J.J., Ahrens, M.B., & Heatherton, T.F. (2001). Effect of seeing tobacco use in films on trying smoking among adolescents: Cross sectional study. *British Medical Journal, 323*: 1–6.

[72] Heatherton, T.F., & Sargent, J.D. (2009). Does watching smoking in movies promote teenage smoking? *Current Directions in Psychological Science, 18*(2): 63–67.

[73] World Health Organization. (2015). *Smoke-free movies: From evidence to action* (3rd ed.). Accessed on May 3, 2016, from http://apps.who.int/iris/bitstream/10665/190165/1/9789241509596_eng.pdf?ua=1

[74] Centers for Disease Control and Prevention. (2017). Tobacco use in top-grossing movies—United States, 2010–2016. *MMWR, 66*(26): 681–86.

[75] Dalton, M.A., Sargent, J.D., Beach, M.L., Titus-Ernstoff, L., Gibson, J.J., Ahrens, M.B., Tickle, J.J., & Heatherton, T.F. (2003). Effect of viewing smoking in movies on adolescent smoking initiation: A cohort study. *The Lancet, 362*(9380): 281–85.

[76] Heatherton, T.F., & Sargent, J.D. (2009). Does watching smoking in movies promote teenage smoking? *Current Directions in Psychological Science, 18*(2): 63–67.

[77] World Health Organization. (2016). Films showing smoking scenes should be rated to protect children from tobacco addiction. Accessed on May 3, 2016, from http://www.who.int/mediacentre/news/releases/2016/protect-children-from-tobacco/en/

[78] Dalton, M.A., Sargent, J.D., Beach, M.L., Titus-Ernstoff, L., Gibson, J.J., Ahrens, M.B., Tickle, J.J., & Heatherton, T.F. (2003). Effect of viewing smoking in movies on adolescent smoking initiation: A cohort study. *The Lancet, 362*(9380): 281–85.

[79] Wagner, D.D., Cin, S.D., Sargent, J.D., Kelley, W.M., & Heatherton, T.F. (2011). Spontaneous action representation in smokers when watching movie characters smoke. *Journal of Neuroscience, 31*(3): 894–98.

[80] Eriksen, M., Mackay, J., Schluger, N., Gomeshtapeh, F.I., & Drope, J. (2015). *The tobacco atlas* (5th ed.). Atlanta, GA: American Cancer Society.

[81] Nova Online. (2001). Anatomy of a cigarette. Accessed on April 11, 2013, from http://www.pbs.org/wgbh/nova/cigarette/anat_text.html

[82] Wagner, H.L. (2003). *Nicotine*. Philadelphia: Chelsea House Publishers.

[83] Ibid.

[84] Connolly, G.N., Alpert, H.R., Wayne, G.F., & Koh, H. (2007). Trends in nicotine yield in smoke and its relationship with design characteristics in US cigarette brands, 1997–2005. *Tobacco Control, 16*(5): e5.

[85] Kozlitina, J., Risso, D., Lansu, K., Olsen, R.H.J., & Sainz, E., et al. (2019). An African-specific haplotype in MRGPRX4 is associated with menthol cigarette smoking. *PLoS Genetics*, https://doi.org/10.1371/journal.pgen.1007916.

[86] Ibid.

[87] Truth Initiative. (2019). Accessed on May 1, 2020, from https://truthinitiative.org/sites/default/files/media/files/2020/02/Truth_E-Cigarette_FactSheet 202019_Update_010920.pdf

[88] Time to address a burning issue. (2019). *Nature, 570*: 415

[89] Truth Initiative. (2019). Accessed on May 1, 2020, from https://truthinitiative.org/sites/default/files/media/files/2020/02/Truth_E-Cigarette_FactSheet 202019_Update_010920.pdf

90 Kaplan, S. (2021). Juul to pay $40 million to settle N.C. vaping case. *The New York Times*. Accessed on June 29, 2021 from https://www.nytimes.com/2021/06/28/health/juul-vaping-settlement-north-carolina.html

91 Richtel, M. (2021). Youth vaping declined sharply for second year, new data show *The New York Times*. Accessed on October 1, 2021 from https://www.nytimes.com/2021/09/30/health/youth-vaping-decline.html?referringSource=articleShare.

92 Sleiman, M., Logue, J.M., Montesinos, V.N, Russell, M.L., Litter, M.I., et al. (2016). Emissions from electronic cigarettes: Key parameters affecting the release of harmful chemicals. *Environmental Science and Technology, 50*(17): 9644–51.

93 Krishnan-Sarin, S., Morean, M., Kong, G., Bold, K.W., Camenga, D.R., et al. (2017). E-cigarettes and "dripping" among high-school youth. *Pediatrics, 139*(3): e20163224.

94 Lundback, M., Antoniewicz, L., Brynedal, A., & Bosson, J. (2017). Acute effects of active e-cigarette inhalation on arterial stiffness. *European Respiratory Journal, 50*: OA1979. DOI: 10.1183/1393003.congress-2017.OA1979

95 Park, S.J., Walser, T.C., Perdomo, C., Wang, T., Pagano, P.C., et al. (2014). The effect of e-cigarette exposure on airway epithelial cell gene expression and transformation. *Clinical Cancer Research, 20*: B16.

96 Food and Drug Administration. (2010). E cigarettes: Questions and answers. Accessed on April 26, 2013, from http://www.fda.gov/forconsumers/consumerupdates/ucm225210.htm

97 SAMHSA. (2020). *Results from the 2019 national survey on drug use and health*. Rockville, MD: Center for Behavioral Health Statistics and Quality.

98 Benowitz, N.L., & Henningfield, J.E. (2013). Reducing the nicotine content to make cigarettes less addictive. *Tobacco Control, 22*(suppl 1): i14–i17.

99 Leao, R.M., Cruz, F.C., Vendruscolo, L.F., de Guglielmo, G., Logrip, M.L., et al. (2015). Chronic nicotine activates stress/reward-related brain regions and facilitates the transition to compulsive alcohol drinking. *Journal of Neuroscience, 35*(15): 6241–53.

100 Kandel, E.R., & Kandel, D.B. (2014). A molecular basis for nicotine as a gateway drug. *New England Journal of Medicine, 371*(10: 932–43.

101 Feduccia, A.A., Chatterjee, S., & Bartlett, S.E. (2012). Neuronal nicotinic acetylcholine receptors: Neuroplastic changes underlying alcohol and nicotine addictions. *Frontiers in Molecular Neuroscience, 5*: 83.

102 Hibbs, R.E., & Zambon, A.C. (2011). Agents acting at the neuromuscular junction and autonomic ganglia. In L.L. Brunton, B.A. Chabner, & B.C. Knollman, (Eds.), *Goodman & Gilman's The pharmacological basis of therapeutics* (12th ed.). New York: McGraw Hill.

103 McClernon, F. J., Hiott, F. B., Westman, E. C., Rose, J. E., & Levin, E. D. (2006). Transdermal nicotine attenuates depression symptoms in nonsmokers: A double-blind, placebo-controlled trial. *Psychopharmacology, 189*: 125–33.

104 Salin-Pascual, R.J., & Drucker-Colin, R. (1996). A novel effect of nicotine on mood and sleep in major depression. *Neuroreport, 9*(1): 57–60.

105 Cole, D.M., Beckmann, C.F., Long, C.J., Matthews, P.M., Durcan, M.J., et al. (2010). Nicotine replacement in abstinent smokers improves cognitive withdrawal symptoms with modulation of resting brain network dynamics. *NeuroImage, 52*(2): 590–99.

106 Potter, A.S., & Newhouse, P.A. (2008). Acute nicotine improves cognitive deficits in young adults with attention-deficit/hyperactivity disorder. *Pharmacology, Biochemistry, and Behavior, 88*(4):407–17.

107 Eriksen, M., Mackay, J., Schluger, N., Gomeshtapeh, F.I., & Drope, J. (2015). *The tobacco atlas* (5th ed.). Atlanta, GA: American Cancer Society.

108 CDC. (2019). Smoking and tobacco use: Fast Facts. Accessed on May 4, 2020, from https://www.cdc.gov/tobacco/data_statistics/fact_sheets/fast_facts/index.htm

109 Zeltner, T., Kessler, D.A., Martiny, A., & Randera, F. (2000). *Tobacco company strategies to undermine tobacco control activities at the World Health Organization*. Report of the Committee of Experts on Tobacco Industry Documents. Geneva: WHO.

110 Centers for Disease Control and Prevention. (2015). Health effects of cigarette smoking. Accessed on October 22, 2015, from http://www.cdc.gov/tobacco/data_statistics/fact_sheets/health_effects/effects_cig_smoking/

111 U.S. Department of Health and Human Services. (2020). Smoking cessation: A report of the Surgeon General. Atlanta, GA: U.S. Department of Health and Human Services, Centers for Disease Control and Prevention, National Center for Chronic Disease Prevention and Health Promotion, Office on Smoking and Health.

112 CDC. (2018). Tobacco related mortality. Accessed on May 4, 2020, from https://www.cdc.gov/tobacco/data_statistics/fact_sheets/health_effects/tobacco_related_mortality/index.htm

113 Naff, C.F. (2007). *Nicotine and tobacco*. San Diego, CA: Reference Point Press.

114 Verhovek, S.H. (1998, January 4). Word for word/last meals: For the condemned in Texas, cheeseburgers without mercy. *The New York Times*. Accessed on May 3, 2016, from http://www.nytimes.com/1998/01/04/weekinreview/word-for-word-last-meals-for-the-condemned-in-texas-cheeseburgers-without-mercy.html

115 U.S. Department of Health and Human Services. (2014). *The health consequences of smoking—50 years of progress: A report of the Surgeon General*. Atlanta, GA: Centers for Disease Control and Prevention.

116 Eriksen, M., Mackay, J., & Ross, H. (2012). *The tobacco atlas* (4th ed.). Atlanta, GA: American Cancer Society.

117 Morita, A. (2007). Tobacco smoke causes premature skin aging. *Journal of Dermatological Science, 48*: 169–75.

118 Centers for Disease Control and Prevention. (2017). Leading causes of death. Accessed on May 4, 2020, from https://www.cdc.gov/nchs/fastats/leading-causes-of-death.htm

119 Siegel, R.L., Jacobs, E.J., Newton, C.C., Feskanich, D., Freedman, N.D., et al. (2015). Deaths due to cigarette smoking for 12 smoking related cancers in the U.S. *JAMA Internal Medicine, 175*(9): 1574–76.

120 Gately, I. (2001). *Tobacco: A cultural history of how an exotic plant seduced civilization*. New York: Grove Press.

121 Alexandrove, L.B., Ju, Y.S., Haase, K., Loo, P.V., Martincorena, I., et al. (2016). Mutational signatures associated with tobacco smoking in human cancer. *Science, 354* (6312): 618–22.

122 Ye, Y.N., Liu, E.S., Shin, V.Y., Wu, W.K., Luo, J.C., & Cho, C.H. (2004). Nicotine promoted colon cancer growth via epidermal growth factor receptor, c-SRC, and 5-lipoxygenase-mediated signal pathway. *Journal of Pharmacology and Experimental Therapeutics, 308*(1): 66–72.

123 Natori, T., Sata, M., Washida, M., Hirata, Y., Nagai, R., & Makuuchi, M. (2003). Nicotine enhances neovascularization and promotes tumor growth. *Molecules & Cells, 16*(2): 143–46.

124 Siegel, R.L., Jacobs, E.J., Newton, C.C., Feskanich, D., Freedman, N.D., et al. (2015). Deaths due to cigarette smoking for 12 smoking related cancers in the U.S. *JAMA Internal Medicine, 175*(9): 1574–76.

125 SAMHSA. (2020). *Results from the 2019 national survey on drug use and health*. Rockville, MD: Center for Behavioral Health Statistics and Quality.

126 Ibid.

127 Chang, G-Q., Karatayev, O., & Leibowitz, S.F. (2013). Prenatal exposure to nicotine stimulates neurogenesis or orexigenic peptide expressing neurons in hypothalamus and amygdala. *Journal of Neuroscience, 33*: 13600–11.

[128] Gately, I. (2001). *Tobacco: A cultural history of how an exotic plant seduced civilization.* New York: Grove Press.

[129] Levinthal, C.F. (2005). *Drugs, behavior and modern society* (4th ed.). New York: Pearson.

[130] Sleiman, M., Gundel, L.A., Pankow, J.F., Jacob, P., Singer, B.C., & Destaillats, H. (2010). Formation of carcinogens indoors by surface-mediated reactions of nicotine with nitrous acid, leading to potential thirdhand smoke hazards. *PNAS, 107*(15): 6576–81.

[131] Centers for Disease Control and Prevention. (2018). Secondhand smoke. *CDC vital signs.* Accessed on May 5, 2020, from https://www.cdc.gov/tobacco/basic_information/secondhand_smoke/index.htm

[132] Ibid.

[133] Ibid.

[134] Kawachi, I., Colditz, G.A., Speizer, F.E., Manson, J.E., Stampfer, M.J., Willett, W.C., & Hennekens, C.H. (1997). A prospective study of passive smoking and coronary heart disease. *Circulation, 95*: 2374–79.

[135] Oberg, M., Jaakkola, M.S., Woodward, A., Peruga, A., & Pruss-Ustun, A. (2011). Worldwide burden of disease from exposure to second-hand smoke: A retrospective analysis of data from 192 countries. *The Lancet, 377*(9760): 139–46.

[136] Asomaning, K., Miller, D.P., Liu, G., Wain, J.C., Lynch, T.J., et al. (2008). Second-hand smoke, age of exposure, and lung cancer risk. *Lung Cancer 61*(1): 13–20.

[137] Barnes, D.E., & Bero, L.A. (1998). Why review articles on the health effects of passive smoking reach different conclusions. *JAMA, 279*(19): 1566–70.

[138] Tong, E.K., & Glantz, S.A. (2007). Tobacco industry efforts undermining evidence linking secondhand smoke with cardiovascular disease. *Circulation, 116*(6): 1845–54.

[139] Centers for Disease Control and Prevention. (2009). Reduced hospitalizations for acute myocardial infarction after implementation of a smoke-free ordinance—City of Pueblo, Colorado, 2002–2006. *MMWR, 57*(51 & 52): 1373–77.

[140] Naiman, A., Glazier, R.H., & Moineddin, R. (2010). Association of anti-smoking legislation with rates of hospital admission for cardiovascular and respiratory conditions. *CMAJ, 182*(8): 761–67. DOI: 10.1503/cmaj.091130.

[141] Gahlinger, P. (2004). *Illegal drugs: A complete guide to their history, chemistry, use, and abuse.* New York: Plume.

[142] Ksir, C., Hart, C.L., & Ray, O. (2006). *Drugs, society, and human behavior* (11th ed.). Boston: McGraw Hill.

[143] DiFranza, J.R., Rigotti, N.A., McNeill, A.D., Ockene, J.K., Savageau, J.A., St. Cyr, D., & Coleman, M. (2000). Initial symptoms of nicotine dependence in adolescents. *Tobacco Control, 9*: 313–19.

[144] Scragg, R., Wellman, R.J., Laugesen, M., & DeFranza, J.R. (2008). Diminished autonomy over tobacco can appear with the first cigarette. *Addictive Behaviors, 33*(5): 689–98.

[145] Naff, C.F. (2007). *Nicotine and tobacco.* San Diego, CA: Reference Point Press.

[146] Hayashi, T., Ko, J.H., Strafella, A.P., & Dagher, A. (2013). Dorsolateral prefrontal and orbitofrontal cortex interactions during self-control of cigarette craving. *PNAS, 110*(11): 4165–66.

[147] U.S. Department of Health and Human Services. (2020). Smoking cessation: A report of the Surgeon General. Atlanta, GA: U.S. Department of Health and Human Services, Centers for Disease Control and Prevention, National Center for Chronic Disease Prevention and Health Promotion, Office on Smoking and Health.

[148] Gallup Poll. (2016). Tobacco and smoking. Accessed on December 16, 2016, from http://www.gallup.com/poll/1717/tobacco-smoking.aspx

[149] U.S. Department of Health and Human Services. (2020). Smoking cessation: A report of the Surgeon General. Atlanta, GA: U.S. Department of Health and Human Services, Centers for Disease Control and Prevention, National Center for Chronic Disease Prevention and Health Promotion, Office on Smoking and Health.

[150] Drope, J., Schluger, N., Cahn, Z., Drope, J., & Hamill, S., et al. (2018). The Tobacco Atlas, 6th edition. Atlanta: American Cancer Society and Vital Strategies.

[151] Kotz, D., Brown, J., & West, R. (2014). Real-world effectiveness of smoking cessation treatments. *Addiction, 109*(3): 491–99.

[152] Global Nicotine Cessation Market. (2019). Accessed on May 6, 2020, from https://www.prnewswire.com/news-releases/global-nicotine-cessation-market-report-2019-market-was-valued-at-usd-15-77-billion-in-2018-and-is-expected-to-grow-at-a-cagr-of-14-37-300956588.html.

[153] Bullen, C., Howe, C., Laugesen, M., McRobbie, J., Parag, V., et al. (2013). Electronic cigarettes for smoking cessation: A randomized controlled trial. *The Lancet, 382*(9905): 1629–37.

[154] Brown, J., Beard, E., Kotz, D., Michie, S., & West, R. (2014). Real-world effectiveness of e-cigarettes when used to aid smoking cessation: A cross-sectional population study. *Addiction, 109*(9): 1531–40.

[155] Hajek, P., Phillips-Waller, A., Przulj, D., Pesola, F., & Smith, K.M., et al. (2018). A randomized trial of e-cigarettes versus nicotine-replacement therapy. *New England Journal of Medicine, 380*: 629–37.

[156] Grana, R., Benowitz, N., & Glantz, S.A. (2014). E-cigarettes: A scientific review. *Contemporary Reviews in Cardiovascular Medicine, 129*: 1972–86.

[157] Grana, R.A., Popova, L., & Ling, P.M. (2014). A longitudinal analysis of electronic cigarette use and smoking cessation. *JAMA Internal Medicine, 174*(5): 812–13.

[158] Vickerman, K.A., Carpenter, K.M., Altman, T., Nash, C.M., & Zbikowski, S.M. (2013). Use of electronic cigarettes among state tobacco cessation quitline callers. *Nicotine and Tobacco Research, 15*(10): 1789–91.

[159] Weaver, S.R., Huang, J., Pechacek, T.F., Heath, J.W., & Ashley, D.L., et al. (2018). Are electronic nicotine delivery systems helping cigarette smokers quit? Evidence from a prospective cohort study of U.S. adult smokers, 2015–2016. *PLoS One, 13*(7): e0198047.

[160] Tavernese, S. (2014, February 22). A hot debate over e-cigarettes as a path to tobacco, or from it. *The New York Times.* Accessed on February 24, 2014, from http://www.nytimes.com/2014/02/23/health/a-hot-debate-over-e-cigarettes-as-a-path-to-tobacco-or-from-it.html?_r=0

[161] The Truth Initiative. (2019). Accessed on May 1, 2020, from https://truthinitiative.org/sites/default/files/media/files/2020/02/Truth_E-Cigarette_FactSheet 202019_Update_010920.pdf

[162] Levinthal, A.M., Strong, D.R., Kirkpatrick, M.G., Unger, J.B., Sussman, S., et al. (2015). Association of electronic cigarette use with initiation of combustible tobacco product smoking in early adolescence. *JAMA, 314*(7): 700–07.

[163] Goldenson, N.I., Leventhal, A.M., Stone, M.D., et al. (2017). Associations of electronic cigarette nicotine concentration with subsequent cigarette smoking and vaping levels in adolescents. *JAMA Pediatrics, 171*(12): 1192–99.

[164] Jorenby, D.E., Hays, J.T., Rigotti, N.A., Azoulay, S., Watsky, E.J., et al. (2006). Efficacy of varenicline, an α4β2 nicotinic acetylcholine receptor partial agonist vs placebo or sustained-release bupropion for smoking cessation. *JAMA, 296*(1): 56.

[165] Wagner, H.L. (2003). *Nicotine.* Philadelphia: Chelsea House Publishers.

[166] Johnson, M.W., Garcia-Romeu, A., & Griffiths, R.R. (2017). Long-term follow-up of psilocybin-facilitated smoking cessation. *American Journal of Drug and Alcohol Abuse, 43*(1): 55–60.

[167] Kotz, D., Brown, J., & West, R. (2014). Real-world effectiveness of smoking cessation treatments. *Addiction, 109*(3): 491–99.

168 Carmody, T.P., Duncan, C., Simon, J.A., Sokowitz, S., Huggins, J., Lee, S., & Delucchi, K. (2008). Hypnosis for smoking cessation: A randomized trial. *Nicotine and Tobacco Research, 10*(5): 811–18.

169 Primack, B.A., Gold, M.A., Land, S.R., & Fine, M.J. (2006). Association of cigarette smoking and media literacy about smoking among adolescents. *Journal of Adolescent Health, 39*: 465–72.

170 Brewer, N.T., Hall, M.G., Noar, S.M., Paraa, H., Stein-Seroussi, A., et al. (2016). Effect of pictorial cigarette pack warnings on changes in smoking behavior: A randomized clinical trial. *JAMA Internal Medicine, 176*(7): 905–12.

171 Bower, B. (2014). The addiction paradox. *Science News, 185*(6). Accessed on March 10, 2015, from https://www.sciencenews.org/article/addiction-paradox

172 Wagner, H.L. (2003). *Nicotine.* Philadelphia: Chelsea House Publishers.

CHAPTER 11

1 Weinberg, B.A., & Bealer, B.K. (2002). *The world of caffeine: The science and culture of the world's most popular drug.* New York: Routledge.

2 Ibid.

3 Ibid.

4 National Coffee Association. (2020). National coffee data trends report. Accessed on May 18, 2020, from https://www.ncausa.org/Industry-Resources/Market-Research/NCDT.

5 Weinberg, B.A., & Bealer, B.K. (2002). *The world of caffeine: The science and culture of the world's most popular drug.* New York: Routledge.

6 Breed, T. (2010). Tea consumers, tea trade, and colonial cultivation. Accessed on February 17, 2016, from https://www.lib.umn.edu/bell/tradeproducts/tea

7 Weinberg, B.A., & Bealer, B.K. (2002). *The world of caffeine: The science and culture of the world's most popular drug.* New York: Routledge.

8 Ibid.

9 Fredholm, B.B., Battig, K., Holmen, J., Nehlig, A., & Zvartau, E.E. (1999). Actions of caffeine in the brain with special reference to factors that contribute to its widespread use. *Pharmacological Reviews, 51*(1): 83–133.

10 Ibid.

11 Euromonitor. (2013). The top 50 coffee consuming countries. Accessed on December 15, 2016, from http://www.caffeineinformer.com/caffeine-what-the-world-drinks

12 Ferdman, R.A. (2014). Where the world's biggest tea drinkers are. Accessed on December 15, 2016, from http://qz.com/168690/where-the-worlds-biggest-tea-drinkers-are/#int/words=dinner_supper&smoothing=3

13 World Atlas. (2016). Countries with the highest levels of soft drink consumption. Accessed on December 15, 2016, from http://qz.com/168690/where-the-worlds-biggest-tea-drinkers-are/#int/words=dinner_supper&smoothing=3

14 McCarthy, N. (2015). The world's biggest chocolate consumers. Accessed on December 15, 2016, from http://www.forbes.com/sites/niallmccarthy/2015/07/22/the-worlds-biggest-chocolate-consumers-infographic/#39d5d13e12b8

15 Weinberg, B.A., & Bealer, B.K. (2002). *The world of caffeine: The science and culture of the world's most popular drug.* New York: Routledge.

16 Mitchell, D.C., Knight, C.A., Hockenberrry, J., Teplansky, R., & Hartman, T.J., (2014). Beverage caffeine intakes in the U.S. *Food and Chemical Toxicology, 63*: 136–42.

17 Ibid.

18 Frary, C.D., Johnson, R.K., & Wang, M.Q. (2005). Food sources and intakes of caffeine in the diets of persons in the United States. *Journal of the American Dietetic Association, 105*: 110.

19 Weinberg, B.A., & Bealer, B.K. (2002). *The world of caffeine: The science and culture of the world's most popular drug.* New York: Routledge.

20 Mitchell, D.C., Knight, C.A., Hockenberrry, J., Teplansky, R., & Hartman, T.J., (2014). Beverage caffeine intakes in the U.S. *Food and Chemical Toxicology, 63*: 136–42.

21 Reyes, C.M., & Cornelis, M.C. (2018). Caffeine in the diet: Country-level consumption and guidelines. *Nutrients, 10*(11): 1772.

22 Statista. (2020). Soft Drinks. Accessed on May 18, 2020, from https://www.statista.com/outlook/20020000/109/soft-drinks/united-states#market-revenue

23 Statista. (2020). Per capita consumption of coffee beans in US, in pounds. Accessed on May 19, 2020, from https://www.statista.com/statistics/184212/per-capita-consumption-of-coffee-in-the-us-since-2000/

24 Ahluwalia, N., Herrick, K., Moshfegh, A., & Rybak, M. (2014). Caffeine intake in children in the United States and 10-year trends: 2001–2010. *American Journal of Clinical Nutrition,* DOI: 10.3945/ajcn.113.082172

25 Ahluwalia, N., & Herrick K. (2015). Caffeine intake from food and beverage sources and trends among children and adolescents in the United States: Review of national quantitative studies from 1999 to 2011. *Advances in Nutrition, 6*(1): 102–11.

26 Beans, J. (2020). Coffee Statistics. Accessed on May 17, 2020, from https://myfriendscoffee.com/usa-coffee-statistics/

27 Statista. (2020). Coffee market in the U.S.—statistics and facts. Accessed on May 16, 2020, from https://www.statista.com/topics/1248/coffee-market/

28 Miller, K.E. (2008). Energy drinks, race, and problem behaviors among college students. *Journal of Adolescent Health, 43*: 490–97.

29 Arria, A.M., Caldeira, K.M., Bugbee, B.A., et al. (2017). Trajectories of energy drink consumption and subsequent drug use during young adulthood. *Drug and Alcohol Dependence, 179*: 424–32.

30 Weinberg, B.A., & Bealer, B.K. (2002). *The world of caffeine: The science and culture of the world's most popular drug.* New York: Routledge.

31 Wright, G., Baker, D., Palmer, M., Stabler, D., Power, E., Borland, A., & Stevenson, P. (2013). Caffeine in floral nectar enhances a pollinator's memory of reward. *Science, 339*(6124): pp. 1202–04.

32 Ibid.

33 McKim, W.A., & Hancock, S. (2012). *Drugs and behavior: An introduction to behavioral pharmacology* (7th ed.). New York: Pearson.

34 Tea Association of the U.S.A. (2015). Tea fact sheet. Accessed on May 24, 2016, from http://www.teausa.com/14655/tea-fact-sheet

35 Generali, J.A. (2013). Energy drinks: Food, dietary supplement, or drug? *Hospital Pharmacy, 48*(1): 5–9.

36 Weinberg, B.A., & Bealer, B.K. (2002). *The world of caffeine: The science and culture of the world's most popular drug.* New York: Routledge.

37 Yang, A., Palmer, A.A., & de Wit, H. (2010). Genetics of caffeine consumption and responses to caffeine. *Psychopharmacology, 211*: 245–57.

38 Fredholm, B.B., Battig, K., Holmen, J., Nehlig, A., & Zvartau, E.E. (1999). Actions of caffeine in the brain with special reference to factors that contribute to its widespread use. *Pharmacological Reviews, 51*(1): 83–133.

39 Nehlig, A., Daval, J.L., & Debry, G. (1992). Caffeine and the central nervous system: mechanisms of action, biochemical, metabolic, and psychostimulant effects. *Brain Research Review, 17*(2): 139–70.

40 Weinberg, B.A., & Bealer, B.K. (2002). *The world of caffeine: The science and culture of the world's most popular drug.* New York: Routledge.

41 Seppa, N. (2015). The beneficial bean: Coffee reveals itself as an unlikely health elixir. *ScienceNews, 188*(7): 16–19.

42. Bellar, D., Kamimori, G.H., & Glickman, E.L. (2011). The effects of low-dose caffeine on perceived pain during a grip to exhaustion task. *Journal of Strength Conditioning Research, 25*(5): 1225–28.

43. Cai, L., Ma, D., Zhang, Y., Liu, Z., & Wang, P. (2012). The effect of coffee consumption on serum lipids: A meta-analysis of randomized controlled trials. *European Journal of Clinical Nutrition, 66*(8): 872–77.

44. Kim, T-W., Shin, Y-O., Lee, J-B., Min, Y-K., & Yank, H-M. (2010). Effect of caffeine on the metabolic responses of lipolysis and activated sweat gland density in human during physical activity. *Food Science and Biotechnology, 19*(4): 1077–81.

45. Venables, M.C., Hulston, C.J., Cox, H.R., & Jeukendrup, A.E. (2008). Green tea extract ingestion, fat oxidation, and glucose tolerance in healthy humans. *The American Journal of Clinical Nutrition, 87*(3): 778–84.

46. Nardi, A.E., Lopes, F.L., Freire, R.C., Veras, A.B., Nascimento, I., et al. (2009). Panic disorder and social anxiety disorder subtypes in a caffeine challenge test. *Psychiatry Research, 169*(2): 149–53.

47. Fredholm, B.B., Battig, K., Holmen, J., Nehlig, A., Zvartau, E.E. (1999). Actions of caffeine in the brain with special reference to factors that contribute to its widespread use. *Pharmacological Reviews, 51*(1): 83–133.

48. Lara, D.R. (2010). Caffeine, mental health, and psychiatric disorders. *Journal of Alzheimer's Disease, 20*: S239–48.

49. Weinberg, B.A., & Bealer, B.K. (2002). *The world of caffeine: The science and culture of the world's most popular drug.* New York: Routledge.

50. Ibid.

51. Cappalletti, S., Piacentino, D., Fineschi, V., Frati, P., & Cipolloni, L., et al. (2018). Caffeine-related deaths: Manner of deaths and categories at risk. *Nutrients, 10*(5): 611.

52. Grosso, G., Godos, J., Galvano, F., & Giovannucci, E.L. (2017). Coffee, caffeine, and health outcomes: An umbrella review. *Annual Review of Nutrition, 37*: 131–56.

53. Tsujimoto, T., Kajio, H., & Sagiyama, T. (2017). Association between caffeine intake and all-cause and cause-specific mortality: A population-based prospective cohort study. *Mayo Clinic Proceedings, 92*(8): 1190–202.

54. Pourshahidi, L.K., Navarini, L., Petracco, M., & Strain, J.J. (2016). A comprehensive overview of the risks and benefits of coffee consumption. *Comprehensive Reviews in Food science and Food Safety, 15*(4): 671–84.

55. Salazar-Martinez, E., Willett, W.C., Ascherio, A., Manson, J.E., Leitzmann, M.F., et al. (2004). Coffee consumption and risk for type 2 diabetes mellitus. *Annals of Internal Medicine, 140*: 1–8.

56. Ding, M., Bhupathiraju, S.N., Chen, M., van Dam, R.M., & Hu, F.B. (2014). Caffeinated and decaffeinated coffee consumption and risk of type 2 diabetes: A systematic review and a dose-response meta-analysis. *Diabetes Care, 37*(2): 569–86.

57. Pereira, M.A., Parker, E.D., & Folsom, A.R. (2006). Coffee consumption and risk of type 2 diabetes mellitus: An 11-year prospective study of 28,812 postmenopausal women. *Archives of Internal Medicine, 166*: 1311–16.

58. Jiang, X., Zhang, D., & Jiang, W. (2014). Coffee and caffeine intake and incidence of type-2 diabetes mellitus: A meta-analysis of prospective studies. *European Journal of Nutrition, 53*(1) 25–38.

59. Huxley, R., Lee, C.M.Y., Barzi, F., Timmermeister, L., Czernichow, S., et al. (2009). Coffee, decaffeinated coffee, and tea consumption in relation to incident type 2 diabetes mellitus. *Archives of Internal Medicine, 169*(22): 2053–63.

60. Eskelinen, M.H., Ngandu, T., Tuomilehto, J., Soininen, J., & Kivipelto, M. (2009). Midlife coffee and tea drinking and the risk of late-life dementia: A population based CAIDE study. *Journal of Alzheimer's Disease, 16*: 85–91.

61. Van Dieren, S., Ulterwaal, C.S.P.M., van der Schouw, Y.T., van der A, D.L., Boer, J.M.A., et al. (2009). Coffee and tea consumption and risk of type 2 diabetes. *Diabetologia, 52*: 2561–69.

62. Huxley, R., Lee, C.M.Y., Barzi, F., Timmermeister, L., Czernichow, S., et al. (2009). Coffee, decaffeinated coffee, and tea consumption in relation to incident type 2 diabetes mellitus. *Archives of Internal Medicine, 169*(22): 2053–63.

63. Crichton, G.E., Elias, M.F., & Aklerwi, A. (2016). Chocolate intake is associated with better cognitive function: The Maine-Syracuse Longitudinal Study. *Appetite, 100*: 126–32.

64. Neves, J.S., Leitao, L., Magrico, R., Vieira, M.B., & Dias, C.V., et al. (2018). Caffeine consumption and mortality in diabetes: An analysis of NHANES 1999–2010. *Frontiers in Endocrinology, 9*: 547.

65. Seppa, N. (2015). The beneficial bean: Coffee reveals itself as an unlikely health elixir. *ScienceNews, 188*(7): 16–19.

66. Modi, A.A., Feld, J.F., Park, Y., Kleiner, D.E., Everhart, J.E., et al. (2010). Increased caffeine consumption is associated with reduced hepatic fibrosis. *Hepatology, 51*(1): 201–09.

67. Tverdal, A., & Skurtveil, S. (2003). Coffee intake and mortality from liver cirrhosis. *Annals of Epidemiology, 13*: 419–23.

68. Molloy, J.W., Calcagno, C.J., Williams, C.D., Jones, F.J., Torres, D.M., et al. (2012). Association of coffee and caffeine consumption with fatty liver disease, nonalcoholic steatohepatitis, and degree of hepatic fibrosis. *Hepatology, 55*(2): 429–36.

69. Barnia, C., Lagiou, P., Jenab, M., Trichopoulou, A., Fedirko, V., et al. (2015). Coffee, tea, and decaffeinated coffee in relation to hepatocellular carcinoma in a European population: Multicentre, prospective cohort study. *International Journal of Cancer, 136*(8): 1899–908.

70. Jin, X., Zheng, R-H., & Li, Y-M. (2008). Green tea consumption and liver disease: A systematic review. *Liver International, 28*(7): 990–96.

71. De Gottardi, A., Berzigotti, A., Seijo, S., D'Amico, M., Thormann, W., et al. (2012). Postprandial effects of dark chocolate on portal hypertension in patients with cirrhosis: results of a phase 2, double-blind, randomized controlled trial. *The American Journal of Clinical Nutrition, 96*(3): 584–90.

72. Arendash, G.W., & Cao, C. (2010). Caffeine and coffee as therapeutics against Alzheimer's disease. *Journal of Alzheimer's Disease, 20*(suppl 1): 117–26.

73. Eskelinen, M.H., Ngandu, T., Tuomilehto, J., Soininen, J., & Kivipelto, M. (2009). Midlife coffee and tea drinking and the risk of late-life dementia: A population based CAIDE study. *Journal of Alzheimer's Disease, 16*: 85–91.

74. Marques, S., Batalha, V.L., Lopes, L.V., & Outeiro, T.F. (2011). Modulating Alzheimer's disease through caffeine: A putative link to epigenetics. *Journal of Alzheimer's Disease, 24*: 161–71.

75. Nurk, E., Refsum, H., Drevon, C.A., Tell, G.S., Nygaard, H.A., et al. (2008). Intake of flavonoid-rich wine, tea, and chocolate by elderly men and women is associated with better cognitive test performance. *The Journal of Nutrition, 139*(1): 120–27.

76. Ng, T-P., Feng, L., Niti, M., Kua, E-H., & Yap, K-B. (2008). Tea consumption and cognitive impairment and decline in older Chinese adults. *American Journal of Clinical Nutrition, 88*(1): 224–31.

77. Mancini, R.S., Wang, Y., & Weaver, D.F. (2018). Phenylindanes in brewed coffee inhibit amyloid-beta and tau aggregation. *Frontiers in Neuroscience, 12*:1–14.

78. Eskelinen, M.H., Ngandu, T., Tuomilehto, J., Soininen, J., & Kivipelto, M. (2009). Midlife coffee and tea drinking and the risk of late-life dementia: A population based CAIDE study. *Journal of Alzheimer's Disease, 16*: 85–91.

79. Ng, T-P., Feng, L., Niti, M., Kua, E-H., & Yap, K-B. (2008). Tea consumption and cognitive impairment and decline in older Chinese adults. *American Journal of Clinical Nutrition, 88*(1): 224–31.

80. Johnson-Kozlow, M., Kritz-Silverstein, D., Barrett-Connor, E., & Morton, D. (2002). Coffee consumption and cognitive function among older adults. *American Journal of Epidemiology, 156*(9): 842–50.

81 Laitala, V.S., Kaprio, J., Koskenvuo, M., Raiha, I., Rinne, J.O., et al. (2009). Coffee drinking in middle age is not associated with cognitive performance in old age. *American Journal of Clinical Nutrition, 90*(3): 640–46.

82 Nurk, E., Refsum, H., Drevon, C.A., Tell, G.S., Nygaard, H.A., et al. (2008). Intake of flavonoid-rich wine, tea, and chocolate by elderly men and women is associated with better cognitive test performance. *The Journal of Nutrition, 139*(1): 120–27.

83 Crichton, G.E., Elias, M.F., & Aklerwi, A. (2016). Chocolate intake is associated with better cognitive function: The Maine-Syracuse Longitudinal Study. *Appetite, 100*: 126–32.

84 Ng, T.-P., Feng, L., Niti, M., Kua, E-H., & Yap, K-B. (2008). Tea consumption and cognitive impairment and decline in older Chinese adults. *American Journal of Clinical Nutrition, 88*(1): 224–31.

85 Crichton, G.E., Elias, M.F., & Aklerwi, A. (2016). Chocolate intake is associated with better cognitive function: The Maine-Syracuse Longitudinal Study. *Appetite, 100*: 126–32.

86 Hu, G., Bidel, S., Jousilaht, P., Antikainen, R., & Tuomilehto, J. (2007). Coffee and tea consumption and the risk of Parkinson's disease. *Movement Disorders, 22*(15): 2242–48.

87 Weinreb, O., Mandel, S., Amit, T., & Youdim, M.B.H. (2004). Neurological mechanisms of green tea polyphenols in Alzheimer's and Parkinson's diseases. *The Journal of Nutritional Biochemistry, 15*(9): 506–16.

88 Ross, G.W., Abbott, R.D., Petrovitch, H., Morens, D.M., et al. (2000). Association of coffee and caffeine intake with the risk of Parkinson disease. *JAMA, 283*(20): 2674–79.

89 Liu, R., Guo, X., Park, Y., Huang, X., Sinha, R., et al. (2012). Caffeine intake, smoking, and risk of Parkinson disease in men and women. *American Journal of Epidemiology, 175*(11): 1200–07.

90 Ding, M., Bhupathiraju, S.N., Satija, A., van Dam, R.M., & Hu, F.B. (2014). Long-term coffee consumption and risk of cardiovascular disease: A systematic review and a dose-response meta-analysis of prospective cohort studies. *Circulation, 129*(6): 643–59.

91 Kim, B., Nam, Y., Kim, J., Choi, H., & Won, C. (2012). Coffee consumption and stroke risk: A meta-analysis of epidemiologic studies. *Korean Journal of Family Medicine, 33*(6): 356–65.

92 Larsson, S.C., & Orsini, N. (2011). Coffee consumption and risk of stroke: A dose-response meta-analysis of prospective studies. *American Journal of Epidemiology, 174*(9): 993–1001.

93 Mostofsky, E., Schlaug, G., Mukamai, K.J., Rosamond, W.D., & Mittleman, M.A. (2010). Coffee and acute ischemic stroke onset: The Stroke Onset Study. *Neurology, 75*(18): 1583–88.

94 Crichton, G.E., Elias, M.F., & Aklerwi, A. (2016). Chocolate intake is associated with better cognitive function: The Maine-Syracuse Longitudinal Study. *Appetite, 100*: 126–32.

95 Tai, J., Cheung, S., Chan, E., & Hasman, D. (2010). Antiproliferation effect of commercially brewed coffees on human ovarian cancer cells in vitro. *Nutrition and Cancer, 62*(8): 1044–57.

96 Seppa, N. (2015). The beneficial bean: Coffee reveals itself as an unlikely health elixir. *ScienceNews, 188*(7): 16–19.

97 Je, Y., Hankinson, S.E., Tworoger, S.S., DeVivo, I.M., & Giovannucci, E. (2011). Consumption and risk of endometrial cancer over a 26-year follow-up. *Cancer Epidemiology Biomarkers, and Prevention, 20*: 2487.

98 Schmit, S.L., Rennert, H.S., Rennert, G., & Gruber, S.B. (2016). Coffee consumption and the risk of colorectal cancer. *Cancer Epidemiology Biomarkers, and Prevention, 25*: 634.

99 Hildebrand, J.S., Patel, A.V., McCullough, M.L., Gaudet, M.M., Chen, A.Y., et al. (2013). Coffee, tea, and fatal oral/pharyngeal cancer in a large prospective US cohort. *American Journal of Epidemiology, 177*(1): 50–58.

100 Shrubsole, M.H., Lu, W., Chen, Z., Shu, X.O., Zheng, Y., et al. (2009). Drinking green tea modestly reduces breast cancer risk. *Journal of Nutrition, 139*(2): 310–16.

101 Freedman, N.D., Park, Y., Abnet, C.C., Hollenbeck, A.R., & Sinha, R. (2012). Association of coffee drinking with total and cause-specific mortality. *New England Journal of Medicine, 366*: 1891–904.

102 Saito, E., Inoue, M., Sawada, N., Shimazu, T., Yamaji, T., et al. (2015). Association of coffee intake with total and cause-specific mortality in a Japanese population: The Japan Public Health Center-based prospective study. *American Journal of Clinical Nutrition, 101*(5).

103 Zhao, Y., Wu, K., Zheng, J., Zuo, R., & Li, D. (2015). Association of coffee drinking with all-cause mortality: A systematic review and meta-analysis. *Public Health Nutrition, 18*(7): 1282–91.

104 Grosso, G., Godos, J., & Galvano, F., et al. (2017). Coffee, caffeine, and health outcomes: An umbrella review. Annual Review of Nutrition, 37: 131–56

105 Tsujimoto, T., Kajio, H., & Sagiyama, T. (2017). Association between caffeine intake and all-cause and cause-specific mortality: A population-based prospective cohort study. *Mayo Clinic Proceedings, 92*(8): 1190–202.

106 Liu, J., Sui, X., Lavie, C.J., Hebert, J.R., Earnest, C.P., et al. (2013). Association of coffee consumption with all-cause and cardiovascular disease mortality. *Mayo Clinic Proceedings, 88*(10): 1066–74.

107 Juliano, L.M., & Griffiths, R.R. (2004). A critical review of caffeine withdrawal: Empirical validation of symptoms and signs, incidence, severity, and associated features. *Psychopharmacology, 176*:1–29.

108 Leviton, A. (1991). Study on PMS and caffeine consumption flawed. *American Journal of Public Health, 81*(12): 1673–75.

109 Spiller, G.A., & Bruce, B. (2010). Coffee, tea, cancer, and fibrocystic breast disease. In G.A. Spiller (Ed.), *Caffeine.* London: CRC Press.

110 Frary, C.D., Johnson, R.K., & Wang, M.Q. (2005). Food sources and intakes of caffeine in the diets of persons in the United States. *Journal of the American Dietetic Association, 105*: 110.

111 Weinberg, B.A., & Bealer, B.K. (2002). *The world of caffeine: The science and culture of the world's most popular drug.* New York: Routledge.

112 Boylan, S., Cade, J.E., Dolby, V.A., et al. (2008). Maternal caffeine intake during pregnancy and risk of fetal growth restriction: A large prospective observational study. *BMJ, 3*(337): a2332.

113 Kuczkowski, K.M. (2009). Caffeine in pregnancy. *Archives of Gynecology and Obstetrics, 280*(5): 695–98.

114 Grosso, G., Godos, J., & Galvano, F., et al. (2017). Coffee, caffeine, and health outcomes: An umbrella review. Annual Review of Nutrition, 37: 131–56

115 Rhee, J., Kim, R., Kim, Y., Tam, M., & Lai, Y., et al. (2015). Maternal caffeine consumption during pregnancy and risk of low birth weight: A dose-response meta-analysis of observational studies. *PLoS One, 10*(7): 1–18.

116 Li, J., Zhao, H., Song, J-M., & Zhang, J. (2015). A meta-analysis of risk of pregnancy loss and caffeine and coffee consumption during pregnancy. *International Journal of Gynecology and Obstetrics, 130*(2): 116–22.

117 Peck, J.D., Leviton, A., & Cowan, L.D. (2010). A review of the epidemiologic evidence concerning the reproductive health effects of caffeine consumption: A 2000–2009 update. *Food and Chemical Toxicology, 48*: 2549–76.

118 Brent, R.L., Christian, M.S., & Diener, R.M. (2011). Evaluation of the reproductive and developmental risks

of caffeine. *Birth Defects Research Park B, Developmental and Reproductive Toxicology, 92*(2): 152–87.

119 van der Hoeven, T., Browne, J.L., Uiterwaal, C.S.P.M., van der Ent, C.K., & Grobbee, D.E., et al. (2017). Antenatal coffee and tea consumption and the effect on birth outcome and hypertensive pregnancy disorders. *PLoS One, 12*(5): e0177619.

120 Wikoff, D., Welsh, B.T., Henderson, R., Brorby, G.P., & Britt, J., et al. (2017). Systematic review of the potential adverse effects of caffeine consumption in healthy adults, pregnant women, adolescents, and children. *Food and Chemical Toxicology, 109*(1): 585–648.

121 Peck, J.D., Leviton, A., & Cowan, L.D. (2010). A review of the epidemiologic evidence concerning the reproductive health effects of caffeine consumption: A 2000–2009 update. *Food and Chemical Toxicology, 48*: 2549–76.

122 Weinberg, B.A., & Bealer, B.K. (2002). *The world of caffeine: The science and culture of the world's most popular drug.* New York: Routledge.

CHAPTER 12

1 National Institutes of Health. (2013). Alcohol use disorders. *NIH Medline Plus, 7*(4): 23.

2 McKenzie, J.F., & Pinger, R.R. (2014). *An introduction to community and public health* (8th ed.). New York: Jones & Bartlett.

3 Esser, M.B., Sherk, A., Liu, Y., Naimi, T.S., & Stockwell, T. et al. (2020). Deaths and years of potential life lost from excessive alcohol use—United States, 2011–2015. *MMWR, 69*(30): 981–87.

4 Dudley, R. (2014). *The drunken monkey: Why we drink and abuse alcohol.* Los Angeles: University of California Press.

5 Vallee, B.L. (1998). Alcohol in the Western world. *Scientific American, 278*(6): 80–85.

6 Ibid.

7 Weil, A., & Rosen, W. (2004). *From chocolate to morphine: Everything you need to know about mind altering drugs.* Boston: Houghton Mifflin.

8 Gately, I. (2008). *Drink: A cultural history of alcohol.* New York: Gotham Books.

9 Ibid.

10 Ibid.

11 *Mourt's Relation*, 1622, commonly attributed to colonists William Bradford and Edward Winslow.

12 Gately, I. (2008). *Drink: A cultural history of alcohol.* New York: Gotham Books.

13 Furnas, J.C. (1965). *The life and times of the late demon rum.* New York: G.P. Putnam's Sons.

14 Black, R. (2010). *Alcohol in popular culture: An encyclopedia.* Westport, CT: Greenwood Publishing Group.

15 Gately, I. (2008). *Drink: A cultural history of alcohol.* New York: Gotham Books.

16 Goode, E. (2007). *Drugs in American society* (7th ed.). New York: McGraw Hill.

17 Gately, I. (2008). *Drink: A cultural history of alcohol.* New York: Gotham Books.

18 Ibid.

19 Gahlinger, P. (2004). *Illegal drugs: A complete guide to their history, chemistry, use, and abuse.* New York: Plume.

20 Ibid.

21 Ibid.

22 Ibid.

23 Ibid.

24 Schlosser, E. (2003). *Reefer Madness: Sex, drugs, and the cheap labor in the American black market.* Boston: Houghton Mifflin.

25 Whitebread, C.H. (2000). "Us" and "them" and the nature of moral regulation. *Southern California Law Review, 74*(2): 364.

26 Gately, I. (2008). *Drink: A cultural history of alcohol.* New York: Gotham Books.

27 Ibid.

28 Rotskoff, L. (2001). *Love on the rocks: Men, women, and alcohol in post-World War II America.* Chapel Hill: University of North Carolina Press.

29 Musto, D.F. (1996). Alcohol in American history. *Scientific American, 274*(4): 78–83.

30 Slater, M.E., & Alpert, H.R. (2020). Apparent per capita alcohol consumption: National, state, and regional trends: 1977–2018. Arlington, VA: NIAAA Surveillance Report.

31 Rose, M.E., & Cherpitel, C.J. (2011) *Alcohol: Its history, pharmacology, and treatment.* Center City, MN: Hazelden.

32 Goode, E. (2007). *Drugs in American society* (7th ed.). New York: McGraw Hill.

33 World Health Organization. (2018). Global status report on alcohol and health, 2018. https://apps.who.int/iris/bitstream/handle/10665/274603/9789241565639-eng.pdf

34 Social Issues Research Centre. (1998). *Social and cultural aspects of drinking: A report to the European Commission.* Oxford: The Social Issues Research Centre.

35 Ibid.

36 LaVallee, R.A., Kim, T., & Yi, H-Y. (2014). *Apparent per capita alcohol consumption: National, state, and regional trends, 1977–2012.* NIAAA Surveillance Report #98. Washington, DC: National Institutes of Health.

37 Substance Abuse and Mental Health Services Administration (SAMHSA). (2020). *Results from the 2019 national survey on drug use and health.* Rockville, MD: Center for Behavioral Health Statistics and Quality.

38 Ibid.

39 Stahre, M., Roeber, J., Kanny, D., Brewer, R.D., & Zhang, X. (2014). Contribution of excessive alcohol consumption to death and years of potential life lost in the United States. *Prevention of Chronic Diseases, 11*: 130293.

40 Ibid.

41 Substance Abuse and Mental Health Services Administration (SAMHSA). (2020). *Results from the 2019 national survey on drug use and health.* Rockville, MD: Center for Behavioral Health Statistics and Quality.

42 White, A.M., Castle, I-J.P., Hingson, R.W., & Powell, P.A. (2020). Using death certificates to explore changes in alcohol-related mortality in the United States, 1999 to 2017. *Alcoholism: Clinical and Experimental Research, 44*(1): 178–87.

43 Substance Abuse and Mental Health Services Administration (SAMHSA). (2020). *Results from the 2019 national survey on drug use and health.* Rockville, MD: Center for Behavioral Health Statistics and Quality.

44 DeJong, W. (2003). Definitions of binge drinking. *JAMA, 289*(13): 1635.

45 Hanson, D.J. (1998). Binge drinking. Accessed on October 10, 2013, from http://www2.potsdam.edu/hansondj/BingeDrinking.html#.UlapAiSoV-Y

46 DeJong, W. (2003). Definitions of binge drinking. *JAMA, 289*(13): 1635.

47 Miech, R.A., Johnston, L.D., O'Malley, P.M., Bachman, J.G., & Schulenberg, J.E., et al. (2021). *Monitoring the Future: National survey results on drug use 1975–2020.* Ann Arbor: Institute for Social Research, The University of Michigan.

48 Anderson, P., de Bruijn, A., Angus, K., Gordon, R., & Hastings, G. (2009). Impact of alcohol advertising and media exposure on adolescent alcohol use: A systematic review of longitudinal studies. *Alcohol and Alcoholism, 44*(3): 229–43.

49 Miller, J.W., Naimi, T.S., Brewer, R.D., & Jones, S.E. (2007). Binge drinking and associated health risk behaviors among high school students. *Pediatrics, 119*(1): 76–85.

50 Hanson, G.R., Venturelli, P.J., & Fleckenstein, A.E. (2012). *Drugs and society* (11th ed.). Burlington, MA: Jones and Bartlett Learning.

51 CORE Institute Survey. (2013). CORE alcohol and drug survey. Southern Illinois University. Accessed on October 5, 2013, from http://core.siu.edu/results.html

52 Ibid.

53 SAMHSA. (2020). *Results from the 2019 national survey on drug use and health*. Rockville, MD: Center for Behavioral Health Statistics and Quality.

54 Keeling, R.P. (2002). Binge drinking and the college environment. *Journal of American College Health, 50*: 197–201.

55 Wechsler, H., Lee, J.E., Kuo, M., Seibring, M., Nelson, T.F., & Lee, H. (2002). Trends in college binge drinking during a period of increased prevention efforts. *Journal of American College Health, 50*(5): 203–17.

56 Task Force of the National Advisory Council on Alcohol Abuse and Alcoholism. (2002). *A call to action: Changing the culture of drinking at U.S. colleges*. Washington, DC: National Institutes of Health.

57 Rose, M.E., & Cherpitel, C.J. (2011) *Alcohol: Its history, pharmacology, and treatment*. Center City, MN: Hazelden.

58 Grossbard, J.R., Lee, C.M., Neighbors, C., Hendershot, C.S., & Larimer, M.E. (2007). Alcohol and risky sex in athletes and nonathletes: what roles do sex motives play? *Journal of Studies on Alcohol and Drugs, 68*(4): 566–74.

59 Reed, E., Prado, G., Matsumoto, A., & Amaro, H. (2010). Alcohol and drug use and related consequences among gay, lesbian, and bisexual college students: Role of experiencing violence, feeling safe on campus, and perceived stress. *Addictive Behaviors, 35*: 168–71.

60 Coulter, R.W.S., Marzell, M., Saltz, R., Stall, R., & Mair, C. (2016). Sexual-orientation differences in drinking patterns and use of drinking contexts among college students. *Drug and Alcohol Dependence, 160*: 197–204.

61 Weil, A., & Rosen, W. (2004). *From chocolate to morphine: Everything you need to know about mind altering drugs*. Boston: Houghton Mifflin.

62 Meyer, J.S., & Quenzer, L.F. (2013). *Psychopharmacology: Drugs, the brain and behavior* (2nd ed.). Sunderland, MA: Sinauer Associates.

63 Mumenthaler, M.S., Taylor, J.L., O'Hara, R., & Yesavage, J.A. (1999). Gender differences in moderate drinking effects. *Alcohol Research and Health, 23*: 55–64.

64 Dettling, A., Skopp, G., Graw, M., & Haffner, H. (2008). The influence of sex hormones on the elimination kinetics of ethanol. *Forensic Science International, 177*: 85–89.

65 Edenberg, H.J. (2007). The genetics of alcohol metabolism: Role of alcohol dehydrogenase and aldehyde dehydrogenase variants. *Alcohol Research and Health, 30*(1): 5–13.

66 Edenberg, H.J., Xuei, X., Chen, H-J., Tian, J., Wetherill, L.F., et al. (2006). Association of alcohol dehydrogenase genes with alcohol dependence: A comprehensive analysis. *Human Molecular Genetics, 15*(9): 1539–49.

67 Janiak, M.C., Pinto, S.L., & Duytschaever, G., et al. (2020). Genetic evidence of widespread variation in ethanol metabolism among mammals: Revisiting the "myth" of natural intoxication. *Biology Letters, 16*(4): 1–7.

68 Seitz, J., & Becker, P. (2007). Alcohol metabolism and cancer risk. *Alcohol Research and Health, 30*(1): 38–47.

69 Marchitti, S.A., Brocker, C., Stagos, D., & Vasiliou, V. (2008). Non-P450 aldehyde oxidizing enzymes: the aldehyde dehydrogenase superfamily. *Expert Opinion on Drug Metabolism and Toxicology, 4*(6): 697–720.

70 Scott, D.M., & Taylor, R.E. (2007). Health related effects of genetic variations of alcohol-metabolizing enzymes in African Americans. *Alcohol Research and Health, 30*(1): 18–21.

71 Seitz, J., & Becker, P. (2007). Alcohol metabolism and cancer risk. *Alcohol Research and Health, 30*(1): 38–47.

72 Clapp, P., Bhave, S.V., & Hoffman, P.L. (2008). How adaptation of the brain to alcohol leads to dependence. *Alcohol Research and Health, 31*(4): 310–39.

73 Ibid.

74 O'Brien, C.P., Rukstalis, M.R., & Stromberg, M.F. (2002). Pharmacotherapy of alcoholism. In K.L. Davis, D. Charney, J.T. Coyle, & C. Nemeroff (Eds.), *Neuropsychopharmacology: The fifth generation of progress*. Philadelphia: Lippincott Williams & Wilkins.

75 Ibid.

76 Clapp, P., Bhave, S.V., & Hoffman, P.L. (2008). How adaptation of the brain to alcohol leads to dependence. *Alcohol Research and Health, 31*(4): 310–39.

77 Ibid.

78 O'Brien, C.P., Rukstalis, M.R., & Stromberg, M.F. (2002). Pharmacotherapy of alcoholism. In K.L. Davis, D. Charney, J.T. Coyle, & C. Nemeroff (Eds.), *Neuropsychopharmacology: The fifth generation of progress*. Philadelphia: Lippincott Williams & Wilkins.

79 Ibid.

80 Mundt, M.P., & Zakletskaia, L.I. (2012). Prevention for college students who suffer alcohol induced blackouts could deter high-cost emergency department visits. *Health Affair (Millwood), 31*(4): 863–70.

81 Topiwala, A., Allan, C.L., Valkanova, V., Zsoldos, E., Filippini, N., et al. (2017). Moderate alcohol consumption as risk factor for adverse brain outcomes and cognitive decline: Longitudinal cohort study. *British Medical Journal, 357*: 2353.

82 Ning, K., Zhao, L., Matloff, W., Sun, F., & Toga, A.W. (2020). Association of relative brain age with tobacco smoking, alcohol consumption, and genetic variants. *Scientific Reports, 10*(1): https://doi.org/10.1038/s41598-019-56089-4.

83 Paul, C.A., Au, R., Fredman, L., Massaro, J.M., Seshadri, S., Decarli, C., & Wolf, P.A. (2008). Association of alcohol consumption with brain volume in the Framingham study. *Archives of Neurology, 65*(10): 1363–67.

84 Brien, S.E., Ronksley, P.E., Turner, B.J., Mujamal, K.J., & Ghali, W.A. (2011). Effect of alcohol consumption on biological markers associated with risk of coronary heart disease: systematic review and meta-analysis of interventional studies. *BMJ, 342*: d636.

85 Peugh, J., & Belenko, S. (2001). Alcohol, drugs, and sexual function: A review. *Journal of Psychoactive Drugs, 33*(3): 223–32.

86 George, W.H., Davis, C., Norris, J., Heiman, J.R., & Schacht, R. (2006). Alcohol and erective response: The effects of high dosage in the context of demands to maximize sexual arousal. *Experimental and Clinical Psychopharmacology, 14*(4): 461–70.

87 Battaglia, C., Battaglia, B., Mancini, F., Nappi, R., Paradisi, R., et al. (2011). Moderate alcohol intake, genital vascularization, and sexuality in young, healthy, eumenorrheic women: A pilot study. *Journal of Sexual Medicine, 8*: 2334–43.

88 Jong, E. (1973). *Fear of flying*. New York: NAL.

89 Nasraliah, N.A., Yang, T.W.H., & Bernstein, I.L. (2009). Long term risk preference and suboptimal decision making following adolescent alcohol use. *Proceedings of the National Academy of Sciences, 106*(41): 17600–604.

90 Hoaken, P.N.S., & Stewart, S.H. (2003). Drugs of abuse and the elicitation of human aggressive behavior. *Addictive Behaviors, 28*:1533–54.

91 Chermack, S.T., & Giancola, P.R. (1997). The relation etween alcohol and aggression: An integrated biopsychosocial conceptualization. *Clinical Psychology Review, 17*(6): 621–49.

92 Ibid.

93 Graham, K., West, P., & Wells, S. (2000). Evaluating theories of alcohol-related aggression using observations of young adults in bars. *Addiction, 95*(6): 847–63.

94 Testa, M., Fillmore, M.T., Norris, J., Abbey, A., Curtin, J.J., et al. (2006). Understanding alcohol expectancy effects: Revisiting the placebo condition. *Alcohol Clinical and Experimental Research, 30*(2): 339–48.

95 Chermack, S.T., & Giancola, P.R. (1997). The relation between alcohol and aggression: An integrated biopsychosocial conceptualization. *Clinical Psychology Review, 17*(6): 621–49.

96 Graham, K., West, P., & Wells, S. (2000). Evaluating theories of alcohol-related aggression using observations of young adults in bars. *Addiction, 95*(6): 847–63.

97 Lindman, R.E., & Lang, A.R. (1994). The alcohol-aggression stereotype: A cross-cultural comparison of beliefs. *International Journal of Addiction, 29*(1): 1–13.

98 Chermack, S.T., & Giancola, P.R. (1997). The relation between alcohol and aggression: An integrated biopsychosocial conceptualization. *Clinical Psychology Review, 17*(6): 621–49.

99 Ibid.

100 Exum, M.L. (2006). Alcohol and aggression: An integration of findings from experimental studies. *Journal of Criminal Justice, 34*: 131–45.

101 Lyvers, M.F., & Maltzman, I. (1991). The balanced placebo design: Effects of alcohol and beverage instructions cannot be independently assessed. *International Journal of Addiction, 26*: 963–72.

102 Testa, M., Fillmore, M.T., Norris, J., Abbey, A., & Curtin, J.J., et al. (2006). Understanding alcohol expectancy effects: Revisiting the placebo condition. *Alcohol Clinical and Experimental Research, 30*(2): 339–48.

103 Howland, J., Rohsenow, D.J., Allensworth-Davies, D., Greece, J., Almeida, A., Minsky, S.J., Arnedt, J.T., & Hermos, J. (2008). The incidence and severity of hangover the morning after moderate alcohol intoxication. *Addiction, 103*: 758–65.

104 Ibid.

105 Rose, M.E., & Cherpitel, C.J. (2011) *Alcohol: Its history, pharmacology, and treatment.* Center City, MN: Hazelden.

106 Howland, J., Rohsenow, D.J., Allensworth-Davies, D., Greece, J., Almeida, A., Minsky, S.J., Arnedt, J.T., & Hermos, J. (2008). The incidence and severity of hangover the morning after moderate alcohol intoxication. *Addiction, 103*: 758–65.

107 Mitchinson, A. (2009). Hangovers: Uncongenial congeners. *Nature, 462*(7276): 992.

108 Rohsenow, D.J., Howland, J., Arnedt, J.T., Almeida, A.B., Greece, J., Minsky, S., Kempler, C.S., & Sales, S. (2009). Intoxication with bourbon versus vodka: Effects on hangover, sleep, and next-day neurocognitive performance in young adults. *Alcoholism: Clinical and Experimental Research, 34*(3): 509–18.

109 Jackson, K.M., Rohsenow, D.J., Piasecki, T.M., Howland, J., & Richardson, A.E. (2013). Role of tobacco smoking in hangover symptoms among university students. *Journal of Studies on Alcohol and Drugs, 74*: 41–49.

110 Millwood, I.Y., Walters, R.G., Mei, X.W., Guo, Y., & Yang, L., et al. (2019). Conventional and genetic evidence on alcohol and vascular diseases aetiology: A prospective study of 500,000 men and women in China. *The Lancet, 393*(10183): 1831–42.

111 Jackson, K.M., Rohsenow, D.J., Piasecki, T.M., Howland, J., & Richardson, A.E. (2013). Role of tobacco smoking in hangover symptoms among university students. *Journal of Studies on Alcohol and Drugs, 74*: 41–49.

112 Fillmore, J.M., Stockwell, T., Chikritzhs, T., Bostrom A., & Kerr, W. (2007). Moderate alcohol use and reduced mortality risk: Systematic error in prospective studies and new hypotheses. *Annals of Epidemiology, 17*(suppl 5): S16–23.

113 Stockwell, T., Zhao. J., Panwar, S., Roemer, A., Naimi, T., & Chikritzhs, T. (2016). Do "moderate" drinkers have reduced mortality risk? A systematic review and meta-analysis of alcohol consumption and all-cause mortality. *Journal of Studies on Alcohol and Drugs, 77*(2): 185–98.

114 Fillmore, J.M., Stockwell, T., Chikritzhs, T., Bostrom A., & Kerr, W. (2007). Moderate alcohol use and reduced mortality risk: Systematic error in prospective studies and new hypotheses. *Annals of Epidemiology, 17*(suppl 5): S16–23.

115 Stockwell, T., Zhao. J., Panwar, S., Roemer, A., Naimi, T., & Chikritzhs, T. (2016). Do "moderate" drinkers have reduced mortality risk? A systematic review and meta-analysis of alcohol consumption and all-cause mortality. *Journal of Studies on Alcohol and Drugs, 77*(2): 185–98.

116 GBD 2016 Alcohol Collaborators. (2018). Alcohol use and burden for 195 countries and territories, 1990–2016: A systematic analysis for the global burden of disease study 2016. *The Lancet, 392*(10152): 1015–35.

117 Ibid.

118 Weafer, J., & Fillmore, M.T. (2012). Acute tolerance to alcohol impairment of behavioral and cognitive mechanisms related to driving: Drinking and driving on the descending limb. *Psychopharmacology, 220*: 697–706.

119 Wenger, J.R., Tiffany, T.M., Bombardier, C., Nicholls, K., & Woods, S.C. (1981). Ethanol tolerance in the rat is learned. *Science, 213*(4507): 575–77.

120 WHO. (2018). Global status report on alcohol and health. Accessed on May 22, 2020 from https://www.who.int/substance_abuse/publications/global_alcohol_report/en/

121 GBD 2016 Alcohol Collaborators. (2018). Alcohol use and burden for 195 countries and territories, 1990–2016: A systematic analysis for the global burden of disease study 2016. *The Lancet, 392*(10152): 1015–35.

122 White, A.M., Castle, I-J.P., Hingson, R.W., & Powell, P.A. (2020). Using death certificates to explore changes in alcohol-related mortality in the United States, 1999 to 2017. *Alcoholism: Clinical and Experimental Research, 44*(1): 178–87.

123 Martinez, P., Kerr, W.C., Subbaraman, M.S., & Roberts, S.C.M. (2019). New estimates of the mean ethanol content of beer, wine, and spirits sold in the U.S. show a greater increase in per capita alcohol consumption than previous estimates. *Alcohol: Clinical and Experimental Research, 43*(3): 509–21.

124 Wood, A.M., Kaptoge, S., Butterworth, A.S., Willeit, P., & Warnakula, S., et al. (2018). Risk thresholds for alcohol consumption: Combined analysis of individual-participant data for 599,912 current drinkers in 83 prospective studies. *The Lancet, 391*: 1513–23.

125 Harper, C., & Matsumoto, I. (2005). Ethanol and brain damage. *Current Opinions in Pharmacology, 5*: 73–78.

126 Zahr, N.M., Kaufman, K.L., & Harper, C.G. (2011). Clinical and pathological features of alcohol-related brain damage. *Nature Reviews Neurology, 7*(5): 284–94.

127 Harper, C., & Matsumoto, I. (2005). Ethanol and brain damage. *Current Opinions in Pharmacology, 5*: 73–78.

128 Brey, R.L. (2012). The adolescent brain. *Neurology Now, December 2011, January 2012*: 9.

129 Squeglia, L.M., Jacobus, J., & Tapert, S.F. (2009). The influence of substance use on adolescent brain development. *Clinical EEG Neuroscience, 40*(1): 31–38.

130 Wood, A.M., Kaptoge, S., Butterworth, A.S., Willeit, P., & Warnakula, S., et al. (2018). Risk thresholds for alcohol consumption: Combined analysis of individual-participant data for 599,912 current drinkers in 83 prospective studies. *The Lancet, 391*: 1513–23.

131 Szabo, G. (1997). Alcohol's contribution to compromised immunity. *Alcohol Health and Research World, 21*(1): 30–41.

132 Bala, S., Marcos, M., Gattu, A., Catalano, D., & Szabo, G. (2014). Acute binge drinking increases serum endotoxin and bacterial DNA levels in healthy individuals. *PLoS ONE, 9*(5): e96864.

133 White, A.M., Castle, I-J.P., Hingson, R.W., & Powell, P.A. (2020). Using death certificates to explore changes

in alcohol-related mortality in the United States, 1999 to 2017. *Alcoholism: Clinical and Experimental Research, 44*(1): 178–87.

[134] Centers for Disease Control and Prevention. (2017). Deaths: Final data for 2017. National Vital Statistics Reports, 68(9).

[135] Nelson, D.E., Jarman, D.W., Rehm, J., Greenfield, T.K., Rey, G., et al. (2013). Alcohol-attributable cancer deaths and years of potential life lost in the United States. *American Journal of Public Health, 103*(4): 641–48.

[136] White, A.M., Castle, I-J.P., Hingson, R.W., & Powell, P.A. (2020). Using death certificates to explore changes in alcohol-related mortality in the United States, 1999 to 2017. *Alcoholism: Clinical and Experimental Research, 44*(1): 178–87.

[137] Seitz, J., & Becker, P. (2007). Alcohol metabolism and cancer risk. *Alcohol Research and Health, 30*(1): 38–47.

[138] Ibid.

[139] Morch, L.S., Johansen, D., Thygesen, L.C., Tjonneland, A., & Lokkegaard, E., et al. (2007). Alcohol drinking, consumption patterns, and breast cancer among Danish nurses: A cohort study. *European Journal of Public Health, 17*(6): 624–29.

[140] Seitz, J., & Becker, P. (2007). Alcohol metabolism and cancer risk. *Alcohol Research and Health, 30*(1): 38–47.

[141] Ibid.

[142] Nelson, D.E., Jarman, D.W., Rehm, J., Greenfield, T.K., & Rey, G., et al. (2013). Alcohol-attributable cancer deaths and years of potential life lost in the United States. *American Journal of Public Health, 103*(4): 641–48.

[143] Peugh, J., & Belenko, S. (2001). Alcohol, drugs, and sexual function: A review. *Journal of Psychoactive Drugs, 33*(3): 223–32.

[144] Ibid.

[145] May, P.A., Chambers, C.D., & Kalberg, W.O., et al. (2018). Prevalence of fetal alcohol spectrum disorders in 4 U.S. communities. *JAMA, 319*(5): 474–82.

[146] National Institute on Alcohol Abuse and Alcoholism. (2000). Fetal alcohol exposure and the brain. *Alcohol Alert, 50.* Washington, DC: National Institute on Alcohol Abuse and Alcoholism. http://pubs.niaaa.nih.gov/publications/aa50.htm

[147] Armstrong, E.M. (2008). *Conceiving risk, bearing responsibility: Fetal alcohol syndrome and the diagnosis of moral disorder.* Baltimore: Johns Hopkins University Press.

[148] Substance Abuse and Mental Health Services Administration (SAMHSA). (2020). *Results from the 2019 national survey on drug use and health.* Rockville, MD: Center for Behavioral Health Statistics and Quality

[149] Ikonomidou, C., Bittigau, P., Ishimaru, M.J., Wozniak, D.F., & Koch, C., et al. (2000). Ethanol-induced apoptotic neurodegeneration and fetal alcohol syndrome. *Science, 287*: 1056–60.

[150] Valenzuela, C.F., Morton, R.A., Diaz, M.R., & Topper, L. (2012). Does moderate drinking harm the fetal brain? Insights from animal models. *Trends in Neuroscience, 35*(5): 284–92.

[151] Maier, S.E., & West, J.R. (2001). Patterns and alcohol-related birth defects. *Alcohol Research and Health, 25*(3): 168–74.

[152] Ibid.

CHAPTER 13

[1] Moore, T.J., & Mattison, D.R. (2016). Adult utilization of psychiatric drugs and differences by sex, age, and race. *JAMA Internal Medicine, 177*(2): 274–75. DOI:10.1001/jamainternmed.2016.7507.

[2] Stuart, J. (2006). Media portrayal of mental illness and its treatments: What effect does it have on people with mental illness? *CNS Drugs, 20*(2): 99–106.

[3] Ibid.

[4] Advokat, C.D., Comaty, J.E., & Julien, R.M. (2014). *Julien's primer of drug action* (13th ed.). New York: Worth Publishers.

[5] Gauthier, G., Mucha, L., Shi, S., & Guerin, A. (2019). Economic burden of relapse/recurrence in patients with major depressive disorder. *Journal of Drug Assessment, 8*(1): 97–103.

[6] Ledford, J. (2014). If depression were cancer. *Nature, 515*: 182–84.

[7] Bromet, E., Andrade, L.H., Hwang, I., Sampson, N.A., Alonso, J., et al. (2011). Cross-national epidemiology of DSM-IV major depressive episode. *BMC Medicine, 9*(90). DOI: org/10.1186/1741-7015-9-90.

[8] Kessler, R.C., & Bromet, E.J. (2013). The epidemiology of depression across cultures. *Annual Review of Public Health, 34*: 119–38.

[9] Hasin, D.S., Sarvet, A.L., Meyers, J.L., Saha, T.D., & Ruan, W.J., et al. (2018). Epidemiology of adult DSM-5 major depressive disorder and its specifiers in the United States. *JAMA Psychiatry, 75*(4): 336–46.

[10] Substance Abuse and Mental Health Services Admin_istration (SAMHSA). (2020). *Results from the 2019 national survey on drug use and health.* Rockville, MD: Center for Behavioral Health Statistics and Quality.

[11] Ibid.

[12] Martin, L.A., Neighbors, H.W., & Griffith, D.M. (2013). The experience of symptoms of depression in men vs women: Analysis of the National Comorbidity Survey Replication. *JAMA Psychiatry, 70*(10): 1100–106.

[13] Twenge, J.M., Cooper, A.B., Joiner, T.E., Duffy, M.E., & Binau, S.G. (2019). Age, period, and cohort trends in mood disorder indicators and suicide-related outcomes in a nationally representative dataset, 2005–2017. *Journal of Abnormal Psychology, 128*(3): 185–99.

[14] Substance Abuse and Mental Health Services Administration (SAMHSA). (2020). *Results from the 2019 national survey on drug use and health.* Rockville, MD: Center for Behavioral Health Statistics and Quality.

[15] Ibid.

[16] Twenge, J.M., Cooper, A.B., Joiner, T.E., Duffy, M.E., & Binau, S.G. (2019). Age, period, and cohort trends in mood disorder indicators and suicide-related outcomes in a nationally representative dataset, 2005-2017. *Journal of Abnormal Psychology, 128*(3): 185–99.

[17] Twenge, J.M., Joiner, T.E., Rogers, M.L., & Martin, G.N. (2018). Increases in depressive symptoms, suicide-related outcomes, and suicide rates among U.S. adolescents after 2010 and links to increased new media screen time. *Clinical Psychological Science, 6*(1): 3–17.

[18] Substance Abuse and Mental Health Services Administration (SAMHSA). (2020). *Results from the 2019 national survey on drug use and health.* Rockville, MD: Center for Behavioral Health Statistics and Quality.

[19] Martin, L.A., Neighbors, H.W., & Griffith, D.M. (2013). The experience of symptoms of depression in men vs women: Analysis of the National Comorbidity Survey Replication. *JAMA Psychiatry, 70*(10): 1100–106.

[20] Luby, J.L., Si, X., Belden, A.C., Tandon, M., & Spitznagel, E. (2009). Preschool depression. *Archives of General Psychiatry, 66*(8): 897–905.

[21] Dunlop, D.D., Song, J., Lyons, J.S., Manheim, L.M., & Chang, R.W. (2003). Racial/ethnic differences in rates of depression among pre retirement adults. *American Journal of Public Health, 93*(11): 1945–52.

[22] Mezuk, B., Rafferty, J.A., Kershaw, K.N., Hudson, D., Abdou, C.M, et al. (2010). Reconsidering the role of social disadvantage in physical and mental health: Stressful life events, health behaviors, race, and depression. *American Journal of Epidemiology, 172*(11): 1238–49.

[23] Mojtabai, R.J. (2013). Clinician-identified depression in community settings: Concordance with structured-interview diagnoses. *Psychotherapy and Psychosomatics, 82*(3): 161–69.

24 Whitaker, R. (2010). *Anatomy of an epidemic.* New York: Broadway Paperbacks.

25 Fava, G.A. (2003). Can long-term treatment with antidepressant drugs worsen the clinical course of depression? *Journal of Clinical Psychology, 64*: 123–33.

26 Posternak, M.A., Solomon, D.A., Leon, A.C., Mueller, T.I., & Shea, M.T., et al. (2006). The naturalistic course of unipolar major depression in the absence of somatic therapy. *The Journal of Nervous and Mental Disease, 194*(5): 324–29.

27 Ronalds, C., Creed, F., Stone, K., Webb, S., & Tomenson, B. (1997). Outcome of anxiety and depressive disorders in primary care. *British Journal of Psychiatry, 171*: 427–33.

28 Goldberg, D., Privett, M., Ustun, B., Simon, G., & Linden, M. (1998). The effects of detection and treatment on the outcome of major depression in primary care: A naturalistic study in 15 cities. *British Journal of General Practice, 48*(437): 1840–44.

29 Hyde, C.L., Nagle, M.W., Tian, C., Chen, X., Paciga, S.A., et al. (2016). Identification of 15 genetic loci associated with risk of major depression in individuals of European descent. *Nature Genetics, 48*: 1031–36. DOI: 10.1038/ng.3623

30 Ibid.

31 Major Depressive Disorder Working Group of the Psychiatric GWAS Consortium. (2013). A mega-analysis of genome-wide association studies for major depressive disorder. *Molecular Psychiatry, 18*: 497–511.

32 Wray, N.R., Ripke, S., Mattheisen, M., Trzaskowski, M., & Byrne, E.M., et al. (2018). Genome-wide association analyses identify 44 risk variants and refine the genetic architecture of major depression. *Nature Genetics, 50*: 668–81.

33 Whitaker, R. (2010). *Anatomy of an epidemic.* New York: Broadway Paperbacks.

34 Arnone, D., McIntosh, A.M., Ebneier, K.P., Munafo, M.R., & Anderson, I.M. (2012). Magnetic resonance imaging studies in unipolar depression: Systematic review and meta-regression analyses. *European Neuropsychopharmacology, 22*(1): 1–16.

35 Shabel, S.J., Proulx, C.D., Piriz, J., & Malinow, R. (2014). Mood regulation: GABA/glutamate co-release controls habenula output and is modified by antidepressant treatment. *Science, 345*(6203): 1494–98.

36 Advokat, C.D., Comaty, J.E., & Julien, R.M. (2014). *Julien's primer of drug action* (13th ed.). New York: Worth Publishers.

37 Ota, K.T., Liu, R.J., Voleti, B., Maldonada-Aviles, J.G., Duric, V., et al. (2014). REDD1 is essential for stress-induced synaptic loss and depressive behavior. *Nature Medicine, 20*(5): 531–35.

38 Anacker, C., Zunsain, P.A., Cattaneo, A., Carvalho, L.A., Garabedian, M.J., et al. (2011). Antidepressants increase human hippocampal neurogenesis by activating the glucocorticoid receptor. *Molecular Psychiatry, 16*(7): 738–50.

39 Duman, R.S., Nakagawa, S., & Malberg, J. (2001). Regulation of adult neurogenesis by antidepressant treatment. *Neuropsychopharmacology, 25*(6): 836–44.

40 Malberg, J.E., Eisch, A.J., Nestler, E.J., & Duman, R.S. (2000). Chronic antidepressant treatment increases neurogenesis in adult rat hippocampus. *The Journal of Neuroscience, 20*(24): 9104–110.

41 Nokia, M.S., Lensu, S., Ahtiainen, J.P., Hohansson, P.P., Koch, L.G., et al. (2016). Physical exercise increases adult hippocampal neurogenesis in male rats provided it is aerobic and sustained. *Journal of Physiology, 594*(7): 1855–73. DOI: 10.1113/JP271552.

42 Duman, R.S. (2004). Depression: A case of neuronal life and death? *Biological Psychology, 56*: 140–45.

43 Nemeroff, C.B. (1998, June). The neurobiology of depression. *Scientific American, 276* (6) 42–49.

44 Canli, T. (2014). Reconceptualizing major depressive disorder as an infectious disease. *Biology of Mood and Anxiety Disorders, 4*(10). DOI:HYPERLINK"//dx.doi.org/10.1186%2F2045-5380-4-10"10.1186/2045-5380-4-10

45 Benros, M.E., Waltoft, B.L., Nordentoft, M., Ostergaard, S.D., Eaton, W.W., et al. (2013). Autoimmune diseases and severe infections as risk factors for mood disorders. *JAMA Psychiatry, 70*(8): 812–20.

46 Dowlati, Y., Hermann, N., Swardfager, W., Liu, H., Sham, L., et al. (2010). A meta-analysis of cytokines in major depression. *Biological Psychiatry, 67*(5): 446–57.

47 Liu, Y., Ho, R.C., & Mak, A. (2012). Interleukin (IL)-6, tumour necrosis factor alpha (TNF-a) and soluble interleukin-2 receptors (sIL-2R) are elevated in patients with major depressive disorder: A meta-analysis and meta-regression. *Journal of Affective Disorders, 139*(3): 230–39.

48 Yirmiya, R., Rimmerman, N., & Reshef, R. (2015). Depression as a microglial disease. *Trends in Neurosciences, 38*(10): 637–58.

49 Kappelmann, N., Lewis, G., Dantzer, R., Jones, P.B., & Khandaker, G.M. (2016). Antidepressant activity of anti-cytokine treatment: A systematic review and meta-analysis of clinical trials of chronic inflammatory conditions. *Molecular Psychiatry, 21*(8): 1130–36. DOI: 10.1038/mp.2016.167.

50 Engstrom, D. (2013). Obesity and depression. Accessed on November 20, 2014, from http://www.obesityaction.org/educational-resources/resource-articles-2/obesity-related-diseases/obesity-and-depression

51 Luppino, F.S., de Wit, L.M., Bouvy, P.F., Stijnen, T., Cuijpers, P., et al. (2010). Overweight, obesity, and depression. *JAMA Psychiatry, 67*(3): 220–29.

52 Ibid.

53 Maes, M., Kubera, M., Leunis, J.-C., Berg, M., Geffard, M., et al. (2013). In depression, bacterial translocation may drive inflammatory responses directed against O&NS-damaged neoepitopes. *Acta Psychiatrica Scandinavica, 127*(5): 344–54.

54 Dinan, T.G., Stanton, C., & Cryan, J.F. (2013). Psychobiotics: A novel class of psychotropic. *Biological Psychiatry, 74*: 720–26.

55 Tetro, J. (2013). Forget Prozac, psychobiotics are the future of psychiatry. Accessed on November 21, 2013, from http://www.popsci.com/blog-network/under-microscope/forget-prozac-psychobiotics-are-future-psychiatry

56 Naseribafrouei, A., Hestad, K., Svershina, E., Sekelja, M., Linlokken, A., et al. (2014). Correlation between the human fecal microbiota and depression. *Neurogastroenterology & Motility, 26*(8): 1155–62.

57 Kearney, C.A., & Trull, T.J. (2012). *Abnormal psychology and life: A dimensional approach.* Belmont, CA: Cengage.

58 Makin, S. (2013). New theory of antidepressants could help predict patients' response. *Scientific American.* January 2014.

59 Kearney, C.A., & Trull, T.J. (2012). *Abnormal psychology and life: A dimensional approach.* Belmont, CA: Cengage.

60 Bradley, R.G., Binder, E.B., Epstein, M.P., Tang, Y., Nair, H., et al. (2008). Influence of child abuse on adult depression. *JAMA Psychiatry, 65*(2): 190–200.

61 Almeida, J., Johnson, R.M., Corliss, H.L., et al. (2008) Emotional Distress Among LGBT Youth: The Influence of Perceived Discrimination Based on Sexual Orientation. *Journal of Youth and Adolescence, 38*(7): 1001–14.

62 Kearney, C.A., & Trull, T.J. (2012). *Abnormal psychology and life: A dimensional approach.* Belmont, CA: Cengage.

63 Kramer, P.D. (1993). *Listening to Prozac: The landmark book about antidepressants and the remaking of the self.* New York: Viking.

64 Chentsova-Dutton, Y.E., Ryder, A.G., & Tsai, J. (2014). Understanding depression across cultural context. In I. Gotlib & C. Hammen (Eds.), *Handbook of depression* (3rd ed.) (pp. 337–52). New York, NY: Guilford Press.

65 Simon, G.E. (2000). Long-term prognosis of depression in primary care. *Bulletin of the World Health Organization, 78*(4): 439–45.

66 Colman, I., Naicker, K., Zeng, Y., Ataullahjan, A., Senthilselvan, A., et al. (2011). Predictors of long-term prognosis of depression. *CMAJ, 183*(17): 1969–76.

67 Ibid.

68 Simon, G.E. (2000). Long-term prognosis of depression in primary care. *Bulletin of the World Health Organization, 78*(4): 439–45.

69 Tavernese, S. (2016, April 22). U.S. suicide rate surges to a 30-year high. *The New York Times.*

70 Dobbs, D. (2013, June 24). Clues in the cycle of suicide. *The New York Times.* http://well.blogs.nytimes.com/2013/06/24/clues-in-the-cycle-of-suicide/?_r=0

71 Parker-Pope, T. (2013, May 3). Suicide rates rise sharply in U.S. *The New York Times.* http://www.nytimes.com/2013/05/03/health/suicide-rate-rises-sharply-in-us.html

72 CDC. (2020). Leading causes of death. Accessed on November 11, 2020, from https://www.cdc.gov/nchs/fastats/leading-causes-of-death.htm

73 Substance Abuse and Mental Health Services Administration (SAMHSA). (2020). *Results from the 2019 national survey on drug use and health.* Rockville, MD: Center for Behavioral Health Statistics and Quality.

74 Nemade, R., Reiss, N.S., & Dombeck, M. (2014). Depression: Major depression and unipolar varieties. Accessed on November 24, 2014, from http://www.gracepoint-wellness.org/5-depression/article/12995-historical-understandings-of-depression

75 Jacobs, B.L. (2004). Depression: The brain finally gets into the act. *Current Directions in Psychological Science, 13*(3): 103–106.

76 Olfson, M., & Marcus, S.C. (2009). National patterns in antidepressant medication treatment. *Archives of General Psychiatry, 66*(8): 848–56.

77 Pratt, L.A., Brody, D.J., & Gu, Q. (2017). Antidepressant use among persons age 12 and over: United States, 2011-2014. *NCHS Data Brief, no 283.* Hyattsville, MD: National Center for Health Statistics.

78 Ibid.

79 Barber, C. (2008). The medicated Americans: Antidepressant prescriptions on the rise. *Scientific American Mind, 19*(1): 44–51.

80 Advokat, C.D., Comaty, J.E., & Julien, R.M. (2014). *Julien's primer of drug action* (13th ed.). New York: Worth Publishers.

81 Lin, K.M., & Poland, R.E. (1995). Ethnicity, culture, and psychopharmacology. In F.E. Bloom & D.J. Kupfer (Eds.), *Psychopharmacology, the fourth generation of progress,* New York: Raven Press.

82 Davies, J., & Read, J. (2019). A systematic review into the incidence, severity and duration of antidepressant withdrawal effects: Are guidelines evidence-based? *Addictive Behaviors, 97:* 111–21.

83 Santarelli, L. (2003). Requirement of hippocampal neurogenesis for the behavioral effects of antidepressants. *Science, 301*(5634): 805–809.

84 Advokat, C.D., Comaty, J.E., & Julien, R.M. (2014). *Julien's primer of drug action* (13th ed.). New York: Worth Publishers.

85 Bahrick, A.S. (2008). Persistence of sexual dysfunction side effects after discontinuation of antidepressant medications: Emerging evidence. *The Open Psychology Journal, 1:* 42–50.

86 Clayton, A.J., Pradko, J.F., Croft, J.A., Montano, C.B., Leadbetter, R.A., et al. (2002). Prevalence of sexual dysfunction among newer antidepressants. *Journal of Clinical Psychiatry, 63*(4): 357–66.

87 Bridge, J.A., Iyengar, S, Salary, C.B., Barbe, R.P., Birmaher, B., et al. (2007). Clinical response and risk for reported suicidal ideation and suicide attempts in pediatric antidepressant treatment. *JAMA, 297*(15): 1683–96.

88 Friedman, R.A. (2014). Antidepressants' black-box warning—10 years later. *New England Journal of Medicine, 371:* 1666–68.

89 Ibid.

90 Gold, C.M. (2014). The antidepressant: Suicide link ten years post black box warning. Accessed on November 24, 2014, from http://www.boston.com/lifestyle/health/childinmind/2014/08/the_antidepressant suicide_link_1.html

91 Lu, C.Y., Zhang, F., Lakoma, M.D., Madden, J.M., Rusinak, D., et al. (2014). Changes in antidepressant use by young people and suicidal behavior after FDA warnings and media coverage: Quasi-experimental study. *British Medical Journal, 348:* g3496.

92 Bouvy, P.F., & Liem, M. (2012). Antidepressants and lethal violence in the Netherlands 1994–2008. *Psychopharmacology, 222*(3): 499–506.

93 Gibbons, R.D., Brown, C.H., Hur, K., Marcus, S.M. Bhaumik, D.K., et al. (2007). Early evidence on the effects of regulators' suicidality warnings on SSRI prescriptions and suicide in children and adolescents. *American Journal of Psychiatry, 164:* 1356–63.

94 Warden, D., Rush, A.J., Trivedi, M.J., Fava, M., & Wisnewski, S.R. (2007). The STAR*D project results: A comprehensive review of findings. *Current Psychiatry Reports 9*(6): 449–59.

95 Kirsch, I., Moore, T.J., Scoboria, A., & Nicholls, S.S. (2002). The emperor's new drugs: An analysis of antidepressant medication data submitted to the U.S. Food and Drug Administration. *Prevention and Treatment, 5*(1): 23a.

96 Kirsch, I., Deacon, B.J., Huedo-Medina, T.B., Scoboria, A., Moore, T.J., et al. (2008). Initial severity and antidepressant benefits: A meta-analysis of data submitted to the Food and Drug Administration. *PLoS Medicine, 5:* e45.

97 Kirsch, I., Moore, T.J., Scoboria, A., & Nicholls, S.S. (2002). The emperor's new drugs: An analysis of antidepressant medication data submitted to the U.S. Food and Drug Administration. *Prevention and Treatment, 5*(1): 23a.

98 Kirsch, I., Deacon, B.J., Huedo-Medina, T.B., Scoboria, A., Moore, T.J., et al. (2008). Initial severity and antidepressant benefits: A meta-analysis of data submitted to the Food and Drug Administration. *PLoS Medicine, 5:* e45.

99 LeNoury, J., Nardo, J.M., Healy, D., Jureidini, J., Raven, M., Tufanaru, C., & Ab-Jaoude, E. (2015). Restoring study 329: Efficacy and harms of paroxetine and imipramine in treatment of major depression in adolescence. *BMJ, 351:* h4320.

100 Sharma, T., Guski, L.S., Freund, N., & Gotzsche, P.C. (2016). Suicidality and aggression during antidepressant treatment: Systematic review and meta-analyses based on clinical study reports. *BMJ, 352:* i65.

101 Geddes, J.R., Carney, S.M, Davies, C., Furukawa, T.A., Kupfer, D.J., Frank, E., & Goodwin, G.M. (2003). Relapse prevention with antidepressant drug treatment in depressive disorders: A systematic review. *Lancet, 361:* 653–61.

102 Kramer, P.D. (1993). *Listening to Prozac: The landmark book about antidepressants and the remaking of the self.* New York: Viking.

103 Carey, B. (2008, January 17). Antidepressant studies unpublished. *The New York Times.* Accessed on December 2, 2014, from http://www.nytimes.com/2008/01/17/health/17depress.html?_r=0

104 Turner, E.H., Matthews, A.M., Linardatos, E., Tell, R.A., & Rosenthal, R. (2008). Selective publication of antidepressant trials and its influence on apparent efficacy. *New England Journal of Medicine, 358*(3): 252–60.

105 Wilson, D., & Singer, N. (2009, September 11). Ghostwriting is called rife in medical journals. *The New York Times.* http://www.nytimes.com/2009/09/11/business/11ghost.html

106 Ebrahim, S., Bance, S., Athale, A., Malachowski, C., & Ionnidis, J.P.A. (2016). Meta-analyses with industry involvement are massively published and report no caveats for antidepressants. *Journal of Clinical Epidemiology, 70:* 155–63.

107 Harvey, M. (2013, March 14). Your tap water is probably laced with antidepressants. *Salon.* Accessed on September 15, 2016, from http://www.salon.com/2013/03/14/your_

tap_water_is_probably_laced_with_anti_depressants_partner/

[108] Thomas, M.A., & Klaper, R.D. (2012). Psychoactive pharmaceuticals induce fish gene expression profiles associated with human idiopathic autism. *PLoS ONE, 7*(6): e32917.

[109] Rabin, R.C. (2014, September 1). Possible risks of SSRI antidepressants to newborns. *The New York Times.* Accessed on September 9, 2014, from http://well.blogs.nytimes.com/2014/09/01/possible-risks-of-s-s-r-i-antidepressants-to-newborns/?_r=0

[110] Venkatesh, K.K., Riley, L., Castro, V.M., Perlis, R.H., & Haimal, A.J. (2016). Association of antenatal depression symptoms and antidepressant treatment with preterm birth. *Obstetrics and Gynecology, 127*(5): 926–33.

[111] Armstrong, C. (2009). Use of psychiatric medications during pregnancy and lactation. *ACOG Practice Bulletin, 7*(3): 385–400.

[112] Venkatesh, K.K., Riley, L., Castro, V.M., Perlis, R.H., & Haimal, A.J. (2016). Association of antenatal depression symptoms and antidepressant treatment with preterm birth. *Obstetrics and Gynecology, 127*(5): 926–33.

[113] Carek, P.J., Laibstain, S.E., & Carek, S.M. (2011). Exercise for the treatment of depression and anxiety. *Psychiatry in Medicine, 41*(1): 15–28.

[114] Alderman, B.L., Olson, R.L., Brush, C.J., & Shors, T.J. (2016). MAP training: Combining meditation and aerobic exercise reduces depression and rumination while enhancing synchronized brain activity. *Translational Psychiatry, 6*: e726.

[115] Francis, H.M., Stevenson, R.J., Chambers, J.R., Gupta, D., & Newey, B., et al. (2019). A brief diet intervention can reduce symptoms of depression in young adults—a randomized controlled trial. *PLoS ONE, 14*(10): e0222768.

[116] Kuyken, W., Warren, F.C., Taylor, R.S., Whalley, B., Crane, C., et al. (2016). Efficacy of mindfulness-based cognitive therapy in prevention of depressive relapse. *JAMA Psychiatry, 73*(6): 565–74.

[117] Beetz, A., Uvnas-Moberg, K., Julius, H., & Kotrschal, K. (2012). Psychosocial and psychophysiological effects of human-animal interactions: The possible role of oxytocin. *Frontiers in Psychology, 3*: 234.

[118] Cohen, I.V., Makunts, T., Atayee, R., & Abagyan, R. (2017). Population scale data reveals the antidepressant effects of ketamine and other therapeutics approved for non-psychiatric indications. *Scientific Reports, 7*(1): 1450.

[119] Greener, M. (2013). Beyond serotonin: New approaches to the management of depression. *Progress in Neurology and Psychiatry* 17 (4), 23–25.

[120] DiazGranados, N., Ibrahim, L.A., Brutsche, N.E., Ameli, R., & Henter, I.D., et al. (2010). Rapid resolution of suicidal ideation after a single infusion of an N-methyl-D-aspartate antagonist in patients with treatment-resistant major depressive disorder. *Journal of Clinical Psychiatry, 71*(12): 1605–11.

[121] Zarate, C.A., Singh, J.B., Carlson, P.J., Brutsche, N.E., & Ameli, R., et al. (2006). A randomized trial of an N-methyl-D-aspartate antagonist in treatment-resistant major depression. *Archives of General Psychiatry, 63*: 856–64.

[122] Diamond, P.R., Farmery, A.D., Atkinson, S., Haldar, J., Williams, N., et al. (2014). Ketamine infusions for treatment-resistant depression: A series of 28 patients treated weekly or twice weekly in an ECT clinic. *Journal of Psychopharmacology, 28*(6): 536–44.

[123] Zanos, P., & Gould, T.D. (2018). Mechanisms of ketamine action as an antidepressant. *Molecular Psychiatry, 23*(4): 801–11.

[124] Greener, M. (2013). Beyond serotonin: New approaches to the management of depression. *Progress in Neurology and Psychiatry, 17*(4): 23–25.

[125] Duman, R.S., & Aghajanian, G.K. (2012). Synaptic dysfunction in depression: Potential therapeutic targets. *Science, 338*(6103): 68–72.

[126] Abdallah, C.G., Adams, T.G., Kelmendi, B., Esterlis, I., & Sanacora, G., et al. (2016). Ketamine's mechanism of action: A path to rapid-acting antidepressants. *Depression and Anxiety, 33*(8): 689–97.

[127] Yang, Y., Cui, Y., Sang, K., Dong, Y., & Ni, Z., et al. (2018). Ketamine blocks bursting in the lateral habenula to rapidly relieve depression. *Nature, 554*(7692): 317–22.

[128] Nogrady, B. (2019). Antidepressant approvals could herald new era in psychiatric drugs. *The Scientist.* Accessed on July 7, 2020, from https://www.the-scientist.com/bio-business/antidepressant-approvals-could-herald-new-era-in-psychiatric-drugs-66475.

[129] Carhart-Harris, R.L., Roseman, L., & Bolstridge, M, et al. (2017). Psilocybin for treatment-resistant depression: fMRI-measured brain mechanisms. *Scientific Reports, 7*: 13187.

[130] Carhart-Harris, R.L., Bolstridge, M., Day, C.M.J., Rucker, J., & Watts, R., et al. (2018). Psilocybin with psychological support for treatment-resistant depression: Six-month follow-up. *Psychopharmacology, 235*: 399–408.

[131] Johnson, M.W., Griffiths, R.R., Hendricks, P.S., & Henningfield, J.E. (2018). The abuse potential of medical psilocybin according to the 8 factors of the Controlled Substances Act. *Neuropharmacology, 142*: 143–66.

[132] Carhart-Harris, R.L., Bolstridge, M., Rucker, J., Day, C.M.J., & Erritzoe, D., et al. (2016). Psilocybin with psychological support for treatment-resistant depression: An open-label feasibility study. *The Lancet Psychiatry, 3*(7): 619–27.

[133] Baumeister, D., Barnes, G., Giaroli, G., & Tracy, D., (2014). Classical hallucinogens as antidepressants? A review of pharmacodynamics and putative clinical roles. *Therapeutic Advances in Psychopharmacology, 4*(4): 156–69.

[134] Osher, Y., & Belmaker, R.H. (2009). Omega-3 fatty acids in depression: A review of three studies. *CNS Neuroscience Therapy, 15*(2): 128–33.

[135] Sanmukhani, J., Satodia, V., Trivedi, J., Patel, T., Tiwari, D., et al. (2013). Efficacy and safety of curcumin in major depressive disorder: A randomized controlled trial. *Phytotherapy Research, 28*(4): 579–85.

[136] Anthes, E. (2014). A change of mind. *Nature, 515*: 185–87.

[137] Carlson, N.R. (2005). *Foundations of physiological psychology* (6th ed.). Boston: Allyn and Bacon.

[138] Leiknes, K.A., Jarosh-von Schweder, L., & Hoie, B. (2012). Contemporary use and practice of electroconvulsive therapy worldwide. *Brain Behavior, 2*(3): 283–344.

[139] Lanzenberger, R., Baldinger, P., Hahn, A., Ungersboeck, J., Mitterhauser, M., et al. (2012). Global decrease of serotonin-1A receptor binding after electroconvulsive therapy in major depression measured by PET. *Molecular Psychiatry, 18*(1): 93–100.

[140] Belluck, P. (2013, February 11). Promising depression therapy. *The New York Times.* Accessed on February 13, 2013, from http://well.blogs.nytimes.com/2013/02/11/promising-depression-therapy/?_r=0

[141] Brunoni, A.R., Moffa, A.H., Sampaio-Junior, B., Borrione, L., & Moreno, M.L., et al. (2017). Trial of electrical direct-current therapy versus escitalopram for depression. *New England Journal of Medicine, 376*: 2523–33.

[142] Loo, C.K., Husain, M.M., McDonald, W.M., Aaronson, S., & O'Reardon, J.P., et al. (2018). International randomized-controlled trial of transcranial Direct Current Stimulation in depression. *Brain Stimulation, 11*(1): 125–33.

[143] Yokoi, Y., Narita, Z., & Sumiyoshi, T. (2018). Transcranial direct current stimulation in depression and psychosis: A systematic review. *Clinical EEG and Neuroscience, 49*(2): 93–102.

144 Brunoni, A.R., Moffa, A.H., Fregni, F., Palm, U., & Padberg, F., et al. (2016). Transcranial direct current stimulation for acute major depressive episodes: Meta-analysis of individual patient data. *British Journal of Psychiatry, 208*(6): 522–31.

145 Boodman, S.G. (2012, February 2). Antipsychotic drugs grow more popular for patients without mental illness. *The Washington Post.* Accessed on December 18, 2014, from http://www.washingtonpost.com/national/health-science/antipsychotic-drugs-grow-more-popular-for-patients-without-mental-illness/2012/02/02/gIQAH1yz7R_story.html

146 Moreno, C., Laje, G., Blanco, C., Jiang, H., Schmidt, A.B., & Olfson M. (2007). National trends in the outpatient diagnosis and treatment of bipolar disorder in youth. *Archives of General Psychiatry, 64*(9): 1032–39.

147 Rowland, T.A., & Marwaha, S. (2018). Epidemiology and risk factors for bipolar disorder. *Psychopharmacology, 8*(9): 251–69.

148 Barnett, J.H., & Smoller, J.W. (2009). The genetics of bipolar disorder. *Neuroscience, 164*(1): 331–43.

149 Arnone, D., Cavanaugh, J., Gerber, D., Lawrie, S.M., Ebmeier, K.P., et al. (2009). Magnetic resonance imaging studies in bipolar disorder and schizophrenia: Meta-analysis. *British Journal of Psychiatry, 195*(3): 194–201.

150 Parboosing, R., Bao, Y., Shen, L., Schaefer, C.A., & Brown, A.S. (2013). Gestational influenza and bipolar disorder in adult offspring. *JAMA Psychiatry, 70*(7): 677–85.

151 Ibid.

152 Jamison, K.R. (1993). *Touched with fire: Manic-depressive illness and the creative temperament.* New York: The Free Press

153 Santosa, C.M., Strong, C.M, Nowakowska, C., Wang, P.W., Rennicke, C.M., & Ketter, T.A. (2007). Enhanced creativity in bipolar disorder patients: A controlled study. *Journal of Affective Disorders, 100*(1–3): 31–39.

154 Kyaga, S., Lichtenstein, P., Borman, M., Hultman, C., Langstrom, N., et al. (2011). Creativity and mental disorder: Family study of 300,000 people with severe mental disorder. *British Journal of Psychiatry, 199*(5): 373–79.

155 Smith, M., & Segal, J. (2014). Bipolar disorder signs and symptoms. Accessed on December 3, 2014, from http://www.helpguide.org/articles/bipolar-disorder/bipolar-disorder-signs-and-symptoms.htm

156 Ibid.

157 Pompili, M., Gonda, X., Serafini, G., Innamorati, M., Sher, L., et al. (2013). Epidemiology of suicide in bipolar disorders: A systematic review of the literature. *Bipolar Disorders, 15*(5): 457–90.

158 Ibid.

159 Kleinman, L.S., Lowin, A., Flood, E., Gandhi, G., Edgell, E., et al. (2003). Costs of bipolar disorder. *PharmacoEconomics, 21*(9): 601–622.

160 Malhi, G.S., Tanious, M., Das, P., Coulston, C.M., & Berk, M. (2013). Potential mechanisms of action of lithium in bipolar disorder: Current understanding. *CNS Drugs, 27*(2): 135–53.

161 Martin, P.-M., Stanley, R.E., Ross, A.P., Freitas, A.E. Moyer, C.D., et al. (2016). DIXDC1 contributes to psychiatric susceptibility by regulating dendritic spine and glutamatergic synapse density via GSK3 and Wnt/β-catenin signaling. *Molecular Psychiatry,* DOI: 10.1038/mp/2016.184.

162 Schrauzer, G.N., & Shrestha, K.P. (1990). Lithium in drinking water and the incidences of crimes, suicides, and arrests related to drug addictions. *Biological Trace Element Research, 25*(2): 105–113.

163 Memon, A., Rogers, I., Fitzsimmons, S.M.D.D., Carter, B., & Strawbridge, R., et al. (2020). Association between naturally occurring lithium in drinking water and suicide rates: Systematic review and meta-analysis of ecological studies. *British Journal of Psychiatry,* https://doi.org/10.1192/bjp.2020.128

164 Whitaker, R. (2010). *Anatomy of an epidemic.* New York: Broadway Paperbacks.

165 Huxley, N., & Baldessarini, R.J. (2007). Disability and its treatment in bipolar disorder patients. *Bipolar Disorders, 9:* 183–96.

166 Advokat, C.D., Comaty, J.E., & Julien, R.M. (2014). *Julien's primer of drug action* (13th ed.). New York: Worth Publishers.

167 Toyoshima, M., Akamatsu, W., Okada. Y., Ohnishi, T., Balan, S., et al. (2016). Analysis of induced pluripotent stem cells carrying 22q11.2 deletion. *Translational Psychiatry, 6*(11): e934. DOI: doi.org/10.1038/tp.2016.206

168 Saha, S., Chant, D., Welham, J., & McGrath, J. (2005). A systematic review of the prevalence of schizophrenia. *PLoS Medicine, 2*(5): e141.

169 McGrath, J., Saha, S., Welham, J., El Saadi, O., & MacCauley, C., et al. (2004). A systematic review of the incidence of schizophrenia: The distribution of rates and the influence of sex, urbanicity, migrant status, and methodology. *BMC Medicine, 2:* 13.

170 Schizophrenia Working Group of the Psychiatric Genomics Consortium. (2014). Biological insights from 108 schizophrenia-associated genetic loci. *Nature, 511*(7510): 421–27.

171 Toyoshima, M., Akamatsu, W., Okada. Y., Ohnishi, T., Balan, S., et al. (2016). Analysis of induced pluripotent stem cells carrying 22q11.2 deletion. *Translational Psychiatry, 6*(11): e934. DOI: doi.org/10.1038/tp.2016.206.

172 Pocklington, A.J., Reese, E., Walters, J.T.R., Han, J., Kavanagh, D.H., et al. (2015). Novel findings from CNVs implicate inhibitory and excitatory signaling complexes in schizophrenia. *Neuron, 86*(5): 1203–214.

173 Sekar, A., Bialas, A.R., de Rivera, H., Davis, A., & Hammond, T.R., et al. (2016). Schizophrenia risk from complex variation of complement component 4. *Nature, 530:* 177–83.

174 Carlson, N.R. (2005). *Foundations of physiological psychology* (6th ed.). Boston: Allyn and Bacon.

175 Walker, E.F., Grimes, K.E., Davis, D.M., & Smith, A.J. (1993). Childhood precursors of schizophrenia: Facial expressions of emotion. *American Journal of Psychiatry, 150*(110): 1654–60.

176 Pocklington, A.J., Reese, E., Walters, J.T.R., Han, J., Kavanagh, D.H., et al. (2015). Novel findings from CNVs implicate inhibitory and excitatory signaling complexes in schizophrenia. *Neuron, 86*(5): 1203–214.

177 Hyman, S.E. (2013). Psychiatric drug development: Diagnosing a crisis. *Cerebrum,* Mar–Apr: 5.

178 Whitaker, R. (2010). *Anatomy of an epidemic.* New York: Broadway Paperbacks.

179 Stepniak, B., Papiol, S., Hammer, C., Ramin, A., Everts, S., et al. (2014). Accumulated environmental risk determining age at schizophrenia onset: A deep phenotyping-based study. *Lancet Psychiatry, 1*(6): 444–53.

180 Kearney, C.A., & Trull, T.J. (2012). *Abnormal psychology and life: A dimensional approach.* Belmont, CA: Cengage.

181 Palmer, C.G.S., Mallery, E., Turunen, J.A., Hsieh, H-J, Peltonen, L., et al. (2008). Effect of Rhesus D incompatibility on schizophrenia depends on offspring sex. *Schizophrenia Research, 104:* 135–45.

182 Kendell, R.E., & Adams, W. (2001). Unexplained fluctuations in the risk for schizophrenia by month and year of birth. *British Journal of Psychiatry, 158*(6): 758–63.

183 Gurillo, P., Juahaar, S., Murray, R.M., & MacCabe, J.H. (2015). Does tobacco use cause psychosis? Systematic review and meta-analysis. *The Lancet Psychiatry, 2*(8): 718–25.

184 Rowland, T.A., & Marwaha, S. (2018). Epidemiology and risk factors for bipolar disorder. *Psychopharmacology, 8*(9): 251–69.

185 Kearney, C.A., & Trull, T.J. (2012). *Abnormal psychology and life: A dimensional approach*. Belmont, CA: Cengage.

186 Chaudhury, P.K., Deka, K., & Chetia, D. (2006). Disability associated with mental disorders. *Indian Journal of Psychiatry, 48*(2): 95–101.

187 Hjorthoj, C., Sturup, A.E., McGrath, J.J., & Nordentoft, M. (2017). Years of potential life lost and life expectancy in schizophrenia: A systematic review and meta-analysis. *Lancet Psychiatry, 4*(4): 295–301.

188 Hor, K., & Taylor, M. (2010). Suicide and schizophrenia: A systematic review of rates and risk factors. *Journal of Psychopharmacology, 24*(4 supp): 81–90.

189 Advokat, C.D., Comaty, J.E., & Julien, R.M. (2014). *Julien's primer of drug action* (13th ed.). New York: Worth Publishers.

190 Stahl, S.M. (2014). Antipsychotic agents. *Essential psychopharmacology online*. Accessed on December 12, 2014, from http://stahlonline.cambridge.org/essential_4th_chapter.jsf?page=chapter5_summary.htm&name=Chapter%205&title=Summary

191 Raggi, M.A., Mandrioli, R., Sabbioni, C., & Pucci, V. (2004). Atypical antipsychotics: Pharmacokinetics, therapeutic drug monitoring and pharmacological interactions. *Current Medicinal Chemistry, 11*(3): 279–96.

192 Arana, G.W. (2000). An overview of side effects caused by typical antipsychotics. *Journal of Clinical Psychiatry, 61*(suppl 8): 5–13.

193 Baldessarini, R.J. (1996). Drugs and the treatment of psychiatric disorders: Psychosis and anxiety. In *Goodman & Gilman's The pharmacological basis of therapeutics* (9th ed.). New York: McGraw Hill.

194 Advokat, C.D., Comaty, J.E., & Julien, R.M. (2014). *Julien's primer of drug action* (13th ed.). New York: Worth Publishers.

195 Arana, G.W. (2000). An overview of side effects caused by typical antipsychotics. *Journal of Clinical Psychiatry, 61*(suppl 8): 5–13.

196 Morrison, A.P., Turkington, D., Pyle, M., Spencer, J., Brabban, A., Dunn, G., et al. (2014). Cognitive therapy for people with schizophrenia spectrum disorders not taking antipsychotic drugs: A single-blind randomized controlled trial. *Lancet, 383*: 1395–403.

197 Meyer, J.S., & Quenzer, L.F. (2005). *Psychopharmacology: Drugs, the brain and behavior*. Sunderland, MA: Sinauer Associates.

198 Lieberman, J.A, Stroup, T.S., McEvoy, J.P., Swartz, M.S., Rosenheck, R.A., et al. (2005). Effectiveness of antipsychotic drugs in patients with chronic schizophrenia. *New England Journal of Medicine, 353*(12): 1209–23.

199 Leucht, S., Cipriani, A., Spineli, L., Mavridis, D., Orey, D., et al. (2013). Comparative efficacy and tolerability of 15 antipsychotic drugs in schizophrenia: A multiple treatments meta-analysis. *Lancet, 382*: 951–62.

200 Boodman, S.G. (2012, February 2). Antipsychotic drugs grow more popular for patients without mental illness. *The Washington Post*. Accessed on December 18, 2014, from http://www.washingtonpost.com/national/health-science/antipsychotic-drugs-grow-more-popular-for-patients-without-mental-illness/2012/02/02/gIQAH1yz7R_story.html

201 Friedman, R.A. (2012, September 25). A call for caution on antipsychotic drugs. *The New York Times*. Accessed on December 18, 2014, from http://www.nytimes.com/2012/09/25/health/a-call-for-caution-in-the-use-of-antipsychotic-drugs.html?_r=0

202 Grohol, J.M. (2019). *Top 25 psychiatric medication prescriptions for 2018*. PsychCentral. https://psychcentral.com/blog/top-25-psychiatric-medications-for-2018/

203 Speilmans, G.I. (2015). Atypical antipsychotics: Overrated and overprescribed. *The Pharmaceutical Journal, 294*(7851). DOI: 10.1211/PJ.2015.20067929.

204 Ibid.

205 Smith, B.L. (2012). Inappropriate prescribing. *American Psychological Association, 43*(6): 36.

206 Ibid.

207 Government Accountability Office. (2015). Antipsychotic drug use. Accessed on March 9, 2015, from http://www.gao.gov/products/GAO-15-211

208 Whitaker, R. (2010). *Anatomy of an epidemic*. New York: Broadway Paperbacks.

209 Dreifus, C. (2008, September 16). Using imaging to look at changes in the brain. *The New York Times*. Accessed on November 10, 2014, from http://www.nytimes.com/2008/09/16/health/research/16conv.html

210 Freeman, D., & Freeman, J. (2014, March 7). At last, a promising alternative to antipsychotics for schizophrenia. *The Guardian*. Accessed on November 7, 2014, from http://www.theguardian.com/science/blog/2014/mar/07/treat-schizophrenia-antipsychotics-drugs-cognitive-therapy

211 Seikkula, J., Aaltonen, J., Alkare, B., Haarakangas, K., & Keranen, J., et al. (2006). Five-year experience of first-episode nonaffective psychosis in open-dialogue approach: Treatment principles, follow-up outcomes, and two case studies. *Psychotherapy Research, 16*(2): 214–28.

212 Linscott, R.J., & van Os, J. (2013). An updated and conservative systematic review and meta-analysis of epidemiological evidence on psychotic experiences in children and adults: On the pathway from proneness to persistence to dimensional expression across mental disorders. *Psychological Medicine, 43*(6): 1133–49.

213 Peet, M., Laughame, J.D.E., Mellor, J., & Ramchand, C.N. (1996). Essential fatty acid deficiency in erythrocyte membranes from chronic schizophrenic patients, and the clinical effects of dietary supplementation. *Prostaglandins, Leukotrienes, and Essential Fatty Acids, 55*(1–2): 71–75.

214 Amminger, G.P., Schafer, M.R., Schlogelhofer, M., Klier, C.M., & McGorry, P.D. (2015). Longer-term outcome in the prevention of psychotic disorders by the Vienna omega-3 study. *Nature Communications, 6*(7934): PMID: 26263244

215 Chaudry, I.B., Hallak, J., Husain, N., Minhas, F., Richardson, P., et al. (2012). Minocycline benefits negative symptoms in early schizophrenia: A randomized double-blind placebo-controlled clinical trial in patients on standard treatment. *Journal of Psychopharmacology, 26*(9): 1185–93.

216 Liu, F., Guo, X., Wu, R., Ou, J., Zheng, Y, et al. (2014). Minocycline supplementation for treatment of negative symptoms in early-phase schizophrenia: A double blind, randomized, controlled trial. *Schizophrenia Research, 153*(1–3): 169–76.

217 Kessler, R.C., Petukhova, M., Sampson, N.A., Zaslavsky, A.M., & Wittchen, H-U. (2012). Twelve-month and lifetime prevalence and lifetime morbid risk of anxiety and mood disorders in the United States. *International Journal of Methods in Psychiatric Research, 21*(3): 169–84.

218 Williams, A. (2017, June 10). Prozac Nation is now the United States of Xanax. *The New York Times*. Accessed on August 14, 2017, from https://www.nytimes.com/2017/06/10/style/anxiety-is-the-new-depression-xanax.html

219 American Psychiatric Association. (2013). *Diagnostic and statistical manual of mental disorders* (5th ed.). Washington, DC: American Psychiatric Association.

220 Anxiety and Depression Association of America. (2014). Facts and statistics. Accessed on March 16, 2016, from http://www.adaa.org/about-adaa/press-room/facts-statistics

221 Meier, S.M., & Deckert, J. (2019). Genetics of anxiety disorders. *Current Psychiatry Reports, 21*(16).

222 Ressler, K.J. (2010). Amygdala activity, fear, and anxiety: Modulation by stress. *Biological Psychiatry, 67*(12): 1117–19.

223 Monk, C.S., Telzer, E.H., Mogg, K., et al. (2008). Amygdala and ventrolateral prefrontal cortex activation to masked angry faces in children and adolescents with generalized anxiety disorder. *Archives of General Psychiatry, 65*(5): 568–76.

224 Marchand, W.R. (2010). Cortico-basal ganglia circuitry: A review of key research and implications for functional connectivity studies of mood and anxiety disorders. *Brain Structure and Function, 215*(2): 73–96.

225 Luhrmann, T.M. (2015, July 19). The anxious Americans. *The New York Times.* Accessed on March 17, 2016, from http://www.nytimes.com/2015/07/19/opinion/sunday/the-anxious-americans.html?_r=0

226 Shannon, S., Lewis, N., Lee, H., & Hughes, S. (2019). Cannabidiol in anxiety and sleep: A large case series. *The Permanente Journal, 23*: 18–041.

227 DeWall, C.N., MacDonald, G., Webster, G.D., Masten, C.L., & Powell, C., et al. (2010). Acetaminophen reduces social pain: Behavioral and neural evidence. *Psychological Science, 21*(7): 931–37.

228 Mithoefer, M.C., Wagner, M.T., Mithoefer, A.T., Jerome, L., & Doblin, R. (2010). The safety and efficacy of 3,4-methylenedioxymethamphetamine-assisted psychotherapy in subjects with chronic, treatment-resistant posttraumatic stress disorder: The first randomized controlled pilot study. *Journal of Psychopharmacology, 25*(4): 439–52.

229 Multidisciplinary Association for Psychedelic Studies. (2015). Frequently asked questions. Accessed on September 15, 2016, from http://www.mdmaptsd.org/faq.html

230 Mithoefer, M.C., Wagner, M.T., Mithoefer, A.T., Jerome, L., Martin, S.F., Yazar-Klosinski, B., Michel, Y., Brewerton, T.D., & Doblin, R. (2012). Durability of improvement in posttraumatic stress disorder symptoms and absence of harmful effects of drug dependency after 3,4-methylenedioxymethamphetamine-assisted psychotherapy: A prospective long-term follow-up study. *Journal of Psychopharmacology, 27*(1): 28–39. DOI: 10.1177/0269881112456611.

231 Mithoefer, M.C., Feduccia, A.A., Jerome, L., Mithoefer, A., & Wagner, M., et al. (2019). MDMA-assisted psychotherapy for treatment of PTSD: Study design and rationale for phase 3 trials based on pooled analysis of six phase 2 randomized controlled trials. *Psychopharmacology, 236*(9): 2735–45.

232 Ot'alora G., M., Grigsby J., Poulter, B., Van Derveer, J.W., & Giron S.G., et al. (2018). 3,4-methylenedioxymethamphetamine-assisted psychotherapy for treatment of chronic posttraumatic stress disorder: A randomized phase 2 controlled trial. *Journal of Psychopharmacology, 32*(12): 1295–1307.

233 Jerome, L., Feduccia, A.A., Wang, J.B., Hamilton, S., & Yazar-Klosinski, B., et al. (2020). Long-term follow-up outcomes of MDMA-assisted psychotherapy for treatment of PTSD: a longitudinal pooled analysis of six phase 2 trials. *Psychopharmacology.* https://doi.org/10.1007/s00213-020-05548-2.

234 Ledford, J. (2014). If depression were cancer. *Nature, 515*: 182–84.

235 Ibid.

236 Hyman, S.E. (2013). Psychiatric drug development: Diagnosing a crisis. *Cerebrum,* Mar–Apr: 5.

237 Sanders, L. (2013). No new meds. *ScienceNews.* Accessed on December 10, 2014, from https://www.sciencenews.org/article/no-new-meds.

238 Hyman, S.E. (2013). Psychiatric drug development: Diagnosing a crisis. *Cerebrum,* Mar–Apr: 5.

CHAPTER 14

1 Goldman, B. (1984). *Death in the locker room.* New York: Penguin.

2 Cohen, J., Collins, R., Darkes, J., & Gwartney, D. (2007). A league of their own: Demographics, motivations, and patterns of use of 1,955 male adult non-medical anabolic steroid users in the United States. *Journal of the International Society of Sports Nutrition, 4*: 12.

3 Sjoqvist, F., Garle, M., & Rane, A. (2008). Use of doping agents, particularly anabolic steroids, in sports and society. *Lancet, 371*: 1872–82.

4 Bowers, L.D. (1998). Athletic drug testing. *Clinics in Sports Medicine, 17*(2): 299–318.

5 Beamish, R. (2011). *Steroids: A new look at performance enhancing drugs.* Santa Barbara, CA: Praeger.

6 Mphil, D.S., Molde, H., Andreassen, C.S., Torsheim, T., & Pallesen, S. et al. (2014). The global epidemiology of anabolic-androgenic steroid use: A meta-analysis and meta-regression analysis. *Annals of Epidemiology, 24*: 383–98.

7 Pope, H.G., Kanayama, G., Athey, A., Ryan, E., Hudson, J.I., et al. (2014). The lifetime prevalence of anabolic-androgenic steroid use and dependence in Americans: Current best estimates. *The American Journal on Addictions, 23*: 371–77.

8 Huang, G., & Basaria, S. (2018). Do anabolic-androgenic steroids have performance-enhancing effects in female athletes? *Molecular and Cellular Endocrinology, 464*: 56–64.

9 Pope, H.G., Kanayama, G., Athey, A., Ryan, E., Hudson, J.I., et al. (2014). The lifetime prevalence of anabolic-androgenic steroid use and dependence in Americans: Current best estimates. *The American Journal on Addictions, 23*: 371–77.

10 Elliot, D.L., Cheong, J.W., Moe, E.L., & Goldberg, L. (2007). Cross-sectional study of female students reporting anabolic steroid use. *Archives of Pediatrics and Adolescent Medicine, 161*(6): 572–77.

11 Kann, L., Kinchen, S., Shanklin, S.L., Flint, K.H., & Hawkins, J., et al. (2014). Youth risk behavior surveillance—United States, 2013. MMWR, 63(4): 1–172.

12 Kann, L., McManus, T., Harris, W.A., Shanklin, S.L., & Flint, K.H., et al. (2019). Youth risk behavior surveillance—United States, 2017. MMWR, 67(8): 1–174.

13 Meich, R.A., Johnston, L.D., O'Malley, P.M., Bachman, J.G., & Schulenberg, M.E., et al. (2021). *Monitoring the Future: National results on adolescent drug use 1975–2020.* Ann Arbor: Institute for Social Research, The University of Michigan.

14 McCabe, S.E., Brower, K.J., West, B.T., Nelson, T.F., & Wechsler, H. (2007). Trends in non-medical use of anabolic steroids by U.S. college students: Results from four national surveys. *Drug and Alcohol Dependence, 90*(2–3): 243–51.

15 Ibid.

16 Cohen, J., Collins, R., Darkes, J., & Gwartney, D. (2007). A league of their own: Demographics, motivations, and patterns of use of 1,955 male adult non-medical anabolic steroid users in the United States. *Journal of the International Society of Sports Nutrition, 4*: 12.

17 Kanayama, G., & Pope, H.G. (2018). History and epidemiology of anabolic androgens in athletes and non-athletes. *Molecular and Cellular Endocrinology, 464*: 4–13.

18 Cohen, J., Collins, R., Darkes, J., & Gwartney, D. (2007). A league of their own: Demographics, motivations, and patterns of use of 1,955 male adult non-medical anabolic steroid users in the United States. *Journal of the International Society of Sports Nutrition, 4*: 12.

19 Cooper, C.J., Noakes, T.D., Dunne, T., Lambert, M.I., & Rochford, K. (1996). A high prevalence of abnormal personality traits in chronic users of anabolic-androgenic steroids. *British Journal of Sports Medicine, 30*: 246–50.

20 Kanayama, G., Pope, H.G., Cohane, G., & Hudson, J.I. (2003). Risk factors for anabolic-androgenic steroid use among weightlifters: A case-control study. *Drug and Alcohol Dependence, 71*: 77–86.

21 NIDA. (2006). Why do people abuse anabolic steroids? Accessed on August 28, 2014, from http://www.drugabuse.gov/publications/research-reports/anabolic-steroid-abuse/why-do-people-abuse-anabolic-steroids

[22] ProCon.org. (2013). Drug use in sports: Pros and cons. Accessed on August 29, 2014, from http://sportsanddrugs.procon.org/view.timeline.php?timelineID=000017.

[23] Cohen, J., Collins, R., Darkes, J., & Gwartney, D. (2007). A league of their own: Demographics, motivations, and patterns of use of 1,955 male adult non-medical anabolic steroid users in the United States. *Journal of the International Society of Sports Nutrition, 4*: 12.

[24] McBride, J.A., Carson, C.C., & Coward, R.M. (2016). The availability and acquisition of illicit anabolic androgenic steroids and testosterone preparations on the Internet. *American Journal of Men's Health*: 1352–57.

[25] Zorpette, G. (2007). The chemical games. In Scientific American (Eds.), *Building the elite athlete*. Guilford, CT: Lyons Press.

[26] Cohen, J., Collins, R., Darkes, J., & Gwartney, D. (2007). A league of their own: Demographics, motivations, and patterns of use of 1,955 male adult non-medical anabolic steroid users in the United States. *Journal of the International Society of Sports Nutrition, 4*: 12.

[27] Ibid.

[28] Oberlander, J.G., & Henderson, L.P. (2012). The *sturm und drang* of anabolic steroid use: Angst, anxiety, and aggression. *Trends in Neuroscience, 35*(6): 382–92.

[29] Cheung, A.S., & Grossmann, M. (2018). Physiological basis behind ergogenic effects of anabolic androgens. *Molecular and Cellular Endocrinology, 464*: 14–20.

[30] Goldman, A., & Basaria, S. (2018). Adverse health effects in androgen use. *Molecular and Cellular Endocrinology, 464*: 46–55.

[31] Sjoqvist, F., Garle, M., & Rane, A. (2008). Use of doping agents, particularly anabolic steroids, in sports and society. *Lancet, 371*: 1872–82.

[32] Hartgens, F., & Kuipers, J. (2004). Effects of androgenic-anabolic steroids in athletes. *Sports Medicine, 34*(8): 513–54.

[33] Ibid.

[34] Ibid.

[35] Kanayama, G., Pope, H.G., Cohane, G., & Hudson, J.I. (2003). Risk factors for anabolic-androgenic steroid use among weightlifters: A case-control study. *Drug and Alcohol Dependence, 71*: 77–86.

[36] Bahrke, M.S., & Yesalis, C.E. (2004). Abuse of anabolic-androgenic steroids and related substances in sport and exercise. *Current Opinion in Pharmacology, 4*(6): 614–20.

[37] Hartgens, F., & Kuipers, J. (2004). Effects of androgenic-anabolic steroids in athletes. *Sports Medicine, 34*(8): 513–54.

[38] Shahidi, N.T. (2001). A review of the chemistry, biological action, and clinical applications of anabolic-androgenic steroids. *Clinical Therapeutics, 23*(9): 1355–90.

[39] Goldman, A., & Basaria, S. (2018). Adverse health effects in androgen use. *Molecular and Cellular Endocrinology, 464*: 46–55.

[40] Estrada, M., Varshney, A., & Ehrlich, B.E. (2006). Elevated testosterone induces apoptosis in neuronal cells. *Journal of Biological Chemistry, 281*: 25492–501.

[41] Kanayama, G., Kean, J., Hudson, J.I., & Pope, H.G. (2013). Cognitive deficits in long-term anabolic-androgenic steroid users. *Drug and Alcohol Dependence, 130*: 208–14.

[42] Marshall-Gradisnik, S., Green, R., Brenu, E.W., & Weatherby, R.P. (2009). Anabolic androgenic steroids effects on the immune system: A review. *Central European Journal of Biology, 4*(1): 19–33.

[43] Pope, H.G., & Brower, K.J. (2009). Anabolic-androgenic steroid-related disorders. In B.J. Sadock, V.A. Sadock, & P. Ruiz (Eds.), *Kaplan and Sadock's Comprehensive Textbook of Psychiatry* (9th ed.). Philadelphia: Lippincott Williams & Wilkins.

[44] Ibid.

[45] Ibid.

[46] Tricker, R., Casaburi, R., Storer, T.W., Clevenger, B., Berman, N., Shirazi, A., & Bhasin, S. (1996). The effects of supraphysiological doses of testosterone on angry behavior in healthy eugonadal men—A clinical research center study. *Journal of Clinical Endocrinology and Metabolism, 81*(10): 3754–58. https://doi.org/10.1210/jcem.81.10.8855834

[47] Pope, H.G., Kouri, E.M., & Hudson, J.I. (2000). Effects of supraphysiologic doses of testosterone on mood and aggression in normal men. *Archives of General Psychiatry, 57*: 133–40.

[48] Pagonis, T.A., Angelopoulos, N.V., Koukoulis, G.N., & Hadjichristodoulou, C.S. (2006). Psychiatric side effects induced by supraphysiological doses of combinations of anabolic steroids correlate to the severity of abuse. *European Psychiatry, 21*: 551–62.

[49] Pagonis, T.A., Angelopoulos, N.V., Koukoulis, G.N., Hadjichristodoulou, C.S., & Toli, P.N. (2006). Psychiatric and hostility factors related to use of anabolic steroids in monozygotic twins. *European Psychiatry, 21*: 563–69.

[50] Sjoqvist, F., Garle, M., & Rane, A. (2008). Use of doping agents, particularly anabolic steroids, in sports and society. *Lancet, 371*: 1872–82.

[51] Pagonis, T.A., Angelopoulos, N.V., Koukoulis, G.N., Hadjichristodoulou, C.S., & Toli, P.N. (2006). Psychiatric and hostility factors related to use of anabolic steroids in monozygotic twins. *European Psychiatry, 21*: 563–69.

[52] Sjoqvist, F., Garle, M., & Rane, A. (2008). Use of doping agents, particularly anabolic steroids, in sports and society. *Lancet, 371*: 1872–82.

[53] Rosenthal, M.S. (2013). *Human sexuality from cells to society*. Belmont, CA: Wadsworth Publishing/Cengage Learning.

[54] Bjorkqvist, K., Nygren, T., Bjorklund, A.C., & Bjorkqvist, S.-E. (1994). Testosterone intake and aggressiveness: Real effect or anticipation? *Aggressive Behavior, 20*: 17–26.

[55] Eisenegger, C., Naef, M., Snozzi, R., Heinrichs, M., & Fehr, E. (2010). Prejudice and truth about the effect of testosterone on human bargaining behavior. *Nature, 463*(7279): 356–59.

[56] Hartgens, F., & Kuipers, J. (2004). Effects of androgenic-anabolic steroids in athletes. *Sports Medicine, 34*(8): 513–54.

[57] Pope, H.G., Kanayama, G., Athey, A., Ryan, E., Hudson, J.I., et al. (2014). The lifetime prevalence of anabolic-androgenic steroid use and dependence in Americans: Current best estimates. *The American Journal on Addictions, 23*: 371–77.

[58] Kanayama, G., & Pope, H.G. (2018). History and epidemiology of anabolic androgens in athletes and non-athletes. *Molecular and Cellular Endocrinology, 464*: 4–13.

[59] Hartgens, F., & Kuipers, J. (2004). Effects of androgenic-anabolic steroids in athletes. *Sports Medicine, 34*(8): 513–54.

[60] Kanayama, G., & Pope, H.G. (2018). History and epidemiology of anabolic androgens in athletes and non-athletes. *Molecular and Cellular Endocrinology, 464*: 4–13.

[61] Zorpette, G. (2007). The chemical games. In Scientific American (Eds.), *Building the elite athlete*. Guilford, CT: Lyons Press.

[62] Anawalt, B.D. (2018). Detection of anabolic androgenic steroid use by elite athletes and by members of the general public. *Molecular and Cellular Endocrinology, 464*: 21–27.

[63] Woolf, J., Rimal, R.N., & Sripad, P. (2014). Understanding the influence of proximal networks on high school athletes' intentions to use anabolic-androgenic steroids. *Journal of Sport Management, 28*(1): 8–20.

[64] Ibid.

[65] Dodge, T., & Clarke, P. (2015). Influence of parent–adolescent communication about anabolic steroids on adolescent athletes' willingness to try performance-enhancing substances. *Substance Use and Misuse, 50*(10): 1307–15.

[66] Woolf, J., Rimal, R.N., & Sripad, P. (2014). Understanding the influence of proximal networks on high school athletes' intentions to use anabolic-androgenic steroids. *Journal of Sport Management, 28*(1): 8–20.

[67] Goldberg, L., Elliot, D., Clarke, G.N., MacKinnon, D.P., & Moe, E., et al. (1996). Effects of a multidimensional

anabolic steroid prevention intervention: The Adolescents Training and Learning to Avoid Steroids (ATLAS) Program. *JAMA*, 276(19): 1555–62.

68 Connor, J., Woolf, J., & Mazanov, J. (2013). Would they dope? Revisiting the Goldman dilemma. *British Journal of Sports Medicine*, 47(11): 697–700.

69 Wolraich M.L., Wibbelsman C.J., Brown T.E., Evans S.W., Gotlieb E.M., & Knight J.R. et al. (2005) Attention-deficit/hyperactivity disorder among adolescents: A review of the diagnosis, treatment, and clinical implications. *Pediatrics, 115*(6): 1734–46.

70 Barbaresi, W.J., Colligan, R.C., Weaver, A.L., Boigt, R.G., Killian, J.M., & Katusic, S.K. (2013). Mortality, ADHD, and psychosocial adversity in adults with childhood ADHD: A prospective study. *Pediatrics, 131*(4): 1–8.

71 Danielson, M.L., Bitsko, R.H., Ghandour, R.M., Holbrook, J.R., & Hogan, M.D., et al. (2018). Prevalence of parent-reported ADHD diagnosis and associated treatment among U.S. children and adolescents, 2016. *Journal of Clinical Child and Adolescent Psychology*, 47(2): 199–212.

72 American Psychiatric Association. (2013). *The diagnostic and statistical manual of mental disorders* (5th edition). Arlington, VA: American Psychiatric Publishing.

73 Ibid.

74 D'Agostino, R. (2014). The drugging of the American boy. *Esquire*. Accessed on July 22, 2020, from https://www.esquire.com/news-politics/a32858/drugging-of-the-american-boy-0414/

75 Danielson, M.L., Bitsko, R.H., Ghandour, R.M., Holbrook, J.R., & Hogan, M.D., et al. (2018). Prevalence of parent-reported ADHD diagnosis and associated treatment among U.S. children and adolescents, 2016. *Journal of Clinical Child and Adolescent Psychology*, 47(2): 199–212.

76 Chiedi, J.M. (2019). *Many Medicaid-enrolled children who were treated for ADHD did not receive recommended followup care*. OEI-07-17-00170 U.S. Department of Health and Human Services.

77 Mascarelli, A. (2013, October 28). Despite years of ADHD research, diagnosis remains tricky and treatment, more so. *The Washington Post*. Accessed on August 5, 2015, from http://www.washingtonpost.com/national/health-science/despite-years-of-adhd-research-diagnosis-remains-tricky-and-treatment-more-so/2013/10/28/a668337a-3a6a-11e3-b6a9-da62c264f40e_story.html

78 Danielson, M.L., Bitsko, R.H., Ghandour, R.M., Holbrook, J.R., & Hogan, M.D., et al. (2018). Prevalence of parent-reported ADHD diagnosis and associated treatment among U.S. children and adolescents, 2016. *Journal of Clinical Child and Adolescent Psychology*, 47(2): 199–212.

79 Ibid.

80 Ibid.

81 Quinn, P.O., & Madhoo, M. (2014). A review of Attention-deficit/hyperactivity in women and girls: Uncovering this hidden diagnosis. *Primary Care Companion: CNS Disorders*, 16(3). DOI: 10.4088/PCC.13r01596.

82 Schwarz, A., & Cohen, S. (2013, April 1). ADHD seen in 11% of U.S. children as diagnoses rise. *The New York Times*. Accessed on August 5, 2015, from http://www.nytimes.com/2013/04/01/health/more-diagnoses-of-hyperactivity-causing-concern.html?_r=0

83 Carroll, L. (2013). ADHD in kids jumps 24% in a decade, study shows. *NBC News*. Accessed on August 5, 2015, from http://vitals.nbcnews.com/_news/2013/01/21/16628054-adhd-in-kids-jumps-24-percent-in-a-decade-study-shows?lite

84 Hinshaw, S., & Scheffler, R. (2014). *The ADHD explosion: Myths, medication, money, and today's push for performance*. London and New York: Oxford University Press.

85 Centers for Disease Control and Prevention. (2016). State-based prevalence data of parent reported ADHD diagnosis by a health care provider. Accessed on August 29, 2016, from http://www.cdc.gov/ncbddd/adhd/prevalence.html

86 Hinshaw, S., & Scheffler, R. (2014). *The ADHD explosion: Myths, medication, money, and today's push for performance*. London and New York: Oxford University Press.

87 Wolraich M.L., Wibbelsman C.J., Brown T.E., Evans S.W., Gotlieb E.M., & Knight J.R., et al. (2005) Attention-deficit/hyperactivity disorder among adolescents: A review of the diagnosis, treatment, and clinical implications. *Pediatrics, 115*(6): 1734–46.

88 Schwarz, A. (2014, May 17). Thousands of toddlers are medicated for ADHD, report finds, raising worries. *The New York Times*. Accessed on August 5, 2015, from http://www.nytimes.com/2014/05/17/us/among-experts-scrutiny-of-attention-disorder-diagnoses-in-2-and-3-year-olds.html

89 Ibid.

90 Schwarz, A. (2013, December 15). The selling of attention deficit disorder. *The New York Times*. Accessed on August 6, 2015, from http://www.nytimes.com/2013/12/15/health/the-selling-of-attention-deficit-disorder.html?pagewanted=all

91 Polanczyk, G.V., Willcutt, E.G., Salum, G.A., Kieling, C., & Rohde, L.A. (2014). ADHD prevalence estimates across three decades: An updated systematic review and meta-regression analysis. *International Journal of Epidemiology*, 43(2): 434–42.

92 Piper, B.J., Ogden, C.L., Simoyan, O.M., Chung, D.Y., & Caggiano, J.F., et al. (2018). Trends in use of prescription stimulants in the United States and territories, 2006 to 2016. *PLoS One, 13*(11): e0206100.

93 Bruchmuller, K., Margraf, J., & Schneider, S. (2012). Is ADHD diagnosed in accord with diagnostic criteria? Overdiagnosis and influence of client gender on diagnosis. *Journal of Consulting and Clinical Psychology 80*(1): 128–38.

94 Thapar, A., Cooper, M., Eyre, O., & Langley, K. (2013). Practitioner review: What have we learnt about the causes of ADHD? *Journal of Child Psychology and Psychiatry*, 54(1): 3–16.

95 Burt, S.A. (2009). Rethinking environmental contributions to child and adolescent psychopathology: A meta-analysis of shared environmental influences. *Psychology Bulletin, 135*: 608–37.

96 Faraone, S.V., & Mick, E. (2010). Molecular genetics of attention-deficit/hyperactivity disorder. *Psychiatric Clinics of North America, 33*(1): 159–80.

97 Franke, B., Faraone, S.V., Asherson, P., Buitelaar, J., & Bau, C.H.D., et al. (2012). The genetics of attention deficit/hyperactivity disorder in adults: A review. *Molecular Psychiatry, 17*(10): 960–87.

98 Thapar, A., Cooper, M., Eyre, O., & Langley, K. (2013). Practitioner review: What have we learnt about the causes of ADHD? *Journal of Child Psychology and Psychiatry*, 54(1): 3–16.

99 Ibid.

100 Del Campo, N., Fryer, T.D., Hong, Y.T., Smith, R., & Brickard, L., et al. (2013). A positron emission tomography study of nigro-striatal dopaminergic mechanisms for underlying attention: Implications for ADHD and its treatment. *Brain, 136*: 3252–70.

101 Hoogman, M., Bralten, J., Hibar, D.P., Mennes, M., & Zwiers, M.P., et al. (2017). Subcortical brain volume differences in participants with attention-deficit/hyperactivity disorder in children and adults: A cross-sectional mega-analysis. *Lancet Psychiatry*. 2017 Apr;4(4): 310–19. DOI: 10.1016/S2215-0366(17)30049-4.

102 Fone, K.C.F., & Nutt, D.J. (2005). Stimulants: Use and abuse in the treatment of attention deficit hyperactivity disorder. *Current Opinion in Pharmacology, 5*: 87–93.

103 Volkow, N.D., Wang, G-J., Kollins, S.H., Wigal, T.L., & Newcorn, J.H., et al. (2009). Evaluating dopamine reward pathway in ADHD: Clinical implications. *JAMA*, 302(10): 1084–91.

104 Del Campo, N., Fryer, T.D., Hong, Y.T., Smith, R., & Brickard, L., et al. (2013). A positron emission tomography study of nigro-striatal dopaminergic mechanisms for underlying attention: Implications for ADHD and its treatment. *Brain, 136*: 3252–70.

105 Bonuck, K., Freeman, K., Chervn, R.D., & Xu, L. (2012). Sleep-disordered breathing in a population-based cohort: Behavioral outcomes at 4 and 7 years. *Pediatrics, 129*(4): e857–65.

106 Cortese, S, Faraone, S.V., Konofal, E., & Lecendreaux, M. (2009). Sleep in children with attention-deficit/hyperactivity disorder: Meta-analysis of subjective and objective studies. *Child and Adolescent Psychiatry, 48*(9): 894–908.

107 Hansen, B.J., Skirbekk, B., Oerbeck, B., Wentzel-Larsen, T., & Kristensen, J. (2014). Associations between sleep problems and attentional and biobehavioral functioning in children with anxiety disorders and ADHD. *Behavioral Sleep Medicine, 12*(1): 53–68.

108 Hvolby, A. (2014). Associations of sleep disturbance with ADHD: Implications for treatment. *ADHD Attention Deficit and Hyperactivity Disorders, 7*: 1–18.

109 Padron, A., Galan, I., Garcia-Esquinas, E., Fernandez, E., Ballbe, M., et al. (2015). Exposure to secondhand smoke in the home and mental health in children: A population-based study. *Tobacco Control, 25*(3): 307–12. DOI: 10.1136/tobaccocontrol-2014–052077.

110 Thapar, A., Cooper, M., Eyre, O., & Langley, K. (2013). Practitioner review: What have we learnt about the causes of ADHD? *Journal of Child Psychology and Psychiatry, 54*(1): 3–16.

111 Ibid.

112 Ji, Y., Azuine, R.E., Zhang, Y., Hou, W., & Hong, X., et al. (2019). Association of cord plasma biomarkers of in utero acetaminophen exposure with risk of attention-deficit/hyperactivity and autism spectrum disorder in childhood. *JAMA Psychiatry, 77*(2): 180–89.

113 Khalife, N., Glover, V., Taanila, A., Eveling, H., Jarvelin, M-R., et al. (2013). Prenatal glucocorticoid treatment and later mental health in children and adolescents. *PLoS ONE, 8*(11): e81394.

114 Zoega, H., Valdimarsdottir, U.A., & Hernandez-Diaz, S. (2012). Age, academic performance, and stimulant prescribing for ADHD: A nationwide cohort study. *Pediatrics, 130*(6): 1012–18.

115 Chen, M-H., Lan, W-H., Bai, Y-M., Huang, K-L., & Su, T.-P., et al. (2016). Influence of relative age on diagnosis and treatment of attention-deficit/hyperactivity disorder in Taiwanese children. *Journal of Pediatrics, 172*(May): 162–67. doi: 10.1016/j.jpeds.2016.02.012

116 Elder, T.E. (2010). The importance of relative standards in ADHD diagnoses: Evidence based on exact birth dates. *Journal of Health Economics, 29*(5): 641–56.

117 Ibid.

118 Layton, T.J., Barnett, M.L., Hicks, T.R., & Jena, A.B. (2018). Attention deficit-hyperactivity disorder and month of school enrollment. *New England Journal of Medicine, 379*: 2122–30.

119 Morrow, R.L., Garland, E.J., Wright, J.M., Maclure, M., & Taylor, S., et al. (2012). Influence of relative age on diagnosis and treatment of attention-deficit/hyperactivity disorder in children. *Canadian Medical Association Journal, 184*(7): 755–62.

120 Goodman, D.W. (2007). The consequences of attention-deficit/hyperactivity disorder in adults. *Journal of Psychiatric Practice, 13*: 318–27.

121 Faraone, S.V., Sergeant, J., Gillberg, C., & Biederman, J. (2003). The worldwide prevalence of ADHD: Is it an American condition? *World Psychiatry, 2*(2): 104–13.

122 De Graaf, R., Kessler, R.C., Fayyad, J., ten Have, M., & Alonso, J., et al. (2008). The prevalence and effects of adult attention-deficit/hyperactivity disorder (ADHD) on the performance of workers: Results from the WHO World Mental Health Survey Initiative. *Occupational and Environmental Medicine, 65*: 835–42.

123 Harpin, V.A. (2005). The effect of ADHD on the life of an individual, their family, and community from preschool to adult life. *Archives of Disease in Childhood, 90*: i2–7. DOI: 10.1136/adc.2004.059006.

124 Goodman, D.W. (2007). The consequences of attention-deficit/hyperactivity disorder in adults. *Journal of Psychiatric Practice, 13*: 318–27.

125 Eldred, S.M. (2013). ADHD doesn't go away. *Discovery News*. http://news.discovery.com/human/health/adhd-neurobehavioral-disorder-age-130304.htm

126 Ibid.

127 Barbaresi, W.J., Colligan, R.C., Weaver, A.L., Boigt, R.G., Killian, J.M., & Katusic. S.K. (2013). Mortality, ADHD, and psychosocial adversity in adults with childhood ADHD: A prospective study. *Pediatrics, 131*(4): 1–8.

128 Hinshaw, S.P., Owens, E.B., Zalecki, C., Huggins, S.P., & Montenegro-Nevado, A.J., et al. (2012). Prospective follow-up of girls with attention-deficit/hyperactivity disorder into early adulthood: Continuing impairment includes elevated risk for suicide attempts and self-injury. *Journal of Consulting and Clinical Psychology, 80*(6): 1041–51.

129 Faraone, S.V., Sergeant, J., Gillberg, C., & Biederman, J. (2003). The worldwide prevalence of ADHD: Is it an American condition? *World Psychiatry, 2*(2): 104–13.

130 Goodman, D.W. (2007). The consequences of attention-deficit/hyperactivity disorder in adults. *Journal of Psychiatric Practice, 13*: 318–27.

131 Wolraich M.L., Wibbelsman C.J., Brown T.E., Evans S.W., Gotlieb E.M., Knight J.R.(2005) Attention-deficit/hyperactivity disorder among adolescents: A review of the diagnosis, treatment, and clinical implications. *Pediatrics, 115*(6): 1734–46.

132 Hinshaw, S.P., Owens, E.B., Zalecki, C., Huggins, S.P., & Montenegro-Nevado, A.J., et al. (2012). Prospective follow-up of girls with attention-deficit/hyperactivity disorder into early adulthood: Continuing impairment includes elevated risk for suicide attempts and self-injury. *Journal of Consulting and Clinical Psychology, 80*(6): 1041–51.

133 Cortese, S., Olazagasti, M.A.R., Klein, R.G., Castellanos, F.X., & Proal, E., et al. (2013). Obesity in men with childhood ADHD: A 33-year controlled, prospective, follow-up study. *Pediatrics, 131*(6): e1731–38.

134 Schwartz, B.S., Bailey-Davis, L., Bandeen-Roche, K., Pollak, J., & Hirsch, A.G., et al. (2014). Attention deficit disorder, stimulant use, and childhood body mass index trajectory. *Pediatrics, 133*(4): 668–76.

135 Sroufe, L.A. (2012, January 29). Ritalin gone wrong. *The New York Times*. Accessed on August 6, 2015, from http://www.nytimes.com/2012/01/29/opinion/sunday/childrens-add-drugs-dont-work-long-term.html

136 Substance Abuse and Mental Health Services Administration (SAMHSA). (2020). *Results from the 2019 national survey on drug use and health*. Rockville, MD: Center for Behavioral Health Statistics and Quality.

137 Schwarz, A. (2012, June 10). Risky rise of the good-grade pill. *The New York Times*. Accessed on August 7, 2015, from http://www.nytimes.com/2012/06/10/education/seeking-academic-edge-teenagers-abuse-stimulants.html

138 Lillienfeld, S.O., & Arkowitz, H. (2013, May). Are doctors diagnosing too many kids with ADHD? *Scientific American*. http://www.scientificamerican.com/article/are-doctors-diagnosing-too-many-kids-adhd/

139 Schwarz, A. (2013, December 15). The selling of attention deficit disorder. *The New York Times*. Accessed on August 6, 2015, from http://www.nytimes.com/2013/12/15/health/the-selling-of-attention-deficit-disorder.html?pagewanted=all

140 Volkow, N.D., Wang, G-J., Tomasi, D., Kollins, S.J., & Wigal, T.L., et al. (2012). Methylphenidate-elicited dopamine increases in ventral striatum are associated with long-term symptom improvement in adults with attention deficit hyperactivity disorder. *Journal of Neuroscience, 32*(3): 841–49.

141 Fone, K.C.F., & Nutt, D.J. (2005). Stimulants: Use and abuse in the treatment of attention deficit hyperactivity disorder. *Current Opinion in Pharmacology, 5*: 87–93.

142 Wilens, T.E., Faraone, S.V., Biederman, J., & Gunawardene, S. (2003). Does stimulant therapy of attention-deficit/hyperactivity disorder beget later substance abuse? A meta-analytic review of the literature. *Pediatrics, 111*: 179–85.

143 Humphreys, K.L., Eng, T., & Lee, S.S. (2013). Stimulant medication and substance use outcomes: a meta-analysis. *JAMA Psychiatry, 70*(7): 740–49.

144 Morton, W.A., & Stockton, G.G. (2000). Methylphenidate abuse and psychiatric side effects. *Primary Care Companion Journal of Clinical Psychiatry, 2*(5): 159–64.

145 Ibid.

146 Gould, M.S., Walsh, B.T., Munfakh, J.L., Kleinman, M., & Duan, N., et al. (2009). Sudden death and use of stimulant medications in youths. *American Journal of Psychiatry, 166*(9): 992–1001.

147 Baughman, F.A., & Hovey, C. (2006). *The ADHD fraud: How psychiatry makes "patients" of normal children*. Bloomington, IN: Trafford Publishing.

148 Sroufe, L.A. (2012, January 29). Ritalin gone wrong. *The New York Times*. Accessed on August 6, 2015, from http://www.nytimes.com/2012/01/29/opinion/sunday/childrens-add-drugs-dont-work-long-term.html

149 Langberg, J.M., & Becker, S.P. (2012). Does long-term medication use improve the academic outcomes of youth with attention-deficit/hyperactivity disorder? *Clinical Child and Family Psychology Review, 15*(3): 215–33.

150 Scheffler, R.M., Brown, T., Brent, F., Hinshaw, S.P., Levine, P., et al. (2009). Positive association between attention-deficit/hyperactivity disorder medication use and academic achievement during elementary school. *Pediatrics, 123*(5): 1273–79.

151 Langberg, J.M., & Becker, S.P. (2012). Does long-term medication use improve the academic outcomes of youth with attention-deficit/hyperactivity disorder? *Clinical Child and Family Psychology Review, 15*(3): 215–33.

152 Parker, J., Wales, G., Chalhoub, N., & Harpin, V. (2013). The long-term outcomes of interventions for the management of attention-deficit hyperactivity disorder in children and adolescents: A systematic review of randomized controlled trials. *Psychology Research and Behavior Management, 6*: 87–99.

153 MTA Cooperative Group. (1999). A 14-month randomized clinical trial of treatment strategies for attention-deficit/hyperactivity disorder. The MTA Cooperative Group Treatment Study of Children with ADHD. *Archives of General Psychiatry, 56*(12): 1073–86.

154 Currie, J., Stabile, M., & Jones, L.E. (2013). Do stimulant medications improve educational and behavioral outcomes for children with ADHD? NBER Working Paper 19105. *Journal of Health Economics, 37*: 58–69.

155 Sharpe, K. (2014). The smart-pill oversell. *Nature, 506*: 146–48.

156 Cropsey, K.L., Schiavon, S., Hendricks, P.S., Froelich, M., & Lentowicz, I., et al. (2017). Mixed-amphetamine salts expectancies among college students: Is stimulant induced cognitive enhancement a placebo effect? *Drug and Alcohol Dependence, 178*(1): 302–09.

157 Advokat, C., & Scheithauer, M. (2013). Attention-deficit hyperactivity disorder (ADHD) stimulant medications as cognitive enhancers. *Frontiers in Neuroscience, 7*: 82.

158 Sprich, S.E., Burbridge, J., Lerner, J.A., & Safren, S.A. (2015). Cognitive-behavioral therapy for ADHD in adolescents: Clinical considerations and a case series. *Cognitive Behavioral Practice, 22*(2): 116–26.

159 Schoenberg, P.L., Hepark, S., Kan, C.C., Barendregt, H.P., Buitelaar, J.K., & Speckens, A.E. (2014). Effects of mindfulness-based cognitive therapy on neurophysiological correlates of performance monitoring in adult attention-deficit/hyperactivity disorder. *Clinical Neurophysiology, 125*(7): 1407–16.

160 Pelham, W.E., Fabiano, G.A., Waxmonsky, J.G., Greiner, A.R., & Gnagy, E.M., et al. (2016). Treatment sequencing for childhood ADHD: A multiple-randomization study of adaptive medication and behavioral interventions. *Journal of Clinical Child and Adolescent Psychology, 45*(4): 396–415. DOI: 10.1080/15374416.2015.1105138.

161 Huss, M., Völp, A., & Stauss-Grabo, M. (2010). Supplementation of polyunsaturated fatty acids, magnesium and zinc in children seeking medical advice for attention-deficit/hyperactivity problems—An observational cohort study. *Lipids in Health and Disease, 9*: 105. http://doi.org/10.1186/1476-511X-9-105

162 Cormier, E., & Elder, J.H. (2007). Diet and child behavior problems: Fact or fiction? *Pediatric Nursing, 33*(2): 138–43.

163 Centers for Disease Control and Prevention. (2007). School Health Policies and Programs Study. Accessed on August 2, 2015, from http://www.cdc.gov/healthyyouth/shpps/2006/factsheets/pdf/FS_PhysicalEducation_SHPPS2006.pdf

164 Hoza, B., Smith, A.L., Shoulberg, E.J., Linnea, K.S., & Dorsch, T.E., et al. (2015). A randomized trial examining the effects of aerobic physical activity on attention-deficit/hyperactivity disorder symptoms in young children. *Journal of Abnormal Child Psychology, 43*: 655–67.

165 Pontifex, M.B., Saliba, B.J., Raine, L.B., Picchietti, D.L., & Hillman, C.H. (2013). Exercise improves behavioral, neurocognitive, and scholastic performance in children with attention-deficit/hyperactivity disorder. *Journal of Pediatrics, 162*(3): 543–51.

166 Smith, A.L., Hoza, B., Linnea, K., McQuade, J.D., & Tomb, M., et al. (2013). Pilot physical activity intervention reduces severity of ADHD symptoms in young children. *Journal of Attention Disorders, 17*(1): 70–82.

CHAPTER 15

1 Consumer Healthcare Products Association. (2021). Statistics on OTC use. Accessed on July 5, 2021, from http://www.chpa.org/marketstats.aspx

2 Sapp, A.J. (2015). Over-the-counter drugs. In N.L. Keltner & D. Steele (Eds.), *Psychiatric Nursing* (7th ed.). St. Louis: Elsevier.

3 Henderson, M.L. (2012). Self-care and nonprescription pharmacotherapy. In D. Krinsky (Ed.), *Handbook of Nonprescription Drugs* (17th ed.). Washington, DC: American Pharmacists Association.

4 Consumer Healthcare Products Association. (2021). Statistics on OTC use. Accessed on July 5, 2021, from https://www.chpa.org/MarketStats.aspx.

5 Ibid.

6 Li, J.J. (2006). *Laughing gas, Viagra, and Lipitor: The human stories behind the drugs we use*. New York: Oxford University Press.

7 Food and Drug Administration. (2015). Code of Federal Regulations Title 21. Accessed on July 14, 2016, from http://www.accessdata.fda.gov/scripts/cdrh/cfdocs/cfcfr/CFRSearch.cfm?fr=330.10

8 Ibid.

9 Henderson, M.L. (2012). Self-care and nonprescription pharmacotherapy. In D. Krinsky (Ed.), *Handbook of Nonprescription Drugs* (17th ed.). Washington, DC: American Pharmacists Association.

10 Consumer Healthcare Products Association. (2021). Statistics on OTC use. Accessed on July 5, 2021, from https://www.chpa.org/MarketStats.aspx.

11 Ibid.

12 Ibid.

13 Ibid.

14 Li, J.J. (2006). *Laughing gas, Viagra, and Lipitor: The human stories behind the drugs we use.* New York: Oxford University Press.

15 Sneader, W. (2000). The discovery of aspirin: A reappraisal. *BMJ, 321*: 1591–94.

16 Zhou, Y., Boudreau, D.M., & Freedman, A.N. (2014). Trends in the use of aspirin and nonsteroidal anti-inflammatory drugs in the general U.S. population. *Pharmacoepidemiology and Drug Safety, 23*(1): 43–50.

17 Agrawal, S., & Khazaeni, B. (2020). Acetaminophen toxicity. In: StatPearls. Treasure Island (FL): StatPearls Publishing.

18 Conaghan, P.G. (2012). A turbulent decade for NSAIDs: Update on current concepts of classification, epidemiology, comparative efficacy, and toxicity. *Rheumatology International, 32*(6): 1491–502.

19 Solomon, D.H. (2016). NSAIDs: Mechanism of action. Accessed on May 12, 2016, from http://www.uptodate.com/contents/nsaids-mechanism-of-action.

20 Li, J.J. (2006). *Laughing gas, Viagra, and Lipitor: The human stories behind the drugs we use.* New York: Oxford University Press.

21 Conaghan, P.G. (2012). A turbulent decade for NSAIDs: Update on current concepts of classification, epidemiology, comparative efficacy, and toxicity. *Rheumatology International, 32*(6): 1491–502.

22 Mallet, C., Daulhac, L., Bonnefont, J., Ledent, C., Etienne, M., Chapuy, E., Libert, F., & Eschalier, A. (2008). Endocannabinoid and serotonergic systems are needed for acetaminophen-induced analgesia. *Pain, 139*(1): 190–200.

23 Klinger-Gratz, P.P., Ralvenius, W.T., Neumann, E. Kato, A., & Nylias, R. et al. (2018). Acetaminophen relieves inflammatory pain through CB1 cannabinoid receptors in the rostral ventromedial medulla. *Journal of Neuroscience, 38*(2): 322–34.

24 Sharma, C.V., & Mehta, V. (2017). Paracetamol: Mechanisms and updates. *Continuing Education in Anesthesia, Critical Care, and Pain, 14*(4): 153–58.

25 Algra, A.M., & Rothwell, P.M. (2012). Effects of regular aspirin on long-term cancer incidence and metastasis: A systematic comparison of evidence from observational studies versus randomized trials. *The Lancet, 13*: 518–27.

26 Baron, J.A., Cole, B.F., Sandler, R.S., & Haile, R.W. (2003). A randomized trial of aspirin to prevent colorectal adenomas. *New England Journal of Medicine, 348*: 891–99.

27 Rothwell, P.M., Wilson, M., Price, J.F., Belch, J.F.F., Meade, T.W., et al. (2012). Effect of daily aspirin on risk of cancer metastasis: A study of incident cancers during randomized controlled trials. *The Lancet, 379*: 1591–601.

28 Rothwell, P.M., Price, J.F, Fowkes, F.G. R., Zanchetti, A., Roncaglioni, M.C., et al. (2012). Short-term effects of daily aspirin on cancer incidence, mortality, and non-vascular death: Analysis of the time course of risks and benefits in 51 randomized controlled trials. *The Lancet, 379*: 1602–12.

29 Friedrich, M.H. (2011). Aspirin cuts cancer risk. *JAMA, 305*(3): 243.

30 In't Veld, B.A., Ruitenberg, A., Hofman, A., Launer, L.J., van Duijn, C.M., et al. (2001). Nonsteroidal anti-inflammatory drugs and the risk of Alzheimer's disease. *New England Journal of Medicine, 345*(21): 1515–21.

31 Breitner, J.C., Baker, L.D., Montine, T.J., Meinert, C.L., Lyketsos, C.G., et al. (2011). Extended results of the Alzheimer's disease anti-inflammatory prevention trial. *Alzheimer's Dementia, 7*(4): 402–11.

32 Dokmeci, D. (2004). Ibuprofen and Alzheimer's disease. *Folia Med, 46*(2): 5–10.

33 Zhang, C., Wang, Y., Wang, D., Zhang, J., & Zhang, F. (2018). NSAID exposure and risk of Alzheimer's disease: An updated meta-analysis from cohort studies. *Frontiers in Aging Neuroscience, 10*: 83.

34 In't Veld, B.A., Ruitenberg, A., Hofman, A., Launer, L.J., van Duijn, C.M., et al. (2001). Nonsteroidal anti-inflammatory drugs and the risk of Alzheimer's disease. *New England Journal of Medicine, 345*(21): 1515–21.

35 Szekely, C.A., & Zandi, P.P. (2010). Nonsteroidal anti-inflammatory drugs and Alzheimer's disease: The epidemiological evidence. *CNS & Neurological Disorders, 9*(2): 132–39.

36 Gorelick, P.B. (2010). Role of inflammation in cognitive impairment: Results of observational epidemiological studies and clinical trials. *Annals of the New York Academy of Sciences, 1207*: 155–62.

37 Consumer Reports. (2013). Best buy drugs. Accessed on June 3, 2016, from http://consumerhealthchoices.org/wp-content/uploads/2012/02/BBD-NSAIDs-Full.pdf

38 Cayley, W., & Alper, B.S. (2007). Acetaminophen poisoning. *Cortlandt Forum, 20*(5): 63–64.

39 Conaghan, P.G. (2012). A turbulent decade for NSAIDs: Update on current concepts of classification, epidemiology, comparative efficacy, and toxicity. *Rheumatology International, 32*(6): 1491–502.

40 Clark, L., Savarie, P.J., Shivik, J.A., Breck, S.W., & Dorr, B.S. (2012). Efficacy, effort, and cost comparisons of trapping and acetaminophen-baiting for control of brown treesnakes on Guam. *Human-Wildlife Interactions, 6*(2): 222–36.

41 Johnson, M.A. (2013). Two thousand mice dropped on Guam by parachute—to kill snakes. Accessed on May 2, 2016, from http://www.nbcnews.com/news/other/two-thousand-mice-dropped-guam-parachute-kill-snakes-f2D11685572

42 Grosser, T., Smyth, E.M., & FitzGerald, G.A. (2011). Anti-inflammatory, antipyretic, and analgesic: Pharmacotherapy of gout. In L.L., Brunton, B.A. Chabner, & B.C. Knollman (Eds.), *Goodman & Gilman's The pharmacological basis of therapeutics* (12th ed.). New York: McGraw-Hill.

43 Schafer, A.I. (1995). Effects of nonsteroidal anti-inflammatory drugs on platelet function and systemic hemostasis. *Journal of Clinical Pharmacology, 35*: 209–19.

44 Aghababian, R.V. (2010). *Essentials of emergency medicine.* Sudbury, MA: Jones & Bartlett.

45 Forman, J.P., Rimm, E.B., & Curham, G.C. (2007). Frequency of analgesic use and risk of hypertension among men. *Archives of Internal Medicine, 167*: 394–99.

46 Levy, S., & Volans, G. (2001). The use of analgesics in patients with asthma. *Drug Safety, 24*(11): 829–41.

47 Singh, S.P., Sharma, S.K., Singh, L., Goyal, S., & Gawad, J.B. (2013). An overview of NSAIDs used in anti-inflammatory and analgesic activity and prevention gastrointestinal damage. *Journal of Drug Discovery and Therapeutics, 1*(8): 41–51.

48 Harirforoosh, S., & Jamali, F. (2009). Renal adverse effects of nonsteroidal anti-inflammatory drugs. *Expert Opinions in Drug Safety, 8*(6): 669–81.

49 Mayo Clinic. (2016). Stevens-Johnson syndrome. Accessed on September 19, 2016, from http://www.mayoclinic.org/diseases-conditions/stevens-johnson-syndrome/basics/definition/con-20029623

50 Glasgow, J.F.T. (2006). Reye's syndrome. *Drug Safety, 29*(12): 1111–21.

51 Cayley, W., & Alper, B.S. (2007). Acetaminophen poisoning. *Cortlandt Forum, 20*(5): 63–64.

52 Durso, G.R.O., Luttrell, A., & Way, B.M. (2015). Over-the-counter relief from pains and pleasures alike: Acetaminophen blunts evaluation sensitivity to both negative and positive stimuli. *Psychological Science, 26*(6): 750–58.

53 Mischkowski, D., Crocker, J., & Way, B.M. (2016). From painkiller to empathy killer: Acetaminophen

(paracetamol) reduces empathy for pain. *Social, Cognitive, and Affective Neuroscience, 11*(9): 1345–53.

54 Rebordosa, C., Kogevinas, M., Horvath-Puho, E., Norgard, B., Morales, M., et al. (2008). Acetaminophen use during pregnancy: Effects on risk for congenital abnormalities. *American Journal of Obstetrics and Gynecology, 198*(2): 178.

55 Stergiakouli, E., Thapar, A., & Smith, G.D. (2016). Association of acetaminophen use during pregnancy with behavioral problems in childhood. *JAMA Pediatrics, 170*(10): 964–70.

56 Ji, Y., Azuine, R.E., Zhang, Y., Hou, W., & Hong, X., et al. (2019). Association of cord plasma biomarkers of in utero acetaminophen exposure with risk of attention-deficit/hyperactivity disorder and autism spectrum disorder in childhood. *JAMA Psychiatry, 77*(2): 180–89.

57 Lee, W.M. (2004). Acetaminophen and the U.S. acute liver failure study group: Lowering the risks of hepatic failure. *Hepatology, 40*(1): 6–9.

58 Agrawal, S., & Khazaeni, B. (2020). Acetaminophen toxicity. In: *StatPearls*. Treasure Island (FL): StatPearls Publishing.

59 James, L., Sullivan, J.E., & Roberts, D. (2011). The proper use of acetaminophen. *Pediatrics and Child Health, 16*(9): 544–47.

60 Consumer Reports. (2013). Best buy drugs. Accessed on June 3, 2016, from http://consumerhealthchoices.org/wp-content/uploads/2012/02/BBD-NSAIDs-Full.pdf

61 Consumer Healthcare Products Association. (2021). Statistics on OTC use. Accessed on July 5, 2021, from http://www.chpa.org/marketstats.aspx

62 Schroeder, K., & Fahey, T. (2002). Systematic review of randomized controlled trials of over-the-counter cough medicines for acute cough in adults. *BMJ, 324*(7333): 329–31.

63 Dealleaume, L., Tweed, B., & Neher, J.O. (2009). Do OTC remedies relieve cough in acute URIs? *Journal of Family Practice, 58*(10): 559a–c.

64 Halfdanarson, T.R., & Jatoi, A. (2007). Chocolate as a cough suppressant: Rationale and justification for an upcoming clinical trial. *Supportive Cancer Therapy, 4*(2): 119–22.

65 Usmani, O.S., Belvisi, M.G., Patel, H.J., Crispino, N., & Birrell, M.A. (2005). Theobromine inhibits sensory nerve activation and cough. *The FASEB Journal, 192*: 231–33.

66 Krouse, J.H. (2006). Allergic and nonallergic rhinitis. In B.J. Bailey, J.T. Johnson, & S.D. Newlands (Eds.), *Head and neck surgery—Otolaryngology* (4th ed.). Philadelphia: Lippincott Williams & Wilkins.

67 Consumer Healthcare Products Association. (2021). Statistics on OTC use. Accessed on July 5, 2021, from https://www.chpa.org/OTCsCategory.aspx

68 Gillson, S. (2016). How many people have acid reflux? Accessed on June 13, 2016, from https://www.verywell.com/how-many-people-have-acid-reflux-1743035.

69 Dunbar, K.B., Agoston, A.T., Odze, R.D., Huo, Z., Pham, T.H., et al. (2016). Association of acute gastroesophageal reflux disease with esophageal histologic changes. *JAMA, 315*(19): 2104–12.

70 Food and Drug Administration. (2011). FDA drug safety communication: Possible increased risk of fractures of the hip, wrist, and spine with the use of proton pump inhibitors. Accessed on September 19, 2016, from http://www.fda.gov/Drugs/DrugSafety/PostmarketDrugSafetyInformationforPatientsandProviders/ucm213206.htm

71 Rao, S.S.C., & Go, J.T. (2010). Update on the management of constipation in the elderly: new treatment options. *Clinical Interventions in Aging, 5*: 163–71.

72 Grosser, T., Smyth, E.M., & FitzGerald, G.A. (2011). Anti-inflammatory, antipyretic, and analgesic: Pharmacotherapy of gout. In L.L. Brunton, B.A. Chabner, & B.C. Knollman (Eds.), *Goodman & Gilman's the pharmacological basis of therapeutics* (12th ed.). New York: McGraw Hill.

73 Sanchez, M.I.P., & Bercik, P. (2011). Epidemiology and burden of chronic constipation. *Canadian Journal of Gastroenterology, 25*(suppl B): 11B–15B.

74 Consumer Healthcare Products Association. (2021). Statistics on OTC use. Accessed on July 5, 2021, from https://www.chpa.org/OTCsCategory.aspx

75 Coffey, F. (1997). *Complete idiots guide to Elvis*. New York: Alpha Books.

76 Rao, S.S.C., & Go, J.T. (2010). Update on the management of constipation in the elderly: New treatment options. *Clinical Interventions in Aging, 5*: 163–71.

77 World Health Organization. (2020). Obesity and overweight. Accessed on July 25, 2020, from https://www.who.int/news-room/fact-sheets/detail/obesity-and-overweight.

78 Hales, C.M., Carroll, M.D., Fryar, C.D., & Ogden, C.L. (2020). Prevalence of obesity and severe obesity among adults: United States, 2017–2018. *NCHS Data Brief No. 360.*

79 Ward, Z.J., Bleich, S.N., Cradock, A.L., Barrett, J.L., & Giles, C.M., et al. (2019). Projected U.S. state-level prevalence of adult obesity and severe obesity. *New England Journal of Medicine, 381*: 2440–50.

80 Tiggemann, M., & Rothblum, E.D. (1988). Gender differences in social consequences of perceived overweight in the United States and Australia. *Sex Roles, 18*: 75–86.

81 Puhl, R.M., & Latner, J.D. (2007). Stigma, obesity, and the health of the nation's children. *Psychological Bulletin, 133*(4): 557–80.

82 Fikkan, J., & Rothblum, E. (2005). Weight bias in employment. In K.D. Brownell, R.M. Puhl, M.B. Schwartz, & L. Rudd (Eds.), *Weight bias: Nature, consequences, and remedies* (pp. *15–28*). New York: Guilford Press.

83 Puhl, R., & Brownell, K.D. (2001). Bias, discrimination and obesity. *Obesity Research, 9*: 788–805.

84 Flegal, K.M., Kit, B.K., Orpana, H., & Graubard, B.I. (2013). Association of all-cause mortality with overweight and obesity using standard body mass index categories: A systemic review and meta-analysis. *JAMA, 309*(1): 71–82.

85 Ofri, D. (2012, May 10). An endless quest for weight-loss pills. *The New York Times*. Accessed on May 14, 2012, from http://well.blogs.nytimes.com/2012/05/10/an-endless-quest-for-weight-loss-pills/?_php=true&_type=blogs&_r=0

86 Lauer, M.S. (2012). Lemons for obesity. *Annals of Internal Medicine, 157*(2): 139–40.

87 Wong, D., Sullivan, K., & Heap, G. (2011). The pharmaceutical market for obesity therapies. *Nature Reviews Drug Discovery, 11*(9): 669.

88 Research and Markets. (2019). United States weight loss and diet control market report 2019: 2018 results and 2019–2023 forecasts-top competitors ranking with 30-year revenue analysis. Accessed on July 24, 2020, from https://www.prnewswire.com/news-releases/united-states-weight-loss--diet-control-market-report-2019-2018-results--2019-2023-forecasts---top-competitors-ranking-with-30-year-revenue-analysis-300803186.html.

89 GAO. (2019). Obesity drugs. Few adults used prescription drugs for weight loss and insurance coverage varied. Accessed on July 24, 2020, from https://www.gao.gov/assets/710/700815.pdf

90 Lauer, M.S. (2012). Lemons for obesity. *Annals of Internal Medicine, 157*(2): 139–40.

91 GlaxoSmithKline. (2013). From page 12 of Alli Companion Guide: "Treatment effects can be an incentive to keep from eating more fat than you really intend to." Accessed on September 19, 2016, from https://www.myalli.com/content/dam/global/Alli/PDF/Alli_CompanionGuide_RP.pdf

92 Consumer Healthcare Products Association. (2021). Statistics on OTC use. Accessed on July 5, 2021, from

https://www.chpa.org/about-consumer-healthcare/research-data

93 Brzezinski, A., Vangel, M.G., Wurtman, R.J., Norrie, G., Zhdanova, I., et al. (2005). Effects of exogenous melatonin on sleep: A meta-analysis. *Sleep Medicine, 9*: 41–50.

94 Council for Responsible Nutrition. (2020). Accessed on July 25, 2020, from https://www.crnusa.org/newsroom/dietary-supplement-use-reaches-all-time-high

95 Food and Drug Administration. (2016). Dietary supplements: What you need to know. Accessed on June 14, 2016, from http://www.fda.gov/Food/ResourcesForYou/Consumers/ucm109760.htm

CHAPTER 16

1 Hill, C. A. (1997). The distinctiveness of sexual motives in relation to sexual desire and desirable partner attributes. *The Journal of Sex Research, 34*(2): 139–53.

2 Meston, C.M., & Buss, D.M. (2007). Why humans have sex. *The Archives of Sexual Behavior, 36*: 477–507.

3 Trussell, J. (2004). Contraceptive efficacy. In R.A. Hatcher, J. Trussell, F. Stewart, A. Nelson, W. Cates, F. Guest, & D. Kowal (Eds.), *Contraceptive technology* (18th ed.). New York: Ardent Media.

4 Guttmacher Institute. (2020). Contraceptive use in the United States. Accessed on August 20, 2020, from https://www.guttmacher.org/sites/default/files/fact-sheet/fb_contr_use_0.pdf

5 Daniels, K., & Abma, J.C. (2018). Current contraceptive status among women aged 15–49: United States, 2015–2017. NCHS Data Brief no. 327. https://www.cdc.gov/nchs/data/databriefs/db327-h.pdf

6 United Nations, Department of Economic and Social Affairs, Population Division. (2019). Contraceptive use by method 2019: Data booklet. Accessed from https://www.un.org/development/desa/pd/sites/www.un.org.development.desa.pd/files/files/documents/2020/Jan/un_2019_contraceptiveusebymethod_databooklet.pdf

7 Rosenthal, M.S. (2013). *Human sexuality from cells to society.* Belmont, CA: Wadsworth Publishing/Cengage Learning.

8 Connell, E.B. (2002). *The contraception sourcebook.* New York: Contemporary Books.

9 Tone, A. (2001). *Devices and desires: A history of contraceptives in America.* New York: Hill and Wang (FSG).

10 Nikolchev, A. (2010). A brief history of the birth control pill. Accessed on January 8, 2015, from http://www.pbs.org/wnet/need-to-know/health/a-brief-history-of-the-birth-control-pill/480/

11 Rosenthal, M.S. (2013). *Human sexuality from cells to society.* Belmont, CA: Wadsworth Publishing/Cengage Learning.

12 Trussell, J. (2018). Contraceptive efficacy. In R.A. Hatcher, J. Trussell, F. Stewart, A. Nelson, W. Cates, F. Guest, & D. Kowal (Eds.), *Contraceptive technology* (21st ed.). New York: Managing Contraception LLC.

13 Hatcher, R.A., & Nelson, A. (2011). The pill: Combined hormonal contraceptive methods. In R.A. Hatcher, J. Trussell, A.L. Nelson, W. Cates, D. Kowal, & M.S. Policar (Eds.), *Contraceptive technology* (20th ed.). New York: Ardent Media.

14 Ibid.

15 Ibid.

16 Hannaford, P.C., Iversen, L., Macfarlane, T.V., Elliott, A.M., Angus, V, & Lee, A.J. (2010). Mortality among contraceptive pill users: Cohort evidence from Royal College of General Practitioners' oral contraception study. *British Medical Journal, 340*(c927): 1–9.

17 Guttmacher Institute. (2015). Contraceptive use in the United States. Accessed on August 30, 2016, from https://www.guttmacher.org/fact-sheet/contraceptive-use-united-states#5a

18 Hou, M.Y., Hurwitz, S., Kavanagh, E., Fortin, J., & Goldberg, A. (2010). Using daily text-message reminders to improve adherence with oral contraceptives: A randomized controlled trial. *Obstetrics and Gynecology, 116*(3): 633–40.

19 Trussell, J. (2018). Contraceptive efficacy. In R.A. Hatcher, J. Trussell, F. Stewart, A. Nelson, W. Cates, F. Guest, & D. Kowal (Eds.), *Contraceptive technology* (21st ed.). New York: Managing Contraception LLC.

20 DeRossi, S.S., & Hersh, E.V. (2002). Antibiotics and oral contraceptives. *Dental Clinics of North America, 46*(4): 653–64.

21 Dickinson, B.D., Altman, R.D., Nielsen, N.H., Sterling, M.L., et al. (2001). Drug interactions between oral contraceptives and antibiotics. *Obstetrics and Gynecology, 98*(5 pt 1): 853–60.

22 Ibid.

23 McClave, A.K., Hogue, C.J., Brunner, L.R., & Ehrlich, A.C. (2010). Cigarette smoking women of reproductive age who use oral contraceptives: Results from the 2002 and 2004 behavioral risk factor surveillance systems. *Women's Health Issues, 20*(6): 380–85.

24 Rosenthal, M.S. (2013). *Human sexuality from cells to society.* Belmont, CA: Wadsworth Publishing/Cengage Learning.

25 Zimmerman, Y., Eijkemans, M.J.C., Bennink, H.J.T, Blankenstein, M.A., & Fauser, B.C.J.M. (2014). The effect of combined oral contraception on testosterone levels in healthy women: A systematic review and meta-analysis. *Human Reproduction Update, 20*(1): 76–105.

26 Panzer, C., Wise, S., Fantini, G., Kang, D., Munarriz, R., et al. (2006). Impact of oral contraceptives on sex hormone-binding globulin and androgen levels: A retrospective study of women with sexual dysfunction. *J Sex Med 3* (May 2006): 567.

27 Althous, F. (2000). Despite their elevated risk, very few women who use oral contraceptives will experience an ischemic stroke. *Family Planning Perspectives, 32*(5): 261.

28 Goldstein, L.B., Bushnell, C.D., Adams, R.J., Appel, L.J., Braun, L.T., et al. (2011). Guidelines for the primary prevention of stroke. *Stroke, 42*: 517–84.

29 McGinley, M., Morales-Vidal, S., Biller, J., & Levine, S.R. (2015). Hormonal contraception and stroke. *MedLink Neurology.* Accessed on August 30, 2016, from http://www.medlink.com/article/hormonal_contraception_and_stroke

30 Skovlund, C.W., Morch, L.S., Kessing, L.V., & Lidegaard, O. (2016). Association of hormonal contraception with depression. *JAMA Psychiatry, 73*(11): 1154–62.

31 Rosenberg, L., Zhang, Y., Coogan, P.F., Strom, B.L., & Palmer, J.R. (2009). A case-control study of oral contraceptive use and incident breast cancer. *American Journal of Epidemiology, 169*(4): 473–79.

32 Kahlenborn, C., Modugno, F., Potter, D.M., & Severs, W.B. (2006). Oral contraceptive use as a risk factor for premenopausal breast cancer: A meta-analysis. *Mayo Clinic Proceedings, 81*(10): 1290–302.

33 Marchbanks, P.A., McDonald, J.A., Wilson, H.G., Folger, S.G., et al. (2002). Oral contraceptives and the risk of breast cancer. *New England Journal of Medicine, 346*(26): 2025–32.

34 Casey, P.M., Cerhan, J.R., & Pruthi, S. (2008). Oral contraceptive use and the risk of breast cancer. *Mayo Clinic Proceedings, 83*(1): 86–91.

35 Iodice, S., Barile, M., Rotmensz, N., Feroce, I., Bonanni, B. et al. (2010). Oral contraceptive use and breast or ovarian cancer risk in BRCA1/2 carriers: A meta-analysis. *European Journal of Cancer, 46*(12): 2275–94.

36 Rosenthal, M.S. (2013). *Human sexuality from cells to society.* Belmont, CA: Wadsworth Publishing/Cengage Learning.

37 Guttmacher Institute. (2015). Contraceptive use in the United States. Accessed on August 30, 2016, from

https://www.guttmacher.org/fact-sheet/contraceptive-use-united-states#5a

[38] Ismail, H., Mansour, D., & Singh, M. (2006). Migration of Implanon. *Journal of Family Planning and Reproductive Health Care, 32*(3): 157–59.

[39] Croxatto, H.B., Urbancsek, J., Massai, R., Bennink, H.C., van Beek, A., et al. (1999). A multicentre efficacy and safety study of the single contraceptive implant Implanon. *Human Reproduction, 14*(4): 976–81.

[40] Hohmann, H. (2009). Examining the efficacy, safety, and patient acceptability of the etonogestrel implantable contraceptive. *Patient Preference and Adherence, 3:* 205–11.

[41] Goldberg, A.B., & Grimes, D.A. (2008). Injectable contraceptives. In R.A. Hatcher, J. Trussell, A.L. Nelson, W. Cates, F.H. Steward, & D. Kowal, (Eds.), *Contraceptive technology* (19th ed.). New York: Ardent Media.

[42] Mangan, S.A., Larsen, P.G., & Hudson, S. (2002). Overweight teens at increased risk for weight gain while using depot medroxyprogesterone acetate. *Journal of Pediatric and Adolescent Gynecology, 15*(2): 79–82.

[43] The faculty of sexual and reproductive healthcare. (2019). Overweight, obesity, and contraception. file:///Users/macmartharosenthal/Downloads/1overweight-obesity-and-contraception-guideline-april-2019.pdf

[44] Bonny, A.E., Ziegler, J., Harvey, R., Debanne, S.M., Secic, M., & Cromer, B.A. (2006). Weight gain in obese and nonobese adolescent girls initiating depot medroxyprogesterone, oral contraceptive pills, or no hormonal contraceptive method. *JAMA Pediatrics, 160*(1): 40–45.

[45] Ibid.

[46] Ibid.

[47] Mansour, D., Gemzell-Danielsson, K., Inki, P., & Jensen, J.T. (2011). Fertility after discontinuation of contraception: A comprehensive review of the literature. *Contraception, 84:* 465–77.

[48] Guttmacher Institute. (2015). Contraceptive use in the United States. Accessed on August 30, 2016, from https://www.guttmacher.org/fact-sheet/contraceptive-use-united-states#5a

[49] National Survey of Family Growth. (2017). Key statistics from the National Survey of Family Growth: Emergency Contraception. Accessed on August 27, 2020, from https://www.cdc.gov/nchs/nsfg/key_statistics/e.htm

[50] Glasier, A.F., Cameron, S.T., Fine, M., Logan, S.J.S., & Casale, W., et al., (2010). Ulipristal acetate versus levonorgestrel for emergency contraception: A randomized non-interiority trial and meta-analysis. *Lancet, 375:* 555–62.

[51] Croxatto, H.B., Brache, V., Pavez, M., Cochon, L., Forcelledo, M.L., Alvarez, F., Massai, R., Faundes, A., & Salvatierra, A.M. (2004). Pituitary-ovarian function following the standard levonorgestrel emergency contraceptive dose or a single 0.75-mg dose given on the days preceding ovulation. *Contraception, 70*(6): 442–50.

[52] Haeger, K.O., Lamme, J., & Cleland, K. (2018). State of emergency contraception in the U.S., 2018. *Contraceptive and Reproductive Medicine, 3:*20.

[53] Noe, G., Croxatto, H.B., Salvatierra, A.M., Reyes, V., Villarroel, C., et al. (2010). Contraceptive efficacy of emergency contraception with levonorgestrel given before or after ovulation. *Contraception, 81*(5): 414–20.

[54] Trussell, J. Raymond, E.G., & Cleland, K. (2016). Emergency contraception: A last chance to prevent unintended pregnancy. Accessed on August 30, 2016, from http://ec.princeton.edu/questions/ec-review.pdf

[55] Wood, S.F. (2006, March 1). When politics defeats science. *The Washington Post.* Accessed March 6, 2006, from http://www.washingtonpost.com/wp-dyn/content/article/2006/02/28/AR2006022801027.html

[56] Trussell, J., Raymond, E.G., & Cleland, K. (2016). Emergency contraception: A last chance to prevent unintended

pregnancy. Accessed on August 30, 2016, from http://ec.princeton.edu/questions/ec-review.pdf

[57] Glasier, A., Cameron, S.T., Blithe, D., Scherrer, B., Mathe, H., et al. (2011). Can we identify women at risk of pregnancy despite using emergency contraception: Data from randomized trials of ulipristal acetate and levonorgestrel. *Contraception, 84*(4): 363–67.

[58] The faculty of sexual and reproductive healthcare. (2019). Overweight, obesity, and contraception. file:///Users/macmartharosenthal/Downloads/1overweight-obesity-and-contraception-guideline-april-2019.pdf

[59] Haeger, K.O., Lamme, J., & Cleland, K. (2018). State of emergency contraception in the U.S., 2018. *Contraceptive and Reproductive Medicine, 3:*20.

[60] Nisen, M. (2013). The long-term, extremely positive effects of birth control in America. *Business Insider.* Accessed on January 15, 2015, from http://www.businessinsider.com/positive-effects-of-birth-control-2013–10

[61] Guttmacher Institute. (2020). Refusing to provide health services. Accessed on August 27, 2020, from https://www.guttmacher.org/state-policy/explore/refusing-provide-health-services

[62] United Nations, Department of Economic and Social Affairs, Population Division. (2019). Contraceptive use by method 2019: Data booklet. Accessed from https://www.un.org/development/desa/pd/sites/www.un.org.development.desa.pd/files/files/documents/2020/Jan/un_2019_contraceptiveusebymethod_databooklet.pdf

[63] Rehman, J. (2013). Where's the male pill? Accessed on January 15, 2015, from http://aeon.co/magazine/society/why-is-there-still-no-pill-for-men

[64] Rosenthal, M.S. (2013). *Human sexuality from cells to society.* Belmont, CA: Wadsworth Publishing/Cengage Learning.

[65] Long, J.E., Lee, M.S., & Blithe, D.L. (2019). Male contraceptive development: Update on novel hormonal and nonhormonal methods. *Clinical Chemistry, 65*(1): 153–60.

[66] Wang, C., Festin, M.P.R., & Swerdloff, R.S. (2016). Male hormonal contraception: Where are we now? *Family Planning, 5:*38–47.

[67] Mannowetz, N., Miller, N.R., & Lishko, P.V. (2017). Regulation of the sperm calcium channel CatSper by endogenous steroids and plant triterpenoids. *PNAS, 114*(5): 201700367.

[68] Syeda, S.S., Sanchez, G., Hong, K.H., Hawkinson, J.E., & Georg, G.I., et al. (2018). Design, synthesis, and in vitro and in vivo evaluation of ouabain analogues as potent and selective Na,K-ATPase a4 isoform inhibitors for male contraception. *Journal of Medical Chemistry, 61*(5): 1800–20.

[69] Syeda, S.S., Sanchez, G., & McDermott, J.P. (2020). The Na⁺ and K⁺ transport system of sperm (ATP1A4) is essential for male fertility and an attractive target for male contraception. *Biology of Reproduction,103*(2): 343–56.

[70] Amory, J.K., Muller, C.H., Shimshoni, J.A., Isoherranen, N., Paik, J., et al. (2011). Suppression of spermatogenesis by bisdichloroacetyldiamines is mediated by inhibition of testicular retinoic acid biosynthesis. *Journal of Andrology, 32*(1): 111–19.

[71] Thoma, M.E., McLain, A.C., Louis, J.F., King, R.B., Trumble, A.C., et al. (2013). Prevalence of infertility in the United States as estimated by the current duration approach and a traditional constructed approach. *Fertility and Sterility, 99*(5): 1324–31.

[72] Homburg, R. (2005). Clomiphene citrate—End of an era: A mini-review. *Human Reproduction, 20*(8): 2043–51.

[73] Ecochard, R., Mathieu, C., Royere, D., Blache, G., Rabilloud, M., et al. (2000). A randomized prospective study comparing pregnancy rates after clomiphene citrate and human menopausal gonadotropin before intrauterine insemination. *Fertility and Sterility, 73*(1): 90–93.

74 Diamond, M.P., Legro, R.S., Coutifaris, C., Alvero, R., Robinson, R.D., et al. (2015). Letrozole, gonadotropin, or clomiphene for unexplained infertility. *New England Journal of Medicine, 373*: 1230–40.

75 Kulkarni, A.D., Jamieson, D.J., Jones, J.W., Kissin, D.M., Gallo, M.F., et al. (2013). Fertility treatments and multiple births in the United States. *New England Journal of Medicine, 369*: 2218–25.

76 Melby, M.K., Lock, M., & Kaufert, P. (2005). Culture and symptom reporting at menopause. *Human Reproduction Update, 11*(5): 495–512.

77 Rice, P.L. (1995). "*Pog laus, tsis coj khaub ncaws lawm:* The menopause in Hmong women." *Journal of Reproductive and Infant Psychology, 13*: 79–92.

78 Zandi, P.P., Carlson, M.C., Plassman, B.L., Welsh-Bohmer, K.A., et al. (2002). Hormone replacement therapy and incidence of Alzheimer disease in older women: The Cache County Study. *JAMA, 288*(17): 2123–29.

79 Paganini-Hill, A., & Henderson, B.E. (1996). Estrogen replacement therapy and risk of Alzheimer disease. *Archives of Internal Medicine, 156*(19): 2213–17.

80 Fackelmann, K. (1995). Forever smart: Does estrogen enhance memory? *Science News, 147*: 74–75.

81 Wysowski, D.K., Golden, L., & Burke, L. (1995). Use of menopausal estrogens and medroxyprogesterone in the United States, 1982–1992. *Obstetrics & Gynecology, 85*: 6–10.

82 Rossouw, J.E., Anderson, G.L., Prentice, R.L., LaCroix, A.Z., Kooperberg, C., et al. (2002). Risks and benefits of estrogen plus progestin in healthy postmenopausal women. Principal results from the Women's Health Initiative Randomized Controlled Trial. *JAMA, 288*(3): 321–33.

83 Martin, K.A., & Barbieri, R.L. (2020). Treatment of menopausal symptoms with hormone therapy. *UpToDate.* Accessed on August 30, 2020, from https://www.uptodate.com/contents/treatment-of-menopausal-symptoms-with-hormone-therapy

84 Vigen, R., O'Donnell, C.I., Baron, A.E., Grunwald, G.K., Maddox, T.M., et al. (2013). Association of testosterone therapy with mortality, myocardial infarction, and stroke in men with low testosterone levels. *JAMA, 310*(17): 1829–36.

85 Bandari J., Ayyash, O.M., Emery, S.L., Wessel, C.B., & Davies, B.J. (2017). Marketing and testosterone treatment in the USA: A systematic review. *Eur Urol Focus,3*(4–5):395–402.

86 Layton, J.B., Li, D., Meier, C.R., Sharpless, J.L., & Sturmer, T., et al. (2014). Testosterone lab testing and initiation in the United Kingdom and the United States, 2000 to 2011. *Journal of Clinical Endocrinology & Metabolism, 99*(3): 835–42.

87 Vigen, R., O'Donnell, C.I., Baron, A.E., Grunwald, G.K., & Maddox, T.M., et al. (2013). Association of testosterone therapy with mortality, myocardial infarction, and stroke in men with low testosterone levels. *JAMA, 310*(17): 1829–36.

88 Budoff, M.J., Ellenberg, S.S., Lewis, C.E., Mohler, E.R., & Wenger, N.K., et al. (2017). Testosterone treatment and coronary artery plaque volume in older men with low testosterone. *JAMA, 317*(17): 708–16.

89 Roy, C.N, Snyder, P.J., Stephens-Shields, Artz, A.S., & Bhasin, S., et al. (2017). Association of testosterone levels with anemia in older men: A controlled clinical trial. *JAMA Internal Medicine, 177*(4): 480–90.

90 Snyder, P.J., Kopperdahl, D.L., Stephens-Shields, A.J., Ellenberg, S.S., & Cauley, J.A., et al. (2017). Effect of testosterone treatment on volumetric bone density and strength in older men with low testosterone: A controlled clinical trial. *JAMA Internal Medicine, 177*(4): 471–79.

91 Resnick, S.M., Matsumoto, A.M., Stephens-Shields, A.J., Ellenberg, S.S., & Gill, T.M., et al. (2017). Testosterone treatment and cognitive function in older men with low testosterone and age-associated memory impairment. *JAMA, 317*(17): 717–12.

92 Finkle, W.D., Greenland, S., Ridgeway, G.K., Adams, J.L., & Frasco, M.A., et al. (2014). Increased risk of nonfatal myocardial infarction following testosterone therapy prescription in men. *PLoS ONE, 9*(1): e85805.

93 Unger, C.A. (2016). Hormone therapy for transgender patients. *Translational Andrology and Urology, 5*(6): 877–84.

94 Ibid.

95 Hughto, J.M.W., & Reisner, S.L. (2016). A systematic review of the effects of hormone therapy on psychological functioning and quality of life in transgender individuals. *Transgender Health, 1*(1): 21–31.

96 Kessler, A., Sollie, S., Challacombe, B., Briggs, K., & Van Hemerlrijck. (2019). The global prevalence of erectile dysfunction: A review. *BJU International, 124*(4): 587–99.

97 Rowland, D.L., & Burnett, A.L. (2000). Pharmacotherapy in the treatment of male sexual dysfunction. *Journal of Sex Research, 37*(3): 226–43.

98 Hatzimouratidis, K., Amar, E., Eardley, I., Guiliano, F., & Hatzichristou, D., et al. (2010). Guidelines on male sexual dysfunction: Erectile dysfunction and premature ejaculation. *European Urology, 57*: 804–14.

99 Capogrosso, P., Colicchia, M., Ventimiglia, E., Castagna, G., & Clementi, M.C., et al. (2013). One patient out of four with newly diagnosed erectile dysfunction is a young man—Worrisome picture from the everyday clinical practice. *Journal of Sexual Medicine, 10*(7): 1833–41.

100 Rosenthal, M.S. (2013). *Human sexuality from cells to society.* Belmont, CA: Wadsworth Publishing/Cengage Learning.

101 Kim, N.N. (2003). Phosphodiesterase type 5 inhibitors: A biochemical and clinical correlation survey. *International Journal of Impotence Research, 15*(suppl 5): S13–S19.

102 McGwin, G. (2010). Phosphodiesterase type 5 inhibitor use and hearing impairment. *Archives of Otolaryngology Head and Neck Surgery, 136*(5): 488–92.

103 Boyce, E.G., & Umland, E.M. (2001). Sildenafil citrate: A therapeutic update. *Clinical Therapeutics, 23*(1): 2–23.

104 Tiefer, L. (2002). Beyond the medical model of women's sexual problems: A campaign to resist the promotion of "female sexual dysfunction." *Sexual and Relationship Therapy, 17*(2): 127–35.

105 Jaspers, L., Feys, F., Bramer, W.M., Franco, O.H., & Leusink, P., et al. (2016). Efficacy and safety of flibanserin for the treatment of hypoactive sexual desire disorder in women. *JAMA Internal Medicine, 176*(4): 453–62.

106 Joffe, H.V., Chang, C., & Sewell, C., Easley, O., & Nguyen, C., et al. (2016). FDA approval of flibanserin—treating hypoactive sexual desire disorder. *New England Journal of Medicine, 374*: 101–104.

107 Simon, J.A., Kingsberg, S.A., Portman, D., Williams, L.A., & Krop, J., et al. (2019). Long-term safety and efficacy of bremelanotide for hypoactive sexual desire disorder. *Obstetrics and Gynecology, 134*(5): 909–17.

108 Rosenthal, M.S. (2013). *Human sexuality from cells to society.* Belmont, CA: Wadsworth Publishing/Cengage Learning.

109 Kotta, S., Ansari, S.H., & Ali, J. (2013). Exploring scientifically proven herbal aphrodisiacs. *Pharmacognosy Review, 7*(13): 1–10.

110 Lee, H.-G., Kim, Y.-C., Dunning, J.S., & Han, K.-A. (2008). Recurring ethanol exposure induces disinhibited courtship in *Drosophila. PLoS ONE, 3*(1): e1391. DOI:10.1371/journal.pone.0001391.

111 Friedman, R.S., McCarthy, D.M., Förster, J., & Denzler, M. (2006). Automatic effects of alcohol cues on sexual attraction. *Addiction, 100*: 672–81.

112 Weatherby, N.L., Shultz, J.M., Chitwood, D.D., McCoy, H.V., McCoy, C.B., et al. (1992). Crack cocaine use and sexual activity in Miami, Florida. *Journal of Psychoactive Drugs, 24*(4): 373–80.

113 Bang-Ping, J. (2007). Sexual dysfunction in men who abuse illicit drugs: A preliminary report. *Journal of Sexual Medicine, 6*(4): 1072–80.

114 Amateau, S.K., & McCarthy, M.M. (2004). Induction of PGE$_2$ by estradiol mediates developmental masculinization of sex behavior. *Nature Neuroscience, 7*(6): 643–50.

115 Centers for Disease Control and Prevention. (2020). HPV vaccine safety and effectiveness. Accessed on August 31, 2020, from https://www.cdc.gov/vaccines/vpd/hpv/hcp/safety-effectiveness.html

116 Centers for Disease Control and Prevention. (2019). Supplemental information and guidance for vaccination providers regarding use of 9-valent HPV. Accessed on August 31, 2020, from https://www.cdc.gov/hpv/downloads/9vhpv-guidance.pdf

117 Centers for Disease Control and Prevention. (2019). HPV-associated cancer statistics. Accessed on August 31, 2020, fromhttps://www.cdc.gov/cancer/hpv/statistics/#:~:text=Based%20on%20data%20from%202012,and%20about%2019%2C000%20among%20men.

118 Markowitz, L.E., Liu, G., & Hariri, S., et al. (2016). Prevalence of HPV after introduction of the vaccination program in the United States. *Pediatrics, 137*(3): e20151968.

119 Guo, F., Cofie, L.E., & Berenson, A.B. (2018). Cervical cancer incidence in young US females after human papillomavirus vaccine introduction. *American Journal of Preventive Medicine,55*(2): 197–204.

120 Shimabukuro, T.T., Su, J.R., & Marquez, P.L., et al. (2019). Safety of the 9-valent human papillomavirus vaccine. *Pediatrics, 144*i(6): e20191791.

121 Centers for Disease Control and Prevention. (2009). *Sexually transmitted disease surveillance, 2008.* Atlanta, GA: Department of Health and Human Services.

CHAPTER 17

1 Verges, A., Haeny, A.M., Jackson, K.M., Bucholz, K.K., Grant J.D., et al. (2013). Refining the notion of maturing out: results from the National Epidemiologic Survey on Alcohol and Related Conditions. *American Journal of Public Health, 103*(12): e67–73.

2 Winick, C. (1962). Maturing out of narcotic addiction. *UNODC, 1*: 1–7.

3 Sobell, L.C., Sobell, M.B., Toneatto, T., & Leo, G.I. (1993). What triggers the resolution of alcohol problems without treatment? *Alcoholism: Clinical and Experimental Research, 17*: 217–24.

4 Hester, R.K., Delaney, H.D., & Campbell, W. (2011). ModerateDrinking.com and Moderation Management: Outcomes of a randomized clinical trial with non-dependent problem drinkers. *Journal of Consulting and Clinical Psychology, 79*(2): 215–24.

5 Hester, R.K., Delaney, J.D., Campbell, W., & Handmaker, N. (2009). A web application for moderation training: Initial results of a randomized clinical trial. *Journal of Substance Abuse and Treatment, 37*(3): 266–76.

6 Kosik, A. (2006). The Moderation Management programme in 2004: What type of drinker seeks controlled drinking? *International Journal of Drug Policy, 17*(4): 295–303.

7 Ritchie, H. & Roser, M. (2019). Drug use. *Our World in Data.* Accessed on September 8, 2020, from https://ourworldindata.org/drug-use

8 Anthony, J.V., Warner, L.A., & Kessler, R.C. (1994). Comparative epidemiology of dependence on tobacco, alcohol, controlled substances and inhalants: Basic findings from the National Comorbidity Survey. *Experimental and Clinical Psychopharmacology, 2*: 244–68.

9 Hilts, P.J. (1994, August 2). Is nicotine addictive? It depends on whose criteria you use. *The New York Times.* http://www.drugsense.org/tfy/addictvn.htm

10 Koob, G.F., Arends, M.A., & Le Moal, M. (2014). *Drugs, addiction, and the brain.* New York: Elsevier.

11 Nutt, D.J., King, L.A., & Phillips, L.D. (2010). Drug harms in the UK: A multicriteria decision analysis. *Lancet, 376*(9752): 1558–65.

12 Ritchie, H. & Roser, M. (2019). Drug use. *Our World in Data.* Accessed on September 8, 2020, from https://ourworldindata.org/drug-use

13 Substance Abuse and Mental Health Services Administration (SAMHSA). (2020). *Results from the 2019 national survey on drug use and health.* Rockville, MD: Center for Behavioral Health Statistics and Quality.

14 Grant, B.F., Goldstein, R.B., Saha, T.D., Chou, P., Jung, J., et al. (2015). Epidemiology of DSM-5 alcohol use disorder: Results from the national epidemiological survey on alcohol and related conditions III. *JAMA Psychiatry, 72*(8): 757–66.

15 Substance Abuse and Mental Health Services Administration (SAMHSA). (2020*). Results from the 2019 national survey on drug use and health.* Rockville, MD: Center for Behavioral Health Statistics and Quality.

16 Ibid.

17 Grant, B.F., Goldstein, R.B., Saha, T.D., Chou, P., Jung, J., et al. (2015). Epidemiology of DSM-5 alcohol use disorder: Results from the national epidemiological survey on alcohol and related conditions III. *JAMA Psychiatry, 72*(8): 757–66.

18 Substance Abuse and Mental Health Services Administration (SAMHSA). (2020). *Results from the 2019 national survey on drug use and health.* Rockville, MD: Center for Behavioral Health Statistics and Quality.

19 Ibid.

20 Elinson, Z. (2015, March 16). Aging baby boomers bring drug habits into middle age. *The Wall Street Journal.* Accessed on August 1, 2016, from http://www.wsj.com/articles/aging-baby-boomers-bring-drug-habits-into-middle-age-1426469057

21 Substance Abuse and Mental Health Services Administration (SAMHSA). (2020). *Results from the 2019 national survey on drug use and health.* Rockville, MD: Center for Behavioral Health Statistics and Quality.

22 Wu, L-T. & Blazer, D.G., (2011). Illicit and nonmedical drug use among older adults: A review. *Journal of Aging and Health, 23*(3): 481–504.

23 Substance Abuse and Mental Health Services Administration (SAMHSA). (1998). *Substance abuse among older adults: An invisible epidemic.* Treatment Improvement Protocol series 26. Rockville, MD: Center for Behavioral Health Statistics and Quality.

24 Substance Abuse and Mental Health Services Administration (SAMHSA). (2020). *Results from the 2019 national survey on drug use and health.* Rockville, MD: Center for Behavioral Health Statistics and Quality.

25 Becker, J.B., Perry, A.N., & Westenbroek, C. (2012). Sex differences in the neural mechanisms mediating addiction: A new synthesis and hypothesis. *Biology of Sex Differences, 3*(1): 14.

26 Zilberman, M.L., Tavares, J., Blume, S.B., & el-Guebaly, N. (2003). Substance use disorders: Sex differences and psychiatric comorbidities. *Canadian Journal of Psychiatry, 48*(1): 5–13.

27 Ibid.

28 Bower, B. (2014, March 7). The addiction paradox. *Science News, 185*(6). Accessed on March 10, 2015, from https://www.sciencenews.org/article/addiction-paradox

29 Verges, A., Haeny, A.M., Jackson, K.M., Bucholz, K.K., Grant J.D., et al. (2013). Refining the notion of maturing out: results from the National Epidemiologic Survey on Alcohol and Related Conditions. *American Journal of Public Health, 103*(12): e67–73.

30 Winick, C. (1962). Maturing out of narcotic addiction. *UNODC, 1*: 1–7.

31 Sobell, L.C., Sobell, M.B., Toneatto, T., & Leo, G.I. (1993). What triggers the resolution of alcohol problems without treatment? *Alcoholism: Clinical and Experimental Research, 17*: 217–24.

32 Ritchie, H. & Roser, M. (2019). Drug use. *Our World in Data*. Accessed on September 8, 2020, from https://ourworldindata.org/drug-use

33 Koob, G.F., Arends, M.A., & Le Moal, M. (2014). *Drugs, addiction, and the brain*. New York: Elsevier.

34 Gahlinger, P. (2004). *Illegal drugs: A complete guide to their history, chemistry, use, and abuse*. New York: Plume.

35 Koob, G.F., Arends, M.A., & Le Moal, M. (2014). *Drugs, addiction, and the brain*. New York: Elsevier.

36 Griffiths, M. (2005). A "components" model of addiction within a biopsychosocial framework. *Journal of Substance Use, 10*(4): 191–97.

37 Kosovski, J.R., & Smith, D.C. (2011). Everybody hurts: Addiction, drama, and the family in the reality television show *Intervention*. *Substance Abuse and Misuse, 46*(7): 852–58.

38 Ibid.

39 Dawson, D.A., Goldstein, R.B., & Grant, B.F. (2007). Rates and correlates of relapse among individuals in remission from DSM-IV alcohol dependence: A 3-year follow-up. *Alcoholism: Clinical and Experimental Research, 31*(12): 2036–45.

40 American Psychiatric Association. (2013). *The diagnostic and statistical manual of mental disorders* (5th ed.). Arlington, VA: American Psychiatric Publishing.

41 Koob, G.F., Arends, M.A., & Le Moal, M. (2014). *Drugs, addiction, and the brain*. New York: Elsevier.

42 Scully, J.L. (2004). What is a disease? *EMBO Reports, 5*(7): 650–53.

43 Szalavitz, M. (2016, June 26). Can you get over an addiction? *The New York Times*. Accessed on August 9, 2016, from http://www.nytimes.com/2016/06/26/opinion/sunday/can-you-get-over-an-addiction.html?_r=0

44 Becker, J.B., Perry, A.N., & Westenbroek, C. (2012). Sex differences in the neural mechanisms mediating addiction: A new synthesis and hypothesis. *Biology of Sex Differences, 3*(1): 14.

45 Koob, G.F. & Volkow, N.D. (2016). Neurobiology of addiction: A neurocircuitry analysis. *Lancet Psychiatry, 3*(8): 760–73.

46 The addicted brain. (2004). *Harvard Mental Health Letter, 21*(1): 1–4.

47 Crews, F.T., & Boettiger, C.A. (2009). Impulsivity, frontal lobes, and risk for addiction. *Pharmacology, Biochemistry, and Behavior, 93*(3): 237–47.

48 Hayashi, T., Ko, J.H., Strafella, A.P., & Dagher, A. (2013). Dorsolateral prefrontal and orbitofrontal cortex interactions during self-control of cigarette craving. *PNAS, 110*(11): 4165–66.

49 Everitt, B.J. (2014). Neural and psychological mechanisms underlying compulsive drug seeking habit and drug memories: Indications for novel treatments of addiction. *European Journal of Neuroscience, 40*: 2163–82.

50 Salamone, J.D., Correa, M., Farrar, A., & Mingote, S.M. (2007). Effort-related functions of nucleus accumbens dopamine and associated forebrain circuits. *Psychopharmacology, 191*: 461–82.

51 Tamir, D.I., & Mitchell, J.P. (2012). Disclosing information about the self is intrinsically rewarding. *PNAS, 109*(21): 8038–43.

52 Crews, F.T., & Boettiger, C.A. (2009). Impulsivity, frontal lobes, and risk for addiction. *Pharmacology, Biochemistry, and Behavior, 93*(3): 237–47.

53 Hayashi, T., Ko, J.H., Strafella, A.P., & Dagher, A. (2013). Dorsolateral prefrontal and orbitofrontal cortex interactions during self-control of cigarette craving. *PNAS, 110*(11): 4165–66.

54 Koob, G.F. (2009). Brain stress systems in the amygdala and addiction. *Brain Research, 1293*: 61–75.

55 Koob, G.F. & Volkow, N.D. (2016). Neurobiology of addiction: A neurocircuitry analysis. *Lancet Psychiatry, 3*(8): 760–73.

56 Everitt, B.J. (2014). Neural and psychological mechanisms underlying compulsive drug seeking habit and drug memories: Indications for novel treatments of addiction. *European Journal of Neuroscience, 40*: 2163–82.

57 Everitt, B.J., Dickinson, A., & Robbins, T.W. (2001). The neuropsychological basis of addictive behavior. *Brain Research Reviews, 36*: 129–38.

58 Xue, Y-X., Luo, Y-X., Wu, P., Shi, H-S., Xue, L-F, et al. (2012). A memory retrieval-extinction procedure to prevent drug craving and relapse. *Science, 336*(6078): 241–45.

59 Volkow, N.D., Fowler, J.S., & Wang, G-J. (2004). The addicted human brain viewed in the light of imaging studies: Brain circuits and treatment strategies. *Neuropharmacology, 47*(1): 3–13.

60 Everitt, B.J. (2014). Neural and psychological mechanisms underlying compulsive drug seeking habit and drug memories: Indications for novel treatments of addiction. *European Journal of Neuroscience, 40*: 2163–82.

61 Robinson, T.E., & Berridge, K.C. (2000). The psychology and neurobiology of addiction: An incentive-sensitization view. *Addiction, 95*(2): S91–117.

62 Ibid.

63 Salamone, J.D., & Correa, M. (2012). The mysterious motivational functions of mesolimbic dopamine. *Neuron, 76*(3): 470–85.

64 Salamone, J.D., Correa, M., Mingote, S.M., & Weber, S.M. (2005). Beyond the reward hypothesis: Alternative functions of nucleus accumbens dopamine. *Current Opinion in Pharmacology, 5*: 34–41.

65 Robinson, T.E., & Berridge, K.C. (2000). The psychology and neurobiology of addiction: An incentive-sensitization view. *Addiction, 95*(2): S91–117.

66 Qi, J., Zhang, S., Wang, H-L., Want, J., Buendia, J., et al. (2014). A glutamatergic reward input from the dorsal raphe to ventral tegmental area dopamine neurons. *Nature Communications, 5*: 5390.

67 Jones, S., & Bonci, A. (2005). Synaptic plasticity and drug addiction. *Current Opinion in Pharmacology, 5*: 20–25.

68 Heinz, A., Mann, K., Weinberg, D.R., & Goldman, D. (2001). Serotonergic dysfunction, negative mood states, and response to alcohol. *Alcoholism: Clinical and Experimental Research, 25*(4): 487–95.

69 Johnson, B.A., Seneviratne, C., Want, X-Q., Nassim, A.D., Li, M.D. (2013). Determination of genotype combinations that can predict the outcome of the treatment of alcohol dependence using the 5-HT3 antagonist ondansetron. *American Journal of Psychiatry, 170*(9): 1020–31.

70 Clapp, P., Bhave, S.V., & Hoffman, P.L. (2008). How adaptation of the brain to alcohol leads to dependence. *Alcohol Research and Health, 31*(4): 310–39.

71 Koob, G.F. (2003). Alcoholism: Allostasis and beyond. *Alcoholism: Clinical and Experimental Research, 27*(2): 232–43.

72 Bevilacqua, L., & Goldman, D. (2009). Genes and addictions. *Clinical Pharmacology and Therapeutics, 85*(4): 359–61.

73 Li, M.D., & Burmeister, M. (2009). New insights into the genetics of addiction. *Nature Reviews: Genetics, 10*(4): 225–31.

74 Bevilacqua, L., & Goldman, D. (2009). Genes and addictions. *Clinical Pharmacology and Therapeutics, 85*(4): 359–61.

75 Kendler, K., & Prescott, C. (1998). Cocaine use, abuse, and dependence in a population-based sample of female twins. *British Journal of Psychiatry, 173*: 345–50.

76 Kendler, K., & Prescott, C. (1998). Cannabis use, abuse, and dependence in a population-based sample of female twins. *American Journal of Psychiatry, 155*(8):1016–22.

77 Rose, M.E., & Cherpitel, C.J. (2011) *Alcohol: Its history, pharmacology, and treatment.* Center City, MN: Hazelden.

78 Agrawal, A., & Lynskey, M.T. (2008). Are there genetic influences on addiction: Evidence from family, adoption, and twin studies. *Addiction, 103*: 1069–81.

79 Ibid.

80 Van den Bree, M., Johnson, E., Neale, M., & Pickens, R. (1998). Genetic and environmental influences on drug use and abuse/dependence in male and female twins. *Drug and Alcohol Dependence, 52*(3): 231–41.

81 Verweij, K.J.H., Zietsch, B.P., Lynskey, M.T., Medland, S.E., Neale, M.C., et al. (2010). Genetic and environmental influences on cannabis use initiation and problematic use: A meta-analysis of twin studies. *Addiction, 105*(3): 417–30.

82 Tsuang, M.T., Lyons, M.J., Meyer, J.M., Doyle, T., Elsen, S.A., et al. (1998). Co-occurrence of abuse of different drugs in men: The role of drug specific and shared vulnerabilities. *Archives of General Psychiatry, 55*(11): 967–72.

83 Bevilacqua, L., & Goldman, D. (2009). Genes and addictions. *Clinical Pharmacology and Therapeutics, 85*(4): 359–61.

84 Goodwin, D.W., Schulsinger, F., Hermansen, L., Guze, S.B., & Winokur, G. (1973). Alcohol problems in adoptees raised apart from alcoholic biological parents. *Archives of General Psychiatry, 28*: 238–43.

85 Bohman, M. (1978). Some genetic aspects of alcoholism and criminality: A population of adoptees. *Archives of General Psychiatry, 35*: 269–76.

86 Cadoret, R.J., Cain, C.A., & Grove, W.M. (1979). Development of alcoholism in adoptees raised apart from alcoholic biologic relatives. *Archives of General Psychiatry, 37*: 561–63.

87 Zhou, Z., Karlsson, C., Liang, T., Xiong, W., Kimura, M., et al. (2013). Loss of metabotropic glutamate receptor 2 escalates alcohol consumption: Genomic discovery and functional validation. *PNAS, 110*(42): 16963–68.

88 Werner, C.T., Mitra, S., Martin, J.A., Stewart, A.F., & Lepack, A.E., et al. (2019). Ubiquitin-proteasomal regulation of chromatin remodeler INO80 in the nucleus accumbens mediates persistent cocaine craving. *Science Advances, 5*(10): eaay0351.

89 Caspi, A., Sugen K., Moffitt, T.E., Taylor, A., Craig, I.W., Harrington, H.L., McClay, J., Mill, J., Martin, J., Braithwaite, A., & Poultri, R. (2003). Influence of life stress on depression, moderation by a polymorphism in the 5-HTT gene. *Science, 301*(5631): 386–89.

90 Daw, J., Shanahan, M., Harris, K.M., Smolen, A., Haberstick, B., et al. (2013). Genetic sensitivity to peer behaviors: 5HTTLPR, smoking, and alcohol consumption. *Journal of Health and Social Behavior, 54*(1): 92–108.

91 Bevilacqua, L., & Goldman, D. (2009). Genes and addictions. *Clinical Pharmacology and Therapeutics, 85*(4): 359–61.

92 Vassoler, F.M., & Sadri-Vakili, G. (2014). Mechanisms of transgenerational inheritance of addictive-like behaviors. *Neuroscience, 264*: 198–206.

93 Lo, C-L., Lossie, A.C., Liang, T., Liu, Y., Xuei, X., et al. (2016). High resolution genomic scans reveal genetic architecture controlling alcohol preference in bidirectionally selected rat model. *PLoS Genetics, 12*(8): e1006178.

94 Youngentob, S.L., & Glendinning, J.I. (2009). Fetal ethanol exposure increases ethanol intake by making it smell and taste better. *PNAS, 106*(13): 5359–64.

95 Slutske, W.S., Heath, A.C., Madden, P.A.F., Bucholz, K.K., Statham, D.J., & Martin, N.G. (2002). Personality and the genetic risk for alcohol dependence. *Journal of Abnormal Psychology, 11*(1): 124–33.

96 LoCastro, J., Spiro, A., Monnelly, E., & Ciraulo, D. (2000). Personality, family history, and alcohol use among older men: The VA normative aging study. *Alcoholism: Clinical and Experimental Research, 24*(4): 501–11.

97 Ritchie, H. & Roser, M. (2019). Drug use. *Our World in Data.* Accessed on September 8, 2020, from https://ourworldindata.org/drug-use

98 Koob, G.F., Arends, M.A., & Le Moal, M. (2014). *Drugs, addiction, and the brain.* New York: Elsevier.

99 Grant, B.F., Stinson, F.S., Dawson, D.A., Chou, S.P., Dufour, M.C., et al. (2006). Prevalence and co-occurrence of substance use disorders and independent mood and anxiety disorders. *Archives of General Psychiatry, 29*(2): 107–210.

100 Kuhn, C., Swartzwelder, S., & Wilson, W. (2008). *Buzzed: The straight facts about the most used and abused drugs from alcohol to ecstasy* (3rd ed.). New York: W.W. Norton & Company.

101 Rose, M.E., & Cherpitel, C.J. (2011) *Alcohol: Its history, pharmacology, and treatment.* Center City, MN: Hazelden.

102 Griffin, K.W., & Botvin, G.J. (2011). Evidence-based interventions for preventing substance use disorders in adolescents. *Child and Adolescent Psychiatric Clinics of North America, 19*(3): 505–26.

103 Chen, C-Y., Storr, C.L., & Anthony, J.C. (2009). Early-onset drug use and risk for drug dependence problems. *Addictive Behavior, 34*(3): 319–22.

104 Nation, M., & Heflinger, C.A. (2006). Risk factors for serious alcohol and drug use: The role of psychosocial variables in predicting the frequency of substance use among adolescents. *American Journal of Drug and Alcohol Abuse, 32*: 415–33.

105 Chen, C-Y., Storr, C.L., & Anthony, J.C. (2009). Early-onset drug use and risk for drug dependence problems. *Addictive Behavior, 34*(3): 319–22.

106 Koob, G.F., Arends, M.A., & Le Moal, M. (2014). *Drugs, addiction, and the brain.* New York: Elsevier.

107 Hingson, R.W., Heeren, T., & Winter, M.R. (2006). Age at drinking onset and alcohol dependence. *Archives of Pediatric and Adolescent Medicine, 160*(7): 739–46.

108 SAMHSA. (2014). *Results from the 2013 national survey on drug use and health: Summary of national findings.* NSDUH Series H-41, HHS Publication no (SMA) 11–4658. Rockville, MD: Center for Behavioral Health Statistics and Quality.

109 National Center of Addiction and Substance Abuse. (2003). *The national survey of American attitudes on substance abuse VIII: Teens and parents.* New York: Columbia University.

110 Elder, R.W., Lawrence, B., Ferguson, A., Naimi, T.S., Brewer, R.D., et al. (2010). The effectiveness of tax policy interventions for reducing excessive alcohol consumption and related harms. *American Journal of Preventive Medicine 38*(2): 217–29.

111 Czeisler, M.E., Lane, R.I., Petrosky, E., Wiley, J.F., & Christensen, A., et al. (2020). Mental health, substance use, and suicidal ideation during the COVID-19 pandemic—United States, June 24–30, 2020. *MMWR, 69*: 1049–57.

112 Dubey, M.H., Ghosh, R., Chatterjee, S., Biswas, P., & Chatterjee, S., et al. (2020). COVID-19 and addiction. *Diabetes and Metabolic Syndrome, 14*(5): 817–23.

113 NIDA. (2020). COVID-19 resources. Accessed on September 10, 2020, from https://www.drugabuse.gov/drug-topics/comorbidity/covid-19-resources

114 Montagne, M. (2011). Drugs and the media: An introduction. *Substance Use and Misuse, 46*: 849–51.

115 Sargent, J.D., Beach, M., Adachi-Mejia, A., et al. (2005). Exposure to movie smoking: its relation to smoking initiation among US adolescents. *Pediatrics, 116*(5): 1183–91.

116 Koordeman, R., Anschutz, D.J., & Engels, R.C. (2012). Alcohol portrayals in movies, music videos, and soap operas and alcohol use of young people: Current status and future challenges. *Alcohol and Alcoholism, 47*(5): 612–23.

[117] Engels, R.C.M E., Hermans, R., van Baaren, R.B., Hollenstein, T., & Bot, S.M. (2009). Alcohol portrayal on television affects actual drinking behavior. *Alcohol and Alcoholism, 44*(3): 244–49.

[118] Primack, B.A., Douglas, E., & Kraemer, K. (2010). Exposure to cannabis in popular music and cannabis use among adolescents. *Addiction, 105*: 515–23.

[119] Barry, C.L., McGinty, E.E., Pescosolido, B.A., & Goldman, H.H. (2014). Stigma, discrimination, treatment, effectiveness, and policy: Public views about drug addiction and mental illness. *Psychiatric Services, 65*(10): 1269–72.

[120] Corrigan, P.W., Kuwabara, S.A., & O'Shaughnessy, J.A. (2009). The public stigma of mental illness and drug addiction. *Journal of Social Work, 9*(2): 139–47.

[121] Hatgis, C., Friedmann, P.D., & Wiener, M. (2008). Attributions of responsibility for addiction: The effects of gender and type of substance. *Substance Use and Misuse, 43*(5): 700–708.

[122] Ibid.

[123] Ibid.

[124] Ibid.

[125] Broadus, A.D., Hartje, J.A., Roger, N.A., Cahoon, K.L., & Clinkinbeard, S.S. (2010). Attitudes about addiction: A national study of addiction educators. *Journal of Drug Education, 40*(3): 281–98.

[126] Ibid.

[127] Rao, H., Mahadevappa, H., Pillay, P., Sessay, M., Abraham, A., & Luty, J. (2009). A study of stigmatized attitudes towards people with mental health problems among health professionals. *Journal of Psychiatric and Mental Health Nursing, 16*(3): 279–84.

[128] Barry, C.L., McGinty, E.E., Pescosolido, B.A., & Goldman, H.H. (2014). Stigma, discrimination, treatment, effectiveness, and policy: Public views about drug addiction and mental illness. *Psychiatric Services, 65*(10): 1269–72.

[129] Substance Abuse and Mental Health Services Administration (SAMHSA). (2014). *Results from the 2013 national survey on drug use and health: Summary of national findings.* NSDUH Series H-41, HHS Publication no (SMA) 11–4658. Rockville, MD: Center for Behavioral Health Statistics and Quality.

[130] Esser, M.B., Hedden, S.L., Kanny, D., Brewer, R.D., Gfroerer, J.C., & Naimi, T.S. (2014). Prevalence of alcohol dependence among U.S. adult drinkers, 2009–2011. *Preventing Chronic Disease, 11*(E206).

[131] DeJong, W. (2003). Definitions of binge drinking. *JAMA, 289*(13): 1635.

[132] Black, D.W., Kehrberg, L.L.D., Flumerfelt, D.L., & Schlosser, S.S. (1997). Characteristics of 36 subjects reporting compulsive sexual behavior. *American Journal of Psychiatry, 154*(2):243–49.

CHAPTER 18

[1] Substance Abuse and Mental Health Services Administration (SAMHSA). (2015). *Behavioral health trends in the United States: Results from the 2014 national survey on drug use and health.* NSDUH Series H-50. Rockville, MD: Center for Behavioral Health Statistics and Quality.

[2] National Institute on Drug Abuse. (2020). Costs of substance abuse. Accessed on September 21, 2020, from https://www.drugabuse.gov/drug-topics/trends-statistics/costs-substance-abuse

[3] Bower, B. (2014). The addiction paradox. *Science News, 185*(6). Accessed on March 10, 2015, from https://www.sciencenews.org/article/addiction-paradox

[4] Institute of Medicine. (1994). *Reducing risks for mental disorders: Frontiers for preventive intervention research.* Committee on Prevention of Mental Disorders, Division of Biobehavorial Sciences and Mental Disorders. Washington, DC: National Academy Press.

[5] National Research Council and Institute of Medicine Committee on the Prevention of Mental Disorders and Substance Abuse among Children, Youth, and Youth Adults. (2009). Preventing mental, emotional, and behavioral disorders among young people: Progress and possibilities. In M.E. O'Connell, T. Boat, and K.E. Warner (Eds.). *National Academies.* Washington DC: National Academies Press.

[6] Broning, S., Kumpfer, K., Kruse, K., Sack, P-M., Schaunig-Busch, I., et al. (2012). Selective prevention programs for children from substance-affected families: A comprehensive systematic review. *Substance Abuse, Treatment, Prevention, and Policy, 7*: 23.

[7] Conrod, P.J., O'Leary-Barrett, M., Newton, N., Topper, L., Catellanos-Ryan, N., et al. (2013). Effectiveness of a selective, personality-targeted prevention program for adolescent alcohol use and misuse. *JAMA Psychiatry, 70*(3): 334–42.

[8] United Nations Office on Drugs and Crime. (2015). International standards on drug use prevention. Accessed on August 3, 2016, from https://www.unodc.org/documents/prevention/UNODC_2013_2015_international_standards_on_drug_use_prevention_E.pdf

[9] Shin, H.S. (2001). A review of school-based drug prevention program evaluations in the 1990s. *American Journal of Health Education, 32*(3): 139–47.

[10] Ibid.

[11] United Nations Office on Drugs and Crime. (2015). International standards on drug use prevention. Accessed on August 3, 2016, from https://www.unodc.org/documents/prevention/UNODC_2013_2015_international_standards_on_drug_use_prevention_E.pdf

[12] Grim, R. (2009). *This is your country on drugs: The secret history of getting high in America.* Hoboken, NJ: John Wiley and Sons.

[13] Pan, W., & Bai, H. (2009). A multivariate approach to a meta-analytic review of the effectiveness of the DARE program. *International Journal of Environmental Research and Public Health, 6*(1): 267–77.

[14] Rosenbaum, D.P., & Hanson, G.S. (1998). Assessing the effects of school-based drug education: A six-year multilevel analysis of project D.A.R.E. *Journal of Research in Crime and Delinquency, 35*: 381.

[15] Hecht, M.L., Graham, J.W., & Elek, E. (2006). The drug resistance strategies intervention: Program effects on substance use. *Health Communication, 120*(3): 267–76.

[16] Caputi, T.L., & McLellan, A.T. (2017). Truth and D.A.R.E.: Is D.A.R.E.'s new Keepin' It REAL curriculum suitable for American nationwide implementation? *Drugs: Education, Prevention and Policy, 24*(1): 49–57.

[17] Lee, M.A. (2012). *Smoke signals: A social history of marijuana—Medical, recreational, and scientific.* New York: Scribner.

[18] United Nations Office on Drugs and Crime. (2015). International standards on drug use prevention. Accessed on August 3, 2016, from https://www.unodc.org/documents/prevention/UNODC_2013_2015_international_standards_on_drug_use_prevention_E.pdf

[19] Ibid.

[20] Cuijpers, P. (2002). Effective ingredients of school-based drug prevention programs: A systematic review. *Addictive Behaviors, 27*(6): 1009–23.

[21] Griffin, K.W., & Botvin, G.J. (2011). Evidence-based interventions for preventing substance use disorders in adolescents. *Child and Adolescent Psychiatric Clinics of North America, 19*(3): 505–26.

[22] Shin, H.S. (2001). A review of school-based drug prevention program evaluations in the 1990s. *American Journal of Health Education, 32*(3): 139–47.

[23] Stigler, M.H., Neusel, E., & Perry, C.L. (2011). School-based programs to prevent and reduce alcohol use among youth. *Alcohol Research and Health, 34*(2): 157–62.

24 Johnston, L.D., O'Malley, P.M., Bachman, J.G., & Schulenberg, J.E. (2012). *Monitoring the future: National results on adolescent drug use.* Ann Arbor: Institute for Social Research, The University of Michigan.

25 Ibid.

26 Primack, B.A., Sidani, J., Carroll, M.V., & Fine, M.J. (2009). Associations between smoking and media literacy in college students. *Journal of Health Communication, 14:* 541–55.

27 Ibid.

28 Jeong, S-H., Cho, J., & Hwang, Y. (2012). Media literacy interventions: A meta-analytic review. *Journal of Communication, 62*(3): 454–72.

29 Pinkleton, B.E., Austin, E.W., Cohen, M., Miller, A., & Fitzgerald, E. (2007). A statewide evaluation of the effectiveness of media literacy training to prevent tobacco use among adolescents. *Health Communication, 21*(1): 23–34.

30 Banerjee, S.C., & Greene, K. (2007). Antismoking initiatives: Effects of analysis versus production media literacy interventions on smoking-related attitude, norm, and behavioral intention. *Health Communication, 22*(1): 37–48.

31 Kupersmidt, J.B., Scull, T.M., & Austin, E.W. (2010). Media literacy education for elementary school substance use prevention: Study of media detective. *Pediatrics, 126*(3): 525–31.

32 Scull, T.M., Kupersmidt, J.B., & Weatherholt, T.N. (2017). The effectiveness of online, family-based media literacy education for substance abuse prevention in elementary school children: Study of the Media Detective Family program. *Journal of Community Psychology, 45*(6): 796–809.

33 Kaestle, C.E., Chen, Y., Estabrooks, P.A., Zoellner, J., & Bigby, B. (2013). Pilot evaluation of a media literacy program for tobacco prevention targeting early adolescents shows mixed results. *Tobacco Control, 27*(6): 366–69.

34 Griffin, K.W., & Botvin, G.J. (2011). Evidence-based interventions for preventing substance use disorders in adolescents. *Child and Adolescent Psychiatric Clinics of North America, 19*(3): 505–26.

35 Hecht, M.L., & Miller-Day, M. (2007). The Drug Resistance Strategies project as translational research. *Journal of Applied Communication Research, 35*(4): 343–49.

36 Hecht, M.L., Colby, M., & Miller-Day, M. (2010). The Dissemination of Keepin' It REAL through D.A.R.E. America: A lesson in disseminating health messages. *Health Communication, 25*(6–7): 585–86.

37 Hecht, M.L., Marsiglia, F.F., Elek, E., Wagstaff, D.A., & Kulis, S., et al. (2003). Culturally grounded substance use prevention: An evaluation of the Keepin' It REAL curriculum. *Prevention Science, 4:* 233–48.

38 Botvin, G.J., Griffin, K.W., & Williams, C. (2015). Preventing daily substance use among high school students using a cognitive-behavioral competence enhancement approach. *World Journal of Preventive Medicine, 3*(3): 48–53.

39 Spoth, R., Trudeau, L., Shin, C., Ralston, E., Redmond, C., et al. (2013). Longitudinal effects of universal preventive intervention on prescription drug misuse: Three randomized controlled trials with late adolescents and young adults. *American Journal of Public Health, 103*(4): 665–72.

40 Spoth, R.L., Randall, G.K., Trudeau, L., Shin, C., & Redmond, C. (2008). Substance use outcomes 5½ years past baseline for partnership-based family-school preventive interventions. *Drug and Alcohol Dependence, 96:* 57–88.

41 Botvin, G.J., Baker, E., Dusenbury, L., Botwin, E.M., & Diaz, T. (1995). Long-term follow-up results of a randomized drug abuse prevention trial in a white middle-class population. *JAMA, 273*(14): 11106–12.

42 Botvin, G.J., Schinke, S.P., Epstein, J.A., Diaz, T., & Botvin, E.M. (1995). Effectiveness of culturally focused and generic skills training approaches to alcohol and drug abuse prevention among minority adolescents: Two-year follow-up results. *Psychology of Addictive Behaviors, 9*(3): 183–94.

43 Botvin, G.J., Griffin, K.W., & Williams, C. (2015). Preventing daily substance use among high school students using a cognitive-behavioral competence enhancement approach. *World Journal of Preventive Medicine, 3*(3): 48–53.

44 Ibid.

45 Wan, W. (2017). Cigarette taxes are the best way to cut smoking, scaring Big Tobacco. *The Denver Post.* Accessed on December 16, 2017, from http://www.denverpost.com/2017/10/21/cigarette-taxes-reduce-smoking/

46 Ibid.

47 Arria, A.M., Caldeira, K.M., Allen, H.K., Bugbee, B.A., & Vincent, K.B., et al. (2017). Prevalence and incidence of drug use among college students: An 8-year longitudinal analysis. *The American Journal of Drug and Alcohol Abuse, 43*(6): 711–18.

48 National Institute on Alcohol Abuse and Alcoholism. (2002). *A call to action: Changing the culture of drinking at U.S. colleges.* Task force of the National Advisory Council on Alcohol Abuse and Alcoholism. Washington, DC: National Institutes of Health. U.S. Department of Health and Human Services.

49 Ibid.

50 Ibid.

51 Ibid.

52 Davis, J.H. (2017). Trump declares opioid crisis a "health emergency" but requests no funds. *The New York Times.* Accessed on December 14, 2017, from http://www.nytimes.com/2017/10/26/us/politics/trump-opioid-crisis.html

53 Fishbein, M., Hall-Jamieson, K., Zimmer, E., von Haeften, I., & Nabi, R. (2002). Avoiding the boomerang: Testing the relative effectiveness of antidrug public service announcements before a national campaign. *American Journal of Public Health, 92*(2): 238–45.

54 Grim, R. (2009). *This is your country on drugs: The secret history of getting high in America.* Hoboken, NJ: John Wiley and Sons.

55 Hornik, R., Jacobsohn, L., Orwin, R., Piesse, A., & Kalton, G. (2008). Effects of the National Youth Anti-Drug Media Campaign on youths. *American Journal of Public Health, 98*(12): 2229–36.

56 Ibid.

57 Ibid.

58 Grim, R. (2009). *This is your country on drugs: The secret history of getting high in America.* Hoboken, NJ: John Wiley and Sons.

59 Leinwand, D. (2006, August 28). Anti-drug advertising campaign a failure, GAO report says. *USA Today.* Accessed on August 18, 2016, from http://usatoday30.usatoday.com/news/washington/2006-08-28-anti-drug-ads_x.htm

60 Werb, D., Mills, E.J., DeBeck, K., Kerr, T., Montaner, J.S.G., & Wood, E. (2011). The effectiveness of anti-illicit-drug public service announcements: A systematic review and meta-analysis. *Journal of Epidemiology and Community Health, 65:* 834–40.

61 Slater, M.D., Kelley, K.J., Lawrence, F.R., Stanley, L.R., & Comella, M.L.G. (2011). Assessing media campaigns linking marijuana non-use with autonomy and aspirations: Be under your own influence and ONDCP's Above the Influence. *Prevention Science, 12*(1): 12–22.

62 National Cancer Institute. (2008). *The role of the media in promoting and reducing tobacco use.* National Cancer Institute Tobacco Control Monographs Series. Washington, DC: National Institutes of Health.

63 Farrelly, M.C., Davis, K.C., Haviland, L., Messeri, P., & Healton, C.G. (2005). Evidence of a dose-response relationship between "truth" antismoking ads and youth

smoking prevalence. *American Journal of Public Health, 95*(3): 425–31.

64 Minton, M. (2019). Blame anti-tobacco advocates for youth vaping "epidemic." Competitive Enterprise Institute. Accessed on September 24, 2020, from https://cei.org/blog/blame-anti-tobacco-advocates-youth-vaping-epidemic

65 Hasse, J. (2019). Drug testing at work is a thing of the past, study finds. Accessed on September 24, 2020, from https://www.forbes.com/sites/javierhasse/2019/08/05/drug-testing-at-work/#7af02a03fa72

66 Grim, R. (2009). *This is your country on drugs: The secret history of getting high in America.* Hoboken, NJ: John Wiley and Sons.

67 Wylie, M. (2018). Surprising stats on drugs in the workplace. Accessed on September 25, 2020, from https://www.psychemedics.com/blog/2018/01/surprising-stats-drugs-workplace/

68 Sznitman, S.R., & Romer, D. (2014). Student drug testing and positive school climates: Testing the relation between two school characteristics and drug use behavior in a longitudinal study. *Journal of Studies on Alcohol and Drugs, 75*(1): 65–73.

69 Yamaguchi, R., Johnston, L.D., & O'Malley, P.M. (2003). Relationship between student illicit drug use and school drug-testing policies. *Journal of School Health, 73*(4): 159–64.

70 Ibid.

71 United Nations Office on Drugs and Crime. (2015). International standards on drug use prevention. Accessed on August 3, 2016, from https://www.unodc.org/documents/prevention/UNODC_2013_2015_international_standards_on_drug_use_prevention_E.pdf

72 Gomez, A.M., & Israel, J. (2019). Accessed on September 25, 2020, from https://archive.thinkprogress.org/states-cost-drug-screening-testing-tanf-applicants-welfare-2018-results-data-0fe9649fa0f8/

73 Alvarez, L. (2012, April 18). No savings are found from welfare drug tests. *The New York Times,* A14.

74 Covert, B., & Israel, J. (2015). What 7 states discovered after spending more than $1 million drug testing welfare recipients. Accessed on March 3, 2015, from http://thinkprogress.org/economy/2015/02/26/3624447/tanf-drug-testing-states/

75 Hasse, J. (2019). Drug testing at work is a thing of the past, study finds. Accessed on September 24, 2020, from https://www.forbes.com/sites/javierhasse/2019/08/05/drug-testing-at-work/#7af02a03fa72

76 Quest Diagnostics. (2020). Positivity rates by testing reason. Accessed on November 12, 2020, from https://www.questdiagnostics.com/home/physicians/health-trends/drug-testing/table4/

77 Hasse, J. (2019). Drug testing at work is a thing of the past, study finds. Accessed on September 24, 2020, from https://www.forbes.com/sites/javierhasse/2019/08/05/drug-testing-at-work/#7af02a03fa72

78 LabCorp Drug Abuse Reference Guide. (2016). Accessed on August 5, 2016, from https://www.labcorp.com/wps/wcm/connect/24b476804b65af7fb49cb5dc8b9b0898/L1123-0216-5.pdf?MOD=AJPERES&CACHEID=24b476804b65af7fb49cb5dc8b9b0898&CACHEID=457e14004b2a17b4ba21bb1199be625c&CACHEID=457e14004b2a17b4ba21bb1199be625c

79 Verstraete, A.G. (2004). Detection times of drugs of abuse in blood, urine, and oral fluid. *The Drug Monitor, 26*(2): 200–204.

80 Gryczynski, J., Schwartz, R.P., Mitchell, S.G., O'Grady, K.E., & Ondersman, S.J. (2014). Hair drug testing results and self-reported drug use among primary care patients with moderate-risk illicit drug use. *Drug and Alcohol Dependence, 141*: 44–50.

81 Joseph, R.E., Su, T., & Cone, E.J. (1996). In vitro binding studies of drugs into hair: Influence of melanin and lipids on cocaine binding to Caucasoid and Africoid hair. *Journal of Analytical Toxicology, 20*(6): 338–44.

82 Maltby, L. (2012, March). Latest research reveals new problems with drug testing. *National Workrights Institute.* Accessed on July 26, 2016, from http://workrights.us/wp-content/uploads/2012/03/NewInformationDrugTesting.pdf

83 Taggart, R.W. (1989). Results of the drug testing program at work at Southern Pacific Railroad. In S.W. Gust & J.M. Walsh (Eds.), *Drugs in the workplace: Research and evaluation data.* Washington, DC: National Institute on Drug Abuse. NIDA Research Monograph. 91: 97–108

84 American Civil Liberties Union. (1999). Drug testing: A bad investment. Accessed on March 3, 2015, from https://www.aclu.org/files/FilesPDFs/drugtesting.pdf

85 Holding, R. (2006, July 7). Whatever happened to drug testing? *Time Magazine.* Accessed on August 3, 2015, from http://content.time.com/time/nation/article/0,8599,1211429,00.html

86 Ramchand, R., Pomeroy, A., & Arkes, J. (2009). *The effects of substance use on workplace injuries.* Arlington, VA: The Rand Corporation.

87 Ibid.

88 James-Burdumy, S., Goesling, B., Deke, J., Einspruch, E., & Silverberg, M. (2010). *The effectiveness of mandatory-random student drug testing: Executive Summary (NCEE 2010–4026).* Washington, DC: National Center for Education Evaluation and Regional Assistance, Institute of Education Sciences, U.S. Department of Education.

89 Yamaguchi, R., Johnston, L.D., & O'Malley, P.M. (2003). Relationship between student illicit drug use and school drug-testing policies. *Journal of School Health, 73*(4): 159–64.

90 United Nations Office on Drugs and Crime. (2015). International standards on drug use prevention. Accessed on August 3, 2016, from https://www.unodc.org/documents/prevention/UNODC_2013_2015_international_standards_on_drug_use_prevention_E.pdf

91 Substance Abuse and Mental Health Services Administration (SAMHSA). (2020). *Results from the 2019 national survey on drug use and health.* Rockville, MD: Center for Behavioral Health Statistics and Quality.

92 Ibid.

93 Ibid.

94 Ibid.

95 Ibid.

96 Hecht, A. (2011). *Understanding drugs: Cocaine and crack.* New York: Chelsea House.

97 Prochaska, J.O. (2008). Decision making in the transtheoretical model of behavior change. *Medical Decision Making, 28*(6): 845–49.

98 Prochaska, J.O., DiClemente, C.C., & Corcross, J.C. (1992). In search of how people change: Applications to addictive behaviors. *American Psychologist, 47*(9): 1102–14.

99 O'Brien, C.P. (1996). Drug addiction and drug abuse. In *Goodman & Gilman's The pharmacological basis of therapeutics* (9th ed.). New York: McGraw Hill.

100 Rose, M.E., & Cherpitel, C.J. (2011) *Alcohol: Its history, pharmacology, and treatment.* Center City, MN: Hazelden.

101 Litten, R.Z., Ryan, M.L., Fertig, J.B., Falk, D.E., Johnson, B., et al. (2013). A double-blind, placebo-controlled trial assessing the efficacy of varenicline tartrate for alcohol dependence. *Journal of Addiction Medicine, 7*(4): 277–86.

102 Johnson, M.W., Garcia-Romeu, A., & Griffiths, R.R. (2017). Long-term follow-up of psilocybin-facilitated smoking cessation. *American Journal of Drug and Alcohol Abuse, 43*(1): 55–60.

103 Johnson, B.A., Seneviratne, C., Want, X-Q., Nassim, A.D., & Li, M.D. (2013). Determination of genotype combinations that can predict the outcome of the treatment of alcohol dependence using the 5-HT3 antagonist

ondansetron. *American Journal of Psychiatry, 170*(9): 1020–31.

[104] Clapp, P., Bhave, S.V., & Hoffman, P.L. (2008). How adaptation of the brain to alcohol leads to dependence. *Alcohol Research and Health, 31*(4): 310–39.

[105] O'Brien, C.P., Rukstalis, M.R., & Stromberg, M.F. (2002). Pharmacotherapy of alcoholism. In K.L. Davis, D. Charney, J.T. Coyle, & C. Nemeroff (Eds.), *Neuropsychopharmacology: The fifth generation of progress.* Philadelphia: Lippincott Williams & Wilkins.

[106] Maisel, N.C., Blodgett, J.C., Wilbourne, P.L., Humphreys, K., & Finney, J.W. (2013). Meta-analysis of naltrexone and acamprosate for treating alcohol use disorders: When are these medications most helpful? *Addiction, 108*(2): 275–93.

[107] Krebs, T.S., & Johansen, P-O. (2012). Lysergic acid diethylamide (LSD) for alcoholism: Meta-analysis of randomized controlled trials. *Journal of Psychopharmacology, 26*(7): 994–1002.

[108] Sessa, B. (2017). Why MDMA therapy for alcohol use disorder? And why now? Neuropharmacology, 142: 83–88.

[109] Bowen, M.T., Peters, S.T., Absalom, N., Chebib, M., Neumann, I.D., et al. (2015). Oxytocin prevents ethanol actions at the δ subunit-containing GABAA receptors and attenuates ethanol-induced motor impairment in rats. *PNAS, 112*(10): 3104–09.

[110] Pedersen, C.A., Smedley, K.L., Leserman, J., Jarskog, L.F., Rau, S.W., et al. (2013). Intranasal oxytocin blocks alcohol withdrawal in human subjects. *Alcoholism: Clinical and Experimental Research, 37*(3): 484–89.

[111] Pettinati, H.M., O'Brien, C.P., Rabinowitz, A.R., Wortman, S.P., Oslin, D.W., Kampman, K.M., & Dackis, C.A. (2006). The status of naltrexone in the treatment of alcohol dependence: Specific effects on heavy drinking. *Journal of Clinical Psychopharmacology, 26*(6): 610–25.

[112] D'Onofrio, G., O'Connor, P.G., Pantalon, M.V., Chawarski, M.C., Busch, S.H., et al. (2015). Emergency department-initiated buprenorphine/naloxone treatment for opioid dependence: A randomized clinical trial. *JAMA, 313*(16): 1636–44.

[113] Heidbreder, C.A., & Hagan, J.J. (2005). Novel pharmacotherapeutic approaches for the treatment of drug addiction and craving. *Current Opinion in Pharmacology, 5*: 107–11.

[114] Gaidos, S. (2016). Addiction protection. *Science News, 190*(1): 22.

[115] Xiaoshan, T., Junjie, Y., Wenqing, W., Yunong, Z., & Jiaping, L., et al. (2020). Immunotherapy for treating methamphetamine, heroin, and cocaine use disorders. *Drug Discovery Today, 25*(3): 610–19.

[116] Gaidos, S. (2016). Addiction protection. *Science News, 190*(1): 22.

[117] Schlosburg, J.E., Vendruscolo, L.F., Bremer, P.T., Lockner, J.W., Wade, C.L., et al. (2013). Dynamic vaccine blocks relapse to compulsive intake of heroin. *PNAS, 110*(22): 9036–41.

[118] Glaser, G. (2015, April). The irrationality of Alcoholics Anonymous. *The Atlantic.* Accessed on August 10, 2016, from http://www.theatlantic.com/magazine/archive/2015/04/the-irrationality-of-alcoholics-anonymous/386255/

[119] Ibid.

[120] Polcin, D.L., Korcha, R., & Galloway, G. (2010). What did we learn from out study on sober living houses and where do we go from here? *Journal of Psychoactive Drugs, 42*(4): 425–33.

[121] Polcin, D.L., Korcha, R.A., Bond, J., & Galloway, G. (2010). Sober living houses for alcohol and drug dependence: 18-month outcomes. *Journal of Substance Abuse Treatment, 38*(4): 356–65.

[122] Mericle, A.A., Mahoney, E., Korcha, R., Delucchi, K., & Polcin, D.L., et al. (2019). Sober living house characteristics: A multilevel analysis of factors associated with improved outcomes. *Journal of Substance Abuse Treatment, 98*: 28–38.

[123] McHugh, R.K., Hearon, B.A., & Otto, M.W. (2010). Cognitive-behavioral therapy for substance use disorders. *Psychiatric Clinics of North America, 33*(3): 511–25.

[124] Magill, M., & Ray, L.A. (2009). Cognitive-behavioral treatment with adult alcohol and illicit drug users: A meta-analysis of randomized controlled trials. *Journal of Studies of Alcohol and Drugs, 70*(4): 516–27.

[125] Jhanjee, S. (2014). Evidence based psychosocial interventions in substance use. *Indian Journal of Psychological Medicine, 36*(2): 112–18.

[126] McHugh, R.K., Hearon, B.A., & Otto, M.W. (2010). Cognitive-behavioral therapy for substance use disorders. *Psychiatric Clinics of North America, 33*(3): 511–25.

[127] Szalavitz, M. (2016, June 26). Can you get over an addiction? *The New York Times.* Accessed on August 9, 2016, from http://www.nytimes.com/2016/06/26/opinion/sunday/can-you-get-over-an-addiction.html?_r=0

[128] Petry, N.M. (2011). Contingency management: What it is and why psychiatrists should want to use it. *The Psychiatrist, 35*(5): 161–63.

[129] Goodnough, B. (2020). This addiction treatment works. Why is it so underused? *The New York Times.* Accessed on October 27, 2020, from https://www.nytimes.com/2020/10/27/health/meth-addiction-treatment.html

[130] Ibid.

[131] De Crescenzo, F., Cibattini, M., D"Alo, G.L., De Giorgi, R., & Del Giovane, C., et al. (2018). Comparative efficacy and acceptability of psychosocial interventions for individuals with cocaine and amphetamine addiction: A systematic review and network meta-analysis. *PLoS Medicine, 15*(12): e1002715.

[132] DePhilippis, D., Petry, N.M., Bonn-Miller, M.O., Rosenbach, S.B., & McKay, J.R. (2018). The national implementation of Contingency Management (CM) in the Department of Veterans Affairs: Attendance at CM sessions and substance use outcomes. *Drug and Alcohol Dependence, 185*: 367–73.

[133] Meyers, R.J., Roozen, H.G., & Smith, J.E. (2011). The community reinforcement approach. *Alcohol Research and Health, 33*(4): 380–88.

[134] Rose, M.E., & Cherpitel, C.J. (2011) *Alcohol: Its history, pharmacology, and treatment.* Center City, MN: Hazelden.

[135] Gately, I. (2008). *Drink: A cultural history of alcohol.* New York: Gotham Books.

[136] Rose, M.E., & Cherpitel, C.J. (2011) *Alcohol: Its history, pharmacology, and treatment.* Center City, MN: Hazelden.

[137] Kelly, J.F., Abry, A., Ferri, M., & Humphreys, K. (2020). Alcoholics Anonymous and 12-step facilitation treatments for alcohol use disorder: A distillation of a 2020 Cochrane Review for clinicians and policy makers. *Alcohol and Alcoholism, 55*(6): 641-51.

[138] Kaskutas, L.A. (2009). Alcoholics Anonymous effectiveness: Faith meets science. *Journal of Addictive Diseases, 28*: 145–57.

[139] Walitzer, K.S., Dermen, K.H., & Barrick, C. (2009). Facilitating involvement in Alcoholics Anonymous during outpatient treatment: A randomized clinical trial. *Addiction, 104*: 391–401.

[140] Humphreys, K., Blodgett, J.C., & Wagner, T.H. (2014). Estimating the efficacy of Alcoholics Anonymous without self-selection bias: An instrumental variables re-analysis of randomized clinical trials. *Alcoholism: Clinical and Experimental Research, 38*(11): 2688–94.

[141] Kaskutas, L.A. (2009). Alcoholics Anonymous effectiveness: Faith meets science. *Journal of Addictive Diseases, 28*: 145–57.

[142] Moos, R.H. (2008). Active ingredients of substance use focused self-help groups. *Addiction* 103(3): 387–96.

[143] Dodes, L., & Dodes, Z. (2015). *The sober truth: Debunking the bad science behind 12-step programs and the rehab industry.* Boston: Beacon Press.

[144] Glaser, G. (2015, April). The irrationality of Alcoholics Anonymous. *The Atlantic.* Accessed on August 10, 2016, from http://www.theatlantic.com/magazine/archive/2015/04/the-irrationality-of-alcoholics-anonymous/386255/

[145] Rose, M.E., & Cherpitel, C.J. (2011) *Alcohol: Its history, pharmacology, and treatment.* Center City, MN: Hazelden.

[146] Ibid.

[147] Hester, R.K., Delaney, H.D., & Campbell, W. (2011). ModerateDrinking.com and Moderation Management: Outcomes of a randomized clinical trial with non-dependent problem drinkers. *Journal of Consulting and Clinical Psychology, 79*(2): 215–24.

[148] Hester, R.K., Delaney, J.D., Campbell, W., & Handmaker, N. (2009). A web application for moderation training: Initial results of a randomized clinical trial. *Journal of Substance Abuse and Treatment, 37*(3): 266–76.

[149] Kosik, A. (2006). The Moderation Management programme in 2004: What type of drinker seeks controlled drinking? *International Journal of Drug Policy, 17*(4): 295–303.

[150] Glaser, G. (2015, April). The irrationality of Alcoholics Anonymous. *The Atlantic.* Accessed on August 10, 2016, from http://www.theatlantic.com/magazine/archive/2015/04/the-irrationality-of-alcoholics-anonymous/386255/

[151] Esser, M.B., Hedden, S.L., Kanny, D., Brewer, R.D., Gfroerer, J.C., & Naimi, T.S. (2014). Prevalence of alcohol dependence among U.S. adult drinkers, 2009–2011. *Preventing Chronic Disease, 11:* E206.

[152] Davis, A.K., & Rosenberg, H. (2012). Acceptance of non-abstinence goals by addiction professionals in the United States. *Psychology of Addictive Behaviors, 27*(4): 1102–09.

[153] Sobell, L.C., Sobell, M.B., Toneatto, T., & Leo, G.I. (1993). What triggers the resolution of alcohol problems without treatment? *Alcoholism: Clinical and Experimental Research, 17:* 217–24.

[154] Verges, A., Jackson, K.M., Bucholz, K.K., Grant, J.D., & Trull, T.J. (2012). Deconstructing the age-prevalence curve of alcohol dependence: Why "maturing out" is only a small piece of the puzzle. *Journal of Abnormal Psychology, 12*(2): 511–23.

[155] Verges, A., Haeny, A.M., Jackson, K.M., Bucholz, K.K., Grant J.D., et al. (2013). Refining the notion of maturing out: results from the National Epidemiologic Survey on Alcohol and Related Conditions. *American Journal of Public Health, 103*(12): e67–73.

[156] National Institute on Drug Abuse. (2012). *Principles of drug addiction treatment: A research-based guide* (3rd ed.). Washington, DC: National Institutes of Health. https://d14rmgtrwzf5a.cloudfront.net/sites/default/files/podat_1.pdf

[157] Hecht, A. (2011). *Understanding drugs: Cocaine and crack.* New York: Chelsea House.

[158] Heyman, G.M. (2013). Quitting drugs: Quantitative and qualitative features. *Annual Review of Clinical Psychology, 9:* 29–59.

[159] Bower, B. (2014). The addiction paradox. *Science News, 185*(6). Accessed on March 10, 2015, from https://www.sciencenews.org/article/addiction-paradox

[160] Moos, R.H., & Moos, B.S. (2006). Rates and predictors of relapse after natural and treated remission from alcohol use disorders. *Addiction, 101*(2): 212–22.

[161] Seo, D., Lacadie, C.M., Tuit, K., Hong K-I., Constable, R.T., & Sinha, R. (2013). Disrupted ventromedial prefrontal function, alcohol craving, and subsequent relapse risk. *JAMA Psychiatry, 70*(7): 727–39.

[162] Voss, J.P. (2009). Relapse after long-term sobriety. *GPSOLO, 26*(7): 1–5.

Credits

Figure 00 Alamy ID: EC2KM7

Figure A Alamy ID: DER4MC

Figure B http://lowres.cartoonstock.com/health-beauty-scientist-dietician-nutritionist-company-misleading-wmi100422_low.jpg

Figure C1 Alamy ID: BC4NNB

Figure C2 Alamy ID: AHRTM4

Figure D http://www.fotosearch.com/photos-images/brain-scan.html#comp.asp?recid=54724501&xtra=

Figure E Alamy ID: DA1F19

Figure F https://slideplayer.com/slide/9804170/ *OR* Image courtesy of Marcus E. Raichle, Department of Radiology, Washington University School of Medicine, St. Louis, Missouri

Figure G Bennett, C.M., Baird, A.A., Miller, M.B., & Wolford, G.L. (2010). Neural Correlates of Interspecies Perspective Taking in the Post-Mortem Atlantic Salmon: An Argument For Proper Multiple Comparisons Correction. Journal of Serendipitous and Unexpected Results, 1(1): 1-5.

Figure H n/a

Figure I n/a

Figure J Alamy ID: C036T3

Figure 1-0 Alamy ID: BH6EP6

Figure 1-1A–1-1I http://bryanlewissaunders.org/contact/

Figure 1.2 United Nations Office on Drugs and Crime. (2020). World drug report, 2020. United Nations publication, sales no. E.20.XI.6. https://wdr.unodc.org/wdr2020/en/index.html

Figure 1.3 World Health Organization. (2018). Global status report on alcohol and health, 2018. *World Health Organization*. https://apps.who.int/iris/handle.10665/312318

Figure 1.4 SAMHSA. (2020). *Results from the 2019 National Survey on Drug Use and Health: Detailed Tables*. Rockville, MD: Center for Behavioral Health Statistics and Quality.

Figure 1.5 Jones, C.M., Clayton, H.B., Deputy, N.P., Roehler, D.R. & Ko, J.Y., et al. (2020). Prescription opioid misuse and use of alcohol and other substances among high school students—Youth Risk Behavior Survey, United States, 2019. *MMWR*, 69(1): 38-46.

Creamer, M.R., Jones, S.E., Gentzke, A.S., Jamal, A., & King, B.A. (2020). Tobacco product use among high school students—Youth Risk Behavior Survey, United States, 2019. *MMWR*, 69(1): 56-63.

Figure 1.6 SAMHSA. (2020). *Results from the 2019 National Survey on Drug Use and Health: Detailed Tables*. Rockville, MD: Center for Behavioral Health Statistics and Quality.

Figure 1.7 SAMHSA. (2020). *Results from the 2019 National Survey on Drug Use and Health: Detailed Tables*. Rockville, MD: Center for Behavioral Health Statistics and Quality.

Figure 1.8 http://www.cartoonistgroup.com/store/add.php?iid=7942

Figure 1.9A Alamy ID: FDMN5J

Figure 1.9B Shutterstock ID: 58766284

Figure 1.10 n/a

Figure 1.11 Alamy ID: GYHD3H

Figure 1.12 Friedman, R.A. (2016). What drug ads don't say. New York Times. http://www.nytimes.com/2016/04/24/opinion/sunday/what-drug-ads-dont-say.html?_r=0

Figure 2-0 Shutterstock ID: 544897837

Figure 2.1 The Sentencing Project. (2020). Trends in U.S. Corrections. https://www.sentencingproject.org/wp-content/uploads/2020/08/Trends-in-US-Corrections.pdf

Figure 2.2 SAMHSA. (2020). Results from the 2019 national survey on drug use and health: Detailed tables. Rockville, MD: Center for Behavioral Health Statistics and Quality.

Figure 2.3 Data from: NABCA. (2014). Wet and dry counties: Control and license states. http://www.nabca.org/assets/Docs/Research/December%202014%20WetDry%20Counties.pdf

Figure 2.4 World Drug Report. (2020). Annual prevalence of drug use. Accessed on November 5, 2020 from https://wdr.unodc.org/wdr2020/International Comparators. (2014). https://www.gov.uk/government/publications/drugs-international-comparators

UNODC. (2012). World drug report, 2011. Vienna, Austria. https://www.unodc.org/documents/data-and-analysis/WDR2011/World_Drug_Report_2011_ebook.pdf

Figure 2.5 World Prison Brief: International Center for Prison Studies. (2020). https://www.prisonstudies.org/world-prison-brief-data

Figure 2.6 The Sentencing Project. (2020). Trends in U.S. Corrections. https://www.sentencingproject.org/wp-content/uploads/2020/08/Trends-in-US-Corrections.pdf

Figure 6.3 Johnston, L.D., Miech, R.A., O'Malley, P.M., Bachman, J.G., & Schulenberg, J.E., et al. (2020). Monitoring the future: National survey results on drug use 1975-2019. Ann Arbor: Institute for Social Research, University of Michigan.

Figure 6.4A Alamy ID: B1YJ2R

Figure 6.4B Shutterstock ID: 63063511

Figure 6.4C https://erowid.org/chemicals/lsd/images/archive/lsd_microdots1.jpg

Figure 6.5 http://en.wikipedia.org/wiki/File:Psilocybe.mexicana.Xico.JPG

Figure 6.6 Shutterstock ID: 100556044

Figure 6.7 Shutterstock ID: 64081936

Figure 6.8 Shutterstock ID: 307708301

Figure 6.9 Shutterstock ID: 339414725

Figure 6.10A Shutterstock ID: 345395984

Figure 6.10B Alamy ID: BKANCM

Figure 6.11A Shutterstock ID: 335327426

Figure 6.11B Alamy ID: BN3XBD

Figure 6.11C Alamy ID: CFNKM1

Figure 6.12 http://www.apimages.com/metadata/Index/Associated-Press-Domestic-News-Texas-United-Sta-/895494d8fde6da11af-9f0014c2589dfb/5/0

Figure 6.13 n/a

Figure 6.14 n/a

Figure 6.15 n/a

Figure 6.16 n/a

Figure 6.17 Image courtesy of Dr. GA Ricaurte, Johns Hopkins University School of Medicine. https://d14rmgtrwzf5a.cloudfront.net/sites/default/files/imagecache/content_image_landscape/eslide17.gif

Figure 7.0 Alamy ID: C48BWW

Figure 7.1 Getty ID: 515143796

Figure 7.2 Alamy ID: EXPKC3

Figure 7.3 CDC (2019). U.S. opioid prescribing rate maps. Accessed on December 3, 2019 from https://www.cdc.gov/drugoverdose/maps/rxrate-maps.html

Figure 7.4 Substance Abuse and Mental Health Services Administration (SAMHSA). (2020). Results from the 2019 National Survey on Drug Use and Health: Detailed tables. Rockville, MD: Center for Behavioral Health Statistics and Quality

Figure 7.5 (SAMHSA). (2020). Results from the 2019 National Survey on Drug Use and Health: Detailed tables. Rockville, MD: Center for Behavioral Health Statistics and Quality

Figure 7.6 Shutterstock ID: 103532333

Figure 7.7 Shutterstock ID: 409643212

Figure 7.8 n/a

Figure 7.9A http://www.apimages.com/metadata/Index/Medical-Prize/d0d6569e43c-34fa0a511d8bff2efe8ea/4/0

Figure 7.9B http://candacepert.com/contact/

Figure 7.10 n/a

Figure 7.11 Centers for Disease Control and Prevention. (2020). Drug overdose deaths in the United States, 1999-2018. NCHS Data Brief, no 356. Hyattsville, MD: National Center for Health Statistics.

Figure 7.12 Shutterstock ID: 96566023

Figure 7.13 n/a

Figure 7.14A http://www.brucekalexander.com/articles-speeches/rat-park/148-addiction-the-view-from-rat-park

Figure 7.14B http://www.brucekalexander.com/articles-speeches/rat-park/148-addiction-the-view-from-rat-park

Figure 8.0 Getty ID: 78366977

Figure 8.1 http://www.goretro.com/2014/08/mothers-little-helper-vintage-drug-ads.html

Figure 8.2A https://www.sciencesource.com/Doc/TR1_WATERMARKED/0/6/0/9/SS2499947.jpg?d63642453236

Figure 8.2B https://www.sciencesource.com/Doc/TR1_WATERMARKED/0/b/f/8/SS2499963.jpg?d63642453263

Figure 8.3 n/a

Figure 8.4 n/a

Figure 8.5 Shutterstock ID: 30929875

Figure 8.6A Alamy ID: DT59HN

Figure 8.6B Getty ID: 51149545

Figure 8.7 NIDA. (2020). Overdose death rates. Accessed on February 22, 2020 from https://www.drugabuse.gov/related-topics/trends-statistics/overdose-death-rates

Figure 8.8 Alamy ID: D58AA0

Figure 8.9 n/a

Figure 8.10A Getty ID: 3223156

Figure 8.10B Getty ID: 3222816

Figure 8.11A Alamy ID: GFWPB4

Figure 8.11B Alamy ID: D5RTPA

Figure 8.12 Alamy ID: A3A0YW

Figure 8.13 Rosenberg, N. (2012). NIDA Research Report (NIH 05-3818). https://teens.drugabuse.gov/sites/default/files/inhalantsrrs.pdf

Figure 9.0 Alamy ID: A68E5M

Figure 9.1A Alamy ID: FAWDJN

Figure 9.1B Alamy ID: FAWHMY

Figure 9.2 National Conference of State Legislatures. (2020). State medical marijuana laws. https://www.ncsl.org/research/health/state-medical-marijuana-laws.aspx

Figure 9.3 SAMHSA. (2020). Results from the 2019 national survey on drug use and health. Rockville, MD: Center for Behavioral Health Statistics and Quality.

Figure 9.4 Johnston, L.D., Meich, R.A., O'Malley, P.M. Bachman, J.G., & Schulenberg, J.E., et al. (2020). Monitoring the Future: National survey results on drug use 1975-2019. Ann Arbor: Institute for Social Research, The University of Michigan.

Figure 9.5 Gallup poll. (2020). Support for legal marijuana inches up to new high of 68%. Accessed on November 9, 2020 from https://news.gallup.com/poll/323582/support-legal-marijuana-inches-new-high.aspx

Figure 9.6 Pew Research Center. (2019). Two-thirds of Americans support marijuana legalization. https://www.pewresearch.org/fact-tank/2019/11/14/americans-support-marijuana-legalization/

Figure 9.7 https://deadline.com/wp-content/uploads/2019/11/weeds-1.jpg?crop=0px%2C176px%2C3000px%2C1681px&resize=681%2C383

Figure 9.8 http://binaryapi.ap.org/5d97e0f19e804812b818ee65c6556382/preview/AP507420537123.jpg?wm=api&ver=0

Figure 9.9 Getty ID: 542896615

Figure 9.10A Shutterstock ID: 135662744

Figure 9.10B Shutterstock ID: 98154770

Figure 9.10C Shutterstock ID: 198662528

Figure 9.10D Shutterstock ID: 309467420

Figure 9.11 n/a

Figure 9.12 n/a

Figure 9.13 n/a

Figure 9.14 http://binaryapi.ap.org/d2205150761e438ea10e51b064cbddce/preview/AP405191522308.jpg?wm=api&ver=0

Figure 9.15 Anthony, J.V., Warner, L.A., & Kessler, R.C. (1994). Comparative epidemiology of dependence on tobacco, alcohol, controlled substances and inhalants: Basic findings from the National Comorbidity Survey. Experimental and Clinical Psychopharmacology, 2:244–268. Nutt, D.J., King, L.A., Phillips, L.D. (2010). Drug harms in the UK: A multicriteria decision analysis. Lancet, 376(9752): 1558-65.

Figure 10.0 Alamy ID: CEWCG4

Figure 10.1 Alamy ID: FF82Y9

Figure 10.2 U.S. Department of Health and Human Services. (2014). The Health Consequences of Smoking—50 Years of Progress: A Report of the Surgeon General. Atlanta, GA: Centers for Disease Control and Prevention.

Figure 10.3 Wang, T.W., Asman, K., Gentzke, A.S., Cullen, K.A., & Holder-Hayes, E., et al. (2018). Tobacco product use among adults—United States, 2017. MMWR, 67: 1225-32.

Figure 10.4 SAMHSA. (2020). Results from the 2019 National Survey on Drug Use and Health. Rockville, MD: Center for Behavioral Health Statistics and Quality.

Figure 10.5 SAMHSA. (2020). Results from the 2019 National Survey on Drug Use and Health. Rockville, MD: Center for Behavioral Health Statistics and Quality.

Figure 10.6 SAMHSA. (2016). 2015 Survey on drug use and health: Detailed tables. Center for behavioral health statistics and quality, Rockville, MD.

Figure 10.7 SAMHSA. (2020). Results from the 2019 National Survey on Drug Use and Health. Rockville, MD: Center for Behavioral Health Statistics and Quality.

Figure 10.8 Johnston, L.D., Miech, R.A., O'Malley, P.M., Bachman, J.G., & Schulenberg, J.E., et al. (2020). Monitoring the future: National survey results on drug use 1975-2019. Ann Arbor: Institute for Social Research, The University of Michigan.

Figure 10.9 Hirsig, R.J. (2009). Cigarette taxes, prices, and sales. Sacramento, CA: State Board of Equalization. http://www.boe.ca.gov/news/cigarette_price_effects_d2.pdf
Holmes, J. (2015). What a pack of cigarette costs, in every state. https://theawl.com/what-a-pack-of-cigarettes-costs-in-every-state-173b6cb1fb9#.68nhupjk3
World Population Review. (2020). Cigarette prices by state, 2020. Accessed on May 1, 2020 from https://worldpopulationreview.com/states/cigarette-prices-by-state/

Figure 10.10 Alamy ID: EXT0AE

Figure 10.11 Alamy ID: B8N147

Figure 10.12 https://www.amazon.com/Scarlett-Johansson-Smoking-Cigarette-Aluminum/dp/B01GAG5NAE

Figure 10.13 Shutterstock ID: 43261138

Figure 10.14 n/a

Figure 10.15 n/a

Figure 10.16A Alamy ID: BKG2RE

Figure 10.16B Alamy ID: CWB2KB

Figure 10.16C Alamy ID: CWARMG

Figure 10.17 CDC. (2018). Tobacco related mortality. Accessed on May 4, 2020 from https://www.cdc.gov/tobacco/data_statistics/fact_sheets/health_effects/tobacco_related_mortality/index.htm

Figure 10.18 SAMHSA. (2020). Results from the 2019 National Survey on Drug Use and Health. Rockville, MD: Center for Behavioral Health Statistics and Quality.

Figure 10.19 Alamy ID: BHHC98

Figure 11.0 Alamy ID: CWJJ8G

Figure 11.1 Shuttertock ID: 100467259

Figure 11.2 Alamy ID: EKYEDX

Figure 11.3 World Atlas. (2018). The top coffee consuming countries. Accessed on May 17, 2020 from https://www.worldatlas.com/articles/top-10-coffee-consuming-nations.html
Ferdman, R.A. (2014). Where the world's biggest tea drinkers are. http://qz.com/168690/where-the-worlds-biggest-tea-drinkers-are/#int/words=dinner_supper&smoothing=3
Nag, O. (2018). Which countries eat the most chocolate? Accessed on May 18, 2020 from https://www.worldatlas.com/articles/which-countries-eat-the-most-chocolate.html
Worldatlas. (2016). Countries with the highest levels of soft drink consumption. http://qz.com/168690/where-the-worlds-biggest-tea-drinkers-are/#int/words=dinner_supper&smoothing=3

Figure 11.4 Mitchell, D.C., Knight, C.A., Hockenberrry, J., Teplansky, R., & Hartman, T.J., (2014). Beverage caffeine intakes in the U.S. Food and Chemical Toxicology, 63: 136-42.

Figure 11.5 Shutterstock ID: 113774812

Figure 11.6 Shutterstock ID: 123643447

Figure 11.7 Shutterstock ID: 82062700

Figure 11.8 Alamy ID: CP8T16

Figure 11.9 Shutterstock ID: 301874270

Figure 11.10 Shutterstock ID: 114201487

Figure 11.11 n/a

Figure 11.12 – Freedman, N.D., Park, Y., Abnet, C.C., Hollenbeck, A.R., & Sinha, R. (2012). Association of coffee drinking with total and cause-specific mortality. NEJM, 366:1891-1904.

Figure 12.0 Shutterstock ID: 191447648

Figure 12.1 n/a

Figure 12.2 Alamy ID: CWA5P4

Figure 12.3 Goode, E. (2007). Drugs in American Society, 7th edition. New York: McGraw Hill.
Slater, M.E. & Alpert, H.R. (2020). Apparent per capita alcohol consumption: National, state, and regional trends: 1977-2018. Arlington, VA: NIAAA Surveillance Report.

Figure 12.4 WHO. (2018). Global status report on alcohol and health, 2018. https://apps.who.int/iris/bitstream/handle/10665/274603/9789241565639-eng.pdf

Figure 12.5 n/a

Figure 12.6 SAMHSA. (2020). Results from the 2019 national survey on drug use and health. Rockville, MD: Center for Behavioral Health Statistics and Quality.

Figure 12.7 SAMHSA. (2020). Results from the 2019 national survey on drug use and health. Rockville, MD: Center for Behavioral Health Statistics and Quality.

Figure 12.8 Shutterstock ID: 448397416

Figure 12.9 n/a

Figure 12.10 n/a

Figure 12.11 n/a

Figure 12.12 n/a

Figure 12.13 Alamy ID: CWK5FN

Figure 12.14A Getty ID: 514976950

Figure 12.14B https://blog.singulart.com/en/2021/01/29/10-things-to-know-about-jackson-pollock/

Figure 12.14C Alamy ID: BH1W0B

Figure 12.14D Alamy ID: B4WE67

Figure 12.15 WHO. (2018). Global status report on alcohol and health. https://www.who.int/substance_abuse/publications/global_alcohol_report/en/

Figure 12.16 Zahr, N.M., Kaufman, K.L., & Harper, C.G. (2011). Clinical and pathological features of alcohol-related brain damage. Nature Reviews Neurology, 7(5): 284-94.

Figure 12.17 https://www.sciencesource.com/Doc/TR1_WATERMARKED/1/4/8/b/SS2393361.jpg?d63642081626

Figure 12.18 Shutterstock ID: 1869185

Figure 13.0 Getty ID: 184591777

Figure 13.1A Alamy ID: FKJBWA

Figure 13.1B Alamy ID: BP7DNM

Figure 13.1C Alamy ID: BNPK67

Figure 13.2 Alamy ID: ECG9PP

Figure 13.3A Shutterstock ID: 100134854

Figure 13.3B Shutterstock ID: 118586734

Figure 13.3C Shutterstock ID: 117263020

Figure 13.4 (SAMHSA). (2020). Results from the 2019 national survey on drug use and health. Rockville, MD: Center for Behavioral Health Statistics and Quality.

Figure 13.5 n/a

Figure 13.6 Robot Hugs provided a hi-res version for the 1e in 2017 for $20 contact@robot-hugs.com

Figure 13.7 Shutterstock ID: 255372655

Figure 13.8 Brody, D.J., & Gu, Q. (2020). Antidepressant use among adults: United States, 2015-2018. NCHS Data Brief, no 377. Hyattsville, MD: National Center for Health Statistics.

Figure 13.9A Shutterstock ID:-54157723

Figure 13.9B Shutterstock ID: 128768372

Figure 13.9C Shutterstock ID: 362153849

Figure 13.9D Alamy ID: BJ0EJD

Figure 13.10A Alamy ID: GD2HG5

Figure 13.10B Alamy ID: G9EMFG

Figure 13.10C Alamy ID: C13CE8

Figure 13.10D Alamy ID: H0JAT0

Figure 13.11 picked up from Lambert/Biological Psychology (figure 13.6, p. 381)

Figure 13.12 n/a

Figure 13.13 http://en.wikipedia.org/wiki/Antipsychotic#mediaviewer/File:Thorazine_advert.jpg

Figure 13.14A Shutterstock ID: 243837430

Figure 13.14B Shutterstock ID: 506904517

Figure 13.14C Alamy ID: C4F172

Figure 14.0 http://media.istockphoto.com/photos/steroid-use-in-weightlifting-concept-picture-id503845420

Figure 14.1 Bureau of Labor Statistics. (2020). May 2019 national occupational employment and wage estimates United States. https://www.bls.gov/oes/current/oes_nat.htm#43-0000

Figure 14.2A Alamy ID: DDM967

Figure 14.2B Alamy ID: S17XTK

Figure 14.3 Alamy ID: CWHNDD

Figure 14.4 Kann, L., McManus, T., Harris, W.L., Shanklin, S.L., & Flint, K.H., et al. (2018). Youth risk behavior surveillance—United States, 2017. MMWR, 67(8): 58-59.

Figure 14.5 n/a

Figure 14.6 Alamy ID: AC9YR8

Figure 14.7 https://s3.amazonaws.com/lowres.cartoonstock.com/business-commerce-attention_spans-breaks-office_job-paper_pusher-focus-bven577_low.jpg

Figure 14.8 Hinshaw, S. & Scheffler, R. (2014). The ADHD Explosion: Myths, medication, money, and today's push for performance. New York: Oxford University Press.

Figure 14.9 Volkow, N.D., Wang, G-J., Kollins, S.H., Wigal, T.L., & Newcorn, J.H., et al. (2009). Evaluating dopamine reward pathway in ADHD: Clinical implications. JAMA, 302(10): 1084-91.

Figure 14.10 Danielson, M.L., Bitsko, R.H., Ghandour, R.M., Holbrook, J.R., & Hogan, M.D., et al. (2018). Prevalence of parent-reported ADHD diagnosis and associated treatment among U.S. children and adolescents, 2016. Journal of Clinical Child and Adolescent Psychology, 47(2): 199-212.

Figure 14.11A Alamy ID: C4M7PH

Figure 14.11B Getty ID: 94626696

Figure 14.12 n/a

Figure 15.0 Alamy ID: CRM7N3

Figure 15.1 n/a

Figure 15.2 https://www.policymed.com/2019/08/fda-proposes-updates-to-labeling-with-two-draft-guidances.html

Figure 15.3 Getty ID: 167061574

Figure 15.4 https://www.flickr.com/photos/28650594@N03/3811874089

Figure 15.5A-B Hales, C.M., Carroll, M.D., & Fryar, C.D., et al. (2020). Prevalence of obesity and severe obesity among adults: United States, 2017-2018. NCHS Data Brief No. 360.
Fryar, C.D., Carroll, M.D., & Ogden, C.L. (2018). Prevalence of overweight, obesity, and severe obesity among adults age 20 and over: United States, 1960-1962 through 2015-2016.

Figure 15.6 Alamy ID: E4TJBR

Figure 15.7 n/a

Figure 16.0 Shutterstock ID: 244260187

Figure 16.1 n/a

Figure 16.2A Alamy ID: BM8E8H

Figure 16.2B Alamy ID: CWBT7F

Figure 16.2C https://www.granger.com/wmpix/por4/mkk/0068193-KATHERINE-D-McCORMICK-1875-1967-American-womens-rights-and-birth-control-advocate.jpg

Figure 16.3 Nikolchev, A. (2010). A brief history of the birth control pill
Daniels, K., Mosher, W.D., & Jones, J. (2013). Contraceptive methods women have ever used: United States, 1982-2010. National health statistics reports, no 62. Hyattsville, MD: National Center for Health Statistics
Daniels, K., Daugherty, J., Jones, J., & Mosher, W. (2015). Current contraceptive use and variation by selected characteristics among women aged 15-44: United States, 2011-2013. National Health Statistics Reports, 86. Washington, DC: NCHS
Tyrer, L. (1999). Introduction of the pill and its impact. Contraception, 59(suppl 1): 11S-16S.

Figure 16.4 n/a

Figure 16.5– Alamy ID: ECE0C5

Figure 16.6A Alamy ID: D3GXCP

Figure 16.6B Alamy ID: AYBBPF

Figure 16.6C Alamy ID: ATDKB3

Figure 16.6D Alamy ID: B6MA6G

Figure 16.7 Alamy ID: E48GFM

Figure 16.8 Shutterstock ID: 70077391

Figure 16.9 Alamy ID: DTTAFK

Figure 16.10A Alamy ID: B3XE7H

Figure 16.10B Shutterstock ID: 78077164

Figure 16.11 http://mms.business-wire.com/media/20151215006910/en/500758/5/2427684_2168747_GARDASIL-9-Package-and-Vial.jpg

Figure 17.0 http://media.istockphoto.com/photos/prescription-drugs-addiction-picture-id169967028

Figure 17.1 Rose, M.E. & Cherpitel, C.J. (2011) Alcohol: Its history, pharmacology, and treatment. Center City, Minnesota: Hazelden.
Substance Abuse and Mental Health Services Administration (SAMHSA). (2020). Results from

the 2019 national survey on drug use and health. Rockville, MD: Center for Behavioral Health Statistics and Quality.

Figure 17.2A Shutterstock ID: 108469235

Figure 17.2B Shutterstock ID: 424089664

Figure 17.2C Alamy ID: F2J7AW

Figure 17.2D Getty ID: 608870770

Figure 17.2E Shutterstock ID: 309476945

Figure 17.2F Shutterstock ID: 91241030

Figure 17.3 (SAMHSA). (2020). Results from the 2019 national survey on drug use and health. Rockville, MD: Center for Behavioral Health Statistics and Quality

Figure 17.4 (SAMHSA). (2020). Results from the 2019 national survey on drug use and health. Rockville, MD: Center for Behavioral Health Statistics and Quality

Figure 17.5 n/a

Figure 17.6 n/a

Figure 17.7 https://openi.nlm.nih.gov/detailedresult?img=PMC2851068_SPP-03-2-4-g009&req=4

Figure 17.8 n/a

Figure 17.9 Ritchie, H. (2019). Mental health disorders as risk factors for substance use. Accessed on September 11, 2020 from https://ourworldindata.org/mental-health-disorders-as-risk-for-substance-use

Figure 17.10A Alamy ID: RWDWEP

Figure 17.10B Alamy ID: W3KRWE

Figure 17.10C Shutterstock ID: 480604309

Figure 17.11 Barry, C.L., McGinty, E.E., Pescosolido, B.A., & Goldman, H.H. (2014). Stigma, discrimination, treatment, effectiveness, and policy: Public views about drug addiction and mental illness. Psychiatric Services, 65(10): 1269-72.

Figure 18.0 Alamy ID: F3FK27

Figure 18.1 n/a

Figure 18.2 Alamy ID: HG0AJR

Figure 18.3 Alamy ID: F7JH6K

Figure 18.4 https://www.bestadsontv.com/ad/22421/Above-the-Influence-campaign-Human-Puppet

Figure 18.5 http://www.nytimes.com/2016/08/08/business/media/this-is-your-brain-on-drugs-tweaked-for-todays-parents.html?_r=0

Figure 18.6 Shutterstock ID: 173756831

Figure 18.7 Getty ID: 112942446

Figure 18.8 (SAMHSA). (2020). Results from the 2018 national survey on drug use and health. Rockville, MD: Center for Behavioral Health Statistics and Quality.

Figure 18.9 n/a

Figure 18.10 Alamy ID: CFH1NB

Figure 18.11 Alamy ID: B9HH74

Figure 18.12 Alamy ID: B8TDHJ

Figure 18.13 n/a

Figure 18.14 Bower, B. (2014). The addiction paradox. Science News, 185(6).

Index

Page numbers followed by *f* and *t* refer to figures and tables, respectively.

Blood brain barrier (BBB), 60f, 60, 77
  alcohol use and, 297
Blood clotting, 379, 380
Blood doping, 351t, 352, 353
Blood tests, for drugs, 453
Blood thinners, 411
Blood transfusions, 353
Body image disorders, 351
Boldenone (Equipoise), 352t
Bongs, 217, 217f
Bootleggers, 288
Botulinum toxin (Botox), 51t, 61t, 64–65
Brain
  and ADHD, 363–64, 364f
  alcohol's effect on, 300–301, 301f, 308f, 308–9
  cocaine addiction, 430f
  and depression, 322
  dopaminergic pathways of, 336
  and drug abuse/addiction, 428–31
  hallucinogens' effect on, 132f, 132
  inhalants' effect on, 200f, 200
  marijuana's effect on, 220, 220f
  methamphetamine's effect on, 111f
  myths about, 59
  nicotine's effect on, 251t
  pleasure center of, 429
  and schizophrenia, 334, 335f, 336f
  See also Central nervous system (CNS)
Brain imaging, xli–xliii, xliiif
Brain injuries, treatment of, 227–28
Brainstem, 58, 61
Brand names (trade names), 13
Brandy, 295t
Breaking Bad (television series), 109f
Breast disease, 280
Bremelanotide (Vyleesi), 411–12, 412t
Bromopheniramine (phenylephrine) (Dimetapp), 374t
Buccal administration, 74t, 75
Bufotenine, 122t, 123t, 125–26, 126f
Bulk-forming laxatives, 387
Buprenorphine (Butrans, Subutex), 81, 147, 153, 154t, 156, 170t, 171, 375, 457t, 458
Bupropion (Zyban, Wellbutrin), 258–59, 327t, 327, 328, 329, 454, 457t, 457
Butane, 197t
Butyl nitrate, 197t, 198
Butyrylcholinesterase (BChE), 106
BZDs. See Benzodiazepines (BZDs)

C
Caffeine, 263–81
  acute effects of, 274–76, 275f, 385
  addiction to, 420, 422t, 426
  chronic effects of, 280–81
  and cocaine, 99
  drug interactions with, 273, 374
  and drug schedules, 15
  history of, 264–67
  mechanism of action of, 273–74
  medical and therapeutic uses of, 276–80, 277t
  and menopause, 409
  as performance-enhancing drug, 351t, 352
  pharmacodynamics of, 84f, 84, 85
  pharmacokinetics of, 2, 74t, 77, 273
  prevalence of use, 2, 267–69
  quantity ingested, 272
  quitting, 281
  risk of death with, 35f
  source and forms of, 269–72
Caffeinism, 276
Calcitonin, 74t
Calcium bicarbonate (Tums, Rolaids), 386
California, price of cigarettes in, 241f, 241
Camcolit. See Lithium salts
Campral (acamprosate), 457t, 458
Cancer, 277t, 278, 379
  alcohol use and, 310
  cigarette smoking related, 255
  marijuana for, 226–27
Cannabidiol (CBD), 215, 215–17, 219–24
  effects on selected receptors, 218t
  medical uses, 226–27
Cannabidiolic acid (CBDA), 215
Cannabinoids
  acute effects of, 219–25
  and alcohol, 300
  chronic effects of, 228–29

drugs' effects on, 51t
  endocannabinoids, 218f, 219
  medical/therapeutic effects of, 225–28
  and pharmacokinetics, 216–17
  phytocannabinoids, 215
  receptors, 66
  synthetic, 216
  testing for, 451
  See also Endocannabinoids
Cannabis, 204–29
  acute effects of, 219–25
  addiction to, 422t, 426
  chronic effects of, 228–29
  defined, 205
  drug laws and prevalence of use, 30f, 30
  history, 205–09
    legal and cultural issues, 210–13
    level of harm associated with, 36f
    mechanism of action, 218–19
    medical/therapeutic effects of, 225–28
    pharmacodynamics of, 218
    pharmacokinetics of, 74t, 216–17
    prevalence of use, 209f, 209–10
    sources and forms, 214–16
    synthetic cannabinoids vs., 216
    testing for, 452t
    types of, 214–15, 227
    See also Marijuana
Cannabis indica, 214
Cannabis products, 215–16
Cannabis sativa, 214f, 214
Cantharidin, 413
Capsaicin, 103
Captopril, 12
Capture ratio, 421f, 421
Carbamazepine (Tegretol), 79, 334
Carbonic anhydrase inhibitors, 86
Cardiac arrest, 102
Cardiovascular disease, 254, 277t, 278
  alcohol use and, 306
Cardiovascular system
  alcohol's effects on, 301, 308f, 309
  anabolic-androgenic steroids and, 356
  caffeine's effect on, 274
  marijuana's effect on, 220, 220f
  nicotine's effect on, 251f, 251, 254
  non-narcotic analgesics and, 379, 380
  opioids' effect on, 160
  sedatives' and hypnotics' effect on, 183
Carfentanil, 156
Casanova, 3
Catalepsy, 122, 127
Cataplexy, 195
Catapres. See Clonidine
Catecholaminergic neurons, 63
Catecholamines, 62–63
Cathinone (khat), 111–12
CatSper, 406
Causation, xxxviii, 34, 142, 201, 279, 304, 357
CBD. See Cannabidiol
CBD (Cannabidiol), 215
CBDA (cannabidiolic acid), 215
CBT. See Cognitive-behavioral therapy
Cefotan, 86
Celexa. See Citalopram
Cellular tolerance, 88, 89f, 164–65, 191, 253, 306
Central Intelligence Agency (CIA), 118–19
Central nervous system (CNS), 51f, 53–60
  areas of, 53t
  caffeine's effects on, 273, 274
  components of, 53–58
  defined, 50
  drugs' effects on, 177, 251
  neurotransmitters in, 64
  opioids' effects on, 159–60
  protection of, 58, 60
  stimulants of, 352
  See also Brain
Cerebellum, 53t, 53, 54f, 58, 66, 301f
Cerebral cortex, 53t, 54
Cerebrum, 53, 54
Cetirizine (Zyrtec), 374t
Chantix. See Varenicline
Chapstick, 375
"Charlotte's Web" cannabis strain, 227, 227f
Cheese, 86, 328
Chemical imbalance theory, 343
Chemical trigger zone (area postrema), 60, 77
Chemotherapeutic drugs, 3

Chewing tobacco, 247, 255
Children, opioid exposure, 160
China, 147–48, 238
Chloral hydrate, 77, 177
Chlordiazepoxide (Librium), 179, 181t, 182
Chloroform, 76, 196
Chlorpheniramine (phenylephrine) (Actifed), 374t, 385
Chlorpromazine (Thorazine), 334, 338f, 338t
Chocolate
  beneficial compounds in, 274
  caffeine in, 270–71, 272
  cocoa beans, 271f
  consumption rates, 267, 268f, 269
  and dogs/cats, 269
  drug interactions with, 86
  history of, 266
  medical benefits of, 276, 277t, 278
  metabolism of, 273
Cholecystokinin (CCK), 83
Cholesterol-lowering drugs, 13
Cholinergic receptors, 64
Chronic drug use, 11, 87–90
Chronic obstructive pulmonary disease (COPD), 254–55
CIA (Central Intelligence Agency), 118–19
Cialis. See Tadalafil
Cigarette packs, warnings on, 259f, 259
Cigarette smoking, 245–46
  acute effects of, 251–52
  chronic effects of, 252–57
  economic/social issues with, 241–45
  history of, 235–37
  pharmacokinetics of nicotine in, 248–49
  by pregnant women, 255f, 255–56
  prevalence of, 234, 238f, 238
Cigar smoking, 238, 246
Cimetidine (Tagamet, Pepcid), 86, 374t, 386
Circular reasoning, xlv
Cirrhosis, alcoholic, 310f, 310
Citalopram (Celexa), 327t, 327, 375, 413–14
Citrucel (methyl cellulose), 387
Claritin (Loratadine), 374t, 385
Clinical stage (drug development), 15–16
Clomifene (Clomid, Serophene), 407
Clomipramine (Anafranil), 327t, 327
Clonazepam (Klonopin), 179, 181t, 181
Clonidine (Catapres), 51t, 170, 457t
Clonidine (Kapvay), 365, 366t
Clozapine (Clozaril), 338t
Cluster headaches, 138
CNS. See Central nervous system
Coca Cola, 266–67
Cocaethylene (CE), 103
Cocaine (cocaine hydrochloride), 94–106
  acute effects of, 101f, 101–3
  as aphrodisiac, 413
  chronic effects of, 103–4
  classification of, 11, 12
  and crime, 34
  dependence on and addiction to, 104–5, 228, 420, 421f, 422t, 424f, 430f, 435
  drug interactions with, 223, 328
  drug policy on, 24
  history of, 94–97
  mechanism of action of, 100–101, 101f
  media portrayals of, 8
  and nervous system, 51t, 53t, 61t, 63
  overdose deaths, 103f, 103
  penalties for trafficking, 28t
  as performance-enhancing drug, 348, 351t, 352
  pharmacodynamics of, 85, 88, 89
  pharmacokinetics of, 74t, 75, 77, 78t, 80, 99–100
  and pregnancy, 41
  prevalence of use, 5f–7f, 26f, 97
  quitting, 465f, 465
  reasons for using, 10
  risk of death/level of harm associated with, 34, 35f, 36f
  in soft drinks, 267
  source and forms of, 97f, 97–99, 98f
  testing for, 451, 452t
  and tobacco use, 249
  treating addiction to, 105–6, 125, 139
  vaccines to prevent addiction to, 459
  See also Crack
Coca leaves, 97–98, 98f
Codeine (codeine sulfate), 146, 153
  acute effects of, 162, 384, 414